An Introduction to
Health Psychology

Third edition
Val Morrison and Paul Bennett

PEARSON

Harlow, England • London • New York • Boston • San Francisco • Toronto • Sydney • Auckland • Singapore • Hong Kong
Tokyo • Seoul • Taipei • New Delhi • Cape Town • São Paulo • Mexico City • Madrid • Amsterdam • Munich • Paris • Milan

Pearson Education Limited
Edinburgh Gate
Harlow
Essex CM20 2JE
England

and Associated Companies throughout the world

Visit us on the World Wide Web at:
www.pearson.com/uk

First published 2006
Second edition 2009
Third edition 2012

© Pearson Education Limited 2006, 2012

ISBN 978-0-273-73519-9

British Library Cataloguing-in-Publication Data
A catalogue record for this book is available from the British Library

Library of Congress Cataloguing-in-Publication Data
A catalog record for this book is available from the Library of Congress

10 9 8 7 6 5 4 3 2
16 15 14 13

Typeset in 9.75/13pt Minion by 35
Printed and bound by Svet Print d.o.o.

Contents

Supporting resources

Visit **www.pearsoned.co.uk/morrison** to find valuable online resources

Companion Website for students

- Multiple choice questions for self-testing
- Links to useful, up-to-date websites
- Searchable glossary to explain key terms
- Flashcards to test knowledge of key terms and definitions

For instructors

- A printable test bank of multiple choice questions for use in a classroom setting
- Tutorial ideas
- Downloadable PowerPoint slides
- Suggestions for essay questions to test deeper understanding of the subject

Also: The Companion Website provides the following features:

- Search tool to help locate specific items of content
- E-mail results and profile tools to send results of quizzes to instructors
- Online help and support to assist with website usage and troubleshooting

For more information please contact your local Pearson Education sales representative or visit **www.pearsoned.co.uk/morrison**

List of figures

List of tables

List of plates

Preface

Background to this book

Health psychology is a growth discipline at both under-graduate and postgraduate level; it is also an exciting, challenging and rewarding subject to study, with career opportunities developing within health care as well as within academic settings. We wrote this book because we believed that a comprehensive European-focused textbook was required that didn't predominantly focus on health behaviours, but which gave equal attention to issues in health, in illness, and in health-care practice and intervention. Someone must have read our first two editions because we have been asked to produce this third one, so thank you! We have maintained our comprehensive coverage of health, illness and health care, while updating and including reference to significant new studies, refining some sections, restructuring others, and basically we have worked towards making this new edition distinctive and (even) stronger than the last!

At the outset of this venture in 2005, we believed that, for psychologists and those studying psychology as part of medical or health-care training, textbooks should be led by psychological theory and constructs, as opposed to being led by behaviour or by disease. Diseases may vary clinically, but, psychologically speaking, they share many things in common – for example, potential for life or behaviour change, distress, challenges to coping, potential for recovery, involvement in health care and involvement with health professionals. We still believe this, reviewers of the previous editions seemed to concur, and so we have stuck to this format in this third edition. We very much hope that you enjoy what we have put together.

Aims of this textbook

The overall aim of this textbook is to provide a balanced, informed and comprehensive UK/European textbook with sufficient breadth of material for introductory students, but which also provides sufficient research depth to benefit final year students or those conducting a health psychology project. In addition to covering mainstream health psychology topics such as health and illness beliefs, behaviour and outcomes, we include topics such as socio-economic influences on health, biological bases, individual and cultural differences and psychological interventions in health, illness and health care, as these are all essential to the study of health psychology. We know from our feedback and sales in the UK and in several other European countries that our text is contributing to medical education; in fact one of us (VM) recently presented to a large class of Dutch medical students where our text is the core text used on their Psychology course! We value this hugely as it helps bridge the biomedical world with the biopsychosocial (see Chapter 1!) in a way that can only benefit us as patients, now or in the future. So we welcome all our readers and hope that our book is accessible to you whether you are a psychologist or not!

In this edition, we have stuck to the format whereby chapters follow the general principle of issue first, theory second, research evidence third, and finally the application of that theory and, where appropriate, the effectiveness of any intervention. We first examine factors that contribute to health, including societal and behavioural factors, and how psychologists and others can improve or maintain individuals' health. We then examine the process of becoming ill: the physiological systems that may fail in illness, psychological factors that may contribute to the development of illness, how we cope with illness, and how the medical system copes with us when we become ill. Finally, we examine a number of psychological interventions that can improve the well-being and perhaps even health of those who experience health problems. For example, in Chapter 3 we describe associations between illness and behaviour such as smoking; in Chapter 5 we examine the empirical evidence of psychosocial explanations of smoking behaviour based on general theories such as social learning theory and specific models such as the Theory of Planned Behaviour, then in Chapter 6 and Chapter 7 we show how this evidence can be put to use in both individual and group-targeted interventions. Describing, predicting and then intervening are primary goals of health psychologists.

This text is intended to provide comprehensive coverage of the core themes in current health psychology but it also addresses the fact that many individuals neither stay healthy, nor live with illness, in isolation. The role of family is crucial and therefore while acknowledging the role of significant others in many chapters, for example in relation to influencing dietary or smoking behaviour, or in providing support during times of stress, we also devote a large part of Chapter 15 to the impact of illness on significant others. Another goal of ours in writing this textbook was to acknowledge that Western theorists should not assume cross-cultural similarity of health and illness perceptions or behaviours. Therefore from the first edition to this current edition we have integrated examples of theory and research from non-Westernised countries wherever possible. Throughout this text runs the theme of differentials, whether culture, gender, age/developmental stage, or socio-economic, and as acknowledged by reviewers and readers of the first two editions, our commitment to this is clearly seen in the inclusion of a whole chapter devoted to socio-economic differentials in health.

Structure of this textbook

We have made no sweeping structural changes to this third edition although we have added new features – each chapter starts with a contemporary headline topic, and several chapters include interviews with relevant professionals to highlight health psychology in practice. We have also strengthened our cross-referencing between chapters and have added a symbol to denote other chapters where the content is addressed. Throughout this textbook, we have drawn from both qualitative and quantitative studies, from cross-sectional data, but wherever possible and if available (which is not always the case) from good quality longitudinal studies.

The textbook continues to be structured into three broad sections. The first, *Being and Staying Healthy*, contains seven chapters, which first examine factors that contribute to health, including societal and behavioural factors, and then describe how psychologists and others can improve or maintain individuals' health. Chapter 1 considers what we actually mean when we talk about 'health' or 'being healthy' and presents a brief history to the mind–body debate which underpins much of our

research. We fully consider the important influence of current health status, lifespan, ageing and culture on health, and in doing so illustrate better the biopsychosocial model which underpins health psychology. Chapter 2 describes how factors such as social class, income and even postcode can affect one's health, behaviour and access to health care. Indeed, the health of the general population is influenced by the socio-economic environment in which we live and which differs both within and across countries and cultures. We have tried to reflect more of this diversity in the present volume.

Many of today's 'killer' illnesses, such as some cancers, heart disease and stroke, have a behavioural component. Chapters 3 and 4 describe how certain behaviours such as exercise have health-enhancing effects whereas others, such as non-adherence to medicines, smoking or the use of illicit drugs, have health-damaging effects. More detail has been added regarding two groups of behaviours – over-eating, and illicit drug use. As well as updating the epidemiological statistics regarding such health behaviours and outlining current health policy and targets where they exist, we continue to provide evidence of lifespan, cultural and gender differentials in health behaviours. These behaviours have been examined by health and social psychologists over several decades, drawing on several key theories such as social learning theory and socio-cognitive theory. In Chapter 5 we describe several models which have been rigorously tested in an effort to identify which beliefs, expectancies, attitudes and normative factors contribute to health or risk behaviour. More coverage of adherence behaviour has been added; also greater discussion of some of the broader determinants of behaviour. This chapter has also been reworked to include more critical reflection. This section of the book, therefore, presents evidence of the link between behaviour and health and illness, and highlights an area where health psychologists have much to offer in terms of understanding or advising on individual factors to target in interventions. The section ends with two chapters on intervention. Chapter 6 presents evidence of successful and less successful approaches to changing individual behaviours that increase risk for disease, while Chapter 7 applies the same review and critique to population approaches such as health education and promotion.

The second section, *Becoming Ill*, contains six chapters which take the reader through the process of becoming ill: the physiological systems that may fail in illness, the psychological factors that may contribute to the development of illness, how we then cope with illness, and how the medical system copes with us when we become ill. We start therefore with a whole chapter dedicated to describing biological and bodily processes relevant to the physical experience of health and illness (Chapter 8). In this third edition, this chapter covers a broader range of illnesses as well as some individual case study examples and more signposts to relevant psychological content to be found elsewhere in the book. Chapter 9 describes how we perceive, interpret and respond to symptoms, highlighting individual, sociocultural and contextual factors that influence these processes, and has seen general updating in the current edition in order that studies addressing the dynamic and changing nature of illness perceptions and responses are addressed. Also in this third edition you will find expanded critique and coverage of issues such as the social construction of illness. In Chapter 10 presenting to, and communicating with, health professionals is reviewed with illustrations of 'good' and 'not so good' practice. The role of patient involvement in decision making is an important one in current health policy and practice and the evidence as to the benefits of patient involvement is reviewed here. Chapters 11 and 12 take us into the realm of stress, something that very few of us escape experiencing from time to time! We present an overview of stress theories, where stress is defined either as an event, a response or series of responses to an event, or as a transaction between the individual experiencing and appraising the event, and its actual characteristics. For the third edition we have added greater coverage of occupational stress and have further detailed the growing field of study that is psychoneuroimmunology, (i.e. the study of how the mind influences the body via alterations in immunological functioning, which then influences health status). To make this section clearer and even more up to date we have added a new diagram of one of the key processes involved here and have also strengthened coverage of neuroendocrine responses. Chapter 12 presents the research evidence pertaining to factors shown to 'moderate' the potentially negative effect of seemingly stressful events, from distal antecedents such as socioeconomic resources, social support and aspects of personality which we have increased coverage of (e.g. optimism, conscientiousness), to specific coping styles and strategies. Social comparison is introduced for the third edition as is much more coverage of the growing movement of 'positive psychology' – in fact positive beliefs are a recurring theme, also seen in Chapters 14 and 15. Chapters 11 and 12 highlight the complexity of the relationship between stress and illness and lead nicely into Chapter 13 which turns to methods of alleviating stress, where it becomes clear that there is not one therapeutic 'hat' to fit all, as we describe a range of cognitive, behavioural and cognitive-behavioural approaches.

In the third section, *Being Ill*, we turn our attention to the impact of illness on the individual and their families across two chapters. In the first of these (Chapter 14), we define and describe what is meant by 'quality of life', clarifying in this edition that which is subjective vs. objective and describe research which has shown how QoL is challenged or altered by illness. In Chapter 15 we address other illness outcomes, both the negative, such as patient depression or carer strain, and the positive, such as the new sections on post-traumatic growth and caregiver gains. Perhaps unique to this textbook is the large section devoted to the impact of providing care for a sick person within the family. This third edition further highlights research that considers the dyad (patient–spouse most typically), demonstrating how such studies can add to our understanding of illness experiences and health outcomes. One of the many new research-focus sections found in this third edition highlights this area of study. Chapter 16 addresses a phenomenon that accounts for the majority of visits to a health professional – pain – which has been shown to be much more than a physical experience. This chapter is the only disease-specific chapter in our text, but we chose to contain a chapter on pain and place it at this point towards the end of our book because, by illustrating the multidimensional nature of pain, we draw together much of what has preceded (in terms of predictors and correlates of illness, health-care processes etc.). Pain illustrates extremely well the biopsychosocial approach health psychologists endeavour to uphold. In a similarly holistic manner Chapter 17 looks at ways of improving health-related quality of life by means of interventions such as stress management training, the use of social support, and illness management programmes.

Finally, we close the third edition of this text in the same way as we closed previously, with Chapter 18, which we have called Futures. This chapter has changed significantly in that it now has three key foci: (i) how a number of psychological theories can be integrated to guide psychological interventions, (ii) how the profession of health psychology is developing in a variety of countries and the differing ways it is achieving growth, and (iii) how psychologists can foster the use of psychological interventions or psychologically informed practice in areas (both geographical and medical) where they are unused. This ends our book therefore by highlighting areas where health psychology research has or can perhaps in the future 'make a difference'.

Hence this third edition contains much of what will be familiar to readers of the previous two, but rather than simply update our material (actually updating is often harder than writing from scratch!), we have, with an eye on the extremely constructive feedback from several excellent European reviewers, in summary, done the following:

- kept the same basic structure but introduced some new features to help cross-referencing between chapters;
- continued to construct sections and chapters within them on the basic principle of issue first, theory second, research evidence third and, where appropriate, interventions fourth;
- added political and social commentary where relevant;
- increased our emphasis on critical psychology, in terms of casting a more critical eye over some of the dominant models in health psychology;
- increased use of case studies in an attempt to make the experiences of trying to maintain health or becoming ill more accessible, from both the personal and professional standpoint;
- added more of the old features where they proved popular with readers and reviewers (e.g. What do YOU think?, Research focus) and added some new ones which we hope you will like, e.g. highlighted cross-referencing, opening headline, interviews with professionals;
- increased the within-text referencing and also the recommended reading at the end of each chapter;
- provided internet websites at the end of most chapters that link to both academic and health-care-related sites, providing an easy link to a wide range of resources and interesting issues beyond the present text.

We hope you enjoy reading the book and learn from it as much as we learned while writing it. Enjoy!

Acknowledgements

This project has been a major one which has required the reading of literally thousands of empirical and review papers published by health, social and clinical psychologists around the globe, many books and book chapters, and many newspapers to help identify some hot health issues. The researchers behind all this work are thanked for their contribution to the field.

On a more personal level, several key researchers and senior academics also acted as reviewers for our chapters, some of whom have been with us from the first edition and have shown great commitment and forbearance! At each stage they have provided honest and constructive feedback and their informed suggestions have made this a better book than it might otherwise have been! They also spotted errors and inconsistencies that are inevitable with such a large project, and took their role seriously.

Many thanks also to the indomitable editorial team at Pearson Education, with several development editors having taken their turn at the helm and guided us through a few bad patches where academic demands and our own research prevented us from spending time on 'the book': originally Morten Fuglevand, the Acquisitions Editor, Jane Powell, Paula Parish and David Cox; for the second edition Catherine Morrissey and Janey Webb; for the third Janey Webb again, Jane Lawes and Tim Parker. They have pushed, pulled, advised and cajoled us up to this point where we hand over to the production team. We owe continued thanks to Morten who secured Pearson's agreement to 'go colour'; we think it makes a difference and hope you do too. To those more hidden to us, the design team, photo acquisitions people, cartoonist and publicist, thanks for enhancing our text with some excellent features. We are grateful to you all.

Finally, to those that have made the coffee in the wee small hours, brought us wine, or otherwise kept us going while we hammered away at our computers in the North and the South of Wales, heartfelt thanks. To my husband Dave, who suddenly added to the heart attack statistics in December 2006, to my big sister who lost a brave fight against ovarian cancer in 2008, and to my baby sister who has hopefully banished breast cancer in 2010, your faces have been in many pages of the papers I read – I hope this book makes a difference somehow to others affected by illness. To Gill who stoically coped with my absences during both day and night . . . I think you noticed them! Love and thanks for looking after me.

Val Morrison and Paul Bennett
March 2012

Salt

Salt intake is also a target of preventive health measures, with high salt (sodium chloride) intake, much of it coming from an increasing overreliance on processed foods, being implicated in those with persistent high blood pressure, i.e. hypertension. The detrimental effects of high salt intake on blood pressure appear to persist even when levels of physical activity, obesity and other health behaviour are controlled (Law *et al.* 1991), and thus educational interventions have attempted to modify intake.

A systematic review and meta-analysis of intervention trials assessed the impact of lowering salt intake in adults who were either normo-tensive (i.e. 'normal' blood pressure), who had high blood pressure that was not being treated, or who had high blood pressure that was being treated using drug therapy (Hooper *et al.* 2002). Overall, the results of the reviewed trials were somewhat mixed in that salt reduction resulted in reduced **systolic** and **diastolic blood pressure**; however, the degree of reduction in blood pressure was not related to the amount of salt reduction. In addition, the trials had no impact on the number of heart disease-related deaths seen in follow-ups lasting from seven months to seven years, with deaths equally distributed across the intervention and control groups. The authors therefore concluded that interventions targeting salt intake provide only limited health benefits.

In spite of such mixed findings, guidelines exist as to recommended levels of salt intake. High salt intake is considered to be in excess of 6 g per day for adults, and over 5 g per day for children aged 7 to 14 (British Medical Association 2003a). While it is perhaps difficult to establish the unique health benefits of a reduced-salt diet when examining individuals engaged in more general dietary change behaviour, the BMA guidelines raise awareness of the need to monitor salt intake from early childhood onwards.

---

systolic blood pressure
the maximum pressure of blood on the artery walls, which occurs at the end of the left ventricle output/contraction (measured in relation to **diastolic blood pressure**).

diastolic blood pressure
the minimum pressure of the blood on the walls of the arteries between heart beats (measured in relation to **systolic blood pressure**).

Obesity

We include obesity in this section even though it is not a behaviour, because of growing international concern about its increasing prevalence and because it is contributed to by a combination of poor diet and a lack of exercise, both health behaviours which are relevant to this and the next chapter.

How is obesity defined?

Obesity is generally measured in terms of an individual's body mass index (BMI), which is calculated as a person's weight in kilograms divided by their height in metres squared (weight/height^2). An individual is considered to be:

- 'normal weight' if their BMI is between 20 and 24.9;
- mildly obese or 'overweight' (grade 1) if their BMI is between 25 and 29.9;
- moderate or clinically obese (grade 2) if their BMI falls between 30 and 39.9;
- severely obese (grade 3) if their BMI is 40 or greater.

BMI does not however take age, gender or body frame/build into consideration (although BMI cut-offs are based on being 20 per cent above the height–weight chart standards for a person of 'medium' frame), and so the index should only be used as a guide in context with these other factors. As well as considering BMI, it has become clear that waist circumference, ratio of waist to hip size, and fat deposited around the abdomen (often referred to as being 'apple-shaped') further increase the implications of overweight and obesity for heart attack in both men (Smith *et al.* 2005) and women (Iribarren *et al.* 2006), for type 2 diabetes and all-case mortality in women (Hu 2003) and for some forms of cancer (Williams and Hord 2005).

Negative health consequences of obesity

As noted earlier, being underweight is the largest global cause of mortality, yet a growing number of people, predominantly in Western or developed countries, are at risk from the opposite problem – obesity. Obesity is a

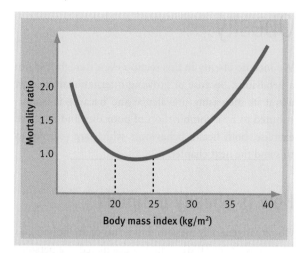

Figure 3.2 The relationship between body mass index and mortality at 23-year follow-up (Framingham heart study)

Source: Wilson, P.W.F. *et al.* (2002).

major risk factor in a range of physical illnesses, including, for example, hypertension, heart disease, type 2 diabetes, osteoarthritis, respiratory problems, lower back pain, and some forms of cancer.

The relative risk of disease appears to increase proportionately in relation to the percentage overweight a person is, although evidence as to this linear relationship remains mixed. The longitudinal Framingham heart study shows a relationship between obesity and mortality which appears over the long term (two–three decades), with the risk of death within twenty-six years being increased by 1 per cent per extra pound in weight in those aged between 30 and 42, and by 2 per cent per extra pound in those aged 50 to 62. Being overweight confers slightly more risk than 'normal' weight but the J-shaped curve shown in Figure 3.2 also reminds us of the risk of being underweight, with the lowest mortality in those within the ideal weight range (body mass index 20–24.9). Obesity is also implicated in psychological ill health including low self-esteem and social isolation (British Medical Association 2003a; Strauss 2000), and being overweight as a child has been associated with poorer health-related quality of life (Williams *et al.* 2005) and even earlier mortality (Bjørge *et al.* 2008).

Prevalence of obesity

In 1999, The European Commission estimated that 31 per cent of the EU adult population was overweight,

with a further 10 per cent reaching weights defined as clinically obese. More recently, however, the proportions of adults defined as obese were as high as 18 per cent, among both men and women in the UK and Greece, for example (Boniol and Autier 2010). In fact, the World Health Organization collation of epidemiological data provides evidence of a three-fold increase in obesity rates in parts of North America, Australasia and China, and within the UK over the past three decades. Sadly this increase was predicted in the 1980s (Department of Health 1995). Alarmingly, excess body weight has been identified as the most common child disorder in Europe (International Obesity Taskforce and European Association for the Study of Obesity 2002) and within the UK, English data points to an 9 per cent increase in the prevalence of overweight children aged between 2 and 10 years between 1995 and 2005 (Health Survey for England 2008). Obesity affects all age groups; however, in younger populations the particular concerns are about the early implications of obesity for psychological health and psychosocial development, whereas with aging, as with middle-aged and older adults, the effects on physical health begin to be seen.

Lower social class has been related to increased obesity for young females, but not for males, and as obese children tend to grow up to be obese adults (Magarey *et al.* 2003), interventions need to start early. To be successful, interventions need to first understand the factors associated with the development of obesity, and to do this researchers have considered the influences on food choice, intake and, crucially, overeating behaviour. These factors fall within **social learning theory**, e.g. the powerful influence of significant others' behaviour or communications – peers, siblings, parents, the media – or within theories of associative learning where food choice and eating behaviours are associated with the receiving of intrinsic or extrinsic rewards or **reinforcers**, such as pleasure, or perceived stress reduction. As well as considering these developmental theories, health psychologists have also

social learning theory
a theory that has at its core the belief that a combination of outcome expectancy and outcome value will shape subsequent behaviour. Reinforcement is an important predictor of future behaviour.

applied cognitive theories to behaviour change with regards to overeating (see Chapter 5 ☞). As with all human behaviour, there is no one explanation! As obesity has the strongest association with disease, we turn briefly to a consideration of influences on that as it is not necessarily all about overeating.

What causes obesity?

A simple explanation of obesity is that it is a condition that results from an energy intake that grossly exceeds the energy output (Pinel 2003). However, early twin studies and studies of adopted children (e.g. Meyer and Stunkard 1993; Price and Gottesman 1991) proposed some hereditary explanations to obesity, which are generally one of three types:

1. Obese individuals are born with a greater number of fat cells: evidence of this is limited. For example, the number of fat cells in a person of average weight and in many mildly obese individuals is typically 25–35 million. The number of cells is dramatically increased in a severely obese person, implying the formation of *new* fat cells.

2. Obese individuals inherit lower metabolic rates. However, evidence shows that obese people are not consistently found to have lower metabolic rates than comparable thin persons.

3. Obese individuals may have deficiencies in a hormone responsible for appetite control, or lack of control: more potential as a contributing factor.

This last explanation has received attention since the 1950s, when a gene mutation was identified in some laboratory mice that had become highly obese (Coleman 1979). Subsequent cloning of this mutated gene found that it was only expressed in fat cells and that it encoded a protein hormone called leptin (Zhang *et al.* 1994). Leptin is produced by fatty (adipose) tissue and is one of several signals to the hypothalamus of the central nervous system that help to regulate weight. Low leptin levels suggest low fat stores which then prompts the signal to eat, to reestablish fatty stores needed for energy (see Chapter 8 ☞). However, Pinel (2003) describes how research has not found similar genetic mutation in all obese humans and how increasing leptin by means of injection has not consistently reduced eating behaviour or body fat in the obese. More recently, exciting research

showing the effects of common FTO (fat mass and obesity associated) gene variants, on BMI, weight, waist circumference and body fat (e.g. Frayling *et al.* 2007), have been brought into the limelight by preliminary evidence that genetic susceptibility to obesity could be reduced or even negated by means of vigorous physical activity (Rampersaud *et al.* 2008).

Another avenue of research has identified that serotonin, a neurotransmitter (see Chapter 8 ☞), is directly involved in producing satiety (the condition where hunger is no longer felt). Early animal experiments investigating the effects on hunger of administering a serotonin **agonist** have had their findings confirmed in humans, where the introduction of serotonin agonists into the body induced satiety, and reduced the frequency and quantity of food intake and body weight (Halford and Blundell 2000).

Such lines of research hold promise for future intervention; however, it is likely that genetic and biological explanations alone are insufficient, given the recent upsurge in obesity in developed countries. This increase is more plausibly attributed to an interaction between such factors and environmental factors such as sedentary lifestyle and behaviour patterns. People of all ages increasingly pass their time indoors, and there is evidence that activities such as watching television or computing can even reduce a person's metabolic rate, so that their bodies burn up existing calories more slowly. Lack of physical activity in combination with overeating or eating the wrong food types are associated with obesity, and it is unclear which is the primary causal factor.

People eat for different reasons. For many, eating carries positive incentives, such as the intrinsic rewards of taste enjoyment (sensory eating), and extrinsic rewards

> ### reinforcers
> factors that reward or provide a positive response following a particular behaviour or set of behaviours (positive reinforcer); or enable the removal or avoidance of an undesired state or response (negative reinforcer).
>
> ### agonist
> a drug that simulates the effects of neurotransmitters, such as the serotonin agonist fluoxetine, which induces satiety (reduces hunger).

such as the pleasure of social eating (Pinel *et al.* 2000). Eating styles have been identified (van Strien *et al.* 1986; and see What do you think? below) whereby some may eat when they catch sight of food or food cues (external eating), or simply when their body signals hunger (internal eating); others may eat when they are bored, irritated or stressed (emotional eating). Overeating also occurs for these same varied reasons (O'Connor *et al.* 2008; Snoek *et al.* 2007; van Strien *et al.* 2007). With regards to eating when stressed, it seems that it is not only the volume of food that may increase, but the type of food selected, for example food with high sugar or fat content (Oliver *et al.* 2000), and furthermore that the type of eating behaviour may differ depending on the nature of the stressor (O'Connor *et al.* 2008).

Effective interventions which aim to make our currently 'obesogenic' environments (BMA 2003a) and behaviour more healthy need therefore to address a complexity of factors. Similarly, interventions to increase exercise behaviour, the other major contributor to reduced obesity, are also high on the public health agenda (see Chapters 6 and 7 ☞). Exercise behaviour is discussed more fully in Chapter 4 ☞.

WHAT DO YOU THINK?

What style of eating do you have? Are you likely to eat when something looks or smells good even if you have recently eaten and don't actually feel hungry? ('external/sensory eating') Are you easily swayed by others simply eating in front of you? ('external eating') Can you exercise restraint over what and when you eat? For example if you think you have eaten more than usual over the weekend, do you try to eat less the next day? ('restraint eating'). What about your mood, does that make a difference to when and what you eat? Some people eat less when depressed, others eat more and seek out certain food types – usually sweet or fatty foods. If you're angry, frustrated or impatient do you snack or nibble more? ('emotional eating').

Styles of eating reported by those with obesity have been 'matched' to different obesity treatments. If you are interested in reading further about this use the references above and also Google the DEBQ (the Dutch Eating Behaviours Questionaire), a screening tool used in many studies of eating styles and which has been shown to have good construct validity and internal reliability.

A final thought on obesity

A word of caution is drawn from the BMA report (2003a) referred to previously: we as individuals, and as a society, must be careful not to over-focus on the weight of individual children – while obesity is on the increase, so too is extreme dietary behaviour and eating disorders; several recent studies point to increasing body dissatisfaction among children and adolescents, particularly females (e.g. Ricciardelli and McCabe 2001; Schur *et al.* 2000). Body dissatisfaction can lead to dietary restraint which can potentially have adverse physical and psychological consequences, including, conversely, overeating (although this is not universally accepted: van Strien *et al.* 2005, 2007) or in terms of eating disorders (e.g. Stice *et al.* 2002).

Smoking

After caffeine and alcohol, nicotine is the next most commonly used psychoactive drug in society today. While smoking behaviour receives a vast amount of negative publicity arising from the death toll attached to it, nicotine is a legal drug, with sale of nicotine-based substances (cigarettes, cigars) providing many tobacco companies and many governments (as a result of tobacco tax) with a vast income (as does alcohol). A shift in how society views smoking has slowly taken shape, with worksite bans, legislation regarding smoking in public places, and restrictions on tobacco advertising having some effect (e.g. Wakefield *et al.* 2000), but smoking prevalence remains high. Smoking prevalence in western countries is only falling slowly, thus reducing smoking behaviour continues to be a public health target. In developing countries, or in the developed East (e.g. China) smoking prevalence, particularly among men, has increased rather than plateaud or decreased.

Negative health effects of smoking

A 1990 report estimated that approximately three million people worldwide die each year as a result of their use of tobacco cigarettes and, to a lesser degree, cigars (Peto and Lopez 1990). By 2008, smoking-attributable deaths had risen to approximately 5 million per year worldwide, with a prediction that over 1 billion people this century

> **chronic obstructive airways disease**
>
> a persistent airway obstruction associated with combinations of chronic bronchitis, small airways disease, asthma and emphysema.

will die from tobacco-related causes (World Health Organization 2008). Such figures are staggering.

Smoking is the key modifiable risk factor for cardio-vascular disease across all age groups. Tobacco products contain carcinogenic tars and carbon monoxide, which are thought to be responsible for approximately 30 per cent of cases of coronary heart disease, 75 per cent of cancers (90 per cent of lung cancer) and 80 per cent of cases of **chronic obstructive airways disease**. In addition, passive smoking is considered to account for 25 per cent of lung cancer deaths among non-smokers. Passive smoking also carries risks to unborn babies.

Carbon monoxide reduces circulating oxygen in the blood, which effectively reduces the amount of oxygen feeding the heart muscles; nicotine makes the heart work harder by increasing blood pressure and heart rate; and together these substances cause narrowing of the arteries and increase the likelihood of thrombosis (clot formation). Tars impair the respiratory system by congesting the lungs,

and this is a major contributor to the highly prevalent chronic obstructive pulmonary disease (COPD: e.g. emphysema) (Julien 1996; see also Chapter 8 ☛). Overall, the evidence as to the negative health effects of smoking tobacco is indisputable. Furthermore, the evidence as to the negative effects of passive smoking has grown over the past decade or so, with associations being shown between occupational exposure to smoke and significantly increased risk of developing a range of illnesses, including lung cancer and cardiovascular disease (USDHHS 2006).

Prevalence of smoking

Worldwide, almost 9 per cent of deaths are attributed to tobacco use. In developed countries tobacco creates the largest disease burden (closely followed by blood pressure, and then alcohol, cholesterol and being overweight). There have been some positive signs of a slight downturn in the prevalence and uptake of smoking over the past 50 years; however, there are signs that any downturn is slowing to a point where still over 20 per cent of the UK population smoke (West and Shiffman 2007). For example, approximately 80 per cent of men and 40 per cent of women smoked in the UK during the 1950s, with men reducing significantly to 51 per cent but women remaining stable at 41 per cent in 1974, whereas by 2002 these

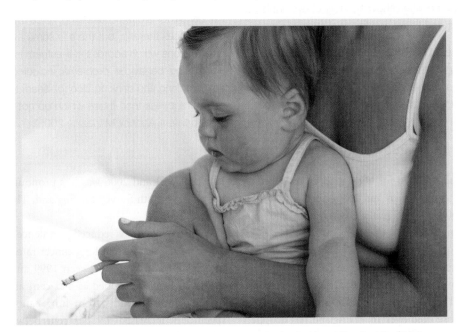

Plate 3.1 Young mother smoking with her baby sitting on her lap looking at the cigarette. This is an emotive example of passive smoking

Source: Alamy Images/Richard Newton.

IN THE SPOTLIGHT

Smoking, drinking and teenage pregnancy

Studies of adolescent girls have pointed to the importance of self-concept (i.e. concept of what one 'is') and self-esteem (i.e. concept of one's 'value' or 'worth') in determining involvement or non-involvement in risk behaviours. Some theorists further suggest that a significant amount of adolescent behaviour is motivated by the need to present oneself to others (primarily peers) in a way that enhances the individual's reputation, their social identity (Emler 1984). In some social groups the 'reputation' that will help the individual 'fit' with that social group will involve risk-taking behaviours (Odgers et al. 1996; Snow and Bruce 2003). Snow and Bruce (2003) found female smokers to have less self-confidence, to feel less liked by their families, and to have lower physical and social self-concepts, while their peer self-concept surprisingly did not differ from that of non-smokers. In relation to becoming pregnant as a teenager, low self-esteem and a negative self-concept may again be implicated, as teenage mothers often show a history of dysfunctional relationships and social and financial strain.

Alcohol appears to play a significant role in early sexual activity likely to lead to becoming pregnant, rather than being necessarily a problem during pregnancy. For example, alcohol consumption and being 'drunk' or 'stoned' is a commonly cited reason for first having sex when a teenager (e.g. Duncan et al. 1999; Wellings et al. 2001) and for subsequently having unprotected sex and risking both pregnancy and sexually transmitted diseases (Hingson et al. 2003). In contrast, there is some evidence that teenagers are less likely to drink during pregnancy than older mothers, thus placing their unborn child at lower risk of foetal alcohol syndrome (California Department of Health Services 2003). However, teenage mothers are more likely than older mothers to have a poor diet and smoke during pregnancy and, combined with their often physical immaturity, these behaviours may contribute to the higher rates of miscarriage, premature birth and low birthweight babies (Department of Health 2003; Horgan and Kenny 2007). Horgan and Kenney further note that the death rate for babies and young children born to teenage mums is 60 per cent higher than that for those born to older mothers, and younger mums are also three times more likely to suffer from post-natal depression.

Teenage substance use therefore has the potential to create significant long-term problems for the individual and potentially their child. However, changing adolescent risk behaviour is often challenging, given the complexity of influences thereon, but there is some evidence that interventions which address self-esteem issues before addressing 'behaviour' problems, including under-age sex, smoking and drinking alcohol, seem to meet with greater success than those which do not (e.g. Health Development Agency Magazine 2005).

percentages had declined for both genders, to approximately 28 per cent of men and 26 per cent of women (Peto et al. 2000, World Health Organization 2003). A less encouraging finding is that the downturn is slower in women, and among young girls, who in fact show a greater increase in smoking initiation (Blenkinsop et al. 2003; Department of Health 2000; Office for National Statistics 2001). The prevalence of males currently smoking in those aged over 16 in England has dropped from 41 per cent in 1976 to 28 per cent in 1996 (*General Household Survey*: Thomas et al. 1998) and further downwards to 24 per cent in 2006. For females, the decline between 1993 and 2006 was less pronounced (26 to 21 per cent) (Health Survey for England, The Information Centre, 2006).

While, overall, this reduced prevalence has been associated with a decrease in lung cancer rates, for example, in England and Wales between 1999 and 2009 cancer deaths for males dropped 15 per cent and for females by 13 per cent, deaths from lung cancer for females specifically increased 4.9 per cent between 2004 and 2009 (Office for National Statistics 2010) . The full benefits of decreased smoking, or negative consequences of any increase, will continue to be seen in mortality figures of

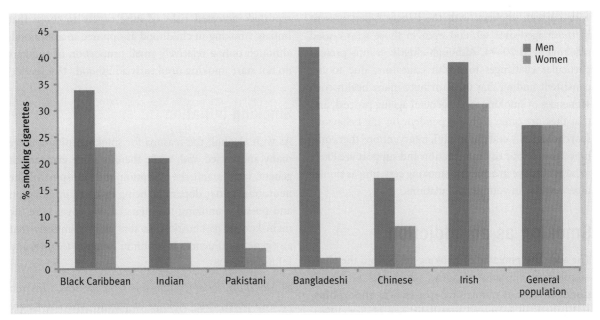

Figure 3.3 Cigarette smoking by gender and ethnic group, England, 1999

Source: www.heartstats.org

future decades. The increased incidence of lung cancer among women over the past two decades is, in part, traceable to the increased prevalence of women smoking since the Second World War, and this worrying upturn is likely to continue if recent survey figures are considered. Ethnic differences in smoking prevalence have also been reported (British Heart Foundation 2004, www.heart stats.org). While overall ethnic minority group figures suggest a lower smoking prevalence than among the total UK population (UK 2005 General Household Survey figures, see Goddard 2006), there are some subgroup exceptions. For example, Bangladeshi men have been found to be at greater risk of coronary heart disease than other groups, and this has been attributed in part to their tendency to exercise less and smoke more than their white counterparts (Nazroo 1997; Health Education Authority 1997). To illustrate this further, Figure 3.3 presents data from a survey conducted in 1999, which found that 42 per cent of Bangladeshi males smoked, in comparison with 27 per cent of males across the general population. In contrast, the percentage of Bangladeshi, Indian and Pakistani women smoking is significantly below the general population norm. Aboriginal and Torres Strait islanders have been shown to have one of the highest prevalences of smoking recorded – with 51 per cent of these indigenous populations aged over 15 years smoking (Australian Bureau of Statistics 2005).

As well as culture, there are age differences in smoking prevalence: smoking remains at high levels among the elderly – a population that initiated smoking before the medical evidence as to the health-damaging effects of the behaviour was clear and publicly available. Bratzler *et al.* (2002) review the impact of smoking on the elderly in terms of increased **morbidity**, disability and death, and provide a strong argument for the continued need for health promotion efforts to target smoking cessation in order to enhance the quality of life and longevity of older individuals. Evidence of the health gains of smoking cessation have been demonstrated: the American Cancer Society Cancer Prevention Study II, for example, reported a significant decrease in **age-specific mortality** rates for former smokers compared

> ### morbidity
> costs associated with illness such as disability, injury.
>
> ### age-specific mortality
> typically presented as the number of deaths per 100,000, per annum, according to certain age groups, for example comparing rates of death from cancer in 2001 between those aged 45–54 with those aged 55–64.

with current smokers, with the benefit being present in those aged over 60, and even in those who ceased smoking aged 70–74. Although elderly groups present particular challenges to health educators, due to the consistent finding that they attribute many health consequences of smoking to the general ageing process, and that they are often highly dependent on the behaviour (psychologically and physically), interventions that combine age-relevant risk information and support are likely to be as effective in achieving smoking cessation as similar interventions in younger populations.

Smoking as an addiction

The addictive potential of smoking arises from the pharmacological substance, nicotine, which acts as a brain stimulant, releases our natural opiates, beta-**endorphins**, and causes an increased metabolic rate (Julien 1996). Physical dependence arises when an individual develops tolerance to the effects of nicotine and smokes more to attain the same effects or to avoid the withdrawal effects that follow a diminished bloodstream nicotine level (e.g. cravings, insomnia, sweating, increased appetite: e.g. West 1992). In this way, smoking can become self-reinforcing. Psychological symptoms of withdrawal such as anxiety, restlessness and irritability are often so pronounced that individuals may recommence smoking in a deliberate attempt to eliminate these symptoms, which are distressing not only for them but also for those around them! Resuming smoking provides reinforcement in terms of the avoidance of any further withdrawal symptoms.

Why do people smoke?

Smoking behaviour is generally adopted in youth, and there are a significant number of young people smoking and accumulating lung and airway damage that will, for many, create significant health problems in the future (Walker and Townsend 1999). Doll and Peto (1981)

reported increased risks of lung cancer in those that initiate smoking in childhood as opposed to adulthood, although only a relatively small proportion of smokers do not start smoking until early adulthood (19+ years).

Smoking initiation

As with alcohol, the reasons for smoking initiation are many and varied and, while there is some evidence of genetic factors and the reception and transport of the neurotransmitter dopamine being involved in initiation and possibly smoking maintenance, we cover here the main known psychosocial factors as it is unlikely that any genetic influences function in isolation (Munaf and Johnstone 2008).

● *Modelling, social learning and reinforcement.* Children with peers, elder siblings or parents who smoke are indeed more likely to imitate such behaviour than children with non-smoking significant others. Family behaviour and dynamics are important socialisation processes, and some authors have suggested that smoking parents increase the 'preparedness' of their children towards smoking by establishing positive attitudes towards the behaviour and by possibly reducing perceptions of risk. The further influence of smoking peers can result in this preparedness turning into action (e.g. Jarvis 2004), with smoking siblings being perhaps even more influential (Mercken *et al.*, 2007).

● *Social pressure.* Social or peer pressure, where smoking behaviour is positively encouraged (including in the media) and reinforced by the responses of significant others, has commonly been cited as a reason for smoking initiation, reflecting either social contagion or influence that a person conforms to. Interestingly, however, Denscombe (2001) reported that young people aged 15–16 years rejected the idea of 'peer pressure' being responsible for smoking initiation, preferring to see the behaviour as something they selected to do themselves. This fits with the notion of smoking initiation being tied up with seeking reputation and status.

● *Image* and reputation is important during adolescence, and wanting to 'fit' in and have status within one's social group is considered important to social functioning (Snow and Bruce 2003; Stewart-Knox *et al.* 2005; Tyas and Pederson 1998). Gender differences may exist here.

---

endorphins

naturally occurring opiate-like chemicals released in the brain and spinal cord. They reduce the experience of pain and can induce feelings of relaxation or pleasure. Associated with the so-called 'runner's high'.

Michell and Amos (1997), for example, found that young males were more ambivalent than females about smoking, with their 'status' in the pecking order being conferred by fitness, whereas for girls high status was attached to appearing cool and sophisticated or rebellious, and for some, this may be achieved through smoking.

- *Weight control.* Weight control has been identified as a motive for smoking initiation and maintenance more often among young girls than among young males (e.g. Crisp *et al.* 1999; French *et al.* 1994), although males are not immune from this strategy (Fulkerson and French 2003). In this American study Native American and Asian American males cited weight control as a reason for smoking more often than males from other ethnic groups. Underlying differences in motivation for smoking are crucial to our understanding of why national statistics vary by factors such as gender and ethnicity. It would seem that the concern about body image and weight needs to be addressed in parallel with perceptions of smoking if smoking behaviour is to be reduced.

- *Risk-taking.* Smoking has been found to be a common feature of those engaged in a larger array of 'risk-taking' or problem behaviour, such as truancy, petty theft or under-age drinking (Sutherland and Shepherd 2001). Low family cohesion has also been associated with higher levels of smoking and drinking among adolescents and young adults aged 12 to 22 (Bourdeaudhuij 1997; Bourdeaudhuij and van Oost 1998), although these studies assessed adolescents and adults at one time point only: thus it is not possible to establish the direction of the effects reported.

- *Health cognitions.* There is evidence that beliefs such as 'unrealistic optimism' regarding the potential of experiencing negative health consequences of smoking (and of other health-risk behaviours) are common: i.e. 'It won't happen to me as I smoke less than other people my age' – see Chapter 5 ☛.

- *Stress and distress.* Stress is often cited as a factor which maintains smoking (see below), and there is also evidence of a role for stress in smoking initiation (see RESEARCH FOCUS). The recent National Longitudinal Study of Adolescent Health has also pointed to a role of depressive symptomatology in smoking onset (McCaffery *et al.* 2008).

Smoking maintenance

Reasons for continuing to smoke are not necesarily the same as reasons given for initiation. There is clear evidence of the biologically addictive properties of smoking, due to tobacco's active ingredient, the alkaloid, nicotine, which activates 'reward pathways' involving the neurotransmitter dopamine in the brain, thus perpetuating the need to repeatedly intake nicotine to avoid 'withdrawal' symptoms (Jarvis 2004).

However people who continue to smoke report psychological reasons for continuing such as:

- pleasure or enjoyment of the behaviour, taste and effects reinforces positive attitudes towards smoking;
- smoking out of habit (this could reflect psychological and/or physical dependence);
- smoking as a form of stress self-management/coping, anxiety control;
- a lack of belief in their ability to stop smoking.

Smoking is very much a learned behaviour and the psychological dependence that results for most, if not all, regular smokers is highly complex and depends greatly on the rewards and incentives received by smoking, and on the motivations and expectations that a person places on their smoking behaviour. For example, Cox and Klinger (2004) describe a motivational model of substance use based on consistent findings that people's decisions about substance use, including tobacco, are not necessarily rational but involve a range of motivational and emotional components. For example, a person considering their smoking behaviour may do so in relation to other aspects of their lives that they may or may not derive satisfaction from. Individuals without commitment to healthy life goals or the motivation to work towards attaining them are less likely to perceive their substance use as a problem and consider themselves as less able to change the behaviour.

Stopping smoking

Even people who stop smoking when aged between 50 and 60 can avoid most of their subsequent risk of developing lung cancer or other smoking-related disease or disability (Bratzler *et al.* 2002) and quitting at 55 can gain a male on average 5 life years (based on 50 years of follow-up of a sample of British male doctors, Doll *et al.*

RESEARCH FOCUS

Does perceived stress influence adolescent smoking?

Byrne, D.G. and Mazanov, J. (2003). Adolescent stress and future smoking behaviour: a prospective investigation. *Journal of Psychosomatic Research*, 54: 313–21.

Smoking behaviour generally commences in adolescence, and research has revealed an array of influences on its uptake, as described above and in Chapter 2 👉, in terms of socio-economic influences. The experience of stress has been associated with the maintenance of adult smoking, but little work has explored this association in adolescence. Furthermore, if general and specific aspects of stress were found to predict smoking onset in young people, this would have important implications for preventive interventions. Byrne and Mazanov (2003) therefore set out to examine whether stress was a factor in smoking initiation among Australian adolescents. In order to address this causal question, they employed a **longitudinal design** and hypothesised that adolescent non-smokers at baseline who experienced stress in an intervening year would be more likely to become smokers than non-stressed non-smokers.

Method

Over 2,600 school pupils aged approximately 16 (range 14–18) entered the study having been recruited from 15 Australian schools who agreed to support the study (out of 29 schools invited). Twelve schools remained in the study, and 64 per cent of the sample completed a follow-up (mean age 17, 16-month range 15–19) assessment twelve months later. This resulted in 1,419

> ### longitudinal (design)
> responses assessed in a study that have been taken on more than one occasion over time, either prospectively (future-oriented) or retrospectively (based on recall of past events). Prospective longitudinal studies are more powerful, and such methods are important to studies where assessment of change is important.

participants, of whom 21 per cent of boys and 26 per cent of girls were current smokers. In terms of measures employed, participants completed a battery of questionnaires, addressing: socio-demographic variables; smoking behaviour, and patterns and contexts in which smoking took place (for smokers only); sources and intensity of stress using a measure previously developed by the authors which consists of seven subscales addressing potential sources of stress (school; family conflict; parental control; school performance; future uncertainty; perceived educational irrelevance; interactions with opposite sex); and a measure of psychological distress, the GHQ12 (Goldberg 1997).

Parental approval had to be given in order for students under 18 years old to participate, but the authors do not note how many failed to obtain this approval and thus were unable to take part. The study was carried out in school time at Time 1, with questionnaires being mailed out only at T2 to participants who were not in school at the time of data collection. The school did not have access to individual data, thus student confidentiality was maintained.

Results

The authors present an array of descriptive analyses including data showing that there were significant gender differences in both distress and stress, whereby girls reported higher distress and stress from family conflict, parental control, school performance, future uncertainty and opposite sex interactions. The authors do point out, however, that the actual levels of distress and stress were not likely to be clinically significant in this sample. It would have helped the reader to see this, had maximum possible scores been presented for each of the stress subscales, as this is an important finding.

Only a small number of non-smokers at T1 had become smokers by T2 (25 boys, 5.4 per cent; 15 girls, 3.4 per cent) and the percentage of smokers in both genders was less at T2. The authors note that attrition, i.e. drop-out from the study, was higher among smokers than non-smokers, which possibly explains this finding. Pupils who failed to complete the follow-up also reported a significantly higher number of friends who smoked at T1 than did those who took part in both phases of the study.

Even though the numbers who became smokers were limited, the authors tested their hypothesis that stress levels would precede smoking onset. Interesting gender differences emerged. For boys, only the stress of attending school distinguished between those who remained non-smokers at both time points, and those who commenced smoking between time points, with smoking uptake being associated with higher stress of attending school. In contrast, reporting higher stress from attending school, family conflict, parental control, and perceived educational irrelevance distinguished those who started smoking from those who remained non-smokers.

Discussion

The authors rightly note that the loss to follow-up of a significant proportion of the sample (47.2 per cent of boys and 44.4 per cent of girls), with evidence of greater incidence of smoking, friends who smoked, and low parental educational levels among those who failed to complete the follow-up, has some bearing on the generalisabiity of their findings. In spite of this, however, the sample size remains large enough to test their main hypothesis. The hypothesis that stress is associated with smoking uptake was not upheld for

boys. The weak association with stress of attending school, the authors suggest, may reflect low academic ability or low attainment in the family, both factors associated with smoking uptake generally. Among girls, however, the evidence is stronger, with associations between commencing smoking and all but two of the stress subscales (but not the distress measure). More girls in this sample smoked: however, only 3.4 per cent became smokers between T1 and T2 and so these results should perhaps be interpreted with more caution than the authors exhibit. However, the findings of this study are consistent with other surveys of gender and stress, and gender and smoking, and so the authors conclude that the implications of their findings are for the provision of stress management strategies for girls at a stage before smoking has been adopted, in order to potentially prevent smoking uptake.

Curiously, the authors do not consider the role of social background (e.g. the child's academic ability or parental educational attainment) in explaining the association between stress and smoking shown for girls as they do when explaining the finding for boys. As we have seen in Chapter 2 ☛, socio-economic correlates and predictors of health behaviour exist for both genders (and see Payne 2006 for a review), and therefore is likely to be implicated also on the findings for girls in this paper. Stress is likely to be only one of many possible causes of smoking uptake.

2004). Better still, stopping when aged 30 leads to more than 90 per cent of lung cancer risk being avoided (Peto et al. 2000) and approximately 10 life years gained (Doll et al. 2004). Attempts to help people to stop smoking are generally viewed positively by the public, and in fact the majority of smokers themselves wish to stop smoking. For example, two-thirds of smokers surveyed in 1996 as part of the UK General Household survey reported wanting to give up (Office for National Statistics 1998). It has been found that stopping smoking is more likely among individuals of a higher socio-economic status (dispelling expectations of significant downturns in smoking among those of lower socio-economic status caused by continual increases in cigarette prices). In addition, a 6.5-year follow-up study of over 1,300 smokers in the Netherlands found that the higher the level of

education, the greater the success rates for smoking cessation (Droomers et al. 2002). Whether this effect is directly attributable to higher levels of knowledge and understanding about potential health consequences, or whether it is confounded by social class (perhaps quitters in higher social classes have fewer smoking acquaintances and friends than non-quitters), remains unclear. Various studies have shown that smoking networks are associated with quitting to a larger degree than health beliefs, whereby not being part of a smoking network facilitates cessation (e.g. Rose et al. 1996). Barriers to cessation, including for some, a fear of weight gain (for example, a study of Danish adults aged between 30 and 60, Pisinger and Jorgensen 2007), are considered in Chapter 5 ☛. Chapters 6 and 7 ☛ describe interventions aimed at promoting smoking cessation.

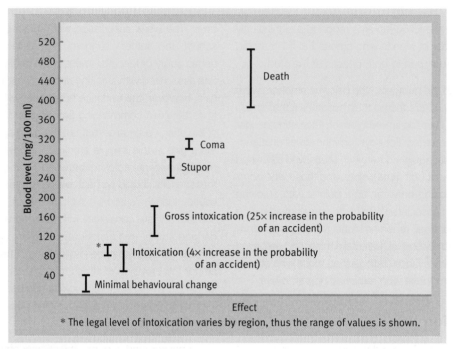

Figure 3.4 The particular consequences correlated with different levels of alcohol in a person's bloodstream

Source: adapted from Julien (1996: 109).

Alcohol consumption

Alcohol (ethanol) is 'the second most widely used psycho-active substance in the world (after caffeine)' (Julien 1996: 101). In Westernised cultures it is also considered an integral part of many life events, such as weddings, birthdays and even funerals, and its social use is widespread. Rarely does a day go by in the British media without reports of an association between antisocial behaviour and binge drinking. While the under-25s do tend to 'binge' drink more than older individuals, the social problems caused by drinking are by no means confined to this age group. For example, a recent poll of 2,221 adults (YouGov poll commissioned by the British Society of Gastroenterology in 2010), and reported in the media in February 2011, points to a high degree of social consequences of drinking behaviour (loss of relationships, domestic violence, work absenteeism) and of personal injury: for example 27 per cent of 18–24-year-olds, and 31 per cent of 25–34-year-olds reported injuring themselves while drunk.

While it has been reported (EC 2006) that 55 million adults drink at harmful levels in the EU, only a small number of people will, however, become dependent

on alcohol (perhaps one in ten). This challenges the dominant theory in this domain, which is that of a dependence model. It is not the case that all alcohol-related problems arise from situations of dependency: in fact the majority do not.

Negative health effects of excessive alcohol consumption

Although alcohol is commonly perceived as a stimulant, it is in fact a central nervous system depressant. Low doses cause behavioural disinhibition, while high levels of intoxication lead to a 25-fold increase in the likelihood of an accident, and extremely high doses severely affect respiratory rate, which can cause coma and even death (see Figure 3.4). It is not only alcohol dependence that causes health problems; so too can acute or prolonged episodes of heavy drinking. Patterns of drinking, as well as the volume consumed, is therefore relevant to health outcomes. Heavy alcohol consumption is implicated in accidents (while driving or operating machinery, for example); in behavioural problems (aggression, suicide, marital disharmony, etc.), and in diseases such as liver cirrhosis, liver and oesophageal cancer, stroke and epilepsy. Hart *et al.* (1999) carried out a 21-year follow-up study among 5,766 Scottish men and found that those who consumed more than 35 units of alcohol a week were at twice the risk of death from stroke than men whose drinking was at light or moderate levels. However, if the amounts of alcohol consumed are low to moderate and the pattern of drinking does not include binges, the World Health Report states that alcohol's relationship to CHD, stroke and diabetes mellitus, is in fact a beneficial one (WHO 2002). (See also IN THE SPOTLIGHT on p. 71.)

There is significant variation across Europe and elsewhere in terms of the volumes of alcohol consumed (World Health Organization 2003, and in the percentage of total liver cirrhosis mortality that is attributed to alcoholic liver cirrhosis. Between 1987 and 1995, for example, a massive 90 per cent of Finnish male cirrhosis deaths were attributed to alcohol-related liver cirrhosis, as opposed to 56 per cent among French males, 45 per cent among UK males, 33 per cent among Irish males (a third of a relatively low number as seen above), and 10 per cent among Spanish males.

Culture and social policy are extremely important in predicting drinking behaviour. Consider, for example, Finland, where strict legislation on alcohol sales and consumption was liberalised in the mid-1970s and where cirrhosis deaths showed subsequent increases in the 1980s and 1990s.

Table 3.1 Deaths from selected alcohol-related causes per 100,000 (all ages) for selected countries

	Males	Females
UK 1990	91.95	37.61
UK 2000	71.95	30.68
UK 2005	73.51	31.61
Spain 1990	175.23	47.45
Spain 2000	91.89	24.43
Spain 2005	79.82	21.73
Poland 1990	236.18	58.20
Poland 2000	149.19	39.66
Poland 2005	149.64	36.24
Netherlands 1990	79.25	36.35
Netherlands 2000	60.97	27.62
Netherlands 2005	n.a.	n.a.
Finland 1990	221.40	62.75
Finland 2000	139.03	46.08
Finland 2005	143.77	44.39

Liver cirrhosis is not the only cause of death attributed to alcohol. The European Commission estimates that 195,000 deaths across the EU each year are due to alcohol-related liver disease, accidents or violence, and in fact 1 in 4 deaths for young men aged 15–29 and 1 in 10 deaths for young women in this age range are attributed to alcohol (EC 2006). The WHO describe a selection of alcohol-related causes including: cancer of oesophagus and larynx, alcohol dependence syndrome, chronic liver disease and cirrhosis. Separate data on liver cancer deaths were not available and so the figures below (Table 3.1) should be viewed as rough indicators of alcohol-related deaths.

Table 3.1 shows that when examining these data for the years 1990, 2000 and 2005, a decrease in alcohol-related deaths per 100,000 can be seen across the decade between 1990 and 2000; however, this reduction is not maintained in all selected countries and, worryingly, in the UK a slight increase can be seen between 2000 and 2005, among both genders (Leon and McCambridge 2006). In fact the gradual increase in alcohol-related deaths seen in annual figures collated in the UK since the early 1990s now reflects a doubling in deaths between 1991 and 2007 (ONS 2010). Males are twice as likely to die from alcohol-related causes generally defined than are females.

Recommended levels of drinking

Different individuals respond differently to the same amount of alcohol intake, depending on factors such as body weight, food intake and metabolism, the social context in which the drinking occurs, and the individual's cognitions and expectations. It is therefore difficult to determine 'safe' levels of drinking alcohol. While the recommended guidelines on 'safe' levels of alcohol consumption vary from country to country, the UK government's recommended limit for weekly consumption has recently been raised from 21 units of alcohol to 28 units for males, and from 14 to 21 units of alcohol for females (where half a pint of normal-strength lager or a standard single measure of spirit (1/6 gill) or wine of average strength (11–12 per cent alcohol) = 1 unit). The lower level of these guidelines had been in existence since 1986, and although the move to increase the guidelines to 28 and 21 units for males and females, respectively, came in 1995 (Royal College of Physicians 1995), many health advisers continue to use the 21/14 limits. Some guidelines also recommend one or two alcohol-free days per

Table 3.2 International definitions of what comprises a 'standard' drink (alcohol in g)

Austria	6
Ireland and UK	8
Iceland	9.5
Netherlands	9.9
Italy, Australia, Spain	10
Finland	11
Denmark, France	12
Canada	13.5
Portugal, USA	14
Hungary	17
Japan	19.75

Source: International Center for Alcohol Policies (1998).

week. There is some confusion internationally as to what constitutes a 'standard' measure or 'unit'. Does it mean the strength of the alcohol or the volume? For example, a standard drink in Japan is defined by government guidelines as 19.75 g alcohol, whereas in the UK a standard drink would contain 8 g, and there are many variations in between, as seen in Table 3.2. The European Commission refer to safe levels as being under 40 g of alcohol a day for men (about 4 standard drinks) and under 20 g per day for women (about 2 standard drinks).

Prevalence of drinking alcohol in the young

A survey of over 7,000 English 11–15-year-olds (2000 Survey DoH 2000a, National Centre for Social Research) showed a significant increase in the amount of alcohol consumed in this age group over a ten-year period, from 5.3 units per week in 1990 to 10.4 units in 2000. The authors suggest that the growth in marketing and sale of alcopops (alcoholic drinks with sweetening and flavourings, marketed with a trendy appearance) played a role in the increased consumption pattern of these young people. Twenty-four per cent of this sample had had an alcoholic drink in the previous week: 5 per cent of 11-year-olds and 48 per cent of 15-year-olds. Children in Wales (where both authors of this textbook are based!) top the European league for the numbers who drink weekly and get drunk (Paton 1999).

There is concern about adolescent drinking in many European countries. Sweden, a country with historically high government control over alcohol production and sale, actively campaigns for non-consumption of alcohol among teenagers. However, an impressive survey of nearly 13,000 16-year-olds found that about 80 per cent had consumed alcohol, 25 per cent of whom had drunk illegal, smuggled alcohol, and 40 per cent had drunk home-distilled alcohol. Although levels of consumption are not clear, alcohol is clearly not outwith the grasp of these teenagers (Romelsjo and Branting 2000). Also of concern is the evidence of a relationship between alcohol consumption, unprotected sexual intercourse (Conner *et al.* 2008) and teenage pregnancy (see IN THE SPOTLIGHT in the Smoking section on page 62).

Are there positive effects of drinking alcohol?

It is generally accepted that there is a linear relationship between the amount of alcohol consumed over time

Plate 3.2 The increase in teenage binge drinking is of concern, particularly amongst females

Source: Alamy Limited/ACE STOCK LIMITED.

IN THE SPOTLIGHT

Is drinking red wine . . . and eating chocolate . . . good for your health?

For some time, it has been known that fruit and vegetable consumption is associated with a reduced rate of some cancers, in particular cancer of the gastrointestinal tract (e.g. Potter *et al.* 1993). This has been attributed to the presence of **antioxidant** compounds known as 'polyphenols', such as the flavonoids (specifically flavonol), and in the case of tomatoes, lycopene.

Red wine, being derived from red grapes, contains many different polyphenolic compounds including flavonol, and its moderate intake has been associated with reduced cardiovascular deaths (e.g. German and Walzem 2000; Wollin and Jones 2001). It appears that by reducing oxidation these substances (derived from fruits, vegetables, but also tea and ginger) protect arteries from the damaging effects of high levels of circulating serum cholesterol and can protect therefore against CHD (Engler and Engler 2006). More recently, it has been proposed that red wine polyphenols may also be beneficial by inhibiting the initiation of **carcinogenesis** due to their antioxidative or anti-inflammatory properties. Additionally, polyphenols may act as suppressing agents by inhibiting the growth of mutated cells or by inducing apoptosis, i.e. cell death. Recent laboratory and animal studies (e.g. Briviba *et al.* 2002) have shown that polyphenols

isolated from red wine did in fact inhibit the growth of different colon carcinoma cells, but not breast cancer cells.

Chocolate also contains flavonoids, particularly that with a high cocoa content, i.e. dark chocolate (Engler and Engler 2006). This is not to say that over-indulgence is recommended, but a small amount of dark chocolate, eaten alone or together with a small glass of red wine, may in fact be good for you!

Medical authorities and public health officials are wary of announcing health 'benefits' of behaviours usually portrayed as detrimental to health, and results of this nature need to be carefully checked and double-checked. Even the authors of one of the research studies, finding a positive effect of alcohol on HDL level, underplayed the implications of their findings (Linn *et al.* 1993: 811). It is unlikely that many individuals presenting to their GPs with health concerns around a family history of heart disease are told to increase their light alcohol consumption to moderate, and instead will most likely be advised to follow a low-fat diet, yet the protection offered is similar! When the most recent findings relating to cancer reached the attention of the media, it resulted in the kind of headlines that would lead you to believe a cure for cancer had been found! However, there remains a need for further research among human samples, with tight controls over other contributory factors. It will be some years before the evidence as to the effects of red wine drinking on people already with cancer becomes clear. In relation to coronary heart disease, however, the evidence is of longer standing, and it would appear that moderate ingestion of alcohol, and not solely red wine, has health-protective effects (e.g. Nestlé 1997).

antioxidants

oxidation of low-density lipoprotein (LDL or 'bad') cholesterol has been shown to be important in the development of fatty deposits in the arteries; antioxidants are chemical properties (polyphenols) of some substances (e.g. red wine) thought to inhibit the process of oxidation.

carcinogenesis

the process by which normal cells become cancer cells (i.e. carcinoma).

Things to think about and research yourself

● Does red wine differ from white wine in terms of its potential effects on health, and if so, how?

● How might some people interpret these kinds of findings – what beliefs might be reinforced?

and the accumulation of alcohol-related illness. However, there are a few question marks around the level of drinking that is damaging. There is now evidence that moderate alcohol consumption may be health-protective, with a J-shaped relationship found between alcohol consumption and CHD risk whereby abstinence confers a higher risk than moderate drinking, although not as high as risk conferred by heavy drinking (Doll *et al.* 1994), and, even reduced mortality (Klatsky 2008). This surprising finding has emerged from both cross-sectional and prospective studies. The consensus view is that light to moderate alcohol intake reduces circulating low-density lipoprotein (LDL) levels (high levels are a known risk factor for CHD) (e.g. Shaper *et al.* 1994; see IN THE SPOTLIGHT on p. 71). However, there are problems in concluding from this, and from studies of non-drinkers where risk of CHD was found to be higher than average, that not drinking confers increased risk. Non-drinkers may choose not to consume alcohol because they are already in poor health, or because they are members of particular religious or ethnic groups that forbid such use: these factors may hide some other 'cause' of CHD. It is safer to conclude only that heavy drinking has negative effects on health that increase in line with consumption; that moderate levels of drinking may not increase risk and may in fact be protective against CHD (although the protective effects are lost on people who smoke); and that the effects of not drinking at all need further exploration.

Why do some people develop drinking problems?

The reasons why young people start to drink alcohol are, as with most social behaviours, many and varied, with genetics and environment playing important roles. Two commonly cited reasons for having that first drink of alcohol are curiosity and sociability (e.g. Morrison and Plant 1991), but curiosity, unlike sociability, is unlikely to be cited as the reason for continued use. For most people, drinking does not become a problem; much research is conducted to distinguish individuals who maintain safe levels of drinking from those who develop problem drinking. The main aspects considered are:

● Genetics and family history of alcohol abuse: children of problem drinkers are more likely to develop problem drinking than children of non-problem

drinkers (e.g. Heather and Robertson 1997). Evidence is inconclusive as parent–child drinking tendencies could also be socialised (see below), although adoptee studies support evidence of heredity to an extent.

● The pre-existence of certain psychopathology: mood disorders, anxious **predisposition**, sensation-seeking personality tendencies (e.g. Clark and Sayette 1993; Khantzian 2003; Zuckerman 1979, 1984), although evidence as to personality's role in drinking, or indeed in other substance-use behaviour, remains controversial (Morrison 2003).

● The social learning experience: social learning theory considers alcohol abuse or dependence to be a socially acquired and learned behaviour that has received reinforcement (internal or external, physical, social or emotional rewards). Addiction may result from repeatedly seeking the pleasurable effects of the substance itself (e.g. Wise 1998).

Among older people, evidence points to lower levels of alcohol consumption, and in elderly samples, problem drinking has been shown to be influenced by physical health, access to social opportunities and financial status, with the affluent elderly having higher rates of drinking problems (Livingston and Hinchliffe 1993). For some individuals, however, an increase in alcohol consumption can be attributed in part to loneliness, bereavement or physical symptomatology (e.g. Atkinson 1994).

Alcohol dependence

Alcohol problems and how those with such problems are viewed by society have changed over time, from being seen as the immoral behaviour of weak individuals, unable to exert personal control over their consumption during the seventeenth–eighteenth centuries, to being the behaviour of passive victims of an evil and powerful substance in the nineteenth century. The earlier 'moral' view considered individuals as responsible for their

---

predisposition

predisposing factors increase the likelihood of a person engaging in a particular behaviour, such as genetic influences on alcohol consumption.

behaviour and therefore the ethos of treatment was punishment. The latter view considered the individual to have less control over their behaviour, and as such the prohibition of alcohol sales (as seen in the USA) was considered an appropriate societal response, and treatment was offered to those 'victims' who 'succumbed'. The medical treatment of individuals with alcohol problems reflects the beginnings of a disease concept of addiction where the drug was seen as being the problem. However, by the early twentieth century, it was clear that prohibition had failed and the model of alcoholism developed into one that placed responsibility back on to the individual. In 1960, Jellinek described alcoholism as a disease but considered both the nature of the substance and the pre-existing characteristics of the person who used it. While it became accepted that alcohol could be used by the majority without any resulting harm, a minority of individuals developed alcohol dependence, and for these individuals pre-existing genetic and psychological 'weaknesses' were acknowledged. Addiction was seen as an acquired, permanent state of being over which the individual could regain control only by means of abstinence, and treatment reflected this: for example, the self-help organisation, Alcoholics Anonymous, founded in 1935, had the primary goal of helping individuals to achieve lifelong abstinence.

However, in psychology during the early twentieth century, the growth of **behaviourism** brought with it new methods of treatment for those with drinking problems that drew from the principles of social learning theory and conditioning theory. These perspectives consider behaviour to result from learning and from the reinforcement that any behaviour receives. Excessive alcohol consumption, according to these theories, can be 'unlearned' by applying behavioural principles to treatment. Such treatment would aim to identify the cues for an individual's drinking behaviour and the type of reinforcement individuals receive for their behaviour (see Chapter 6 ☛). These approaches therefore consider the individual, their drinking behaviour and the social environment. Nowadays, at least in the UK and elsewhere in Europe, abstinence is considered as one possible treatment outcome among others, such as controlled drinking. In controlled drinking, individuals are encouraged to restrict their consumption to certain occasions/settings/ times of day, or to control the alcoholic content of drinks consumed by, for example, switching to low-alcohol alternatives (Heather and Robertson 1997).

> **behaviourism**
> the belief that psychology is the study of observables and therefore that behaviour, not mental processes, is central.
>
> **primary prevention**
> intervention aimed at changing risk factors prior to disease development.

Patterns of heavy drinking laid down in late childhood and early adulthood tend to set the pattern for heavy drinking in adulthood, and alcohol-related health problems such as liver cirrhosis tend to accumulate in middle age. It should not be assumed, however, that heavy or problem drinking is more common in those less well educated or of lower socio-ecnomic status as evidence in this regard is quite mixed. The better educated have often been shown more likely to engage in various forms of risky behaviour but to be less likely to develop problem drinking (e.g. Caldwell *et al.* 2008). However, a recent study (Huerta and Borgonovi 2010) using a large sample of almost 10,000 individuals aged 34 years at the time of the study (all drawn from the British Cohort Study, which is a sample of all those born in a specific week in 1970) found that higher educational attainment was associated with increased odds of daily alcohol consumption and with problem drinking, particularly among females. However, this is a very specific cohort of those in their mid-30s and so we cannot assume from such findings that relationships do not exist at other ages, for example in teenage, or for other forms of drinking, such as binge drinking.

Health promotion efforts therefore have two targets: **primary prevention** in terms of educating children about the risks of heavy drinking and about 'safe' levels of consumption; and secondary prevention in terms of changing the behaviour of those already engaged in heavy drinking. Examples of these are described in Chapters 6 and 7 ☛.

Illicit drug use

As Figure 3.1 showed at the start of this chapter, the 'burden' of disability-adjusted life years attributed to the use of illicit drugs is significantly less than that attributed to alcohol, smoking, or even to a lack of exercise. However, the mere mention of illicit use of drugs (some legally obtained e.g. valium, some not e.g. heroin), can cause anxiety in teachers, parents, the police, the government, and in young people themselves. The statistics, however, at least for health and disease consequences perhaps do not support this. Why then is so much negative feeling attached to illicit drug using behaviour?

In part this can be explained by perceptions of such drug use which are driven by one of two models – a dependence model where illicit drug users are thought to be addicted, possibly ill and out of control; or a criminal model, where they are seen as irresponsible, delinquent and even dangerous. However, it is not the case that the use of all illicit drugs leads to dependency, for example Ecstacy, even though there are health risks attached to use; and it is likewise not the case that all those who engage in illicit drug use turn to theft or become violent as a result. The method of ingestion, perhaps more than the substance itself, has led people to associate some forms of drug use – injecting drug use – with serious diseases including HIV and Hepatitis C.

While about a third of UK resident individuals aged between 16 and 59 years old (British Crime Survey, Hoare and Flatley 2008) will try an illegal drug at least once in their lifetime, unlike in the case for alcohol very few go on to use such substances regularly. Cannabis is top of the list, but has itself a relatively low prevalence in terms of use 'in the past year' (7.6 per cent).

As with drinking alcohol or smoking tobacco when underage (also illegal behaviour), there are a range of psychological and social influence on a person's first use of an illegal drug, and a range of factors that contribute to behaviour maintenance. Whether influenced by peers, reacting to stress or availability, motivated by a desire to escape negative thoughts, emotions or situations, the prevention of initiation to illicit drug use can and should be treated in the same way as alcohol use or smoking. In terms of reducing use among regular users, however, for a minority there will be, as with alcohol, issues of physical and psychological dependence to deal with. To a large extent the treatment of alcohol dependence will be exactly the same as the treatment for opiate dependence, at least in terms of any cognitive or motivational therapy. What will differ will have been people's responses to the individuals concerned and how, perhaps, they have been treated by health and social care services.

It is not the purpose of this book to do anything more than to raise, for the reader, the question of societal judgement and how society can sometimes wrongly make a special case of some behaviours over others. It is worth reflecting on whether equal attention and resources could be allocated towards the more prevalent and potentially more harmful behaviours such as alcohol and tobacco smoking.

Unprotected sexual behaviour

Negative health consequences of unprotected sexual intercourse

Notwithstanding unwanted pregnancy (see IN THE SPOTLIGHT on p. 62), unprotected sexual intercourse carries with it several risks: infections such as chlamydia and HIV. Sexual behaviour as a risk factor for disease has received growing attention since the 'arrival' of the human immunodeficiency virus (HIV) in the early 1980s and the recognition that AIDS affects heterosexually active populations as well as homosexual populations and injecting drug users who share their injecting equipment. Unlike the other behaviours described in this chapter, sexual practices are not inherently individual behaviour but behaviour that occurs in the context of an interaction between two individuals. Sex is fundamentally 'social' behaviour (although drinking behaviour may also be considered 'social', the actual physical act of drinking is down to the individual). As such, researchers studying sexual practices and the influences upon them, and health educators attempting to promote safer sexual practices such as condom use, face particular challenges. However, it is worth persevering, given the findings of a Cochrane Review of the evidence as to the effectiveness of condom use in reducing heterosexual transmission of HIV (Weller and Davis-Beaty 2007). This review concluded that consistent use of condoms (defined as use for all acts of penetrative vaginal intercourse) led to an 80 per cent reduction in HIV incidence.

HIV prevalence

The World Health Organization (1999, 2002) had estimated that about 40 million people had been infected with HIV, of whom about 14 million had died. More recently the UNAIDS survey of cases up to the end of 2009 reported that between 31 and 35 million people are currently infected, with between 2.3 and 2.8 million being diagnosed in 2009 alone. While 70 per cent of HIV cases are concentrated in Africa, there is cause for concern in Eastern European and Central Asian countries where figures have tripled since 2000 (although some of this may be due to increased openness in reporting).

It is estimated that the UK (end of 2009) has 86,500 people living with HIV and with population prevalence therefore around 0.1 per cent the situation is not dissimilar to that found elsewhere in northern Europe, such as in Germany, the Netherlands and Scandinavia. However, the southern European countries of Spain, France, Portugal and Italy have much higher infection figures, attributed in large part to the prevalence of injecting drug use (PHLS Communicable Disease Surveillance Centre 2002).

In many countries, unprotected heterosexual sex has to a large extent taken over from homosexual sex and injecting drug use (IDU) as a route of infection, initially appearing to add weight to research findings of behaviour change among homosexual men (Katz 1997) and offering support to the effectiveness of syringe-exchange schemes for injecting drug users. For example, although needle sharing still occurs, in the UK diagnoses of HIV among IDUs have shown a steady decline over the past two decades or more since figures were first collated in 1985 (588 cases), to 211 diagnoses in 1995, 143 new diagnoses in 2001 and 149 in 2008. By June 2010 about 5 per cent of

all cases were attributed to IDU in compari[...] for heterosexually acquired infection an[...] male homosexually acquired infection (H[...] Agency 2010 (see also Figures 3.5 and 3.6)). In fact, male homosexually acquired infection has increased gradually year on year since 2003, providing support for findings of an upturn in the practice of unprotected anal sex (e.g. Chen *et al.* 2002; Dodds and Mercey 2002). Part of this downturn in the practice of safer sex may be attributable to the fact that people consider AIDS a disease for which there are a growing number of treatments, and thus the perceived lethality of the disease, and the implicit requirement to practise safer sex, may have been undermined. Additionally, individuals' perceptions of risk may be wrong.

Heterosexual infection has greater implications for women (as the 'receptors' of semen during sexual intercourse) than men, and in the USA this is evidenced in increased female HIV figures (e.g. Wortley and Fleming 1997; Logan *et al.* 2002). The prevalence of HIV infection in pregnant women is relatively low in Europe, but monitoring has found cases to have risen, suggesting an urgent need for development of further antenatal screening services.

Chlamydia, HPV and other sexually transmitted diseases

Of growing concern is the upturn in figures relating to the sexually transmitted diseases or infections (STD/

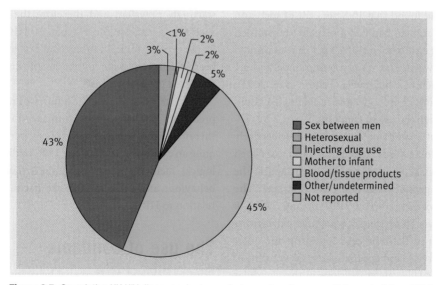

Figure 3.5 Cumulative UK HIV diagnoses by transmission route, all years until the end of June 2010

Source: from www.avert.org/uk-transmission-route.htm, reproduced with permission from AVERT.

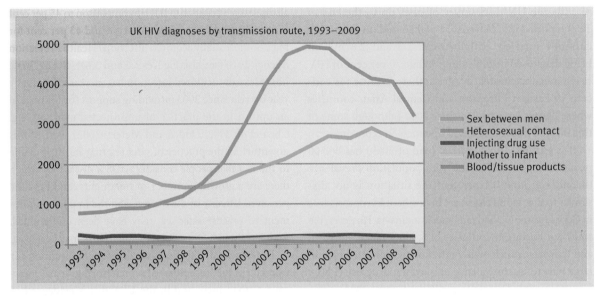

Figure 3.6 UK HIV diagnoses by transmission route, 1993–2009

Source: from www.avert.org/uk-transmission-route.htm, reproduced with permission from AVERT.

STIs) of chlamydia, genital herpes simplex and genital warts, most common among adolescents and young adults. Chlamydia is a curable disease and is also the most preventable cause of infertility: however, a recent national screening survey of prevalence in young people found that 13.8 per cent of those under 16 years old, 10.5 per cent of those aged 16–19 and 7.2 per cent of those aged 20–24 had this infection (Moens *et al.* 2003). Another survey of sexual behaviour, among 11,161 adults aged 16–44, carried out urine testing on half of the sample and found that 10.8 per cent of men and 12.6 per cent of women had had a sexually transmitted infection, 3.6 per cent of men and 4.1 per cent of women had had genital warts, and 1.4 per cent of men and 3.1 per cent of women had chlamydia (Fenton *et al.* 2001). These are worrying figures, given that chlamydia could be avoided through the use of condoms.

A subgroup of a family of viruses known collectively as Human Papilloma Virus (HPV) have been associated with abnormal tissue and cell growth implicated in the development of genital warts and cervical cancer. The high-risk type viruses labelled HPV-16 and HPV-18 together cause over 70 per cent of squamous cell cancers (cancer develops in flat-type cells found on the outer surface of the cervix), and approximately 50 per cent of adenocarcinomas (the cancer develops in the glandular cells which line the cervix). About 95 per cent of cervical cancers are squamous cell type and about 5 per cent are adenocarcinomas. There are also low-risk type of HPV viruses which are associated with the development of genital warts, which do not cause cervical cancer in themselves but which are a sexually transmitted infection which cause significant discomfort. HPV is not contagious as such, but can be transmitted from a single act of sexual intercourse with an infected person.

While condom use reduces the risk of infection, HPV 'lives' on the whole genital area and therefore a condom alone is insufficient to prevent transmission. HPV is startingly prevalent and therefore the discovery of a vaccination against those types of HPV which cause 70 per cent of cervical cancers (but not genital warts) has been billed as a major public health discovery. This is discussed in Chapter 4 ☞.

It is likely that we will see a flurry of research into the predictors of uptake and non-uptake of vaccination and, therefore, from a health psychology perspective, this is quite an exciting time. Chapter 5 ☞ outlines key psychological factors and sociocognitive models of health behaviour and these models are likely to be tested in relation to HPV.

The use of condoms

Prior to HIV and AIDS, sexual behaviour was generally considered to be 'private' behaviour and somewhat under-researched (with the exception of clinical studies of individuals experiencing sexual difficulties). The lack of information as to the sexual practices of the general population made it initially extremely difficult to assess the potential for the spread of HIV infection. One notable survey that was triggered by this need for information was the National Survey of Sexual Attitudes and Lifestyles, conducted with nearly 19,000 adults (aged 16–59) living in Britain in 1990–91 (Wellings *et al.* 1994). It was found that:

- Young people use condoms more commonly than older people.

- Females tend to use condoms less often than males.

- For both males and females condom use was greatest with a 'new' sexual partner (34 and 41 per cent of males and females, respectively, used condoms on all occasions of sex with a single new partner).

- Condom use declined dramatically in those who reported having had multiple new partners (17.5 and 10 per cent, respectively).

- The rate of condom use was lowest in males who had multiple partners who were not new sexual partners (only 5.7 per cent always used a condom).

- Female condom use was less affected by whether multiple partners were 'new' to them or not (14.3 per cent always used a condom with not new multiple partners).

This survey was repeated in 2001 with over 11,000 men and women aged 16–44 years and with a deliberate intention of boosting the cultural mix of the sample which also over-represented London (NATSAL II; Erens *et al.* 2003). Although not as representative a national sample as the first survey, results regarding condom use (any use in the year prior to interview) were encouraging (Cassell *et al.* 2006). A significant increase in usage was reported in both males (from 43.3 per cent in 1990 to 51.4 per cent in 2000) and females (from 30.6 per cent in 1990 to 39.1 per cent in 2000). As in the first survey, condom use was highest among younger respondents and for those for whom the last sexual partner was 'new'. One important finding was the rate of condom use among those with multiple partners – those 'high-risk' individuals were the most likely to report condom use. Non-white ethnicity and being of a non-Christian religion was also found to be associated with greater condom use, highlighting the importance of ensuring representation across differing cultural and religious groupings. Among the heterosexual sample, the prevention of pregnancy was given as the primary reason for condom use, although in the younger sub-sample (16–24-year-olds) prevention of HIV and other STIs was of equal or greater concern. This may reflect increased awareness of HIV and sexual health in the decade between the two surveys, and provide support to those offering health education and health promotion (see Chapters 6 and 7 (☞).

Safer sex practices were not influenced solely by concerns about STIs but also by the type, number and length of sexually active relationships a person is engaged in. Condom use commonly begins to decline after six months within any given relationship. Many other factors have been been reported to act as barriers against safer sex behaviour, as we describe in the next section (see also Chapter 5 (☞).

Barriers to condom use

Alcohol intake has been found to reduce condom use in both younger and older individuals, heterosexuals and homosexuals (e.g. Gillies 1991), an effect sometimes attributed to the disinhibitory effects of alcohol. However, this author notes that alcohol use may simply be an indicator of general risk-taking behaviour (which includes non-use of condoms), and that further research is required to ascertain whether alcohol itself plays a direct causal role.

In terms of women and HIV prevention, many interpersonal, intrapersonal, cultural and contextual factors have been shown to interact and affect whether or not the woman feels able to control the use of condoms in sexual encounters (e.g. Bury *et al.* 1992; Sanderson and Jemmot 1996). In general, surveys of condom use among young women have found that while females share some of the negative attitudes towards condom use found among male samples (such as that condoms reduce spontaneity of behaviour or reduce sexual pleasure), and that they also tend to hold unrealistically optimistic estimates of personal risk of infection with STDs or HIV, women face additional barriers when considering condom use (Bryan *et al.* 1996, 1997; Hobfoll *et al.* 1994). These can include:

- anticipated male objection to a female suggesting condom use (denial of their pleasure);

- difficulty/embarrassment in raising the issue of condom use with a male partner;

● worry that suggesting use to a potential partner implies that either themselves or the partner is HIV-positive or has another STD;

● lack of self-efficacy or mastery in condom use.

These factors are not simply about the individual's own health beliefs and behavioural intentions regarding avoiding pregnancy, STDs or AIDS; they also highlight that sexual behaviour is a complex interpersonal interaction. Safer sexual behaviour perhaps requires multiple-level interventions that target not only individual health beliefs (such as those described in Chapter 5

☞) but also their interpersonal, communication and negotiating skills (see Chapters 6 and 7 ☞). Individual behaviour, where positively or negatively associated with health, can be a sensitive issue, with some people preferring to keep their practices and motivations to themselves. This can create many challenges for those interested in measuring health or risk behaviour with a view to developing understanding of it. While measurement issues are not confined to studies of health behaviour, they are particularly pertinent in this domain (see ISSUES below).

ISSUES

The challenge of measuring health behaviour

The research tradition assumes that the objects of study, e.g. health, illness, or in the context of this chapter, behaviour, remain as fixed entities in people's minds. However, without a researcher actually being present and observing the individual behaving over long periods of time, it is difficult to know whether what a person reports to the researcher (or clinician) accurately reflects their actual behaviour. Obtaining valid measures of behaviour is made increasingly difficult when one is interested in behaviour that is perhaps considered 'undesirable' (e.g. excessive alcohol or drug use), or when it is private (e.g. sexual behaviour). Researchers also face the challenge of knowing how best to define the behaviours under study, and yet it is only through appropriate definition that measurement becomes possible. For example, rather than defining exercise in terms of organised activity, it could be defined as any physical activity that requires energy expenditure; or in terms of drinking alcohol, whether a 'drink' is defined and counted in terms of standard 'units' (see alcohol section), or size of glass, or strength of alcohol. The definition adopted will influence the questions asked and, furthermore, questions need to address not just the type of behaviour performed but also aspects such as the frequency, duration, intensity, and even social context in which it is performed.

Where direct observation and/or objective measurement (for example, taking blood or urine sample) are not possible, researchers have to rely on *self-report*. When studies are interested in the frequency with which certain behaviour is performed, it is commonplace to ask study participants to complete a diary, for example of cigarettes/alcohol/foods consumed or activities undertaken. Participants in such studies are generally required to either record the relevant activity daily for a period of a week (any longer places high demand on participants), or to reflect back on the previous week's activity (a retrospective diary – RD). The latter has obvious memory demands – could you accurately recall how many units of alcohol you drank seven days ago? While there is no evidence of a systematic bias towards overestimation or underestimation (Maisto and Connors 1992; Shakeshaft *et al.* 1999), some studies attempt to cross-validate behavioural self-reports by obtaining observer ratings or blood samples. However, observation is not always ethical, and biochemical tests are intrusive and costly. Other studies rely on asking participants about their 'typical or average' behaviour: for example, they report the typical amount of alcohol consumed (quantity), and the 'typical or average' number of days on which they consume alcohol (frequency) (e.g. Norman *et al.* 1998). This method known as a quantity/frequency index (QFI) may, however, provide over-general information. Shakeshaft and colleagues (1999) compared an RD method with a

QFI, and found that the RD method elicited higher reported levels of weekly alcohol consumption than did the QFI. In fact, neither way may be totally accurate.

One way of minimising inaccuracies in reporting is by using continuous *self-monitoring techniques*, such as smoking or food consumption diaries, with short recording periods, e.g. hourly. This can be a useful method of establishing patterns of behaviour and the circumstances in which they occur. For example, food diaries commonly instruct the person completing them to note not only the time at which each meal or snack is consumed but also the location, whether anyone else was present, whether any particular 'cue' existed and the reasons for consumption. Some studies invite the person to note also whether they are currently experiencing positive or negative emotions. A potential limitation of self-monitoring is that it can be reactive; in other words, it acts as an intervention itself, with participants modifying their consumption on the basis of their increased awareness of their intake. Behaviour that is seen as undesirable is likely to decrease while being monitored, whereas desirable behaviour is likely to increase. This may be useful in a clinical context, where the intention of self-monitoring *is* behaviour change, but in a research context it may be obstructive: for example, it may prevent researchers from obtaining reliable baseline measurement of behaviour against which to evaluate the efficacy of an intervention programme. Reliance on self-monitoring data can also create problems clinically; for example, Warren and Hixenbaugh (1998) reviewed evidence that people with diabetes make up their self-monitored blood glucose levels and found that, in some studies, individuals did so in order to present a more positive clinical profile to their medical practitioner (i.e.

self-presentation bias/**social desirability bias**). This behaviour could potentially disadvantage treatment efficacy or disease management and outcomes.

Self-monitoring techniques are not the only data-collection technique which could potentially elicit self-presentation bias, as there is evidence that collecting data via *face-to-face interviews* can also elicit reporting bias. Face-to-face interviews enable researchers to seek more explanation for a person's behaviour by using open-ended questions such as 'Think back to your first under-age drink of alcohol. What would you say motivated it? How did you feel afterwards?' Interviews also facilitate the building of rapport with participants, which may be particularly important if the study requires participants to attend follow-up interviews or complete repeated assessments. Rapport may increase commitment to the study and improve retention rates; however, the interview process, content and style may also influence participants' responses. Some people may simply not report their 'risk behaviour' practices (e.g. illicit drug use, unprotected sexual intercourse) or lack of preventive behaviour practices (e.g. toothbrushing, exercising) in the belief they will be judged to be 'deviant', in poor health, or simply as being careless with their health (e.g. Davies and Baker 1987). Impression management is common; i.e. people monitor and control (actively construct) what they say in order to give particular impressions of themselves (or to achieve certain effects) to particular audiences (Allport 1920 first noted this in the domain of social psychology).

So how can you tell whether health behaviour data that are collected provide a true representation of behaviour or simply the outcome of self-presentational processes? It is probably best to assume that they are a bit of both, and when reading statistics regarding the prevalence of particular behaviour, stop to consider the methods used in generating the data and ask yourself what biases, if any, may be present.

---

social desirability bias

the tendency to answer questions about oneself or one's behaviour in a way that is thought likely to meet with social (or interviewer) approval.

SUMMARY

This chapter has defined health behaviour as those behaviours associated with health status, whether or not they are performed with the explicit goal of health protection, promotion or maintenance in mind. The behaviours addressed in this chapter are sometimes referred to as 'behavioural pathogens' or health-risk behaviour and includes smoking, heavy consumption of alcohol, unprotected sexual behaviour and an unhealthy diet. 'Behavioural immunogens' or health-enhancing behaviours, such as exercise, a balanced diet, health screening and immunisation behaviours are discussed in the next chapter.

This chapter has described behaviours with clear associations with prevalent illnesses, and as such they account for a vast amount of research enquiry within health psychology. A significant body of work has addressed the complexity of social, emotional and cognitive factors that contribute to the uptake and maintenance of health-damaging behaviour, and a range of theories and models of health behaviour which have been developed and tested are described in Chapter 5 ☞.

We concluded this chapter by bringing to the reader's attention some of the challenges to effective measurement of health behaviours and, as elsewhere in this text, we encourage readers to stop and think about the data on which a lot of the evidence we review is built, and to do this they may need some further individual reading.

Further reading

Connor, M., Sutherland, E.D., Kennedy, F. *et al.* (2008). Impact of alcohol on sexual decision-making: intentions to have unprotected sex. *Psychology and Health*, 23: 909–34.

This paper is worth a look because it reports three studies where the effects of alcohol intoxication on sexual decision-making depends on gender as well as on behaviourally relevant attitudes and beliefs.

Engler, M.B. and Engler, M.M. (2006). The emerging role of flavonoid-rich cocoa and chocolate in cardiovascular health and disease. *Nutrition Reviews*, 64: 109–18.

All too often we read about what we shouldn't do; this paper gives you a flavour for something you can do – eat chocolate! It is a nicely written paper summarising the current state of knowledge regarding flavonoids.

Orford, J. (2001). *Excessive Appetites: A Psychological View of Addictions*, 2nd edn. Chichester: Wiley.

For a thorough exploration of 'appetitive' behaviour including smoking, drinking, eating and sexual behaviour, this book is a classic read. Orford addresses both the changed societal views of health behaviour thought to be addictive and the psychological and physiological explanations of such behaviour.

Wardle, J. and Johnson, F. (2002). Weight and dieting: examining levels of weight concern in British adults. *International Journal of Obesity*, 26: 1144–9.

This paper points to the fact that many normal weight women wish to weigh less, thus buying in to the idea of 'thinner is better'. In spite of this, we still face an obesity epidemic and those who are overweight face being judged against this perceived 'ideal'.

For a useful overview of current Department of Health survey statistics pertaining to health behaviour and illness (UK):

www.doh.gov.uk/stats

For a copy of the recent UK survey of adolescent health and health behaviour, including recommendations for interventions:

www.bma/org.uk

For information about the HPV vaccination programme, look at this website. It offers a health encyclopedia to members of the public in order to provide up-to-date information about health conditions and their treatments:

www.nhsdirect.nhs.uk/articles/article.aspx?articleId=2336

For information regarding worldwide HIV and AIDS figures, campaigns and news:

http://www.avert.org/

Visit the website at **www.pearsoned.co.uk/morrison** for additional resources to help you with your study, including multiple choice questions, weblinks and flashcards.

Chapter 4
Health-protective behaviour

Learning outcomes

By the end of this chapter, you should have an understanding of:

- the behaviour found to have health-enhancing or health-protective effects

- the relevance of adherence to medicine and treatments, healthy diet, exercise, screening and immunisation to health across the lifespan

- the range and complexity of influences upon the uptake and maintenance of health-enhancing behaviour

Brain and body training treats ME, UK study says (BBC News, 18 Feb 2011)

Chronic Fatigue Syndrome, also known as ME, affects approximately a quarter of a million people in the UK, with symptoms incuding severe fatigue, poor concentration and memory, disturbed sleep, muscle and joint pain. A paper published in the highly respected medical journal, *The Lancet* (White *et al.* 2011), elicited a feature on the BBC News, as their findings regarding the most effective treatment contradicted that recommended by patients' organisations and the Action for ME charity. Following a randomised controlled trial with 641 individuals with ME receiving either standard specialist medical care (the control group), cognitive behavoural therapy (CBT), a graded exercise programme or adaptive pacing therapy (planning activity to avoid fatigue), the researchers conclude that fatigue and physical functioning improved most (over 12 months) when treated with CBT or with graded exercise, whereas the charity claim their survey findings from almost 3,000 individuals support adaptive pacing therapy.

For the majority of people reading or hearing the media coverage, the scientific paper is not accessible, nor will many be aware of the difference in the quality of evidence gained from a controlled trial versus a questionnaire survey. The contradictory information such features contain can create anxiety in those individuals living with this condition as they may feel they are not being treated 'properly'. For now, they should probably carry on doing what they are doing to manage their symptoms – if it is currently working for them. Generally there is a significant time lag between new findings and any policy or practice change. What happens next is that NICE (the National Institute for Health and Clinical Excellence) will analyse the trial results in more detail before deciding whether there is a clinical need to update their treatment guidelines. However, if those affected by ME wish, they can discuss other treatment possibilities with their own doctors. As we will see in this chapter, there are many beneficial effects of exercise: it may be that this new evidence has revealed further benefit.

Chapter outline

As shown in the previous chapter, behaviour is linked to health. However, not all our behaviour has potentially negative effects on our health; much of what we do can benefit our health, and indeed protect against illness. These are sometimes called 'behavioural immunogens'. This chapter provides an overview of the evidence pertaining to an array of such health-protective behaviour, including medication or treatment adherence, healthy diet, exercise behaviour, health screening and immunisation. The scientific evidence pertaining to the health benefits of each behaviour is considered, and where available, some national guidelines in relation to the practice of each behaviour are illustrated. A broad array of influences on the uptake or maintenance of specific health-enhancing behaviour is introduced to the reader here in order to provide a foundation for Chapter 5 ☞, where psychosocial theories of health behaviour and health behaviour change are described. The behaviours summarised in this chapter are common targets of educational and health promotion endeavours worldwide, as discussed in Chapters 6 and 7 ☞.

Individual behaviour can both undermine (Chapter 3 ☞) and act to protect and maintain health (this chapter). In a society where chronic disease is prevalent and where the population is ageing, it is increasingly important to take positive steps towards healthy living and healthy ageing. While media coverage and public health campaigns can raise awareness of the beneficial effects of certain behaviours on health, it is important to remember that people do not behave as they do solely to protect their health or to reduce their risk of illness. As health psychologists, it is important to develop an understanding not only of the consequences of certain behaviour for health but also of the many psychosocial factors that influence its performance (both health-risk and health-protective behaviours). That is what we hope to achieve in this chapter, with the dominant psychosocial theories applied and tested in this regard being described in Chapter 5 ☞. We start the chapter with a look at adherence behaviour, focusing on medication and treatment adherence, however many points have relevance also to adhering to behaviours addressed in the preceding chapter (e.g. smoking cessation) or in this chapter (e.g. healthy eating or exercise).

Adherence behaviour

Definitions

Depending on whether you are reading from medical literature, pharmacological literature or psychological literature, you will come across the terms 'compliance', 'concordance' or 'adherence' being used to refer to the act of acquiring prescriptions and taking medicines appropriately, or carrying out other illness self-management behaviours such as rehabilitation exercises. Although often used interchangeably these terms impart different meaning about the relationship between a patient and a health-care professional and so we provide brief definitions here, and then we adopt the term 'adherence' in the remainder of this section (unless it is assessed as compliance in the study referred to) as it is most closely aligned with both a health psychology stance and the literature.

- Compliance: most often used in medical literature, this term suggests patient medicine taking behaviour which conforms with 'doctor's orders', 'the extent to which the patient's behavior coincides with the clinical prescription' (Sackett and Haynes 1976). The term 'patient compliance' was introduced in 1975 as an official Medical Subject Heading (MeSH term) in the United States National Library of Medicine.

- Concordance: introduced by the Royal Pharmaceutical Society of Great Britain in 1995, this term is more often used in a pharmacological or therapeutic literature, and suggests cooperation by means of an agreement between physician and patient as to what is the appropriate behaviour.

- Adherence: most often used in health psychology and behavioural medicine, this terms suggest that a person sticks to, or cooperates with advice about medication (or lifestyle changes, behaviours) (NICE 2009a). Adherence is viewed as a behavioural process influenced by individual and environmental factors including health-care practices and system influences, and 'medication adherence' became a MeSH term only in 2009.

Reflecting these differences, the World Health Organization's own definitions (WHO 2003) of adherence have changed from being 'the extent to which the patient's behavior coincides with the clinical prescription', to 'the extent to which the patient's behavior coincides with the agreed recommendation from a health provider'.

To be defined as 'non-adherent' also varies across studies, with thresholds (the amount to be taken appropriately in order *not* to be categorised as non-adherent) ranging from 70–100 per cent depending on the disease and the treatment concerned (this is discussed further below). This makes comparison of findings difficult, but the consensus is that a clinically relevant cut-off should be used wherever possible (Vitolins *et al.* 2000), thus if 60 per cent of a medicinal product is needed to be taken daily for a drug to be effective, then any less than that should be defined as non-adherence.

Why do definitions matter? They matter because if we are to measure the nature and extent of adherence or non-adherence, we have to know what it is we are assessing and how to word our assessments! Conceptual overlap and conceptual confusion is not helpful if one is to synthesise a literature, something some of you may discover if you carry out research in this domain. One attempt to assist in this is the ongoing work of the ABC (Ascertaining Barriers to Compliance) group, a multinational group of researchers from Poland, the UK, Belgium and Switzerland, where a systematic review of terminology as used in papers published prior to April 2009 led to the proposal of a new taxonomy of medication therapy management, where 'medication adherence' is the preferred term and, within that, initiation, implementation (the extent to which the patients actual dosing corresponds to the prescribed regimen) and discontinuation is specified. The work of this EU-funded group is ongoing, and includes a 12-country survey of health psychology and health economic predictors of adherence behaviour in people with hypertension (see www.abcproject.eu).

Do people adhere?

Hippocrates (*c* 400 BC) was the first documented recorder of the finding that patients did not take medicines as prescribed, and that they even complained when they didn't seem to get better! More recently (!) consensus is that between a third and a half of all medicines prescribed for long-term conditions are not taken as prescribed, but rates vary depending on many factors. For example, a meta-analysis of data from those with cardiovascular disease found an average adherence of 77 per cent (DiMatteo 2004a), reflecting a non-adherence level similar to that reported amongst adult organ transplant patients in relation to their taking of essential immunosuppressant drugs (22.6 per cent, Dew *et al.* 2007); however, non-adherence among some chronic disease groups (e.g. arthritis, HIV) is lower, and in others it is higher (e.g. diabetes, asthma) (DiMatteo 2004a; see also Chapter 10 ☞). The reasons for variation across conditions is likely to be in part due to treatment complexity and in part due to many other factors which we list below.

Two key challenges facing adherence researchers is (a) how adherence and non-adherence are defined and (b) how adherence is measured. In terms of the first of these, non-adherence can range from not filling a prescription in the first place (estimated occurrence in between 14–21 per cent), skipping an occasional dose, through to skipping many doses, and these differing forms of non-adherence carry differing consequences. For example, Sherr *et al.* (2010) report that although as many as 57 per cent of their sample of HIV-infected adults in receipt of a prescription for HAART (Highly Active Antiretroviral Therapy, also known as ART) had taken a tablet at the wrong time in the previous week, it was the 10 per cent who reported having missed two or more dosages within the past week who risked a worse disease prognosis as a result. Related to what we described earlier in terms of setting clinically meaningful thresholds for defining non-adherence, this finding suggests that adherence to this treatment (if once per day) requires 70 per cent or better (i.e. 5 doses of 7).

In terms of the second challenge, i.e. of measuring adherence, statistics are often derived from individual patient self-report which, while more reliable than asking the health professional involved in their care (who generally overestimate adherence), is also subject to recall and reporting bias. Some studies therefore gather data on adherence using mixed methods, combining self- and other-report, with biological measurements (e.g. urine or blood testing), or pill counts, including using electronic monitoring systems (MEMS, where counters are in the lids of pill bottles to record timing of openings); however, all methods have their limitations and, as it stands, no gold standard measure exists (diMatteo 2004a).

The costs of non-adherence

It has been shown that patients themselves recognise the costs of non-adherence, with Annema *et al.* (2009) reporting that one-third of patients with heart failure described improvement in their adherence to their treatment regimes as the most important factor preventing hospital readmission. Few patients, however, probably realise the actual financial costs of non-adherence. For example, within the UK it has been estimated that individual non-adherence to prescribed medicines costs the UK NHS approximately £196 million *per year* due to repeat admissions to hospital, but a further £4 billion may be wasted also due to not taking medicines as prescribed. It is hard to ascertain what further costs can be attached to non-adherence to recommended behaviour change following illness events, such as dietary change or smoking cessation following a heart attack, but they are likely to add further to this huge figure.

Why do people not adhere to medical recommendations and prescriptions?

The reasons for non-adherence to medicines or other recommended treatments are as many and varied as the reasons described already in this chapter regarding other health-protective or health-enhancing behaviours, but they can be considered as falling into the following groupings (Sabaté 2003):

● *Patient-related factors*: e.g. culture, age, personality, knowledge, personal and cultural beliefs, attitudes towards illness and medicines, self-**efficacy** beliefs (see Chapter 5 ☞).

● *Condition-related factors*: e.g. symptom type, perceived severity (NOT actual severity, diMatteo *et al.* 2007), presence or absence of pain, presence of comorbidities, prognosis.

● *Treatment-related factors*: e.g. the number, type, timing, frequency and duration of dosage of medications, presence and extent of side-effects, expense.

● *Socioeconomic factors*: low educational level, costs of treatment (relates also to socio-economic equalities associated with ethnicity), access to dispensing pharmacy, social isolation.

---

efficacy
Bandura's technical term analogous to confidence.

• *System-related factors*: communications with healthcare provider regarding medicines necessity or function, presence of traditional healing beliefs and systems (see RESEARCH FOCUS).

For most people non-adherence will be influenced by a mixture of the above, not all non-adherence will be intentional, and not all non-adherence carries the same risks to health. Research tends to distinguish between intentional non-adherence (e.g. 'I stopped taking my pills as they made me feel sick/are too expensive') and unintentional non-adherence (e.g. 'Sometimes I forget to take a dose if I'm busy'), sometimes described as

the distinction between perceptions and practicalities (Horne 2001). Chapter 10 ☛ describes some of the efforts made to maximise adherence and, given evidence of generally moderate impact (see Haynes *et al.* 2008 for a Cochrane review and meta-analysis), some of the challenges faced.

Influences on adherence therefore can be considered as going from the micro-level, which includes personality (for example, the association between neuroticism and medication non-adherence in older adults, Jerant *et al.* 2011), to the macro and meso level, such as culture and social systems. These latter influences are addressed in RESEARCH FOCUS.

RESEARCH FOCUS

Structural barriers to medication adherence

Kagee, A. and Deport, T. (2010). Barriers to adherence to antiretroviral treatment: the perspectives of patient advocates. *Journal of Health Psychology*, 15: 1001–11 .

As described in this chapter, non-adherence to appropriately prescribed medicines, whether intentional or unintentional, is a significant cause of additional illness events, hospitalisations, and poor clinical outcomes including avoidable deaths. The increased health and social care costs of non-adherence are phenomenal. While a significant body of research, some of which is presented in this chapter and elsewhere in this text, has identified individual characteristics such as age or social class (Chapters 2 ☛ and 10), and psychological characteristics such as attitudes and expectancies (Chapter 5 ☛), which are associated with non-adherence, few studies have explored the wider 'structural' influences on adherence behaviour, such as the social, cultural, economic and political influences. Few studies have in fact explored non-adherence in non-Western populations where health threats such as HIV infection are endemic. Sub-Saharan Africa accounts for a staggering 67 per cent of the global total of those living with HIV infection, with an adult prevalence of 18.1 per cent in South Africa in 2008. Antiretroviral Therapy (ART) can reduce AIDS deaths,

which, given that an estimated 350,000 South African adults and children died of AIDS-related illnesses in 2007, offers an important lifeline. ART, however, needs to be taken fully and properly to be effective.

This study addresses both these gaps by focusing on structural barriers to ART adherence reported by patient advocates in South Africa. Drawing from Ecological Systems Theory (Bronfenbrenner 1972), the study explores micro- (the person's immediate environment, family, school, work), macro- (the cultural and political context) and meso- (social institutions such as healthcare systems transport systems, local ecomony) system influences on adherence.

Method

Ten patient advocates (PA) – laypersons employed by non-governmental organisations (NGO), hospitals or provincial health departments to provide support, mentoring and counselling to patients with HIV – were invited to take part in a qualitative study. These PAs visit patients in their home both before and after HIV testing to offer voluntary counselling, may accompany them to clinics and are thought to gain unique perspectives into the patients' experience of accessing and negotiating ART treatment. As such, they link the patient, their home and the clinic staff and environment and thus were thought to have access to both the micro- and meso-level factors.

All ten PAs recruited were women aged between 25 and 55, all had attended high school (eight did not graduate), had training in ART awareness-training basic counselling, and one was HIV positive. To recruit these women the research team, having obtained relevant ethical approvals, made contact with the medical staff, and subsequently the specific NGO associated with the Infectious Diseases Clinic of a large peri-urban hospital in South Africa. All PAs invited agreed to take part (although the invitation was made by the PA Coordinator and it is unclear if s/he selected who s/he invited). Two focus groups took place at the University, followed by 8/10 individual interviews with those still available at the NGO offices. Both types of session were audio recorded and transcribed for analysis. Two facilitators took part in each focus group, and these and the interviews were conducted bilingually (English/Afrikaans). Focus groups asked for PAs to discuss what they thought the experience of patients was with the health-care system, and the ART clinic more specifically, and what problems they thought patients faced in attending appointment, and taking ART medication specifically. The interviews followed up on issues raised in the focus groups. In terms of analysis, detail of how the focus group data is handled is not presented; however, interviews were examined for emerging themes and categorised using grounded theory (Strauss and Corbin 1998). In reading the transcripts the authors' focus was on identifying 'structural barriers', and examples were sought which suggested related processes, actions, assumptions and consequences. The use of metaphor was also explored but not presented, particularly in this paper.

Results

Nine themes were identified as barriers to adherence and grouped into three categories: poverty-related, institutional, and cultural–social. The nine themes within these broader categories are not fully outlined, perhaps reflecting the challenge qualitative researchers face in presenting their data fully within the word restrictions of most journals), and the sub-themes identified by my reading do not add to nine, however:

Poverty-related factors:

● the prohibitive cost and poor transport infrastructure left many patients, PAs felt, being reluctant to walk to clinic because of distance and also because of illness symptoms such as fatigue (even taxis act as buses and do not typically deliver passengers to their specific destination);

● food costs meant stomachs were often empty and patients would not take their medication on empty stomachs due to intolerable side-effects;

● disability grants for those with low immune function (a low CD4 count – see Chapter 8 (☞) acted as a disincentive to taking medicine which would improve cell counts and thus cause the cessation of grant income, suggesting that, for some, non-adherence was intentional, and PAs felt that the government should change the criteria for receiving the grant.

Institutional factors:

● Negative perceptions of the experience in terms of waiting time, overcrowding and lack of privacy were seen by PAs to put patients off.

● Negative behaviour of clinic staff to patients, particularly 'rude' or 'rough' mannered nurses was inferred by some PAs to have racial or socio-economic undertones. Several PAs felt empathy with the patients as they themselves were considered of lower social status: '*they are white people, they are treated respectably but we know, those that live on the outside, we just, we are just spoken to harshly*'. While overwork and understaffing was acknowledged, PAs felt that a better attitude to patients would improve patient well-being.

● Health literacy was thought to be a barrier to both attendance and pill-taking. A lack of information and knowledge meant that some '*do not understand well what HIV is about*', or '*not know how important it is to take your ARVs*', which led to myths and misperceptions, such as tuberculosis leading to HIV. Poor services and neglected education in Black areas during Apartheid were thought to have caused poor overall literacy, thus undermining comprehension of health-related information.

- The lack of services to deal with underlying problems such as alcohol or drug abuse was thought to undermine PAs' efforts to support patients during ART treatment.

Cultural and social factors:

- The unique cultural aspects of the patient community within which the PAs worked was seen to interact with the socio-economic dynamics of the healthcare system.

- Strong religious beliefs that taking ART showed a lack of faith in God was thought to be encouraged by some charismatic preachers and this interpretation of faith led to some patients substituting medication with prayer (in fact getting infected by HIV within this culture is sometimes interpreted as a sign of disobedience to the church). PAs related the following of this belief as a further consequence of poor health literacy. Religious leaders in socially and economically marginalised groups such as this seem to represent 'hope of delivery'.

- Traditional healing and a belief in ancestral powers is a powerful barrier – '*its like a struggle, because of this ancestor and this beliefs that they are having, this person will make them right and that person will make them right. That's why most of them, some of them just died in South Africa, because of not taking medication*'.

- The presence of stigma and the fact that some patients had not disclosed their status to family made medication taking difficult, and, even if disclosed to family, the diagnosis was still associated with shame and guilt which meant some did not want to be seen at clinic.

Discussion

The authors review their findings and contextualise them within a wider literature on HIV and ART adherence; however, for the purposes of this RESEARCH FOCUS, I highlight mainly those which differ with data gathered within Western cultures. Some of the sub-themes in the data resonate with findings of other adherence studies conducted in sub-Saharan Africa: for example, the cost and quality of transport services from rural or peri-urban communities to clinics. Walking for hours, sometimes days, to receive treatments (for example, in the case of child vaccinations) has been well documented and serves to highlight differences in transport infrastructure and poverty between developed and the developing or under-developed nations. Food insecurity is a major concern to those rolling out national treatment programmes, as the individual choice will be to avoid the unpleasant side-effects of medicating on an empty stomach, yet there are no easy solutions to poverty and associated food deprivation. This is one factor that rarely appears cited as a barrier to medication use in Western samples.

In contrast perhaps, the issue of the apparent disincentivising nature of some welfare grants has also been raised in the UK – for example, unemployment benefit and associated grants such as for child care, are often cited by UK recipients as providing greater income than employment, thus maintaining people outwith a productive workforce. In the current data deliberately staying less well in order to receive disability grants is made more understandable by the fact that the authors cite evidence that social grants, including the specific disability grant referred to in their data, can account for almost half of a household's income. The authors could perhaps have reflected on how to help individuals realise that, with regards to non-adherence in order to keep the money, this disability grant could in the end cost them – their lives! However, politically this issue is almost impossible to win, in any country.

In terms of institutional barriers, those cited are not unique to South Africa – waiting times for treatment, crowded waiting rooms, lack of privacy, dissuade individuals in many countries from attending services where perhaps there is an element of stigma or shame (mental health services, genito-urinary medicine or STD clinics, for example). However, the racial overtones assumed by PAs to be present in nurse–patient communication are less well documented.

Perhaps the most interesting and unique findings of this study come from suggestions that strong faith, religious and spiritual beliefs worsen the already influential effects of low levels of health literacy. While a lack of knowledge and comprehension has been reported from Western samples, this religious and spirituality factor adds a further dimension that interventions would need to address sensitively, possibly, the authors suggest, by building spiritual beliefs into adherence counselling. Stigma and shame attached to HIV seem to remain high, perhaps surprising in a culture where HIV is so prevalent, and so the PAs point to a need for confidential and individually delivered services so that patients can maintain secrecy around their medication if they wish, although community education may also be effective here.

In drawing their conclusions, the authors point to a need to tackle structural barriers to adherence. They make a clear call for greater resources, at an educational level and also in terms of more, more accessible, better staffed, integrated and confidential services. A further intervention would be to enable patients

themselves to negotiate with and tackle the structural barriers, perhaps with support from PAs. Moving beyond the individual as the level of analysis to the systems that enhance or detract from adherence behaviour is shown by these data to be necessary, at least in this Black South African culture.

In terms of limitations, the authors do not record the ethnicity of the PAs, which is likely to be relevant in their shaping and interpreting of the patient experience; it may be that only the Black PAs, for example, noted staff communication as a barrier to the patients, and that they were more knowledgeable about the failing of education for Black patients. Also, while the interpretations of the PAs are useful, given their interface between patient and health system, this data would be all the richer if some patients had also been able to contribute their views.

This section has highlighted the contribution of both macro (societal) and micro (individual) influences on behaviour and that theme continues below and in our exploration of influences on other health behaviours (Chapter 5 ☞).

Healthy diet

As described in the previous chapter, what we eat plays an important role in our long-term health and illness status, with diet having both direct and indirect links with illness. For example, fat intake is directly linked to various forms of heart disease by a range of physiological mechanisms, and indirectly related to disease by virtue of its effects on weight control and, in particular, obesity. The World Health Organization (WHO 2002) states that low intake of fruit and vegetables as part of diet is responsible for over three million deaths a year, worldwide, from cancer or cardiovascular disease. The World Health Report (WHO 2002) attributed between 3.5 and 7.6 per cent of total mortality in the year 2000 to low fruit and vegetable intake, with the highest percentage being in the developed world including Europe and America, and the lowest attributable percentage being in high-mortality developing countries including many parts of Africa. Furthermore, 35 per cent of cancer deaths

are attributable, in part, to poor diet, particularly high intake of fats and salt and low levels of fibre (American Cancer Society, 2008; see also Chapter 3 ☞). Given these reports, it is no surprise that government bodies, health ministers and medical authorities are producing guidelines on how to eat healthily, and that health researchers are working towards identifying factors that facilitate the adoption of these guidelines in our daily lives.

The health benefits of fruit and vegetable consumption

Fruit and vegetables contain, among other things, vitamins, folic acid, antioxidants (for example, lycopene in the red pigment of tomatoes, polyphenols in red grapes) and fibre, all of which are essential to a healthy body. They may also offer protection against diseases such as some forms of cancer, heart disease and stroke. Lock *et al.* (2005) estimated that worldwide, if people ate the amounts of fruit and vegetables recommended, the incidence of several forms of cancer would reduce significantly: oesophageal cancer 20 per cent, stomach cancer 19 per cent, lung cancer 12 per cent, colorectal cancer 2 per cent. For this latter cancer, fibre in the diet is thought to be crucial. Evidence to date does not, however, suggest that vegetarianism is protective against all types of cancer, although a large **meta-analysis** of data involving 76,000 men and women did find that vegetarianism reduced the risk of dying of **ischaemic heart disease** (Key *et al.* 1998). However, in this study, vegetarians also reported lower rates of smoking and lower levels of alcohol consumption than non-vegetarians, and although these factors were controlled for in the analyses, other unidentified but important differences may also have existed between the two groups that may further explain the health differences.

Research evidence across individual studies is fairly consistent in finding positive health benefits of fruit and vegetable intake (e.g. Ness and Powles 1997; World Health Organization 2003). While evidence of an association with lowered rates of some forms of cancer is available (see Marmot *et al.* 2007), in relation to coronary heart disease risk, however, a recent review (Dauchet *et al.* 2009) concluded that, 'Controlled nutritional prevention trials are scarce and the existing data do not show any clear protective effects of fruit and vegetables on coronary heart disease'.

Recommended fruit and vegetable intake

Current recommendations are to eat five or more portions of fruit and vegetables a day (one 'portion' is defined as 80 g); however, data from the Health Survey for England 2006 (The Information Centre 2008) found that only 19 per cent of boys and 22 per cent of girls aged 5 to 15 were found to be eating at least 5 portions per day. While this is an increase since the earlier surveys in 2001 and 2004, this is still a small proportion of children. There is also substantial evidence that while increases are being seen, the majority of adults are also not following these recommendations, particularly young adults and males (e.g. Baker and Wardle 2003; Henderson *et al.* 2002). Much of the research carried out with regards to healthy

eating focuses on young people and their food choices and eating behaviours, and, while this makes sense in relation to the growing prevalence of obesity (see Chapter 3 (☞) and in light of the fact that health behaviours set down in childhood can contribute towards adult health state, our society is an increasingly ageing one and therefore a greater focus on 'healthy ageing' is also required. A loss of appetite and reduced energy is often associated with growing older, but those are not inevitable consequences and may reflect social factors (such as experiencing a loss of interest in food caused by eating alone), physical factors (access to shops, physical mobility) or personal factors such as lack of skill. It may be that older males, when widowed, face a particular challenge when having to shop and cook for themselves, as among much of the older population such roles have commonly been adopted by women. Hughes *et al.* (2004) carried out a questionnaire and interview study of 39 older men and found that only five (13 per cent) consumed five portions of fruit and vegetables a day, that 64 per cent consumed less energy than appropriate even when controlling for BMI, activity, and age, and most had lower intake of essential nutrients than they should. What is novel about this study is that it relates these intake characteristics to the individuals' cooking skills. Good cooking skills (food preparation and cooking) was associated with higher vegetable intake but with lower energy/calorie intake. Men with poorer cooking skills, ate less vegetables but they did tend to eat more calorie-dense foods which, although it was at levels in line with calorie intake guidelines, is not necessarily a good thing as energy-dense foods are not always nutritious. The implications of such findings is that interventions could be quite practical, tying up cooking skills with both appropriately calorific and nutritious food (a new project for TV chef, Jamie Oliver, perhaps?!)

Why do people not eat sufficient fruit and vegetables?

In spite of growing public awareness of the link between eating and health, fruit and vegetables tend not to be the food of choice of many young people. For example, the National Diet and Nutrition Survey (Food Standards Agency 2009) found that the foods most frequently consumed by British young people (aged 4 to 18 years) were white bread, savoury snacks (e.g. crisps), biscuits, potatoes and confectionery, although an encouraging

---

meta-analysis

a review and re-analysis of pre-existing quantitative datasets that combines the analysis so as to provide large samples and high statistical power from which to draw reliable conclusions about specific effects.

ischaemic heart disease

a heart disease caused by a restriction of blood flow to the heart.

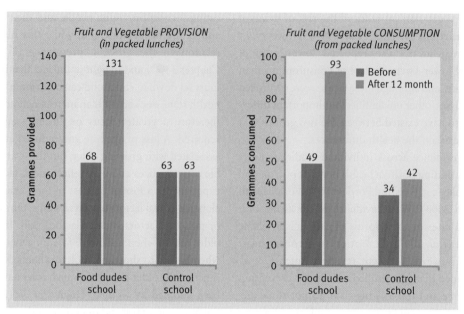

Figure 4.1 Ireland Experimental Evaluation

Source: Horne *et al*. (2009) Increasing parental provision and children's consumption of lunchbox fruit and vegetables in Ireland: the Food Dudes intervention. *Eur. J. Clin. Nutr*. 63, p613–618.

trend was seen in terms of increased fruit intake compared to previous years. Although the average vitamin intake was not deficient, intake of some minerals was low. These food preferences can in part be understood by the findings of another survey of British young people (Haste 2004), which found that children gave 'It tastes good' (67 per cent) and 'It fills me up' (43 per cent) as the top two reasons for their favourite food choice, above 'Because it is healthy' (22 per cent) and 'It gives me energy' (17 per cent).

Unfortunately, tasting 'good' often appears to correlate with sugar and fat content rather than with healthy food, and preconceptions exist about healthy food that can work against a person making healthy food choices. For example, 37 per cent of Haste's sample agreed with the statement 'Healthy food usually doesn't taste as good as unhealthy food'. Where do these preferences and perceptions come from?

Food preferences

Parents play a major role in setting down patterns of eating, food choices and leisure activities inasmuch as they develop the rules and guidelines as to what is considered appropriate behaviour. For example, parental permissiveness was associated with less healthy eating behaviour among adolescents and young adults aged 12 to 22 (Bourdeaudhuij 1997; Bourdeaudhuij and van

Oost 1998). Food preferences are generally learned through socialisation within the family, with the food provided by parents to their children often setting the child's future preferences for:

Plate 4.1 'We are what we eat?' The importance of providing positive norms for healthy eating in children

Source: Bangor University, School of Psychology.

- *cooking methods*: e.g. home-cooked/fresh vs. ready-made/processed;
- *products*: e.g. high-fat vs. low-fat, organic vs. non-organic;
- *tastes*: e.g. seasoned vs. bland, sweet vs. sour;
- *textures*: e.g. soft–crunchy, tender–chewy;
- *food components*: e.g. red/white meat, vegetables, fruit, grains, pulses and carbohydrates.

Various interventions have targeted the fruit and vegetable intake of young people, such as the Food Dudes programme developed in North Wales, which targets pre-school and primary-school children in the UK and Ireland (Tapper *et al.* 2003; Horne *et al.* 2004; 2009). This programme draws on established learning theory techniques of increased taste exposure to fruit and vegetables, modelling of healthy behaviour through cartoon youth characters, and reinforcement by means of child-friendly rewards (e.g. stickers, crayons) for eating the fruit and vegetables provided at snack and meal times (Lowe *et al.* 2004). Long-term effectiveness of a peer-modelling and rewards-based intervention on the fruit and vegetable consumption of children was found (see Figure 4.1), with particular gains among those children who ate less fruit and vegetables at the study outset (Horne *et al.* 2009).

However, an exposure-only study, a randomised controlled trial of having fruit 'tuck shops' in primary schools, did not find an increase in fruit consumption (Moore *et al.* 2000; Moore 2001), suggesting that availability alone is insufficient to motivate change.

Given the challenge of increasing fruit and vegetable intake, ISSUES below raises the question of whether supplementing a person's diet with antioxidant vitamins (e.g. vitamins A, C and E; beta-carotene; folic acid) has benefits in terms of reducing disease risk.

ISSUES

Do vitamins protect us from disease?

Research has suggested that a lack of vitamins A, C and E, beta-carotene and folic acid in a person's diet plays a role in blood vessel changes that potentially contribute to heart disease, and low beta-carotene has been linked with certain cancers including mouth, throat and lung. Beta-carotene is a form of vitamin A found in the cell wall of carrots and sweet potatoes, and we now understand that cooking these vegetables releases this more easily for absorption than eating them raw (at least carrots!). Folate, a component of vitamin B, has also been linked to reduced risk of pancreatic cancer, and selenium, found in grain products but also available as a supplement, has been associated with reduced cancer incidence, albeit in men only (see Bardia *et al.* 2008, for a systematic review and meta-analysis). Such associations are attributed to the antioxidant properties of these vitamins (i.e. they reduce the oxidated products of metabolism which can cause cell damage). Additionally, vitamins C and E have anti-inflammatory effects, and both inflammation and oxidation have been linked with cognitive decline and progression towards dementia. Naturally, such findings stimulate media and public interest, and taking vitamin supplements as a means of protecting one's health became commonplace, in the USA and more recently across Europe.

However, what is the evidence base as to their effectiveness? The United States Preventive Services Task Force (USPSTF: an expert group formed to review research evidence in order to make informed health recommendations) conducted two large-scale reviews of studies of vitamin supplements published between 1966 and 2001. One reviewed the evidence regarding reduced risk of cardiovascular disease (USPSTF 2003) and the other reviewed evidence in relation to reduced risk of breast, lung, colon and prostate cancer (Morris and Carson 2003). They found that even well-designed randomised controlled trials comparing vitamin supplements with an identical-looking placebo pill, in terms of subsequent development of disease, were inconclusive in their findings. Bardia *et al.* (2008) reviewed 12 randomised trials (9 had high methodological quality; overall related to 104,196 individuals) of antioxidant supplementation specifically in relation to primary cancer incidence and mortality. They concluded that there was no effect on overall cancer incidence or mortality. While vitamin E also had no effects, selenium had beneficial effects (among men only) both in terms of incidence and mortality, although conclusive evidence was hampered by methodological and sampling variability.

More worryingly, both reviews report evidence of slightly increased cancer risk (pointing to lung cancer in the USPSTF review, but also head and neck and upper gastrointestinal tract in Bardia *et al.*'s) in those taking beta-carotene supplements, with higher risk seen among smokers. However, Bardia notes that the evidence regarding mortality is limited because not all trials analysed mortality data by whether their sample smoked or not.

It is worth highlighting that less rigorously designed studies tend to be those which report associations between vitamin supplementation and reduced disease risk. For example, **observational studies** reporting reduced breast cancer risk related to vitamin A intake generally failed to control for other aspects of their sample's behaviour, such as general dietary intake or exercise behaviour. Other evidence, such as reduced risk of colon cancer among those taking folic acid supplements, was based on retrospective reports of those affected/not affected rather than on long-term prospective follow-up studies of initially healthy individuals. Such findings therefore need to be interpreted with caution. Also, Bardia reminds us, these vitamins are made up of several antioxidant components and also micro- and macro-nutrients, and as different studies focus on different compounds taken in differing amounts and rarely explore the interactions between components (for example, between selenium and lycopene), detailed comparisons and conclusions are difficult.

observational studies

research studies which evaluate the effects of an intervention (or a treatment) without comparison to a control group and thus such studies are more limited in their conclusions than randomised controlled trials.

In terms of vitamin C and E supplements and their potential in halting cognitive decline, the evidence is more preliminary as well-designed randomised controlled trials (comparing those taking vitamins with those taking a placebo) are still required (Haan 2003). One study pointed to beneficial effects of vitamins C and E (when taken together, not separately) on the verbal fluency and verbal memory scores of healthy elderly women, the loss of which are implicated in the development of dementia (Grodstein *et al.* 2003). However, other evidence is less encouraging. For example, Plassman *et al.* (2010) reviewed 127 observational studies, 22 randomised controlled trials, and 16 systematic reviews in terms of a range of factors associated with cognitive decline (nutritional, medical and medications; social, economic, or behavioral factors; toxic environmental exposures; and genetic factors), and found insufficient evidence to support an association for any of these, but most relevant here not for nutritional factors (examined in only 7 of all studies reviewed). It may be that effects are confined to specific populations, however. For example, in women with pre-existing cardiovascular disease or cardiovascular disease risk factors, overall antioxidant supplementation did not slow cognitive change over a 5-year period, but evidence of a late effect of vitamin C or beta carotene intake among those who had low dietary intake levels was reported (Kang *et al.*, 2009). While findings of global effects are therefore mixed, more rigorous and focused studies with less varied populations may well be worthy of further study, given that cognitive decline and dementias are increasingly prevalent in an ageing society.

Overall, therefore, current research no longer supports the taking of antioxidant supplements, except perhaps where natural food sources are lacking. It would appear that eating a healthy diet with these vitamins contained within the foodstuffs, and maintaining a healthy body weight is more relevant to reducing disease risk than relying on supplements. Finally, and importantly, there is reasonably consistent evidence that the specific supplement of beta carotene may even be detrimental to the health of smokers and this information should perhaps be contained on packaging of relevant products.

Exercise

The physical health benefits of exercise

Exercise is generally considered as health-protective physical activity, reducing an individual's risk of developing diseases such as cardiovascular disease, type 2 diabetes mellitus, osteoporosis, and obesity, and some forms of cancer, including colorectal and breast cancer (Kohl 2001; Kriska 2003; World Health Organization 2002). In addition, exercise has benefits for those already with disease, for example, increased strength and function, reduced fatigue, reduced side-effects of cancer treatments and increased quality of life (Cramp and Daniel 2008; Perna *et al.* 2008).

We use the term 'exercise' broadly here, encompassing both planned physical activity such as going swimming or to the gym and that which is simply physical activity generated by body movement in the pursuit of one's daily life essentials such as going shopping, walking the dog. The majority of research studies investigating the health benefits of exercise focus on the presence of purposeful exercise; however, interventions or public health promotion increasingly highlight the need to simply avoid being sedentary (i.e. encourage any physical activity).

An early pointer towards the benefits of moderate to high levels of exercise came from a longitudinal study of the lifestyles of 17,000 former graduates of Harvard University. This study reported 1,413 deaths between 1962 and 1978 and noted that significantly more deaths had occurred among those who had reported leading a sedentary life. Those who exercised the equivalent of 30–35 miles running/walking a week faced half the risk of premature death of those who exercised the equivalent of five miles or less per week. Moderate exercisers were defined as exercising the equivalent of 20 miles per week, and these individuals also showed health benefits in that on average they lived two years longer than the low-exercise group (<5 mile equivalent) (Paffenbarger *et al.* 1986). A similar follow-up study of an elderly male sample (61–81 years) found that the 12-year death rate was halved in those who walked more than two miles per day compared with those who walked less (Hakim *et al.* 1998). Furthermore, these authors found that the incidence of cancer and heart disease was also lower among those who walked more, and that this effect remained even when other common risk factors such as alcohol consumption and blood pressure were controlled for. All individuals who participated in this study were non-smokers, and smoking behaviour therefore did not need to be controlled for; however, this otherwise careful study did not control for an individual's dietary behaviour, which may in part be implicated in the findings.

A review of evidence from several prospective observational studies has suggested that regular physical activity can reduce the risk of coronary heart disease associated with excessive body weight (Blair and Brodney 1999). For example, one study found that overweight individuals – a body mass index (BMI, see Chapter 3 ☞) of 25.0 or more – who were active, had a lower rate of heart attacks (1.3/1,000 man years) than non-active normal weight (BMI less than 24.9) individuals (heart attack rate 5.5/1,000 man years) (Morris *et al.* 1990). Being 'fat' does not inevitably mean being 'unfit'. Exercise does not have to be structured and formal either; there is clear evidence from a meta-analysis of randomised controlled trials that simply regular walking can reduce the risk of cardiovascular disease, particularly among older people (Murphy *et al.* 2007).

Regular exercise is also protective against the development of osteoporosis, a disease characterised by a reduction in bone density due to calcium loss, which leads to brittle bones, a loss of bone strength and an increased risk of fractures. It is estimated that, in the UK, someone experiences a bone fracture due to osteoporotic bones every three minutes, and that one in three women and one in twelve men over the age of 50 will have this condition. Regular exercise, particularly low-impact exercise or weight-bearing exercise such as walking and dancing, is not just important to bone development in the young but is also important to the maintenance of peak levels of bone density during adulthood. Additional benefits to muscle strength, coordination and balance can be gained from resistance-strengthening exercise, which in turn can benefit older individuals by reducing the risk of falls and subsequent bone fractures.

In general, therefore, regular exercise is an accepted means of reducing one's risk of developing a range of serious health conditions; furthermore, it is associated with a significant downturn in all-cause mortality among both men (Myers *et al.* 2002) and women (Manson *et al.* 2002). There is also some suggestion that adult health and disease risk is influenced by the level of childhood activity (Hallal *et al.* 2006), although there is need for more longitudinal research to confirm the pathways through which any effects may be achieved (Mattocks *et al.* 2008). It may be that active youngsters maintain activity in adulthood, but it may also be that active youngsters' lifestyles vary in other (healthy) ways as they grow older.

Once a relationship between behaviour and a health outcome has been established, it is important to ask 'how' this relationship operates. In terms of exercise and reduced heart disease risk, it appears that regular performance of exercise strengthens the heart muscle and increases cardiac and respiratory efficiency; it also tends to reduce blood pressure, and people who exercise regularly have a lesser tendency to accumulate body fat (e.g. Department of Health, 2004). Exercise therefore helps to maintain the balance between energy intake and energy output and works to protect physical health in a variety of ways. A 'dose–response' relationship is seen to exist in relation to reduced risk of cardiovascular disease, type 2 diabetes and some forms of cancer, whereby the greater the level (frequency and intensity) of exercise, the greater the benefits. There is some note of caution in relation to this dose–response association, however: extreme exercise dependence is sometimes associated with a poor body image and with other compulsive disorders including eating disorders (e.g. Cook and Hausenblas 2008; Hamer and Karageorghis 2007), and there is also the risk of injury and musculo-skeletal damage.

The psychological benefits of exercise

Exercise has also repeatedly been associated with psychological benefits in terms of elevated mood among clinical populations, such as those suffering from depression (Glenister 1996) and decreased risk of anxiety, depression and low self-esteem or body-image among non-clinical populations (Lox *et al.* 2006). The evidence is, however, less strong for preventative effects than it is for therapeutic effects (Department of Health 2004). It is not simply that regular exercise brings about such long-term benefits to mood as a result of improved body-image or increased physical fitness: single episodes or limited-frequency aerobic exercise also has benefits,

for example upon mood, self-esteem and **prosocial behaviour** (Biddle *et al.* 2000; Lox *et al.* 2006). These psychological benefits of exercise have been attributed to various biological mechanisms, including:

● exercise-induced release of the body's own natural opiates into the blood stream, which produce a 'natural high' and act as a painkiller;

● stimulation of the release of **catecholamines** such as **noradrenaline** and **adrenaline**, which counter any stress response and enhance mood (Chapters 8 and 12 (☛));

● muscle relaxation, which reduces feelings of tension.

However, the relationship between exercise and positive mood states is perhaps not as simple as these biological routes suggest. For example, evidence exists of an inverse relationship between exercise intensity and adherence, whereby individuals are less likely to maintain intense exercise than moderate exercise, possibly because it is experienced as adverse (Brewer *et al.* 2000). This suggestion that, beyond a certain level, exercise may in fact

---

prosocial behaviour
behavioural acts that are positively valued by society and that may elicit positive social consequences.

catecholamines
these chemical substances are brain neurotransmitters and include **adrenaline** and **noradrenaline**.

noradrenaline
this **catecholamine** is a neurotransmitter found in the brain and in the **sympathetic nervous system**. Also known as norepinephrine.

adrenaline
a neurotransmitter and hormone secreted by the adrenal medulla that increases physiological activity in the body, including stimulation of heart action and an increase in blood pressure and metabolic rate. Also known as epinephrine.

sympathetic nervous system
the part of the autonomic nervous system involved in mobilising energy to activate and maintain arousal (e.g. increased heart rate).

be detrimental to mood has been explored further by Hall *et al.* (2002). They examined the **affective** response of 30 volunteers to increasing levels of exercise intensity and found not only that intense exercise caused negative mood but also that the timing of mood assessments (pre- and post-exercise assessment, compared with repeated assessment during exercise) profoundly changed the nature of the relationship found between exercise and mood. Studies measuring mood before exercise, and again after exercise has ended and the person has recovered, generally report positive affective responses. However, Hall and colleagues' data clearly show considerable mood deterioration as exercise intensity increases, with mood rising to more positive levels only on exercise completion. These authors propose that remembering the negative affective response experienced during exercise is likely to impair an individual's future adherence, and that this may explain why some studies report poor exercise adherence rates. In a subsequent study (Ekkekakis *et al.* 2008) these interesting findings were replicated and extended, and overall their work leads one to suggest that methodological factors play a role in whether or not exercise is associated with positive mood. Additionally, other factors such as cognitive distraction or actual physical removal from life's problems, or social support gained from exercising with friends, may further combine with biological factors to influence the affective experience reported. Even the exercise environment itself can play a role in mood outcomes, such as room temperature, the presence and type of music, and the presence of mirrors – the latter being associated with negative well-being (Martin Ginis *et al.* 2007). Mood is a complex phenomenon!

Moderate regular exercise appears to offer various routes to well-being. For some individuals, self-image and self-esteem may be enhanced as a result of exercise contributing to weight loss and control. Rightly or wrongly, we live in a society where trim figures are judged more positively (by others as well as by ourselves) than those that are considered to be overweight. Another potential route to well-being may be seen in those who use exercise as a means of coping with stress. Exercise for these individuals may act as a positive distraction from negative and stressful

> **affective**
> to do with affect or mood and emotions.

appraisals, or as time out from work or other demands. During exercise, a person may focus on aspects of the physical exertion or on the heart-rate monitor, they may distract themselves by listening to music or planning a holiday, or they may use the time to think through current stressors or demands and plan their coping responses (see Chapter 12 ☞). Finally, exercise can have psychological benefits for those experiencing cognitive decline as a result of ageing or dementia. Cotman and Engesser-Cesar (2002) recently reported that physical activity was associated with delays in the age-related neuronal dysfunction and degeneration that underlies the types of cognitive decline often associated with Alzheimer's disease, such as memory lapses and not paying attention.

In summary, engaging in regular physical activity is considered to be beneficial for both physical and psychological health, and possibly even for survival, but as with much behaviour, it may be that moderation is required.

The negative consequences of exercise

Paradoxically, excessive reliance on exercise to the extent that exercise becomes a compulsion and produces dependence (evidenced by, for example, experience of withdrawal effects, guilt and irritability when an exercise period is missed) is also an area of investigation by health psychologists (e.g. Hausenblaus and Symons Downs 2002; Ogden *et al.* 1997). Experimental studies have shown that depriving regular exercisers of exercise can lead to reductions in mood and to irritability (e.g. review by Biddle and Murtrie 1991), with mood restored when exercise is reinstated. The long-term physical consequences of excessive exercising relate to muscle wastage and weight loss rather than to any specific disease; however, these findings are a reminder that moderate levels of behaviour – even behaviour considered health-protective – are better than extreme levels.

Recommendations to exercise

Specific recommendations regarding physical activity for adults suggest at least 30 minutes of moderate intensity exercise on at least five days of each week, and for children and young people the recommendations are higher, suggesting 60 minutes of at least moderate intensity exercise a day, every day (e.g. Department of Health

2004). The aim of such guidelines is to set activity targets with the potential to reduce blood pressure and the incidence of diabetes, osteoporosis, coronary heart disease and obesity, as well as improving general well-being. Guidelines are not intended to be set so high as to be beyond the reach of the average individual, and certainly the advice for a previously inactive individual is to build up their exercise levels gradually, rather than making dramatic changes to both the frequency and intensity of exercise performance. Furthermore, where a pre-existing health complaint exists, plans to become more active should first be discussed with a medical professional.

In spite of obvious health benefits and active campaigning on the part of many health authorities and the media to encourage people of all ages to become more active, exercise levels in some parts of Europe remain low.

Levels of exercise

Less than half of the British adult population do some form of exercise at least once a month, and a similar percentage fail to exercise to current recommended levels, with percentages dropping with age (Department of Health 2004). Norman et al. (1998) estimated that only about 25 per cent of this population exercise with sufficient regularity to obtain any protective effects of exercise behaviour. This pattern is not only evident in Britain: for example, a survey conducted across 21 European countries found that approximately one-third of 18–30-year-olds did not engage in regular physical activity (Steptoe et al. 1997). Gender and age differences have also been reported, with women generally found to be more inactive than men, and older women being less active than younger women (e.g. Stephenson et al. 2000). Further evidence of an age effect on participation in regular physical activity was reported by Skelton et al. (1999), who found that while 18 per cent of men and 20 per cent of women aged 50–54 were participating in activity at least once a week, only 9 per cent of men and 4 per cent of women aged 80 or more were doing so. The proportions exercising to a level thought likely to produce health benefits is significantly less again. Data on the behaviour of the 'very old' (i.e. 85+) are limited as many surveys simply compare people who are under 65 years of age with those aged over 65. In older populations exercise behaviour is likely to be influenced by factors such as current health status and physical functioning, access to facilities, and even personal safety concerns (in terms of walking alone, or of accidents at the gym). However, a person's lifespan (longevity) may be predicted by the extent to which a person is physically active. For example, Hakim and colleagues (Hakim et al. 1998) followed a cohort of 61–81-year-old men over a period of 12 years and monitored the amount of walking they did. Men who walked more than two miles a day lived significantly longer than those who walked less (21.5 per cent died over the 12 years, compared with 43 per cent).

While a greater percentage of younger adults (16 to 24 years, Department of Health 2004) do appear to meet current recommended physical activity levels than older adults, the prevalence of inactivity is high in younger samples. For example, a World Health Organization study of 162,000 young people aged 11, 13 and 15 in 35 countries across Europe and North America found that only 35 per cent of 15-year-old boys and only 22 per cent of girls engage in at least one hour of moderate or heavier exercise five days a week, with huge geographical as well as gender differences (www.euro.who.int) (see Figure 4.2).

Many large-scale studies report a gender difference in exercise frequency, with boys generally found to be more active from an early age than girls, and with differences being maintained through adolescence. Cultural differences in the frequency of physical activity have also been reported. For example, the activity levels of Bangladeshi, Indian, Pakistani and Chinese men and women aged over 55 living in the UK was lower than levels reported by white respondents (Joint Health Surveys Unit 2001). Various studies have identified common clusters of reasons for choosing to exercise or not to exercise, although the extent to which this evidence is used to usefully inform intervention programmes has been questioned (e.g. Brunton et al. 2003).

Although guidelines exist based on evidence of exercise effectiveness, there is some suggestion that levels lower than national guidelines can still be beneficial: for example, a large-scale study of almost 40,000 healthy females aged over 45 concluded that the minimum level of exercise required to reduce heart disease risk may be as little as 20–60 minutes of purposeful walking per week (Lee et al. 2001). In contrast, others argue that governmental guidelines mislead by suggesting that 'moderate' intensity exercise is better for your health than more vigorous exercise (BBC News, 9 October 2007), but this may be due to how broadly health is defined (i.e. fitness and well-being, disease protection).

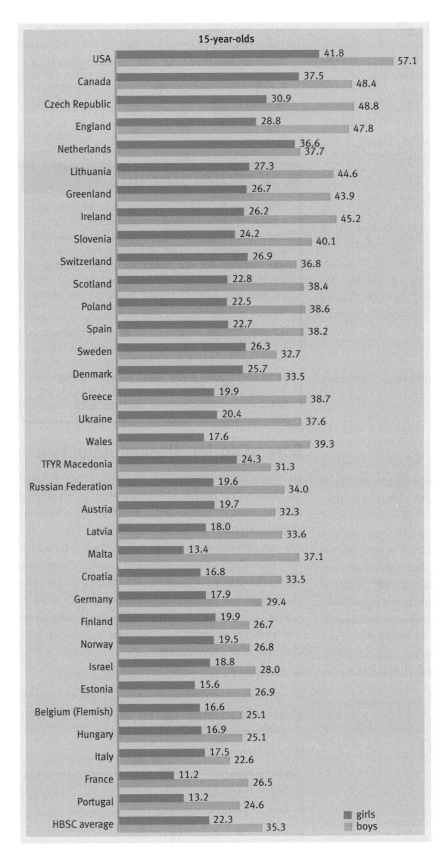

15-year-olds

Country	girls	boys
USA	41.8	57.1
Canada	37.5	48.4
Czech Republic	30.9	48.8
England	28.8	47.8
Netherlands	36.6	37.7
Lithuania	27.3	44.6
Greenland	26.7	43.9
Ireland	26.2	45.2
Slovenia	24.2	40.1
Switzerland	26.9	36.8
Scotland	22.8	38.4
Poland	22.5	38.6
Spain	22.7	38.2
Sweden	26.3	32.7
Denmark	25.7	33.5
Greece	19.9	38.7
Ukraine	20.4	37.6
Wales	17.6	39.3
TFYR Macedonia	24.3	31.3
Russian Federation	19.6	34.0
Austria	19.7	32.3
Latvia	18.0	33.6
Malta	13.4	37.1
Croatia	16.8	33.5
Germany	17.9	29.4
Finland	19.9	26.7
Norway	19.5	26.8
Israel	18.8	28.0
Estonia	15.6	26.9
Belgium (Flemish)	16.6	25.1
Hungary	16.9	25.1
Italy	17.5	22.6
France	11.2	26.5
Portugal	13.2	24.6
HBSC average	22.3	35.3

Figure 4.2 Proportion of 15-year-olds across a selection of 35 countries who engage in recommended exercise levels (at least one hour of moderate or higher-intensity activity on five or more days per week)

Source: WHO (2004); www.euro.who.int

Why do people exercise?

People who choose to exercise cite a variety of reasons for doing so, including, most commonly:

● desire for physical fitness;
● desire to lose weight, change body shape and appearance;
● desire to maintain or enhance health status;
● desire to improve self-image and mood;
● as a means of stress reduction;
● as a social activity.

However, it is not to be inferred that choosing *not* to exercise reflects an absence of the types of desire and goals listed above. Many perceived barriers exist that contribute to people's reasons for not exercising, even when they simultaneously report, for example, a desire to lose weight. Barriers commonly mentioned include:

● lack of time;
● cost;
● lack of access to appropriate facilities and equipment;
● embarrassment;
● lack of self-belief;
● lack of someone to go with to provide support.

Differences have been found in the beliefs and attitudes towards exercise held by those who are active and those who are not active. For example, individuals who exercise regularly are more likely to perceive (and report) positive outcomes of exercise than those who do not, perceive fewer barriers to exercising, and believe that exercising is under their own control. These individual health cognitions are discussed in more detail in Chapter 6 (☛. There is also some evidence that parental activity during a child's younger years (when child is approximately 2 years old) has a modest effect on increased child activity by the age of 11–12, thus suggesting a role for parental modelling and some scope for parental intervention (Mattocks *et al.* 2008).

Health-screening behaviour

Screening is a growing part of preventive medicine across the industrialised world, with genetic testing becoming the 'hot issue' for the twenty-first century;

however, screening is not without its challenges, as we shall describe below.

There are two broad purposes of health screening:

1. to detect early asymptomatic signs of disease in order to treat;
2. identification of risk factors for illness to enable behaviour change.

WHAT DO YOU THINK?

What type of health screening behaviour do you engage in? Do you attend dental check-ups? Do you attend even when you have had six months without any symptoms of tooth decay? If not, consider your reasons for not doing so. If you receive a 'clean bill of health', how do you feel? Do you relax the way you look after your teeth due to feeling reassured that they are 'healthy'?

Do you engage in any form of self-examination (breasts, testes)? If so, what made you start doing this? What would influence whether or not you would go to your doctor if you found something atypical? Chapter 9 (☛ further discusses symptom perception and responses such as seeking health care.

Screening for disease detection

Screening for the purpose of disease detection is based on a biomedical model, which states that by identifying abnormalities in cell or organ functioning as early as possible, treatments can be implemented prior to the onset or advancement of disease symptoms. This is basically secondary prevention in that a specific screening test is offered to individuals identified as being at moderate to high risk of a certain condition on the basis of factors such as family history or, in terms of some forms of population screening, age. The best-known examples of this form of screening are:

● screening for breast cancer (**mammography**);
● screening for cervical cancer (cervical smear or Pap test);
● antenatal screening, e.g. for Down's syndrome or spina bifida;
● bone density screening.

---

mammography
a low-dose X-ray procedure that creates an image of the breast. The X-ray image can be used to identify early stages of tumours.

Screening programmes for breast and cervical cancer are based on the fact that incidence of the former is high, and that although cervical cancer is less common than breast cancer (it is about the eighth most common form of cancer in women), identifying the disease at a pre-invasive stage, or at an early invasive stage can enable early treatment with significant reductions to the associated mortality (Hakama *et al.* 2008). The mortality rate associated with untreated cancer of the cervix is high (about 40 per cent). Cervical cancer is in fact the top-ranked cancer in females under the age of 35, with regular 'smear tests' (Pap tests) being advocated from early adulthood. Most Western countries have a programme of routine invitation of adult women (aged over 18) to cervical screening every five years, with older women (aged 60 or over) being invited every three years in some countries. Recently evidence has emerged that a large proportion of young, newly sexually active young women, acquire a viral infection (HPV: human papilloma virus) which is itself a risk factor for cervical cancer. An HPV vaccination is now available and is discussed in the Screening section below. For men prostate cancer is the most common form of cancer, with a lifetime risk of about 1:9 and with the majority (75 per cent) of UK cases seen in men aged over 65 years. Screening is available in the form of digital rectal examination, which can be uncomfortable, but also by means of a less invasive method, PSA testing – this involves a test to assess levels and density of Prostate Specific Antigen (PSA) in the blood, which is one possible indicator of this common, treatable (if detected early) cancer. However, a lack of **sensitivity** (fails to detect disease in about 15 per cent of cases where it is present) and **specificity** (about two-

thirds of men with an elevated PSA won't have prostate cancer, but have other conditions which also influence PSA) means that as yet this screening is only available on a case-by-case basis and not routinely available to the wider population (Cancer Research UK 2011). Results of a 20-year follow-up of a large Swedish trial (Sandblom *et al.* 2011) conclude that no survival advantage was found for men aged between 50 and 69 routinely screened every 3 years for 20 years. Thus it may be some time before we see research into psychological factors associated with uptake of prostate screening.

Antenatal procedures such as amniocentesis also screen for disease by checking whether maternal serum alphafoetoprotein levels are indicative of spina bifida or Down's syndrome. In this instance, screening is routinely offered, at least in the UK, to pregnant women over the age of 30. If screening proves positive, there are no treatment options, but rather decisions to be made regarding continuation or termination of the pregnancy. Another example of screening for disease detection is most common among the middle-aged and consists of screening to check for signs of bone density deterioration and osteoporosis. In this case, an individual receiving a result indicating early signs of bone disease can take action in terms of increased calcium intake or increased weight-bearing exercise. It is worth noting that in relation to population screening for these conditions the individuals are invited to screening while they generally consider themselves healthy. In contrast, being invited for screening on the basis of family history may mean that individuals already perceive themselves as being 'at risk'. As psychologists, the differences between these two groups are worthy of consideration.

Screening for risk factors

Screening for risk factors in those individuals thought to be healthy is based on the principle of susceptibility and, as such, it aims to identify an individual's personal level of risk for future illness (and in the case of genetic testing, also in their offspring) in order to offer advice and information as to how to minimise further health risk, or to plan further investigation and treatment. Examples include:

- screening for cardiovascular risk (cholesterol and blood pressure assessment and monitoring);
- eye tests to screen for diabetes, glaucoma or myopia;
- prenatal genetic screening;

---

sensitivity (of a test)

the ratio of true positive tests to the total number of positive cases expressed as a percentage; for example, a sensitive test may have 95 per cent success in detecting a disease among patients known to have that disease. A test with high sensitivity has few false negatives.

specificity (of a test)

the ratio of true negative tests to the total number of negative cases expressed as a percentage; for example, healthy people are correctly identified as not having the condition being tested for. A test with high specificity has few false positives.

● antenatal screening;

● genetic testing for carrier status of the cystic fibrosis, or Huntington's disease gene, in those with a family history;

● genetic testing for breast, ovarian or colon cancer, in those with a family history.

Bearing testimony to the importance of primary prevention, some community or worksite-based programmes offer blood pressure and cholesterol testing, along with an assessment of lifestyle factors and family history of heart disease. These assessments generate an index of general susceptibility, or personal 'risk score' related to potential morbidity and if a person's risk of disease is thought to be moderate or high, preventive measures can be suggested, such as dietary change or smoking cessation. In order for screening to be of public health (societal) benefit as well as individual benefit, many of those identified as being at risk of future disease would be required to change their behaviour. It will become evident in later chapters that predicting behaviour change is highly complex (see Chapter 5 (☛)), and thus interventions to change individuals' risk behaviour face many challenges (see Chapters 6 and 7 (☛)).

Genetic screening

A range of diseases have a genetic component: for example, cystic fibrosis which results from mutation to a single gene; Downs syndrome which results from chromosomal disorder; type 1 diabetes, breast and ovarian cancer, which have a multifactorial cause in that genetic damage may have an acquired cause (e.g. diet) as well as being inherited. With advances in the diagnostic technology for carrier status of genes predisposing to a range of conditions, such as breast cancer (e.g. genes BRCA1 and BRCA2) (see Sivell *et al.* 2007 for a review) or obesity (e.g. gene MC4R), brought about by programmes of scientific research such as the Human Genome Project which ended in 2003, screening has perhaps become more controversial. Stone and Stewart (1996: 4) had stated that 'the benefits of large-scale genetic screening to individuals, families or society as a whole remain largely theoretical. There is scant evidence to support the view that the public at large perceives a need for carrier screening'. A decade later, in contrast, Braithwaite *et al.* (2002) conclude from their review of studies pertaining to specific genetic testing for hereditary cancer that

between 60 and 80 per cent of the general population samples studied report high levels of interest. Even more recently Ropka *et al.* (2006) conducted a systematic review, which included 18 actual uptake decision groups as well as 40 hypothetical studies, and found actual uptake to be just less than the hypothesised uptake (59 per cent vs. 66 per cent). An Australian study assessed interest in genetic testing for colorectal cancer among 300 Ashkenazi Jews, a population who have a higher risk of this multifactorial condition, and found that 94 per cent would have the predictive test, and a majority would make this decision out of a desire for information for their families as well as to decrease their own cancer risk through potentially changing lifestyle factors (Warner *et al.* 2005). Findings such as these show that interest is in fact high and this is perhaps not that unexpected given the increased risk such genes can carry. The two genes identified for breast cancer, BRCA1 and BRCA2, are associated with a 56–85 per cent risk of developing breast cancer, and a 20–60 per cent risk of developing ovarian cancer (Patenaude *et al.* 2002). Compared to lifetime risk in those without the gene(s), of 12 per cent for breast cancer and 1.4 per cent for ovarian cancer, this is a significant increase (National Cancer Institute, *SEER Cancer Statistics Review*, 1975–2005, retrieved 20 April 2009 from: http://seer.cancer.gov/csr/1975_2005/index.html). Studies have shown that positive test results cause significant distress (Meiser 2005) and that receipt of a negative test sometimes fails to reassure the individual (Michie *et al.* 2003), possibly because it does have to be explained by the genetic counsellor that there are remaining risk factors, including the individual's health behaviours or obesity, which mean that they cannot consider themselves at 'no risk' whatsoever, and also that there may be other mutations involved that have not as yet been identified (Ropka *et al.* 2006). In this systematic review, older age, being not married and having either a personal or family history of cancer increased the actual uptake in several of the included studies, although findings were not unanimous.

Griffith *et al.* (2009) examined whether healthy adults formed an interest in, or intention to seek, genetic testing for breast cancer on the basis of the perceived pros and cons of such testing. Making decisions in this way is sometimes referred to as 'utility maximisation': i.e. it is assumed that a person weighs up the pros and cons of a choice and then selects the option that provides them either with the greatest perceived benefit, or alternatively, the least undesirable consequences. To test whether or not utility maximisation does occur, this study used an experimental design to manipulate the understanding of genetic testing among 142 undergraduate students. Information about testing was provided in three different ways: Positive information only; Positive followed by Negative; Negative followed by Positive. A fourth group acted as a control and this group received information irrelevant to the genetic-testing decision questions. Pre- and post-manipulation assessments were taken regarding the perceived pros and cons of testing, and the interest in, and likelihood of, testing. The experimental information was found to influence the ratio of pros to cons, although the direction of change was not consistent with the ordering of the information: i.e. provision of positive information only did not increase the weighting of pros in relation to cons. Likewise, the information provision manipulation significantly changed the interest in, and likelihood of, testing reported, but again the ordering did not have the expected effect. Finally, these authors report a non-significant assocation between the weighted ratio of pros–cons and the post-manipulation interest and

likelihood scores. This finding suggests that utility maximisation was *not* occurring and that models of decision making need to look beyond simply the pros and cons of behaviour. This can be seen in the many models of behaviour and health behaviour utilised by health psychologists (see Chapter 5 ☞).

WHAT DO YOU THINK?

What does it mean when a person has been tested for carrier status of a particular gene? Do you know? It has been found that the general public commonly do not understand the issues of heritability (Figure 4.3), recessive genes or gene penetrance. There is an obvious and growing need for education and information about these very issues as more and more genes are identified that predispose us to various diseases.

What thoughts do you have about genetic testing? Write down a list of pros and cons, for example in relation to breast or prostate cancer testing. Consider what your decision may be if testing were to become more widely available.

Figure 4.3 A genetic family tree

Source: © Dorling Kindersley.

The costs and benefits of screening

While screening programmes for both disease detection and risk factor status have proliferated, questions remain as to whether there are as many benefits to the individuals undergoing screening as there are to wider society. Furthermore, some findings call into question whether the benefits of screening – in terms of eliciting behaviour change that reduces disease risk to the individual, or in terms of enabling early disease symptoms to be treated and subsequently the threat of disease progression to be reduced or removed – justify the financial costs of implementing large-scale screening programmes.

In order to try to maximise the benefits of screening to both the individual and to society, some researchers have set out what they consider to be necessary criteria for effective screening programmes.

Criteria for establishing screening programmes

Austoker (1994: 315) describes several criteria on which the introduction of screening programmes aimed at early detection of prostrate, ovarian and testicular cancer should be based. These criteria can usefully be applied to all forms of screening for disease detection, and many also apply to genetic testing:

- The condition should be an important health problem: i.e. prevalent and/or serious.
- There should be a recognisable early stage to the condition.
- Treatment at an early stage should have clear benefits to the individual (e.g. reduced mortality) compared with treatment at a later stage.
- A suitable test with good sensitivity and specificity should be available.
- The test should be considered acceptable by the general population.
- Adequate facilities for diagnosis and treatment should be in place.
- Issues of screening frequency and follow-up should be agreed.
- The costs (individual and health care) should be considered in relation to the benefits (individual and public health).
- Any particular subgroups to target should be identified.

This list of criteria remains in place currently (see Holland and Stewart 2005).

However, it is difficult to conclude whether some screening programmes meet the criteria of benefits outweighing costs: for example, while public health, disease prevention and detection and monitoring concerns are being addressed by screening, it is important not to lose sight of the individual. Marteau and Kinmouth (2002: 78) note that:

> a traditional public health approach to screening regards the population benefits of reduced morbidity and mortality as inherent, not to be appraised by individuals before they decide whether or not to participate. In keeping with this, the information accompanying the invitation (to screening) tends to be brief, emphasising the general health benefits of participation.

This suggests that the requirement that an individual is fully informed prior to making a decision is not being fully met and these authors further note that doing so would require informing potential patients about the possible adverse outcomes of screening and the limited prognostic benefits of some treatments (if any are available) for some individuals. This may affect the uptake of screening by some of those who would in fact have benefited from early detection and treatment, thus posing a dilemna for screening professions.

In the case of genetic testing, for example to identify whether an individual carries the gene that predisposes towards the development of Huntington's disease (an adult-onset disease), there is actually nothing that can be done to change the individual's risk, and therefore some question the value of screening other than preparing the individual for their future. In contrast, some individuals, when identified as carrying the BRCA1 or BRCA2 gene for breast cancer, opt for prophylactic surgery (i.e. breast removal) in order that disease cannot manifest itself (Kauff *et al.* 2002; Lerman *et al.* 2000) and in this group there is evidence of psychological benefit (Braithwaite *et al.* 2004).

Individuals considering any form of health screening will not approach solely health professionals for information, and health professionals cannot control where individuals receive health information from. For example, in the EU an average of 23 per cent of the population use the internet for health information, and in some countries, such as Denmark, that figure doubles (Jørgensen and

Gøtzsche 2004). Jørgensen and Gøtzsche undertook a large-scale review of the nature of information about breast cancer screening mammography presented on the websites of international and national organisations. They found that in many cases the information was unbalanced and biased towards screening uptake, and provided limited clear information about the possibility of false positive and false negative results or about the adverse effects of screening, such as over-diagnosis and over-treatment. Few websites informed readers of the limited evidence of a reduction in risk of mortality in those screened compared with unscreened individuals (which is in fact only about 0.1 per cent reduction in relative risk of breast cancer over ten years). Overstating the benefits of screening, or understating potential risks or adverse consequences of screening results, is not providing the individual with fully informed choice, and while most people will cope with the screening process and its outcomes, for some the emotional and behavioural consequences are significant (Anderson *et al.* 2007).

Some types of screening form long-term goals of public health, such as mass screening for the gene for cystic fibrosis among couples during pregnancy (Stone and Stewart 1996). Screening, for whatever risk factor or disease, is not as yet compulsory, and therefore the generally low level of uptake of screening opportunities plays an important part in whether people go on to develop diseases that they may have been able to avoid or reduce their risk of developing. In relation to the procedures described above, screening generally involves an individual attending an appointment; however, other forms of health screening rely on an individual performing the screening themselves.

Self-screening behaviour

Self-examination behaviour is most commonly advocated and studied in relation to early detection of breast cancer, although testicular self-examination and skin self-examination are getting increasing attention. Among women, breast cancer is the most common cause of cancer death (although the incidence of lung cancer in women is growing, Office for National Statistics 2010), and despite increasing numbers of screening programmes available in health-care settings, up to 90 per cent of all breast cancers are first detected through self-examination. However, there has in fact been some controversy over

the efficacy of breast self-examination (BSE) in saving lives. One study contributing to this controversy is a large randomised trial carried out in Shanghai, China (Thomas *et al.* 2002), whereby BSE was either taught or not taught to a huge sample (266, 064) of women factory workers aged 30+ to examine whether reduced breast cancer mortality could be found in those instructed in, monitored at least twice yearly in years 1–5, and reminded to keep practising BSE. Over a 10-year follow-up, rigorous data was gathered including factory records of a breast lump being found, referral to hospital, and medical confirmation of whether a cancer was present and at what stage of spread. All assessments were 'blind' as to whether the woman was in the control group (CG) or the intervention group (IG). Analyses also controlled for other known breast cancer risk factors. There was no effect on survival of the BSE training. An identical percentage of women developed breast cancer and died in both groups (0.10 per cent). What further adds to controversy about the value of BSE is that the women in the IG detected more lumps, with a larger number being found to be harmless (benign). The costs of health-care visits and biopsies for those individuals were significant and again counter the value of recommending BSE. One limitation of this otherwise rigorous study is that data on the specific frequency of BSE practice is absent; thus the study may attest more to the failure of teaching BSE than to the failure of BSE practice. Further research is needed to address this question.

Among men, testicular cancer is the most frequently occurring form of cancer and the second leading cause of death among those aged 15 to 35. Surviving testicular cancer is possible in 95–100 per cent of cases if the disease is detected early; however, over 50 per cent of cases present to health professionals after the early, treatable, stage has passed. Men are, however, less likely to engage in self-examination than women (Courtenay 2000).

Likewise, skin cancer incidence is also increasing, particularly in those aged 20 to 40, yet early detection of skin lesions of the more harmful type (malignant melanoma) through self-examination can lead to high cure rates. In spite of rising incidence of this cancer, Ness *et al.* (1999) have noted that 'lay epidemiology' (i.e. the general perception within society) considers sun exposure to be healthy, and in some instances this is correct (e.g. positive effect of sun exposure on well-being and mood, on vitamin D production and bone strengthening). This presents a real challenge to health educators who seek to increase sun protection behaviours (e.g. use of sunscreen, avoidance of sunbeds) from an early age as they have to counter this evidence with evidence of a clear association between sun exposure and malignant melanoma, particularly in fair-haired, light-skinned and blue-eyed individuals. In Australia, where the majority of studies on skin self-examination and skin protection behaviour have originated, the incidence of skin cancer is high. It might therefore be expected that skin protection behaviour, as well as skin examination, is normative; however, while such behaviours are certainly more prevalent, health education interventions generally have short-lived effects (Aitken *et al.* 2006). There is also some evidence of gender differences in tanning behaviours, with, for example, female British students being more prepared to protect their skin than males while also placing higher value on sunbathing (Eiser *et al.* 1993). Such differences suggests that interventions should address the value placed on a particular 'risk behaviour', as this will likely affect the intervention's effectiveness (see Chapter 3 ☛ for the same point in relation to smoking).

Uptake of screening behaviour

Psychology, particularly health and social psychology, has a large part to play in helping to identify predictors of the uptake of screening programmes, such as individual attitudes and beliefs about illness, about screening, and about preventive behaviour. While the increasing availability of screening programmes for many diseases and disease risk factors seems to have increased uptake, generally uptake remains at a lower level than is considered optimal in terms of disease reduction at a societal level.

Factors associated with screening behaviour

A range of factors have been found to be associated with the non-uptake of screening opportunities or self-examination behaviour, including:

● lower levels of education and income;

● age (e.g. younger women tend not to attend risk-factor screening);

● lack of knowledge about the condition;

● lack of knowledge about the purpose of screening;

● lack of knowledge about potential outcomes of screening;

● embarrassment regarding the procedures involved;

● fear that 'something bad' will be detected;

● fear of pain or discomfort during the procedure;

● lack of self-belief (self-efficacy, see Chapter 5 ☛) in terms of being able to practise self-examination correctly.

In terms of self-screening behaviour, knowledge of testicular cancer and the practice of self-examination have generally been found to be at a low level. Studies of breast self-examination have found that even among women who do perform it, many do not do so correctly (i.e. it should ideally be carried out mid-menstrual cycle, in an upright position as well as when lying down, and should include examination of all tissue in the breast, nipple and underarm areas). Worryingly, a study by Steadman and Quine (2004) confirmed low levels of knowledge among young adult males about testicular cancer and regarding the potential benefits of self-examination. This study went on to demonstrate that a simple intervention, which required half of the participants to write down and visualise when, where and how they would self-examine their testes over the forthcoming three weeks, led to a significantly higher proportion of them self-examining than that found in the control group who did not form such plans. This study demonstrates the relative ease with which behaviour can be changed, although a longer-term follow-up would be beneficial to check whether self-examination practices were maintained beyond the study period. This intervention focused specifically on making an individualised plan for action, referred to in health psychology as forming an 'implementation intention'. This construct, and further research supporting its practical utility in developing interventions, is described in the next chapter. ☛

Immunisation behaviour

The purpose of immunisation

Public health policy is to provide vaccinations that provide long-lasting protection against specific disease without adverse consequences to the individual, and with the costs of providing the vaccination being outweighed by the costs of having to treat the disease if no vaccination were to be provided. Vaccination is the oldest form of immunisation, in which immunity is provided to an individual by introducing a small amount of an **antigen** into their body (either orally, intramuscularly or intra-dermally (injecting into the skin)), which triggers off the development of antibodies to that specific antigen. Some vaccinations, such as orally administered polio vaccine, measles, mumps and rubella, use live components, while others, such as hepatitis B or swine flu (available since 2009) use inactivated components. Vaccinations against infectious disease have been credited with the virtual eradication of diseases that in previous centuries caused widespread morbidity and mortality, such as smallpox, diptheria and polio (e.g. Woolf 1996), although com-pulsory administration of any vaccine is generally not supported (Blume 2006).

Immunisation against infectious disease is considered beneficial to the individual and, where uptake is wide-spread, beneficial to the wider community when 'herd immunity' is achieved. Public health specialists consider vaccines both safe and successful and, at least in developed countries, the incidence of many common, predominantly childhood diseases, such as measles, is low. However, infectious diseases still account for approximately 17 million deaths in developing countries and half a million deaths in industrialised countries (BMA 2003a). Although immunisation is offered to various subgroups in the population, such as influenza vaccination to the elderly or to those with pre-existing conditions that increase their vulnerability to infection (e.g. asthma), the main emphasis of immunisation has been on the prevention of childhood disease. It is policy in the UK to advise parents to immunise their child, as shown in Table 4.1

However, immunisation coverage varies in different parts of the world and even in different regions within countries; there is growing concern that some diseases, such as whooping cough and measles, may re-emerge as uptake has not reached saturation level.

A subgroup of a family of viruses known collectively as **human papillomavirus (HPV)** have been associated with abnormal tissue and cell growth implicated in the development of genital warts and cervical cancer. The dis-covery of a vaccination against those types of HPV which cause 70 per cent of cervical cancers (but not genital warts) has been billed as a major public health discovery, with clinical trials finding the vaccine to be effective in

Table 4.1 Immunisation policy in the United Kingdom*

Age	Vaccine	Means of administration
2–4 months	Polio	By mouth Combined injection Injection
12–15 months	Measles, mumps and rubella (MMR)	Combined injection
3–5 years	Polio	By mouth Combined injection
	Measles, mumps and rubella (MMR)	Combined injection
10–14 years	Rubella (girls)	Injection
12 years +	HPV*	3 injections over 6 months
15–18 years	Tetanus booster	Injection

*HPV: Human Papilloma Virus, vaccination available since September 2008 in the UK government vaccination programme.

both adults and children, with 90 per cent effectiveness in those who have not already acquired infection (Lo 2006, 2007; Steinbrook 2006). As a result, from September 2008 the UK government has run a vaccination programme targeted at girls aged 12–13 years, on the basis that the vaccination needs to be given before sexual activity commences. Also a 'catch-up' programme in 2009/10 targeted 15–17-year-olds, and so by the end of 2010 it is hoped that all girls under 18 will have been offered the vaccine. The vaccination requires three injections over a six-month period and will be made available in second-

antigen

unique process found on the surface of a pathogen that enables the immune system to recognise that pathogen as a foreign substance and therefore produce antibodies to fight it. Vaccinations introduce specially prepared viruses or bacteria into a body, and these have antigens.

human papillomavirus (HPV)

a family of over 100 viruses, of which 30 types can cause genital warts and be transmitted by sexual contact. While most genital HPV come and go over the course of a few years, two specific HPV types markedly elevate the risk for cancer of the cervix.

ary schools. Parental permission will of course be required in order for the vaccination to be given.

Costs and benefits of immunisation

Over the past century, the widescale benefits of childhood vaccination programmes have become apparent. It is now rare for a child living in the Western world, and increasingly in developing countries where vaccination programmes are being promoted, to die from measles, diphtheria or polio. The World Health Organization set a target for almost universal vaccination by 2000, and in 1997 there were high hopes of achieving population immunity against measles following the introduction of a vaccine in 1988, at least in Britain, with initial uptake high (97 per cent, Bellaby 2003).

However, widespread publicity following a 1998 study (see IN THE SPOTLIGHT opposite) that reported adverse effects of the combined MMR vaccination has largely been 'credited' with the downturn in immunisation uptake, to an average 81 per cent in 2004. Rates varied hugely: for example, uptake ranged from 59 to 98 per cent between 2002 and 2004 in one study of 257 general medical practices in one region of England (Lamden and Gemmell 2008). A lack of public confidence and debate about vaccine safety has been at its most vociferous in relation to the MMR vaccine. However, there are encour-aging signs of change: for example, in Scotland where quarterly statistics (ISD Scotland, September 2008) hit the target of having 95 per cent of five-year-olds in Scotland immunised with at least one dose of the MMR vaccine for the first time since the target was introduced

Plate 4.2 Immunisation behaviour is crucial to public health, yet is influenced by many cultural, social, emotional and cognitive factors. Here, a queue of mothers take up the first opportunity of vaccination for their child against measles to be offered in their village

Source: Getty Images/Jacob Silberberg.

in September 2006; and those having a second dose by age five had also risen, from 81.1 per cent to 87.4 per cent. Uptake rates for the majority of other childhood immunisations in Scotland remain above 95 per cent.

While socio-economic variables such as low educational attainment have sometimes been found to influence the uptake of vaccination (see Chapter 2 ☞), not all studies report this (Lamden and Gemmell 2008). Evidence more consistently points to emotional and cognitive predictors of uptake: for example, Bennett and Smith (1992) studied the vaccination status of 300 children aged 2 to $2^{1}/_{2}$ in Wales and found that those parents who did not have their child vaccinated exhibited anxiety about the risks of vaccination as well as low perceptions of the potential benefits of vaccination. Risk perceptions and outcome expectancies and the research evidence as to their utility in explaining health behaviour are examined in Chapter 5 ☞.

IN THE SPOTLIGHT

Immunisation debate and the MMR vaccination

In order to achieve population immunity, the required uptake of a measles vaccine is between 92 and 95 per cent (BMA 2003b). In the UK, at least, General Practitioners are financially rewarded if they hit the World Health Organization target of 95 per cent. While an upturn in MMR uptake has been reported since 2008, it is still lower than that recorded for other vaccinations. Data for 2009–10 show that in England the proportion of children having at least one dose of the vaccine by the time they reach the age of 2 increased from 79.9 per cent to 88.2 per cent between 2004 and 2010; in Wales 92.2 per cent of children have been vaccinated, in Scotland 93.7 per cent and in Northern Ireland it's 92.2 per cent. However, to varying extents all countries fall short of target (NHS Information Centre 2010).

Why is one immunisation being taken up less commonly than another? It is likely that this is in part due to differing perceptions of the illnesses concerned (meningitis is almost universally feared, whereas measles may be considered a less serious illness); in part due to the manner in which health professionals advocate the different vaccines (e.g. New and Senior 1991) and in part due to the nature of publicity attracted by the different diseases/vaccines. This has been the case with the MMR vaccine, which lost public confidence following a paper published in 1998 suggesting a link between the measles, mumps and rubella (MMR) vaccine and autism, and to a lesser degree (at least in terms of publicity) inflammatory bowel disease (IBD).

This paper led to a great deal of media attention, increased public and parental concerns, and has been blamed for the resultant decline in the percentage of children being immunised against these diseases. Although published over 12 years ago, Wakefield *et al.*'s (1998) paper, published in the highly respected medical journal, *The Lancet*, is still cited today as a contributing factor in parental anxiety about this combined vaccination. What is not always pointed out in media coverage is that the speculated link between autism was made on the basis of their finding that among 12 children referred for gastroenterological investigation, 9 manifested varying degrees of behavioural problems that had received autistic spectrum diagnoses, and in 8 cases parents attributed the onset of symptoms to a time following the MMR vaccine. However, this study was seriously limited by its small sample size, and findings disseminated perhaps inappropriately. In fact, this research has since been discredited and Dr Wakefield was struck off the medical register in May 2010, after the General Medical Council ruled he had acted 'dishonestly and irresponsibly'.

What the media at the time neglected to publicise were findings from several larger-scale and more rigorous studies such as Peltola *et al.*'s (also 1998), which found no evidence of a link between MMR, autism or IBD in spite of conducting a 14-year prospective study; or Taylor *et al.*'s (1999) study, which reviewed 500 children with autism born between 1979 and 1994 and found no sudden increase in autism cases associated with the introduction of the MMR vaccine in 1988 and no difference in the age of autism diagnosis between those who had been immunised and those who had not (Taylor *et al.* 1999). Furthermore, Taylor and colleagues subsequently confirmed these findings in a population study conducted in five health districts in England (Taylor *et al.* 2002).

The stance then, and now, of the World Health Organization and thus the medical authorities globally is that there is no link between MMR and autism or IBD as evidenced by methodologically valid studies. However, parental fears, once raised, are hard to reduce, and lay perceptions of risks attached to this vaccination remain even now. One option proposed to address concerns that the combined vaccine was problematic, was to provide measles, mumps and rubella vaccines singly. However, the World Health Organization advised against this on the grounds that the extended period of time necessary to provide three separate injections increases overall levels of non-adherence to the vaccination programme, which then exposes children to infection and increases the likelihood of epidemics occurring. Concerned parents point to the fact that some countries, such as France, provide the vaccines singly to babies aged 9–12 months (although it is usually given in combined MMR form subsequently)

and use this as support for the argument that the MMR vaccine is unsafe.

What the history of the MMR debate highlights is the power of the media. While it is indeed important that the media stimulate debate through their presentation of evidence, it is also important that the general public are informed objectively and in an evidence-based manner. Health professionals also, in communicating with their patients, need to present both sides of the evidence so as to enable informed decisions.

Things to think about and research yourself

Do you think that you would provide your child(ren) in the future with vaccination protection? Would you consider all vaccines as equally important or would you weigh up the pros and cons for each one independently? Where can people find reliable evidence of the pros and cons of immunisation?

How do you think health professionals could better convince the public as to the benefits of immunisation? Where do policy makers and public health speakers go 'wrong' in communicating the need for immunisation?

SUMMARY

This chapter has provided an overview of a range of behaviour often described as 'behavioural immunogens': behaviour that acts in ways that protect or enhance an individual's health status. A lack or low level of 'immunogens' is also detrimental to health, as is reflected in the rising obesity figures (see Chapter 3 ☞) attributed in large part to low levels of physical activity. Given the convincing evidence of a behaviour–disease association reviewed in this and the previous chapter, we could perhaps be

forgiven for expecting that the majority of people would behave in a manner that protects their health. However, as you will have seen, this is not borne out by statistics. It is increasingly evident that there is a complexity of influences on health behaviour practices and this is what we now turn attention to in Chapter 5 ☞, where the key psychosocial theories and models of health behaviour employed in health psychology research are described.

Further reading

Di Matteo, M.R (2004a). Variations in patients' adherence to medical recommendations: a quantitative revew of 50 years of research. *Medical Care*, 42: 200–9.

A useful review of over 500 studies, this provides a summary of the relative contributions made by individual and illness-related factors.

Sivell, S., Iredale, R., Gray, J. and Coles, B. (2007). Cancer genetic risk assessment for individuals at risk of familial breast cancer. *Cochrane Database of Systematic Reviews* issue 2, art. no.: CD003721.

This useful paper provides a review of randomised controlled trials relating to the impact of genetic risk assessment in cancer. Addresses many issues raised a decade earlier by Hopwood and shows how science has progressed.

Department of Health (2004). *Choosing Health: Making Healthy Choices Easier*.

This UK government White Paper sets out the key principles for supporting the public to make healthier and more informed choices in regards to their health. The DoH website is a useful site for accessing many such policy and discussion documents.

This link will take you to useful downloads including the above:

www.dh.gov.uk/en/Publicationsandstatistics/Publications/PublicationsPolicyandGuidance/DH_4094550

Commission of the European Communities (2007). White Paper. *Together for Health: A Strategic Approach for the EU 2008–2013*.

On 23 October 2007 the European Commission adopted a new Health Strategy which aims to provide an overarching strategic framework spanning core issues in health (e.g. in relation to ageing, child health, health behaviours, occupations) at the European level. This and other documents can be downloaded from:

http://ec.europa.eu/health/ph_overview/strategy/health_strategy_en.htm

Visit the website at **www.pearsoned.co.uk/morrison** for additional resources to help you with your study, including multiple choice questions, weblinks and flashcards.

Chapter 5
Explaining health behaviour

Learning outcomes

By the end of this chapter, you should understand and be able to describe:

- how demographic, social, cognitive and motivational factors influence the uptake of health or risk behaviour

- the components of several key psychosocial models of health behaviour and health behaviour change

- how 'continuum' or 'static' models differ from 'stage' models in terms of how they consider behaviour change processes

- the research evidence that supports or refutes the models in terms of which factors are predictive of health behaviour and health behaviour change

Girls behaving badly

'The scourge of the "ladette" has spread to girls as young as ten, shocking figures reveal today'. This is the opening sentence of the story headlined in the *Daily Mail*, 3 October 2010 as 'More binge-drinking teenage girls now end up in hospital than boys'. Young British girls are not doing too well in these figures collated by Alcohol Concern, a national charity. Twenty-eight per cent more girls aged under 18 years old (23,347) than boys (18,159) were admitted to Accident and Emergency hospital services for alcohol-related causes in 2009, an increase of a third since figures in 2004. While some of this difference can perhaps be explained by lower levels of alcohol tolerance among females, there are likely to be other factors at play here. The article cites 'ludicrously cheap' prices and a professor who considers each case as reflecting 'a child in need and a teachable moment in a child's family', but as we will see in the forthcoming pages there are many factors which interact to affect our behaviour, not all of which a teenager's family may be aware nor able to influence. Binge drinking is likely to be influenced by different factors than alcohol-dependent drinking and thus as a behaviour it highlights the need for psychologists and health professionals to not expect that one model or explanation 'fits all'.

Chapter outline

The previous two chapters have described behaviour that is associated with health and illness: positive or health-protective behaviours such as exercise and health screening, and health-risk behaviours, such as smoking or unsafe sex. This chapter aims to describe the key theoretical models that have been proposed and tested in terms of their ability to explain and predict why people engage in health-risk or health-protective behaviour. Personality, beliefs and attitudes play an important role in motivating behaviour, as do our goals and intentions, social circumstances and social norms. The key psychological models and their components are described and critiqued, drawing on evidence from studies of an array of health behaviours. While our understanding of health behaviour remains incomplete due to the complexity of influences upon human behaviour generally, the empirical studies described have identified many significant and modifiable influences upon health and health behaviour that offer potential targets for future health promotion and health education, as described in Chapters 6 and 7 ☛.

Distal influences on health behaviour

One way of considering the factors predictive of health behaviour generally is to view some influences as 'distal', such as culture, environment, ethnicity, socio-economic status, age, gender and personality, and others as 'proximal' in their influence, such as specific beliefs and attitudes towards health-risk and health-protective behaviour. This division is somewhat arbitrary but is intended to reflect the fact that some influences operate on behaviour indirectly, by means of their effects on other factors, such as a person's attitudes, beliefs or goals. These variables are therefore potential **mediator**s of, for example, the effect of socio-economic status on health. To illustrate this further, there is reasonably consistent evidence that people in the lower socio-economic groups drink more, smoke more, exercise less and eat less healthy diets than those in the higher socio-economic groups, in both the UK and elsewhere in the European Union (e.g. Cavelaars *et al.* 1997; Choinière

et al. 2000). This evidence of a distal influence does not, however, explain 'how' or 'why' this is the case, (see Chapter 2 ☛ for a full discussion of socio-economic inequalities in health). Further explanation can be offered from evidence showing that social class affects health beliefs (see Chapter 1 ☛), which in turn may then affect behaviour. These perceptions or beliefs can be considered 'closer' to the behaviour (more proximal) and offer a more feasible target for intervention than would an intervention aimed at altering a person's social class. Beliefs may therefore **mediate** the effects of more distal influences, and this hypothesis can be tested statistically. Another term you may come across when reading about relationships between

---

mediate/mediator

mediating variables explain how or why a relationship exists between two other variables: for example, the effects of age upon behaviour may be mediated by health beliefs; thus age effects would be said to be indirect, rather than direct.

variables is **moderation**. Moderating variables explains the conditions under which a relationship exists, for example the relationship between a predictor and an outcome may vary according to categories of another variable (e.g. male/female, under 65, over 66). The models described in this chapter all acknowledge the role of these 'distal' influences, but are limited in the extent to which they propose specific associations between these and the more proximal factors, or vary in the extent to which their hypothesised associations have been tested. Before turning to the models, we therefore present some of the evidence regarding the specific distal influences of demographic characteristics of age, gender, and personality. For a fuller discussion of socio-economic and cultural influences on health behaviour, see Chapter 2 ☞.

Demographic influences

In terms of age, the health behaviours that receive the majority of attention from educational, medical and public health specialists (i.e. smoking, alcohol consumption, unprotected sexual activity, exercise and diet) are patterns of behaviour set down in childhood or early adulthood. For example, according to the Global Youth Tobacco Survey Collaborative Group (2002) the majority of smokers took up the habit as teenagers. Attitudes also change at this time when adolescents generally begin to seek autonomy (independence) from their parents. This may include making health-related decisions for themselves: for example, whether or not to start smoking or drinking alcohol, whether or not to brush their teeth before bed. Influences on decisional processes, attitudes and behaviour change during these years, with more credence being given to the attitudes, beliefs, values and behaviour of one's peers (and in fact siblings) than to the advice or attitudes of parents or teachers (e.g. Chassin *et al.* 1996; Hendry and Kloep 2002; Mercken *et al.* 2007). While establishing a sense of identity among

---

> **moderator/moderation**
>
> moderating variables explains the conditions under which a relationship between two other variables may exist: for example, the relationship between individual beliefs and behaviour may be different depending on gender or health status.

---

one's peer group and attempting to 'fit in', it is perhaps not surprising that, for some adolescents, this will include the initiation of 'risk' behaviour as part of rebelling against authority or because the behaviour is considered to be 'cool' and grown-up (Michell and Amos 1997). Gender has been shown to exert a significant influence on the nature and performance of health-protective or health-risk behaviours, as we have described in the two preceding chapters. What is necessary is better understanding of why this is the case, given, for example, concerns highlighted in the opening feature regarding increased binge drinking among young females. Perceptions of health and the meanings attached to health and health behaviours offer a partial explanation, with males seeming to engage in risk behaviours such as drinking alcohol as a projection of their masculinity (Visser and Smith 2007). Conversely they may also engage in the health-enhancing activity – exercise – for similar reasons (Steffen *et al.* 2006), and they may avoid health care for related reasons, for example to be seen as being 'strong' (Marcell *et al.* 2007). Visser and Smith (2007) present qualitative material which beautifully illustrates the linkages made between health-risk behaviour and social constructions of masculinity, and how other factors, such as sporting success, can 'compensate' for the reduced perceived masculinity assumed from lower levels of drinking. Selected quotes from males aged 18–21 include:

> . . . really icons of masculinity who go out and booze, and get in fights, and get lots of women and stuff like that, they are regarded as . . . the prime kind of, you know, specimens of maleness . . . because I was better than most of the players, they didn't, like, pressure me into drinking, because . . . you know, it was kind of like I could say to them 'Forget it' or whatever. Um . . . that was, that's personally me, but then I have friends who . . . weren't quite as experienced as me at hockey, but just to kind of get into the group I think they felt the need to partake in that [drinking].

However, there were exceptions to this association between masculinity and drinking behaviour. Ethnicity and religion exerted stronger influences on the behaviour of some black and Asian Muslim interviewees than did the need to be seen as 'masculine'.

> I'm a Muslim guy, you know, and if you are a Muslim you are not allowed to drink. And I'm a guy that, you know I pray, you know. I pray and so I don't drink. I never, never tried to drink either.

The broader influences of age, gender and ethnicity need to be acknowledged to a greater extent than is often the case in studies of health behaviour and health behaviour change. Individuals also operate in varying social worlds, each with their own systems and norms which exert influence on individual beliefs and behaviours. We try to highlight these wider influences wherever possible.

A further influence on behaviour that is not consistently operationalised or tested in studies of health behaviour change, although it is usually included in the diagrammatic representation of the models (see below), is that of personality.

Personality

Personality, generally speaking, is what makes individuals different from one another, in that each of us thinks and behaves in a characteristic manner, showing traits that are particularly enduring regardless of situation. Different scientists have proposed different numbers of key traits or dimensions of personality; two of the major examples are presented here.

Eysenck's three-factor model

1. *Extroversion* (outgoing social nature): dimensionally opposite to *introversion* (shy, solitary nature).
2. *Neuroticism* (anxious, worried, guilt-ridden nature): dimensionally opposite to *emotional stability* (relaxed, contented nature).
3. *Psychoticism* (egocentric, aggressive, antisocial nature): dimensionally opposite to *self-control* (kind, considerate, obedient nature).

According to Eysenck (1970, 1991), individual personality is reflected in an individual's scores along these three dimensions; for example, one individual may score positively and high on neuroticism and extroversion but negatively on psychoticism, whereas another may score positively and high on neuroticism, and negatively and high on extroversion and psychoticism. These three factors received significant empirical support and are considered to be valid and robust personality factors (Kline 1993). However, another model, the five-factor model (McCrae and Costa 1987, 1990), identifies five primary dimensions of personality – the 'big five' – and it is this model which has received the most attention and support within health psychology research (see also Chapter 12 ☞ for more detailed discussion of personality and responses to stress).

McCrae and Costa's five-factor model

The Big Five traits include:

1. neuroticism
2. extroversion
3. openness (to experience)
4. agreeableness
5. conscientiousness.

Four of these five have been validated in different cultures (with the exception of conscientiousness) and at different points in the lifespan from age 14 to 50+ (McCrae *et al.* 2000), and are considered therefore relatively stable and enduring. Many associations between these personality traits and health have been reported (see Vollrath 2006 for a review); however, less attention has been directed at whether individual behaviours mediate this association. There is some evidence that increased risk-taking behaviour is seen among individuals scoring high on extroversion, neuroticism or openness, with less risk-taking seen among those scoring higher on agreeableness and conscientiousness (e.g. Nicholson *et al.* 2005; Terraciano and Costa 2004). Similar directional associations have been reported with health-protective behaviours. For example, Goldberg and Strycker (2002) carried out a large-scale community survey of the associations between personality and dietary behaviour and found that openness predicted low meat fat consumption and high fibre intake. This is consistent with the findings of Steptoe *et al.* (1995), where openness was associated with a willingness to try novel situations, including new food tastes and types. In general, conscientiousness is associated with health-protective behaviour (for a meta-analysis see Bogg and Roberts 2004) whereas neuroticism tends to associate with health-risk behaviour (Goldberg and Strycker 2002; Booth-Kewley and Vickers 1994), including dietary 'pickiness' (fussiness) and **neophobia** among a sample of 451 Scottish children aged between 11 and 15 (MacNicol *et al.* 2003).

In seeming contradiction to this negative influence of neuroticism, it has also been associated with greater health-care use. This is attributed to the tendency of highly neurotic individuals to report greater attention to

---

neophobia
a persistent and chronic fear of anything new (places, events, people, objects).

bodily sensations and to label them as a potential threat or 'symptom' of disease more than people lower in neuroticism (Cameron and Leventhal 2003; Jerram and Coleman 1999; and see Chapter 9 ☞). However, Friedman (2003) concluded that there is no consistent evidence that people scoring high on neuroticism engage in a greater range or frequency of health-protective behaviour or in less damaging health behaviour than those people with low neuroticism, and that 'healthy neurotics' may exist as well as 'unhealthy neurotics'. This suggests therefore that personality traits such as neuroticism offer insufficient explanation for health or risk behaviour.

What may add to the predictive utility of personality factors is some exploration of how personality traits effect the motivations for carrying out behaviour. Self-determination theory (Deci and Ryan 2000) distinguishes between intrinsic and extrinsic motivation, whereby a person is motivated to behave in a certain way for the inherent personal satisfaction or rewards it produces, such as feelings of competence or autonomy, or because of other externally situated rewards, such as peer approval. Testing this theory in relation to the safer sexual behaviour of students, Ingledew and Ferguson (2007) found that students scoring high on agreeableness or conscientiousness had intrinsic, autonomous or self-determined motivations to perform safer sex (e.g. 'Personally, I would practise safe sex because . . . I personally believe it is the best thing for my health'), rather than extrinsic, external or controlled motivations (e.g. 'Personally, I would practise safe sex because . . . I feel pressure from others'). This cross-sectional study cannot, however, ascertain whether the identified motives predict behaviour over time. Evidence pointing to a relationship between personality and behavioural motives is provided by Cooper *et al.* (2000) who found that neurotic individuals drank to reduce negative mood states whereas extroverted individuals drank to enhance their positive mood. Such studies make useful contributions to an area of research where understanding of the processes by which personality achieves its effects on health behaviour, and ultimately health, remains limited.

Other aspects of personality

Another commonly investigated aspect of personality is generalised **locus of control** (LoC) beliefs (Rotter 1966). Rotter originally considered individuals to have either an internal LoC orientation (i.e. they place responsibility

for outcomes on themselves and consider that their actions affect outcomes) or an external orientation, which suggests that they place responsibility for outcomes at the door of external factors such as luck. A sense of internal control was thought to be adaptive. In order to test this assumption in relation to health outcomes, Kenneth Wallston and colleagues (Wallston *et al.* 1978) developed a LoC scale specific to health beliefs. This scale, the MHLC (multidimensional **health locus of control**) scale, identified three statistically independent dimensions:

1. *Internal*: strong internal beliefs consider the individual themselves as the prime determinant of their health state. Theoretically associated with high levels of health-protective behaviour and with Bandura's self-efficacy construct (see below).

2. *External/chance*: strong external beliefs consider that external forces such as luck, fate or chance determine an individual's health state, rather than their own behaviour.

3. *Powerful others*: strong beliefs on this scale consider health state to be determined by the actions of powerful others such as health and medical professionals.

Wallston argued that these dimensions become relevant only if an individual values their health. This reflects the theoretical underpinning to locus of control, that of social learning or social cognitive theory (Bandura 1986), whereby an individual acts on the expectancy of certain valued outcomes. If individuals do not value their health, it is thought that they are unlikely to engage in health-protective behaviour (even if they believe in personal control over health), simply because health is not prioritised (e.g. Wallston and Smith 1994). Individuals with an internal, or even a powerful others HLC who do

---

locus of control

a personality trait thought to distinguish between those who attribute responsibility for events to themselves (i.e. internal LoC) or to external factors (external LoC).

health locus of control

the perception that one's health is under personal control; controlled by powerful others such as health professionals; or under the control of external factors such as fate or luck.

value their health are therefore more likely to behave in a health-protective manner. In the case of internal LoC, this might be seen in a person commencing a healthy eating programme, or in the case of a powerful others HLC, going to a local health clinic for dietary advice. Powerful others beliefs can, however, detract from an individual taking active responsibility for behaviour, with such individuals being over-reliant on medical 'cures'. Such generalised LoC dimensions have proved, however, to be only a modest, or indeed weak, predictor of behaviour (see Norman and Bennett's 1996 review). A weak association was confirmed in a large-scale survey of over 13,000 healthy individuals where positive health behaviour was weakly correlated with higher internal control, and even more weakly associated with lower external and powerful others control beliefs (Norman *et al.* 1998). Given this modest influence researchers turned their attention to more behaviourally specific and proximal constructs, such as **perceived behavioural control** (see theory of planned behaviour on p. 126) and **self-efficacy** (Bandura 1977 and see the health action process approach model on p. 141). Interestingly, though, a study by Armitage (2003) has suggested that dispositional or generic control beliefs might in fact influence these more specific proximal control beliefs. He found that generalised internal control beliefs independently predicted the relationship between perceived behavioural control and intention. In other words, the ability of perceived behavioural control beliefs to explain intention was strongest among those individuals with high generalised internal LoC. Such findings suggest that interventions aiming to enhance specific perceived behavioural control beliefs may be most effective if targeted at those with an internal locus of control.

Other personality characteristics may also affect proximal predictors of behaviour. Linda Cameron has shown, following a study of beliefs about skin cancer risk, that beliefs in low personal control over cure of the disease were associated with greater risk perception (perceived likelihood of developing skin cancer) and lower intention to engage in prevention (Cameron 2008). She suggested that this association may reflect underlying personality such as **dispositional pessimism** or anxiety, as other studies have found these to influence susceptibility beliefs (e.g. Gerend *et al.* 2004).

Overall, we have suggested in this section that the personality–health behaviour relationship is one which warrants further consideration. Perhaps one reason why

health psychologists have played relatively less attention to personological predictors of behaviour than cognitive, emotional or even some social factors is that personality is considered fixed and unchangeable (as the definition of 'trait' suggests). While this may be the case, personality shapes the beliefs which cognitive interventions address and thus contribute to the whole picture.

Social Influences

Humans are fundamentally social beings. Our behaviour is a result of many influences: the general culture and environment into which we are born; the day-to-day culture in which we live and work which generally has a set of shared norms and expectations; the groups, subgroups and individuals with whom we interact; and our own personal emotions, beliefs, values and attitudes, all of which are influenced by these wider factors. We learn from our own positive and negative experience, but we also learn 'vicariously' through exposure to, and observation of, other people's expectancies, behaviour and experiences. The behaviour of people, past and present, in our culture or smaller social groups, creates a perceived 'social norm', which suggests implicit (or explicit) approval for certain behaviour. For example, a four-year follow-up study of nearly 10,000 American high school students found that 37 per cent of non-smokers at high school had started smoking by college follow-up; 25 per cent of original 'experimental' smokers had increased their smoking behaviour; and the remaining students had stayed the same (either non-smokers, experimenting with smoking (none in last month), current smokers or

---

perceived behavioural control
one's belief in personal control over a certain specific action or behaviour.

self-efficacy
the belief that one can perform particular behaviour in a given set of circumstances.

dispositional pessimism
having a generally negative outlook on life and a tendency to anticipate negative outcomes (as opposed to dispositional optimism).

ex-smokers) (Choi *et al.* 2003). Clear differences were found in the factors that explained initiation to smoking from non-smoking (i.e. white, rebellious students who did not like school) and progression from experimental (irregular, social, short-term) smoking to current smoker. Those who progressed in their smoking behaviour perceived peer approval for their smoking and perceived experimental smoking as safe. Additionally, perceived parental approval was a more important influence on starting smoking than on progression. College and university students similarly have been found to make assumptions about what constitutes 'typical' alcohol intake, and thus, for some, their problematic drinking can be judged as 'normal' when it may not be (Perkins *et al.* 2005).

In relation to health-risk behaviour, broader social influence is seen in the many sources of information that a person is exposed to: for example, televised advertisements graphically illustrating the negative consequences of smoking; an older sibling or parent appearing to be healthy in spite of regular binge drinking episodes; a classroom workshop on how to 'just say no' to the first offer of a cigarette or other drug; a friend who smokes telling you that smoking is cool. There is consistent evidence to show that the credibility, similarity to self and even the attractiveness of the source of information influences whether or not attitudinal change or behaviour change occurs as a consequence (e.g. Petty and Cacioppo 1986, 1996; see Chapter 7 ☞ for further discussion of influences on the effectiveness of health promotion).

Goals and self-regulation of behaviour

We need to address the fact that health-protective and risk behaviours are generally performed for a reason. **Social cognition** theory assumes that behaviour is motivated by **outcome expectancies** and goals (both

> ### social cognition
> a model of social knowledge and behaviour that highlights the explanatory role of cognitive factors (e.g. beliefs and attitudes).
>
> ### outcome expectancies
> the outcome that is expected to result from behaviour, e.g. exercise will make me fitter.

Plate 5.1 Social norms have been found to be important predictors of whether or not a person initiates specific health behaviours, in this instance smoking and drinking alcohol

Source: Rex Features/SUTTON-HIBBERT.

short- and long-term goals), i.e. behaviour is viewed as being goal-directed (e.g. Fiske and Taylor 1991; Carver and Scheier 1998). Ingledew and McDonagh (1998) have shown that health behaviour serves coping functions (which may be considered as short-term goals of the behaviour): for example, for some individuals smoking may serve the function of coping with stress. These authors identified five coping functions attached to health behaviour: problem solving, feeling better, avoidance, time out and prevention – for example, exercise behaviour loaded on to a 'prevention with problem-solving' function, but also on to a 'time out with problem-solving' function. Such findings highlight that there are many reasons why individuals behave in the way that they do; in this case, individuals exercised as a means of preventive health behaviour but also as a means of time out or relaxation. The implication therefore is that interventions designed to reduce 'unhealthy' behaviour need to take account of the coping functions or goals that individual behaviour serves for each individual – it is these goals that will motivate the behaviour (see also Chapter 6 ☞).

Processes of **self-regulation**, the cognitive and behavioural processes by which individuals guide, control, modify or adapt his or her responses, enable an individual to achieve desired outcomes or reduce undesired outcomes, i.e. their goals. Goals focus our attention and direct our efforts, with more valued, and more specific, goals leading to greater and more persistent effort (Locke and Latham 2002). Cognitive regulation (i.e. controlling or modifying our thoughts) is required as well as emotion regulation (controlling or modifying our emotions) if we are to successfully organise and execute goal-directed activity. An inability to control thoughts and evaluate decision options and potential outcomes or regulate emotions (for example, when drunk!) may increase impulsivity and risk-taking behaviour (Magar et al. 2008). There is some suggestion that women use such self-regulation more than men: for

example, in relation to planning for exercise uptake (Hankonen et al. 2010) and healthy eating (Renner et al. 2008). Attentional control, an aspect of dispositional self-regulation, is also required in order to achieve desired goals. Luszczynska et al. (2004) developed a scale to assess attentional control, defined as the extent to which a person can focus on activities and goals and avoid being distracted by competing goals, demands, or even negative arising emotions, such as anxiety about failure, that might interfere with goal attainment or, at least, return to goal-directed activity after the distraction has passed or been dealt with.

Thinking more broadly about our goal-directed behaviour, existential theory (Frankl 1946/2006) states that individuals need to be able to find meaning in their lives if they are to achieve mental health. A sense of meaning or purpose in life is derived from achieving one's goals and feeling that one's activities are worthwhile. Having a weak sense of meaning or purpose in life has been associated with greater likelihood of risk behaviours such as smoking (Konkolÿ Thege et al. 2009) and drinking alcohol (Marsh et al. 2003).

WHAT DO YOU THINK?

What is important to you in your current life? Think of three aspects of your life that you currently value highly. Why do you value them? What meaning do they have? What function do they serve?

What goals do you hope to achieve over the next six months? Over the next ten years? If you engage in any specific health or risk behaviour, how does it 'fit' with your current values and your short- and long-term goals?

Now, project your mind ahead to when you reach middle age (or if you have already reached this, think of your post-retirement years!). What do you think will be important to you then? Will the areas of importance change, and why do you think this? Do you think your goals and behaviour will change and, if so, in what way and why?

---

self-regulation
the process by which individuals monitor and adjust their behaviour, thoughts and emotions in order to maintain a balance or a sense of normal function.

Humans are inconsistent

Inconsistencies in the factors associated with health behaviours include the following:

- Different health behaviours are controlled by different external factors: e.g. smoking may be socially discouraged, while exercise may be supported; however, cigarettes are readily available, whereas access to exercise facilities may be limited.

- Attitudes towards health behaviour vary within and between individuals.

- In the same individual, health behaviour may be motivated by different expectations: e.g. a person may smoke to relax, exercise to improve appearance and consume alcohol to socialise.

- Differences between individuals can in part be explained by life stage: e.g. a teenager may diet for fashion reasons, while a middle-aged man may diet to reduce the risk of having a heart attack.

- Motivating factors may change over time: e.g. drinking alcohol when under age may be a form of rebellion but may later be considered essential to social interaction.

- Triggers and barriers to behaviour are influenced by context: e.g. smoking may be banned in the workplace, and alcohol consumption may be restricted in front of parents or colleagues in comparison with peers.

The next part of the chapter addresses a range of theories and models that have been developed in an attempt to explain and thereby predict health behaviour.

Sociocognitive models of health behaviour

First, it is important to remind the reader that by adopting healthy habits, we are only reducing the statistical risks of ill health, not guaranteeing that we will lead a long, healthy life. Furthermore, we should not expect that by examining human behaviour and the motives for it, we shall ever be able to fully explain the huge variations in people's health. Behaviour is not the only factor that causes disease. We can, at best, offer a partial (social, cognitive and behavioural) explanation of illness, and an evidence-based conclusion as to how to intervene to prevent or reduce the likelihood of illness in some individuals. In this section we first address some of the features common to many models of health behaviour

and health behaviour change before providing the reader with more detailed examples of leading models.

Early theories as to why we changed our behaviour were based on the simplistic assumption that:

Information → Attitude change → Behaviour change

These were found to be naive. Although many past, and sometimes current, health education campaigns still draw upon this simplistic premise, the evidence regarding predictors of behaviour change show that things are much more complex: simply providing information, for example about the the value of a low-cholesterol diet or the health risks of smoking, may not change a person's attitudes towards this behaviour and even if attitudes do change, it is not inevitable that this will lead to increased perception of personal risk and thus a change in behaviour (e.g. Eagly and Chaiken 1993; Ruiter and Kok 2005). More than information about a health threat is required to motivate behaviour change although attitudes and risk perceptions do play a significant role.

Attitudes

What is an attitude? Attitudes are thought to be the common-sense representations that individuals hold in relation to objects, people and events (Eagly and Chaiken 1993). Some theorists have described attitudes as a single component based on affective evaluation of an object/event (i.e. you either like something/someone or you do not; e.g. Thurstone 1928); others have presented a two-component model, where attitude is defined as an unobservable and stable predisposition or state of mental readiness that influences evaluative judgements (e.g. Allport 1935). From the 1960s onwards, there has been growing acceptance of a three-component model of attitude, whereby attitudes are considered as relatively enduring and generalisable and made up of three related parts – thought (cognition), feeling (emotion) and behaviour:

1. *Cognitive*: beliefs about the attitude-object – e.g. cigarette smoking is a good way to relieve stress; cigarette smoking is a sign of weakness.

2. *Emotional*: feelings towards the attitude-object – e.g. cigarette smoking is disgusting/pleasurable.

3. *Behavioural* (or intentional): intended action towards the attitude-object – e.g. I am not going to smoke.

Early attitudinal theorists considered the three components to be generally consistent with each other and likely to predict behaviour; however, the empirical evidence to support a direct association between attitudes and behaviour is inconclusive. This is in part because an individual may hold several different, sometimes conflicting, attitudes towards a particular attitude-object, depending on social context and many other factors. I may, for example, enjoy the taste of a cream cake but be worried about the negative health implications of high fat/high calorie intake. Such contradictory thoughts can produce what is known as 'dissonance', which many people will attempt to resolve by bringing their thoughts into line with one another. However, some individuals maintain a dissociation between attitudes and behaviour: for example, so-called dissonant smokers, who continue to smoke despite holding a number of negative attitudes towards smoking. This conflict is sometimes referred to as **ambivalence**, where a person's motivation to change could potentially be undermined by the holding of ambivalent attitudes or competing goals, such as believing low-fat food to be a healthy option that they would like to increase intake of while not wanting to appear obsessive about their diet (e.g. Sparks *et al.* 2001). Attitudes alone are insufficient. Many factors can shape, challenge or change initial attitudes, cause them to be ignored, or increase the likelihood of them being acted upon. An important influence on attitude is that of personal relevance and perceived risk.

Risk perceptions and unrealistic optimism

People often engage in risky or unhealthy behaviour because they do not consider themselves to be at risk or facing any harm. This can be as a result of unawareness of risk a behaviour carries or by a lack of understanding or acceptance of threat information received. While some of us may process threat information systematically and rationally, there is evidence that, for many, information is processed in a way that best fits with how one sees oneself: i.e. any information has to have relevance, and thus some information processing is defensive and self-affirming (Good and Abraham 2007; Wright 2010).

For some, their risk perceptions may be inaccurate, with individuals believing, for example, that 'I do not smoke as much as "person X" and therefore won't be at risk of cancer compared with them'. Weinstein (1984) named this biased risk perception, which he found to be common, '**unrealistic optimism**' – 'unrealistic' because quite obviously not everyone can be at low risk. He noted that individuals engage in forms of social comparison that reflect best on themselves (comparative optimism/optimistic bias) (Weinstein and Klein 1996; Weinstein 2003): for example, in relation to HIV risk, 'I may sometimes forget to use a condom, but at least I use them more than my friends do'. He found that the negative behaviour of peers is focused on more when making these judgements than is the same peers' positive health behaviour. Such selective attention can lead to unrealistically positive appraisals regarding personal risk.

Weinstein (1987) identified four factors associated with unrealistic optimism:

1. a lack of personal experience with the behaviour or problem concerned;

2. a belief that their individual actions can prevent the problem;

3. the belief that if the problem has not emerged already, it is unlikely to do so in the future: e.g. 'I have smoked for years and my health is fine, so why would it change now?';

4. the belief that the problem is rare: e.g. 'Cancer is quite rare compared with how common smoking is, so it is pretty unlikely I'll develop it'.

There is some evidence that unrealistic optimism is associated with greater belief in control over events (e.g. 'I am at less risk than others because I know when to stop drinking') and that such beliefs are associated with risk-reducing behaviour (Hoorens and Buunk

---

ambivalence

the simultaneous existence of both positive and negative evaluations of an attitude-object, which could be both cognitive and emotional.

unrealistic optimism

also known as 'optimistic bias', whereby a person considers themselves as being less likely than comparable others to develop an illness or experience a negative event.

1993; Weinstein 1987). However, Schwarzer (1994) refers to unrealistic optimism as 'defensive optimism' and suggests instead that the relationship between such optimism and behaviour is likely to be negative because individuals underestimate their risk and thus do not take precautions against the risk occurrence. There remains a need to explore further the actual relationship between these constructs and health behaviour. Risk perceptions within health psychology are often defined (and assessed) as individually generated cognitions, i.e. the extent to which a person considers themselves as facing potential harm, and they are assessed as such in several of our theoretical models of health behaviour and health behaviour change (see, for example, the health belief model below – not covered in this chapter). However, risk perceptions are also influenced by the current social and cultural context: for example, if I (VM) were to perceive my risk of contracting TB (tuberculosis) high while living in North Wales, this would likely be considered as being unrealistically pessimistic, whereas it may be the case that I work with homeless populations where TB is still present, or that I make regular trips to countries where incidence is high (for malaria example, see Morrison *et al.* (1999). Assessing the context in which beliefs arise, wax and wane is important if interventions to change beliefs are to have optimal effect.

Self-efficacy

The construct of self-efficacy is defined as 'the *belief* in one's capabilities to organize and execute the sources of action required to manage *prospective* situations' (Bandura 1986). For example, believing that a future action (e.g. weight loss) is within your capabilities is likely to generate other cognitive and emotional activity, such as the setting of high personal goals (losing a stone rather than half a stone), positive outcome expectancies and reduced anxiety. These cognitions and emotions in turn affect actions, such as dietary change and exercise, in order to achieve the goal. As Bandura (1997: 24) states: 'It is because people see outcomes as contingent on the adequacy of their performance, and care about those outcomes, that they rely on efficacy beliefs in deciding which course of action to pursue and how long to pursue it'. Success in attaining a goal also feeds back in a self-regulatory manner to further a person's sense of self-efficacy (Bandura 1997) and to further their efforts to attain goals (Schwarzer 1992). In situations where

competence of one's own performance is unrelated or less closely tied to outcome (for example, the outcome of physical recovery following a head injury will depend to a large degree on the extent of neurological damage), self-efficacy, as with other control constructs, will be less predictive of outcome.

However, personal performance is relevant to individual health behaviour change and maintenance of change, therefore unsurprisingly efficacy beliefs often emerge as an important predictor. Thus several of the dominant models include some measure of personal efficacy beliefs (see below).

It should be clear by now that many factors influence health behaviour and while not all are psychological, health and social psychologists have developed theoretical models which aim to test how these factors combine empirically to explain a wide range of behaviour. The dominant models which have been applied to behaviour change (initiation, maintenance or cessation) are presented below.

Sociocognitive models of behaviour change

The health belief model

An early and well-known model of health behaviour change is the health belief model (HBM) (Rosenstock 1974; Becker 1974; Becker and Rosenstock 1984). The HBM proposes that the likelihood that a person will engage in particular health behaviour depends on demographic factors: e.g. social class, gender, age and four beliefs that may arise following a particular internal or external cue to action (see Figure 5.1). These beliefs encompass perceptions of threat (risk perception, see above) and evaluation of the behaviour in question, with cues to action and health motivation added at a later date.

Specific examples will best illustrate how the various components fit together:

● Perception of threat:
  ○ I believe that coronary heart disease (CHD) is a serious illness contributed to by being overweight: *perceived severity*.
  ○ I believe that I am overweight: *perceived susceptibility*.

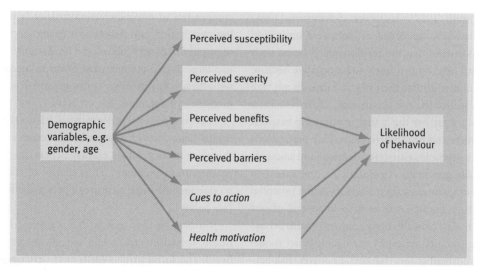

Figure 5.1 The health belief model (original, plus additions in italics)

● Behavioural evaluation:
  ○ If I lose weight my health will improve: *perceived benefits* (of change).
  ○ Changing my cooking and dietary habits when I also have a family to feed will be difficult, and possibly more expensive: *perceived barriers* (to change).
● Cues to action (added in 1975; Becker and Maiman):
  ○ That recent television programme on the health risks of obesity worried me (*external*).
  ○ I am regularly feeling breathless when I climb stairs, so maybe I should lose some weight (*internal*).
● Health motivation (added in 1977; Becker *et al.*):
  ● It is important to me to maintain my health.

The HBM has been applied to a wide range of behaviour over many years, as illustrated below.

The HBM and preventive behaviour

The consensus finding in the breast self-examination (BSE) literature is that many people do not practise it at all, that adherence rates are low and that practice decreases with age, even though the incidence of breast cancer increases with age. The health belief model has been widely used for predicting BSE. Both in terms of predicting intention to perform BSE (e.g. Savage and Clarke 1996) and actual BSE behaviour, it appears that perceiving benefits of self-examination

and few barriers to its performance are most consistently and most highly correlated, with perceived seriousness of breast cancer, perceived susceptibility and being motivated towards health (e.g. seeking health information and generally engaging in health-promoting activity) also predictive (e.g. Champion 1990; Ashton *et al.* 2001). In fact, health motivation distinguished between low, medium and high BSE performers, and predicted BSE over a one-year follow-up period (Champion and Miller 1992). This supports the need to assess health motivation rather than assume that all people value health or are equally motivated to pursue it.

Components of the HBM have been shown to be influenced by ethnicity and by the behaviour under study. With regards to ethnicity, an American study (Chen *et al.* 2007) found that while uptake of an influenza vaccination was strongly related to beliefs in influenza seriousness and personal susceptibility in the whole sample, these factors were much more strongly associated among African American and European American adults than among Hispanic Americans who were more influenced by perceived barriers to vaccination. In terms of different components of the HBM being more or less salient, depending on the behaviour under study, a review of 13 HBM studies by Curry and Emmons (1994) found that the uptake of breast cancer screening was explained by perceived susceptibility beliefs, low perceived barriers, and cues to action, whereas Pakenham *et al.* (2000) did not find susceptibility beliefs to be predictive of mammography uptake.

Perceived benefits have been shown to be important predictors of a range of preventive behaviours, including exercise (e.g. Saunders *et al.* 1997) and attendance at antenatal care (Letherman *et al.* 1990), whereas perceiving barriers is (perhaps unsurprisingly) generally associated with low levels of the preventive behaviour, such as low dietary adherence among cardiac patients (Koikkalainen *et al.* 1996). Norman and Brain (2005) found in longitudinal data that the best predictors of BSE, using an extended HBM, was past BSE behaviour, emotional barriers and self-efficacy barriers. Past behaviour is also consistently found predictive across a range of behaviours. However, following a lifestyle intervention, reduced perceptions of barriers to exercise did not predict exercise initiation nor maintenance among older adults with hypertension (Burke *et al.* 2007).

The HBM and reducing-risk behaviour

In terms of HBM components being useful in predicting change in risk behaviour such as smoking cessation, or condom use to avoid HIV infection, one might expect that successful behaviour change would occur when the perceived benefits of change outweigh the perceived benefits of continued risk-taking, However, the evidence of this is mixed. In relation to smoking, this is likely to be because smoking is a dependency-producing behaviour and thus the impulse to smoke can occur independent of our conscious cognitive efforts (Hofmann *et al.* 2008) – thus our models do not work in the same way (see Vangeli and West 2008). In relation to safer sex practices, Abraham *et al.* (1996) found that HBM variables were not significantly predictive of consistent condom use among sexually active adolescents once a measure of previous condom use had been taken into consideration. This suggests that one of the best predictors of what we do in the future is what we have done in the past. For example, previous failed attempts to quit smoking can become a barrier to future change, possibly because this elicits poor self-efficacy beliefs for future quitting attempts. It is now more common for research studies based on the HBM and other theoretical models to include measures of previous behaviour in their design (e.g. Norman and Brain 2005; Yzer *et al.* 2001).

Abraham *et al.* (2002) also concluded from a review of the evidence prior to a further study of condom use that 'threat perceptions are weaker correlates of condom use than action-specific cognitions, such as attitudes towards condom use, perceived self-efficacy in relation to condom use, the social acceptability of condom use and condom use intentions' (p. 228). One must also add to this list the consideration of the context of condom use: i.e. it is not a behaviour involving the individual alone.

Limitations of HBM

As the evidence reviewed above would suggest, the HBM components appear to be more relevant to predicting the initiation of health preventive behaviours than perhaps reducing health-risk behaviour. However, across these studies, problems exist in how the HBM has been applied and even what its basic content is. Different authors operationalise the components in differently worded items and not all HBM studies include an assessment of cues to action and health motivation (Harrison *et al.* 1992; Sheeran and Abraham 1996). Further limitations include:

- Rosenstock (1966) did not specify the manner in which the different variables interact with one another or combine to influence behaviour. He implied that components could usefully be added to each other, yet many studies have examined components independently (e.g. Abraham *et al.* 1996).

- Strecher and Rosenstock (1997) suggested that adding or multiplying susceptibility scores with severity scores to get an overall 'perceived threat' score may enable greater prediction than using each independently; that cues to action and perceived benefits and barriers may better predict behaviour in situations where perceived threat is high; and that the model may be better tested against intention than actual behaviour. Few of these hypotheses have been tested empirically (Armitage and Conner 2000).

- Becker *et al.* (1977) suggested that perceived benefits were weighted against perceived barriers, but they did not specify how the combined score was to be calculated (i.e. do you subtract the number of barriers from the number of benefits reported, or vice versa? Do all benefits and barriers carry equal weight to an individual?

- Steadman and colleagues (2002) have shown that highly salient beliefs (i.e. those that hold high importance to the individual) may enhance the prediction of outcomes beyond a model which employs modal beliefs.

- The HBM may overestimate the role of 'threat'. Perceived susceptibility is not consistently predictive of health behaviour change. It is important that health promotion messages do not overuse fear arousal as this can be counter-productive to behaviour change (Albarracín *et al.* 2005) particularly among those who lack the resource to change (e.g. Ruiter and Kok 2006).

- The HBM takes limited account of social influences on behaviour, which as we will see later is an important factor.

- The HBM fails to consider whether the individual feels able to initiate the behaviour (or behaviour change) required. Protection motivation theory (Rogers 1983; Rogers and Prentice-Dunn 1997), which is not discussed in this chapter, is very similar to the HBM in terms of how it considers threat appraisals, but it adds coping appraisals, response-efficacy and costs, and self-efficacy to the factors they consider influence behaviour change. Perceived behavioural control and self-efficacy constructs also contribute to two of the models discussed next (the theory of planned behaviour and the HAPA).

- A further barrier to behaviour is mood or negative affect, found, for example, to be inversely associated with exercise behaviour among women with breast cancer (Perna *et al.* 2008).

- The HBM is a static model, suggesting that beliefs occur simultaneously in a 'one-off' assessment. This does not allow for staged or dynamic processes such as changing or oscillating beliefs over time.

Given these limitations, it is perhaps not surprising that studies employing the HBM have found that its components account for only a small proportion of variance in behaviour change (see meta-analysis of adult studies by Harrison *et al.* 1992). By initially failing to consider the interactions between its components, the role of social norms and influences, and the factors that can turn beliefs into more proximal (close-up) determinants of behaviour (such as self-efficacy), it provided only a limited account of human action, and more extensive models were developed and adopted.

The theory of planned behaviour

While the HBM is predominantly a cognitive model derived from **subjective expected utility theory** (i.e. individuals are active and generally rational decision makers who are influenced by the perceived utility (usefulness to them) of certain actions or behaviour (cf. Edwards 1954), the theory of reasoned action (TRA) and its successor, the theory of planned behaviour (TPB), are social cognition models. These models assume that social behaviour is determined by a person's beliefs about behaviour in given social contexts and by their social perceptions and expectations (cf. social learning theory: Bandura 1986) and not simply by their cognitions or attitudes.

Underlying the development of these models is the assumption (Ajzen and Fishbein 1970; Fishbein 1967) that individuals behave in a goal-directed manner and that the implications of their actions (outcome expectations) are weighed up in a rational manner before the decision is taken whether to engage in the behaviour or not. The TPB aims to explore and develop the psychological processes involved in making a link between attitude and behaviour by incorporating wider social influences, beliefs in personal behavioural control, and the necessity of intention formation. IN THE SPOTLIGHT (p. 128) highlights that understanding of factors associated with and predictive of behavioural intention is going to be important in a generation facing new vaccinations for newly publicised conditions. Behaviour is thought to be proximally determined by intention, which in turn is influenced by a person's attitude towards the object behaviour (*outcome expectancy beliefs*, e.g. positive outcome expectancy: if I stop smoking, exercising will become easier for me; negative outcome expectancy: if I stop smoking, I will perhaps gain weight; and *outcome value*: it is important for me to be healthier) and their perception of social pressure regarding the behaviour (e.g. my friends and parents really want me to stop smoking) (known as a

> ### subjective expected utility (seu) theory
> a decision-making model where an individual evaluates the expected utility (cf. desirability) of certain actions and their outcomes and selects the action with the highest seu.

subjective norm). The extent to which they wish to comply or fall into line with the preferences or norms of others is known as motivation to comply (I would like to please my parents and friends). The model states that the importance of the person's attitudes towards the behaviour is weighted against the subjective norm beliefs, whereby a person holding a negative attitude towards behaviour change (I don't really like dieting) may still develop a positive intention to change in situations where their subjective norm promotes dieting and they wish to comply with their significant others (e.g. all my friends eat more healthily than I do, and I would like to be more like them).

The third influence on intention is that of perceived behavioural control, added to the TRA to create the TPB (Ajzen 1985, 1991; see Figure 5.2). Perceived behavioural control (PBC) is defined as a person's belief that they have control over their own behaviour in certain situations, even when facing particular barriers (e.g. I believe it will be easy for me not to smoke even if I go to the pub in the evening). The model proposes that PBC will directly influence intention and thus, indirectly, behaviour. A direct relationship between PBC and behaviour is also considered possible if perceptions

of control were accurate, meaning that if a person believes that they have control over their diet they may well intend to change it and subsequently do so, but if the preparation of food is in fact under someone else's control, behavioural change is less likely even if a positive intention had been formed) (Rutter and Quine 2002: 12). PBC beliefs themselves are influenced by many factors, including past behaviour and past successes or failures in relation to the behaviour in question, and in this way the PBC construct is very similar to that of self-efficacy. For example, a person who has never tried to stop smoking before may have lower PBC beliefs than a person who has succeeded in stopping previously and who therefore may believe that it will be relatively easy to do so again.

With Ajzen (1991) reporting a mean correlation between PBC and intention of 0.71, it is clear that this construct has been an important addition, although intention remains a stronger predictor of subsequent behaviour than PBC is directly. It has been suggested that PBC may be most powerful when it is considered in interaction with the other components of the model, such as attitudes and motivations (Eagly and Chaiken 1993) and even more dispositional measures of locus of control (e.g. Armitage 2003). However, Armitage et al. (1999) compared the predictive utility of self-efficacy beliefs with perceived behavioural control beliefs in relation to the use of legal and illegal drugs and found that self-efficacy beliefs were more strongly associated with behaviour than were PBC beliefs. Self-efficacy is central to the HAPA model (see later section).

In a large-scale meta-analysis of studies employing the TPB, its variables accounted for between 35 and

> ### subjective norm
>
> a person's beliefs regarding whether important others (referents) would think that they should or should not carry out a particular action. An index of social pressure, weighted generally by the individual's motivation to comply with the wishes of others.

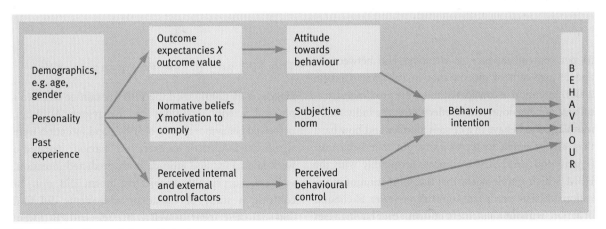

Figure 5.2 The theory of planned behaviour

IN THE SPOTLIGHT

Have you heard of HPV – Human papillomavirus?

Human papillomavirus is a highly prevalent sexually transmitted infection, thought to be present in about 30 per cent of sexually active females at any one time, with an estimated lifetime risk of 75–80 per cent. HPV is implicated in cervical cancer, i.e. it is referred to as a 'necessary cause', and although only a small proportion of HPV infections do actually develop into cancer, HPV is found in about 70 per cent of cervical cancer cases (Kuper *et al.* 2000). A preventive vaccine was developed and licensed in June 2006 in the USA, and subsequently elsewhere, and vaccination policy has developed accordingly in each country. In the UK since September 2008, vaccination is offered to teenage girls aged 12 to 13, with a two-year catch-up programme from 2009 to vaccinate those under 18 missed by the new programme. Parental consent is required, which is controversial, given the implicit acknowledgement of sexual activity. In order to achieve what is known as 'herd immunity', i.e. the whole population is protected, it may be that the vaccination programme will need to be extended to males, but in the first instance teenage girls are targeted. One early Dutch study reporting intention to have the HPV vaccination explored whether a sample of 1,367 adult women would have a '10 year old (grand) daughter' vaccinated. The women were not told that

HPV is a sexually transmitted infection. Intention was at a high level with no significant difference between a random sample of women invited for a Pap smear test (76 per cent 'yes'), women who had had an abnormal Pap smear (81 per cent), women who had survived cervical cancer themselves (77 per cent) and a random group of women not invited for cervical screening within the previous two years (78 per cent). Having children did not make any difference to hypothetical intention. Intention was, however, affected by age – those under 50 were significantly more likely to agree to vaccination of their hypothetical '(grand)daughter'. An earlier and smaller study conducted in the UK found a lower level of intention among a sample more directly involved in the decision – 317 parents of 11–12-year-olds. In this study only 38 per cent 'certainly' agreed to vaccination, although a further 43 per cent stated they would probably agree (Brabin *et al.* 2006).

Crucially, studies which assess actual uptake behaviours are needed if health promotion efforts are to be targeted effectively. However, to date, studies have focused on predicting intention, for example showing that the method of presenting (visual vs. textual) risk/benefit information to parents is important (Cox *et al.* 2010).

How do you think you would respond to a similar question were you to have a teenage daughter? Consider the reasons behind your decision.

---

50 per cent of variance in *intentions* and between 26 and 35 per cent of the variance in *behaviour* (Sutton 2004). Intention is considered to be the proximal determinant of behaviour, and it reflects both the individual's motivation to behave in a certain manner and how hard they are prepared to try to carry out that behaviour (Ajzen 1991: 199). This compares favourably with the HBM, which simply stated that a combination of motivational beliefs predicted a greater or lesser likelihood of action, without a statement of intent ever having been formed.

The TPB and preventive behaviour

Hagger *et al.* (2001) used the TPB to examine children's physical activity intentions and behaviour. Attitudes, perceived behavioural control (PBC) and intention were significant influences on exercise behaviour assessed a week later. PBC and attitude both predicted intention, whereas, surprisingly, subjective norm did not. In contrast, a study of Canadian adolescents did find that subjective norm (as well as attitudes and PBC) were significant predictors of intention to eat fruit and vegetables daily, engage in regular physical activity and be smoke-free over a one-month period (Murnaghan *et al.* 2010; see RESEARCH FOCUS on next page). This reflects a previously reported inconsistency in the strength of influence played by normative beliefs (Conner and Sparks 2005). An explanation here may be in the age of the children, with the Canadian sample being older adolescents (ranged 12–16 years) who are perhaps more responsive to social influence than younger adolescents (range 12–14 year in Hagger's study). Molloy and colleagues in Scotland (Molloy *et al.* 2010) examined predictors of university students' physical activity and found that this older group, particularly females, benefited from social support for physical activity and that the influence of social support on subsequent physical activity was partially mediated by both PBC and coping planning.

The TPB has also been used to study physical activity intentions and behaviour among individuals with chronic diseases. For example, Eng and Martin-Ginis (2007) found that the leisure time physical activity of 80 men and women with chronic kidney disease was predicted by PBC assessed a week previously. Among adolescent survivors of cancer, intentions to be physically active on a regular basis were predicted by affective attitudes towards physical activity (e.g. enjoyable–unenjoyable) and instrumental attitudes (useful–useless), but not by any of the other TPB components (34 per cent of variance explained in total). Physical activity itself was explained by intention (19 per cent variance explained) and by self-efficacy (added a further 10 per cent). This study assessed both PBC and self-efficacy and note that it is the latter that emerged significant (Keats *et al.* 2007). That different components of the TPB explain intention and actual exercise behaviour is consistent with findings of a meta-analysis of exercise behaviour among healthy populations (Hagger *et al.* 2002).

Other preventive behaviours studied extensively using the TPB include the uptake of screening opportunities for cervical cancer and breast cancer. As is typical, different TPB variables explain intention than explain actual behaviour. For example, Rutter (2000) found that intention to attend screening was predicted by attitude, PBC and subjective norm, although only attitude and subjective norm were predictive of actual uptake of screening. Studies of self-screening, in terms of breast or testicular self-examination, report similar differences in predictors of intention compared with predictors of actual behaviour, but more longitudinal studies are

crucial if a causal relationship is to be confirmed. One prospective longitudinal study of predictors of mammography uptake among 1,000 women addressed whether individual normative belief were better predictors than modal beliefs (Steadman *et al.* 2002). Generally, subjective norm is assessed by asking individuals to state what they believe the norms and expectancies of a range of listed other people are in relation to the behaviour in question. In this method of questioning, an individual is prompted to think of many people or many influences and a 'modal' belief is what is analysed. The same applies to calculations of attitudes, as totals are used rather than examining the strength and **salience** of individual attitudes therein. Steadman and colleagues argue that in modal beliefs there may be one or more highly salient belief that holds high importance to the individual, and that prediction of outcomes may be improved if such salient beliefs are analysed rather than modal beliefs. The results only partially confirmed the authors' hypotheses. There was not a stronger association between individual beliefs and intention or attendance behaviour than between modal beliefs and intention or attendance. However, there was evidence of individual beliefs adding to the prediction of attendance, a result not found in terms of modal SN (subjective norm) beliefs. Previous studies have not reported an effect of SN on mammography uptake behaviour, and this may be, as the authors conclude, because 'an individually generated subjective norm is a more sensitive and accurate estimate of the true effect of normative pressure' (p. 327). It is worth noting that while the removal of data for those who could not identify a normative influence on their behaviour was necessary for this study, this group of women are an interesting group in that their decisions about screening uptake are likely to be made on a very individual basis.

Hunter *et al.* (2003) examined the predictors of intention to seek help from a GP for breast cancer symptoms among a general population sample of women. Attitudes towards help seeking (e.g. 'Making an appointment to see my doctor for a symptom that might be cancer would be good/bad, beneficial/harmful, pleasant/unpleasant, wise/foolish, necessary/unnecessary') and

salience
strength and importance.

RESEARCH FOCUS

Predictors of physical activity, healthy eating and being smoke-free in teens: a theory of planned behaviour approach.

Murnaghan, D.A., Blanchard, C.M., Rodgers, W.M. *et al.* (2010). *Psychology & Health*, 25: 925–941.

As we have described in Chapters 3 and 4 ☞, smoking, unhealthy diets or overeating and obesity and lack of physical activity are among the leading public health concerns in Western society today. As all of these health-risk behaviours are primarily developed in childhood or adolescence the following paper has been selected to illustrate the role adolescent beliefs play in such behaviour. This study focuses on beliefs regarding physical activity (PA), fruit and vegetable intake and remaining smoke-free, among grades 7–9 in a Canadian school (12–16-year-olds), and bases the assessment of beliefs on the theory of planned behaviour,

Aims and method

The study had two phases of data collection.

1. The authors acknowledge from the outset that *different* beliefs are often predictive of different behaviour, thus they used qualitative methods to first elicit and develop context specific beliefs. They carried out a series of interviews and a focus group with six school students (two per grade year) where a TPB questionnaire was completed, reviewed and discussed, and also 18 students (six per grade year, equal gender distribution) were randomly selected to take part in a belief elicitation interview. These students were excluded from the later fully quantitative study. The key beliefs about the three behaviours under study were identified and prioritised, using the TPB concepts as a categorising aid, i.e. 'data were coded according to the behavioural, normative and control belief conceptual definitions'. Then two TPB experts carried out content analysis and reached agreement on those beliefs that were common to all three behaviours (e.g. normative beliefs included

siblings, parents, friends and teacher for all), and those that were behaviour-specific (e.g. normative beliefs for exercise included sports coaches).

2. The second phase/study was to establish whether the identified TPB variables did indeed explain significant variation in the three behaviours which were assessed twice within a one-month period. Hypotheses were TPB-derived, i.e. that behaviour would be predicted by intention which itself was predicted by attitudinal, normative and control beliefs. A total of 287 pupils took part in the first assessment, with a third lost to follow-up due to a clash of the study with a school band concert! As well as being collected for demographic information, the TPB variables were all assessed, using Likert scale responses for:

○ *attitudes* – two items per behaviour, e.g. 'During the next four weeks, for me to . . . eat five servings of fruit and vegetables each day . . . will be (a) on a scale of 1 (extremely unenjoyable) to 7 (extremely enjoyable); (b) on a scale of 1 (extremely good) to 7 (extremely bad)'.

○ *perceived behavioural control* – two items per behaviour, e.g. 'During the next four weeks (a) I am confident that I will be able to . . . be smoke free . . . on a scale of 1 (extremely not confident) to 7 (extremely confident); (b) it is completely up to me whether or not I am . . . smoke free on a scale of 1 (strongly disagree) to 7 (strongly agree)'.

○ *subjective norm* – one item per behaviour, e.g. 'During the next four weeks, most people important to me think I should . . . eat five servings of fruit and vegetables each day/be smoke free/engage in regular physical activity, on a scale of 1 (strongly disagree) to 7 (strongly agree)'.

○ *intention* – two items asked separately for each behaviour, e.g. 'During the next four weeks I intend to (a) eat five servings of fruit and vegetables; (b) be smoke-free, and (c) engage in regular PA, rated on a scale of 1 (strongly disagree) to 7 (strongly agree)'.

In addition, behavioural, normative and control beliefs generated in the first study were included and were rated from 1 (strongly disagree) to 7 (strongly agree): for example, *behavioural beliefs* – 'Being smoke free for the next four weeks, would. . . . prevent me from getting yellow teeth and fingers, help me achieve better health, make it easier for me to make friends, etc.'; 'Eating five servings of fruit and vegetables over the next four weeks I would . . . have more energy, lose or maintain my weight . . . etc.'; 'Participating in regular physical activity over the next 4 weeks, I would . . . feel better, keep in shape, be more awake etc.'; *normative beliefs* – 'The following people think I should (a) eat five servings of fruits . . . (b) be smoke-free (c) engage in regular PA, over the next four weeks'. *Control beliefs* were included regarding aspects of the environment which exerted control over a teenager's behaviour: for example, for fruit and vegetable intake the list included TV commercials, preparation time; for physical activity it included bad weather, homework, no access to equipment; and for being smoke-free control items elicited included the risk of suspension if caught, that it looks gross, anti-smoking ads on TV. Control items were preceded by 'Would it be more easy or more difficult (1 extremely difficult, 7 extremely easy) for you to eat five servings of fruits and vegetables each day/be smoke free/engage in regular PA over the next four weeks, if the above were present?'

Finally, *behaviour* was measured in terms of participants writing how many days in the past 30 days they had (a) been smoke-free, (b) eaten five servings of fruits and vegetables. For PA, they were asked how many days in the past seven days they had participated in moderate physical activity for 60 mins a day and the same question but for vigorous activity a duration of 30 minutes.

Results

The results were tested in terms of the amount of variance in each behaviour that could be explained by the TPB items. Path analysis followed correlational analyses and because a gender and year grade effect was found on the performance of all three behaviours, these were controlled for. Finally a series of multiple

regression analyses were carried out. Key findings were as follows:

The beliefs elicited in phase 1 were correlated with (a) a global construct consisting of attitude and subjective norm, controlling for covariates of gender and grade, (b) intention controlling for covariates of gender and grade, and (c) each specific behaviour controlling for covariates and intention.

For *fruit and vegetable consumption* all the behavioural and normative beliefs were significantly correlated with global beliefs, intention and behaviour, but there were a few non-significant relationships between the controlling factors (eating in a restaurant, low availability of fruit and vegetables at home, school cafeteria choices, and being teased for eating fruit and vegetables) and the global construct, and between cafeteria fruit and vegetable choices and actual consumption.

For *physical activity*, all behavioural and normative constructs were associated with global beliefs, intention and behaviour, but there was more non-significant findings than significant ones when it came to the control factors, particularly limited in relation to the global construct and actual behaviour. However, weather, lack of access, wanting to play on a computer, concern that others will see you exercising, and wanting to watch TV all correlated with low intention. Only wanting to play on the computer or watch TV reduced actual PA.

For *being smoke-free*, again all behavioural and normative constructs were associated with global beliefs, intention and behaviour, with one exception whereby, perhaps not surprisingly given the adolescent sample, teacher norms were not associated with smoke-free behaviour. Only two control beliefs (can't smoke on school property, anti-smoking ads on TV) were negatively associated with global beliefs. However, all control beliefs were associated with intention, but there were absolutely none associated between these and actual smoke-free behaviour.

In the ensuing path analyses, the global constructs assessing attitudes, subjective norm and PBC were significant predictors of all three behaviours and accounted for between 50 and 56 per cent of intention, and intention accounted for between 25 per cent (being smoke-free) and 40/41 per cent (eating fruit and vegetables/PA) of the variance in actual behaviour. The indirect effects of attitude, subjective norm and PBC could be seen in significant relationships with intention in all cases.

Discussion

In the first phase it was interesting to see what emerged as generic and what emerged as behaviour-specific items regarding self-efficacy for the three behaviours under study. The differential associations that subsequently emerged with the global attitude and subjective norm construct, with intention, and with actual behaviour, points to the importance of using more qualitative means to elicit questionnaire items that are relevant to the behaviour in question.

The relationship between a young person's attitude and both the intention to eat fruits and vegetables and engage in regular PA were moderately large, but small–moderate for being smoke-free. In contrast, perceived behavioural control beliefs had a large effect on being smoke-free and only a moderate–large

effect on the other two behaviours. Intention, perhaps unsurprisingly, had a large effect on the performance of all three behaviours.

As the authors note, these findings are consistent in the main with that previously reported, with the exception perhaps of a larger than often reported effect of subjective norms. This relates to what was discussed at the outset of this chapter – the changing influence of other people's norms on our behaviour. This study sampled from adolescents who are generally found to be more responsive to social influences.

Overall, this study supports the tenets of the TPB while highlighting the differential salience of some components depending on the behaviour in question. This is important and has implications for interventions to encourage healthy eating, exercise, and being smoke-free. While behavioural specific factors need to be addressed, school-based interventions targeting multiple behaviours are also indicated, where a focus on common influences, such as subjective norms and perceived behavioural control would be fruitful.

perceived behavioural control (e.g. 'There is nothing I could do to make sure I got help for a breast cancer symptom': agree–disagree (seven-point scale)) explained a small but significant amount of variance in intention (7.1 per cent). Subjective norms were not predictive of intention to seek help for such symptoms (but given the point above about measuring individual and not modal subjective norm beliefs, this is perhaps not surprising). It is important to note that the authors also examined participants' perceptions of cancer (**illness representations**; see Chapter 9 (☞) and entered these variables into the regression analysis before the TPB variables. Illness

representations explained 22 per cent of the variance in intention, and the TPB variables added a further 7.1 per cent thereafter. This highlights the importance of considering individuals' perceptions of the illness that the behaviour in question is related to. For example, when examining smoking behaviour, perhaps perceptions of cancer or COPD should be more fully addressed. Additionally, perceptions of treatment may influence the health behaviour of adherence, as suggested in studies of the beliefs in the necessity of medicine and concerns about taking them (e.g. Clifford *et al.* 2008 and see also Chapter 9 (☞).

Ethnic differences in how certain conditions are perceived may also affect help-seeking behaviour, as suggested in a Hawaiian study comparing beliefs held about alcoholism and emotional problems by Caucasian, Philipino, Japanese and native Hawaiian adults. Caucasians perceived significantly fewer barriers to disclosing alcohol or emotional problems than the three ethnic minority groups. The perceived barriers showed interesting ethnic differences: for example, ethnic minority

---

illness representations

beliefs about a particular illness and state of ill health – commonly ascribed to the five domains described by Leventhal: identity, timeline, cause, consequences and control/cure.

groups more often perceived barriers relating to low awareness of where to go for help for alcohol problems, and greater barrier of shame of others finding out about an emotional problem (Takeuchi *et al.* 1988). In our multicultural society it should not be assumed therefore that beliefs about conditions, or about relevant preventive health behaviours, are the same.

The TPB and risk behaviour

Two different examples of behaviour will be illustrated here: smoking and unprotected sexual intercourse. Smoking is fundamentally an individual behaviour requiring one person only for its performance, whereas unprotected sexual intercourse is a behaviour that involves two people in a social encounter or interaction. Smoking is talked about frequently but as a behaviour is increasingly becoming marginalised, whereas unprotected sexual intercourse is rarely discussed in public! A further difference is in the potential for dependence – from high (smoking) through to rare (sexual behaviour) (although sexual addiction does exist; see Orford 2001). There are sufficient differences between these behaviours to perhaps expect that the predictors of each may differ.

Godin *et al.* (1992) reported that the frequency of smoking behaviour over a six-month period among a general population sample could be explained primarily by low perceived behavioural control over quitting beliefs. Norman *et al.* (1999) applied the TPB to smoking cessation and found that the best predictor of intention to quit was not only perceived behavioural control, but also beliefs in one's susceptibility to the negative health consequences of continued smoking. Few studies have actually applied the TPB to smoking cessation, acknowledging that addictive behaviour is subject to different controlling and contributing factors than is behaviour of a more volitional nature. In saying that, however, beliefs in control over the behaviour, and in particular self-efficacy beliefs (as defined in the HAPA, below), have been found to be salient.

Factors associated with condom use include previous use of condoms, a positive attitude towards use, subjective norms of use by others, self-efficacy in relation to both the purchase and use of condoms, and intentions (see Sheeran *et al.* (1999) for a meta-analysis of studies). One limitation of this area of research is that many studies have been conducted with educated young adult populations (e.g. students) rather than in more 'chaotic' populations such as injecting drug users, who are at above average risk of HIV infection (e.g. Morrison 1991a) and for whom behaviour change is crucial. Interestingly, perceiving a risk of not using a condom (HIV, STDs) does not necessarily follow actual risky practices: for example, MacKellar *et al.* (2007) found that young men who had sex with men were overly optimistic about their HIV risk. It is important to address also whether sexual partners are long-term or casual, as this will also affect real and possibly perceived risk as well as, potentially, attitudes towards the need for, and importance of, 'safe sex'. These factors are likely to influence whether or not the issue of using condoms is raised with a potential partner. It has been suggested that for some individuals the non-use or the use of condoms is less governed by intention (and by implication the cognitive processes that the TPB claims precede intention) than by habit, and, as such, interventions should be targeted very early in a sexual career so as to facilitate the development of 'safer sex' habits (cf. Yzer *et al.* 2001).

Limitations of the TPB

- The TPB does not acknowledge likely transactions between predictor variables (attitudes and subjective norms) and outcome variables, either intention or behaviour. Behaviour itself may shape attitudes. Only prospective longitudinal studies will enable the changing relationships between variables over time to be examined.

- The research evidence supporting a link between intention and subsequent behaviour is limited by an over-reliance on cross-sectional studies. The prediction of behaviour from the TPB variables is significantly lower than the prediction of intention, providing strong evidence for the need to identify further variables that move an individual from intention to action. Other factors which have emerged include affective (emotional) variables and those that relate to planning processes involved in the initiation of action following intention formation. These are described below.

- The TPB, as with most models of health behaviours, assumes that the same factors and processes predict the initiation of a behaviour and the maintenance or change of that behaviour. In fact the majority of studies focus on behaviour initiation. This may be why interventions based on such findings fail to have long-term effects on behaviour change maintenance (van Stralen *et al.* 2009).

Potential additions to the TPB

From rigorous review and evaluation of the short-comings of the TPB emerged several other potential predictors of behaviour, such as self-efficacy, anticipatory regret and implementation intentions, all of which have been added to many empirical studies and tested to establish what they can add to the explanation of behaviour change.

● '*Moral norms*': rather than a behaviour being influenced by subjective social norms, it has been recognised that some intentions and behaviour may be partially motivated by moral norms, particularly behaviours that directly involve others, such as condom use or drink driving (e.g. Armitage and Conner 1998; Evans and Norman 2002; Manstead 2000).

● *Anticipatory regret* (Bell 1982; Triandis 1977): while outcome expectancies have been addressed in the TPB, one specific anticipated consequence that warrants more attention is that of regret. Regret is anticipated when a certain behavioural decision is thought to have an undesireable future outcome. For example, regarding unprotected sexual intercourse, anticipatory regret (i.e. I would really regret it if she got pregnant/If I got an STD) increased an individual's intention to use condoms (e.g. Richard *et al.* 1996; van der Pligt and de Vries 1998). In relation to a single occasion of heavy drinking, anticipating negative affect (e.g. hangover) was not, however, associated with changes in drinking intentions or behaviour (Murgraff *et al.* 1999). This suggests that the type of behaviour and how it is perceived (e.g. risky unprotected sex/less risky drinking) may moderate the effect of anticipatory regret. Perugini and Bagozzi (2001) propose that anticipatory emotions (including regret) arise from a person's consideration of the likelihood of attaining (success) or not attaining (failure) the desirable outcomes of the behaviour. Dunton and Vaughan (2008) have shown that anticipating positive emotion is more likely at a pre-intentional stage in the behaviour

change process, and negative emotions more likely post-intentionally (see discussion of stage models below).

● *Self-identity*: how one perceives and labels oneself may influence intention above and beyond the effect of core TPB variables. For example, self-identifying as a 'green consumer' and valuing this self increased intention to eat organic vegetables (Sparks and Shepherd 1992), suggesting that we behave in a manner that affirms our self-image. For self-affirmation as an intervention tool, whereby people are encouraged to reflect on cherished values or attributes of themselves as a means of enhancing risk information processing and acceptance, resulting in greater behaviour change, see Epton and Harris (2008) (fruit and vegetable intake), van Koningsbruggen *et al.* (2009) (caffeine intake)).

● *Implementation intention* (II): forming an II is thought to be part of the process involved in turning an intention into action, i.e. filling the intention–behaviour gap highlighted by limitations in behavioural prediction by TPB studies (see below).

Implementation intentions

One of the reasons why people may not always translate their intentions into action is that they have not made adequate plans as to how, when and where they will implement their intention. Gollwitzer suggests that individuals need to shift from a mindset typical of the motivation (pre-doing) phase towards an implementational mindset, which is found in the **volition** (doing) phase (Gollwitzer 1999; Gollwitzer and Oettingen 1998; Gollwitzer and Schaal 1998). Individuals need to make a specific 'when, where and how' plan that commits them to a certain time and place and to using a particular method of action. For example, rather than stating, as is typical in the TPB measures, how strongly I intend to stop smoking, an implementation intention would require me to state that I intend to stop smoking first thing next Sunday morning, at home, using a nicotine

---

volition

action or doing (the post-intentional stage highlighted in the HAPA model of health behaviour change).

replacement patch. Although Ogden (2003) argues that this method of questioning is manipulative rather than descriptive and serves a different purpose to that of simply asking questions about one's attitudes or beliefs (i.e. it has the purpose of intervention and not description), many studies now include a measure of II.

Goal intentions can be distinguished from implementation intentions, for example:

- goal intention: 'I intend to go on a diet' (motivational, part of TPB);

- implementation intention: 'I intend to go on a diet on Monday after my party weekend' (planning, not part of TPB).

Implementation intentions have been shown to increase a person's commitment to their decision and the likelihood of their attaining a wide variety of specified health-related goals by carrying out the intended action (meta-analysis, Gollwitzer and Sheeran 2006). For example, Orbell *et al.* (1997) assessed the attitudes, social norms and intentions of women to perform breast self-examination and then instructed half of the sample to form an II as to when and where they would carry it out. This half of the sample showed a significantly higher rate of subsequent self-examination than the sample that had not formed an II. Commonly reported barriers to attaining goals or implementing intended behaviour, such as forgetting or being distracted from it, can be overcome by committing the individual to a specific course of action when the environmental conditions specified in their II are encountered (Rutter and Quine 2002: 15). Illustrating this, Gollwitzer and Brandstätter (1997) describe how an II creates a mental link between the specified situation (e.g. next Monday) and the behaviour (e.g. starting a diet). It seems likely that IIs obtain their effects by making action more automatic, i.e. in response to a situational stimuli set down in the II. This *reflexive* action control is automatic initiation of goal-directed behaviour which can be contrasted with deliberative and *reflective* processes in which a person might procrastinate and think 'When will I do this?' type thoughts that prevent many intentions being put into action (Mendoza *et al.* 2010).

Gollwitzer (1999) also notes that while forming proximal (more immediate) goals leads to better goal attainment than forming distal (long-term) goals, IIs do show persistence over time. For example, forming

an II to take vitamin pills persisted over a three-week period in Sheeran and Orbell's (1999) study. Such findings could have implications for a range of groups; for example, hospitalised patients could be encouraged to form IIs about their home-based rehabilitation in order to improve exercise adherence (and hence recovery) post-discharge. While some people spontaneously form IIs when they form the motivational intention ('I intend to exercise'), many others do not and therefore the encouragement of the formation of IIs offers a fruitful avenue for health education and intervention (see Chapter 6 ☞). However, de Vet and colleagues (de Vet *et al.* 2011) rightly point out that much of the evidence of positive effects of II formation on behaviour comes from research studies where assistance was given to the individuals in forming their II. This face-to-face assistance is not available to individuals in real life: for example, when considering safer sex practices. They examined the quality of IIs developed independently by young single females aged between 16 and 30 years regarding 'preparing' to buy a condom and actually using' the condom. Results showed that IIs were of better quality (sufficiently complete and precise) in relation to preparation than for action, but in fact IIs were not predictive of all preparatory behaviours (buying, having at home, discussing with potential partner). In spite of some sample restrictions, such findings serve to highlight that effective planning for condom-use behaviour is complex and perhaps IIs for preparatory action should be encouraged in health promotion campaigns rather than targeting use directly. In doing this, the goals of the behaviour can be highlighted. Generally, goal attainment is influenced by the value placed on the likely outcome; by the belief that the goal is attainable through the person's actions, i.e. self-efficacy; and by the receipt of feedback on progress made (particularly important where long-term goals, such as weight loss, are involved) (Locke and Latham 2002). It is becoming clear that models of health behaviour change need to address personal goals more effectively.

So far in this chapter, we have reviewed static or continuum models, which describe additive components whereby perceptions or beliefs (or sets of them) are used in combination to try to predict where an individual will lie on an outcome continuum such as an intention or behaviour. We turn our attention now to stage models, i.e. models of behaviour change which consider individuals

ISSUES

How the wording and ordering of questions may influence the data obtained

It has been suggested that studies reporting evidence of unrealistic optimism (UO) in a sample may actually be witnessing a measurement artefact, i.e. UO may be appearing as a result of the manner in which the questions are asked (Harris and Middleton 1994). Weinstein originally asked one simple question to establish the presence of UO: 'Compared with others of my sex/age . . . my chances of developing "disease *x*" are . . . (great/average/low)'. Other studies, however, ask two questions: the first generating a rating for personal risk, the second generating a rating for the risk of similar others (see, for example, Perloff and Fetzer 1986; van der Velde *et al.* 1992). UO is considered to be present when the second rating is higher than the first. Hoorens and Buunk (1993) manipulated the ordering of these two questions and also the comparison group that their sample of adolescents were required to think of when making their risk judgements. They found significant effects of ordering whereby those rating personal risk first, and then comparative others' risk, exhibited lower levels of UO than those receiving the questions in the opposite order.

In an early study further illustrating ordering effects, Budd (1987) conducted an experiment where the order of theory of reasoned action items was muddled across different versions of a questionnaire. Budd found that muddling significantly altered the inter-correlations between perceptions of threat, attitude, normative beliefs and intention to either smoke, brush teeth three times per day, or exercise for twenty minutes. Sheeran and Orbell (1996) tried to replicate this using *protection motivation theory* (PMT) components in relation to different behaviour – that of condom use and dental flossing. While fewer effects of ordering were found, correlation strengths between some key cognitive variables did change. These authors also report that scores on a social desirability scale, along with the perceived salience of the behaviour being addressed, had small but reliable effects on the associations between the health beliefs assessed in the PMT.

In addition to ordering effects, we are faced with the likelihood of 'mere measurement effects' (Morwitz *et al.* 1993, as cited in Godin *et al.* 2008: 179), whereby the very questions that we ask likely effect subsequent behaviour. For example, a questionnaire assessing perceived susceptibility to a particular illness may increase awareness of an issue or may cause the individual to reflect upon their own behaviour and change their belief structure. Potentially, these changed beliefs may alter subsequent behaviour. In our own study examining beliefs and intentions about future, hypothetical genetic testing uptake for breast cancer (e.g. Morrison *et al.* 2010), participants rated their attitudes towards genetic testing, their outcome expectancies, perceived benefits of, or barriers to testing, and their intention to undertake testing were it to become available. For some individuals, this type of questioning probably caused them to think about something they may not have done previously. The questions provide information to the participant about the behaviour: e.g. 'To what extent do you think that genetic testing will: reduce uncertainty about my long-term risk of breast cancer; enable me to make positive decisions about my future', and this information could potentially change beliefs and attitudes. In other studies effects may be seen in changed behaviour; for example, answering questions about one's drinking behaviour may cause reflection and change, or as Godin *et al.* (2008) found, those (n = 2900 adults) who were asked a question about intention to donate blood within a TPB questionnaire were significantly more likely to register for donation and subsequently donate blood than a control group (n = 1772) who did not receive a questionnaire. In effect, the questionnaire itself acted as an intervention (and a relatively cheap one at that!)

Such findings suggest that the direction of behaviour change could be manipulated by changing the wording of the questions, in the same way as other studies attempt to change beliefs by manipulating the nature of information provided. While this may be desirable in certain circumstances, this issue of questions as interventions requires greater attention in research designs and greater acknowledgement in the discussion of findings (see also Ogden (2003) for a review of this issue in relation to 47 empirical studies based on the social cognition models discussed in this chapter).

as being at 'discrete ordered stages', each one denoting a greater inclination to change outcome than the previous stage (Rutter and Quine 2002: 16).

Stage models of behaviour change

According to Weinstein (Weinstein, Rothman and Sutton 1998; Weinstein and Sandman 2002) a stage theory has four properties:

1. *A classification system to define stages*: it is accepted that the stage classifications are theoretical constructs, and although a prototype is defined for each stage, few people will perfectly match this ideal.

2. *Ordering of stages*: people must pass through all the stages to reach the end point of action or maintenance, but progression to the end point is neither inevitable nor irreversible. For example, a person may decide to quit smoking but not do so; or may quit smoking but lapse back into the habit sometime thereafter.

3. *Common barriers to change facing people within the same stage*: this idea would be helpful in encouraging progression through the stages if people at one stage have to address similar issues: for example, if low self-efficacy acted as a common barrier to the initiation of dietary change.

4. *Different barriers to change facing people in different stages*: if the factors producing movement to the next stage were the same regardless of stage (e.g. self-efficacy), the same intervention could be used for all, and the stages would be redundant. Ample evidence exists that barriers are different in the different stages (see below).

The transtheoretical model (TTM)

This model was developed by Prochaska and di Clemente (1984) to address intentional behavioural change. Initially applied mostly to smoking cessation (e.g. di Clemente *et al.* 1991), the existence of 'stages of change' have now been reported in many behaviours (e.g. smoking cessation, cocaine use cessation, taking up exercise, consistent condom use, sunscreen use, weight control, radon testing,

reduction of dietary fat intake, mammography screening, and even the modification of delinquent behaviour: Prochaska 1994; Prochaska *et al.* 1994). The model makes two broad assumptions: that people move through stages of change; and that the processes involved at each stage differ and are independent, thus it meets several of the requirements outlined by Weinstein.

Stages of change

The stages of change proposed by the TTM are stages of motivational readiness and are outlined below, using dietary behaviour as an illustration:

- *Pre-contemplation*: a person is not currently thinking of dieting, no intention to change dietary intake in next six months, may not consider that they have a weight problem.

- *Contemplation*: e.g. 'I think I need to lose a bit of weight, but not quite yet' reflects awareness of a need to lose weight and consideration of doing so. Generally assessed as planning to change within next six months.

- *Preparation*: a person is ready to change and sets goals, such as planning a start date for the diet (within three months). Stage includes thoughts and action, and people make specific plans about change.

- *Action*: for example, a person starts eating fruit instead of biscuits; overt behaviour change.

- *Maintenance*: keeps up with the dietary change, resists temptation.

While the above stages are the five most commonly referred to, there are also:

- *Termination*: where behaviour change has been maintained for adequate time for the person to feel no temptation to lapse and who believe in their total self-efficacy to maintain the change.

- *Relapse*: di Clemente and Velicer (1997) acknowledged that relapse (where a person lapses into earlier behaviour patterns and returns to a previous stage) is common and can occur at any stage, i.e. this is not a final stage or alternative to termination.

People do not necessarily move smoothly from one stage to another. For example, some individuals may go from preparation back to contemplation and stay there for months or even years before re-entering the preparation phase and successfully moving on to action. For others action can fail, maintenance may never be achieved, and relapse is common. The model therefore allows for 'recycling' from one stage to another and is sometimes referred to as a 'spiral' model (e.g. Prochaska *et al.* 1992). The first two stages are generally considered to be defined by intention or motivation; the preparation stage combines intentional and behavioural (volitional) criteria, whereas the action and maintenance stages are purely behavioural (Prochaska and Marcus 1994).

To help understand factors that influence progression through the stages, the model outlines independent psychological 'processes of change' that are considered to be at play in the different stages (with some being important in more than one stage). These processes include the covert or overt activities that people engage in to help them to progress: for example, seeking social support and avoiding settings that 'trigger' the behaviour, as well as more 'experiential' processes that individuals may go through emotionally and cognitively, such as weighing up pros and cons of changing; self re-evaluation or consciousness raising. These processes are the targets of intervention efforts to 'move' individuals through the stages towards effective and maintained behaviour change (see Chapter 6 ☞).

● In the pre-contemplation stage, individuals are more likely to be using denial and/or may report lower self-efficacy (to change) beliefs and more barriers to change.

● In the contemplation stage, people are more likely to seek information and may report reduced barriers ('cons') to change and increased benefits, although they may still underestimate their susceptibility to the health threat concerned.

● In the preparation stage, people start to set their goals and priorities, and some will make concrete plans (similar to implementation intentions as described in an earlier section) and small changes in behaviour (e.g. joining a gym). Some may be setting unrealistic goals for success, or underestimating their own ability to succeed. Motivation and self-efficacy are crucial if action is to be elicited.

● In the action stage, realistic goal setting is crucial and perception of 'cons' lower. The use of social support provides reinforcement that will help to maintain the lifestyle change.

● Many individuals, for example up to 80 per cent of smokers who quit (Oldenburg *et al.* 1999), will not

succeed in maintaining behavioural change and will relapse or 'recycle' back to contemplating a future attempt to change. Maintenance can be enhanced by self-monitoring and reinforcement.

There is evidence that several motivational factors vary across these stages: for example, perceived behavioural control and attitudes to activity (Lorentzen *et al.* 2007), outcome expectancies and anticipated affective consequences (Dunton and Vaughan 2008), and the perception of barriers and benefits, or 'pros and cons'. For example, one meta-analysis of the pros and cons relative to 48 different behaviours found that pros were greater in number in the action stage than in the pre-contemplation stage, and that 'cons' are lower in this action stage than in the contemplation stage (Hall and Rossi 2008). An individual in the contemplation stage is likely to focus on both the pros and cons of change, but the 'cons' or barriers may be weighted more heavily (e.g. 'Even if I get healthier in the long term, I am probably going to gain weight if I stop smoking'), whereas someone in the preparation stage is likely to focus more on the pros of change (e.g. 'Even if I gain weight in the short term, it will be worth it to start feeling healthier'). The relative weight between pros and cons is referred to as **decisional balance**.

The TTM and preventive behaviour

De Vet and colleagues (2007) compared whether a previously described 'static' model variable of 'intention' (TPB) was more or less predictive of fruit intake (action) than the stages of change, and in fact intention did better. However, much support for interventions based on staged models exists; for example, Cox *et al.* (2003) conducted a longitudinal trial of an exercise behaviour change programme among sedentary Australian women aged 40–65. The intervention was either exercise centre or home-based and promoted either 'moderate' or 'intense' exercise levels. The study assessed participants' 'stage of change' regarding exercising and also explored the role

---

decisional balance
where the costs of behaviour are weighed up against the benefits of that behaviour.

of self-efficacy and decisional balance in relation to changes in exercise behaviour observed over time, as these factors likely mediate the relationship between the processes of change and progress through the stages, (cf. Prochaska and Velicer 1997). Women were reassessed after eighteen months. Increased activity levels were seen in those who had received either intervention, almost independently of the stage of readiness that women had been in following the intervention. (This finding that the place of delivery is unimportant psychologically has important implications for intervention delivery costs.) Additionally, the intervention produced increases in self-efficacy in line with the 'stage of change' achieved (i.e. self-efficacy increased as the stage progressed towards action) and appeared to be critical, whereas decisional balance findings were inconclusive.

The TTM and risk-reducing behaviour

In general, the notion of stages of change has received support (Dijkstra *et al.* 2006); however, several studies have questioned whether the change processes outlined are in fact useful predictors of change. For example, Segan *et al.* (2002) examined the changes in specific behavioural and experiential processes, self-efficacy and decisional balance among a sample of 193 individuals who were preparing to stop smoking and making the transition to the action stage. Results suggested that some changes in TTM components resulted *from* the transition to action, rather than preceded it: for example, increases in situational confidence and counter-conditioning (where positive behaviour is substituted for smoking). The main findings for the effect of behavioural and experiential processes were not reported, even though the TTM claims that these act as 'catalysts' for change. Furthermore, although self-efficacy was associated with making a quit attempt, it did not predict the success or failure of that attempt. As with the study of exercise prediction described in the previous section, decisional balance was not predictive of any behaviour change (from quitting to remaining quit or relapsing). Although a relatively small study, these findings have further questioned the validity of the TTM stages and processes as a model of change. However, such findings do further reinforce the central role of self-efficacy, which is addressed fully in our discussion of a further model, the HAPA, below.

Limitations of the TTM

- Prochaska and di Clemente suggested a time-frame within which they distinguish contemplaters from preparers (i.e. thinking of changing but not in the next six months versus thinking of changing within the next three months). There is, however, little empirical evidence that these are qualitatively different or differ in terms of the attitudes or intentions of stage members (e.g. Godin *et al.* 2004; Kraft *et al.* 1999) which has implications for the likely effectiveness of stage-tailored interventions (Herzog 2008).

- Past behaviour has been found to be a powerful predictor of future behaviour change efforts, which calls into question the usefulness of stages, where readiness or intentions to change are assumed to be key (Sutton 1996; Sutton 2001). For example, Godin *et al.* (2004) present a model which combines recent past behaviour with future intentions to produce four 'clusters' of individuals with different attributes in terms of current behaviour and future intention to exercise. They find that attitudes and perceived behavioural control associate more strongly with membership of these staged clusters than with membership of the five stages of change that do not consider past behaviour. Such findings, if replicated longitudinally, would suggest that we should be assessing both intentions and current or recent behaviour.

- The validity of five independent stages of 'readiness to change' has been further questioned on the basis of data that did not succeed in allocating all participants to one specific stage (e.g. Budd and Rollnick 1996). This suggests that a continuous variable of 'readiness' may be a better description of this construct than one considered in discrete stages (Sutton 2000).

- The model, as with many mainstream psychological models, insufficiently addresses the social aspects of much health behaviour, such as drinking behaviour (Marks *et al.* 2000).

- The model does not allow for some people not knowing about the behaviour or the issue in question. This is likely when a rare or new illness is being considered (such as when HIV/AIDS or BSE (bovine spongiform encephalopathy) emerged), or when the risk concerned is related to a 'new' behaviour: e.g. mobile phone use, or to newly identified risk factors such as human papillomavirus or HPV (see IN THE

SPOTLIGHT on p.128). This is acknowledged in a less commonly employed model, the precaution adoption process model (Weinstein 1988; Weinstein and Sandman 1992), which is addressed below.

To address some of these proposed limitations of the TTM, researchers have attempted to test both the stages and the processes within and between them by conducting intervention studies (e.g. Quinlan and McCaul 2000; see Chapter 6 ☛), where targeting the processes of change hypothesised by the TTM has not resulted in the anticipated movement between stages. A systematic review of the findings of 37 controlled interventions studies provided limited support for stage-appropriate interventions (Bridle *et al.* 2005), thus leading to calls for an end to TTM-based interventions (e.g. Sutton 2005; West 2005); however, other studies do continue to provide support (Dijkstra *et al.* 2006; Hall and Rossi 2008). The debate continues!

The precaution adoption process model (PAPM)

Weinstein and colleagues (Weinstein 1988; Weinstein and Sandman 1992) developed the PAPM as a framework for understanding deliberate actions taken to reduce health risks and was intended to meet the criteria for a stage theory described by Weinstein himself (see above). Weinstein's model has seven stages, and highlights important omissions in the TTM (and indeed omissions in other models) (Table 5.1). Some factors

Table 5.1 Stages in the transtheoretical model and the precaution adoption process model

Stage	Transtheoretical model	Precaution adoption process model
1	Pre-contemplation	Unaware of issue
2	Contemplation	Unengaged
3	Preparation	Considering whether to act
4	Action	Deciding not to act (and exit the model)
5	Maintenance	Deciding to act (and proceed to next stage)
6		Action
7		Maintenance

that 'move' people from one stage to another are also proposed and similar to the TTM. While the model asserts that people pass through stages in sequences, no time limit within which to reach the action stage is specified. The major difference then between this model and the TTM is that the PAPM gives greater consideration to the pre-action stages.

● *Stage 1*: a person is basically 'unaware' of the threat to health posed by a certain risk behaviour or the absence of a protective behaviour, e.g. unaware of their insufficient exercise activity); they have no knowledge and therefore are not aware of a risk.

● *Stage 2*: termed 'unengaged', here a person has become aware of the risks attached to a certain behaviour but believes that the levels at which they engage in it is insufficient to pose a threat to their health ('I know smoking causes various diseases, but I don't smoke enough for them to be a threat'). This is seen as an 'optimistic bias' and led to Weinstein's development of the construct of unrealistic optimism (see earlier).

● *Stage 3*: people become engaged for some reason (includes internal and external triggers). They enter a 'consideration' stage, akin to pre-contemplation and are deciding whether or not to act. So many things compete for our attention that a fair amount can be known about a hazard before this decision-making phase is entered. Three decisions can be reached, they can stay where they are in stage 3, or make one of two opposing decisions taking them to either stage 4 or 5.

● *Stage 4*: although perceived threat and susceptibility may be high, some people actively 'decide not to act', which is very different from intending to act but then not doing so. These individuals may not progress further, or may do so at a later date.

● *Stage 5*: some enter a 'decide to act' stage, similar to intention/preparation. There are important differences between people with a definite stance who have decided to act and those who are undecided (stage 3). Individuals in stage 3 may be more open to information and persuasion than those with a definite stance (decided not to act as in stage 4 or decided to act as in stage 5). As noted previously, stating an intention to act does not inevitably lead to action. Perceived susceptibility beliefs are considered necessary here to motivate progression to action. Moving from stage 5 to stage 6 relates to moving from motivation to volition.

- *Stage 6*: the action stage, when a person has initiated what is necessary to reduce their risk.
- *Stage 7*: this final stage is not always required/relevant as it is about maintenance and, unlike with smoking cessation, some health behaviour processess are not long-lasting, for example deciding whether or not to have a vaccination or a mammogram.

Weinstein applied the PAPM to studies of home testing for radon, an invisible odourless radioactive gas produced by the decay of naturally occurring uranium in soil in some geographical areas. It enters homes through cracks in foundations, and although little heard of, it is the second leading cause of lung cancer after smoking (Weinstein and Sandman 2002). Perceived susceptibility (or vulnerability) was found to be crucial in the transition between stage 3 (trying to decide) and stage 5 (deciding to act). Although a stage-matched intervention, as with those based on the TTM, was not as successful in moving 'decided to act' stage 5 participants into action (buying a home radon-testing kit), as it was in shifting the undecided participants into making a decision to act (but not action necessarily), participants receiving either of these stage-matched interventions did significantly better than control participants (Weinstein *et al.* 1998), showing support for matched interventions.

Limitations of the PAPM

The PAPM has been tested less extensively than ι TTM, although both models suffer from a lack of longitudinal testing. However, the PAPM does progress thinking to include the issue of awareness and pre-decisional processes.

The health action process approach (HAPA)

The HAPA is a hybrid model having both 'static' and staged qualities. The HAPA has really taken on board the issue of stages and attempts to fill the 'intention–behaviour gap', crucially by highlighting the role of post-motivational (or volitional) self-efficacy and action planning factors not addressed by the TPB or PMT (Schwarzer 1992; Schwarzer *et al.* 2008). The HAPA model is particularly influential because it suggests that the adoption, initiation and maintenance of health behaviour must be explicitly viewed as a process that consists of at least a pre-intentional motivation phase and a post-intentional volition phase (where a conscious choice or decision is made) which leads to the actual behaviour (Figure 5.3). Schwarzer (2001) further divided self-regulatory processes into sequences of planning, initiation, maintenance, relapse management and disengagement; however, the first three of these are where the model has been best tested.

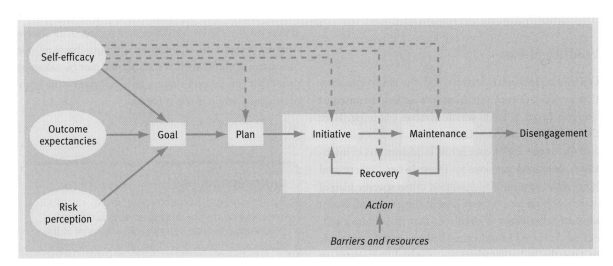

Figure 5.3 The health action process approach model

Source: Schwarzer (1992); http://userpage.fu-berlin.de/~health/hapa.htm

Motivation phase

As we have seen in models such as the TPB, individuals form an intention to either adopt a precautionary measure (e.g. use a condom during sexual intercourse) or change risk behaviour (e.g. stop smoking) as a result of various attitudes, cognitions and social factors. The HAPA proposes that self-efficacy and outcome expectancies are important predictors of goal intention (as in the TPB perceived behavioural control construct). Perceptions of threat severity and personal susceptibility (perceived risk) are considered a distal influence on actual behaviour, playing a role only in the motivation phase. In terms of 'ordering' of self-efficacy and outcome expectancies, the latter may precede the former (e.g. an individual probably thinks of the consequences of their action before working out if they can do what is required). Under conditions where individuals have no previous experience with the behaviour they are contemplating, the authors suggest that outcome expectancies may have a stronger influence on behaviour than efficacy beliefs.

Intention in the motivation phases is considered as a goal intention: e.g. 'I intend to stop smoking to become healthier'. Schwarzer also proposes phase-specific self-efficacy beliefs which is consistent with Bandura's findings (1997). Self-efficacy in the motivational stage is defined as 'task/pre-action self-efficacy': e.g. 'I can succeed in eating a healthy diet even if I have to change my lifestyle a bit'. At this stage, it is important for an individual to imagine successful outcomes and be confident in their ability to achieve them.

Volition phase

Once an intention has been formed, the HAPA proposes that in order to turn intention into action, a conscious decision to act is made which involves planning. Here the model incorporates Gollwitzer's (1999; Gollwitzer and Oettingen 2000) concept of implementation intentions, described previously. These 'when, where and how' plans turn the goal intention into a specific plan of action. Schwarzer proposes that at this stage a different kind of self-efficacy is involved, that of *initiative* self-efficacy, whereby an individual believes that they are able to take the initiative when the planned circumstances arise (e.g. the morning of the planned diet arrives and the

individual needs to believe that they can then implement their plan). Once the action has been initiated, the individual next needs to try to maintain the new, healthier behaviour. At this stage *coping* (or *maintenance*) self-efficacy is considered important to success (e.g. 'I need to keep going with this diet even if it is hard at first'). This form of self-efficacy describes a belief in one's ability to overcome barriers and temptations (such as being faced with a birthday celebration) and is likely to enhance resilience, positive coping (such as drawing upon social support) and greater persistence. If, as many do, the individual suffers a setback and gives in to temptation, for example as often reported in the case of addictive behaviours such as smoking or **drug dependence**, the model proposes that *recovery* self-efficacy is necessary to get the individual back on track (Renner and Schwarzer 2003).

Findings based on the HAPA are encouraging. For example, in a longitudinal study of breast self-examination behaviour among 418 women, pre-actional self-efficacy and positive outcome expectancies (and not risk perception) were significant predictors of (goal) intention. Self-efficacy beliefs also predicted planning. In terms of actual BSE behaviour, by the time of follow-up (twelve–fifteen weeks later), planning was, as hypothesised, highly predictive, with maintenance and recovery self-efficacy also predicting greater frequency of the behaviour (Luszczynska and Schwarzer 2003). Although it is perhaps surprising that risk perception was not predictive (given findings from HBM or TPB-based studies), it may well be that risk perceptions influenced participants *before* they were assessed for the study, and therefore effects on the HAPA variables had passed. It is always hard in research to establish an absolute 'baseline' for measurement, and such results should not be taken as proof that risk perceptions are not important – the body of evidence would prove otherwise.

---

drug dependence

usually a progression from drug abuse. Involves dependence on the drug to achieve a desired psychological state, withdrawal symptoms in the absence of the drug, and social and work-related problems.

Further longitudinal evidence of the importance of phase-specific self-efficacy has been found among those undergoing cardiac rehabilitation and needing to adhere to a programme of exercise rehabilitation (Sniehotta *et al.* 2005; Schwarzer *et al.* 2008). In these studies, believing in one's ability to resume activity after failure or illness was a significant predictor of planning and of actual behaviour. These proximal predictors open up avenues to quite different intervention than those that address risk perceptions, generally not found to be significant in studies employing the HAPA.

Limitations of the HAPA

The limitations of this model could in fact be attributed to any of the preceding models and thus are raised briefly here and more generally in ISSUES below.

- Renner *et al.* (2007) found that the HAPA modelled the behaviour of middle-aged and older people better than it did that of younger people (although this could be culture-specific as their sample was composed of South Koreans). This theme of the global utility of models of behaviour is continued in ISSUES below.

- More is still needed in terms of our understanding of volition-action. De Vries and colleagues (2006) distinguish between distal pre-motivational determinants (e.g. threat perception), motivational determinants (e.g. self-efficacy, perceived behavioural control, outcome expectancies, and intention) and proximal post-motivational determinants (e.g. action planning and control, goal setting, coping planning and control, implementation intentions). The latter of these are volitional concepts which are only now receiving the research attention they deserve (Schwarzer and Luszczynska 2008).

- Insufficient attention is given to non-conscious processes. Rivis *et al.* (2010) distinguish between four modes of action control: intentional control (i.e. conscious self-instruction); reactive control (i.e. a non-rational willingness to perform a certain behaviour in some circumstances, e.g. not use a condom if partner is unhappy to); habitual control (acting out of habit, often on cue and non-conscious) and stereotype activation control (non-conscious stereotyping or acting by prototype – 'smoking is typical for my age group'). Their findings from a study of adolescent smoking confirmed all but intentional control as predictive.

Plate 5.2 Preparing for healthy eating by making the purchases will increase the likelihood of action

Source: Pearson Education Ltd.

The need for including self-regulatory processes

The models described in this chapter differ in some aspects but share a common goal – to aid our understanding of correlates and predictors of behaviours associated with health, whether positively or negatively. Recently, some authors have linked their consideration of sociocognitive models to wider thinking regarding behavioural (and emotional) self-regulation, i.e. what we do deliberately, reflectively and consciously in order to achieve goals or desired outcomes (Hofmann *et al.* 2008 as cited in Sutton 2010: 58; Hagger *et al.* 2009; Hagger 2010). Self-regulation requires self-control, and individuals likely vary in that regard (Cameron and

ISSUES

Are models of health behaviour globally useful?

Health models such as described in this chapter have brought our understanding of behaviour a long way. However, we are still far from being able to predict all behaviour (perhaps thankfully), and we are further still from successfully developing and implementing interventions that will maximise the adoption or maintenance of healthy lifestyles. It has proven important to acknowledge that different factors determine behaviour initiation than behaviour maintenance or change (see van Stralen *et al.* 2009 for a review of the differential determinants of physical activity initiation and maintenance in the over-40s). We do not yet fully understand the differential influences, partly because studies based on the models described in this chapter tend to focus on behaviour change initiation (e.g. beginning to stop smoking, adopting a low fat diet) rather than the maintenance of that behaviour. Interventions, such as those described in Chapter 6 ☞ need to acknowledge this.

Furthermore, when attempting to explain or motivate change in dependency-producing behaviour such as smoking, it needs to be acknowledged that the impulse to smoke can occur independently of our conscious cognitive efforts, thus challenging models which rely on conscious processes and decision making (Hofmann *et al.* 2008; Vangeli and West 2008).

It is worth noting, as do Renner *et al.* (2007) above, that models and their components might 'work better' in some samples than do others. For example, a recent study by Hankonen *et al.* (2010) address the question of whether late middle-aged males and females experience the same psychosocial processes in relation to self-efficacy, planning and use of social support. Interestingly and perhaps surprisingly, men reported greater social support and women reported more planning for exercise. Both sexes had significant associations between self-efficacy and exercise increase. While these models have been employed in numerous studies, many, particularly in relation to the TPB, have been conducted among young healthy populations. The prolific use of student samples, for example, enables theories to be tested and built, and

interesting questions to be addressed. For example: what influences students' drinking behaviour and, given its normative function, can it be changed? What factors influence non-regular use of condoms, and does drinking alcohol interfere with even the best of intentions? However, the findings of studies such as these may not translate across to prediction of behaviour among older populations, less educated individuals, or to those leading less structured lives, such as the homeless drinker or drug user; or even to those who are attempting to change behaviour as a response to a life-threatening condition, such as dietary change following a heart attack or physical activity among those with diabetes (Plotnikoff *et al.* 2010). Other social, environmental, cognitive and emotional factors are likely to play a role in these populations. Sallis *et al.* (2007), for example, highlight the important role played by environmental influences, such as perceived crime and traffic safety or perceived access to facilities, on the initiation and maintenance of physical activity among the over-50s. Perceived safety is not often cited as an exercise determinant among student samples.

The models of health behaviour primarily used in health psychology research focus more on individual cognitions than perhaps is warranted. Behaviour is influenced hugely by context, by socio-economic resources, by culture and by laws, sanctions and habits, and we have highlighted these at various points in this chapter, but also in detail in Chapters 1 and 2 ☞ and in most other chapters.

Therefore, given all the above, if you are planning some research of your own you should consider:

● Different factors are salient in relation to some behaviours but not others (for example, subjective norm may be more important to smoking initiation than vitamin intake).

● The salience of certain factors may vary by age or gender (e.g. attitude to medicines may predict intention to adhere to medication in adults, but not in children, where adherence is more under parental control).

● The role of culture, ethnicity and religion may significantly influence beliefs about health and preventive health. For example, an individual of the Muslim

- faith who drinks heavily will likely face very different emotional and normative pressures than someone of Christian faith.
- Cognitive models may not account very well for habitual behaviours, particularly those with dependency potential, e.g. smoking, drug use, where physiological cues take on salience and create impulses which may override rational thought.
- All of the models reviewed here assume that human beings are rational decision makers. We need to take much more account of non-rational processes, such as impulsivity (Strack and Deutsch 2004). People differ in the extent to which they can, or even wish to, control their impulses. When drunk, angry or tired, for example, we may reflect less on our behaviours or on the decision-making process, or be biased in what cues we attend to (Wiers and Hofmann 2010). Health psychologists perhaps need to consider more the influence of context on the shifting balance between reflection, attentional processes and impulse.
- There may be bias in self-reports of 'illegal' behaviour or of those perceived to be 'unconventional' . For example, the incidence of teenage drug use as self-reported was significantly discrepant from that 'proven' in hair sample bioassays (Delaney-Black *et al.* 2010).
- We also need to consider the influence of nonconscious processes, such as control of behaviour by stereotype activation or habit (Rivis *et al.* 2010).

Leventhal 2003)! Self-regulation is associated with motivational factors such as self-efficacy which we have seen, for example, in the TPB in the form of perceived behavioural control, or in the HAPA. However, it is also closely associated with post-motivation (volitional) factors such as intention and planning. Self-regulation is, in effect, a wider process that affects our behaviour and, in relation to health behaviour change, newer constructs such as 'action control' (e.g. Rivis *et al.* 2010), 'implementation intentions' (e.g. Sniehotta *et al.* 2005) and behavioural monitoring are highly pertinent. Research adopting a self-regulatory perspective in relation to health behaviour change is, relative to studies employing sociocognitive theories, new and complex, and thus interested readers are referred to further reading. For example, Hall and Fong (2007) describe a specific theory called 'temporal self-regulation', and the resulting commentaries published in a Special Issue of *Health Psychology Review* (September 2010) are worth a look at. In addition, Hagger *et al.* (2010) discuss a 'strength' model of self-regulatory failure (i.e. when an individual fails to elicit an intended change or relapses following change. It is likely that these papers will provide much food for thought.

SUMMARY

Many proximal and distal factors influence our behaviour and our health behaviour. More emphasis is required on the wider influences on health behaviour such as culture and group processes. However, as psychologists, our focus has tended to be more on the individual to date.

Continuum models like the HBM and the TPB have demonstrated the importance of social and cognitive factors in predicting both intention to act and action, although the static nature of these models does not facilitate understanding of the processes of change. Stage models like the TTM, PMT and the HAPA address processes of change and have gone some way towards filling the gap between intention and behaviour, by highlighting the distinction between motivational and volitional, planning processes. Perceived susceptibility and self-efficacy are identified as relatively important and consistent predictors of change. As such, they carry intervention potential. Tailored interventions for different stages are more costly than a 'one size fits all' approach, and evidence is mixed as to their success.

Finally, research is needed which examines the social cognitive, emotional and behavioural processes that occur once a person engages in health behaviour change in order to better inform interventions that maximise maintained change (see Chapters 6 and 7 for examples ☞).

Further reading

Conner, M. and Norman, P. (eds) (2005). *Predicting Health Behaviour: Research and Practice with Social Cognition Models*, 2nd edn. Buckingham: Open University Press.

An excellent text that provides comprehensive coverage of social cognition theory and all the models described in this chapter (with the exception of the HAPA). A useful resource for sourcing measurement items for components of the models if you are designing a questionnaire.

Cameron, L.D. and Leventhal, H. (eds) (2003). *The Self-regulation of Health and Illness Behaviour*. London: Routledge.

This excellent book considers both health and illness behaviour and thus has relevance also to Chapters 9 and 10. As the title suggests, the theoretical underpinning to this book is self-regulation theory – a theory increasingly applied to health behaviour initiation and change.

Visser, de R.O. and Smith, J.A. (2007). Alcohol consumption and masculine identity among young men. *Psychology and Health*, 22: 595–614.

In additon to highlighting masculinity as an 'explanation' of drinking behaviour, this qualitative paper raises the important influence of culture and/or religous norms.

Visit the website at **www.pearsoned.co.uk/morrison** for additional resources to help you with your study, including multiple choice questions, weblinks and flashcards.

Chapter 6
Reducing risk of disease – individual approaches

Learning outcomes

By the end of this chapter, you should have an understanding of:

- the costs and benefits of screening programmes for the early detection of risk of disease or disease itself

- the impact of information provision on health-related behaviour following screening for disease risk

- the use of the 'stages of change model' in developing more complex interventions likely to be most effective following detection of risk behaviour

- the process and outcomes of strategies to increase motivation to change behaviour

- the nature and use of problem-solving approaches and implementation planning in facilitating behavioural change

- how modelling and practice may increase the likelihood of behavioural change

- the use of cognitive-behavioural techniques to facilitate risk factor change

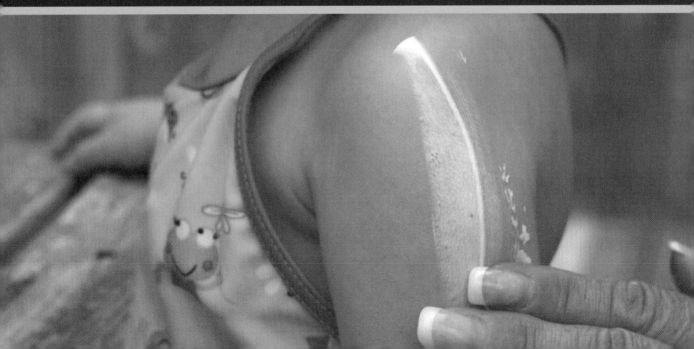

Health education doesn't work!

Doctors today reported that a number of health education programmes failed to achieve any impact on people's behaviours including safer sex, smoking and attending hospital health clinics. Resorting to scare tactics made things even worse. There is an interesting assumption implicit in many government or health service strategies designed to change our behaviour that if they tell us what to do, then we are likely to do it, especially if the message carries a slightly worrying health message. Yet, there is repeated evidence that simple factual or scary information does not work. Of note in this respect was the repeated provision of information about AIDS, the prevention of AIDS, and scary (indeed, terrifying) videos depicting death and hell as a consequence of enjoying unprotected sex people in the UK experienced over a 10–15-year period in the late 1980s and 90s. Reported condom use over this time revealed absolutely no change in response to any of these programmes. The public appeared utterly impervious to the potentially catastrophic consequences of AIDS and remained obstinately fixed in their old behaviours. Clearly, relevant information is necessary to instigate change, but many other factors contribute to the likelihood of change, and the simple repetition of health information (scary or otherwise), however accurate, is unlikely to influence change significantly.

Chapter outline

This chapter considers strategies used to encourage individuals with no evidence of disease to adopt health-enhancing behaviour or stop health-damaging activities. It starts by considering the simplest approach to this issue – screening people for risk of disease as a consequence of either their genetic make-up or their behaviour, and whether this is sufficient to motivate or sustain changes in risk behaviour.

The chapter then considers a number of more complex ways of motivating and maintaining behavioural change based on the degree of motivation an individual may have to achieve change. The first approach we examine is known as motivational interviewing. As its name implies, this has been used particularly with people with low levels of motivation to change their behaviour. The chapter then considers how effective educational programmes are in facilitating change, before examining approaches based on planning and problem-solving techniques, modelling and rehearsing new behaviours, and cognitive-behavioural strategies. The principles of each approach are outlined, and evidence of their effectiveness is considered.

Promoting individual health

How we live our lives has important implications for how long we live, and the degree of physical well-being we enjoy while alive (see Chapters 1 and 2 ☞). Awareness of these issues, and also the financial consequences of an increasingly elderly population, has led governments across the world to invest significant resources in programmes designed to prevent illness and promote higher levels of fitness and health among the population as a whole. In the 1960s and 1970s, when health promotion became a serious issue for governments and health care, most programmes targeted behaviours known to increase our risk for disease. Fortuitously, perhaps, one of the most widely prevalent diseases, CHD, is also the one most strongly linked to lifestyle factors such as smoking or a sedentary lifestyle. The emerging role of these behaviours in the development of some cancers (see Chapter 3 ☞) reinforced the need to promote healthy lifestyles, and was accompanied by an increasing emphasis on encouraging safer sex behaviour following the emergence of HIV infection and AIDS. Biomedical advances have also contributed to the type of preventive services now provided by many health-care services. The ability to identify people at risk of a number of cancers and CHD as a consequence of their genetic make-up has led to programmes designed to identify whether individuals carry the genes that result in increased risk of these diseases, although how that risk is managed once identified is perhaps less clear.

Two broad approaches to facilitating risk factor change can be identified. The first assumes that if we inform people of their risk for certain diseases, this will result in them engaging in long-term preventive behaviour. This model has resulted in screening programmes for risk factors for diseases such as CHD being established throughout the world. More recently, more complex behaviour change technologies have been used to facilitate behavioural change. The next sections of this chapter consider the impact of screening programmes on our physical and psychological health, before considering some of the more complex strategies that have been used to facilitate health-related behavioural change.

Screening programmes

A number of different types of screening programme now exist (see Table 6.1). These include:

- screening for genetic risk of diseases such as cancer or conditions such as high cholesterol;
- screening for risk of disease as a result of health damaging behaviours including smoking, poor diet, and lack of exercise; and
- screening to detect the early stages of disease when it is most easily treatable and curable.

Each carries significant implications for those involved and brings particular benefits and challenges:

- Women identified as carrying the gene mutations that increase risk for breast cancer may choose to take preventive action, such as breast removal (mastectomy) before the onset of disease, and will have to live with the knowledge of their risk for many years.
- People identified as having high cholesterol or high blood pressure may be placed on drugs for the rest of their lives.
- Those found to have behavioural risk factors for disease may choose to make lifestyle changes that have implications for both them and their family.

Genetic risk of disease

We have now identified the genes linked to a number of significant diseases. Here, we focus on the implications of screening for just one of them – mutations to the BRCA1 and BRCA2 genes that increase risk of breast and ovarian cancer. These gene mutations are responsible for breast and ovarian cancer in approximately 40–45 per cent of

individuals with an inherited susceptibility to the disease (Hodgson and Maher 1999). Fortunately, while the risk of cancer associated with them is high, they are relatively rare within the population, and only 4–5 per cent of cases of breast cancer result from these mutations.

The Cancer Genetic Service for Wales (CGSW: Brain *et al.* 2000) provides an example of how a programme identifying genetic risk of developing breast cancer and BRCA gene mutations can work. In this programme, both men and women whose doctors think they may be at heightened genetic risk for breast cancer are referred to the service. Referral is followed by a letter to the patient from the service asking them to complete and return a family history questionnaire, which would give detailed information about their family history of cancer. Once returned, this is scored by medical geneticists, who identify participants' level of risk for developing cancer: the same as the general population, moderate, or high risk. Patients are informed of their risk level by letter and through telephone contact.

- Women at high risk are invited for further counselling and formal genetic testing involving taking blood and looking for the BRCA gene mutation. They are offered annual mammography to detect breast lumps that may be tumours, or preventive mastectomy.
- Women in the moderate risk level are offered annual mammography.
- Women in the population risk group are discharged from the service.

Knowledge of being at moderate or high risk has significant impact for the individual – and their children, who may also be at genetic risk. With these profound implications, one may expect participation in the testing process to be stressful. However, most people seem to

Table 6.1 Some of the common types of screening programme

Type of screening	Example of detection	Possible outcomes of screening
Genetic risk for disease	BRCA1, BRCA2 gene mutations for risk of breast and ovarian cancer	Routine subsequent screening for early detection of disease Preventive surgical procedures
Early detection of disease or its precursors	Cervical screening Mammography Hypertension	Medical or surgical treatment of any abnormalities found
Behavioural risk for disease	Smoking Sedentary lifestyle Poor diet	Behavioural change

cope with no great anxieties, although about a quarter of those assessed report high levels of distress during their risk assessment (Brain *et al.* 2000). Of particular concern is that this may not be a short-term phenomenon. Bennett *et al.* (2010) found that about one-third of women identified as being at moderate risk of developing breast or ovarian cancer by the CGSW were still experiencing frequent and significant worries about their genetic status some six years after their initial risk assessment. Nor does being assigned a population risk level necessarily result in low levels of distress. Geirdal *et al.* (2005) found that many women found to have no genetic mutations reported higher anxiety and depression levels than many women at a higher risk for cancer.

It appears that once some people are alerted to their potential risk for cancer, this becomes a long-term worry. We are not sure why this is the case. Perhaps some individuals who are naturally prone to worry find it difficult to tolerate the idea of *any* level of risk. Certainly, the beliefs people hold about the implications of their risk level are associated with anxiety. Bennett *et al.* (2008), for example, found that levels of anxiety following risk provision were associated with feelings of hopelessness about future health and having little control over developing cancer. Family members may also experience significant anxiety in the context of the testing process. Lodder *et al.* (2001) found that 20 per cent of the women found to carry the gene mutation and 35

IN THE SPOTLIGHT

A different viewpoint on emotional reactions to health screening

Most studies of the emotional effects of cancer genetic screening have focused on measures of anxiety and depression. Studies with these *outcome* measures include those of Brain *et al.* (2000) described in the main text. An alternative model of anxiety or worry as a *motivator* to engage in testing is exemplified by studies such as Glanz *et al.* (1999), who sent a questionnaire to first-degree relatives of patients diagnosed with colorectal cancer, assessing their willingness or intentions to attend counselling for risk of colorectal cancer. While 45 per cent indicated an interest in taking it up, 26 per cent said they definitely would when testing was available. Strength of intentions was predicted by the degree of cancer worry and perceived risk of cancer.

Despite these and similar studies, the wider emotional responses to cancer genetic screening have been largely ignored. One may go even further to suggest that screening programmes are viewed through a psychopathological perspective – asking what harm we do to people who go through them rather than what benefits people gain. This is clearly a very important issue, but such data present only a partial picture

of the emotional response to cancer genetic testing, which may be more positive. Women are unlikely to take part in the testing process unless they have some positive expectation of benefit – evident perhaps through emotional states such as hope or optimism. Similarly, they may feel relief if the testing shows them to be at population risk.

What evidence there is suggests that many individuals with a family history of cancer seek to clarify their genetic risk partly to *reduce* anxiety (Hopwood 1997). Many enter the process with high levels of optimism and hope. In one of the few studies to examine these positive emotional responses to screening, one of the authors (Bennett *et al.* 2008) followed a cohort of women going through genetic risk assessment, measuring their emotions at the beginning of the process and following risk information provision. The overall picture for these women was that, although they felt anxious about their test results, they also felt optimistic about the testing process. After being told their risk level, all the women regardless of the genetic risk assigned were more relieved, calm and hopeful and less anxious and sad when they thought about the testing process and their risk for cancer than when they entered the testing process.

per cent of their partners reported high anxiety levels. Levels of anxiety were lower but still significant among the couples in which the woman was found not to carry the genetic mutation: 11 per cent of these women and 13 per cent of their partners were clinically anxious. Despite this focus on negative emotions in response to risk assessment, most people do benefit emotionally from the testing process – something we consider in IN THE SPOTLIGHT.

Reducing the anxiety associated with genetic risk assessment is not easy. Most people going through the risk assessment process have little or no direct contact with health professionals, and it would be prohibitively expensive to provide stress or anxiety management to all those who experience some distress. For this reason, alternatives including self-help interventions may be of some benefit. In one study aiming to reduce distress in women undergoing assessment of risk for breast/ovarian cancer, Bennett *et al.* (2007) sent a simple leaflet encouraging participants to plan where and when they would think about issues related to their risk assessment, and to use simple distraction techniques to prevent intrusive worries about the process at other times. The leaflet proved effective in reducing the frequency of such worries in those who were experiencing them during the assessment process. Addressing the longer-term needs of women who have already completed the risk assessment process, Appleton *et al.* (2004) found short-term reductions in anxiety in women who had known themselves at risk for several years following provision of a combination of medical information and psychological strategies for managing any distress they were experiencing.

Early detection of disease

Breast cancer is the most common cancer in women and the second leading cause of death in women. Mammography provides a means of detecting early cancers before they become obvious to the woman involved. Of those who take part in this type of screening, less than one per cent are found to have an early cancer (Moss *et al.* 2005). Nevertheless, there is good evidence that this detection rate can significantly reduce rates of disease. Sarkeala *et al.* (2008), for example, found a 22 per cent reduction in deaths from breast cancer among Finnish women who were invited to mammography compared to those who had not received such an invitation. In

the UK, the age limits of mammography in the absence of any particular risk for disease involve women aged between 50 and 70 years. Screening younger women appears to be less beneficial, partly because of the lower frequency of tumours in this population, and partly because their higher density of breast tissue makes it difficult to identify small lumps within it.

Despite these benefits, mammography brings a number of concerns and anxieties, particularly for women who consider themselves to be at high risk for breast cancer. Such women frequently report high levels of anxiety both before and after testing – even when their mammogram is found to be normal (Absetz *et al.* 2003). Unfortunately, mammography is not an exact science, and women may be called back for a second mammogram or an **ultrasound** scan, which provides a more accurate view of the breast if the results of the initial mammogram are not clear. Where lumps in the breast *are* found, some women may have a small operation involving a **fine needle aspiration** or a **biopsy** to identify the nature of any lump. Following this procedure, women may be told that the lump is benign (known as a **false positive result**) or that it is cancerous and requires some form of medical or surgical intervention (a true positive). This

---

ultrasound

the use of ultra-high-frequency sound waves to create images of organs and systems in the body.

fine needle aspiration

entails placing a very thin needle into a mass within the breast and extracting cells for microscopic evaluation. It takes seconds, and the discomfort is comparable with that of a blood test.

biopsy

the removal of a small piece of tissue for microscopic examination and/or culture, usually to help to make a diagnosis.

false positive result

a situation in which an individual is told that they may have a disease or are at risk of disease, but subsequent tests show that they are not at risk or do not have the disease.

process is clearly stressful, and while some women may be reassured following these various procedures, others appear to remain anxious for a long time. Jatoi *et al.* (2006), for example, found that in their general population sample of nearly 10,000 US women, 8 per cent had experienced a false positive result at some time. These women were more likely to report feeling sad, restless, worthless, and that everything was an effort than those with no such experience. In addition, they were more likely to have seen a mental health professional in the year before the survey and had higher mental distress scores. So strong is the anxiety triggered by the assessment process, it may prevent many women attending subsequent mammography screening, although Brewer *et al.* (2007) reported interesting cross-cultural findings. US women who were given a false positive mammography result were more likely to return for routine screening than those who received normal results; the false positive had no effect on European women's attendance, while Canadian women were less likely to return for routine screening.

A number of studies have tried to find out how best to reduce the stress associated with this type of testing. One approach has involved compressing all the testing procedures into one day rather than over a period of days or even weeks – a process known as 'one-stop testing'. This approach is generally effective at reducing anxiety. Dey *et al.* (2002), for example, found lower levels of anxiety in women that went through the one-stop process around the time of their screening, but no differences over the following year. By contrast, Harcourt *et al.* (1998) found that the psychological outcomes may depend on the medical outcome. Women found to have no breast problems (about 90 per cent of those referred) appeared to benefit from it emotionally. By contrast, women found to have breast abnormalities did less well than those who took part in a testing and reporting process that took several days. Perhaps a longer time period allowed the affected women to adjust to the possibility of there being problems more than a relatively rushed process that occurred in one day.

A different type of intervention targeted at women given false positive results was assessed by Bowland *et al.* (2003). They randomly allocated women who had been called back for further investigations and then found to be free of disease into one of three conditions: face-to-face counselling, telephone counselling and usual care. In the counselling sessions, they were encouraged to express their distress, given relevant information and helped to develop solutions to any problems they had. The session took up to one hour. When all the outcome data were analysed, no differences were found between the conditions. However, when the analysis was restricted to just those people who actually took part in the counselling process, these individuals scored better on measures of psychological and physical functioning than those who received the usual care.

Increasing uptake

Despite the potential health benefits of mammography, uptake levels remain lower than optimal. In the USA, for example, the percentage of women aged 40 or more who took part in mammography screening rose between 1987 and 1992 (Martin *et al.* 1996), but over 80 per cent of eligible women still did not take part in any screening programme. Many programmes are advertised through television advertisements, leaflets in general practitioner surgeries, and so on. More complex interventions to try and increase uptake have also been used. One of the more impressive interventions was reported by Allen *et al.* (2001), who recruited a number of volunteers from the workforces of 13 US worksites. These women talked about their own positive experiences of screening, gave breast and cancer information to their co-workers, and provided social support to women thinking of, or going to, mammography. In addition, they each led a number of small-group discussion sessions, which provided information about screening, how to talk to health-care professionals, and how to set goals for health. They also ran two high-profile educational campaigns. Participants in control worksites had no such interventions. Despite these efforts, the percentage of women to have a mammogram increased only marginally in the worksites that ran the intervention over the course of the programme – from 5.6 to 7.2 per cent: a non-significant difference. Similar small gains were achieved by aggressive follow-up and contact with non-attenders in a UK Primary Care Trust (Kearins *et al.* 2009). By contrast, Rutter *et al.* (2006) found that the simple act of inviting women to plan how they would overcome up to three previously identified barriers to attending mammography resulted in a significantly higher uptake than not doing so (see further discussion of this approach later in the chapter and in Chapter 5 ☞).

RESEARCH FOCUS

Falling numbers of falls

Logan, P.A., Coupland, C.A.C., Gladman, J.F.R. *et al.* (2010). Community falls prevention for people who call an emergency ambulance after a fall: randomised controlled trial. *British Medical Journal*, 340: c2102.

Falls in older people can result in significant disability, particularly if major bones are broken. Where bones are already fragile, a fall may result in substantial breaks causing personal suffering, significant medical costs and, in some, cases long-term disability. This study involved an assessment of the effectiveness of a service designed to reduce the frequency of falls in a group of older adults (aged over 60 years old) who had called for an ambulance as a consequence of a fall at their home or in a local authority care home, and which resulted in no injury. It compared this service, described below, with a control condition which involved participants being advised by letter to use existing social and medical services 'as usual'.

The intervention

The intervention was provided by four community teams in the person's own home or the care home where the incident occurred. The interventions were provided by a physiotherapist who provided six training sessions in strength and balance. In addition, an assessment of any hazards in the home and their remediation was made by a team member, who could be a nurse or occupational therapist. Participants were given equipment such as chair raisers, grab handles, improved lighting, and removal of items from the floor. They were also taught how to get up from the floor by the occupational therapist. Away from the home, participants attended twelve sessions, spread over a six-week period, held in a local community hall. In these, they received one hour of muscle strengthening and balance training, and an hour of education and practice in 'functional activities'. The sessions also covered advice on nutrition, pacing (maintaining an appropriate – neither excessive not too limited – level of exercise), strategies for coping with activities of daily living, hazards in the home, equipment, footwear, and how to get up from the floor.

Method

Two hundred and four participants who were involved in an ambulance call-out following a fall that required no admission to hospital were identified from Ambulance Service records and randomly allocated, using a remote computer-generated randomisation procedure to either intervention or control condition.

Participants completed a number of measures at baseline (before the intervention) and at twelve-month follow-up. However, the main outcome measure was a monthly diary of the number of falls. Participants were sent the diary each month, recorded any falls, and then sent it back to the researchers in a stamped addressed envelope. They received a further diary in the post. Falls were defined as any slip or trip in which they lost their balance and landed on the floor or ground. Questionnaires completed at baseline and follow-up include: the Barthel Activities of Daily Living Index, the Nottingham Extended Activities of Daily Living Scale, and a falls self-efficacy questionnaire to measure their fear of falling.

Results

A total of 98 participants in the intervention condition received the intervention (3 declined to participate, 1 died before assessment, 6 did not require an intervention). Of those treated, 79 received the intervention entirely at home; 19 also attended group sessions. A total of 73 participants received seven or more (of twelve) sessions. Only 1 participant in the control group received a falls prevention provided through 'usual care'.

In all, 98 participants in the intervention group and 99 in the control group returned one or more fall diaries: 80 and 75 respectively returned all diaries (a non-significant difference). Analysis was conducted on all the available diaries. Of the 956 falls recorded in the diaries, 649 were in the control group – 307 were in the intervention group. This averaged at 3.46 falls 'per person years' in the control group, and 7.68 falls per person years in the control group. These differences were significant at the 0.001 level, and were not influenced by the age of participants nor the number of previous falls. In addition, the onset of falls was significantly delayed in the intervention group in comparison with those from the control condition. The median time to the first fall in the intervention group was 166 days, the same figure in the control group was 21 days. In all, 6 people in the control group and 3 in the intervention group (a non-significant difference) were admitted to hospital with bone fractures.

Questionnaires were completed by 82 participants in the intervention group and 75 in the control group. At follow-up, participants in the intervention group recorded significantly higher levels of fall self-efficacy (median score 76 versus 57; p < 0.001) and higher scores on the Nottingham activities of living scale (median scores 6 versus 8; p < 0.001). The authors also claimed that the median scores of the Barthel Index differed significantly between the two groups (p = 0.021), although the medians reported in their results table were identical (15 versus 15).

Discussion

This was a single-centre study with a limited number of professionals involved, dependent on self-report data for its main outcome. This means that the impact of the intervention could be attributable to the quality and enthusiasm of the therapists involved and biases in reporting by a group of participants who were keen to show that the intervention they had received was of benefit. Nevertheless, the results indicate the potential for this type of approach to prove an effective intervention. Future research needs to examine the effectiveness of this type of approach in a larger group of patients and health professionals, use validated outcome measures (for example, falls diaries completed by partners), and examine whether the difference in the frequency of fractures is sufficient to make this a cost-effective intervention.

Behavioural risk for disease

Screening programmes targeted at changing health behaviour have generally focused on risk behaviour for CHD: smoking, high-cholesterol diet, low levels of exercise, and so on. Many of the early programmes were established in the UK in the 1990s, the best known of which was developed by the OXCHECK group (OXCHECK Study Group 1994). In this, all adults in participating primary care practices around Oxford who went to their doctor for any reason were invited to attend a 'health check' conducted by a nurse. This involved an interview to identify risk behaviour for CHD as well as measurement of blood pressure and cholesterol levels. Where appropriate, participants were advised to stop smoking, eat a low-cholesterol diet and increase their exercise levels, as well as given medical treatment for hypertension and high cholesterol levels. Unfortunately, the outcome of this procedure was only measured some time after the intervention – at the one- and three-year follow-ups – and we therefore cannot be sure about the short-term effects of the intervention. Nevertheless, at both times there was evidence that some people had benefited from the screening programme. At one-year follow-up, participants' blood pressure levels were lower than those of people who did not take part in the screening programme, as were the cholesterol levels of women, but not men. There were no differences between the groups on measures of smoking or **body mass index**. By the three-year follow-up (OXCHECK Study Group 1995), cholesterol levels, systolic blood pressure and body mass index of both men and women who took part in the programme were lower than those of the controls. Smoking levels remained the same in both groups. It is difficult to disentangle from their results how much any changes in blood pressure and cholesterol were the result of behavioural change, and how much they resulted from the use of medication. However, the lack of change in smoking levels and, to a lesser extent, body mass index suggests that long-term behavioural changes were difficult to achieve. Indeed, the authors concluded that although the programme proved of benefit, changing difficult-to-change behaviours such as smoking may require a more specialised intervention.

> **body mass index**
> a measurement of the relative percentages of fat and muscle mass in the human body, in which weight in kilograms is divided by height in metres and the result used as an index of obesity.

Considering just one coronary risk behaviour, smoking, Stead *et al.*'s review of the relevant literature (2008) concluded that quit rates with no intervention are around 2 to 3 per cent: a brief advice intervention by a doctor can increase quitting by a further 1 to 3 per cent. Only one study determined the effect of smoking advice on mortality. This study found no statistically significant differences in death rates at 20 years follow-up. Of note also, were the findings of Gilpin *et al.* (1993) who found that the first advice was the most important determinant of quitting. Giving advice in further sessions did not result in further quit attempts. In addition, despite many years of smoking, people over 50 years old still appear to both benefit from, and to have positive attitudes towards, physician advice (Ossip-Klein *et al.* 2000). Of course, this type of intervention only works if physicians actually provide the impetus to quit smoking. And this may not always be the case. This was certainly the finding of Unrod *et al.* (2007) who found that most of their sample of general practitioners were neither actively encouraging their patients to stop smoking nor following simple guidelines on how this may be achieved. However, when these doctors were given specific training in smoking cessation techniques and a one-page leaflet suggesting personalised strategies for how to stop smoking to give to their patients, they found abstinence rates of 12 per cent among the intervention group and 8 per cent among those who received standard physician encounters.

WHAT DO YOU THINK?

Combining genetic counselling and attempts at coronary risk factor change, Audrain *et al.* (1997) fed back to participants their level of genetic risk for developing lung cancer in an attempt to motivate smoking cessation. They randomly allocated smokers to either a counselling intervention or counselling combined with level of genetic risk. The risk factor information seemed to increase the motivation of some smokers to change, with almost a doubling of initial cessation rates in this group in comparison with the no-risk information condition. By one-month follow-up, however, any between-condition differences had dissipated, and there were no longer any differences in cessation rates between the groups. The authors noted that those who received the risk information were initially more depressed than those who did not, but these differences also dissipated over time.

Given that high levels of fear typically do not lead to long-term behavioural change (see Chapter 7 (☞)) and may result in depression and learned helplessness (and may also result in long-term health anxieties), is it fair or ethical to use genetic risk factor information to motivate difficult behaviour change?

Plate 6.1 Providing easy access to 'Stop Smoking' clinics may increase their effectiveness

Source: Alamy Images/Stephen Dorey.

Strategies for changing risk behaviour

The evidence reviewed above suggests that while some people will strive to change their behaviour once they are aware of being at risk for an illness such as CHD, many will not, or will not be able to sustain any changes that they make. It has become increasingly obvious that making people aware of their risk status may not be enough to foster mid- to long-term behavioural change. As a consequence, more sophisticated interventions have been developed to achieve these goals, some of which are considered in this section.

Historically, most one-to-one psychological interventions have been targeted at people who are relatively motivated to change their behaviour. Clinics are held in hospitals, out-patient departments or primary care centres, and the people who take the trouble to attend them are usually motivated to take an active part in any programme of change. However, this is not always the case. The introduction of screening programmes in primary care, for example, has resulted in the identification of many people who are not particularly motivated to change their behaviour. In response to this, efforts have been made to develop interventions that take into account people's differing levels of motivation to change rather than a 'one intervention fits all' approach. This targeted approach has generally been based on a stage model of change developed by Prochaska and di Clemente (1986). Their transtheoretical, or **stages of change model**, identified a series of five stages through which they considered an individual passed when considering change:

1. *pre-contemplation*: they are not considering change;
2. *contemplation*: they are considering change but have not thought through its exact nature or how it can be achieved;
3. *preparation*: they are planning how to achieve change;
4. *change*: they are actively engaged in change;
5. *maintenance or relapse*: they are maintaining change (for longer than six months) or relapsing.

The model is thought to be applicable to virtually any decision relating to change, from giving up cigarettes to buying a new car. Prochaska and di Clemente noted that the factors that may shift an individual from one stage to another – and they can move back and forth along the change continuum or even skip stages – can differ enormously. As a consequence, the model does not attempt to specify what these factors are – merely that they occur and that they can shift the individual from stage to stage. Accordingly, a smoker may shift from pre-contemplation to contemplation as a result of developing a chest infection, move to preparation and action after seeing a book on giving up smoking in the local library, and relapse after being tempted to smoke while out for a beer with friends.

Although the transtheoretical model is not without its critics (e.g. Weinstein, Rothman and Sutton 1998), the model does appear to predict behaviour with some degree of accuracy. Fahrenwald and Walker (2003), for example, found that measures of the stage of change were predictive of low-income mother's exercise behaviours, including daily physical energy expenditure and daily minutes of moderate to very hard physical activity, as well as their beliefs supporting or against exercise, and decisional balances related to exercise. Similar findings were reported by Cardinal *et al.* (2009) in a group of South Korean and US college students. A diet including appropriate levels of fruit and vegetable intake among urban and immigrant US African American men was also predicted by individual's stage of change: those eating healthy levels of fruit and vegetables were more likely to be in the action rather than contemplation/preparation stage (Wolf *et al.* 2008). Finally, in an exercise programme designed for the 'over 50s' (Nifty After Fifty), Miller and Miller (2003) found that contemplators were more likely to have read about the programme, rung its phone number, contacted a class, and participated in physical activity than non-contemplators.

The stages of change approach has been particularly useful from an intervention perspective in that it has focused consideration on what is the best type of intervention to conduct at each stage of change. The most obvious implication of the model is that there is little point in trying to show people *how* to achieve change if

> ### stages of change model
> developed by Prochaska and di Clemente, this identifies five stages through which an individual passes when considering behavioural change: pre-contemplation, contemplation, preparation, change and maintenance/relapse.

they are in the pre-contemplation or possibly the con-templation stage. Such individuals are unlikely to be sufficiently motivated to attempt change, and will bene-fit little from being shown how to do so. By contrast, an individual in the planning or action stage may benefit from this type of approach.

The pre-contemplation stage: motivational interviewing

The intervention generally considered most likely to be effective for people who are unmotivated to change their behaviour is known as **motivational interviewing** (Miller and Rollnick 2002). Its goal is to increase an individual's motivation to consider change – not to show them how to change. If the interview succeeds in motiva-ting change, only then can any intervention proceed to considering ways of achieving that change.

Motivational interviewing is designed to help people explore and resolve any ambivalence they may have about changing their behaviour. The approach assumes that when an individual is facing the need to change, they may have beliefs and attitudes that both support and counter change. Prior to the interview, thoughts that counter change probably predominate – or else the person would be actively seeking help to achieve change. Nevertheless, the goal of the interview is to elicit both sets of beliefs and attitudes and to bring them into sharp focus ('I know smoking does damage my health', 'I enjoy smoking', and so on). This is thought to place the individual in a state of **cognitive dissonance** (Festinger 1957), which is resolved by rejecting one set of beliefs in favour of the other. These may (or may not) favour behavioural change. If an individual decides to change their behaviour, the intervention will then focus on consideration of how to achieve change. If the individual still rejects the possibility of change, they would typically not continue in any programme of behavioural change.

The motivational interview is deliberately non-confrontational. Miller and Rollnick (2002) consider the process of motivational interviewing to be a philosophy of supporting individual change and not attempting to persuade an individual to go against their own wishes, rather than a set of specific techniques. Nevertheless, a few key strategies can be identified. Perhaps the key questions in the interview are:

- What are some of the good things about your present behaviour?
- What are the not so good things about your present behaviour?

The first question is perhaps slightly surprising but important, as it acknowledges that the individual is gaining something from their present behaviour and is intended to reduce the potential for resistance. Once the individual has considered each issue (both for and against change), they are summarised by the counsellor in a way that highlights the dissonance between the two sets of issues. Once this has been fed back to the individual, they are invited to consider how this infor-mation makes them feel. Only if they express some interest in change should the interview then go on to consider how to change. Other key elements and strategies include:

- expressing **empathy**;
- avoiding arguments by assuming that the individual is responsible for the decision to change;
- rolling with resistance rather than confronting or opposing it;
- supporting self-efficacy and optimism for change.

Given that the goal of motivational interviewing is to motivate people to consider change, it is perhaps sur-prising that most outcome studies have not examined this issue at all. Instead, they have focused largely on whether it can alter behaviour in the mid to long term.

---

motivational interview

developed by Miller and Rollnick, a set of procedures designed to increase motivation to change behaviour.

cognitive dissonance

a state in which conflicting or inconsistent cognitions produce a state of tension or discomfort (dissonance). People are motivated to reduce the dissonance, often by rejecting one set of beliefs in favour of the other.

empathy

an understanding of the situation from the individual's viewpoint.

WHAT DO YOU THINK?

We all have bad habits or do less of the things we 'ought to do' than we should. Or at least, most of us do. Think of a behaviour you would like to change or could change – to either do more of . . . or less. Then consider the issue in the light of the motivational process. What stage of the motivational process are you in: pre-contemplation, contemplation? Try out a motivational interview on yourself. What are the good things about the status quo? What would you gain if you were to change things? Write down a 'decisional balance sheet', listing the pros and cons of change. Did you expect to write what you did? Did it motivate you to change, or simply accept the status quo? Was it harder to think of reasons for change than reasons to maintain the status quo? It often is!! How did the process feel, and how easy would this be to do with someone else?

However, those studies that *have* examined this issue have found the interview to be at least as good if not better at encouraging participation than more direct attempts at persuasion. K. Carroll *et al.* (2001) found that individuals referred to a treatment programme for **drug abuse** were most likely to continue attending after an initial session that involved a motivational interview: 59 per cent of referrals attended at least one further session following a motivational interview compared with 29 per cent following a standard first session.

Initially, motivational interview techniques were used to help people who presented with substance misuse problems. More recently, the approach has been used with an increasing range of other behaviours. In the context of smoking, Lai *et al.*'s (2010) meta-analysis comparing the effectiveness of motivational interviewing against brief advice revealed a 25 per cent higher quit rate among those receiving motivational interviewing. The approach was most beneficial when delivered by primary care physicians, who achieved a three times higher quit rate following the use of motivational interviewing than simple advice or no intervention.

In an attempt to increase consumption of fruit and vegetables and exercise levels among older adults (aged over 66 years), Campbell *et al.* (2009) examined the effectiveness of either written information or information combined with a brief motivational telephone contact.

They compared the interventions in two groups: people who had survived cancer and a group with no evidence of disease. The combined intervention was more effective than the simple provision of information in facilitating changes in diet – but only in the healthy group. The intervention had no impact on exercise levels. A second, more complex intervention also targeted healthy eating. Resnicow *et al.* (2001) examined the impact of the 'Eat for Life' programme conducted among church-attending African Americans. They compared the effect of two interventions in trying to increase fruit and vegetable intake in the target group. These involved either a self-help intervention with a telephone call to encourage use of the programme, or this approach combined with three telephone calls using motivational interviewing techniques. At one-year follow-up, participants in the second group were eating more fruit and vegetables than those in the self-help only group, who in turn were eating more than a no-treatment control group. Whether this was due to the increased attention given to the combined intervention group, or to the motivational elements is not clear. However, when motivational techniques were simply integrated into another therapy, in this case a behavioural weight loss programme, Carels *et al.* (2007) found this led to an increase in weight loss among people experiencing difficulties in achieving significant weight loss.

Problem-solving approaches

Problem-focused interventions provide one form of strategy for considering *how*, rather than *whether*, to change. They are best used for people who are willing to consider changing their behaviour and need help working out how to do this. Perhaps the most clearly described **problem-focused counselling** approach was developed by Egan (e.g. 2006). His form of problem-

---

drug abuse

involves use of a drug that results in significant social or work-related problems.

problem-focused counselling

a counselling approach developed by Gerard Egan that attempts to foster a collaborative and structured approach between counsellor and client to solving life problems.

focused counselling is complex in parts but has an elegantly simple basic framework. It emphasises the importance of appropriate analysis of the problem the individual is facing as a critical element of the counselling process. Only when this has been achieved can an appropriate solution to the problem be identified. A further element of Egan's approach is that the job of the counsellor is not to act as an expert solving the person's problems. Instead, their role is to mobilise the individual's own resources both to identify problems accurately and to arrive at strategies of solution. Counselling is problem-oriented. It is focused specifically on the issues at hand and in the 'here and now', and it has three distinct phases:

1. *problem exploration and clarification*: a detailed and thorough exploration of the problems an individual is facing: breaking 'global insolvable problems' into carefully defined soluble elements;

2. *goal setting*: identifying how the individual would like things to be different. Setting clear, behaviourally defined, and achievable goals (or sub-goals);

3. *facilitating action*: developing plans and strategies through which these goals can be achieved.

Some people may not need to work through each stage of the counselling process. Others may be able to work through all the phases in one session. Still others may require several counselling sessions. However, it is important to deal with each stage sequentially and thoroughly. Flitting from stage to stage serves only to confuse both the counsellor and the individual being counselled.

Case history: Mrs T

Mrs T provides a good example of how the problem-solving approach may lead to issues and interventions far from those that might be expected. Mrs T took part in a regular screening clinic held at her local GP's surgery, where she was found to be obese and to have a raised serum cholesterol level. Following standard dietary advice, Mrs T agreed to a goal of losing two pounds a week over the following months. She was given a leaflet providing information about the fat and calorific content of a variety of foods and a leaflet describing a number of 'healthy' recipes.

On her follow-up visits, her cholesterol level and weight remained unchanged – so she saw a counsellor to provide her with more help. The counsellor used the problem-focused approach of Egan. In the first session, she explored why Mrs T had not made use of the advice she had previously been given. Mrs T explained that she already knew which were 'healthy' and 'unhealthy' foods. Indeed, she had been on many diets before – without much success. Together, she and the counsellor began to explore why this was the case. At this point, a number of problems became apparent. One important factor was that she was not receiving support from her family, and in particular her two grown-up sons. Mrs T was the family cook, in a family that often demanded 'fry-ups'. She accepted this role but had difficulty in not nibbling the food as she cooked it. Although she actually ate quite small (and low-fat) meals, her nibbling while cooking significantly increased her calorie and cholesterol intake.

Mrs T's husband supported her attempts to lose weight and was prepared to change his diet to help her. However, her sons often demanded meals when they got back from the pub, late at night and often the worse for drink. The upshot of this was that Mrs T often started to cook late at night at the end of what may have been a successful day of dieting. She then nibbled high-calorie food while cooking. This had two outcomes. First, she increased her calorie input at a time when she did not need calories. Second, she sometimes catastrophised ('I've eaten so much, I may as well abandon my diet for today') and ate a full meal at this time. It also reduced her motivation to follow her diet the following day.

Once this specific problem had been identified, Mrs T set a goal of not cooking late night fry-ups for her sons. She decided that, in future if her sons wanted this, they could cook it themselves. Once the goal was established, Mrs T felt a little concerned about how her sons would react to her no longer cooking for them, so she and the counsellor explored ways in which she could set about telling them – and sticking to her resolution. She finally decided she would tell them in the coming week, explaining why she felt she could no longer cook for them at that time of night. She even rehearsed how she would say it. This she did, with some effect, as she did start to lose weight.

WHAT DO YOU THINK?

Think about how you react if someone asks you for advice. Do you sit and listen to the causes of the problems, invite your friend to consider their options for change, and then decide which one to adopt? Or are you quick to give advice, without really knowing the issues from the perspective of your friend? Most people fit into the latter category, so you are not alone if you came to that conclusion. But how effective is your advice giving likely to be?

Despite the generally acknowledged effectiveness of the problem-focused counselling approach, there has been surprisingly little empirical examination of its effectiveness in **primary health promotion**.

In one of the few such studies, Gomel *et al.* (1993) screened hundreds of factory workers for risk factors for coronary heart disease (CHD), assigning them to one of three groups if at least one risk factor was found:

1. risk factor education,

2. problem-focused counselling, and

3. no intervention control.

Participants in the educational programme received standard advice on the lifestyle changes needed to reduce their risk of CHD (following an information provision model) and some videos showing how to modify these risk factors. Participants in the problem-solving programme first went through an exercise based on motivational interviewing techniques. Following this, they identified a number of high-risk situations in which they were likely to engage in CHD-risk behaviour (such as smoking or eating high-fat meals) or which would prevent them from engaging in health-promoting behaviours (such as lack of planning, leaving no time for exercise). They were then encouraged to think through how they could minimise their effect. This more complex intervention

proved the most effective. Participants in this condition had greater reductions in blood pressure, body mass index and smoking than those in either the education-only intervention or no-intervention control.

In a study targeted more specifically at reducing blood pressure, Elmer *et al.* (1995) also reported the outcome of a programme that incorporated an element of problem solving. Participants were taught to recognise environmental or psychological cues that led to over-eating and to plan how to change or cope with them as well as considering how to begin and maintain an exercise programme. They also worked with their partners to develop a joint strategy to support any lifestyle changes they made. One year after the programme started, the intervention appeared to be a success. By this time, 70 per cent of the participants had significantly reduced their alcohol intake and increased their exercise levels. As a consequence, they had achieved significant weight loss over the year, and their blood pressure had fallen significantly.

More sophisticated approaches have integrated motivational interviewing and problem-focused approaches. Steptoe *et al.* (1999) adjusted their intervention to suit the stage of change of participants in a screening programme to identify and reduce risk for CHD. They identified individuals at risk of CHD as a consequence of one or more modifiable risk factors: regular cigarette smoking, high cholesterol levels, and high body mass index combined with low physical activity. Practice nurses then provided brief behavioural counselling on the basis of the stages of change model, using elements of motivational interviews for those who were in pre-contemplation and developing strategies of change for participants who were considering the possibility of change. Compared to no intervention, some benefits were achieved, with modest reductions in dietary fat intake and cigarettes smoked per day, and increased regular exercise at 4- and 12-month follow-up assessments. However, no differences were found between groups on measures of total serum cholesterol concentration, weight, body mass index, or smoking cessation. It seems that more sustained support and counselling may have been necessary to achieve long-term behavioural change with these difficult-to-change behaviours. We consider several additional studies in the context of secondary prevention that have found problem-focused interventions to be more effective than educational interventions in Chapter 17 ☞.

primary health promotion

health promotion targeted at preventing the onset of disease. Contrasts with secondary health promotion, which aims to prevent the further progression of disease.

Smoking cessation as a form of problem solving

Although they may not explicitly state it, many other behavioural change programmes have within them an element of problem identification and resolution. The example of smoking cessation can illustrate this point. Smoking is driven by two processes:

1. a conditioned response to a variety of cues in the environment – picking up the telephone, having a cup of coffee, and so on – the so-called habit cigarette;

2. a physiological need for nicotine – to top up levels of nicotine and prevent the onset of withdrawal symptoms.

Nicotine is an extremely powerful drug. It acts on the **acetylcholine** system, which, in part, mediates levels of attention and activation in the brain and muscle activity in the body. Its activity is bi-phasic: that is, short, sharp inhalations increase activity in this system as the nicotine bonds with the acetylcholine receptors and activates the neurons – resulting in increased alertness. Long inhalations, by contrast, result in the nicotine remaining in the post-synaptic acetylcholine receptors, preventing further uptake of nicotine or acetylcholine by the receptors – leading to feelings of relaxation. Accordingly, when an individual stops smoking, they may have to deal with:

- the loss of a powerful means of altering mood and level of attention;
- withdrawal symptoms as a consequence of a biological dependence on nicotine;
- the urge to smoke triggered by environmental cues.

The best smoking cessation programmes address each of these issues. Following a 'quit day', most call for complete cessation of smoking, following which the individual may have to cope with varying degrees of urges to smoke as a result of withdrawal symptoms or encountering cues that previously were associated with smoking.

> **acetylcholine**
> a white crystalline derivative of choline that is released at the ends of nerve fibres in the parasympathetic nervous system and is involved in the transmission of nerve impulses in the body.

Any withdrawal symptoms may take up to two or three weeks to subside, and be at their worst in the first two to three days following cessation. Accordingly, there is an acute period of high risk for relapse following cessation that may be driven by the immediate psychological and physiological discomfort associated with quitting.

Many programmes prepare ex-smokers to cope with these problems. Each set of strategies involves a degree of problem solving, as the smoker has to identify both the particular problems they may face and individual solutions to those problems (see Table 6.2). The strategies may involve:

- how to cope with cues to smoking – this may involve avoiding them completely or working out ways of coping with temptation triggered by smoking cues;

Table 6.2 Some strategies that smokers may use to help them to cope in the period immediately following cessation

Avoidant strategies	Coping strategies
Sit with non-smoking friends at coffee breaks	If you feel the urge to smoke, focus attention on things happening around you – *not* on your desire for a cigarette
Drink something different at coffee breaks – to break your routine and not light up automatically	Think distracting thoughts – count backwards in sevens from 100
Go for a walk instead of smoking	Remember your reasons for stopping smoking – carry them on flashcards and look at them if this helps
Chew sugar-free gum or sweets at times you would normally smoke	
Move ashtrays out of sight	
Try to keep busy, so you won't have time to think of cigarettes	

Make it difficult to smoke	Cognitive re-labelling
Don't carry money – so you can't buy cigarettes	These horrible symptoms are signs of recovery
Avoid passing the tobacconist where you usually buy your cigarettes	

● how to reduce the possibility of giving in to cravings should they occur;

● how to cope with any withdrawal symptoms.

One strategy for coping with any withdrawal symptoms involves the use of **nicotine replacement therapy (NRT)**, either as a gum or, more recently, as a **transdermal patch**. The development of NRT was initially seen as a major breakthrough that would prevent the need for any psychological intervention to help people to stop smoking. This has not proved to be the case. Indeed, most manufacturers of nicotine replacement products now recommend using a number of problem-solving strategies along with the NRT – a recommendation clearly supported by the outcome of clinical trials of their use. As Moore *et al.* (2009) concluded following a meta-analysis of the relevant data, NRT is an effective intervention in achieving sustained abstinence, achieving six-month quit rates of nearly 7 per cent (double that of placebo control conditions). However, most of the evidence came from trials with regular behavioural support, and it is not clear whether using NRT without regular contact would be as effective.

One interesting study took regard of the type of smoker who entered their programme. Hall *et al.* (1985) identified smokers as being primarily nicotine-dependent or primarily habit smokers and assigned half of each type of smoker to either a problem-focused programme, which should be of maximum benefit for habitual smokers, nicotine gum aimed at nicotine-dependent participants, and a combination of both approaches. Each group did indeed fare better from the intervention targeted at their particular problem, although only the nicotine-dependent group benefited from the combined

intervention. In a further comparison of extended CBT or nicotine replacement therapy in older smokers, Hall *et al.* (2009) found that extending a cognitive behavioural intervention over a period of 40 weeks (with 11 meetings) beyond a standard smoking cessation programme resulted in high and stable cigarette abstinence rates among both men and women. Cessation rates at six months after the intervention were 58 per cent: at one- and two-year follow-up they were 55 per cent. An extended NRT programme proved of no additional benefit to the initial programme.

Implementing plans and intentions

A number of interventions have identified the last of Egan's stages as the key therapeutic element. Based on the social cognitive models of the health action process approach (HAPA; Schwarzer and Renner 2000) and implementation intentions (Gollwitzer and Schaal 1998; see Chapter 5 ☞), both of which identified planning as an important determinant of behavioural change, these approaches have simply encouraged individuals to plan how they will engage in their behaviour of choice. Some interventions have targeted relatively simple or short-term behavioural change. De Nooijer *et al.* (2006) found that writing plans to eat an extra serving of fruit per day for one week resulted in a higher intake of fruit than a no-treatment condition. Sheeran and Orbell (2000) found implementation plans resulted in a higher attendance at a cervical screening clinic than a no-treatment condition. Even more impressively, Conner and Higgins (2010) found forming implementation plans resulted in a higher rate of quitting smoking than no intervention among adolescents, while Luszczynska *et al.* (2007) found that they significantly enhanced the effectiveness of a weight loss programme for obese women. Women who were on a standard commercial weight loss programme achieved a weight loss of 2.1 kilograms over a two-month period, while those given the implementation planning intervention achieved a weight loss of 4.2 kilograms over the same period. Gratton *et al.* (2007) found an intervention based on implementation plans to be equally effective as one designed to enhance motivation in relation to children's fruit and vegetable consumption. On a more cautious note, Michie *et al.* (2004) carried out a study of an intervention aimed at increasing antenatal screening uptake among women who had expressed the intention to do so. Eighty-eight

---

nicotine replacement therapy (NRT)

replacement of nicotine to minimise withdrawal symptoms following the cessation of smoking. Delivered in a variety of ways, including a transdermal patch placed against the skin, which produces a measured dose of nicotine over time.

transdermal patch

a method of delivering a drug in a slow release form. The drug is impregnated into a patch, which is stuck to the skin and gradually absorbed into the body.

pregnant women were allocated to either standard care or a group asked to write down an action plan for attending or making the screening appointment. No difference in subsequent attendance was found. In the intervention group itself, however, only 63 per cent actually made an action plan, and these women *were* more likely to attend screening (84 per cent of them attended) than the women in this group who had not done so (47 per cent attended). So, a crucial element of any intervention may be to clearly facilitate the planning process.

Modelling change

Problem-focused and 'planning'-based interventions can help individuals to develop strategies of change. However, achieving change can still be difficult, particularly where an individual lacks the skills or confidence in their ability to cope with the demands of change. Egan himself noted that it may be necessary to teach people the skills to achieve any goals they have set or to change the social norms in which such behaviours occur.

One way that these deficits can be remedied is by learning skills or appropriate attitudes from observation of others performing them – a process known as **vicarious learning**. Bandura's (2001) social cognitive theory (see Chapter 5 ☛) suggested that both skills and confidence in the ability to change (self-efficacy) can be increased through a number of simple procedures, including observation of others performing relevant tasks (vicarious learning), practice of tasks in a graded programme of skills development, and active persuasion. The effectiveness of learning from observation of others can be influenced by a number of factors. However, the optimal learning and increases in self-efficacy can generally be achieved through observation of people similar to the learner succeeding in relevant tasks. This may be further enhanced by the use of what Bandura termed coping models, in which those being observed demonstrate a skill or other behaviour in a way that does not leave the observer feeling de-skilled or incapable of gaining the skills. Where complex skills are being taught, behaviour may be shaped by observation of the progressive learning of skills by the models.

One way that this approach can work is through the use of video – an approach that has proven particularly effective in modifying sexual behaviour. Sanderson and Yopyk (2007), for example, found that young sexually active people reported stronger intentions to engage in protected sex, higher self-efficacy in refusing to have unprotected sex, and higher levels of condom use four months after seeing videos providing positive attitudes about condom use and modelling appropriate strategies for negotiating their use. Higher intentions may translate into behavioural change and better health. Warner *et al.* (2008) compared the effect of a waiting room video depicting couples overcoming barriers to safer sex behaviours with that of a standard, no video, waiting room in a number of sexually transmitted disease (STD) clinics in three US cities. At an average of 15 months later, they followed up over 2,000 patients, and found a 10 per cent reduction in new infections among those that had seen the video compared to the control group (5.7

Plate 6.2 Both watching others, and practice, increases the chances of people purchasing and using a condom

Source: Corbis/Image 100.

> **vicarious learning**
> learning from observation of others.

per cent versus 4.9 per cent infection rates). Despite these positive findings, the results of Jenkins *et al.* (2000) provide a more cautionary message. They found that watching an interactive video increased their participants' intentions to abstain from sex and to change risky partner behaviour in the short term, but that these changes were no longer evident at follow-up. They concluded that risky sexual behaviour was particularly resistant to change but that the single-session intervention had some impact, and could be viewed as a 'priming' effect that could enhance multi-session interventions.

Mathews *et al.* (2002) reported a different, and important, use of video in the context of HIV infection. They used it to teach attenders at an STD clinic in Kwazulu Natal in South Africa how to tell their sexual partners, who they may have infected with HIV, about the need to check their sexual health status. This is important as it would allow these individuals to be treated and to prevent further spread of HIV. As a consequence of the intervention, attenders' confidence in their ability to notify their sexual partners rose, as did the rate of sexual contacts who subsequently attended the clinic.

Behavioural practice

A further addition or alternative to problem-solving or implementation-based strategies involves the actual practice of new behaviour. Here, solutions to problems as well as skills needed to achieve change can be worked out and taught in an educational programme – increasing both skills and self-efficacy. In one study of this approach, again in the context of sexual behaviour, Kelly *et al.* (1994) reported on the effectiveness of an intervention to reduce risky sexual behaviour among women at high risk of HIV infection who had attended an STD clinic. The programme included risk education, training in condom use and practising sexual assertiveness skills such as negotiating the use of a condom. This was compared with a standard education-based programme. The complex intervention proved the most effective. While the women in both groups did not reduce their number of sexual partners, those in the complex intervention reported that more of their partners used condoms on more occasions over the three months following the intervention. Even a simple behavioural element in an intervention can be remarkably effective. As part of an AIDS workshop run for young adults, Weisse *et al.* (1995) asked half the participants to buy a condom from a local shop. Following the workshop, while all participants knew more about HIV infection prevention, only those who took part in the behavioural exercise reported less embarrassment than before while purchasing condoms.

The effectiveness of video intervention can also be enhanced by adding other behavioural change techniques. O'Donnell *et al.* (1995), for example, compared the effectiveness of either a video condition alone or combined with a problem-solving skill-building session with a no-treatment control condition, in attempting to promote safer sexual behaviour among attenders at an STD clinic. One way of directly assessing the impact of their intervention was to provide all of the study participants with a voucher that they could exchange at a local pharmacy for free condoms; 40 per cent of the people who took part in the combined intervention made use of this service, compared with 28 per cent of those in the video condition alone and 21 per cent of the no-intervention control group. It seems that while learning how to do things from a video can be effective, it can still be enhanced by active practice in the skills required to achieve change.

One interesting development of the behavioural practice approach has been on modifying drink driving. 'Fatal Vision goggles' simulate the visual impairment caused by alcohol or other drugs. According to the manufacturers, 'Viewing through the goggles is rather clear, but confusing to the mind. The wearer experiences a loss of equilibrium, which is one of the effects of intoxication'. Different goggles simulate four levels of intoxication. They are now frequently used in drink-driving education programmes in the USA, with wearers using a driving simulator while wearing the goggles. This approach has achieved some modest effects, at least in the short term (Jewell and Hupp 2005). Unsurprisingly, perhaps, they appear to work best with young people who drink significant amounts of alcohol and who believe that this may impair their driving (Hennessy *et al.* 2006).

Cognitive interventions

The interventions so far considered can be thought of as behavioural interventions, in that they attempt to directly influence behaviour. They may also result in cognitive change – increasing an individual's confidence in their ability to make and maintain any lifestyle changes, and so on. But this is an indirect effect. By contrast, cognitive strategies attempt to change cognitions directly – in particular, those that drive an individual to engage in behaviours that may be harmful to their health or prevent them making appropriate behavioural changes. From a health psychology perspective, various categories of relevant cognitions have been identified, including our attitudes towards the behaviour and any relevant social norms (Ajzen 1985), our beliefs about the costs and benefits of disease prevention and behavioural change (Becker 1974), our self-efficacy expectations (Bandura 2001) and beliefs about an illness or condition and our ability to manage it (Leventhal *et al.* 1984; see Chapter 9 ☞). The need to change cognitions is based on the premise that we do not have relevant information or somehow have developed distorted or inappropriate beliefs about a relevant issue, and that changing these beliefs will result in more appropriate (and health-promoting) behaviour. The simplest form of intervention may involve the provision of appropriate education – particularly when an individual is facing a new health threat or is unaware of information that may encourage appropriate behavioural change. Such education is likely to be optimal if it targets factors known to influence health-related behaviours. It can educate individuals about the nature of their risk, show them how to change their behaviour, and so on (see the discussion on theory and behavioural change in Chapter 18 ☞).

The OXCHECK programme described above provides a good example of a programme based on information provision. Such programmes have frequently been based on the assumption that people will make necessary changes if they are informed of the need to change and the nature of the changes they need to make. Many small-scale health education programmes are still premised on this assumption. However, the relatively low impact of such interventions, as well as an increasing awareness and use of psychological theory, has led to a recognition that any information provision about *what* to change may be significantly enhanced by information about *how* to change and encouraging appropriate planning. A good example of this transition can be found in leaflets on smoking cessation available in the UK, the emphasis of which has shifted from a major emphasis on disease and damaged lungs to consideration of planning and implementing strategies of change. Booklets explaining the need to stop smoking have been added to by step-by-step programmes showing the

individual *how* to stop and teaching any skills that may benefit them: e.g. cut down till you smoke about 12 cigarettes a day, choose a quit day, work out strategies to cope with habit cigarettes such as not carrying them with you, and so on. The next chapter considers a number of information-based approaches in the context of health promotion, while Chapter 17 ☞ considers their use in individuals who have already developed an illness.

More complex interventions may be required to change inappropriate beliefs that have been developed and reinforced over time. Beliefs that encourage substance use or abuse, for example, may include 'I cannot cope with going to a party without a hit' or 'Drinking makes me a more sociable person'. At the beginning of a history of drug use, positive beliefs such as 'It will be fun to get high' may predominate. As the individual begins to rely on the drug to counteract feelings of distress, more dependent beliefs may predominate: 'I need a drink to get me through the day'. Cognitive interventions may be of benefit where such thoughts interfere with any behavioural change. Key to any intervention is that the beliefs we hold about illnesses, our health, events that have happened or will happen in the future, and so on, are *hypothetical*. Some of these guesses may be correct; some may be wrong. In some cases, because maladaptive beliefs ('I need a shot of whisky to get through this') come readily to mind, they are taken as facts, and alternative thoughts ('Well, I might be able to cope without') are not considered. The role of cognitive therapy is to teach the individual to treat their beliefs as hypotheses and not facts, to try out alternative ways of looking at the situation and to have different responses to it based on these new ways of thinking ('Well, I used to cope in this situation before without having a drink. Perhaps I can do the same this time'). One way in which this can be achieved involves a process known as **Socratic dialogue** or guided discovery (Beck 1976). In this, beliefs about particular issues are identified and questioned by the therapist in order to help the individual to identify distorted thinking patterns that are contributing to their problems. It encourages them to consider and evaluate different sources of information that provide evidence of

Socratic dialogue

exploration of an individual's beliefs, encouraging them to question their validity.

the reality or unreality of the beliefs they hold. Once they can do this in the therapy session, they can be taught to identify and challenge these automatic thoughts in the real world and to replace thoughts that drive inappropriate behaviour with those that support more appropriate behaviour. An example of their use is provided by this extract from a session adapted from Beck *et al.* (1993) using a technique known as the downward arrow technique designed to question the very core of an individual's beliefs – in this case their assumptions about their drinking.

> **Therapist** You feel quite strongly that you need to be 'relaxed' by alcohol when you go to a party. What is your concern about being sober?
>
> **John** I wouldn't enjoy myself and I wouldn't be much fun to be with.
>
> **Therapist** What would be the implications of that?
>
> **John** Well, people wouldn't talk to me.
>
> **Therapist** And what would be the consequence of that?
>
> **John** I need to have people like me. My job depends on it. If I can't entertain people at a party, then I'm no good at my job.
>
> **Therapist** So, what happens if that is the case?
>
> **John** Well, I guess I lose my job!
>
> **Therapist** So, you lose your job because you didn't get drunk at a party?
>
> **John** Well, put like that, perhaps I was exaggerating things in my head.

Here, the downward arrow technique has been used both to identify some of the client's core beliefs and to get them to reconsider the accuracy of those beliefs.

A second strategy is to set up homework tasks that directly challenge any inappropriate cognitive beliefs that individuals may hold. An example of this can be found in the case of the individual who believes that they cannot go to a party without drinking, and who may be set the homework task of trying to remain sober at a party – directly challenging their belief that they need to drink alcohol to be socially engaging (and the exaggerated ultimate belief that they will lose their job if they remain sober). Clearly, such challenges should be realistic. If a person attempts a task that is too hard and fails to achieve it, this may maintain or even strengthen the pre-existing beliefs. Accordingly, they have to be

chosen with care and mutually agreed by both the individual concerned and the therapist. However, success in these tasks can bring about long-term cognitive and behavioural changes.

The complexities of these types of intervention, which fall under the rubric of cognitive-behavioural therapy, mean that they are used infrequently in the context of primary prevention, and more frequently with people who have already developed health problems (see Chapter 17 (☛)). However, it can be a useful form of therapy with people who engage in difficult-to-change behaviours such as addiction to alcohol or other drugs that may be harmful to health. In such cases, cognitive-behavioural therapy has proved to be an effective intervention, although whether it is more effective than some alternatives is not clear. Balldin *et al.* (2003) found it to be superior to supportive therapy. However, it may be no more effective than other active interventions. This is perhaps best exemplified by the results of Project MATCH (Project MATCH Research Group 1998). This large study compared three treatment approaches in over 1,500 American problem drinkers:

- twelve-step facilitation (based around **Alcoholics Anonymous** and involving total abstinence);

- a combination of cognitive and behavioural techniques;

- motivational enhancement therapy (similar to but not the same as motivational interviewing).

By the end of treatment, 41 per cent of people who received the cognitive-behavioural therapy and the same percentage of those in the twelve-step programme were abstinent or drank moderately, while 28 per cent of the motivational enhancement group achieved the same criteria. However, by one- and three-year follow-up, there were few differences between the three groups.

Alcoholics Anonymous

a worldwide self-help organisation for people with alcohol-related problems. Based on the belief that alcoholism is a physical, psychological and spiritual illness and can be controlled by abstinence. The twelve steps provide a framework for achieving this.

SUMMARY

This chapter has reviewed two broad sets of issues. First, it examined the implications of programmes that set out to identify genetic or behavioural risk factors for disease or, in the case of mammography, to identify diseases at a sufficiently early stage that they can be treated before they became life-threatening. Second, it considered a number of methods by which people found at risk of disease can be encouraged and helped to change any health-compromising behaviour.

The first section considered three kinds of screening programme:

1. screening for genetic risk of disease;
2. screening for the early detection of disease or its precursors;
3. screening for behaviour that places an individual at risk of disease.

Each approach can be particularly stressful, although most people who go through these screening programmes benefit emotionally from them.

One of the outcomes of screening is that an individual may be asked to change any health behaviour that places them at particular risk of disease. A number of approaches to behavioural change in which the health-care professional can work on a one-to-one basis were considered, each of which is likely to be optimally effective in people with differing levels of motivation or ability to change. The approaches considered were:

● *Motivational interviewing*: a process of increasing motivation when people are not thinking of change or are not strongly motivated to consider change.

● *Problem-focused counselling*: a structured approach to identifying causes of problems or elements that are preventing change, identifying new goals, and developing strategies through which to achieve those goals. This works best in people who are motivated to address particular issues.

● *Implementation intentions*: simply encouraging people to plan how they will change can be sufficient to encourage change in some contexts.

● *Modelling and rehearsal of change*: these can both increase the belief that an individual has in their ability to achieve change (self-efficacy) and provide them with the skills needed to achieve change if they do not have them.

● *Cognitive-behavioural approaches*: these address cognitions that may be preventing an individual from working on change, and they provide a structured approach to achieving change.

Each of these various approaches can be used either jointly or singly depending on the nature and magnitude of the problems an individual faces.

Further reading

Carlsson, S., Aus, G., Wessman, C. *et al.* (2007). Anxiety associated with prostate cancer screening with special reference to men with a positive screening test (elevated PSA): results from a prospective, population-based, randomised study. *European Journal of Cancer*, 43: 2109–16.

Men, apparently, don't feel very anxious when they find they have a high PSA score. Or are we not good at measuring their anxiety?

Miles, A. and Wardle, J. (2006). Adverse psychological outcomes in colorectal cancer screening: does health anxiety play a role? *Behaviour Research and Therapy*, 44: 1117–27.

An interesting study further studying the role of psychological factors that may moderate our response to health information following screening – and in particular the role of health anxiety.

Sivell, S., Iredale, R., Gray, J. and Coles, B. (2007). Cancer genetic risk assessment for individuals at risk of familial breast cancer. *Cochrane Database of Systematic Reviews*: CD003721.

A review of the psychological impact of cancer genetic risk assessment. As usual with Cochrane reviews, the review is limited to randomised controlled trials (the authors eliminated 54 of the 58 papers they initially thought relevant), and therefore excludes longitudinal studies of the impact of genetic risk assessment where no-intervention trial was conducted, but it does summarise some of the literature well.

Martins, R.K. and McNeil, D.W. (2009). Review of motivational interviewing in promoting health behaviors. *Clinical Psychology Review*, 29: 283–93.

An excellent critique of where we are at with the practice of motivational interviewing in the context of health behaviours.

Miller, W. and Rollnick, S. (2002). *Motivational Interviewing: Preparing People to Change Addictive Behaviour.* New York: Guilford Press.

A guide to motivational interviewing from its originators. The book shows motivational interviewing in its present form, which now synthesises elements of 'pure' motivational interviewing (as described in the chapter) with a problem-focused approach. Later chapters provide evidence of its effectiveness in a variety of settings.

www.motivationalinterview.org/

Those wanting to explore the world of MINTies would do worse than going to this page, set up by Miller himself, with the goal of providing resources for clinicians, researchers and trainers in relation to motivational interviewing.

Egan, G. (2009). *The Skilled Helper, international edition.* Pacific Grove, CA: Brooks/cole.

One of the bibles of problem-focused counselling. It shows the process to be rather more complex than the 'Egan-lite' described in the chapter.

Rutter, D. and Quine, L. (2002). *Changing Health Behaviour: Intervention and Research with Social Cognition Models.* Buckingham: Open University Press.

An edited text describing a number of interventions each of which is either derived from or involves measures relevant to a number of social cognition theories, including the health action process and theory of reasoned action, among others.

Conner, M. and Higgins, A.R. (2010). Long-term effects of implementation intentions on prevention of smoking uptake among adolescents: a cluster randomized controlled trial. *Health Psychology*, 29: 529–38.

One of the more recent studies of the use of implementation intentions.

Wilson, R. and Branch, R. (2005). *Cognitive Therapy for Dummies*. Chichester: Wiley.

As good an introduction to cognitive-behavioural therapy as you are likely to get (23 five-star reviews in Amazon). Useful as background reading for Chapters 16 and 17 as well.

Visit the website at **www.pearsoned.co.uk/morrison** for additional resources to help you with your study, including multiple choice questions, weblinks and flashcards.

Chapter 7
Population approaches to public health

Learning outcomes

By the end of this chapter, you should have an understanding of:

- the benefits and limitations of using the mass media

- the elaboration likelihood model and its use in media campaigns

- how the environment may be used to influence health-related behaviours

- the outcomes of interventions targeting whole populations' heart and sexual health

- the nature and effectiveness of interventions targeted at more specific populations: worksite and school health-promotion initiatives

- the emerging use of the internet as a change agent, and some of the limitations of its present use

Saving money *and* health

Saving lives is good. Spending money on doing so is not so good. When resources are tight, the amount of money governments spend on health has clear implications for other areas in which money could be spent – including reducing university fees or increasing maintenance grants! So, the amount spent on either enhancing the health of the nation or treating sickness is relevant to us all. Treating illness is an obvious requirement of any health-care system. But should the system also attempt to prevent ill health and, if so, should it not seek the most cost-effective way of doing so? And if we could encourage other people to bear the cost burden of change, would this not be even better? In an attempt to encourage industry and others to bear some of the cost of enhancing population health, the UK government has developed spreadsheets accessible by employers that allow them to work out the cost savings to their organisation if they were to initiate programmes encouraging people to engage in appropriate health behaviours – such as stopping smoking. The Public Health Interventions Cost Effectiveness Database (PHICED: www.yhpho.org.uk/nphl/nphlresults.asp) also provides guidance relevant to these issues to the wider planning and local authority sector. They have, for example, provided guidelines for organisations such as local transport authorities, education, and transport planners on how to develop cost-effective interventions to increase physical activity within the general population by manipulating environmental factors. Ironically, getting non-health-related organisations involved in health may impact more on preventive health and at much less cost to the government than traditional health promotion programmes.

Chapter outline

In the last chapter, we considered how we can influence health-related behaviour through individually based interventions. While these may be effective, no government or body involved in public health has the resources to intervene at a one-to-one level with the entire population – nor would people in the population want to be involved in any attempt to do so. So attempts to influence the health-related behaviour of large groups of people or entire populations necessarily involve other approaches. Perhaps the most obvious means through which health promoters attempt to influence our behaviour is through media campaigns. However, there are a number of other potential routes through which our behaviour can be influenced, including economic and environmental influences. This chapter considers the strengths and limits of the use of mass media approaches to health promotion, before considering some of the other approaches that have been used. We look at the effectiveness of influencing behaviour through the use of environmental factors in the workplace and school, and the use of peer education. Finally, we consider the emerging use of the internet as an agent of behavioural change. Theories relating to each approach are considered as well as the effectiveness of interventions based on them.

Promoting population health

In the previous chapter, we considered a number of one-to-one or small-group interventions that have been used to change health-related behaviour. Many proved reasonably effective, so from the viewpoint of their absolute effectiveness, they could generally be considered 'a good thing'. However, they are expensive to provide, and achieve change in relatively few individuals. Accordingly, from a cost-effectiveness perspective, they are perhaps less impressive. They are also impractical to provide on a large-scale basis. As a result of this, a parallel set of theories and studies have considered how to change the behaviour of large groups of individuals. Approaches that target whole populations are likely to be less effective in achieving change in any one individual than one-to-one interventions. Nevertheless, because of the large number of individuals who may be reached through this type of intervention, they may still achieve significant change over an entire population. A one-to-one inter-vention that achieved change in, say, 5 per cent of those who took part would be considered ineffective. A large-scale intervention that targeted hundreds of thousands if not millions of individuals and achieved a similar success rate could be considered highly effective, at least in terms of the resources and costs necessary to achieve any changes. That is, such interventions have the potential to be highly cost-effective.

Using the mass media

Perhaps the most obvious contribution of psychology to public health initiatives can be found in the design and implementation of mass media campaigns. The earliest media campaigns adopted a 'hypodermic' model of behavioural change, which assumed a relatively stable link between knowledge, attitudes and behaviour (something we now know to be somewhat optimistic: see Chapter 5 (☞). The approach assumed that if we could 'inject' appropriate information into the recipients, this would change their attitudes and in turn influence their behaviour. This approach, led by people such as McGuire (e.g. 1985), suggested that the key to success was to make the information persuasive and for it to come from appropriate sources. Defining each of these elements is not easy. What is persuasive for one person may not be for another. Good sources of information may be an 'expert', 'someone like you', a neutral individual or someone clearly linked to the issue, such as a doctor providing health information. Seeing someone affected by a particular condition or who has achieved significant behavioural change can be a much more potent source of information than a neutral person or even an expert. It is much more powerful to see a 34-year-old man explain how smoking caused his lung cancer, for example, than to have the risks of developing lung cancer explained by a doctor who has not been personally affected by the condition. In one study of this phenomenon, Scollay et al. (1992) reported that a lecture to a school audience about the risks of unsafe sex by someone known to be HIV-positive resulted in greater increases in knowledge, less risky attitudes and safer behavioural intentions than a neutral source.

Despite the popularity of media campaigns, a key issue is whether they result in any behavioural change. This cannot be taken for granted – nor can the fact that the target audience even notices the campaign. Isolated health campaigns may have little impact. In one such programme, focusing on attempting to increase levels of exercise in the community, Wimbush et al. (1998) assessed the effect of a mass media campaign in Scotland designed to promote walking. Although 70 per cent of those asked about the campaign were aware of its existence, it had no impact on behaviour. Such limited outcomes have led some to argue that media campaigns are best used to raise awareness of health issues rather than as attempts to engender significant behavioural change (Stead et al. 2002), and that behavioural change is most likely when media campaigns form one element of a multi-modal intervention, or when the target behaviour is a one-off or episodic behaviour, such as attending a vaccination or screening clinic (Wakefield et al. 2010).

More positively, the cumulative effects of repeated media campaigns may influence attitudes and behaviour. One example of this can be found in US anti-smoking media advertising which has campaigned against smoking consistently over many years. Such advertising has two key goals: first, to be noticed, and second, to influence knowledge, attitudes and behaviour. The programmes seem to have achieved both goals

(see a meta-analysis reported by Bala et al. 2008). In Massachusetts, for example, over half the population noticed anti-smoking advertisements at least weekly for a period of three years (Biener et al. 2000). Exposure to anti-smoking advertising at this level was associated with increases in the perceived harm of smoking, and stronger intentions not to smoke (Emery et al. 2007). It may also impact on smoking rates. McVey and Stapleton (2000) calculated that an 18-month long British anti-smoking advertising campaign resulted in a 1.2 per cent reduction in smoking levels. Again showing the benefits of long-term advertising, Hyland et al. (2006) found a 10 per cent increase in the likelihood that people would quit smoking for every '5000 units of exposure' to anti-smoking television advertising over a two-year period. Even more dramatic results have been reported in programmes specifically targeted at young people and which place the advertising within a more complex intervention. Zucker et al. (2000) reported that their US 'truth' (anti-tobacco marketing) campaign, which involved 'in-school education, enforcement, a schoolbased youth organisation, community based organisations, and [. . .] an aggressive, well funded, counter-advertising programme' resulted in a 19 per cent reduction in smoking among middle-school students, and an 8 per cent reduction among high-school students. It seems that the level of exposure is highly influential in terms of its impact.

Despite, or perhaps because of, these successes, those involved in using the media to influence behaviour have adopted a number of methods to maximise its effectiveness, including:

- refining communication to maximise its influence on attitudes;
- the use of fear messages;
- information framing;
- specific targeting of interventions.

Refining communication

Different people may be influenced by different types of information or sources of information – they may also be more or less motivated to consider any information they encounter. We considered this issue in relation to working with individuals in our discussion of the stages of change model (Prochaska and di Clemente 1984) in the previous chapter. Media campaigns can also adopt different arguments depending on the stage of change of

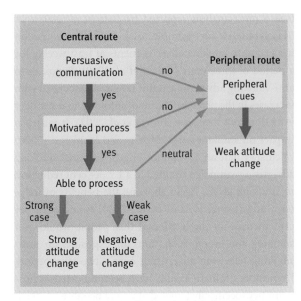

Figure 7.1 The elaboration likelihood model of persuasive communication

people in its target audience. They can provide motivating messages, show how to achieve change, and even encourage people to plan change. An alternative method of refining communication for those more or less motivated to consider change is provided by a theoretical model known as the elaboration likelihood model (ELM) developed by Petty and Cacioppo (1986; see Figure 7.1). This suggests that attempts to influence people who are not interested in a particular issue by rational argument will not work (nor will they succeed if the arguments for change are weak). Only those individuals with a pre-existing interest in the issue are likely to attend to such information and, perhaps, act on it. In their jargon, individuals are more likely to 'centrally process' messages if they are 'motivated to receive an argument' when:

● it is congruent with their pre-existing beliefs;

● it has personal relevance to them;

● recipients have the intellectual capacity to understand the message.

Such processing involves evaluation of arguments, assessment of conclusions, and their integration into existing belief structures. According to the ELM, any attitude change resulting from such deliberative processes is likely to be enduring and predictive of behaviour. However, given that health promotion is often targeted at individuals who are not interested in an issue and who are not motivated to process messages, how then do we attempt to influence them? According to the ELM, influence here is

less reliable but still possible. The model suggests that this can be achieved through what it terms 'peripheral processing'. This is likely to occur when individuals:

● are not motivated to receive an argument;

● have low issue involvement;

● hold incongruent beliefs.

Peripheral processing involves maximising the credibility and attractiveness of the source of the message using indirect cues and information. Attempts, for example, to influence middle-aged women to take part in exercise may involve a technical message about health gains that can be achieved following exercise (the central route) and also include images associated with exercise that appeal to the target audience, such as making friends while engaging in gentle exercise and wearing attractive clothes in the gym (the peripheral route). Similarly, the importance of a message can be emphasised by a senior person, such as a medical professor presenting information. According to the ELM, any attitude change fostered by the peripheral route is likely to be transient and not predictive of behaviour.

A good example of combining the central and peripheral routes with a credible source can be found in a series of UK television advertisements targeted at smokers. These involved real people who had serious smoking-related illnesses – we were told that one person died soon after filming – talking about the adverse outcomes of their smoking. The film was black and white, and the images involved the people sitting in a chair with a very sparse background. The message was that smoking kills, and the peripheral cues associated with the image were downbeat and gloomy. It did not encourage the viewer to take up smoking! Of course, one danger of this negative portrayal is that viewers may find it too depressing and simply disengage from the adverts – either mentally by thinking about something else, or physically by switching the television to another channel (see discussion of fear appeals in the next section). To avoid such an outcome, and in order to find the maximally persuasive approach, it is necessary to develop media campaigns based on sound psychological theory and also to include a testing process, discussing them with their target population – perhaps through the use of focus groups – to fine-tune the finished product.

The ELM has been subject to a number of experimental tests, most of which (e.g. Agostinelli and Grube 2002) suggest that information containing carefully chosen peripheral cues can facilitate attitudinal change in people who are relatively unmotivated to consider particular issues, or that combining central processing with peripheral cues can enhance the effectiveness of some interventions. Kirby *et al.* (1998), for example, showed African American women two health messages about mammography involving both central and peripheral cues. They systematically varied the number of each type of cue over four messages embedded as advertisements in a television talk show. Women who reported a high involvement in the issue reported stronger intentions to seek mammography than those with low involvement, regardless of the presence of central arguments or peripheral cues. By contrast, women with a low involvement in the issue were more likely to report strong intentions to seek mammography if they had been exposed to high levels of favourable peripheral cues than if they had not. Whether these attitudinal changes result in behavioural change is less clear. Drossaert *et al.* (1996) found this not to be the case. Again, in the context of attempts to increase attendance at mammography, they made two versions of a leaflet designed to increase attendance. The main arguments were the same in each leaflet, but one leaflet had low levels of peripheral cues and the other had high levels. Attendance rates of women exposed to the differing leaflets sent out with the invitation to attend did not differ, suggesting that there was little or no benefit from adding peripheral cues to their leaflets. Perhaps this is the real limitation of the ELM and other models of attitude change. They can suggest means of maximising attitudinal change, but many other factors will influence whether any attitudinal change or even behavioural intentions are translated into action (see Chapter 5 ☞ for a discussion of the relationship between attitudes and behaviour).

The use of fear

A second potential approach to increasing the influence of mass media communication is through the use of fear messages. This has proven popular among both health promoters and politicians, as well as the recipients of such advertising (Biener *et al.* 2000), who consider fear (and sadness) engendering advertisements to be more effective than humour. Despite this support, high levels of threat have proven relatively ineffective in engendering behavioural change. The problems with this approach can be demonstrated in both the UK and Australian governments' early attempts to change sexual practices in response to the development of HIV/AIDS. Both countries used high-fear messages, including visual images of the chipping of a gravestone with the words AIDS (in the UK) and a celestial bowling alley in which a 'grim reaper' representing HIV bowled down families and children (in Australia). These were associated with portentous messages declaring the need to avoid HIV infection and to use safer sex practices. The Australian advert can be watched on YouTube (key words, AIDS Grim Reaper: www.youtube.com/watch?v=U219eUIZ7Qo). Both campaigns increased HIV-related anxiety in audiences that saw them, but they did not increase knowledge about HIV/AIDS or trigger any behavioural change (Rigby *et al.* 1989; Sherr 1987). Subsequent fear-based messages have also failed to promote appropriate behavioural change, and may even increase feelings of shame and scepticism relating to the issues being addressed (Slavin *et al.* 2007).

One explanation of this effect may be found in protection motivation theory (Rogers 1983; see Chapter 5 ☞). This suggests that individuals will respond to information in either an adaptive or maladaptive manner depending on their appraisal of both threat *and* their own ability to minimise that threat (their self-efficacy judgements). The theory suggests that an individual is most likely to behave in an adaptive manner in response to a fear-arousing health message if they have evidence that engaging in certain behaviour will reduce any threat and they believe they are capable of engaging in it. This approach has been further developed by Witte's (1992) extended parallel process model which states that individuals who are threatened will take one of two courses of action: danger control or fear control. Danger control involves reducing the threat, usually by actively focusing on solutions. Fear control seeks to reduce the perception of the risk, often by avoiding thinking about the threat. For danger control to be selected, a person needs to consider that an effective response is available (response efficacy) and that they are capable of engaging in this response (self-efficacy). If danger control is not selected, then fear control becomes the dominant coping strategy. Both these theories suggest that the most persuasive messages are those that:

● arouse some degree of fear – 'Unsafe sex increases your risk of getting HIV';

● increase the sense of severity if no change is made – 'HIV is a serious condition';

● emphasise the ability of the individual to prevent the feared outcome (efficacy) – 'Here are some simple safer sex practices you can use to reduce your risk of getting HIV'.

These theoretical notions have been reinforced by a number of meta-analyses of the relevant research. Witte and Allen (2000), for example, concluded that high threat/fear appeal should be accompanied by an equally high efficacy message, and that the stronger the levels of fear evoked, the more likely the individual is to produce strong fear-defensive responses – the outcome of which is the maintenance of the old behaviour rather than behavioural change. Further cautionary data stem from Earl and Albarracin's (2007) meta-analysis of HIV-specific fear appeals from a sample including 150 treatment groups. These data indicated that receiving fear-inducing arguments increased perceptions of risk but decreased knowledge and condom use. By contrast, resolving fear through HIV counselling and testing both decreased perceptions of risk and increased knowledge and condom use.

Information framing

A less threatening approach to the development of health messages involves 'framing' the message. Health messages can be framed in either positive (stressing positive outcomes associated with action) or negative terms (emphasising negative outcomes associated with failure to act). While some have argued that negative frames are more memorable (Newhagen and Reeves 1987), others have suggested that positive messages enhance information processing. This may particularly be the case when time is short and individuals are not highly motivated to receive a message (Isen 1987). But the evidence can be conflicting, and complex to interpret. Evidence supporting the use of positive framing, for example, was illustrated by a study reported by Bigman *et al.* (2010), who found that this resulted in a 40 per cent difference in the perceived effectiveness of the human papillomavirus (HPV) vaccine in comparison to negatively framed messages. In addition, participants exposed to the positively framed message were more likely to support the public availability of the vaccine. By contrast, Gerend and Shepherd (2007) found that negatively framed messages were more likely than positively framed messages to increase intentions of young women to have the human papillomavirus vaccine – but only among those who had multiple sexual partners and who infrequently used condoms. Finally, Considine *et al.* (2007) found no effect of type of framing on attendance at breast screening.

Overall, these data suggest that we can make no strong *a priori* judgements about what type of framing will affect particular populations – emphasising the need to test out any intervention as a pilot before it is finally aired in public. These conclusions have been supported by a number of meta-analyses which have found non-significant differences in the effectiveness of either loss- or gain-framed approaches in changing behaviours as varied as safer-sex behaviours, skin cancer prevention behaviours, or diet and nutrition behaviours (e.g. O'Keefe and Jensen 2007).

Audience targeting

Early attempts to influence behaviour via the mass media frequently targeted whole populations. This meant that the messages received by the target population were more or less relevant, and the message had to be so broad that it had some potential relevance to all those who received it. As a consequence, health messages were frequently so diluted that they had little relevance to those who received them. Media attempts to influence sexual behaviour illustrate the point. Early media approaches promoting safer sex, as noted above, were based on fear messages, and the same messages were received by all, whether they were elderly, non-sexually active widows and widowers or young sexually active gay men enjoying multiple partners. The outcome of such an approach was the raising of unnecessary fears among a group of people for whom HIV/AIDS had little immediate relevance, while not speaking the language of, or giving relevant advice to, the groups for whom it was most relevant. Now, media messages on sexual behaviour are more carefully targeted and use the language of their differing target audiences, making them much more effective.

Audience targeting can be based on a number of factors, including behaviour, age, gender and socio-economic status – each of which is likely to influence the impact of any message (Flynn *et al.* 2007). They may even be developed in part by the target audience. Toroyan and Reddy (2005–6), for example, described how young South Africans were involved in the development of photo-comics addressing issues around HIV/AIDS and other sexually transmitted diseases. Similarly, Bethune and Lewis (2009) aimed to increase Maori women's use of cervical screening services. In order to best target their media campaign, they ran focus groups with 'priority women' and other key informants to identify the key messages likely to influence their behaviour. The intervention worked, and resulted in an increase in screening uptake from 7 to 13 per cent over a one-year period. Contrast this with the high intensity programme targeted at women within one worksite discussed in the previous chapter (Allen *et al.* 2001) that resulted in similar, or slightly less, gains. The relative cost-effectiveness of this intervention is clear. A simple example of the social targeting process is afforded by the Terrence Higgins Trust leaflet in Plate 7.1, which would be considered outrageous by many, but fits the profile of its target audience – young, sexually active, gay men – well.

Audiences may also be segmented along more psychological factors such as their motivation to consider change. A worksite exercise programme reported by Peterson and Aldana (1999), for example, involved attempts to increase levels of participation in exercise among 527 corporate employees who either received written messages tailored to their reported stage of change or general information about exercise. Six weeks after the material was received, participants who received the tailored, staged-based messages increased their activity by 13 per cent and were more likely to shift towards contemplating change (as well as actual change) than those receiving general information. A similar intervention reported a comparable effect one year after the intervention, but only in women (Plotnikoff *et al.* 2007). An interesting study reported by Griffin-Blake and DeJoy (2006) compared a stage-matched intervention and a social cognitive intervention focusing on self-

Plate 7.1 An example of a health promotion leaflet targeted at gay men – with a sense of humour – encouraging them to have three vaccinations against hepatitis, produced by the Terrence Higgins Trust

Source: Terrence Higgins Trust.

efficacy, outcome expectancies and goal satisfaction (see Chapter 5 (☛). Both interventions proved equally effective in increasing physical activity in their target group (college employees).

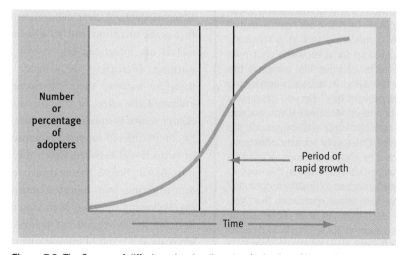

Figure 7.2 The S curve of diffusion, showing the rate of adoption of innovations over time

Environmental influences on health behaviour

Behaviour and behaviour change do not occur in isolation from the environment in which they occur. The environment may contribute directly to risk of disease (see Chapter 2 ☞). It can indirectly affect health, by influencing the ease with which health-promoting or health-damaging behaviour can be conducted. However keen young single mothers may be to exercise, not having someone to look after their child while they are doing so may prevent them from exercising; asking people to eat healthily at work may not be possible unless they are offered healthy choices in the work canteen; and so on. The health belief model (Becker *et al.* 1977; see Chapter 5 ☞) provides a simple guide to key environmental factors that can be influenced in order to encourage behavioural change. In particular, the model suggests that an environment that encourages healthy behaviour should:

● provide cues to action – or remove cues to unhealthy behaviour;

● enable healthy behaviour by minimising the costs and barriers associated with it;

● maximise the costs of engaging in health-damaging behaviour.

WHAT DO YOU THINK?

This next section concerns environmental and social issues that can facilitate or inhibit our health-related behaviour. Before considering this in a relatively theoretical way, consider for a moment your own behaviour. What parts of your life increase the possibility of you behaving in a health-enhancing way? What factors prevent this? Do you have easy access to sports or leisure facilities? If you wanted to, would you feel safe cycling or walking around the area where you live? Does your locality offer easy access to good-quality shops, or does accessing them require a car or bus ride? Does this restrict your (or other people's) access to healthy foodstuffs? What about people with fewer resources than you – or with higher demands on their time: single mothers with limited income, for example. How does the environment influence their health choices?

Cues to action

Much of our behaviour is routine, based on habit. Accordingly, we rarely think about change. Cues to action, things that remind us to behave healthily or to change our unhealthy behaviour, can remind us of the need to change our behaviour. Two key areas where this has been used involve health warnings on cigarettes and nutritional information on food. These approaches may be of some benefit, although the evidence suggests that they reinforce existing behaviour rather than prompt consideration of behavioural change. Part of this lack of effect may be due to poor understanding of the issues raised and/or the low visibility of such cues. Cowburn and Stockley (2005), for example, in a review of over a hundred relevant papers, reported that many people in the general public, and particularly those on low incomes, did not understand or were uninterested in the nutritional information on food packaging. One South African study (Jacobs *et al.* 2010), for example, reported that the vast majority of the respondents to their survey only took notice of the expiry date of the food. Nutritional information was considered far less important, with participants favouring taste and price over nutritional content. In addition, many participants did not understand the information provided and were therefore unable to use it to inform health-related decisions. Similarly, Krukowski *et al.* (2006) found that just under half their sample of US college students looked at food labels, or said they would use the information of food labels even if available.

Interestingly, the design of advertising may actually discourage looking at health warnings on tobacco advertisements. A clear delineation between the picture that grabs attention and its associated health warning that is not integrated into it may inhibit reading the warning. Increasing the salience of such cues may therefore increase their effectiveness. Borland (1997) evaluated the effect of the introduction of larger and clearer health warnings on cigarette packets in Australia by comparing self-reported responses to health warnings in two surveys between which the new warnings were introduced. Before the changes were initiated, 37 per cent of respondents reported noticing the health warning. Following increases in its size, 66 per cent reported noticing it. The equivalent figures for refraining from smoking as a result of the warning rose from 7 to 14 per cent. A significant impact can also be obtained by using graphic imagery rather than written text (Thrasher *et al.* 2007; O'Hegarty *et al.* 2006). Cues reminding people to engage in health-promoting behaviours may also be of value. One simple example can be found in posters reminding people to use stairs instead of lifts or escalators. Webb and Eves (2007) found that posters encouraging people to use the stairs instead of a nearby escalator in a shopping centre resulted in a near doubling of stair use. The same research team (Eves *et al.* 2006) found that overweight individuals were more likely to respond to the signs than individuals of more average weight, suggesting this may be a simple but effective way of increasing fitness among this group. In addition, these individuals may then act as models, encouraging others to climb the stairs rather than use the escalator (Webb *et al.* 2010).

Environmental cues not only act as prompts to healthy behaviour, they can also act as reminders to behave in unhealthy ways. Frequent exposure to relevant advertising, for example, has been shown to increase perceptions of the prevalence of smoking (Burton *et al.* 2010) as well as smoking itself (Sargent *et al.* 2000) and levels of alcohol consumption (Smith and Foxcroft 2009) among young people. Accordingly, those involved in public health frequently strive to limit and legislate against such things as tobacco and alcohol advertising. The UK government, for example, banned television advertising of tobacco in 1965 and totally banned its advertising from 2003. How effective this approach has been appears to differ across countries. Quentin *et al.* (2007) reported that total bans on advertising of tobacco products were associated with mixed reductions in consumption. Of the 18 studies they reviewed from various countries, only 10 reported a significant reduction in smoking following the ban; two studies suggested that a partial ban on advertising had little or no effect. Of course, advertising is not the only media influence on attitudes about health-related behaviour. Many young people consider images in magazines to portray smokers as attractive, reassuring and sociable (MacFadyen *et al.* 2002). In addition, in limited experimental conditions, alcohol consumption portrayed in films has been shown to increase consumption during the film (Koordeman *et al.* 2009). The net impact of these images and messages is that any health advertising is competing against a background of complex and influential processes. Any gains should therefore be applauded.

Minimising the costs of healthy behaviour

The environment in which we live can either facilitate or inhibit our level of engagement in health-related behaviour. Poor street lighting, busy roads and high levels of pollution may inhibit some inner-city dwellers from taking exercise such as jogging or cycling; shops that sell healthy foods but which are a long way from housing estates may result in more use of local shops that sell less healthy foodstuffs, and so on. Making the environment safe and supportive of healthy activity presents a challenge to town planners and governments. Such an environment should promote safety, provide opportunities for social integration and give the population control over key aspects of their lives.

A number of projects, under the rubric of the 'Healthy Cities movement' (World Health Organization 1988), have attempted to design city environments in ways that promote the mental and physical health of their inhabitants. The movement initially involved cities in industrialised countries, but is now expanding to include cities in industrialising countries such as Bangladesh, Tanzania, Nicaragua and Pakistan. To be a member of the movement, cities have to develop a city health profile and involve citizen and community groups. Priorities for action include attempts to reduce health inequalities as a result of socio-economic factors (see Chapter 2 ☛), traffic control, tobacco control, and care of the elderly and those with mental health problems (Kickbusch 2003). Unfortunately, while very laudable, this rather broad set of strategies has proved difficult to translate into measurable and concrete action. Indeed, as recently as 2006, O'Neill and Simard (2006) were still writing discussion papers on how to evaluate the effectiveness of the, by then, twenty-year-old programme, while Ison (2009) reported the recent introduction of a common measure of health impact to be used in its assessment. Nevertheless, where appropriate measures have been used and appropriate environmental changes made, this does seem to influence health behaviour. Jago *et al.* (2005), for example, found that levels of light intensity exercise were greater among male adolescents when there was good street lighting, safe areas for jogging or walking, well-maintained pavements, and the presence of trees.

More specific studies have shown that environmental manipulations aimed at minimising the costs of engaging in exercise may result in significant change. Linegar et al. (1991), for example, took advantage of the unusual context of a completely closed community of a naval base to manipulate both its physical and organisational environment. They established cycle paths, provided exercise equipment, and organised exercise clubs and competitions within the base. In addition, they gave workers 'release time' from other duties while they participated in exercise. Not surprisingly, perhaps, this combination of interventions resulted in significant increases in exercise, even among people who had not previously exercised. This combination of approaches is rarely possible, but the results indicate what is possible when there is the freedom to manipulate a wide range of environmental factors. A more 'doable' programme, intended to increase levels of exercise among women in a suburb of Sydney, was reported by Wen et al. (2002). It targeted women aged between 20 and 50 through a marketing campaign and increasing opportunities for participation in exercise. The marketing included establishing community walking events, and initiating walking groups and community physical activity classes. Local council members were invited on to the project group to raise the profile of the project with council members and to ensure that the project fitted within the council's social and environmental plans. Pre- and post-project telephone surveys indicated a 6.4 per cent reduction in the proportion of sedentary women in the local population, as well as an increased commitment to promoting physical activity by the local council. Overall, programmes including those establishing and improving cycle lanes, alone or in combination with high-profile cycling initiatives do seem to achieve modest increases in the level of cycling across many countries (Yang et al. 2010).

Another area where the costs of healthy behaviour have been considered is that of needle-exchange schemes for injecting drug users. Needle-exchange schemes exchange old for new needles, preventing the need for sharing and reducing the risk of cross-infection of blood-borne viruses, including HIV and hepatitis. Where syringes cannot legally be obtained elsewhere, they are effective. Kerr et al. (2010), for example, reported reductions in needle borrowing from 20 to 9 per cent of respondents in a sample of 1,228 injecting drug users in British Columbia, which was associated with a significantly lower risk of contracting HIV. Despite the overwhelmingly positive findings from needle-exchange programmes, one study (Taylor et al.

2001) had a more cautionary message. This Scottish study reported a reduction in the use of shared needles between 1990 and 1992 in Scotland following the introduction of needle-exchange schemes, but then a gradual increase in sharing in the following years despite their continued provision. These changes mirror some of the changes in risk behaviour in other populations at risk for HIV, where initial changes towards safer behaviour have dwindled, and riskier behaviour has returned over time (e.g. Dodds et al. 2004). The reasons for this are unclear but may relate to the relatively low profile given to HIV/AIDS awareness, at least in the UK, and increasing (inappropriate) beliefs that AIDS can be 'cured'.

Increasing the costs of unhealthy behaviour

Making unhealthy behaviour difficult in some way (often through pricing) can act as a barrier to unhealthy behaviour and a facilitator of healthy behaviour. Economic measures related to public health have been largely confined to taxation on tobacco and alcohol. The price of alcohol impacts on levels of consumption, although its impact is greater among moderate than heavy drinkers – nevertheless, even among this group, price still does have a modest impact on consumption (Wagenaar et al. 2009).

Increases in tobacco taxation may also be the most effective measure in reducing levels of cigarette smoking. Hu et al. (1995) modelled the relative effectiveness of taxation and media campaigns on tobacco consumption in California. They estimated that a 25 per cent tax increase would result in a reduction in sales of 819 million cigarette packs, compared with 232 million packs as a result of media influences. Taxation seems to be a particularly effective deterrent among young people, who are three times more likely to be affected by price rises than older adults (Ding 2003). However, these findings must now be interpreted against attempts to avoid these costs. In the UK, for example, increasing levels of smuggled tobacco and alcohol from the continent (where tax levels are much lower) compete against higher prices in formal outlets.

While prohibition may be seen as a necessary barrier by some, others have called for more modest barriers to availability. One approach involves restricting the number of outlets for drugs such as alcohol. This increases transaction 'costs' as people have to travel further and make more effort to purchase their alcohol, and in reduced cues to consumption from advertising in shop windows and other signs. Connor *et al.* (2010) found this to be the case at least to a limited degree, with more geographically widespread off-sales outlets across New Zealand being associated with less binge drinking and alcohol related harm – although there was no association between outlet density and frequency of 'sensible' drinking. By contrast, increasing availability – as has occurred relatively recently in Sweden through the Saturday opening of alcohol retail shops – may result in an increase in consumption (Norström and Skog 2005).

A more direct form of control over smoking has been the introduction of smoke-free work and social areas. These clearly reduce smoking in public places – and may impact on smoking elsewhere. Heloma and Jaakalo (2003) found that secondary smoke inhalation levels fell among non-smokers, while smoking prevalence rates at work fell from 30 per cent to 25 per cent following a national smoke-free workplace law. Following a ban on smoking in Norwegian bars and restaurants, Braverman *et al.* (2007) reported significant reductions in the prevalence of daily smoking, daily smoking at work by bar workers, number of cigarettes smoked by continuing smokers, and the number of cigarettes smoked at work by continuing smokers. Restaurants and bars have expressed some concern that smoking bans will reduce their profits. Countering this claim, Stolzenberg and D'Alessio (2007) reported a small, 4 per cent, reduction in profits in restaurants immediately following the smoking ban in California, but that over time profits again rose, and there was no long-term reduction in profits or consumption in any bar or restaurant. Even more encouraging are emerging data suggesting that such bans can positively impact on health. Although they do not provide absolute proof of an association between reduced smoking and reduced disease, a number of studies have now shown reductions in the number of admissions to hospital with myocardial infarction both in the USA (e.g. Herman and Walsh 2010) and Europe (Cesaroni *et al.* 2008) since the ban was implemented. Of particular note is that there appears to be a reduction in smoking-related conditions among people, such as bar staff directly affected by the ban (e.g. Larsson *et al.* 2008), and even indirectly affected by it. Mackay *et al.* (2010) found that rates of admissions for childhood asthma in Scotland have also fallen significantly following the ban. The mechanisms for these changes are unclear, but the data provide some reassurance that the costs of being in a smoky atmosphere are not simply being transferred to others, such as children, in the home.

IN THE SPOTLIGHT

The binge drinking epidemic

Despite some reductions in the consumption of alcohol throughout the population, many countries have recently reported significant increases in binge drinking, particularly among young people. This phenomenon has been reported, for example, in the UK, New Zealand, Australia, an area known as the vodka belt (Russia and other countries where vodka is the primary drink), but is less prevalent in South America and southern Europe. The causes of this behaviour are not fully understood, but the availability of cheap alcohol in supermarkets, clubs and pubs – and the culture of drinking while standing – is widely recognised as contributing to the phenomenon. The drinking culture contributes to significant personal harm, as well as having a substantial economic and social impact on the affected communities. Some cities have increased policing in response to the social problems. Some have made bars contribute to the cost of this policing. But one French town took their approach a stage further. They bought the bars! The city of Renne, in Brittany, has bought two bars in the centre of town and converted one into a DVD shop, and one into a restaurant in an attempt to reduce alcohol consumption in its centre. Time will tell whether this impacts on alcohol consumption . . . but you have to admit, it's a pretty bold approach to health promotion!

Health promotion programmes

So far, we have looked at some broad approaches to behavioural change in large populations, and some of the underlying principles that underpin them. The next sections of this chapter examine how these, and some other, approaches have been used in health promotion programmes targeted at whole populations and more specific target groups within them. We consider a number of differing target populations, the approaches that have been used to change their behaviour, the theoretical models that have guided the interventions, and their effectiveness.

Targeting coronary heart disease

Some of the first health promotion programmes targeted at whole towns aimed to reduce the prevalence of key risk factors for CHD – smoking, low levels of exercise, high fat consumption and high blood pressure – across the entire adult population. The first of these, known as the Stanford Three Towns project (Farquhar *et al.* 1977), provided three towns in California with three levels of intervention.

The first town received no intervention. The second received a year-long media campaign targeting CHD-related behaviour. Although the media programme preceded the stages of change model (Prochaska and di Clemente 1984; see Chapter 6 ☞) by some years, it followed a programme very similar to that suggested by that model. It started by alerting people to the need to change their behaviour (itself a relatively novel message in the early 1970s). This was followed by a series of programmes modelling behaviour change – for example, by broadcasting films of people attending a smoking cessation group or showing cooking skills. These were based on social learning theory (Bandura 1977; see Chapters 5 and 6 ☞) and were aimed at teaching skills and increasing recipients' confidence in their ability to change and maintain change of their own behaviour. This phase was followed by further slots reminding people to maintain any behavioural changes they had made, and showing images of people enjoying the benefits of behavioural change such as a family enjoying a healthy picnic (potentially impacting on attitudes and perceived social norms). In the third town, a group of individuals at particularly high levels of risk for CHD and their partners received one-to-one education on risk behaviour change and were asked to disseminate their knowledge through their social networks. This strategy was used to provide

Plate 7.2 For some, environmental interventions may be far from complex. Simply providing clean water may prevent exposure to a variety of pathogens in dirty water

Source: © Comic Relief UK, reproduced courtesy of Comic Relief UK.

Table 7.1 The three levels of intervention in the Stanford Three Towns project

Approach	What it involved	Expected effect
Ongoing health promotion activity	A minimal intervention 'comparison' town	+/−
Year-long media campaign	Phase 1: alerting people to the need to change Phase 2: modelling change Phase 3: modelling continued change	+
Media campaign + high-risk intervention	Media as influence combined with dissemination of knowledge from lay experts	++

another channel for disseminating information – through the use of people given the role of opinion leaders – and increasing motivation in both high-risk people and the general public.

Accordingly, there were three levels of intervention, each of which was expected to result in a step-wise increase in effectiveness (see Table 7.1). The expected outcomes were found. By the end of the one-year programme, scores on a measure of CHD-risk status based on factors including blood pressure, smoking and cholesterol level indicated that average risk scores among the general population actually rose in the control town, while they fell significantly among the general population who received the media campaign alone, and to an even greater extent among those who lived in the town that received the combined intervention. After a further year, risk scores in the intervention towns were still significantly lower than those of the control town, although because scores in the media-only town continued to improve, there was no difference between the two intervention towns (Farquhar *et al.* 1990a).

The European equivalent of this programme was established in North Karelia in Finland (Puska *et al.* 1985). This five-year programme differed slightly from the Stanford approach in that, in addition to a media approach, it also changed environmental factors, encouraging local meat manufacturers and butchers to promote low-fat products, encouraging 'no smoking' restaurants, and so on. It was generally considered to be a success, with reductions in a number of risk factors including blood pressure, cholesterol levels and smoking among men. However, its final summary paper showed that these reductions in risk factors were not consistently better than those in a control area, which received no intervention.

Unfortunately, this apparent lack of success has been repeated in a number of subsequent large-scale interventions. A second study conducted around Stanford, called the Five City project (Farquhar *et al.* 1990b), for example, combined its previous media approach with an increased emphasis on community-initiated education and environmental interventions similar to the Karelia intervention. In a cohort followed for the duration of the intervention, the general population in the intervention area showed improvements in cholesterol levels, fitness and rates of obesity in the early stages of the intervention. However, by its end, the only differences between a comparison area that did not receive the intervention and the intervention areas were on measures of blood pressure and smoking (the latter being perhaps the most important risk behaviour due to its links with so many other diseases). On this criterion, the intervention could be considered a modest success. Unfortunately, on a series of cross-sectional studies comparing control and intervention areas over time, smoking and risk levels for CHD did not differ at any time during the course of the programme – questioning the success of the intervention.

A final US intervention to be considered here used virtually all the approaches so far considered in this and the previous chapter. The Minnesota Heart Health programme (Jacobs *et al.* 1986) used the mass media to promote awareness and to reinforce other educational approaches. In addition, the programme established large-scale screening programmes in primary care settings, as well as a number of other interventions including telephone support, classes in the community and worksite, self-help materials and home correspondence programmes. Environmental interventions included healthy food labelling (low fat, high fibre, etc.), establishing healthy menus in restaurants, smoke-free areas in public and work areas, and increased physical recreation facilities. Despite this complex and sophisticated approach, the programme had surprisingly little impact on health and health behaviour. Levels of smoking in the intervention areas, for example, differed little from those in the control areas, while the average adult weight in both control and intervention areas rose over the course of the study by seven pounds. Similar findings were found for another intervention known as the Community Intervention Trial for Smoking Cessation (COMMIT Research Group 1995), which did not change heavy smokers' behaviour and had only a marginal effect on light smokers.

At first glance, these data appear disappointing. Indeed, they provide little encouragement to suggest that the approaches they used should be continued. However, before they are dismissed, it is important to contextualise their findings. First, apart from the original Stanford study, they occurred at a time when there were significant changes in health behaviour and disease throughout the countries in which the studies were conducted. Rates of CHD fell by 20 per cent over the time they were running (Lefkowitz and Willerson 2001), and there was a general increase in health-promoting behaviour and a concomitant fall in health-damaging behaviour such as smoking. Why did these changes occur, and what implications do they have for interpretation of the results of the large-scale programmes considered above?

Perhaps the experiences of the five-year Heartbeat Wales programme (Tudor-Smith *et al.* 1998) sum up those of all the programmes so far considered. This programme combined health education via the media with health screening and environmental changes designed to promote behavioural change. These included some of the first food labelling (low fat, low sugar, etc.) in the UK, establishing exercise trails in local parks, no-smoking areas in restaurants, the promotion of low-alcohol beers in bars, and so on. It also used doctors and nurses as opinion leaders within their own communities to argue the case for adopting healthy lifestyles. Remember that the interventions in each programme were compared with 'control' areas – areas that did not receive the intervention. However, these were not true 'control' areas in the sense that they received no intervention at all. They received whatever local health education programmes were being conducted at the time. In addition, any innovations conducted by these major research programmes could not be guaranteed to remain only in the intervention area. In the case of Heartbeat Wales, for example, its 'control' area was in the northeast of England, which itself was subject to large-scale heart health programmes conducted in England at the same time as Heartbeat Wales. It was certainly not a 'no intervention' control. In addition, innovations such as food labelling, originally conducted just in Wales, spread through to England via supermarkets such as Tesco over the course of the programme. It is perhaps not surprising, therefore, that although levels of risk factors for CHD fell in Wales over the five-year period of Heartbeat Wales, they did not fall any further than levels in the control area. The research programme essentially compared the effectiveness of two fairly similar interventions. In addition, the majority of health promotion affecting the population with regard to CHD is now probably provided by the mass media as part of its general reporting – through reporting and discussion of healthy diets, issues such as men's health, and so on. It is therefore increasingly difficult for any health promotion programme to add further to this information and result in a meaningful reduction in risk for CHD.

Reducing risk of HIV infection

In contrast to interventions targeted at CHD, those targeted at sexual behaviour in relation to HIV and AIDS appear to have been more successful (Merzel and D'Afflitti 2003). Summing up some of the key data, the US Centers for Disease Control and Prevention (1996) reported significant increases in rates of condom use with main or casual partners in areas that received interventions across a number of US cities in comparison with control areas that had not. In addition, they reported significant increases in the rates of carrying condoms both among those at whom the intervention was targeted and among community members as a whole. In the intervention areas, an average 74 per cent increase in condom carrying was reported. In addition, among injecting drug users, although both intervention and control communities reported a similar rise in the use of bleach to clean their needles and other equipment, those who lived in the intervention areas who were not using bleach were more likely to be considering its use.

Many of these positive outcomes have been achieved using an approach called peer education. In this, opinion leaders and others from specific communities are involved in projects and form a key part of the programme.

The approach draws upon social learning cognitive theory (Bandura 1986: see Chapter 5 ☞), as these individuals provide particularly strong role models of change. Using people known and respected within a particular community makes their message salient and shows that appropriate change can be achieved. In one of the first studies using this approach, Kelly *et al.* (1992) tried to increase levels of safer sexual behaviour among patrons of gay bars in three small southern US cities. They identified and recruited key individuals in these bars and trained them to talk to patrons on issues of risk behaviour change and to distribute relevant health education literature. Following this intervention, levels of high-risk sexual behaviour fell by between 15 and 29 per cent. In a larger community trial conducted by the same team in eight US cities (Kelly *et al.* 1997), levels of unprotected anal intercourse fell from 32 to 20 per cent among men frequenting gay bars in the intervention group – in contrast to a 2 per cent rise among those in the control cities. Amirkhanian *et al.* (2005) found this approach translated to East Europe, examining its impact in Russia and Bulgaria, with similar results to those found in the US. In addition, more formal peer counselling, within clinics and involving a formal referral process has also been found to reduce sexually risky behaviour (McKirman *et al.* 2010).

Merzel and D'Afflitti (2003) noted that the HIV/AIDS prevention programmes have been markedly more successful than those targeted at CHD. Why this should be the case is unclear. Perhaps the most obvious difference between the interventions was the use of peers by those involved in HIV prevention – working with specific groups of people rather than trying to impose change from without. This may have been a crucial factor. Janz *et al.* (1996), for example, conducted a process evaluation of 37 AIDS prevention programmes and concluded that the use of trained community peers whose life circumstances closely resembled those of the target population was one of the most important factors influencing acceptance of health messages. Merzel and D'Afflitti speculated that a second reason for these differences may lie in the natural history of the diseases that each programme was trying to influence. Coronary heart disease develops over time, and there is no marked increase in risk as a result of particular behaviour – 'One bar of chocolate won't do me any harm'. It is therefore relatively easy to minimise risk and put off behaviour change. By contrast, the risks associated with unsafe sex

are highly salient. It can take relatively few (or just one) unsafe sexual encounters to contract HIV, and the consequences can be catastrophic – so the imperatives of change are much more salient than in CHD.

While the above studies allow comparison of interventions within the same culture, it should not be forgotten that AIDS is a global issue. Given the devastating impact of HIV/AIDS in Africa, interventions here and in other parts of the developing world are of paramount importance. Some approaches mirror those in other countries. Galavotti *et al.* (2001), for example, described a model known as the Modeling and Reinforcement to Combat HIV (MARCH), which was used in Africa and was modified from a pre-existing US media approach. The intervention model had two main components:

1. use of the media;
2. local influences of change.

It used the media to provide role models in 'entertainment that educates'. Interventions included testimonials from people living with HIV/AIDS, and peer education. These provided information on how to change, and model steps to change in sexual behaviour. Serial dramas on television were also used to educate, because they involved the viewer emotionally with the action on the screen, increased its salience and encouraged viewing. Interpersonal support involved the creation of small media materials such as flyers depicting role models progressing through stages of behaviour change for key risk behaviour, mobilisation of members of the affected community to distribute media materials and reinforce prevention messages, and the increased availability of condoms and bleacher kits for injecting drug users. In one study of effectiveness of the media elements of this approach (Vaughan *et al.* 2000), Radio Tanzania aired a radio soap opera called *Twende Na Wakati* ('Let's go with the times'). This soap played twice weekly for two years with the intention of promoting reproductive health and family planning, and preventing HIV infection. In comparison with an area of Tanzania that did not receive national radio at the time of the study, people who lived in areas where the radio programme was received reported greater commitment to family planning and higher uptake of safer sex practices. In addition, attendance at family planning clinics increased more in the intervention than control area.

Other approaches, both in Africa and other countries, have gone beyond using the media. Asamoah-Adu *et al.*

(1994) engaged prostitutes in Ghana to provide peer education and distribute condoms to their fellow prostitutes, resulting in a significant reduction in unsafe sex. Overall, the women who took part in the intervention were more likely to use a condom than they were prior to the intervention. In addition, three years after the end of the formal programme, women who maintained contact with the project staff were more likely than those who disengaged from them to have continued using them. Other, varied, interventions have included legal interventions including the mandatory use of condoms in brothels in Thailand, and economic measures enhancing empowerment of women in a number of African countries in order to reduce their economic dependence on men and increase their ability to negotiate decisions such as the use of contraceptives (see Ross *et al.* 2006).

RESEARCH FOCUS

Changing whole population's behaviour – or trying to

Rissel, C.E., New, C., Wen, L.M. *et al.* (2010). The effectiveness of community-based cycling promotion: findings from the *Cycling Connecting Communities* project in Sydney, Australia. *International Journal of Behavioral Nutrition and Physical Activity*, 7: 8. doi: 10.1186/1479-5868-7-8.

Regular cyclists typically have lower levels of mortality than non-cyclists, as well as lower levels of obesity and diabetes. Despite these benefits, only one per cent of journeys in Australia involve use of a bicycle. There has been little research into the effects of infrastructure and environmental changes in increasing population levels of cycling, but what studies have been done show they can increase levels of exercising. However, these studies have failed to determine whether these increases reflect increased cycling by existing cyclists or whether they attract new people to cycling. The *Cycling Connecting Communities (CCC)* project aimed to address both these issues.

Methods

The CCC project was supported through an advisory committee, including representatives of local government. The project involved increasing the visibility of existing cycle paths through production of a booklet addressing concerns of potential cyclists, a map of the routes, water bottles and reflective wrist bands. In addition, they established a number of free training cycling courses, ran hour-long presentations at local community or workplaces. A National Ride to Work Day included a highly marketed community breakfast. Four community rides were organised throughout the year, but with a particular focus during the New South Wales Bike Week. Councils and other organisations were encouraged to run these events in safe and supported environments. Free bicycle hire was established in lower socio-economic areas to allow local people to take part in the rides.

Evaluation

Hypotheses of the intervention were evaluated in two ways:

● *Telephone survey*: was there a significant increase in cycle path use for cycling or walking or in the percentage of cyclists who used the cycle paths in the previous month? Did the campaign result in an increase in awareness of the cycle paths? Did the intervention result in a significant increase in cycling commuting or recreational cycling? Measures were taken from 1,450 interviews at baseline (start of the study), and a lower number (86 per cent who agreed to be re-interviewed) 24 months later.

● *Bike count monitoring*: trafficorders (recording devices that monitored the number of cycles and their speed to cross a rubber tube laid over the pathway) were set up on the cycle paths and measured usage for 24 hours during each monitoring period. Data from these records were compared over the 24 months of the project.

Findings

There were some differences between the intervention area and a control area not receiving the intervention at baseline, with the intervention area having a higher level of bicycle ownership, a greater use of bicycle paths, and non-significant likelihood of having cycled more recently.

At follow-up, 25.8 per cent of respondents in the intervention group had cycled in the last year compared with 19.4 per cent of respondents in the comparison area. However, this difference was largely explained by the baseline differences between the two groups. More positively, significantly more (11.5 per cent) of these respondents described themselves as novice or beginner riders compared than those in the comparison area (1.4 per cent: χ^2 p = 0.013). In addition, significantly more participants in the intervention area (28.3 per cent) than in the comparison area (16.2 per cent) had used the bicycle paths (χ^2 p < 0.001), and more were likely to use the paths in the future (28.6 per cent) compared with the comparison area (17.8 per cent) (p < 0.001).

In the intervention area, those who had ridden in the past week reported a slight decrease in the mean minutes cycling for recreation or exercise (169.5 minutes to 152.1 minutes per week), but also reported a large increase in the mean minutes cycling for transport (76.9 minutes to 174.2 minutes per week). In the comparison area there was a much bigger drop in the mean minutes of recreational cycling (190.3 minutes to 121.3 minutes per week) and a large drop in mean minutes of cycling for transport (197.6 minutes to 71.7 minutes per week).

Discussion

The intervention achieved modest gains, although the authors note that the absence of an increase in cycling in the intervention area was disappointing. However, they also note that this stable level of cycling was at a time that levels of cycling were decreasing in other areas of Sydney, and followed a period of reduced bicycle use in the intervention area. They also concluded that increases in cycling (and in particular leisure cycling) were most likely to occur if there were more changes to the infrastructure and the paths could take people to places of interest – the lack of such areas was seen as a significant barrier to use of the paths in a pre-intervention survey. Nevertheless, with a relatively simple and cheap intervention it appears that use of cycle paths can be increased, in particular for commuting, and that new people can be persuaded to use cycling.

Worksite health promotion

One response to the problems encountered by the large-scale population interventions has been to target smaller, more easily accessible target groups, and the past few decades have seen the development of many impressive health promotion programmes in the workplace. The majority of these have been conducted in the USA, perhaps because enhancing the health of the workforce reduces the cost of workers' health insurance – often paid by the employer – and therefore benefits the company as well as the individuals in it. Worksite programmes have targeted a range of health-related behaviour, including diet, exercise, smoking and stress (generally focusing on risk factors for CHD and cancer). Because the worksite offers a wide possibility of interventions, these have utilised a variety of formats, some extremely innovative. Approaches include:

- screening for risk factors for disease;
- providing health education;
- provision of healthy options, such as healthy food in eating areas;
- providing economic incentives for risk behaviour change;
- manipulating social support to facilitate individual risk behaviour change;
- provision of no-smoking areas (and more recently smoking rooms) in the work environment.

Although a number of screening programmes similar to those described in the previous chapter have failed to be of benefit, Sorensen et al. (2010) achieved some success when they provided a bespoke four-month long education plus telephone counselling programme designed to reduce tobacco use and enhance weight management among blue-collar workers in 17 US ports. Before running the programme, they ran a number of focus groups to identify particular issues relevant to their work environment which they incorporated into the recruitment materials and intervention messages and, when possible, in the counselling calls. Of 542 workers invited to participate, half agreed to participate and received at least the first telephone call. By ten-month follow-up, the quit rate was significantly higher among those in the counselling programme than those who did not participate (39 versus 9 per cent). However, they did not make concomitant gains in the weight management programme.

Other more contextual programmes have met with mixed success. Perhaps the simplest intervention has simply been to provide information on the nutritional and calorific content of the food being provided in the dining areas. Unfortunately, there is no evidence that this simple approach is likely to be successful (Engbers et al. 2006). Accordingly, a number of studies have developed more complex interventions. The Well Works programme reported by Sorensen et al. (1998) recorded modest improvements in fat and fruit and vegetable consumption following a programme in which they combined health education programmes and provided healthy food options. The prevalence of smoking, a second target of the intervention, did not change. Similarly, the Health Works for Women programme (Campbell et al. 2002) targeted blue-collar women employed in small- to medium-sized workplaces. They provided information on healthy lifestyle behaviour and suggestions on how to change to it, using information tailored to individual participants' needs, determined by questionnaires completed before the intervention. The programme also worked at developing peer support from social networks among the workforce. Despite these complex interventions, they found no long-term changes in fat intake, smoking or physical activity levels among the intervention group. Their only gain was modest increases in self-reported fruit and vegetable intake.

Acknowledging the potential influence of the home as well as work on diet and health, the Treatwell programme (Sorensen et al. 1999) compared two interventions with a minimal intervention control group. An in-work programme involved classes and food demonstrations open to factory workers to teach them about healthy eating, and provided healthy options and food labelling in their worksite eating areas. A second approach combined the in-work programme with a family intervention designed to encourage healthy eating within the home. Total fruit and vegetable intake increased by 19 per cent in the worksite-plus-family group, 7 per cent in the worksite intervention group and 0 per cent in the control group.

The worksite provides more than an opportunity for the provision of health education and healthy food options. It gives the opportunity to exert more influence over behaviour than can be achieved elsewhere. One way that employers can influence their workforce is to provide financial incentives for change – to provide an external reward system for appropriate behavioural change rather than relying on employees' personal motivation. These have proved quite successful. Glasgow et al. (1993) offered monthly lottery prizes to people in a factory workforce who quit and maintained their no-smoking status for up to one year: 19 per cent of smokers in the workforce took part in the intervention, 20 per cent of whom remained abstinent by the end of the programme. By contrast, Hennrikus et al. (2002) found that financial incentives alone increased levels of entry into a smoking cessation programme, but successful quitting was only achieved if further support, such as telephone counselling was given. The worksite can also provide strong social support for those involved in behavioural change. Koffman et al. (1998), for example, compared a multi-component smoking cessation programme similar to that described in the previous chapter with a combination of this programme and financial incentives for abstinence and a team competition in which groups supported each other in the weeks and months following cessation. Six months after the initiation of the programme, 23 per cent of those in the multi-component group were abstinent, in comparison with 41 per cent of those who also received the incentive and competition programme. By the one-year follow-up, the equivalent figures were 30 and 37 per cent, respectively. Summarising the data so far, Leeks et al. (2010) found that this type of multi-component intervention, combining incentives with other approaches, including education, smoking cessation groups, and telephone support, to be more successful than incentives alone – and cost-effective for the companies that ran the projects as they reduced the costs of tobacco-related illnesses.

Just as preventing smoking in bars appears to reduce smoking-related harm, preventing people smoking at the worksite will necessarily reduce levels of secondary exposure to cigarette smoke among non-smokers. In addition, the discomfort associated with smoking outside buildings may provide a disincentive for many smokers, which may impact on smoking levels. Longo *et al.* (2001) certainly found such an effect. They studied the smoking habits of employees in hospitals that became smoke-free and those that continued to permit smoking over a period of three years, and found that twice as many smokers in the non-smoking hospitals quit smoking than did in the hospitals that continued to allow smoking.

School-based interventions

School brings to mind traditional education, and a number of health promotion initiatives have used this type of model. James *et al.* (2007), for example, reported short- but not long-term gains following a series of educational lessons targeted at health nutrition and weight control. It also provides a context in which health professionals can access students and act as agents of change. Pbert *et al.* (2006), for example, found that a smoking cessation intervention involving school nurses working with school students resulted in greater (self-report) abstinence rates than with no intervention. School also brings connotations of discipline and control – but whether attempts at control, however harsh, impact on health behaviours is questionable. Evans-Whipp *et al.* (2010), for example, found that school policies that incorporated a comprehensive smoking ban, harsh and remedial penalties for those caught smoking, as well as more positive strategies had no impact on smoking levels in schools in the USA and Australia.

At a higher, more positive and systemic level, simple one-target interventions may be effective, particularly if they target pupils early in school life. In the Netherlands, for example, the Schoolgruiten project gave 9–10-year-old pupils a free piece of fruit or ready-to-eat vegetables (tomatoes or baby carrots) twice a week in their mid-morning break (thereby not competing with the unhealthy food that is often preferred by children, often with the support of their parents, available at mealtimes; Moore *et al.* 2010). The aim of this regular exposure was to both directly increase consumption, but also to encourage a taste preference for fruit. A year after the inception of the project, children in the intervention group reported a higher vegetable intake – a finding not replicated in parental reports. By two-year follow-up (Tak *et al.* 2009), both children and parents reported higher levels of fruit intake than those in the control condition, although there were no differences in vegetable intake. Finally, the children in the intervention condition were more knowledgeable than those in the control condition.

A more complex systemic approach, advocated by the World Health Organization (1996) has met with more mixed results. The WHO Health-promoting schools initiative states that schools should prioritise the health of their pupils and develop an integrated approach to enhancing health, preventing uptake of unhealthy behaviour and educating pupils about health-promoting activities. This removes health education from simply being a taught part of the curriculum to something central to the aims of the school, around which the school activities and infrastructure are based. The framework around which schools involved in this sort of programme includes:

- school health policies – developing policies for school behaviour, such as a 'no helmet, no bike at school' policy for cycle safety or an Australian 'no hat, no play' policy (to avoid sunburn), as well as more traditional policies such as no smoking on school premises and no tolerance of bullying;
- establishing a safe, healthy physical and social environment;
- teaching health-related skills;
- providing adequate health services within the school;
- providing healthy food;
- school-site health-promotion programmes for staff;
- availability of school counselling or psychology programmes;
- a school physical education programme.

This approach has met with limited success, partly perhaps as a result of it being so complex and achieving only a mixed uptake and implementation in schools where it has been advocated. In a study evaluating the impact of this mixed uptake in Hong Kong, A. Lee *et al.* (2006) compared a number of schools according to measures of success in implementing a health-promoting schools policy, and found that those schools who had most successfully implemented the various elements of the healthy schools evidenced improvements in diet and antisocial behaviour relative to those who were less successful. Of particular note was that the scheme was more influential in primary rather than secondary schools. Less optimistically, M. Schofield, *et al.* (2003) established an intervention involving formal education addressing the health risks associated with smoking, information leaflets and bi-weekly school newsletters for parents, letters to tobacco retailers, smoke-free school policy development, encouragement of non-smoking parents, peers and teachers as role models, peer influence programmes and incentive programmes. When compared to schools that had not implemented these elements, no differences in smoking rates were found over a period of two years.

WHAT DO YOU THINK?

Effective sex education provides a powerful influence on sexual behaviour. Countries where sex education is central to the curriculum, starts early and focuses on the social as well as physical aspects of sexual relations have lower unwanted pregnancy rates than countries where the sex education is less central and starts later in the academic curriculum. In the UK, sex education is not compulsory, occurs late in the curriculum and is often taught in one or two lessons independently of the wider curriculum by teachers lacking in relevant expertise. The UK has one of the highest teenage pregnancy rates in Europe. Are these two factors related? Or is there a third (or fourth) hidden factor that explains this association? How would you teach sex education?

Out-of-school activities

One alternative to school-based programmes is provided by a programme known as Smokebusters. This is a community – deliberately not school-based – intervention aimed at preventing young people smoking. It involves a series of clubs throughout Europe, each of which emphasises the positive aspects of non-smoking rather than the negative aspects of smoking. They are 'fun clubs', where non-smoking is portrayed as the norm and smokers as the minority. The intention is to develop strong social peer groups of non-smokers, intended to assist in self-empowerment and development of rejection skills. Events established by the clubs include discos and outdoor events, and they often provide discount schemes for local shops. Being a non-smoker is often rewarded by free membership of the club. The programme is considered to be more attractive to many smokers, who may reject the authoritarian context of school-based programmes. Bruce and van Teijlingen (1999) summarised the reports of 36 Smokebuster clubs throughout the UK. As community-based programmes with no particular research remit, only 3 had attempted to measure long-term effects of the club on knowledge, attitudes and smoking behaviour. One such study evaluated the effects of a North Yorkshire-based programme. They measured smoking levels, knowledge and attitudes in 866 primary and secondary schoolchildren – only half of whom had subsequent access to the club – before and one year after a local Smokebusters club had been established. Over this time, levels of regular smoking rose in both groups, but less so in the group of young people who had access to the club: an 11 per cent versus 3 per cent rise in smoking prevalence. Similar gains were reported by the two other studies to report smoking prevalence levels (Bruce and van Teijlingen 1999). More disappointingly, intentions to smoke in the future did not differ consistently across the studies: the intervention may have delayed rather than prevented smoking – although some have argued that this is a significant benefit.

Peer education

One final approach to health education in schools involves peer education. As in the social interventions to reduce the spread of HIV described earlier in the chapter, this typically involves training influential pupils in a school about a particular health issue such as smoking, alcohol consumption or HIV education and encouraging them to educate their peers about the issues, hopefully in a way that encourages healthy behaviour. The methods used vary considerably. They may involve teaching whole classes, informal tutoring in unstructured settings, or one-to-one discussion and counselling. In one study of this type, Lotrean *et al.* (2010) examined the impact of involving peer-led discussions combined with teaching cigarette refusal skills in their smoking prevention programme targeted at 13–14-year-old Romanian school pupils. Compared to a control group who did not receive the intervention, the percentage of pupils to take up smoking was halved up to nine months following the intervention (4.5 versus 9.5 per cent).

A much more informal approach to peer education in the context of smoking was reported by Campbell *et al.* (2008). In their study, pupils aged 12–13 years were asked to identify particularly influential people within their social group. From this, the intervention team identified a group of people who were particularly influential among the target population – some of whom may not have been the choice of their form teachers! Volunteers from this group were then taken to a hotel for two days, where they were given training in their peer education role. The training gave them information about short-term risks to young people of smoking, and the health, environmental, and economic benefits of remaining smoke-free. It also used role-play and small group work to enhance their communication skills, including verbal and non-verbal communication skills and conflict resolution. It also aimed to enhance students' personal development, including their confidence and self-esteem, empathy and sensitivity to others, and assertiveness. Following their training days, the peer educators were then asked to talk to their friends and anyone else they felt appropriate about smoking, sharing information and advice over a period of 10 weeks. This model of uncontrolled dissemination contrasts strongly with some of the more formal methods adopted by other programmes. In their evaluation of the programme, Campbell *et al.* reported that the odds of becoming a smoker (at this age, they were trying to prevent or delay the uptake of smoking more than smoking cessation) were significantly higher among a control group who did not receive the intervention at one- and two-year follow-up, both among all pupils, and a subgroup of pupils they considered particularly at risk of taking up smoking. However, these differences may reflect baseline differences. At baseline, 6.59 per cent of the control group had smoked in the previous week, compared to 4.78 per cent of the intervention group. The corresponding figures immediately after the intervention were 8.48 versus 6.6 per cent respectively, and at one-year follow-up were 15.13 and 12.49 per cent. A subsequent unpublished study of this approach on alcohol consumption, unfortunately, failed to have any positive impact.

In the field of HIV/AIDS prevention, peer-led education appears to have a number of benefits over teacher-led education. Perhaps the strongest is that peer-led education is more acceptable to pupils than teacher-led teaching, and may result in greater gains in knowledge and attitude change. In a study of Chinese school pupils, for example,

Ye *et al.* (2009) reported no differences in knowledge between teacher-led and peer-led programmes, but those in the peer-led programme reported more positive attitudes towards those people with HIV/AIDS and stronger intentions to use a condom. In Canada, Caron *et al.* (2004) found significantly greater changes on a number of attitudinal and efficacy measures following a peer-led HIV educational programme than one led by teachers, but no significant differences in behaviour whether this was to postpone sex or use a condom. Similar findings were reported by Borgia *et al.* (2005) in Italy, who found modest differences in knowledge (favouring peer education) and no differences in sexual behaviour when comparing the outcomes of peer- and teacher-led educational programmes. Some reports of behavioural as well as attitudinal change have been found, although both were (perhaps inevitably) based on self-report. A Chinese research programme followed pupils for up to one year following either a teacher- or peer-led programme, and found that self-report condom use was higher among the peer-led group (Cai *et al.* 2008), while in South Africa, Visser (2007) found a peer-led programme resulted in modest delays in sexual activity, but no difference in condom use when compared to no treatment. In sum, peer-led teaching consistently leads to high levels of acceptability, more attitudinal change than when provided by teachers, but only inconsistent behavioural change.

Using the Web

The internet provides a simple means of communicating with vast numbers of individuals, and has been eagerly appropriated by many of those involved in health promotion. The early stages of this research and the difficulties in measuring outcomes and conducting randomised controlled trials in this research context means that many papers simply report usage rather than outcomes. McNeill *et al.* (2007), for example, gave access to a site giving nutritional information to 52 residents of a multi-ethnic working class area for six weeks. More than half of the participants owned a computer, and 75 per cent of them logged on to the website at least once. Those who visited the site averaged four visits and viewed an average of 25 pages on each occasion. Usage declined over the study period, but increased following email reminders. Nearly three-quarters of the participants viewed information on goal setting, 72 per cent viewed information on dietary tracking, and 56 per cent searched for main course recipes.

In a more formal evaluation of outcomes as well as usage, Swartz *et al.* (2006) conducted a randomised controlled trial of the use of an internet-based smoking cessation programme. Participants were engaged from a variety of workplaces and were randomly assigned to receive the programme either immediately or after a period of 90 days. The intervention involved a video-based internet programme that presented current strategies for smoking cessation and motivational materials tailored to the user's ethnicity, sex and age. At follow-up, the cessation rate at 90 days was 24 per cent for the treatment group and 8 per cent for the control group. Winett *et al.* (2007) combined an internet programme designed to improve nutrition and exercise levels alone or in combination with 'live' support. The programme was made available to overweight individuals in a variety of churches. They found a hierarchical effect with the internet condition resulting in significant improvements in reported diet compared to a no-treatment control, but with only the internet plus support resulting in changes in both exercise and diet.

It can be easy for modern health promoters to be attracted by the technology of the internet and ignore more traditional approaches. But does this result in better outcomes? Cook *et al.* (2007) compared the effectiveness of a web- and paper-based intervention designed to improve dietary practices, reduce stress and increase physical activity. The web-based programme was more effective than print materials in producing improvements in the areas of diet and nutrition but was no more effective in reducing stress or increasing physical activity. Marshall *et al.* (2003) found no difference in the effectiveness of written or internet-based programmes designed to increase physical activity, while Marks *et al.* (2006) found that printed materials were more effective than the internet in changing exercise levels. It should be noted, however, that none of these programmes utilised the Web and its potential interactivity to its maximum. There was no interaction between the users and the programme and no use of prompts or other strategies that can be used with modern multimedia approaches. Simply emailing reminders to action – easy via the internet but more difficult and expensive to send its paper equivalent – may be sufficient to prompt action among its recipients (Plotnikoff *et al.* 2005).

SUMMARY

This chapter has examined a number of issues related to interventions targeted at improving the health of whole populations. The key targets examined have been those aiming to change incremental risk of disease, in this case CHD, and behaviour that may result in diseases after being enacted on one occasion – those related to safer sex and HIV infection.

The prime method of influence has been use of the media. Three methods of optimising its use were considered:

1. refining communication to maximise their influence on attitudes through the use of differing channels depending on recipients' motivation to consider the information presented;

2. the use of fear messages – and how these may be optimised not only by raising health anxiety but also by providing an easy way of reducing it;

3. more specific targeting of interventions – targeting at groups within society, categorised by such

indices as behaviour, social class and prevailing attitudes.

The environment may also be manipulated to make health behaviour more salient, to make it easier to engage in and to reward those who engage in it. In particular, environmental manipulations can:

● provide cues to action – or remove cues to unhealthy behaviour;

● enable health behaviour by minimising the costs and barriers associated with it;

● increase the costs of engaging in health-damaging behaviour.

Interventions using these various principles (and some considered in the previous chapter) have proved reasonably successful at changing behaviour in large and more defined populations such as those in worksites or schools.

Early interventions targeted at changing CHD-related behaviour proved successful, although their very success may have reduced the apparent intervention-specific success of subsequent interventions. By contrast, interventions targeted at safer sex behaviour appear to have been particularly successful.

Interventions in the worksite have had mixed success, although the ability of the worksite to offer financial rewards and to establish peer support makes it a useful arena for influencing public health. Innovative attempts to change working practice may also reduce stress in the workforce.

Schools appear to be the key to establishing health behaviour. 'Healthy schools' appear to benefit the health of children – if their implementation is not half-hearted. Peer education may also have some benefits, although many children may find it difficult to act as health educators, reducing the effectiveness of the approach.

Finally, the internet provides a key medium for future health-promotion programmes, but probably needs to be interactive and engaging to be maximally useful.

Further reading

Acheson, D. (1998). *Independent Inquiry into Inequalities in Health*. Report. London: HMSO.

Looks at some alternative approaches to health promotion, particularly in relation to economic inequalities.

www.dh.gov.uk/en/Publicationsandstatistics/Publications/PublicationsPolicyAndGuidance/DH_4094550

This link takes you to a 'free to download' series of links in which you can access the UK government's document called 'Choosing health: making healthy choices easier', which examines how health and social policy can influence our lifestyles and health, making healthy behaviours easy to adopt.

Merzel, C. and D'Afflitti, J. (2003). Reconsidering community-based health promotion: promise, performance, and potential. *American Journal of Public Health*, 93: 557–74.

An excellent, readable account of the pros and cons of community-based interventions.

Sangani, P., Rutherford, G., Wilkinson, D. (2004). Population-based interventions for reducing sexually transmitted infections, including HIV infection. *Cochrane Database of Systematic Reviews*, CD001220. doi: 10.1002/14651858. CD001220.

As with all Cochrane reviews it is thorough.

Naidoo, J. and Wills, J. (2000). *Health Promotion: Foundations for Practice*. London: Bailliere Tindall.

A good review of the practice of health promotion from theoretical and practitioner perspective.

White, J. and Bero, L.A. (2004). Public health under attack: the American Stop Smoking Intervention Study (ASSIST) and the tobacco industry. *American Journal of Public Health*, 94: 240–50.

A reminder that the health promotion agenda is not adopted by all.

www.kingsfund.org.uk/health_topics/public_health.html

The King's Fund is a UK 'think tank' that considers health policy in a number of arenas. This link takes you to their public health web page, where there is a wealth of information about community and environmental approaches to health promotion.

Katz, D.L., O'Connell, M., Yeh, M.C. *et al.* Task Force on Community Preventive Services (2005). Public health strategies for preventing and controlling overweight and obesity in school and worksite settings: a report on recommendations of the Task Force on Community Preventive Services. *Morbidity and Mortality Weekly Report. Recommendations and Reports*, 54: 1–12.

A thorough review of interventions in both worksite and school, freely available on the Web.

van den Berg, M.H., Schoones, J.W. and Vliet Vlieland, T.P. (2007). Internet-based physical activity interventions: a systematic review of the literature. *Journal of Medical Internet Research*, 9: e26.

A good review of internet health-promotion programmes designed to increase exercise levels.

Norman, G.J., Zabinski, M.F., Adams, M.A., *et al.* (2007). A review of eHealth interventions for physical activity and dietary behaviour change. *American Journal of Preventive Medicine*, 33: 336–45.

This one also tackles dietary change.

 www.pearsoned.co.uk/morrison for additional resources to help you with your study, including multiple choice questions, weblinks and flashcards.

Part II
Becoming ill

Chapter 8
The body in health and illness

Learning outcomes

In this chapter, we outline the physiology and pathology underpinning a number of chronic diseases, as well as the experiences of people who develop them. This is intended to support the chapters considering the impact of disease on the individual (Chapters 14 and 16) and their family (Chapter 15) as well as interventions designed to help people cope more effectively with the symptoms and psychological sequelae of chronic illness (Chapter 17). Readers who already have an understanding of the nature of the illnesses described here may choose to skip the chapter. By the end of it, you should have an understanding of:

- the basic anatomy and function of:
  - specific parts of the brain
  - the autonomic nervous system
- the immune system and key disorders that can result from immune dysfunction
- the basic anatomy, physiology and disorders of:
  - the digestive system
  - the cardiovascular system
  - the respiratory system
- the experiences of people with a number of chronic diseases

Bad health costs money!

At any one time in the USA, an astonishing 17 per cent of individuals within the country will have some type of lung disease. A further four per cent will have some form of cancer or diabetes, and nearly 7 per cent will have heart disease. Together, these chronic diseases cost the nation around $1.5 trillion each year as a consequence of treatment costs and lost productivity. In the UK, over two million people either have or have recovered from cancer, and a further 3 per cent of the population develops cancer each year. Over 6 per cent of men and 4 per cent of women have heart disease – and treating these individuals costs around £3.5 billion a year, with additional economic costs due to absence from work, caring for others with the disease, and so on adding a further cost of £3.1 billion to the economy. Clearly, chronic diseases are highly prevalent and extremely costly to the nation. Oh, and the personal experience of long-term illness can be emotionally and physically 'costly' as well.

Chapter outline

This chapter provides an introduction to the basic anatomy and physiology of key organ systems within the body. Each section considers the basic anatomy and physiology of each system, and describes some of the disease processes, and their treatment, that may occur within them. These may be diseases that are associated with particular risk behaviours or other psychological processes – usually stress. Others include diseases that present individuals with particular challenges. Later chapters consider how people can prevent or cope with these diseases, and in some cases the psychological interventions that may help them do this. As well as being a chapter to read on its own, it also forms a reference providing basic information on the illnesses and treatments we refer to in other chapters of the book.

We start by examining two systems that influence the whole body:

1. the brain and autonomic nervous system
2. the immune system.

We then go on to examine three other organ systems:

1. the digestive system
2. the cardiovascular system
3. the respiratory system.

The behavioural anatomy of the brain

The brain is an intricately patterned complex of nerve cell bodies. It is divided into four anatomical areas (see Figures 8.1 and 8.2):

1. *Hindbrain*: contains the parts of the brain necessary for life – the medulla oblongata, which controls blood pressure, heart rate and respiration; the reticular formation, which controls alertness and wakefulness; and the pons and cerebellum, which integrate muscular and positional information.

2. *Midbrain*: contains part of the reticular system and both sensory and motor correlation centres, which integrate reflex and automatic responses involving the visual and auditory systems and are involved in the integration of muscle movements.

3. *Forebrain*: contains key structures that influence mood and behaviour, including:

   ● *Thalamus*: links the basic functions of the hindbrain and midbrain with the higher centres of processing, the cerebral cortex. Regulates attention and contributes to memory functions. The portion that enters the limbic system (see below) is involved in the experience of emotions.

   ● *Hypothalamus*: regulates appetite, sexual arousal and thirst. Also appears to have some control over emotions.

   ● *Limbic system*: (Figure 8.3) a series of structures including a linked group of brain areas known as the Circuit of Papez (the hippocampus–fornix– mammillary bodies–thalamus–cingulate cortex–

hippocampus). The hippocampus–fornix–mammillary bodies circuit is involved in memory. The hippocampus is one site of interaction between the perceptual and memory systems. A further part of the system, known as the amygdala, links sensory information to emotionally relevant behaviour, particularly responses to fear and anger.

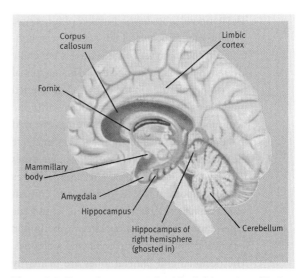

Figure 8.3 The major components of the limbic system. All of the left hemisphere apart from the limbic system has been removed

Source: Carlson, N. (2005), © 2005, reproduced by permission of Pearson Education, Inc.

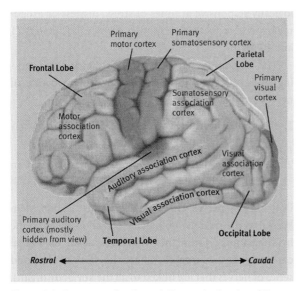

Figure 8.1 A cross-section through the cerebral cortex of the human brain

Source: Carlson, N. (2005), © 2005, reproduced by permission of Pearson Education, Inc.

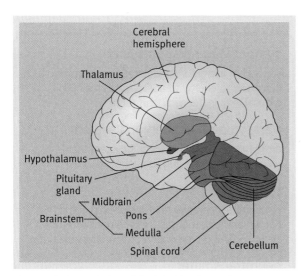

Figure 8.2 A lateral view of the left side of a semi-transparent human brain with the brainstem 'ghosted' in

Source: Carlson, N. (2005), © 2005, reproduced by permission of Pearson Education, Inc.

It has been called the 'emotional computer' because of its role in coordinating the process that begins with the evaluation of sensory information for significance (i.e. threat) and then controls the resulting behavioural and autonomic responses (see below).

4. *Cerebrum*: the most recently evolved part of the brain includes:
   - *Basal ganglia*: responsible for complex motor coordination.
   - *Cortex*: the convoluted outer layer of grey matter comprising nerve cell bodies and their synaptic connections. It is divided into two functional hemispheres linked by the corpus callosum, a series of interconnecting neural fibres, at its base and is divided into four lobes: frontal, temporal, occipital and parietal:
     ○ The frontal lobe has an 'executive' function, as it coordinates a number of complex processes, including speech, motor coordination and behavioural planning. The frontal lobes also influence motivation. The pre-frontal lobes are connected to the limbic system via the thalamus and motor system within the cortex. Links between the pre-frontal cortex and the limbic system are activated during rewarding behaviour.

○ The temporal lobes have a number of functions. In right-handed people, at the risk of oversimplification, the main language centre is generally located in the left hemisphere, and visuo-spatial processing is located in the right. In left-handed individuals, there is less localisation within the hemispheres. The temporal lobes are also involved in the systems of smell and hearing. They integrate the visual experience with those of the other senses to make meaningful wholes. The temporal lobes have an important role in memory and contain systems that preserve the record of conscious experience. Finally, they connect to the limbic system and link emotions to events and memories.

○ The occipital and parietal lobes are primarily involved in the integration of sensory information. The occipital lobe is primarily involved in visual perception. Links to the cortex permit interpretation of visual stimuli.

The autonomic nervous system

The autonomic nervous system is responsible for control over levels of activity in key organs and organ systems in the body. Many organs have some degree of control over their functioning. The heart, for example, has an intrinsic rhythm of 110 beats per minute. However, this level of activity may not be appropriate at all times. The heart may have to beat more at times of exercise, less at times of rest. The autonomic nervous system overrides local control to provide this higher level of coordinated control across most of the bodily systems in response to the varying demands being placed on the body. Its activity is controlled by a number of brain areas, the most important of which is the hypothalamus. The hypothalamus receives information about the demands being placed on the body from a variety of sources, including:

● information about skin temperature from the reticular formation in the brainstem;

● information about light and darkness from the optic nerves;

● receptors in the hypothalamus itself provide information about the ion balance and temperature of the blood.

The hypothalamus also has links to the cortex and limbic systems of the brain, which are involved in the processing of cognitive and emotional demands. This allows the autonomic system to respond to psychological factors as well as physical demands being placed on the body. Accordingly, the autonomic nervous system can initiate sweating in high temperatures, increase blood pressure and heart rate during exercise, and also make us physiologically responsive at times of stress, distress or excitement (we discuss these responses further in Chapters 11 and 13 ☛).

The autonomic nervous system controls these varying levels of activity through two opposing networks of nerves (see Figure 8.4):

1. the **sympathetic nervous system**: involved in activation and arousal – the fight–flight response;

2. the **parasympathetic nervous system**: involved in relaxation – the rest–recover response.

Both sets of nerves arise in an area in the brainstem known as the medulla oblongata (which is linked to the hypothalamus). From this, they pass down the spinal cord to various **synapses**, where they link to a second series of nerves that are linked to all the key body organs, including the heart, arteries and muscles (Figure 8.4). For the sympathetic arm, the **neurotransmitter** involved at the synapse between the spinal cord nerves and the nerve to the target organ is acetylcholine. Activity at the synapse between this second nerve and the end

---

sympathetic nervous system
the part of the autonomic nervous system involved in mobilising energy to activate and maintain arousal (e.g. increased heart rate).

parasympathetic nervous system
arm of the autonomic nervous system that is responsible for rest and recuperation.

synapse
junction between two neurons or between a neuron and target organ. Nerve impulses cross a synapse through the action of neurotransmitters.

neurotransmitter
a chemical messenger (e.g. adrenaline, acetylcholine) used to communicate between neurons and other neurons and other types of cell.

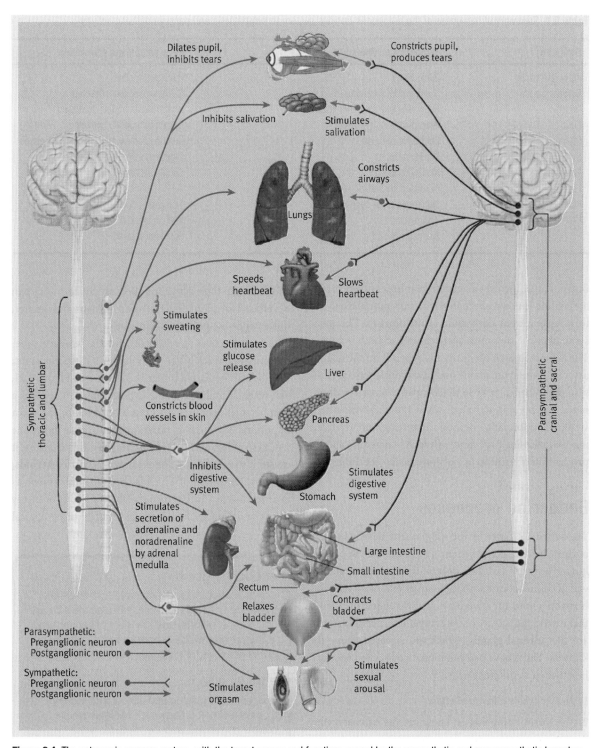

Figure 8.4 The autonomic nervous system, with the target organs and functions served by the sympathetic and parasympathetic branches

Source: Carlson, N. (2005), © 2005, reproduced by permission of Pearson Education, Inc.

Table 8.1 Summary of responses of the autonomic nervous system to sympathetic and parasympathetic activity

Structure	Sympathetic stimulation	Parasympathetic stimulation
Iris (eye muscle)	Pupil dilation	Pupil constriction
Salivary glands	Saliva production reduced	Saliva production increased
Heart	Heart rate and force increased	Heart rate and force decreased
Lung	Bronchial muscle relaxed	Bronchial muscle contracted
Stomach	Peristalsis reduced	Gastric juice secreted; motility increased
Small intestine	Motility reduced	Digestion increased
Large intestine	Motility reduced	Secretions and motility increased
Liver	Increased conversion of glycogen to glucose	
Kidney	Decreased urine secretion	Increased urine secretion
Bladder	Wall relaxed	Wall contracted
	Sphincter closed	Sphincter relaxed

organ mainly involves a neurotransmitter known as nor-adrenaline (known alternatively as norepinephrine) and to a lesser extent adrenaline (epinephrine). The para-sympathetic system uses acetylcholine at both synapses. The activity in each of the organs depends on the relative activity in the sympathetic and parasympathetic nervous systems. When activity in the sympathetic system domi-nates, the body is activated: when the parasympathetic system is dominant, the body is resting and relatively inactive, allowing basic functions such as digestion and the production of urine to occur more easily (see Table 8.1).

Endocrine processes

The activity initiated by the sympathetic nervous system is short-lived. A second system is therefore used to provide longer-term arousal. This system uses **endocrine glands**, which communicate with their target organs by releasing hormones into the bloodstream. The endocrine glands that extend the activity of the sympathetic nervous system are the **adrenal glands**, which are situated above the kidneys. These have two functional areas, each of which is activated in different ways:

1. the centre or *adrenal medulla*;

2. the surrounding tissues, known as the *adrenal cortex*.

The adrenal medulla is innervated by the sympathetic nervous system. Activity in this system stimulates the adrenal medulla to release the hormonal equivalent of the neurotransmitter noradrenaline into the bloodstream, in which it is transported to the organs in the body. Receptors in the target organs respond to the hormone

and maintain their activation. Because the hormone can be released for a longer period than the neurotransmitter, this extends the period of activation.

A second activating system involves the pituitary gland, the activity of which is also controlled by the hypothalamus. This lies immediately under the brain (see Figure 8.2), and when stimulated by the hypothalamus, it releases a number of hormones into the bloodstream, the most important of which is adrenocorticotrophic hormone (ACTH). When the ACTH reaches the adrenal cortex, it causes it to release hormones known as **corticosteroids**, the most important of which is **cortisol** – also known as hydrocortisone. Cortisol increases the availability of energy stores and fats to fuel periods of high physiological

---

endocrine glands

glands that produce and secrete hormones into the blood or lymph systems. Includes the pituitary and adrenal glands, and the islets of Langerhans in the pancreas. These hormones may affect one organ or tissue, or the entire body.

adrenal glands

endocrine glands, located above each kidney. Comprises the cortex, which secretes several steroid hormones, and the medulla, which secretes noradrenaline.

corticosteroids

powerful anti-inflammatory hormones (including cortisol) made naturally in the body or synthetically for use as drugs.

activity. It also inhibits inflammation of damaged tissue. We discuss the sympathetic nervous system again in Chapter 11 ☞.

The immune system

Components of the immune system

The immune system is very sophisticated and complex, and is designed to help the body to resist disease. It provides a variety of protective mechanisms that respond to attacks from bacteria, viruses, infectious diseases and other sources from outside the body – collectively known as **pathogens** or antigens. In this section, we first identify and briefly describe the role of different elements of the immune system. We then go on to look at the links between them and how they combine to combat invading pathogens and the development of cancers.

A number of organs and chemicals form the front line of the system. These include:

● *Physical barriers*: provided by the skin.

● *Mechanical barriers*: cilia (small hairs in the lining of the lungs) propel pathogens out of the lungs and respiratory tract – coughs and sneezes achieve the same goal more dramatically. Tears, saliva and urine also push pathogens out of the body.

● *Chemical barriers*: acid from the stomach provides an obvious chemical barrier against pathogens. Sebum, which coats body hairs, inhibits the growth of bacteria and fungi on the skin. Saliva, tears, sweat and nasal secretions contain lysozyme, which destroys bacteria. Saliva and the walls of the gastrointestinal tract also contain an **antibody** known as immunoglobulin A (IgA).

● *'Harmless pathogens'*: a variety of bacteria live within the body and have no harmful effects on us. However, they defend their territory and can destroy other bacteria that invade it.

● *Lymph nodes*: secondary organs at or near possible points of entry for pathogens. This system includes the tonsils, Peyer's patches in the intestines, and the appendix. They have high levels of **lymphocytes** (see below), ready to attack any invading pathogens.

As well as these relatively static defences against attack, there are a number of cells that circulate around the body. This can be through the circulatory system or a parallel system known as the lymphatic system. This carries a fluid called lymph and transports cells important to the destruction of antigens to the sites of cellular damage and the waste products of this destruction away from them.

Two groups of cells in the circulatory and lymphatic systems provide protection against a variety of pathogens. **Phagocytes** (sometimes called white blood cells) circulate within the circulatory system. They are created in the bone marrow and attract, adhere to and then engulf and destroy antigens – a process known as phagocytosis. The immune system has a number of phagocytes, including:

● *Neutrophils* have a short life of a few hours to days. They provide the major defence against bacteria and the initial fight against infection by engulfing and digesting them. They are followed by macrophages about three to four hours later.

---

cortisol

a stress hormone that increases the availability of energy stores and fats to fuel periods of high physiological activity. It also inhibits inflammation of damaged tissue.

pathogens

a collective name for a variety of challenges to our health and immune system, including bacteria and viruses.

antibodies

immunoglobulins produced in response to an antigen.

lymphocyte

a type of white blood cell. Lymphocytes have a number of roles in the immune system, including the production of antibodies and other substances that fight infection and disease. Includes T and B cells.

phagocyte

an immune system cell that can surround and kill micro-organisms and remove dead cells. Phagocytes include macrophages.

● *Macrophages* are long-lived and are best at attacking dead cells and pathogens capable of living within cells. Once a macrophage destroys a cell, it places some of its own proteins on its surface. This allows other immune cells to identify cells as invaders and to attack them.

A second group of cells known as lymphocytes circulate in the blood (where they are also known as white blood cells) and lymph system. These include **T cells** and **B cells**:

● *Cytotoxic T cells* bind on to antigens, including virus-infected cells and tumour cells. They form pores in the target cell's plasma membrane, allowing ions and water to flow into the target cell, making it expand, then collapse and die.

● *Helper T cells* trigger or increase an immune response. They identify and bind to antigens, then release chemicals that stimulate the proliferation of cytotoxic T and plasma B cells (see below). Helper T cells are also known as **CD4+ cells** because of their chemical structure.

● *Plasma B cells* destroy antigens by binding to them and making them easier targets for phagocytes. They attack antigens in the blood system before they enter body cells.

● *Memory B cells* live indefinitely in the blood and lymphatic systems. They result from an initial attack by a novel antigen. In their initial response to such attacks, memory B cells 'learn' the chemical nature of such antigens and are able to deal with them more effectively should they encounter them again.

A third group of attacking cells are **natural killer (NK) cells**, which move in the blood and attack cancer cells and virus-infected body cells.

Central nervous system links with the immune system

The immune system is intimately linked to the central nervous system. The influence of these two interacting systems affects the development and activity of the phagocytes, and the B, T and NK cells. Lymphocytes also have adrenal and cortisol receptors, which are affected by hormones from both the adrenal cortex and medulla (see above). The influence of these neurotransmitters and hormones is complex. Increases of adrenaline in response

to short-term stress can stimulate the spleen to release phagocytes into the bloodstream and increase NK cell counts, but decrease the number of T cells. Cortisol release decreases the production of helper T cells and ingestion of cells by macrophages. These issues are complex and differ over the time course of stress and the nature of the stressor. However, it is generally recognised that chronic stress significantly impairs the effectiveness of the immune system, leaving us less able to ward off infection (see Chapter 11 ☛ for further discussion of this issue).

Immune dysfunction

Human immunodeficiency virus infection

The human immunodeficiency virus (HIV) is the cause of a potentially fatal condition known as Acquired ImmunoDeficiency Syndrome (AIDS). The virus belongs to a subgroup of viruses known as 'slow viruses', which have a long interval between initial infection and the onset of serious symptoms – potentially up to 10 years and beyond. The virus affects the T helper (CD4+) cells. In response to a virus or other pathogens, healthy CD4+ cells replicate and send messages to B and T cells to also replicate and attack the pathogen. When infected with HIV, CD4+ cells still replicate in response to pathogens, but the replicated CD4+ cells are infected with the virus, are unable to activate their target B and T cells,

---

T cell

a cell that recognises antigens on the surface of a virus-infected cell, binds to that cell and destroys it.

B cell

a form of lymphocyte involved in destruction of antigens. Memory B cells provide long-term immunity against previously encountered pathogens.

CD4+ cells

otherwise known as helper T cells, these are involved in the proliferation of cytotoxic T cells as part of the immune response. HIV infection impairs their ability to provide this function.

natural killer (NK) cells

cells that move in the blood and attack cancer cells and virus-infected body cells.

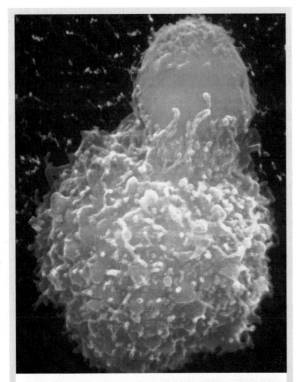

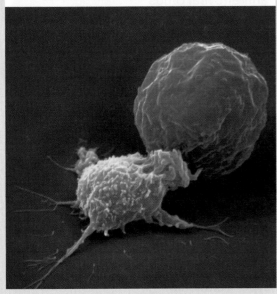

Plates 8.1 and 8.2 Here we see two cells, a virus and cancer cell, being attacked and either engulfed by B cells (8.1) or rendered inert by NK cells (8.2)

Source: Dr Andrejs Liepins/Science Photo Library (8.1) and Eye of Science/Science Photo Library (8.2).

and eventually die. Initially, the non-infected CD4+ cells still provide an effective response against pathogens. However, over time, proliferation of infected CD4+ cells in response to pathogens results in an increase in infected CD4+ cells in circulation. These will eventually die, but before doing so may bind with healthy CD4+ cells, resulting in their death. In addition, the immune system may recognise the virus-laden cells as invasive, and begin to attack its own CD4+ cells. Together, these processes result in a gradual reduction in the number of circulating CD4+ cells, reducing the immune system's ability to defend itself effectively against viruses, bacteria and some cancers. When the CD4+ cell count falls below $500/mm^3$, approximately half the immune system reserve has been destroyed. At this point minor infection such as cold sores and fungal infections begin to appear. Once the CD4+ cell count falls below $200/mm^3$, life-threatening opportunistic infections and cancers typically occur. AIDS, the end point of HIV disease, occurs when the CD4+ cell count is less than $200/mm^3$ or when the individual develops potentially life-threatening infections such as pneumonia or cancers such as **Kaposi's sarcoma**.

Treatment for HIV infection involves three classes of drugs:

- *Reverse transcriptase inhibitors*: HIV uses reverse transcriptase to copy its genetic material and generate new viruses. Reverse transcriptase inhibitors disrupt the process and thereby suppress its growth.

- *Protease inhibitors*: these interfere with the protease enzyme that HIV uses to produce infectious viral particles.

- *Fusion inhibitors*: these interfere with the virus's ability to fuse with the cellular membrane of other CD4+ cells, blocking entry into the host cell.

These drugs do not cure HIV infection or AIDS. They can suppress the virus, even to undetectable levels, but are unable to completely eliminate HIV from the body. Accordingly, infected individuals still need to

> **Kaposi's sarcoma**
> a malignant tumour of the connective tissue, often associated with AIDS. The tumours consist of bluish-red or purple lesions on the skin. They often appear first on the feet or ankles, thighs, arms, hands and face.

take **antiretroviral drugs**. In addition, as HIV replicates itself, different strains of the virus emerge, some of which are resistant to antiretroviral drugs. For this reason, treatment guidelines state that HIV-positive individuals take a combination of antiretroviral drugs known as Highly Active Antiretroviral Therapy (HAART or ART). This strategy, which typically combines two different classes of antiretroviral drugs, has been shown to effectively suppress the virus when used appropriately. Unfortunately, strict adherence to the HAART regimen presents a significant challenge to the individual taking the medication, both in terms of taking the medication at the correct time and the side-effects that they may experience (see Chapters 10 and 17 ☞).

Autoimmune conditions

The immune system is able to identify cells that are part of the body ('self') and those that are 'non-self': antigens, developing cancers, and so on. On occasion, this process breaks down and the immune system treats cells within the body as non-self and begins to attack them. This can result in a number of **autoimmune conditions**, including diabetes, rheumatoid arthritis and multiple sclerosis.

Diabetes

Two types of **diabetes** have been identified. In **type 1 diabetes**, the body does not produce sufficient insulin within the islets of Langerhans in the **pancreas**. Its onset is frequently triggered by an infection, often by one of the Coxsackie virus family. This virus expresses a protein similar in structure to an enzyme involved in the production of insulin, and the immune response to this virus can also destroy the insulin-producing cells within the pancreas. Insulin normally attaches itself to glucose molecules in the circulatory system, permitting it to be taken up by the various body organs which need it to provide them with energy. Without insulin, these glucose molecules cannot be absorbed, leading to high levels of glucose within the blood which the body cannot use. This can lead to a life-threatening coma known as diabetic ketoacidosis, which requires hospitalisation and immediate treatment to avoid death. Less dramatic symptoms include increased thirst and urination, constant hunger, weight loss, blurred vision and extreme fatigue.

Treatment typically involves between one and four injections of insulin a day, meal planning to avoid sudden peaks of glucose being released into the bloodstream, weight control, and exercise. Treatment is a balancing act, aimed at achieving appropriate levels of circulating blood glucose. Too much food and/or too little insulin can result in ketoacidosis. Too little food and/or too much insulin can result in a condition known as hypoglycaemia, characterised by symptoms including a period of confusion and irritability, followed by a fairly rapid loss of consciousness. Immediate treatment is to give oral glucose where possible, or intravenously if the individual has lost consciousness. Good day-to-day control over diabetes reduces but does not obviate long-term complications including poor circulation which can lead to loss of sight, heart disease, skin ulcers, loss of limbs and nerve damage.

A second form of the condition is known as **type 2 diabetes**. In this, the body produces sufficient insulin (or close to sufficient), but the cells that take up the glucose-

---

antiretroviral drugs

drugs that prevent the reproduction of a type of virus known as a retiovirus. Most well known in the treatment of the HIV.

autoimmune conditions

a group of diseases, including type 1 diabetes, Crohn's disease and rheumatoid arthritis, characterised by abnormal functioning of the immune system in which it produces antibodies against its own tissues – it treats 'self' as 'non-self'.

diabetes (type 1 and 2)

a lifelong disease marked by high levels of sugar in the blood and a failure to transfer this to organs that need it. It can be caused by too little insulin (type 1), resistance to insulin (type 2), or both.

type 1 diabetes

see **diabetes**.

pancreas

gland in which the islets of Langerhans produce insulin. Also produces and secretes digestive enzymes. Located behind the stomach.

type 2 diabetes

see **diabetes**.

insulin molecules become 'resistant' to them, and no longer absorb them. Type 2 diabetes often develops later in life, and is associated with obesity – a person's chances of developing type 2 diabetes increases by 4 per cent for every pound of excess weight. The symptoms of type 2 diabetes develop gradually, and their onset is not as sudden as in type 1 diabetes. They may include fatigue or nausea, frequent urination, unusual thirst, weight loss, blurred vision, frequent infections and slow healing of wounds or sores. Some people have no symptoms. First-line treatment involves weight loss and exercise – although many people find it hard to adhere to such regimens (Vermeire *et al.* 2007). Second-line treatment involves treatment with oral medication designed to variously stimulate the beta cells in the pancreas to release more insulin, decrease the amount of glucose produced by the liver and enhance the effectiveness of naturally produced insulin, and lower glucose levels by blocking the breakdown of starches in the gut. We discuss the impact of diabetes on the individual and family in Chapter 15 ☛ and interventions designed to increase adherence to insulin and appropriate behavioural change in Chapter 17 ☛.

Rheumatoid arthritis

Rheumatoid arthritis (RA) may be triggered by viruses in individuals with a genetic tendency for the disease. It is a systemic disease that affects the entire body (and can impact on internal organs including lungs, heart and eyes) characterised by inflammation of the membrane lining the joints (the synovium). Any joint may be affected, but the hands, feet and wrists are the most frequently involved. It is a chronic, episodic condition, with 'flare-ups' and periods of remission. During flare-ups, people with the condition experience significant pain, stiffness, warmth, redness and swelling in affected joints – as well as fatigue, loss of appetite, fever and loss of energy. Over the long term, inflammatory cells in the synovium release enzymes that digest bone and cartilage, leading to joints losing their shape and alignment, and pain and restricted movement within the joint. Rheumatoid arthritis is more common in women than in men, and affects relatively young people: the age of onset is usually between 25 and 50 years.

There is no known cure for RA. The goal of treatment is to reduce joint inflammation and pain, maximise joint function, and prevent joint destruction and deformity. Treatment involves both medication and self-care: rest,

joint strengthening exercises and joint protection. Two types of medications are used in treating rheumatoid arthritis: fast-acting 'first-line drugs' and slow-acting 'second-line drugs'. First-line drugs, such as aspirin and cortisone (corticosteroids), are used to reduce pain and inflammation. Slow-acting second-line drugs, such as gold, methotrexate and hydroxychloroquine promote disease remission and prevent progressive joint destruction. As can be seen in the example of Mrs K (see p. 210), people with RA may also benefit from a number of aids to help them engage in many everyday behaviours. Mrs K recounts a typical day which may not be different to many people's day, but which is characterised by small (and not so small) frustrations due to her condition.

We examine the impact of arthritis on the individual and their family in Chapters 14 and 15 ☛, treatment of the pain associated with arthritis in Chapter 16 ☛, and self-management programmes to help people minimise the negative impact of arthritis on their lives in Chapter 17 ☛.

Multiple sclerosis

Multiple sclerosis (MS) is a neurological condition involving repeated episodes of inflammation of the central nervous system (brain and spinal cord). This results in the slowing or blocking of the transmission of nerve impulses. As this may occur in any part of the brain or spinal cord, symptoms can differ markedly across individuals, and include loss of limb function, loss of bowel and/or bladder control, blindness due to inflammation of the optic nerve, and cognitive impairment. Muscular spasticity is a common feature, particularly in the upper limbs. Around 95 per cent of people with MS experience debilitating fatigue, which can be so severe that about 40 per cent of people with the condition are unable to engage in sustained physical activity: 30 to 50 per cent require walking

---

rheumatoid arthritis
a chronic autoimmune disease with inflammation of the joints and marked deformities.

multiple sclerosis
a disorder of the brain and spinal cord caused by progressive damage to the myelin sheath covering of nerve cells.

Case history: Mrs K

I am a 42-year-old wife and mother of two young children. I have had severe rheumatoid arthritis for nearly eight years. This has caused deformities in my hands and feet. My fingers are gnarled. My wrists have nearly fused. My toes have bent upwards. My knees and many of the small joints of my knuckles are swollen.

I am usually very stiff when I wake up, so I get up slowly. After sitting at the side of the bed, I stand slowly, then slowly walk to the kitchen to prepare breakfast and school lunches for my children. Because my grip has been impaired with my deformities, I use a knife with an oversized grip handle to make sandwiches. I use a lid gripper pad to open jars. I take my tablets with my breakfast.

After breakfast, it's time for my morning washing routine. I have a raised toilet seat to avoid straining my joints sitting down and getting up. I shower while waiting for the morning tablets to start working. Washing my hair is difficult with my hands and I have adapted a scrubbing brush to help me wash it. I am careful getting in and out of the shower because the instability of my legs puts me at risk of falling.

Getting dressed is not easy. I am too clumsy to use buttons, so most of my shirts are pullover or have velcro attachments. My bra can be fastened in front and reversed or I ask my husband to fasten it for me. Most of my trousers have elastic waistbands and do not require buttoning or zipping. My shoes are especially wide and I usually wear running shoes for comfort. I dress for comfort – not for 'fashion'!

I drive the kids to school. Getting into and out of the car is painful and slow. I have a special key enlarger attachment for my car and house keys, which makes it easier to turn them. I can drive, but it makes my wrists hurt.

I try to exercise every day. I start with stretching exercises, then either ride a stationary bike or go on a walk. Once a week, I go for a swim. Exercise makes me feel good and gives me a sense of control over my body. Housework also always needs doing. I make good use of attachments to the vacuum cleaner that help me get to places that are hard to reach. Our door handles are levers instead of knobs so that it is easier for me to turn them. I can't do the ironing. When I cook, I use special grippers to hold the handles of pots and pans, and an electric can opener.

At bedtime, undressing can be as challenging as dressing. My husband frequently assists me with the undressing. My wrists are frequently painful by the evening, so I strap on my wrist splints before reading a few chapters of my novel, and calling it a night.

---

aids or a wheelchair for mobility. During acute symptomatic episodes, patients may be hospitalised.

The course of MS differs across individuals. Twenty per cent of people with the condition have a benign form of the disease in which symptoms show little or no progression after the initial episode. A few people experience malignant MS, resulting in a swift and relentless decline, with significant disability or even death occurring shortly after disease onset. Onset of this type of MS is usually after the age of 40 years. The majority of people have an episodic condition, known as remitting–relapsing MS, with acute flare-ups followed by periods of remission. Each flare-up, however, is usually followed by a failure to recover to previous levels of function, resulting in a slowly deteriorating condition. Death is usually due to complications of MS including choking, pneumonia and renal failure. As well as physical problems, nearly half the people with MS experience some degree of cognitive impairment and memory problems. In addition, about half the people who develop MS will be clinically depressed at some time during the course of the illness (Siegert and Abernethy 2005). Whether this is a direct result of neuronal damage or a reaction to the experience of the disease is not clear. It may, of course, be both.

One chemical within the immune system, called gamma-interferon, is particularly implicated in MS. This stimulates production of cytotoxic T cells, which are responsible for attacking and destroying diseased or damaged body cells. In MS, the activated cytotoxic T cells wrongly identify the **myelin sheath** of nerve cells within the brain and spinal column as 'non-self', and attempt to destroy it. Viral infections may act as a trigger to the production of gamma-interferon, and the onset of MS may follow a viral infection. One approach to the treatment of MS involves a different type of interferon. Beta interferon appears to inhibit the action of gamma

---

myelin sheath

a substance that contains both protein and fat (lipid) and surrounds all nerves outside the brain. It acts as a nerve insulator and helps in the transmission of nerve signals.

---

interferon and prevents the T cells attacking the myelin sheath. Unfortunately, interferons have to be regularly injected, and are responsible for the fever, muscle aches, fatigue and headache experienced during illnesses such as influenza. These also form the side-effects of taking them as medication, and as a consequence many patients avoid their use. There is increasing evidence that cannabis can be effective in reducing pain and muscle spasticity associated with MS. But the treatment has to counter the problems of its legal status. It is legally prescribed, for example, in the Netherlands and Canada but is not legally available in the UK or USA. Its status is under review in Australia.

Ms F provides an insight into what it feels like to have MS. At the time of our talk (see Bennett 2006) she

Case history: Ms F

I developed MS about four years ago. It was odd to start with. I didn't think I had anything serious, although you do worry about symptoms you don't understand. It started when I had some problems with my sight. I couldn't see as well as I used to be able to – it came on suddenly so I didn't think it was age or anything normal. I think at the time I was also a bit more clumsy than I had been – nothing obvious, but I dropped things a bit more than before. Nothing really that you'd notice unless other things were happening as well. I went to my GP about my eyes and he sent me to see a neurologist. He tried to reassure me that there was nothing too badly wrong and that he wanted to check out a few symptoms. But I began to worry then . . . you don't get sent on to see the hospital doctors unless there is anything really wrong with you. He suggested that he thought it might be MS, which was why he was not sending me to an eye specialist.

I got to see the neurologist pretty quickly and she ran a few tests over a few weeks – testing my muscle strength, coordination, scans and so on . . . sticking needles into me at various times. The upshot of this was that I was diagnosed as having MS. My consultant told me and my husband together, and allowed us to ask questions about things. We also got to speak to a specialist nurse who has helped us over the years. She was able to take the time to tell us more than the doctor about what to expect and what support we could have. Although I think it was nice to hear the diagnosis from the doctor.

I must admit that I found it really hard to deal with things at the beginning – you don't know what to expect and perhaps you expect the worst. You hear all sorts of horror stories about people dying with MS and that. And no one can really reassure you that you won't have problems . . . Over the last few years, I've got to know my body and seen things getting worse. But it happens gradually and a lot of the time there are no changes. So that is reassuring – that things aren't going to collapse too quickly and I won't be left incontinent and unable to feed myself for a long time – hopefully not ever!

The worse thing is the tiredness and clumsiness. My eyes have actually got better, thank goodness. I use sticks to get around the house. Sometimes I can walk a little out of the house. Often I have to take the wheelchair. I just get exhausted too quickly, there isn't a lot of point trying to walk, because I cannot go far . . .

I hate having MS. I used to take part in sports, go out, be lively. Now I can't do any of that. I'm tired . . . down a lot of the time. I think the two often go together. My memory was never that good, but now it seems to be worse than ever. I can hold conversations, but keeping my concentration up for a long time is difficult. So, people find you difficult to deal with. I know my husband feels that way. He married a lively, sporty, slim woman . . . now I'm lethargic, down, putting on weight because I eat and don't exercise – even though they tell me not to, so I can keep mobile and not develop skin problems. I don't go out very much because it's such a hassle in my wheelchair . . . cities were not designed for people in wheelchairs . . . and people don't like people in wheelchairs. You are ignored . . . and just want to say, 'Hey, I'm here. I have a brain you know . . .' I know this sounds sorry for myself. And sometimes I feel more positive. But I find living with uncertainty difficult. Will I have a bad day today? Will I have a flare-up – have to go to hospital, take megasteroids, come out worse than when I went in? I guess you have to live for the day . . . but it can be difficult.

was taking antidepressants for her depression and, as you will read, was having problems coming to terms with her illness.

We examine the impact of multiple sclerosis on caregivers in Chapter 15 ☛ and some interventions designed to reduce the problems of living with MS in Chapter 17 ☛.

The digestive system

The digestive tract (see Figure 8.5) is the system of organs responsible for the ingestion of food, absorption of nutrients from that food, and finally the expulsion of waste products from the body. It comprises a number of connected organs, each with a different role:

- *Mouth*: here, food is masticated by chewing, causing the release of enzymes in the saliva and beginning the process of digestion.
- *Oesophagus*: this transports food from the mouth to the stomach, compressing it in the process.
- *Stomach*: here, food is churned and mixed with acid to decompose it chemically.
- *Small intestine*: this is responsible for mixing the bowel contents with chemicals to break it into its constituent parts and then absorb them into the bloodstream for transportation to other organs. Chemicals involved in this process include **bile**, which is made by the liver and stored in the **gallbladder** and digests fats, and enzyme-rich juices released from the pancreas.

- *The large bowel* (colon): this is largely responsible for reabsorption of water from the bowel contents and expulsion of the unused bowel contents. Movement between and along these various organs is controlled by a process known as peristalsis. This involves smooth muscle within the walls of the organs narrowing and the narrow sections moving slowly along the length of the organ in a series of waves, pushing the bowel contents forward with each wave.

---

bile

a digestive juice, made in the liver and stored in the **gallbladder**. Involved in the digestion of fats in the small intestine.

gallbladder

a structure on the underside of the liver on the right side of the abdomen. It stores the bile that is produced in the liver before it is secreted into the intestines. This helps the body to digest fats.

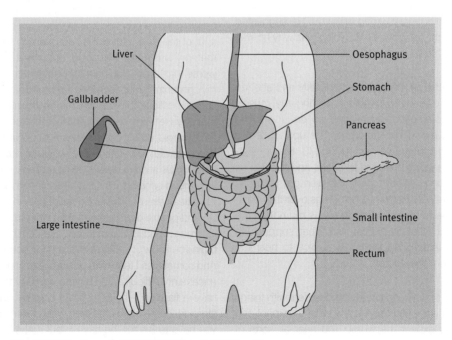

Figure 8.5 The large and small intestine and related organs.

Controlling digestion

Each of these digestion processes is controlled by both hormone and nerve regulators. Hormones are produced and released by cells in the mucosa (lining) of the stomach and small intestine at key stages in the digestive process. Among other roles:

- Gastrin causes the stomach to produce its acid.
- Secretin causes the pancreas to produce a fluid that is rich in bicarbonate and enzymes to break down food into its constituent proteins, sugars and so on. The bicarbonate is alkaline and prevents the bowel wall from being damaged as the highly acidic stomach contents are released into the small intestine. Secretin also stimulates the liver to produce bile, the acid that aids fat digestion.
- Cholesystokinin triggers the gallbladder to discharge its bile into the small intestine.

Activity in the digestive system is also controlled by a complex local nervous system known as the enteric nervous system, in which:

- Sensory neurons receive information from receptors in the mucosa and muscle. Chemoreceptors monitor levels of acid, glucose and amino acids. Sensory receptors respond to stretch and tension within the wall of the gut.
- Motor neurons, whose key role is to control gastrointestinal motility (including peristalsis and stomach motility) and secretion, control the action on smooth muscle in the wall of the gut.

Key neurotransmitters involved in the activity of the enteric nervous system are noradrenaline and acetylcholine: the former provides an activating role, the second an inhibitory role. The enteric nervous system works independently of the central nervous system. However, the gut also has links to the central nervous system, providing sensory information (such as fullness) to the hypothalamus and allowing the gut to respond to the various excitatory or inhibitory processes of the autonomic nervous system. In general, sympathetic stimulation inhibits digestive activities, inhibiting gastrointestinal secretion and motor activity, and contracting gastrointestinal sphincters and blood vessels. The latter may be experienced as feelings of 'butterflies in the stomach' – and also some other, perhaps even more obvious, symptoms! Conversely, parasympathetic activity typically stimulates digestive activities.

Disorders of the digestive system

Gastric ulcer

Gastric ulcers are ulceration of the lining of the stomach (mucosa), which can result in a number of symptoms, the most common of which is abdominal discomfort or pain. This typically comes and goes for several days or weeks, occurs two to three hours after eating, is relieved by eating, and may be at its worst during the night – when the stomach is empty following a meal. Other symptoms include poor appetite, weight loss, bloating, nausea and vomiting. If the disease process is not treated, the ulcer may erode through the stomach wall, resulting in the potentially fatal outflow of its contents into the abdomen.

Until relatively recently, gastric ulcers were thought to be a consequence of stress, which was thought to increase acid secretion in the stomach. More recent evidence, however, has shown that a bacterium known as *Helicobacter pylori* is responsible for 70 per cent of cases of the disorder. *Helicobacter pylori* infection is thought to weaken the protective mucous coating of the stomach and duodenum, and allow acid to reach the sensitive lining beneath. It may also increase the amount of stomach acid secreted. Both acid and bacteria irritate the stomach lining and cause the ulcer. However, stress may still be implicated in the development and maintenance of gastric ulcers as it may increase risk behaviours such as smoking or alcohol consumption, as well as adversely affecting the immune system's ability to influence levels of *H. pylori* in the gut.

Treatment involves suppressing acid secretion and, if appropriate, eradicating the *H. pylori* bacteria. Various types of drugs may be used to achieve this effect. Reductions in acid production can be achieved by histamine blockers (e.g. Cimetidine) and drugs known as hydrogen pump antagonists (e.g. Omeprazol). Drugs which eradicate *H. pylori* include antibiotics such as tetracycline or amoxicillin which are frequently given in combination with histamine blockers or hydrogen pump antagonists. Only rarely is surgery used in the treatment of gastric ulcers, and this usually when the ulcer has eroded through the stomach wall and has led to life-threatening haemorrhage.

Inflammatory bowel disease

Inflammatory bowel disease (IBD) is a group of inflammatory conditions of the large and, in some cases, small intestine. The main forms of IBD are:

● Crohn's disease

● ulcerative colitis.

Crohn's disease

Crohn's disease can involve any part of the gastrointestinal tract. It is an inflammatory condition characterised by episodes of severe symptoms followed by periods of remission. Its key symptoms are chronic, and occasionally severe, diarrhoea and disrupted digestion. Over time, the inflammation process can result in a thickening of the bowel wall, which may result in the diameter of the bowel becoming so constricted that food cannot pass through these damaged sections. These may require surgical excision. Unfortunately, as the disease tends to recur at these sites, the constriction may reoccur and require further surgery within a few years. For this reason, surgery is often considered the treatment of last resort. There is some evidence that the condition may have a genetic basis, although a diet high in sugar and fats, smoking and stress have also been implicated in its aetiology. The usual age of onset is between 15 and 30 years of age, with no difference in prevalence between men and women. Its symptoms include:

● abdominal pain;

● changes in bowel movements – faeces may vary between solid and watery;

● periods of mild fever, sometimes with blood in the stools, and pain in the lower right abdome;

● loss of appetite;

● unintentional weight loss;

● boils and **fistulas**;

● general malaise.

At times of acute symptoms, individuals become severely dehydrated and are unable to digest food and absorb necessary nutrients, resulting in the need for significant medical care. At such times, a number of drugs designed to reduce inflammation and antibiotics may be necessary.

Ulcerative colitis

Ulcerative colitis is similar to Crohn's disease, but usually affects the terminal part of the large intestine and rectum. It may develop into cancer after many years of the disease. For this reason, patients have regular check-ups for the beginning of cancer or even have preventive removal of segments of the bowel. This may result in the affected individual needing a **colostomy**. Its severity can be graded as:

● *Mild*: fewer than four stools daily, with or without blood. There may be mild abdominal pain or cramping.

● *Moderate*: more than four stools daily. Patients may be anaemic and have moderate abdominal pain and low grade fever.

● *Severe*: more than six bloody stools a day, and evidence of systemic disease such as fever, **tachycardia**, or anaemia.

● *Fulminant*: ten bowel movements daily, continuous bleeding, abdominal tenderness and distension. Patients will require blood transfusion and their colon may perforate, resulting in the gut content being released into the abdomen. Unless treated, fulminant disease will soon lead to death.

The goals of treatment with medication are to treat acute episodes and to maintain remission once achieved. Treatment is similar to that of Crohn's disease, and involves

---

inflammatory bowel disease

a group of inflammatory conditions of the large intestine and, in some cases, the small intestine. The main forms of IBD are **Crohn's disease** and **ulcerative colitis**.

Crohn's disease

autoimmune disease that can affect any part of the gastrointestinal tract but most commonly occurs in the ileum (the area where the small and large intestine meet).

fistulas

formation of small passages that connect the intestine with other organs or the skin.

ulcerative colitis

a chronic inflammatory disease of the large intestine, characterised by recurrent episodes of abdominal pain, fever and severe diarrhoea.

colostomy

a surgical procedure that creates an opening (stoma) in the abdomen for the drainage of stool from the large intestine (colon). It may be temporary or permanent.

tachycardia

high heart rate – usually defined as greater than 100 beats per minute.

steroids to reduce inflammation and immunomodulators which suppress the body's immune processes that are contributing to the condition. An interesting fact is that risk of developing ulcerative colitis appears to be higher in non-smokers and in ex-smokers, and some patients may actually improve when treated with nicotine.

Irritable bowel syndrome

Irritable bowel syndrome (IBS) is a condition of the bowel involving a period of at least three months abdominal discomfort or pain, with two or more of the following features:

- pain, relieved by defaecation;
- pain associated with a change in the frequency of bowel movements;
- change in the form of the stool (loose, watery, or pellet-like).

Also central to a diagnosis of IBS is that these symptoms occur in the absence of any obvious physical pathology. Because of this lack of physical pathology, IBS was at one time considered to be the archetypal psychosomatic disorder. Indeed, Latimer (1981) went so far as to suggest that anxiety and IBS were the same condition, with IBS symptoms reported by people who were unwilling or unable to attribute their symptoms to psychological factors. However, evidence of this link to stress is not as strong as was previously thought, and other factors have now been linked with IBS. These include food hypersensitivities and the presence of bacteria such as *Blastocystishominis* and *Helicobacter pylori* (see Singh *et al.* 2003). Spence and Moss-Morris (2007) argued that the initial trigger to IBS may be an infection (an episode of gastroenteritis), with the condition maintained in the longer term by high levels of anxiety and/or stress. Whatever its cause, psychological treatment using cognitive-behavioural therapy or a form of relaxation known as autogenic training, in which patients are given specific instructions of visualising and feeling warm and relaxed in the gut appears to be effective forms of treatment (see Chapter 17 ☛). Medical treatment involves the use of smooth muscle relaxants to reduce gut motility, adding or reducing fibre to the diet (depending on the level of fibre already in the diet), drugs which 'bulk' up stools to reduce diarrhoea and, on occasion, anxiolytic or anti-depressant drugs. While IBS may be unpleasant, and some people may be restricted by the pain they experience or the fear of not being able to get to a toilet in time if they were to have diarrhoea, it is not a life-threatening condition nor as debilitating as the previously described conditions. We examine psychological treatments for IBS in Chapter 17 ☛, and the role of stress in the development of bowel disorders in Chapter 11 ☛.

Colorectal cancer

Colorectal cancer is the third most common cancer in men and women. Risk for the condition is increased by both biological and behavioural factors, including genetic factors, pre-existing inflammatory conditions including ulcerative colitis, and a diet high in fat and low in fibre. Symptoms of the disorder are often unnoticed because they are relatively mild, and include: bleeding, constipation or diarrhoea, and unformed stool. One early symptom may be a general tiredness and shortness of breath as a consequence of anaemia caused by long-term, but unnoticed, bleeding within the gut. For this reason, the cancer may be quite advanced before people seek medical help. It is nevertheless generally treatable with a combination of surgery to remove the cancer followed by chemotherapy. Radiotherapy is rarely used except in cases of rectal cancer. As with many cancers, the condition can be described in terms of its stages, with the higher stage being more difficult to treat and having a poorer **prognosis**:

- *Stage 1*: the cancer is limited to the inside of the bowel.
- *Stage 2*: the cancer penetrates through the wall of the bowel to the outside layers.
- *Stage 3*: the cancer involves the lymph glands in the abdomen.
- *Stage 4*: the cancer has metastasised to other organs.

> **irritable bowel syndrome**
> a disorder of the lower intestinal tract. Symptoms include pain combined with altered bowel habits resulting in diarrhoea, constipation or both. It has no obvious physiological abnormalities, so diagnosis is by the presence and pattern of symptoms.
>
> **prognosis**
> the predicted outcome of a disease.

IN THE SPOTLIGHT

Cancer

Hundreds of genes play a role in the growth and division of cells. Three classes of gene control this process and may contribute to the uncontrolled proliferation of cells, which is cancer:

1. *Oncogenes* control the sequence of events by which a cell enlarges, replicates its DNA, divides and passes a complete set of genes to each daughter cell. When mutated, they can drive excessive proliferation by producing too much – or an overactive form – of a growth-stimulating protein.
2. *Tumour suppressor genes* inhibit cell growth. Loss or inactivation of this gene may produce inappropriate growth by losing this inhibitory control.
3. *Checkpoint genes* monitor and repair DNA, which is often damaged prior to reproduction and needs to be repaired before cell division. Without these checking mechanisms, a damaged gene will become replicated as a permanent mutation. One of the most notable checkpoint proteins is known as p53, which prevents replication of damaged DNA in the normal cell and promotes **cell suicide** in cells with abnormal DNA. Faulty p53 allows cells carrying damaged DNA to replicate and survive and has been found to be defective in most human cancers.

Other factors are also important in tumour development. Growing tumours are dependent on a good blood supply. To promote this, local tissues may be transformed into blood vessel cells, allowing the tumour to establish its own blood supply. Some modern treatments of cancer attack this blood supply as well as the tumour mass itself. Tumours also acquire the ability to migrate and invade other tissues, forming tumour masses at different sites in the body. This process is known as metastasis – and in some cases these secondary tumours may be more deadly than the original tumour.

> **cell suicide**
>
> a form of cell death in which a controlled sequence of events (or programme) leads to the elimination of cells without releasing harmful substances into the surrounding area.

The cardiovascular system

The main function of the cardiovascular system is to transport nutrients, immune cells and oxygen to the body's organs and to remove waste products from them. It also moves hormones from their point of production within the body to their site of action. The transport medium used in this process is the blood; the pumping system that pushes the blood around the body involves the heart and various types of blood vessel:

● *Arteries*: transport blood away from the heart. These vessels have a muscular sheath that allows them to contract or expand slightly. This activity is controlled by the autonomic nervous system.

● *Arterioles*: these are small arteries, linking the large arteries to the organs of the body.

● *Veins*: these transport blood back to the heart once the oxygen and nutrients have been absorbed from it and replaced by carbon dioxide, and a variety of waste products. They are thinner than arteries, and because they are so far from the heart have much lower pressures than the arteries. Blood is pushed through them partly by the pressure of the pulse of blood from the heart, partly through the action of the moving muscles. As large muscle groups contract during everyday activities, they push blood through the veins. To prevent back flow of blood they have a series of valves, which allow the blood to flow in only one direction. When the muscles are inactive, blood may no longer flow freely in the veins and may even stagnate and begin to clot – a deep vein thrombosis that may occur after long-haul flights or other periods of inactivity in some susceptible individuals.

The heart

The heart has two separate pumps operating in parallel. The right side of the heart is involved in the transportation of blood to the lungs; the left side pumps blood to the rest of the body (Figure 8.6). Each side of the heart has two chambers (Figure 8.7), known as atria and ventricles. The right atrium takes deoxygenated blood from veins known as the superior and inferior vena cava and pumps it into the right ventricle. Blood is then pumped into the pulmonary artery, taking it to the lungs, where it picks up oxygen in its **haemoglobin** cells. Oxygen-laden blood then returns to the heart, entering through the left atrium. It is then pumped into the left ventricle, and then into the main artery, known as the **aorta**, which carries blood to the rest of the body.

The rhythm of the heart is controlled by an electrical system. It is initiated by an electrical impulse generated in a region of the right atrium called the sinoatrial node. This impulse causes the muscles of both atria to contract. As the wave of electricity progresses through the heart muscle and nerves, it reaches an area at the junction of the atria and ventricles known as the atrio-ventricular node. This second node then fires a further electrical discharge along a system of nerves including the Bundle of His and Purkinje fibres (see Figure 8.7), triggering the muscles of both ventricles to contract, completing the cycle. Although the sinoatrial node has an intrinsic rhythm, its activity is largely influenced by the autonomic nervous system.

An electrocardiogram (ECG) is used to measure the activity of the heart. Electrodes are placed over the heart

---

haemoglobin

the main substance of the red blood cell. When oxygenated in the lungs, it is converted to oxyhaemoglobin, thus allowing the red blood cells to carry oxygen from the air in our lungs to all parts of the body.

aorta

the main trunk of the systemic arteries, carrying blood from the left side of the heart to the arteries of all limbs and organs except the lungs.

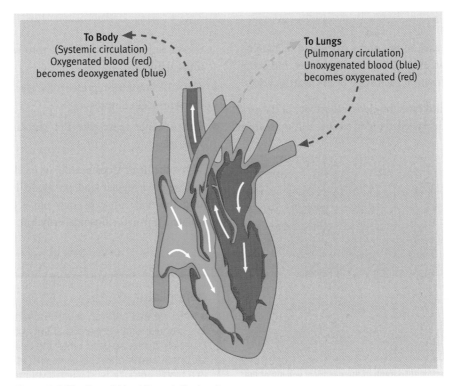

Figure 8.6 The flow of blood through the heart

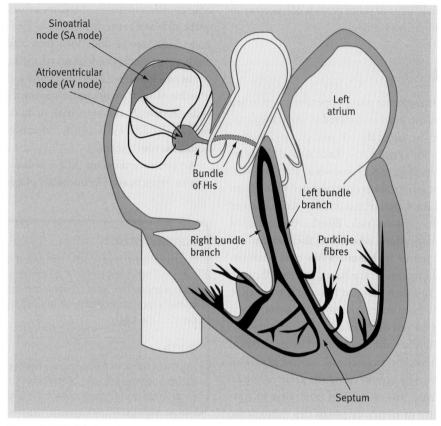

Figure 8.7 Electrical conduction and control of the heart rhythm

and can detect each of the nodes firing and recharging. Figure 8.8 shows an ECG of a normal heart, indicating the electrical activity at each stage of the heart's cycle.

● The P wave indicates the electrical activity of the atria firing – the time needed for an electrical impulse from the sinoatrial node to spread throughout the atrial musculature.

● The QRS complex represents the electrical activity of the ventricles compressing.

● The T wave represents the repolarisation of the ventricles.

When the heart stops beating or its electrical rhythm is completely irregular and no blood is being pushed around the body, doctors may use a **defibrillator** to stimulate a normal (sinusoidal) rhythm.

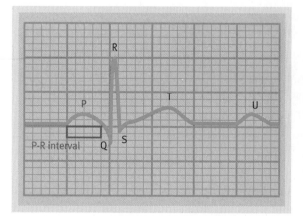

Figure 8.8 An electrocardiograph of the electrical activity of the heart (see text for explanation)

defibrillator

a machine that uses an electric current to stop any irregular and dangerous activity of the heart's muscles. It can be used when the heart has stopped (**cardiac arrest**) or when it is beating in a highly irregular (and ineffective) manner.

Blood

The body usually contains about five litres of blood. Its constituents include a fluid known as plasma and a variety of cells. As well as the various **exogenous** cells carried in the blood (nutrients, oxygen, etc.), it produces its own cells. These are manufactured by **stem cells** in the bone marrow. Three different types of cell are produced:

1. **Erythrocytes** (or red blood cells) transport oxygen around the body. In them, oxygen combines with haemoglobin in the lungs and is transported to cells in need of oxygen, where it is released, allowing cell respiration.

2. Phagocytes and lymphocytes (or white blood cells; see above) include the immune system's B cells and T cells described earlier in the chapter.

3. **Platelets** are cells that respond to damage to the circulatory system. They aggregate (form a clot) around the site of any damage and prevent loss of blood from the system. They are also involved in repair to damage within the arteries themselves and contribute to the development of atheroma. We consider this process later in the chapter.

Blood pressure

Blood pressure has two components:

1. the degree of pressure imposed on the blood as a result of its constriction within the arteries and veins – known as the diastolic blood pressure (DBP);

2. an additional pressure as the wave of blood pushed out from the heart flows through the system (our pulse) – known as the systolic blood pressure (SBP).

This pressure is measured in millimetres of mercury (mmHg), representing the height of a tube of mercury in millilitres that the pressure can push up (using a now old-fashioned sphygmomanometer). Healthy levels of blood pressure are an SBP below 130–140 mmHg and a DBP below 90 mmHg (written as 130/90 mmHg: see also the discussion of hypertension later in the chapter).

A number of physiological processes are involved in controlling blood pressure. Those of particular interest to psychologists involve the autonomic nervous system. The brainstem receives continuous information from pressure-sensitive nerve endings called **baroreceptors** situated in the **carotid arteries** and aorta. This information is relayed

to a centre in the brainstem known as the vasomotor centre, and then on to the hypothalamus. Reductions in blood pressure or physical demands such as exercise that require increased blood pressure causes activation of the sympathetic nervous system. Sympathetic activation results in an increase in the strength and frequency of heart contractions (via the activity of the sinoatrial and atrioventricular nodes) and a contraction of the smooth muscle in the arteries. Together, these actions increase in blood pressure, and allow sustained flow of blood to organs such as the muscles at times of high activity. Parasympathetic activity results in an opposing reaction.

Diseases of the cardiovascular system

Hypertension

Hypertension is a condition in which resting blood pressure is significantly above normal levels (see Table 8.2).

---

exogenous
relating to things outside the body.

stem cell
a 'generic' cell that can make exact copies of itself indefinitely. In addition, such cells have the ability to produce specialised cells for various tissues in the body, including blood, heart muscle, brain and liver tissue. Found in the bone marrow.

erythrocyte
a mature blood cell that contains haemoglobin to carry oxygen to the bodily tissues.

platelets
tiny bits of protoplasm found in the blood that are essential for blood clotting. These cells bind together to form a clot and prevent bleeding at the site of injury.

baroreceptors
sensory nerve endings that are stimulated by changes in pressure. Located in the walls of blood vessels such as the carotid sinus.

carotid artery
the main artery that takes blood from the heart via the neck to the brain.

Table 8.2 Typical blood pressure readings in normal and hypertensive individuals

	Diastolic (mmHg)	Systolic (mmHg)
Normal	≤90	≤140
Mild hypertension	90–99	140–159
Hypertension	≥100	≥160

Two broad causes of hypertension have been identified:

1. *Secondary hypertension*: here, hypertension is the result of a disease process usually involving the kidneys, adrenal glands or aorta. This type of hypertension accounts for about 5 per cent of cases.

2. *Essential (primary) hypertension*: in the majority of cases, there is no known disease process that causes the problem. It seems to be the 'normal' consequence of a number of risk factors, such as obesity, lack of exercise and a high salt intake. It is a progressive condition, and people with the condition usually experience a gradual rise in blood pressure over a period of years, with no obvious symptoms.

Psychological stress may contribute to the development of essential hypertension. At times of stress, sympathetic activity increases muscle tone in the arteries and the strength of the heart's contractions – both of which contribute to short-term increases in blood pressure, which then falls as parasympathetic activity follows a period of stress. If the stress is sustained or frequent, however, the activity of the sympathetic nervous system begins to dominate and gradually pushes blood pressure up for longer periods until the individual develops chronically raised blood pressure.

Hypertension may be present and remain unnoticed for many years, or even decades. It is usually considered to be a syndrome with few if any symptoms, and many cases of hypertension are detected during routine screening (see Chapter 6 ☞). If high blood pressure has no symptoms, why bother treating it? At low levels of high blood pressure – mild hypertension – some have argued that medical treatment may actually be of little benefit, and that the side-effects of treatment may outweigh its benefits (although this position is now being challenged as new drugs are used to treat the condition: see Weber and Julius 1998). However, as blood pressure rises, so too does the amount of damage it can do. High blood

pressure increases the risk of a heart attack (myocardial infarction (MI) – see below), stroke, kidney failure, eye damage and **heart failure**. It also contributes to the development of atheroma. Hypertension is usually treated with anti-hypertensive drugs with a variety of actions, including **ACE inhibitors**, **diuretics** and **beta-blockers**, all of which have been proven effective in reducing blood pressure.

Coronary heart disease

Like hypertension, coronary heart disease (CHD) may develop over many years before becoming evident. Indeed, people may have quite significant CHD and never be aware of their condition. The long-term, and silent, element of CHD is the development of atheroma in the blood vessels. This may result in more obvious manifestations of CHD, including an MI and angina (see below).

Atherosclerosis

Atherosclerosis is a disease in which atheroma builds up on lining of the arteries. The main constituent of atheroma is cholesterol. This is a waxy substance that is present in

heart failure

a state in which the heart muscle is damaged or weakened and is unable to generate a cardiac output sufficient to meet the demands of the body.

ACE inhibitors

angiotensin II causes the muscles surrounding blood vessels to contract and thereby narrows the blood vessels. Angiotensin Converting Enzyme (ACE) inhibitors decrease the production of angiotensin II, allowing blood vessels to dilate, and reduce blood pressure.

diuretics

elevates the rate of bodily urine excretion, reducing the amount of fluid within the cardiovascular system, and reducing pressure within it.

beta-blockers

block the action of adrenaline and noradrenaline on β-adrenergic receptors, which mediate the 'fight or flight' response, within the heart and in muscles surrounding the arteries. In doing so, they reduce increases in blood pressure associated with sympathetic activation.

IN THE SPOTLIGHT

The life and (heroic) death of John Henry

John Henry was born a slave in the USA in the 1840s or 1850s. So what has he got to do with modern-day psychology? Well, legend has it that he was a giant of a man, who rose to any challenge he faced – a characteristic that eventually resulted in his death. He died while working as a labourer on the railroad tunnelling through a mountain in West Virginia. One of his jobs was to pound holes into rock, which were then filled with explosives and used to blast through tunnels. When the railroad owners brought in steam drills to do the same job more quickly and cheaply, he challenged the steam drill to a contest. He won the contest but died of exhaustion soon after. His name has now become synonymous with a process, initially at least, thought to drive hypertension in black males – John Henryism.

Hypertension is particularly prevalent among African Americans. Black people in the USA are up to four times more likely than whites to develop hypertension by the age of 50 (Roberts and Rowland 1981). One of the reasons for this is thought to be that they are more frequently placed in situations in which they have to respond to difficult psychological stressors – poverty, racism, and so on – more than their white counterparts (see Chapter 2 👉). Those people who have strong emotional or behavioural responses to such stressors typically experience sustained increases in heart rate and blood pressure. This overcomes the body's homeostatic processes and pushes the resting blood pressure increasingly up until they develop long-term hypertension. Although initially viewed as an issue for black men, the process is increasingly being seen as the outcome of the stresses associated with low socio-economic position – and may account for some of the health inequalities considered in Chapter 2 👉.

blood plasma and in all the body's cells. Without it, cells could not maintain the integrity of their walls, and we would become seriously ill or die. Too much cholesterol, on the other hand, may be harmful. To get to cell walls in order to repair and maintain them, cholesterol must be transported through the body – via the bloodstream. However, it is insoluble in the blood. To allow such transport, it is therefore attached to groups of proteins called lipoproteins. **Low-density lipoproteins** (LDLs) transport cholesterol to the various tissues and body cells, where it is separated from the lipoprotein and is used by the cell. It can also be absorbed into atheroma on the inner surface of the blood vessels. **High-density lipoproteins** (HDLs) transport excess or unused cholesterol from the tissues back to the liver, where it is broken down to bile acids and then excreted. LDLs are therefore characterised as 'harmful' cholesterol; HDLs are considered to be health-protective. Although some cholesterol is absorbed from our food through the gut, about 80 per cent of cholesterol in our bodies is produced by the liver. The development of atherosclerosis involves a series of stages:

- *Early processes*: atheroma usually occurs at sites of disturbed blood flow, such as bifurcations of the arteries. It forms as part of the repair process to damage of the

low-density lipoprotein (LDL)

the main function of LDL seems to be to carry cholesterol to various tissues throughout the body. LDL is sometimes referred to as 'bad' cholesterol because elevated levels of LDL correlate most directly with coronary heart disease.

high-density lipoprotein (HDL)

lipoproteins are fat protein complexes in the blood that transport cholesterol, triglycerides and other lipids to various tissues. The main function of HDL appears to be to carry excess cholesterol to the liver for 're-packaging' or excretion in the bile. Higher levels of HDL seem to be protective against CHD, so HDL is sometimes referred to as 'good' cholesterol.

artery wall caused by the disturbed blood flow. In this process, inflammatory monocytes, which are precursors to macrophages (see the section on the immune system earlier in the chapter), absorb LDL cholesterol from the circulating blood to become what are known as foam cells. These form a coat over the lining of the damaged artery. As the foam cells die, they lose their contents of LDL, resulting in pools of cholesterol forming between the foam cells and the artery wall. The presence of foam cells may trigger the growth of smooth muscle cells from the artery wall to cover them. In this way, the walls of the artery become lined with lipids, foam cells and finally a wall of smooth muscle. This repeated process results in a gradual reduction of the diameter of the artery.

● *Acute events*: at times, more acute events may occur, and clots of cholesterol and foam cells may be pulled out of the artery wall. This may result in a clot blocking an artery in a key organ such as the heart, resulting in a myocardial infarction (MI) (see below).

The distribution of atheroma within the circulatory system is not uniform throughout the body. It is most developed around the junctions of arteries because disturbances in blood flow at such points can facilitate these processes, but the heart arteries are also one of the areas most likely to be affected. High levels of cholesterol may be treated with drugs known as statins, if dietary changes are insufficient to lower cholesterol to safe levels. They work by blocking an enzyme (HMG-CoA reductase) the liver needs to make cholesterol. They may also help reabsorb cholesterol that has accumulated in atheroma on the artery walls.

Myocardial infarction

As we noted in the last section, an important end point of CHD is when a clot is pulled off an artery wall and enters the circulating blood. This may prove a harmless event, with no health implications for the individual. However, if the circulating clot has a greater diameter than the blood vessels it is passing through, it will inevitably block the blood vessels and prevent the flow of blood beyond them. This blockage (occlusion) may result in significant health problems if it occurs in the arteries supplying oxygen and nutrients to the heart. Unless rapidly treated, the cells of the heart muscle beyond the occlusion no longer receive their nutrients and oxygen and die – a myocardial infarction (MI). The severity of the MI is determined by how large

a blood vessel is affected (larger is worse) and which parts of the heart are damaged.

The classic symptoms of an MI include what is often described as 'crushing chest pain'. The affected individual may feel like their chest is trapped in a vice. Other symptoms include shortness of breath, coughing, pain radiating down the left arm, dizziness and/or collapse, nausea or vomiting, and sweating. However, an MI may also be much less dramatic. Indeed, many people delay seeking help for an MI as their symptoms are vague, may be confused with heartburn or indigestion, and the affected individual hopes that the symptoms will go away without treatment. Perhaps the strangest symptom that can rarely be indicative of an MI is toothache – although we would not recommend you visit your local hospital complaining of a heart attack should you be unfortunate enough to develop this problem!

Approximately 45 per cent of people will die of their MI immediately or in the week or so following the event. The majority of people go on to make a good recovery. This may be aided by treatment with drugs known as '**clot busters**'. These drugs dissolve the clot causing the blocked artery and, if given within an hour or so of the infarction, can prevent permanent muscle damage. Longer-term treatment now frequently involves a procedure known as an angioplasty (or its longer formal name, Percutaneous Transluminal Coronary Angioplasty: PTCA) in which a long narrow catheter is inserted into the femoral artery (near the groin) and, guided by X-rays, is pushed along the arteries until it reaches the coronary arteries. After reaching the site of the MI, a small balloon is inflated which pushes against the occluded artery wall, increasing the diameter of the artery and allowing normal blood flow through it. A small wire mesh tube (known as a stent) is then frequently left in position at the site to maintain the patency of the artery. Long-term contributors to CHD, including high cholesterol or blood pressure, are treated with appropriate lifestyle changes (see Chapters 6, 7 and 17 ☛) and medication if necessary.

---

clot busters
drugs which dissolve clots associated with myocardial infarction and can prevent damage to the heart following such an event. Are best used within one hour of the infarction.

Angina

The key symptom of **angina** is similar to that of an MI. It is a central chest pain that may radiate to the left shoulder, jaw, arm or other areas of the chest. Some patients may confuse arm or shoulder pain with arthritis or indigestion pain. Unlike an MI, however, it is a temporary condition which occurs when the heart muscle needs more oxygen than can be provided by the heart arteries, and stops once these demands are reduced. It is frequently precipitated by exertion or stress, and may result from two underlying causes:

1. atheromatous lesions of the coronary arteries reduce their diameter and limit the blood flow through them;

2. **vasospasm** of the coronary arteries results in a temporary reduction in their diameter;

3. a combination of both.

Classic angina (or angina pectoris) is associated with high levels of atheroma in the coronary arteries which limits the amount of blood they can carry to the heart muscle. Physical exertion, emotional stress and exposure to cold are among the triggers for this type of angina. In a second type of angina known as unstable angina, people with the condition experience angina symptoms after relatively little effort (such as just taking a few steps) or even when they are resting. It is usually the result of a severe narrowing in a coronary artery, and may lead to an MI if it is not treated. As with an MI, treatment involves interventions to reduce the immediate symptoms of angina

and to prevent the underlying disease progress. Symptomatic relief can be achieved through the use of Glyceryl-Trinitrate (GTN: otherwise known as nitroglycerin!). This comes as a spray (sprayed into the mouth) or tablets (placed under the tongue) to take when an angina episode starts, and results in an immediate widening of the arteries and relief from symptoms. If the level of disease warrants it, patients with angina may also be given PTCA, or a **coronary artery bypass graft** (CABG), in which blood vessels are taken from the legs or the chest and used to bypass the diseased artery. Treatment of underlying conditions may involve the use of statins or hypertensive medication. In Chapter 17 (☛, we describe the case of Mr Jones, whose angina was so severe that on two occasions he believed he was having an MI and went to the emergency department of the local hospital. We also show how we helped him adjust better to his condition.

The respiratory system

The respiratory system delivers oxygen to and removes carbon dioxide from the blood. The exchange of oxygen and carbon dioxide occurs in the lungs. The system comprises:

- the *upper respiratory tract*, including the nose, mouth, larynx and trachea;

- the *lower respiratory tract*, including the lungs, bronchi, bronchioles and alveoli. Each lung is divided into upper and lower lobes – the upper lobe of the right lung contains a third subdivision known as the right middle lobe.

The bronchi carry air from the mouth to the lungs. As they enter the lungs, they divide into smaller bronchi, then into smaller tubes called bronchioles (see Figure 8.9). The bronchioles contain minute hairs called cilia, which beat rhythmically to sweep debris out of the lungs towards the pharynx for expulsion and thus form part of the mechanical element of the immune system – see earlier in the chapter. Bronchioles end in air sacs called alveoli – small, thinwalled 'balloons', which are surrounded by tiny blood capillaries. As we breathe in, the concentration of oxygen is greater in the alveoli than in the haemoglobin in the blood travelling through the capillaries. As a result, oxygen diffuses across the alveolar walls into the haemoglobin.

---

angina
severe pain in the chest associated with a temporary insufficient supply of blood to the heart.

vasospasm
a situation in which the muscles of artery walls in the heart contract and relax rapidly, resulting in a reduction of the flow of blood through the artery.

coronary artery bypass graft
surgical procedure in which veins or arteries from elsewhere in the patient's body are grafted from the aorta to the coronary arteries, bypassing blockages caused by atheroma in the cardiac arteries and improving the blood supply to the heart muscle.

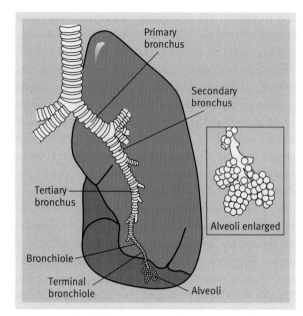

Figure 8.9 Diagram of the lungs, showing the bronchi, bronchioles and alveoli

As we breathe out, carbon dioxide concentration in the blood is greater than that in the alveoli, so it passes from the blood into the alveoli and is then exhaled.

Respiration is the act of breathing:

● *Inspiration*: two sets of muscles are involved in inhalation. The main muscle involved is the diaphragm. This is a sheet of muscle that divides the abdomen and is found immediately below the lungs. Contraction of this muscle pulls the lungs down and sucks air into them. The second set of muscles is known as the intercostal muscles. These are found between the ribs and can expand the chest – again pulling air into the lungs.

● *Expiration*: relaxation of the diaphragm and intercostal muscles allows the lungs to contract, decreases lung volume, and pushes air out of them. The air then passively flows out.

The rate of breathing is controlled by respiratory centres in the brainstem. These respond to:

● the concentration of carbon dioxide in the blood (high carbon dioxide concentrations initiate deeper, more rapid breathing);

● air pressure in lung tissue. Expansion of the lungs stimulates nerve receptors to signal the brain to 'turn off' inspiration. When the lungs collapse, the receptors

give the 'turn on' signal, known as the Hering–Breuer inspiratory reflex.

Other automatic regulators include increases in blood pressure, which slows down respiration; a fall in blood acidity, which stimulates respiration; and a sudden drop in blood pressure, which increases the rate and depth of respiration.

Diseases of the respiratory system

Chronic obstructive airways disease

Chronic obstructive pulmonary disease (COPD) is a group of lung diseases characterised by limited airflow through the airways resulting from damage to the alveoli. Its most common manifestations are **emphysema** and **chronic bronchitis**.

Emphysema

Emphysema results from the destruction of the alveoli, resulting in reduced lung elasticity and reductions in the surface area on which the exchange of oxygen and carbon dioxide can occur. People with the condition experience chronic shortness of breath, an unproductive cough (which produces no phlegm), and a marked reduction in exercise capacity. The condition typically results from exposing the alveoli to irritants, whether as a result of direct or passive smoking or living or working in a polluted environment. About 15 per cent of long-term smokers

---

emphysema

a late effect of chronic infection or irritation of the bronchial tubes. When the bronchi become irritated, some of the airways may become obstructed or the walls of the tiny air sacs may tear, trapping air in the lung beyond them. As a result, the lungs may become enlarged, at the same time becoming less efficient in exchanging oxygen for carbon dioxide.

chronic bronchitis

an inflammation of the bronchi, the main air passages in the lungs, which persists for a long period or repeatedly recurs. Characterised by excessive bronchial mucus and a cough that produces sputum for three months or more in at least two consecutive years.

will develop COPD (Mannino 2003). More rarely, an enzyme deficiency called alpha-1 anti-trypsin deficiency can cause emphysema in non-smokers. Treatment of emphysema involves a number of approaches: drugs known as bronchodilators widen the air passages and relax smooth muscle tissue in the lungs. Some individuals may need continuous oxygen therapy. Finally, as people with emphysema are prone to lung infections, they may require treatment with antibiotics. What is it like to live with emphysema? Well, here is a quote from someone (Gary Bain) with the condition taken from a self-help website (www.emphysema.org):

> Sit down somewhere and relax a little and when you feel comfortable, take your right or left hand and with your thumb and forefinger, hold your nose shut. While holding your nose shut, cover your mouth tightly with the rest of your hand so you can just barely breathe through your fingers. Now, walk for about 40 steps and turn around and come back while still breathing through your hand. Now, do you see how hard it is to breathe? Especially when you try to walk around? That is what emphysema is . . .

Chronic bronchitis

Chronic bronchitis results from inflammation and a consequent narrowing of the airways. Bronchitis is considered to be chronic when it persists for three months or more for at least two consecutive years. People with the condition experience shortness of breath and have excessive mucus within the bronchial tree and a 'wet' cough. They may also experience wheezing and fatigue. As with emphysema, it is caused predominantly by smoking and second-hand smoke. Allergies, outdoor and indoor air pollution, and infection may exacerbate the condition. Treatment involves the use of bronchodilators, and for some people, oxygen therapy. Corticosteroids may also be used at times of acute severe episodes of breathing difficulty when other treatments are ineffective.

Self-help for people with COPD

Unfortunately, the way many people cope with their COPD may inadvertently add to their problems. Understandably, people who become out of breath when they exercise stop doing so. It makes sense: breathlessness is both unpleasant and frightening. Unfortunately, this avoidance results in a decrease in lung function and a worsening of symptoms. As patients' contribution to their lung health has become more evident, a number of programmes have now been developed and implemented to teach people how best to cope with COPD. Often referred to as pulmonary rehabilitation, these provide advice on 'lung health' and coping with breathlessness, and a gentle physical exercise programme designed to increase fitness and lung capacity.

Lung cancer

Lung cancer is the second most common cancer affecting both sexes. Its symptoms include a dry non-productive cough, shortness of breath, coughing up sputum with signs of blood in it, an ache or pain when breathing, loss of appetite, fatigue and losing weight. The main cause of lung cancer is smoking, and as women have taken up smoking following the Second World War, rates of lung cancer among this group have risen, while those among men have fallen (Tyczynski *et al.* 2004). Other risk factors involve exposure to carcinogens, including asbestos and radon, and scarring from tuberculosis. There is some evidence of a genetic risk also.

Two different types of lung cancer have been identified:

1. *Small cell cancer*: the main treatment is radiotherapy or chemotherapy. The overall survival rate depends on the stage of the disease. For limited-stage small cell cancer, cure rates may be as high as 25 per cent, while cure rates for extensive-stage disease are less than 5 per cent.

2. *Non-small cell cancer* (between 70 and 80 per cent of cases): the main treatment for this type of cancer involves removal of the cancer through surgery. Where the tumour is small and has not spread, up to 50 per cent of people with the condition may survive. The prognosis is worse the larger the tumour. Where the tumour has spread and lymph nodes are involved, the disease is almost never cured, and the goals of therapy are to extend life and improve quality of life (Beadsmoore and Screaton 2003).

We examine how people respond to having lung cancer in Chapter 9 ☞, and some interventions designed to help people with lung diseases in Chapter 17 ☞.

SUMMARY

This chapter reviewed some of the anatomy and physiology relevant to health psychology and other chapters of this book. In the first section, it briefly described key functions of the brain and their situation within it. Key functional areas include:

● the medulla oblongata, which controls respiration, blood pressure and heartbeat;

● the hypothalamus, which controls appetite, sexual arousal and thirst. It also exerts some control over our emotions;

● the amygdala, which links situations of threat and relevant emotions such as fear or anxiety, and controls the autonomic nervous system response to such threats.

One of the key systems controlled by the brain is the autonomic nervous system. This comprises two parallel sets of nerves:

1. The sympathetic nervous system is responsible for activation of many organs of the body.

2. The parasympathetic nervous system is responsible for rest and recuperation.

The highest level of control of the autonomic nervous system within the brain is the hypothalamus, which coordinates reflexive changes in response to a variety of physical changes, including movement, temperature and blood pressure. It also responds to emotional and cognitive demands, providing a link between physiological systems and psychological stress.

Activation of the sympathetic nervous system involves two neurotransmitters – adrenaline and noradrenaline – which stimulate organs via the sympathetic nerves themselves. Sustained activation is maintained by their hormonal equivalents, released from the adrenal medulla. A second system, controlled by the hypothalamus and pituitary gland, triggers the release of corticosteroids from the adrenal cortex. These increase the energy available to sustain physiological activation and inhibit inflammation of damaged tissue.

The immune system provides a barrier to infection by viruses and other biological threats to our health. Key elements of the system include phagocytes, such as macrophages and neutrophils, which engulf and destroy invading pathogens. A second group of cells, known as lymphocytes, including cytotoxic T cells and B cells, respond particularly to attacks by viruses and developing tumour cells. Both groups of cells can collaborate in the destruction of pathogens through a complex series of chemical reactions.

Slow viruses, including HIV, attack the immune system – by infecting CD4+ cells – and prevent the T and B cell systems from responding effectively. This leaves the body open to attack from viruses and cancers, either of which may result in life-threatening conditions.

The immune system may, itself, cause problems by treating its own cells as external invading agents. This can result in diseases such as multiple sclerosis, rheumatoid arthritis and type 1 diabetes.

The digestive tract is responsible for the ingestion, absorption and expulsion of food. Activity within it is controlled by the enteric nervous system, which is linked to the autonomic nervous system. Activity in the system is therefore responsive to stress and other psychological states. That said, some conditions thought to be the result of stress are now thought to be the result of physical as well as psychological factors. Gastric ulcers are thought to result from infection by *Helicobacter pylori*, while irritable bowel syndrome is no longer seen as entirely the result of stress but as having a multi-factor aetiology of which stress is but one strand.

The cardiovascular system is responsible for carrying oxygen, nutrients and various other materials around the body. Its activity is influenced by the autonomic nervous system. Two long-term 'silent' conditions that may lead to acute illnesses such as myocardial infarction or stroke are hypertension and atheroma. Both involve long-term processes. One way in which long-term hypertension may develop is by repeated short-term increases in blood pressure through the action of the autonomic nervous system in response to stress. Atheroma develops as a result of repair processes to the artery wall. Two obvious outcomes of this process are myocardial infarction, in which an artery supplying the heart muscle is blocked and dies. Angina presents with similar symptoms but is the result of spasm of the arteries and is reversible.

Finally, the respiratory system is responsible for inspiring and carrying oxygen around the body, and the expulsion of carbon dioxide. It is prone to a number of disease processes, including chronic obstructive airways disease and lung cancer, all of which are significantly exacerbated by cigarette smoking.

Further reading

Lovallo, W.R. (2004). *Stress and Health. Biological and Psychological Interactions*. Thousand Oaks, CA: Sage.

A relatively easy introduction to the autonomic and immune systems, as well as how stress can influence their activity.

Kumar, P.J. and Clark, K.L. (2009). *Clinical Medicine*. Oxford: W.B. Saunders.

At 1,464 pages, this is not a textbook you may want to buy. But if you want to know more about the development of various diseases, this is an excellent starting point.

Vedhara, K. and Irwin, M. (eds) (2005). *Human Psycho-neuroimmunology*. Oxford: Oxford University Press.

A readable guide to psychoneuroimmunology, written for those people who do not want to plough through £250, 400-page tomes (or so say the editors).

You can also find a wealth of information about illnesses and their treatment from the internet. Three excellent sites are:

medlineplus.gov/ – this is a free service provided by the US National Library of Medicine and the National Institutes of Health

www.netdoctor.co.uk/ – provides similar information and is also free.

www.patient.co.uk/ – as does this site.

In addition, many sites provide information on specific illnesses, including:

www.heartfoundation.org.au/index.htm – the Australian Heart Foundation

www.ulcerativecolitis.org.uk/ – the Ulcerative Colitis Information Centre

www.lunguk.org/ – the British Lung Foundation.

In fact, simply using the name of an illness as a search term in any search engine will undoubtedly allow you to access all the information you are likely to need about that illness and its treatment.

Visit the website at **www.pearsoned.co.uk/morrison** for additional resources to help you with your study, including multiple choice questions, weblinks and flashcards.

Chapter 9
Symptom perception, interpretation and response

Learning outcomes

By the end of this chapter, you should have an understanding of:

- key theoretical models of symptom perception, interpretation and response
- contextual, cultural and individual influences upon symptom perception
- the core dimensions upon which illness can be represented
- a broad range of influences upon symptom interpretation
- factors that influence delay in seeking health-care advice for symptoms

First impressions can be wrong

'Gosh, he's hot,' says Mum to Dad when putting baby Josh into his cot. 'Not surprised given all the layers you have him wrapped in,' says Dad, Dan. Having unwrapped the six-month old baby a little from his cocoon of vest, Baby-Grow, and three blankets, the parents return downstairs to watch *Silent Witness*. Unusually Josh has settled by nine so they have a rare chance to watch their favourite drama. Two hours later they are heading for bed and check on Josh, who is restless, hot, but sleepy. When Mum leans over to kiss him goodnight, she sees he is flushed on the face and looks a bit blotchy. Rather than disturb him further, she loosens his covers a bit more and wonders if it's time for the first tooth to start worrying away at his wee gums. She tells herself to check her parenting book in the morning, and to buy some teething gel.

Three hours later she awakens to Josh moaning and crying. She puts on the side light, looks over to the cot and seeing his blankets are all over the place, goes over. 'Best to check his nappy,' mutters Dan. So she lifts Josh, who is so sleepy he is a bit floppy, puts him on the changing unit and undoes his Baby-Gro. 'Aah, clever boy, no messy nappy,' she murmurs. While refastening his clothing, she notices a rash on his tummy and when she touches it, he feels clammy. He isn't crying any more but neither is he really watching her as he usually does. She picks him up, He is REALLY hot and kind of limp.

'Dan, wake up, something's not right with Joshy.' 'DAN, wake UP.' She goes over to the bed and puts on the light at Dan's side. 'Look at this rash Dan . . . what do you think it is?'

'He is probably just too hot, I told you not to wrap him up too much.'

'I had taken half his covers off when we came to bed, it can't be that Dan.'

'He's maybe teething?' Dan sits up in bed and looks at Josh. 'They're just pinpricks, looks like a heat rash to me. He's a bit spaced out, he's still half asleep poor lad, put him back down and see if he settles.'

'Nah, I'm not happy, he is spaced out, and he has a rash, go and get a glass.'

'Oh God, to test his rash like it says to do for meningitis? I think you're over-reacting, it doesn't have to be THAT,' says Dan as he gets out of bed.

'Yeah, OK, I know I probably am but I'm phoning NHS Direct to ask them what they think,' says Jane as Dan goes to get a glass, tucking Josh under his arm. She is waiting for an answer when Dan yells up, 'Forget that, call an ambulance quickly, he is really out of it and these spots don't disappear!'

Forty minutes later they are in ICU at the local hospital. Josh is going through all sorts of tests and soon it is confirmed, Josh is seriously ill with meningitis.

'Thank god we came in when we did Jane, they say if we had left him till morning he may not be with us still,' sobs Dan.

Chapter outline

How do we know if we are getting ill? Do we all react in the same way to symptoms? What influences how we perceive and interpret symptoms of illness? Do beliefs about illness differ across the lifespan? Do illness perceptions and their interpretation influence health-care seeking? These types of question are important to our understanding of how people cope with illness and of differentials in health-care-seeking behaviour. They are questions that you need to ask yourself when thinking about the study of health and illness, whether as a future health psychologist or health-care practitioner.

How do we become aware of the sensations of illness?

Illness generates changes in bodily sensations and functions that a person may perceive themselves or perhaps have pointed out to them by another person who says, for example, 'You look pale'. The kind of sign that is likely to be noticed by the individual themselves includes changes in bodily functions (e.g. increased frequency of urination, heartbeat irregularities), emissions (such as blood in one's urine), sensations (e.g. numbness, loss of vision) and unpleasant sensations (e.g. fever, pain, nausea). Other people may not notice these changes but would perhaps notice changes in bodily appearance (weight loss, skin pallor) or function (e.g. paralysis, limping, tremor). Radley (1994) distinguishes, as did MacBryde and Blacklow in a key early paper (1970), between 'bodily signs' and 'symptoms of illness'. The former can be objectively recognised, but the latter requires interpretation; for example, a person has to decide whether a raised temperature (a bodily sign) is symptomatic of illness (e.g. influenza) or simply a sign of physical exertion.

While some diseases have visible symptoms, others do not and instead involve a subjectively sensed component of bodily responses, e.g. feeling sick, feeling tired, being in pain, which cannot be seen *per se*. Many people regularly experience symptoms, but there is huge variability between individuals when it comes to attending to, or reporting, symptoms. Although 70 to 90 per cent of us have, at some time, a condition that could be diagnosed and treated by a health professional, only about one-third will actually seek medical attention. Health psychologists are interested in why this is the case.

As described in Chapter 1 ☞, people's views about health are shaped by both their prior experience of illness and their understanding of medical knowledge, whether expert or lay. People therefore learn about health in the same way as they learn about everything else – through experience, either their own or of other people's. People 'fall ill against a background of beliefs about good and poor health' (Radley 1994: 61). Furthermore, Radley notes, people's lives are 'grounded in *activity*', i.e. on the everyday activities or behaviour that depends upon the body, whether they be instrumental activities such as being able to run for a bus or expressive activities like being able to look attractive. Illness can therefore challenge a person at a fundamental level.

Illness or disease?

Cassell (1976) used the word 'illness' to stand for 'what the patient feels when he goes to the doctor', i.e. the experience of not feeling quite right as compared with one's normal state; and 'disease' to stand for 'what he has on the way home from the doctor's office'. Disease, then, is considered as being something of the organ, cell or tissue that suggests a physical disorder or underlying pathology, whereas illness is what the person experiences. People can feel ill without having an identifiable disease (think of a hangover!), and importantly, people can have a disease and not feel ill (for example, well-controlled asthma or diabetes, early stage HIV infection). A routine medical check-up may lead to a person who thought themselves healthy finding out that they are in fact 'officially' ill as indicated by the result of some routine

test. By providing a diagnosis, doctors mark the entry of a person into the health-care system.

How does a person know if they are getting ill? This chapter will attempt to answer this by describing the processes underlying three stages of response:

1. perceiving symptoms;
2. interpreting symptoms as illness;
3. planning and taking action.

WHAT DO YOU THINK?

The chapter opening 'headline' perhaps made you think about how you would have responded in such a situation. We may in fact respond differently, quicker, to symptoms in our child than to our own symptoms. How many of the symptoms below have you experienced in the last two weeks? Of those experienced, how many have you seen a health professional about? Think of the reasons why you did, or did not, seek medical advice about your symptoms.

- fever
- nausea
- headache
- tremor
- joint stiffness
- excessive fatigue
- back pain
- dizziness
- stomach pains
- visual disturbance
- chesty cough
- sore throat
- breathlessness
- chest pain.

Symptom perception

Many different stimuli compete for our attention at any given moment, so why do certain sensations become more salient than others? Why do we seek medical

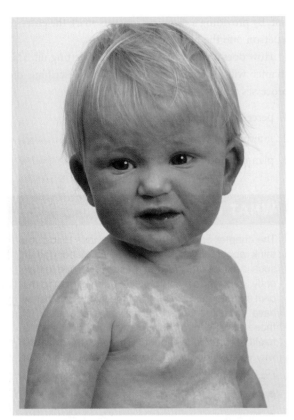

Plate 9.1 This rash looks unpleasant, but is it a heat rash or something more serious?

Source: Alamy Images/Bubbles Photo Library.

attention for some symptoms when we perceive them and not for others? While an early study of American college students found that they had experienced an average of 17 different symptoms per month (Pennebaker and Skelton 1981), few will have sought medical attention. This is partly because most symptoms are transient and pass before we think too much about them, but also because people are not necessarily the best judges of whether their own perceived symptoms are in fact signs of illness.

There are several models of symptom perception. The attentional model of Pennebaker (1982) describes how competition for attention between multiple internal or external cues or stimuli leads to the same physical sign or physiological change going unnoticed in some contexts but not in others. The cognitive–perceptual model of Cioffi (1991) focuses more on the processes of interpretation of physical signs and influences upon their attribution as symptoms while also acknowledging the role of selective attention (Cioffi 1991). Overall, research has highlighted an array of biological, psychological and contextual influences upon symptom perception (see Figure 9.1), with bottom–up influences upon perception arising from the physical properties of a bodily sensation, and top–down influences being seen in the influence of attentional processes or mood.

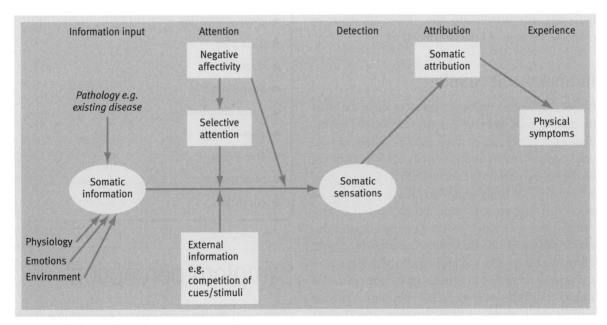

Figure 9.1 A simplified symptom perception model

Source: adapted from Kolk, Hanewald, Schagen *et al.* (2003).

Characteristics of bodily signs that increase likelihood of symptom perception

Bodily signs are physical sensations that may or may not be symptoms of illness: for example, sweating is a bodily sign, but it may not indicate fever if the person has simply been exerting themselves. Signs can be detected and identified, for example, blood pressure, whereas symptoms are what is experienced and as such are more **subjective**, e.g. nausea. (MacBryde and Blacklow 1970). Symptoms generally result from physiological changes with physical (somatic) properties, but the fact that only some will be detected by the individual highlights that biological explanations of symptom perception are insufficient. Those receiving attention and interpretation as a symptom are likely to be:

● *Painful or disruptive*: if a bodily sign has consequences for the person, e.g. they cannot sit comfortably, vision is impaired, or they can no longer perform a routine activity, then the person is more likely to perceive this as a symptom (Cacioppo *et al.* 1986, 1989).

● *Novel*: subjective estimates of prevalence have been shown to significantly influence (1) the perceived severity of a symptom and (2) whether the person will seek medical attention (e.g. Ditto and Jemmott 1989; Jemmott *et al.* 1988). Experiencing a 'novel' symptom (new to oneself or believed not to have been experienced by others) is likely to be considered indicative of something rare and serious, whereas experiencing a symptom thought to be common leads to assumptions of lower severity and a reduced likelihood to seek out health information or care. For example, tiredness among students may be normalised and interpreted as a sign of late nights studying or partying, where it may, for some, reflect underlying disease.

● *Persistent*: a bodily sign is more likely to be perceived as a symptom if it persists for longer than is considered usual or if it persists in spite of self-medication.

● *Pre-existing chronic disease*: having a chronic disease increases the number of other symptoms perceived and reported. Past or current illness experience has a strong influence upon somatisation (i.e. attention to bodily states) (e.g. Chapman and Martin 2011; Kolk *et al.* 2003).

There are many trivial symptoms which do not require medical attention and which could be self-managed successfully without the costs associated with seeking health care (e.g. most flu episodes), but there are also some illnesses with few initial symptoms, such as cancer; therefore symptoms alone are 'unreliable indicators of the need for medical attention' (Martin *et al.* 2003: 203).

Attentional states and symptom perception

Individual differences exist in the amount of **attention** people give to their internal state and external states (Pennebaker and Skelton 1981; Pennebaker 1982, 1992). Pennebaker discovered that somatic sensations are less likely to be noticed when a person's attention is engaged externally than when they are not otherwise distracted. Think, for example, of an athlete going on to win a race in spite of having sustained a leg injury. On the other hand, individuals are more likely to notice tickling sensations in their throats and start coughing towards the end of lectures as attention begins to wane than at the beginning of the lecture or during highly interesting sections! Individuals are limited in their attentional capacity, so internal and external stimuli have to compete for attention. This 'competition of cues theory' (Pennebaker 1982) explains why a bodily sign that may be noticed immediately in some contexts may remain undetected in others. (This also points to findings that

subjective

personal, i.e. what a person thinks and reports (e.g. excitement) as opposed to what is **objective**. Subjective is generally related to internal interpretations of events rather than observable features.

objective

i.e. real, visible or systematically measurable (e.g. adrenaline levels). Generally pertains to something that can be seen, or recorded, by others (as opposed to subjective).

attention

generally refers to the selection of some stimuli over others for internal processing.

manipulating attentional focus, through cognitive or behavioural distraction, can be a useful form of symptom management; see Chapter 13 (☞.)

A high degree of attention increases a person's sensitivity to new, or different, bodily signs. Consider the effects of well-publicised outbreaks of illnesses, infections or toxins on symptom perception, for example outbreaks of Swine flu or of *E. coli*, identification of new diseases such as SARS in 2003, or chemical leaks. Attendance at doctors' increases massively at such times and in extreme circumstances can lead to what is called 'mass psychogenic illness'. This response illustrates the powerful effect of anxiety and suggestion on our perceptions and behaviour. Worry about even tenuous links to the source of infection heightens a person's attention to their own bodily signs and can produce the belief that they have contracted the illness. However, many people who seek medical attention at such times will find that there is no organic explanation for their symptoms. Another example of external stimuli altering attention to, and processing of, bodily signs can be seen in what has been described as 'medical student's disease' (Mechanic 1962). In this case the increased knowledge about disease-specific symptoms obtained during medical lectures increased the self-reported experience of exactly these symptoms among over two-thirds of the medical students studied!

Brown (2004) has distinguished between two attentional systems which are proposed to influence how symptom information is processed. The first, the primary attentional system (PAS), is proposed to operate below the level of consciousness and acts on stored representations, such as illness schema which it automatically selects from when a person for whatever reasons, over-attends to somatic (bodily) experiences. This can thus lead a symptom to be wrongly matched to a pre-existing schema, such as might happen in cases of 'mass psychogenic illness' or 'medical student's disease' referred to above. The secondary attentional system (SAS) on the other hand is considered more amenable to executive control, i.e. attention here can be manipulated by conscious thoughts and cognitive processes, such as those we describe later in this chapter. However, this process is hampered if PAS has already dictated where the person's attention is focused on and a 'label' has already been assigned to the symptoms. The example Brown uses is chronic fatigue syndrome (CFS), a condition where there is currently no medically identified pathology to explain the reported symptoms. A whole special issue of the journal *Clinical Psychology Review* addressed the issue of 'medically unexplained symptoms' in 2007 and articles point to an array of influences including genetic, psychophysiological and social as well as those cognitive processes of attention and memory, which we refer to here.

Social influences on symptom perception

It has been shown that people hold stereotypical notions about 'who gets' certain diseases and that this can interfere with perception and response to initial symptoms. For example, Martin *et al.* (2003) describe studies showing that the general public associate males with vulnerability to heart disease and not females, and that among heart attack patients, females less often recognised their initial bodily signs as symptoms of heart disease. The implications for health-care-seeking behaviour are obvious.

Our motivation to attend to and detect signs or symptoms of illness will depend on the context at the time the symptom presents itself. As referred to above, people tend not to notice internal sensations when their environment is exciting or absorbing, but a lack of alternative distraction may increase perception of symptoms. Furthermore, situations bring with them varying expectations of physical involvement, as illustrated in Figure 9.2. Bodily signs, for example muscle spasms,

	Production of bodily disturbance	
	High	**Low**
Requirement to contain signs **High**	Sport	Attending lecture
Requirement to contain signs **Low**	Giving birth	Watching TV at home

Figure 9.2 Situational differences in the production and containment of physical symptoms

Source: adapted from Radley (1994: 69).

when playing sport or giving birth are expected and thus would not generally be taken as symptomatic of illness; however, these two situations differ in the extent to which they would expect a person to suppress the pain caused by the spasms (very few people give birth silently!). As another example of the importance of context on both perception and expression, few bodily signs are expected when sitting in lectures or watching TV, and unless the bodily sign (e.g. lower back pain) can be attributed to something like posture, then it may be interpreted as a symptom of illness. In terms of expression, the home and the lecture setting also differ significantly, with suppression of physical discomfort by means of motivated distraction being more likely in the lecture setting (e.g. listening to the lecturer) than pain expression (e.g. moaning out loud) which may occur if at home.

Individual differences affecting symptom perception

The same bodily sign may, or may not, be perceived as a symptom on the basis of individual difference variables such as gender, life stage, emotional state or personality traits, and the effect such factors have on attentional states. Research has tried to identify whether differences in symptom perception exist that may help us understand differences seen in health-seeking behaviour (see later section).

Gender

It is often proposed that gender **socialisation** provides women with a greater readiness to attend to and perceive bodily signs and symptoms; however, the evidence appears to vary according to the symptoms explored (Baum and Grunberg 1991; Macintyre 1993). A recent qualitative study of the symptom perception and reporting behaviour of men with prostate disease found that four themes emerged from interview data: 'living up to the image'; 'normal or illness?' (re symptom interpretation); 'protecting the image'; 'engaging with the system'. These themes encompass men's accounts of learning to ignore symptoms out of a need to be seen to be strong and masculine, point to a lack of understanding about prostate problems being symptoms of illness as opposed to part of ageing, and highlight men's unwillingness or anxiety about taking 'embarrassing' symptoms

to a health-care professional (Hale *et al.* 2007). In keeping with this, Gijsbers van Wijk and Kolk (1997) suggest that as male-directed media is less inclined to provide health advice than women's media, less developed illness cognitions may exist in males which reduces the likelihood of them perceiving a bodily sign as a 'symptom' and limits their reporting behaviour. Hale and colleagues' studies also find evidence of men 'avoiding' information about illness even when they are faced with it in the media. Thus, in considering gender differences in symptom perception, there are many overlapping explanations. It may also be that physiological differences arising from puberty and menstruation influence **pain thresholds** in the first place, or perhaps the evidence that women attend health care more does not reflect so much a gender difference in symptom perception as one in reporting behaviour (see later section). While no full explanation can be expected of such a complex human behaviour as symptom perception, it is generally acknowledged that differences exist in the extent to which males and females are 'allowed' to respond to bodily signs.

Life stage

With age comes experience and increasing awareness of one's internal organs and their functions and sensations. While there are age differentials in definitions and perceptions of the meaning of health and illness (Chapter 1 ☞), do age differences in whether or not bodily signs are perceived as symptoms of illness contribute to identified differentials in health-care-seeking behaviour (Grunfeld *et al.* 2003; Ramirez *et al.* 1999; see Chapter 2 ☞)? Ageing populations certainly bear the burden of many chronic or life-threatening diseases, such as heart disease, stroke, arthritis and breast cancer,

socialisation

the process by which a person learns – from family, teachers, peers – the rules, norms and moral codes of behaviour that are expected of them.

pain threshold

the minimum amount of pain intensity that is required before it is detected (individual variation).

but does this mean they pay less attention to their bodily states and perceive fewer symptoms? There is little evidence of this. However, it does appear that older adults *interpret* and respond differently to perceived symptoms (see later section).

Children develop a conceptual understanding of illness during the course of their cognitive development and socialisation, but whether children perceive specific symptoms differently to adults is less known, and the limited language of very young children presents challenges to parents, researchers and health professionals alike. Crying, rubbing or other behaviour is relied upon by adults as indicators of symptom experience in the very young, with pain, for example, being exhibited rather than reported. It is likely, however, that symptom perception is influenced by similar attentional, contextual, individual and emotional influences as seen in adults. One study which measured children's record of their daily symptoms and compared these data to peak expiratory flow rates found that symptom perception was inaccurate in a substantial number of children with asthma, independent of clinical severity, age, gender and use of preventative medication (Cabral *et al.* 2002). It has also been shown that the presence of problems in attention, concentration and impulsivity may be related to symptom perception and asthma outcomes (Koinis-Mitchell *et al.* 2009; McQuaid *et al.* 2007).

Emotions and personality traits

Generally, mood is crucial. People who are in a positive mood have been found to rate themselves as more healthy and indicate fewer symptoms, whereas people in negative moods report more symptoms, are more pessimistic about their ability to act to relieve their symptoms and believe themselves to be more susceptible to illness (Leventhal *et al.* 1996). Negative emotional states, particularly anxiety or depression, may increase symptom perception by means of its effect on attention, as well as by increasing the recall of prior negative health events, which makes it more likely that new bodily signs will be viewed as symptoms of further illness (Cohen *et al.* 1995; Watson and Pennebaker 1989; see Chapter 16 ☞). Another emotion associated with symptom perception is that of fear, which can work in either a positive or negative direction. For example, fear of pain and fear of recurrence can increase a person's attention and responsiveness to

bodily signs, seen among heart attack survivors who often become increasingly vigilant of their internal states in the hope of detecting, at an early stage, signs of possible recurrence. In contrast, fear of being seriously ill can reduce a person's attention to and consideration of possible meanings of their symptoms, such as reported among men with prostate problems who downplayed symptoms out of fear of finding disease (Hale *et al.* 2007, and see also their subsequent study in relation to men seeking medical help in RESEARCH FOCUS on p. 255).

Neuroticism (N) can be described as a trait-like tendency to experience negative emotional states and is related to the broader construct '**negative affectivity**' (NA). NA can manifest itself either as a state (situation-specific) or a trait (generalised). While state NA can incorporate a range of emotions, including anger, sadness and fear, trait NA, like neuroticism, has been found to affect the perception, interpretation and reporting of symptoms. In terms of perceptual style, neurotics and those high in trait NA are more introspective and attend more negatively to somatic information and thus they perceive more frequent symptoms and are more likely to misattribute them to underlying disease (Williams 2006) and more likely to report them (Bennett *et al.* 1996; Deary *et al.* 1997; Watson and Pennebaker 1989, 1991). It is worth noting that, while such traits appear associated with retrospectively reported symptom experience, the support for longitudinal effects of negative affectivity on symptom perception is mixed. For example, trait NA did not predict symptom complaints over time among an elderly sample (e.g. Diefenbach *et al.* 1995; Leventhal *et al.* 1996). Quite often, studies examining neuroticism in relation to symptom perception have implied a link between N and hypochondriasis, where there is a preoccupation with having illness based on misattributions and

---

neuroticism

a personality trait reflected in the tendency to be anxious, feel guilty and experience generally negative thought patterns.

negative affectivity

a dispositional tendency to experience persistent and pervasive negative or low mood and self-concept (related to **neuroticism**).

misinterpretations of bodily signs as symptoms (Ferguson 2000). This suggests that the symptom perception is unfounded in terms of actual physical symptoms. However, Williams (2006) in a chapter reviewing this area points to a body of evidence where neuroticism is associated with greater physiological reactivity to stress, including elevated levels of stress hormones such as cortisol (see Chapter 11 ☞). In some circumstances, therefore, there may be a 'real' or objective pathway between this personality trait and increased symptom experience.

Cognitions and coping style

How people characteristically think and respond to external or internal events can also influence symptom perception. For example, there is some evidence that

---

type A behaviour (TAB)

a constellation of characteristics, mannerisms and behaviour including competitiveness, time urgency, impatience, easily aroused hostility, rapid and vigorous speech patterns and expressive behaviour. Extensively studied in relation to the aetiology of coronary heart disease, where hostility seems central.

repression

a defensive coping style that serves to protect the person from negative memories or anxiety-producing thoughts by preventing their gaining access to consciousness.

comparative optimism

initially termed 'unrealistic optimism', this term refers to an individual's estimate of their risk of experiencing a negative event compared with similar others (Weinstein and Klein 1996).

monitors

a generalised coping style that involves attending to the source of stress or threat and trying to deal with it directly, e.g. through information gathering/ attending to threat-relevant information (as opposed to **blunters**).

blunters

a general coping style that involves minimising or avoiding the source of threat or stress, i.e. avoiding threat-relevant information (as opposed to **monitors**).

---

individuals characterised by time urgency, impatience, hostility and competitive drive (i.e. **type A behaviour**: Friedman and Rosenman 1959; Rosenman 1978) are less likely to perceive symptoms, perhaps because they are highly focused on the task in hand or because they avoid paying attention to signs of self-weakness. Their desire for control, on the other hand, is associated with prompt health-care-seeking behaviour once a severe health threat is acknowledged (Matthews *et al.* 1983). It has also been shown that people who cope with aversive events by using the cognitive defence mechanism of **repression** are less likely to experience symptoms than non-repressors (Ward 1988; Myers 1998), with repression being associated with higher levels of **comparative optimism** regarding controllable health threats such as tooth decay and skin cancer (Myers and Reynolds 2000). Both repressive coping and comparative optimism have previously been related to poor physical health (Weinstein and Klein 1996).

A further distinction has been drawn between monitoring and blunting coping styles (Miller *et al.* 1987). **Monitors** deal with threat by monitoring their situation for threat-relevant information, whereas **blunters** ignore or minimise external and internal stimuli. Where one stands on this dimension will influence symptom perception as well as determine how quickly a person uses health services (see below).

Symptom interpretation

Once a symptom has been perceived, people do not generally consider it in isolation but relate it to other aspects of their experience and to their wider concepts of illness. Symptoms are more than labels for the various changes that happen to the body; they not only derive from medical classifications of disease but can also influence how we think, feel and behave. Culture will influence the meanings and labels that individuals ascribe to symptoms (Stainton Rogers 1991), as will gender, life stage, past experience, illness beliefs and representations. While information about illness and symptoms of illness are increasingly woven into popular television programmes and other media, we know little about how this information is processed by children.

Cultural influences

We have heard in earlier chapters about cultural varia-tions in health behaviours and in terms of prevalence of certain diseases (e.g. higher prevalence of diabetes among Asian populations, for example). It has also been shown that cultural variation exists in the extent to which individuals show readiness to respond to perceived physical symptoms, although findings are mixed in the extent to which differences can truly be ascribed to culture, given the range of other influences that are not always controlled for (e.g. age, illness experience, etc.). For example, several American studies have compared samples of pain patients by virtue of their Jewish, Italian, Irish or 'old' American (those of Anglo-Saxon descent) origin. Stereotypic explanations were often provided whereby Jewish and Italian American men expressed pain more readily than Irish or 'old' Americans. Although pain expression was similar, the aim of their pain expression differed, with Italian Americans complaining about pain discomfort, while Jewish Americans typically expressing worries about what the pain might mean in terms of their underlying and future health. A further difference was found in terms of willingness to complain about pain at home: Italian Americans felt that they lacked the freedom to complain about their pain at home as they wanted to project the image of being the strong 'head of the family', whereas Jewish American men did not see pain expression at home as a sign of weakness. These differences in pain expression and interpretation were associated with group differences in the willingness to accept treatment. Italian American men were more likely to trust the doctor and accept pain medication where Jewish American men were more cynical as to the benefits of analgesics. The 'old' Americans differed in expression, not displaying their feelings but instead reporting their pain in a factual way. These men saw emotional expression as a likely hindrance to the doctor's knowledge, skill and efficiency in treating them. At home, the 'old' American men withdrew from other people if their pain got too severe, and their wives reacted with either embarrassment or concern if they saw their husbands express emotional responses to their pain. Irish Americans were found to stoically accept or deny the pain, again reflecting a socialised gender phenomenon. Zborowski (1952) states that such cultural variations are learned during socialisation, where peo-ple's ideas about what is acceptable pain to bear and

express is shaped. The lengthy illustration above shows that not only do pain perception and expression differ, but they also have a social function in terms of influencing treatment expectations or even the reactions of others (see also Chapter 16 ☛). What this illustration also highlights is some of the gendered responses we described in the section on symptom perception.

Individual difference influences

Some individuals can maintain their everyday activities when experiencing what would be perceived as debilitat-ing symptoms of illness by another person. Why? This is because of **individual differences** in how symptoms are interpreted.

Gender

Somatisation disorder, i.e. the experience of multiple unexplained symptoms, is more common in females (Noyes 2001) and thought to overlap with the presence of hypochondriasis, and women tend also to score higher on measures of neuroticism (Williams 2006). For these reasons, and others explored in an earlier section such as general socialisation, it is thought more likely that a woman will interpret a bodily sign as symptomatic of underlying illness than men. Evidence commonly bears this out inasmuch as women are seen to present to health services more frequently (Eurostat 2007). Few studies have explicitly compared men and women matched in terms of other influences on symptom inter-pretation such as personality, social context and such like, with gender often being controlled for in analysis rather than focused on. Where gender differences are highlighted, such as in some studies of illness percep-tions, we have included them.

Life stage

It is likely that young children are distinct from adolescents in their cognitive awareness of illness and its implications by virtue of the stage of cognitive development attained

> **individual differences**
> aspects of an individual that distinguish them from other individuals or groups (e.g. age, personality).

(Bibace and Walsh 1980; see Chapter 1 ☞) but also by virtue of the difference in life or illness experience and knowledge accumulated (Eiser 1990; Goldman *et al.* 1991). As described earlier in this chapter, studying the illness perceptions and interpretations of very young ill children is challenging, for various reasons, including ethical issues in submitting sick children to the demands of face-to-face interviews, methodological issues such as the limited availability of child-validated assessment tools, or the challenges of limited linguistic and cognitive skills. Young people with diabetes, both pre-adolescent and adolescent, have been described as having 'a basic understanding of the nature, cause and timeline of their illness and treatment recommended' (Standiford *et al.* 1997, cited in Griva *et al.* 2000); however, there is convincing evidence that children have similar multidimensional illness representations to adults, with illness consequences and issues of control being highlighted in both quantitative and qualitative studies. Multidimensional illness constructs have been reported among children and young adults considering their own serious and chronic conditions, such as CFS (Gray and Rutter 2007), asthma and eczema (Walker *et al.* 2006), and illness in others, such as their mother's cancer (Forrest *et al.* 2006). In this latter study, children aged 6 to 18 years talked about their mother's breast cancer, and mothers also talked about how they thought their child perceived the cancer and its treatment. Children's ideas about cancer included seeing it as common, as rare, as a killer, as treatable, as something that can be genetic, caused by smoking, worsened by stress; and ideas about treatment included thinking that the more treatment received the worse the cancer, but the less likely it would be to come back. Mothers were not always aware of how much their child understood about the illness and its treatment and, indeed, many found communicating about treatment implications or potential life-threatening consequences of the cancer difficult. When illness is in the family (Chapter 15 ☞), communication and shared understanding of symptoms or treatment is an important factor in aiding adaptive coping with illness, both for the 'ill' person and for those affected by it. Other evidence of differences in parental and child perceptions of a child's illness can be seen in a small-scale study of nine asthmatic children aged 12–15 years, and eleven of their parents (Morrison *et al.* 2000a). While no significant differences emerged in the perceived severity of the illness, parents had higher perceptions of control over the child's asthma than what the children themselves reported. Fuller exploration is needed as to the implications of such differences, for example on adherence or coping behaviours.

Personality

As well as influencing symptom perception, personality and emotional characteristics can affect how symptoms are interpreted. For example, those high in N or NA commonly exhibit heightened symptom perception and, although there is some evidence that there may be a physical explanation for this, the consensus view still remains that neurotic or trait NA individuals over-attend to their internal states and exaggerate the meaning and implications of perceived symptoms. As a result of their negative interpretations of symptoms, individuals high in neuroticism are more likely to seek health care than those low in N. However, neuroticism is not all bad: there is evidence that moderate levels of neuroticism can benefit health, for example in terms of better adherence to treatment or quicker presentation to medical services following actual illness events (see Williams 2006 for a fuller discussion).

Illness experience

Prior experience affects interpretation of and response to symptoms in that having a history of particular symptoms or vicarious experience (e.g. experience of illness in others) leads to assumptions about the meaning and implications of some symptoms. Also, as previously stated, symptoms considered to be rare in either one's own experience, or in that of others, are more likely to be interpreted as serious than a previously experienced or widespread symptom (Croyle and Ditto 1990). Believing symptoms to be 'just a bug that's going round' can mean that people sometimes ignore potentially dangerous 'warning signals'. A knowledge of which bodily signs are associated with particular behaviour or illnesses (e.g. sweats and flu, sweats and exercise) will enable interpretation and attachment of a meaning to the symptom. These reserves of knowledge are known as 'disease prototypes'.

Illness/disease prototypes

Even when a physical sensation or bodily sign is perceived as a 'symptom', what is it that leads a person to believe they are sick? This arises when the symptoms a person is experiencing 'fit' a model of illness retrieved from their memory and it is here that health psychology draws from models dominant in cognitive psychology. People have disease prototypes that help them to organise and evaluate information about physical sensations that might not otherwise be interpretable. Symptoms are placed in the context of a person's past knowledge and experience, which has led to the development of protypical expectations of certain illnesses. Matching or not matching symptoms to a disease prototype (also referred to as cognitive 'schemata') shapes how a person perceives and responds to bodily signs, influences whether bodily signs are perceived to be symptoms of illness or not, and influences how it is then interpreted and responded to.

Illnesses that have clear sign-sets (symptoms) associated with them are more likely to be easily recognised in self-diagnosis: for example, a person experiencing serious abdominal pains may quickly consider appendicitis, and another person experiencing mild chest pain may quickly consider indigestion. It would be easy to assume therefore that a lump found in the breast would, generally, prompt concerns that it may signify cancer and result in health-care seeking, and this is generally the case (see Chapter 4 ☛ for a discussion of influences on breast-screening behaviour). However, there are other symptoms of breast cancer, such as breast pain or skin scaling around the nipple, that may not be in a person's 'prototype', and thus such symptoms may go unidentified. This inability to correctly identify various potential breast cancer symptoms predicted help-seeking delay among a general population sample of 546 women (Grunfeld *et al.* 2003). Relevant to this, Caciopco *et al.* (1989) pointed to the notion of 'salience' i.e. some symptoms will be 'tagged' to strong and emotive labels in our memory stores, e.g. cancer, heart attack, whereas others will be less so, e.g. menstrual cramps, indigestion. He reports data whereby women with gynaecological cancers had initially been more likely to consider less threatening explanations for their symptoms, e.g. menopause, than they were the most negative interpretation of their symptoms, i.e. cancer, and had only accepted cancer as a possibility (this leading them to seek health care) when symptoms had worsened. In this early and influential paper Caciopco also notes that the 'more nondescript the sign or symptom, the greater the number of potential matches in long-term memory and the greater tends to be the likelihood of making errors when linking

these bodily events to a particular physiological condition' (p. 260). Similarly, Perry *et al.* (2001) report that when heart attack symptoms do not 'match' the existing illness prototype in terms of severity, delay in seeking medical attention is greatest. In addition, there is evidence that a failure of a symptom to fit a protypical image of the 'likely victim' of one possible explanation for the symptom can lead to misinterpretation or delay. For example, Martin and colleagues (2004) found that women were less likely to attribute chest pain to a possible heart attack, as their stereotypical image of a heart attack victim was male.

These prototypes have given rise to what is often described as 'common-sense models of illness', examples of which are contained in Table 9.1. A vast amount of health psychology research has developed this thinking into what is often referred to as 'illness representation' research.

Illness representations and the 'common-sense model' of illness

Many different terms are employed, sometimes interchangeably, by authors discussing illness models: for example, cognitive schemata (Pennebaker 1982);

Table 9.1 Disease prototypes

	Influenza	AIDS
Identity	Runny nose, fever, shivery, sneezing, aching limbs	Weight loss, swollen glands, fever, skin lesions, pneumonia
Cause	Virus	Virus
Consequences	Rarely long-term or serious (except if new 'strain')	Long-term ill health, death, uncertainty
Timeline	24 hours to a week	Months to years
Cure	Time and self-medication	None, multiple treatments to delay progression
Type of person	Anybody	High-risk groups of injecting drug users; increasingly anyone via unprotected sexual intercourse

<table>
<tr><td>

illness cognition

the cognitive processes involved in a person's perception or interpretation of symptoms or illness and how they represent it to themselves (or to others) (cf. Croyle and Ditto 1990).

</td></tr>
</table>

illness cognition (Croyle and Ditto 1990); common-sense models of illness and illness representations (Lau and Hartman 1983; Lau *et al.* 1989; Leventhal *et al.* 1980; Leventhal *et al.* 1984); personal models (Hampson *et al.* 1990; Lawson *et al.* 2007) and illness perceptions (Weinman *et al.* 1996). One well-known model is the self-regulatory model of illness and illness behaviour proposed by Howard Leventhal and colleagues (see Figure 9.3). In this model, illness cognitions are defined as 'a patient's own implicit common-sense beliefs about their illness' (e.g. Leventhal *et al.* 1980; Leventhal *et al.* 1992). This 'common-sense model' states that mental representations provide a framework for understanding and coping with illness, and help a person to recognise what to look out for. What Leventhal and his colleagues proposed is a dual-processing model, which considers in parallel the objective components of the stimuli, e.g. the symptom is painful (cognitive), and the subjective response to that stimulus, e.g. anxiety (emotional). This model suggests that people actively process this information, which then elicits a coping response thought to be

appropriate. Coping efforts, if subsequently appraised as being unsuccessful, can be amended, or alternatively the initial representation of the stimuli/health threat can be revisited and amended. For example, if a person experiences a headache that they believe is a hangover, they are unlikely to be too worried about it and may simply self-medicate and wait for the symptoms to pass. If the symptoms persist, however, they may rethink their coping response (e.g. go to bed), or rethink their initial perception (e.g. maybe this isn't a hangover) and thus alter their coping response (e.g. go to the doctor's). The existence of feedback loops from coping to representations and back again contributes to the model being called 'self-regulatory', with self-regulation simply meaning that an individual makes efforts to alter their responses in order to achieve a desired outcome. Feedback loops enable responsiveness to changes in situations, appraisals or coping responses and thus maximise the likelihood of coping in a way that facilitates a return to a state of 'normality' (for that individual).

Mental representations of illness (illness representations – IRs – as they are called by those working within Leventhal's framework) emerge as soon as a person experiences a symptom or receives a diagnostic label. At this point they start a memory search to try to make sense of the current situation by retrieving pre-existing illness schemata with which they can compare (Petrie and Weinman 2003). IRs are acquired through the media, through personal experience and from family

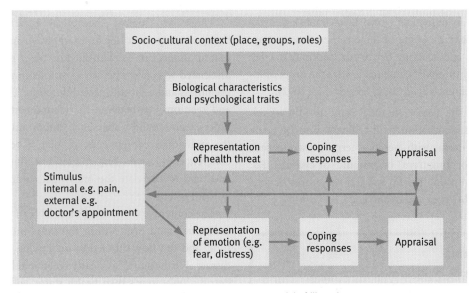

Figure 9.3 The self-regulation model: the 'common-sense model of illness'

Source: Leventhal, Diefenbach and Leventhal (1992: 147).

and friends and, as prototypes, they can be vague, inaccurate, extensive or detailed. IRs are thought to exist in memory from previous illness experience, generally that of common illness such as a cold or flu, and the new symptom may be matched to a pre-existing model or 'prototype' of illness that the person holds. Obviously, 'matching' chest pain erroneously to previously experienced indigestion could be dangerous if it is in fact a heart attack.

Early work leading to this model asked open-ended questions of people suffering from a range of common conditions, including the common cold (Lau *et al.* 1989), cancer or diabetes (Leventhal *et al.* 1980) and found five consistent themes in the content of IRs reported. These were:

1. *Identity*: variables that identify the presence or absence of the illness. Illnesses are identified by label, concrete signs and concrete symptoms. For example, 'I feel shivery and my joints ache, I think I have flu'.

2. *Consequences*: the perceived effect of illness on life: physical, emotional, social, economic impact or a combination of factors. May be short-term or long-term. For example, 'Because of my illness I won't be able to go to the gym today' or 'Because of my illness I will have to take early retirement'.

3. *Cause*: the perceived cause(s) of illness. May be biological (e.g. germs), emotional (e.g. stress, depression), psychological (e.g. mental attitude, personality), genetic or environmental (e.g. pollution), or as a result of an individual's own behaviour (e.g. overwork, smoking). Some of these causes may overlap, e.g. stress and smoking behaviour, and may overlap with **attributions** of cause made after the onset of illness (e.g. French *et al.* 2001; French *et al.* 2002).

4. *Timeline*: the perceived time-frame for the development and duration of the illness. Can be acute (or short-term, with no long-term consequences), chronic (or long-term) or episodic (or cyclical). For example, 'I think my flu will last only three or four days' or 'My pain comes and goes'.

---

attributions

a person's perceptions of what causes beliefs, feelings, behaviour and actions (based on attribution theory).

---

5. *Curability or controllability*: Lau and Hartmann (1983) added questions to assess the extent to which individuals perceive they, or others, can control, treat or limit progression of their illness. For example, 'If I take this medicine it will help to reduce my symptoms' or 'The doctor will be able to cure this'. This dimension may be particularly relevant for those facing chronic disease.

The dimensions identified by Leventhal are captured in a quantitative scale developed by John Weinman and colleagues (Weinman *et al.* 1996), the illness perception questionnaire (IPQ), which has been validated across a range of illnesses in a wealth of studies. A child-specific version (CIPQ, Walker *et al.* 2006) has also been developed for children aged 7–12 with asthma and eczema, although in the reported pilot study the cure–control scale did not show acceptable internal consistency, suggesting that perhaps children of this age did not fully understand the concept of personal control or potential for cure. Interestingly, however, it was often this subscale that performed less consistently in adult studies and the control/cure items became a main target of IPQ revisions. The new scale, the IPQ-R, distinguished between beliefs about personal control and beliefs about treatment control of the illness (Moss-Morris *et al.* 2002; Moss-Morris and Chalder 2003; see ISSUES on p. 247) and also added two further dimensions – emotional representations and illness coherence. These are yet to be tested in a child sample.

There are logical theoretical interrelationships between component IRs: for example, strongly believing that an illness can be controlled or cured is likely to be associated with fewer perceived serious consequences of the illness and a short expected duration. The clustering and relationships between the component parts of an illness representation may be as important in fact than the individual components, in that it reflects illness coherence; however, few studies test this statistically and tend to correlate the individual components with outcomes separately.

The content and organisation of IRs can vary between individuals and even within the same individual over time, and can be attributed to underlying beliefs about disease. Furthermore, as clearly illustrated by Buick and Petrie (2002), one's own health status will affect one's beliefs regarding illness. These authors compared the perceptions of breast cancer and post-surgical treatment, mood and coping responses of 78 women who had received surgery for breast cancer with the perceptions and anticipated responses among 78 healthy women, matched on age, marital status and educational attainment. Healthy women overestimated the number, severity and frequency of patient symptoms (identity component), rated patient health as poorer, believed more strongly in chance, patient-related internal (e.g. behaviour), genetic and environmental causes of breast cancer, believed that breast cancer had a longer timeline, that its consequences were worse and that treatment offered less cure or control. Healthy women also had more negative perceptions of how a woman with breast cancer would cope, thinking, for example, that patients would engage in generally avoidant coping such as mentally and behaviourally disengaging from treatment, venting emotion, using denial, alcohol and drugs, religion and restraint coping to a higher degree than patients themselves reported. The healthy women thought that patients were less likely to use positive reappraisal and acceptance than other strategies, yet in reality these were the two most common strategies reported by patients (who also did not report using alcohol or drugs)! Given these differences, it was not surprising that healthy women also overestimated the emotional impact of breast cancer treatment.

It is a sad fact that most people will encounter cancer at some point in their lives, either personally or through a family member or friend, and thus most of us non-oncologists have, to varying extents, a 'lay model' of this condition. Perceiving internal, or more specifically the person's behaviour, to be the cause of the illness may limit a healthy person's expression or provision of support for the ill person. Furthermore, if a societal perception of cancer is that patients best cope by avoidance, then healthy members of that society may consider any attempts to discuss the illness with the affected person to be unhelpful. These mismatched perceptions have obvious implications in terms of responses to people with cancer, but they also hold implications for healthy individuals. For example, if the lay perception is that treatments offer little hope of cure, preventive health practices such as screening behaviour may be undermined. Therefore identifying the illness perceptions of healthy individuals is highly relevant, not only due to their influences on their own behaviour but also as a means of increasing professionals' understanding of supportive behaviours towards those affected by illness.

While Moss-Morris and colleagues (2002) confirmed the validity and reliability of the dimensions of the IPQ-R across eight different health conditions, many illnesses were not included (e.g. cancer). It is important to confirm the domains of IRs held in the illness under study, given evidence that while the domains of IR may exist in different groups, their salience can vary. For example, a Dutch study using the original IPQ (Heijmans and de Ridder 1998) compared the IRs of patients with either chronic fatigue syndrome (CFS) or Addison's disease (AD), both chronic illnesses with common symptoms of fatigue and weakness. While AD, exemplified by gastrointestinal complaint, responds to medication, CFS is generally a more limiting condition and has no well-established treatment. Within each disease group the illness perceptions were similarly interrelated – identity (frequency and symptom seriousness) was positively associated with timeline and consequences, and negatively with control/cure (i.e. those reporting more symptoms perceived more consequences and a longer timeline, and less control over their illness), and a chronic timeline was associated with low perceptions of control or cure and more serious consequences. However, differences existed *between* illness groups: CFS patients viewed their illness more negatively than AD patients, reporting more frequent and serious consequences and less positive future expectation of control or cure. Therefore, although IR components were robust in terms of how they related to each other, illnesses differed in the specific strengths of each component. In a similar vein, a recent confirmatory factor analysis of the IPQ-R completed by a large sample (N = 587) of oesophageal cancer patients found that the domains of the IPQ-R model 'fitted' the data adequately but that some of the questionnaire items, in particular those relating to timeline beliefs, needed further consideration (Dempster and McCorry 2011). For example, one timeline factor was more closely aligned to the treatment control factor, suggesting that believing the illness will improve in time is, quite intuitively perhaps, related to treatment beliefs in this cancer sample. In addition, two acute/chronic items acted independently, suggesting that these patients can believe in both an acute illness model (it will last only a short time) but also in a chronic or permanent illness (i.e. perhaps something that will be with them till an imminent death perhaps). It is these differences which highlight the need for communications or interventions with patients to have specific focus, and not rely solely on generic observations drawn from other populations.

The influence of self-identity on symptom interpretation

It has been suggested that the medical sociological tradition of assessing lay models of health and illness (e.g. Blaxter's study – see Chapter 1 ☛), which takes a broader view of illness beliefs and knowledge shaped by social factors such as social class, cultural or economic environment, and the health psychological model of individual cognitions, should be merged. Levine and Reicher (1996) proposed an account of symptom evaluation based on self-categorisation theory (e.g. Turner *et al.* 1987), which highlights the importance of **social identity**. Most people have several social identities depending on context (e.g. student/partner/daughter), and it is proposed that the interpretation of symptoms differs depending on a person's current salient social identity. For example, they found that female teacher-training students specialising in PE (physical education) evaluated illness and injury scenarios differently depending on whether they were in a condition that identified them by gender or as a PE student. The extent to which the illness scenario details were perceived as threatening their salient identity was important. These findings were explored in two further studies, one involving female secretaries and the other involving rugby-playing males. In the secretary sample, different scenarios (based around threat to attractiveness, occupation or emotionality) elicited different responses depending on whether the women were in the 'gender-identity' group or the 'secretary-identity' group. Perceived illness severity was highest when the scenario posed an attractiveness threat to the gender-identity group, or an occupational performance threat (e.g. hand injury) to the secretary-identity group. The study of male rugby players introduced two hypothetical comparison groups, telling the men that their results would be compared with either females or 'new men'. This allowed the research team to explore the effect of context on symptom representations

and self-identity. The scenarios presented threatened physical attractiveness, emotionality or physicality. Attractiveness threat led to greater illness severity perceptions when the comparator group was females, and the threat to emotionality led to less serious perceptions of the illness when compared with 'new men'. There was no difference in the perceived severity of illness when the threat was to physicality.

What this shows is that social identity may alter illness and injury perceptions and, as such, perhaps models of illness representation commonly applied in health psychology research should expand to consider such influences. Although participants in Levine's studies were dealing with hypothetical illness/injuries in an artificial experimental setting, the reality is that most people fulfil a variety of social roles, and therefore it is logical to suppose that salient identity may differ in different contexts, with potential effects upon symptom perception and interpretation.

Causal attributions of illness

Attributional models are all about where a person locates the 'cause' of an event (Heider 1958) or, as here, symptoms and/or illness. We make attributions in order to attempt to make unexpected events more understandable or to try and gain some sense of control – if we know 'why' something has happened, we can elicit coping efforts. Of course, attributions can be wrong and thus coping efforts misguided, as we will discuss later.

The majority of attributional research in health psychology has addressed 'ill populations', such as those who have suffered a heart attack (myocardial infarction) (e.g. Affleck *et al.* 1987; Gudmunsdsdottir *et al.* 2001), or those diagnosed with cancer (Costanzo *et al.* 2005; Costanzo *et al.* 2011; Salander 2007). In relation to heart attack, attributions of cause – stress, work, it being in the family, smoking, eating fatty foods – were recorded regardless of whether attributions were *spontaneous* (patients asked to describe what they think about their illness), *elicited* (asked directly about their ideas of what may have caused their heart attack) or *cued* (asked to respond 'yes', 'no' or 'might have' to a list of 34 causes) (Gudmundsdottir *et al.* 2001). A review of studies of attributions for heart disease concluded that lifestyle factors and stress were the most common attributions made, with the latter more likely to come from heart attack patients than from healthy individuals, suggesting a form of self-preservation bias (French *et al.* 2001).

> ### social identity
> a person's sense of who they are at a group, rather than personal and individual, level (e.g. you are a student, possibly a female).

This bias in perceived cause is also reported in a rare longitudinal study of lung cancer patients (Salander 2007). It is relatively well-established fact that smoking accounts for about 80 per cent of the incidence of lung cancer (Chapter 3 ☞), yet among the 16 smokers interviewed repeatedly (of a sample of 23), the two most common attributions of 'cause of their illness' was 'don't know' and 'environmental toxins/pollution'. A total of 14 did not consider smoking as a probable cause, and the author points to this as a defence mechanism or 'disavowal', potentially useful for a sample at a relatively late stage in their illness. Lung cancer patients in other studies have been found to attribute partial cause to their smoking behaviour (e.g. Faller *et al.* 1995), but studies of this patient group are rare and methodologies and timing of sampling generally differ. Another disease with a strong association to smoking is COPD (chronic obstructive pulmonary disease) and, in contrast to Salander's study of lung cancer patients, in this sample the vast majority (93 per cent of 394 patients with a smoking history) agreed or strongly agreed in smoking as a cause, with workplace/environmental pollution, and infection/pneumonia also common (48.5 and 3.5 per cent respectively). These patients, however, were not newly diagnosed (Hoth *et al.* 2011).

When attributions were examined at an earlier stage in illness experience, i.e. at the time of symptom perception, Swartzman and Lees (1996) found that the dimensions of controllability, locus (internal physical/external non-physical cause) and stability described by attributional theorist Weiner (1986), and consistently reported in studies of illness attribution and coping (Roesch and Weiner 2001), were only partially supported. Symptoms addressed primarily reflected physical discomfort and were found to be attributed to either a physical (e.g. age, exertion)–non-physical (e.g. stress, mood) dimension; a high–low personal controllability dimension; and a dimension thought to reflect controllability by health professional/treatable versus stability/not treatable, although this dimension was less clear. Attributions of causes of symptoms (rather than attributions of cause of a confirmed illness) may be an area worth further exploration. Perceiving a cause of discomfort as being non-physical, under high personal control and stable/not treatable may lead to very different interpretation, response and health-care-seeking behaviour than a cause of discomfort with physical, low personal control and treatable attribution.

As described in this chapter, attributions of cause can be affected by one's own illness experience and can potentially affect how we respond to illness in others; they can also influence how we respond to our own illness: for example, perceiving diet as a causal factor in breast cancer increases the likelihood of dietary change following treament (Costanzo *et al.* 2011). Unfortunately however, they can sometimes be wrong. For example, a woman may attribute joint pain to excessively high-heeled shoes rather than to the first signs of arthritis, and she may fail to seek medical advice. Other risks of misattributed cause is failure to adhere to essential medication: for example, a study of women with HIV infection found that drug treatment was wrongly attributed as causing their symptoms, leading to reductions in, or cessation of, medication adherence (Siegel and Gorey 1997).

The influence of culture

Culture influences illness at many levels in that it shapes both how it is perceived, understood and experienced (Adams and Salter 2009). For example, as described in Chapter 1 ☞, there is significant variation in the extent to which members of specific cultures believe in supernatural causes of illness, e.g. evil spirits, divine punishment or in spiritual explanations. In terms of the latter, it has been described how Chinese women made sense of their cancer experiences by attributing their cancer to '*tien ming*' (the will of Heaven, a concept from the Chinese Confucian and Daoist traditions) and to 'karma' (a Buddhist concept of cause and effect that cannot be changed through human effort) and as a result showed acceptance and 'going with the flow' ('*ping chang xin*') (Leung *et al.* 2007). These findings equate to that reported by non-Eastern research participants explaining the effects of a Buddhism-derived intervention (mindfulness-based cognitive therapy) on their living with cancer (Ingram *et al.* 2008).

Cultural differences have also been reported in terms of other illness representation dimensions. For example, a study of perceptions of diabetes held by South Asians, Europeans and Pacific Islanders found that perceived illness identity, timeline beliefs, consequences and emotional representations differed between groups (Bean *et al.* 2007). Pacific Islanders perceived more symptoms of diabetes, greater consequences and were affected more emotionally by the condition. The Europeans differed from the other two groups only in terms of perceiving a longer timeline. Illness coherence and personal or treatment control beliefs did not differ. The differences in beliefs identified related to poorer metabolic control and aspects of self-care, highlighting a need for health professionals to address illness perceptions when trying to improve a person's self-management of symptoms or health condition such as diabetes, or indeed many other controllable conditions such as hypertension, epilepsy or asthma.

It is likely that cultural and religious factors will indirectly influence health and illness outcomes via their effects on health and illness beliefs and behaviours. However, research evidence from cross- and within-culture comparisons is relatively limited, at least within Western Europe. One study pointing to this is that of Swami *et al.*'s (2009) where Malaysian Muslim participants were found to believe more strongly than Malaysian Buddhist or Malaysian Catholic participants that their likelihood of becoming ill was uncontrollable and that fate played a role in recovery. If pursued into a longitudinal study, such differences may well be reflected in different health behaviours (such as health-risk behaviours or seeking health care) and personal engagement in recovery from illness (cf. French *et al.* 2006). We turn now to broader consideration of the effects of illness representations and health outcomes.

Illness representations and outcomes

While proposed in Leventhal's theoretical model to affect illness outcome via effects on coping (i.e. a mediated effect of IRs), illness representations have also been shown to have direct effects on a wide range of outcomes, including, for example:

- seeking and using/adhering to medical treatment (Horne and Weinman 2002; Leventhal *et al.* 1992; Scharloo *et al.* 1998);
- engagement in self-care behaviour or behaviour change (Costanzo *et al.* 2011; Petrie *et al.* 2007);
- attitudes towards the use of brand-specific vs. generic medicines, and treatment choices (Figueiras *et al.* 2010);
- illness-related disability and return to work (Heijmans 1998; Petrie *et al.* 2002);
- caregiver anxiety and depression (Parveen and Morrison 2011a);
- quality of life (Gray and Rutter 2007).

In terms of predicting attendance at health-care clinics, a recent study (Lawson *et al.* 2007) found that among patients with type 1 diabetes, perceived treatment effectiveness was a significant predictor along with the coping strategy of seeking instrumental support. In this study, treatment controllability is assessed within a 'personal models' questionnaire which is specific to diabetes but which fits into Leventhal's conceptualisation of illness representations.

The pattern of association reported between illness representations and quality of life outcomes in adults with chronic fatigue syndrome (Heijmans 1998) was also seen in children and young adults: i.e. low identity beliefs and perceived treatment efficacy was associated with better QoL (Gray and Rutter 2007). Interestingly, there was greater evidence of coping responses mediating the effect of IRs on outcome in this younger sample, than is commonly reported in adult samples, suggesting perhaps that coping plays a greater role in outcomes of younger patients, although why this may be the case needs further exploration.

Unfortunately many studies exploring the role of illness representations in explaining illness outcomes, including the Gray and Rutter study above, are limited by their **cross-sectional design**, i.e. they report only concurrent associations. One exception is the study of Llewellyn and colleagues (Llewellyn *et al.* 2007) where illness and treatment beliefs assessed prior to treatment for head and neck cancer were *not* found to be predictive of health-related QoL, generic QoL or mood, in spite of many associations between IRs and coping at both a 1-month follow-up and at the final 6–8-month follow-up. Chronic timeline beliefs at baseline were predictive of depression 6–8 months after treatment, with this being a direct effect as there was no relationship to the 1-month coping strategies. In predictive analyses, coping and satisfaction with information received pre-treatment are more predictive of these outcomes. Although longitudinal, these analyses are limited by a sample size of less than 50 patients and therefore statistical tests of the

> **cross-sectional design**
> a study that collects data from a sample on one occasion only. Ideally, the sample should be selected to be representative of the population under study.

effects of change in key variables over time were not possible. More recently, efforts have been made to test associations over a changing illness course. For example, a longitudinal study of 87 patients with COPD who were taking part in a rehabilitation programme (Fischer *et al.* 2010), found that timeline and personal control beliefs significantly increased after rehabilitation, and that in both cases the higher levels could be partially explained by earlier beliefs and perceptions of rehabilitation goal achievement. In relation to changes in perceived control beliefs, the time since diagnosis was also predictive (longer time since diagnosis, less perceived control). A longitudinal study of informal caregivers found that, over a nine-month period, perceptions of illness conse-quence increased, and that this was predictive of anxiety. Furthermore, decreases in perceived control beliefs and increased emotional representations were predictive of depression (Parveen and Morrison 2011c) and increased illness coherence was predictive of caregiver gains (Parveen and Morrison 2011b). Such findings confirm the dynamic nature of Leventhal's model and also point to the importance of achieving goals for recovery or illness management in the shaping of subsequent illness beliefs and, potentially, outcomes.

Support for the contribution of illness representations to coping and illness outcomes was found following a meta-analysis of 45 empirical studies, many of which, however, were cross-sectional (Hagger and Orbell 2003). Generally speaking, perceived controllability was associated with adaptive outcomes including psychological well-being and social functioning, whereas perceptions of high symptom identity, chronicity and serious consequences were negatively associated with such outcomes.

While many existing studies confirm statistical associations between the variables (i.e. illness repres-entations, coping, illness outcomes) specified in the common-sense model of illness described in this chapter, they have been primarily quantitative in nature. It could be said that they are thus limited in the extent to which they develop our understanding of what lies *within or behind* the representations presented. Consider, for example, the following quotes from cancer patients, one regarding cause and the other regarding consequences:

> . . . to begin with, it just didn't sink in that I was really sick. I had a lot of difficulty in grasping it, because . . . we have lived pretty – soundly I think . . . outdoors a lot. And that, that I have heart problems also. I just don't really understand that it has turned out like this . . . And just that one should exercise a lot and try to eat properly and I've done that, largely because you don't want to gain weight either, but no – I don't under-stand it.
>
> (woman with lung cancer reflecting on the onset of her condition, Leveälahti *et al.* 2007: 468)

> I remember sitting in this mound of grass overlooking the bay and just feeling completely in the moment, and completely at peace; this is wonderful, this is one of the best times in my life . . . so in some ways it (the cancer) has given me quite a lot because it's given me that appreciation of living now, living every day . . . I still hold onto that kernel, of this is the only life I've got, today may be the only day I've got, so I think that's a very valuable thing to come from it, a positive thing, and I don't think I've ever had that before, that appreciation.
>
> (woman with breast cancer talking about the conse-quences of her condition, Ingram *et al.* 2008)

The depth of emotion, including positive emotion, seen in these words, would be hard to capture quantita-tively (see ISSUES for further discussion of methods of assessing illness representations).

ISSUES

Measuring illness representations

Opinions vary about how best to elicit and assess individuals' privately held illness perceptions and beliefs. The use of open-ended interviews as a method of eliciting illness representations (as used in Leventhal and colleagues' early work) has led to the criticism that questions such as 'To what extent when thinking about your illness do you think about its consequences?' may well be leading. Furthermore, interviews are very time-consuming and generally restrict sample size, although some studies have managed to successfully employ open-ended questioning (using prompts where necessary) (e.g. Forrest *et al.* 2006; Hampson *et al.* 1990; Hampson *et al.* 1994).

While Leventhal's model provides a useful framework on which to base studies of illness perceptions, early studies tended to focus on specific component beliefs, for example perceived control over illness (e.g. Multidimensional Health Locus of Control Scale, Wallston *et al.* 1978). The ability to assess all five constructs was made easier with the development of the illness perception questionnaire (IPQ) by a team of UK- and New Zealand-based researchers (Weinman *et al.* 1996). A meta-analysis of 45 empirical studies using the IPQ in a wide range of illness populations across varying time-spans (Hagger and Orbell 2003) found it to have both construct and predictive validity (although a call was made for further longitudinal confirmation), and provided support for all IR domains except for 'cause' representations. The multitude of overlapping causal attributions made meta-analysis problematic, and measurement of the cause dimension requires further refinement.

The IPQ was revised in 2002 (IPQ-R) to address some of these limitations. The IPQ-R distinguishes personal control over illness from outcome expectancies and from perceived treatment control; strengthens the timeline component by adding items regarding cyclical illnesses as well as acute/chronic timeline items; assesses emotional responses to illness such as fear and anxiety (part of Leventhal's self-regulatory model not well addressed in the original IPQ), and finally, examines the extent to which a person feels they understand their condition, defined as illness coherence (Moss-Morris *et al.* 2002). The IPQ-R was tested among 711 people representing eight different illness conditions, and found to have a reliable and valid dimensional structure. However, the illnesses represented did not include cancer, and a burgeoning field of psycho-oncology therefore welcomes recent confirmation that the structure offered a 'good fit' to an oesophageal cancer population (Dempster and McCorry 2011). These authors importantly draw our attention to the fact that this, and all other studies using the IPQ-R, including those in non-Western populations (e.g. Chen *et al.* 2008) have found that

emotional representations are highly correlated with perceived consequences (high perceived negative consequences associated with high anxiety representation). This highlights that cognitions and emotions are hard to disentangle causally, as acknowledged by Lazarus and colleagues (Chapter 11 ☞), and also that our conceptual models, in this author's (VM) view, could benefit from working together when exploring predictors of stress or illness outcome and the underlying proceses.

While Leventhal's framework dominates the study of illness perceptions and outcome within health psychology, other models do exist. For example, the implicit models approach utilises a questionnaire (IMIQ; Turk *et al.* 1986) which, when administered to three groups (diabetic patients, diabetic educators, college students), found four slightly different dimensions to those described by Leventhal: seriousness, personal responsibility, controllability and changeability. However, these results emerged when asking participants to *compare* two diseases, suggesting perhaps that their dimensions are more what discriminates *between* illnesses, rather than domains like Leventhal's, which relate to perceptions of individual illnesses. It may in fact be impossible to have a model or measure to fit all illnesses; for example, the potential for cure or treatment simply does not exist for all conditions and therefore this dimension is likely to lack validity in such situations.

The existence of commonly employed and reasonably well-validated quantitative assessment tools should not detract from the important contribution made by more open-ended methods of eliciting IRs. Understanding the sources and salience of beliefs and perceptions, and the reasons behind these, could be crucial to the development of targeted interventions. The value of qualitative enquiry can be highlighted by the findings of a study exploring cultural differences in illness perceptions regarding 'fatigue' between European American women and South Asian immigrant women (Karasz and McKinley 2007). Using a case vignette of a woman suffering from fatigue, conceptions were elicited which revealed that, while some conceptions of fatigue were shared (e.g. perceiving both physical and psychological general causes), there were significant differences. For example, European Americans referred more often to genetic causes, medicalised/somatised the condition more and considered it a chronic condition, whereas South Asian women tended to think fatigue was temporary, caused by something transient and less needing of medical treatment. In exploring reasons for these differences, the qualitative accounts exemplify differing models of illness – a biomedical 'disease' model (European Americans) and a more socially oriented 'depletion' model which also drew on traditional 'humoral' concepts of illness (see Chapter 1 ☞). It is worth noting that the similarities and differences between groups may not hold for other symptoms or, indeed, for other comparison groups. Culture, these authors note, is more than simply a demographic variable, and only through this type of study can we begin to explore 'the structures, contexts, cond-itions, ideologies, and processes through which culture shapes illness cognition and illness behaviour' (p. 614). One limitation of this study, however, is that participants were invited to respond to the vignette in a way that addressed predetermined IR dimensions. It would have been interesting to have assessed spontaneous responses to the vignette scenario in order to ascertain whether the dimensions outlined by Leventhal and others were implicit in the models of illness portrayed.

Thus, what we hope to have shown here is that there are various ways in which a person's perceptions of illness can be elicited, and measured, and it is for the individual researcher to decide which is most suited to their questions and their population. Perhaps mixed methods would be more informative than either alone.

Planning and taking action: responding to symptoms

As this chapter has described, the first step towards seeking medical care begins with a person recognising that they have symptoms of an illness, and it may take some time for this step to occur. In many cases, people choose to treat an illness themselves by self-medicating with pharmaceutical, herbal or non-proprietary products, and others will rest or go to bed and wait to see whether they recover naturally. A number of surveys have suggested that less than one-quarter of illnesses are seen by a doctor.

Kasl and Cobb (1966a) refer to the behaviour of those who are experiencing symptoms but who have not yet sought medical advice and received a diagnosis as **illness behaviour**. Illness behaviour includes lying down and resting, self-medication and seeking sympathy, support and informal advice in an attempt to determine one's health status. Many people are reluctant to go to the doctor on the initial experience of a symptom and instead first seek advice from a **lay referral system**, generally including friends, relatives or colleagues (Croyle and Barger 1993). Symptoms are therefore not always sufficient to motivate a visit to the doctor.

Once people recognise a set of symptoms, label them and realise that they could indicate a medical problem, they therefore have the option of:

- ignoring the symptoms and hoping they recede;
- seeking advice from others;
- presenting themselves to a health professional.

Some people will do all three over time.

---

illness behaviour

behaviour that characterises a person who is sick and who seeks a remedy, e.g. taking medication. Usually precedes formal diagnosis, when behaviour is described as **sick role behaviour**.

lay referral system

an informal network of individuals (e.g. friends, family, colleagues) turned to for advice or information about symptoms and other health-related matters. Often but not solely used prior to seeking a formal medical opinion.

Plate 9.2 Making screening accessible by means of such mobile screening units outside workplaces or supermarkets may increase the likelihood of screening uptake. How would finding a lump be interpreted?

Source: © Health Screening (UK) Ltd.

One might expect that the recognition that one has symptoms would be a sufficient condition for deciding that one is sick, but Radley (1994: 71) suggests that one must question that assumption. Think of your own experience – symptoms do not necessarily precede sickness – sometimes being deemed to be sick (by virtue of receiving a diagnosis) is an important element in appearing symptomatic, and perhaps adopting what is termed **sick role behaviour** (Parsons 1951; Kasl and Cobb 1966b).

Our response even to serious symptoms may still involve some delay to see whether things improve or whether attempts at self-care will improve the situation. A dramatic example of this was reported by Kentsch *et al.* (2002), who found that over 40 per cent of patients who thought they were having a heart attack, *and who considered this to be potentially fatal*, waited over one hour before calling for medical help. This delay would have had a significant impact on the outcome of their illness. Treatment with 'clot-busting' drugs, which dissolve the clot that causes an MI and minimise damage to the heart, are at their most effective when given within an hour of the onset of problems. An example of delay in a more chronic but equally serious condition was reported by Prohaska *et al.* (1990), who found that the first response of over 80 per cent of their sample of patients with colorectal cancer was the use of over-the-counter medication. Patients waited an average of seven months before seeking medical help. Cockburn *et al.* (2003) also found significant evidence of our ability to ignore important symptoms. In a survey of over a thousand adults, they found that 23 per cent of their sample reported having had blood in their stools (a potential symptom of bowel cancer) – but only one-third had ever reported these symptoms to a doctor. Perhaps more encouraging was the reporting of breast lumps by women in a study by Meechan *et al.* (2002). They found that of their sample of women who identified breast lumps following breast self-examination, 40 per cent had seen their doctor within seven days, 52 per cent within

> ### sick role behaviour
> the activities undertaken by a person diagnosed as sick in order to try to get well.

fourteen days, 69 per cent within thirty days, and only 14 per cent had waited over ninety days. However, it should be noted that even among this group of health-aware women who took active steps to identify and prevent disease, a significant proportion still delayed significantly in reporting their symptoms to their doctor.

> **morbidity**
>
> costs associated with illness such as disability, injury.

WHAT DO YOU THINK?

Health is one of our most precious attributes. Yet many people who fear they have an illness – in some cases one they think may be fatal – delay in seeking medical help. Interestingly, people who are in the presence of someone else they know when their symptoms occur are more likely to call for help than people who are alone at the time they experience their symptoms. It seems that by talking with this person they are given 'permission' to call for medical aid. Why should this be the case? Are people frightened that their fears, perhaps of having cancer, will be justified, or that the treatment they may receive will be ineffective or too difficult to cope with? Can you think of any factors that might distinguish between those who do seek medical help at the onset of symptoms and those who don't? Think of your own illness experience and that of those close to you.

Delay behaviour

Delay behaviour in this instance refers to an individual's delay in seeking health advice as opposed to delays inherent in the health-care system itself (see IN THE SPOTLIGHT, Chapter 8 ☞ for suggestions as to how to reduce such delay in the delivery of treatment for heart attack). Studies of cancer patients have shown that delay in presenting symptoms for medical attention is highly related to outcomes of **morbidity** and mortality (e.g. Andersen *et al.* 1995; Richards *et al.* 1999), and thus it is important to gain an understanding of the factors that influence delay behaviour.

Safer *et al.* (1979) developed a model of delay behaviour, defined as the time between recognising a symptom and seeking help for it. They described three decision-making stages (see Figure 9.4) and point out that a person will enter treatment only after all three stages have been gone through and the questions in each stage have been answered positively.

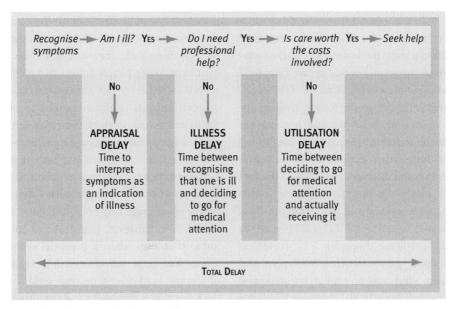

Figure 9.4 The delay behaviour model

Source: adapted from Safer, Tharps, Jackson and Leventhal (1979).

In the first stage, a person infers that they are ill on the basis of perceiving a symptom or symptoms – the delay in reaching this decision is termed 'appraisal delay'. Next, the person considers whether or not they need medical attention, and the time taken to decide this is termed 'illness delay'. The final stage covers the time taken between deciding one needs medical attention and actually acting on that decision and making an appointment or presenting to a hospital. This is termed 'utilisation delay'.

To illustrate these three stages, let us imagine that on Sunday you wake up with a sore throat (recognise symptoms); by Tuesday you decide you are sick (appraisal delay); on Wednesday you decide to see your doctor (illness delay); on Friday you actually see the doctor (utilisation delay). The latter delay may not be under the individual's control if it includes time to the actual appointment (referred to as a 'scheduling delay'), as opposed to the time taken to *make* the appointment. The length of each delay period is likely to vary for different symptoms and illnesses, with, for example, appraisal delays being long for embarrassing personal symptoms such as rectal bleeding but scheduling delays likely to be short. It becomes obvious therefore that appraisals are crucial in getting the help-seeking process moving along, particularly when symptoms are potentially lethal. It follows therefore that if the potential for the appropriate cognitive appraisal is diminished through intellectual or cognitive impairment, appraisal and illness delays are likely to be exacerbated. There are many other reasons for delaying seeking treatment, including social class and educational level (the lower one's level of education and income, the greater the delay; see Chapter 2 (☛), age, gender, ignorance of the meaning of the symptoms, getting used to the symptoms, feeling invulnerable (cf. unrealistic optimism), believing that nothing can be done (relates to treatment perceptions, see below) and, commonly, fear. Earlier sections on influences on symptom perception and interpretation are also relevant here. Table 9.2 presents a summary of reasons that distinguished between seeking and not seeking medical consultation among a sample of 215 Chinese adults suffering from functional dyspepsia – a condition manifested by upper gastrointestinal tract pain and excessive belching, which has no underlying structural or biochemical cause (Cheng 2000). This table highlights many of the reasons for and against health-care-seeking; however, factors *external* to the individual, such as

Table 9.2 Reasons consulters sought, and non-consulters did not seek, a medical consultation

Reason	N	%
Consulters (N = 109)		
Sought information about symptoms	46	42
Sought explanation for causes of symptoms	37	34
Sought advice to cure symptoms	26	24
Non-consulters (N = 106)		
Do not have time	29	27
Think the symptoms will disappear very soon	27	25
Do not want to take sick leave from work	21	20
Think the symptoms are a normal part of busy city life	10	10
Have uncomfortable feelings about hospitals	9	8
Think it is OK or not a problem	6	6
Other	4	4

Source: Cheng, C. (2000). *Psychosomatic Medicine*, 62: 844–52.

aspects of the condition, of ones' social network, or even beliefs about the health professional's response (see RESEARCH FOCUS on p. 255), nor reasons *within* the individual, such as demographic characteristics or personality, were explored. We address these later.

Symptom type, location, perceived prevalence

As described in the symptom perception section, symptoms that are visible, painful, disruptive, frequent and persistent generally (but not always) lead to action. If the symptom is easily visible to oneself and others, for example a rash, then one will delay less in seeking treatment. When people believe that their symptoms are serious (whether or not subsequently confirmed by the doctor), unusual (e.g. no one else seems to have had them) and that they can be controlled or treated through medical intervention, they are more likely to take action. The effects of symptoms are also important. When symptoms threaten normal relations with friends and family, or when they disrupt regular activity or interaction, people usually seek help (Peay and Peay 1998; Ringstrom *et al.* 2007). However, Grunfeld and colleagues (2003) found that even when a potential symptom of breast cancer had been self-identified, a significant number of women aged 35–54 delayed seeking health care in the belief that seeking help and potentially entering protracted treatment would be disruptive to their lifestyle! Not seeking help for such symptoms could result in an illness and treatment regime significantly more disruptive than presenting to health care early.

The location of the symptom also influences use of a lay referral system and/or going to a doctor: for example, persistent headaches may be discussed with friends and family before seeking medical help, whereas detection of a lump in the genital region, or irritable bowel symptoms, may not be – certain parts of the body seem more open to discussion than others. The attributes associated with some diseases may also influence ease of reporting; Hale *et al.* (2007), for example, noted that shame or embarrassment about the likely need for rectal examinations contributed significantly to delayed reporting of symptoms subsequently found to be associated with prostate cancer. This is also one of the reasons that many testicular cancers are diagnosed late, with potentially serious consequences (for cancer screening issues, see Chapter 4 (☞).

Furthermore, it has been shown that people make judgements about the prevalence of symptoms and disease that influence their interpretation and whether medical attention is sought. Diseases that a person has experience of have been found to be judged as more prevalent by both students *and* by physicians, and diseases considered prevalent tend to become normalised and viewed as less serious or life-threatening (Jemmott *et al.* 1988). Thankfully, however, it has been shown that presenting with symptoms of a condition that one reports a family history for predisposes the emergency services to respond in an urgent manner (Hedges *et al.* 1998).

Financial reasons for delay

For some, seeking refuge in the sick role following a formal diagnosis might be an attractive option as it can allow a person time out from normal duties and responsibilities. However, some people do not want to be declared sick because of the implications it may have for them socially ('If I am sick how can I attend that party?'); occupationally ('If I am off sick my work will pile up and await my return or will someone else get my job?'); or financially ('I cannot afford to lose wages or overtime payments by being sick.' 'I cannot afford to pay for tests or medicines'). In the USA, some people delay seeking medical care when money for the anticipated treatment is limited; these people are generally among the 16 per cent of American citizens (predominantly Hispanic and

black people) who do not have health insurance (USBC 1999). This is not always the case, however: for example, following a heart attack many of those who delayed seeking treatment did have medical insurance (Rahimi *et al.* 2007, see Chapter 2 (☞). Luckily, other countries have health-care systems that make personal finance less of a barrier to treatment, for example the National Health Service in the UK.

Cultural influences on delay behaviour

Westernised cultures have been found to promote an independent sense of responsibility, i.e. the individual has supreme importance, whereas African cultures (e.g. Chalmers 1996; Morrison *et al.* 1999), and Chinese and Japanese cultures (e.g. Heine and Lehman 1995; Tan and Bishop 1996) have been shown to perceive health and illness more collectively and interdependently, in terms of the effects of health and illness on group function. As a result, different cultures may exhibit broadly different belief systems and different attitudes towards, and responses to, illness. To illustrate this, Bishop and Teng's (1992) study of Singaporean Chinese students found that, while severity and contagiousness were commonly used dimensions of illness perception (as found among Western students), an additional dimension existed whereby illness was tied to behaviour and to blocked *qi* – the source of life and energy. These beliefs were associated with the use of traditional and Western health care, where it appeared that when dual health-care systems operate in parallel in a society, they are used differentially depending on the specific illness and illness perceptions (Heine and Lehman 1995; Quah and Bishop 1996; Lim and Bishop 2000). African studies (Chalmers 1996) have shown that the use of traditional medicine such as faith healers remains strong even as Westernised health-care availability increases. These kind of findings suggest that delays in seeking professional medical help may in part result from holding specific cultural beliefs about illness causation that do not 'fit' biomedical views of illness and treatment (Pachter 1994). In these cases, individuals will seek culturally relevant cures, including, for example, herbal or animal-based treatments, acupuncture, faith healing, and so on. In some cases, this may be associated with a parallel seeking of medical help – in others, seeking Westernised medical treatment may be considered only if the condition fails to respond to the more traditional remedies (Chalmers 1996; Heine and Lehman 1995; Lim and Bishop 2000; Quah and Bishop 1996).

Minority status, which includes ethnicity, but also gender, sexuality and so forth, may also contribute to delayed help-seeking where health-care consultations are seen as holding potential for humiliation or discrimination (Wamala *et al.* 2007). Economic differentials can mean that the cost of treatment is also a factor to be considered when seeking health care in countries other then the UK. For example, one American study employing focus groups to identify delay in relation to heart attack symptoms, found that African-Americans were more likely than White or Hispanic American participants to report delaying calls to emergency services out of concerns about the costs and location of care (Finnegan *et al.* 2000).

A fuller discussion of the influence of ethnicity on health-care-seeking behaviour, and access to services, is covered in Chapter 2 (☛).

Age and delay behaviour

The young and the elderly use health services more often than other age groups (see Chapter 2 (☛). Acute onset of severe symptoms tends to result in quicker seeking of medical attention by everyone, although particularly among the middle-aged. Elderly people generally present to their doctors more quickly regardless of symptom severity and in spite of the fact that many symptoms are commonly attributed initially to ageing (Prohaska *et al.* 1987). The quicker presentation of older individuals to health-care professionals has been interpreted as a need to remove uncertainty, whereas middle-aged individuals may attempt to minimise their problems, often relying on self-medication, until they worsen or fail to disappear naturally (Leventhal and Diefenbach 1991). In terms of a symptomatic child, the responsibility for acting on, interpreting symptoms and subsequently seeking health care (or not) lies often with the parent or guardian, and it may be expected that delay would be minimal. However, this is not inevitable, and presenting a child to health care may be subject to similar influences as presenting oneself. For example, a Nepalese study found that, even when presenting a child to health care, the speed of seeking health care depended on maternal educational level, family income, and the number and perceived severity of symptoms (Sreeramareddy *et al.* 2006). In late adolescence the decision to attend moves away from some parents and these young people can

become reluctant to seek medical attention, particularly if their symptoms are something they wish to conceal from their parents. For example Meyer-Weitz *et al.* (2000) interviewed 292 South African adolescent and young adults (aged under 20 years) about the influences on their seeking health care for a sexually transmitted disease. The majority presented within 6 days of symptoms (56 per cent), 23 per cent waited 7–10 days, and 21 per cent waited more than 10 days. The reasons given for those seeking health care early were perceived seriousness of the symptoms, absence of any self-treatments and positive attitudes to autonomy and, perhaps surprisingly, to condoms. Adolescents may also delay in seeking health care out of a sense of invulnerability and a resulting optimism about susceptibility to health problems (see Chapter 3 (☛).

Gender and delay behaviour

Women generally use health services more than men and we have already explored whether this may reflect greater attention being paid to internal states and bodily signals or gender socialisation. Perhaps women make better use of their social support and lay referral networks, which promote health care-seeking behaviour (Krantz and Orth 2000). However, a study conducted in France (Melchior *et al.* 2003) found that occupational status, and not gender, influenced social support usage, with those with low social status reporting better support. This contradicts American and British findings (Marmot *et al.* 1998; Stansfeld *et al.* 1998), where low socio-economic status was associated with less social support. The interaction between gender, socio-economic status, social support and health-care use is not yet fully understood (see Chapter 2 (☛) and any explanation is likely to be multifaceted, given the range of potential influences described in this section.

Gender differences in seeking medical help may occur as a result of different meanings given to health-related behaviour by the two sexes (Courtenay 2000). The differences, they propose, reflect issues of masculinity, femininity and power. Men show their masculinity and power by engaging in health-risking behaviour and not showing signs of weakness – even when ill. Women, conversely, experience no such issues and are more willing to seek medical help. It may be that women are more willing to confront the implications of any symptoms than men; this can be seen in the context of testicular, bowel and prostate cancer, for example, where women are often highly influential in encouraging their male partners to attend for doctor consultations (e.g. Hale *et al.* 2007; Gascoigne *et al.* 1999).

Finally, parenthood (motherhood has been studied more extensively to date than fatherhood) may also influence seeking help. Perhaps surprisingly, it has been shown that self-help or medical aid may be sought more willingly for symptoms perceived as minor than for those perceived as serious, perhaps suggesting avoidance of diagnoses that may interfere with the parenting role (Timko and Janoff-Bulman 1985).

RESEARCH FOCUS

What do male doctors think of men who contact GP services?

Hale, S., Grogan, S., and Willott, S. (2010). Male GPs' views on men seeking medical help: a qualitative study. *British Journal of Health Psychology*, 15: 697–713.

Background

Women on average live five years longer than men, with males having a higher mortality rate at all ages. Social class and occupational status plays a role in mortality for both genders and so it is thought that a strong explanation for men's poorer longevity is their lower rate of usage of health services, from seeing their local GP to attending screening or routine health (Including dental and eyesight) checks. A significant body of work has sought to identify reasons for men's lower levels of contact with health care and explanations include that they perceive and interpret fewer symptoms than women (see earlier sections in this chapter), or that they in fact perceive and interpret symptoms similarly, but fail to bring them to medical attention, as they consider this inconsistent with a masculine identity or with their expected social roles (as we have discussed previously). This study explores a less commonly explored route, focusing instead on the role played by the practitioners' own gender and how male GPs themselves view the self-referral behaviour of male patients. Previously it has been shown that male patients prefer to see female GPs when presenting with 'personal' or 'sexual' problems, although the evidence is inconsistent. It is speculated that female doctors are more empathic and reassuring in their communications with male patients. This type of study addresses the interesting issue of gender stereotyping and suggests that lay people as well as professionals are guilty of that, but is this the case? In earlier work the authors of the current paper had found that males believed that male GPs made judgements about their attending; however, the actual views of male GPs were not sought. The current study sets out to explore the experiences of male GPs specifically in relation to their male patients' help-seeking behaviour, but also explores the GPs' own helath-care behaviours and any influence this has on their views about male patients.

Method

Procedure

Using semi-structured interviews, ten male GPs (aged 35–53 years) were recruited by means of snowball sampling, i.e. two initially recruited GPs then invited their colleagues to participate. Interviews were conducted individually and each followed an interview guide which started broadly, with questions about the type of problems and patients seen in daily practice, and then moved on to perceptions of men's health and male patient self-referreal paterns and perceptions thereof. Questions about GPs' own behaviour came at the end of the interviews which typically lasted 30–40 minutes.

Data analysis

Interviews were tape-recorded and transcribed verbatim. Analysis was by means of IPA-Interpretative Phenomenological Analysis (cf. Smith 1995; 1996), whereby repeated reading seeks to elicit themes that reflect the participants' own perceptions and experience, and by drawing the individual accounts and themes together a sense of the 'shared meanings' the topic has for all the participants is gathered. Some themes were directly related to the interview topics but others arose from spontaneously elicited concerns or reflected common ways of thinking which emerged. (The paper presents a useful and clear account of the process of data analysis in a flow chart which the interested reader may wish to view (p. 703).)

In order to assess internal reliability and validity of the emergent data, this type of analysis relies on internally consistent and a 'backed up by data' argument and a second researcher who 'audits' the initial researchers' account and evidence (interview quotes are the data here).

Results

Three superordinate themes emerged which the authors detail using selected quotes from the transcripts. These themes are 'managing demand'; 'men in consultation'; and the curiously labelled, 'men first, doctors second'. For reasons of length we only present a brief account of the data here, and focus on the issue of most relevance to this chapter – that of male GPs' perceptions of male patients health-seeking behaviour. The authors note from the outset that themes are interrelated.

Managing demand

This theme is least relevant to our chapter in that it reflects GPs' anxiety about their escalating workload, not considered to be due, perhaps as we might have expected, to a growing elderly population but rather a more health-aware younger population, but doesn't include a discussion of male patients specifically. One sub-theme of importance, however, is that the younger patients were considered by GPs to have higher expectations of life and broader definitions of what they believed was 'health-illness' relevant, and thus had unrealistic expectations of what GPs could help them with, e.g. 'We often say that we have a generation of you know 18–25-year-olds who are totally irresponsible in the demands they sometimes place on your service . . . now if you look at them in 30 years'

time we will be overwhelmed as a country with a whole generation of middle-aged hypochondriacs . . .'. Somewhat unsympathetic a view perhaps, but the authors' material highlights how these GPs perceive a gulf between what patients and GPs consider as 'medical problems'.

Men in consultation

This theme narrows down the broader preceding theme to GPs' perceptions specifically about male patients, acknowledged by 9 of 10 GPs as seen less by them than women. All GPs attributed the lower self-referral rate among men to reflect their need to be seen as 'brave and manly', particularly in those of lower socio-economic status. Interestingly, GPs felt this group only presented when perhaps the need was genuine – consider this quote: 'Working men, for instance, we don't see as many of them, unless they've got a real health problem . . .' suggesting that other patient groups, including non-working men, and women, may present with non-real problems. 'The working guys come in with stuff that stops them from working, so really bad chest infections . . . significant bowel problems . . . You've got the non-working men who've got the attendance profile that you associate with non-working women'.

This is taken as suggesting also that self-referral is feminine behaviour. Furthermore, there was some indication that GPs felt it was more acceptable by women than it was for men. For older men who also were thought to be more frequent attenders, the view seemed also unsympathetic, with suggestions that this group presented inappropriately to 'overcompensate for all the years of neglect'. However, many disease processes emerge in those of post-retirement age and the GPs here do not seem to acknowledge this. Sadly, the transcripts suggest that male GPs are more supportive of males who do not present than those who do, even though we know from, for example, cancer statistics that late presentaton causes significant morbidity and increased mortality!

Some of the participants transcripts suggested that male patients' wives or partners were behind the self-referral behaviour of many men, and this was treated with some humour by the GPs and by the male patients themselves – by presenting because 'someone else said I should come' helps men preserve their masculine image as someone who 'doesn't fuss about his health'. This does portray men as somewhat passive, and furthermore presenting late in the course of illness also adds to this notion of not fussing or not malingering.

Men first, doctors second

This final theme highlights how the male GPs' attitudes towards illness and how they coped with it was similar to how they described that of their male patients. The GPs described themselves as stoic in the face of their own illness, and as working men themselves some of the quotes highlighted that they too avoided seeing their own GP! This next quote highlights how even GPs can behave in a non-recommended manner: 'I haven't checked my blood pressure for years I don't think five, ten years, haven't done anything . . . should do probably . . . but I'm sure it's normal . . . better not to know sometimes, isn't it?'.

Some of the GPs admitted to, after a period of self-treatment, bypassing their own GP and directly approaching a specialist if they did believe something was wrong, and also admitted to NOT engaging in age-relevant screening (e.g. for prostate cancer) on the basis of knowing too much about the unpleasant follow-up tests. The theme seemed to be that they would recommend certain treatments or actions to their patients that they would not undergo themselves!

Overall, this theme highlighted that male GPs, at least in this sample, shared some of the same beliefs as their male patients about the need for males to be 'strong', but that when it came to treatment, they did not always practise what they preached.

Discussion

This paper was quite fascinating in terms of accessing the voices of male GPs with regards to how they considered those who sought their treatment – not just male patients, but women, those in and out of work, those retired. The authors of this qualitative paper quite rightly include a lot of discussion with the interpretation of data in the results section, but in the discussion highlight several key points. In relation to the first theme where GPs seem overwhelmed by demands of increased consultations, the conclusion drawn is that low rates of self-referral by males is probably just as well as GPs are already struggling to cope!

In the second theme we see an implicit judgement being made about what and who comes to a GP with a 'real' reason for self-referral and what and who does not. Non-working males were equated with females by some in that they attended their GP more often than working males. Males could avoid the 'malingerer' label or accusation of having too much time on their hands, if they attributed their presence to a female partners' pressure to do so, or had waited until symptoms were more serious. Although this study cannot test this, it is likely that these judgements infuence the non-verbal, if not the verbal, behaviour of the GPs towards these male patients who over-refer. Hale refers back to their earlier findings that males 'feel' that male Gs have negative attitudes towards them – this data would suggest that it is perhaps the case. In the case of male patients maintaining the masculine stereotype by maintaining that they were pressured into attending, the GPs' response seems to be one of humour rather than overt criticism; however, it does serve to undermine the male role in their own health.

In the final theme we see that male GPs themselves act in a manner congruent with male stereotypes, and that as working males they tend to under-refer to medical care! Overall, while certainly producing interesting findings and evidence of stereotypic thinking and behaviour among both male patients and male GPs, further research needs to compare these attitudes with those held by female GPs – they too may judge male patients differenty to female patients, and they too may make judgements about who over-attends and why. Inappropriate attendance is a challenge to medical services whatever the gender of the patient. It is also important to know whether patients' perceptions of critical judgements being made of them by GPs is borne out, as the GP is our first line of approach for many crucial screening and treatment options known to minimise more serious illness. Are GPs ambivalent to the referrals of certain types of patient? If so, does it affect any aspects of their communication or treatment actions? These issues are controversial, but nonetheless need to be addressed.

Limitations

The authors themselves acknowledge the limitations of snowball sampling whereby two initial GPs in effect invite their colleague/GP friends to participate – this is likely to introduce bias by restricting the sample diversity; however, other methods of recruiting GPs (by post) failed, and thus the approach taken is a pragmatic and understandable one, given the difficulty of reaching this population.

Influence of others on delay behaviour

People often take action only when they are encouraged to do so by others in their lay referral network or when they realise that others with the same problem sought help in the past. It appears that many people look for 'permission' to call for help from their friends or family members – and are more reluctant to call for help in its absence (Finnegan *et al.* 2000; Kentsch *et al.* 2002). Related to this are delays as a result of 'not wanting to bother anybody'.

Discussing symptoms with others can be helpful. For example, Turk *et al.* (1985) found that discovering the presence of a family history of the symptoms currently being experienced led to health-care contact being made. Such disclosures of family history or of others' illness experiences are a likely outcome of conversations within a lay referral network, and having a family history is associated with seeking health care (Petrie and Weinman 1997). However, not all social networks are helpful: some people consulted may distrust doctors after negative experiences of their own; others may believe in alternative treatment or therapies rather than traditional medical routes; yet others may decide that the symptoms reflect something else going on, their friend/relative being stressed, for example (Leventhal and Crouch 1997). The use of lay referral networks can therefore work for or against delays in the seeking of health care.

Treatment beliefs and delay behaviour

Horne (Horne 1999; Horne and Weinman 1999) suggests an extension to Leventhal's self-regulation model (described earlier in the chapter) whereby, in addition to illness perceptions predicting illness responses, the perceived benefits that an individual foresees of any treatments they may obtain as a result of seeking medical help are also predictive. For example, believing that one has a serious illness but that it can be cured with treatment is more likely to result in seeking medical help than the opposite cluster of beliefs. The identification of treatment representations (Horne and Weinman 1999) highlights perceptions of medicines as restorative, as symptom relievers, or as disruptive, harmful or addictive. Representations of medication and knowledge about treatment rationale have been associated with treatment adherence among adult populations (e.g. McElnay and McCallion 1998; Horne and Weinman 1999, 2002), and this is a growing area of research. A further effect of beliefs about treatment might be an effect on decisions to seek or not seek health professional advice for a symptom.

Perhaps due to growing concerns about some traditional medical treatments (e.g. antiobiotics, steroids, HRT – hormone replacement therapy), an increasing number of individuals are utilising what are known as complementary therapies, involving both physical and non-traditional pharmaceutical interventions, such as acupuncture, chiropractice, homeopathy and traditional Chinese herbal medicine. Interestingly, those who use such treatments tend to be among the more highly educated and more economically well-off groups in society (Astin 1998).

Emotions, traits and delay behaviour

Fear and anxiety have been inconsistently associated with delay in seeking health care. O'Carroll *et al.* (2001), for example, found that people who had relatively high scores on a measure of dispositional anxiety were more likely to seek help quickly following the onset of symptoms than their less anxious counterparts. While fear of doctors, treatment procedures or medical environments can delay health-care-seeking, and trait anxiety, neuroticism and negative affectivity generally increase health-care utilisation, illness-specific anxiety appears to be less influential. For example, delay in seeking medical care was not significantly associated with anxiety among a study of individuals with head and neck cancer (Tromp *et al.* 2004).

Emotion itself may be insufficient to determine health-care-seeking behaviour, given the previously described importance of illness prototypes, symptom perception and interpretations and treatment beliefs, all of which act together to shape a person's response to a health threat. For example, a person who is highly anxious about a symptom and believes it signifies a terminal illness for which there is no treatment is less likely to seek medical attention quickly than someone who is equally anxious but believes that the symptom may be an early warning sign of a condition for which preventive or curative treatment is available.

One further response to health threats is that of denial. It has been shown that people who engage in denial generally show reduced symptom perception and report, and greater delay in seeking help (Jones 1990; Zervas *et al.* 1993). Unrealistically optimistic beliefs about health status or illness outcomes were thought to reduce symptom report and preventive health behaviour by means of increasing the presence of denial. However, neither of these relationships was upheld in a study of symptom report among those with either multiple sclerosis or insulin-dependent diabetes (de Ridder *et al.* 2004). Aspinwall and Brunhart (1996) have pointed out that optimism is not necessarily unrealistic and maladaptive, but that optimistic beliefs may actually benefit symptom report by enabling people to attend to symptoms without perceiving them as a threat. Tromp *et al.* (2004) offer support for this from a study of predictors

> **health hardiness**
> the extent to which a person is committed to and involved in health-relevant activities, perceives control over their health and responds to health stressors as challenges or opportunities for growth.

of delay among patients with head and neck cancer, where delay was found to be greater (> three months) in those scoring low on optimism, as well as low on active coping, the use of social support and low **health hardiness**.

There is a limited literature examining the influence of personality traits on health-care-seeking behaviour (Williams 2006), and what there is tends to focus on optimism, as discussed above, or neuroticism. Neurotic individuals, as described earlier, tend to over-attend to internal bodily signs and over-interpret and over-report symptoms; this means that they generally exhibit shorter delays in seeking help than those less neurotic individuals (O'Carroll *et al.* 2001). However, it has been suggested that their consulting style, of elaborate symptom description, for example, works against them being seen as credible and potentially undermines the medical care they receive (Ellington and Wiebe 1999).

Finally, following diagnosis, Kasl and Cobb describe how people engage in sick role behaviour, as the symptoms have been validated (and may increase once a label has been attached to them; Kasl and Cobb 1966b). People are then working towards getting better or preserving health such as avoiding activity or further injury. Seeking health care does not inevitably lead a person into the sick role, however, as effective treatment may be provided that rids them of their symptoms and enables them to carry on as usual.

SUMMARY

This chapter has described the various processes that people go through before deciding that they might be getting ill. We have described how people may or may not become aware of certain bodily signs, depending upon the context in which they are experienced or upon individual characteristics such as neuroticism. Both internal and external factors influence the extent to which a person attends to their bodily states, and how they subsequently interpret bodily signs as symptoms. We have described how, upon interpreting bodily signs as symptoms of some underlying illness, a person compares them with pre-existing illness prototypes derived from their personal experience or from external sources of information. People's beliefs about illness have commonly been found to cluster around five domains: perceived identity (label), timeline, consequences, cure–control and cause. These ways of thinking about illness are relatively stable across various patient groups, but specific beliefs can differ from that of a healthy person. Finally, we have described a range of personal, social and emotional factors that influence whether a person responds to their symptoms by seeking the advice of a health-care professional. The journey from a bodily sign perceived as a symptom to the doctor's door is often a long one, and delay in seeking health care can itself be damaging to one's health. Health psychology therefore has an important role to play in identifying the factors that contribute to this journey in order to maximise the likelihood of positive health outcomes for patients. How people communicate with health professionals and engage in their treatment is discussed in the following chapter.

Further reading

Brown, R. (2004). Psychological mechanisms of medically unexplained symptoms: an integrative conceptual mode. *Psychological Bulletin*, 130: 793–813.

An interesting model of cognitive and attentional processes is presented that brings cognitive psychology thinking to the domain of medically unexplained symptoms, such as those seen in chronic fatigue syndrome. See also his editorial in a Special Issue of *Clinical Psychology Review*:

Brown, R.J. (2007). Introduction to The special issue on medically unexplained symptoms: background and future directions. *Clinical Psychology Review*, 27: 769–80.

Buick, D. and Petrie, K. (2002). 'I know just how you feel': the validity of healthy women's perceptions of breast cancer patients receiving treatment. *Journal of Applied Social Psychology*, 32: 110–23.

This paper highlights the fact that personal experience shapes one's perceptions of a particular illness and that discrepant perceptions between lay and 'patient' populations has implications for societal and carer responses.

Fischer, M., Scharloo, M., Abbink, J., van't Hul, A., van Ranst, D. *et al.* (2010). The dynamics of illness perceptions: testing assumptions of Leventhal's common-sense model in a pulmonary rehabilitation setting. *British Journal of Health Psychology*, 15: 887–903.

This paper is worth a read as it acknowledges the dynamic nature of illness representation components of Leventhal's Self Regulation model of illness. They examine what influences change in illness perceptions.

Martin, R. and Leventhal, H. (2004). Symptom perception and health-care seeking behavior. In J.M. Raczynski and L.C. Leviton (eds), *Handbook of Clinical Health Psychology*, Vol. 2. Washington, DC: American Psychological Association, pp. 299–328.

This chapter, contained in an excellent and well-resourced text, provides a clear overview of theory and findings regarding the illness-related and personal influences on how people interpret and act upon symptoms.

Parveen, S. and Morrison, V. (2011c). Predicting caregiver anxiety and depression (in review).

This paper continues the theme referred to in relation to the Fischer *et al.* (2010) paper above, and further tests Leventhal's dynamic constructs by examining how change in illness representations influences emotional outcomes among family caregivers.

Williams, P.G. (2006). Personality and illness behaviour. In M.E. Vollrath (ed.), *Handbook of Personality and Health*. Chichester: Wiley, pp. 157–73.

This chapter provides an overview of evidence regarding the role of personality in illness behaviour, from symptom perception to health-care-seeking behaviour. It also highlights key gaps in current knowledge and highlights why personality research offers exciting opportunities to develop our theoretical models of illness behaviour.

Visit the website at **www.pearsoned.co.uk/morrison** for additional resources to help you with your study, including multiple choice questions, weblinks and flashcards.

Chapter 10
The consultation and beyond

Learning outcomes

By the end of the chapter, you should have an understanding of:

- the process of the medical consultation
- the movement towards 'shared decision making' and the issues it creates
- factors that contribute to effective and ineffective consultations with health professionals
- issues related to 'breaking bad news'
- issues in medical decision making
- factors that influence adherence to medical treatments and behavioural change programmes
- interventions to improve adherence to medication and behavioural regimens

Doctor error causes heart attack death

This is a headline that could probably be written in the newspapers every day. But this error was not the fault of long waiting lists, giving the wrong drugs, or poor surgery. Rather, it was the result of the doctor's communication with the patient – or rather their lack of it. Mr Jones who had a history of anxiety went to his General Practitioner about a mild pain in his chest that had been going on for some hours. Unfortunately, for him, Mr Jones was what doctors sometimes call a 'heart sink' patient – the doctor's heart sinks when they see them come in the door, because they know the patient will make several complaints of a very general nature that they will not be able to treat, and the patient will return in the next few weeks with new complaints – which will again be untreatable. Even more unfortunately, the doctor then acted on her assumption that this was the case rather than trying to get a full picture of Mr Jones's symptoms and without conducting relevant tests. The doctor took charge of the consultation, asking closed questions about the symptoms, and confirmed to her satisfaction that the symptoms were psychosomatic in nature. She gave some reassuring words to Mr Jones, who left feeling somewhat disappointed by the relatively brief consultation and still doubtful that his symptoms were not more serious. However, he followed the doctor's advice and did not seek further medical help. Later that day, he died of a heart attack at home. In this chapter we cover the two key issues that may have contributed to this outcome: the doctor adopting a medically led interview style that did not allow the patient to volunteer information they considered relevant to the case, and their use of faulty diagnostic heuristics. Together, they proved fatal.

Chapter outline

Conversations between health-care providers and patients are one of the most important means through which both groups give and receive information relevant to medical decisions, treatment and self-care. As such, the consultation remains one of the most important aspects of medical care. Good communication enhances the effectiveness of care; poor communication can lead doctors to make poor diagnoses and treatment decisions and leave patients feeling dissatisfied and unwilling or unable to engage appropriately in their own treatment. This chapter considers a number of factors that contribute to the quality of the consultation, and how doctors and patients act on information gained from it. It starts by examining the process of the consultation – what makes a 'good' or a 'bad' consultation. It then considers how doctors use the information given in the consultation to inform their diagnostic decisions. Finally, the chapter considers how factors in the consultation and beyond influence whether and how much patients follow medical treatments or behavioural programmes recommended in it.

The medical consultation

The nature of the encounter

Consultations are a time in which doctors and other health professionals can obtain information to inform their diagnostic and treatment decisions, and patients can gain information about their condition, its treatment, and discuss issues relevant to them . They typically include five phases (Byrne and Long 1976):

1. The doctor establishes a relationship with the patient.

2. The doctor attempts to discover the reason for the patient's attendance.

3. The doctor conducts a verbal or physical examination or both.

4. The doctor, or the doctor and the patient, or the patient (in that order of probability) considers the condition.

5. The doctor, and occasionally the patient, considers further treatment or further investigation.

These phases appear to hold for most consultations – although, as we consider later, what happens within each 'stage' can vary significantly. Another way of exploring the consultation is to consider the key elements that make for a successful interview. Ford *et al.* (2003) identified six factors considered to be important to a 'good' medical consultation by a variety of informants including general practitioners, hospital doctors, nurses and lay people. They involve the health professional:

1. having a good knowledge of research or medical information and being able to communicate this to the patient;

2. achieving a good relationship with the patient;

3. establishing the nature of the patient's medical problem;

4. gaining an understanding of the patient's understanding of their problem and its ramifications;

5. engaging the patient in any decision-making process – treatment choices, for example, are discussed with the patient;

6. managing time so that the consultation does not appear rushed.

Who has the power?

The consultation involves both patient and health professional: and both can contribute to its outcome. The nature of the meeting, however, means that the health professional usually has more power over the consultation than the patient. This power differential can be exacerbated by the patient's behaviour and expectations within the consultation. They may often defer to the professional and be reluctant to ask questions or challenge any conclusions they may make. Such behaviour is more likely to occur in consultations with doctors than with other health professionals, such as nurses. Nevertheless, all health professionals have significant responsibility for determining the style and outcome of the consultation. This can result in approaches differing from 'doctor knows best', the professional-centred approach identified by Byrne and Long (1976), to a more patient-centred approach pioneered by Pendleton (1983) and others.

Characteristics of the professional-centred approach include:

- The health professional keeps control over the interview.
- They ask questions in order to gain information. These are direct, closed (allow yes/no answers), and refer to medical or other relevant facts.
- The health professional makes the decision.
- The patient passively accepts this decision.

Characteristics of the patient-centred approach include:

- The professional identifies and works with the patient's agenda as well as their own.
- The health professional actively listens to the patient and responds appropriately.
- The communication is characterised by the professional encouraging engagement and seeking the patient's ideas about what is wrong with them and how their condition may be treated.
- The patient is an active participant in the process.

Over the past decade, there has been a gradual shift from the professional-centred model to the patient-centred approach. Increasingly, both health professionals and patients are seen as collaborators in decisions concerning patient health care. This is perhaps most strongly expressed in a movement among health professionals towards a process of 'shared decision making' (see Edwards and Elwyn 2009), in which the patient and health professional have an equal share (and responsibility) in any treatment decision. Its advocates note that this approach is not relevant to all medical encounters, and may only truly occur where there is no dominant choice of treatment – a situation referred to as equipoise. This may occur in the context of very important health issues – such as a woman with breast cancer deciding whether or not to conserve a breast with a **lumpectomy** or to have more radical surgery and remove the whole affected breast. Here, there is no differential medical benefit from either approach (i.e. equipoise), and the choice may be more determined by factors such as the patient's concerns over their appearance or their desire to minimise the risk of recurrence. Although the health professional may provide information to inform patient choice, or even offer an opinion about that choice, the final decision should be reached jointly. Where equipoise does not exist, for example, in the case of a request for antibiotics for the treatment of a viral condition (where they will be of no benefit), the health professional may educate the patient to accept their choice of treatment, and so arrive at a 'joint decision', but not a truly shared decision.

These issues are taken into account in Elwyn *et al.*'s (2000) consultation approach which involves the following steps:

1. Explore the patient's ideas about the nature of the problem and potential treatments.
2. Identify how much information the patient would prefer, and tailor information to meet these needs.
3. Check the patient's understanding of potential treatment options and their expectations and concerns in relation to them.
4. Assess the patient's decision-making preference (joint, doctor, or patient-led) – and adopt their preferred mode.
5. Make, discuss or defer decisions.
6. Arrange follow-up.

> ## lumpectomy
> a surgical procedure in which only the tumour and a small area of surrounding tissue are removed. Contrasts with mastectomy in which the whole breast is removed.

Both shared and joint decision-making approaches are now advocated by, among others, the British National Health Service (NHS) which has called for 'active partnerships' between health professionals and patients (NHS Executive 1996). Despite this enthusiasm, there are often power differentials between high status health professionals (particularly doctors) and patients within the consultation. The health professional, for example, typically has more relevant knowledge than the patient. The appearance of equality can therefore be an illusion rather than reality, and both health professionals and patients may find it difficult to move away from this implicit power structure. Indeed, many patients *prefer* this asymmetry and resist moves to 'empower' them into a decision-making role. Some patients may be distressed and worried if a health-care professional admits there is no clear evidence about the best choice of intervention, or that the evidence is mixed or premised on poor methodology. By contrast, being prescribed a particular treatment by an expert health professional may confer certainty and reassurance in the treatment of disease that cannot be found when the patient is asked to make choices about a number of uncertain treatment options.

Empirical research confirms some of these cautions. Lee *et al.* (2002) asked over a thousand patients with either breast cancer or who were receiving **stem cell transplants** to identify their preferred consultation style. Only a minority of individuals opted for the shared decision-making approach. Patients' preferred decision-making processes were:

- Physician makes treatment decisions — 10 per cent
- Physician makes decisions following discussion with patient — 21 per cent
- Shared decision making — 42 per cent
- Patient makes decision following discussion with doctor — 22 per cent
- Patient makes decision — 5 per cent

> **stem cell transplant**
>
> procedure in which stem cells are replaced within the bone marrow following radiotherapy or chemotherapy or diseases such as leukaemia where they may be damaged.

Women, older people, those with an active coping style, and people with more education and a severe health problem are most likely to want to be engaged in the decision-making process (Arora and McHorney 2000). Paradoxically, Arora and McHorney found that people who placed the highest value on their health were least likely to want to be engaged in the decision-making process – perhaps because they considered this to be such an important issue that they did not want to question the expert opinion of the doctor. Whatever their preference, most patients do not appear to be engaged in shared decision making. Keating *et al.* (2002), for example, found that most patients (64 per cent) in their sample of over a thousand women with breast cancer desired a collaborative role in decision making, but only 33 per cent reported having had such a role when they discussed treatments with their surgeons. Even worse, Bensing *et al.*'s (2006) analysis of Dutch family doctors' consulting styles revealed that over the 15 years before their report, consultations had become increasingly medically-led and interrupted by frequent recording of information on computer.

These relatively low levels of joint decision may reflect doctors' difficulties in adopting a collaborative role in the hurly-burly of busy medical life – particularly when faced with patients who do not or cannot easily engage in the process. To reduce this problem, a number of clinicians (e.g. Lee *et al.* 2010; Waljee *et al.* 2007) have developed written or computer-based 'decision aids' to help patients make decisions about their treatment in the light of complex health information. These typically provide patients with information both for and against a number of treatment options, encouraging them to score each item of information in terms of its desirability or lack of desirability, and to achieve a total plus or minus score in relation to each potential treatment.

Consultations which involve patients in decision making are likely to result in high levels of patient satisfaction, confidence in health-care recommendations, improvements in self-care and well-being, and, on occasion, fewer drug prescriptions and less demand for inappropriate surgical treatments. They also appear to have similar, but no better, medical outcomes to more traditional consultation approaches (e.g. Bieber *et al.* 2006; Krones *et al.* 2008). Indeed, medical outcomes may not always be optimal. Kinmonth *et al.* (1998), for example, found that patients who were given a patient-centred approach to the treatment of their type 2 diabetes

Doctor–patient communication: are things improving

Langewitz, W.A., Loeb, Y., Nübling, M. *et al.* (2009). From patient talk to physician notes – comparing the content of medical interviews with medical records in a sample of outpatients in Internal Medicine. *Patient Education and Counseling*, 76: 336–40.

Two key roles of the consultation are to obtain and record relevant information. Good medical care involves achieving both goals with a high degree of effectiveness and accuracy. This study set out to investigate whether doctors in a general out-patient department of a University Hospital in Switzerland achieved both these goals.

Method

Interviews with 20 patients by 11 physicians were randomly selected for analysis from 56 interviews videoed for another unrelated research project. Each interview involved an individual who had presented at the hospital with symptoms they thought warranted medical investigation, but had no known diagnosis. The interviews were assessed by three independent assessors in order to identify a variety of elements:

- The type of information mentioned by patient: medical, therapeutic, lifestyle, psychosocial – new, or repeated.

- The type of utterance made by the doctor (measured using the Roter Interaction Analysis System), rated as waiting, echoing, mirroring, summarising

(indicating a patient-centred interview style), showing empathy (broken down into the sub-categories of: naming emotions ('You seem sad'), understanding the emotion ('I can well understand you feel this way'), respecting ('I can appreciate how you have tried to . . . ')

- Note was also taken of the time physicians spent silently taking notes or reading material brought by patients to the consultation.

Results

The interviews lasted an average of 37 minutes, and in total contained 9,002 utterances.

The combined score of the 'waiting', 'echoing', 'mirroring', and 'summarising' (WEMS) measures in the videos was correlated with the total amount of information gathered from patients. The correlations were largely significant: WEMS and amount of medical information ($r = 0.57$, $p = 0.009$), WEMS and therapeutic information ($r = 0.41$, $p = 0.07$), WEMS and psychosocial information ($r = 0.52$, $p = 0.02$), and WEMS and lifestyle information ($r = 0.64$, $p = 0.003$). Table 1 provides a summary of the frequency of key utterance classifications by doctors within each interview.

A key analysis involved investigation of how much information that was gained in the interview was then noted in the medical notes. As can be seen in Figure 1a, there was a large discrepancy between the

Table 1 The mean number of various utterance types by physicians during assessment interviews

Utterance type	Frequency	Utterance type	Frequency
Closed medical question	36.25	Gives respect	0.55
Open medical question	19.35	Echoing	23.0
Gives medical information	6.25	Summarising	9.80
Closed lifestyle question	10.6	Naming	0.05
Open lifestyle question	7.90	Personal	1.45
Gives lifestyle information	0.45		
Closed psychosocial question	1.30		
Open psychosocial question	175		
Gives psychosocial information	0.15	Taking notes	24.10

amount of information given (in this case medical information) and information recorded in the notes. The only 100 per cent agreement in the two was for patient number 2. The more information given in the interview, the greater the discrepancy between this and the amount of information recorded in the notes. The authors note also that at no point did any of the doctors check with the patients that their edited version of the information given was appropriate. As can be seen in Figure 1b, the disparities between information given and information recorded in relation to lifestyle factors (and not recorded here, for psychosocial and therapeutic information) was greater than that related to medical information.

Discussion

The authors note the positive relationship between the number of active communication skills used (such as reflection, mirroring, and so on – the WEMS) and the amount of information gained within the interviews. They take this to suggest that the active engagement

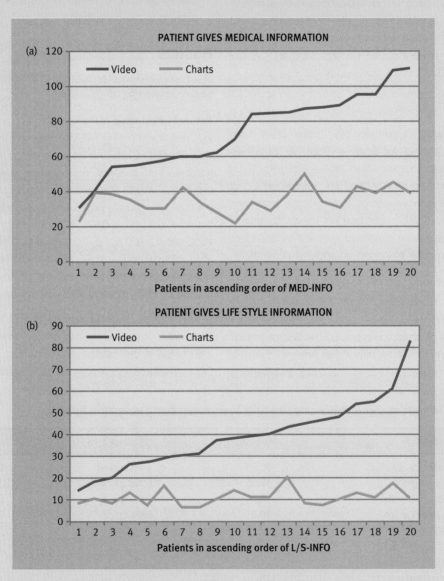

Figure 1 Disparities between the amount of information given by each patient, and the amount of information recorded in patients' medical notes.

of the doctor, evident through the use of reflection, mirroring, and so on, results in higher levels of patient disclosure of information. Alternatively, there may be a third variable here – the duration of the interview – that may both increase the time for such utterances, and the amount of information given during the interview. The authors also suggest that the gap between medical information given and recorded may reflect the synthesis of various elements of medical information into clear medical entities: temperature, coughing, sore throat, running nose, etc. may be condensed to upper respiratory tract infection. This explanation is unlikely to account, however, for the gap between psychosocial, lifestyle, and therapeutic information. Indeed, in 12 of the interviews, they note that patients revealed psychosocial information, but none was recorded. Thus, there appears to be two different criteria of importance. Patients tell physicians about things they deem important for the physician to know; physicians filter this out, and essentially record medical information they deem appropriate. Whether this affects subsequent care is as yet unknown.

expressed higher levels of satisfaction with their communication with health professionals, greater treatment satisfaction, and greater well-being than patients who received a standard health-professional-led consultation. However, they were less careful in sticking to the calorie-controlled diet necessary to maximise control over their condition. This may not be a bad outcome, of course. Rather, it implies that patients had knowingly opted to have a higher day-to-day quality of life rather than one constrained by medical 'necessities'. Ultimately, it is their life, and fully informed decisions such as this need to be supported.

Factors that influence the process of consultation

Working together

A variety of factors may influence the behaviour of health professionals, some of which may be of no immediate medical relevance. Gerbert (1984), for example, found that health professionals gave more information to patients that they liked than those they disliked. Encounters may also be influenced by the time available, the type of problem being dealt with, and so on. Patients and health professionals may also hold different agendas and expectations of the consultation. Patients are frequently concerned about issues such as pain and how an illness may interfere with their everyday lives. Health professionals are often more concerned with understanding the severity of the patient's condition and developing their treatment plan. These differing agendas may mean that health professionals and patient fail to appreciate important aspects of any information given and received. They may also impact on the outcome of the consultation.

The findings of Zachariae *et al.* (2003) typify those found in studies of this phenomenon. They found that patients' ratings of how well they considered the physician understood their feelings during the consultation, whether they attempted to gain an understanding of their viewpoint, and the quality of their contact with the doctor were as important as their confidence in their doctor's ability to handle the medical aspects of their care in predicting satisfaction with the interview, their confidence in their ability to cope with their illness, and levels of emotional distress. Of note also was that doctors who evidenced poor communication skills were least aware of the patients' responses and level of dissatisfaction with the interview.

The type of health professional

As well as these subtle differences in skills and personal characteristics, more obvious factors may also influence the style of the encounter. The style of interaction appears to differ across professions. Nurses, for example, are generally seen as more nurturing, easier to talk to and better listeners than doctors. These different roles were highlighted by Nichols (2003) who suggested that doctors may find it difficult to become emotionally involved or to know their patients as people when they are involved in life and death decisions or actions such as surgery. With this in mind, he suggested that nurses should provide the main 'caring' role and be more involved in

Plate 10.1 Being a friendly face and expressing empathy can help patients cope with bad news. Here an occupational therapist discusses therapy options with someone with a progressive muscular disorder in a completely informal and 'non-medical' manner

Source: Pearson Education Ltd.

holistic care of the individual. For this reason, nurses typically address more psychosocial concerns than doctors, and have different styles of talking to patients. Collins (2005), for example, found that nurses' communication frequently involved responding to patients' contributions: doctors' communication involved leading the consultation and addressing matters important to them. In addition, nurses' explanations began from the viewpoint of patients' responsibilities and behaviour; doctors' explanations began from the viewpoint of biomedical intervention.

Gender of the health professional

The gender of the health professional may also influence the nature of the consultation. Hall and Roter (2002), for example, concluded from their meta-analysis of seven relevant studies that patients spoke to female physicians more than male physicians, reported more medical and personal information, and made more positive statements. Patients also appeared more assertive and interrupted more when being interviewed by female doctors than by their male counterparts. Interestingly, perhaps, the gender of the doctor did not influence the degree to which

emotional issues, such as concern, worries and personal feelings, were discussed. Some of these differences may be a consequence of the doctors' behaviour: female physicians tend to ask more questions and make more active efforts to build a relationship with their patients than male physicians – behaviours that lead to higher levels of disclosure than would otherwise occur. Interestingly, satisfaction with female doctors is likely to be high only when they adopt what are perceived to be gender-role congruent communication styles (Schmid Mast *et al.* 2007). What may also be important is the concordance or lack of concordance between the gender of health professionals and patients. Beran *et al.* (2007), for example, found that both men and women were more likely to report being treated disrespectfully by doctors of the opposite gender than when they saw someone of the same gender.

Culture and language

Culture and language are inextricably linked in the context of the consultation, and there is clear evidence that people from differing cultures and languages will experience differing styles of consultation (see also Chapter 2 ☞).

One UK research group (Neal *et al.* 2006) found that South Asians fluent in English had the shortest consultations with their family doctors; South Asians not fluent in English had the longest. White patients discuss more emotional problems than the South Asian patients, and are more active during the consultations than either of the Asian groups. In the Netherlands, consultations with immigrant patients (especially those from Turkey and Morocco) are likely to be significantly briefer, and the power distance between patient and doctor greater than those with Dutch patients. Doctors invest more effort in trying to understand immigrant patients, while they show more involvement and empathy with those that are Dutch (Meeuwesen *et al.* 2006). Problems in communication may result in doctors experiencing difficulties in reaching appropriate diagnoses (e.g. Okelo *et al.* 2007) and patients misunderstanding information given in the consultation (e.g. B. Jones *et al.* 2007). The likelihood of these communication errors may be increased as a consequence of many health professionals' overestimation of the level of language understanding these patients have (Kelly and Haidet 2007), and exacerbated further by many health professionals' expectations of how patients expect to be treated. Fagerli *et al.* (2007), for example, found that their sample of Norwegian health professionals thought that Pakistani-born patients preferred an authoritarian health-worker style. In fact, they preferred empathy and care. This disparity resulted in a lack of trust between patients and professionals.

The type of information and the way it is given

One obvious factor that will influence the degree to which patients understand what is said in a consultation is the language used within it. Technical or medical language can be confusing unless appropriately explained. Words such as arthritis, jaundice, anti-emetic, dilated and haemorrhoids are not understood by nearly half the population (Ley 1997). Lobb *et al.* (1999) found significant misunderstandings of information given to women diagnosed with breast cancer. Not surprisingly, perhaps, 73 per cent of their sample did not understand the term 'median survival' – nor did the term 'good prognosis' carry a clear meaning. In a study of patients' understandings of words used to describe 'lumps', Chadha and Repanos (2006) found that a majority of patients were unaware of the meaning of words such as 'sarcoma' and 'lipoma'. While this confusion may be expected, 19 per cent of patients thought that a 'benign' lump was a malignant cancer – a serious misunderstanding. Not surprisingly, the use of jargon may result in significant anxiety. Abramsky and Fletcher (2002), for example, found that the words rare, abnormal, syndrome, disorder, anomaly and high risk in the context of genetic screening were particularly worrying to patients. They also found that risk for developing a disorder expressed as '1 in X' evoked more worry than when the same information was expressed as a percentage. These subtle uses of language show how careful health-care professionals need to be when talking to patients.

The way information is given within consultations is also important. Of particular importance may be whether information is framed in a positive or negative way. Edwards *et al.* (2001) noted the 'paucity of evidence' relating to the effects of framing of information and health behaviour but noted that some early evidence suggested framing may act as important influence on patient and even health professional behaviour. As an example of this research, McNeil *et al.* (1982) found that patients, medical students, and even surgeons were more likely to opt for a hypothetical surgical operation when the risks associated with the operation were presented with a positive rather than negative frame (i.e. a 40 per cent likelihood of survival versus a 60 per cent risk of dying). More recent work with 'real life' issues has, however, found framing to be relatively modest in its influence – and the optimal approach is not always obvious. Carling *et al.* (2010), for example, found that both positive *and* negative framing resulted in higher uptake of antihypertensive medication than neutrally framed information. In addition, while framing may influence intentions, it may not always impact on behaviour. Van't Riet *et al.* (2010) found that computer-generated feedback on fitness plus gain-framed messages resulted in stronger intentions to be physically active than the same feedback with loss-framed messages, but did not result in greater levels of exercise. Similarly, Park *et al.* (2010) found message framing had no effect on attendance for screening for type 2 diabetes. Accordingly, any interventions using message framing need to assess its impact on behaviour in pre-intervention pilot studies, to ensure the optimal approach is being used.

Patient factors

Patient factors will also significantly influence the consultation. High levels of anxiety or distress during the interview, a lack of familiarity with the information discussed, a failure to actively engage with the interview, and not having considered issues to be discussed within the consultation may minimise patients' level of engagement. Patients may not think through what information they want, or realise only after the interview what they could have asked. They may also be reluctant to ask questions of doctors and other health professionals who are still frequently seen as of a higher status than them (Schouten *et al.* 2003). Perhaps for these reasons, people who are well educated and of high socio-economic status tend to gain more information and to have longer consultations than people with low levels of education and less economic status (Stirling *et al.* 2001).

Breaking bad news

One type of consultation for which the necessary skills have received particular attention is called the 'bad news' interview. As its name implies, these interactions are typically those in which patients and/or their partners are told that they have a serious illness or that they may die of their illness. Clearly, such interviews are stressful for both patients and health-care professionals. Historically, information about the likelihood of dying has frequently been withheld from patients – although their relatives were frequently told, placing a significant burden of knowledge on these people. However, this is no longer considered ethical – patients are now considered to have the right to be told their prognosis.

There is consistent evidence that the way in which bad news is given will impact on patient well-being (P. Schofield *et al.* 2003). Unfortunately, there is little evidence about the best methods of doing so, and most guidelines are based on opinion and basic principles of good communication rather than empirical data. Buckman (1992) suggested a six-step protocol for the process:

1. Give the news in person, in private, with enough time and without interruptions.

2. Find out what the patient knows about their diagnosis.

3. Find out what the patient wants to know.

4. Share the information: start with a 'warning shot' and then a small amount of information in simple language at a pace the patient can cope with.

5. Respond to the patient's feelings, including acknowledging and validating their emotional reaction to the news.

6. Plan and follow-through: includes planning next steps, summarising what has been said, identifying sources of support, and making an early follow-up appointment.

When these, or similar, guidelines are followed, patients appear to benefit. M. Schofield *et al.* (2003), for example, asked patients to recall a **bad news interview** in which they received information about a 'life threatening' **melanoma**. They were asked questions about how their diagnosis was given, whether they received as much information as they wanted about their diagnosis, its treatment options, and its prognosis, and how the interview was conducted. They examined the relationship between their responses and levels of anxiety and depression at the time of diagnosis, 4 and 13 months later. Factors associated with low levels of anxiety included the health professional preparing the patient for their diagnosis, giving as much information as required, providing written information, talking about the patient's feelings, being reassuring, and the presence of other (supportive) people while being given the diagnosis. Practices associated with low levels of depression included encouraging the patient to be involved in treatment-related decisions and discussing the severity of the diagnosis and how it may affect other aspects of their life. The importance of non-specific factors within the interview was highlighted by the findings of Roberts *et al.* (1994), who found that the physician's caring attitude was more important in aiding psychological adjustment to a diagnosis of breast cancer than the information given during the interview.

---

bad news interview
conversation between health professional (usually a doctor) and patient in which they are told 'bad news', usually that their illness has a very poor prognosis and they may die.

melanoma
a form of skin cancer. Usually begins in a mole and has a poor prognosis unless treated early.

Many doctors considered it a kindness not to tell patients when they were dying – a belief that also obviated *their* need to go through this painful process (see below). Indeed, so common was this practice that a rule of thirds was often cited as relevant to this situation. That is, two-thirds of patients were assumed to wish to know their prognosis – and two-thirds of doctors did not want to tell them. It is now considered a patient's right to know they are dying, and the practice of telling the relatives and not the patient is no longer acceptable – and many patients know they are dying without being told.

Patients may be upset, or even distraught, when given such information. However, knowledge of a poor prognosis can allow patients to prepare for death – from the most prosaic preparation such as making sure bills are paid to dealing with relationship issues and other important aspects of their lives. When death is not immediate, patients may prepare life goals that they wish to achieve before they die, and so on. So there are both positive and negative issues to be considered. Do the benefits outweigh the costs? Perhaps this decision can only be made on an individual basis. But on what grounds? Or perhaps all patients should be told whatever their circumstances?

Having identified 'best practice', a number of studies have examined how well physicians actually give bad news. Farber *et al.* (2002) found that over half their sample of junior doctors reported always or frequently performing 10 of 11 emotionally supportive strategies (e.g. ask about patients' worries, fears and concerns) and engaging 6 of 9 environmental supports (e.g. ensure that the patient has a support person present). Similarly, Chadha and Repanos (2006) found that 64 per cent of their sample of surgeons felt confident in their ability to break bad news (compared to 91 per cent who felt confident in gaining consent to surgery and 40 per cent who felt confident in discussing 'do not resuscitate' decisions). These optimistic self-ratings may be contrasted with the findings of Ford *et al.* (1996), who used audiotapes of consultations to analyse cancer specialists' bad news interviews with their patients and found that the majority of time in their interviews was spent giving biomedical information with relatively little emphasis on empathic responses or acknowledgment of distress. In addition, the doctors exerted significant levels of control over the interview, moving away from the patient-led interview that the guidelines indicate as being optimal. Another observational study by the same group (Fallowfield *et al.* 1990) found that surgeons did not detect 70 per cent of instances of emotional distress in women being diagnosed with breast cancer.

Despite the clear need for skills in breaking bad news, many senior doctors (around one half of consultants surveyed in the UK by Barnett *et al.* (2007)) receive no formal training in doing so. Most considered such training to be of value: an expectation that is justified by empirical studies. Back *et al.* (2007), for example, measured bad news skills in what they termed standardised patient encounters, which involved the use of actors playing patients. They found that physicians made significant gains in their ability to give bad news following a four-day workshop. Most changes were substantial: for example, 16 per cent of participants used the word 'cancer' when giving bad news before the workshop; 54 per cent used it at the end of the workshop. However, it is not clear how these skills translated to their day-to-day work.

Before ending this section, it should be acknowledged that the bad news interview is stressful for health professionals as well as patients. Ptacek and Eberhardt (1996) mapped out patient and doctor stress in relation to the interview (see Figure 10.1), suggesting that doctors experience significant anticipatory stress before the consultation, peaking during the 'clinical encounter', while patients' levels of stress typically peak following the interview. Many clinicians experience a range of emotions including sorrow, guilt, and feeling a failure (Fallowfield and Jenkins 2004). The stress associated with giving bad news can last as long as three days or more

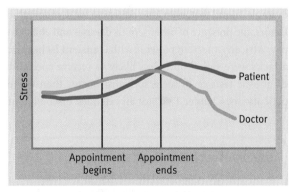

Figure 10.1 The timescale of stress experienced by health-care professionals and patients in relation to the bad news interview

Source: adapted from Ptacek and Eberhardt (1996).

(Ptacek *et al.* 2001), and can result in significant increases in blood pressure and impaired immune (NK cell) response (Cohen *et al.* 2003).

Moving beyond the consultation

A key goal of the consultation is to allow health-care professionals and patients to receive and provide information relevant to medical decision making and treatment. The next part of the chapter considers two outcomes of this process: one involving the health-care professional, and one involving the patient.

Medical decision making

Health-care decisions do not happen in a neutral context – and may be influenced by a wide variety of factors. They may be biased by health-care professionals' expectations of their patients, their fellow professionals, and the sheer pressure of making decisions in a short time – often without all the information necessary to make a fully informed decision. Doctors' own views about the nature of health care may also influence their decisions. Some doctors, for example, may only be willing to treat patients who are actively involved in maintaining their own health. Such doctors may refuse to provide expensive curative treatment for smoking-related diseases in patients who are unwilling to give up smoking. Other biases may be less conscious, or may be motivated by non-health related issues. Mitchell *et al.* (2000), for example, found that, even after adjusting for demographic factors, the presence of other serious diseases and ability to pay, African American patients with **transient ischaemic attacks** were significantly less likely to receive specialist diagnostic tests or to see a specialist doctor than white patients (see Chapter 2 ☛ for an extended discussion of

> **transient ischaemic attacks**
> short periods of reduced blood flow to the brain resulting in symptoms including short periods of confusion, weakness and other minor neurological symptoms.

this issue). Gender differences may also influence the care people receive in hospital. Nurses are more likely to offer pain medication to women than to men, at least in casualty departments (Raftery *et al.* 1995). By contrast, more men than women are likely to be offered a place on cardiac rehabilitation programmes following an MI (Allen *et al.* 2004).

A key area of medical decision making involves diagnosing the illness with which patients present. Elstein and Schwarz (2002) identified a number of ways that doctors achieve this:

● *Hypothesis testing*: the so-called 'gold star' level of decision making. This involves a logical sequencing of establishing and testing hypotheses about the nature of the diagnosis. Hypotheses are established, tested, and when they fail are replaced by further hypotheses until a final 'correct' hypothesis is established.

● *Pattern recognition*: compares patterns of symptoms with disease prototypes. This may be a good way of reaching easy diagnoses, with the hypothesis-testing approach being utilised for more complex decisions.

● *Opinion revision or 'heuristics and biases'*: perhaps the least reliable approach to making diagnoses: involves making decisions based on partial evidence as a result of using rules of thumb or heuristics.

Clearly, most of the diagnoses assigned by doctors are accurate. However, their decision making may be prone to error, particularly when the third of these approaches is used. This may sometimes be inevitable in the context of medical decision making where rapid decisions without optimal information may need to be made. Such situations may push doctors towards the use of diagnostic short-cuts. But the use of these short-cuts may happen in other, less demanding, situations as well. Tversky and Kahneman (1981) suggested that because we can only handle limited amounts of information when making decisions, we often take short-cuts known as heuristics or 'rules of thumb'. Those that are most useful for medicine may be 'fast and frugal' (Elstein and Schwarz 2002): that is, they aid quick decision making on the basis of minimal information. They allow doctors to make decisions at times of uncertainty and when information is lacking, but may lead to errors because they are based on assumptions which may or may not be relevant to particular situations. In a qualitative study of this process, André *et al.* (2002) asked a number of family doctors to describe some of their decision-making processes. One doctor stated that she was so used to 40-year-olds presenting with chest pain having had an MI that she no longer tested for alternative diagnoses (as is recommended practice). Another doctor stated that if he thought a condition was psychosomatic, 'I begin to try to tie down the idea right away. I won't start with physical examination before talking about the possibility that it could be something emotional . . .' – a process that may miss a physical disease process.

A key problem with the use of heuristics is that they limit thinking through the full diagnostic possibilities, and may be biased by a number of factors (Elstein and Schwarz 2002). These include:

- *Availability*: diseases that receive considerable media attention are frequently thought to be more common than they actually are, even by doctors. Assuming a high probability of finding a condition may lead to it being diagnosed in error. A similar factor may occur if the diagnosing doctor has knowledge of previous diagnoses given by colleagues.

- *Representativeness*: here, errors can occur because a set of symptoms is compared to a prototype set of symptoms and matched to one of two conditions without taking into account the likelihood of each of the two conditions being present. If these vary in prevalence within the population, the likelihood is that the condition being diagnosed will be the more prevalent disease. Heuristics that do not take this aspect into account may result in the physician not challenging their initial diagnosis through strict hypothesis testing.

- *Potential 'pay off' of differing diagnoses*: if a diagnosis is unclear, the diagnosis assigned may be the one that carries the least cost and most benefit for the individual. When doctors are presented with a young child complaining of abdominal pain of no obvious origin, for example, a diagnosis of appendicitis and treatment of appendicectomy may be made, as treating the appendicitis successfully may be considered to outweigh the risks of an unnecessary operation.

Examples of these types of heuristic errors were provided by Vickrey *et al.* (2010) who described several cases of misdiagnosis by a number of neurologists. One occurred as a result of the doctor inappropriately focusing on the onset of a disease in Mexico – excluding alternatives that were not based on the place of onset (a framing effect of geography); a repeated misdiagnosis of depression-related neurological difficulties that was made as an initial diagnosis but was then repeated by several clinicians despite evidence of no benefit from antidepressant medication (bias as a result of the 'anchoring' effect of the first diagnosis), and a diagnosis of cobalamin deficiency made as a result of a superficial similarity of the presenting symptoms to a recently treated case of this very rare problem (the availability heuristic).

One method of improving decision making involves the use of computerised programmes that support doctors in their decision making. One web-based programme was evaluated by Ramnarayan *et al.* (2006). The programme was a 'diagnostic reminder system that provided rapid advice with free text data entry' that participants could access if they were unsure of a diagnosis. To evaluate its impact, trainee doctors who used the system to diagnose children with acute disorders noted the initial diagnosis they made without the programme and then (when they felt necessary) following its use. These diagnoses were then compared to the diagnosis the child was given prior to discharge from hospital. Before using the programme, 45 per cent of their diagnoses were considered 'unsafe'; following its use, this figure fell to 33 per cent. In an analogue study of a similar programme, using simulated patients, the same team (Ramnarayan *et al.* 2006) found that the diagnostic accuracy of all grades of doctors, including experienced hospital consultants, improved following the use of such a system.

Compliance, adherence and concordance

A key determinant of the success of any medical intervention is whether patients actually follow the recommended medical regime – whether this involves taking tablets or making more complex behavioural changes. Initially, research into this issue focused on what was termed treatment compliance, which implied a doctor- or health-professional-led process in which the patient was expected to comply with whatever instructions they were given. After several years, the more politically correct term 'adherence' was introduced, implying that patients were more involved in the decision-making process – although how this increase in patient independence was achieved was not always clear. More recently still, the

IN THE SPOTLIGHT

More heads make worse decisions

Decisions may be affected by a number of factors beyond the consultation. Christensen *et al.* (2000) examined the effect of group diagnostic decision making involving small teams of junior doctors and medical students. Information given to the groups was manipulated by asking the physicians to individually watch videos of actors acting as patients, offering the same information to all those in the group, and some information unique to each viewer, including one viewer who was given information crucial to making a correct diagnosis.

Their results were interesting in that, once convened, the groups discussed the information common to all those involved more than they discussed the unique information held by each group member. As a result they actually made *more* diagnostic errors than a control group of individual doctors given the same information. These data are particularly pertinent to making difficult diagnoses that may involve discussion by several doctors with information gleaned from a variety of different consultations or to some medical specialties (particularly those involved in mental health) where information from many sources may be used to arrive at a diagnosis.

Plate 10.2 Some decision-making contexts are more difficult than others. Joint decisions, particularly if led by a powerful consultant, may not always be correct

Source: Rex Features/TM & 20th Century Fox/Everett.

term 'concordance' has been introduced reflecting a further development in this process. Here, both doctor and patient reach a jointly determined agreement concerning the treatment regimen. This joint decision requires a patient to be fully informed of the benefits and costs (in terms of side-effects, treatment benefits, etc.) of following a particular treatment regimen. Full concordance between health professional and patient is assumed to increase the likelihood of patients following a treatment plan – although patients may of course change their decision or not follow the agreed treatment for a number of other reasons.

Taking the tablets

The most frequent medical treatment involves patients taking prescribed medication at times and in sufficient quantities to provide a therapeutic dose. This may not be a simple task. Taking HIV antiretroviral medication known as HAART (Highly Active Antiretroviral Therapy, or ART as it frequently now called: see Chapter 8 (☛)), for example, is an extremely important and complex issue. People taking this medication not only have to take tablets on a daily basis, but they also have to take them within very tight time limits during the day. HAART medications may require different dosing schedules – some at twelve-, eight-, six-, or four-hour intervals. Some tablets need to be taken with food, some with fatty foods, some with non-fatty foods and some on an empty stomach. Many result in serious side-effects that require taking further medication, and other medications may be required to treat secondary opportunistic infections. Not only is the required regimen for taking HAART complex, but it may also take place in the absence of symptoms. Indeed, it may cause more short-term symptoms than it appears to prevent. Failure to keep to this regime, however, can result in the virus mutating – with serious implications for both the individual involved and any person to whom they may pass the mutated virus. Nevertheless, adherence levels may be far from ideal. Sherr et al. (2010), for example, found that 57 per cent of their UK sample had taken a tablet at the wrong time in the previous week, 21 per cent had missed one dosage, and 10 per cent had missed two or more dosages within the previous week. Using measures of viral status, they determined that the third level of non-adherence was sufficient to worsen these people's prognosis.

The complexity of taking the anti-HIV regimen perhaps makes this a special case. However, the percentage of people to follow the optimal medical regimen required in many chronic illnesses can be low. It has been estimated that, on average, only half of those who are prescribed pharmacological therapies take sufficient medication to experience a therapeutic benefit (Haynes et al. 1996), resulting in about 10 per cent of hospital admissions (Schlenk et al. 2004). Looking at more specific disorders,

Cramer (2004) reported that between 36 and 93 per cent of patients with type 2 diabetes followed the recommended regimen of **oral hypoglycaemic agents** for between 6 and 24 months. Between 50 to 70 per cent of people are thought to take all their anti-hypertensive medication (Caro et al. 1999). Krigsman et al. (2007) reported that 42 per cent of their sample were under-using their asthma medication, while 23 per cent were overusing it. Similarly, Bernal et al. (2006) reported that 43 per cent of patients with inflammatory bowel disease admitted to missing medication; 20 per cent of patients admitted to self-medicating.

Given the importance of taking these medications, one may wonder why people fail to do so. One simple explanation is that many people forget to take their medication or find their treatment regimen too complicated to cope with effectively. This may be particularly pertinent in the complex medical regime associated with the treatment of HIV. Maggiolo et al. (2002) found that 60 per cent of failures to follow the recommended medical regimen were associated with forgetfulness, 50 per cent with being away from home, while 38 per cent of failures were associated with problems with the drug schedule. A wider range of other factors have also been found to predict sub-optimal use of medication in general (e.g. Chesney 2003) including:

- *social factors*: including low levels of education, unemployment, concomitant drug use, low levels of social support;
- *psychological factors*: including high levels of anxiety and depression, use of emotion-focused coping strategies such as denial, a belief that continued use of a drug will reduce its effectiveness, taking drug holidays to prevent 'harm' as a consequence of long-term drug use;
- *treatment factors*: including misunderstandings regarding treatment, complexity of the treatment regimen, high numbers of side-effects, little obvious benefit from taking medication, poor relationship between patient and health-care provider, poor health professional–patient communication.

---

oral hypoglycaemic agents
various drug types, all of which reduce circulating blood glucose levels.

To these issues, patients prescribed HAART medication may add those of fear of disclosure, suspicions of treatment, the sheer number of pills required, decreased quality of life, and problems of access to medication (Mills *et al.* 2006).

Another contextual factor that may affect adherence with medical regimens, particularly in children, involves the family system. Tubiana-Rufi *et al.* (1998), for example, found that diabetic children from families characterised as rigid, with low levels of cooperation and communication between family members, were more than six times less likely to adhere to their insulin regimes than children from families with more positive dynamics. From a different perspective, Mellins *et al.* (2004) found that children's non-adherence with HAART was significantly associated with high caregiver stress, and poor parent–child communication, caregiver quality of life and caregiver cognitive functioning. Older people also appear less adherent to recommended treatment regimens than younger people. However, any age issues may be more apparent than real. Edelmann (1999) contended that because older people tend to have more chronic diseases than younger people, apparent differences in medication adherence may reflect the problems of taking multiple prescriptions rather than being an age-related phenomenon.

A more theoretical perspective on adherence to medication is based on a combination of the illness representations (Leventhal *et al.* 1992; see Chapter 9 ☞) and health belief (Rosenstock 1974; see Chapter 5 ☞) models. Horne (1997) suggested that adherence to medication is predicated upon a combination of patients' beliefs about the nature of their illness and the treatment they are being given to treat it. Illness beliefs include understandings of the nature of the illness, its severity, cause, time-frame, likely prognosis, and its 'treatability'. Illnesses that are seen as minor, short-term and likely to self-remit may result in less use of active treatments than conditions which are seen as long-term and likely to benefit from treatment. The second arm of this deliberation involves an evaluation of the costs and benefits of taking any medication. These include consideration of how likely the treatment is to cure the condition and how 'costly' this is likely to be. Cost here includes, but is not limited to, consideration of the likely side-effects of the medication. Applying this model to a condition such as hypertension may explain why adherence to anti-hypertensive medication is frequently so low. Many people believe hypertension to be a short-term condition. It is symptom-free, so it is not clear to the patient that it is present for much of the time. Accordingly, people prescribed such medication may not see the necessity to take any medication over a long period of time. Add in a number of side-effects associated with this type of medication, such as dizziness or light-headedness, dry mouth, constipation, drowsiness, headache and impotence, and the result is a scenario that involves patients taking medication for a condition they are not aware of having, which provides no obvious benefit, and which brings with it some unpleasant side-effects. Little wonder that adherence to such medication can be so low. Even in severe conditions such as HIV infection, these issues also hold. Siegel *et al.* (1999) found that HIV-positive men and women stopped taking their antiretroviral medication if they considered it either made them sicker than their condition itself or carried greater risks than benefits. Reassuringly, a subsequent study found that HAART medication was viewed more positively than previous antiretroviral treatments, and its benefits were usually seen as outweighing any problems it caused (Schrimshaw *et al.* 2005).

Interestingly, the Horne model may not hold in all circumstances. When a medical condition is severe, some patients may actually welcome a treatment that brings high levels of side-effects. Leventhal *et al.* (1986) found that some women who received chemotherapy for the treatment of breast cancer found the *absence* of side-effects distressing: their expectation was that treatment of serious illnesses involved serious side-effects, and the lack of them implied that the drug used was not sufficiently potent to cure their condition. Other factors may be quite idiosyncratic to the individual. Gamble *et al.* (2007), for example, found that adherence to asthma medication was largely influenced by the fear of side-effects such as weight gain, anxiety, irritability and depression. However, participants also described feelings of 'not being themselves' and personality changes, resulting in a loss of their role within relationships when taking the medication.

Maximising the appropriate use of medication

Maximising the likelihood of an individual taking medication can be increased by a few simple strategies within the consultation.

Achieving concordance

One key factor that may increase adherence to a recommended regimen is that both patient and prescriber have discussed the various treatment options and agreed to follow a treatment regimen. The discussion of shared decision making earlier in this chapter provided an outline of the steps within the consultation that will lead to shared decisions/concordance between doctor and patient. A number of factors that enhance this process can also be identified from the previous discussion, including the doctor providing relevant information in a language understandable to the patient, and the doctor listening and responding to the patient in ways that encourage engagement in the decision-making process. Concordance is unlikely to be achieved by health professionals who adopt a strong biomedical stance within the consultation and who pay little regard for the social and emotional concerns that patients may bring to the consultation.

Maximising understanding

A further key aspect of both achieving concordance and, more generally, ensuring patients fully understand the nature and implications of any medication they are being prescribed involves the health professional using language appropriate to the particular patient. However, patients can also improve their understanding of an issue by preparing questions to ask in the consultation. Many patients leave a consultation without the information they want – for a variety of reasons discussed earlier in the chapter. To avoid this occurring, a number of studies have examined whether preparing patients before a consultation can help them ask relevant questions within it. In one study, Clayton *et al.* (2007) randomly allocated patients with advanced cancer to either a standard consultation or a consultation augmented by a prompt sheet. This comprised a list of questions prepared by the patient before the consultation that they wanted to ask within it. Patients took the prompt sheet into the consultation to remind them which questions to ask as it progressed. Clayton and colleagues evaluated the programme by examining audiotapes of the consultation as well as by patient-completed questionnaires. Their results were impressive. Patients given the prompt sheet asked more than twice as many questions than patients in the control group. In addition, they discussed 23 per cent more issues, asked more prognostic questions and discussed more end-of-life issues. Their consultations

with the doctors were longer, and they left the consultation with fewer unmet-information needs. These and other data suggest that encouraging patients to be actively involved in the consultation by prompting them to voice opinions or to ask clarifying questions will result in them achieving a greater understanding of their health problems and how these may best be treated. Advice given to people by the University of Michigan (www.mcare.org/healthathome/doctorpa.cfm) summarised how patients can actively involve themselves in the consultation, and gain maximum understanding of issues relevant to them:

- Plan what you will say about your problem ahead of time.
- Repeat in your own words what the health professional has told you. Use simple phrases like, 'Do I hear you say that . . . ?' or 'My understanding of the problem is . . .'.
- Take notes on what is wrong and what you need to do.
- If you are confused by medical terms, ask for simple definitions. There is no need to be embarrassed by this. When a medication is prescribed, ask about its possible side-effects, its effectiveness, and how long it must be taken. If your health professional discusses surgery, ask about alternatives, risks and a second opinion.
- Don't be afraid to voice your fears about what you've heard. The health professional may be able to clarify any misconceptions.

Maximising memory

Memory for information given in consultations is often surprisingly poor. Summing up the relevant evidence, Ley (1997) suggested that 75 per cent of information given in four statements is likely to be retained – only 50 per cent of information given in ten statements will be. In time, patients may even forget even their own actions. Montgomery *et al.* (1999), for example, reported that nearly a quarter of patients undergoing radiotherapy for the treatment of cancer could not recall having signed a consent form to permit the treatment – despite there being clear evidence that they had. Of those who did remember providing consent, a quarter could not remember being told about the side-effects of the treatment, while half could not remember its most frequent side-effect of feelings of exhaustion. Such poor outcomes are not always found, though. In a study of this phenomenon in the African country of Benin, Kelly *et al.* (2007) reported very high retention of information given during consultations, even when the amount of information given was high and the majority of the recipients were illiterate. People in the study were given an average of 39 points of information designed to improve their management of their child's illness. Immediately following the consultation, they were able to accurately recall an average of 90 per cent of the information points given. One day later, this had fallen to 82 per cent of the information points.

Despite this optimistic finding, there is a need for health professionals to help maximise patients' memories of information they are given during the consultation. One simple strategy involves giving information in a structured manner. According to Ley (1998), the most important information should be given early or late in the flow of information to maximise primacy and recency effects and its importance should be emphasised. Further strategies include repetition and the use of specific rather than general statements. This may be augmented by asking patients to repeat key messages during the consultation to ensure understanding and increase memory consolidation.

A second strategy involves providing some form of permanent record of key information. This may involve pre-prepared information or a record of the information given during a consultation. In one examination of the latter approach, Stephens *et al.* (2008) provided patients with oesophageal cancer a tape recording of the consultation in which they were given their diagnosis. Patients in this group were more likely to retain information given in the consultation, but were no more likely to be depressed or anxious than those in a comparison group who did not receive the tape.

When information is given in written form, many people read it: Nathan *et al.* (2007), for example, found that 70 per cent of patients read patient-information leaflets when given new medication. Of course, written information should take into account the same issues as those that relate to spoken information – it needs to be clear, jargon-free, and not so complex that readers will be unable to understand it. Unfortunately, this requirement is not always met. Less than 30 per cent of the population would understand the leaflets given to patients with head injuries in Scotland (Macdonald *et al.* 2010). Similarly, Freda (2005) found that 41 of 74 patient-education brochures produced by the American Academy of Pediatrics had readability levels beyond the majority of their readers. At the other end of the scale, some innovative methods have been used to increase the readability of leaflets. One approach has involved the use of pictograms in addition to text to help people with limited literacy skills. This has proven surprisingly difficult to do. Knapp *et al.* (2005), for example, found that only 30 per cent of pictograms used in medication leaflets were understood by 85 per cent of the population.

THE INTERVIEW

Here PB interviews Joanna Harris, a health psychologist working with doctors to improve their communication skills. She works in the academic department of General Practice within a UK medical school

PB: Thanks for talking with me. Can you tell us about your work here in the department?

JH: Yes, of course. I have a couple of roles within the department. Part of my time is spent working as a member of the team teaching communication skills to medical students and qualified doctors. The rest is spent as a researcher supporting a large randomised controlled trial looking at the effectiveness of patient-focused intervention in patients with type 1 diabetes.

PB: Could you tell us a bit about the communication skills training you are involved in.

JH: Of course. The communication training is actually quite good fun. I didn't start working on this, but it has developed while I have been working in the department. When I came to the Unit, I was no expert on communication myself, so I have had to read quite a lot and spend some time in role-play and watching the clinical psychologists give feed-back before I was able to do so myself. At the beginning I was more involved in organising and helping out with the sessions. But now I am fully involved, and it is really good fun.

We work as a team, with myself, a couple of General Practitioners, and a group of other people such as GPs or local clinical psychologists working in the medical school who we rope in to help us. There is also a group of actors whose role it is to play the patients in the interviews. There are about a dozen of them. They are mostly all retired people, although there are some younger people among them. The medics teach them the basic medical information associated with a number of diagnoses – mostly those you would come across in General Practice, not people that are acutely and desperately ill. We also teach them to be easy patients or less helpful patients using role-play and videoed practice. The medical students come into the Unit as part of a course on obtaining patient histories and medical symptoms. We see them for a week or so in their third year of training (before they actually encounter real patients), and then occasionally in the following years. For each student, we run a teaching pro-gramme in lectures about how to talk to patients, the doctors teach them about how to conduct a basic initial assessment and to gain a history of the medical programme. Then we unleash them on the pseudo-patients. The communication practice involves working in small groups with the students. One person plays the role of doctor and interviews the 'patient' while being observed by their fellow students and videoed. The interview usually involves the doctor introducing themselves to the patient and then using questions to gain an understanding of the patient's symptoms. Although the actors play the role of a patient with a particular diagnosis, the goal of the exercise is to be patient-centred and appropriate in

their questioning style rather than to necessarily identify what the condition is – although they always like to work it out! Following the interview, one of the doctors or clinical psychologists, and now me, go through the video discussing good and less good interactions, how things could be improved, and so on. The medical students really enjoy the sessions and want to be good communicators, so they are motivated to work hard but have fun doing so.

PB: How did you come to work in the department of General Practice in the first place?

JH: I finished my degree some years ago, and tried to get work as a clinical psychology assistant. But I couldn't get any of the jobs, and ended up working as a nursing assistant at a large psychiatric hospital. I then had to rethink my career. I thought about becoming a psychiatric nurse, but wanted to use my psychology more, so applied and was then accepted on a master's course in health psychology. And it was such a good decision, because I really like the opportunities it has given me. I came to the department originally as a research assistant and found that, while the department was happy to use my research skills, they also allowed me to experiment and work in a couple of other places in the depart-ment – not very much time, and I had to do all my work as a researcher. But this allowed me to look at other parts of the role of health psychogists I could get involved with. I drifted into the communication skills workshops as the doctors were looking – as usual – for a pair of hands to help run all the various small groups they were running. I really enjoyed it, and although I could not work there all the time, began to help out when necessary. When my research contract ran out, I applied for a part-time research post and the department agreed to part fund me working in the CSU. So, it pays to be a bit enterprising and get yourself known . . . because I now really love this part of my job.

Keep taking the tablets

Whatever transpires within the consultation, patients have to be motivated and remember to take their medi-cation or follow other advice in the hurly-burly of their

everyday life. Any intervention designed to maximise adherence has also to take these contextual issues into account. McDonald *et al.* (2002) examined the effective-ness of 39 interventions which did so and were designed to enhance adherence to medication in a variety of chronic health problems including CHD, hypertension, asthma, COPD, HIV infection, rheumatoid arthritis and epilepsy. They concluded that the most effective interventions were generally complex and involved combinations of:

● convenient timing of drug taking;

● providing relevant information;

● reminders to take medications;

● self-monitoring (i.e. noting down when and where medication is taken);

● reinforcement of appropriate use of medication;

● family therapy.

They also noted that even the most effective interventions had 'modest' effects.

The simplest methods involve ensuring that the prescribed medical regimen places as little demand on memory as possible. Nachega *et al.* (2010), for example, noted significant increases in adherence and measures of viral load in people with HIV whose HAART regimen was simplified to one tablet a day. Other approaches involve helping patients to select contextual cues to help them remember to take medication (take with food or other daily routines) or placing medicine in plastic medication boxes with compartments that are filled with the tablets to be taken at each time during the week. These are often used by older people, and can be filled by health-care professionals or family members.

More complex procedures involve the use of reminders sent via the post, text, or telephone. In one study of the effectiveness of this approach, Chatkin *et al.* (2006) found that 74 per cent of people with asthma followed the recommended treatment regimen while receiving bi-weekly reminders; 52 per cent of those in a standard treatment (no reminders) group achieved the same level of adherence. Puccio *et al.* (2006) contacted young people newly diagnosed with HIV by telephone when their medication was required. While the calls continued, adherence remained high. However, as the calls were tapered and then stopped over a period of several weeks, so did levels of adherence, and levels of viral suppression decreased. It seems that once initiated, prompting may need to continue in the long term. This may be because a dependency on prompts has been established; it may reflect a lack of carry-over effect following cessation. One even more hi-tech approach has involved the use of microelectronic devices in tablet containers that meas-

ure whether the container is moved or opened (e.g. Wu *et al.* 2006). Failure to do so within certain time limits can result in electronic notification of health-care providers who then contact the patient to remind to take their medication.

A second group of interventions involves self-management programmes based around the self-regulation model (Chapter 9 ☛) and similar to those discussed in Chapter 17 ☛. Here we consider self-management programmes specifically developed to increase adherence to one of the more complex regimens – HAART medication. Safren *et al.* (2001) compared two different interventions in this context. The first intervention involved self-monitoring and use of a pill diary to record when each tablet was taken, combined with visits to the clinic to provide feedback on medication usage. A more active intervention, known as Life-Steps, involved a single-session intervention involving an educational video, motivational interview (see Chapter 6 ☛), training in planning medication schedules, cues to pill taking, and the use of imagery involving successful adherence in response to daily cues. This may seem an overly complex process. However, it should be remembered that taking HAART medication can involve planning different types of meals and being in particular places at set times. Patients may even be taught skills to take pills surreptitiously so that no one knows they are taking them. With this in mind, this sort of training programme may not seem so excessive. Adherence was measured at 2 and 12 weeks following the intervention. The researchers also examined a number of personal and social predictors of adherence. Both interventions led to improvements in adherence. However, among people with low levels of adherence, the Life-Steps programme achieved these more quickly than the self-monitoring condition. It also appeared to improve adherence more than the self-monitoring programme in those people who were depressed – a particularly important finding, as depression was the one person-factor they found to be independently associated with non-adherence.

In contrast to these positive results, a warning that some people can be particularly difficult to influence was provided by Martin *et al.* (2001). They compared the effect of an educational plus counselling intervention with counselling alone to enhance adherence to HAART therapy. A total of 74 per cent of those approached (many of whom were injecting drug users) refused to take part in the programme: 59 per cent of those who refused to take part did so for 'personal reasons', while 33 per cent did so because of trouble in their jobs. Those who were poor adherers to their HAART were most likely not to want to take part in the programme. Similar null effects have been reported elsewhere, including a report by Simoni *et al.* (2007) in an intervention involving peer support to a group largely comprising 'indigent' men and women from the Bronx. Despite the dire effects of non-adherence, there are many societal groups who find it difficult to follow recommended treatment programmes, and who are not helped by even quite substantial and sophisticated interventions.

Changing behaviour

Many medical interventions require more significant behavioural change than taking medication, and it is to these we turn now. Measuring adherence to behavioural change programmes can be difficult. Measurement of daily diet, smoking or exercise levels is notoriously difficult to achieve accurately. However, one measure of adherence is relatively simple to achieve – whether patients attend clinics and other appointments. In this context, non-attendance can be high – and rises as the demands on the patient increase. Kosminder *et al.* (2009) reported that 21 per cent of patients treated for colorectal cancer failed to attend one or more outpatient appointments. More complex programmes typically have lower attendance rates. Only 56 per cent of the patients taking part in Jolly *et al.*'s (2007) cardiac rehabilitation programmes attended five or more hospital sessions – in programmes lasting between 9 and 21 sessions. Similarly, Al-Moamary (2008) found that 26 per cent of those invited to the first session in a pulmonary rehabilitation programme did not attend. Among those who did attend 43 per cent did not change their behaviour as a result of attending the programme.

Smoking is one of the hardest behaviours to change, as a result of a number of factors including its addictive nature and the strong associations built up between smoking and various contexts such as feeling under stress and social occasions. Not surprisingly, therefore, adherence to medical advice to stop smoking is often low. Among patients with no evident illness, cessation rates of between 3 and 12 per cent have been found following advice to quit and provision of a leaflet (Russell *et al.* 1979; Unrod *et al.* 2007). Following more sophisticated programmes, involving drug plus counselling,

adherence rates increase to around 30–35 per cent six months following the intervention (e.g. Swan *et al.* 2010). Among people with smoking-related diseases, initial quit rates may be higher, but these fall over time and are no higher than among the healthy population. Hajek *et al.* (2002), for example, found that six weeks following a myocardial infarction (MI), 60 per cent of previous smokers reported not smoking. One year after their MI, this figure had dropped to 37 per cent.

Changes in exercise levels may also be modest and reduce over time in both patient and non-patient populations. Lear *et al.* (2003) reported that few cardiac patients had achieved any changes on measures of leisure-time exercise and treadmill performance one year after a standard cardiac rehabilitation programme (see Chapter 17 (☞) which gave recommended exercise levels. In a more extended programme, involving monthly prompts to exercise and provision of heart rate monitors and exercise diaries, Dolansky *et al.* (2010) reported that less than 37 per cent of their sample of cardiac patients adhered to a three-times-a-week exercise programme one year following attending a general cardiac rehabilitation programme. Planned exercise programmes in sedentary individuals are also likely to have low attendance rates. In a review of the outcomes of exercise prescription programmes in which family doctors prescribed attendance at group exercise programmes to sedentary but otherwise healthy individuals, Williams *et al.* (2007) reported that only between 12 and 42 per cent of those starting completed their 10–12 week programmes. These data are not unusual. Overall non-adherence rates of physiotherapist-led exercise programmes are as high as 70 per cent (Sluijs *et al.* 1993).

Maintaining dietary change is also not easy, both in patient populations and those people without evident disease who would benefit from losing weight. In cardiac patients, Leslie *et al.* (2004) found that 65 per cent of their dietary counselling programme achieved the target of five portions of fruit and vegetables per day. Only 31 per cent of their control group achieved this goal. The percentage of those eating healthily in the intervention group fell over a one-year follow-up period and did not differ from the control group by this time. Luszczynska and Cieslak (2009) found even lower levels of adherence in their group of cardiac patients: following rehabilitation, only 20 per cent were following recommended guidelines for fruit and vegetable intake, and this figure fell to 12 per cent at one-year follow-up. Long-term intervention programmes also show significant declines in adherence over time. An example of this can be found in a detailed study of a one-year behavioural weight-loss programme in healthy but overweight individuals. Acharya *et al.* (2009) made weekly records of the percentage of overweight patients who attended their group sessions, monitored their food intake, followed an exercise plan, and limited fat and calorie intake. In the first session after goals had been set, 90 per cent of the people attended the session, 82 per cent had adhered to the self-monitoring element, 72 per cent had exercised, while only 28 per cent had kept to the calorie and fat requirements. At the six-month mark, the respective percentages were 50 per cent (attendance), 45 per cent (self-monitor), 30 per cent (exercise and calorie target), and 20 per cent (fat intake). By one year, these figures had fallen to 50 per cent attendance, 25 per cent self-monitoring, 20 per cent calorie target and exercise, and 5 per cent fat intake. Overall, just as in adherence to medication, adherence to behavioural programmes is far below optimal, and may benefit from programmes designed to enhance them.

Reasons for non-adherence

Reasons for poor or non-adherence vary considerably across behaviour and contexts. A number of studies have assessed non-adherence from an a theoretical perspective. Low adherence with the leg exercises and elevation required in the treatment of leg ulcer, for example, was found to be associated with pain, discomfort and lack of clarity concerning what exercises and other precautionary behaviours patients could engage in to improve their ulcers (Van Hecke *et al.* 2009). A study of Kuwaiti patients (Serour *et al.* 2007) at high risk of cardiac disease revealed some interesting and culturally idiosyncratic reasons for non-adherence to a number of lifestyle changes. The main predictors of non-adherence to a low fat diet were lack of motivation, difficulties in adhering to a diet different to that of the rest of the family, and social gatherings. The main barriers to adherence to exercise were lack of time, coexisting diseases, and adverse weather conditions (presumably heat, not rain!). Factors influencing adherence to lifestyle measures in general were the high fat and calorie content of traditional Kuwaiti food, stress, a high consumption of fast food, high frequency of social gatherings, an 'abundance of maids', and excessive use of cars.

One key issue of relevance is that of motivation, or lack of motivation, and competing demands on time. In the context of exercise, for example, both Jones *et al.* (2007) in cardiac patients and Casey *et al.* (2010) in people with type 2 diabetes, found this to be the primary reason for non-adherence. Both found that the presence of other health problems also impacted on engagement with the exercise programme. Family and social support, whether from friends or professionals, are also important factors. In the context of diet, Luszczynska and Cieslak (2009) found that intake of fruit and vegetables in cardiac patients was predicted by the presence of family support, while the type 2 diabetics of Casey *et al.* (2010) appreciated the monitoring, encouragement and accountability provided by programme staff, and when this was withdrawn frequently reduced the levels of exercise they took. From a series of qualitative studies, Huberty *et al.* (2008) found that the key factors associated with continuing physical activity following completion of a structured exercise programme were participants' self-worth, motivation, activity enjoyment, priorities, body image, ability to access support, and self-regulation skills such as planning and/or coping with obstacles to exercise and so on.

From a more theoretical perspective, the cost–benefit analysis of the health belief model or Horne's extension of this model in relation to medication may also hold in the case of prescribed behavioural change. Bourbeau and Bartlett (2008), for example, found that adherence to exercises to improve lung function and stopping smoking in patients with chronic obstructive pulmonary disease (COPD: see Chapter 8 ☛) were predicted by patients' perceptions of the disease, their confidence in their ability to control their health, and anticipating serious consequences should they not adhere to the treatment programme. In the context of adhering to appropriate self-care behaviours such as taking medication, meal planning, regular exercise, and testing blood glucose by type 2 diabetics (see Chapter 8 ☛), Daly *et al.* (2009) found that key predictors of adherence to an appropriate regime were cost, the belief that type 2 diabetes is a serious problem, being married, and greater self-reported adherence-satisfaction with taking medication and testing blood glucose. Depression was independently predictive of non-adherence.

A second theoretical model that has proven highly predictive of adherence is the self-regulation model (Leventhal *et al.* 1980). Just as in adherence to medication, so variables within this model predict behavioural adherence. In a review of the psychological factors that contributed to adherence to exercise programmes by cardiac patients, Petter *et al.* (2009) found the most consistent predictors were: confidence in the ability to exercise (including dealing with obstacles to exercise and other indirect issues), intentions to exercise, perceived control over exercise, belief in the benefits of previous physical activity, perceived barriers to exercise, and action planning – all of which fall within the self-regulation or Health Action Process models discussed in Chapters 5 and 9 ☞.

Improving adherence

The work of Petter *et al.* suggests that programmes to enhance adherence to behavioural programmes may advantageously be based on self-regulation theory. In a test of whether such an approach could be more effective than a standard educational approach in the context of exercise, Sniehotta *et al.* (2006) allocated patients who had already completed a cardiac rehabilitation programme into one of three conditions:

1. standard care involving check-ups with physicians but with no therapeutic input;

2. developing action plans on when, where, and how to exercise; or

3. action planning plus developing coping plans on how to deal with anticipated barriers to exercise.

Participants in the combined planning group did significantly more physical exercise two months post-discharge than those in the other groups. An alternative, and perhaps simpler, intervention reported by Arrigo *et al.* (2008) involved patients writing a diary of physical activities complemented by quarterly group meetings. In comparison to a standard care group, significantly more patients adhered to regular physical activity (73 vs. 40 per cent) at one-year follow-up.

A differing approach, based on social cognitive theory (Bandura 1986), involves a structured and gradual increase in the degree of behavioural change achieved. Steps in behaviour change should be sufficient to leave the participant feeling they are making acceptable progress, but small enough to ensure that they are achievable. This approach should result in increases in change self-efficacy and be sufficiently rewarding to maintain or enhance

motivation. An example of this approach was reported by Pisters *et al.* (2010), who compared the effectiveness of graded increases in activity against usual care involving less structured advice to exercise in patients with osteoarthritis of the hip or knee. The active intervention group received 18 sessions of behavioural graded activity over 12 weeks and up to 7 booster sessions over the next year. The control group received 18 sessions of usual care over 12 weeks. So, there was some inequality of input between the two groups. However, 13 weeks after the start of the programme, when both groups had received a similar level of professional input, those in the active intervention were more likely to adhere to the recommended exercise regimen. Based on evidence such as this, the ERIC database (www.ericdigests.org/pre-9219/exercise.htm) suggested a number of components that should be central to any programme of behavioural change. These can be divided into self-regulation and motivational strategies (although there are fuzzy edges to these categories, and some strategies may achieve both goals).

● *Self-control strategies*: participants are more likely to adhere to a programme if they attribute any successful behavioural change to their own efforts rather than those of health professionals. This can be enhanced by teaching self-management skill such as self-monitoring, goal setting, planning, and so on. Early goals should be relatively easy to achieve so that there is immediate success and the rewards and confidence that come from success. Goals should be both behaviourally ('I will run for 20 minutes after work on Monday, Wednesday and on Saturday morning') and outcome (' I will lose 2lbs a week') defined. Participants should write plans down where they will act as regular reminders, and make visible measures of progress.

● *Relapse prevention:* this involves identifying high-risk situations that may result in 'relapse' back to previous behaviours, and planning how to avoid or cope with them. It may also involve planning how to re-engage with any behavioural change following a 'relapse'.

● *Motivational strategies:* these may include a stepwise progression in the degree of behaviour change made, using social support where available, using a structured but flexible approach, setting achievable personal goals and measuring successes in reaching them, rewarding oneself for success – with concrete rewards, not simply the satisfaction of having achieved change.

● *Make change habitual:* change should be continuous and sustained, not intermittent. Rewarding appropriate dietary choice with, for example, an occasional high-

calorie 'take way' meal prevents the establishment of long-term habits, which are the key to long-term change.

We consider more of the evidence related to these and similar interventions designed to maximise adherence to behavioural change programmes in Chapter 17 ☛.

SUMMARY

The chapter has reviewed a number of issues related to how health professionals interact with patients, and how this can influence the outcome of any treatment they may recommend.

In the first section we considered the shift from the paternal 'doctor knows best' type of consultation to more patient-centred approaches, and the ultimate outcome of this shift – shared decision making. It was noted that while this has many benefits, many patients are cautious in adopting it, as it raises concerns over the apparent expertise of health professionals and may place a responsibility on patients for their treatment that they are unwilling to carry.

We went on to consider some other elements of the consultation that may influence its outcome, including:

● the gender of the health professional – women appear more empathic and caring, factors usually associated with greater satisfaction with the interview;
● the 'spin' given to information;
● the input of the patient: people who ask more questions tend to gain more information from the consultation.

Breaking bad news involves telling patients that they have a serious illness, and that they may die from it. It is a stressful process for both patient and health professional. Key factors in optimising this process include:

● Give the news in person, in private, with enough time and without interruptions.
● Find out what the patient knows about their diagnosis.
● Find out what the patient wants to know.

● Share the information, starting with a 'warning shot'.
● Respond to the patient's feelings.
● Plan and follow through.

Medical decision making can be influenced by a number of factors. Doctors often employ heuristics to help them arrive at a diagnosis. This can speed the process up, but increases the risk of diagnostic errors. Typical errors are those of:

● availability;
● representativeness;
● differing pay-offs of differing diagnoses.

Adherence to recommended medical treatments is influenced by a number of factors, including:

● social factors;
● psychological factors;
● treatment factors;
● family dynamics;
● beliefs about the nature of the illness and its treatment regimen.

Adherence may be enhanced by:

● the use of patient-centred approaches and shared decision making;
● maximising satisfaction with the process of treatment;
● maximising understanding of the condition and its treatment;
● maximising memory for information given.

Beyond the consultation, these factors may be added to be a number of strategies, including:

- convenient timing of drug taking;
- relevant information;
- reminders to take medications;
- self-monitoring (i.e. noting down when and where medication is taken);
- reinforcement of appropriate use of medication.

Adherence to behavioural programmes is also far from maximal. This may result from a variety of factors, including cost–benefit analysis of change, low motivation, and difficulties in planning or executing consistent change. Key theoretical variables associated with adherence to behavioural programmes are:

- confidence in the ability to exercise;
- intentions to exercise;
- perceived control over exercise;
- belief in the benefits of previous physical activity;
- perceived barriers to exercise;
- action planning.

Self-regulation-based interventions that take these factors into account appear to be the most effective means of achieving sustained behavioural change.

Further reading

Here are a number of reviews of issues dealt with in the chapter. Most of them are 'as it says on the tin', in that the title shows the content of the paper.

Brédart, A., Bouleuc, C. and Dolbeault, S. (2005). Doctor–patient communication and satisfaction with care in oncology. *Current Opinions in Oncology*, 17: 351–4.

Coderre, S., Mandin, H., Harasym, P.H. *et al.* (2003). Diagnostic reasoning strategies and diagnostic success. *Medical Education*, 37: 695–703.

Elstein, A.S. and Schwarz, A. (2002). Clinical problem solving and diagnostic decision making: selective review of the cognitive literature. *British Medical Journal*, 324: 729–32.

A useful insight into medical decision making.

Elwyn, G., Edwards, A., Kinnersley, P. and Grol, R. (2000). Shared decision making and the concept of equipoise: the competences of involving patients in healthcare choices. *British Journal of General Practice*, 50: 892–9.

A paper on the process of shared decision making by the leading UK research group.

Grime, J., Blenkinsopp, A., Raynor, D.K. *et al.* (2007). The role and value of written information for patients about individual medicines: a systematic review. *Health Expectations*, 10: 286–98.

Mast, M.S. (2007). On the importance of nonverbal communication in the physician–patient interaction. *Patient Education and Counseling*, 67: 315–18.

Tackles an important issue not looked at in the chapter – the role of non-verbal behaviour during the doctor consultation.

Elmore, J.G., Ganschow, P.S. and Geller, B.M. (2010). Communication between patients and providers and informed decision making. *Journal of the National Cancer Institute Monographs*, 41: 204–9.

Considers the role of doctor–patient communication in decision making in relation to patients with cancer.

van Dulmen, S., Sluijs, E., van Dijk, L. *et al.* (2007). Patient adherence to medical treatment: a review of reviews. *BMC Health Service Research*, 7: 55.

Free on the internet, and a good review to boot.

Visit the website at **www.pearsoned.co.uk/morrison** for additional resources to help you with your study, including multiple choice questions, weblinks and flashcards.

Chapter 11
Stress, health and illness: theory

Learning outcomes

By the end of this chapter, you should have an understanding of:

- stress as a stimulus (stressors)
- stress as a result of an interaction between an event and an individual
- the critical role of cognitive appraisal
- the nature of acute and chronic stress
- physiological processes invoked by the stress experience
- how stress manifests itself in various diseases

Here comes another bride

Will the dress fit? Will Auntie Janet and Uncle Alan do the conga? Will her big day be overshadowed by that other lot up the road? A royal wedding day bride charts the agonising run-up to her marriage (Friday, 29 April 2011, *The Guardian*, guardian.co.uk © Guardian News and Media Limited 2011)

This article provides a highly entertaining account of the 'not so' royal wedding of Jude Rogers and her fiancé Dan. You may recall when reading this that the date above was when HRH Prince William and Kate Middleton got married with an audience of many millions across the world. Whether a royalist or a republican, I hope you will see the relevance of this selection to the topic of this chapter – stress. I select part of the article below where Jude illustrates a typical conversation she has with her partner:

'We are in the midst of Invitegate.'

'We seem to have 347 guests.'

'Well, we can't have all of those.'

'We need matt finish for the invites.'

'Well, I can't find any online for less than £4,392.'

'You've spelt the name of the pub wrong – or should I say, "pbub".'

'Do you mind if I paper-cut myself to death, dear? You go first.'

'A company promising stress-free invitations delivers bent cards, bleeding edges and a finish so glossy that the reflection of my gritted teeth nearly blinds my fiancé. We finally get it sorted, amazingly without cancelling the wedding.'

The above reflects the simple fact that even a positive event such as marrying someone you love (a usual prerequisite!) can present challenges. We see in the text selected above, challenges of capacity (number of guests), quality and

▶

▶ cost (of invites), literacy (in getting spelling correct), handling (of paper edges), and of keeping calm and communicating clearly one's needs and wishes (even if through gritted teeth!). We see in the conversation the need to communicate, use technology, spend money, all of which need certain skills or resources. Although the ultimate goal, the marriage, is a positive one, the build-up to the wedding day presents an array of demands and stimulates an array of responses – cognitive, emotional, behavioural and physiological. This chapter and Chapter 12 ☞ considers both the stimuli and the responses and what factors contribute to either being described as 'stressful'.

Source: from 'Here comes another bride', *The Guardian*, 29/04/2011 (guardian.co.uk), © Guardian News and Media Limited 2011, Jude Rogers.

Chapter outline

The beginning of this chapter outlines the main thinking about stress in terms of nature and definition and highlights three main ways in which stress is studied: as a stimulus, as a transaction between a stimulus event and an individual's appraisal of it, and as a biological and physiological response. The second of these reflects a psychological model of stress proposed by Richard Lazarus and his colleagues and is described in detail to illustrate the central role of cognitive appraisal. This is done by examining how stress impacts upon us all in our living and working lives, and by examining acute and chronic stressors. The final part of the chapter provides evidence as to the physiological processes by which stress and our responses to it exert an influence on physical health, focusing particularly, but not solely, on cancer, CHD and HIV. By the end of the chapter, the nature of stress and the processes by which it may impact on illness should be clear.

Concepts of stress

The term 'stress' is used very widely and with several meanings: everyone probably thinks they know what the term means, but few people define it in exactly the same way.

Stress has generally been examined in one of three ways: as a stimulus or event external to the individual; as a psychological transaction between the stimulus event and the cognitive and emotional characteristics of the individual; or as a physical or biological reaction. Each of

WHAT DO YOU THINK?

What does stress mean to you? What causes you to feel stressed?

Think of some recent events that you have experienced as stressful. Why was this? Reflect on your answers to these questions as the chapter progresses.

these perspectives and their accompanying methodologies have their own strengths and weaknesses, which are outlined in the forthcoming sections.

Stress as a stimulus

In thinking of stress as a stimulus, researchers focus on stressful events themselves and on the external environment; i.e. a person will attribute their tension to an event or events such as moving house or getting married. The event and its properties are considered amenable to objective definition and measurement: for example, the event can be labelled (e.g. wedding) and aspects of it such as its proximity (e.g. next week, next year) can be assessed. Researchers taking this approach have studied the impact of a wide variety of stressors on individuals or groups, including *catastrophic events* such as earthquakes, floods or plane crashes, and more commonly, *major life events* such as losing one's job or starting a new job, getting married or divorced, giving birth, being bereaved, or even going on holiday. Life events such as these are considered to require significant adjustment on the part of the person experiencing them, and can include both positive and negative events.

Life events theory

The major proponents of this approach were Holmes and Rahe, who in 1967 proposed their **life events** theory. They proposed that naturally occurring life events did not simply have unitary consequences for a person but cumulative effects; in other words, the more life events one experienced, for example within the past year, the greater the likelihood of physical health problems. Furthermore, they claimed that specific kinds of event could be weighted against each other. To make these claims, Holmes and Rahe had carried out a series of interesting studies. First, they invited over 5,000 participants to generate a list of events that they found most stressful; from this, they generated a representative list of 43 commonly mentioned events, including positive, negative, frequent and rare events. Holmes and Rahe then asked a new sample of almost 400 people to rank

the listed events in order of the degree of disruption the event, if experienced, had caused them. Furthermore, they asked participants to rate each event against marriage, which had arbitrarily been given a value of 500 by the researchers. For example, if divorce was considered by a respondent as requiring twice as much adjustment as marriage, it was given a value of 1,000. By averaging the ratings received for each event item and then ranking them, Holmes and Rahe produced a scale known as the social readjustment rating scale (SRRS; Holmes and Rahe 1967; see Table 11.1), with values ranging from 11 (minor violations of law) to 100 (this maximum value was assigned to death of a spouse, which averaged out as the event requiring greatest adjustment). The values were called life change units (LCU). Social readjustment was defined as 'the intensity and length of time necessary to accommodate to a life event, *regardless of the desirability of this event*' (Holmes and Masuda 1974: 49), highlighting the fact that both positive events (e.g. marriage) and negative events (e.g. redundancy) would require some adjustment on the part of the individual. A subsequent study of 88 physicians (Rahe 1974) found that the greater the LCU score the higher the risk of ill health. Of the 96 major health changes reported by the participants,

Table 11.1 Representative life event items from the social readjustment rating scale and their LCUs

Event	LCU rating (1–100)
Death of a spouse	100
Divorce	75
Death of a close family member	63
Personal injury or illness	53
Marriage	50
Being fired from work	47
Retirement	45
Sex difficulties	39
Death of a close friend	37
Change to a different job	36
Foreclosure of mortgage or loan	30
Son or daughter leaving home	29
Outstanding personal achievement	28
Begin or end school	26
Trouble with boss	23
Change in residence	20
Change in social activities	18
Vacation	13
Christmas	12

Source: Holmes and Rahe (1967).

life events

a term used to describe occurrences in a person's life which may be viewed positively or negatively but which inherently require some adjustment on the part of the person (e.g. marriage, loss of job). Such events are implicated in the experience of stress.

89 took place in individuals scoring over 150 LCUs; and when LCU scores exceeded 300, over 70 per cent of the physicians reported subsequent ill-health. Those individuals scoring less than 150 LCUs tended to report good health. Holmes and Masuda (1974) defined a *mild life crisis* as scoring between 150 and 199 LCUs, a *moderate life crisis* as scoring between 200 and 299 and a *major life crisis* as scoring over 300. They drew not only on their own work but also on that of other researchers of the time to support their hypothesis that life change could cause ill health (see review by Tennant 2002). For example, more recently, Lorenz *et al.* (2006) found negative health impacts of divorce upon women divorcees both in the short term but also in the decade following, and in the Netherlands, Feldman *et al.* (2007) report health consequences of stress, prejudice and change experienced by refugees.

Limitations of life events measurement

The evidence of the associations between LCUs and ill health (physical and/or mental) has been questioned (e.g. Dohrenwend and Dohrenwend 1982), as a result of various methodological or sampling limitations. For example, many studies reporting moderate to strong associations between LCU's, health and illness (including many of Holmes and colleagues'), relied on retrospective assessment: i.e. participants who were already ill were asked to report whether or not they had experienced any life events prior to the onset of illness. In contrast, studies employing prospective designs found much weaker or non-existent relationships. Other weaknesses exist in terms of the items included in the scale. For example, depending on your age, many of the listed events may not be applicable (divorce, childbirth, etc.). Some of the listed events may simply not occur with sufficient frequency to enable many individuals to report them or for their effects on health to be experienced (e.g. moving house), and others may be intertwined and may cancel out or enhance the effects of one another (for example, marriage requiring positive adjustments but coinciding with a negatively perceived house move). Other events listed are vague and ambiguous: for example, reporting a 'change in social activities' could mean many things brought about for many different reasons. Finally, and perhaps most importantly for psychologists, allocating LCUs to events assumes that all people rank events in a similar way. However, think of moving house. For some people this will be a positive outcome of increased financial resources, while for others it will be a devastating consequence of repossession by a bank following prolonged failure to pay a mortgage or rent. The life events approach to stress therefore fails to systematically address the many internal and external factors that may moderate the relationship between events and stress or illness outcomes. Psychological theories of stress illustrated in this chapter highlight the importance of such factors (which are then described in Chapter 12 (☛)).

In spite of many limitations, this body of work shows that major life events can and do impact on people's lives in a variety of ways. For example, prospective longitudinal studies often assess the life event experience of those studied on the basis that it may influence other variables of interest: for example, adjustment to an illness may be undermined by the occurrence of other major life changes.

Life hassles

In addition to major and often rare life events, research has highlighted the stressful nature of daily *hassles*. Kanner *et al.* (1981: 3) defined hassles as 'irritating, frustrating, distressing demands that to some degree characterize everyday transactions with the environment' and measured such things as not having enough money for food or clothing, losing things, being overloaded with responsibilities, making silly practical mistakes, or having a row with a partner. Unlike major life events, hassles do not generally require major adjustment on the part of the person experiencing them but their impact was thought to be particularly evident if they were frequent, chronic or repeated over a particular period of time. To test this proposal, Kanner and colleagues developed a tool to assess daily hassles and found that they strongly associated with negative mental and physical outcomes even when controlling for major life events. This association has been confirmed in many studies using either Kanner's original scale or a shorter version developed by De Longis *et al.* (1988) (e.g. Bouteyre *et al.* 2007 – a study of first-year psychology students!). It is worth noting that stronger associations have in fact been found between hassles and health outcomes (including psychological health) than between life events and health outcomes (e.g. Kanner *et al.* 1981; Lazarus 1984; Searle and Bennett 2001).

In these measures, positively rated events, described as 'uplifts' (e.g. getting away with something, completing a task, getting or giving a compliment, having a laugh) were acknowledged more thoroughly than in life events theory. For both hassles and uplifts, Kanner found effects of life stage/role and gender on how events were perceived and appraised. For example, Kanner studied three groups of people – middle-aged, professionals and students – and found that these groups differed in the importance they attached to particular events, in particular the importance they attached to economic concerns, work and time pressures, and social hassles. In terms of uplifts, the groups differed in their weighting of having good health, spending time with family, and hedonistic items such as socialising and having fun. Kanner also found that women experienced psychological symptoms following uplifts as well as hassles, whereas men were unaffected by uplifts, suggesting perhaps that women are affected by 'change' in either a positive or negative direction. These findings highlight that two people could experience the same number of events and weight them equally but experience very different health outcomes. Why could this be? This question obviously moves us away from considering stress simply in terms of the stimulus. We return to this later and also in Chapter 12 ☞ where moderators of the stress experience are discussed.

It has also been suggested that only negatively rated events or hassles lead to adverse outcomes and that positive events or uplifts may 'moderate' the impact of negative events (e.g. Thoits 1995), which is consistent with both stress theory and positive psychology thinking whereby the experience of positive emotions (a likely consequence of experiencing an uplift such as receiving a compliment, getting a good grade) enhances coping appraisals (e.g. Lazarus et al. 1980; Folkman 2008; Fredrikson 1998, 2001). However, the evidence for this is inconclusive as few studies explore the prospective interactions between positive and negative events, and those that have predominantly report weak associations between hassles and uplifts, and weak or no relationship between uplifts and mental health outcomes (Barrett and Heubeck 2000).

If health outcomes are indeed affected by major events or an accumulation of minor events, what are the processes (psychophysiological or behavioural) by which this occurs? The stress-as-a-stimulus approach has proved attractive to many research scientists, who aim to identify the effects of a common stressful event among both general and specific populations on adverse health outcomes. For example, studies of the effects of unemployment have been carried out in terms of the morbidity and mortality of a general population (e.g.

House et al. 1982) as well as among refugees (e.g. Schwarzer et al. 1994). However, such studies do not tell us *how* unemployment affects illness or even death rates, or *why* it may in some people but not others (Marmot and Madge 1987). To answer the 'how' question leads us to consider physiological theories of stress (stress manifest in biological responses), whereas to answer the 'why' question requires consideration of sociological explanations (see, in part, Chapter 2's ☞ discussion of social inequalities in health) and psychological theories of stress (involving cognitive appraisal and emotion). We turn here to the psychological explanations.

Stress as a transaction

According to psychological theory, stress is a subjective experience, an internal state of being that may or may not be considered by an outside observer as being appropriate to the situation that evoked the response. As John Milton (1608–74) put it when he wrote *Paradise Lost*: 'The mind is its own place, and in itself can make a heaven of hell, a hell of heaven'. This points to what has become the central tenet of psychological theories of stress: that appraisal is central to whether or not an event is deemed to be a stressor or not. The key figure in this domain is Richard Lazarus, who with colleagues (e.g. Lazarus and Launier 1978; Lazarus and Folkman 1984) proposed what is called a cognitive transactional model of stress (Figure 11.1). Evidence of the importance of psychological processes was drawn from early experimental studies of Lazarus and colleagues (e.g. Speisman et al. 1964), which quite simply exposed student participants to stressful films while monitoring self-reported stress levels and physiological arousal (i.e. heart rate and skin conductance). One example included a gruesome video about tribal initiation rites that included genital surgery. Before the film, participants were divided into four experimental conditions, each of which received different introductions and soundtracks. One group heard an intellectual description of the rites from a cultural perspective (to mimic a **distancing response**); another heard a lecture

---

distancing response

taking a detached view, often a scientific view, of an event or stimulus in order to reduce emotional activation.

that de-emphasised the pain the 'willing' initiates were experiencing and emphasised the excitement they were feeling (to mimic a **denial response**); another heard a narrative that emphasised the pain and trauma the initiates were undergoing (to emphasise the perceived threat); and a control group received no information or soundtrack. Results showed quite clearly that the introductions influenced the way in which the film was seen, reflected in both self-reported stress and skin conductance, with the first and second groups (distancing and denial) showing significantly less stress than group 3. While these classic studies were initially intended to address the idea of 'ego defences' (i.e. what people do to protect themselves from threat), Lazarus realised that appraisal processes were mediating stress responses, and hence he subsequently developed a theory of stress that remains one of the most influential in health psychology.

According to Lazarus, stress is a result of an interaction between an individual's characteristics and appraisals, the external or internal event (stressor) environment, and the internal or external resources a person has available to them. Motivational and cognitive variables are considered central. Lazarus's initial model maintained that when individuals confront a new or changing environment they engage in a process of **appraisal**, which is of two types: primary and secondary.

Primary appraisal processes

In primary appraisal, a person considers the quality and nature of the stimulus event. Lazarus distinguished three kinds of possible stressor: those that pose harm, those

> **denial response**
> taking a view that denies any negative implications of an event or stimulus. If subconscious, it is considered a defence mechanism.
>
> **appraisals**
> interpretations of situations, events or behaviour that a person makes.

that threaten and those that set a challenge. Harm is considered as damage that has already been done, i.e. a loss or failure; threat is the expectation of future harm; and challenge results from demands that are appraised as opportunities for personal growth or opportunities that a person is confident about dealing with. Events that are not appraised as either harm, threat or challenge are considered to be benign events that require no further action. The questions asked of oneself are along the lines of 'Is this event something I have to deal with?' 'Is it relevant to me?' 'If so, what is at stake?' 'Is it a positive, negative or neutral event? If potentially or actually negative, then is it posing me harm/threat or challenge?' Simultaneously to making these appraisals, emotions may arise that elicit various physiological responses, as we shall describe later.

Secondary appraisal processes

At the same time as carrying out primary appraisals, Lazarus proposed that secondary appraisals are initiated

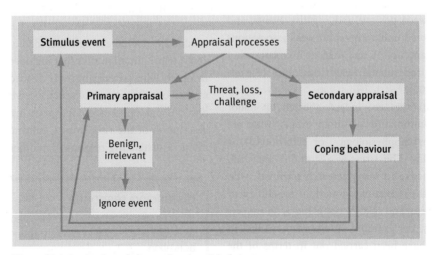

Figure 11.1 Lazarus's early transactional model of stress

Source: adapted from Lovallo (1997: 77).

whereby one assesses one's resources and abilities to cope with the stressor (coping potential). The questions asked of oneself at this stage are of the type: 'How am I going to deal with this?' 'What can I use or call upon to help me?' Resources can be either internal (e.g. strength, determination) or external (e.g. social support, money).

Using forthcoming exams as an example, various appraisal judgments may be made, for example:

- 'There is no way I can possibly deal with this. I simply know I will fail' (threat + no resources = stress).

- 'This will be really hard. I just am not as clever as the other students' (threat = limited internal resources = stress).

- 'Maybe I can manage this if I revise really hard' (challenge + possible internal resources = less stress).

- 'I could perhaps do it if I get some help from my friends' (challenge + external resources = less stress).

- 'This isn't a problem. I know the material really well' (benign).

- 'I managed to pass the last time, I'll be okay this time' (benign).

Lazarus maintained that stress would be experienced when perceived harm or threat was high but perceived coping ability was low, whereas when perceived coping ability was appraised to be high (i.e. resources were considered to be available to deal with the threat), then stress was likely to be minimal. In other words, stress arose from a mismatch between perceived demands and resources, both of which could change over time. It is important that stress is viewed as a dynamic process.

Developments in Lazarus's framework

In the 1990s, Lazarus increasingly considered the stress process as part of the wider domain of emotions and modified his cognitive appraisal theory of stress accordingly (Lazarus 1991a). He also collaborated with an eminent colleague at this time (Smith and Lazarus 1993), although the two academics differed slightly in the components of appraisal proposed. Smith proposed that primary appraisal consists of two sequential assessments: one of *motivational relevance*, i.e. the extent to which the event is considered relevant to one's current goals or commitments; the other of *motivational congruence*, i.e. the extent to which the situation is perceived to be

congruent with current goals. Stress was likely in situations where relevance was high and congruence was low. This is illustrated below:

APPRAISAL	
motivational relevance	motivational congruence
'The proposed class test is important to my studies'	*'I would prefer to party'*
high relevance	low congruence

Lazarus included in primary appraisal an appraisal of *ego involvement*, whereby appraisals of threat to one's sense of self or social esteem would elicit anger, events violating one's moral codes would result in guilt, and any existential threat would create anxiety.

Removing threat/challenge and harm/loss appraisals from the core cognitive definition of primary appraisal and instead attaching them to emotion types is important to how we think about stress. Prior to this, it had often been overlooked that appraisals associate with emotions, yet it makes intuitive sense. For example, appraising an event as a threat is likely to precede the emotion of fear, whereas a loss appraisal is likely to precede the emotion of sadness (Smith and Lazarus 1993). Less well articulated are the appraisals associated with positive emotions, but positive appraisals such as that of benefit, gain or challenge may precede emotions such as joy or hope (Snyder *et al.* 1991; Folkman 2008). An early stress researcher, Hans Selye (1974), generally known for his work on physiological responses to stressful stimuli (more later), distinguished between good and bad stress; between 'eustress', i.e. stress associated with positive feelings or healthy states (seen perhaps in sporting activities or in the performing arts, where the stress gives you focus or a competitive edge perhaps), and 'distress', i.e. the bad kind of stress associated with negative feelings and disturbed bodily states. Although he did not detail how these two types of stress differed in terms of physiological response, their distinction remains an important one, and research attempts such as those examining the emotions attached to different forms of stress appraisal (e.g. nursing students on placement described experiential learning as eustress in a recent study by Gibbons *et al.* 2008) go some way towards addressing this distinction.

Also in working with Smith, secondary appraisal became more complex, consisting of four assessments (Smith) or three (Lazarus):

Plate 11.1 This is a good example of 'eustress', something positive and controlled, but nonetheless often considered stressful

Source: Pearson Education Ltd.

Table 11.2 Appraisal-related emotions

● *Loss/harm*: sadness, depression, despair, hopelessness
● *Threat*: anxiety, fear, anger, jealousy
● *Challenge*: worry, hope, confidence

1. *Internal/external accountability ('blame/credit', Lazarus)*: concerned with attributing responsibility for the event; is seen to distinguish between emotions of anger (other-blame) and guilt (self-blame). Credit is less often studied but may associate with emotions such as pride.

2. *Problem-focused coping potential*: considers the extent to which the situation is perceived as changeable by instrumental (practical, problem-focused) coping options. If not perceived as changeable, the emotions of fear and anxiety will be elicited.

3. *Emotion-focused coping potential*: concerned with perceiving an ability to cope emotionally with the situation. Perceptions of not being able to cope are associated with fear, anxiety or sadness.

4. *Future expectancy concerning situational change*: refers to perceived possibilities of the situation being changeable. Sadness is associated with perceptions of unchangeability.

Lazarus merged the second and third assessment, referring simply to 'coping potential'.

The important factor to hold on to from these developments in Lazarus's theory is that the role of emotions is being addressed as well as the cognitions, with both aspects interlinked in an ongoing and dynamic transaction. Furthermore, this theory proposes that emotional impressions of events are stored in memory and will influence how we appraise the same event in any future encounters.

Criticism of Lazarus's framework

There appear to be many advantages of the transactional approach and its cognitive appraisal theory: it is compatible with both biological and social models, acknowledging as it does the role of the stimulus, of emotional and behavioural responses, of individual differences and of the external environment. Certainly, in the psychological literature, there is a large body of supporting empirical evidence, and few studies of coping with stress or illness are conducted without acknowledging the central role of individual difference variables and appraisals. This will become quite evident in the subsequent chapter. However, no model or theory escapes without criticism, as this is one way in which academic understanding is advanced. Some have criticised Lazarus's framework for its circularity. For example, limited research has attempted to examine the nature of interaction between primary and secondary appraisals, i.e. between perceived demands and perceived coping resources. Demand and coping capacity are not defined separately, leading to claims of the model being tautological (Hobfoll 1989) – put simply, this means that whether an event is demanding or not depends on perceived coping capacity, and whether coping capacity is perceived as adequate or not is dependent on perceived demand! Furthermore, it is unclear whether both primary and secondary appraisal are necessary; for example, Zohar and Dayan (1999) found positive mood outcomes in their sample to be affected mainly by coping potential variables and not by primary appraisal variables. Additionally, they found that stress arose and increased as the stakes or motivational relevance of an event increased, even in situations where coping potential was not restricted. They noted that any slight uncertainty about coping potential modified the effect of 'stakes' (primary appraisal) on stress. Imagine, for example, a situation where a person believes that their forthcoming mid-term examination is a 'mock' and does not count towards their final grade, but on turning up to the exam they are told that it is not a 'mock' but a 'real' exam. In spite of having revised the subject seriously and having no major concerns about their ability to answer the questions, this new situation is likely to be appraised differently because its value has changed (raised stakes), and the stress experience will therefore also change (increase), even though their resources (secondary appraisals of coping potential) have not. Further research is required to investigate the interaction between primary and secondary appraisals, and whether the assumption that demands need to outweigh resources in order for stress to be experienced can be upheld.

> ### WHAT DO YOU THINK?
>
> Which do you think comes first – the thought (appraisal) or the emotion? Is it possible to order them? Think of a recent event that you were happy about – what thoughts were 'attached' to that happiness? Did your feelings about the event change over time and, if so, did your thoughts also change? What about an event that made you unhappy – WHY did it make you unhappy? Consider the thought processes. Does Lazarus's model make sense to you?

What factors influence appraisal?

While the nature of stimulus events/potential stressors varies hugely – from, for example, receiving a final demand for an unpaid bill to being a victim of a natural disaster, from having a head cold to receiving a diagnosis of a life-threatening illness – certain features of all events have been found to increase the likelihood of their being appraised as stressful:

- events that are *imminent* (e.g. medical results due the next day; driving test that afternoon);
- events that occur at an *unexpected time* in life (e.g. being widowed in one's 40s compared with when in one's 70s; the death of a child);
- events that are *unpredictable* in nature (e.g. being made redundant; sudden bereavement);
- events that are *ambiguous* in terms of
  - ○ personal role (e.g. starting a new job);
  - ○ potential risk or harm involved (e.g. undergoing surgery, taking new medication);
- events that are *undesirable* (e.g. having to move house because of financial loss);
- events over which the individual perceives *no control* (behavioural or cognitive, e.g. noisy neighbours);
- events that elicit high amounts of *life change* (e.g. childbirth, relocation).

Further distinction has been drawn (e.g. Sapolsky 1994: 5) between acute physical stressors, which demand immediate physiological adaptation (e.g. being attacked); chronic physical stressors (e.g. being ill or surviving in a hostile environment); long-term physiological demands that we are not so good at dealing with, such as pain; and psychosocial stressors, which involve our cognitions, emotions and behavioural responses as well as the physiological arousal that will be triggered. Many psychologists would argue that all these are in fact psychosocial as they involve more than simply the event or stimulus. Chapter 12 ☞ will deal with the personal and interpersonal influences on appraisals and stress responses.

Lay theories of stress

Before moving on to describing types and potential sources of stress, it is worth stopping to reflect on what has been made clear in the above review of scientific study of stress. Stress is the subject of significant scientific enquiry, yet as a subjective construct it is hard to define. As discussed in Chapter 9 ☞, in relation to symptom perception and interpretation, lay models of illness are important to understanding what occurs between symptom perception and response. Similarly in relation to stress, we need to acknowledge the role played by what the layperson considers to be the causes and consequences of stress – stress as a concept exists not only in scientific study but also in our everyday language.

Several authors have studied these understandings in relation to work stress (e.g. Furnham 1997; Rystedt *et al.* 2004; Kinman and Jones 2005; Jones *et al.* 2006) and some have studied understanding of stress in relation to specific illnesses, such as heart attack (e.g. Clark 2003). In Clark's study of 14 Scottish heart attack survivors, while the understanding of social, personal and situational influences on what was considered to be 'stress' varied significantly between individuals, there was a common view that the stress was a more salient cause of their heart attack than even smoking or diet. This type of understanding and attribution could of course be self-serving! In relation to work stress, lay theories were similarly multifaceted and variable. Interestingly in Kinman and Jones's (2005) study, we find an example of rank or position in a company making a difference (see later discussion of police stress). In this instance it is seen in the differential understanding of the impact of stress – lower-level workers considered the impact of occupational stress to be more personal and requiring of joint efforts by themselves and the organisation if stress is to be managed, whereas managerial workers considered that the responsibility for stress management lay at the feet of the individual workers – in spite of agreeing that many causes of stress were organisational! Such lay beliefs are important, given that evidence of their longitudinal effects on worker stress, including mental strain (Rystedt *et al.* 2004) and certainly lay theorising about why stress has occurred and what its likely consequences are, holds implications for stress management interventions (Chapter 13 ☛).

Now, we turn our attention to potential sources of stress: 'potential' sources because, as described above, the role of appraisal is brought to bear on the stimulus and it is this situation – person interaction – that determines whether stress, as a response, results.

Types of stress

Stress and resource loss

Hobfoll (1989) proposed a 'conservation of resources' model of stress whereby individuals are assumed to work to conserve or protect their valued resources (e.g. objects, roles, personal characteristics such as self-esteem, energy, time, money, skills). Hobfoll suggests that stress will result when there is actual or threatened loss of resources or a lack of gain after investing resources. Resources are thought to be quantifiable and 'real' and therefore 'mean' the same to all people when they are lost. This therefore de-emphasises the role of individual appraisal, central to Lazarus's model. Hobfoll states that the more resources are lost, the more difficult it becomes to replace them, and the greater the resulting stress. This quantification of resources fits with the kind of evidence discussed in Chapter 2 ☛, i.e. that of socio-economic deprivation, unemployment and poverty, all of which are found to associate with illness, independent of the individual's appraisals. By focusing on loss of quantifiable entities rather than appraisals, this model avoids any difficulties in distinguishing appraisals from responses. However, Marks *et al.* (2000) point out that the loss and resource constructs are not particularly well defined or easy to measure, and that many questions remain unanswered by this model. For example, how permanent must loss be for a person to experience stress? Does the speed and extent of resource loss matter? Is resource gain never stressful? (Some lottery winners would perhaps challenge this.)

Hobfoll (1991) found that rapid and extensive depletion of valued resources, such as that experienced following a natural disaster, was associated with traumatic stress responses. Natural disasters are generally acute-onset stressors, but many may have long-term consequences. Examples of other acute stressors are given below.

Acute stress

Studies of acute-onset stress generally distinguish between stimulus events that are rare but cataclysmic and more common acute stressors, such as exams.

Cataclysmic events

Earthquakes, hurricanes and air disasters are rare events that allow a person little or no preparation time. Natural catastrophes, such as the Asian tsunami in 2004, Hurricane Katrina in 2005, and technological disasters such as the nuclear meltdown at Chernobyl in 1986 and Japan, 2011, produce intense physical and psychosocial suffering for victims and for the 'worried well', i.e. those not actually in the disaster but affected by it in that it raises issues for them about their own personal safety and future. Environmental stress theory (Fisher *et al.* 1984; Baum 1990) considers stress to be a combined psychological and physiological response to demands, and support for this can be found in the many psychological and physical symptoms reported in survivors of a natural calamity. These include:

- initial panic
- anxiety
- phobic fear
- vulnerability
- guilt (survivor guilt)
- isolation
- withdrawal (including some suicide attempts)
- anger and frustration
- interpersonal and marital problems
- disorientation
- lack of attachment
- loss of sense of security
- sleep disturbances
- eating disturbances.

The severity and duration of these effects seem to depend on the magnitude of the loss. In addition to this long list of possible outcomes, some people continuously relive

> ### post-traumatic stress disorder
> a disorder that forms a response to experiencing a traumatic event. The key elements are unwanted repetitive memories of the event, often in the form of flashbacks, attempts at avoidance of such memories, and a generally raised level of arousal.
>
> ### coping self-efficacy
> the belief that one can carry out a particular coping response in a given set of circumstances.

the event in distressing dreams and/or suffer from 'flashbacks'. Such symptoms may lead to the individual being diagnosed as suffering from **post-traumatic stress disorder** (PTSD; see Chapter 13 ☞).

Hobfoll's 'conservation of resources' model of stress was applied in a study of lost resources or 'losses' among 135 individuals assessed following Hurricane Andrew in the United States (Benight *et al.* 1999). This study also investigated the extent to which **coping self-efficacy** (cf. Bandura 1986) determined stress responses and the ability of individuals to recover from their losses by employing their remaining coping resources. Coping self-efficacy was specific to the ability to meet needs

Plate 11.2 Environmental events, such as the Asian tsunami, have devastating short-term effects, but also have serious long-term effects on survivors, some of whom will experience post-traumatic stress disorder (PTSD)

Source: Getty Images: Athit Perawongmetha.

following the hurricane, and losses were focused on loss of material resources rather than psychological resources, although both were assessed. Overall, the results confirmed a positive association between loss of resource, coping self-efficacy and subsequent distress. Resource loss was positively associated with long-term distress, with active coping efforts mediating this relationship and reducing the distress experienced (see Chapter 12 ☞).

This study highlights that quantifiable resource loss is in itself distressing, but that appraisals related to coping ability also play a significant role: thus the conservation of resources model has to extend to consider such factors. It is clear that acute-onset stressors can have chronic effects on a person's psychological well-being and interventions to minimise distress therefore need to be targeted appropriately. For example, in the case of hurricane survivors, interventions may maximise their effectiveness if they target both the lost resources (e.g. restoration of housing, water, clothing) and the emotions and cognitions (e.g. self-efficacy) of the victims. Stress management and coping-based interventions are discussed fully in Chapter 13 ☞.

Exam stress

Cohen *et al.* (1986) found that high levels of perceived stress can impair people's memory and attention during cognitive activities. For example, many students report the experience of having the answer to questions on the tip of their tongue, and even memories of revising it the night before, but being unable to remember it once in the exam setting. Others will misread and misinterpret clearly written questions. It has been found that there is an optimum level of arousal necessary to maintain attention and memory, but that too little arousal, or too much, can be detrimental to one's performance. This is known as the Yerkes–Dodson law, first described in 1908 (see Figure 11.2). An exam in a subject where the result is desired and valued will generally elicit more arousal than an exam that is not valued, and the key to good performance lies in not becoming over-aroused so that all the learning goes to waste and the mind empties in the exam room!

Exam stress has been associated with increased smoking, increased alcohol consumption, poor eating, increased caffeine intake, and less physical activity, and was attributed to a breakdown in self-control, particularly among

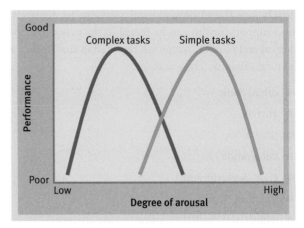

Figure 11.2 The Yerkes–Dodson law
Source: Rice (1992: 5).

those with poor study skills, as evidenced in a study of Australian students (Oaten and Cheng 2006). This association between stress and behaviour is an indirect route by which stress can be considered to influence illness status. Exam stress has also been found to affect bodily responses, such as blood pressure, which was found to increase among medical students on the day of their exams (Sausen *et al.* 1992). This kind of study is required to continuously assess physical indices of **stress reactivity** (such as blood pressure, see later section on physiological responses) in order to achieve multiple baselines against which to assess increases and decreases in blood pressure over time and during different activities. To obtain such data, Sausen and colleagues employed ambulatory monitoring techniques whereby devices attached to individual participants activated at set and regular intervals to read blood pressure.

A link between acute stressors such as exams and actual illness (rather than focusing on physiological reactivity, which is generally short-lived and poses no danger to the individual unless it is maintained; Brosschot *et al.* 2005) has been proposed following findings that students exhibit increased prevalence of infections at exam periods compared with during non-assessment periods. These studies often include blood sampling and have examined immunological markers that have led to the conclusion

> **stress reactivity**
> the physiological arousal, such as increased heart rate or blood pressure, experienced during a potentially stressful encounter.

that for many individuals, exams, and the build-up to them which is often accompanied by anxiety and changed behaviours, are sufficiently stressful to increase susceptibility to illness, via immunosuppressant effects (e.g. Kiecolt-Glaser et al. 2002; Vedhara and Irwin 2005; see also the later section on stress as a physiological response).

Chronic stress

Occupational stress

The workplace is a good environment in which to study the chronic effects of stress, although many other environmental situations have been studied, for example traffic jams and road rage, noise pollution and over-crowding on public transport (Evans and Stecker 2004; Fisher et al. 1984). Loss of control in these situations, particularly when demands are also high, appears to play a crucial role in the stress experienced (e.g. Wang et al. 2007, 2008) (for discussion of this construct see Chapter 12 ☞). Most working individuals will experience workplace stress at some point, and while for many it is short-lived or manageable, for others it is chronic and damaging, being accompanied, for example, by changes in eating or sleep patterns, fatigue or relationship strain. Undergraduate students are of course not exempt from stress, and in fact a report by the Royal College of Psychiatrists (2003) found that undergraduates have a higher prevalence of mental health problems than age-matched non-students, and that these problems disrupt performance. Given the current political and economic climate and changes to fee structures in British universities, more students may experience mental, emotional and physical ill health, given evidence of their higher levels among those experiencing financial pressures (e.g. Jessop et al. 2005).

One possible outcome of prolonged chronic occupational stress has been described as 'burn-out' (Maslach 1982, 1997). Burn-out is similar to the final stage of Selye's general adaptation syndrome: i.e. exhaustion, both mental and physical (see later section on stress response). Maslach (1997) defined burn-out as a three-part syndrome of emotional exhaustion, depersonalisation and reduced personal accomplishment that occurs among individuals who work with people in some capacity, and which can be associated with both physical and mental ill health.

For example, hospital consultants (e.g. Taylor et al. 2005), nurses (e.g. Allan et al. 2009; Jones and Johnston 2000; McVicar 2003), and those working with cancer patients (e.g. Barnard et al. 2006; Isikhan et al. 2004; Trufelli et al. 2008) have shown a high incidence of burn-out and stress. However, it is worth noting that not all studies have found an association between workload itself and levels of burn-out, (e.g. Healy and McKay 2000; Payne 2001, and see McVicar 2003 for a review). One of the reasons for such differences between study findings is likely to lie in the sample or setting differences (e.g. registered general nurses vs. palliative or hospice nurses), although another likely factor is that of the vary-ing responses made to the demands, i.e. coping (see Chapter 12 ☞ for a full discussion of coping). For one study which found that workload-specific stress factors was more strongly associated with mood disturbance than nurses' coping responses (Healy and McKay 2000), organisational interventions aimed at reducing work-load may be appropriate and of more potential benefit than interventions targeting individuals' coping strate-gies. This contrasts with the conclusion of McVicar following his review of 21 studies, where he states (p. 640) that 'Development of preventative strategies will be hindered until employers enable individualized coping strategies, and research enables understanding of per-sonal and workplace interactions and provides a means of assessing the intensity of distress experienced by individuals.' Related to burn-out is the concept of carer strain or carer burden, identified among many individuals who provide care for dependent relatives (due to chronic illness or disability). (See Chapter 15 ☞, where we explore the impact of illness on family and friends.)

What is it about some jobs that makes them so stressful? One possible explanation for stress in the work environment is offered by person–environment fit theories (cf. French et al. 1982), or the 'goodness-of-fit' approach described by Lazarus (1991b). Such approaches suggest that stress arises because of a mismatch between environmental variables (demands) and person variables (resources). 'Fit' is considered as dynamic rather than static, in that demands and resources can change over time. Early work focused more on environmental features of the workplace than on individual difference variables, a primary example of this being the job demand–control (JDC) model of occupational stress, or job strain, put forward by Karasek and colleagues (1979, 1981, 1990). The job features identified as leading to stress included:

- demand
- controllability
- predictability
- ambiguity.

Each of these broad features can be assessed with specific questions, as illustrated in Table 11.3. Chronic ongoing stressors such as permanently excessive workload demands are thought to create stress in employees, as are sudden, unexpected requests or interruptions, being pushed to make a decision, not having the latitude to take decisions, or being unclear as to what is expected of one. Interestingly, underload, as well as overload, has been found stressful, with frustration and boredom proving as stressful for some employees as overload. This highlights a point central to the study of stress: it is subjective and each individual will construct their own definition of what is stressful 'for them'. This is seen in the findings of an idiographic study of the meaning of stress to five health professionals (neurological consultant – NC, ophthalmology assistant – OA, paediatrician – P, psychiatrist – PS and theatre nurse – TN) where aspects listed as most stressful included work environment factors such as monotonous tasks (NC), maintaining cleanliness (TN), time pressures (NC, TN), full waiting room (P), overload (NC), poor pay or conditions (OA) as well as external factors such as family pressure (PS, P) (Kirkcaldy *et al.* 2000). Think back to your own responses to the 'What

do YOU think?' at the start of the chapter, and perhaps discuss and compare with your fellow students.

Karasek's model proposed that a combination of demand and control would determine whether or not the employee experienced stress (high demand and low control contributing to higher stress–strain than would situations of high demand and high control) (Karasek and Theorell 1990). Karasek's model has been tested and proven useful in many studies. However, while it was initially thought that perceived or actual control acted as a moderator of demand (in other words, that control 'buffered' the negative effects of demands), reviews of studies using the JDC model between 1979 and 1997 (van der Doef and Maes 1998, 1999) found only minimal evidence that control moderated the negative impact of high work demands upon well-being, or upon burn-out (Rafferty *et al.* 2001). It appears that demand and control have independent and direct effects on stress outcomes.

Critics suggested that the control component needed to be specified better and that social support, or lack of it, needed to be added to the model (see Searle *et al.* 2001; Van der Doef and Maes 1999 for discussion of the job demand–control–support model (JDCS)). Increasing attention is being paid to aspects of the individual that are potentially more amenable to intervention, such as skills, self-belief or the use of social support. Attempts to challenge or resolve issues of overload, underload or ambiguity of role are not always easy or feasible in many

Table 11.3 Examples of items to assess work-related stress

	Never	Rarely	Sometimes	Often	Most times
Demand					
● My workload is never-ending					
● Job deadlines are constant					
● My job is very exciting					
Control					
● I have autonomy in carrying out my duties					
● There are too many bosses					
Predictability					
● My job consists of responding to emergencies					
● I am never sure what will be expected of me					
Ambiguity					
● My job is not very well defined					
● I am not sure about what is expected of me					

Source: adapted from Rice (1992: 188–2).

workplaces, nor are coping responses which increase engagement in health-damaging behaviour such as excessive alcohol consumption, or avoidance through absenteeism, as such responses carry huge costs for employers in terms of loss of productivity, staffing shortages and accidents in the workplace (Cooper and Payne 1988).

Addressing such factors are several studies carried out among staff in the police force (in a range of countries, e.g. Germany: Kirkcaldy and Cooper 1992; Britain: Brown et al. 1996; Wales: V. Morrison et al. 2002; New Zealand: Stephens et al. 1997; Scotland: Biggam et al. 1997; the Netherlands: Kop et al. 1999), an occupation considered to be inherently stressful due to operational, bureaucratic and interpersonal demands. Morrison et al. (2002) investigated the personal and occupational sources of stress among 699 police officers and 230 support personnel in North Wales, and explored whether personal resource variables of self-efficacy and optimism and home- and workplace-based support moderated perceived stress and emotional distress. We found that perceived stress and emotional distress were significantly associated with low levels of dispositional optimism, low self-efficacy and low levels of social support at home and in the workplace. Levels of stress and distress were high in both support staff and police officers with those employed in mid-high ranks, such as sergeants and above, reporting higher stress than junior-ranked constables. Rank was also significantly correlated with levels of support used in the workplace, with higher ranks reporting lower levels of access to, and use of, workplace support. Home support was associated with lower stress among support staff, whereas work-based and home support were important to reduced stress among police staff. The personal resources of self-efficacy and optimism were found to moderate stress levels, with females benefiting particularly from high self-efficacy (although as a group females had lower self-efficacy than male colleagues). Support staff generally had lower levels of self-efficacy beliefs than police staff. Occupational stressors were generally identified as being bureaucracy-associated (increased paperwork, poor communication with managers) among mid-low-ranked staff and additionally job-overload related in terms of increasing levels of unpaid overtime and the need to take work home among higher-ranked personnel.

The above findings show quite complex effects of rank on the personal resources of self-efficacy and social-support use and on the stress experienced. Some occupations, such as the police force, or in health-care professions, may also have strong internal sanctions against exhibiting symptoms of stress, given the level of contact required with the public, which may bring additional challenges. While rank may not be so explicit in other occupations, except perhaps the Armed Forces, an implicit hierarchy exists in most workforces. The effects of status on interactions between personnel is a factor that needs considering in any studies of occupational stress. Illustrating this, conflict with or harassment by other colleagues has been associated with a significant level of staff absenteeism, to the stage where the Royal College of Nursing (RCN 2002) has acknowledged a need to improve interprofessional and intraprofessional communication and management style.

An alternative model to that of Karasek's which we have described above is the Effort/Reward Imbalance model (Siegrist et al. 2004). This model highlights what the individual 'puts in' to their work and highlights how a lack of recognition or return for effort can be stressful (see review of studies using this model in van Vegchel et al. 2005). For example, an over-commitment to work has been associated with increased blood pressure (Steptoe et al. 2004); job strain and an effort/reward imbalance significantly predicted risk of CVD mortality over 25 years of the Whitehall 11 Study (Kivimaki et al. 2002); and along with low levels of support was associated with reduced immune function in a study of German factory workers (Bosch et al. 2009).

The commonly employed models of occupational stress described here have therefore succeeded in integrating what the individual brings to the workplace (personal characteristics, cognitions, effort), their support resources and the environmental features. Workplace-based interventions targeting both the work environment as well as individuals stress responses have shown considerable success in enhancing physical and emotional well-being and also productivity – outcomes of importance to both employee and employer (e.g. Brabantia Work Health Program, Maes and van der Doef 2004). Some occupational specific findings may point to the need for differing interventions (Chapters 2 and 13 ☞), but the common themes are evident of demands, appraisals and the cognitive, emotional and behavioural responses of both the employee and the employer.

For many, stress may be maintained by repeatedly rethinking past events and worrying about future ones, a process known as rumination (e.g. Nolen-Hoeksema 1991;

Nolen-Hoeksema *et al.* 2008), a type of, as Brosschot and colleagues (Brosschot *et al.* 2006) call it, perseverative cognition. While Brosschot and colleagues have conducted some interesting studies of the effects of perserverative cognition on physiological stress responses, RESEARCH FOCUS describes the consequences of rumination for mood among those facing the real-life stressor of a cancer diagnosis.

RESEARCH FOCUS

Rumination and mood in cancer patients

Morrison, V., Henderson, B.J., Soulsby, J., Williams, M., Doody, M., Williams, R., Parry, H., Tapping, H. and Stuart, N. (in review). Anxiety and depression in cancer patients: the role of rumination, appraisal and coping.

Introduction

Rumination has been defined as a stable coping style/trait, where an individual engages in passive, repetitive and self-focused thinking about their negative emotional states and the implications and consequences of these states (Nolen-Hoeksema 1991). Rumination has been related to many 'negative' states including anxiety and depression, has been shown to exacerbate negative future thinking and contribute to poorer problem solving and is thought to be 'stress-reactive' (Alloy *et al.* 1999; Robinson and Alloy 2003) as well as a general coping 'style'. Although rumination has been consistently associated with negative emotions, cognitive models of emotional distress in chronic physical illness have not yet included rumination (Soo *et al.* 2009). This is unfortunate given that it has been found to be amenable to intervention (e.g. Segal *et al.* 2002). Thus to address this gap and with a thought to future intervention, this study set out to explore the extent and correlates of rumination in those with a diagnosis of cancer within the past five years.

Aims and objectives

The study aims were to examine psychological responses to a range of cancer diagnoses, with a specific focus on the level of rumination patients engage in and the association between this and distress.

Methods

Eligible patients were those previously determined by consultants at team meetings as being fit enough to be interviewed, and not having a life expectancy of less than three months, cognitive or communicative impairment, illiteracy or an inability to comply with the requirements of the study and/or give informed consent. On receipt of consent (a 58 per cent response rate was achieved), questionnaires were administered by a researcher to patients over the age of 18, with a diagnosis of malignant disease, from two months post-diagnosis to five years post-initial-diagnosis, attending for an appointment at a day clinic at the local general hospital. A total of 123 cancer outpatients completed a questionnaire in clinic which included measures of rumination, stress appraisal, adjustment to cancer, and two measures of mood state. The measure of rumination used here has 22 items which reflect a general (i.e. not a cancer-specific measure) ruminative style of response that are either self-focused (e.g. 'I analyse recent events to try to understand why I am depressed'), symptom-focused (e.g. 'I think about how hard it is to concentrate') or focused on the cause and consequences of negative mood (e.g. 'I think I wont be able to do my job if I don't snap out of this').

Findings

For the purposes of this RESEARCH FOCUS, we present mainly those findings concerning rumination; however, the paper includes fuller analysis of appraisal, coping and mood relationships.

Levels of distress were found to be similar to other studies with this population, with 26 per cent of participants having clinically significant anxiety and 12 per cent having clinically significant depression. Overall, participants reported that they rarely ruminated, and they appraised their illness as being mildly stressful. Age, cancer site and current clinical status were related to psychological responses, but gender was not.

The table below summarises the regression analyses for two outcomes, anxiety and depression where, if you look at the coefficients accompanied by **s (reflecting significance), rumination, a high stress appraisal and (for anxiety only) anxious preoccupation coping are positively associated with negative mood.

Table (extract): Summary of hierarchical regression analyses for anxiety and depression

	Generalised anxiety				Generalised depression			
	R	Adj R^2	$R^2 \Delta$	F Δ	R	Adj R^2	$R^2 \Delta$	F Δ
Step 1 Gender	.07	−.00	.01	.56	.10	.00	.01	1.2
Step 2 Age	.22	.03	.04	4.9*	.12	−.01	.00	.34
Step 3 Cancer site	.38	.06	.10	1.5	.37	.05	.12	1.8
Step 4 Current clinical status	.40	.04	.01	.39	.43	.06	.05	1.3
Step 5 Rumination	.71	.43	.35	67.2**	.71	.42	.32	60.3**
Step 6 Stress appraisal	.73	.46	.03	5.9*	.74	.48	.06	11.8**
Step 7 Coping	.78	.52	.07	3.4**	.76	.47	.02	.79

The table only reproduces the findings for two of the eight emotions addressed, using the two subscales of the Hospital Anxiety and Depression scale. The Profile of Mood States (POMS) measure was also used and predictors of fatigue-inertia; tension-anxiety, vigour-activity; anger-hostility, depression-dejection, and confusion-bewilderment are also reported. Using the language of regression analyses, rumination explained the majority of variance in each mood variable (67.2 per cent of anxiety variance; 60.3 per cent of depression variance), with stress appraisal also explaining a smaller, but significant amount. Coping did not predict variance in depression (nor fatigue or vigour, see paper), but did contribute in a small, but significant way, to the explanation of variance in the other mood outcomes.

Discussion

An important finding in terms of implications for intervention is that psychological variables were more closely related to patient distress than socio-demographic or clinical factors, which are generally unalterable. Patients in this sample as a whole were not engaged in particularly high levels of rumination; however, those that engaged in this type of 'perseverative cognition', reflecting on symptoms, negative emotions or past events or brooding about the future, were more likely to experience negative mood in terms of both general anxiety and depression and in terms of the more transient mood states. Although based on cross-sectional data, the authors' findings are consistent with stress-appraisal theory, with appraisals explaining emotional outcome (doing 'better' than coping perhaps in this regard), but they also point to a crucial role of cognitive processing of a ruminative type that has been neglected in many studies of responses to stress.

It is likely that different aspects of rumination exist which have different effects, for example, Morris and Shakespeare-Finch (2010) distinguish between a deliberate reflective rumination which reappraises the situation to seek benefits, a life purpose rumination which revisits past events and losses and ponders one's purpose in life since the cancer, and an intrusive rumination which is when unwanted thoughts of the negative experience regularly intrude into consciousness. In a study also of cancer survivors, these authors find that intrusive and life purpose rumination were associated with negative emotions, whereas the former type was associated with post-traumatic growth.

What the two cancer studies here point to is the potential for intervention where 'ruminative cycles' are

decreased. One example Morrison suggests is that of mindfulness-based interventions which have already shown promise in cancer populations (e.g. Ramel *et al.* 2004; Foley *et al.* 2010), and mindfulness is also described more in our chapter (Chapter 13 ☞) on stress management. We also know from other studies that depression itself is predictive of poorer cancer outcomes, and thus longitudinal studies could perhaps explore whether rumination mediates this association.

We have thus far established that stress responses arise from events and from appraisals of these events, but we have not yet described what happens following these cognitive or emotional processes. Lazarus's transactional model of stress posits that appraisals and their attached emotions lead to cognitive and behavioural coping efforts, and in Chapter 12 ☞ coping theory and the role of coping in moderating stress outcomes is discussed fully. However, in addition to these psychological stress responses, stress can also trigger biological and physiological responses, and it is to these that we now turn our attention.

Stress as a physiological response

Thinking of stress as a response takes us into the domain of seeking biological or physiological explanations of how stress affects the body and potentially illness; the assumption here is that stressors place demands on the person that are manifested in some response; in physics, this response would be termed 'strain'. Proponents of the 'response' model of stress describe how individuals react to danger or potentially harmful situations or even pleasant demands with a coordinated physiological and behavioural response (e.g. Cassel 1974, cited in Leventhal and Tomarken 1987). Initially, an event has to be appraised, and this involves the **central nervous system**

> **central nervous system**
> that part of the nervous system consisting of the brain and spinal cord.

(CNS). The sensory information and the appraisal of the event combine to initiate autonomic (the autonomic nervous system is part of the peripheral nervous system and contains both the sympathetic and the parasympathetic NS, see below) and endocrine (hormone) responses. These feed back to the cortex and limbic system, which in turn links with the hypothalamus and brainstem. It has been found that, for example, appraising an event as *unpredictable* in nature affects various aspects of physiological activation (Zakowski 1995).

These processes are summarised below, although Chapter 8 ☞ provides greater physiological definition and detail.

Early work on the stress response

An early researcher, Walter Cannon (1932), outlined the role of catecholamines (adrenaline and noradrenaline), which, when released from the adrenal glands of the sympathetic nervous system as hormones, heighten arousal in order to facilitate the 'fight or flight' response. When faced with imminent danger or a high level of threat (such as when being charged at by an angry dog), the options are to face the challenge or escape it. This natural response of physical arousal – dry mouth, increased heart rate, rapid breathing – signifies the release of adrenaline, a hormone that enlarges the autonomic responses (e.g. breathing deeply, a rapid heart rate) and facilitates the release of stored fuels for energy, which enables either running away or fighting the threat. This 'fight or flight syndrome', Cannon reasoned, was *adaptive* because it enabled quick responses to threat but also *harmful* because it disrupted emotional and physiological functioning. If prolonged, such responses were thought to contribute to many medical problems, (based on early animal studies whereby dogs and monkeys were exposed to prolonged periods of stress causing excessive hydrochloric acid to build up in the stomach, thus contributing to ulcer formation). In other words, in situations of chronic or ongoing stress, this fight–flight response would not be adaptive.

Subsequent to Cannon, another physiologist, Hans Selye (1956), discovered (quite accidentally while conducting animal research into the sex hormones) that a triad of responses commonly followed the unpleasant injecting procedures used – the adrenal glands enlarged, the thymus gland shrank and ulcers developed in the digestive tract. He followed up his early findings with over forty years of research using different aversive stimuli (injections, heat, cold, exercise), and came to the conclusion that there were universal and non-specific responses to stress: i.e. the same physiological responses followed a range of stimuli, whether pleasant or unpleasant, and that the 'fight–flight' response was only the first stage of response to stress (e.g. Selye 1974). Selye's model of stress is known as the **general adaptation syndrome**. The response to stress was seen to be an innate drive of living organisms to maintain internal balance, i.e. homeostasis, and he proposed that it did so in a three-stage process:

1. *Alarm reaction*: the awareness of a stressor is the initial response that can cause a downturn in bodily defences, and blood pressure and heart rate may initially decrease before rising to higher than normal levels. Selye stated that this arousal could not be maintained for long periods. He attributed his stress response to activitation of the anterior–pituitary–adrenal cortex system, although exact physiological processes only became clear some years later (Pinel 2003; Selye 1991; and see later section).

2. *Stage of resistance*: the next stage is where the body tries to adapt to a stressor that has not subsided in spite of resistance efforts made during the acute/alarm stage. Arousal decreases from that seen in the alarm stage but is still higher than normal, and Selye noted that this stage of mobilisation of bodily defences could not last indefinitely without the organism becoming vulnerable to illness.

3. *Stage of exhaustion*: exhaustion would occur if the resistance stage lasts too long, resulting in a depletion of bodily resources and energy. At this stage, the ability to resist the stress declines, and Selye proposed the increased likelihood of 'diseases of adaptation' such as cardiovascular disease, arthritis and asthma.

Later work on stress responses

Cannon's and Selye's work stimulated a huge amount of research into the physiology of stress. Much of it has not confirmed Selye's proposed 'non-specific response', as different physiological responses have been found to be associated with different kinds of stressor. Evidence for this comes from consistent findings of experimental studies carried out in the 1980s; for example, an experimental study that exposed participants to different types of challenge (mental or physical) and took continuous blood samples during exposure found that blood levels of adrenaline were increased during mental stress, whereas noradrenaline increased during physical stress (Ward *et al.* 1983, cited in Rice 1992).

However, there is a large and growing body of evidence that shows that adverse events (and positive events) produce physiological changes. Typical stress responses (e.g. rapid and deeper breathing, increased heart rate, sweating or shaking) result not just from activation of the anterior–pituitary–adrenal cortex system as Selye thought but also from increased activity of the sympathetic branch of the autonomic nervous system (ANS). The ANS can be divided into two connected systems – the sympathetic nervous system (SNS) and the parasympathetic nervous system (PNS) – which 'exist in a state of dynamic but antagonistic tension' (Rice 1992: 126). The SNS is involved in arousal and expenditure of energy (such as during a 'fight–flight' response), whereas the PNS is involved in reducing arousal and in restoring and conserving the body's energy stores (such as during rest) (see Chapter 8 ☞). Both systems control the actions of many internal organs, such as the heart and skeletal muscles, with their activity initially mediated by the neurotransmitter acetylcholine. Acetylcholine links the neurons of the spinal synapse to the brainstem, where

---

general adaptation syndrome
a sequence of physiological responses to prolonged stress, from the alarm stage through the resistance stage to exhaustion.

the nerves then act on their target organs. Mediation in the sympathetic branch is provided by noradrenaline (adrenergic fibres) and, to a lesser degree, adrenaline; whereas in the parasympathetic branch, acetylcholine (cholinergic fibres) makes this final link.

The stress response is maintained following short-lived sympathetic arousal by neuroendocrine (combining the nervous and the endocrine systems i.e. electrical/chemical and hormonal) responses resulting from activation of the sympathetic–adrenomedullary system (SAM) and release of the catecholamines adrenaline (epinephrine) and noradrenaline (norepinephrine), those in brackets being the US terms, from the adrenal glands. This activation of the adrenal medullary system by the hypothalamus which sends nerves signals down to the adrenal medulla via the spinal cord, in conjunction with the more crucial action of the hypothalamus in activating the pituitary–adrenal cortex (the hypothalamic–pituitary–adrenocortical (HPA) system), enables our bodily organs to alter their usual function to facilitate an adaptive response to both internal and external stresses even where the stress is prolonged.

The HPA system (see Figure 11.3) originates in the hypothalamus, which releases its own hormone, corticotrophin-releasing factor (CRF), which controls the anterior pituitary gland in its secreting of adrenocorticotrophic hormone (ACTH). ACTH then travels to the adrenal gland, where the hormones adrenaline and noradrenaline are released, and secretion of glucocorticoids, particularly the hormone cortisol, is stimulated from the adrenal cortex. While Cannon's early model described the role of adrenaline, Selye was more interested in such adrenocortical responses. We now know that circulating glucocorticoids provide energy for the 'alarm phase' as the release of glucocorticoids into the bloodstream regulates the levels of glucose in the blood from which energy can be drawn. Almost every cell in the human body contains glucocorticoid receptors, and hormones such as cortisol affect every major organ system in the body. For example, cortisol inhibits glucose and fat uptake by tissue cells so that more can be drawn on for immediate energy, it increases blood flow, it suppresses immune function by inhibiting the action of phagocytes and lymphocytes, and it inhibits inflammation of any damaged tissue that is sustained during the fight or 'flight' (e.g. Antoni 1987; Kemeny 2003). Blood cortisol levels are at their peak 20–40 minutes after a stressor and thus their levels have been used as stress indices in many studies.

The duration of some of the physiological responses to stress, such as the release of cortisol, influences whether the responses are beneficial to the organism or not. Prolonged release of cortisol can actually have negative feedback effects on the HPA axis functioning and the suppression of the immune system caused by increased blood-circulating cortisol (serum or s-cortisol) can make a person vulnerable to infection. Furthermore, McEwen notes (2008: 174) that 'it is not clear whether prolonged stress for many months or years may have irreversible effects on the brain'. McEwen describes the 'wear and tear' resulting from chronic or repeated stress as 'allostatic load' whereby the process of 'allostasis' – a process of response and adaptation to stress where appropriate activation levels are maintained outside the normal range (Sterling and Eyer 1988) – is overloaded, challenged and fails. Increased or dysregulated allostasis, referred to by McEwen as being 'stressed out' can indirectly lead to illness by virtue of behavioural and physiological responses to this state, e.g. health-damaging behaviour such as smoking, excessive comfort eating, sleep loss (e.g. Segestrom and Miller 2004). Cortisol levels are known to be elevated in those with sleep deprivation and, as mentioned above, excessive cortisol can cause its own problems (see also IN THE SPOTLIGHT on p. 311). Prolonged release of adrenaline and noradrenaline can also have negative results, including suppressed cellular immune function, increases in heart rate and blood pressure, heartbeat irregularities (arrhythmia) and, potentially, hypertension and heart disease (Fredrickson and Matthews 1990; Clow 2001).

HPA activation also elevates the production of growth hormones and prolactin, beta endorphins and encephalin, which are also found in the brain in response to stress and are thought to play a role in immune-related disease and in problems such as depression. Beta endorphins have a useful analgesic (pain-killing) function and, as such, may explain why people can endure high levels of pain until they succeed in escaping stressful situations or completing demanding tasks: for example, soldiers with extreme injuries have been known to crawl long distances to receive help, and athletes can complete races in spite of damaged muscles (e.g. Wall 1979).

The SAM and HPA systems could therefore be thought of as providing total coverage, one via adrenaline for acute responses such as fight or flight, and one via cortisol for more sustained responses. These responses within

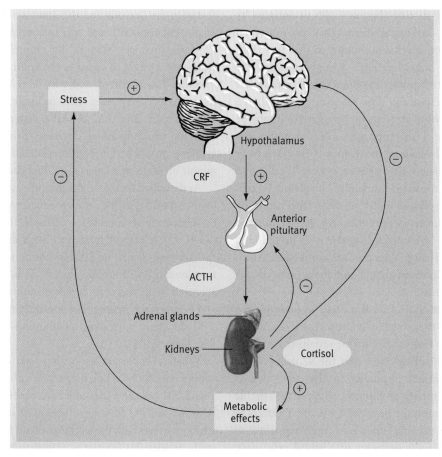

Figure 11.3 The HPA Axis : a schematic diagram where stimulatory and inhibitory paths are indicated by the arrows and + or − signs respectively. CRF represents corticotropin − releasing factor and ACTH represents adrenocorticotropic hormone

Source: adapted from Lenbury, Y. and Pornsawad, P. (2005). *Mathematical Medicine and Biology*, 22, 15–33.

the autonomic nervous system and the endocrine system work together to prepare our bodies to meet the demands of our environment. Our autonomic nervous system may work 'behind the scenes', but its functions are essential to basic human responses.

The need for combined psychological and physiological understanding of stress can be seen in the subsequent sections where evidence of an association between stress and physiological pathways is considered and then explored in relation to various illness conditions.

Stress and immune function dysregulation

Declines or alterations in immune function have frequently been associated with the experience of stressful life events (e.g. Ader 2001; Glaser and Kiecolt-Glaser 2005; Salovey *et al.* 2000). The immune system (see Chapter 8 ☞) is the body's defence against disease. It operates by producing certain types of cell that operate against foreign organisms (e.g. bacteria, poisons, viruses, parasites) and abnormal cells (e.g. cancer cells) in the blood and lymphatic systems. These potential threats to the body are known as antigens, and their threat can be met by either a general and rapid-response first line of defence (natural immunity), or a slower, more specifically targeted defence (specific immunity). Immune cells are white blood cells of two major types, lymphocytes and phagocytes, which can be found in the lymphatic system, in the lymph nodes, spleen and in the blood circulation. The second of these, phagocytes, are attracted to sites of infection due to tissue releasing chemical messengers, and when they reach their destination they destroy abnormal cells or antigens by engulfing and consuming them. They provide what is known as 'non-specific immunity' in that they offer a first general line of defence. Lymphocytes on the other hand offer 'specific immunity' which follows the first natural responses. This involves 'cell-mediated immunity' via lymphocyte action (triggered by a subtype of phagocytes, a macrophage) where lymphocytes consist of T cells made in the thymus (CD4+ T cells or helper T cells, and CD8+ cells or cytoxic T cells) and also 'humoral-mediated immunity' involving B cells (memory and plasma cells). B cells label invading antigens in order to identify them for destruction and also 'remember' the antigen to enable early detection of future attacks. Their plasma produces antibodies, which remain in the blood circulation until the germ or disease is no longer present.

Natural killer (NK) cells also occur in body plasma and slow down the growth of abnormal cells (in cancer, for example) so that other immune responses can form an attack. As with phagocyte action, the NK cells provide non-specific natural immunity in that they defend against a wide variety of antigens, whereas the specific and acquired immunity provided by B and T cells is to those antigens to which they have been sensitised to (see Table 11.4 for a summary of T and B cell roles). Both the natural and the specific systems, involving NK, B and T cells, interact and help one another in the fight against infection or the growth of abnormal cells (see Chapter 8 ☞ for further details of the action of these cell types, and for consideration of some conditions associated with 'faulty' immune system function, i.e. diabetes, rheumatoid arthritis, multiple sclerosis). T-helper cells also produce the chemical messengers

Table 11.4 Specific immunity and cell types

Humoral immunity: B cells	Cell-mediated immunity: T cells
Operate in the bloodstream	Operate at level of the cell
Work by releasing antibodies, which then destroy the antigen	Include memory, killer (NK), helper (CD4+) and suppressor T cells
Include memory cells	Mature in the thymus and not the bone marrow as other white blood cells do

(between the nervous and the immune system) known as pro-inflammatory and anti-inflammatory cytokines. Pro-inflammatory cytokines (for example interleukin-1 (IL-1) are thought to signal to the brain when injury or infection has occurred and play a role in triggering inflammatory responses that facilitate, for example, wound repair. The SAM and HPA systems are involved here as catecholamines increase pro-inflammatory cytokine production and glucocorticoids are known to inhibit it (see IN THE SPOTLIGHT opposite).

As described therefore, the immune system is affected by the workings of the sympathetic nervous system and the endocrine responses; for example, the HPA system causes the release of hormones such as cortisol from the adrenal glands, and these hormones are thought to stimulate the immune system. It is now generally accepted that there is communication both within and between the neuroendocrine and immune systems, with the brain providing an immuno-regulatory role (e.g. Blalock 1994).

What is important to health psychologists is that studies have found a link between the proliferation of B, T and NK cells and the subjective experience of stress; in other words, they have shown that psychological stress interferes with the workings of our body. One early study by Kiecolt-Glaser *et al.* (1984) found a significant reduction in NK cell activity among students prior to important end-of-term exams compared with those tested in mid-term. In addition, those students who reported feelings of loneliness plus a high number of recent stressful life events showed significantly less NK cell activity at both times than those students who were low in life events and low in loneliness. The findings of such experimental studies took a long time to be accepted, because they necessitated a paradigm shift from where the body was thought to operate independently of the mind to acceptance of the fact that psychological factors could influence immuno-competence (i.e. the degree to which our immune system functions effectively). Since the late 1970s, work in the area of psychoneuroimmunology (the study of how psychosocial factors interact with the central and peripheral nervous system and the immune system) has gone from strength to strength, with improvements in technologies leading to even greater developments in the twenty-first century (compare the classic reviews of Herbert and Cohen 1993 and Cohen and Herbert 1996 with more recent work, e.g. Vingerhoets and Perski 2000; Vedhara and Irwin 2005; Ader 2007).

IN THE SPOTLIGHT

Cortisol

While playing a crucial role in the regulation of key physiological systems and the stress response as described above, cortisol production over long periods of time can actually damage immunity. Animal research has shown that long-term exposure to such gluco-corticoids damaged neurons in the hippocampal formation (Antoni 1987; Coburn-Litvak et al. 2003; Sapolsky 1996), an area of the brain crucial to learning and memory, with a link being proposed with ageing (Sapolsky et al. 1986; Magri et al. 2006). Magri and colleagues interpret the increased cortisol levels found in older individuals as evidence of reduced abiilty to adapt to stress, and possibly related to cognitive declines associated with dementia. Although more research with humans is required to address such associations further (prolonged chronically elevated cortisol is seen in those with both major depression and Cushing's disease, typified by bloating, atypical facial hair, for example). In both of these conditions, however, the duration of the illness and not the age of the subjects predicts a progressive reduction in volume of the hippocampus, determined by structural magnetic resonance imaging (McEwen 2008).

In terms of immune function, cortisol also plays a role. Pro- and anti-inflammatory cytokines are produced by many cells in the body, for example B and T-helper cells of the immune system, and they are part of the signalling process to the brain that enables the stress responses. Their production is regulated by glucocorticoids and catecholamines, but while catecholamines increase pro-inflammatory cytokine production, glucocorticoids are known to inhibit it, with consequences of reducing immunity, i.e increasing susceptibility to infection or impairing wound healing (Sapolsky et al. 2000; Gouin et al. 2008).

Finally, Steptoe and colleagues (2005) have shown evidence of a relationship between positive psychology and lower (better) cortisol levels, i.e. they gathered data on daily 'moments' where positive affect had been experienced and found an association between the aggregated experiences, lower cortisol production and higher heart rate variability (showing higher parasympathetic activity), in response to a mental stress test. In contrast, in an earlier study the same group (Steptoe et al. 2004b) found that people with low self-esteem had larger cortisol responses to wakening in the morning, and higher natural killer (NK) cell responses to a mental stress test, as well as sleep problems.

Thus in these brief examples we can get a sense of the dual aspect of neuroendocrine responses, essential and valuable bodily responses, but which have a limit, described by some as 'allostatic load', but in lay terms as 'wear and tear'. The role of individual differences in these responses, including possibly genetic influences, is an interesting avenue for future research.

Age and immune function

It is generally accepted that immune function declines with age. This is sometimes referred to as 'immuno-senescence' whereby the innate system of an immediate immune response to invading germs, and also the slower-acting immune resistance response, declines (Gomez et al. 2008). There is evidence, from animal and human studies, suggesting that NK cell function becomes less efficient even though they are increased in number in older people, and that pro-inflammatory cytokine activity is also increased. The importance of these findings lies in the fact that they place older people at greater risk of severe reactions to infections, as seen in the influenza mortality statistics, for example, or in the complications of inflammation following wounds or surgery and slower healing. Additionally, Graham et al. (2006), in a review of the current evidence, suggested that in young adults stress can mimic the effects of aging, and in older adults, stress can exaggerate the effects of aging on immune competence. While this is a relatively under-researched area, studies of caregivers are certainly pointing to significant associations, with Alzheimer's caregivers, for example, showing slower wound healing than age-matched non-caregivers, and reduced antibody responses to immunisation (Kiecolt-Glaser et al. 1995; Damjanovic et al. 2007; Pederson-Fischer et al. 2009) (see also Chapter 15 ☞).

IN THE SPOTLIGHT

Can stress prevent your wounds healing?

Janice Kiecolt-Glaser and Ronald Glaser have spent many years researching the mind–body relationship, in particular the relationship between the experience of stress and immune function. While this chapter has presented evidence of the physiological pathways underlying stress responses, you may not have stopped to consider how stress might affect you, not just in terms of potentially increasing your risk of diseases such as heart disease but also in terms of more day-to-day health challenges, such as wounds received while participating in sporting activities. The Glasers have shown in many studies of elderly carers of people with Alzheimer's disease that healing of experimentally induced tissue wounds took significantly longer among carers than among healthy age-matched control participants. However, this may in part be due to coexisting ageing processes, so further studies have explored whether similar effects can be found in younger samples. Vedhara and colleagues in Bristol (2003) examined the healing rates of foot ulcers among 60 adults with type 2 diabetes. They found that healing was reduced in those who had shown high anxiety, depression or stress. Importantly, similar effects of stress have been found on the healing rates of otherwise healthy students who are given a small experimental skin wound at two different times, one during the summer holiday, the other prior to sitting exams. The wound inflicted before exams took on average three days longer to heal, and this was reflected by decreases in immunological status (Marucha *et al.* 1998). Broadbent *et al.* (2003) have confirmed the impairing effects of high stress and worry levels on wound healing where wounds were not experimental but real, i.e. participants were recovering from hernia surgery.

Why do such findings matter? Think of your own stress levels; think of your likelihood of becoming wounded in sport or other activity; or of the potential of facing surgery in the future. Think of current concern about MRSA (methicillin-resistant *Staphylococcus aureus*) and *C difficile* infections in hospitals and in the community. Effectively dealing with your own stress is important, not only in keeping you healthy but also in helping you to heal and recover when and if you become ill or injured or require surgery.

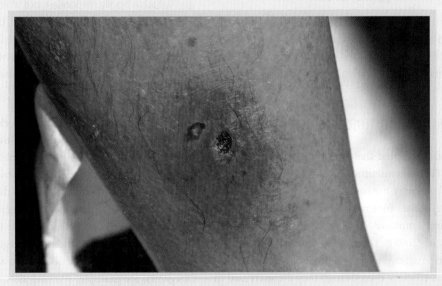

Plate 11.3 Stress has been shown to influence the healing process

Source: Alamy Images/Andrew Holt.

Stress and cardiovascular reactivity

There is also a reasonably consistent body of psychobiological evidence showing that stress can cause alterations in physiological responses, with arousal of the sympathetic nervous system being greater in some people than in others. This 'reactivity hypothesis' first proposed by Krantz and Manuck (1984) describes how genetic or environmental factors combine to influence a person's vulnerability to a physiological response following stress and to negative emotions that can be detrimental to their health, particularly their arterial health implicated in heart disease. Reactivity, for example periods of elevated heart rate or blood pressure, is seen in both laboratory settings where individuals are exposed to acute or repeated stress, such as mental arithmetic tasks or public speaking, and in real-life settings where people face occupational challenge or marital conflict, for example. There are some pointers towards ethnic variations in reactivity, for example, that African Americans tend to show greater reactivity where Asian or European Americans may not, although whether this is biologically or environmentally explained remains unclear. Whether or not this CVR (cardiovascular reactivity) is related to the development of disease, or indeed disease progression, is something of great interest to psychobiologists and psychologists alike (e.g. Johnston 2007; Linden *et al.* 2003). However, attention more recently has also addressed the whole process of physiological arousal, from before an event (e.g. anticipatory responses), during (as suggested by reactivity work), and after, in terms of perseverative thoughts or ruminative responses that may maintain physiological changes (Brosschot *et al.* 2006). We discussed this earlier in the chapter, but the main point here is that reactivity, which is thought to occur during an event (laboratory or real-life stressor), is perhaps only part of the physiological story.

Evidence of the influence of psychological stress upon immune function, or upon cardiovascular reactivity has provided scientists with the opportunity to assess 'objective' indices of the stress response alongside, and in relation to, subjective stress reports. For example, V. Burns *et al.* (2003) examined the effects of minor and major life events on the antibody response to influenza vaccination among a sample of undergraduate students. Students were followed up over five months and results found that participants with low antibody levels at five months reported having experienced significantly more life events in the intervening time following vaccination. Similar findings have been reported among those caring for a spouse with Alzheimer's disease (a chronic stressor), whereby their antibody responses to flu vaccination are lower than that of non-carer controls (e.g. Kiecolt-Glaser *et al.* 1996; Vedhara *et al.* 1999), although studies of younger carers have not consistently supported such findings (e.g. Vedhara *et al.* 2002). Such findings have implications for the success of vaccination programmes.

Evidence of physiological correlates of occupational stress have also been reported, for example Clays *et al.* (2007) found that the ambulatory blood pressure at work, home and even while asleep was significantly higher in workers with high job strain than in those with lower strain. Students are often used as participants in this area of research due to the 'occupational hazard' of exposure to potentially stressful patterns of assessment and examinations. Chandrashekara *et al.* (2007), for example, found that medical students with high anxiety and poorer emotional adaptability about end-of-term exams showed lower levels of an inflammatory cytokine (tumour necrosis factor alpha – TNF-α) than students with lower anxiety and greater emotional adaptability. The effect was not seen for mid-term exams, similar to that reported in the 1984 study of Kiecolt-Glaser *et al.* mentioned above. Such situation-specific responses contrasts with other findings where exposure to non-academic stressors contributed to a delayed *increase* in circulating cytokine levels (Steptoe *et al.* 2001). More research on these responses is warranted, particularly studies which contrast stressor types and contexts, as well as consider other individual difference variables that may contribute to stress reactivity (see Chapter 12 ☞). In terms of the implications of such findings for psychological intervention (see Chapter 13 ☞), there is some evidence that individuals can be 'trained' using classical or operant conditioning procedures to alter their immune response to threat (see Miller and Cohen 2001 for a meta-analytic review of 85 studies of psychological interventions and immune functioning). However, further work, including better controlled studies that also address potential mediators of any shown effects, is needed.

It should therefore have become clear during the course of this chapter that stress is not a unitary process but a highly complex one. The experience of stress is, to varying degrees, dependent on stimulus events (acute or chronic, physical or psychological), on internal representations of events, including a person's appraisals and emotional responses, and on the nature and extent of physiological and behavioural activation that follows. Stress indisputably has a strong psychological component, and furthermore stress responses change over time as a person adjusts (or not) to their situation. Given all the evidence reviewed above, it is hardly surprising that measuring stress is complex, as described in ISSUES below.

ISSUES

Can stress be measured?

As with any concept, how stress is defined influences how it is measured or assessed. We have described three broad ways of thinking about stress – as a stimulus, as the result of cognitive appraisal and as a physiological response – and each of these views leads to different forms of assessment.

Measuring stress as a stimulus is problematic, given what was described earlier as weaknesses in the life events approach to stress – if many of the life events are irrelevant to the responder because of their age or life stage, does this mean that they are less stressed because their potential total scores are reduced? Additionally, people generally search for explanations for how they feel or for events that have happened to them – it is common, for example, for people to report many life events in the lead up to a heart attack – so measuring retrospective accounts of life events or even smaller 'hassles' may in this instance lead to inflated estimates of the role that stress plays in illness. Some researchers argue for greater validity of measures, taking a daily hassles (and uplifts) approach rather than a time-lagged retrospective. However, daily assessment places many demands on respondents, and in fact reviews of findings from studies using a life events approach has found the SSRS to have good predictive utility in terms of stress-related symptoms (Scully et al. 2000).

Stress is based upon appraisal, which involves stimulus, cognition and emotion, and therefore it is necessary to measure, not only the events, but also people's appraisals of the event, their emotions, their perceived resources and their perceived coping potential. Stress appraisals tend to be assessed by simply asking people how they feel or getting them to complete a standardised psychometric assessment. One commonly employed example is the Perceived Stress Scale, which assesses the degree to which life situations are appraised as stressful (Cohen et al. 1983). Examples include 'In the last month, how often have you been upset because of something that happened unexpectedly?' and 'In the last month, how often have you found that you could not cope with all the things you had to do?' (scored as 0 = never; 1 = almost never; 2 = sometimes; 3 = fairly often; 4 = very often). Higher scores are indicative of greater perceived stress. The stressor, or the event being considered, is not specified in the standard wording of this scale, thus general appraisals are assessed only. Some studies, however, reword the PSS to record event-specific stress appraisals, e.g. 'In the last weeks since receiving your diagnosis . . .'.

In order to assess secondary appraisal processes central to Lazarus's model, measures of personal resource, such as self-efficacy or perceived social support, which are thought to moderate, mediate or 'buffer' the stress–outcome relationship, can be employed (see Chapter 12 ☛). Regardless of the number of assessment tools used, however, there are inherent limitations in assessing an experience as subjective as stress. For example, distress is likely to bias the answers one gives to questions regarding the nature of the stressor, or regarding the number of recent life events experienced, and is also likely to influence the resources one considers to have available. Given that aspects of the stress experience interact, it is necessary for research studies to disentangle precursors of a stress response from the stress response itself and this is challenging without well-designed longitudinal studies.

In terms of assessing individual responses considered to be indicative of stress, a measure of distress or more specific mood states (e.g. anger, depression or anxiety), for example, the general health questionnaire (GHQ; Goldberg and Williams 1988) is commonly used. There are various GHQs, which vary in the number of items included. The 28-item version measures a combination of emotional states (anxiety, insomnia, social dysfunction, severe depression and somatic symptoms), whereas the more common, and perhaps more user-friendly in terms of time demands on participants, 12-item version does not distinguish between each of these. The GHQ-12, still provides a sensitive measure of psychiatric disorder. Respondents indicate whether they have experienced a particular symptom or behaviour 'less than usual', 'no more than usual', 'rather more than usual' or 'much more than usual', and example items include 'have you recently . . . been able to concentrate on whatever you're doing? . . . been feeling unhappy and depressed? . . . felt constantly under strain?'.

Stress as a response can be measured using physiological and physical indices such as heart rate, blood pressure, galvanic skin response, levels of adrenaline, noradrenaline and cortisol levels in the blood, urine, or saliva, other indicators of increased cortisol levels such as reflected decreases in salivary secretory immunoglobulins (Sig-A), or other immune responses such as described earlier in relation to helper T cells, B or NK cell activity. Measurement of these aspects of the stress experience require specific skills and expertise in their collection, storage, analysis and interpretation (see Vedhara et al. 2001) and are more often gathered in laboratory-based stress research than

perhaps in naturalistic settings, although ambulatory measures of blood pressure or heart rate are available. Even these so-called 'objective' measures of stress are open to question, however, as some people may be more 'stress-responsive' or 'stress-reactive' than others (Felsten 2004; Johnston 2007) and thus, for example, the extent of heart-rate or blood-pressure increase seen in response to threat is not universal, due to genetic differences, variations in central nervous system activity (Lovallo 1997) or individual differences such as personality (appraisals and past experience, Lazarus 1999; see Chapter 12 ☞ for a review of such factors).

In spite of challenges of measurement, a vast amount of research is conducted in this field that acknowledges that since stress is a subjective experience, measuring it cannot be expected to be an exact science. As Kasl (1996: 21) stated: 'What we have, at best, are indirect and partial indicators of the stress process, and these indicators tend to measure both too much and not enough'. As an illustration of this, he refers to the perceived stress scale, which measures 'too much' in that it correlates significantly with depression and measures 'not enough' in that it does not assess secondary appraisal processes, emotions or indicators of physiological reactivity. As this chapter has shown, stress is by its very essence complex, and you will discover through your wider reading that many empirical research studies have acknowledged this by adopting multiple methods of assessment. This itself has costs, however, in terms of participant demands and so, often, studies will focus on only part of the picture.

The final challenge in the domain of stress research is that of establishing causality between stressful events and illness, ideally via immune or other physiological pathways. The concluding section of this chapter therefore describes some of the evidence that stress is associated with the development of illness.

described in some detail and the reader was introduced to common diseases associated with these bodily systems. This final section takes a closer look at the role of stress in activating these systems with resulting implications for the development of illness. First, however, it is worth reminding ourselves that there are different ways of viewing the relationship between stress and illness.

The stress and illness link

In Chapter 8 ☞, the workings of the nervous, respiratory, digestive, cardiovascular and immunological systems were

The direct route

As described above, stress can produce physiological changes that may lead to the development of illness, particularly in instances where the stress is chronic (Cacioppo *et al.* 1998; Johnston 2007; Smith *et al.* 2003). However, there is so much individual variation in responding to stressors that the direct route is not a straightforward one, as reviewed below.

The indirect routes

● People, by virtue of their behavioural responses to stress such as smoking, eating habits and drinking, predispose themselves to disease (see Chapter 3 ☞).

● People, by virtue of certain personality traits, predispose themselves to disease by the manner in which they respond to stress (see Chapter 12 ☞).

● People experiencing stress are more likely to use health services than people who are not under stress. Stress can produce symptoms such as anxiety, fatigue, insomnia and shakiness, which people seek treatment for but which are not in themselves illnesses (see Chapter 12 ☞).

However, we should bear in mind a quote of Sapolsky's while reading the next sections: 'everything bad in human health now is not caused by stress, nor is it in our power to cure ourselves of our worst medical nightmares merely by reducing stress and thinking healthy thoughts full of courage and spirit and love. Would it were so. And shame on those who sell this view' (1994).

There is a moderate relationship between stress and illness and we address a selected few of the many illnesses that have been found to have an association with stress below, with the psychosocial influences upon, or moderators of, the stress response being discussed in Chapter 12 ☞.

Stress and the common cold

Various researchers (Cohen *et al.* 1993a, 1993b; Cohen 2005; Stone *et al.* 1993) have conducted experiments where volunteers submit themselves to artificial exposure to respiratory rhinoviruses of the common cold (using nasal drops mainly). Participants then remain in a controlled environment for varying lengths of time while researchers wait to see whether colds or infections develop more often among those who received viral drops than among the control subjects, who received saline drops. Volunteers who had reported more chronic negative life events, perceived stress, negative affect and poor coping responses prior to the experiment were

more likely to develop signs of respiratory infection and subsequent colds than both control subjects and experimental subjects with low-level life stress. This is known as a dose-response relationship. In Cohen's studies perceived stress and negative affect predicted infection rates, whereas negative life events did not predict infection itself but predicted the probability of illness among those who became infected. These associations persisted when health behaviour such as smoking and alcohol consumption or personality variable such as self-esteem and introversion–extroversion were controlled for (Cohen *et al.* 2003). It also emerged that longer duration of the event was more likely to be followed by infection than severe but short-lived stress (Cohen *et al.* 1998).

Although the studies above were predominantly lab-based using artificially induced viruses, there is reasonably convincing evidence of a relationship between chronic stress (as opposed to severity) and upper respiratory infections – the common cold, and influenza (Marsland *et al.* 2002; Takkouche *et al.* 2001). Takkouche and colleagues importantly considered the naturally acquired common cold in a one-year prospective cohort study among the faculty and staff of a Spanish university (N = 1,149). Like the laboratory-based work before it, they found that the occurrence of stressful life events, perceived stress, and positive and negative affect were all related to the occurrence of common cold.

There is still some way to go before full understanding of how stress operates in real-life environments. Prospective studies with clinical populations facing 'natural' stressors will inevitably improve our understanding of the stress–immune function–illness link. While some evidence exists that stress-mediated physiological changes play a role in the initial onset of disease among healthy individuals (such as coronary heart disease), there is more evidence that stress experienced by 'ill' individuals can affect further progression of their symptoms or disease, as we describe below.

Stress and coronary heart disease

Coronary heart disease (CHD) is a disease of the **cardiovascular** system that develops over time in response to a

> **cardiovascular**
> pertaining to the heart and blood vessels.

range of factors, such as family history and lifestyle factors (e.g. smoking and diet; see Chapter 3 (☞). As described in Chapter 8, ☞ the cause of CHD is a gradual narrowing of blood vessels that supply the heart. In situations of acute stress, activation of the sympathetic nervous system causes increased cardiac output and the blood vessels to constrict, thus restricting blood flow, so blood pressure increases. This can cause damage to the artery walls, a process that is contributed to further by stress-induced adrenaline and noradrenaline output. If blood pressure remains raised for prolonged periods of time, a person is said to have hypertension, a contributory factor in CHD.

Repeated or chronic stress also activates the sympathetic nervous system's release of fatty acids into the bloodstream, which, if not utilised for energy expenditure, are metabolised by the liver into cholesterol. A build-up of cholesterol is highly implicated in the 'furring up' of arteries or atheroma (the laying down of fatty plaques on artery walls), and a key feature of heart disease is this atherosclerosis. Furthermore, the release of catecholamines during the stress process also increases the stickiness of blood platelets (thrombocytes), which elevates the risk of a clot forming or thrombosis as they adhere to the artery walls with the fatty plaques, thus making the 'passageway' narrower for blood to flow through. Inflammatory processes, involving pro-inflammatory cytokines such as IL-6 (interleukin-6), are also implicated in this process (see Chapter 12 in relation to hostility (☞). If reduced blood flow causes a clot to form, it could then travel through a person's arteries until it becomes so big as to form a blockage (occlusion) and, depending on whether it blocks an artery to the brain or to the heart, this will lead to either a stroke or a heart attack – both major causes of mortality worldwide (see Chapter 8 (☞). In terms of acute coronary syndromes such as heart attack and stroke, the evidence that stress plays a role in precipitating the event is good. For example, work and home stress, financial problems and past year major life events were significantly associated with heart attack in a huge cross-cultural, 52-country, study of more than 11,000 heart attack survivors and over 13,000 controls, the INTER-HEART study (Rosengren *et al.* 2004). In terms of processes by which this may be achieved, other studies have found that among those with pre-existing CVD, an acute stressor, for example an anger outburst, or a depressive episode, may trigger the rupture of atherosclerotic plaques, which disrupt blood flow and cause a heart attack or a stroke (Sheps 2007).

In terms of the development of CHD, stress does appear to contribute to various related conditions, such as hypertension, elevated serum lipids (fats in the blood) and smoking behaviour, an acknowledged risk factor (e.g. Ming *et al.* 2004). Cardiovascular reactivity during acute stress (i.e. the extent to which a stressor produces cardiac arousal such as increased heart rate or blood pressure) has been implicated in various disease processes, such as the extent and progression of carotid artery atherosclerosis, and the emergence of coronary heart disease itself (Smith *et al.* 2003). Reactivity, however, in itself is not 'disease', but a risk factor (Johnston 2007). Experimental studies of reactivity in response to aversive or rewarding stimuli have speculated that the individuals who responded to aversive tasks with sizeable heart-rate and blood-pressure increases (high reactives) but who showed no difference from controls in subjective ratings of the tasks, had greater activation of the hypothalamic system and neuroendocrine responses such as those described earlier. Indeed, high-reactive participants showed larger noradrenaline increases in response to both types of task than low-reactive participants, and larger cortisol increases to the aversive task but not to the reward task (Lovallo *et al.* 1990). This highlights the importance of considering the type of task. Also important is finding that effects persist outwith the artificial laboratory setting, as found, for example, by Johnston and colleagues (Johnston 2007). In this study laboratory-based reactivity was reflected in similar increases in heart-rate reactivity when individuals were exposed to the real-life stressor of public speaking. Furthermore, in relation to ongoing stress of an occupational nature, job strain was linked to progression of coronary atherosclerosis over a three-year period in a large sample of women employees (Wang *et al.* 2007). In another study, ambulatory blood pressure at work and at home (and even while asleep!) was significantly higher in workers with high job strain than in those with lower strain (Clays *et al.* 2007). It is worth noting that most research into the physical consequences of carer stress (see also Chapter 15 (☞) have examined the increased vulnerability to disease resulting from immune changes rather than actual disease development; however, raised levels of the pro-inflammatory cytokine Interleukin-6 found among caregivers is actually at a level considered a risk factor for cardiovascular disease (Kiecolt-Glaser *et al.* 2003).

The findings reviewed here point to a need to distinguish between the role stress plays in triggering or maintaining certain risk behaviours which provide the 'indirect' link with chronic manifestations of CHD, e.g. smoking and arterial disease; the role chronic stress plays in the activation of physiological risk factors and in progression of existing disease; and the role played perhaps by more acute stress events in the potentiating of acute coronary events, such as heart attacks (Johnston 2002, 2007; Strike and Steptoe 2005; Sheps 2007).

Speculation as to the role of stress in the development of actual disease has abounded for many years; for example, Rosch (1994), in an editorial in the journal *Stress Medicine*, pointed to the importance of distinguishing between causal factors and contributing factors when considering disease, arguing that the 'true cause' of any disease is biomedical and that behavioural or social factors such as smoking or stress are not 'true' causes but contributors. This conclusion has received some challenges from longitudinal research in the years since – with some evidence of a causal role for stress reactivity, inflammatory responses, and also negative emotions (depression primarily) in relation to acute coronary events and to CHD. For example, in the field of occupational stress Kuper and Marmot (2003) found, within a cohort of over 10,000 UK civil servants, that those with low decision latitude and high demands were at the highest risk of developing CHD over 11 years. However, an American study with a ten-year follow up found no association between job strain and CHD (Eaker *et al.* 2004). A review of studies (including those two referred to above) with long-term follow-ups ranging from 5 to almost 20 years (Byrne and Espnes 2008) suggests that overall findings are persuasive, but that more rigorous and prospective research is required.

Finally, just as reactivity can be considered as a 'psychophysiological trait' that is stable within any given individual across time and events, it can also be considered as a moderator, in that evidence suggests that being reactive or not will moderate any effect of stress upon disease risk: in other words, stress poses a greater threat to the health of high-reactive individuals than it does low-reactive individuals (Segerstrom and Smith 2006). Furthermore, as discussed in Chapter 12 ☛, stress reactivity can itself be influenced by other traits, such as anger, and therefore reactivity is considered within a broader personological model. However reactivity is considered, it is a factor that seems unwise to ignore, and perhaps we need also to extend our consideration of it to beyond the event/stimulus phase as described earlier. We know from many years of research that the mind and body interact, and if into this we add individual 'risk' or 'protective' behaviours (see Chapters 3–4 ☛), we can begin to understand the complexity of influences upon disease processes such as those subsumed under the broad heading of 'heart disease'.

Stress and cancer

Cancer, like heart disease, develops slowly and begins with mutation of cells and the development of generally undetectable neoplasms, which eventually develop into spreadable tumours (i.e. the cells metastasise). Predominantly animal research has demonstrated associations between environmental stressors (electric shocks, surgery) and increased susceptibility to tumour development; however, human evidence is limited. Forms of cancer vary hugely in terms of rates of growth, spread and prognosis; in terms of their sensitivity to neuroendocrine or immune system changes (Greer 1999), and in terms of available treatment options. Accordingly, it is perhaps unwise to expect stress to exert uniform effects, if any, on different forms of cancer and in fact the general consensus is that there is no clear link. For example a meta-analysis of 46 studies investigating the association between psychosocial factors, including life event stress, and the development of breast cancer concluded that life events were not predictive, but rather a combination of risk factors and psychosocial factors were (McKenna *et al.* 1999). This is consistent with findings of a meta-analysis specifically examining the predictive role of life events in breast cancer development (Petticrew *et al.* 1999).

However, studies have addressed whether stress plays any role in cancer progression or outcomes. Caution has been advised regarding overstating the role of the individual and their cognitions, emotions and stress or coping responses in cancer progression (Spiegel 1992); however, there is some evidence of direct and indirect effects. For example, stress may directly affect tumour cell mutation by slowing down the cell repair process, possibly by virtue of stress effects on hormonal activation and the release of glucocorticoids, or by influences on the immune system's production of lymphocytes (see Rosch 1996 for a review of both animal and human research). Furthermore, a review of 24 studies reported that 19 studies showed an association between depression and faster breast cancer progression (Spiegel and Giese-Davis 2003). Note therefore that 5 did not show an association. In terms of life events and progression, Palesh *et al.* (2007) presented data from 94 women with metastatic or recurrent breast cancer tumours and found that those with no retrospective reports of traumatic life events, or lesser stressful events, had a significantly longer disease-free interval than women with experience of traumatic events, or of stressful events (median of 62 months as compared to median of 31 months). The women who had experienced traumatic events, or lesser stressful events, did not significantly differ from those reporting no stress events, in terms of current age, age at diagnosis, medical history, relationship status, cortisol levels, site of metastases, and disease status indicators that may have offered alternative explanations for the findings. It is worth noting, however, that the reported events had not necessarily occurred in the intervening time period (i.e. between first diagnosis and recurrence) and therefore some had potentially played a role in the initial cancer. The authors had hypothesised that the mechanisms through which stress exerted any effect on recurrence was likely to relate to HPA function, yet cortisol did not differ between groups. However, this study is limited by its retrospective nature and in fact a five-year prospective study of women diagnosed with breast cancer found that recurrence was not increased in those who had experienced one or more extremely stressful events in the year prior to diagnosis or in the five years subsequently (Graham *et al.* 2002). This finding is perhaps more robust, given that their study involves a larger sample of women, is prospective in nature, and more clearly controls for biological prognostic indicators such as tumour size and the extent to which the cancer involved the lymph nodes.

Many other studies have explored whether personality, coping style (particularly one that is passive and indicative of helplessness and hopelessness) and mood affect cancer outcome (Walker *et al.* 1999; and see Spiegel 2001 for a brief discussion of the literature). These issues have provoked some controversy and are addressed more fully in Chapter 12. ☞

Stress and bowel disease

Two diseases of the bowel have been investigated in terms of their association with the experience of stress. In both, stress is examined as an exacerbating factor rather than one involved in the aetiology of the condition (see also Chapter 8 ☞). First, *irritable bowel syndrome* (IBS) is a disorder of the lower large intestine characterised by abdominal pain and prolonged periods of either diarrhoea or constipation, although no organic disease is identifiable.

Naliboff *et al.* (1998) noted that during stressful episodes, the reactivity of the gut is greater and symptoms such as bloatedness, pain or diarrhoea increase, and, more recently, Spence and Moss-Morris (2007) support the role of anxiety and/or stress in maintaining symptoms. A second bowel disease is *inflammatory bowel disease* (IBD), which can be subdivided into Crohn's disease (CD) and ulcerative colitis (UC). Both these diseases are typified by pain and diarrhoea, which worsen and improve in an alternating and disruptive manner, but UC typically involves inflammation of the lower colon, whereas CD can occur anywhere in the gastrointestinal tract and is seen as inflammation of the outer intestinal wall (☞ Chapter 8). Both diseases, as with IBS, were originally thought to be psychosomatic, with some limited evidence that stress plays a role in their aetiology. More likely, however, is that stress may exacerbate the condition. For example, Duffy *et al.* (1991) examined exposure to stressful events among 124 individuals with IBD and found that over a period of six months, those exposed to stress showed a two- to fourfold increase in clinical disease episodes compared with those participants who did not report stressful incidents. When disease-related and disease-unrelated events were distinguished (on the basis of patient report), the relationship between stress and illness was clearest when the reported events were health-related but not necessarily IBD-specific. However, when the authors examined the time lag between the event and disease activity (i.e. a stressful event preceding disease activity), they found that concurrent relationships were strongest and, in fact, disease activity was predictive of subsequent levels of stress rather than vice versa. Such bidirectional relationships between variables makes the disentangling of issues of cause and effect difficult, although other evidence of stress being associated with symptom 'flare-ups' does exist (Searle and Bennett 2001).

In addition, individual variation in stress-responsivity/ reactivity may explain mixed research findings. Illustrating this point, Dancey *et al.* (1998) used repeated measures of daily stress and daily symptomatology obtained from 31 IBS patients to examine the associations between stress and symptoms over time and found that only in half of the sample was an association evident between stress and the onset or exacerbation of symptoms. As described in Chapter 9 ☞, symptom perception and reactivity can also be influenced by personal characteristics of somatisation and attention to internal organs, features often associated with neuroticism.

Stress and HIV/AIDS

Over the past 25 or so years, AIDS has spread throughout the world to become a major cause of death in Africa and a leading cause of death elsewhere (see Chapter 3 ☞). AIDS (acquired immune deficiency syndrome) is a syndrome characterised by opportunistic infections and other malignant diseases, and until the HIV (human immunodeficiency virus) was identified in 1984, the cause of such immunosuppression was unclear. The nature of the HIV virus and how it infiltrates the body is described in Chapter 8 ☞, but, crucially, in terms of potential stress for the sufferer, as a lentivirus (i.e. slow-acting) it can be many years before an HIV-infected individual develops AIDS. As well as being life-threatening, the disease label itself can be psychologically stressful due to the continued social stigma attached to the disease (due primarily to its early associations with homosexuality, drug abuse and sexual promiscuity). Petrak *et al.* (2001) found that self-disclosure of HIV status to family (53 per cent of sample had told their family) and to friends (79 per cent had told close friends) was significantly influenced by wanting to protect others from distress and out of fear of discrimination. Living with this illness is inherently stressful, and although there is only limited suggestion that stress influences the likelihood of infection when exposed to the virus (Marks *et al.* 2000), there is evidence that stress plays an influential role in disease progression.

Evidence is particularly strong when moderating variables such as depression, social support and coping responses are taken into consideration. For example, a meta-analysis (Zorrilla *et al.* 1996) suggested that depressive symptoms, but not stress experience, were associated with increased speed of symptom onset in HIV-positive individuals, and that stress, but not depressive symptoms, was associated with reduced NK cell count. Similarly, progression to AIDS was found to be quicker in those experiencing a build-up of stressful life events, depressive symptoms and low social support (Leserman *et al.* 1999). Associations have been shown between baseline depression and a CD4+ cell decline (Burack *et al.* 1993) and in the same sample nine years later, faster progression to AIDS (Page-Shafer *et al.* 1996), and a meta-analysis of cognitive behavioural interventions targeting such negative emotions found benefits for individual immune status, (Crepaz *et al.* 2008) suggesting that progression could perhaps be slowed by appropriately targeted psychological intervention.

Finally, within this disease group, a sad reality is that many individuals will face the loss of a partner through AIDS, which itself has been found to impact upon disease progression over subsequent years (Kemeny *et al.* 1994). Social support, or lack or loss of it, is discussed in Chapter 12 ☞; however, social support in the form of providing care to a loved one is considered in Chapter 15 ☞.

SUMMARY

This chapter set out to provide a definition of stress and has shown that there is no such thing as a simple definition of this phenomenon. Stress is generally examined in one of three ways: as a stimulus that focuses on the external event (stressors); as a transaction between the external event and the individual experiencing it; and as an array of physiological responses that are manifested when an individual faces demanding events. The transactional psychological model of stress highlighted the crucial role of appraisal, and points to the importance of considering the individual in the stress experience. Many different events may be appraised as stressful, and stressor events can be acute or chronic in their manifestation and in the responses they require. Examples of these were presented, with particular emphasis on occupational stress, something that most of us will experience at some time. The physiological pathways by which stress has been shown to affect health status were examined, and these processes were explored further in relation to evidence (or not) of their direct role in diseases such as coronary heart disease and cancer. While some evidence of a direct effect of stress on the development of illness exists, many of stress's effects are either indirect, for example via an influence on behaviour, or are more evident during the illness experience, when individual differences in personality, cognitions and social resources become important to outcome. These moderating variables are the focus of the next chapter.

Further reading

Key texts

Sapolsky, R.M. (2002). *Why Zebras Don't Get Ulcers*. New York: Henry Holt & Co.

Although dated in terms of empirical material covered, this is a well-written and engaging book with excellent coverage of both physiological and psychological theories of stress. You will, however, need to supplement reading of this book with reading of up-to-date empirical studies such as those referred to in this chapter!

Vedhara, K. and Irwin, M. (eds) (2005). *Human Psychoneuroimmunology*. Oxford: Oxford University Press.

In this rapidly developing area of understanding, this remains an excellent resource for those interested in past and current thinking in pschoneuroimmunology.

Ader, R. (2007). *Psychoneuroimmunology*, 4th edn. New York: Academic Press.

This is an essential read for any student wanting to get to grips with the fundamental science of psychoneuroimmunology (the processes, mechanisms and effects of behavioural, neural, endocrine and immune responses) while not getting put off by hard-core biological language. Written for an interdisciplinary audience including behavioural scientists, psychobiologists, neuroscientists and immunologists, this book is an accessible and well-informed review of the current state of knowledge.

Key articles

Lazarus, R.S. (1993). From psychological stress to the emotions: a history of changing outlooks. *Annual Review of Psychology*, 44: 1–21.

This article provides a useful account of the transactional model of stress and the developments in thinking about appraisal in terms of relations with emotions. Although from the 1990s, this remains a key theoretical paper.

Byrne, D.G. and Espnes, G.A. (2008). Occupational stress and cardiovascular disease. *Stress & Health*, 24: 231–8.

This review paper is found in a special issue addressing 'Stress and the Heart'. This paper reviews evidence of the role played by work stress and coronary risk, hypertension and heart disease and concludes that 'Taken broadly, the evidence is supportive of postulated links', although further prospective evidence would be welcome.

Graham, J.E., Christian, L.M., Segestrom, S.C. and Miller, G.E. (2004). Psychological stress and the human immune system: a meta-analytic study of 30 years of enquiry. *Psychological Bulletin*, 130: 601–30.

This paper brings together the data of many studies in a meta-analysis which shows substantial empirical support for the relationship between stress, particularly chronic stress, and decreased immune function.

Kiecolt-Glaser, J.K. (2006). Stress, age and immune function: toward a lifespan approach. *Journal of Behavioral Medicine*, 29: 389–400.

This well-written paper catalogues the key findings relating to the relationship between age and immune function, stress and immune function (considering both acute and chronic stressors), and the interaction between stress, age and the immune function, with a particular, but not exclusive, focus on older adults.

The International Labour Organization website:

www.ilo.org/public/english/protection/safework/stress/nursing.htm

Provides access to a wealth of global materials regarding occupational stress. The link above takes you specifically to details of a manual on stress prevention which was commissioned by the ILO specifically to consider nursing stress. The full report can be ordered via this website and is referenced below:

Cox, T., Griffith, A. and Cox, S. (1996). Work-related stress in nursing: controlling the risk to health. CONDIT/T/WP 4/1996, available from ILO as detailed above.

Visit the website at **www.pearsoned.co.uk/morrison** for additional resources to help you with your study, including multiple choice questions, weblinks and flashcards.

Chapter 12
Stress and illness moderators

Learning outcomes

By the end of this chapter, you should have an understanding of:

- coping theory, definitions and the distinction between coping styles, coping strategies, and coping goals

- how coping responses influence the manner in which stress may affect health outcomes

- aspects of personality, such as conscientiousness, neuroticism, hostility and optimism, which influence stress appraisal, coping response and illness outcomes

- aspects of individual cognitions, such as personal control, efficacy and hope, which influence stress appraisal, coping response and illness outcomes

- aspects of emotion, such as depression and emotional expression, which influence stress appraisal, coping response and illness outcomes

- the nature and function of social support and how it influences stress appraisal, coping responses and illness outcomes

The search for happiness

At an individual level, most of us would confess to a desire to be happy. Even the UK government seems to be looking for it, or wanting to measure it in all of us – even if they can't perhaps take much credit for creating it! In November 2010 the UK government announced that until April 2011 a consultation led by the Office of National Statistics will consider what is important in our lives that creates psychological (and environmental) well-being or happiness. The idea is that the next General Household Survey, a national survey which generates statistics used to help inform government policy, will assess well-being and possibly illustrate that economic growth is not necessarily in a direct and linear relationship with a population's well-being (by implication the powers that be can then perhaps be forgiven the economic crisis, asserting that crisis does not inevitably create unhappiness). It is intended that the nation's well-being 'scores' will be used to inform planning and policy in conjunction with more traditional, and more objective, social and economic indicators that highlight social inequalities. This proposal has elicited many critics who consider socio-economic indicators more valid, and critics observe that happiness is a complex and multidimensional concept which may be impossible to measure in any meaningful way at such a 'mass' level. While final decisions are yet to be taken on how this construct will be assessed and how it will be used, it has stimulated much debate. Through describing factors that influence how we respond to external or internal events (potential stressors), this chapter will hopefully illustrate that individual variation in personality, emotion, cognition and coping, as well as in social relationships and resources, are all likely contributors to outcomes such as well-being or happiness, and that nothing is quite as simplistic as perhaps some would like to believe!

Chapter outline

The preceding chapter established that stress can be considered as both an objective and subjective experience, and evidence was provided as to physiological and immunological pathways by which stress may influence health and illness status. However, not all people will become ill when exposed to stressful events, which raises questions of great fascination to health psychologists. What aspects of the individual, their stress responses, or their stress-coping resources moderate or influence the negative impact of stress on health? This chapter will present evidence of psychosocial factors crucial to stress appraisals, responses and outcomes. Individual differences in personality, cognitions and emotions (both positive and negative) have direct and indirect effects on stress outcomes. Indirectly, such factors affect outcome via their influence upon cognitive and behavioural responses to stressful demands placed on us – these efforts are known as coping. In addition, aspects of social relationships and social support act as external resource variables, which directly and indirectly influence the negative impact of stress. Evidence as to the direct and/or moderating role of such variables will be presented and their importance examined. By the end of the chapter, the complexities of the relationship between stress, health and illness should be clear.

In Chapter 11 ☛ we described stress theories, acute and chronic stressors and the broad theoretical links between stress and disease. We also presented evidence relating to direct pathways by which physiological and immune processes affect the stress–disease relationship. As there is so much individual variation in responding to stressors, this chapter focuses more on the indirect routes introduced in Chapter 11 ☛, i.e. how different personalities, beliefs and emotions influence the stress–illness relationship, either directly, or via an effect on cognitive and behavioural coping responses.

It is unlikely that anyone can avoid stress and, certainly, as indicated previously, some stress is good

for us in that it enhances performance (eustress e.g. Gibbons *et al.* 2008). However, stress is more commonly considered as negative appraisals and negative emotions, which elicit a desire to reduce such thoughts and feelings in order to restore a sense of harmony or balance in our lives. Lazarus's transactional model of stress and coping (Lazarus 1966; Lazarus and Folkman 1984) was introduced in the previous chapter and highlights the crucial role of appraisal of events. Individual differences in appraisal in turn influences the cognitive, emotional and behavioural response to them, i.e. the coping response. What exactly do we mean by coping?

Coping defined

Although over thirty definitions of coping exist, Lazarus's transactional model (see Figure 11.1) has had the most profound impact on the conceptualisation of coping (cf. Lazarus 1993a, 1993b; Lazarus and Folkman 1984). According to this model, psychological stress results from an unfavourable person–environment fit: in other words when there is a perceived mismatch between demands and resources as perceived by an individual in a specific situation (Lazarus and Folkman 1984; Lazarus 1993a). Individuals are required to alter either the stressor or how they interpret it in order to make it appear more favourable. This effort is called coping.

Coping involves a constellation of cognitions and behaviour that arise from the primary and secondary appraisals of events, and the emotions attached to them (see Chapter 11 ☛). Coping is *anything* a person does to reduce the impact of a perceived or actual stressor, and because appraisals elicit emotions, coping can operate to either alter or reduce the negative emotions, or it can directly target the 'objective' stressor. Coping does not inevitably succeed in eliminating the stressor, but it may manage the stressor by various means, for example through mastering new skills to deal with it, tolerating it, reappraising it or minimising it. The goal of coping therefore is to try to achieve adaptation, and it is consequently a dynamic, learned (we hopefully learn from past coping succeses and failures) and purposeful process.

Cohen and Lazarus (1979) described five main coping functions, each of which contribute to successful adaptation to a stressor:

1. reducing harmful external conditions;

2. tolerating or adjusting to negative events;

3. maintaining a positive self-image;

4. maintaining emotional equilibrium and decreasing emotional stress;

5. maintaining a satisfactory relationship with the environment or with others.

Coping responses may succeed in one or more of these goals, but adaptation may not necessarily be long-lived, depending upon the context and the nature of the stressor. It is unlikely that any person would cope with influenza in the same way as they would a diagnosis of cancer, or would cope with failing a driving test the second time in the same way as they coped with failing the first time.

Coping can be cognitive or behavioural, active or passive, with many different, often overlapping, terms being used in the coping literature. Two of the main coping taxonomies are summarised in Table 12.1: firstly those which differentiate between problem-focused and emotion-focused coping (cf. Folkman and Lazarus 1980, 1985); and secondly those which distinguish between approach-oriented coping and avoidance (cf. Roth and

Table 12.1 Coping dimensions

---

1. **Problem-focused coping (problem-solving function)**, i.e. instrumental coping efforts (cognitive and/or behavioural) directed at the stressor in order to either reduce the demands of it or increase one's resources. Strategies include: planning how to change the stressor or how to behave in order to control it; suppressing competing activities in order to focus on ways of dealing with the stressor; seeking practical or informational support in order to alter the stressor; confronting the source of stress; or showing restraint.

Versus

Emotion-focused coping (emotion-regulating function), i.e. mainly, but not solely, cognitive coping efforts directed at managing the emotional response to the stressor: for example, positively reappraising the stressor in order to see it in a more positive light; acceptance; seeking emotional support; venting anger; praying.

2. **Attentional/approach, monitoring, vigilant, active**, i.e. concerned with attending to the source of stress and trying to deal with the problem by, for example, seeking information about it, or making active cognitive or behavioural efforts to manage the stressor (see also coping styles).

Versus

Avoidant, blunting, passive, i.e. concerned with avoiding or minimising the threat of the stressor; sometimes emotion-focused, sometimes involves avoiding the actual situation: for example, distraction by thinking of pleasant thoughts or distraction by engaging in other activities to keep one's mind off the stressor; disengagement through substance use.

Cohen 1986; Suls and Fletcher 1985). Within each of the broad dimensions described in Table 12.1 are a variety of coping subscales, generally derived from factor analysis of a large number of coping items in an attempt to identify statistically meaningful 'clusters' of items that can then be used in a new measurement scale. Folkman and Lazarus (1988), in the popular Ways of Coping scale, distinguish eight subscales that address the two dimensions of problem-focused and emotion-focused coping: confrontive coping, distancing, self-controlling, seeking social support, accepting responsibility, escape–avoidance, planned problem solving and positive reappraisal. Carver and colleagues (1989) distinguish 13, and subsequently 15, subscales: planning, active coping, suppressing competing activities, acceptance, turning to religion, venting emotions, seeking instrumental support, seeking emotional support, humour, positive reinterpretation, restraint coping, denial, mental disengagement, behavioural disengagement, alcohol or drug use (COPE scale). In contrast, Endler and colleagues (Endler and Parker 1993; Endler *et al.* 1998) assess across three dimensions: *emotion-oriented* (person-oriented strategies such as daydreaming, emotional response or self-preoccupation); *task-oriented* (strategies to solve, minimise or reconceptualise the problem) and *avoidance-oriented* (includes distraction or social diversion (CISS scale). Krohne (1993) described vigilance and cognitive avoidance as two coping 'superstrategies' which he considered were orthogonal dimensions of attention orientation and likely to reflect underlying personality, therefore being indicative of a coping 'style' as opposed to situational specific coping 'strategies'

Coping styles or strategies

Coping styles are generally considered as unrelated to the specific context or stressor stimulus; instead, they are trait-like forms of coping that people have a tendency to adopt when facing a potentially difficult situation. If you think about your own behaviour you will probably know whether you tend to duck and avoid stressors or whether you face them head-on! One example of a coping style dimension is that of 'monitoring versus blunting' (Miller 1987; Miller *et al.* 1987). Monitoring reflects an approach style of coping, where threat-relevant information is sought out and processed, for example asking about treatments and side-effects, or seeking information about forthcoming exam content. Blunting reflects a

general tendency to avoid or distract oneself from threat-relevant information, such as by sleeping or daydreaming, or engaging in other activities to avoid thinking about forthcoming exams. Van Zuuren and Dooper (1999) examined the relationship between monitoring and blunting coping styles and engagement in disease detection (e.g. attending doctor if frequently feeling tired, having blood pressure checked) and preventive behaviour (e.g. eating low-fat diet, exercising regularly). Monitoring was modestly, but significantly, associated with both detection and preventive behaviour, and individuals with a dominant blunting style were less likely to engage in protective behaviour than those where blunting was less dominant. In contrast, among a sample of women with cancer, monitoring was associated with negative responses of increased feelings of vulnerability and elevated distress, and the authors propose that this tendency to scan for and amplify threatening cues can be counter-productive (Miller *et al.* 1999). The conflicting outcomes of a monitoring style of coping shown by these two studies highlights the importance of context – a person's coping style may not 'fit' the situation and as a result may be counter-adaptive. This is where the adoption of situation-specific coping strategies is important.

Coping strategies (see Table 12.1 for examples of commonly employed coping subscales) derive from an approach that considers stress and coping as a dynamic process that varies according to context, event and the person's personal resources, mood, and so on (see Figure 12.1). Coping at any one time might include a range of seemingly oppositional strategies. For example, Lowe *et al.* (2000) found that in the months following a heart attack, people used both passive coping (e.g. acceptance, positive reappraisal) and active, **problem-focused coping** simultaneously. In a similar vein, Macrodimitris and Endler (2001) found that a combination of instrumental and distraction coping strategies were employed by people with diabetes. Also, in a rarely studied population of those aged over 85 years old living in the community (i.e. not in institutions), Johnson and Barer (1997) found that both acceptance of change (in oneself cf. dependency) as well as disengagement from stressful roles, were common.

> **problem-focused coping**
> a style of coping that involves active planning and dealing with any source of stress.

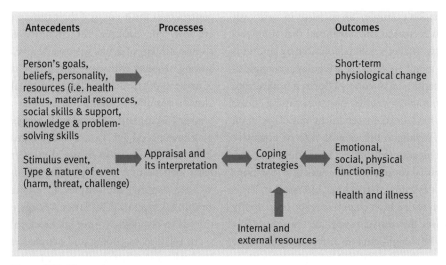

Figure 12.1 The coping process

Source: adapted from Lazarus (1999: 198).

This study also highlighted that for the oldest-old, giving up some control was beneficial, whereas this is not the case in studies of the younger-old where fighting to retain aspects of self and independence alive are common (Rothermund and Brandstädter 2003). There is some evidence that individual differences in aspects of personality influence the extent to which people are flexible in their choice of coping strategy (see later section).

While coping research in the field of health psychology more commonly assesses coping strategies than styles, the two approaches can be addressed simultaneously. For example, studies adopting repeated assessment periods can examine the nature and consistency of coping strategies over time, with consistent use of specific strategies suggesting a 'style' of coping (e.g. Tennen *et al.* 2000). Other studies can explore explicit associations between aspects of trait personality and specific coping responses (for example, the effects of neuroticism and extroversion, see D. Watson *et al.* 1999) or of optimism (e.g. Carver and Scheier 2005) on coping. These issues are addressed later in this chapter.

What is adaptive coping?

Lazarus's model of coping suggests that it is hard to predict which coping strategies will be effective in which situations, as both problem-focused and emotion-focused strategies are interdependent and work together to create the overall coping response in any situation (Lazarus

> ### WHAT DO YOU THINK?
>
> Everyone experiences stress at some point in their lives. Think of a recent stressful experience you have faced. What strategies did you adopt in order to deal with this event and what were you hoping to achieve through the use of these strategies? Would you describe some of the strategies you adopted as 'problem-focused' and others as 'emotion-focused'? Did they coexist? Did different strategies have different intended goals and, if so, which were effective and which were not?
>
> In revisiting that experience, can you think of anything in your personal background, your character or outlook on life that influenced how you responded to that event? Keep the experience you have just been thinking about in mind as you continue reading this chapter and consider whether any of the influences on stress and coping that we describe are relevant to how you dealt with that event in particular, or with stress generally.

1993b). Tennen *et al.* (2000) confirmed this in an impressive longitudinal study of pain patients where daily measures of coping were taken. They found that emotion-focused coping strategies were 4.4 times more likely to be used on a day when problem-focused strategies were also used than on days where problem-focused strategies were not used. They also report that day-to-day pain symptomatology influenced the coping strategies used on a daily basis; for example, 'an increase in pain over yesterday's pain increased the likelihood that problem-focused coping yesterday would be followed by emotion-focused coping today' (p. 632). This highlights the role of appraisal and reappraisal of coping efforts: modifications are made depending on whether previous coping efforts are thought to have been successful or not. Troy *et al.* (2010) further highlight the critical role of cognitive reappraisal as a means of emotional regulation, i.e. regulating the emotional coping that often exists in situations of high stress. They found that at high, but not low, levels of stress, women with a high cognitive reappraisal ability experienced fewer depressive symptoms than those low in this ability. This highlights an individual difference factor that may explain why in highly stressful situations some people appear to adjust emotionally better than others (see later section for further discussion of such (di)stress moderators).

Coping is highly contextual – to be effective it has to be amenable to change (see Figure 11.1 in the previous chapter, where there are arrows feeding back from coping to (re)appraisal, and also Figure 12.1). If the stressor event is starting a new job and this is eliciting anxiety, coping can either deal with the 'job' (make contacts with new colleagues, research the company and its products), or it can deal with the anxiety (engage in meditation, talk with a friend, get drunk). The person may in fact do all the above and thus it should not be assumed that coping in a way which addresses the problem directly (researching the new role) is inherently more adaptive than coping which does not (getting drunk). Maintaining distinctions between emotion-focused and problem-focused coping is sometimes difficult, as movement between them is ever-present.

Generally, it is considered that problem-focused or attentional coping is more likely to be adaptive when there is something that can be done to alter or control the stressor event. Focusing one's thoughts on aspects of the situation and planning how to deal with each would be an example of a cognitive problem-focused coping strategy, whereas seeking helpful information about the event would be a behavioural problem-focused coping strategy. Individuals who are typically problem-focused, vigilant or attentional in their coping with stress may find that in some circumstances this is counter-productive. When facing life-changing surgery for example, or on receipt of a diagnosis of a life-threatening illness, emotion-focused coping may be more adaptive (Lazarus and deLongis 1983) if, in such events, the individual has little control over the event or if their resources to deal with it are low. For example, the cognitive emotion-focused coping strategy of denial was an effective coping response among women with a recent breast cancer diagnosis (Carver *et al.* 1993; Greer *et al.* 1990) although, among Greer's sample, ongoing denial was associated with poorer 15-year survival outcomes, suggesting that denial may have a good 'fit' (Lazarus and Folkman 1984; Lazarus 1999) to the situation in the short term but not long term. Behavioural examples of emotion-focused coping include venting and displaying emotion, or seeking emotional support. This latter strategy is generally considered to be adaptive – see later section.

In relation to coping and adaptation, Stanton *et al.* (2000) have pointed out that emotions can have adaptive coping functions rather than disruptive functions (as often implied in the emotion-focused coping distinction). In a series of studies, they examined 'emotional-approach coping' and distinguished between 'emotional processing' (active attempts to understand the emotions experienced) and 'emotional expression'. Both forms of coping associated with indicators of positive psychological adjustment (see later section on emotional expression). In support of this, emotion-focused coping is shown to be adaptive, for example positive reappraisal of one's responses to an event (e.g. 'It could have been worse, at least I did my best') can elicit positive emotion (e.g. pride, satisfaction) (Fredrickson 1998; Folkman and Moskowitz 2004).

One psychological coping response known as 'fighting spirit' (e.g. 'I am determined to beat this disease') was in early studies found to be associated with improved outcomes and long-term survival among breast cancer patients (Greer *et al.* 1979; Greer *et al.* 1990). In contrast, feelings of hopelessness and helplessness (e.g. 'I feel there is nothing I can do to help myself') were associated with poorer survival among this same population (M. Watson *et al.* 1999a) and among stroke patients (Lewis *et al.* 2001). These coping responses of fighting spirit and helplessness differentially associated with either active, problem-focused or passive, **avoidant coping** behaviour.

> **avoidant coping**
>
> a style of coping that involves emotional regulation by avoiding confrontation with a stressful situation. Analagous to emotion-focused coping.

Fighting spirit was thought to reflect a kind of realistic optimism and determination, with people high in fighting spirit facing illness head-on rather than avoiding it (Spiegel 2001). These early findings elicited hope for interventions that could enhance disease outcomes by targeting such attitudes and coping responses, for example increasing fighting spirit while decreasing feelings of helplessness. However, a review and meta-analysis of 26 studies investigating the effects of fighting spirit or hopelessness/helplessness and cancer survival or recurrence concluded that many of the reported predictive associations between these variables were limited by restricted sample sizes or poor methodological quality of the studies (Petticrew *et al.* 2002). Furthermore, a subsequent study involving a ten-year follow-up of 578 women with early-stage breast cancer conducted by the original research team also failed to replicate long-term predictive associations for fighting spirit, although helpless/hopelessness coping remained predictive of survival outcome (Watson *et al.* 2005).

Finally, in relation to forms of coping, Folkman and Moskowitch describe what they call a 'previously unaddressed aspects of coping', that of *meaning-focused coping*. This is typified by coping strategies which draw on a person's values and beliefs and encompasses goal revision, reordering priorities and focusing on strengths in order to obtain personal and possibly existential meaning within a negative and stressful situation (Park and Folkman 1997). Meaning-focused coping is thought to regulate the experience of positive emotion, such as hope (Folkman 2010) and is akin to the growing literature on benefit-finding and growth (see Chapter 14 ☞, and also Helgeson *et al.* 2006).

Coping goals

Coping intentions or goals (cf. Cohen and Lazarus 1979 (see earlier); Laux and Weber 1991) are likely to influence the coping strategies employed in any given situation and their likely success. Few studies have explicitly addressed goals (such as a desire to return to 'normalcy' after a trauma or illness) in relation to the specific strategies which are selected in an attempt to achieve that goal.

Why do people choose to cope in the way that they do? The reason for selecting one (or more) strategy to deal with a perceived stressor is related to past experience with that coping response, but more importantly it is related to the anticipated outcomes of that coping response, i.e. coping is a purposeful or motivational process (Lazarus 1993b). The general purpose or goal of coping, i.e. to manage a situation so as to make it less distressing, brings with it an inherent need to maintain one's self-esteem and self-image, and to maintain good relations with others. To illustrate this, a study of arguments between married couples found that anger and attack coping responses arose when one or the other party felt that their self-esteem was under threat and their coping goal was therefore one of self-defence. In contrast, when couples were in a situation where there was a shared anxiety about some external event, anger was more often suppressed and supportive forms of coping used instead, as the goal in such instances was that of resolving shared concerns (Laux and Weber 1991).

As Coyne and Racioppo note (2000: 658) 'Coping checklist research has paid scant attention to differences in goals and agendas across situations and persons, and coping effectiveness cannot be evaluated without attention to these considerations.' In other words, unless we know 'why' a person choses to cope in a particular way in terms of what they hoped to achieve – reduced distress, more support, less pain etc., etc. – we cannot tell whether or not that particular coping strategy has been effective. People use different coping strategies, often simultaneously, perhaps because each one is aiming for a different goal and some goals may be short-term (e.g. reduce pain) and others may be longer-term (e.g. to manage to walk independently). More research needs to assess coping goals if we are to progress our understanding of coping and how and why it changes over time. Furthermore, if coping interventions are to succeed, the practitioners need to know what the participants' coping goals are in order that the intervention can be appropriately targeted.

Stress, personality and illness

What is personality? Personality can be defined as the 'dynamic organization within the individual of those psychophysical systems that determine his characteristic behavior and thought' (Allport 1961: 28). This definition reflects a trait approach to personality (see also Chapter Five), which considers a person's personality profile in terms of stable and enduring dimensions such as sensitivity, conscientiousness or neuroticism. Eysenck (1970) argued for two dimensions, neuroticism and extroversion, with psychoticism added at a later stage; however, the theory adopted most widely in health psychology is the Big Five theory which, as its name suggests, conceptualises and assesses personality using five dimensions (Costa and McCrae 1992a, 1992b):

- agreeableness, i.e. cooperative;
- conscientiousness, i.e. responsible;
- extroversion, i.e. sociable;
- neuroticism, i.e. tense, anxious;
- openness, i.e. imaginative, open to new experiences.

Each of these factors has been considered as a set of traits that enable both individuals and groups to adapt to demands of life, and many associations between these relatively stable personality traits, stress, coping and health outcomes have been reported (see Vollrath 2006; Semmer 2006 for more detailed reviews).

Personality traits provide a helpful means for us to typify behaviour patterns, with clusters of traits often providing 'typologies'; for example, an extroverted 'type' of person will generally exhibit sociable, adventurous and impulsive traits, while a psychotic 'type' will exhibit egocentric, aggressive, cold and impulsive characteristics (Eysenck 1982). Note that impulsivity features in both 'types', yet overall the two types differ in terms of clustered traits.

There are various possible models of association between personality variables and health and illness that have differing degrees of 'directness':

- Personality may promote unhealthy behaviour predictive of disease (e.g. smoking), thereby having an indirect effect on disease risk (see Chapter 5 ☞).

- General aspects of personality may influence the manner in which an individual appraises or copes with stress or illness events (e.g. pessimistic individuals may not use social support effectively), thereby having an indirect effect on illness progression or outcomes.

- Personality may simply be predictive of disease onset (e.g. Friedman and Booth-Kewley 1987). This is the notion of a generic 'disease-prone personality' which underpins the psychosomatic tradition.

- Specific clusters of personality traits may predispose to specific illnesses (e.g. Type A behaviour pattern and heart disease, Type C and cancer, see later section).

One likely route of such effects is physiological: for example, angry personalities may be more physiologically stress-reactive (see Chapter 11 ☞). Thus this route is also indirect.

Studies employing five-factor models have found that each has differential associations with health behaviour (e.g. Booth-Kewley and Vickers 1994; Goldberg and Strycker 2002; Nicholson *et al.* 2005; Terraciano and Costa 2004), symptom perception (Feldman *et al.* 1999; Cameron and Leventhal 2003), coping (e.g. David and Suls 1996; Cooper *et al.* 2000) and illness behaviour (e.g. Korotkov and Hannah 2004).

Neuroticism and negative affectivity

As one of the three personality dimensions identified by Eysenck (1982), and one of the 'Big Five', it is not perhaps surprising that neuroticism (N) has received the most research attention in relation to illness. Neuroticism is considered a trait which is relatively unchangeable and is a broad dimension characterised by the tendency to experience negative emotions and to exhibit associated beliefs and behaviours (Costa and McCrae 1987; McCrae 1990). Individuals high on neuroticism often display anxious beliefs and behaviour disproportionate to the situation (Suls and Martin 2005, and see also Chapter 9 ☞ in terms of attention to internal states and increased somatic complaints). In trying to explain this, it has been suggested that neurotics by virtue of their character become exposed to more negative stressors (Suls and Martin 2005). It is hard to address this and to disentangle actual events from subjective reports of events as most studies rely on self-report; it may in fact be an appraisal or reporting bias of those high in neuroticism. In terms of responding to events appraised as stressful, research has suggested that neurotic individuals employ more different types of coping strategies (perhaps searching for one that works) and that these tend to be maladaptive and emotion-focused coping strategies (see Semmer 2006).

Related to neuroticism is a pervasive trait known as negative affectivity (NA), proposed by Watson and Clark (1984) to play a central role in the stress–health relationship. High-NA individuals are characterised by a generalised negative outlook, greater introspection, low affect (mood) and low self-concept. In studies of a range of adult samples, NA was also found to be associated with lower self-rated health, greater health complaints, but generally not with objective ill-health indicators (Cohen *et al.* 1995; Watson and Pennebaker 1989; Evers *et al.* 2003). However, in terms of the ultimate health indicator – death – this was predicted by neuroticism in a 21-year prospective cohort of 5,424 UK adults, specifically death from cardiovascular diseases, even when controlling for known risk factors (Shipley *et al.* 2007). This effect was found to be partially mediated by sociodemographic, health behaviour and physiological factors, and lessened when mood state was considered, reflecting the close association between N and mood.

In the absence of understanding of the mechanisms by which N and NA affect outcomes, these variables have been described as 'nuisance factors' (Watson and Pennebaker 1989: 248) which make it necessary for researchers to interpret self-reported outcomes of health complaints, stress or distress, with caution, as the relationship 'found' between stress and illness may be inflated by reporting bias of participants high in N/NA. However, there is some evidence that neuroticism and NA contribute to immune suppression. For example, NA has been associated with cortisol production (e.g. van Eck *et al.* 1996); and neuroticism associated with interleukin-6 (Il-6) in older samples (implicated in depression also) (e.g. Bouhuys *et al.* 2004). Given that stress has also been shown to have immune effects as we have described in Chapter 11 ☞, it may be that personality adds to this already negative relationship.

Conscientiousness and the other Big Five traits

Conscientiousness, defined as being of a responsible and dependable character, following social norms, having foresight, being persistent and self-disciplined, has shown a consistent relationship to positive health outcomes, including longevity, in the relatively small number of studies which have assessed it (relative to neuroticism). A meta-analysis of 20 independent samples, representing child samples, middle-aged samples, as well as those with chronic disease, found a modest, but nonetheless significant correlation of 0. 11 between this trait and longevity (Kern and Friedman 2008). Two studies of centenarians also find conscientiousness to be protective (Masui *et al.* 2006; Martin *et al.* 2006). This general effect across a range of samples and cultures is therefore notable and

may be attributable to findings of fairly robust associations between conscientiousness and positive health behaviours (e.g. Bogg and Roberts 2004; Nicholson *et al.* 2005; Paunonen and Ashton 2001; Terraciano and Costa 2004; see Chapter 15 ☞). In responding to stress, those high in conscientiousness have been shown to use problem-focused coping (Bartley and Roesch 2011) and their characteristic persistence is considered beneficial to self-regulatory efforts such as when trying to control one's response to stress (Hagger *et al.* 2010; Soldberg Nes *et al.* 2011).

It has also been suggested that while extraversion and neuroticism are more closely associated with emotional well-being (e.g. happiness), conscientiousness is more closely aligned to cognitive and evaluative aspects of well-being (e.g. satisfaction) (De Neve and Cooper 1998; Hayes and Joseph 2003). Of the other 'Big Five' personality traits, agreeableness is generally considered adaptive in terms of flexible coping response to stressors, and extraversion has been found to be positive in some regards, e.g. appraisal, active coping, and emotional well-being (Hayes and Joseph 2003), but less so in relation to exposure to health-risk behaviours, given their tendency to seek stimulation (see Chapter 5 ☞). Extraversion has also emerged as protective for mortality generally among centenarians (Masui *et al.* 2006; Martin *et al.* 2006) and also for specifically respiratory-disease-related death (Shipley *et al.* 2007), possibly explained by enhanced immune function by way of increased Natural Killer cells (Bouhuys *et al.* 2004). These positive effects contradict associations with risk behaviours such as smoking (see Chapter 3 ☞); however, it is worth noting that Shipley's study controlled for such risk factors, and therefore the mechanism through which extraversion operates, remains unclear.

Besides the Big Five, other personality traits have been identified that have 'general' positive effects on stress responses and health, and we turn attention now to these 'personal resource' variables.

Optimism

One 'protective' resource is that of dispositional optimism, i.e. having a generally positive outlook and positive outcome expectations. Scheier and colleagues (Scheier *et al.* 1986; Scheier and Carver 1992) proposed that dispositional optimists are predisposed towards believing that desired outcomes are possible, and that this motivates

Table 12.2 Measuring optimism: the life orientation test

Please be as honest and accurate as you can be throughout. Try not to let your response to one statement influence your responses to other statements. There are no 'correct' or 'incorrect' answers. Answer according to your *own* feelings rather than how you think 'most people' would answer. Using the scale below, write the appropriate letter in the box beside each statement.

	A I agree a lot	B I agree a little	C I neither agree nor disagree	D I disagree a little	E I disagree a lot
1. In uncertain times, I usually expect the best					☐
2. It's easy for me to relax*					☐
3. If something can go wrong for me, it will					☐
4. I always look on the bright side					☐
5. I'm always optimistic about my future					☐
6. I enjoy my friends a lot*					☐
7. It's important for me to keep busy*					☐
8. I hardly ever expect things to go my way					☐
9. Things never work out the way I want them to					☐
10. I don't get upset easily*					☐
11. I'm a believer in the idea that 'every cloud has a silver lining'					☐
12. I rarely count on good things happening to me*					☐

*These are 'filter' items, which have the function of disguising the focus of the test.

optimistic individuals to cope more effectively and persistently with stress or illness events, thus reducing their risk of negative outcomes. Dispositionally optimistic persons are less likely to make internal ('It is my fault'), stable ('It is an aspect of my personality that I cannot change') and global attributions for negative events: i.e. they are more likely to appraise stress as changeable and specific and coming from external sources that are potentially more changeable or ignorable than internal ones. Pessimism, on the other hand, is a generalised negative outlook associated with denial and distancing responses to stress. Pessimism among cancer patients, for example, was found to have independent effects to optimism and was associated with mortality among younger patients even when controlling for the related construct of depression (Schulz *et al.* 1996).

In a meta-analysis of studies using the life orientation test (the measure of optimism developed by Scheier and Carver 1985; see Table 12.2), Andersson (1996) reports that optimism was significantly associated with active coping, with reduced symptom reporting and with reduced negative mood or depression, with this latter relationship being strongest. This has been confirmed more recently in another meta-analysis where a positive association with approach type coping and a negative association with avoidance type coping was confirmed (Solberg Nes and Segestrom, 2006). Optimism was

found to have benefits for both healthy populations dealing with stressful events (e.g. Steptoe *et al.* 2008) and patient populations dealing with various aspects of their illness (e.g. Fournier *et al.* 2002).

It is thought that optimism promotes better functioning and outcomes because optimistic people appraise events in a way that makes it more likely that they will employ problem-focused coping strategies, i.e. they expect positive outcomes. For example:

● Optimistic patients with fibromyalgia were less likely to give up on goals even when pain made this challenging (Affleck *et al.* 2001).

● Optimism following cancer diagnosis predicted more positive adjustment in the subsequent 12 months, possibly by reducing disease-related threat appraisals and avoidant coping (Schou *et al.* 2005).

● Optimistic children (as assessed using the Youth-Life Orientation Test) reported more hope in relation to goal attainment, greater global and social self-competence, and fewer depressive symptoms (Ey *et al.* 2005).

● Optimistic law students exhibited less avoidance coping than non-optimistic students (Segestrom *et al.* 1998).

It is worth noting that in this latter study optimists also reported lower perceived stress; however, this

Plate 12.1 How optimistic are you? Is this glass half-empty or half-full?

Source: Tanya Louise Robinson.

In an attempt to reveal how dispositional optimism is related to the two constructs of unrealistic optimism and self-efficacy (see Chapter 5 ☞, and also the section on control beliefs in this chapter) and explore whether each have independent effects on adaptation to illness, Fournier *et al.* (2002) examined predictors of self-care in people with either insulin-dependent diabetes or multiple sclerosis (MS). They hypothesised that people with diabetes – a disease generally controllable by self-management – would have better mood and self-care if they were high on positive self-efficacy and dispositional optimism, as this would lead to better self-care strategies, perceived positive benefits to their condition and thus lower levels of anxiety and depression. In contrast, positive efficacy expectations in the MS patients were thought to be less important to self-care, as this disease is less controllable. In MS patients, it was hypothesised that unrealistic optimism would instead benefit mood, because these beliefs were maintained in the face of health deterioration, and therefore the individual is not facing negative feedback from unrealistically optimistic expectations and attempts to control their illness. Both hypotheses were confirmed by their data, highlighting the fact that optimistic beliefs work in different ways, depending on context and the controllability of the disease. They also report that dispositional optimism and self-efficacy beliefs remained relatively stable over the 12-month follow-up period in comparison with unrealistic optimism, which decreased over time. Stable, dispositional variables such as optimism may offer more limited opportunity for intervention than do cognitions, such as situational and unrealistic optimism or perceptions of control. Folkman and Moskowitz (2000) have suggested that optimistic beliefs can be maintained by successful coping outcomes which leads to a consideration of whether coping-skills training and positive feedback on successful efforts may build optimism. If so, optimism would then become closer to self-efficacy.

However, one recent study points to the possibility that the beneficial effects of optimism in chronically or multiply challenging situations may be less clear than one might assume. Solberg Nes *et al.* (2011) found that while there were beneficial effects of optimism on task persistence of those with chronic multi-symptom illness (and control participants), the association was weakened in the patient sample when self-regulatory fatigue was experienced. This suggests perhaps that when facing multiple challenges to self-regulation and where

association was with situationally specific optimism rather than the general trait, or dispositional optimism. Further highlighting this important distinction, these different measures of optimism predicted different outcomes – situational optimism predicted elevated mood and immune function, whereas dispositional optimism did not.

Another construct related to dispositional optimism is that of unrealistic optimism, i.e. the view that unpleasant events are more likely to happen to others than to oneself, and that pleasant events are more likely to happen to oneself than to others (Weinstein 1982; see Chapter 5 ☞). Sometimes referred to as 'defensive optimism' (Schwarzer 1994), this way of thinking may operate as an emotional buffer against the recognition or acceptance of possible negative outcomes, i.e. it may protect people from a depressing reality.

'self-regulatory fatigue' is present, optimism may fail to maintain its positive influence. Further research is needed to explore this interesting finding.

Hardiness

The concept of hardiness was identified and tested by Kobasa (1979) when searching for factors that might differentiate those who respond to stress by becoming ill from those who stay healthy. Hardiness can be considered more perhaps as a belief system than part of personality, given that it was defined as an aspect of a person arising from having experienced rich, varied and rewarding experiences in childhood, and manifest in feelings of:

- *Commitment*: a person's sense of purpose or involvement in events, activities and with people in their lives. Committed individuals would view potentially stressful situations as meaningful and interesting.

- *Control*: a person's belief that they can influence events in their lives. Individuals high on control were thought to view stressors as potentially changeable.

- *Challenge*: a person's tendency to view change as a normal aspect of life and as something that can be positive. Individuals scoring high on the challenge dimension would view change as an opportunity for growth rather than as a threat to security.

Rather than exerting a direct effect on health, it is thought that by possessing each of these characteristics, a hardy person would be buffered against the experience of stress, thus enabling them to remain healthy. Kobasa's first study reported correlations between the scores of male executives on the Holmes and Rahe's life events scale (see Chapter 11 ☞) and their self-reported checklist of symptoms and illness events, and these findings were upheld in subsequent longitudinal prospective studies (Kobasa *et al.* 1982). The buffering effects are presented in Figure 12.2, where it is evident that hardiness has more effect in situations of high stress than in situations of low stress, i.e. a 'buffering' effect. This was supported by findings of Beasley *et al.* (2003) in a study of 187 university students who retrospectively reported life stress. In addition to a direct relationship between hardiness and reduced distress, hardiness buffered the effects of negative life events on the psychological health of female participants, i.e. the effects of negative life events were less for females higher in hardiness. For both

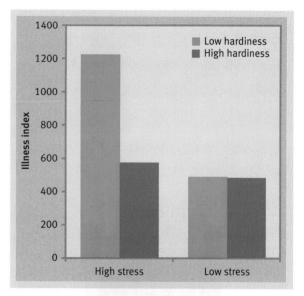

Figure 12.2 The buffering effects of hardiness

Source: adapted from Kobasa *et al.* (1982).

genders, the negative effect of emotion-oriented coping on distress was less in those scoring high on the hardiness measure. However, this study was cross-sectional and, in fact, several prospective studies have failed to find evidence of buffering effects of hardiness. Some have concluded that a lack of hardiness is important, rather than the presence of it, in terms of how this might affect appraisals. This has led to suggestions that non-hardiness may reflect underlying trait neuroticism (Funk 1992) and certainly there is a relationship between the two (see review by Semmer 2006).

Trait views dominated research until the late 1960s, but when traits failed to explain observed behaviour sufficiently well, attention turned to the role of external or situational variables and the existence of state-like characteristics (e.g. anxiety specific to a situation). Research has produced a wealth of findings pertaining to these more specific associations and some of these are described next.

Type A behaviour and personality

Coronary heart disease (CHD), and its outcomes (heart attack, angina, cardiac death) have been studied extensively in relation to personality variables and to emotion (see later section). The search for a coronary-prone personality led to the discovery of a constellation of behaviour labelled Type A behaviour (TAB) (Friedman and Rosenman 1959, 1974; Rosenman 1978). TAB is a multidimensional concept combining action and emotion and is manifest in individuals showing the following:

- competitiveness;
- time-urgent behaviour (trying to do too much in too little time);
- easily annoyed/aroused hostility and anger;
- impatience;
- achievement-oriented behaviour;
- a vigorous speech pattern.

In the 1960s and 1970s, TAB was found to modestly but consistently increase the risk of CHD and MI (heart attack) mortality when compared with persons showing a Type B behaviour pattern (the converse of Type A, i.e. relaxed with little aggressive drive) (e.g. the Western Collaborative Group study (WCGS) – Rosenman et al. 1976; and the Framingham heart study – Haynes et al. 1980). Yet most subsequent research, including longer-term (22 years) follow-up of the WCGS participants, failed to confirm these early associations (e.g. Booth-Kewley and Friedman 1987; Hollis et al. 1990; Orth-Gomér and Undén 1990; Ragland and Brand 1988). In fact, some of these studies found very different results to what was expected; for example, Ragland and Brand's 22-year follow-up of the WCGS cohort found that Type Bs with prior CHD experienced a second heart attack sooner than Type As with prior CHD, and healthy Type As were no more likely than healthy Type Bs to have experienced a fatal heart attack. Some of these contradictory findings may be explained by differences in the methods of assessment of TAB (for example, structured face-to-face interviews versus self-completed questionnaires) or by sampling differences (some studies used healthy samples, others used heart attack survivors or those with other risk factors, such as smoking). Or perhaps, as a meta-analysis of studies suggests (Myrtek 2001), contradictory findings arise from differences in the heart disease outcome assessed (e.g. heart attack event, heart attack death, angina, arterial disease), with studies reporting positive findings predominantly using self-reported angina as the indice of CHD, with obvious limitations.

While evidence of a TAB–coronary illness link may be less consistent than it was once considered, there is some evidence suggesting that Type As respond more quickly and in a stronger emotional manner to stress, and that

they exhibit a greater need for control than non-Type A individuals (Furnham 1990). These features of Type A may actually increase the person's likelihood of encountering stress, as they are likely to influence their interactions with others (Smith 1994) and result in the individual experiencing a more 'stressful' environment. Type As also show greater physiological reactivity than Type Bs, although this appears to be task-dependent and evident when tasks are competitive or challenging rather than in tasks that are irrelevant to the TAB character, such as simple perceptuo-motor tasks (e.g. Krantz et al. 1982). As described in the previous chapter, cardiovascular reactivity during stress has been implicated in various disease processes, such as the extent and progression of carotid artery atherosclerosis and the emergence of coronary heart disease (Smith et al. 2003), and therefore it is this reactivity that may provide the mechanism by which personality or Type A characteristics influence disease. Part of Type A personality therefore is seen in behavioural responses to provocative situations where the core component appears to be antagonistic, or hostile attitudes and behaviour. This likely key trait of hostility emerged from a review where the collapsing of findings across 83 different studies of the links between Type A and CHD found small but consistently significant correlations between the hostility component and total CHD outcomes (Booth-Kewley and Friedman 1987). In fact hostility was the only aspect of TAB that showed this association, although anger showed some associations with subcategories of outcomes. After a subsequent review almost a decade later confirmed this conclusion (T. Miller et al. 1996), Type A research had all but been replaced by hostility and anger research.

Hostility and anger

Hostility emerged as an important predictor of illness from various large-scale studies (e.g. the MRFIT study – Houston et al. 1992; the Western Collaborative Group study – Dembrowski et al. 1989; and see T. Miller et al. 1996 for a meta-analysis of the findings of 45 studies). While links were being established, so too were investigations of the pathways through which hostility might be having its effects on health status, and several possible mechanisms have been explored.

First, hostile individuals have been found to engage in health-risk behaviour which may itself be risk factors for illnesses such as heart disease, for example excessive

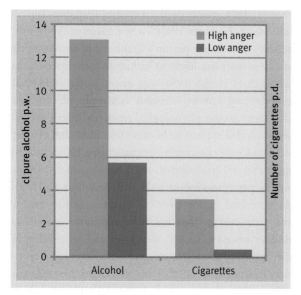

Figure 12.3 Anger and health behaviour

Source: Vögele (1998).

smoking or alcohol intake (e.g. Lipkus *et al.* 1994; Whiteman *et al.* 1997). Vögele (1998) has also found that anger is associated with increased intake of alcohol and cigarettes (see Figure 12.3). It is therefore essential that studies investigating the hostility–disease link control for such risk factors, so that the actual extent to which hostility independently contributes to disease outcomes becomes clear.

Secondly, hostile individuals have been found to have a lower capacity to benefit from psychosocial resources or interpersonal support and thus they are less 'buffered' against the negative effects of stressful or challenging events (T. Miller *et al.* 1996). This has been termed a 'psychosocial vulnerability hypothesis', whereby hostility is considered to be a moderator of the relationship between stressful environmental characteristics and health problems (Kivimäki *et al.* 2003). Their large-scale study of Finnish adults found that, for men only, hostility influenced the relationship between unemployment and ill health, with hostile men having a high prevalence of health problems regardless of employment status, whereas non-hostile men had better health if employed. This paper also highlights a commonly reported, but unsatisfactorily explored, gender difference in the associations between hostility and health outcomes (although at least studies conducted in the 1990s onwards tend to include women as well as men, where many earlier studies did not).

Thirdly, experimental studies have shown that hostile individuals are generally more stress-reactive than non-hostile individuals. Reduced 'buffers' plus a tendency to greater stress reactivity among hostile individuals makes them vulnerable to coronary heart disease, and even acute events such as heart attack (Strike and Steptoe 2005). For example, in a series of experimental studies, Suarez and colleagues (e.g. Suarez and Williams 1989; Suarez *et al.* 1998) found that persons scoring high in cynical hostility on the Cook–Medley hostility scale produced larger blood-pressure responses and greater neuroendocrine responses (e.g. raised cortisol levels) than non-hostile participants did when performing a task either during or immediately after an encounter with a rude and harassing laboratory assistant. Similar evidence from Everson *et al.* (1995) showed that individuals scoring high in hostility had increased cardiovascular activation during a task performed after a staged interruption and that, furthermore, hostile individuals differed in their evaluations of the experiment and the person who interrupted them than did low-hostility participants (e.g. they manifest more irritation and anger, and feelings of being personally insulted). As described in Chapter 11 ☛, prolonged or repeated episodes of elevated blood pressure may cause damage to the walls of vessels carrying blood to the heart (the coronary arteries).

Enough evidence was amassed from systematic reviews and meta-analyses to conclude that hostility is a likely risk factor for development of CHD (see Whiteman 2006 for a review), with several authors suggesting that the association is most evident in younger samples (aged 60 or under) (Kop and Krantz 1997; T. Miller *et al.* 1996; Smith *et al.* 2003). However, there have been inconsistencies in findings (see Myrtek's review 2001) and so, similar to that which happened with Type A research, studies have also addressed the component parts to try and establish whether there is a key component. Hostility has been defined as a trait made up of emotional, cognitive and behavioural components. Trait anger is the central emotional component that is both experienced by the individual and manifested in aggressive or antagonistic actions or expressions; cognitive components include having a cynical view of the world, a negative general attitude and negative expectations (cynicism, mistrust and denigration) about the motives of others; and behaviourally, hostile individuals may appear overtly aggressive or angry.

Finally, investigations of the pathways through which hostility affected health status have highlighted one of its core features – trait anger. Studies of psychosocial factors in blood pressure and hypertension have consistently identified associations with both inhibited anger (anger-in) and anger expression (anger-out), and interventions to reduce hostility have been associated with reductions in blood pressure (e.g. Davidson *et al.* 2007). Some studies have reported an increased CHD risk among participants with high anger expression (e.g. Rosenman 1996; Suls *et al.* 1995; Williams *et al.* 2000), with anger inhibition or suppression more associated with hypertension risk (Vögele and Steptoe 1993; Vögele *et al.* 1997). The UK-based Caerphilly study, however, found that low anger expression and suppressed anger significantly increased CHD risk (Gallacher *et al.* 1999). Such mixed findings are likely to be due to differences in measures used. Researcher have studied the possible immunological effects of hostility and anger, and findings point to an association with pro- and anti-inflammatory cytokines, discussed previously in relation to stress responses and potential associations with heart disease (e.g. among healthy male military personnel, Mommersteeg *et al.* 2008).

Finally, some authors suggest that risk 'characteristics' such as hostility may be created by certain social contexts that undermine an individual's ability to attain goals or financial security, and that hostility may be less of a trait than a coping response (e.g. Taylor *et al.* 1997). This view raises the question of whether hostility is also indirectly associated with disease by virtue of a relationship with social deprivation (see Chapter 2 ☞).

Type C personality

The search for a disease-prone personality in relation to CHD which led to identification and examination of Type A and hostility, stimulated research into whether or not there was a cancer-prone personality type. Earlier work that considered the existence of disease-prone personality types (e.g. Eysenck 1985; Grossarth-Maticek *et al.* 1985) identified four personality 'types'. Their 'cancer-prone personality', type 1, was characterised by suppression of emotion and inability to cope with interpersonal stress, leading to feelings of hopelessness, helplessness and finally depression, whereas a CHD-prone personality, type 2, was characterised by strong reactions of frustration, anger, hostility and emotional arousal (similar to TAB described above). Eysenck and Grossarth-Maticek (1989), following a large-scale community survey in Yugoslavia, reported evidence to show that type 1 increased individual risk of cancer by 120 times and type 2 increased CHD risk 25 times. These figures obviously suggest that phenomenal amounts of risk can be conferred on personality variables, for example greater risk than that elicited even by smoking. Their claims inevitably led to much scrutiny of their work, and the survey and its findings have now been heavily criticised on the grounds of inappropriate analyses, insufficient methodological detail being provided in their paper, and a general inability of others to replicate their findings in either CHD studies or cancer studies (Amelang and Schmidt-Rathjens 1996; Pelosi and Appleby 1992, 1993; Smedslund and Rundmo 1999).

In contrast, Temoshok's typology (Temoshok and Fox 1984; Temoshok 1987), following a 15-year follow-up of women with breast cancer, did generate a robust finding of an association between passive and helpless coping style and poor disease prognosis. They described a **Type C personality** as having the following characteristics:

- cooperative and appeasing;
- compliant and passive;
- stoic;
- unassertive and self-sacrificing;
- tendency to inhibit or repress negative emotions, particularly anger.

While several early studies offered support for the Type C typology and elevated cancer risk (e.g. Shaffer *et al.* 1987), larger, better designed studies and recent reviews of the role of Type C characteristics (and in fact any psychosocial factor) and cancer onset suggest that effects are limited and weak (e.g. Garssen 2004; Stürmer *et al.* 2006).

Personality as a factor that influences appraisal of, and response to cancer, has also been explored in terms of outcomes such as recurrence and survival. Generally, support for the predictiveness of characteristics of Type

---

Type C personality

a cluster of personality characteristics manifested in stoic, passive and non-emotionally expressive coping responses. Thought to be associated with an elevated cancer risk.

C is limited (Garssen 2004), and this is true also of studies examining effects of other personality characteristics such as neuroticism or extroversion (e.g. Canada *et al.* 2005). There is mixed evidence of survival benefits of aspects of personality best described as 'coping styles', for example of 'fighting spirit' (see 'What is adaptive coping?' above), and of helplessness–hopelessness.

Type D personality

More recent than research into elevated CHD risk through Type A behaviour and hostility is the notion of a **Type D personality**, considered to be detrimental to cardiovascular disease prognosis and outcomes (Denollet and Potter 1992; Denollet 1998; Denollet *et al.* 2006). This personality type is best described as a 'distressed' personality, with individuals scoring highly on negative affectivity (NA) and social inhibition (SI, defined as 'the avoidance of potential dangers involved in social interaction such as disapproval or nonreward by others', Denollet 1998: 209). Type D individuals therefore are thought to experience negative emotions but inhibit them while also avoiding social contact. There is evidence that these characteristics associated with increased mortality following a heart attack or other **cardiac event**, even when controlling for other biomedical risk factors, or for concurrent symptoms of stress. (e.g. Denollet *et al.* 2006). The effect was found in both women and men who had pre-existing heart disease. A meta-analysis of six studies (Reich and Schatzberg 2010) found that Type D was associated with worse cardiac outcomes in all cases (two studies related to heart transplant surgery) although the extent to which risk factors were controlled for is unclear.

In an attempt to identify physiological correlates of Type D personality, Habra *et al.* (2003) examined cardiovascular reactivity (blood pressure, heart rate, salivary cortisol levels) of students completing a mental arithmetic task while being harassed. Socially inhibited males showed heightened blood pressure reactivity; negative affectivity was associated with dampened heart-rate changes during the task in males; and salivary cortisol levels were positively associated with both Type D dimensions (but not in final, more stringent analyses). Unlike Denollet's studies, where NA and SI were only predictive jointly, Habra's findings suggested that NA and SI operated independently. These differences may be due to clear differences in the samples (older adults with CHD versus healthy undergraduate students); however, they also point to a need to further explore what this construct is. A final point regarding the process through which any effect of Type D may be achieved is preliminary evidence relating to psychoneuroimmunological responses, including that of increased pro-inflammatory cytokine activity (see Chapter 11 ☞).

Stress and cognitions

Perceived control

Early work on the construct of control considered it to be a personality trait. Locus of control, derived from Rotter's social learning theory, proposed LoC as a generalised belief that would influence behaviour as greater reinforcements (e.g. rewarding outcomes) were expected when responsibility for events was placed internally rather than externally (Rotter 1966). Furthermore, internal locus of control beliefs would only predict behaviour in situations where the rewards/outcomes were valued. LoC therefore refers to the trait-like expectation that personal actions will be effective in controlling or mastering the environment, with individuals falling on the side of either internality or externality. An 'internal' individual would take responsibility for what happens to them; for example, they would attribute successes to their own efforts and their failures to their own laziness. An 'external' individual would be more likely to believe that outside forces or chance circumstances control their lives, and both success and failures would be likely to be attributed to luck or chance. These beliefs would therefore influence a person's behaviour. It is considered that internal individuals have more efficient cognitive systems and that they expend energy on obtaining information that will enable them to influence events of personal

---

Type D personality

a personality type characterised by high negative affectivity and social inhibition.

cardiac event

generic term for a variety of end points of coronary heart disease, including a myocardial infarction, angina and cardiac arrest.

importance. In other words, internally oriented individuals would engage in more problem-focused coping efforts when faced with personal or social stressors. Highlighting this, Henselmanns *et al.* (2010) demonstrated in a longitudinal study of breast cancer patients that threat appraisals (primary appraisal) were greater and secondary appraisals of coping ability were lower in women who reported low perceptions of control over events and situations in life (using Pearlin and Schoolers 1978 mastery measure) pre-diagnosis, and that this impacted on these women's greater distress. This shows how internal resources/beliefs and appraisals interact in a dynamic manner, and furthermore, suggests a protective role for a general sense of personal control, or mastery (as assessed in this study).

There is a large body of evidence relating locus of control to physical and psychological health, and much of it has employed a scale specific to health developed by Kenneth Wallston and colleagues (e.g. Wallston *et al.* 1978) – the multidimensional health locus of control scale. The MHLC assesses the extent to which a person believes that they themselves, external factors or 'powerful others' (e.g. friends, health professionals) are responsible for their health and health outcomes. This measure therefore has three subscales and includes items such as:

● 'I am in control of my health' – internal;

● 'No matter what I do, if I am going to get sick I will get sick' – external; ·

● 'Regarding my health, I can only do what my doctor tells me to do' – powerful others.

Scores on these subscales have been found to be associated with a range of coping, emotional and behavioural outcomes (including health behaviour itself). For example, among two longitudinal studies of patients with lower back pain, internal HLC was associated with reduced physical disability at follow-up, and patients with stronger internal control beliefs gained more from their treatment and exercised more often (distress was associated with poorer exercise behaviour) (Fisher and Johnston 1998; Härkäpää *et al.* 1991). Using an HLC measure specific to recovery from disability (the recovery locus of control scale; Partridge and Johnston 1989), Johnston *et al.* (1999) also found that perceptions of internal control predicted better recovery from disability (measured in terms of the ability to perform a range of activities such as walking, dressing and toileting) six months after

an acute stroke, although this was not achieved by means of an influence on exercise behaviours, as reported by the Finnish study (Härkäpää *et al.* 1991). Importantly, Johnston and colleagues reassessed their stroke survivors after three years to examine whether the beneficial effects of perceived control persisted long term, and confirmed that perceived-control beliefs, as assessed at baseline (10–20 days post-stroke onset) were significantly predictive of long-term physical recovery, but not emotional recovery in terms of reduced distress (Johnston *et al.* 2004; Morrison *et al.* 2005). The importance of this type of finding is that, unlike neurological impairment or age (both predictors of outcome following stroke), control beliefs can be modified with simple (e.g. Fisher and Johnston 1996b) or more intensive (e.g. Johnston *et al.* 2007) intervention.

Few studies have found perceived control to be predictive of disease course, for example cancer relapse or survival (DeBoer *et al.* 1999). Furthermore, there is evidence that encouraging patients or research participants to increase internal control may not always be popular (e.g. Joice *et al.* 2010) nor adaptive. Unrealistic perceptions of control could potentially lead to unrealistic optimism, although the direction of causality is unclear (do optimists perceive control, or does perceiving control make you optimistic? e.g. Klein and Helweg-Larsen 2002). Furthermore, maintaining beliefs in internal control in situations where such beliefs are unrealistic (e.g. severe and permanent disability following traumatic brain injury), may lead to problem-focused coping efforts that fail. This perceived failure may contribute to feelings of depression and helplessness, whereas accepting the reality of having no control could encourage more adaptive emotion-focused coping responses (Folkman 1984; Thompson 1981). However, rather than accept an absence of control, Folkman (2010) notes that by revising one's goals a sense of hope can be maintained for new, more realistic or attainable goals and that this may help provide a sense of control and sustain a person's well-being.

This highlights the importance of asking ourselves what we are trying to measure, i.e. 'Control over what?' Various types of control have been described:

● *Behavioural*: the belief that one can perform behaviours likely to reduce the negative impact of a stressor, e.g. using controlled breathing techniques prior to and during a painful dental procedure.

- *Cognitive*: the belief that one has certain thought processes or strategies available that would reduce the negative impact of a stressor, e.g. distracting oneself from surgical pain by focusing on pleasant thoughts of a forthcoming holiday.

- *Decisional*: having the opportunity to choose between options, e.g. having a local anaesthetic prior to a tooth extraction (bearing in mind that the after-effects can last for hours!) or having the tooth removed without anaesthetic.

- *Informational*: having the opportunity to find out about the stressor; i.e. the what, why, when, where, likely outcomes, possibilities, etc. Information allows preparation (see Chapter 13 ☛).

- *Retrospective*: attributions of cause or control of an event made after it happens: i.e. searching for the meaning of an event can give some sense of order in life; e.g. blaming a birth defect on a defective gene (internal) may be more adaptive than attributing blame externally, although this is not clear-cut.

Each of these types of control can reduce the stressfulness of an event by altering the appraisal a person makes of the stressor, by reducing emotional arousal or by influencing the coping responses adopted. Even in generally uncontrollable circumstances, for example in terms of disease progression, believing in control over one's day-to-day symptoms rather than over the disease as a whole, has been associated with better adjustment (Schiaffino and Revenson 1992) and reduced distress (Thompson *et al.* 1993; Stanton *et al.* 2007). Therefore while control over outcome may not be realistic, finding or retaining control over some aspects of an event or one's responses to it is generally considered beneficial (Montpetit and Bergeman 2007).

In a recent study of cancer caregivers, however, Fitzell and Pakenham (2010) found that perceived control over caregiving demands was not a significant predictor of any outcome, positive or negative (in spite of modest correlations with positive affect and subjective health status). They investigated caregiver appraisals of demand (stress, challenge) and resources (personal control, social support) in relation to both positive, and negative, caregiver adjustment. In the final regression analyses, while perceived control was not predictive, perceived stress (assessed as a single item) was a significant predictor of all outcomes in the expected direction; a more robust five-item measure of perceived challenge was predictive

only of life satisfaction; and the 'resource' variable of satisfaction with social support also added significantly to the prediction of all outcomes. The authors suggest the lack of prediction of control beliefs (and also in fact of most of the coping subscales they assessed) may be due to using items which referred to control over caregiving challenges generally, rather than specific demands/caregiving tasks. This issue of whether to assess generically or specifically is an important one which we address at various points throughout this text.

Self-efficacy and perceived locus of control are the two main control concepts used in health psychology, and they could be considered as spanning different phases of the coping process; for example, locus of control is an appraisal of the extent to which an individual believes they can control outcomes, whereas self-efficacy addresses appraisal of the resources and skills an individual believes they can use in order to achieve desired outcomes. Also related to control beliefs are **causal attributions**. In a review of 64 data sets exploring associations between attributions of cause in a wide range of conditions (including arthritis, cancer, heart disease, burns, AIDS, infertility, stroke and pregnancy loss) and adjustment (Hall and Marteau 2003), 80 per cent of studies reported no association between internal (behavioural self-blame) attributions or external (other-blame) attributions and adjustment. In fact, no particular attribution was strongly associated with achieving a better outcome. Characterological self-blame (e.g. 'It is something in my nature that I can't change that caused me to become ill') was most often associated with poorer outcomes. This type of self-blame has been associated with negative emotions such as depression.

Importantly, there is evidence that social class influences the extent of an individual's belief in personal control (see Chapter 2 ☛). Examining two control-related constructs in a large sample of adults aged 25–75 years, Lachmann and Weaver (1998) found that personal mastery beliefs (e.g. 'I can do just about anything I really set my mind to') and perceptions of constraints in one's

---

causal attribution

where a person attributes the cause of an event, feeling or action to themselves, to others, to chance or to some other causal agent.

life (e.g. 'Other people determine most of what I can and cannot do') differed according to their indice of social class–household income. Mastery was lower and constraints higher among those with lower incomes, but when lowest-income participants reported a high sense of control, their health and well-being became comparable with the higher-income groups. Control therefore moderated the effect of low income on both physical (self-rated health, functional limitations) and psychological (life satisfaction, depressed mood) outcomes.

WHAT DO YOU THINK?

While findings such as those described above make general conclusions, there are obviously individuals who differ from the mean (in other words, some people of low socio economic status (SES) will report high mastery, and some of high SES will report low mastery). However, thinking of the overall picture, stop and ask yourself why many people of a lower SES have a lower sense of control and greater perceptions of constraints in their lives than people of higher SES. Do you think they are right in having such views, i.e. might such beliefs be adaptive in certain circumstances? Refer back to Chapter 2 ☞ when thinking about these issues.

Hope

Snyder (1989) introduced 'hope theory' to the study of cognitive–motivational processes involved in explaining human behaviour. Relevant to the study of stress and coping, hope was defined as 'a positive motivational state that is based on an interactively derived sense of successful (a) agency (goal-directed energy) and (b) pathways (planning to meet goals)' (Snyder *et al.* 1991: 287). For Snyder, hope was fundamentally the person's belief that they can set, plan and attain goals – it was about goal-directed thinking and was believed to have both trait and state-like aspects. There is some conceptual overlap between the hope construct and other constructs, such as dispositional optimism and self-efficacy, both of which have been associated with positive physical and emotional well-being. Snyder *et al.* (2006) acknowledge that all three constructs focus on individual 'resources', but point out that hope is about the

motivation (agency) and route (pathway) to achieving goals (outcomes), whereas optimism is about generalised positive outcome expectancies that are not founded solely on agency and pathway thinking, and self-efficacy is less a generalised belief than a situation and goal-specific belief that depends on various contingencies (i.e. I can do 'a' even if the situation is 'b'). (Some might question this, given that self-efficacy theories do also propose a more generalised construct.) Snyder further supports his argument that the three constructs differ by describing how a hope-based intervention would differ from an optimism or a self-efficacy-based intervention; however, the differences have not been fully tested.

More recently, Folkman (2010) has described how 'Hope, like stress, is appraisal based, it waxes and wanes, is contextual, and is complex' (p. 902). For Folkman, hope is about more than goals; it is motivational but it is also in a bidirectional and active relationship with coping and is about emotion and finding meaning (Folkman and Moskowitz 2000). For example, when faced with a life-threatening illness, people may revise their goals in order to find those more possible or within their control which they can then imbue with hope. Hope in some contexts can have faith-like or existential qualities, for example, when coping with an uncertain future or a changing reality following an HIV or terminal cancer diagnosis (e.g. hope to find peace). Whether closely tied to goals, or more broadly defined, the construct of hope is hard to capture empirically. As Folkman acknowledges, we, as behavioural and social scientists 'cannot capture all of its aspects. However, what we do learn from those aspects we are able to study can be used to help people sustain well-being through difficult times' (p. 907). There does, however, still remain a need for empirical studies to establish whether the measurable aspects of hope adds any 'unique' explanation in terms of health outcomes, than that offered by assessment of other personal 'resource' variables such as optimism and personal control.

The constructs reviewed in this section are often referred to within a field of study known as 'positive psychology', i.e. where a person's strengths, resources and abilities are focused on and harnessed rather than their pathology, limitations or negative cognitions and emotions. IN THE SPOTLIGHT below highlights this growth area, but then in the subsequent section we address the more negative emotions found to be associated with stress responses and outcomes.

Positivity and meaningful lives

There has been a growth in studies in what is being called 'positive psychology' (Folkman and Moskowitz 2000: Seligman and Csikszentmihalyi 2000; Snyder and Lopez 2005). Basically, what these authors, among others, are suggesting is that we need to move away from a focus on the negatives (inability as a result of illness pathology, lack of resources, negative thoughts and emotions) and turn more attention towards the benefits to health and well-being offered by thinking and acting positively. The premise of positive psychology is that 'positive affect in the context of stress has important adaptational significance of its own (Folkman and Moskowitch 2000: 648). For example, in addition to optimism and hope, which we have discussed earlier, happiness and joy are thought to contribute to what Seligman, in a special edition on positive psychology in *The Psychologist* (2003), calls desirable lives: the pleasant life, the good life and the meaningful life. A pleasant life arises from one that pursues positive emotions about present, past and future experiences and involves the simple pleasures and gratifications or rewards that we get out of life. A good life arises from 'being' as well as 'doing' and by being involved in life and all its activities, in order to get the best out of it. A meaningful life is when we use our strengths and skills to benefit more than just ourselves.

To feel that life is pleasant, good or meaningful would imply that a person would therefore be happy. However, little research has actually addressed positive appraisal and emotions such as happiness in relation to health outcomes, with subjective 'well-being', (which may not be quite the same), often being used to indicate happiness. Veenhoven (2003) states that happiness can be defined and measured and that by simply asking people about their levels of happiness we could explore questions such as: is quality of life associated with happiness or can we have a quality of life without it? What makes a good life? This relates to the chapter opener.

Think about your own life and what makes you happy – some would suggest it may help you live longer, but while that is yet to be proven, it seems reasonable to expect that it won't do you any harm!

Stress and emotions

Depression and anxiety

The role of depression in increasing the incidence/likelihood of disease experience is controversial and depends on the disease concerned. The Alameda County study discussed in Chapter 3 ☞ (where we listed the seven types of 'healthy behaviour') did not find any effect of depressed mood upon CHD incidence; however, other studies have associated depression with hypertension, even when taking other risk factors into consideration. As early examples, the Framingham Heart Study found that depression, as well as anxiety, predicted 20-year incidence of hypertension even controlling for age, smoking and obesity (Markovitz *et al.* 1993), and in relation to cancer, a major study showed that recurrent major depression among an elderly sample predicted a higher incidence of breast cancer (Penninx *et al.* 1998).

In relation to CHD there have been several reviews and meta-analyses over the decades where significant association between depression and CHD outcomes (heart attack, angina, cardiac death, as well as global CHD) have been found (Booth-Kewley and Friedman 1987; Hemingway and Marmot 1999). In the latter review 11 out of 11 longitudinal prospective studies in healthy populations presented results supportive of a role of depression and/or anxiety in the aetiology (development) of CHD, and 6 out of 6 prospective studies among CHD patients reported a significant prognostic role for depression. More recently, a large UK study (Surtees *et al.* 2008) found that of almost 20,000 CHD-free participants followed up on average 8.5 years, those diagnosed as having major depression were 2.7 times more likely to die from ischaemic heart disease than those who were not. This relationship existed even after all behavioural and demographic risk factors were controlled for.

A significant association between depressed mood and mortality from heart attack (myocardial infarction, MI) has also been reported (Bush *et al.* 2001). Frasure-Smith *et al.* (1995) concluded that depression was more predictive of death than was either the degree of heart damage or having had a previous heart attack and subsequent work has found similar effects. For example, a longitudinal study of 237 healthy men found that 45 per cent of those with a depressive episode at or before the baseline assessment were dead by the time of follow-up – a massive 55 years later – compared with only 5 per cent of those who had not experienced such an episode (Vaillant 1998). Neither depression nor anxiety were predictive of (non-) survival in two longitudinal studies of stroke patients carried out in Scotland (Johnston *et al.* 2004; Lewis *et al.* 2001; Morrison *et al.* 2005), although other studies with longer follow-ups have found a significant relationship (Morris *et al.* 1993).

Depressed mood may reflect an underlying state of negative affectivity (see earlier section). Studies by Denollet and colleagues (Denollet and de Potter 1992; Denollet 1998) have found that cardiovascular disease outcomes (recovery, death, further heart attacks) can be partially explained by high NA scores combined with social inhibition ('Type D personality'; see earlier section). It is likely that for some individuals, psychosocial risk factors cluster together; for example, stress plus hostility plus depression plus social isolation would confer compounded risk. It is also notable that anxiety and depression themselves are interrelated (Suls and Bunde 2005) and, although depression is perhaps more commonly found to be associated with CHD, and in fact all-cause mortality, anxiety also plays a role (Grossardt *et al.* 2009).

While the evidence of a role of depression on CHD onset and outcome is reasonably consistent, this is less the case in terms of the evidence of emotions associated with increased cancer risk. Early findings of the Western Electric study (WES; Persky *et al.* 1987), which conducted 17- and 20-year follow-ups, were that those participants who initially scored highly on the global depression subscale of the MMPI (Minnesota multiphasic personality inventory) had a greater incidence of cancer at follow-up. However, this was later attributed to environmental factors, and indeed the large-scale longitudinal Alameda County study found no relationship (Kaplan and Reynolds 1988). In the 1990s, two longitudinal studies of healthy,

but older, samples over six years found inconsistent results, one finding an association between chronic depression and cancer incidence (Penninx *et al.* 1998), the other, finding no relationship (Whooley and Browner 1998). Notably, the latter study was conducted in a women-only sample and an association was in fact found with CHD and all-cause mortality. Both these studies were among older individuals, however, and therefore such findings may not hold for middle-aged or younger samples.

Although there is some suggestion that feelings of hopelessness and helplessness associated with depression are implicated in cancer onset (Everson *et al.* 1996), the evidence appears to be, as with CHD, more strongly in support of depression influencing outcomes rather than aetiology (Petticrew *et al.* 2002). Depression as an outcome of illness is addressed in Chapter 14 ☞.

When considering pathways by which depression may affect health outcomes, there are, as with personality, various possible routes. First, depression and anxiety have been shown to influence the appraisals that individuals make when facing stressful events (appraisals of threat, as opposed to appraisals of challenge), thus influencing the coping actions a person engages in. For example, Lowe *et al.* (2003), drawing from the stress–emotion–coping framework of Smith and Lazarus (1993; see Chapter 11 ☞ for theoretical explanation), examined whether the emotion of depression was attached to secondary appraisals of low problem-focused coping potential and pessimistic future expectations, and whether anxiety was attached to appraisals of low emotion-focused coping potential. Results from 148 women with suspected breast cancer confirmed expectations in relation to stress appraisals and also found that confrontation coping, avoidance coping and acceptance–resignation coping were all positively associated with anxiety, whereas depression was negatively associated with confrontation and not related to the other two coping responses.

The second route is also indirect, i.e. via a person's behaviour. Depression is seen to reduce the likelihood of healthy behaviour or cessation of unhealthy behaviour. For example, people who had experienced a heart attack (MI) and who exhibited subsequent depression had lower rates of smoking cessation than those who did not show signs of depression five months after the MI (Huijbrechts *et al.* 1996). Depressed individuals were also less likely to attend cardiac rehabilitation classes than non-depressed individuals (Lane *et al.* 2001), and generally research findings suggest that adherence to therapeutic interventions or treatments such as exercise or medication is lower among depressed individuals than those who are not depressed (e.g. DiMatteo *et al.* 2000; Wing *et al.* 2002). Such non-adherent behaviour can expose individuals to adverse health outcomes, such as future illness, poorer recovery from illness, or even mortality (McDermott *et al.* 1997).

Thirdly, there may be physiological pathways through which depression exerts its effects. Pointing to this, individuals with elevated depressive symptoms but without a history of coronary disease were twice as likely as their non-depressed counterparts to have **carotid plaques** (a significant risk factor for CHD), and this association also controlled for baseline risk factors (Haas *et al.* 2005), suggesting that this association was not solely attributable to behaviours such as smoking. A link has also been made between depression and increased pro-inflammatory cytokines in older people with cancer (Spolentini *et al.* 2008), suggesting a further possible mechanism of effect, although causality certainly needs to be disentangled here.

Finally, depression may also interfere with a person's ability to seek, or benefit from, social support and supportive interactions (see later section on support).

Emotional disclosure

One possible moderator of coping receiving increased attentions in recent years is that of emotional disclosure – the opposite of emotional suppression, or repressive coping, commonly found to be detrimental to health (see earlier 'Type C personality' section). A leading figure in this area is Pennebaker (e.g. Pennebaker *et al.* 1988; Pennebaker 1993), who with various colleagues has developed a paradigm whereby writing (typically for 15 minutes, for several consecutive days) about one's feelings regarding a recent trauma is shown to have long-term benefits in terms of reduced stress (Zakowski *et al.* 2004), immune functioning, including wound healing (Pennebaker *et al.* 1988; Petrie *et al.* 2004; Weinman *et al.* 2008) and healthcare use (Pennebaker and Beall 1986). A large meta-analysis of 146 such studies supports the potential of this low-cost intervention (Frattaroli 2006).

Disclosure of emotional experiences is not to be confused with work on **expressed emotion** (EE; can include the venting of negative as well as positive emotion) which, although studied using a similar writing paradigm, has

been associated with poorer prognosis among psychiatric populations and is showing contradictory findings among the physically ill (interested readers can see a meta-analysis by Panagopoulou *et al.* 2002). It is thought that venting negative emotion may maintain the emotion by virtue of increasing the attention paid to it; it can also interfere with the potential to receive social support (Semmer 2006). For example, Coyne and colleagues (2003) found that EE among couples where one had experienced **congestive heart failure** was associated with poorer marital quality and increased distress. Other authors suggest that EE assists in emotional self-regulation by allowing the person to develop greater mental control over the stressor and a coherent narrative of events in their head, which facilitates 'closure' and reduces distress (Niederhoffer and Pennebaker 2005). There is evidence that the style of expression (antagonistic vs. constructive expression of anger) influences whether the outcome of expression is positive or not (e.g. Davidson *et al.* 2000).

Social support and stress

So far in this chapter we have focused on aspects of the individual that influence how they respond to stress. We now turn attention to include those beyond the individual – to social support. Evidence exists that people who have strong (in both size and usage) networks of

---

carotid plaque

a plaque is a thick waxy coating which forms on blood vessel walls and restricts blood flow, in this instance in the carotid artery.

expressed emotion

the disclosure of emotional experiences as a means of reducing stress; often achieved by describing the experience in writing.

congestive heart failure

a disorder in which the heart loses its ability to pump blood efficiently. As a consequence, many organs do not receive enough oxygen and nutrients, leading to the potential for them to become damaged and, therefore, not work effectively.

social support are healthier and live longer than the socially isolated (Cacioppo and Patrick 2007; Cohen 2004). Being in a social network and receiving support from it is available to most people at some points in their lives, but is not experienced by all people at all times (see also Chapter 15 ☛).

What is meant by the term 'social support'?

Definition, types and functions of social support

Social support can be actual (received support) or perceived. People with social support believe they are loved and cared for, esteemed and valued, and part of a social network of communication and mutual obligation, such as that often shared with family, friends or members of a social organisation. Sources of support can include anyone from partners, close family and friends, to colleagues, to health and social care professionals and support grops. Social support is generally considered in terms of two interacting components – its structure (i.e. type of support, size of networks) and the function(s) they serve (Uchino 2006). The social network facilitates the provision of goods, services and mutual defence in times of need or danger (Cobb 1976). However, people may vary in the extent to which they participate in these networks and this will be reflected in the extent of social integration a person has. A lack of intergration, also referred to as social isolation, is a recognised risk factor for poor well-being. In studying social support, one must be aware of the interconnectedness of the above terms and perspectives that are 'social support', social networks' and 'social integration' (Gottlieb and Bergen 2010).

Table 12.3 presents examples of types of social support and their functions in terms of what the social support provider provides and in terms of what is received by the recipient. Some support may be global (i.e. from people generally) or specific to one event or support person. Five basic types have been described, although the most common distinction is between instrumental, emotional and informational. Most studies do not attempt to record what the recipient actually 'gets' from the support but instead assume that it is all helpful. (Chapter 15 ☛ challenges this assumption when carer and patient relationships are examined). Furthermore, some studies assess perceived support which is a person's belief that support is available to them, whereas others address actual received support, and there is evidence that this is an important distinction, particularly where there is a mismatch between what is expected and what is received (e.g. Cutrona and Russell 1990). Perceived support is often more predictive of outcome than actual received support, and in fact having to seek it out rather than receive what was anticipated spontaneously can have a negative impact (E. Lawrence *et al.* 2008).

Social support is considered within Lazarus's stress and coping framework as a resource variable that when perceived as being available will affect how individuals appraise and respond to, i.e. cope with, events. Individuals who perceive support levels as high are likely to appraise events as less stressful than individuals who do not perceive they have any support (i.e. social support acts as a 'buffer' against stress). Evidence of the association between social support and health outcomes is reviewed below, followed by consideration of some of the likely mechanisms of action.

Table 12.3 Types and functions of social support

	Provider	Recipient
Emotional support	Empathy Caring Concern	Reassurance sense of comfort and belongingness
Esteem support	Positive regard Encouraging person Positively comparing	Builds self-worth Sense of competence Being valued
Tangible/instrumental support	Direct assistance financial/practical aid	Reduces strain/worry
Informational support	Advice, suggestions feedback	Communication self-efficacy/self-worth
Network (or 'companionate', cf. Gottlieb and Bergen 2010) support	Welcoming Shared experiences	Sense of belonging Affiliation

Social support and mortality

Many years have been spent trying to establish whether social support is causally implicated in mortality. Early support was obtained from the Alameda County study (Berkman and Syme 1979), with almost a twofold increased risk of mortality for both men and women with fewest social ties, even when health status and self-reported health-risk behaviour were controlled for. Social isolation (low levels of social support and social activity) was associated with heart disease mortality among middle-aged men followed up for ten years (Orth-Gomér *et al.* 1988), and similarly in an impressive 15-year follow-up of 2,603 adults (Vogt *et al.* 1992), social 'networks' (assessed by size, number of supportive domains (scope) and frequency of use) strongly predicted mortality from ischaemic heart disease, cancer and stroke. These are important findings, given the evidence that socio-economic and cultural factors can shape the extent to which individuals can access social networks which facilitate support provision and receipt (Chaix *et al.* 2007; Parveen *et al.*, 2011).

Social support and disease

Evidence of a relationship between life stress and health status has pointed to social support as a moderator (for a review see Taylor 2007). For example, Rosengren *et al.* (1993) found that among middle-aged men, the association between an accumulation of critical life changes and subsequent heart attack was moderated by the quality of social support. Among individuals suffering from rheumatoid arthritis, social support in terms of a limited social network was predictive of disease activity three years later, even when coping behaviour was controlled for (Evers *et al.* 2003). Among healthy samples, for example a large sample of French employees (Melchior *et al.* 2003), a lack of social support and dissatisfaction with social relationships predicted poor health status. It has been suggested that social relationships are particularly important in diseases where physical dependence on others, and decreased social activity resulting from the disease, are present (Penninx *et al.* 1999).

How does social support influence health status?

We all need support. There is ample evidence that social support effectively reduces distress during times of stress, and furthermore the lack of social support during times of need can itself be very stressful, particularly for people with high needs for social support but insufficient opportunities to obtain it, e.g. the elderly, the recently widowed and other victims of sudden, severe or uncontrollable life events (e.g. Balaswamy *et al.* 2004; Penninx *et al.* 1999; Stroebe *et al.* 2005). Although there is more evidence for the benefit of social support in reducing stress and distress during illness than there is on actually preventing it occurring, Greenwood *et al.* (1996), following a review of empirical studies, also concluded that poor social support had a stronger effect on CHD incidence than did stressful life events.

Two broad theories as to how social support might operate have been proposed (Cohen 1988):

1. *Direct effects hypothesis*: social support is beneficial regardless of the amount of stress people experience, and a lack of social support is detrimental to health even in the absence of stress. High levels of social support provide greater 'ties' to others and a greater sense of belonging and self-esteem than low levels, thus producing a positive outlook and healthier lifestyles. Alternatively, social support has a physiological route to health by virtue of either reduced blood pressure reactivity, thought to arise from positive stress appraisals and emotions, or possibly via enhanced endocrine or immune system functions, although there are less consistent findings in this area. (For a comprehensive review, see Uchino 2006.)

2. *Buffering hypothesis*: social support protects the person against negative effects of high stress. Social support acts as a buffer by either (a) influencing the person's *cognitive appraisals* of a situation so they perceive their resources as being greater to meet threat; or (b) modifying the person's *coping response* to a stressor after it has been appraised as stressful (i.e. they do not cope alone) (Cohen and Wills 1985; Schwarzer and Leppin 1991).

Evidence for direct effect of social support

In terms of direct effects on healthy behaviour, there is reasonably consistent evidence that social support facilitates healthy behaviours such as not smoking and adhering to medication, although as discussed in Chapter 5 ☞ social influence can also be negative. It is likely that social

Plate 12.2 From an early age, social support is a powerful moderator of stress response

support enables the individual, for example, by promoting their self-efficacy (see Chapter 5 ☞) beliefs. For example, when stopping smoking, a supportive person, perhaps someone who has already quit smoking themselves, can provide assurances and enhance the other person's confidence and self-efficacy for change (Schwarzer and Knoll 2007). Many studies have pointed to beneficial effects of social support for psychosocial well-being among both healthy and ill populations. For example, marital support has been shown to benefit partner health, although interestingly the association is stronger for male partners than for females (Kiecolt-Glaser and Newton 2001) possibly reflecting gender differences in ability to seek or provide needed support, and also in the response to it (see also Chapter 15 ☞). Here we consider more the direct effects of social support on physiological rather than behavioural processes.

Uchino (2006) reviews the evidence regarding physiological pathways affected by social support, and highlights both reduced stress reactivity seen in typical measures of cardiovascular reactivity (see Chapter 11 ☞) and also some evidence of neuroendocrine and immune responses, the latter particularly important among older samples. However, this review primarily addresses experimentally manipulated support and we need to consider 'real-world evidence also. Turner-Cobb *et al.* (2000) found that breast cancer patients who assessed social support as being present and helpful had lower morning cortisol levels than those who did not assess social support in this way, suggesting a physiological route by which social support may enact its benefits. As described in Chapter 8 ☞ and Chapter 11 ☞ cortisol has been implicated in immune down-regulation and is perhaps implicated in tumour growth. Cognitive-behavioural interventions that have provided breast cancer patients with group support have also reported reduced cortisol levels (e.g. Creuss *et al.* 2000). A recent review of social support and cardiovascular disease and cancer risk has also highlighted a role for the immune system and biochemical processes of inflammation (involving pro-inflammatory cytokines and interleukins (see also Chapter 11 ☞; Penwell and Larkin 2010). While the evidence is not conclusive, such reviews certainly offer exciting insights into some of the potential mechanisms through which social support achieves its beneficial effects on health.

Proactive coping in the elderly

Greenglass, E., Fiksenbaum, L. and Eaton, J. (2006). The relationship between coping, social support, functional disability and depression in the elderly. *Anxiety, Stress, and Coping*, 19: 5–31.

Background aims

Many studies on stress referred to in this and the previous chapter have addressed young adults facing acute stressors (e.g. students and exams), healthy populations (e.g. adult employees, married couples) or patient populations. Given the global ageing population, society is facing significant increases in numbers of people living, in the community, with functional limitations and disability. A declining ability to perform 'typical' roles and tasks is a stressor that may be associated with depression, which itself can create additional challenges for the individual.

Functional ability itself is thought to be predicted by factors such as described in this chapter – personal resources of health status, age, and social support, and by the manner in which the individual copes with stressful events. While this chapter has focused primarily on situation-specific coping strategies, these authors focus on proactive coping, broadly conceptualised as 'an approach to life in which an individual's efforts are directed towards goal management where demands and different situations are seen more as challenges rather than stressors'. Some of the skills that reflect such proactive coping behaviour (as opposed to more reactive type coping) are planning, goal setting, organisation and mental stimulaton (cf. Aspinwall and Taylor 1997). Social support has been found to promote proactive coping in that resources from one's social network help shape one's choice of coping strategy.

The study proposes a psychosocial model of functional disability (FD) whereby direct and indirect effects of proactive coping are tested. Physical health status is expected to predict FD; however, it is further hypothesised that coping will associate with less FD

and that social support will play a significant role in these relationships, being associated with lower FD, lower depression and greater proactive coping.

Method

A total of 224 community-residing older adults (aged 62–95 years, mean age 75 years) took part in this questionnaire-based cross-sectional study. The majority were female (78.2 per cent), educated to high school level or above (89.6 per cent), 39.8 per cent were married, 50.5 per cent lived alone. Although most (88.3 per cent) were retired, 55 per cent remained involved in voluntary work.

In addition to gathering demographic information, the questionnaire contained several self-report assessments including:

> Functional Disability Scale, e.g. difficulties in washing, dressing, shopping, housework
>
> Proactive Coping subscale of the Proactive Coping Inventory
>
> The Brief Symptom Inventory, an assessment of depression
>
> A checklist of physical health status
>
> Social Support Behaviors Scale

Results

Descriptive results show that physical health was associated with depression and FD as hypothesised, and social support was positively correlated with proactive coping and negatively correlated with depression and FD. In order to 'predict' FD and establish the relative contributions made by the various physical and psychological measures, a hierarchical regression was carried out. A total of 45 per cent of the variance in FD was explained by the model, with demographic factors (age predominantly) contributing 17 per cent to this, poor physical health adding a further 19 per cent to the explanation, and therefore a smaller proportion explained (10 per cent) by proactive coping. The hypothesis that proactive coping would predict less FD was supported. To further test the 'fit' of the model proposed, i.e. where social support leads to FD and proactive coping and depression, and that proactive coping would lead to lower FD and lower depression (see Figure 1), further analysis using path analysis techniques was conducted.

Figure 2 shows the model that provided the best fit for the data, with all connecting arrows significant in the hypothesised direction. However, you will see that the hypothesised direct association between social support and low FD was not supported, and that an association (positive) between depression and FD was.

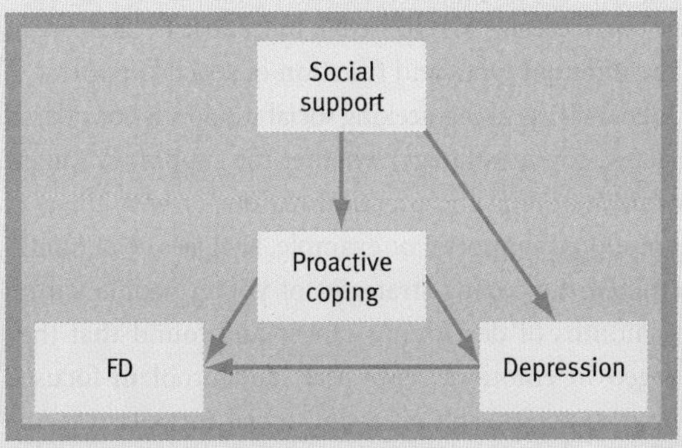

Discussion

This study was selected because it addresses many of constructs described in this chapter as stress mediators or moderators and because it illustrates that resource variables such as social support can have both direct effects and indirect effects via coping (see Figure 2 for indirect and direct effects on depression, but indirect effect only on FD). Social support seems to enhance the proactive coping efforts these elderly

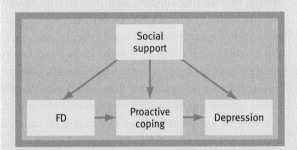

Figure 1 Theoretical model relating proactive coping, FD, social support, and depression

Figure 2 Modified model

participants engage in and, as such, proactive coping can be described as mediating the effects of social support on functional disability and on depression. Coping, in this case, proactive coping, was associated with both less depression and less functional disability, suggesting a positive role for beliefs such as those contained in the proactive coping measure, e.g. 'I always find a way around obstacles, nothing really stops me'. The authors describe how this form of coping relates to self-efficacy.

In spite of the limitation of a cross-sectional design (thus all arrows between constructs could go in either direction really as causality is not established) and a sample perhaps biased towards the more educated elderly person (who may thus have greater resources of all tyes, financial, practical, social, see Chapter 2 ☞), this study highlights the value of an integrative model of social support and coping in relation to emotional and physical outcomes of importance in our ageing society. It also adds to a body of work on proactive coping, which suggest potential opportunities for intervention to enhance such coping, possibly via self-efficacy training.

Evidence for indirect or 'buffering' effect of social support

The effect of perceived and actual social support on the appraisal of stressful events has not perhaps been rigorously studied to date, although there is some evidence that perceiving social support as being available

contributes to more positive outcome expectancies and appraisals of control over the event. Furthermore, perceptions of control in relation to illness outcomes were positively associated with seeking social support in a meta-analysis of 45 empirical studies, albeit not as strongly as might have been expected (Hagger and Orbell 2003). The authors consider that this may in part be due to social support being assessed as part of a generic measure of coping, as opposed to more specific assessment of the different types and function of social support.

Generally speaking, seeking social support is considered an active coping strategy, whether the support is sought for informational and practical reasons or with the goal of emotional support. For example, Kyngaes *et al.* (2001) examined the coping strategies of young people within two months of developing cancer and found that they engaged in emotion-, appraisal- and problem-focused coping strategies, and accessing social support was one of the most common strategies. Different 'functions' of support were seen in that they sought information about their disease and its treatment from health professionals, and emotional support from their families.

Stroebe and colleagues tested the widely held assumption that social support acts as a buffer against the impact of loss following bereavement in their study of 1,532 recently widowed adults aged over 65 years (Stroebe *et al.* 2005). They found limited evidence of support acting as a buffer against loss, or that it facilitated general 'recovery', when assessing participants at 6, 18 and 48 months after bereavement. What they did find, however, is that social support had a beneficial effect on depression levels. This is consistent with findings that social support buffered the impact of depression on mortality following a heart attack (Frasure-Smith *et al.* 2000).

Gender and cultural influences on seeking support

Gender is considered to be a robust predictor of the use of social support, with many empirical studies finding that females have a greater tendency both to seek and provide social support, and as a result tend to report larger social networks than males. Taylor (2006) suggests that female socialisation may generate a 'tend and befriend' response in times of stress, whereby nurturing loved ones or seeking and maintaining supportive networks are characteristic coping behaviours. Within spousal relationships, male partners tend to receive their support from female spouses, whereas female partners tend to receive support from female friends and relatives.

There are consistent findings that cultural differences exist in the norms of support-seeking behaviour and in the perceptions of available support, where Asian cultures, which have a collectivist rather than individualist orientation, tend not to seek or expect support (V.

Lawrence *et al.* 2008; Kim *et al.* 2009). As Kim *et al.* state, 'people in the more collectivistic cultures may be relatively more cautious about bringing personal problems to the attention of others for the purpose of enlisting their help because they share the cultural assumption that individuals should not burden their social networks and that others share the same sense of social obligation' (p. 519). In contrast, Europeans, and Americans, use friends for support as much as, if not sometimes more than, family (Chun *et al.* 2007, Taylor *et al.* 2004; and see review by Parveen 2011). It is consistently found that in Asian samples (including Chinese, Korean, Japanese), for example, carers of those with chronic or disabling illness (see Chapter 15 ☛) report receiving significantly less social support than that reported by white American carers (e.g. Chun *et al.* 2007; McCabe *et al.* 2005; Katbamna *et al.* 2004). Interestingly, however, this difference may only be between Asian and non-Asian; Lincoln *et al.* (2003), for example, found in contrast that African Americans turned to family for support to a greater extent than did European Americans. The difference seems to lie in the 'seeking' of support, with Asian individuals exhibiting reluctance to disrupt relationships by talking of personal problems and seeking explicit support. Taylor *et al.* (2007) found that in Asian cultures the perception of having the 'implicit support' of others was more acceptable than explicitly seeking or receiving support, as it does not necessitate any disclosure of problems to others. Implicit support was both biologically (seen in reduced cortisol responses) and psychologically (seen in reduced stress scores) more beneficial to their Asian American participants, with the reverse actually being true for European Americans for whom explicit support is preferred and more beneficial. A review of studies relating to this important cultural difference is found in Kim *et al.*'s (2009) paper, and strongly highlights the need for cultural norms to be taken into account when, for example, considering any intervention which aims to deliver explicit support.

Can social support be bad for you?

There are some instances where high levels of social support can be detrimental. For example, among pain patients, it was found that high social support in terms of providing practical assistance with everyday tasks caused poor adaptation through operant conditioning (e.g. Gil *et al.* 1987). Over-caring can cause the care recipient to become overly dependent on the carer and overly passive in terms of their own recovery (see Chapter 15 ☞). In addition, the type of social support provided may not always be received as supportive, or, more importantly, the help offered may not match the needs of the patient: e.g. instrumental support is helpful if aspects of the event are controllable; emotional support may be more helpful when things are uncontrollable, e.g. after a death (e.g. Cutrona and Russell 1990).

Finally, there is a caveat in social support research. Given the subjectivity of the construct in that it is defined in terms of 'How much social support do you perceive?', studies have to rely on self-report. As noted elsewhere, there are inherent biases in gathering self-report data, and it is likely that individual difference variables, such as neuroticism, may influence not only an individual's perceptions of the nature and level of social support they have received but also their satisfaction with it. Additionally, personality or emotional state might interfere with social resources and in effect prevent or enhance a person's ability to access support, or gain from it (see discussion of hostility or depression).

SUMMARY

The evidence reviewed in Chapter 11 ☞ suggested that stress can increase the risk of artery damage, which in turn encourages the development of CHD. This is a direct effect proposal, which implies that simply reducing stress exposure would reduce the likelihood of that disease. However, this chapter has shown this to be overly simplistic. Many factors moderate the impact of stress on health, or the impact of stressful illness upon longer-term outcomes such as disability, distress and survival. This chapter has described how factors attributed to a person's personal profile (age, gender, ethnicity), personality, beliefs, emotions, and use of social support can affect stress responses in terms of coping or in terms of physiological responses, and how such responses influence health outcomes. Such variables can be studied in terms of the direct relationships they have with stress outcomes, or as variables that need to be controlled for when examining other predictors. For example, one study might examine whether trait neuroticism predicts psychological distress following surgery, where another study might control for neuroticism in examining the effects of a pre-surgical information sheet on patient distress following surgery. Whatever the research question, it has become increasingly clear that many variables influence how potentially stressful events are appraised and responded to, and that biological, psychological and sociocultural factors work together in the stress–health-illness experience.

Further reading

Jones, F. and Bright, J. (2001). *Stress: Myth, Theory and Research*. Harlow: Prentice Hall.

An accessible and useful book which covers the main theoretical and methodological approaches to the study of stress.

Snyder, C. and Lopez, S.J. (2005). *Handbook of Positive Psychology*. New York: Oxford University Press.

A comprehensive collection of chapters from eminent research academics such as Martin Seligman (positive psychology), Ed Diener (science of happiness), Howard Tennen and Glenn Affleck (benefit-finding). The chapters address the cognitive, emotional, interpersonal, behavioural and biological aspects of positive strengths such as seen in appraisals, coping or social support mechanisms.

Key papers

Adler, N.E. and Matthews, K.A. (1994). Health psychology: why do some people get sick and some stay well? *Annual Review of Psychology*, 45: 229–59.

A classic overview of many of the moderating variables discussed in this chapter which is useful conceptually, although you will definitely need to supplement your reading of this with reading of more recent empirical papers!

De Neve, K.M. and Cooper, H. (1998). The happy personality: a meta-analysis of 137 personality traits and subjective wellbeing. *Psychological Bulletin*, 124: 197–229.

Given the burgeoning field of positive psychology, this review and reanalysis of a wide body of evidence regarding personality and what makes or keeps us happy remains a worthwhile read.

Folkman, S. (2008). The case for positive emotions in the stress process. *Anxiety, Stress and Coping*, 21: 3–14.

Again reflecting the growth in positive psychology, this paper describes, after many years of focusing primarily on the role of negative emotions in stress appraisal, coping and outcomes, the evidence of the significant role played by co-occurring positive emotions.

Semmer, N.K. (2006). Personality, stress, and coping. In M.E. Vollrath (ed.), *Handbook of Personality and Health*. London: Wiley, pp. 73–113.

A clear account of the various processes and mechanisms through which personality may influence stress and coping responses and disease risk, progression or other outcomes.

Taylor, S.E., Welch, W., Kim, H.S. and Sherman, D.K. (2007). Cultural differences in the impact of social support on psychological and biological stress responses. *Psychological Science*, 18: 831–7.

A fascinating and important review of a strong body of evidence pointing to cultural variations in support-seeking coping – read this if you are planning a social support intervention!

Tennen, H., Affleck, G., Armeli, S. *et al.* (2000). A daily process approach to coping: linking theory, research, and practice. *American Psychologist*, 55: 620–5.

An impressive longitudinal study of pain patients where daily measures of coping were taken. While a time-consuming methodology, daily measurement is an excellent way of illustrating dynamic processes such as coping.

Uchino, B.N. (2006). Social support and health: a review of physiological processes potentially underlying links to disease outcomes. *Journal of Behavioral Medicine*, 29: 377–87.

A well-presented review of social support and its effects on cardiovascular, endocrine and immune system functioning. Very useful summaries are provided of key studies.

Weblinks

For personality assessment items based on a scientific collaboration to develop advanced measures of personality and other individual difference variables, go to the International Personality Item Pool at:

http://ipip.ori.org/ipip

Visit the website at **www.pearsoned.co.uk/morrison** for additional resources to help you with your study, including multiple choice questions, weblinks and flashcards.

Chapter 13
Managing stress

Learning outcomes

By the end of this chapter, you should have an understanding of:

- the second and third wave cognitive and behavioural approaches to stress management
- ways of intervening at a population or organisational level to reduce work stress
- interventions of value in helping people to cope with the stress associated with a surgical operation

Stress costs the National Health Service millions of pounds

No surprise in that, we hear you think. And, indeed, stress-related diseases do cost the British National Health Service (NHS) millions of pounds. But these are not the only cause of stress-related financial drain on valuable NHS resources – some can be directly influenced by the health-care system itself. Staff sickness due to stress is estimated to cost the NHS £400 million a year (*Guardian* newspaper, 19 August 2009). Less measurable is the impact of stress on patient recovery. Being in hospital and having an operation are both inherently stressful events: stress that may impact on patients' experience of pain, their use of pain medication, and even the time taken to recover from surgery. Conversely, simple interventions to reduce stress prior to an operation or giving patients control over pain medication have been shown to reduce the amount of pain medication used, and even reduce the time patients spend in hospital. Stress may be an ambiguous term, it may even be inherent in the experience of being a health-care worker or patient, but reducing the stress of both hospital staff and their patients may not only make their lives better but also actually save money.

Chapter outline

Stress, they say, is all around us. Indeed, one of the most frequently reported problems in general practitioners' surgeries is tiredness – often as a symptom of stress. Other chapters in this book comment on the role of stress in the development of illness (Chapter 11 ☞), or how learning to manage stress effectively can enhance mood, improve the outcome of a number of diseases and reduce the experience of pain (Chapters 16, 17 ☞). What they do not consider in any detail is how such changes can be achieved. This chapter addresses this issue from a number of perspectives. It first reviews the basic cognitive-behavioural models of stress, before building on these and more complex models to introduce two distinct approaches to the treatment of stress. The first, commonly referred to as stress management training, adopts a traditional cognitive-behavioural approach to the treatment of stress. The second involves more recent developments in cognitive-behaviour therapy, sometimes referred to as the third wave therapies. This section builds on Chapters 11 and 12 ☞, which examined the relationship between stress, coping and illness and will prepare you for Chapters 16 and 17 ☞, which include sections on how stress management and third wave therapies can help people to cope with illness and pain. The chapter then considers approaches used to minimise stress in healthy individuals, both in the public at large and in the workplace. In this, it complements Chapters 5 and 6 ☞ and their consideration of health-promotion strategies, considering how we can reduce stress through working with both the individual and the wider environment. Finally, we consider how stress may be minimised when people face a specific stressor – in this case a surgical intervention – in hospital, using relatively simple interventions.

Stress theory: a quick review

In this first section, we examine some components of a set of interventions collectively referred to as **stress management training**. They are based on cognitive-

behavioural theories of stress, which consider stress to be the outcome of a variety of environmental and cognitive processes. Stress is seen as a negative emotional and physiological state resulting from our cognitive responses to events that occur around us: that is, stress can be seen as a process rather than an outcome. We discussed appraisal and transactional theories of stress in Chapter 11 ☞. Stress management approaches are in part based on these theories and in part based on more clinical theories, the two most prominent of which are those of Aaron Beck (1976) and Albert Ellis (1977). Both assumed that our cognitive response to events – not the events themselves – determines our mood, and that feelings of distress or other negative emotional states

> **stress management training**
> a generic term for interventions designed to teach participants how to cope with stress.

> **cognitive schemata**
>
> set of unconscious beliefs about the world and ourselves that shape more conscious cognitive responses to events that impinge on us.

are a consequence of 'faulty' or 'irrational' thinking (see Figure 13.1). That is, they considered stress to be the result of *misinterpretations* of environmental events or cognitions that exaggerate the negative elements within them and lose focus on any positive aspects of the situation.

Beck referred to the thoughts that drive negative emotions as automatic negative assumptions. They come to mind automatically as the individual's first response to a particular situation and are without logic or grounding in reality. Despite this, their very automaticity means they are unchallenged and taken as true. He identified two levels of cognition. Surface cognitions are those we are aware of. We can access them and report them relatively easily. Underlying them are a set of unconscious beliefs about ourselves and the world, known as **cognitive schemata** (singular, schema) which influence our surface cognitions and, in turn, influence our emotions, behaviour and physiological arousal. Stress-evoking thoughts, for example, result in an increase in sympathetic nervous system arousal (see Chapter 8 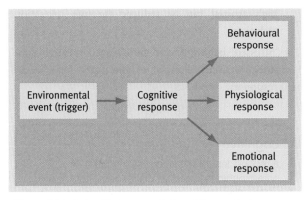), behaviour that may be more or less helpful in resolving the problem an individual is facing, and feelings of anxiety. Beck identified a number of categories of thought that lead to negative emotions, including:

- *Catastrophic thinking*: considering an event as completely negative, and potentially disastrous: 'That's it – I've had a heart attack. I'm bound to lose my job, and I won't be able to earn enough to pay the mortgage.'

- *Over-generalisation*: drawing a general (negative) conclusion on the basis of a single incident: 'That's it – my pain stopped me going to the cinema – that's something else I can't do.'

- *Arbitrary inference*: drawing a conclusion without sufficient evidence to support it: 'The pain means I have a tumour. I just know it.'

- *Selective abstraction*: focusing on a detail taken out of context: 'OK, I know I was able to cope with going out, but my joints ached all the time, and I know that will stop me going out in future.'

A good example of how long-term schemata drive very stressful ways of responding to external events is provided by Price's (1988) cognitive model of Type A behaviour (see Chapter 12). From her clinical work with Type A men, she concluded that the schemata underlying Type A behaviour were low self-esteem and a belief that one can gain the esteem of others only by continually proving oneself as an 'achiever' and a capable individual. These underlying beliefs underpinned more conscious competitive, time-urgent or hostile thoughts.

Surface cognitions associated with Type A behaviour include:

- *Time-urgent thoughts*: 'Come on – we haven't got all day – I'm going to be late! Why is he so slow? Am I the only person who gets things done around here?'

- *Hostile thoughts*: 'That person cut me up deliberately! I'll sort him out. Why is everyone else so incompetent – they really are pretty stupid.'

Deeper (unconscious) schemata include:

- 'I can't say no to her request or I will look incompetent and I will lose her respect.'

- 'I must get to the meeting on time – whatever the cost – or people will think I'm incompetent and I will lose their respect.'

- 'People only respect you for what you do for them – not for who you are.'

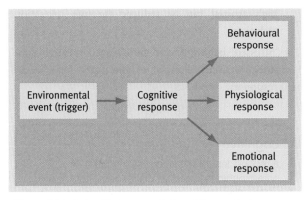

Figure 13.1 A simplified representation of the event–stress process suggested by Beck and other cognitive therapists

The cognitive-behavioural model of stress assumes that stress lies within the individual. Stress arises from the misinterpretation of events that happen to us. But is this really true? It is possible to argue that while some stress may be the result of faulty thinking, stress can also be triggered by truly stressful circumstances. Most people would consider having a surgical operation, for example, to be a stressful event. Theorists such as Hobfoll have argued that many more general factors, such as being a single mother or holding down a demanding job, are universally stressful events. Arguments that socio-economic status influences health through psychological processes discussed in Chapter 2 ☛ also suggest that there are broad differences in the degree of stress experienced across different social groups.

If these assertions are true, then, at least in some cases, stress truly does result from environmental circumstances and not from an individual's interpretation of a situation. Such arguments may lead us to question how relevant stress management techniques based on the cognitive-behavioural models described above can be in these contexts.

The argument that cognitive-behavioural therapists would marshal against this critique is that, even acknowledging that there are environmental factors that influence stress, some people cope with them better than others. There is individual variability in our ability to cope with similar demands placed on us. The role of stress management is not to deny the role of the environment but to help people to cope with the stressful circumstances they face as effectively as they can and with the least possible emotional distress. This seems to be a reasonable argument, but it leaves a number of questions for health psychologists. One particularly pertinent issue is how much effort we should put into changing the sources of stress and how much into changing people's responses to potentially stressful environments. Should we put our emphasis on reducing social inequalities by changing the environment, or on helping people to cope better with the demands of their environment here and now? Should we help some people to cope better with operations, or try to make the processes before and after an operation less stressful for all? Often, teaching people to cope better with stressful situations is easier and cheaper than changing the causes of stress. But is it the best approach?

Stress management training

The model of the stress response described above suggests a series of factors that can be changed in order to reduce an individual's stress. These include:

● environmental events that trigger the stress response – or series of triggers to longer-term stress;

● inappropriate behavioural, physiological or cognitive responses that occur in response to this event.

Most stress management programmes focus on changing people's reactions to events that happen around them or to them. Many simply teach relaxation to minimise the high levels of arousal associated with stress (see Chapter 11 ☛). More complex interventions try to change participants' cognitive (and therefore emotional) reactions to these events. Few address the factors that trigger the stress response in the first place. This can be considered a serious limitation – the most effective way of reducing stress is to prevent it occurring in the first place. Accordingly, we incorporate into our overview of stress management training a process of both identifying and changing triggers to stress as well as strategies for dealing with stressful thoughts, feelings, emotions and behaviour once initiated:

● Triggers can be identified and modified using problem-solving strategies.

● Cognitive distortions can be identified and changed through a number of cognitive techniques, such as **cognitive restructuring** (see below).

● High levels of muscular tension and other signs of high arousal can be reduced through relaxation techniques.

● 'Stressed' behaviour can be changed through consideration and rehearsal of alternative behavioural responses.

cognitive restructuring
a reconsideration of automatic negative or catastrophic thoughts to make them more in line with reality.

Changing triggers

This is an often neglected part of stress management training, perhaps because there is no standard intervention that can be applied. The triggers to each person's stress necessarily differ, as will any strategies they develop to reduce their frequency. Changing them involves first identifying situations that contribute to an individual's stress and then either changing their nature or reducing the frequency with which they occur. A simple strategy to reduce an individual's level of stress or anger while driving to work, for example, may be to start the journey earlier than previously so they feel less pressure during the journey.

One of the most frequently used approaches to identifying and changing triggers to stress was developed by Gerard Egan (1998). His model of problem-focused counselling introduced in Chapter 6 ☞ can be adapted to coping with stress, so stress triggers are dealt with in three stages:

1. *Problem exploration and clarification*: what are the triggers to stress?

2. *Goal setting*: which stress triggers does the individual want to change?

3. *Facilitating action*: how do they set about changing these stress triggers?

Stress may have multiple sources, and some areas of stress may be easier to change than others. It can be helpful to change relatively easy triggers at the beginning of any attempt at change before working towards more difficult-to-change triggers as the individual gains skills or confidence in their ability to change. Some changes can be achieved using the personal resources already available to the individual – once they have planned how they will achieve them, they feel confident in their ability to put the plan into action. Others may require the individual to learn new skills in order to manage their stress more effectively. They may benefit, for example, from learning to relax or reducing the frequency or type of any stress-provoking thoughts that contribute to their stress. It is to these taught skills that we now turn.

Relaxation training

The goal of teaching relaxation skills is to enable the individual to relax as much as is possible and appropriate both throughout the day and at times of particular stress. This contrasts with procedures such as meditation, which often provide a period of deep relaxation and 'time out' as sufficient in themselves. As well as the physical benefits, effective use of relaxation techniques can lead to an increase in actual and perceived control over the stress response. This can be a valuable outcome in itself. Relaxation may also increase access to calm and constructive thought processes, although this is a relatively weak effect, reflecting the reciprocity between each of the different stress components. Relaxation skills are best learned through three phases:

1. learning basic relaxation skills;

2. monitoring tension in daily life;

3. using relaxation at times of stress.

Learning relaxation skills

The first stage involves learning to relax under optimal conditions – a comfortable chair in a quiet room. Ideally, a trained practitioner should teach the process of deep relaxation. This can then be added to by continued practice at home, typically using taped instructions. Regular practice over a period of days, and sometimes weeks, is important at this stage, as the skills need to be well practised and relatively automatic before they can be used effectively in 'real life' contexts.

The relaxation process most commonly taught is based on Jacobson's (1938) deep muscle relaxation technique. This involves alternately tensing and relaxing muscle groups throughout the body in an ordered sequence. Over time, the emphasis of practice shifts towards relaxation without prior tension, or relaxing specific muscle groups while using others, to mimic the use of relaxation in the 'real world'. The order in which the muscles are relaxed varies, but a typical exercise may involve the following stages (the tensing procedure is described in brackets):

- hands and forearms (making a fist);
- upper arms (touching fingers to shoulder);
- shoulders and lower neck (pulling up shoulders);
- back of neck (touching chin to chest);
- lips (pushing them together);
- forehead (frowning);
- abdomen/chest (holding deep breath);
- abdomen (tensing stomach muscles);
- legs and feet (push heel away, pull toes to point at head: not lifting leg).

Time	Situation	Tension	Behaviours	Thoughts
8.32	Driving to work – late!	62	Tense – gripping steering wheel Cutting up other drivers Cursing at traffic lights	Late again!! . . . the boss is bound to notice . . . Come on – hurry up – I haven't got all day! Why do these bloody traffic lights always take so long to change?!
10.00	Presenting work to colleagues	75	Spoke too quickly Rushed	I'm not looking good here . . . why can I never do this properly? They must think I'm a fool! I feel a wreck!

Figure 13.2 Excerpt from a stress diary noting stress triggers, levels of tension and related behaviours and thoughts

At the same time as practising relaxation skills, individuals can begin to monitor their levels of physical tension throughout the day. Initially, this serves as a learning process, helping them to identify how tense they are at particular times and what triggered any excessive tension. This process may also help to identify likely future triggers to stress and provide clues as to when the relaxation procedures may be particularly useful. This frequently involves the use of a 'tension diary', in which the individual records their level of tension on some form of numerical scale (0 = no tension, 100 = the highest tension possible) at regular intervals throughout the day or at times of particular stress. As a prelude to cognitive or behavioural interventions, such diaries may also focus on the thoughts, emotions or behaviour experienced at such times. Figure 13.2 provides an excerpt from a typical stress diary. As the individual begins to use additional strategies to combat their stress, they may add columns measuring their level of tension after the use of relaxation, the thoughts they used to deal with their stressful thoughts, and so on.

After a period of learning relaxation techniques and monitoring tension, individuals can begin to integrate relaxation into their daily lives. At this stage, relaxation involves reducing tension to appropriate levels while engaging in everyday activities. Initially, this may involve trying to keep as relaxed as possible and appropriate at times of relatively low stress and then, as the individual becomes more skilled, using relaxation at times of increasing stress. The goal of relaxation at these times is not to escape from the cause of stress but to remain as relaxed as possible while dealing with the particular stressor. An alternative strategy involves relaxing at regular intervals (such as during coffee breaks) throughout the day.

Cognitive interventions

Two strategies for changing cognitions are frequently employed. The simplest, known as self-instruction training, was developed by Meichenbaum (1985) and is targeted at surface cognitions. It involves interrupting the flow of stressogenic (stress-provoking) thoughts and replacing them with pre-rehearsed stress reducing or 'coping' thoughts – so-called 'positive **self-talk**'. These typically fall into one of two categories. The first are reminders to use any stress-coping techniques the person has learned ('You're winding yourself up here – come on, take it easy, remember to relax, deep breathe, relax your muscles'). The second form of self-instruction acts as a form of reassurance, reminding the individual that they have previously coped effectively with their feelings of distress and will be able to now ('Come on, you've dealt with this before – you should be able to again – keep calm – things will not get out of control'). To make sure these are relevant to the individual, and to help to actually evoke these thoughts at times of stress, Meichenbaum suggested that particular coping thoughts should be rehearsed, wherever possible, before the stressful events occur – whether in a therapy session or minutes before an anticipated stressor is likely to occur. At a minimum, such thoughts interrupt the flow

> **self-talk**
> talking to oneself (internally). Can be negative and thus add to stress. Therapeutically, individuals are taught to use self-talk in a way that helps them to keep calm.

of stressful thoughts; at best, they actively reduce an individual's levels of stress.

A more complex intervention, known as cognitive restructuring, involves first identifying and then challenging the accuracy of stressogenic thoughts. It asks the individual to consider them as hypotheses, not facts, and to assess their validity without bias. This process may involve consideration of both surface cognitions and cognitive schemata – although the latter require significant insight and may best be achieved in the context of therapy. To teach the skill, the therapist typically uses a process known as the Socratic method or 'guided discovery' (Beck 1976), in which the client identifies a number of thoughts, and then challenges their accuracy under the guidance of their therapist. They may challenge their stressful assumptions by asking key questions such as:

- What evidence is there that supports or denies my assumption?
- Are there any other ways I can think about this situation?
- Could I be making a mistake in the way I am thinking?

Once the individual can engage in this process within the therapy session, they are encouraged to use the Socratic process at times when they experience stress in their daily lives (see also the discussion of the downward-arrow technique in Chapter 6 (☞)).

Behavioural interventions

The goal of behavioural change is to help the individual respond to any stress triggers in ways that maximise their effectiveness in dealing with the trigger and cause them minimal stress. Some behaviour can be relatively simple. Behaviour that reduces the stress of driving may involve driving within the speed limits, putting the handbrake on when stopped at traffic lights and taking time to relax, not cutting in front of other cars, and so on. Others may take practice – a person who becomes excessively angry, for example, may role-play assertive responses in therapy sessions to prepare them for doing the same in 'real life'. Still others may have to be thought through at the time of the stress. Here, the goal of stress management training may be to teach the individual to plan their response to any potential stressor to be one that minimises their personal stress. A simple rule of thumb that can be useful

> **stress inoculation training**
>
> a form of stress-reducing intervention in which participants are taught to control stress by rehearsing prior to going into stressful situations. Participants are taught to relax and use calming self-talk. The approach was developed by Donald Meichenbaum.

here is to encourage individuals to stop and plan what they are going to do – even if this takes a few seconds – rather than to jump into action without thought, as this typically leads to more rather than less stress.

Stress inoculation training

In his approach called **stress inoculation training**, Meichenbaum (1985) suggested that the various strands of cognitive therapy described above could be combined so that, when an individual is facing a stressor, they concentrate on:

- checking that their behaviour is appropriate to the circumstances;
- maintaining relaxation;
- giving themselves appropriate self-talk.

In addition, he suggested that, where a particular stressor can be anticipated, the opportunity should be taken to rehearse these actions before the event itself. Once in the situation, the planned strategies should be enacted. Finally, after the situation has occurred, time should be given to review what occurred and successes or failures learned from – rather than treated as triumphs or disasters that should be soon forgotten.

The third wave therapies

Historically, the stress management approach outlined above falls into what has become known as the second wave of cognitive-behavioural therapies. The first wave theories and treatments were based on Pavlov and Skinner's conditioning theories, and did not consider changing cognitions to be relevant to behavioural change. The second wave adopted a much more cognitive approach, viewing cognitions as central to both the development and treatment of emotional problems. Although most stress management interventions are still based on this approach, the so-called third wave of therapies is now gaining increasing empirical validation and use in the treatment of emotional disorders. The key characteristic of the third wave approach can be characterised by the phrase 'Feel the fear, but do it anyway'. It adopts a more behavioural stance, shifting the focus from changing cognitions back to directly changing behaviour.

Proponents of this approach (e.g. Hayes *et al.* 2004; Wells 2000) state that one way in which we become inappropriately anxious or distressed is through the avoidance of difficult or feared situations. As a consequence we fail to learn that many of our fears are exaggerated, and that we could actually cope more effectively in the avoided situation than we believe. The goal of therapy is therefore to encourage the individual to engage in a feared behaviour, cope with the emotional or physiological responses they may experience while doing so, and through successful negotiation of the situation come to learn that there is actually nothing to fear.

The treatment of someone with agoraphobia using second and third wave therapies may illustrate the contrasting principles of the two approaches. Treatment using second wave therapies would involve the use of Socratic dialogue to help the individual both identify and learn to challenge some of the catastrophic beliefs they may hold about leaving the house ('I will faint or collapse and make a fool of myself', 'I will feel so frightened I will not be able to cope', etc.). These beliefs will be challenged and rationalised: 'The last time I went out, I didn't feel too bad. If I feel faint, I can always sit down until I feel better', 'I can use the relaxation to help me get through this, so I will be able to cope', and so on. They may be taught to use coping skills such as relaxation and cognitive challenge when they do go out of the house. Finally, they will engage in a programme of leaving the house into increasingly challenging situations, using these skills to help them cope. The third wave therapies would still involve participants being taught a number of coping skills to help them cope when out of the house. However, these would not involve cognitive challenge or self-talk. Rather, they involve skills such as mindfulness meditation (see below) to help reduce the emotional impact of any negative cognitions rather than trying to rationalise them away. Success is measured by increasing engagement in the behavioural programme and experiencing less emotional distress while doing so.

Metacognitive therapy

The first 'third wave' therapy to be discussed here is the metacognitive therapy of Adrian Wells (e.g. Wells 2000). Wells (2000) argued that the second generation CBT theories focused on the *content* of thoughts and ignored the *form* that such thinking takes and the mechanisms that give dysfunctional thoughts their power. His Self-Regulatory Executive Function (S-REF) model was developed to remedy these deficiencies. The model focuses on both the content of cognitions and the processes associated with them.

According to Wells, emotional distress arises following an appraisal of a disjunction between an actual and desired state ('If I stay here I am going to get really stressed', 'My angina is going to be triggered if I do any exercise'), and the development of plans to reduce or obviate this discrepancy. In the case of stress or anxiety (or the perceived health risk of exercising), these plans may simply involve the avoidance of the situation that causes or contributes to the stress. This may reduce the immediate discrepancy between feeling fearful and the desired state of not being fearful. However, continued use of avoidance as a coping strategy prevents the individual from learning that the feared situation will not actually occur or result in harm. Plans may also involve accessing and attending to beliefs that may be negative and upsetting, and which trigger negative emotional states. The goals of therapy, or metacognitive therapy as Wells refers to it, include:

● teaching individuals to develop more flexible coping strategies to use in stressful situations – to 'unlock' themselves from previous patterns of inappropriate coping responses;

● encouraging participants to engage in feared behaviours or enter feared situations in a graduated process, using skills such as mindfulness to help them cope with difficult thoughts or emotions;

● teaching individuals a 'a higher metacognitive mode' which allows them to process information in ways that do not trigger high levels of distress.

Wells adopted two key supportive strategies to help people achieve any changes they wish to make: mindfulness and active distraction. Both can be used to build tolerance to distressing thoughts or emotions that may arise while they are planning or engaging in new ways of responding to difficult situations.

Mindfulness

According to Buddhist learning, mindfulness is necessary on the road to enlightenment, and is achieved through the meditative process of focusing one's awareness on the present – not memories of the past or possible creations of the future. Through meditation, we can learn that 'thoughts are just thoughts' that may or may not be true. However, we can also learn to ignore particular thoughts or to be aware of them without them evoking an emotional reaction. Bishop *et al.* (2004) proposed a two-component model of mindfulness:

- *Self-regulation of attention*: this involves being fully aware of current experience – observing and attending to changing thoughts, feelings and sensations as they occur, but not elaborating on these experiences. Rather than getting caught up in ruminative thoughts, mindfulness involves a direct non-judgemental experience of events in the mind and body as they occur. This leads to a feeling of being very alert and 'alive'.

- *An orientation toward one's experiences in the present moment characterised by curiosity, openness and acceptance*: the lack of cognitive effort given to the elaboration on the meanings and associations of our various experiences allows the individual to focus more on their present experience. Rather than observing experience through the filter of our beliefs and assumptions, mindfulness involves a direct, unfiltered awareness of our experiences.

Clearly, learning mindfulness is not simple, and most teaching programmes involve attending a number of classes spread over many weeks or months. During meditation, participants learn to focus on a particular physical stimulus, such as a picture, or a sensory stimulus such as the sound of a repeated mantra, and to be aware of, but not focused on, unwanted intrusive sensations, thoughts or emotions. Participants also practise mindfulness during ordinary activities like walking, standing and eating. Wells and Matthews (1996) stated that mindfulness can help people be aware of and change their cognitions and meta-cognitions without being overwhelmed by them. It can also be used at times when potentially distressing thoughts come to mind. Rather than challenge such thoughts, practitioners of mindfulness learn to be aware of them, but only as a small, unattended part of their perceptual awareness – which is still focused on the immediate experiences of the moment.

As well as a component of therapy, mindfulness can form a primary intervention in itself. The most frequently cited method of mindfulness training is the mindfulness-based stress reduction (MBSR) programme of Kabat-Zinn (e.g. 1990). The programme comprises an 8–10-week course for groups who meet weekly for around two hours for instruction and practice in mindfulness meditation skills, together with discussion of stress, coping, and homework assignments. An all-day (7–8-hr) intensive mindfulness session is usually held around the sixth week. Several mindfulness meditation skills are taught. For example, the 'body scan' is a 45-min exercise in which attention is directed sequentially to numerous areas of the body while the participant is lying down with eyes closed. Sensations in each area are carefully observed. In sitting meditation, participants are instructed to sit in a relaxed and wakeful posture with eyes closed and to direct attention to the sensations of breathing. Hatha yoga postures are used to teach mindfulness of bodily sensations during gentle movements and stretching. Participants also practise mindfulness during ordinary activities like walking, standing and eating. Participants in MBSR are instructed to practise these skills outside group meetings for at least 45 minutes a day, for six days per week. Audiotapes are used early in treatment, but participants are encouraged to practise without tapes after a few weeks. For all mindfulness exercises, participants are instructed to focus attention on the target of observation (e.g. breathing or walking), and to be aware of it in each moment. When emotions, sensations, or cognitions arise, they are observed non-judgementally. When the participant notices that their mind has wandered into thoughts, memories or fantasies, their nature or content is briefly noted, if possible, and then attention is returned to the present moment. Even judgemental thoughts (e.g. 'This is a waste of time') are to be observed non-judgementally! An important consequence of mindfulness practice is the realisation that most sensations, thoughts and emotions fluctuate, or are transient, passing by 'like waves in the sea'.

Attention control skills

Attentional training is somewhat easier than mindfulness to master. Unlike mindfulness, it does not help participants to tolerate the experience of distressing thoughts. Rather, it gives the individual 'time-out' from them. Because Wells argues that avoidance of worrisome thoughts is a core contributor to continued distress, he states that distraction is not to be used at times of high distress – at such times mindfulness should be used to help the individual learn to tolerate their distressing thoughts. Rather, it can be used as a time-out to 'reset maladaptive thought processes' at times when the individual is not experiencing particularly high levels of distress. The process is first taught in a therapy session, and then used as homework. It involves initially fixating on a visual stimulus such as a mark on the wall and then focusing attention for several moments on each of a series of different sounds, such as the therapist's voice, tapping, the ticking of a clock. The individual is instructed to focus exclusively on only the sound. The patient then shifts their attention rapidly between the set of sounds, before listening simultaneously to all the sounds, trying to be aware of as many of them as possible. The whole sequence takes between 10 and 15 minutes to enact.

Acceptance and commitment therapy

According to Hayes *et al.* (2004: 143), ACT is a therapy approach that uses acceptance and mindfulness as well as commitment and behaviour change processes to produce a greater psychological flexibility. ACT is rooted in radical behaviourism, as it assumes that psychological events (thoughts, emotions, behaviour) are the result of classical and operant conditioning processes. In addition, ACT does not consider thoughts or feelings direct behaviour. Change can be achieved through changing contextual variables or direct behavioural change rather than attempts to change internal processes such as cognitions, emotions, sensations, and so on.

The goals of ACT

In common with the S-REF model, ACT teaches the individual to be aware of ongoing private events (thoughts), but not to be driven by them: to be in touch with the present moment as fully as possible, and to either change or persist in behaviours in order to achieve valued goals. All ACT interventions aim to increase the individual's flexibility in responding to situations they face. This flexibility is established through a focus on five, related, core processes: acceptance, defusion, contact with the present moment, values, and committed action.

Acceptance

This involves allowing oneself to be aware of thoughts, feelings, and bodily sensations as they occur, but not to be driven by them. Instead, the aim is to experience non-judgemental awareness of these events and actively embrace the experience. Therapy emphasises that attempts at inappropriate control are costly and stressful and frequently maintain the distress one is trying to control: 'control is the problem, not the solution'. Acceptance is taught through a variety of techniques, including mindfulness. Clients learn through graded exercises that it is possible to feel intense emotions or notice intense and bodily sensations without harm.

Cognitive defusion

This involves teaching clients to see that thoughts are simply thoughts, feelings are simply feelings, memories are memories, and physical sensations are physical sensations. None of these private events are inherently damaging. Just as in the second wave of cognitive therapy, clients are taught that our thoughts form just one interpretation of events, and there are many others that may be equally appropriate to any situation. However, rather than attempt to identify incorrect thoughts and change them to a correct interpretation of events, clients are encouraged to accept their presence, and not to try to change or control them.

Contact with the present moment

Contact comprises effective, open and undefended contact with the present moment. There are two features to this process. First, clients are trained to observe and notice what is present in the environment and in private experience (i.e. their thoughts and emotions). Secondly, they are taught to label and describe what is present, without excessive judgements or evaluation. Together these help establish a sense of 'self as a process of ongoing awareness' of events and experiences. Mindfulness is one technique through which this can be achieved.

Values

These relate to the motivation for change. In order for a client to face feared psychological obstacles, there needs to be a purpose for doing so. The aim of ACT is not simply to rid the person of their problems, but to help them build a more vital, purposeful life. This is a central element of ACT. Its goal is to enable the individual to progress towards valued life goals without being prevented from doing so by historical worries, emotions and other private events.

Committed action

This relates to clients developing strategies for achieving desired goals. Once they have begun to understand how fusion and avoidance are preventing them from moving towards such goals, clients are encouraged to define goals in specific areas and to progress towards them. Progress, or lack of it, towards these goals becomes a key part of therapy. Strosahl *et al.* (2004) identified a number of broad strategies to help people make changes in each of the domains. These included:

● helping the client make direct contact with the paradoxical effect of emotional control strategies: i.e. the more you try to avoid painful thoughts, the more they may be experienced, and avoidance of feared situations leads to continued fear;

● using a graded and structured approach to acceptance as assignments: i.e. a form of systematic desensitisation in which they learn acceptance of painful emotions (and other factors) in gradually more demanding situations;

● using various interventions, including mindfulness, to reveal that unwanted private experiences are not toxic and can be accepted without judgement;

● showing the client how to pull away from worries or ruminations and come back to the present moment.

ACT is a complex therapy involving a variety of behavioural methods as well as the use of stories, metaphors and mental exercises to encourage change. As such, the approach cannot be fully considered within the present chapter. Interested readers may find the book edited by Strosahl *et al.* (2004) a useful further reader. However, the key aim of their approach is that the primary process of change is to engage in previously avoided behaviours or refrain from previous ineffective and problematic coping behaviours, to learn to cope or reduce the distress involved in doing this through the use, for example, of mindfulness, and thereby learn that the feared consequences will not occur. As such, despite many differences in philosophy and approach, both the cognitive approach of Wells and the behavioural approach of the ACT therapists have much in common.

Preventing stress

Teaching stress management strategies

There is clear and increasing evidence that second wave stress management programmes can significantly reduce perceived stress and improve well-being. In addition, there is good evidence that they impact on a variety of biological processes known to be affected by stress. Both Storch *et al.* (2007) and Hammerfald *et al.* (2006), for example, found differing stress management programmes to be effective in reducing both perceived stress and levels of the stress hormone, cortisol (see Chapters 8 and 11 ☞). There is also increasing evidence that mindfulness-based interventions can also reduce stress. Shapiro *et al.* (2008), for example, randomly allocated college undergraduates with no evidence of mental health problems to either a mindfulness intervention or a waiting-list control group. Those in the mindfulness group achieved greater reductions in mindfulness, and with it greater gains on measures of perceived stress and rumination. Nyklícek and Kuijpers (2008) also found mindfulness to be more effective in changing measures of well-being, perceived stress, and exhaustion than a no-treatment control condition. Of course, comparison with a no-treatment group in both studies allows the possibility that any gains were a consequence of seeing a therapist or group dynamics rather than the therapy. However, the results are indicative of the potential for mindfulness to be an effective intervention. This is substantiated by the findings of Smith *et al.* (2008), who compared the effectiveness of an eight-week mindfulness-based intervention with a second wave CBT intervention for people recruited from the community. The mindfulness intervention appeared to be most effective, achieving the same level of benefit as second wave CBT on the core measures of well-being, perceived stress and depression, but performing better on measures of mindfulness (perhaps not surprisingly), energy and pain.

We consider the impact of stress management on well-being and biological processes in people with health problems in more detail in Chapter 17 ☞. The next sections, however, examine stress management interventions conducted with healthy individuals in a specific context – the workplace.

Stress management in the workplace

Stress management interventions clearly have the potential to provide significant benefit to those who take part – but only a very small proportion of the public who have the potential to benefit are likely to take the time and trouble to attend workshops or other training programmes. Health psychologists and others have therefore turned to other methods of attempting to reduce the stress of significant parts of the general population. One of the most important approaches they have adopted is to develop strategies for reducing stress in more 'captive audiences', the most important of which has been people at work.

There is significant and rising pressure on employers to provide staff with the skills to manage stress effectively. In the UK, this has become increasingly important as the Health and Safety Executive, which determines safety standards in the workplace, gives employers a legal obligation to protect the emotional as well as physical well-being of their employees. Their reasons for this policy include data from their own sources (e.g. Jones *et al.* 2003), which indicated that:

- in 2002, over half a million individuals in Britain reported experiencing work-related stress at a level that was making them ill, while nearly one in five thought their job was very or extremely stressful;
- work-related stress, depression or anxiety accounts for an estimated 13.5 million lost working days per year in Britain;
- levels of work stress are rising;
- teachers and nurses have particularly high prevalence of work-related stress.

Most published attempts to reduce stress in the workplace have involved running stress management training at the workplace using similar methods to those described earlier in the chapter: that is, they have tried to help attenders to cope more effectively with the demands placed upon them. These appear to be effective. Summarising the relevant data, Richardson and Rothstein (2008) reported a consistent and significant benefit for those attending stress management programmes outlined earlier in the chapter. In one such study, Eriksen *et al.* (2002) randomly allocated a large group of employees to one of three intervention conditions: physical exercise, stress management training, or an integrated health programme involving physical exercise and health information. None of the interventions influenced health complaints, sick leave or job stress. However, each of the interventions did appear to impact on its target. Participants in the physical activity intervention showed improvements in general health and physical fitness, while the stress management group reported reductions in their levels of general stress. A similar result was reported by Mino *et al.* (2006) who found improvements in general mood following a stress management programme, but little effect on the specific stress associated with work.

There have been a number of criticisms of individually targeted stress management programmes within the workplace. Oldenburg and Harris (1996), for example, noted that this type of programme usually attracts only between 10 and 40 per cent of the workforce – and even less if it is not given a 'high profile' in the workplace. In addition, the majority of people who do attend seem to have relatively few stress-related problems, while many anxious individuals do not attend, perhaps because they feel that they will gain little from such courses or do not want to air their problems in front of their colleagues. Noblet and Lamontagne (2006) had more philosophical concerns, as they suggested that the approach can be seen as labelling those with high stress as somehow not coping, and avoids employers having to modify any work-related causes of stress. The failure of Eriksen *et al.* and Mino *et al.* to influence either work-related stress or levels of sick leave highlights the need to influence these issues more directly – by addressing the *causes* of stress.

Identifying organisational causes of stress is more complex than providing stress management classes and can have more significant implications for an organisation. Table 13.1 indicates the variety of potential stressors that may influence the stress of people working in a hospital, some of which are common to many work situations, some of which are unique to working in health-care settings.

Changing any of these factors may impact on the stress of hospital workers, and working out where and how to intervene at an organisational level is not easy. However, the process used by one of the authors (PB) to reduce stress in a group of hospitals provides an example of how this might be done. The process involved:

- identifying causes of stress in the working environment;
- identifying solutions to this stress from those most involved;
- developing a process of change to address the issues raised.

Table 13.1 Some of the sources of stress for hospital workers

Professional issues	Patient issues	Work issues
Over-promotion	Distressed patients or relatives	Shift work
Under-promotion	'Difficult' patients or relatives	Poor working conditions
Interactions with colleagues	Dying patients	Too high a workload
Interactions with management	Complaints made against staff	Work intruding on home time
Working beyond knowledge level		Lack of social support
Lack of management support		Inadequate equipment

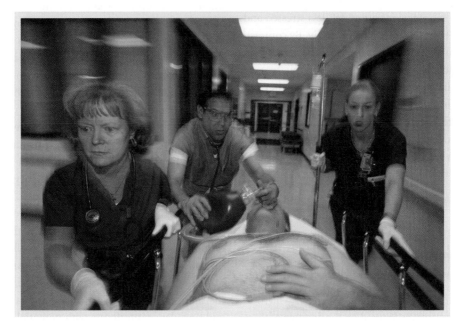

Plate 13.1 Sometimes it can all get too much – a stressed nurse in a busy surgical ward

Source: Alamy Images.

The first two stages of the intervention involved running a series of focus groups with different staff throughout the organisation. These were led by a health psychologist, who worked with the management of the hospital but who was not part of the management team. Many focus groups were run with key hospital staff, including cleaners and porters, nurses, managers, clerical workers, and people from the paramedical professions such as occupational therapists and physiotherapists. In each of these meetings, comprising about six people, attenders were invited to identify factors in their working environments that adversely affected their 'quality of life' at work. If problems were identified – and they inevitably were – they were also asked to identify any solutions to those problems. These meetings were intended to last up to one hour but often went on longer, and were extremely productive.

Each of the issues and solutions put forward in the groups were then arranged into a set of common problems (and perhaps solutions) in a document that formed the basis of the next phase of the intervention. Problems raised included major systemic problems, such as:

- a poor computer network system;
- poor timing of the hospital bus provision (it did not fit in with shift times);
- very poor parking facilities, making transport to and from work difficult;
- inadequate crèche facilities;

- the organisation of various groups of wards in the hospital into competing rather than cooperating units;
- a working culture among management that punished people who did not work significant overtime.

Interestingly, the solutions that some workers had used to manage their stress impacted on other workers by increasing their dissatisfaction and stress. One example of this was that the management team in one hospital had moved its offices away from the wards to avoid what they thought of as too much day-to-day contact with the ward staff and to allow them to concentrate on more long-term planning. As a result, the management group felt less stressed and more able to get on with their job effectively. By contrast, and unbeknown to the management team, the ward nurses were angry and disillusioned as they felt this was an example of management blocking off contact they felt vital to their effective running of the wards.

Once the problems and solutions were documented, these were taken to a small committee of senior managers, which formed a response to the needs. It did so by grouping the issues raised into three broad categories:

1. those likely to have minimal effect, but relatively easy to instigate;
2. those likely to have a significant effect, but more difficult to instigate;
3. those likely to have a significant effect, but impossible to instigate.

Clearly, the interventions focused on the first two of these categories. Changes made included increasing the size of the crèche and lengthening its opening hours so that it was more useful for shift workers, changing the times of the hospital buses to make them more user-friendly, and initiating a new hospital computer system – over a number of years. However, any interventions need not necessarily be on such a large scale. One example of this was provided by a nurse manager, who noted that her staff often arrived late or very close to the time of their morning shift. When she asked them why, she found that these were predominantly single mothers who had to leave their child with a child-minder on their way to work. Because childminders would only take children from a time close to the beginning of the shift, this put these nurses under significant time pressure. If the traffic was good between the childminder's and hospital, they got to work on time; if the traffic was busy or delayed, they were late to work. The simple solution to the problem was to start the shift 15 minutes later.

Do organisational interventions work?

There have been relatively few empirical studies of the effectiveness of this type of intervention. However, those that have been reported suggest they may be of benefit. Maes *et al.* (1990), for example, changed the nature of the working environment by redesigning jobs to avoid short and repetitive performance tasks, giving workers some control over the organisation of work, and enhanced social contact. They also trained managers in communication and leadership skills and encouraged them to develop strategies for reducing stress in their area of work. This intervention resulted in an increase in work quality and lower absenteeism rates in comparison with the control sites, which received no intervention.

A second intervention to use such an approach was reported by Mikkelsen and Saksvik (1999). They intervened in two offices in the Norwegian Post Office. The intention of their intervention was to increase employees' learning opportunities and decision-making authority in order to improve the work environment and health. In order to decide what changes to make, they ran discussion groups with the workers, which 'diagnosed' any problems, then planned and enacted changes to the working environment to remedy them. They reported that work conditions in the larger organisation actually deteriorated over the course of the study, a process that was reversed in one but not both intervention offices. They attribute the failure of the latter to organisational restructuring and turbulence interfering with potential benefits of the intervention. A third, and much simpler, intervention was reported by Dababneh *et al.* (2001). They evaluated the impact of short rest breaks on productivity and well-being in a meat processing factory. In one condition, workers were given 36 minutes of extra breaks by adding to their present breaks – one by adding four nine-minute break schedules distributed evenly throughout the day, the other by adding twelve three-minute breaks. Neither additional break lowered production, but both resulted in significant reductions in psychological discomfort. Workers preferred the nine-minute rest interval. One final intervention involved training Japanese factory supervisors in stress management skills through an online training programme (Takao *et al.* 2006). This was associated with increases in job strain in a control area, but not the intervention worksites, and improvements in work atmosphere in the intervention, but not control worksites.

RESEARCH FOCUS

Changing environmental stressors is not always easy

Haukka, E., Pehkonen, I., Leino-Arjas, P. *et al.* (2010). Effect of a participatory ergonomics intervention on psychosocial factors at work in a randomised controlled trial. *Occupational and Environmental Medicine*, 67: 170–7.

Participatory ergonomics involves involving workers in problem solving, planning and implementation of new, efficient and minimally stressful ways of working (referred to in this paper as 'work processes'), with the support of supervisors and management. This type of intervention is usually targeted at physical tasks, and is generally intended to reduce musculoskeletal strain and disorders. The authors of this paper established a participatory ergonomics programme, and evaluated its effects on both physical and psychosocial variables.

Methods

The intervention involved technical staff and managers working in collaboration with individual kitchen workers in 59 municipal workplaces to develop ways of reducing any physical strain associated with their job.

The intervention involved two phases:

- *The pre-implementation phase*: two five-hour workshops in which workers were taught the principles of ergonomics. They were trained and encouraged to analyse their work tasks and processes in order to recognise strenuous tasks and risk factors for musculoskeletal disorders and to seek solutions to decrease their physical and mental workload. They were given one month to analyse their work and develop ideas to improve ergonomics.

- *The implementation phase*: all workers attended six workshops reflecting particular themes related to ergonomics: working postures, manual materials handling, repetitive work, hurry, physical risk factors, and work safety.

Baseline data including measures of 'lifestyle' factors, morbidity, perceived physical workload were collected before randomisation into the intervention group or a control group (60 kitchens) which did not receive the intervention. After the intervention had been fully implemented in each work area (between 9 and 12 months after the beginning of the implementation phase) a post-intervention assessment was made, involving all participants. A further assessment was made 12 months later. Both comprised a mailed-out questionnaire. Response rates were 99 per cent at baseline, 95 per cent at the end of the intervention, and 92 per cent at 12-month follow-up.

- The following measures involved a single item five-point scale, with the scores dichotomised into no (1–3) and yes (4–5): mental stress during the month, hurry at work, job dissatisfaction, low job control, low skill discretion, poor co-worker relationships, low supervisor support.

- Two additional seven-point scales measured musculoskeletal pain and physical workload.

Results

The results could perhaps be best described as disappointing. Table 1 reports the odds ratios and 95 per cent confidence limits for those within the intervention group having an 'adverse' score on each variable relative to those in the control group. As an example of interpretation, participants in the intervention group were 2.3 times more likely to record high levels of mental stress during the past month than those in the control group. Accordingly, all the findings indicated a worsening of psychosocial factors in the intervention sites or no change relative to the control condition. At 12-month follow-up, these differences were significant on measures of mental stress, job satisfaction and co-worker relationships.

Table 1 Effect of the intervention on psychosocial factors at work among kitchen workers

Outcome	Post intervention OR (95 per cent CI)	12-month follow-up OR (95 per cent CI)
Mental stress during the past month	2.31 (1.15 to 4.66)*	1.22 (0.63 to 2.36)
Mental strenuousness of work	1.31 (0.74 to 2.36)	1.36 (0.75 to 2.46)
Hurry	0.85 (0.51 to 1.40)	1.21 (0.65 to 2.23)
Job dissatisfaction	3.02 (1.08 to 8.45)*	3.03 (1.18 to 7.82)*
Low job control	1.51 (0.84 to 2.69)	1.34 (0.74 to 2.41)
Low skill discretion	1.16 (0.54 to 2.49)	1.85 (0.88 to 3.88)*
Poor co-worker relationships	2.29 (1.00 to 5.22)*	2.03 (0.89 to 4.63)*
Low supervisor support	0.99 (0.56 to 1.74)	1.77 (0.95 to 3.32)

* $p < 0.05$

Discussion

The intervention appears to have had a damaging effect on a number of psychosocial variables. Scores of participants in this group were significantly worse than those in the control group. This is surprising. At worst, one would expect the intervention to have been of no benefit. But why did it have an adverse effect?

The answer perhaps does not lie with the intervention, but with unspecified 'organisational reforms' happening in many of the kitchens in the active intervention area. A disappointing result for what seems to have been an excellent intervention, but one that almost seems typical of this type of research, which is all too frequently compromised by issues beyond the research itself.

IN THE SPOTLIGHT

Ban football . . . save a life!

There may be one stress management approach not detailed in the chapter that could save many lives. Ban football! Or at least, ban watching football. There is now accumulating evidence that high levels of excitement and stress associated with important games of football can trigger a heart attack in vulnerable individuals. Wilbert-Lampen and colleagues (2008), for example, reported in the *New England Journal of Medicine* that three times as many German men had a myocardial infarction (MI) on the days that Germany was playing in the 2008 World Cup than on days they were not

playing. Women were also at increased risk, but slightly less so than men. The peak admission time was in the first two hours after the beginning of each match. But this is not an isolated finding, and it is not restricted to German fans. Similar findings were reported by Carroll and colleagues (2002) amiong English fans during the 1998 World Cup. They found that the risk of admission to hospital with an MI increased by 25 per cent on 30 June 1998 – the day England lost to Argentina in a penalty shoot-out – and the following two days. Dutch, Australian and other fans have also been similarly affected. The moral of the story? If banning football can save one life, it has to be considered!

Minimising stress in hospital settings

Preoperational preparation

Having an operation is a stressful event, whether it is a small operation conducted under local anaesthetic or a larger one involving a period of unconsciousness and a significant period of recovery. It should not be surprising, therefore, that levels of anxiety can be high both before and after an operation. This anxiety is both unpleasant for the individual concerned and can add to the complications they experience. It may increase the amount of painkilling medication they take, the degree to which they need reassurance both before and after the operation, and even the time necessary for them to stay in hospital (Johnston and Vogele 1993). As a consequence, a number of researchers have attempted to identify ways of minimising this distress. While the stress management approaches described above may be appropriate under such circumstances, health-care staff and patients rarely have the time (or the inclination) to teach or learn these strategies (although hypnosis has

been used with some effect with children; Liossi *et al.* 2006). Accordingly, a very different approach has been taken to help people to cope with this specific type of stress.

Many studies have shown that we feel less anxiety when faced with potentially stressful circumstances if we can be given some degree of control over them (e.g. Lok and Bishop 1999). These findings have led health psychologists to examine whether giving patients undergoing surgery some degree of control over their situation will reduce the amount of stress they experience. Clearly, patients cannot have much control over their anaesthetics or surgery – such things really should be left to the experts! So, in this case, 'giving control' has been interpreted as 'keeping people informed about what is happening to them'. This is thought to reduce anxiety by minimising the fear of the unknown. If patients know what to expect, they may understand better and be less alarmed by any experiences they have. If patients are told, for example, that they will experience some pain after their surgery they will be less alarmed and less likely to think that things have gone wrong if they do experience any pain. A number of studies have examined the effectiveness of providing two sorts of information to patients prior to them having surgery:

Plate 13.2 The calming presence of a parent can help children to relax and cope better with any concerns they may have about their operation

Source: Science Photo Library Ltd/John Cole.

> **colonoscopy**
> a minor surgical procedure in which a small piece of bowel wall is cut from the colon. This can then be tested for the presence of malignant cells.

1. *Procedural information*: telling patients about the events that will occur before and after surgery; having a pre-medication injection, waking in the recovery room and having a drip in their arm, and so on.

2. *Sensory information*: telling patients what they will feel before and after surgery: that it is normal to feel some pain following surgery, they may feel confused when they come round from the anaesthetic, and so on.

The overall picture is that these interventions usually work (Johnston and Vogele 1993), although not always. Luck *et al.* (1999), for example, found that showing a video about the procedure a week before patients were given a **colonoscopy** reduced anxiety in the period leading up to the procedure. In a subsequent study of the same procedure, however, they found no such benefit (Pearson *et al.* 2005).

Matching patient needs

One explanation for these mixed findings is that the effect of the intervention is relatively weak, and may not always be found. Another explanation could be that the intervention works for some people, and not others. What may be as important as the type of intervention is matching it to the characteristics of the patients receiving it. Patients who typically cope with stress by using avoidant coping strategies may benefit, for example, from receiving less information than those who typically cope through the use of problem-focused strategies (see Chapter 11 ☞), and vice-versa. This hypothesis was tested by Morgan *et al.* (1998), who gave people identified as primarily 'information seekers' or 'avoiders' either sensory information about the nature of a forthcoming colonoscopy or no information. Patients who were given information congruent with their coping style (i.e. no information for 'avoiders'; information for 'seekers') reported less anxiety prior to the procedure than those who were given incongruent information. They also scored lower on a measure of 'pain behaviour' made by nursing staff during the procedure, although

participants did not report any differences in pain during the procedure, or differ in their use of sedative drugs. These data suggest that:

● People who usually cope using problem-focused strategies benefit from information that helps them to understand their experience and to actively interpret their experience in relation to information they are given.

● People who usually cope using avoidant, emotion-focused, strategies benefit most from not being told what to expect, and perhaps being helped to develop strategies that help them distract from the situation.

Levels of anxiety may also influence the impact of pre-operative preparation. Hathaway (1986), for example, concluded from a meta-analysis that patients with low levels of anxiety benefited most from the provision of procedural information, while those with high levels of anxiety gained most from unstructured discussion. Anxiety inhibits new learning, partly because people who are anxious may not attend to whatever they are being told, partly as a direct inhibition of memory processes. It is possible, therefore, that anxious patients may benefit most when they are given relatively little information, but the information they are given matches their needs.

More complex interventions have taught people cognitive restructuring techniques (see above) to help to minimise anxiety-provoking thoughts both before and after surgery. Ridgeway and Mathews (1982), for example, assigned women having gynaecological surgery to one of three conditions: a placebo condition in which they received general information about the hospital ward; procedural and sensory information; and training in cognitive restructuring methods. Following surgery, there were no differences between the groups on measures of pain, nausea or sleep duration. However, participants in the cognitive restructuring condition used less analgesia while in hospital and reported less pain following discharge from hospital than either of the other groups. Despite the success of the cognitive intervention, the simplicity of the informational-based interventions makes them more likely to be carried out in the 'real world' of a busy ward.

Working with children and parents

Much of the recent work in preparing people for surgery has focused on helping children and their parents. Studies that have focused on children have shown that a variety of techniques may be of benefit. Mahajan *et al.* (1998), for example, randomly allocated young people aged between 6 and 19 years to one of two conditions prior to gastrointestinal endoscopy. The first received routine preparation. The second received procedural preparation, involving a demonstration of materials that would be used during the **endoscopy** and the use of a doll or a book of photographs showing the procedure. Compared with the no-preparation condition, participants in the procedural information condition reported less anxiety both before and during the procedure, used less anaesthetic, and had lower heart rates, suggesting that they were more relaxed. Hatava *et al.* (2000) randomly assigned children and parents to one of two interventions designed to reduce anxiety before an ear, nose or throat (ENT) operation. In the first condition, they were given written or verbal information by a nurse two weeks prior to surgery. This included information about general hospital rules, routines and the date of the operation. This acted as a form of **placebo intervention** as there is little here that would have been expected to reduce anxiety other than meeting the nurse that may be involved in their care. The second group was given a more complex intervention comprising the same information two weeks prior to the operation followed by a visit to the ENT department the day before surgery. During this visit, each child and parent met the anaesthetist who would be at the operation and took part in a group session led by a nurse in which they were shown the operating theatre and lay on the operating table. They were also shown the equipment that would be used during anaesthesia and were encouraged to play with it in order to minimise its threat and increase familiarity. They were then shown the procedure that would occur on the day through role-play using a doll. This complex intervention resulted in significant benefits. Both younger and older children reported less fear and anxiety prior to the surgery. In addition, their parents reported more satisfaction and less anxiety than those who did not receive the intervention.

Jay *et al.* (1995) provided an unusual comparison between medical and psychological methods of reducing distress in children undergoing **bone marrow biopsy** – an excruciatingly painful procedure. It can also be distressing for both the children and parents involved. They compared two approaches to minimising this distress in a sample of children aged between 3 and 12 years. The first was simply to fully anaesthetise the children. While this approach evokes some degree of anxiety, they reasoned that it may be less distressing than experiencing the process while under local anaesthetic. They compared this approach with conducting the procedure under local anaesthetic after teaching the children both relaxation and cognitive restructuring as a means of controlling their distress. One can only imagine that this was taught at a very simple level, particularly to the younger children. Perhaps not surprisingly, the children who received training in stress management methods experienced more distress than those who were anaesthetised at the beginning of the procedure. However, their parents' ratings suggested that they were the least distressed in the following days. Interestingly, neither the children nor their parents showed any preference for either intervention. One final approach used by Liossi *et al.* (2009) compared the effects of a local skin cream anaesthetic alone or combined with the use of self-hypnosis involving suggestions including numbness, topical anaesthesia, and glove anaesthesia (pain free area mirroring that of a glove over a hand) prior to a painful procedure (in this case taking blood). This combined intervention proved superior on measures of anxiety and procedure related pain.

Tackling the issue from another perspective, interventions that target parents may benefit both parent and child. Campbell *et al.* (1992), for example, prepared mothers of pre-school-age children having a cardiac operation during which their child would be conscious in one of three ways: supportive counselling, education about the hospital and procedure, and relaxation and positive self-talk (stress management). The latter interventions proved most

---

endoscopy

the use of a thin, lighted tube (called an endoscope) to examine the inside of the body.

placebo intervention

an intervention designed to simulate a psychological intervention but not believed to be a specific therapy for the target condition.

bone marrow biopsy

usually performed under local anaesthetic by making a small incision into the skin. A biopsy needle is then pushed through the bone and takes a sample of marrow from the centre of the bone. Marrow contains platelets, phagocytes and lymphocytes.

effective. Mothers and children who received the stress management training coped better with the procedure itself, and their children adapted more positively at home following discharge from hospital than those in the other conditions. The women who received the educational intervention reported less anxiety and tension during the procedure than those in the other conditions. Again, it seems that a combination of interventions including education and teaching coping strategies may provide the optimal intervention.

SUMMARY

This chapter has examined a variety of approaches to stress management and contexts in which it has been conducted. Systemic interventions that target whole organisations can be used as a preventive approach. More individual approaches based around specific therapeutic approaches may benefit people experiencing general stress. Finally, simple procedural information may benefit people facing the stress of an operation where there is little time (or need) to use these more complex interventions.

We noted that, while stress management 'classes' based around second and third wave interventions provide a potentially useful intervention, attendance is likely to be limited, and health psychologists and others have targeted larger and more 'captive audiences' in organisations.

Managing stress at this level can involve a variety of approaches depending on the organisational causes of stress. Stress management interventions should follow an audit of stressors, and target environmental issues that both contribute to stress and can realistically be changed in the context of the particular workplace.

Cognitive-behavioural interventions targeted at reducing stress involve changing:

● triggers to stress, using, for example, the problem-focused approach of Egan;

● the cognitive precursors to stress, using the self-instruction and cognitive restructuring approaches of Beck, Meichenbaum and Ellis;

● the physiological response to stress using relaxation methods, including the modified Jacobsen technique;

● the behavioural reactions to stressful situations using Meichenbaum's stress inoculation and role-play techniques.

Mindfulness-based, third wave, approaches to stress management take an opposing view. Rather than directly attempting to change cognitions, they teach participants to acknowledge any stress engendering thoughts they may have, but not to make these the focus of their attention. This can be achieved using mindfulness or acceptance techniques, and allows the individual to engage in previously stressful behaviours, and learn through experience that they can cope while doing so.

Finally, providing relevant information to help people to understand and cope with the stress of hospital procedures such as operations may reduce distress and pain and facilitate rehabilitation following surgery. However, its benefits vary according to individual differences in coping style.

● Patients who are typically problem solvers benefit most from the provision of information.

● Patients who typically cope with stress using avoidant strategies may be helped best by teaching them distraction techniques.

Further reading

Elkin, A. (1999). *Stress Management for Dummies*. New York: Wiley.

A fairly irreverent but useful guide to managing your own stress.

Carlson, R. (1998). *Don't Sweat the Small Stuff . . . and It's All Small Stuff*. London: Hodder Mobius.

Multiple five-star ratings on Amazon; recommended by clients dealing with stress and anger. What better recommendations can you have? It's a self-help book, not an academic text, but it gives good insight into cognitive and other elements of stress management.

Wells, A. (2008). *Metacognitive Therapy for Anxiety and Depression*. New York: Guilford Press.

Harris, R. (2009). *ACT Made Simple: An Easy-to-read Primer on Acceptance and Commitment Therapy*. Oakland, CA: New Harbinger Publications.

Two third wave books with a UK and US flavour

Kabat-Zinn, J. (2006). *Mindfulness for Beginners.* Audio CD: Sounds True Inc.

The zen master speaks directly to you.

Williams, S. and Cooper, L. (2002). *Managing Workplace Stress*. Chichester: Wiley.

A good and practical review of stress management issues at an organisational level. It was sponsored by the 'bosses' (the Confederation of British Industry), so they should know what they are talking about.

Jones, M.C. and Johnston D.W. (2000). Reducing distress in first level and student nurses: a review of the applied stress management literature. *Journal of Advanced Nursing*, 32: 66–74.

It's a little old now, but still the most up-to-date and good review of a variety of systemic and individual interventions to reduce stress among student nurses.

Lamontagne, A.D., Keegel, T., Louie, A.M. *et al.* (2007). A systematic review of the job-stress intervention evaluation literature, 1990–2005. *International Journal of Occupational and Environmental Health*, 13: 268–80.

Still, the most up-to-date review.

Jain, S., Shapiro, S.L., Swanick, S. *et al.* (2007). A randomized controlled trial of mindfulness meditation versus relaxation training: effects on distress, positive states of mind, rumination, and distraction. *Annals of Behavioral Medicine*, 33: 11–21.

An interesting study showing a specific effect of meditation on levels of intrusive worries.

Type 'stress management' or 'stress management training' into any search engine, and you will get thousands of hits. Few are useful resources though, as most are links to commercial sites who want your money before you can access information. You could try this site, though (although no promises!):

www.mindtools.com/smpage.html

Visit the website at **www.pearsoned.co.uk/morrison** for additional resources to help you with your study, including multiple choice questions, weblinks and flashcards.

Part III
Being ill

Chapter 14
The impact of illness on quality of life

Learning outcomes

By the end of this chapter, you should have an understanding of:

- quality of life as a multidimensional, dynamic and subjective construct
- demographic, clinical and psychosocial influences on perceptions of quality of life
- benefits and disadvantages of common methods of assessing quality of life
- the need to consider specific populations when developing measurement tools

Pets enhance your quality of life

As reported by Deborah Wells in *The Psychologist* in March 2011, the idea that pets are beneficial to health has been around for a long time, with animals deliberately used in eighteenth-century asylums to promote good feeling. Research evidence has had a mixed reception when claims are made for benefits such as increased survival following heart attacks. However, more merit can perhaps be attached to findings that having a pet can act as a buffer against stress – not perhaps due to the physiological explanations of reduced stress reactivity seen in lowered blood pressure reported from some experimental studies etc., but perhaps for more straightforward psychosocial reasons. Dogs, for example, provide companionship and enable outings that not only get someone physically active (which is good for physical health), but which may also enhance social relationships (which is good for mental health). If you've ever walked a dog or accompanied someone doing so, you will see how dog owners often greet one another, compare notes on dog behaviour, develop relationships, and even form dog walking groups. Other pets may not require such outings but they do also need to be looked after, whether fish, budgies, cats, rabbits or reptiles; thus a dependency bond develops that can make a person feel useful and provides a sense of purpose. Perhaps the benefits of pet ownership are greater for those living alone, for those for whom 'feeling useful and valued' is important, or for those whom making social contact independently is a challenge, such as the elderly, those with physical disability or impairment. Although the research evidence as to the health benefits of pets is not without its critics, the purpose of bringing this topic to your attention is this: if you think your pet enhances your quality of life, keeps you fit, makes you happier, then that is sufficient. Quality of life is in the eye of the beholder.

Chapter outline

Illness is a dynamic process, beginning with perception of symptoms or a diagnosis and continuing or changing over time as a function of the disease pathology, treatment possibilities and the responses to illness by the person affected and those around them. We have shown in previous chapters that many individual and social factors exist that influence the responses to a stressful experience, and in this chapter we turn our attention to the impact of illness. We address the impact of illness on an individual's emotional well-being and adjustment, on their global and health-related functioning – in other words, their quality of life (QoL). It is first necessary to define this broad construct, before exploring how demographic, disease and treatment, and psychosocial factors can influence perceptions of QoL. Having described what QoL is (if that is fully possible, given the subjectivity of the concept), we turn attention to issues of how to measure this multidimensional, dynamic and subjective concept.

Illness and quality of life

While the primary goal of medicine and health care is to improve health and/or treat and cure illness and its symptoms, in order to reduce morbidity and premature mortality, there is a need to address more global outcomes of health-care treatments and services, such as patient well-being. While clinical outcomes can be assessed in an objective manner (such as observing improved physical functioning, reduced symptomatology), assessing patient well-being requires that the view of the patient be sought, i.e. it is subjective. For example, in clinical trials such as those conducted to test the efficacy of a new drug and intervention studies whether based on psychological or clinical principles and practices, it is not only important to evaluate clinical outcomes but also the individual's perceptions of how the treatment or intervention has influenced their illness experience and their general psychosocial functioning. Quality of life (QoL) research has become a major area of multidisciplinary research for a variety of reasons. One likely reason is that because technological advances in medicine can effectively treat conditions that in previous generations people would

have died from (e.g. major strokes, heart attacks and many forms of cancer), people are living longer, often with some dependency needs or with some aspect of their life restricted. A consequence of this is growing acceptance of the importance of knowing about and understanding the psychosocial as well as the clinical outcomes of treatments or interventions. Having this fuller knowledge has implications for future care, treatment and service provision. As Boini *et al.* (2004: 4) succinctly put it, 'physicians now have the opportunity to add life to years, as well as adding years to life'. Furthermore, patients may derive great benefit from certain treatments or interventions in terms of enhanced quality of life, even though these same treatments or interventions may not extend survival or quantity of life (see IN THE SPOTLIGHT on p. 383).

To illustrate the growth of QoL research in both the psychological and medical literature, Garratt *et al.* (2002) published a review in the *British Medical Journal*, where it was revealed that between 1990 and 1999 there were over 23,000 QoL records in the literature engines searched, 4,000 of which were specifically about scale development and testing. What is this construct that has received so much research attention?

WHAT DO YOU THINK?

How would you define quality of life? Think about you 'now' compared perhaps with your parents and your friends. Do you think you see 'quality of life' differently to them? Consider why this may be. Consider what you see as being important to your quality of life in the future.

What is quality of life?

In general terms, quality of life (QoL) can be referred to as an individual's evaluation of their overall life experience (their situation, experiences, states and perceptions) at a given time (global quality of life), with the term 'health-related QoL' emerging to refer to evaluations of this life experience and how it is affected by symptoms, disease, accidents or treatments, and also by health policy. A health-related quality of life (HRQoL) is therefore associated with 'optimal levels of mental, physical, role (e.g. work, parent, carer) and social functioning, including relationships, and perceptions of health, fitness, life satisfaction and well-being. It should also include some assessment of the patient's level of satisfaction with treatment, outcome and health status and with future prospects' (Bowling 1995a: 3).

According to the World Health Organization Quality of Life (WHOQOL) working group (1993, 1994), QoL is a person's perceptions of their position in life in relation to their cultural context and the value systems of that context in relation to their own goals, standards and expectations. Quality of life is considered to be a broad concept affected by an individual's physical and mental health, level of independence, quality of social relationships, social integration and, added subsequently (WHOQOL 1998), their personal, religious and spiritual beliefs. This working group has produced a generic and cross-culturally valid assessment tool (WHOQOL-100), which addresses 25 different facets of QoL grouped into one of six domains:

1. *physical health*: pain and discomfort; energy and fatigue; sleep and rest;

2. *psychological*: positive feelings; self-esteem; thinking, memory, learning and concentration; bodily image and appearance; negative feelings;

3. *level of independence*: activities of daily living (e.g. self-care); mobility; medication and treatment dependence; work capacity;

4. *social relationships*: personal relationships; practical social support; sexual activity;

5. *relation to environment*: physical safety and security; financial resources; home environment; availability and quality of health/social care; learning opportunities; leisure participation and opportunities; transport; physical environment;

6. *spirituality, religion and personal beliefs.*

This generic tool provides core items for use across all conditions, with disease- and population-specific versions being developed subsequently (see later section on measuring quality of life). Most of the QoL measures available to researchers or clinicians address the multiple dimensions described above, and certainly if you asked someone nowadays what their 'quality of life' was, their answer would reflect many differing aspects of life. However, early studies tended to focus more keenly on physical function as if QoL was reflected fundamentally in this. Certainly one of the aims of assessing QoL is to ascertain the impact of disease on an individual's functioning, and many studies use measures of disease or symptom severity, disability or physical functioning as outcome measures considered to be indicative of quality of life. However, the WHO model of impairment, disability and handicap (see Chapter 1 ☞; WHO 1980) described how illness had more than just physical consequences, by defining handicap as disadvantages and limitations in performing social roles that resulted directly from impairment and/or disability. Johnston and Pollard (2001), in testing the WHO model, further concluded that the linear relationship between impairment, disability and handicap was not inevitable but depended on psychological and social factors. This is reflected in the World Health Organization's revised model of disability, the ICF model (International Classification of Functioning, Disability and Health, WHO 2001). Further support for this is seen, for example, among individuals suffering from rheumatoid arthritis, where the link between pathophysiology and disability outcomes is often indirect and moderated by psychosocial and environmental factors (see Walker *et al.* 2004 for a review), or in stroke patients receiving a workbook intervention targeting their beliefs in control over their recovery, where disability was reduced relative to a control group (Johnston *et al.* 2007).

Rather than considering disease or disability as indicative *of* quality of life, they could therefore be considered as potential influences *upon* it (McKenna *et al.* 2000;

McKenna 2004) that may or may not affect a person's perceived QoL, depending on the extent to which that individual rates them as important to that judgement (e.g. Cox 2003). For some individuals, the inability to perform valued activities as a result of impairment or disability may be considered a 'fate worse than death' (e.g. Ditto *et al.* 1996); however, for others they will continue to find meaning and purpose in life in spite of disablement (e.g. life-threatening disease such as cancer or HIV infection; Tsarenko and Polonsky 2011). IN THE SPOTLIGHT (opposite) raises the question of whether the outcomes important to the person concerned are the same as the outcomes valued by the health profession or, in particular, health economists.

What influences quality of life?

Many factors influence QoL including:

● demographics: e.g. age, culture;

● the condition itself: e.g. symptoms, presence or absence of pain, functional disability, neurological damage with associated motor, emotional or cognitive impairment, sensory or communicative impairment;

● treatment: e.g. its availability, nature, extent, toxicity, side-effects, etc.;

● psychosocial factors: e.g. emotions (anxiety, depression), coping, social context, goals and support.

Age and quality of life

Age has been shown to influence the aspects of life considered to be important to people. While studies of QoL in child populations remains relatively limited and focused on chronic, rather than generally life-threatening illness (e.g. asthma and epilepsy), Matza and colleagues (Matza *et al.* 2004) noted in their review of conceptual, methodological and regulatory issues relevant to HRQoL in children that 'researchers are becoming aware of the unique challenges of assessing pediatric health outcomes, including health-related quality of life' (p. 79). They point to the different contexts which may mediate the impact of illness and its treatments on the child. For example, cancer treatments commonly impact upon school attendance and participation in school activities important to a child's social development (Eiser 2004); childhood epilepsy can impede social functioning,

independence and relationships with peers as well as, in some cases, self-esteem and mood (McEwan *et al.* 2004).

Jirojanakul *et al.* (2003) note that understanding childhood QoL is important because any effects of impaired QoL may be cumulative and affect later development. Given that QoL judgements are made by assessing present lifestyle relative to one's expectations (Eiser and Morse 2001), a fruitful avenue of work might therefore examine whether children with chronic disease modify their future life expectations as a result of QoL being compromised in their childhood. Logically, however, we might expect consequences, given the evidence that negative experiences such as social rejection in childhood (a possible consequence of the non-participation some physical illnesses may create) can have long-term effects. In terms of adolescents, often considered to be a particularly challenging time to be diagnosed with a chronic or serious illness (see Chapter 15 ☛), the evidence is mixed regarding whether or not illness such as cancer has long-term effects on quality of life. For example, Larsson *et al.* (2010) conducted a longitudinal study of 61 individuals diagnosed with cancer in adolescence (mean age 15.5), and compared their QoL over four years with age and gender matched controls. While initially (up to 6 months post-diagnosis) the cancer group had significantly lower mental health and vitality, and greater depression than controls; at 18 and 48 months this was reversed and the cancer group actually reported greater vitality and lower anxiety and depression. Although a small study, such findings confirm other large studies of cancer survivorship following a childhood diagnosis (e.g. Hudson *et al.* 2003) and suggest perhaps that the early experience of illness and its associated treatments lead to a maturation and heightened appreciation of life, and what is sometimes referred to as **post-traumatic growth** (Tedeschi and Calhoun 2004).

While the majority of studies have relied on parental 'proxy' reports of their child's QoL (see the section on measuring quality of life, below), several interesting

---

post-traumatic growth
following a traumatic event, including serious illness, a person may experience positive psychological change, e.g. increased life appreciation, improved relations to self and others, new life values and priorities.

IN THE SPOTLIGHT

Which health outcomes are important to whom?

For most people, the choice between a treatment without major side-effects and a treatment with major side-effects would be an easy decision, i.e. that without the side-effects. However, the decision becomes more complex if the choice is now between a treatment without major side-effects but with only moderate proven success in eradicating or controlling the illness concerned, and a treatment with significant side-effects but with excellent success rates. Which would you choose? These types of decision are faced daily by many cancer patients, who are fighting for survival but facing often toxic treatments in terms of their side-effects. The quantity of life may be added to by these treatments, but what about life quality? These questions raise the issue of which outcomes are best for the individual being treated.

If economics also enters the debate, as it increasingly does in terms of treatment costs, costs of hospital stays, costs of follow-up care, etc., then decisions about which treatment outcomes are best often fall into the hands of doctors and hospital managers who are responsible for the spending. The outcome of mortality has little health-care cost, whereas prolonged morbidity does and therefore treatment efficacy is central to these decisions. The ideal outcome from a medical standpoint is likely to be optimal functioning, but few treatments come with that guarantee and, if they do, then they are likely to be very expensive! Decisions are generally made in terms of weighing up the costs of treatment (e.g. financial costs, costs to the person in terms of side-effects) against the objective benefits of treatment (e.g. financial savings from reduced further treatment needs, projected quantity of life gain for the individual).

Time trade-off techniques used by health economists can examine the utility (importance) attached to health states. Patients can be asked to imagine living with a certain condition for a couple of years, compared with living in better health for a shorter length of time if given a certain treatment, although they may die or be very ill after this time. The actual periods in normal health are adjusted until the person can no longer choose between the states. For example, if you were indifferent to whether you lived in poor health for six months or in optimal health for three months with treatment, then this would indicate the utility of that treatment for that individual. Basically, these kinds of judgement require individuals to consider how much time in terms of current QoL they would be willing to trade for post-treatment QoL; for example, how many days of treatment would you willingly trade for how many months of improved health? (See Bowling 1995a: 12–14 for a fuller discussion of the complexities of such techniques.)

There is evidence that health professionals differ in their ability to communicate about such issues and, furthermore, that they may underestimate patients' HRQoL (Detmar *et al.* 2000). This illustrates the point that such decisions, and the values placed on outcomes such as pain, disability, distress and even death, are subjective: i.e. different individuals value different aspects of life. As this chapter will also show, what is valued may change over the lifespan. For example, will a 75-year-old cancer patient consider the treatment options such as six three-weekly doses of chemotherapy, the anticipated benefits in terms of extended lifespan, and the likely side-effects (nausea, achey limbs, hair loss, etc.) in the same way as a 35–45-year-old parent? This is why it is so important to assess individuals' perceptions of what makes their life 'quality'.

studies have employed **qualitative methods** to elicit domains of importance in QoL and factors that influence it. Focus-group discussions with children have identified a broad range of influences on quality of life, for example among adolescents (aged 11–17) with epilepsy (Cramer

> **qualitative methods**
> concerned with describing (qualifying) the experience, beliefs and behaviour of a particular group of people (see Glossary, **qualitative methodologies**).

et al. (1999, cited in McEwan *et al.* 2004) identified eight subscales related to health-related QoL:

1. general epilepsy impact;

2. memory/concentration problems;

3. attitudes towards epilepsy;

4. physical functioning;

5. stigma;

6. social support;

7. school behaviour;

8. general health perceptions.

Quantitative results from the same study found that seizure severity was the main predictor of health-related quality of life, independent of age of onset of the illness. In other words, the length of time that the illness had been present did not appear to reduce the impact of severe seizures on QoL. In another focus-group study that examined health-related QoL and its relation to distress among children with epilepsy aged 6–12, distress was mainly associated with loss of independence and restrictions in daily activities, concern about the reactions of others to their illness and seizures, treatment by peers, and concerns about the side-effects of medication (Ronen *et al.* 1999, as cited in McEwan *et al.* 2004).

An unusual study of children aged 5–8 either attending school or working alongside construction worker parents in Thailand found, perhaps surprisingly, that generic QoL (note that health-related QoL is not what is assessed here) was less affected by health states (chronic, acute or severe illness) than by socio-economic factors (Jirojanakul *et al.* 2003). Socio-economic variables including parental income, education and occupational status, type of housing and extent of child's extracurricular activities significantly explained QoL whereas health status did not. While this study was conducted in Thailand where cultural variations in health and illness perceptions likely exist (see Chapters 1 and 9 ☞), and among predominantly healthy children, the findings are considered consistent with studies in Western child populations, where current life circumstances (and the expectations they bring with them) are important to QoL (e.g. Eiser and Morse 2001).

The effect of age on QoL ratings is not inevitable. For example, age was not predictive of quality of life in a one-year longitudinal study of stroke survivors ranging from 32 to 90 years old, where other factors, such as physical disability, depressed mood and gender (females

had poorer QoL) were (Carod-Artal *et al.* 2000). It may be that age is less important than 'life stage': i.e. the impact of a disabling illness on QoL might vary according to whether or not it occurs at a time in life when a person is still professionally or reproductively active. Among younger people who have suffered an acute stroke, being unable to return to work has been associated with reduced life satisfaction and subjective well-being (e.g. Vestling *et al.* 2003), whereas this would not concern the majority of stroke patients who are post-retirement age. Referred to as the 'third age', the period of life after retirement can continue to be full of enjoyment and opportunity, whereas the 'fourth age' is when illness and disability present challenges to an older persons' independence (Woods 2008). Maintaining QoL and promoting healthy, positive and successful ageing has become increasingly important, given the ageing population of most societies (Baltes and Baltes 1990; Grundy and Bowling 1999). The goal of healthy ageing approaches is to minimise dependency (physical and/or emotional), which, in turn, it is hoped, will reduce the 'costs' to society of health-care provision for an increasingly ageing population. Studies of older people have found the life domains of importance to be good physical functioning, having relationships with others, and maintaining health and social activity. Compared with younger samples, older people are more likely to mention independence, or the fear of losing it and becoming dependent (Bowling 1995b).

WHAT DO YOU THINK?

Have you ever experienced something which has challenged your quality of life? If so, in what way did it challenge it, and how did you deal with it? Did you find that one domain of QoL took on greater importance than it had previously? Why was this the case? Have the 'weightings' you attach to the different domains returned to their pre-challenge levels or has the event had a long-lasting impact on how you evaluate life and opportunities?

If you are lucky enough not to have experienced any major challenges to your QoL, consider how the loss of some aspect of health seems to have impacted on someone you know. Consider whether you would respond in the same way were you to lose that same aspect of health.

Plate 14.1 Social isolation increases the risk of a reduced quality of life

Source: Corbis/Jerry Cooke.

Blane *et al.* (2004) examined influences on QoL in over three hundred individuals aged between 65 and 75 and found that serious and limiting health problems were most strongly predictive of QoL, whereas non-limiting chronic disease did not affect QoL. They also found housing security, receipt of welfare or non-pension income and (for men only) years out of work to be predictive. As described in IN THE SPOTLIGHT in the very first chapter of this book, (see Chapter 1 ☛), Bowling and Iliffe's (2006) study of the relationship between five 'models' of successful ageing and QoL among 999 adults aged over 65 years found that the broadest model of understanding of what it meant to have 'aged successfully' was most predictive of a person reporting they had a good quality of life, or not 'a not good' one. This broad 'lay model' encompassed biomedical (function), broader biomedical (e.g. roles and function), social functioning (social networks and support), and psychological resources (e.g. self-efficacy, optimism, coping) models, but added in socio-economic (income, capital) and environmental (safety, services, access) factors. Therefore while having a limiting illness influences the domains of importance in terms of judging one's own QoL in that they become more focused on physical functioning and activity, social support and social contact, feeling that you have 'successfully aged' is

about a lot more than that. Furthermore, illness type appears less important than the level of any resultant physical disability, most likely because physical disability challenges many of these other important domains – a person's social, emotional, cognitive, economic, social and environmental functioning.

While being limited in terms of one's activities or roles is commonly a predictor of poorer mental and physical QoL, this is not always the case. Over half of the older people surveyed by Evandrou (2006) who had long-standing limiting illness self-rated their health as good or fairly good, further highlighting the fact that quality of life is about more than just physical health and physical function. In fact Berg *et al.* (2006) highlights that while subjective health ratings of the oldest-old (85 years +) correlate with other self-evaluations such as general well-being or quality of life, anxiety and depression, they tend to be more weakly associated with objective health-related measures. While a key global aim of interventions to enhance QoL, regardless of disease type, is the improvement and maintenance of physical and role functioning, in old age as at all ages QoL continues to be multidimensional. Even among the 'oldest-old', QoL encompasses psychological, social and environmental well-being (Grundy and Bowling 1999) and as Windle and Woods (2004) point out, it is a person's subjective appraisal of their situation which mediates objective circumstances into experienced life quality.

One explanation for why some people with chronic illness report higher than expected QoL, sometimes at levels similar to that of healthy comparator groups, can perhaps be found in studies of adaptation which suggest that when a situation is clear-cut and understood to be a permanent feature of one's life (e.g. bereavement, loss of a limb, an incurable illness), adaptation is easier and better than when one believes their circumstances may change (Herrman and Wortman 1985). This paradoxical suggestion led to a fascinating study which we report in RESEARCH FOCUS.

RESEARCH FOCUS

Does believing loss is permanent make it easier to adapt?

Smith, D.M., Loewenstein, G., Jankovic, A., and Ubel, P.A. (2009). Happily hopeless: adaptation to a permanent, but not to a temporary, disability. *Health Psychology*, 28: 787–91.

Background aims

Related to the topic of this chapter, quality of life, is the concept of well-being, also considered to be a subjective evaluation which reflects in part objective circumstances, including one's health status, employment status and financial security, relationships etc. The assumption that significant illness or disability will reduce one's well-being is not always upheld and, as seen in this chapter and elsewhere in this text, many psychosocial factors can help explain why this is the case. This study examines the common assumption that adaptation to disability will improve over time by arguing that the nature of the loss will influence this. They argue that clear-cut permanent losses which may make a person appear objectively 'less well off' may actually allow better subjective adjustment, whereas temporary losses that carry hope for recovery or change may lead to subjectively poorer well-being. This paradox was be tested in patients who either had a temporary and reversible colostomy (also known as an ileostomy) or a permanent colostomy. In both cases surgery results in the bowel being bypassed so bodily waste is passed via a tube to an external receptacle, and so the 'disability' is the same, but in the reversible condition, there is hope that the procedure could be reversed if the bowel heals and normal function is restored.

Method

A total of 107 patients were contacted who had received this procedure, of whom 96 were deemed eligible on first screening interview and 74 of those agreed to take part. Questionnaires were sent to these participants three times – one week after hospital discharge following surgery, and one and six months later. Three participants stated they did not know whether their surgery was reversible or not (reflects somewhat on doctor–patient communication!), and thus the data from 71 participants is presented. A total of 41 stated their colostomy was reversible, and 30 stated it was permanent. Attrition from the study was considerable but not unexpected, with 59 completing the one-month follow-up (83 per cent) and 45 the six-month follow-up (63 per cent).

Questionnaires sent by post assessed demographics, current symptoms, clinical and treatment questions, and quality of life using two scales thought to reflect this. The first was a life satisfaction scale (Diener *et al.* 1985) where participants indicate how strongly they agree or disagree with five items such as, 'In most ways my life is close to my ideal', and secondly, a Cantril (1967) 'ladder scale' where participants indicate where on a 0–10 ladder they stand currently, with 10 being the top and 0 being the bottom. The top represents the best possible life for them at the present time, the bottom the worst possible life for them at the current time.

Results

It emerged that those with permanent colostomy were more likely to have had a cancer diagnosis and those with temporary colostomy more likely to have an Inflammatory Bowel Disease diagnosis and thus diagnosis was controlled for in analyses. (While this is appropriate, as health psychologists we know that illness beliefs and emotional factors may also differ across diagnostic groups and thus further group differences may exist in this sample that are not controlled for.)

The main hypothesis that QoL would increase more over time for those with permanent colostomy than for temporary colostomy was strongly supported. The reversible group reported higher initial life satisfaction (although not significantly so), but this did significantly decline over time, whereas the permanent group's life satisfaction increased. In terms of the ladder data, while initially similar, the groups diverge after one-month follow-up, with the permanent group's quality of life showing an increase, and the temporary group showing a slight downturn.

A form of analysis known as Hierarchical Linear Modelling tested the interactions suggested in these data (time × group/surgery type) and also controlled for gender, illness and surgery-related symptoms reported at the three time points. In these analyses, both for the life satisfaction data and for the ladder data, a significant positive effect of time was found on QoL/well-being scores for the permanent group, but not for the temporary group. In other words, adaptation over time did not occur for those with temporary colostomies.

Discussion

'These findings are not consistent with models of adaptation that assume that negative reactions fade with time merely because of continued exposure to a negative stimulus (Diener *et al.* 2006)'. Crucially, state the authors, such findings highlight a role for cognitions, particularly expectancies of an improvement in circumstances, which paradoxically may impede adaptation. They argue that motivation to cope, consciously or unconsciously, may vary in these two groups and that looking forward to the potential of surgery being reversed at some point in the future may deter the person from adapting positively to current circumstances, as they are constantly comparing their current state with one yet to be achieved.

I found this a fascinating study which, in spite of a limited sample size and moderate to high levels of drop-out (which the authors do acknowledge and check for effects of in their findings), addresses a very intriguing question. If we believe things to be temporary, expect change or live in the future rather than the present, do we undermine our adjustment to current challenges? It is unfortunate that the study, however, does not explicitly assess these expectations, by using an assessment of hope perhaps, or one of benefit-finding (see the next chapter), nor does it assess the other possible illness-specific beliefs that may also explain life satisfaction and quality of life ratings. However, the conclusions are tempered by an acknowledgement of these limitations, and the paper concludes with implications for health professionals' delivery of information regarding prognosis – being unduly optimistic about change, while easier news to deliver to patients and their families, may instill false hope that is detrimental to patient adjustment. Hopefully, more and larger studies will pursue this research question further before we turn away from the newly burgeoning field of positive psychology (see Chapters 11 and 12 ☞) and accept that no hope may be better than hope – but for now this paper provides food for thought!

Culture and quality of life

Chapter 1 ☞ described how health itself is viewed slightly differently in Western and non-Western cultures, with individualistic Western views and more collectivist Eastern views of health being identified. Yan and Sellick (2004) point out that culture influences many factors relevant to quality of life judgements, such as responses to pain, attitudes towards and use of traditional versus Western medicines and treatments, concepts of dependency, and the culture of communication. While their longitudinal study of Chinese cancer patients revealed many of the same physical, psychosocial and emotional responses to gastrointestinal cancer reported in Western studies, the authors note that their sample differed from Western samples in their emphasis on family support, and in the patients' indirect indication of distress through symptom report rather than through direct interpersonal communication. The role of culture and the underlying values and beliefs about health, illness and QoL must therefore be considered in terms of their influence on self-reported QoL. As Bullinger (1997: 816) observed: 'If disease, as anthropological research suggests, is so very much culture-bound, how could quality of life be culture free?' Conceptually, the meaning of health and illness has been shown to be affected by cultural norms and experiences of health, illness and health care, as well as by different belief systems, such as the Chinese belief in the need to maintain a balance between *yin* and *yang*, or as in some tribal beliefs in the supernatural. Differences have also been found in the extent to which Europeans, Americans, Asians, Africans and Latinas use religious-based coping, with religious beliefs and spirituality also being a component of quality of life for some more than others (e.g. Culver *et al.* 2004). We described many such different beliefs in the opening chapter (see Chapter 1 ☞). Cultural differences also affect how QoL can be assessed (see the section on measuring quality of life, below).

Aspects of the illness and quality of life

There is a reasonably strong body of evidence showing that physical illness has an impact on a person's reported QoL. For example, a review of the pooled data of 118 studies of health related QoL in adults with type 2 diabetes (Norris *et al.* 2011) concluded that diabetes had a negative effect, particularly on physical function and general health domains of QoL, although the authors note that pooled effects obscure the many individual different factors that influence individual experience of QoL. Aspects of the illness also matter: for example, pervasive and persistent pain and disability are generally found to be associated with a lower QoL, for example as reflected in depression levels, disability and use of health care (see Chapter 16 ☞). Ferrucci *et al.* (2000) investigated the extent to which disease severity in stroke, Parkinson's disease (PD) or coronary heart disease (CHD) patients was associated with their health-related QoL. They found that the relationship between disease severity and health-related QoL was non-linear in the stroke and CHD patients, and that only in the least severe stroke and most severe CHD cases was QoL in fact associated. In Parkinson's disease, however, there was a linear relationship reported whereby severe PD associated with lower health-related QoL. In other words, severity of illness is not inevitably or consistently associated with lower health-related QoL, and disease-specific relationships need to be explored.

In those with neurological illnesses such as Parkinson's disease, cognitive dysfunction such as memory impairment or attentional deficits can disrupt key QoL domains such as physical and psychosocial functioning. Furthermore, memory deficits can make it hard for some individuals to evaluate their current status against their former status in order to make meaningful QoL judgements (Murrell 2001). Perhaps for this reason, patients with cognitive impairments have been the subject of less research attention (see also the section on measuring quality of life, below). It is quite common for QoL not to be predicted by objectively determined severity of illness and associated symptoms. Furthermore, among carers, it has also been shown that the severity of symptoms or disability of the cared-for does not inevitably reduce carer QoL. We return to this issue in Chapter 15 ☞. The finding that symptom severity or extent of disability does not consistently predict QoL highlights the subjective nature of this concept, and it should come as no surprise to readers that QoL judgements, as with stress and illness discussed in previous chapters, are influenced by individual differences in the appraisal of, and subsequent coping with, ill health. It also highlights the fact that QoL is by definition about the things that people value in life, and that illness or physical disability may or may not change such perceptions. Most available measures assume that illness will disrupt many domains of QoL, yet, as noted by Carr and Higginson (2001: 1,359): 'if they [standardised measures] do not cover domains that are important to individual patients they may not be valid measures for those patients'. Highlighting the need to make QoL assessment relevant to the population addressed, ISSUES (opposite) addresses the question of whether or not QoL is attainable at the end of life, as a result of either ageing or terminal illness.

Aspects of treatment and quality of life

Treatment itself also influences QoL. Most studies that examine the effects of treatment on QoL do so in order to either determine its impact on specific populations or compare which of several treatment alternatives is associated with the greatest QoL outcomes. In cancer, for example, scores on the POQOLS (pediatric oncology (child cancer) QoL scale; Goodwin *et al.* 1994) differed

ISSUES

End-of-life QoL

While the majority of deaths take place in hospitals, the care of the dying more often takes place in patients' homes, until the point is reached where some home carers can no longer provide the necessary care or medication, and hospitalisation in nursing homes or hospices ensues. Among others, Elizabeth Kubler-Ross (1969) highlighted the psychological and emotional aspects of dying and the need to 'listen to the dying patient'. The hospice movement developed in the late 1960s out of recognition that traditional hospitals with their routines, emphasis on treatment and depersonalised atmosphere were not best placed to provide care to the dying (Saunders and Baines 1983). The hospice movement aimed to provide care that facilitated an optimal QoL for both patients and their families as death approaches. This requires that patients are pain-free, experience little distress, maintain some dignity and control, and can maintain relationships with loved ones in a caring and compassionate environment. A good QoL at the end of life has also been found to encompass patients' need to remain as independent as possible so as not to 'burden' (see later section) their carer (e.g. Gill et al. 2003). It is also important for carers' needs to be supported in order that they are able to provide the patient with whatever support is needed during the final days and weeks of their life (World Health Organization Expert Committee 1990). Importantly, such settings need to acknowledge cultural variations in the 'rituals' that accompany dying and the resultant expectancies family and friends may have. For example, positioning of the deceased to face Mecca is important to those of Muslim faith; the burning of sage by American Indians is an important ritual to prepare a dying person's soul for the afterlife. As Emanuel et al. (2007) note, the dying 'role' encompasses practical, relational and personal elements, all of which are necessary if the person is to move from a 'sick' role to the dying' role and adjust to it. Although taking on this role is emotional and accompanied by feelings of loss and grief, focusing only on the physical needs is insufficient. Do hospices achieve this?

Carers of patients who had died in hospices reported that 'their' patients were more aware that they were dying than did carers of those who had died in hospital, perhaps reflecting the ethos of openness encouraged in hospices (ibid.). This openness regarding dying may enable greater preparation for death and bereavement among patients and spouse carers, which has, in turn, been associated with reduced levels of emotional distress (e.g. Chochinov et al. 2000). The positive differences attributed to hospice care are not consistently reported, however; for example, Seale and Kelly (1997) did not find a difference between hospice and hospital care in terms of the care and support provided to spouses. Thinking positively, this may reflect the changing nature of hospital care towards more holistic, psychosocial care, or thinking less positively, perhaps a growing medicalisation of hospices (Crossley and Small 1998). With increasing emphasis on specialist nurses in hospitals, at least in the UK, we can perhaps infer that hospital care is becoming more holistic. Certainly, within England and Wales the National Institute for Clinical Excellence (NICE) guidance on Improving Supportive and Palliative Care for Adults with Cancer (2004) recommends that 'assessment and discussion of patients' needs for physical, psychological, social, spiritual and financial support should be undertaken at key points (such as at diagnosis; at commencement, during, and at the end of treatment; at relapse; and when death is approaching)' (Key recommendation 2).

Whenever a person is facing death as a result of a long-standing illness, issues such as 'a good death' and 'dying with dignity' become salient and bring with them many ethical and moral debates. Research has consistently shown that older people do not fear death itself, as younger people do, but are more concerned about the process of dying and the fear of dying in pain or without dignity and self-control (e.g. Chochinov et al. 2002; McKiernan 1996; Strang and Strang 2002). Questions are many, and the answers are not simple. When should treatment be stopped? How much can, or should a person endure, and for how long? Should a dying person who has been experiencing great pain or severe dyspnoea (breathlessness) be resuscitated if they become unconscious? Should a person facing a terminal illness and inevitable decline towards death (such as the highly publicised case of Diane Petty, who faced full physical paralysis while remaining mentally intact as a result of motor neurone disease) be allowed to invite assisted suicide? How, and even where, an ill person chooses to die is inevitably a personal decision. Choosing 'when' to die is altogether more contentious. 'Advance directives' are becoming increasingly common, whereby people indicate their wishes for medical intervention (or not) when and if the time comes that they are unable to communicate their wishes. Even in the presence of advance directives, however, health professionals may give priority to family members' views and decisions regarding end-of life care (Mowery 2007).

The practice of non-treatment of a dying person – passive euthanasia – is generally acknowledged as an inevitable part of medicine; however, active euthanasia in terms of carrying out an action that effectively ends that life (such as administering a fatal dose of adrenaline) is much less common. Van der Heide *et al.* (2003) reviewed end-of-life decision-making practices in six European countries and found that the explicit hastening of death varied from less than 1 per cent in Denmark, Italy, Sweden and Switzerland, through to 1.82 per cent in Belgium and 3.4 per cent in the Netherlands. While all low percentages, these differences are significant and in part reflect national differences in the legality of assisted suicide or euthanasia. This varies from being fully prohibited (e.g. Italy) to prohibited except in specific circumstances (e.g. Belgium, the Netherlands). In the Netherlands, GPs have been able

to carry out these practices since 1991 (Onwuteaka-Phillipsen *et al.* 2003) while other countries have yet to make policy on this issue. For example, a study conducted in Wales (Pasterfield *et al.* 2006) asked GPs this question 'Do you think that the law on intentional killing should be changed to allow (a) physician-assisted suicide and (b) voluntary euthanasia?' Of the 1,025 doctors who responded (a very reasonable 65 per cent of those invited into the study), 62.4 per cent did not favour a change in law regarding (a), and 55.8 per cent similarly did not favour a change of law regarding (b). In the face of such findings, it is likely to be some time before this contentious issue is resolved in terms of any legislation, at least in the UK, although public support is reported to be high in the case of those suffering from painful, terminal illness (House of Lords 2005).

Human rights legislation, the desire for control over our lives and the fact that the world is facing an ageing population, many of whom will live many years with chronic ill health, suggests that issues regarding euthanasia are going to remain, and possibly grow, in most parts of the ageing world (Zucker 2007). It is worth noting that a 'good death' in terms of the quality of the death experience is also important to the bereaved, to reduce any lingering anger or resentment and enable the grief process to be a more positive one (Tedeschi and Calhoun 2008).

Have your own personal experiences of death, if you have experienced any, influenced your thoughts on how you would choose to die, if that choice were available? What do you think would provide 'quality of life' at the end of life?

across groups receiving different treatments; for example, children undergoing intensive treatment showed poorer QoL than those in remission (Bijttebier *et al.* 2001).

Many treatment evaluations carried out as part of randomised controlled trials of new or comparable treatments include some indicator of QoL, such as symptomatology, physical functioning or return to work. However, few as yet have adopted 'patient-centred' measures, which invite patients to describe outcomes important to them in terms of their QoL (Carr and

Higginson 2001). However, this is an area of research and evaluation that is becoming more widespread, particularly in studies of cancer or pain. For example, several studies have been carried out to ascertain the impact of bone marrow transplantation in leukaemia patients. In a UK study, Watson *et al.* (2004a) examined the QoL outcomes of a large number (481) of patients who had participated in a randomised trial of one of two types of bone marrow transplantation (BMT) (both preceded by intensive chemotherapy) compared with a course of intensive chemotherapy alone. On following participants up after one year, those patients who received BMT reported greater fatigue, more problems in sexual and social relationships, and disruptions to work and leisure activities. In addition, having BMT from a related sibling had a greater negative impact on the QoL indices than either unrelated donor transplantation or the chemotherapy group. A Dutch study of psychological functioning and QoL following BMT found that a quarter of patients still experienced significant functional limitations when followed up after three years, although almost 90 per cent of the total sample (thus including many of those with functional limitations) reported their quality of life to be good to excellent (Broers *et al.* 2000). Although effects of BMT on quality of life appear from these data to be long-lasting, another study of Dutch patients by Helder *et al.* (2004) found that the majority of QoL domain scores in young adults who had been children (an average age of 11) at the time of their BMT were not significantly lower than that found in a comparison group of healthy young adults. For example, those who had undergone childhood BMT between 6 and 12 years previously did not score lower in terms of physical or role functioning, pain or vitality, mental health, social and emotional functioning than the healthy participants, although their general health was rated lower (using the SF36 measure – see p. 394). These findings would suggest that the childhood experience of a serious illness requiring intensive treatment and a prolonged period of adjustment does not have long-lasting effects into adulthood, although such conclusions have to be tempered by the fact that the study involved a relatively small sample, was cross-sectional and did not assess a number of other factors that may have contributed to the QoL of BMT survivors, such as social support resources.

Psychosocial influences on quality of life

Among physically healthy populations, the presence of anxiety symptoms or disorder has been associated with poor QoL (e.g. Mendlowicz and Stein 2001). Among those with physical illness, emotional responses have also been shown to impact upon quality of life. For example, both depression and anxiety symptoms measured within 15 days of a heart attack were found to predict low QoL at four months, although depression was the strongest predictor (Lane *et al.* 2000). Similarly, among 568 cancer

patients, anxiety and depression were both related to the QoL dimensions of emotional, physical and social functioning, pain, fatigue (depression only), and global QoL, although as in Lane's study, depression was more strongly associated (Skarstein *et al.* 2000).

Studies of the impact of pain on patient well-being may offer some explanation as to why depression is commonly associated with QoL, as pain is strongly associated with depressed mood (see Chapter 16 ☛). One study that examined both pain and depression is that of Rosenfeld *et al.* (1996) who conducted a prospective survey of over four hundred AIDS patients in New York: 63 per cent of participants reported frequent or persistent pain in the preceding two weeks. Comparing scores across a range of QoL indices between those who were and those who were not currently experiencing pain revealed significant differences between the groups in terms of psychological distress, depression, feelings of hopelessness and global QoL. The analyses controlled for other possible influences on the QoL indices, such as age or gender, and social support (which itself was an independent predictor of distress). These results are consistent with many pain studies, showing that pain affects a broad range of psychosocial functioning. Also of importance is the finding that race was significantly related to QoL and distress, with non-white patients reporting poorer QoL and more distress. The authors consider whether this may be due to differences in access to pain management, or whether it reflects other factors not considered in their study, such as socio-economic or life stress, which may be detrimental to the QoL evaluations these individuals made. These findings highlight that several factors need to be taken into account when attempting to establish what 'predicts' QoL: the presence or absence of pain; the presence or absence of depressed mood; levels of social support, ethnicity and other background stressors that may be happening independently of the disease process under study.

In terms of coping response, Carver *et al.* (1992) point out that avoidant coping is likely to be beneficial to QoL in situations where a person is unable to exert control, and they suggest that approach coping in these situations could lead to frustration when control is not forthcoming. Others suggest that maintaining a good QoL in relatively unalterable situations, such as that faced by individuals with chronic pain, may require individuals to cope by means of acceptance coping or positive reinterpretation (McCracken 1998). For example, McCracken and Eccleston (2003), in a study of 230 adults with chronic pain, found that coping was weakly related to pain acceptance and unreliably associated with adjustment, but that among those who did show acceptance of their pain many QoL indicators were higher, including reduced pain symptomatology and disability, less depression and pain-related anxiety, a higher amount of time per day spent up and about, and a greater likelihood to be working. Such findings underscore the fact that, as discussed in Chapter 12 ☛, there is no one coping strategy that is inherently better than another, and coping will change over time and place depending on the demands and resources available to the person.

In terms of resources upon which individuals may draw when faced with stress or the demands of illness, previous chapters have highlighted the crucial role of social support. Perceived social support is generally considered important to personal well-being, and many positive relationships between perceived social support, coping and adjustment to chronic disease have been reported. However, the direction of causality between variables is not always clear. For example, in a study of 210 outpatients receiving treatment for epilepsy, results of regression analyses found that, independently of current physical health status, psychological distress, loneliness, adjustment and coping and stigma perception contributed most significantly to the measures of QoL (Suurmeijer *et al.* 2001). However, disentangling the direction of relationships between mood, resources (or lack of resource if considering loneliness) or coping variables and illness outcomes such as QoL requires studies with several waves of data collection, where change in the levels of support and adjustment, changes in coping responses, etc. can be assessed. In an attempt to do this, Burgoyne and Renwick (2004) assessed 41 Canadian adults with HIV three times over a four-year period and examined whether changes or stability in social support was associated with changes or stability in QoL. Although having a relatively small sample size, this well-designed study considers the dynamic associations between disease symptomatology, social support and QoL and explores the direction of causality between these factors; for example, do changes in social support lead to changes in QoL, or do changes in QoL lead to changes in social support? Slightly contrary to expectations, analyses revealed that both social support and QoL remained relatively stable over the four-year period, although social support did decrease significantly for 40 per cent of the sample (a finding such as this, if obtained in a larger

sample, would have warranted further exploration to try and ascertain 'who' these 40 per cent were, i.e. did they differ from those for whom social support remained stable in terms of any personal or illness characteristics?). Poorer mental functioning QoL scores tended to predict subsequent lower perceived emotional and informational support, but the directional relationship between physical functioning QoL and social support was unclear. Importantly, results did not show any strong longitudinal association between social support and subsequent QoL. Furthermore, results did not reveal that changes in either QoL or social support were linked in the longer term (i.e. from year one to year four), although there was evidence of a link between the first and second year. Certainly the two measures were associated within each time point, with positive or negative changes in social support corresponding to positive or negative changes in QoL domains; however, the disappointing longitudinal predictive results means that social support and its effects on QoL, at least in this disease group, remains open to debate and in need of a similarly designed study to be conducted with a much larger sample.

Goals and QoL

QoL research has sometimes been criticised for the absence of a theoretical model around which to develop and test the QoL concept. One attempt to bring theory to bear has employed Scheier and Carver's self-regulation theory (see Chapter 9 ☛), which describes a process of goal attainment in the face of a disturbance such as illness (1992). It is proposed that the disturbance of personal goal attainment caused by chronic illness and its consequences is likely to influence a person's perceived QoL (e.g. Echteld *et al.* 1998). Within the self-regulatory framework, event appraisal, appraisals of goal disturbance, outcome expectancies, appraisals of resources and coping processes all combine to influence QoL (e.g. Maes *et al.* 1996). Echteld *et al.* (2003), for example, found that among 158 patients who had undergone **coronary angioplasty**, disease-specific quality of life and positive

---

coronary angioplasty

a procedure where a small balloon is inserted into the blocked coronary artery of a person with **atheroma**.

affect three months after surgery were predicted by pre-surgery QoL, low stress appraisals and avoidant coping. Goal disturbance predicted disease-specific QoL and negative affect. Boersma *et al.* (2005b) also found that disturbance in 'higher-order' goals such as fulfilling duties to others, or having fun, following a heart attack was associated with anxiety, depression and a lower health-related quality of life. It may be that goals indirectly influence QoL outcomes by altering the 'meaning' a person attaches to their illness (Taylor 1983; theory of cognitive adaptation to illness, see below). The 'meaning' of illness has been defined as 'an individual's under-standing of the implications an illness has on self, rela-tionships with others, priorities, and future goals', and as such has been shown to influence well-being and adjust-ment, for example among those with cancer (e.g. Fife 1995, cited in Walker *et al.* 2004: 467). Examining per-sonal goals (both day-to-day and higher-order goals) and their attainment or non-attainment as a result of ill health is therefore important if we are to better under-stand why people rate their QoL in the way that they do when given standardised QoL assessment tools.

WHAT DO YOU THINK?

While we have shown that age, illness and culture might affect how we perceive QoL, where you live may also influence the extent to which a 'good' QoL can be achieved. A survey of the economies of 183 countries found that while Britain had the 5th biggest economy in the world, it ranked 17th for quality of life (based on *PocketWorld in Figures*, 2008, published by The Economist):

1. Norway
2. Iceland
3. Australia
4. Ireland
5. Sweden
6. Canada
7. Japan
8. USA
9. Finland, the Netherlands, Switzerland
12. Belgium, Luxemborg
14. Austria
15. Denmark
16. France
17. Italy, United Kingdom
19. Spain
20. New Zealand

Is your own country in the Top 20? Who is above it and who is below? Why do you think the Netherlands does so much 'better' than the UK?

Why do you think Norway and Iceland are top (the weather?)?

If you are living in Britain, it may please you to know that Britain tops the table for attracting foreign investment, although any pleasure at this is short-lived if you then consider the rankings for child well-being – Britain came 21st, where Holland came 1st!

The rankings were actually based on environmental indicators, such as traffic, pollution, the housing market, and on social statistics regarding leisure activities, consumer-good ownership, crime, edu-cational attainment and unemployment, as well as health indicators, and as such provide an 'objec-tive' estimate of 'quality of life'. Whatever you think of league tables generally (for example, Good University guides, school A-level league tables), in the domain of quality of life they are perhaps mis-leading, given how we have shown in this chapter that quality of life is a subjective construct. Should we pay much attention to these rankings? Do they make any difference to how you lead your life? Are they there purely to feed the media with buckshot to fire at our politicians? Or do they raise real con-cerns about the health and social care systems and environmental policies of your country?

Measuring quality of life

Several main reasons have been suggested as to why QoL assessment is a useful clinical practice (e.g. Higginson and Carr 2001). These include:

● *Measure to inform*: to increase understanding about the multidimensional impact of illness and factors that moderate impact, in order to (a) inform inter-ventions and best practice, and (b) inform patients about treatment outcomes or possible side-effects in order that they are mentally 'prepared' for them, or so that supportive resources can be put in place. Descriptive data from QoL studies can also be used to inform patients and their families about likely treatment experiences so that treatment choices can be made. For example, Cocquyt et al. (2003) found that there is no definite evidence that breast-sparing procedures have more favourable QoL and psychosocial outcomes than mastectomy (although some studies do find better body image and sexual functioning in those with breast-conserving therapy). This information can be presented by health-care providers to aid patient decision making.

● *Measure to evaluate alternatives*: QoL measures may be used as a form of clinical 'audit' to identify which interventions have the 'best' outcomes – for the patient, but also often in relation to costs. In medicine (and health economics), a related concept has emerged, called quality-adjusted life years, or QALYs. Different treatments may be considered as increasing length of life and QoL to varying degrees, and if weightings are attached to certain treatments and assessed against the actual cost of the treatment, QALYs can be used to inform medical treatment decisions. For example, two cancer treatments may offer the same survival benefits, but QoL and QALYs may be poorer during and after one treatment than the other; or one treatment may be cheaper than the other where both have the same effect on improved QoL. Brewster et al. (2006) surveyed the influences upon health professionals and general public attitudes towards treating cancer in the elderly and found that hypothetical decisions to offer treatment were most commonly influenced by life gain, followed by quality of life gain, severity of side-effects and finally patient age. The financial cost of treatment was not examined in this study.

● *Measure to promote communication*: while this is unlikely to be the primary motive for conducting a QoL assessment in a clinical setting, engaging patients in QoL assessment may require health professionals to address areas that they may not otherwise have done, for example about treatment satisfaction, family interactions, hobbies or sexual functioning. This will provide health professionals with a more holistic view of the impact that illness or treatment has had upon their patient and may help future treatment decision making or health care to be responsive to any remaining needs or wants the individual may identify.

Whatever the motive for assessing QoL, a major issue faced by researchers or clinicians is which instrument or method of assessment to use. If we accept that QoL is a multidimensional, dynamic and subjective construct, measurement is inevitably going to face many challenges!

Leventhal and Coleman (1997) state that QoL should be considered not only in terms of outcomes but also as a process that is influenced by individuals' perceptions of various domains of their lives, including their perceptions of any illness and its treatment (see Chapter 9 ☞), and the weightings or importance they attach to their perceptions at any given point in time (see also the discussion of 'response shift' below). They do not argue that QoL should be assessed separately from all its possible component parts, e.g. physical, emotional and social functioning, but that each should be seen as separate factors, as possible determinants of QoL. Changes in any of these determinants will influence changes in QoL (see Figure 14.1). This process model has generally been accepted in psychological research studies where multiple measures of determinants are used, as well as generic or specific QoL measures, as will be seen in the discussion of measures below.

Generic versus specific QoL measures

The global domains of QoL described by the WHOQOL group and outlined earlier in the chapter have been supported in many empirical studies; however, a question remains as to whether to adopt a generic, or global, measure of QoL which assesses concepts relevant to all illness groups or to adopt a measure specific to the illness being studied. Commonly employed generic measures include the Medical Outcome study short form 36, usually referred to as the SF36 (Stewart and Ware 1992); the Nottingham Health Profile (NHP; Hunt et al. 1986); and the EUROQOL (Euroqol group 1990). In terms of disease-specific measures, an increasing number are available (see Bowling 2005), such as those developed for people with cancer (e.g. EORTC QLQ-C30; Aaronson et al. 1993; Cocks et al. 2008, or the FACT-G, Cella et al. 1993; Holzner et al. 2004), asthma (e.g. Hyland et al. 1996), arthritis (e.g. AIMS-1, 2; Meenan and Mason 1990) or Parkinson's disease (see review by Marinus et al. 2002).

There are disadvantages and advantages to both types of measure. Generic measures, while allowing for comparison between different illness groups, often fail to address some of the unique QoL issues for that illness.

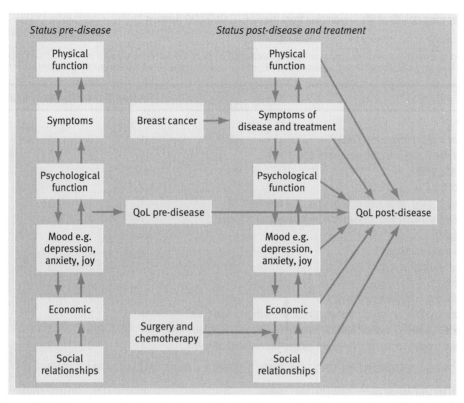

Figure 14.1 The quality-of-life process prior to and subsequent to breast cancer. Baseline QoL is changed by the impact of the disease and treatment upon each of the domains. Changes in functioning post-disease are weighted and will lead to changes in post-disease onset QoL

Source: Leventhal and Coleman (1997: 759).

In cancer, for example, the European Organisation for Research and Treatment of Cancer (EORTC) developed a cancer-specific tool (EORTC QLQ-C30) to assess not only quality of life issues relevant to most people (see Table 14.1) but also including cancer-specific supplementary modules which address fears of recurrence or of treatment side-effects (Aaronson *et al.* 1993). In HIV infection and AIDS, issues such as HIV testing and the results process, concern with symptoms, and disclosure of a positive diagnosis to others, are addressed in a tool developed out of the previously mentioned WHOQOL (the WHOQOL-HIV) (O'Connell *et al.* on behalf of WHOQOL-HIV group 2003).

Disease-specific measures therefore have 'added value', but they do not allow for the same amount of between-illness comparability. This comparability enables questions such as, 'Is the quality of life reduced more by cancer than by heart disease?' to be asked – a question of interest perhaps to those considering research funding allocations or developing community support resources, for example.

Individualised QoL measures

Another option available to health researchers is to take an individualised approach to assessing QoL. Such approaches abandon the dimensions of many generic and disease-specific instruments and allow respondents to choose the dimensions and concerns relevant and of value to them. This does not necessarily require the use of a questionnaire. For example, in an interesting study by Stenner *et al.* (2003), a technique known as 'Q-sort' was adopted whereby 90 healthy participants sorted a collection of 52 statements about QoL (developed from WHOQOL and other sources) into piles according to their importance to them (least important, neutral, most important). They then return to the three piles and sort each item within the piles on a scale ranging from −5 least important, through 0 neutral, to +5 extremely important. Participants then examine their own unique Q-sort and discuss why they ranked some items as more important than others, and whether they believe it is an accurate reflection of their personal view about QoL.

Table 14.1 Assessing quality of life – examples from the EORTC QLQ-C30 (version 3)

(NB: This is NOT the full scale, thus not for use in research)

We are interested in some things abot you and your health. Please answer all of the questions yourself by circling the number that best applies to you. There are no 'right' or 'wrong' answers. The information that you provide will remain strictly confidential.

	Not at all	A little	Quite a bit	Very much
(2 examples of 5)				
Do you have any trouble taking a *long* walk?	1	2	3	4
Do you need to stay in bed or a chair during the day?	1	2	3	4
DURING THE PAST WEEK:				
(10 examples of 23)				
Were you limited in doing either your work or other daily activities?	1	2	3	4
Were you limited in pursuing your hobbies or other leisure-time activities?	1	2	3	4
Have you had pain?	1	2	3	4
Have you had trouble sleeping?	1	2	3	4
Have you lacked appetite?	1	2	3	4
Did you feel tense?	1	2	3	4
Have you had difficulty remembering things?	1	2	3	4
Has your physical condition or medical treatment interfered with your family life?	1	2	3	4
Has your physical condition or medical treatment interfered with your *social* activities?	1	2	3	4
Has your physical condition or medical treatment caused you financial difficulties?	1	2	3	4

FOR THE FOLLOWING QUESTIONS PLEASE CIRCLE THE NUMBER BETWEEN 1 AND 7 THAT BEST APPLIES TO YOU

How would you rate your overall health during the past week?

1   2   3   4   5   6   7
very poor   excellent

How would you rate your overall quality of life during the past week?

1   2   3   4   5   6   7
very poor   excellent

Source: from EORTC Quality of Life group http://groups.eortc.be/qol/questionnaires_qlqc30.htm, For permission to use contact: Quality of Life Department, EORTC European Organisation for Research and Treatment of Cancer, AISBL-IVZW, Avenue E. Mounier, 83/11, 1200 Brussels, BelgiumWebsite: http://groups.eortc.be/qol.

Eight significant factors emerged that were interpreted as reflecting distinct constructs of the meaning and personal relevance of QoL for this sample: happy families; standing on my own two feet; emotional independence; just do it; life as a positive challenge; in God we trust; staying healthy enough to 'bring home the bacon', and 'You can't choose your family'. Interesting demographic differences were seen in which participants contributed to these emergent factors: for example, younger participants rated standing on their own two feet and being independent and in control more highly than older participants; whereas older participants, more often married, rated happy familes and their relationships and support more highly. Many other differences existed: for example, in the extent to which spirituality was considered a self-belief or based on a religion; the extent to which mental well-being was valued in comparison

to physical health; and the extent to which control is considered to be an internal or external resource. Such findings also highlight that the different strands of QoL interact, and causal sequencing seems likely; in other words, psychological aspects may influence the reported social, financial and physical aspects, and vice versa. Interesting differences are suggested for age, gender and educational status, although this study is limited by not including participants over the age of 64, anyone who was unemployed, or anyone not of white English origin. (The influence of ageing on perceived QoL was addressed earlier in the chapter.)

This 'idiographic' approach is also taken in specific assessment instruments. One of the first examples is the schedule for the evaluation of individual quality of life (SEIQoL; O'Boyle *et al.* 1993; Joyce *et al.* 2003). This instrument is not specific to a health condition but invites individuals to identify five aspects of life that are important to them (i.e. 'What are the five most important areas of your life at present – the things that make your life a relatively happy or sad one at the moment . . . the things that you feel determine your quality of life?'). Individuals then rate their current level of functioning on each, attach a weighting of importance to each aspect and rate how satisfied they are currently with that aspect of life. The aspects of life mentioned most often by the hip replacement patients in the original study were family, leisure activities, independence, happiness, finances and religion; with control subjects being very similar, although nominating health more often than patients. Perhaps it was important to the healthy participants to retain health and therefore these participants mentioned it, whereas it featured less strongly in the patient sample, perhaps because they had had to readjust their life goals and values and no longer rated health as one of the most important domains in their lives, although this was not explored in the study.

Another individualised measure, very similar to the SEIQoL but specific to those with a health condition, is the PGI – the Patient Generated Index (Martin *et al.* 2007), which also asks individuals to name the (five) most important areas of their life, but in this case, the five *are* to be those that are affected by their health condition. These are then rated in terms of how badly affected they are on a 0–100 scale (worst imaginable, to no effect, exactly as they would like it to be). This measure also allows for other aspects additonal to the five listed to be noted. Finally, in an interesting and novel way, participants are given 60 points to 'spend' on buying improvement in any of their listed domains, and this spend is multiplied with the rating to get the final score of the weight attached to that domain of QoL. This really highlights the subjective value of different domains to different people. This measure is growing in popularity but was not found to be concurrently associated with illness perceptions in those with head and neck cancer where one would hypothesise an association (see Chapter 9 ☛; Llewelyn *et al.* 2007), and scores on the PGI showed moderate reproducabilty, responsiveness to change and only correlated moderately with other QoL measures in a study of older heart failure patients (Witham *et al.* 2007). Thus further validation work with this newer measure is perhaps required.

While individualised methods of assessment acknowledge the subjectivity of QoL, such methods are time-consuming and relatively complex processes that critics suggest may exclude their use in certain populations. Addressing this point, Jenkinson *et al.* (2001) adopted technology to make QoL assessment quicker, portable and possibly more adaptable to clinical situations. They describe a method of assessment known as the dynamic health assessment (DYNHA) system (see www.qualitymetric.com), which is a short computer-based instrument. Items for assessment are selected from a pool, dependent upon participants' earlier responses to global questions, and currently on offer are assessments for generic Qol based on the SF36, as well as specific measures of the impact of headache, arthritis, pain and pediatric asthma. The benefit of this method is that assessment is more adapted to uniquely individual problems, while the use of SF36 items still enables comparison with other groups assessed with SF36. More studies are required using this method, but results from Jenkinson's study with neurological populations are encouraging.

Practicality of measures

Where assessment circumstances allow, most studies use multiple measures and, as well as assessing generic and/or illness-specific multidimensional QoL, will generally also include unidimensional outcome measures such as assessments of mood, pain or disability that address only one specific aspect of QoL. There is a natural limit to how many questionnaires can be 'inflicted' on an ill individual, and it is important for researchers to be sensitive to this. A good research tool may not be an appropriate tool to administer in a clinical setting. For example, the functional limitations profile (Patrick and Peach 1989) (or its American precursor the sickness impact profile; Bergner *et al.* 1981), while a well-validated and commonly employed outcome measure, has 136 items assessing 12 domains of potential illness impact (e.g. self-care, mobility, social functioning, communication and emotion), and it takes 20–30 minutes to complete, which is potentially impossible in many clinical settings! In fact, it is worth noting that the detection of mood disorders in hospitalised patients, such as clinical levels of depression, is often difficult for front-line nurses (see meta-analysis by Mitchell and Kakkadasam 2011), and this is in part due to the complexity of assessment instruments.

In addition, certain conditions make it difficult to carry out assessments of subjective perceptions, such as QoL. Illnesses that elicit a communication deficit, such as the receptive and expressive aphasias that are common following a stroke, often results in such patients being excluded from self-report studies (e.g. Morrison *et al.* 2005) and the use of proxy measures often results, the limitations of which are described below.

Overall, there has been a proliferation of QoL measures and assessment methods available to researchers in this area, and the choice of which to use will be determined by the aims of the study and by the practicalities offered by the research situation and the population to be studied. This makes it quite difficult to compare across studies, and quite difficult to translate research findings into clinical practice. While the growth of the WHOQOL group measures may go some way towards achieving consistency in measurement, the standardisation of quantitative measures and methods bring with them the risk of losing information as to the very personal and individualised meaning of QoL as seen in the discussion above.

Response shift

Some authors have found individuals with limiting illness to rate their QoL higher than do healthy people (e.g. in diabetes; Hart *et al.* 2003). In trying to interpret this counter-intuitive finding we can either consider simply that it reflects the subjectivity of QoL, or that illnesses do not inevitably limit a person's perceived quality of life. More recently, researchers have begun to consider the idea that illness can bring about changes that create what is described as a **response shift**, i.e. the meaning of the concept being assessed changes in the view of an individual because perhaps their illness causes them to recalibrate their internal standards, reprioritise expectations and life values (Schwartz *et al.* 2004) or reconstruct their identity to accommodate and take ownership of an illness identity (Jones *et al.* 2011 (see RESEARCH FOCUS Chapter 15 (☞); Tsarenko and Polonsky 2011). Yardley and Dibb (2007) nicely illustrated response shift recently in a longitudinal study of 301 individuals with Meniere's disease, a chronic although not life-threatening condition

---

response shift

changes in subjective reports that may result from a reprioritisation of life expectations or recalibration of internal standards so that the construct being assessed is reconceptualised.

---

characterised by severe and disabling vertigo, tinnitus and progressive hearing loss. They found that when the scores obtained on the SF36 quality of life measure obtained at the first study time point were compared with the score given when participants were asked ten months later to look back to that first time point and score their quality of life 'then', there was a significant reduction in the reported level of general health, mental health, role-physical, and role-emotional attributed to the first time point. In other words, when looking back, these participants attributed poorer QoL across all SF36 subscales, except the 'physical health' one, to 'then' than they had reported at the time. The 'then test' was significant whereas the difference between the first time point and the second time point was not, i.e. the ten-month follow-up scores themselves did not differ from the baseline scores. This is response shift and is worth bearing in mind when conducting longitudinal studies. Yardley offers some explanation for this response shift by also showing that scores on a measure of goal orientation relevant to five broad domains of QoL *did* change over time with an improvement in participants' approach. If we are to better understand 'change' over the course of illness, the use of the 'then-test' is likely to be seen in many more studies in future. Qualitative findings have commonly pointed to changes in life expectations, meanings, goals and priorities following diagnosis or during illness (e.g. Ingram *et al.* 2008) and therefore we should not be surprised to find that such 'shifts' in perspective affects how questionnaire items are interpreted and scored at different time points.

Related to this, an interesting study by Sargent-Cox and colleagues (2010) which assessed self-rated health (thought to be a holistic self-rating and thus highly relevant to QoL) in the large Australian Longitudnal Study on Ageing clearly illustrated that these judgements are often made in comparisons to others and that depending on who the comparator is the ratings may vary over time. They found that self-comparative ratings ('Is your health now, better, about the same, or not as good as it was 12 months ago?') declined over time (ten-year follow-up), whereas age-comparative ratings (i.e. 'Would you say your health is better, about the same, or worse than most people your age?') stayed roughly stable for women but became more negative for men. This goes against the expected downward social comparisons (Festinger 1954), whereby contrasting oneself to those worse off at the same age could have utility in that one can then dissociate from the 'ageing' stereotype and increase one's self-esteem (Wills 1981) or contribute to adaptive coping (Buunk *et al.* 2006). *Identifying* downwards (as opposed to *contrasting* downwards), seen particularly in the oldest-old men (85+ years) who compared themselves negatively against age similar peers, is likely to create feelings of threat or anxiety. In contrast, young-old men (65 years) showed the expected increasingly positive age-comparative ratings. A global rating ('How would you rate your overall health at the present time?') which is commonly used in the literature and commonly found to be predictive of many health outcomes, including mortality, significantly declined over time. Such findings have implications for the conclusions we draw from our findings. Unlike in this study where participants are explicitly invited to make comparative ratings, how are we to know whether social comparisons are implicitly enacted in the responses people make to our questions?

Two final factors that warrant consideration in the development of new measures or in the choice made from existing instruments (see Bowling 1995a for coverage of many QoL instruments) is that of participant age and culture.

Culture

Measures of health-related QoL have been developed predominantly in the English language, meaning that for use in non-English-speaking countries, measures have to be translated. Bowden and Fox-Rushby (2003) reviewed the process of translating measures, generally developed in English, in 23 countries across Africa, Asia, Eastern Europe, the Middle East and South America. These authors concluded that in the process of translation the meaning of items may be lost, and that using measures that have been generated predominantly from samples of Western populations assumes that words and concepts have equivalent meaning in different cultures, and that domains have equal salience. Furthermore, the nature of disease varies considerably between countries, with, for example, the authors citing evidence that in Europe only 6 per cent of mortality is attributable to communicable diseases (such as HIV, TB), whereas in Africa and South-east Asia communicable diseases account for 71 and 39 per cent of deaths, respectively. Differences in disease experience such as these are likely to have an effect on illness and QoL expectations. The

WHOQOL group is addressing these culturally relevant questions in its many studies.

In relation to cancer, the commonly employed health-related QoL measure, the FACT-G (Cella *et al.* 1993), has also received cross-cultural validation within a sample of Korean women with breast cancer (Lee *et al.* 2004). While perceptions of illness and health-care-seeking behaviour have been shown to vary between Western and non-Western populations (see Chapter 9 ☞), few studies have addressed specific differences in understanding of QoL. Lee *et al.* find that the FACT-G and its physical, emotional and functional well-being dimensions had good construct validity when the items were entered into factor analysis, but that the social/family well-being subscale was problematic in that items did not load together on to a coherent factor. This subscale assesses closeness to friends and partners, seeking of emotional support from family or friends, family communication, accepting illness on the part of the family, and sex life. The authors interpret these findings as evidence that the Korean women separated out family from friends in terms of what they offered to their well-being, with family communication and closeness fundamental, whereas the cancer was often kept from friends. Such findings have been reported within other Asian cultures and need to be borne in mind when pooling the data obtained from multidimensional measures used within mixed cultural samples. Cultural differences are likely to affect statistical findings and thus the conclusions drawn from the data.

Age

McEwan *et al.* (2004: 4) point out that adapting an adult questionnaire into a child version 'fails to acknowledge important aspects of child and adolescent development and functioning'. The young child may, for example, have cognitive limitations that make it difficult for them to understand abstract questions such as those concerning life satisfaction or global well-being. Developmentally, and consistent with Piagetian thinking (see Chapter 1 ☞), the understanding of the more concrete domains of QoL (such as pain) may emerge as early as between 4 and 6 years of age, for example the Childhood Asthma Questionnaire Form A (French *et al.* 1994), whereas the more abstract domains (such as feelings) emerge from around age 7.

Although some measures have been developed specifically to assess QoL in child populations, not many have been validated, and this fact, alongside a common assumption of cognitive limitation in children, has led to many studies using parents to complete questionnaires on behalf of their children (e.g. Bijttebier *et al.* 2001). This is known as proxy measurement. However, parental 'proxy' reports in effect go against the principle of QoL being a personal subjective belief, as a parent may not share the same views as their child (Matza *et al.* 2004). This point was well illustrated by Eiser and Morse (2001) when they reviewed studies of chronically ill samples where both child reports and parental proxy reports were generated. Parent–child agreement was greater for observable aspects of QoL such as physical functioning but less for emotional or perceived social functioning. In Bijttebier *et al.*'s (2001) study of QoL among young cancer patients (using parental proxy reports), predominantly observable aspects of QoL were assessed in relation to:

● *physical restriction*: e.g. my child has been able to perform as usual;

● *emotional distress*: e.g. my child has anger outbursts;

● *discomfort from medical treatment*: e.g. my child complained of pain after a medical procedure.

As such, the data on child QoL obtained in this study may be more reliable than if 'non-behavioural' aspects of QoL had been assessed; however, whole domains of QoL are not examined.

As further illustration of possible discrepancies between proxy and 'real' reports, a study of 100 children with congenital heart disease and their parents found that while both parents and children reported reduced child motor functioning and autonomy when compared with healthy children, the children reported lower levels of emotional QoL than did their parents. Overall, parents reported that more problems were faced by their children than the children themselves reported (Krol *et al.* 2003). Healthy children, by contrast, have been reported to show less agreement with their parents regarding their physical status than they do in other domains (e.g. Theunissen *et al.* 1998).

Additionally, it has been shown, following a review of findings of six studies where two sets of ratings were obtained, that significant discrepancies exist in the perceptions of patient well-being and QoL during the course of long-term (primarily cancer) treatment reported by their physicians and that reported by the patients themselves or, in the case of children, parental perceptions (Janse *et al.* 2004).

The findings reviewed here highlight that parent–child dyads may converge and diverge in terms of their beliefs, depending on various factors, including the child's current health status. In the context of a child with illness, parental over- or underestimation of a child's problem areas can have implications for parental caring behaviour (see Chapter 15 ☞). Furthermore, we have presented evidence that patient (or parent) ratings often diverge from health professionals' ratings of that patient's QoL, and this could lead to misunderstandings about treatment or its usefulness in terms of QoL gain, which may, as Janse *et al.* note, have implications for non-adherence. Given the above evidence of divergence in reports, it is unclear who researchers should direct their questions to: it may be that assessing both the 'patient' and a significant other will in fact give a more complete picture.

In addition to who the questions are directed to, consideration needs to be given to the content of the questions. As Matza and colleagues note in their very useful review in this area (Matza *et al.* 2004): 'When designing a pediatric HRQoL instrument, it is important to ensure that items correspond to experiences, activities, and contexts that are directly relevant to the age of the sample' (p. 80). There is little to be gained from asking children about the impact of illness on general functioning where a distinction between school, play, at home, and with peers is likely to be needed.

Finally, consideration needs to be given about when and how often HRQoL is assessed, and by whom. This chapter has shown that QoL is an important outcome of illness and treatment and has noted that, increasingly, medical professionals are recognising the scientific evidence regarding the importance of psychosocial outcomes. The potential to take the research evidence back into practice is illustrated in the findings of a recent randomised controlled trial comparing the effects of computerised real-time feedback of patient HRQoL results to physicians (experimental group), versus no feedback (control group), on the HRQoL scores, patient satisfaction and consultation behaviours of 162 liver disease patients (Gutteling *et al.* 2008). While no direct effect of the experiment was found in terms of overall patient QoL (similar to reports from some earlier studies), several interesting interaction effects emerged from more detailed analyses. Older patients who were in the experimental group had a better disease-specific QoL than controls; and both older patients, and males of any age, in the experimental group had better mental QoL than control group patients. In addition, the physicians themselves were seen to have benefited in that those in the experimental group altered their patient management practices in terms of time spent discussing psychosocial issues. While a relatively small study and with a poor response rate, this kind of study is immensely valuable in that it begins to demonstrate how we, as health psychologists, can put our years of studying QoL and how to assess it to good use in clinical practice.

SUMMARY

This chapter has provided evidence that QoL is an important concept that encompasses a person's subjective belief about the quality of various life domains of importance to them. The domains generally considered in quality of life research include:

● physical functioning;

● role functioning;

● emotional functioning;

● social functioning;

● environmental aspects, and, increasingly;

● spiritual functioning.

We have described a range of influences on the experience of quality of life, including aspects of the disease and its treatment, and aspects of the individual such as their age, ethnicity, mood or levels of social support. We have also shown that, in spite of difficulties in clearly defining and measuring QoL, there is a growing recognition of the need to do so, and for research and practice to look beyond traditionally clinical outcomes of illness, such as disability, symptomatology and mortality, to more holistic psychosocial outcomes.

While there is increasing evidence of the inclusion of QoL assessment in clinical trials of treatments or in psychosocial interventions, the debate as to whether it is best assessed objectively or subjectively, generically or specifically remains. There is also the need to be sensitive to the needs of specific populations, for example children, and to address cultural variation in the understanding of QoL. We have described various methods of assessing this subjective construct, including:

● self-report interview;

● self-report questionnaire completion;

● proxy report (either interview or questionnaire).

As with beauty, quality of life is in 'the eye of the beholder', and therefore this presents challenges to interventions based on identified predictors of quality of life, as it is unlikely that 'one size will fit all'. However, this chapter has, it is hoped, presented some of the general influences and is a starting point from which to develop interventions.

Further reading

Bowling, A. (2005). *Measuring Health: A Review of Quality of Life*, 3rd edn. Milton Keynes: Open University Press.

Bowling, A. (2001). *Measuring Disease: A Review of Disease-specific Quality of Life Measurement Scales*, 2nd edn. Milton Keynes: Open University Press.

These two well-written books provide the reader with a comprehensive and invaluable overview of issues in both health- and illness-related quality of life. Additionally, many of the available QoL scales are outlined and useful examples provided. While new scales continue to appear, these books provide essential background reading.

D. Balk, C. Wogrin, G. Thornton and D. Meagher (eds), *Handbook of Thanatology: The Essential Body of Knowledge for the Student of Death, Dying, and Bereavement*. Northbrook, IL: Association for Death Education and Counseling, pp. 93–102.

Although an American text, this book contans many chapters of relevance to our understanding of this emotive topic – death – including coverage of euthanasia debates. The website is also worth a visit – see below.

Key papers

Carr, A.J. and Higginson, I.J. (2001). Are quality of life measures patient centred? *British Medical Journal*, 32: 1357–60.

This brief paper addresses the crucial issues of how to measure QoL, and who should take the measurements – doctors, patients or other proxy reporters? The fact that this paper was published in the *British Medical Journal* was encouraging testimony to the fact that QoL is on the medical profession's agenda.

Matza, L.S., Swensen, A.R., Flood, E.M. *et al.* (2004). Assessment of health-related quality of life in children: a review of conceptual, methodological, and regulatory issues. *Value in Health*, 7: 79–92.

For anyone considering a research project involving assessment of children, this paper is a must, whether you are assessing QoL or some other construct. Matza and colleagues clearly describe issues regarding the timing, content and scoring of QoL measures in children, and debate the issues of proxy measurement and response bias. They also provide a useful table of selected child QoL measures.

Weblink

Type 'quality of life' into any search engine and you will get thousands of hits, some from health-professional pages, some from academia, while others will be papers from economists, policy makers and even governmental bodies. It is clear that QoL is a term in use in many domains outside psychology!

The Association for Death Education and Counseling website is produced by one of the oldest multidisciplinary organisations studying policy, practice and related evidence in the field of death and dying:

www.adec.org

Visit the website at **www.pearsoned.co.uk/morrison** for additional resources to help you with your study, including multiple choice questions, weblinks and flashcards.

Pain in the absence of pain receptors

Perhaps the most obvious evidence to counter these simple biological models is the evidence that many people experience pain in the absence of any nerve pain receptors. The most dramatic example of this phenomenon is known as 'phantom limb pain', which involves sensations, sometimes extremely painful, that feel located in a patient's missing limb following amputation. Up to 70 per cent of amputees report phantom limb pain a week after amputation, and over half of these people continue to experience phantom limb pain for many months or even years after their surgery (Dijkstra *et al.* 2002). Two years following amputation, nearly a third of patients who initially experienced phantom limb pain still experience significant pain despite using strong opiate medication (Mishra *et al.* 2007). Interestingly, people who have their upper limb amputated are far less likely to experience phantom limb pain than those who have had a leg amputated. Similar experiences are reported by people with spinal cord injuries and paralysis. Unfortunately, phantom limb pain is difficult to treat and can have a significant negative impact on those with the condition.

'Pain receptors' that do not transmit pain

A second physical phenomenon that presents problems for these early theories stems from the experiences of people with CUIP referred to above. Individuals with this condition may experience painless bone fractures and ulceration to their hands and feet, which may go unnoticed. They may also fail to identify pain as a symptom of severe disease and sustain dramatic injuries as a result of a failure to respond to danger signals. Some people with CUIP may even experience ulceration of the cornea of the eye as they fail to protect against strong sunlight (Nagasako *et al.* 2003). Individuals with CUIP appear to have intact pain pathways, so they present the opposite problem to that posed by phantom limbs: a failure to perceive pain in the presence of an apparently intact pain pathway.

Psychological influences on pain

A number of psychological factors have been found to influence the experience of pain. Three of the key ones are:

1. *Mood*: anxiety and depression reduce pain tolerance and increase the reporting of pain.

2. *Attention*: focusing on pain increases the experience of pain.

3. *Cognitions*: expectations of increases or reductions in pain can be self-fulfilling.

Mood and pain

Mood influences the perception of pain – and pain influences mood. Evidence of the influence of mood on the experience of pain can be found in studies in which participants are asked to rate or tolerate pain until their discomfort is too great to tolerate it any further. These have shown that depressed or anxious participants report the equivalent pain stimulus as more painful than people without any mood disorder (e.g. Mel'nikova 1993) and tolerate pain for significantly less time (Pinerua-Shuhaibar *et al.* 1999).

Short-term mood states may also affect the experience of pain. Fisher and Johnston (1996b), for example, gave patients with lower back pain a simple mood induction procedure in which they were asked either about upsetting aspects of their condition or to report more positive aspects of their condition and how they were coping with it. Before and after this procedure, participants were given a plastic bag into which were placed as many packets of rice as they felt able to tolerate and then held the bag until it felt uncomfortable. In comparison with their performance at baseline, participants who reported the upsetting issues (and were therefore assumed to be more depressed) performed less well. By contrast, those whose mood was improved were able to hold the same weights for a longer period than baseline. This was an important study, as it used real patients faced with a task similar to their everyday activities.

Evidence of a reciprocal relationship between pain and mood has also been reported in a number of studies. Magni *et al.* (1994), for example, followed over two thousand participants for a period of eight years. They found that participants who reported chronic pain at the beginning of the study were nearly three times more likely to become depressed over the follow-up period than those without this problem. By contrast, another group of people who were depressed and free of pain at the beginning of the study were over twice as likely to report having had a significant period of pain over the follow-up period. The authors speculated that depression may predict some 'pain conditions' while some 'pain conditions' may predict depression, although the nature of these two conditions was not clear. Suffice it to say that there is an interaction between pain and mood that can operate in both directions.

Attention and pain

One of the ways that mood may influence our perception of pain is by influencing the attention we pay to any pain sensations. Depressed or anxious people may pay more attention to pain sensations than other people, and this focus may significantly influence their experience of pain. Focusing on pain seems to increase its impact: focusing on other things seems to reduce it. Many people who experience injuries while playing sports requiring effort and concentration, for example, do not notice the extent of any injuries until after the game has finished. Less anecdotally, there is evidence that fewer people experience pain following physical trauma at times of intense stress, such as being on the battlefield, than when similar levels of injury are sustained in less stressful situations (Beecher 1946). This may be because of attentional factors – in the battlefield there are many important distractions from one's own pain. However, other factors may also have been involved. It is possible, for example, that the soldiers were simply pleased to be alive following battle and thought that their injury would result in them being sent away from the battlefield. Civilians would be more likely to view their injuries as unwelcome and likely to interfere with their day-to-day activities. The issue here, therefore, may be the meaning ascribed to the injury and pain as much as the degree of attention paid to it.

Despite these alternative explanations, more controlled evaluations of the relationship between attention and pain have shown that the use of distraction can reduce pain, while experimental manipulations that increase attention to painful stimuli result in increased reporting of pain. James and Hardardottir (2002), for example, asked patients to place their lower arm in freezing cold water (an excruciatingly painful procedure known as the **cold pressor test**) and to either concentrate on a computer-based task or the pain sensations. Those who focused on the pain were least able to tolerate it and pulled their arm out of the water significantly earlier than those in the distraction task.

> **cold pressor test**
> procedure in which participants place their arm in a mixture of water and ice maintaining the water temperature at between 0 and 3°C.

Attentional bias may also explain why some people with acute pain go on to develop chronic pain, while others do not. Vlaeyen *et al.* (1995) suggested that people who develop chronic pain in the absence of any clear physical injury or inflammation may respond to acute pain with a degree of fear, worry about its consequences and begin to check themselves for any pain sensations. Because they are now paying attention to a variety of aches and pains that may pass unnoticed in other people, they label their pain as symptomatic of an underlying problem. They may also stop engaging in activities that

Plate 16.1 The experience of pain differs according to context. Terry Butcher (in photograph) probably experienced no pain when clearly injured while playing football for England. After the match, it may have been a different story

Source: Getty Images/David Cannon.

could trigger an episode of pain. In an experimental study that relates to this process, Nouwen *et al.* (2006) asked patients with chronic pain and individuals with no such problem to focus on the pain experienced during a cold pressor task (and therefore not related to the medical cause of their pain). Patients with chronic pain reported more pain and withdrew their hand from the water earlier than those in the control group. Further evidence of this process is provided by Dehghani *et al.* (2003). Their study, which used the dot probe task to explore attentional bias towards pain-related stimuli, found that people with chronic pain were more attentive to words describing the sensory experience of pain than neutral words or words describing its emotional or behavioural consequences. Their results also indicated that people with high levels of fear of pain both attended to relevant words more quickly and then had difficulty in focusing their attention away from them. Both results support the attentional hypothesis of chronic pain.

A number of theoretical models have elaborated on the role of attention in the experience of, and response to, pain. One example of this is Van Damme *et al.*'s (2010) motivational account of bias towards pain-related stimuli. This suggested we have an evolutionary bias towards automatically attending to pain, at the expense of paying attention to other goals; although as we reported earlier in the chapter, this bias may be overridden at times. In addition, they argued that the individual may consciously elect to prioritise attempts at pain control above other goals. With our limited attentional processing ability, this may mean increasing focus on pain reduction, and reduced attention to other life goals. A similar model was proposed by Eccleston and Crombez (1999) who identified three basic responses to pain. First, the presence of pain initiates escape behaviours. Secondly, pain demands and captures attention. Thirdly, the ability of pain to capture attention and interrupt other on-going activities is influenced by a number of characteristics of the pain: its intensity, novelty, and any emotion such as fear that it may be associated with. Pain interrupts other ongoing goal-related behaviour, with chronic pain resulting in the long-term interruption of attention towards other goals.

Cognition and pain

Mood may influence pain by influencing our thoughts about the nature and consequences of any pain. The types of thought that may influence the pain experience include:

- attributions concerning the cause of pain;
- beliefs about the ability to tolerate pain;
- beliefs about the ability to control pain;
- expectations of pain relief – the placebo effect.

A simple example of how attributions concerning the cause of pain may influence the pain experience was described by Cassell (1982) in a case report in which one patient's pain was easily controlled with codeine when they attributed it to **sciatica** but required strong opiate analgesia when they attributed the same pain to having cancer. Walsh and Radcliffe (2002) found that the beliefs of people with chronic back pain influenced their willingness to take part in an exercise programme. Those people who believed their pain was the result of physical damage to their spine were more reluctant to engage in exercise than those who attributed it to 'psychological' factors – because they were afraid that exercise would exacerbate their damaged back and increase their pain. Similarly, Murphy *et al.* (1997) found that the activities of people with lower back pain were more restricted by their expectations of pain than by the actual pain they experienced. They were most restricted when the pain they experienced exceeded the level of pain they expected – presumably because they considered this additional pain to indicate some physical damage as a result of their exercise. Related to this, one particular cognitive response to pain, known as catastrophising (e.g. 'This pain means something is seriously wrong!') is consistently associated with poor outcomes in relation to pain, including reports of preoperative pain (Roth *et al.* 2007), pain following physiotherapy (Hill *et al.* 2007), and restrictions in activity (Voerman *et al.* 2007).

People who feel able to tolerate or manage their pain are less restricted by it. Maly *et al.* (2007) found that patients with osteoarthritis of the knee with high levels of

> **sciatica**
>
> pain down the leg, which is caused by irritation of the main nerve into the leg, the sciatic nerve. This pain tends to be caused where the nerves pass through and emerge from the lower bones of the spine (lumbar vertebrae).

belief in their ability to manage their pain walked more than those with less strong beliefs. Similarly, fit cyclists who believed in their ability to control or manage their pain allowed themselves to experience more painful exercise than those with lower control beliefs (Motl *et al.* 2007). Individuals with high control beliefs may also *experience* less pain. Jensen *et al.* (2001), for example, found that among a group of patients with chronic pain involved in a pain management programme (which would not reduce the objective amount of pain experienced by the attenders), increased perceptions of control over pain were associated with reductions in reported pain. Experimental studies also provide support. In one such study, van den Hout *et al.* (2000) randomly assigned healthy participants to one of three preparatory conditions before they were given a cold pressor task. The preparatory conditions involved a task during which participants were given feedback indicating high levels of control over the task, low levels of control, or no feedback. Despite the fact that the initial task was not pain-related, it seemed to have some carry-over to the cold pressor task. In this, participants who received the high control feedback tolerated the cold pressor task for significantly longer than those who received low control feedback. Perceived control may also influence pain-related behaviour in patient populations. In a partial replication of their study of the effect of mood on pain behaviour described above, Fisher and Johnston (1996) allocated patients with chronic pain to conditions in which their perceptions of control over their pain were experimentally increased or decreased. Control was increased by asking patients to talk about times when they had been in control of their pain and decreased by asking them to recount periods when their control was low. Patients in the increased control condition performed their lifting task for longer than those in the decreased control condition.

Expectations of pain relief: the placebo response

One of the most fascinating phenomena associated with pain is known as the placebo response. If you were to give an inert tablet with no biochemical effects to people experiencing some degree of pain, *tell* them that it will have no effect, a percentage of those individuals (and probably quite a significant percentage) would report some relief from pain as a result of being given the 'tablet'. Red 'tablets' are more effective than blue 'tablets' in this context (Huskisson 1974). There appears to be some benefit to simply being given what appears to be treatment, whether this is a tablet, injection or more culturally diverse form of treatment. This phenomenon is known as the placebo effect.

A placebo (from the Latin, 'I please') is an inert preparation that has no pharmacological effects. Two of hundreds of studies provide examples of its impact. Verdugo and Ochoa (1994) examined the placebo response to an injection of saline (salt water) close to the area of maximum pain in patients with neuropathic pain – that is, pain that seems to be generated by the nerves themselves – which can be difficult to treat with conventional analgesia. Following this simple intervention, nearly two-thirds of the patients reported a 50 per cent or greater reduction in pain. In a similar study, Fine *et al.* (1994) tested a placebo injected into patients with chronic lower back pain. All participants in the study reported significant reductions in pain beginning between fifteen minutes and one hour after the injection and lasting up to several days. These are not unusual findings. Across a range of studies, the percentage of individuals to report at least a 50 per cent reduction in pain following being given a placebo ranges from a lowly 7 per cent to nearly 50 per cent across a variety of conditions and periods of time (McQuay and Moore 2005). Its effect is not limited to pain. The placebo effect can be found in inflammation, the speed of wound healing, immune responses to infection, and the treatment of conditions as diverse as angina, asthma and depression (Humphrey 2002). If a placebo is given following treatment with an active drug, the patient may not only show the degree of benefit in symptom reduction experienced during the active treatment, they may also experience the same side-effects as they did while on the active drug (Suchman and Ader 1992).

Two key mechanisms through which the placebo effect is assumed to have its effect have been posited. The first involves a classical conditioned response, which has been implicated in immune and respiratory responses. A second process, particularly relevant to pain, involves our expectations of pain or pain relief (Price *et al.* 2008). We experience a reduction in pain because we expect a reduction in pain. The logic of this theory (and consistent with explanations of pain experiences described earlier in the chapter) is that if we can somehow change expectations about the efficacy or otherwise of a particular placebo treatment, then the effectiveness of that placebo treatment will also vary. In one of the few studies to attempt this, Fedele *et al.* (1989) found that repeated use of a placebo over several menstrual cycles in women suffering from painful periods resulted in a lowering of the placebo's success in controlling pain. Although they did not directly measure the beliefs and expectations of these women, such a finding is consistent with a gradual change of expectations in the effectiveness of the treatment leading to a reduction in placebo response. Of course, just as positive expectations can lead to a reduction in pain, negative expectations can lead to increases in pain – the nocebo response. Patients recently diagnosed as having a serious illness or patients who distrust their therapy, for example, are likely to report more pain than others (Benedetti *et al.* 2007).

On a slightly tangential note, the placebo effect is considered so important and pervasive that the best trials of the effectiveness of a new intervention involve a comparison with a placebo version of the intervention, for which trial participants have an equal expectation of effectiveness. To simply compare an intervention with no-treatment condition is no longer considered a good test of the effectiveness of an intervention. It must fare significantly better than a placebo to be considered an effective treatment. Medical placebos are relatively easy to construct – usually a tablet or injection identical to the real intervention. Psychological placebos are more difficult to construct, but typically involve as a minimum the same amount of time spent with the participants in some apparently 'psychological' act (e.g. a non-specific discussion of a problem) as the active therapy.

RESEARCH FOCUS

An experimental exploration of factors influencing the pain experience

Lautenbacher, S., Huber, C., Schöfer, D. *et al.* (2010). Attentional and emotional mechanisms related to pain as predictors of chronic postoperative pain: a comparison with other psychological and physiological predictors. *Pain*, 151: 722–31.

The authors note that around 50 per cent of patients experience persistent postoperative pain. Previous predictors of this pain have included depression, anxiety, catastrophising, and possible attentional factors. The aim of this study was to explore further the role of psychological factors in the experience of postoperative pain, focusing on the role of pain hypervigilance, pain catastrophising, pain anxiety, and attentional bias towards pain-related cues.

Method

The 78 participants who completed the study (of 92 at baseline) were men aged 16–37 years given major chest surgery usually involving a 7–10-day period in hospital.

- Baseline (T1): one day prior to surgery: questionnaires including self-rating of pain hypervigilance, pain anxiety, and pain catastrophising; dot probe task comparing reaction times to pain-related, socially threatening, and positive words, experimental pain sensitivity tests, including the cold and heat pain thresholds assessed by asking participants to note the first pain sensation they experienced when a probe was placed against the skin which either became hot or cold. Finally, four salivary cortisol readings taken in the morning, 15, 30, 45 and 60 minutes after wakening (as a physiological measure of psychological stress).

- One week following surgery (T2): assessment of acute postoperative pain.

- Three months after surgery (T3): average intensity of postoperative pain and pain disability across a range of activities during previous four weeks.

- Six months after surgery (T4): average intensity of postoperative pain and pain disability during previous four weeks.

Analyses

Participants were grouped into high and low postoperative pain and disability groups. Low pain intensity participants scored between 0 and 2 on the pain intensity scale, while high intensity participants scored between 3 and 11. Low disability group scores ranged between 0 and 8, while the high disability scores were between 9 and 70. Although there was some overlap between the groups (60 per cent), the authors judged this to be small enough to allow them to use each group as an independent outcome measure. Differences on the predictor variables according to outcome group were assessed using both univariate and multivariate (Structural Equation Modelling) methods. At three months post-surgery, 25 per cent of the sample was reporting some degree of pain; after six months this figure was 14 per cent.

Significant univariate baseline predictors of being in the high pain group were:

● at three months: attentional preference for positive words (i.e. faster reaction time to positive words than socially threatening or pain-related words; Cohen's d = 0.5074, medium effect size), heat pain thresholds (Cohen's d = 0.5240, medium effect size), and morning cortisol levels (Cohen's d = 0.6615, medium effect size);

● at six months: attentional preference for positive words (Cohen's d = 0.6475, medium effect size) and morning cortisol levels (Cohen's d = 0.5074, medium effect size).

Significant baseline predictors of being in the high disability group were:

● at three months: self-rated pain vigilance (Cohen's d = 0.6475, medium effect size);

● at six months: self-rated pain vigilance (Cohen's d = 0.5237, medium effect size), cold pain threshold (Cohen's d = 0.5129), medium effect size, self-rated pain vigilance (Cohen's d = 0.7514, medium effect size), and depression (Cohen's d = 0.5742, medium effect size).

Significant multivariate (SEM) baseline predictors of being in the high pain group were:

● at three months: heat pain threshold (standardised regression weight [SRW] = −0.262, p < 0.05);

● at six months: attentional preference for positive words (SRW = 0.239, p < 0.05).

Significant multivariate (SEM) predictors of being in the high pain disability group were:

● at three months: self-report pain attentional bias (SRW = 0.346, p < 0.01);

● at six months: pressure pain threshold (SRW = −0.295, p < 0.05), cold pain threshold (SRW = 0.464, p < 0.001), depression (SRW = −0.323, p < 0.05).

Discussion

The authors note the apparent paradox between the findings of long-term pain being associated with baseline attentional bias on the dot probe task towards the positive words (and hence, relative avoidance of the pain-related words). They attributed this to the timing of the dot probe task being the day before surgery, suggesting that participants at this time may have been using avoidance coping to help them cope with the expected pain of the operation, and that only sustained pain-related attention over time (which they did not assess) would be associated with longer-term pain. Nevertheless, the finding that an attentional measure did predict pain suggests that attentional processes are involved in coping with pain. Heat pain thresholds were also both predictive of pain – and more so than the measures of anxiety or depression found to predict pain in other studies. The role of attentional processes was further emphasised in the finding that self-report pain attentional bias was associated with long-term disability (at least up to three months), although pain thresholds and depression were more predictive of six-month pain-disability ratings.

A psychobiological theory of pain

The evidence considered previously suggests that two sets of processes are involved in the experience of pain: one involving sensory information from the site of the painful stimulation, the other involving emotional and cognitive processes. The **gate control theory of pain** proposed by Melzack and Wall (e.g. 1965) takes both processes into account and is generally recognised as the best theoretical account of the experience of pain we now have. Melzack and Wall used the analogy of a gate to explain the pain experience. The essence of their gate control theory of pain is that the degree of pain we experience is the result of two sets of processes:

---

gate control theory of pain

a theory of pain developed by Melzack and Wall in which a 'gate' is used as a metaphor for the chemicals, including endorphins, that mitigate the experience of pain.

---

1. Pain receptors in the skin and organs transmit information about physical damage to a series of 'gates' in the spinal column (see Figure 16.1). Within the gates, these nerves link to other nerves along the spinal column that transmit information up to pain centres in the brain.

2. At the same time as we experience physical damage, we also experience related cognitions and emotions – fear, alarm, and so on. This information results in the activation of nerve fibres taking information from the brain down the spinal column to the gate at which the incoming pain signals enter the spinal column.

The degree of pain we experience is a result of differing levels of activation in these two systems. Activation of the sensory nerves from the site of the pain to the spinal column 'opens' the gate. This activates the nerves leading to the pain centres and is recognised as pain – that is the essence of the biological theories of pain described above. However, the downward pathways activated by emotional and cognitive factors can also influence the position of the gate. Anxious thoughts or focusing attention on pain 'open' the gate and increase our experience of pain; calming or distracting thoughts 'close' the gate. This, in effect, prevents neural impulses travelling up through the spinal cord to the brain and reduces the experience

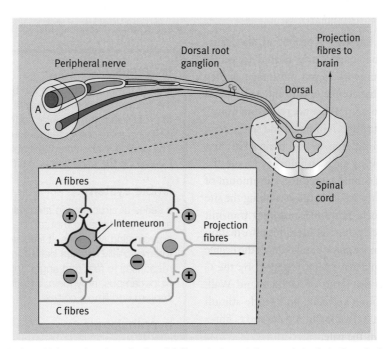

Figure 16.1 The transmission of information along the A and C fibres to the gelatinosa substantia in the spinal cord and upwards to the brain

Source: adapted from Rosenzweig, Leiman and Breedlove (1996: 272).

of pain. The intensity of pain we experience at any time will be a function of these two sometimes competing and sometimes complementary processes.

Pain sensations are transmitted from the site of an injury to the spinal gate by nerves known as nociceptors, three types of which have been identified:

● A delta fibres (types I and II):
  ○ respond to light touch, mechanical and thermal stimuli; carry information about brief sharp pain;
  ○ very strong noxious stimuli related to potential or actual damage to tissues; the experience is short-lasting.
● C polymodal fibres:
  ○ slow conducting; carry information about dull, throbbing, pain – which is experienced for a longer period than that from the A delta fibres.

Perhaps the most important characteristic of these different fibres is that they transmit information at different speeds. As a result, our response to injury usually involves two phases:

1. The first, mediated by A delta fibres, involves the experience of sharp pain.
2. This is followed by a more chronic throbbing pain mediated by the C polymodal fibres.

A second set of nerves, known as A beta fibres, also transmit tactile information, particularly related to gentle touch. These fibres can work to our advantage as they provide information that competes with the A delta and C fibres at the spinal column. When we receive an injury, activation of the A delta fibres is initiated and sends 'pain signals' via the spinal column to the brain. The first instinct we have following such an injury is to rub the site of the injury. This simple act reduces the amount of pain we experience. This occurs because rubbing the site of injury activates A beta fibres. Because they transmit information more quickly than C fibres, this information also reaches the brain more quickly and reduces the degree of activation that would have been triggered by the C fibres alone. Thus, in the terms of Melzack and Wall, activation of A beta fibres to touch and gentle stimuli can close the pain gate. Activation of A delta and C fibres to painful stimuli opens the gate.

The A and C fibres transmit information to areas in the spinal cord known as the substantiagelatinosa. These lie within the dorsal horn of each part of the spinal column (see Figure 16.1). Nerve impulses here trigger the release of a chemical known as substance P into the substantiagelatinosa. This, in turn, activates nerve fibres known as T(ransmitter) fibres, which transmit the sensation of pain to the brain:

● Information from A fibres is taken to the **thalamus** and on to the cortex, where the individual can plan and initiate action to remove them from the source of the pain.
● Information from the C fibres follows a pathway to the **limbic system**, **hypothalamus** and autonomic nervous system (see Chapter 8 ☞). Activity within the limbic system adds an emotional content, such as fear or alarm, to the experience of pain. The hypothalamus controls activity within the autonomic nervous system (see Chapter 8 ☞), which allows us to respond quickly to remove ourselves from harm.

The results of this neural activity are transmitted *down* the spinal column through nerve pathways known as reticulospinal fibres to the spinal gate mechanism (see Figure 16.2). These may trigger the release of a variety of chemicals into the 'soup' of chemicals in the substantiagelatinosa (and brain), the most important of which are naturally occurring opiate-like substances called **endorphins**. These 'close' the gate and moderate the degree of pain experienced. Activity in this system is mediated by a number of factors, each of which influences the release of endorphins. These include:

---

thalamus

area of the brain that links the basic functions of the hindbrain and midbrain with the higher centres of processing, the cerebral cortex. Regulates attention and contributes to memory functions. The portion that enters the limbic system is involved in the experience of emotions.

limbic system

a series of structures in the brain, often referred to as the 'emotional computer' because of its role in coordinating emotions. It links sensory information to emotionally relevant behaviour, in particular responses to fear and anger. Includes the hippocampus, amygdala, anterior thalamic nuclei, septum and limbic cortex.

hypothalamus

area of the brain that regulates appetite, sexual arousal and thirst. Also appears to have some control over emotions.

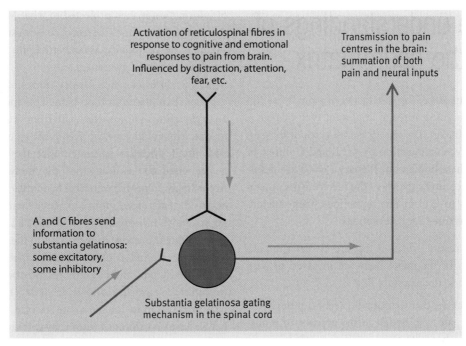

Figure 16.2 A schematic view of the gate control mechanism postulated by Melzack and Wall

- *Focusing on the pain*: worrying, or **catastrophising**, reduces the amount of endorphins released and opens the gate.

- *Emotional and cognitive factors*: feeling optimistic and unconcerned about the 'meaning' of the pain increases endorphin release and closes the gate – anxiety, worry, anger or depression opens the gate.

- *Physical factors*: relaxation increases endorphin release and lessens the experience of pain.

Pain medication will also 'close' the pain gate.

endorphins

naturally occurring opiate-like chemicals released in the brain and spinal cord. They reduce the experience of pain and can induce feelings of relaxation or pleasure. Associated with the so-called 'runner's high'.

catastrophising

the act of constructing **catastrophic thoughts**.

catastrophic thoughts

automatic thoughts that exaggerate the negative aspects of any situation.

WHAT DO YOU THINK?

We have already identified a number of factors that influence our experience of pain. Think how *you* react to pain. Do these factors reflect your own experience of pain? And how do we come to respond to pain in the way we do? Do you rub yourself if you are bruised to ease the pain? If so, why? Did you learn to do it as a response to previous pain experiences – or were you told to do so by a parent or friend? Are you stoic in the face of pain? If so, is this a result of how others have expected you to respond? 'Big boys don't cry': cultural and childhood experiences may encourage different ways of expressing both emotional and physical pain in men and women. Do they affect how you respond to pain? Or do you respond in ways determined by your personality? People who are generally anxious may be more prone to respond to pain with catastrophic thinking, anxiety and high levels of physiological arousal – resulting in a relatively high experience of pain (and other labelling of bodily sensations as 'symptoms' of disease: see Chapter 9 ☞). People who are more relaxed and optimistic may have a less emotional response to pain and experience relatively less pain. Is this the case for you?

Future understandings of pain: the neuromatrix

Despite the success of the gate theory of pain, it has still struggled to account for one important type of pain – phantom limb pain. The theory cannot account for pain in the absence of stimulation by the A and C fibres. In response to these limitations, Melzack (2005) has developed a more complex theory of the mechanisms of pain that attempts to explain this mysterious phenomenon. His model has three key assumptions:

1. The same neural processes that are involved in pain perception in the intact body are involved in pain perception in the phantom limb.

2. All the qualities that we normally feel from the body, including pain, can be felt in the absence of inputs from the body.

3. The body is perceived as a unity and is identified as the 'self', distinct from other people and the surrounding world.

Melzack contended that the anatomical substrate of the 'body-self' is a large, widespread network of neurons linking the thalamus, cortex and limbic system in the brain. He termed this system the 'neuromatrix'. We process and integrate pain-related information within the neuromatrix. Related information about a pain experience (physical elements of the injury, emotional reactions to the injury, and so on) combine to form a 'neurosignature' or network of information about the nature and emotional reaction to a pain stimulus. Neuro-signatures have two components:

1. *the body-self matrix*: processes and integrates incoming sensory and emotional information;

2. *the action neuromatrix*: develops behavioural responses in response to these networks.

Behavioural responses to pain can only occur after information about the nature of the pain, its cause, and physical and emotional consequences have been, at least, partially processed and integrated. We do not move away from a hot object, for example, until we realise that it is the cause of pain and that continuing to be near it will cause further pain and potential injury. We only become consciously aware of pain after this integrated network

of information is then projected to what Melzack terms the 'sentient neural hub': the seat of consciousness. Here, the stream of nerve impulses is converted into a continually changing stream of awareness.

So far, Melzack's new theory does not explain the experience of phantom limb pain. This moves us from an explanation of how we feel pain from external sources to one explaining how we feel pain generated by the body itself. Melzack suggested that the neuromatrix is pre-wired to 'assume' that the limbs can move. Accordingly, in people who have had limbs removed, the body still sends signals to try to move them. When they do not move in response to these signals, stronger and more frequent messages may be sent to the muscles, and these are perceived as pain. Melzack's theory of pain is still relatively new and has only recently been subjected to empirical research. However, what data there are provide broad support for the existence of a neuromatrix, but we have yet to locate it within any particular brain area (Derbyshire 2000). That said, not all the phenomena of phantom limb pain can be explained by the neuromatrix. In particular, it fails to explain why the reduction or elimination of other sensations associated with the experience of the phantom limb is not accompanied by reductions in pain, how phantom limb pain can spontaneously cease, and why not all patients experience this type of pain (Giummarra *et al.* 2007).

Helping people to cope with pain

The first-line treatment for *acute* pain is generally some form of pharmacological treatment – varying in strength from aspirin to some form of opium derivative such as pethidine. Psychological interventions generally form a second-level intervention. The American Agency for Health Care Policy (1992), for example, suggested that these should be used for those who find this type of intervention 'appealing', where patients may benefit from reducing or avoiding pharmacological treatment, have high levels of anxiety, would need prolonged pain relief and/or who have incomplete pain relief following pharmacological intervention. By contrast, increasing numbers of patients with *chronic* pain resulting from conditions as varied as rheumatoid arthritis and lower back pain are being taught to manage their pain using psychological approaches in order to minimise the amount of painkilling medication they need to take and to maintain or improve their quality of life. It is important that the effectiveness of these interventions is evaluated as part of the day-to-day care of patients as well as in research studies. So, before we look at some of the approaches used to treat both acute and chronic pain, we examine some simple, and not so simple, ways of measuring pain.

Measuring pain

The simplest measure of pain involves the use of a simple linear visual analogue or numerical rating scales – typically varying from a score of 0, registering no pain, to 100, rating the most pain you could imagine. This type of measure is quick to administer and score and is frequently used in clinical settings. A limitation of the approach is that patients often find it quite difficult to consider pain in numerical terms. Another simple approach involves patients rating their pain on a series of adjectives denoting increasing pain: mild, distressing, excruciating, and so on. This has the advantage of being more easily comprehensible to patients than numeric scales – it uses concepts patients are more familiar with. However, this approach has its disadvantages, as many patients tend to rate themselves somewhere in the middle of such scales, making them less sensitive to subtle differences in pain than analogue scales.

One important limitation of these measures is that they simply measure the sensation of pain. However, we have already noted that the experience of pain is multidimensional. It involves emotional, cognitive and behavioural responses as well as sensory experiences. A number of measures have tried to address these inadequacies. Perhaps the best known of these is the McGill pain questionnaire (e.g. Melzack 1975). This is more complicated to administer and interpret than the simple scales described above. However, it provides a multidimensional understanding of the nature of the pain that an individual is experiencing. In its various forms, it measures:

- *the type of pain*: including throbbing, shooting, stabbing, cramping, gnawing, hot and tender, using a four-point scale from 'none' to 'severe';
- *the emotional response to the pain*: including tiring, exhausting, fearful and punishing;

- *the intensity of the pain*: on a scale from 'no pain' to 'worst possible pain';
- *the timing of pain*: whether it is brief, continuous or intermittent.

While this measure extends our assessment of pain, it does not address all the responses to it. It does not, for example, measure pain in relation to movement or measure an individual's behavioural response to pain. How much does it restrict their daily life? Can they walk up stairs, or lift heavy weights? These may all have to be measured separately. Turk and Okifuji (1999) suggested that one can also measure the pain behaviour in which an individual engages. They suggested measuring:

- *verbal/vocalisations*: sighs, moans, complaints;
- *motor behaviour*: facial grimacing, distorted gait (limping), rigid or unstable posture, excessively slow or laboured movement, seek help/pain reducing behaviour;
- *treatment behaviours*: taking medication, use of protective device (e.g. cane, cervical collar), visit doctor;
- *functional limitations*: resting, reduced activity.

Each of these may become a target for some of the interventions discussed below.

Treating acute pain

A number of approaches have been used to help people to cope with acute pain. Any procedures used need to be relatively easy to learn and use. Accordingly, most approaches to acute pain control have focused on:

- increasing patients' sense of control over the pain experience and medical procedures that may be causing the pain;
- teaching coping skills, including distraction techniques and relaxation;
- hypnosis.

Some of these are discussed further in the context of preparing people for the experience of surgery in Chapter 10 ☛. Here, we address other ways of achieving these goals.

Increasing control: patient-controlled anaesthesia

The experience of pain following trauma or surgical operations can be made worse by patients' fears that they cannot control their pain. They may be frightened that when they are in significant pain the nurses may be too busy to give them painkillers, that the pain will be so bad that it will not be controlled by the type of painkiller they will be given, and so on. To alleviate such fears, patients may exaggerate reports of pain or pester health-care professionals to give them painkillers in order to avoid periods of inadequate analgesia. This may result in them experiencing unnecessary anxiety and using more medication than necessary.

One way that each of these issues can be addressed is through the use of **patient-controlled analgesia** (PCA). Using this method, the patient controls how much analgesic drug they receive through an intravenous drip – albeit with some controls built into the delivery system so they cannot exceed a specified dosage. It is assumed that because patients can control the timing of their pain relief, they will be less anxious about the control of their pain, be more satisfied with their analgesia and use less analgesic. Systematic reviews of this approach, summarised in *Bandolier* (2003), suggest that this is the case – and its use has even been advocated in patients with a pre-existing opioid dependency (Mehta and Langford 2006). Children can also use PCA systems. Birmingham *et al.* (2003) reported data from over a hundred children for whom PCA was used for acute postoperative pain control. Satisfactory analgesia was obtained in 90 per cent of cases, with no evidence of toxicity or serious adverse effects. It therefore seems a safe, beneficial form of treatment for a wide range of people.

Teaching coping skills

Distraction

We have already noted in the chapter that focusing on pain tends to increase the experience of pain, while distraction decreases it. Given the apparent simplicity of teaching distraction techniques, these would seem to be sensible strategies to teach patients who are in acute pain

---

> ### patient-controlled analgesia (PCA)
> a technique through which small doses of analgesic drugs, usually opioids, are administered (usually by an intravenous drip and controlled by a pump) by patients themselves. It is mostly used for the control of postoperative pain.

---

or who have to undergo painful procedures. The procedure seems to work. Callaghan and Li (2002), for example, taught women undergoing a hysterectomy to distract themselves from worrisome thoughts prior to their operation. Compared with women only given information about the procedure, they reported less pain and evidenced less distress after the operation. Fauerbach *et al.* (2002) also reported success after teaching distraction skills (in this case concentrating on music) – but only if patients actively focused on the music rather than simply trying not to think of the pain. More technologically based interventions, including the use of virtual reality games have also been shown to reduce the pain experienced during a number of medical procedures (Mott *et al.* 2008).

Relaxation

A second relatively simple approach that can be taught to patients is the use of relaxation. This involves teaching people to relax the muscles throughout their body, particularly those close to the site of the pain (see Chapter 13 ☞). This has a number of advantages. First, it can be used to reduce any muscular tension that can contribute to the experience of pain. Secondly, because relaxation instructions may explicitly involve thinking about pleasant images or at least images inconsistent with the painful situation, it may act as a form of distraction. The concentration involved in relaxing may also distract from pain sensations. Finally, there is evidence that relaxation promotes endorphin release and thus has a direct impact on the pain experience. There is ample evidence that relaxation procedures can help reduce levels of pain and distress associated with postoperative pain. Renzi *et al.* (2000), for example, reported that patients undergoing major bowel surgery who used relaxation experienced less pain, less distress and better sleep following surgery than a control group receiving 'standard care'. Similarly, Friesner *et al.* (2006) found that relaxation combined with the use of opiate drugs was superior to opiate drugs alone during a short but painful surgical procedure involving removal of a tube inserted into the chest during coronary artery bypass surgery. The evidence in support of relaxation has been so consistent that the American National Institutes of Health consensus panel (National Institutes of Health Technology Assessment Panel 1996) concluded that relaxation procedures should be adopted for general use.

Hypnosis

Hypnosis is a procedure during which a health professional suggests that a patient experience changes in sensations, perceptions, thoughts or behaviour. The hypnotic context is generally established by an induction procedure. Although there are many different hypnotic inductions, most include suggestions for relaxation, calmness and well-being. Instructions to imagine or think about pleasant experiences are also commonly included in hypnotic inductions. It has been shown to have a reliable and significant effect on acute pain. Lang *et al.* (2006), for example, found self-hypnosis to reduce both pain and anxiety associated with having a needle breast biopsy. Not only can hypnosis reduce pain, but it may also aid patients' physical recovery. Ginandes *et al.* (2003) examined the effects of hypnosis on pain and wound healing following breast surgery. They allocated women to three interventions following surgery: usual care (normal analgesia); sessions with a counsellor providing unstructured support; and hypnosis, in which they focused on relaxation and 'accelerated wound healing' as part of the instructions ('Imagine your wound healing well'). They measured the women's pain and level of wound healing one week and seven weeks following the interventions and found that the wounds of the women in the hypnosis condition healed significantly more quickly than those in the others. They also experienced less pain over the course of their recovery. The benefits of self-hypnosis need not be restricted to adults. Liossi *et al.* (2009) provide an example of the use of hypnosis in the control of pain during venipuncture (blood taken through a needle) in children aged between 6 and 16 years. The children were taught self-hypnosis techniques involving images including a switch to modulate the experience of pain, feelings of numbness, and the experience of anaesthesia across the hand. They were then encouraged to use this approach up to an hour before being experiencing venipuncture. Those who received the hypnosis intervention experienced less anticipatory anxiety as well as less pain during the procedure itself.

Treating chronic pain

Transcutaneous electrical nerve stimulation (TENS)

Before examining psychological interventions to reduce pain, we first consider a popular method of pain control,

based on the electrical stimulation of A beta fibres in order to compete with the pain signals of pain-related nerves (see discussion earlier in the chapter) and stimulate C fibres to result in endorphin release. Transcutaneous electrical nerve stimulation (TENS) involves the use of a small electrical device, about the size of a personal stereo, that is connected by wires to electrodes, placed on the skin in the area of the pain. This allows a small, low-intensity electric charge to be passed across the area. Such stimulation devices are typically used for between 15 to 20 minutes, several times a day, and are controlled by the user. A Canadian review (Reeve *et al.* 1996) in which the authors examined the use of TENS across Canada, was broadly supportive of its use. They surveyed 50 hospitals with 200 or more beds, and estimated that over 450,000 uses of TENS took place in Canadian hospitals each year, with widespread use in the treatment of acute pain (used by 93 per cent of hospitals), pain associated with labour and delivery (43 per cent), and chronic pain (96 per cent).

Unfortunately, a series of subsequent reviews and empirical studies suggest this level of use may not be appropriate. Khadilkar *et al.* (2005), for example, in conducting a Cochrane review of the area found only two studies that were of sufficient methodological rigour to provide a meaningful test of the approach's effectiveness. One study (Cheing and Hui-Chan 1999) found some short-term benefits compared to placebo; another (Deyo *et al.* 1990) found no such benefit. In a review of studies of postoperative pain, Carroll *et al.* (1996b) concluded that TENS was no better than placebo in 15 out of 17 of them. Unfortunately, studies into the effectiveness of TENS are frequently small or uncontrolled. Al-Smadi *et al.* (2003), for example, found that TENS was no better than TENS placebo in the treatment of low back pain in people with multiple sclerosis. However, they randomly allocated only five people to each treatment group – making any statistically significant treatment effect almost impossible to find. Some three years after the first Cochrane review, a second review by Nnoaham and Kumbang (2010) still concluded that due to the lack of well-conducted trials they could not come to any conclusions about the effectiveness of TENS as a stand-alone treatment for acute pain in general; while Robb *et al.* (2009) found few high-quality studies of the use of TENS in cancer patients, and these found no evidence of effectiveness.

Relaxation and biofeedback

Relaxation can be used to relax the whole body or to relax specific muscle groups such as those on the forehead or back, which contribute to headaches and back pain, respectively. The latter may be of particular benefit in some patients. Turk (1986), for example, noted that many patients who were taught general relaxation for the treatment of back pain generally reported reductions in pain. However, one small subgroup of individuals reported either no benefit or even an increase in pain following the intervention. Closer assessment revealed that, while many people in this group had been able to relax most of their muscles, they had been unable to relax the particular muscles in their back that were contributing to their pain. To do this, they needed guidance on relaxing these specific muscles. This can be achieved through the use of **biofeedback** techniques, including electromyographic biofeedback, galvanic skin response and thermal biofeedback:

- *Electromyographic (EMG) biofeedback*: measures the small amount of electrical current in the muscles. The voltage equates with muscle tension: higher voltage = higher tension. Uses electrodes stuck to the skin over specific muscles that contribute to pain.

- *Galvanic skin response (GSR)*: measures general tension in the body by measuring subtle changes in the moisture (sweat) typically of the hand. Increased sweat relates to increased general muscle tension – although the relationship is far from one-to-one.

- *Thermal biofeedback*: based on a theory that warming the skin can reduce the pain of headaches. Skin temperature is measured by a thermistor, often placed on the back of the fingers to avoid sweat and to provide a more accurate gauge of body temperature.

Whatever the mode of measurement, biofeedback helps patients to make changes (relax, increase finger temperature) guided by auditory or visual feedback of any physiological changes they produce. In the case of auditory feedback, for example, a tone may become lower as the person relaxes their muscles. Visual feedback may involve moving an indicator along a scale as they do the same. In this way, changes in physiology that the patient may not recognise are made apparent and the patient can learn how to change their muscle tension.

One area in which biofeedback has been used with some success is in the treatment of chronic headaches. Rains *et al.* (2005), for example, reported that biofeedback interventions resulted in between 35 per cent and 55 per cent improvements in migraine and tension-type headaches. These improvements are about three times as large as any gains following some form of placebo intervention, and the equivalent to gains achieved by medication (Andrasik 2007). So effective is biofeedback in the treatment of tension headache, the European Federation of Neurological Sciences (Bendsten *et al.* 2010) guidelines recommended its use, noting at the same time that cognitive behavioural interventions and relaxation are 'likely' to be effective. However, while biofeedback may be an effective intervention in other forms of pain, it is generally no more effective than relaxation alone. As relaxation is both simpler and cheaper to implement, this should perhaps be the first-line treatment rather than biofeedback – with biofeedback only used under particular circumstances, such as those identified by Turk earlier in this section. If relaxation techniques are to be augmented, it may be better to do so using strategies that address other aspects of the pain experience than the physiological ones.

An alternative strategy has been to combine relaxation with antidepressant medication. No one has fully explained why antidepressant medication helps to reduce pain, but it has consistently been shown to do so. With this in mind, Holroyd *et al.* (2001) compared treatment with antidepressant medication, training in relaxation techniques, a combination of the two, and a placebo drug therapy. The results were encouraging for both interventions. Both antidepressant and cognitive-behavioural techniques proved to be more effective than the placebo on measures including the frequency of headaches, analgesic medication use and restrictions in activity as a result of the headache. Although both single active interventions were equally effective, patients who received the pharmacological medication experienced these changes more quickly than those in the cognitive-behavioural intervention. Nevertheless, the combined therapy proved the most effective. This resulted in clinically significant reductions on a combined index of headache severity in 64 per cent of participants in this condition. This

---

biofeedback
technique of using monitoring devices to provide information regarding an autonomic bodily function, such as heart rate or blood pressure. Used in an attempt to gain some voluntary control over that function.

Plate 16.2 Biofeedback has proven to be an excellent treatment for specific pain due to muscle tension such as headache. However, in many cases, simple relaxation may prove as effective

Source: Science Photo Library/Will & Deni Mcintyre.

compared with 38 per cent of those in the antidepressant condition, 35 per cent of those receiving stress management, and 29 per cent of those in the placebo condition.

Behavioural interventions

The first modern psychological intervention for pain involved behavioural interventions, based on operant conditioning processes. The treatment model, initially developed by Fordyce (1976), is based on the premise that we cannot truly understand the pain experience of others; all we can do is observe 'pain behaviour'. Fordyce argued that this behaviour should, therefore, form the target of any intervention, not the unobservable inner experience. Operant theory states that pain behaviour may be established and controlled not only by the experience of pain but also by how others respond to expressions of pain. Pain behaviour may be as subtle as gentle winces or as obvious as lying down unable to move as a result of apparently unbearable pain. It may be reinforced by expressions of sympathy, being 'let off' tasks about the

home, given analgesia, and so on (see Bokan *et al.* 1981, earlier in the chapter).

The aim of behavioural interventions is to reduce disability by changing the environmental contingencies that influence pain behaviour – to remove the individual from any reinforcement of their pain behaviour. Instead, non-pain-related, adaptive behaviour is reinforced. The methods used include:

- reinforcement of adaptive behaviour such as appropriate levels of exercise;
- withdrawal of attention or other rewards that were previous responses to pain behaviour;
- providing analgesic medication at set times rather than in response to behaviour.

In this way, new forms of behaviour are encouraged through appropriate reinforcement, and older maladaptive behaviour is extinguished through non-reinforcement. The approach may involve both health professionals and others with whom the patient interacts, including their partner or even friends.

Depending on the nature of the presenting problem, these processes may be added to by other interventions. In the case of lower back pain, for example, where disuse may have resulted in a weakening of the back muscles, patients may take part in exercise programmes. In these, patients will typically engage in a number of exercise trials to identify their tolerance for various lifting activities and movements. The programme will then advance them through a series of progressively more difficult steps towards full mobility and strength. Success at each stage of the intervention is positively rewarded by the health-care professionals involved in the treatment programme.

Early studies of this approach were often case histories, as the approaches used to treat individual cases were necessarily quite different. Fordyce (1976), for example, reported a case in which they moved a hospital patient who was engaging in excessive pain behaviour into a single room, the door of which could be closed if necessary. This prevented the patient trying to attract the attention of nurses in the ward. Rewards for non-pain behaviour and 'punishments' for pain-related behaviour were achieved by entering and leaving the room if the patient inappropriately demanded pain medication or staying for social chat if they did not do so. These various case reports indicated the potential for this type of treatment. More recently, the development of standardised behavioural programmes in the treatment of a variety of disorders, including back pain, has meant that their effectiveness can be assessed using group designs. Back pain is frequently treated using behavioural methods, possibly because it is a common disorder that often has no obvious pathology but which can cause significant impairment. They are also very effective in treating the disorder. Van Tulder *et al.* (2003), for example, reported a meta-analysis of the effects of behavioural programmes on lower back pain, and concluded that there was strong evidence that behavioural treatments were of significant benefit on measures of reported pain, improvements in mobility and lifting capacity, and on behaviour away from the clinic. However, the shift from behavioural to cognitive-behavioural interventions in general has also been seen within pain treatment programmes, which now often combine behavioural and cognitive elements.

Cognitive-behavioural interventions

Behavioural interventions clearly work by changing behaviour, but these changes may also influence other parts of the pain experience. Active engagement in activities may distract patients from negative cognitive and emotional responses to pain. Re-engaging in activities previously stopped may increase self-efficacy beliefs and optimism ('Wow – I didn't think I was going to be able to do that. Perhaps I can do some other things I've stopped doing'). That is, behavioural programmes may *indirectly* change pain-related cognitions, and these changes may contribute to any improvements that patients make. Cognitive-behavioural approaches tackle these issues more directly. They focus on the cognitions mediating our emotional and behavioural responses to pain. Cognitions are seen as central to our experience of pain, and our reactions to it. As such, the model does not contradict the model of pain provided by the gate control model – it focuses on one group of variables that influence the gate. The goals of cognitive-behavioural therapy for pain are threefold:

1. To help patients alter their beliefs that their problems are unmanageable. To help them to become 'resourceful problem solvers' and move away from feeling unable to cope with their pain.

2. To help patients identify the relationship between their thoughts, emotions and behaviour, and in particular how catastrophic or other negatively biased thoughts can lead to increased perceptions of pain, emotional distress and psychosocial difficulties.

3. To provide patients with strategies to manage their pain, emotional distress and psychosocial difficulties, and in particular to help them to develop effective and adaptive ways of thinking, feeling and behaving.

Cognitive-behavioural interventions can take the form of both individual and group interventions. Cognitive change is brought about in a number of stages (see also the discussion of stress management skill in Chapter 13 (☛). In these, patients are helped to identify any maladaptive thoughts that are increasing their experience of pain or their disability. This can be achieved by discussion in therapy sessions in which patients reflect back on periods of pain or when they have been frightened to engage in particular behaviour. Any thoughts that occurred at such times are identified and discussed. Patients may also be asked to monitor their thoughts during their day-to-day activities by completing a diary in which they record their level of pain, accompanying thoughts and mood.

Once patients have begun to identify how their thoughts influence the level of pain they experience, their behaviour and their mood, they are taught to change the nature of their thoughts to more adaptive ones. This may involve two types of cognitive intervention. The first is known as self-instruction training. In this, patients are taught to change the commentary in their head at times of worry or concern about their pain or activities to a more positive commentary. This can be pre-rehearsed and thought through with the therapist. Such thoughts include reassuring commentaries, such as *'I've had pain like this before and it didn't do me any harm in the long run'* or *'The pain only means I'm extending myself, not doing myself any damage'*. Other thoughts may involve reminders to use other strategies to help to control the pain: *'OK! When the pain starts, remember to relax so I don't add to it with tension'*, and so on.

A more complex cognitive process involves trying to identify the thoughts that are driving any emotional distress or inhibiting behaviour and challenging them. This involves treating them not as truths but as hypotheses, and challenging the hypotheses by looking for contrary evidence. In practice, these types of challenge may not be that different to the self-instructions, but they may be more targeted at particular worries or concerns:

> Oh no! My back's beginning to hurt again. I know that means I'm going to be in pain for hours – I'd better stop now and take it easy. Hang on! Remember the last time this happened; I didn't feel that bad, particularly after relaxing and slowing down a bit. So take it easy – keep going . . . I'll feel better in myself for trying.

These cognitive interventions are often accompanied by a programme of gradually increasing exercise. This may have a number of advantages. First, and most obviously, it will increase fitness and minimise restriction of activities. In addition, it allows patients to learn from their own experience that they will not be harmed by exercising – and therefore confirm some of the new beliefs that the cognitive therapy is trying to instil.

Other interventions may also be provided. One frequently used intervention involves teaching people to relax their muscles throughout their body and, particularly, close to the site of the pain (see above in the case of acute pain). Hanson and Gerber (1990) summarised a number of strategies for coping with periods of particularly intense pain that can be taught in a cognitive-behavioural programme, including:

- stop and ask myself if I can identify the pain trigger or learn anything from this pain;
- begin slow, deep breathing and remind myself to keep calm; review my alternatives;
- identify some distracting activities – a conversation with my partner about anything but the pain, a crossword puzzle, baking biscuits, etc.;
- take a long, hot shower;
- listen to relaxation or self-hypnosis tape;
- use positive self-talk – 'The pain won't last. I can handle this on my own';
- use pain-modification imagery – 'Imagine a block of ice resting on my back, see my endorphins working to counter the pain', and so on.

Cognitive-behavioural interventions have proven very effective in the treatment of chronic pain – although they may not be the only effective intervention for some types of pain. A systematic review by Chou *et al.* (2007), for example, concluded that cognitive-behavioural interventions were effective in the treatment of low back pain – as were exercise and spinal manipulation. All three outperformed sham therapy or no treatment – but there had been no direct comparison between them. In a broader analysis, Morley and Williams (1999) found 25 trials suitable for meta-analysis that examined their effectiveness in the treatment of pain resulting from medical conditions, including back problems, arthritis and musculoskeletal problems but excluding headaches. Overall, cognitive-behavioural treatments proved more effective than no treatment on measures of reported pain, mood, cognitive coping and appraisals, behavioural activity and social engagement. They proved more effective than pharmacological, educational and occupational therapy interventions on measures of reported pain, cognitive coping and appraisal, and in reducing the frequency of pain-related behaviour. Perhaps surprisingly, however, cognitive-behavioural interventions were no more effective than the others in reducing negative, fearful or catastrophic thoughts. Nor were they more effective in changing mood. This may be because the most important therapeutic process in these interventions was that patients engaged in higher levels of activity than they previously had. As we suggested earlier in the chapter and in Chapter 13 ☞ in discussion of the third wave therapies, this may change their beliefs about their ability to exercise, to control their pain while doing so, and their mood.

Whatever the cause, there is mounting evidence that cognitive change is an important mediator of change in therapy. In a relatively early study of this phenomenon, Burns *et al.* (2003) found that the cognitive changes patients made in the early stages of a cognitive-behavioural programme were strongly predictive of pain outcomes later in therapy. They took measures of catastrophising and pain at the beginning, end and middle of a four-week cognitive-behavioural pain management programme. Early changes on the measure of catastrophising were predictive of pain measures taken at the end of therapy. By contrast, early changes in pain did not predict changes in catastrophising. Turner *et al.* (2007) came to similar conclusions using data from patients with **temporomandibular disorder pain**. In this group, changes in pain beliefs (control over pain, disability and pain signals harm), catastrophising and self-efficacy in relation to managing pain mediated the effects of cognitive-behavioural therapy on pain, activity interference and jaw-use limitations at one year.

One of the difficulties many patients who are referred for cognitive-behavioural therapy experience is that it presents a very different model of pain and its treatment to that which they are used to. Often because patients are frequently offered cognitive-behavioural therapy at the end of a long chain of medical or surgical treatments – most of which have failed – but which have emphasised the medical rather than psychological aspects of their condition (see box).

> ### temporomandibular disorder pain
> a variety of conditions that cause tenderness and pain in the temporomandibular joint (hinge joint of the jaw).

Mindfulness-based interventions

As mindfulness-based interventions are becoming increasingly used in mental health settings, so are they in physical health settings – and with some effect. In one study of older adults, averaging 75 years old, with lower back pain, Morone *et al.* (2008) compared an eight-week long mindfulness programme (MBSR: see Chapter 13 ☛) with a waiting list control group. Participants were experiencing pain of moderate intensity either every other day or daily. The majority of participants completed the intervention and gained on measures of pain acceptance and physical function, but not pain, relative to the control condition. Thus, it seems the intervention did not change perceptions of pain, but did help participants cope more effectively with it. An interesting uncontrolled study was reported by Rosenzweig *et al.* (2010), who as part of a larger study compared the effectiveness of MBSR in patients with a number of different types of pain and found marked differences in effectiveness. Most patients, with conditions as varied as back, and neck pain, showed gains on measures of pain intensity and functional limitations. Patients with fibromyalgia, or tension or migraine headaches reported minimal benefit, while those with arthritis reported the greatest improvements. Of note was that increased use of meditation was not associated with greater gains on measures of pain or quality of life. In a direct comparison of the second and third wave cognitive/behavioural interventions in a group of patients with rheumatoid arthritis, Zautra *et al.* (2008) compared group interventions based on second wave CBT, mindfulness, and education only. Their outcome measures included a measure of pain and inflammation (interleukin-6). Those in the CBT group

Case history: Mr W

I came to this clinic [for cognitive-behavioural therapy] after years of looking for a treatment for my back pain. The doc sends you here, there, everywhere looking for the answer. I've had pain killers, TENS, physiotherapy, manipulation . . . and then surgery. Every time you go to the next treatment, you have that little ray of hope that this will provide the cure! I've even gone to the alternative people in the hope that they would help. The weirdest thing I have had was something called cranial manipulation . . . supposed to relieve the nerves or something. But every one you hope the pain will go . . . even if you

don't believe it quite as strongly with different treatments! But this has been different. Rather than trying to take the pain away, the course has focused on helping me cope with the pain. That was the first shock on the course – and it was disappointing. I expected that you could get rid of it, not keep it . . . and let me cope better! I was quite depressed for a few days when I learned this . . . but I guess I had to stick it out. I don't have much choice. But I must admit, as the course has gone on, it has helped. The relaxation really helps me. I can take myself away from the pain for a while if I imagine stuff. And at least I know I can cope with the pain, and won't let it stop me doing things like I used to . . .

achieved the greatest changes in both measures, although patients with a history of recurrent depression achieved greater changes on a number of measures including joint tenderness and mood following the mindfulness training than did those in the CBT group. Even before there is a large body of evidence to support mindfulness in the treatment of pain, some researchers are evaluating innovative strategies to provide this type of intervention – in ways that are both effective and cost-effective. In one such study, Gardner-Nix *et al.* (2008) compared a mindfulness chronic pain intervention delivered using a group face-to-face format with the same intervention using a videoconferencing facility to patients in their own homes. Outcomes of these two active interventions were compared to those of a waiting list control group. Both groups made more gains on a measure of pain than those in the control condition. However, those who received the face-to-face intervention scored more highly than the remote group on measures of 'usual pain'. A second innovative approach was adopted by Johnston *et al.* (2008), who examined the impact of a self-help book related to acceptance and commitment therapy (see Chapter 13 ☞). Participants read the book and completed related exercises over a period of six weeks, with the support of weekly telephone calls. The intervention had a modest impact on pain, while also resulting in greater changes in acceptance, quality of life, and satisfaction with life.

Pain management clinics

So far, we have considered treatments for pain in isolation, without considering who provides the treatment or where patients may go for treatment. Nowadays, many hospitals provide services specifically for people with chronic pain – of whatever origin. These services will involve a number of people. Doctors, usually anaesthetists, provide expertise in the pharmacological and even surgical treatment of pain. Physiotherapists work with patients to develop exercise programmes that they can realistically expect to be able to engage in. Occupational therapists may work with patients to consider how they can improve their day-to-day activities around the home if their mobility is restricted. Specialist nurses may work with patients to develop pain management plans for individuals or groups of individuals. Psychologists may also contribute to and develop such programmes. Table 16.1 shows the outline of a typical outpatient pain management programme – conducted at the Gloucester Royal Hospital in the UK.

Table 16.1 Outline of a typical pain management programme, in this case run at the Gloucester Royal Hospital in the UK

WEEK 1	Welcome, introduction and housekeeping Pain management philosophy What is chronic pain? – questions answered Introduction to exercise – sitting and standing Pacing everyday activities The stress response and introduction to diaphragmatic breathing
WEEK 2	Recap pacing Goal setting and action plans Introduction to exercise – lying Sitting and chairs Introduction to stretch and relax Video patients doing exercises for comparison at end of group
WEEK 3	How pain works: the gate control theory of pain How pain works: pain pathways Thoughts and feelings about pain Exercises Stretch and relax Action plans
WEEK 4	Recommended use of medication for chronic pain Communication and relationships Pain management graduate perspective talk Exercises Introduction to relaxing your mind Action plans
WEEK 5	Lifting and bending Managing everyday activities Sexual relationships The benefits of exercise Exercise Relaxing your mind Action plans
WEEK 6	Introduction to fitness and fitness equipment Doctor's talk: medication, treatments and surgery for chronic pain, sleeping and beds/positions to ease pain Action plans Relaxation
WEEK 7	Flare-ups and setbacks Helpful sleep habits Video exercises and compare with the beginning of the course Introduction to brief relaxation techniques Reviewing progress, and setting goals for the follow-up sessions

SUMMARY

Pain is a widely prevalent phenomenon. Over 20 per cent of the general population are experiencing chronic pain at any one time, and the personal and social consequences of chronic pain are significant. Various types of pain have been identified:

- *acute*: lasting up to between three and six months;
- *chronic*: lasting more than three to six months; can be further categorised as chronic benign and chronic progressive pain.

Pain can also be defined in terms of its nature: its type, severity and pattern.

The experience of pain is moderated by a variety of physical and psychological factors, including:

- the degree of attention paid to the pain;
- the mood of the individual;
- the person's beliefs about the nature of the pain, including its cause and controllability.

Early specificity and pattern theories that did not take account of these psychological factors proved to be unsuccessful in explaining the various ways in which pain can be experienced. A more complex model developed by Melzack and Wall, known as the gate theory of pain, has superseded these models of pain. This suggests that pain is the outcome of a number of complementary or competing processes. Any model of pain has to take into account how psychological factors affect the perception of pain. The gate theory of pain suggests that:

- Afferent nerves carry pain messages up to the substantiagelatinosa and then through the spinal gate mechanism to the brain.

- At the same time, psychological processes influence the activity of nerves leading from the brain to the spinal gate.
- Activation of both systems results in a variety of chemicals being produced within the gate (substantiagelatinosa), some of which 'open' the pain gate, some of which 'close' it. The main chemicals involved in reducing pain sensations in the substantiagelatinosa are endorphins.

Melzack has developed a more complex neurological model of pain, known as the neuromatrix, which accounts for phenomena previously difficult to account for by the gate theory (including phantom limb pain).

TENS is a physiological intervention based on the gate control theory of pain. Unfortunately, consistent evidence of its effectiveness is lacking.

Biofeedback interventions can help to reduce pain, but their overall effectiveness is no greater than more general relaxation procedures. They may be best used when there are individual muscle groups contributing to the pain that are not relaxed following more general relaxation instructions, or for the treatment of headaches.

Both behavioural and cognitive-behavioural interventions have proved to be effective in the treatment of both acute and more chronic pain. Cognitive changes appear to mediate changes in the experience of pain. Mindfulness has also been shown to reduce pain, and (possibly to an even greater extent) quality of life and acceptance measures. Psychological interventions may be combined (at least in some cases) with antidepressant medication to provide maximal benefit.

Further reading

Melzack, R. and Wall, P.D. (2008). *The Challenge of Pain*. London: Penguin.

A classic. The most up-to-date text by the originators of the gate control theory – and over £200 cheaper than the more recent *Wall and Melzack's Textbook of Pain*. Written in a non-technical way for the interested 'lay' reader.

Two papers from the pain research centre at Bath University are worth a read:

Morley, S., Eccleston, C. and Williams, A. (1999). Systematic review and meta-analysis of randomized controlled trials of cognitive-behavioural therapy and behaviour therapy for chronic pain in adults, excluding headache. *Pain*, 80: 1–13.

A relatively up-to-date review of intervention studies to treat pain.

Crombez, G., Eccleston, C., De Vlieger, P. *et al.* (2008). Is it better to have controlled and lost than never to have controlled at all? An experimental investigation of control over pain. *Pain*, 137: 631–9.

An experimental study of what happens when you first provide control over pain, and then take it away.

Three differing theoretical psychosocial perspectives on pain:

Van Dammme, S., Legrain, V., Vogt, J. *et al.* (2010). Keeping pain in mind: a motivational account of attention to pain. *Neuroscience and Biobehavioral Reviews*, 34: 204–13.

Eccleston, C. and Crombez, G. (1999). Pain demands attention: a cognitive-affective model of the interruptive function of pain. *Psychological Bulletin*, 125: 356–66.

Meredith, P., Ownsworth, T. and Strong, J. (2008). A review of the evidence linking adult attachment theory and chronic pain: presenting a conceptual model. *Clinical Psychology Review*, 28: 407–29.

A number of websites may also provide useful information:

www.jr2.ox.ac.uk/bandolier/booth/painpag/
www.painrelieffoundation.org.uk/
www.nlm.nih.gov/medlineplus/pain.html
www.psychnet-ukk.com/clinical_psychology/clinical_psychology_pain_management.htm

Visit the website at **www.pearsoned.co.uk/morrison** for additional resources to help you with your study, including multiple choice questions, weblinks and flashcards.

Chapter 17
Improving health and quality of life

Learning outcomes

By the end of this chapter, you should have an understanding of a number of psychological interventions that aim to:

- *reduce distress*: focusing on information provision, stress management training and providing social support

- *improve disease management*: focusing on information provision, self-management training, stress management training, facilitating family and social support, and the use of written emotional expression

- *reduce the risk of future disease or disease progression*: focusing on counselling, stress management and providing social support

Every hospital should have one . . . a psychology department, that is

Probably not a headline you will actually read. But it should be. Most general hospitals in most countries, even where there are well-established professions of clinical and health psychology do not have access to psychologists. Read the research papers from countries such as the USA or UK, and you would begin to believe that all hospitals are teaming with psychologists engaging in the interventions the empirical data show to be highly effective. But they are not. So why, if we know that psychology can 'make a difference', are so few hospitals actually employing professional psychologists? Perhaps physicians or surgeons do not think psychology has much, or anything, to offer? Well, they do. When one of the authors (PB) was working as a clinical psychologist in a district general hospital, a number of physicians working in specialties including diabetes, gastroenterology, and renal medicine asked for psychological input into their clinics. They were very keen . . . until they were asked to pay for the service of a psychologist from their budget. At which point, they were much less keen . . . and eventually most decided not to have the psychologist. So, psychology is seen as important, but not central to the provision of quality care. Therefore, when developing interventions, psychologists need to consider not only what is effective but also what is cost-effective. Health-care providers increasingly have to consider the bottom line: how much does it cost? Too much, and they will not pay. Something to consider as you read the chapter . . .

Chapter outline

This chapter focuses on a number of psychological interventions used to help people to cope with and manage serious illnesses. These interventions have a number of goals. Some seek to reduce the distress associated with having a serious illness. Others aim to help people to manage their illness as effectively as possible and to minimise its impact on their daily life. Yet others are designed to prevent the progression of an illness and minimise the risk of further health problems in the future. This chapter considers a number of interventions designed to achieve these goals in the context of a number of chronic diseases, such as cancer, coronary heart disease and arthritis.

Coping with chronic illness

The onset of a serious illness has many implications for both the individual concerned and those around them (see also the discussion in Chapter 12 (☛). Following the onset of symptoms, the person with the illness may experience the anxiety of waiting for and being given a serious diagnosis, the possibility of having to come into hospital, with its associated discomfort and disruption of normal life, and so on. In the longer term, they may have to come to terms with restrictions or handicaps associated with their condition and the possibility of a gradual decline in health. They may have to learn how to manage their condition or take action to prevent their health deteriorating further. Having a chronic illness presents the individual with a number of 'tasks'. People who are HIV-positive have to take many drugs each day at carefully determined times; people with arthritis may benefit from engaging in a variety of exercises to maintain joint mobility; and so on. Other diseases, such as coronary heart disease (CHD), may or may not be apparent on a day-by-day basis. However, changing risk factors such as diet or smoking may help to prevent the disease progressing further. A third issue that patients often have to deal with is the significant emotional distress that may accompany a diagnosis of severe or chronic disease.

The interventions considered in this chapter aim to help people to cope with each of these challenges. This chapter examines the effectiveness of a number of approaches used to help people to reduce any distress they experience, to manage their disease and to prevent it developing further. The therapeutic approaches we consider include:

● providing relevant information;

● stress management training;

● the use of social support;

● self-management training;

● enhancing social support;

● the use of **written emotional expression**.

Each type of intervention may have multiple benefits. Improvements in mood, for example, may increase the likelihood of cardiac patients participating in an exercise programme, and therefore impact on both their well-being and their physical health. Conversely, taking part in such a programme may reduce depression or anxiety as the individual feels they are gaining control

> **written emotional expression**
> a writing technique in which participants write about upsetting incidents either in their past or related to specific issues.

over their illness and their life. Stress management training may simultaneously reduce the distress associated with being HIV-positive and improve its prognosis through its positive impact on immune function. So, separating the specific outcomes of the various interventions is a little artificial. Nevertheless, we try to tease out each of these multiple end points and consider how well each intervention achieves each of these separate goals.

Reducing distress

Information provision

Many people with serious illness experience significant levels of distress. They may have concerns about their prognosis and treatment, the potential effects of their illness on their quality of life, and so on. Levels of distress are perhaps highest in the early stages of an illness or at times when the nature of an illness changes. We discuss these issues in more detail in Chapter 12 ☞. However, as examples of the level of distress many patients experience, about a third of patients with cancer and a quarter of those who have had a myocardial infarction (MI) report clinically significant levels of distress at some time in the course of their illness (e.g. Lane *et al.* 2002b). This can be reduced by various types of information, including information about:

- the nature of a disease and/or its treatment;
- how to cope with disease and/or its treatment;
- how to change behaviour in order to reduce risk of disease or disease progression.

Perhaps the simplest form of information provision involves keeping patients informed about the progress of their condition and its treatment. Uncertainty can increase distress – providing information can reduce it. Wells *et al.* (1995), for example, found that giving information to people with cancer about their chemotherapy, showing them around the clinic in which they were to receive the treatment, and giving them the opportunity to ask questions to a specialist counsellor was highly effective in reducing their levels of distress. A subsequent study reported by Deschler *et al.* (2006) found that patients preferred to be sent such informa-

tion in the post prior to coming into hospital, and that those with high levels of trait anxiety benefited most from this type of intervention.

More complex interventions may also be relevant at the beginning of a serious illness. One particular issue that needs to be dealt with particularly sensitively is telling patients and relatives when they have a disease with a poor or fatal prognosis – a process often known as 'breaking bad news'. The way that this information is given at this time may have important implications for how people cope and come to terms with their prognosis. Clearly, the communication skills of the person giving the bad news are important in the success of this process – we discuss these issues in more detail in Chapter 10 ☞. However, a simple informational strategy may also facilitate this process. Hogbin and Fallowfield (1989) gave patients an audiotape of the consultation in which they were given their 'bad news'. They were encouraged to play the tape in their own time to help them to recall the information given. This simple procedure helped them to recall more information than a control group who did not receive the tape, and to be more confident about telling their family and friends about their illness and prognosis. In a different context, Cope *et al.* (2003) compared the effectiveness of a variety of communication strategies with women having a scan for a potential foetal abnormality. Two weeks after their consultation, women who received an audiotape or letter summarising the information given in the session reported less anxiety than the control group without this information. The groups did not differ on recall of information. Despite these encouraging findings, it should be noted that not all patients may benefit from this approach. McHugh *et al.* (1995) found that patients with a particularly poor prognosis who were given a tape recording of their bad news consultation were more likely to be depressed than those not given a tape.

Providing people with information about how to cope emotionally with medical procedures as well as providing information about their illness or the nature of any medical procedures they will experience is now increasingly found to be of benefit in patient groups as diverse as cancer patients undergoing chemotherapy (Stiegelis *et al.* 2004) and renal patients undergoing dialysis (Devins *et al.* 2003). However, one of the few studies to identify the degree to which this combination enhanced patients outcomes was reported by Marteau

colposcopy

a method used to identify cells that may develop into cancer of the cervix. Sometimes follows a cervical smear if abnormalities are found. A colposcope is a low-power microscope.

cervical smear

smear of cells taken from the cervix to examine for the presence of cell changes indicating risk of cancer.

et al. (1996), who considered the effectiveness of two booklets given to women referred for **colposcopy** following an abnormal **cervical smear**:

1. A coping booklet provided brief information about the procedure they were about to experience, information on the likely outcomes of the procedure, and instructions on relaxation and distraction techniques (see Chapter 13 ☞) they could use to help them to cope before and during the procedure.

2. A medical information booklet provided more details on the nature of cervical abnormalities, the procedure and its likely outcomes than the standard information booklet. However, it did not suggest any coping strategies that the women might use.

The results suggested a specific effect of each aspect of the information given. All patients who received the booklets knew more about issues around the colposcopy than a group of patients who received the standard level of information. However, the women who received the medical booklet did not experience any reductions in anxiety as a consequence. By contrast, those patients given the coping booklet were less anxious when they attended the hospital for their operation than those who received either the medical or no booklet.

Educational programmes whose primary intention is to help people to manage a disease or reduce risk of further disease may also impact on mood. Why this should happen is not clear. It is possible that such interventions provide patients with a sense of control over their illness and reduce anxieties about their long-term health. They may also encourage participants not to overly restrict their lives as a result of their disease. Each may result in improved mood. An early, but influential UK study of rehabilitation of people following an MI, showed evidence

of this effect. In this, Lewin *et al.* (1992) compared the effectiveness of a six-week home-based education package known as the *Heart Manual* with a placebo package of information and informal counselling. The *Heart Manual* focused on guiding patients through a progressive change of risk factors for CHD, including changes in diet, exercise and relaxation techniques. Patients followed the manual at home for a period of six weeks. Over this time, they also received three telephone calls from expert nurses to discuss their progress and any problems they were experiencing. Over the following year, participants who received the *Heart Manual* reported lower levels of anxiety and depression than those in the control group. They were also less likely than people in the control group to go to their doctor with concerns about their heart condition in the first six months following their discharge. In a similar type of programme, Hartford *et al.* (2002) used a telephone contact programme for patients who had had a coronary artery bypass graft and their partners. The programme provided information on a number of issues to aid recovery, including a graded activity and exercise plan, coping with pain, and dealing with psychosocial problems, diet and medication use. The programme began with a meeting between a specialist nurse and the patient and their partner on the day of discharge, when they were provided with information about medication for pain, distances to walk, rest stops on the way home, the nurse's 24-hour telephone number, and a time when they would phone again. This was followed by six telephone calls at increasing intervals over the next seven weeks, during which problems were assessed and relevant information provided. Despite its emphasis on changing behaviour, it also proved effective in reducing both patient and partner levels of anxiety. New technologies may also be used to help the provision of information. Rawl *et al.* (2002) evaluated the effect of a computer-based intervention providing women newly diagnosed with breast cancer with information on the disease, its treatment and strategies for symptom management. This was combined with support from a nurse specialising in the care of people with cancer. Following the intervention, participants reported less depression and anxiety than those who did not receive the intervention, although combining the two elements of the intervention makes it difficult to work out which aspect of the intervention proved the more effective.

Stress management training

Stress management training involves teaching individuals directly how to cope with stress, using strategies including:

- *problem solving*: to prevent or minimise external problems that contribute to stress;
- *cognitive restructuring*: to identify and challenge stress-provoking thoughts which may initiate or exacerbate the stress response;
- *relaxation*: to reduce the physiological arousal that forms part of the stress response.

We discuss these approaches in more detail in Chapter 13 ☞. Given that these strategies are directly targeted at reducing distress, one would hope that they are effective in doing so – and this does seem to be the case. A meta-analysis of 45 studies involving some form of stress management procedure (Meyer and Mark 1995) concluded that the average person was up to 60 per cent better off than those not receiving the intervention. The approach has proven effective at various stages in the process of care, including:

- waiting for a diagnosis;
- during treatment;
- coping with the emotional stress of living with a long-term illness.

Here, we consider examples of the effectiveness of stress management procedures in the context of HIV/AIDS, cancer and heart disease.

Living with HIV is not easy, and the stresses faced by those with the virus may not only impact at a psychological level but also impact adversely on their health and, ultimately, how long they live (see Chapter 8 ☞). Minimising distress should therefore form an important part of any HIV treatment package. Accumulating evidence suggests that stress management interventions achieve this goal. In a series of studies conducted by researchers at the University of Miami, group stress management interventions have been shown to improve cognitive functioning and reduce distress in women with AIDS (Lechner *et al.* 2003), reduce depression in HIV-positive homosexual men (Carrico *et al.* 2005), as well as influencing physiological correlates of stress including cortisol levels (Antoni *et al.* 2000). Using a slightly different approach to managing distress, Chesney

et al. (1996) compared a three-month programme of **coping effectiveness training** (see Chapter 13 ☞) with an education-only group and a waiting-list control group in reducing distress in HIV-positive individuals. The intervention proved effective, with people in the active-intervention group reporting significantly greater reductions in stress and increases in self-efficacy than those in either of the other conditions. The carers of people who are HIV-positive may also experience significant stress and may benefit from being taught stress management techniques. But is it better to work with such people individually, or as part of a couple and include the cared-for person in the intervention? Pakenham *et al.* (2002) addressed this issue, comparing a stress management intervention targeted at carers individually or as a dyad. The intervention included strategies to help the resolution of problems through problem-solving techniques as well as strategies to help participants cope with any distress they experienced. Although working with individuals proved better than no intervention, the most effective intervention involved working with both members of the couple in the programme.

A second group of patients for whom stress management has proven effective is people with a diagnosis of cancer. One early study in this population was reported by Fawzy *et al.* (1993), who compared a stress management programme with usual care in a group of patients with **malignant melanoma** whose tumours had been surgically excised. Only the active-intervention group reported any improvements in mood both immediately after the intervention and at six-month follow-up. We discuss this study again later in the chapter when we consider the effects of this type of intervention on disease progression.

More recently, Antoni *et al.* (2001) found that a stress management programme was more effective than

---

coping effectiveness training

a specialist form of stress management in which participants are taught to alter the nature of their coping efforts to suit the particular type of demands they are facing: using emotion-focused coping where the situation cannot be changed and problem-focused coping where it can.

malignant melanoma

a rare but potentially lethal form of skin cancer.

> **benefit-finding**
>
> a process of finding beneficial outcomes as a consequence of what is normally seen as a negative event, such as developing cancer or being infected with HIV.

a one-day educational seminar in improving measures of depression and '**benefit-finding**' among women with early stage breast cancer. Typical benefits included:

● a greater enthusiasm to live life to the full;

● making positive life choices as a result of illness;

● a greater appreciation of being alive;

● improved relationships with partner.

Similar gains have been made among men following medical treatment of prostate cancer (Penedo *et al.* 2006) and men and women during a course of radiotherapy (Krischer *et al.* 2007).

A third group in which we consider the effectiveness of stress management programmes is cardiac patients. Most such interventions to reduce distress in cardiac patients have proven effective (see, for example, Rees *et al.* 2004). More specific stress management programmes have targeted people with implantable cardioverter defibrillators (ICDs). These are small instruments placed in patients' abdomens with leads leading to the heart. They monitor the heart for potentially fatal changes in heart rhythm, which they correct firstly by 'pacing' the heart and, if necessary, shocking the heart. Pacing involves increasing the heart rate for a short time. The shock is similar to that from an external defibrillator. Patients may not notice the pacing, although many do. They certainly notice the shock, which has been described as similar to being punched hard in the chest. Although most patients never actually experience a shock, they are all aware that it can occur. As a consequence, many people avoid situations that they think may lead to an arrhythmia, such as engaging in exercise or potentially stressful situations. Those that have experienced a shock may experience classically conditioned fear in situations where this has occurred or those similar to it. ICDs are a relatively new technology, but are now being increasingly used, and studies helping people cope with them are now emerging. One such pilot study tested a stress management programme. Sears *et al.* (2007) compared

two active stress management programmes following ICD implantation, one lasting a full day, the other involving six weekly sessions. Both interventions were associated with short-term reductions in anxiety and cortisol levels – although the lack of no-treatment control group allows the possibility that these changes would have occurred naturally as patients adapted to having the ICD.

Mindfulness

Mindfulness training can be considered a form of stress management, as it is often used to help patients manage any stress they are experiencing. And it is proving an effective and easy to learn skill. In a summary of all the research to date, Merkes (2010) identified 15 studies of the effectiveness of mindfulness-based stress reduction (MBSR: see Chapter 13 ☞) in reducing distress in patients with a variety of chronic diseases. They concluded that MBSR is likely to result in patients coping better with their symptoms, improved overall well-being and quality of life, as well as improved health status. Examples of the research included work by Pradhan *et al.* (2007) in patients with rheumatoid arthritis (see Chapter 8 ☞) who reported no immediate benefit following attending an eight-week MBSR course. However, by four-month follow-up before which participants had received a further less intensive intervention, significant gains relative to a no-treatment control group were found on measures of psychological distress and well-being, depressive symptoms, and mindfulness. Finally, Gross *et al.* (2010) compared the effectiveness of MBSR with an education and no-treatment control conditions in patients who were sleeping poorly following organ transplantation. Following initial gains at two-month follow-up, by one year following the intervention, those in the MBSR group continued to report less anxiety and sleep problems than those in either of the other groups.

Enhancing social support

We discussed in Chapter 12 ☞ how social support can improve or maintain both mental and physical health. With this in mind, a number of studies have evaluated the impact of support groups designed to provide social support from people experiencing similar

RESEARCH FOCUS

A new way of treating cardiac patients

Sullivan M.J., Wood L., Terry J. *et al.* (2009). The Support, Education, and Research in Chronic Heart Failure Study (SEARCH): a mindfulness-based psychoeducational intervention improves depression and clinical symptoms in patients with chronic heart failure. *American Heart Journal*, 157: 84–90.

The paper reports on the effectiveness of the Support, Education, and Research in Chronic Heart Failure (SEARCH) study. The study evaluated the impact of an eight-week-long mindfulness-based psycho-educational intervention on depression, quality of life, and clinical outcomes of patients with chronic heart failure (CHF) – a condition in which the heart is unable to pump sufficient blood around the body to meet its metabolic requirements.

Method

Participants were recruited from heart failure pro-grammes at the Duke University and the University of North Carolina Medical Centres, general medical wards, local community practices, and via newspaper advertising. Participants had significant heart failure and no other life-threatening disease. Between November 2000 and February 2003, 217 people entered the study. Of these, 100 people living more than 90 miles from the research centre were enrolled into the control condition, and received the usual care available to them.

- The intervention comprised eight once-weekly meetings, each lasting around two and a quarter hours. It had three components: mindfulness-based stress reduction (MBSR: see Chapter 13 ☞), coping skills training, and expressive support group discussion (see this chapter).

- Baseline measures included: heart failure status, medication use, lifestyle measures.

- Outcome measures included: the CES-D measuring depression, Profile of Mood States (POMS) measuring six mood states (four reported in the paper – tension-anxiety, depression-dejection, anger-hostility, confusion-bewilderment), and the Kansas City Cardiomyopathy Questionnaire (KCCQ), measuring 'disease-specific health status' for patients with heart failure.

Measures were taken at baseline, and 3, 6, and 12 months after treatment began.

Results

Participants had an average age of 61 years, and 70 per cent were male. Their median level of heart failure met the New York Heart Association grade II (Slight limitation of physical activity; comfortable at rest, but ordinary physical activity results in fatigue, palpitation, or shortness of breath).

Treatment effects

CES-D depression and POMS anxiety-tension scores were significantly reduced in the intervention condition at month 3 and 6, but by 12 months levels of depression had increased in both conditions, and they did not differ significantly. Trends in POMS subscales depression-dejection, anger-hostility, and confusion-bewilderment favoured the intervention group, but there were no significant between-group differences at any time. There were gains in the intervention group not reported in the control group on the KCCQ symptom and overall score, at months 3 and 6, but not one-year follow-up. Figure 1 shows the cumulated event-free survival curve over the year following the intervention. This showed no between-group differences over this time. Note that the higher the line on the y axis, the more people survived. Each drop represents one or more deaths. With this in mind, the control group actually did (non-statistically significantly) better than the intervention group until around day 260, when the intervention group showed an (again non-statistical) advantage over the control condition.

Discussion

The results indicated gains on measures of depression and anxiety, and some benefits on measures of health status up to six months after the intervention. These effects may have been overwhelmed by the gradual increase in physical symptoms and physical limitations reported by many patients with heart failure. So-called harder measures of outcome, and in particular how long people lived (evident on the survival curve) showed no benefit of the intervention. It would have been interesting to measure some more direct measures of mindfulness. However, a gain in mood and quality of life even for six months following a relatively brief intervention can be considered a good clinical outcome.

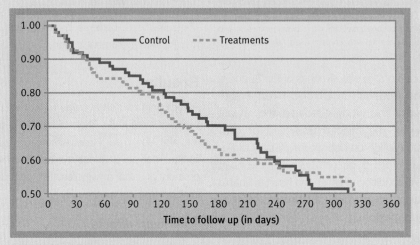

Figure 1 unadjusted event-free survival curve by time and treatment

health problems. Many of these have been led by professionals and include an element of group therapy or working towards group goals. One of the first studies to evaluate the effectiveness of this approach was reported by Spiegel *et al.* (1989). They randomly assigned women with breast cancer to either a usual treatment control or weekly support groups led by health professionals. These focused on a number of issues, including:

● building strong, supportive bonds;

● expressing emotions;

● dealing directly with fears of dying;

● improving relationships within the family;

● active involvement in decisions concerning treatment.

Only those in the active intervention evidenced any improvements on measures of depression and anxiety.

Subsequently, Giese-Davis *et al.* (2002) reported that women who went through the groups reported less suppression of negative moods while also showing less aggressive, inconsiderate, impulsive and irresponsible behaviour in comparison with the no-treatment group.

They therefore concluded that this form of intervention can help women to become more expressive of their emotions without becoming more hostile. Supportive interventions appear to be of benefit to women across a variety of cultures, including Iranian (Montazeri *et al.* (2001) and Japanese (Fukui *et al.* 2000) women. With increasing access to the internet, the need for face-to-face support is changing, and some innovative work is now beginning to measure the benefits associated with online support groups. In a small pilot study of this approach, Vilhauer *et al.* (2010) found that 73 per cent of women with metastatic breast cancer invited to participate in the virtual group did so, and most continued to remain part of the group over a period of two months, accessing it on average six days a week. Although they did not measure mood, another study of this approach by the same group reported that the women reported benefits including: group cohesiveness, information exchange, feelings of being in the same situation as others, hope, catharsis and altruism. Finally, although men may be relatively unwilling to attend support groups, they may still benefit from peer support. Weber *et al.* (2007), for example, found men who had experienced

> **radical prostatectomy**
>
> otherwise known as a total prostatectomy, this involves using surgery to remove all of the prostate as a cure for prostate cancer.

a **radical prostatectomy** benefited more, on measures of depression and self-efficacy from meeting with a fellow patient once a week for eight weeks to discuss any concerns they had and coping strategies they could use, than a control group.

Before leaving this issue, it is important to note that although socially based interventions have proven effective, they are not for all. Pollock *et al.* (2007) found that many patients preferred to turn to friends and families for support, and did not wish to attend more professionally organised support groups. This cautionary note supports an approach in which family and partner skills are strengthened, and provide the support given to the patient. Northouse and colleagues have conducted a number of trials of this type of intervention. In one study, they (Northouse *et al.* 2007) provided a couples-intervention addressing issues such as communication, coping with uncertainty, instilling hope, and symptom management. At four-month follow-up, the partners appeared to have benefited most, reporting less uncertainty, hopelessness, and symptom distress at four-month follow-up. In a previous study, in which they provided a similar intervention to couples in which the patient had recurrent breast cancer, Northouse *et al.* (2005) reported gains on measures of hopelessness and negative appraisal of illness among patients, and a significantly lower negative appraisal of caregiving burden three months (but not six months) following such an intervention among their partners.

Managing illness

A second set of interventions can be used to help people to gain the skills and motivation to manage the symptoms of an illness as effectively as possible: to maintain an exercise and mobility programme in rheumatoid arthritis, an insulin regimen in type 1 diabetes, and so on. The goal of the intervention here is not to prevent the development of a disease but to minimise its negative impact on the affected individual.

Information provision

There is a significant body of evidence showing that patient education programmes can enhance knowledge about a condition or its management, at least in the short term (e.g. Gibson *et al.* 2000; van den Arend *et al.* 2000). However, even where increases in knowledge are achieved, they may not always impact on behaviour or symptom control. Indeed, a number of studies have found only a marginal relationship between educational programmes and behavioural change. In a systematic review of 11 educational programmes for people with asthma, for example, Gibson *et al.* (2000) concluded that, while such programmes increased knowledge, there was no evidence that they impacted on measures of medication use, doctor visits, hospitalisation and lung function. However, the simple addition of an action plan (see discussion of problem-focused counselling and implementation intentions in Chapter 6 (☛) seemed to enhance their effectiveness (Powell and Gibson 2003).

The internet now provides a key source of information for many patients. This provides both formal 'official' sites and 'unofficial' sites, many of which advocate the use of a variety of treatment approaches or condemn them as dangerous and unacceptable. Given the plethora of, often contradictory, information on the internet, access to this information can both benefit patients and carry the potential for confusion and even harm. It also presents significant challenges for doctors when giving information about a particular condition. Witness one anecdotal story in which a UK doctor prescribed tamoxifen, a drug treatment known to significantly reduce the risk of cancer recurrence in women that have had breast cancer (see Buzdar 2004). In the consultation, he described both the benefits and the common side-effects and health risks of taking the drug to one patient. With this knowledge, she decided to take the drug on a preventive basis. The next day she telephoned the doctor to say that she was no longer willing to take the drug as she had searched a number of US websites, and their descriptions of the health risks associated with the drug made her decide against its use. While in one way this may be seen as the power of truly informed consent, what had frightened this woman was reading a list of diseases that had occurred in women taking the drug. What she did not have was the data to contextualise this list, which included many conditions that may have occurred in only a very small percentage of those taking the drug, or they

> **atrial fibrillation**
>
> a heart rhythm disorder (arrhythmia). It involves a very rapid heart rate, in which the atria (upper chambers of the heart) contract in a very rapid and disorganised manner and fail to pump blood effectively through the heart.

may not even have been the result of taking tamoxifen. Mindful of this, Kalichman *et al.* (2006) found that an eight-session training in the appropriate use of the internet given to people living with HIV/AIDS resulted in increased access to health information on the internet, and lower vulnerability to misinformation and fraud.

Another response to this involves health-care providers setting up their own web-based information that patients can easily access and that can provide appropriate information. One of many web-based health information sites is provided by the American Heart Association. Heart Profilers (www.americanheart.org/profilers) provides a web-based interactive tool through which patients can obtain a personalised report of 'scientifically accurate' treatment options, a list of questions to ask their doctor on their next visit (which has been shown to improve doctor–patient communication and patient satisfaction – see Chapter 10 (☛)), and key information they need to participate in their treatment. In the site, menus lead to information related to heart failure and CHD, hypertension, high cholesterol and **atrial fibrillation**. The effectiveness of this type of intervention is difficult to assess. However, people who access health- and illness-related websites are generally more knowledgeable than those who do not (Kalichman *et al.* 2003), although this may be the result of better-informed people being more likely to access internet sites relevant to their illness. Nevertheless, these data suggest that the internet may prove a useful resource for people with many chronic conditions, and as we shall show later, can prove an effective medium of change.

Self-management training

Perhaps the best-known approach to helping patients to gain control over their illness is known as self-management training (Lorig 1996), and those who undertake this form of training are often referred to as 'expert patients'. The approach involves teaching affected individuals how to manage their illness in a way that maximises control over their symptoms and quality of life. It is based on social cognition theory (e.g. Bandura 2001), which suggests that patients can learn self-management skills from practice and watching others, and that success in achieving control leads, in turn, to increased confidence and continued application of new skills. Accordingly, the core of self-management training is a structured, progressive, skills-training programme that ensures success at each stage before progression to the next. Self-management programmes are usually, but not uniquely, run as group interventions, facilitating the process of learning from observation of others. The approach is specifically targeted at the effective management of disease. It does not focus on the emotional sequelae of disease; nor is it intended to be a preventive intervention. Self-management programmes began by focusing on helping people cope with arthritis, typically addressing issues such as:

● exercising with arthritis;

● managing pain;

● eating healthily;

● preventing fatigue;

● protecting joints;

● taking arthritis medication;

● dealing with stress and depression;

● working with the doctor and health-care team;

● evaluating alternative treatments;

● outsmarting arthritis: problem solving.

These programmes proved extremely effective. A review by SuperioCabuslay *et al.* (1996), for example, reported gains in excess of drug treatment alone of:

● 20 to 30 per cent on measures of pain relief;

● 40 per cent in functional ability;

● 60 to 80 per cent in the reduction in tender joint counts.

The original self-management programmes addressed all issues with all people. However, it is possible that some issues were more relevant than others. As a result, a number of programmes have now moved from a 'one size fits all' approach to tailored programmes that provide a number of modules that participants can select according to their particular needs, with significant effect (Iversen *et al.* 2010). Evers *et al.* (2002) evaluated the effectiveness of one such programme targeted at people with rheumatoid arthritis. Modules included those targeted at helping people to cope with fatigue, negative mood and pain, and to maintain or improve social relationships. The programme resulted in mid- to long-term gains on a number of psychological measures, including the use of active coping strategies, mood, fatigue and helplessness in comparison with a no-treatment condition. Gains were also reported in an Australian study reported by Osborne *et al.* (2007) using the same approach. This study found significant reductions in pain and health distress, as well as increases in self-efficacy and exercise – changes which were sustained for at least two years. Adding an exercise component to a specific programme for people with osteoarthritic knee pain led Yip *et al.* (2007) to report significant gains in comparison to a no-treatment control group on measures of arthritis pain, fatigue, duration of weekly light exercise practice and knee flexion.

Following their success with arthritis, self-management programmes are now used to help people to manage a number of long-term conditions. Gifford *et al.* (1998), for example, randomly assigned men with symptomatic HIV or AIDS to either a seven-session group self-management programme or usual care. The intervention used interactive methods to provide information about living with HIV/AIDS and a number of disease self-management skills, including symptom assessment and management, medication use (see Chapter 10 ☞), physical exercise and relaxation skills. Over the course of the study, participants who did not enter the programme reported increases in the number of 'troubling symptoms' they experienced and an increased feeling of loss of control over their health. By contrast, participants in the self-management condition reported more control over their health and fewer 'troubling symptoms'. One other programme (Inouye *et al.* 2001) reported short-term gains on measures of mood, including anger, and increases in perceived control over their condition following an HIV self-management intervention compared with a waiting-list control group.

A further example of a self-management programme involves the control of blood sugar levels in diabetes. Lorig *et al.* (2009) found a classic peer-led self-management intervention to be useful in improving a number of measures relative to a usual care condition. In comparison to this group, participants in the self-management group evidenced gains on measures of depression, symptoms of hypoglycaemia, communication with physicians, healthy eating immediately following the intervention.

However, no change was found on a measure of long-term blood sugar (HbA1C). An older, but interesting study, was reported by Langewitz *et al.* (1997) who provided what they termed 'intensified functional insulin therapy'. Not only did their intervention involve an educational component, but it also taught participants how factors such as additional exercise and eating meals with varying levels of carbohydrate may influence their blood sugar levels by allowing them to experience, and then cope with, these situations within the programme. This approach should provide more realistic learning than conventional approaches and therefore provide more benefit should problems arise. In comparison with baseline measures, participants in the intervention evidenced significant improvements in blood sugar levels and a reduction in the frequency with which they experienced **hypoglycaemic episodes** in the following year.

Self-management programmes need not be delivered live. There are now several examples of graduated skills-based programmes that have translated the key elements of the self-management process into written or computer-based form. The *Heart Manual*, which we described earlier in this chapter, provides a good example of this. The latest evaluation of this approach was reported by Jolly *et al.* (2007). They randomly allocated participants who had experienced an MI from inner-city, ethnically diverse, socially deprived areas of the West Midlands of England to receive either a hospital-based cardiac rehabilitation programme or the Heart Manual used at home. Both involved programmes including exercise, relaxation, education and lifestyle counselling. The *Heart Manual* followed the developmental approach of gradual change and skills learning suggested by Lorig. Significant improvements in total cholesterol, smoking prevalence, anxiety scores, self-reported physical activity and diet were seen in both conditions between baseline and the six-month follow-up. However, no clinically or statistically significant differences were seen between

---

hypoglycaemic episode

occurs when the body's glucose level is too low. It frequently occurs when too much insulin or oral diabetic medication is taken, not enough food is eaten, or following exercise without appropriate food intake. Symptoms include excessive sweating, paleness, fainting and eventually loss of consciousness.

the home- and centre-based groups, suggesting that the home intervention is a viable and effective intervention. In a similar study, Lewin *et al.* (2002) evaluated a written intervention to help patients manage their angina. They compared a standard educational package providing information but no strategies of change with a written behavioural programme showing participants how best to manage their angina and encouraging them to plan new activities and to limit the impact of angina on their lives. Six months after the end of the intervention, patients in the self-management intervention reported lower levels of angina, used drugs to control their angina less frequently, and reported fewer physical restrictions on their activities than patients in the control group.

Self-management programmes can be implemented simply and cheaply using the internet or interactive programmes on computers. It is important to note, though, that such interventions may appeal to specific groups within the population. Several studies, for example, have shown younger people to enjoy and benefit from the use of such technology in managing illnesses such as diabetes (Chan *et al.* 2007) and asthma (e.g. van der Meer *et al.* 2007). But not all patient populations will feel comfortable with such an approach. In an ethnically diverse Californian sample, Sarkar *et al.* (2007), for example, found that 69 per cent of their respondents reported interest in telephone support, 55 per cent wanted group medical visits, while only 42 per cent would use the internet. Unsurprisingly, people who reported themselves as having poor literacy were more likely to be interested in telephone support than the alternative approaches.

Stress management training

A number of interventions have focused on teaching stress management procedures in an effort to control the symptoms of disorders as diverse as rheumatoid arthritis and **atopic dermatitis**. Some of the relevant literature is reviewed below, focusing on the treatment of irritable bowel syndrome (IBS), angina and diabetes.

Although the role attributable to stress in the aetiology of IBS has been downplayed recently (see Chapter 8 ☞), a number of interventions using stress management techniques have been evaluated, and they seem to be reasonably effective – achieving similar outcomes to medical interventions whether conducted face to face (Spiller *et al.* 2007) or through the use of self-help

material augmented by brief telephone contact (Moss-Morris *et al.* 2010). Taking the issue one step further, Kennedy *et al.* (2005) reported a study in which they examined whether stress management could add to the effectiveness of a drug that slows down the gut's activity and is generally used to treat IBS. All the people in the study were first given the drug treatment. Those who continued to have IBS symptoms six weeks later were either entered into a stress management programme or continued on their drug regimen in the hope that additional time on the drug would improve their symptoms. Patients in the cognitive-behavioural programme fared best, reporting significant improvements on a variety of measures of IBS symptoms as well as reductions in measures of emotional distress.

Episodes of angina may be triggered by emotional as well as by physical stresses (see Chapter 8 ☞). Accordingly, a number of studies have explored the potential benefits of stress management procedures in people with this condition. One of the first was reported by Bundy *et al.* (1994), who found that patients who took part in a stress management programme reported greater reductions in the frequency of angina symptoms, were less reliant on medication and performed better on a standardised exercise known as a **treadmill test** than a control group who did not receive the intervention. A much larger study, involving hundreds of participants, was reported by Gallacher *et al.* (1997), who compared a less intensive intervention, involving a stress management programme delivered in booklet form and three group meetings, with a no-treatment control condition. At six-month follow-up, patients in the intervention condition reported significantly fewer episodes of angina triggered by stress, but not exercise – a finding consistent with the intervention impacting directly on the stress mechanisms that led to the episodes of angina.

---

atopic dermatitis

a number of conditions, including eczema, involving an inflammatory response of the skin.

treadmill test

a test of cardiovascular fitness in which participants gradually increase the level of exercise on a treadmill while having their heart monitored with an electrocardiogram.

Case history: Mr P

Mr P provides an interesting case involving the use of stress management and angina. His problems began when he was admitted to hospital following an MI. As with most patients, he spent two days in the coronary care unit before being transferred to a medical ward, and was discharged a few days later following an uneventful time on that ward. Unfortunately, when he went home he developed the symptoms of angina, which on occasion mimicked the symptoms Mr P had experienced at the time of his initial infarction: chest pain, shortness of breath and feeling dizzy. The second of these episodes occurred following a major sale (he was a sales representative) leading to him feeling very excited, after which he walked out of a building into a freezing cold night to go to his car to drive home. The combination of adrenalin-fuelled excitement and sudden exposure to cold air triggered a significant episode of angina. Unfortunately, he found these symptoms extremely frightening and interpreted them as indicating he was having a further MI. This resulted in him hyperventilating, exacerbating his physical symptoms, having a 'full-blown' panic attack, and then calling out an ambulance to be admitted to the same hospital. As on the first occasion, he was discharged from hospital the following day after being told that he had 'only' had an episode of angina.

In an attempt to stop this happening again, he was referred to a clinical psychologist. The challenges of therapy were to help Mr P distinguish (and then control) any panic symptoms from those of his heart disease, and to be able to distinguish any symptoms of angina from symptoms of a true MI. A mistake at any stage in this process could prove, literally, fatal. The intervention proved relatively simple, as Mr P was keen to adopt a psychological approach to managing his problems. The first stage involved working out exactly what was contributing to his feelings of panic. The key issue here was panicky thoughts, in particular thoughts that his heart disease was out of control and that he could die unless he got medical help. This led to increased sympathetic arousal, ironically placing more strain on his heart and increasing his angina, and hyperventilation which added to his feelings of being out of control, and dizziness.

The goal of therapy was to break this circle. This initially involved Mr P learning to relax and to use some simple breathing techniques he could use to slow his breathing when he became anxious. He practised these skills regularly until they became relatively easy to implement. Then, working with the psychologist, he developed a strategy to use if he experienced any angina symptoms. These were:

● Assume that the symptoms were angina, not a heart attack. Use positive self-talk to remind himself that he had experienced the symptoms before and they were not a sign of impending death, that he could control them, and if he used his gtn [glyceryl trinitrate] spray (see Chapter 8 ☞) they would soon go.

● Use relaxation and breathing exercises to bring his symptoms under control.

● Wait 5–10 minutes, to see whether the symptoms reduced as a result of these procedures.

● If they did not, to call an ambulance and seek medical help.

He talked this action plan through during a therapy session, and planned on its use at key times during the day. He used it twice, successfully, in the month following its development. In the next month, he did not experience any panic attacks, and was discharged from psychology services. Another successful case!

The potential benefits of stress management for the control of diabetes are perhaps less obvious than those related to angina. Nevertheless, there are reasons to presume that they could form an effective element in any programme of diabetes control. Stress often precedes periods of reduced adherence to self-care behaviour and may be associated with inappropriate changes in eating patterns (Viner *et al.* 1996). In addition, high levels of stress hormones such as cortisol reduce the body's sensitivity to insulin and may be accompanied by elevations in blood sugar (Surwit and Schneider 1993). As a consequence, some studies have found relaxation to be an effective intervention in keeping blood sugar levels within the optimum range. Attari *et al.* (2006), for example, reported an Iranian study comparing the effectiveness of stress management versus no intervention in the long-term control of high blood sugar levels in people with type 1 diabetes. Their main outcome measure was a substance known as HbA(1c), which indicates levels of blood sugar over the previous three months. Over the course of the three-month intervention, participants in the stress management group had lower levels of HbA(1c) than those in the no-intervention group. Similar gains have also been reported in people with type 2 diabetes (Surwit *et al.* 2002). Interestingly, they found that those people who reported the most stress did not benefit any more than those with lower levels of stress – perhaps because they found the stress management intervention more difficult to implement.

Perhaps the best interventions are those that combine teaching stress management techniques with other strategies to help to control diabetes. Grey *et al.* (2000), for example, compared an intensive diabetes management programme combined with a stress management programme with the diabetes management programme

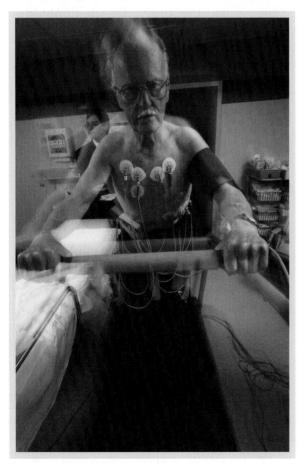

Plate 17.1 The treadmill can provide a good test of cardiac fitness while in the safety of a medical setting

Source: Getty Images/Alvis Upitis.

alone in young people with diabetes. By one-year follow-up, participants in the combined intervention had lower blood sugar levels and a higher belief in their ability to control diabetes and general health than those in the single condition. In addition, participants in the combined intervention were less likely to gain weight than those in the diabetes management programme, and women in this condition were least likely to report hypoglycaemic episodes.

Enhancing social and family support

Despite the widely acknowledged impact that family and friends of people with chronic illnesses may have on their behaviour and emotional well-being (see Chapter 12 ☛), relatively few interventions have targeted such individuals. Those that have have had generally positive results – although among them are also some cautionary findings.

Some programmes have involved peers helping patients cope with chronic conditions. These may involve peer experts showing how best to manage a particular condition. One such programme reported the outcomes among a Hispanic community, with peers teaching strategies for managing a variety of chronic conditions – CHD, lung disease and type 2 diabetes. The intervention proved successful, with attenders reporting better health status, health behaviours and more confidence in their ability to manage their condition than controls who did not attend the sessions for up to one year after the end of the programme. Another project, described by Greco *et al.* (2001), reported outcomes of an intervention in which young people with diabetes and their best friends took part in a group intervention aimed at increasing diabetes-related knowledge in both participants and increasing the friend's support of the patient's diabetes care behaviour. The intervention achieved these goals. In addition, the young people's wider groups of friends understood more about diabetes, and parents reported less diabetes-related conflict. With the development of modern technology, support from peers or fellow patients need to always be live. The internet has become an important means of keeping in touch – although as the results of Lindsay *et al.* (2009) indicated, that if the goal is behavioural change, this is more likely to be achieved if an internet support group 'meeting' is moderated. They evaluated the degree of risk behaviour change in cardiac patients living in an economically deprived area of the UK who were able to access professionally moderated then unmoderated online support groups. During the moderated phase, the group members achieved more changes in diet than a usual care control group. However, during the following unmoderated phase, they not only lost the behavioural gains they had made, but they also made *more* appointments with health-care staff than those in the control condition. Why this would happen is unclear, but the potential for an ummoderated group to spread worry and concern among its members rather than ameliorate is clear.

Involving partners in any intervention may also be of value – and may be done quite simply. Taylor *et al.* (1985), for example, compared the effects of wives' differing levels of involvement in testing the exercise tolerance of cardiac patients. In their study, wives were allocated to one of three conditions:

1. no observation of the test;

2. observing their partners taking part in a treadmill test to assess their cardiac fitness;

3. observing their partners take the test and also taking part in it themselves;

All the women were fully informed of their partners' level of fitness in a counselling session. The key measure in the study was the wives' ratings of their partners' physical and cardiac efficiency. Partners who both observed and took part in the treadmill exercise were more reassured of their husbands' ability to exercise than women in either of the other groups. Although we do not know from the results of this study, it is hoped that this confidence would result in the women being less restrictive of their partners' levels of exercise and less anxious when they did so. However, involving partners in educational programmes may not always be successful. Riemsma *et al.* (2003) reported that when both patients and their partners attended a cardiac group education programme, participants reported *decreases* in self-efficacy and increased fatigue. By contrast, patients participating in group education without partners showed *increases* in self-efficacy and decreased fatigue. More complex family interventions have also proven of benefit in helping young people manage chronic illnesses. Wysocki *et al.* (2007), for example, reported on the outcomes of a programme involving working with whole families to help young people cope

with their diabetes. The intervention changed the family dynamics, for example, by reducing family conflict, and also changed condition-specific factors, such as improving adherence and long-term HbA(1c) levels. Similar benefits have been found in the treatment of other conditions that require young people to be actively involved in the management of their condition, such as asthma (Yorke and Shuldham 2005) and cystic fibrosis (Duff 2001).

Emotional expression

Perhaps the most unexpected therapeutic approach now being developed for people with physical health problems is the variously termed narrative or written emotional expression. The work stems from the findings by Pennebaker in the 1980s (see Pennebaker *et al.* 1990) of the psychological effects of a writing task in which healthy participants, usually students, wrote about an event or issue from the past that had caused them upset or distress in a way that explored their emotional reaction to that event for about 15–20 minutes on three consecutive days. Typical instructions for this exercise were:

1. Find a place where you will not be disturbed. You can write by hand or on a computer – whatever you are most comfortable with. If you don't want to write, you can also talk into a tape recorder.

2. Plan on your writing for a minimum of three days and a minimum of 15 minutes a day. The only rule is that you write continuously. If you run out of things to say, simply repeat what you have already written.

3. Instructions: really let go and write about your very deepest thoughts and feelings about *X*. How does *X* relate to other parts of your life? For example, how do they tie into issues associated with your childhood, your relationship with your family and friends, and the life you have now. How might they be related to your future, your past, or who you are now? Why are you feeling the way you are and what other issues are being brought up by this?

4. You can write about the same general topic every day or a different one each day. Don't worry about spelling or grammar. Your writing is for you and you alone. Many people throw away their writing samples as soon as they are finished. Others keep them and even edit them.

5. Be your own experimenter. Try writing in different ways. If you find that you are getting too upset in your writing, then back off and change directions. Your goal here is to better understand your thoughts and feelings associated with X. See which approach to writing works best for you.

Following this process, participants typically reported short-term increases in depression or distress, but in the mid to long term experienced better mood and, importantly in this context, seemed to have better physical health as measured by immune function and the frequency of visiting a doctor (see Esterling *et al.* 1999). It took some time for this approach to be tested in patient populations. However, the interventions that have been conducted appear to show benefits. Smyth *et al.* (1999), for example, compared the effects of written expressed emotion and a neutral writing task in patients with rheumatoid arthritis and asthma. Those in the intervention condition were asked to write about the 'most stressful experience they had ever undergone'; those in the control group were asked to write about time-management issues as an exercise to reduce stress. Both types of patient in the intervention group fared better than their equivalents in the control group at four-month follow-up: patients with asthma showed improvements in lung function, while patients with rheumatoid arthritis showed improvements on a combined index measuring physician-rated factors such as disease activity, joint swelling and tenderness, and the presence and severity of joint deformities as well as patient reports of any constraints on daily living tasks. Accordingly, the gains reported cannot simply be attributed to changes in self-report of symptoms as a function of improved mood following the intervention: they appear to be 'objective' gains in disease activity. Warner *et al.* (2006) reported similar benefits for young people with asthma, and began to explore what elements of the writing task appeared to mediate the improvements they found. By analysing the content of the participants' writing, they noted that the greatest improvements in asthma were associated with improved insight into the issue the participants were writing about, and the expression of more negative emotions.

In another study examining who benefits most from this approach, Stanton *et al.* (2002b) assigned participants, all of whom were in the early stages of breast cancer,

to write about either: (a) their deepest thoughts and feelings regarding breast cancer (the emotional expression condition), (b) positive thoughts and feelings regarding breast cancer, or (c) facts about their experience of having breast cancer (the neutral task). Once again, the emotional expression seemed to be of benefit. In comparison with the neutral task, participants in the emotional expression condition reported fewer somatic symptoms and fewer visits to the doctor with worries about cancer or related medical conditions. Of interest was that women who typically did not use avoidant coping strategies appeared to benefit most from the emotional expression condition. The positive emotional expression task appeared to benefit those women who were typically avoidant, presumably because it did not force them to confront their fears and other issues raised by their disease. A subsequent paper, with data taken from this study (Low *et al.* 2006) replicated the findings of Warner *et al.* above, as the expression of negative emotions was significantly associated with an improvement in symptoms.

WHAT DO YOU THINK?

The premise of the emotional expression paradigm is that it can be useful to think about, and somehow process, emotional issues. This has proved effective in a number of settings, but are there times when this may not be an optimal, or even a desirable approach? It has been suggested that there may be times when the opposite approach may be of benefit. It was reasoned that people waiting for medical information – some of which may have powerful implications for the individual, such as their HIV status or a diagnosis of cancer – may benefit more by being distracted from any worries they may have than dwelling on them. At this time, they have no information to process emotionally – rather, they are lacking any relevant information. At such times, it may be best to distract from any intrusive worries rather than focus on them using the Pennebaker approach. This finding raises a frequently raised issue concerning the targeting of interventions at appropriate times and at individuals most likely to benefit from them. So what sort of conditions, situations or individuals may be best helped by emotional expression? Are there situations where this approach should be avoided, and other approaches considered?

Despite these positive results, it should be acknowledged that not all interventions involving written expression are effective. Harris *et al.* (2005), for example, found it did not benefit adults with asthma. Similarly, there may be some contexts in which the expression of emotions is actually counter-productive. Panagopoulou *et al.* (2006) found that women who were emotionally expressive were less likely to become pregnant while undergoing *in vitro* fertilisation than those who contained their emotions. The goal of the next phase of research into the written emotional expression is to find out with whom and in what context the approach works best (see the special section of the *British Journal of Health Psychology*, volume 13, part 1, 2008 for a series of papers that address this issue).

Preventing disease progression

Counselling

One particular form of counselling has been used with cardiac patients in an attempt to prevent disease progression – with somewhat mixed results. The Life Stress Monitoring Program (LSMP: Frasure-Smith and Prince 1985) targeted middle-aged men who had experienced an MI and who were struggling to cope in the year following their infarction. In the study, over four hundred and fifty patients were allocated into either a no-intervention control group or a low-contact 'counselling' intervention. In this, they received monthly telephone contact from a nurse for a period of one year, during which they completed a measure of psychological distress. If they scored above a criterion score, indicating significant stress, they were offered a home visit by the nurse. The action taken by this nurse could vary according to the circumstances they encountered: the majority of contacts involving teaching and providing reassurance by supplying information, but the intervention could involve changes in medication and referral to a cardiologist if necessary.

Half the participants in the intervention condition were visited by the nursing team over the period of the intervention, with an average of six hours contact per patient. By the end of the intervention, the total death rate in the control group was 9 per cent, while that of the intervention group was 5 per cent – a significant difference. Four years following baseline, although a similar percentage of patients in the intervention and control groups had a further MI, patients in the intervention group were less likely to have died from their MI, suggesting a smaller but still significant benefit from having taken part in the counselling intervention. Unfortunately this finding may not be as exciting as it first appears. The proportion of white-collar workers in the intervention group was significantly greater than that in the control group. Accordingly, many of those in the intervention group may have been at less risk of re-infarction than those in the control group simply as a consequence of socio-economic differences (see Chapter 2 ☞). As a consequence of methodological constraints, these differences could not be statistically partialled out in their analyses, and the interpretation of the results must therefore be considered with some caution.

Such caution may be justified by the results of a later attempt to replicate these findings by the same team (Frasure-Smith *et al.* 1997). The Montreal heart attack readjustment trial (M-HART) study evaluated the same form of intervention, this time including interventions with women and an older population. Unfortunately, the intervention resulted in no benefits for men – re-infarction rates in the first year were 2.4 per cent in the intervention group and 2.5 per cent in the control group. Worse, women in the intervention group proved to be *more* at risk of re-infarction than those in the control group, with re-infarction rates of 10.3 per cent and 5.4 per cent, respectively – an effect maintained up to five-year follow-up (Frasure-Smith *et al.* 2002). In retrospect, these findings may have been a consequence of inadequately trained nurses attempting to cope with extremely distressed individuals and thus perhaps exacerbating rather than moderating their problems.

Stress management training

The impact of more traditional cardiac rehabilitation programmes that provide some form of intervention to all patients has been reviewed by Dusseldorp *et al.* (1999) and Linden *et al.* (1996), who conducted meta-analyses of the effect of 'psychosocial' and 'psycho-educational' interventions on 23 and 37 programmes, respectively.

> **exercise programme**
> a key element of most cardiac rehabilitation, including a progressive increase in exercise usually starting in a gym, sometimes developing into exercise in the home and beyond.

These interventions typically combined some form of **exercise programme** involving graded increases in activity with an educational programme about risk factor change, medication and other issues relevant to patients being discharged home following an MI. Both reviews came to some positive conclusions. Linden and colleagues, for example, reported that patients who did not enter a psychosocial programme were significantly more likely to die or have further cardiac problems in the two years following their infarction than those who did. After this, any protective effect was weaker. Dusseldorp et al. similarly reported that psycho-educational interventions resulted in a 34 per cent reduction in cardiac mortality, a 29 per cent reduction in recurrence of MI, and significant positive effects on blood pressure, cholesterol, body weight, cigarette smoking, physical exercise and eating habits. However, both reviews did not separate the effects of different psychosocial interventions such as counselling, risk behaviour education and what they term 'stress management trials'.

Perhaps the strongest evaluation of the effectiveness of stress management in the context of cardiac disease was provided by Friedman et al. (1986), who reported on a trial known as the Recurrent Coronary Prevention Program. This targeted men high on a measure of Type A behaviour (see pp. 334–37) who had experienced an MI. Participants were allocated to one of three groups: cardiac rehabilitation, cardiac rehabilitation plus Type A management, and a usual care control. The rehabilitation programme involved small group meetings over a period of four-and-half years, in which participants received information on medication, exercise and diet, as well as social support from the group. The Type A management group received the same information in addition to engaging in a sustained programme of behavioural change involving training in relaxation, cognitive techniques and specific behavioural change plans in which they reduced the frequency of their Type A behaviour. Evidence of the effectiveness of this process was compelling. Over the four-and-a-half years of the

intervention, those in the Type A management programme were at half the risk of further infarction than those in the traditional rehabilitation programme, with total infarction rates over this time of 6 and 12 per cent in each group, respectively. This remains one of the most convincing studies of the effectiveness of stress management on survival following an MI (Schneiderman et al. 2001), although whether most health-care services could provide such an expensive long-term intervention is debatable.

Smaller studies have also shown positive gains following stress management interventions targeted at more general responses to stress. Blumenthal et al. (1997) assigned cardiac patients to either a 'usual care' group involving regular out-patient appointments with a cardiologist, a four-month programme of exercise, or a programme of stress management training. Those in the stress management group were least likely to have a cardiac event over the following year. In a second study examining these issues, the same team (Blumenthal et al. 2005) found both stress management and exercise to be equally effective in changing a number of psychological and physiological markers of disease. More specifically, meditation may prove an effective intervention for people with CHD. Castillo-Richmond et al. (2000), for example, found evidence of a slowing in the development (and even perhaps a modest decrease) in the thickness of atherosclerosis in the carotid artery of hypertensive African Americans who were taught meditation compared to controls who were not.

Depression substantially increases risk of infarction or re-infarction (see Frasure-Smith et al. 1995). Such a relationship suggests that interventions that reduce depression should reduce the risk of re-infarction. However, evidence in support of this hypothesis is still lacking. In one of the first studies to examine this issue, Black et al. (1998) allocated MI patients found to be experiencing significant distress to either usual care or to one to seven sessions of behavioural therapy. They found that 35 per cent of participants in the active intervention were hospitalised with cardiac symptoms in the following year, in comparison with 48 per cent of those in the usual care group. However, whether this difference was a consequence of physiological or psychological changes such as less anxiety over cardiac symptoms is not clear.

Unfortunately, evidence from the largest trial of any form of cardiac rehabilitation, known as the ENRICHD study (Berkman et al. 2003), suggests that interventions targeted at depression may not prove as effective as this early study suggested. The ENRICHD study was a large multicentre study involving 2,481 patients, providing an intervention lasting up to one year for people identified as depressed immediately following their MI. All participants in the active intervention arm received two or three treatment components, each aimed at improving their emotional state:

- group cognitive-behavioural therapy;
- social support enhanced by training participants in the social skills needed to develop their social support network;
- antidepressant medication for people who did not evidence any improvement in mood received.

A comparison group received the usual care provided by the institutions in which the study took place. Unfortunately, the results of the study were disappointing. Although the ENRICHD intervention did result in lower levels of depression than those achieved in the usual care condition, there were no differences in

survival between the two groups over the two years following infarction. These data have led some to claim that there are no benefits to treating depression in MI patients – and they certainly seem to indicate this to be the case. However, the sheer size of the study meant that the investigators had limited control over the interventions received by patients in both arms of the study. This meant that the usual care received by some people in the control condition was, in fact, very similar to that provided by the ENRICHD study. In addition, attendance at the ENRICHD intervention was less than optimal, with most patients attending about eleven sessions – an attendance not that different to many of the control group interventions. Perhaps because of these factors, the differences in levels of depression between the two groups, although statistically significant, were not that great. Accordingly, it remains possible that the reductions in depression in the ENRICHD condition relative to the control condition were not sufficiently large to bring about reductions in risk for further MI.

IN THE SPOTLIGHT

Reading the report of the ENRICHD study, which was published in the prestigious *Journal of the American Medical Association*, it is clear that the readers of this journal had one interest. Did treating depression save lives? This is a question that has excited many health psychologists as well as medical doctors – and it is very important. But because it did not save lives, many psychologists consider the ENRICHD study to be a failure. But was it? Yes, from a biomedical stance, the results of the ENRICHD study were disappointing. But what about a more psychological perspective?

Depression is a potentially disabling condition that has significant implications for the quality of life and rehabilitation outcomes of both patients and the people

involved with them. While psychologists should be involved in the questions of the impact of disease on physiological processes, they should also be careful not to lose sight of other psychological questions and adopting too strong a biomedical stance in the questions they address. Changes in depression are an important outcome in themselves – not just a vehicle to reduce mortality. From this perspective, the ENRICHD intervention proved a costly one that fared moderately better than the care usually provided. As such, it provides a wealth of information about how to identify and treat depression in cardiac patients, with potentially significant benefits to future patients. We should be careful not to throw out the 'psychological baby' when we throw out the 'medical bath water'.

If treating depression does not appear to result in health gains in cardiac patients, treating anxiety in patients with immune-system-mediated diseases does. One condition in which this issue has been explored is that of HIV/AIDS. Antoni *et al.* (2002), for example, followed

the immunological outcomes in 25 HIV-positive men randomly allocated to either a ten-week stress management intervention or a waiting-list control condition. Their measures particularly focused on the impact of the intervention on CD4+ cells (see Chapter 8 ☞). Immediately following the intervention, those who took part had higher CD4+ cell counts than those in the control group, despite there being no pre-treatment differences, suggesting that stress management may slow down the disease progress and reduce the risk of opportunistic infections.

A second set of studies has examined whether stress management procedures can influence the health outcomes of people with cancer. There is evidence that stress management can improve immune function in the short term in people with cancer (e.g. McGregor *et al.* 2004). The key question that then follows is whether these immune changes translate into health gains. The outcomes following the intervention conducted by Fawzy *et al.* (1993) described earlier in the chapter were impressive. In a series of studies, they reported the percentage of people in a stress management group and a no-treatment control group to show progression of malignant melanoma six months, five–six years, and ten years after the intervention. At the first of the long-term follow-up periods, participants were significantly less likely to have died of cancer than those in the control group and were marginally more likely to have had a longer period free of disease. By the ten-year follow-up (Fawzy *et al.* 2003), these differential effects remained. By this time, 11 of the 34 people in the control group had

had recurrences and had died of cancer: 3 others had had non-fatal recurrences. In the stress management group, 9 of 34 had died of cancer, and 2 had survived recurrences. Overall, these differences were not significantly different between the groups. However, after statistically controlling for differences in the severity of the presenting melanoma, more participants who took part in the stress management intervention survived up to ten years after their initial diagnosis than those in the control group. Similar gains following stress management training or similar interventions have been found in two large studies of patients with gastrointestinal cancer (Kuchler *et al.* 1999) and a mixture of cancers (McCorkle *et al.* 2000), although some smaller studies have reported null findings. However, Ross *et al.* (2002) pointed out that the effects of these interventions may have been stronger if patients had been selected for any of the studies as a result of their having some distress to ameliorate rather than simply having a diagnosis of cancer.

Enhancing social support

One of the earliest studies to examine the impact of increasing social support on disease outcomes was reported by Spiegel *et al.* (1981). In a study designed to

Plate 17.2 Social support can help you keep healthy. Sometimes by just having someone to talk to. Sometimes by supporting healthy behaviours – even in difficult circumstances!

improve the quality of life in cancer patients, they randomly assigned women with breast cancer to either an active treatment programme or a no-treatment control. The active intervention involved weekly support groups that emphasised building strong supportive bonds, expressing emotions, dealing directly with fears of dying, improving relationships within the family and active involvement in decisions concerning treatment. To the surprise of the investigators, women in this group lived an average of 18 months longer than those in the no-treatment control, despite being well matched for disease status at the beginning of the trial. These findings generated a great deal of excitement in the research and clinical community when published. Unfortunately, attempts at replication, including a study conducted by Spiegel himself (Spiegel *et al.* 2007), have failed to replicate this finding, and social support has yet to be convincingly shown to impact on illness outcomes in patients with cancer.

SUMMARY

The chapter considered psychological interventions designed to achieve three interacting goals in patients with serious chronic diseases:

- to reduce distress;
- to improve disease management;
- to reduce risk of future disease or disease progression.

A number of approaches have been successfully used in each case.

Reductions in distress have been achieved by the use of:

- appropriate information (including information about a condition or coping strategies to minimise distress or improve control over the condition);
- stress management training while waiting for a diagnosis, during treatment and while coping with the emotional stress of living with a long-term illness;
- providing social support – often in the guise of professionally run support groups.

Improvements in the management of illness have been achieved by:

- providing information – particularly information that provides a structure to achieve symptom control rather than simply providing information about a condition or its treatment;
- training in self-management programmes, with emphasis shifting from the provision of general 'one size fits all' programmes to more bespoke programmes specifically developed to suit participants' needs;
- stress management training in conditions in which stress is involved in their aetiology (e.g. IBS) or may exacerbate symptoms (e.g. angina, diabetes);
- improving social and family support;
- written emotional expression.

Finally, a number of interventions may impact on longer-term health:

- Counselling may be of benefit in cardiac patients, but results of the M-HART study have made people cautious in adopting this model.
- Stress management appears to be of benefit in improving health in a number of conditions, including CHD and HIV/AIDS.
- Treatment of depression in cardiac patients may impact on prognosis, although the ENRICHD study suggests that this approach should be viewed with caution.
- Social support may be of benefit, although the promise of some early studies has not been repeated in later studies.

Overall, there is significant evidence that psychological interventions can be of great value in helping people to come to terms with the emotional consequences of having a serious chronic illness. They may also be of benefit in aiding day-to-day symptoms and even longer-term prognoses in a more limited set of conditions.

Further reading

The entire volume of the *Journal of Consulting and Clinical Psychology* for June 2002 (volume 70, part 3) provides an excellent overview of the types of psychological intervention that may be used with a variety of health conditions. It's a little dated now, but still worth a read.

A section of the February 2008 *British Journal of Health Psychology* considers new evidence in relation to the written emotional expression approach. Edited by two of the leaders in the field (Pennebaker and Smyth); well worth a read.

Fekete, E.M., Antoni, M.H. and Schneiderman, N. (2007). Psychosocial and behavioral interventions for chronic medical conditions. *Current Opinion in Psychiatry*, 20: 152–7.

An up-to-date review of recent evidence by leading researchers in the area.

McGregor, B.A. and Antoni, M.H. (2009). Psychological intervention and health outcomes among women treated for breast cancer: a review of stress pathways and biological mediators. *Brain Behavior and Immunity*, 23: 159–66.

Recent review of outcomes following primarily stress management interventions. Needs a bit of psychoneuroimmunology knowledge, so can be hard work. But worth the read.

Newbould, J., Taylor, D. and Bury, M. (2006). Lay-led self-management in chronic illness: a review of the evidence. *Chronic Illnesses*, 2: 249–61.

One of the most recent reviews of the expert patient (Lorig) approach to self-management of chronic disease as used in the USA and UK. A cautious review.

Joynt, K.E. and O'Connor, C.M. (2005). Lessons from SADHART, ENRICHD, and other trials. *Psychosomatic Medicine*, 67 (Suppl. 1): S63–6.

Critical review of a number of psychological and psycho-pharmacological interventions in the treatment of depression in cardiac patients.

Fann, J.R., Thomas-Rich, A.M., Katon, W.J. *et al.* (2008). Major depression after breast cancer: a review of epidemiology and treatment. *General Hospital Psychiatry*, 30: 112–26.

Up-to-date review of an important issue.

Anderson, A.S. and Klemm, P. (2008). The Internet: friend or foe when providing patient education? *Clinical Journal of Oncology Nursing*, 12: 55–63.

Interesting paper considering the pros and cons of the internet as a means of providing patient education.

There are many expert patient websites. Some, such as the Stanford site, focus on research, and payment is required to access self-help materials. Others, such as the expert patient programme or the British Heart Foundation, offer a little more. The cardiac psychology site is particularly helpful.

www.expertpatients.co.uk/public/default.aspx?load=
PublicHome
http://patienteducation.stanford.edu/
www.bhf.org.uk/
www.cardiacpsychology.com/page/page/4176374.htm

Visit the website at **www.pearsoned.co.uk/morrison** for additional resources to help you with your study, including multiple choice questions, weblinks and flashcards.

Part IV
Futures

Chapter 18
Futures

Learning outcomes

By the end of this chapter, you should have an understanding of:

- the need for theory-led practice

- how psychologists may influence practice, and some of the barriers to the effective development of practice

- the role and training of health psychologists in differing parts of the world

- influences on the uptake (or not) of recommended treatment approaches

British psychology leads the way!

Not a headline we see often these days. But the training of health psychologists in the UK is, at the time of writing, one of the strongest and most professional in the world. It compares with leading programmes in the USA, and its requirement for professional health psychologists to hold a doctoral-level degree is higher than the master's requirement in, say, Australia and New Zealand. Many other countries have yet to recognise the profession of health psychologists. But things are changing, and not perhaps for the better. Until recently, British qualifications in psychology were validated entirely by the British Psychological Society. This charity determined that the qualification required to be a health psychologist was at a doctoral level (in combination with the relevant experience). However, a recently established governmental body, the Health Professions Council (HPC), has determined that the educational requirement for health psychologists is set at master's level (in combination with the relevant experience). In the next few years, it will be possible to follow both training routes – a doctoral programme leading to a BPS validated professional qualification or an MSc programme leading to HPC professional accreditation. The longer-term implications of this lowering of educational requirement could be considered good news, perhaps, as the time taken to qualify as a health psychologist and the costs associated with this training will clearly reduce. But these changes may also have a downside in terms not only of knowledge and skills, but also of the career prospects of those involved. In a professional world in which other psychologists such as clinical psychologists will have a doctoral training, how will health psychologists fare in competition for more senior psychologist posts? And how will master's-trained health psychologists fare when they apply for jobs against people with doctoral training? The short-term gains of gaining a professional qualification in less time are clear, the long-term costs are perhaps less so. British psychology may lead the way in the training of health psychologists at the moment – but will this lead continue?

Chapter outline

This chapter draws together a number of the strands of research and the practice of health psychology. It starts with a reminder of the need for health psychologists not only to develop the practice of health psychology, but also to develop and utilise theory in our practice of health psychology. It provides some examples of how theory may inform practice, before examining who may come to actually use interventions based on health psychology theory. The chapter considers some of the barriers to the dissemination of good health-care practice, whether based on health psychology or input from other disciplines. It also considers the development of health psychology as a health-care profession across a number of health-care settings.

The need for theory-driven practice

In this section we consider how these developing theories can be applied in health-care settings. This book has outlined a wide range of contemporary evidence showing the importance of psychological and psychosocial factors in explaining health, health-related behaviour, and the outcomes of interventions to affect both. Key variables that influence behaviour have been integrated into coherent theories such as the theory of planned behaviour, social cognitive theory, and so on. More complex models, such as the health action process, have further integrated these theories into second-order theories of behavioural acquisition and change. These theories are developing and expanding as a direct result of the theoretical work conducted by many academic health psychologists: the theory of planned behaviour is now, for example, often considered in the context of additional variables such as moral norms and anticipated regret (see Chapter 5 ☞). However, such theories are not only of academic benefit to researchers and other psychologists but also of importance to a range of health-care practitioners,

because they help identify which, out of the vast range of potential factors, are most likely to influence behaviour. They can help us construct interventions that are most likely to be effective in a variety of contexts. An example of this can be found in work on smoking cessation. Ask many health professionals how to help someone stop smoking, and they will probably say that the best way is to scare them into behavioural change. Empirical evidence suggests that such an approach will work for some, but not the majority of smokers. Psychological theory provides a series of alternative factors that may be more influential:

- The *health belief model* suggests that not only do we need to convince smokers that smoking will result in serious illness and that they are at significant risk of developing such illnesses, but we also have to convince them that the benefits of stopping smoking (health, cost, fitness, etc.) outweigh the benefits of continued smoking (avoidance of withdrawal symptoms, loss of social camaraderie, 'It can't happen to me', etc.).

- The *theory of planned behaviour* further emphasises the role of attitudes and beliefs in behaviour change. It also indicates the potential role of peers and other important others in developing personal strategies in stopping smoking. It, and the *health action process*, also clearly indicates the benefit of planning behavioural change, not simply acting on impulse.

● *Social cognition theory* suggests that before people are motivated to stop smoking and/or to continue in any efforts to remain smoke-free they have to believe they have the ability to do so. The principle of vicarious learning suggests we gain both skills and self-efficacy from observation of coping models – and these should form an integral part of smoking cessation programmes. The theory also suggests that although health may be a long-term gain following smoking cessation, we are largely influenced by shorter-term benefits. Accordingly, smoking cessation programmes should highlight the short-term benefits of stopping smoking as well as the long-term health gains.

Finally, the emphasis of theory on the role of environmental triggers to behaviours such as smoking indicates the benefit of modifying the environment in the early days of smoking cessation to either minimise the number of cues to smoking a person may experience, or plan specific strategies on how to deal with any urges to smoke as a consequence of such cues should they occur.

These factors have not designed an intervention programme, but they provide a good framework, based on first principles, on which to base any smoking cessation programme. We now consider how two theories may inform our understanding of an individual's response to a set of symptoms and how they can determine the types of intervention we conduct.

Some of the first theoretically driven interventions involved changing patients' inappropriate responses to their illness – and in particular the pain they were experiencing (see also Chapter 16 ☛). Seminal work by Fordyce (1982) was influenced by learning theory and used operant conditioning techniques to influence patients' pain-related behaviour. Fordyce argued that our response to pain is determined by both internal sensations of pain and the environmental contingencies any pain-related behaviour provokes. He noted that some individuals responded to pain with either an exaggerated response (groans of pain, winces, and so on) or an absence of behaviour (avoidance of behaviours that may result in pain). Both of these responses may result in

poor outcomes. Exaggerated responses may result in over-medication, as carers and health professionals respond to these pain behaviours; avoidance behaviours may result in a reduction in physical capacity. Fordyce argued that rather than treat the pain, which we cannot see and evaluate, we should instead manage the pain-related behaviours by either administering pain relief on a regular basis, ignoring (not reinforcing) pain behaviours, and/or rewarding (reinforcing) appropriate behaviours such as engagement in physical activity. He showed in a series of elegant case reports how these simple interventions could significantly alter quite marked inappropriate use of pain medication.

More recent influences on the practice of health-care practitioners have been based on cognitive models of how we respond to and cope with serious illnesses. Leventhal's self-regulation theory (see Chapter 9 ☛), for example, suggests we generate a set of beliefs, or more technically we appraise the nature of our symptoms in terms of what illness they are associated with, its consequences, curability and so on. As in broader theories of emotion, this appraisal determines our emotional reaction to the illness. Although Leventhal does not specify the appraisal–emotion links, other theories (e.g. Lazarus 1999) make the links for us. Appraisals of an illness as serious and out of our control may be associated with the emotions of anxiety and depression. Appraisals of an illness as serious but controllable may be associated with some anxiety, but also optimism and hope. Appraisals also determine our behavioural response to the illness. Appraisals that an illness is long-term and untreatable, for example, may result in different behaviours to appraisals that the illness will quickly go and is easily treatable. Self-regulation theory also suggests that coping is elicited by our emotional response to a situation – and in particular a negative emotional response. The coping strategies we adopt, whether emotion- or problem-focused, are designed to moderate negative emotions. Accordingly, someone who has had a myocardial infarction may choose to exercise or stop smoking – acts that will both help reduce risk for disease progression and reduce anxieties associated with such risk. Another individual may avoid exercise, as the sensations they experience while doing so remind them of their illness and the threat it carries to their health. The actions we take at this time are triggered by our emotional response, but guided by our cognitive appraisal of the illness. As we have seen in Chapter 11 ☞, where the coping responses match the reality of the situation, they are likely to be effective and appropriate. Where there is a mismatch between appraisals and reality, inappropriate coping strategies may be evoked. Worse, inappropriate coping may lead to poor emotional and health states, and lead to a downward cycle of negative expectations and responses to illness. We need to know more about these various steps. However, the basic framework enables effective theoretically driven interventions. For example, we know that any intervention designed to optimise patients' responses to the onset of illness may benefit from a number of elements, including:

● Identification of illness beliefs and attempts to change them if they are either inadequate or incorrect – see for example, the work of Petrie *et al.* with cardiac patients described in Chapter 17 ☞. The intervention may involve the use of cognitive restructuring techniques described in Chapter 13 ☞.

● Teaching coping skills to help people cope more effectively with the stress of living with a serious illness. Encourage the use of problem-focused coping as appropriate in order to facilitate active attempts to enhance control over the illness and emotion-focused coping strategies or skills such as mindfulness to provide ways of reducing any emotional distress the individual may experience.

● Behavioural hypothesis testing (see Chapter 13 ☞) to disconfirm any inappropriate beliefs an individual may hold.

Again, the theory does not provide an individualised intervention, but it does provide a structure around which such an intervention may be designed.

The wider social and psychological environment may also be invaluable in facilitating and maintaining behavioural change. Such interventions draw on models of family dynamics, as we discuss in Chapter 15 ☞, and may involve a less individualised approach to behaviour change than is usually the case. These models may be particularly pertinent in the context of changing young people's behaviour (although we would argue that sim-

ilar issues could usefully be considered in many interventions to change older people's behaviour). DiMatteo (2004a), for example, highlighted the following factors that should be considered when attempting to do so:

● building trust between health professional, young patient and parent through supportive and sensitive interactions and discussion of perspectives on treatment needs and goals;

● the consideration of specific beliefs and attitudes about treatment needs and goals, including areas of discrepancy between young person and parent, and in particular identifying the young person's health beliefs;

● identification and discussion of norms and expectations in relation to the desired behaviour that the young person is exposed to: for example, parental adherence behaviour and treatment anxieties, cultural and social norms of treatment adherence;

● gaining and encouraging family commitment to treatment and within-family communication if problems with treatment arise by providing social support, possibly via illness-specific support groups;

● working together to overcome barriers and increase belief in the ability of the young person to make any required behavioural changes (self-efficacy);

● tailoring wherever possible the treatment regime to the lifestyles of the family unit.

After reading this text, you may think that the issues raised here are obvious, and surely must be taken into account when health professionals develop their interventions in the 'real world'. But this is far from the case, as we highlight in IN THE SPOTLIGHT and in the following section. Thus, a key future issue for health psychology is to continue developing relevant theories and interventions based upon them – particularly interventions that are 'doable' within the context of busy health professionals (we return to this issue later) – and also to consider ways in which the implementation of these interventions can be encouraged. We turn to this issue in the next section.

IN THE SPOTLIGHT

Who uses research?

As we discuss in the text, one of the key issues in health psychology is how to link theory to practice. This is a particularly salient issue in public health initiatives as relatively few health psychologists work directly in health promotion. Furthermore, much of the research reported by health psychologists is in the journals they read. How much these journals are read by others, such as health promotion practitioners – and how much of what they read is translated into actual practice – is questionable.

This issue was highlighted in a paper published by Abraham *et al.* (2002), who performed a content analysis on safer-sex promotion leaflets used in the UK and Germany. They first identified the types of information that we know from theory and/or empirical data are likely to influence behaviour. They then examined the frequency with which these types of information were presented in their sample of safer-sex leaflets. Of the 20 categories of information they identified as influencing behaviour, only one-quarter of the leaflets used text that referred to more than ten. Two-thirds of the leaflets used two or less of these information categories. These data highlight a key issue facing health psychology – how to influence people involved in the health-care system, whether in prevention or treatment of illness. Without this influence, our research is of little or no benefit to health professionals and those they seek to care for.

Getting evidence into practice

Having considered how psychological theory can guide the development of clinical and preventive interventions, we now consider how health psychologists and others may facilitate the application of these interventions with relevant client groups. Nowadays, clinicians of all types do not have the luxury of trying out or using interventions that they 'like' or 'feel' may be effective. Increasingly, we are constrained by guidelines and limits of acceptable interventions. All clinicians working within modern health-care systems necessarily engage in what is known as evidence-based practice. We use, or at least we should use, interventions or techniques for which there is good evidence of effectiveness. The intervention studies reported in this book have contributed to the knowledge upon which this evidence is based. But simply doing and reporting the research may not be sufficient for psychologists and others to make a contribution to health care. One key issue that all researchers need to address is how our research can effectively influence the process of health care.

The role of health psychologists

In the light of the significant research conducted by health psychologists, it would seem reasonable that health psychologists should be able to apply their theoretical and practical knowledge within the health-care system. Certainly the British Psychological Society (BPS) thought so when it facilitated the development of the profession of health psychologists by first stimulating and then evaluating and accrediting training programmes in this emerging discipline. Of particular note in this context is that a wider body, known as the Health Professions Council (HPC) has also began to accredit and register individuals as practitioner psychologists, with a specialty in health psychology. Thus, in the UK, there are two boards (BPS and HPC) that now confer a professional qualification that allows the individual to work as a health psychologist – albeit one with doctoral level training (through BPS training programmes) and one that requires a master's-level degree plus supervised experience (the HPC route).

The BPS Division of Health Psychology identifies the key roles of health psychologists as people who apply psychological research and methods to:

- the promotion and maintenance of health;
- the prevention and management of illness;

- the identification of psychological factors contributing to physical illness;
- the improvement of the health-care system;
- the formulation of health policy.

They also note that the types of questions addressed by health psychologists include:

- How do people adapt to chronic illness?
- What factors influence healthy eating?
- How is stress linked to heart disease?
- Why do patients often not take their medication as prescribed?

Health psychologists work as applied psychologists, teachers, consultants and researchers within a variety of settings such as the NHS, higher education, health promotion, schools or industry. Prospects, the official UK graduate careers website, states that the typical work activities of health psychologists include:

- using psychological theories and interventions for primary prevention and health-related behaviour change in community and workplace settings to reduce health-damaging behaviour;
- encouraging the uptake of health-enhancing behaviour and psychological approaches to health promotion,

improving communication between health-care professionals and patients;

- investigating cognitive processes, which mediate and determine health and illness behaviours;
- looking at the psychological impact of acute and chronic illness on individuals and their families to improve quality of life and reduce disability.

They also note that there has been a significant increase in the number of lectureships in health psychology, and growth in research into social and behavioural factors in health and health care. To gain a more detailed perspective on the role and type of job conducted by members of the Division of Health Psychology, the division conducted a survey of all its members – of whom roughly one-quarter responded. A total of 58 per cent of the survey responders were chartered (i.e. professionally qualified), and one-quarter were also chartered to another discipline of psychology. Just over half the respondents were currently working within the university sector, while 9 per cent were in the NHS in secondary health-care services (usually hospitals) and clinical (direct patient contact) posts. A further 6 per cent of respondents were working in areas such as the prison service, charities, the civil service, research councils and self-employment. Of those working in the NHS, 37 per cent

Plate 18.1 Get down with it!

Source: Alamy Images/Tetra Images.

were consultant psychologists (of whom many were consultant *clinical* psychologists), 20 per cent were lower-grade qualified psychologists, while 12 per cent were trainees and 4 per cent were psychology assistants. The types of work individuals engaged in differed, of course, according to work setting and grade. Of those in the NHS, over two-thirds conducted a clinical service, mostly in chronic illness management, while others worked in health promotion, consultancy, education and training, health service research, public health and non-physical health-related practice (e.g. mental health, counselling, learning disabilities). Academics were largely involved in research and teaching. Many of the more senior individuals in the NHS were probably clinical psychologists with joint membership of the divisions of clinical and health psychology. As the profession matures, the number of individuals with a solely health psychology qualification is likely to increase. The following case studies are examples of job descriptions of health psychologists provided by the Division of Health Psychology.

The Australian Psychology Society (APS) Division of Health Psychology has a similar training and work type as in the UK – but, interestingly, they include clinical work as a core element of their work (in the UK, clinical skills are seen as an additional rather than a core skill of the profession). The APS notes that health psychologists have knowledge and skills in the following areas:

- the interaction between the physical systems of the body, psychological make-up and social networks of friends and family and how they influence health and illness;
- the amount and type of health problems experienced by various groups in Australia;
- the way that people behave, or the underlying attitudes that put their health at risk and how they might change these behaviours to prevent illness and promote health;
- strategies that people can learn to help them cope with illness or associated problems and how they can involve their friends and family to help them in their recovery; and
- the psychological impact of illness.

They identify the areas of specialism of health psychologists as:

- Health promotion:
  ○ development and provision of programmes that assist in the prevention of illnesses such as heart attacks, stroke, cancer, sexually transmitted diseases, smoking-related illness and dietary-related problems;

CASE STUDY 1

National health service, consultant health psychologist

Location of job: Gloucestershire Hospitals NHS Foundation Trust
Job title: Consultant Health Psychologist

Main roles: Responsible for developing, leading, managing and providing the psychology service to Cardiac Medicine and Renal Medicine. Responsible for the coordination and management of the Health Psychology Department's (HPD) Clinical Governance agenda. Provides highly specialist psychological care (including individual and group interventions, consultative advice and supervision for colleagues, education of colleagues and service-based research) for patients with renal disease and coronary heart disease as part of the multi-disciplinary teams. Provides supervision, teaching and training and consultation to other health-care staff and organisations. Supervises doctoral trainees and newly qualified Clinical and Health psychologists. Member of the HPD Management Team which provides strategic and operational management of Health Psychology Services. Line-manages staff within the Renal and Cardiac Rehabilitation services (currently one Grade A Clinical Psychologist)

Participates in budgetary planning for the Renal and Cardiac Rehabilitation services.

CASE STUDY 2

Chartered health psychologist

Location of job: Working within the Public Health Directorate of an NHS Primary Care Trust
Job title: Head of Stop Smoking Services

Main roles: Managing and developing a stop smoking service. Applying research into practice. Determining levels of stop smoking treatment required according to local demand. Managing service budget. Ensuring that there is appropriate training available for health professionals and others regarding smoking cessation. Ensuring that trained staff receive appropriate ongoing professional development. Evaluating existing services and applying changes as necessary. Chairing the Primary Care Trust steering group for smoking cessation. Managing multi-disciplinary team of stop smoking advisers. Providing a health psychology input for other public health initiatives. Providing treatment services to people expressing an interest in stopping smoking. Liaising with other services within the Health Authority and Region to ensure exchange of information and coordinated service provision. Coordinating Continuing Professional Development provision for stop smoking staff within the Health Authority. Working on Pan-London initiatives to promote stop smoking services.

○ linking up with other health professionals to understand what behaviours might be contributing to illness and how they might be changed, e.g. understanding why some people overeat or eat a high-fat diet;

○ identifying how behaviour is linked with the development of disease and injury;

○ designing public health education programmes in areas such as exercise and alcohol, cigarette and drug consumption;

○ determining the distribution of disease and the health needs of differing communities;

○ working with community members to improve their health.

● Clinical health:

○ developing therapy and education programmes to help people cope with health issues such as weight management, cancer and heart health;

○ using psychological treatment for problems that often accompany ill health and injury, such as anxiety, depression, pain, addiction, sleep and eating problems;

○ understanding how psychological factors such as stress, depression and anxiety might be contributing to illness;

○ helping people with the self-management of chronic illness;

○ understanding how people cope with diagnosis and medical treatment of acute health problems and how they obtain medical care;

○ understanding how people cope with terminal illness, including the impact of grief, bereavement, death and dying;

○ identifying how the relationship between health professionals, such as doctors, nurses and psychologists, and their patients can influence how well they recover from illness and injury;

○ helping people cope with trauma, disability and rehabilitation.

Other countries have less developed professional roles for health psychologists. The Netherlands, for example, despite having a significant number of academic health psychologists, does not have a training programme for health psychologists – although they do have a two-year training programme for generic health professionals who may be involved in some of the work that health psychologists do in other countries. Similarly, in southern European countries such as Spain and Italy, while health psychology still remains a primarily academic subject, there is an increasing move to training health psychologists who can work in applied settings.

THE INTERVIEW

Here, PB talks with Dianne Harcourt, a past Chair of the British Psychological Society's Division of Health Psychology. She tells a little about her own career, before discussing the future of the profession of health psychology in the UK.

PB: Thanks for talking with me. Could you tell me a little bit about yourself.

DH: Thanks. Yes, I am a reader in health psychology at the University of the West of England in Bristol. I both teach health psychology and am co-director (with Nicola Rumsey) of the Centre for Appearance Research at UWE.

PB: Appearance research? How does this relate to health psychology?

DH: Well, my interest in appearance and health stems from my early career research. During my PhD I investigated how women with breast cancer felt when they were either diagnosed with cancer very quickly (in one day) or over a longer period of time. Working with these women, it became evident that very soon after they were diagnosed with cancer, they were being asked what sort of treatment they would like – total mastectomy, reconstructive surgery, and so on. I became interested in how these women made decisions that would affect their appearance in the long term so soon after having to deal with the shock of being diagnosed with cancer. This and other research I have been involved in draws a clear link between issues of both health and appearance.

PB: Thanks. What do you think are the achievements of health psychology in the last five years?

DH: Many! The academic strength of British health psychology is very strong, and I expect it to remain so. Many UK health psychologists are engaged in world leading research – and UK health psychology research has an excellent reputation across the world. Another success is that we now have many health psychology training programmes around the country, and health psychology is gradually raising its profile – lots of people want to do these courses. Another way that we are being successful is by raising the profile of health psychology at high levels such as the Department of Health – people

such as influential politicians and civil servants. We actually have very good links here, and people such as Charles Abrahams, Susan Michie, and Nicky Rumsey have had long-term contracts with the Department to provide advice and consultancy on a range of health psychology-relevant issues on behalf of the Division of Health Psychology. So, we are working to raise the profile of the profession in a number of key areas. One concern we did have was the impact that the development of the Health Professions Council would have on the Division of Health Psychology, the British Psychological Society – would people leave the BPS if they could become health psychologists without being a chartered member? – and the development of health psychology jobs. Well, so far so good! Membership of the Division of Health Psychology and BPS has actually risen over the last year or two. We still have to see the impact on training courses and jobs. Time will tell here.

PB: Thanks. Now the obverse . . . what do you think is the greatest challenge facing health psychology in the UK?

DH: The main challenge is to ensure that these people can get jobs as health psychologists. All of people that came through the UWE doctoral training programme have done well, and they have got jobs that involve psychology, but not many of them can actually call themselves health psychologists. We need to get more people to work in settings such as the NHS as health psychologists, to gain more a foothold so more managers learn about health psychology and are more likely to appoint health psychologists in the future. One way is to work with clinical psychologists – the other is to keep our contacts with the Department of Health – keep the profile of health psychology high. We have a strong practitioner base who are working on raising the profile of the profession in many ways – contacts with health service managers, running workshops and study days on health psychology, and so on. We need to keep the pressure on and to ensure good job prospects for the graduates of our training programmes.

PB: Dianne, thank you very much!

Other people 'do' psychology

Despite the developing profession of health psychologists within a number of health-care systems, all of whom will clearly utilise psychological theory and practice, there are still far too few qualified health psychologists (or other types of psychologist) to provide a service to all patients that may benefit from their work. In addition, there is a clear need for all health-care professionals to adopt psychologically sophisticated ways of working with patients. Accordingly, the application of the principles of care derived from health psychology research is very much in the hands of health professionals with no immediate alliance to psychology. In the absence of health psychologists, how can one ensure that the research conducted by health psychologists is taken into practice in the wider health-care system?

One way this can be achieved is through a key role of health psychologists employed within any health-care system – to teach other professions about the principles of health psychology, so their practice can be influenced by such knowledge. But how else can this information be disseminated? Unfortunately, at the present time, the answer to this question has to be 'With difficulty'. One acknowledged problem in influencing health professionals (including psychologists!) is the communication gap between researchers and practitioners – something that psychological research may particularly suffer from. Most health-care practitioners and managers rarely read journals which provide cutting-edge research on the delivery of health care – even within their own discipline. But, for psychology the communication problem may be even more acute. Nurses tend to read nursing journals, doctors read medical journals, and so on. Walk through most hospital libraries and you will not see a psychology journal. Yet most psychological research is published in psychology journals – not medical journals, and not nursing journals. As Richard Lazarus (2000: 667) noted, 'The lack of collaboration and communication between researcher and clinician . . . is a familiar and painful topic for most psychologists'. He went on to say that 'It is disheartening that so few researchers accept the responsibility of making the relevance of their research clear to the practitioner, and so few clinicians pay attention to such research even when it has implications for clinical practice'. Although Lazarus was referring primarily to the situation in the USA, his comments also reflect the situation elsewhere in the world.

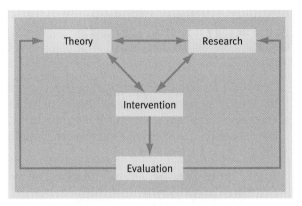

Figure 18.1 From theory to practice and back again.

If reaching and influencing individual health-care professionals is difficult, how *can* psychology influence health care? One way is to publish in relevant journals. Another is through its influence on higher integrative policies. Health-care professionals provide care. But the type of care they provide is constrained by a number of bodies external to them. A number of national psychology and other professional bodies have produced guidelines on psychological care, mostly (it must be admitted) in the treatment of mental health problems or more general therapy issues (working with young people, professional standards, and so on), but some of which may be relevant to the care of people with physical health problems. Even more influential than these, though, may be guidelines for care produced by governments and government-sponsored organisations (to which we provide some useful internet links at the end of the chapter). In the United Kingdom, for example, the National Institute for Health and Clinical Excellence (NICE: www.nice.org.uk/) is responsible for producing treatment guidelines for a variety of health conditions treated within the National Health Service. Still other bodies are responsible for ensuring that these guidelines are followed. These guidelines are the strongest influence on the nature of health care, and can be extremely detailed, noting the types of drugs and dosages that can be given, the types of psychological therapy that are considered effective and should be used (and for how long any form of therapy should last), and so on. Some of these guidelines have a strong focus on the treatment of psychological problems, such as anxiety, depression and PTSD or medical problems where there is an acknowledged role for psychological interventions, such as patients with cardiac disorders. Others deal with clearly medical issues such as anaemia in chronic kidney disease and caesarean section. However, even here psychological factors are acknowledged. The first page of text of the NICE guidelines for the 'treatment of acutely ill patients in hospital' runs as follows:

- This guideline offers best practice advice on the care of adult patients within the acute hospital setting. Treatment and care should take into account patients' needs and preferences. People with an acute illness should, if appropriate, have the opportunity to make informed decisions about their care and treatment, in partnership with their healthcare professionals . . .

- Good communication between healthcare professionals and patients is essential. It should be supported by evidence-based written information tailored to the patient's needs. Treatment and care, and the information patients are given about it, should be culturally appropriate. It should also be accessible to people with additional needs such as physical, sensory or learning disabilities, and to people who do not speak or read English.

- If the patient agrees, carers and relatives should have the opportunity to be involved in decisions about treatment and care. Carers and relatives should also be given the information and support they need.

The research reported in Chapter 10 (☛) has clearly contributed to this emphasis on good communication between health professionals and their patients. Clearly, health psychology has made a contribution, and an acknowledged contribution, to the care of critically ill patients through its influence on care guidelines. It has also contributed to more specific guidelines, including rehabilitation following myocardial infarction and the implantation of ICDs (see Chapter 17 (☛)). As guidelines develop for the care of patients with a variety of disorders, we can confidently expect psychological care and interventions to be integrated into them. But despite this optimism, our contribution may be far from optimal. And there is even evidence to show that inclusion within guidelines does not guarantee the implementation of any form of care.

Implementing (or not) clinical guidelines

Unfortunately, even when a fully informed evidence base and written guidelines of best practice exist, and therefore the gap between research and practice has theoret-

> **bronchiolitis**
>
> inflammation of the bronchioles, the smallest air passages of the lungs. It is a common childhood disorder.

ically been bridged, there is no guarantee that they will actually be implemented by the health professions concerned. Touzet *et al.* (2007), for example, reported on the impact of new guidelines for French doctors on the primary care of **bronchiolitis**. This study showed only a slight increase in adherence to the guidelines for the use of non-validated drugs (6.6 per cent adherence before and 14.3 per cent after), provision of general advice (29.0 per cent adherence before and 57.1 per cent after) and physical therapy (91.9 per cent adherence before and 98.8 per cent after). This finding is by no means unique – even asking staff to engage in relatively simple tasks such as hand-washing following patient contact has proven extremely difficult. The NHS Centre for Reviews and Dissemination report, *Effective Health Care: Getting Evidence into Practice* (1999) noted that 'Unless research-based evidence and guidance is incorporated into practice, efforts to improve the quality of care will be wasted. Implementing evidence may require health professionals to change long-held patterns of behaviour' (NHS Centre for Reviews and Dissemination 1999: 1). They highlighted the following factors that may reduce the uptake of clinical guidelines:

- weaknesses in communicating the evidence base to practitioners;

- conflicting sources of information and opinion being available to practitioners (such as patient preferences, which can contradict global recommendations);

- a tendency to individually tailor responses and make decisions that may not always adhere to guidelines;[1]

- difficulties in getting the right people to work together to implement change (for example, to involve a health promotion adviser in a general practice making changes aimed at improving smoking cessation);

---

[1] An interesting example of this can be found in the clinical work of a professor of general practice known by one of the authors who has written several articles arguing that general practitioners should not prescribe antibiotics to people with a cold, as there is no infection to treat, and the cause is a virus. He nevertheless does occasionally prescribe antibiotics at such a time 'just to be sure', despite no evidence of infection.

● resistance to change, which is amplified by health professionals' stress levels.

Other factors include:

● *personal attitudes and beliefs* regarding the *target behaviour* (their own and/or the patients' behaviour), the *treatment* (for example, attitudes towards HRT – hormone replacement therapy – chemotherapy, child immunisation, abortion) and the *condition* (e.g. obesity, drug use, heart disease, AIDS, chronic fatigue syndrome);

● *personal characteristics of the professional*: age, gender, culture and ethnic values or norms may all impact on the willingness to make any required changes;

● *information content*: any changes will not be implemented if they are not seen as credible or applicable to health professionals, patients or patient groups;

● *information transfer*: deficient communication of information due to the problems of communication within a large and complex organisation such as a hospital or health-care system;

● *transferability*: staff may argue that 'what works in research may not work in practice';

● *environmental/organisational issues*: staff may consider there not to be enough time, staff, or support in making any changes to their practice. They may also consider the changes to be too expensive.

Given these broad-ranging potential weaknesses in the system, it is not surprising that efforts are being made to try to address this situation. However, simply providing research information alone has been shown to be insufficient to alter an individual practitioner's health practice. Oxman *et al.* (1995), for example, reviewed 102 studies of interventions to improve health-care delivery, and found that interventions in which information on 'what to do' was distributed passively to health professionals showed little evidence that the health professionals had adopted the recommended changes to their practice. More recently, things seem to have improved – although performance following more structured interventions is far from optimal. Doherty *et al.* (2007), for example, reported increases in various aspects of the treatment of adults with asthma varying from 0 to 26 per cent (deliver therapy via a spacer device), 66 to 84 per cent (use systemic steroids), and 14 to 82 per cent (use written short-term plans) following a mail-out of guideline

booklets, and placing posters with flow charts in the clinical setting. No changes were found in a hospital which did not receive this intervention. These results show both the existing low levels of adherence to the guidelines and how a relatively simple intervention may markedly increase adherence. In another context, Vikman *et al.* (2004) reported only modest increases in adherence to guidelines for the treatment of high-risk cardiac patients. Nevertheless, the changes that were made did result in improved survival rates.

The need for health psychologists to engage politically

Health psychologists need to engage in appropriate dissemination to health-care practitioners and, ideally, to policy makers – and need to become better at it. Having greater professional 'status', as implied in the British example of stage 2 professional recognition, for example (see companion website), and the increasing presence of health psychology 'practitioners' in health-care settings, will go some way towards making health psychology voices 'heard'. However, there is some concern that psychologists are reluctant to use their carefully collected evidence to provide 'guidelines' for practice. Johnson (1999) suggested that this wariness is, in part, due to psychologists' training in being critically aware of limitations in a knowledge base; for example, we typically encourage students (and subsequently researchers) to become increasingly critical in their thinking and in their interpretation of research methodologies and evidence. Johnson concluded that: 'I sometimes think we spend more time criticizing each other than we do promoting our accomplishments. In the meantime, other health professionals are more than willing to write practice guidelines and identify standards of care in areas where psychology has greater expertise' (p. 330). To 'sell' our findings to practitioners and policy makers, we need to have confidence in both our findings and ourselves.

In addition to learning how to better 'sell' the findings of health psychology research to health professions and policy makers, Murray and Campbell (2003) argued that health psychologists need to engage more effectively at a socio-political level. To do so, they argued, health psychology needs to broaden its approaches to encompass sociocultural, economic and political aspects of health and health care. (This book has acknowledged

Plate 18.2 To make an increasing difference to the health of our nations, health psychologists need to disseminate their findings to a wide audience, including health professionals, educators and policy makers.

Source: Corbis/Dave and Les Jacobs/Blend Images.

this need in a whole chapter addressing social inequalities in health, and integrated elsewhere in the book are many of the criticisms targeted at mainstream health psychologists by critical health psychologists.) The perception of psychology, and by default, health psychology, is that we develop and test our theories and methods at an individual level. This traditional narrowness of focus has, Murray and Campbell noted, held back the effectiveness of strategies to improve health on a large scale (such as reducing HIV infection in sub-Saharan Africa, promoting healthier diets in the West), because salient aspects of the micro and macro socio-economic and political environment that act to maintain inequalities in health are ignored. Health psychology, Murray and Campbell proposed, needs to engage in some reflection in order to move forward in a more 'actionable' manner. Schwarz and Carpenter (1999, cited in Davey-Smith *et al.* 2001) also noted that focusing on individual-level determinants of health instead of macro-level determinants (such as income or poverty levels) leads to individualised interventions that fail to address the question, or the solution, appropriately.

WHAT DO YOU THINK?

So, what do you think? How *should* psychology and psychologists attempt to influence key players both in health care and other spheres? What can individuals do to disseminate good psychological practice? And what should learned and professional bodies do to promote the discipline? Who are the key players psychologists should influence? Should they seek allies in other health professions, such as nurses or occupational therapists, disciplines for which psychology is a core element of their work? Should we influence politicians, leaders of health services, or others? Who would you target as people or positions to influence, and how would you set about this?

Keep it simple

One key element that has only briefly been touched upon in this chapter is that interventions are more likely to be implemented by both health professionals and their clients if they are relatively simple and easy to implement. One of the authors of this book (PB) was made acutely aware of this in a discussion with colleagues in an academic department of General Practice in which he was working at the time. He was thinking of researching a group intervention targeted at depressed cardiac patients to see whether it would reduce both depression and the incidence of recurrent myocardial infarction (see Chapter 17 ☞). The discussion revolved around whether it would be better to run the groups in the weeks immediately after the intervention (and therefore be able to prevent any depression becoming chronic, but also risk treating people who would naturally recover without any intervention) or wait for six months and treat people whose depression had become chronic (and potentially harder to treat). Unfortunately, the debate was rather cut short when one of the GPs noted that even if such an intervention were to work, there are so few psychologists who would be able to run such groups (and no likely funding within the NHS) that no GP would be able to send their patients to it! As a result of this discussion, PB went on to develop a one-page written intervention, based around active distraction, designed to reduce distress in women undergoing genetic risk assessment (Bennett *et al.* 2007).

Whatever the impact of this discussion on PB's career, the discussion held a key truth. Psychologists and others can develop many and complex interventions, but unless they are implementable within the context of a busy, and tightly resourced health-care service (as they all are), they will not be taken up by health-care professionals, and managers will not fund them. Interventions such as the Recurrent Coronary Prevention Program (which worked) and the ENRICHD study (which didn't) described in Chapter 17 ☞ may show the potential impact of complex and extended psychological interventions on health. But even if both had proved enormously successful, neither would be implemented in most existing health services. Interventions such as establishing implementation intentions, as discussed in Chapter 6 ☞, or using simple distraction techniques to reduce worry may be less glamorous than these hugely expensive multi-factorial studies, but they may ultimately be of more benefit. The issue that has to be considered when developing any intervention is not only is it effective, but also is it *cost-effective*? Because only if it is cost-effective will both health-care providers and bodies that provide guidance to health-care providers (such as NICE) endorse the use of such interventions. Accordingly, health psychologists may usefully concentrate on this type of intervention if they want their interventions to be of value in the health-care system.

RESEARCH FOCUS

Theory should guide our interventions

Lopez,, L.M., Tolley, E., Grimes, D.A. *et al.* (2009). Theory-based interventions for contraception. *Cochrane Database of Systematic Reviews* issue 1, art. no.: CD007249. doi: 10.1002/14651858.CD007249.

The authors note that theory-based interventions are likely to be more effective than atheoretical interventions. They also note that while many HIV prevention programmes have been based on theoretical models, many educational interventions addressing contraception in the absence of HIV have not been theoretically based. The review aimed to identify which trials aimed at increasing contraceptive use had or had not used a psychosocial theory to guide their intervention, and to assess their relative effectiveness.

Method

The authors searched computerised databases for trials involving theoretically derived interventions to increase contraceptive use. Databases were: MEDLINE, POPLINE, CENTRAL, PsycINFO, EMBASE, ClinicalTrials.gov, and International Clinical Trials Registry Platform. They also wrote to researchers to identify other trials. Primary outcomes included pregnancy, choice of contraceptive, and adherence to contraceptive regimen. Secondary outcomes included knowledge of, and attitudes toward, contraception. Key search terms included (as examples): contraception/contraception behavior/contraceptive device AND theor*/model/construct AND educat*/randomized controlled trial/clinical trial/.

One author went through all the abstracts this search identified to determine their relevance to the review. A second author checked that the reports identified as relevant fit the criteria for review and analysis. Of those considered relevant to the review, they both independently extracted key data and checked this for accuracy. Data was stored in the Cochrance database programme, RevMan 5. This included: 'dose information' (e.g. length and number of sessions of any intervention), theoretical basis of the intervention (see Table 1), and outcomes (as summarised above). The strength of the research methodology was also rated, based on criteria including: whether or not there was appropriate randomisation, whether allocation to condition was blind, and the numbers of participants dropping out from the study.

Table 1 Examples of studies and theories identified by the search strategy

Study	Theory or model	Principles or constructs
Black 2006	Social cognitive theory	Skills, cultural norms, goal-setting, self-efficacy, modelling, family support and mentoring relationships
Coyle 2006	Social cognitive theory, theory of reasoned action, and theory of planned behaviour	Knowledge, attitudes, norms, self-efficacy, sense of vulnerability, risk, skills
Dilorio 2006	(a) Social cognitive theory (b) Problem behaviour theory	(a) knowledge, skills, environmental supports, values, peer influences, goal-setting (b) Co-occurring behaviours, at-risk behaviours, psychological attributes or predisposition
Floyd 2007	Motivational interviewing; Transtheoretical model	Client-centred, decisional balance, readiness to change, goal statements and change plans, personalised feedback, problem-solving, commitment to change
Ingersoll 2005	Motivational interviewing	Risk behaviour; exercises (decisional balance, development of goal statements and change plans); feedback using 'elicit–provide–elicit strategy'.
Jemmott 2007	Social cognitive theory, adapted	Personal vulnerability, self-efficacy, negotiation, skills
Kiene 2006	Motivational interviewing; Stages of change (from Transtheoretical model)	Information, motivation, behavioural skills, readiness to change, goal-setting
Morrison-Beedy 2005	Information–Motivation–Behavioural skills model	Risk information, motivation, behaviour change, self-efficacy, reinforcement, social norms
Peipert 2008	Transtheoretical model of behaviour change	Stages of change (contemplation, preparation, action, maintenance); decisional balance, self-efficacy, processes of change
Petersen 2007	Motivational interviewing	Empathy, self-efficacy, perceived barriers, motivation, stage of adopting, improving communication
Ross 2007	Social learning theory	Knowledge and beliefs about risks and behaviours, perceived susceptibility, perceived benefits of safer behaviour, self-efficacy, social support, skills acquisition
Roye 2007	Social cognitive theory; Theory of reasoned action; Health belief model	Risk, perceived susceptibility, perceived barriers, role models, skill-building, intention to perform behaviour
Stanton 2004	Protection motivation theory	Threat appraisal: extrinsic and intrinsic rewards, perceived severity and vulnerability; coping appraisal: self-efficacy, response efficacy, response cost
Villarruel 2006	Social cognitive theory; Theory of reasoned action and Theory of planned behaviour	Knowledge, attitudes, behavioural and normative beliefs, self-efficacy, skills, cultural concepts (gender-role expectations and values)

Results

The literature search identified 26 trials, of which 18 randomised participants into various conditions, and 8 assigned participants in a so-called cluster randomised trial. A total of 24 were conducted in the USA, one in Scotland and one in Tanzania. Participants were recruited from a number of sources, including primary care, family planning clinics, schools and universities. Four trials focused on reducing pregnancy, eight focused on preventing Sexually Transmitted Diseases (STDs) or HIV transmission, and thirteen addressed reducing risk for STDs and HIV. One addressed multiple risks associated with sexual risk behaviour. The number of contacts with participants varied between one and four, with eleven studies having six or more sessions. Follow-up ranged from 1 to 36 months, but was most frequently 6–12 months. Comparisons between interventions did not involve meta-analysis, as the interventions grouped under each theoretical approach. However, they grouped similar interventions in smaller analyses where they could. Key results by theoretical basis for intervention are reported:

Social cognitive theory

Of 12 trials with interventions based on SCT, 10 had some positive results for the experimental group (in brackets is the number of studies to report effect):

● Compared to usual care, SCT had fewer second births (1), more contraceptive use (other than condoms) (1), and more reported condom use (4).

● SCT intervention resulted in a greater percentage of sex acts protected in the short-term than minimal or no intervention (1)

● SCT resulted in more condom use than 'health promotion intervention' (2)

● Better condom use was reported for a skill-based program than an information-based one (2)

● Group information was not as effective as individualised information (1)

Motivational interviewing

Of 7 trials using MI, 5 reported positive effects:

● Compared to health promotion, MI group reported more condom use and knowledge (1).

● Compared to minimal information, MI group reported less 'ineffective contraception' (1) and more 'effective contraception' (1).

Discussion

The authors concluded that compared to no-intervention or simple educational interventions, significantly greater change was found in two-thirds of the interventions on measures of condom use and about half of the programmes addressing use of other contraceptives. Unfortunately, some trials used parts of theories or models, while others combined various models, making it hard to determine what may have worked. Due to the small number of trials in each intervention group, combining interventions based on several theories, and the heterogeneity of interventions based on each theory, it proved difficult to make strong conclusions about what the best intervention components were. Further research would benefit from interventions based on only one theory, and with well-defined components. In addition, only two trials were conducted outside of the USA; theory-based interventions should be adapted to other cultural settings. For results to be useful, careful documentation and better reporting are needed on the research design, the theory or principles incorporated, and the intervention implementation.

. . . and finally, be positive

While this textbook has highlighted many of the challenges faced by our discipline (such as definitional clarity, choice of assessment techniques and tools, inclusion and consideration of sociocultural influences on health and illness), it has highlighted the many domains in which health psychology has contributed significantly to understanding (e.g. health behaviour and behaviour change, stress and coping, illness processes and outcomes, psychosocial interventions). There is a lot to be positive about, but clearly not complacent, and many questions remain. For example, do implementation intentions work in clinical samples? Do stage-based activity interventions work in the long term? Does coping really make a difference? Much of health psychology tends to focus on problems – preventing illness, coping with illness, and so on. As well as being optimistic in ourselves, we can also learn from developments in the field of 'positive psychology' (e.g. Seligman and Csikszentmihalyi 2000), which bring with them many other opportunities for health psychology to strengthen its evidence base – see Chapters 11 and 12 ☛. Research in the 'positive psychology' tradition has shown that out of many potentially negative situations come positives (for example, reaffirmed love, or the discovery of unknown personal strengths, caused by entering a spousal caring role), and that positive affect and the finding of 'meaning' in stressful situations can be adaptational (e.g. Folkman and Moscowitz 2000). Underlying many psychosocial interventions to improve adjustment or behavioural change has been the assumption that certain stressors (e.g. illness, caring) inevitably elicit negative affect and cognition, and that these need to be reduced in order to improve outcome. In contrast, positive psychology encourages thinking to turn to enhancement of positive affect (particularly that which is congruent with one's current situation), such as hope or optimism in a situation where goals are attainable, humour or positive reappraisal where goals are not so easily reached. A good example of how health psychology may provide a biased or distorted view of the impact of health problems can be found in the work examining the impact of cancer genetic risk identification. The

work here has consistently found that around one-quarter of the women that undergo assessment for their risk of breast/ovarian cancer experience significant distress (see Chapter 6 ☛). However, a study of this group conducted by one of the authors (PB) found that the most highly endorsed emotional responses to this process included anxiety, but also included the more positive emotions related to hope, challenge and optimism. The neglect of such issues means we run the risk of pathologising many of the phenomena we study, and ignore many of the positive and human aspects they bring. Furthermore, in the area of preventive health, health psychology research has identified 'protective' factors for health as well as risk factors for morbidity. Think, for example, of the research supporting positive associations between social support, or optimism, and positive adjustment to stressful events. Such findings provide opportunities for interventions that are quite different in emphasis from those offered by the findings of negative associations between hostility, stress responses and coronary heart disease. We must not fall into the trap of assuming that we can only advise on 'what not to do'.

Health psychology will not stand still. Its contribution to the health of society is likely to grow as our knowledge base and our confidence in it grows, and as external bodies grow in confidence as to the important role psychology has to play in relation to health. Keep in touch via our website. New developments in the professional and academic practice of this discipline will be highlighted and updated annually on the companion website to this text: www.pearsoned.co.uk/morrison.

SUMMARY

This final chapter has attempted to draw together much of the work described in this book and to give the reader a picture of the ways in which health psychology research can contribute to health practice. Although health psychology is a theory-led discipline, its goals are applied, and we have attempted in this chapter to make the links between theory and practice evident. In addition, we have noted that there is a need for health psychologists to engage more politically and to 'sell' themselves and their (cost-effective) 'goods' more effectively to policy makers and health practitioners. In doing so, we would hope to maximise the impact of health psychology as a discipline upon health psychology as a practice. Our final aim should be to strengthen the links between health psychology and health professional practice in order to benefit all of us, who will at some point in our lives enter the health-care system.

Further reading

De Ridder, D. and de Wit, J. (2006). *Self-regulation in Health Behavior*. New York: Wiley-Blackwell.

This text describes self-regulation theories in relation to both the engagement in various health-related behaviours and interventions based upon these theories and their related assumptions.

Rutter, D. and Quine, L. (2002). *Changing Health Behaviour*. Buckingham: Open University Press.

This well-written text highlights many areas of intervention in which health and social psychologists have been at the forefront. Chapters describe specific theory-based interventions including those directed at safer sex practices, smoking cessation, reduced fat intake, uptake of screening for colorectal or cervical cancer, the use of cycling helmets by schoolchildren and pedestrian safety. It also includes a useful chapter by Steve Sutton that raises some of the difficulties in turning research findings into effective interventions.

The Improved Clinical Effectiveness through Behavioural Research Group (ICEBeRG) (2006). Designing theoretically-informed implementation interventions. *Implementation Science*, 1: 4.

A freely accessible paper examining issues in the translation of psychological theory to psychological practice.

Eccles, M., Grimshaw, J., Walker, A., Johnston, M. and Pitts, N. (2005). Changing the behavior of healthcare professionals: the use of theory in promoting the uptake of research findings. *Journal of Clinical Epidemiology*, 58, 107–12.

Another paper examining how to translate theory to practice in the context of health professional behaviour.

In addition to these static texts, it may be interesting to go to websites describing developments in the profession of health psychology. Some examples of such sites (extant in 2012) are:

The Australian Psychological Society:

www.psychology.org.au/community/specialist/health

The site provides a description of the role of health psychologists, as seen by the APS.

The British Psychological Society:

www.bps.org.uk/careers/accredited-courses/accredited-courses_home.cfm

This takes you to a description of a variety of UK postgraduate courses, including training in health psychology.

Health Psychology Update:

www.health-psychology.org.uk/menuItems/HPUpdate.php

This is the newsletter of the BPS Division of Health Psychology. One step back and you are in the main site of the British Division of Health Psychology, which may be worth keeping up with.

The European Health Psychology Society:

www.ehps.net/

This introductory page to EHPS, leads to information about access to conferences and other potentially relevant information. Of particular note is that it also allows access to the EHPS's newsletter, *The European Health Psychologist*, which regularly presents updates on the professional developments in health psychology within Europe.

The International Society of Behavioral Medicine:

www.isbm.info/

According to the ISBM, 'Behavioral Medicine is the interdisciplinary field concerned with the development and integration of behavioral, psychosocial, and biomedical science knowledge and techniques relevant to the understanding of health and illness, and the application of this knowledge and these techniques to prevention, diagnosis, treatment and rehabilitation.' As such, it has much in common with the applied end of health psychology (and much that is different). The website may be of interest.

Some sources of published clinical guidelines. These are central government resourced guideline resources. Other guidelines may be produced by (usually) specific medical organisations involved in the treatment of specific disorders. Psychology guidelines tend to be more general, and not specific to conditions or types of intervention:

www.nhmrc.gov.au/publications/subjects/clinical.htm (Australia)
www.nice.org.uk/ (England)
www.sign.ac.uk/guidelines/published/index.html (Scotland)
www.guideline.gov/ (USA)

Visit the website at **www.pearsoned.co.uk/morrison** for additional resources to help you with your study, including multiple choice questions, weblinks and flashcards.

Glossary

A

acceptance coping: accepting the reality of a situation and that it cannot easily be changed.

ACE inhibitors: angiotensin II causes the muscles surrounding blood vessels to contract and thereby narrows the blood vessels. Angiotension Converting Enzyme (ACE) inhibitors decrease the production of angiotensin II, allowing blood vessels to dilate, and reduce blood pressure.

acetylcholine: a white crystalline derivative of choline that is released at the ends of nerve fibres in the parasympathetic nervous system and is involved in the transmission of nerve impulses in the body.

adrenal glands: endocrine glands, located above each kidney. Comprises the cortex, which secretes several steroid hormones, and the medulla, which secretes noradrenaline.

adrenaline: a neurotransmitter and hormone secreted by the adrenal medulla that increases physiological activity in the body, including stimulation of heart action and an increase in blood pressure and metabolic rate. Also known as epinephrine.

aetiology (etiology): the cause of disease.

affective: to do with affect or mood and emotions.

age-specific mortality: typically presented as the number of deaths per 100,000, per annum, according to certain age groups, for example comparing rates of death from cancer in 2001 between those aged 45–54 with those aged 55–64.

agonist: a drug that simulates the effects of neurotransmitters, such as the serotonin agonist fluoxetine, which induces satiety (reduces hunger).

Alcoholics Anonymous: a worldwide self-help organisation for people with alcohol-related problems. Based on the belief that alcoholism is a physical, psychological and spiritual illness and can be controlled by abstinence. The twelve steps provide a framework for achieving this.

ambivalence: the simultaneous existence of both positive and negative evaluations of an attitude object, which could be both cognitive and emotional.

ambulatory blood pressure: blood pressure measured over a period of time using an automatic blood pressure monitor which can measure blood pressure while the individual wearing it engages in their everyday activities.

angina: severe pain in the chest associated with a temporary insufficient supply of blood to the heart.

antibodies: immunoglobulins produced in response to an antigen.

antigen: unique protein found on the surface of a pathogen that enables the immune system to recognise that pathogen as a foreign substance and therefore produce antibodies to fight it. Vaccinations introduce specially prepared viruses or bacteria into a body, and these have antigens.

antioxidants: oxidation of low-density lipoprotein (LDL or 'bad') cholesterol has been shown to be important in the development of fatty deposits in the arteries; antioxidants are chemical properties (polyphenols) of some substances (e.g. red wine) thought to inhibit the process of oxidation.

antiretroviral drugs: drugs that prevent the reproduction of a type of virus known as a retrovirus. Most well known in the treatment of HIV.

aorta: the main trunk of the systemic arteries, carrying blood from the left side of the heart to the arteries of all limbs and organs except the lungs.

appraisals: interpretations of situations, events or behaviour that a person makes.

arteriosclerosis: loss of elasticity and hardening of the arteries.

atheroma: fatty deposit in the intima (inner lining) of an artery.

atherosclerosis: formation of fatty plaque in the arteries.

atopic dermatitis: a number of conditions, including eczema, involving an inflammatory response of the skin.

atrial fibrillation: a heart rhythm disorder (arrhythmia). It involves a very rapid heart rate, in which the atria (upper chambers of the heart) contract in a very rapid and disorganised manner and fail to pump blood effectively through the heart.

attention: generally refers to the selection of some stimuli over others for internal processing.

attributions: a person's perceptions of what causes beliefs, feelings, behaviour and actions (based on attribution theory).

autoimmune conditions: a group of diseases, including type 1 diabetes, Crohn's disease and rheumatoid arthritis, characterised by abnormal functioning of the immune system in which it produces antibodies against its own tissues – it treats 'self' as 'non-self'.

avoidant coping: a style of coping that involves emotional regulation by avoiding confrontation with a stressful situation. Analogous to emotion-focused coping.

B

bad news (interview): conversation between health professional (usually a doctor) and patient in which they are told 'bad news', usually that their illness has a very poor prognosis and they may die.

baroreceptors: sensory nerve endings that are stimulated by changes in pressure. Located in the walls of blood vessels such as the carotid sinus.

B cell: a form of lymphocyte involved in destruction of antigens. Memory B cells provide long-term immunity against previously encountered pathogens.

behavioural immunogen: a behavioural practice considered to be health-protective, e.g. exercise.

behavioural pathogen: a behavioural practice thought to be damaging to health, e.g. smoking.

behaviourism: the belief that psychology is the study of observables and therefore that behaviour, not mental processes, is central.

benefit-finding: a process of finding beneficial outcomes as a consequence of what is normally seen as a negative event, such as developing cancer or being infected with the HIV.

beta-blockers: block the action of epinephrine and norepinephrine on ß-adrenergic receptors, which mediate the 'fight or flight' response, within the heart and in muscles surrounding the arteries. In doing so, they reduce increases in blood pressure associated with sympathetic activation.

bile: a digestive juice, made in the liver and stored in the gallbladder. Involved in the digestion of fats in the small intestine.

biofeedback: technique of using monitoring devices to provide information regarding an autonomic bodily function, such as heart rate or blood pressure. Used in an attempt to gain some voluntary control over that function.

biomedical model: a view that diseases and symptoms have an underlying physiological explanation.

biopsy: the removal of a small piece of tissue for microscopic examination and/or culture, usually to help to make a diagnosis.

biopsychosocial: a view that diseases and symptoms can be explained by a combination of physical, social, cultural and psychological factors (cf. Engel 1977).

blunters: a general coping style that involves minimising or avoiding the source of threat or stress, i.e. avoiding threat-relevant information (as opposed to **monitors**).

body mass index: a measurement of the relative percentages of fat and muscle mass in the human body, in which weight in kilograms is divided by height in metres and the result used as an index of obesity.

bone marrow biopsy: usually performed under local anaesthetic by making a small incision into the skin. A biopsy needle is then pushed through the bone and takes a sample of marrow from the centre of the bone. Marrow contains platelets, phagocytes and lymphocytes.

bronchiolitis: inflammation of the bronchioles, the smallest air passages of the lungs. It is a common childhood disorder.

C

carcinogenesis: the process by which normal cells become cancer cells (i.e. carcinoma).

cardiac arrest: situation in which the heart ceases to beat.

cardiac event: generic term for a variety of end points of coronary heart disease, including a myocardial infarction, angina and cardiac arrest.

cardiovascular: pertaining to the heart and blood vessels.

carotid artery: the main artery that takes blood from the heart via the neck to the brain.

carotid plaque: a plaque is a thick waxy coating which forms on blood vessel walls and restricts blood flow, in this instance in the carotid artery.

catastrophic thoughts: automatic thoughts that exaggerate the negative aspects of any situation.

catastrophising: the act of constructing **catastrophic thoughts**.

catecholamines: these chemical substances are brain neurotransmitters and include adrenaline and noradrenaline.

causal attribution: where a person attributes the cause of an event, feeling or action to themselves, to others, to chance or to some other causal agent.

CD4+ cells: otherwise known as helper T cells, these are involved in the proliferation of cytotoxic T cells as part of the immune response. HIV infection impairs their ability to provide this function.

cell suicide: a type of cell death in which the cell uses specialised cellular machinery to kill itself.

central nervous system: that part of the nervous system consisting of the brain and spinal cord.

cervical smear: smear of cells taken from the cervix to examine for the presence of cell changes indicating risk of cancer.

chronic bronchitis: an inflammation of the bronchi, the main air passages in the lungs, which persists for a long period or repeatedly recurs. Characterised by excessive bronchial mucus and a cough that produces sputum for three months or more in at least two consecutive years.

chronic obstructive airways disease: a persistent airway obstruction associated with combinations of chronic bronchitis, small airways disease, asthma and emphysema.

clot busters: drugs which dissolve clots associated with myocardial infarction and can prevent damage to the heart following such an event. Are best used within one hour of the infarction.

cognitive dissonance: a state in which conflicting or inconsistent cognitions produce a state of tension or discomfort (dissonance). People are motivated to reduce the dissonance, often by rejecting one set of beliefs in favour of the other.

cognitive restructuring: a reconsideration of automatic negative or catastrophic thoughts to make them more in line with reality.

cognitive schema (schemata): set of unconscious beliefs about the world and ourselves that shape more conscious cognitive responses to events that impinge on us.

cold pressor test: procedure in which participants place their arm in a mixture of water and ice maintaining the water temperature at between 0 and 3°C.

collectivist: a cultural philosophy that emphasises the individual as part of a wider unit and places emphasis on actions motivated by collective, rather than individual, needs and wants.

colonoscopy: a minor surgical procedure in which a small piece of bowel wall is cut from the colon. This can then be tested for the presence of malignant cells.

colostomy: a surgical procedure that creates an opening (stoma) in the abdomen for the drainage of stool from the large intestine (colon). It may be temporary or permanent.

colposcopy: a method used to identify cells that may develop into cancer of the cervix. Sometimes follows a cervical smear if abnormalities are found. A colposcope is a low-power microscope.

comparative optimism: initially termed 'unrealistic optimism', this term refers to an individual's estimate of their risk of experiencing a negative event compared with similar others (Weinstein and Klein 1996).

congestive heart failure: a disorder in which the heart loses its ability to pump blood efficiently. As a consequence, many organs do not receive enough oxygen and nutrients, leading to the potential for them to become damaged and, therefore, not work effectively.

coping effectiveness training: a specialist form of stress management in which participants are taught to alter the nature of their coping efforts to suit the particular type of demands they are facing: using emotion-focused coping where the situation cannot be changed and problem-focused coping where it can.

coping self-efficacy: the belief that one can carry out a particular coping response in a given set of circumstances.

coronary angioplasty: a procedure where a small balloon is inserted into the blocked coronary artery of a person with **atheroma**.

coronary artery bypass graft: surgical procedure in which veins or arteries from elsewhere in the patient's body are grafted from the aorta to the coronary arteries, bypassing blockages caused by atheroma in the cardiac arteries and improving the blood supply to the heart muscle.

coronary heart disease: a narrowing of the blood vessels that supply blood and oxygen to the heart. Results from a build-up of fatty material and plaque (**atherosclerosis**). Can result in **angina** or **myocardial infarction**.

corticosteroids: powerful anti-inflammatory hormones (including cortisol) made naturally in the body or synthetically for use as drugs.

cortisol: a stress hormone that increases the availability of energy stores and fats to fuel periods of high physiological activity. It also inhibits inflammation of damaged tissue.

Crohn's disease: autoimmune disease that can affect any part of the gastrointestinal tract but most commonly occurs in the ileum (the area where the small and large intestine meet).

cross-sectional design: a study that collects data from a sample on one occasion only. Ideally, the sample should be selected to be representative of the population under study.

D

decisional balance: where the costs of behaviour are weighed up against the benefits of that behaviour.

defibrillator: a machine that uses an electric current to stop any irregular and dangerous activity of the heart's muscles. It can be used when the heart has stopped (**cardiac arrest**) or when it is beating in a highly irregular (and ineffective) manner.

denial response: taking a view that denies any negative implications of an event or stimulus. If subconscious, it is considered a defence mechanism.

diabetes (type 1 and 2): a lifelong disease marked by high levels of sugar in the blood and a failure to transfer this to organs that need it. It can be caused by too little insulin (type 1), resistance to insulin (type 2), or both.

diastolic blood pressure: the minimum pressure of the blood on the walls of the arteries between heart beats (measured in relation to **systolic blood pressure**).

dispositional pessimism: having a generally negative outlook on life and a tendency to anticipate negative outcomes (as opposed to dispositional optimism).

distancing response: taking a detached view, often a scientific view, of an event or stimulus in order to reduce emotional activation.

diuretics: elevates the rate of bodily urine excretion, reducing the amount of fluid within the cardiovascular system, and reducing pressure within it.

drug abuse: involves use of a drug that results in significant social or work-related problems.

drug dependence: usually a progression from drug abuse. Involves dependence on the drug to achieve a desired psychological state, withdrawal symptoms in the absence of the drug, and social and work-related problems.

dualism: the idea that the mind and body are separate entities (cf. Descartes).

E

efficacy: Bandura's technical term analogous to confidence.

egocentric: self-centred, such as in the preoperational stage (age 2–7) of children, when they see things only from their own perspective (cf. Piaget).

empathy: an understanding of the situation from the individual's viewpoint.

emphysema: a late effect of chronic infection or irritation of the bronchial tubes. When the bronchi become irritated, some of the airways may be obstructed or the walls of the tiny air spaces may tear, trapping air in the lung beyond them. As a result, the lungs may become enlarged, at the same time becoming less efficient in exchanging oxygen for carbon dioxide.

empiricism: arising from a school of thought that all knowledge can be obtained through experience.

endocrine glands: glands that produce and secrete hormones into the blood or lymph systems. Includes the pituitary and adrenal glands, and the islets of

Langerhans in the pancreas. These hormones may affect one organ or tissue, or the entire body.

endorphins: naturally occurring opiate-like chemicals released in the brain and spinal cord. They reduce the experience of pain and can induce feelings of relaxation or pleasure. Associated with the so-called 'runner's high'.

endoscopy: the use of a thin, lighted tube (called an endoscope) to examine the inside of the body.

epidemiology: the study of patterns of disease in various populations and the association with other factors such as lifestyle factors. Key concepts include mortality, morbidity, prevalence, incidence, absolute risk and relative risk. Type of question: Who gets this disease? How common is it?

erythrocyte: a mature blood cell that contains **haemoglobin** to carry oxygen to the bodily tissues.

exercise programme: a key element of most cardiac rehabilitation, including a progressive increase in exercise usually starting in a gym, sometimes developing into exercise in the home and beyond.

exogenous: relating to things outside the body.

expressed emotion: the disclosure of emotional experiences as a means of reducing stress; often achieved by describing the experience in writing.

F

false positive result: a situation in which an individual is told that they may have a disease or are at risk of disease, but subsequent tests show that they are not at risk or do not have the disease.

fine needle aspiration: entails placing a very thin needle into a mass within the breast and extracting cells for microscopic evaluation. It takes seconds, and the discomfort is comparable with that of a blood test.

fistulas: formation of small passages that connect the intestine with other organs or the skin.

G

gallbladder: a structure on the underside of the liver on the right side of the abdomen. It stores the bile that is produced in the liver before it is secreted into the intestines. This helps the body to digest fats.

gate control theory of pain: a theory of pain developed by Melzack and Wall in which a 'gate' is used as a metaphor for the chemicals, including **endorphins**, that mitigate the experience of pain.

general adaptation syndrome: a sequence of physiological responses to prolonged stress, from the alarm stage through the resistance stage to exhaustion.

H

haemoglobin: the main substance of the red blood cell. When oxygenated in the lungs, it is converted to oxyhaemoglobin, thus allowing the red blood cells to carry oxygen from the air in our lungs to all parts of the body.

HDL cholesterol: the so-called 'good' cholesterol.

health behaviour: behaviour performed by an individual, regardless of their health status, as a means of protecting, promoting or maintaining health, e.g. diet.

health differential: a term used to denote differences in health status and life expectancy across different groups.

health hardiness: the extent to which a person is committed to and involved in health-relevant activities, perceives control over their health and responds to health stressors as challenges or opportunities for growth.

health locus of control: the perception that one's health is under personal control; controlled by powerful others such as health professionals; or under the control of external factors such as fate or luck.

healthy life expectancy: the WHO provides a fairly vague definition of this phrase: the number of years that a person can expect to live in 'full health' (in contrast to life expectancy, which is how long one would expect to live) by taking into account years lived in less than full health due to disease and/or injury.

heart failure: a state in which the heart muscle is damaged or weakened and is unable to generate a cardiac output sufficient to meet the demands of the body.

high-density lipoprotein (HDL): lipoproteins are fat protein complexes in the blood that transport cholesterol, triglycerides and other lipids to various tissues. The main function of HDL appears to be to carry excess cholesterol to the liver for 're-packaging' or excretion in the bile. Higher levels of HDL seem to be protective against CHD, so HDL is sometimes referred to as 'good' cholesterol.

holistic: root word 'wholeness', holistic approaches are concerned with the whole being and its well-being, rather than addressing the purely physical or observable.

Human papillomavirus (HPV): a family of over 100 viruses, of which 30 types can cause genital warts and be transmitted by sexual contact. While most genital HPV come and go over the course of a few years, some HPV infections may markedly elevate the risk for cancer of the cervix.

hypertension: a condition in which blood pressure is significantly above normal levels.

hypoglycaemic episode: occurs when the body's glucose level is too low. It frequently occurs when too much insulin or oral diabetic medication is taken, not enough food is eaten, or following exercise without appropriate food intake. Symptoms include excessive sweating, paleness, fainting and eventually loss of consciousness.

hypothalamus: area of the brain that regulates appetite, sexual arousal and thirst. Also appears to have some control over emotions.

I

illness behaviour: behaviour that characterises a person who is sick and who seeks a remedy, e.g. taking medication. Usually precedes formal diagnosis, when behaviour is described as **sick role behaviour**.

illness cognition: the cognitive processes involved in a person's perception or interpretation of symptoms or illness and how they represent it to themselves (or to others) (cf. Croyle and Ditto 1990).

illness representations: beliefs about a particular illness and state of ill health – commonly ascribed to the five domains described by Leventhal: identity, timeline, cause, consequences and control/cure.

incidence: the number of new cases of disease occurring during a defined time interval – not to be confused with prevalence, which refers to the number of established cases of a disease in a population at any one time.

individual differences: aspects of an individual that distinguish them from other individuals or groups (e.g. age, personality).

individualistic: a cultural philosophy that places responsibility at the feet of the individual; thus behaviour is often driven by individual needs and wants rather than by community needs or wants.

inflammatory bowel disease: a group of inflammatory conditions of the large intestine and, in some cases, the small intestine. The main forms of IBD are **Crohn's disease** and **ulcerative colitis**.

irritable bowel syndrome: a disorder of the lower intestinal tract. Symptoms include pain combined with altered bowel habits resulting in diarrhoea, constipation or both. It has no obvious physiological abnormalities, so diagnosis is by the presence and pattern of symptoms.

ischaemic heart disease: a heart disease caused by a restriction of blood flow to the heart.

K

Kaposi's sarcoma: a malignant tumour of the connective tissue, often associated with AIDS. The tumours consist of bluish-red or purple lesions on the skin. They often appear first on the feet or ankles, thighs, arms, hands and face.

L

lay referral system: an informal network of individuals (e.g. friends, family, colleagues) turned to for advice or information about symptoms and other health-related matters. Often but not solely used prior to seeking a formal medical opinion.

life events: a term used to describe occurrences in a person's life which may be viewed positively or negatively but which inherently require some adjustment on the part of the person (e.g. marriage, loss of job). Such events are implicated in the experience of stress.

limbic system: a series of structures in the brain, often referred to as the 'emotional computer' because of its role in coordinating emotions. It links sensory information to emotionally relevant behaviour, in particular responses to fear and anger.

locus of control: a personality trait thought to distinguish between those who attribute responsibility for events to themselves (i.e. internal LoC) or to external factors (external LoC).

longitudinal (design): responses assessed in a study that have been taken on more than one occasion over time, either prospectively (future-oriented) or retrospectively (based on recall of past events). Prospective longitudinal studies are more powerful, and such methods are important to studies where assessment of change is important.

low-density lipoprotein (LDL): the main function of LDLs seems to be to carry cholesterol to various tissues throughout the body. LDLs are sometimes referred to as 'bad' cholesterol because elevated levels of LDL correlate most directly with **coronary heart disease**.

lower respiratory tract infection: infection of the parts of the respiratory system including the larynx, trachea, bronchi and lungs.

lumpectomy: a surgical procedure in which only the tumour and a small area of surrounding tissue are removed. Contrasts with mastectomy, in which the whole breast is removed.

lymphocyte: a type of white blood cell. Lymphocytes have a number of roles in the immune system, including the production of antibodies and other substances that fight infection and disease. Includes T and B cells.

M

malignant melanoma: a rare but potentially lethal form of skin cancer.

mammography: a low-dose X-ray procedure that creates an image of the breast. The X-ray image can be used to identify early stages of tumours.

mechanistic: a reductionist approach that reduces behaviour to the level of the organ or physical function. Associated with the **biomedical** model.

mediate/mediator: mediating variables explain how or why a relationship exists between two other variables: for example, the effects of age upon behaviour may be mediated by health beliefs; thus age effects would be said to be indirect, rather than direct.

melanoma: a form of skin cancer. Usually begins in a mole and has a poor prognosis unless treated early.

meta-analysis: a review and reanalysis of pre-existing quantitative datasets that combines the analysis so as to provide large samples and high statistical power from which to draw reliable conclusions about specific effects.

migraine: differs from other headaches because it involves symptoms such as nausea, vomiting or sensitivity to light. Their exact cause is not known. However, they appear to be related to problems with blood flow through parts of the brain. At the start of a migraine, blood vessels in certain areas of the brain constrict, leading to symptoms including visual disturbances, difficulty in speaking, weakness or numbness. Minutes to hours later, the blood vessels dilate, leading to increased blood flow in the brain and a severe headache.

moderator/moderation: moderating variables explains the conditions under which a relationship between two other variables may exist: for example, the relationship between individual beliefs and behaviour may be different depending on gender or health status.

monitors: a generalised coping style that involves attending to the source of stress or threat and trying to deal with it directly, e.g. through information gathering/attending to threat-relevant information (as opposed to **blunters**).

morbidity: costs associated with illness such as disability, injury.

mortality: death. Generally presented as mortality statistics, i.e. the number of deaths in a given population and/or in a given year ascribed to a given condition (e.g. number of cancer deaths among women in 2000).

motivation: memories, thoughts, experiences, needs and preferences that act together to influence (drive) the type, strength and persistence of our actions.

motivational interview: developed by Miller and Rollnick, a set of procedures designed to increase motivation to change behaviour.

multiple sclerosis: a disorder of the brain and spinal cord caused by progressive damage to the myelin sheath covering of nerve cells. This results in decreased nerve functioning, which can lead to a variety of symptoms, including weakness, paralysis, tremor, pain, tingling, numbness and decreased coordination.

myelin sheath: a substance that contains both protein and fat (lipid) and surrounds all nerves outside the brain. It acts as a nerve insulator and helps in the transmission of nerve signals.

myocardial infarction: death of the heart muscle due to a stoppage of the blood supply. More often known as a heart attack.

N

natural killer (NK) cells: cells move in the blood and attack cancer cells and virus-infected body cells.

negative affectivity: a dispositional tendency to experience persistent and pervasive negative or low mood and self-concept (related to **neuroticism**).

neophobia: a persistent and chronic fear of anything new (places, events, people, objects).

neuroticism: a personality trait reflected in the tendency to be anxious, feel guilty and experience generally negative thought patterns.

neurotransmitter: a chemical messenger (e.g. adrenaline, acetylcholine) used to communicate between neurons and other neurons and other types of cell.

nicotine replacement therapy (NRT): replacement of nicotine to minimise withdrawal symptoms following the cessation of smoking. Delivered in a variety of ways, including a transdermal patch placed against the skin, which produces a measured dose of nicotine over time.

noradrenaline: this **catecholamine** is a neurotransmitter found in the brain and in the **sympathetic nervous system**. Also known as norepinephrine.

O

objective: i.e. real, visible or systematically measurable (e.g. adrenaline levels). Generally pertains to something outside the body that can be seen by others (as opposed to **subjective**).

observational studies: research studies which evaluate the effects of an intervention (or a treatment) without comparison to a control group and thus such studies are more limited in their conclusions than randomised controlled trials.

operant conditioning: attributed to Skinner, this theory is based on the assumption that behaviour is directly influenced by its consequences (e.g. rewards, punishments, avoidance of negative outcomes).

oral hypoglycaemic agents: various drug types, all of which reduce circulating blood sugar.

outcome expectancies: the outcome that is expected to result from behaviour, e.g. exercise will make me fitter.

P

pain threshold: the minimum amount of pain intensity that is required before it is detected (individual variation).

pancreas: gland in which the islets of Langerhans produce insulin. Also produces and secretes digestive enzymes. Located behind the stomach.

parasympathetic nervous system: arm of the autonomic nervous system that is responsible for rest and recuperation.

pathogen: a collective name for a variety of challenges to our health and immune system, including bacteria and viruses.

patient-controlled analgesia (PCA): a technique through which small doses of analgesic drugs, usually opioids, are administered (usually by an intravenous drip and controlled by a pump) by patients themselves. It is mostly used for the control of postoperative pain.

perceived behavioural control: one's belief in personal control over a certain specific action or behaviour.

phagocyte: an immune system cell that can surround and kill micro-organisms and remove dead cells. Phagocytes include macrophages.

phantom limb pain: a phenomenon that occurs following amputation of a limb, in which the individual feels like they still have their limb, and the limb is in pain.

placebo intervention: an intervention designed to simulate a psychological intervention but not believed to be a specific therapy for the target condition.

platelets: tiny bits of protoplasm found in the blood that are essential for blood clotting. These cells bind together to form a clot and prevent bleeding at the site of injury.

post-traumatic growth: following a traumatic event, including serious illness, a person may experience positive psychological change, e.g. increased life appreciation, improved relations to self and others, new life values and priorities.

post-traumatic stress disorder: a disorder that forms a response to experiencing a traumatic event. The key elements are unwanted repetitive memories of the event, often in the form of flashbacks, attempts at avoidance of such memories, and a generally raised level of arousal.

predisposition: predisposing factors increase the likelihood of a person engaging in a particular behaviour, such as genetic influences on alcohol consumption.

premature mortality: death before the age it is normally expected. Usually set at deaths under the age of 75.

prevalence: the number of established cases of a disease in a population at any one time. Often described as a percentage of the overall population or cases per 100,000 people.

primary health promotion: health promotion targeted at preventing the onset of disease. Contrasts with secondary health promotion, which aims to prevent the further progression of disease.

primary prevention: intervention aimed at changing risk factors prior to disease development.

problem-focused coping: a style of coping that involves active planning and dealing with any source of stress.

problem-focused counselling: a counselling approach developed by Gerard Egan that attempts to foster a collaborative and structured approach between counsellor and client to solving life problems.

prognosis: the predicted outcome of a disease.

prosocial behaviour: behavioural acts that are positively valued by society and that may elicit positive social consequences, e.g. offering sympathy, helping others.

psychosocial: an approach that seeks to merge a psychological (more micro- and individually oriented) approach with a social approach (macro-, more community- and interaction-oriented), for example, to health.

Q

qualitative methods: qualitative methods are concerned with describing (qualifying) the experience, beliefs and behaviour of a particular group of people. Data elicited is non-numerical, may or may not be generalisable to the wider population, but may generate themes of response that can be examined in further samples. The depth of material gained through qualitative work is great and allows insight into the meaning behind people's responses. Methods may include open-ended interviews, focus group discussions, taped transactions and conversations. Samples are generally small, given the time demands of data collection and analysis.

quantitative methods: unlike **qualitative methods**, quantitative methods are concerned with counting (quantifying), i.e. data describes the frequency with which a set of beliefs are held or behaviour actioned and means of scores can be obtained and compared statistically. Larger and more representative samples can be obtained, as the method of data collection is predominantly paper-based questionnaires that are self-completed (or can be completed in the presence of a researcher). Criticised for reducing data to numerical categories at the expense of breadth of illustrative meaning.

R

radical prostatectomy: otherwise known as a total prostatectomy, this involves using surgery to remove all of the prostate as a cure for prostate cancer.

reinforcers: factors that reward or provide a positive response following a particular behaviour or set of behaviours (positive reinforcer), or enable the removal or avoidance of an undesired state or response (negative reinforcer).

repression: a defensive coping style that serves to protect the person from negative memories or anxiety-producing thoughts by preventing their gaining access to consciousness.

response shift: changes in subjective reports that may result from a reprioritisation of life expectations or recalibration of internal standards so that the construct being assessed is reconceptualised.

rheumatoid arthritis: a chronic autoimmune disease with inflammation of the joints and marked deformities. Something (possibly a virus) triggers an attack of the synovium in the joint by the immune system, which stimulates an inflammatory reaction that can lead to destruction of the joint.

risk ratio: a way of comparing whether the probability of a certain event is the same for two groups. A risk ratio of 1 implies that the event is equally likely in both groups. A risk ratio greater than 1 implies that the event is more likely in the first group. A risk ratio of less than 1 implies that the event is less likely in the first group.

S

salience: strength and importance.

sciatica: pain down the leg, which is caused by irritation of the main nerve into the leg, the sciatic nerve. This pain tends to be caused where the nerves pass through and emerge from the lower bones of the spine (lumbar vertebrae).

self-concept: those conscious thoughts and beliefs about yourself that allow you to feel that you are distinct from others and that you exist as a separate person.

self-efficacy: the belief that one can perform particular behaviour in a given set of circumstances.

self-regulation: the process by which individuals monitor and adjust their behaviour, thoughts and emotions in order to maintain a balance or a sense of normal function.

self-talk: talking to oneself (internally). Can be negative and thus add to stress. Therapeutically, individuals are taught to use self-talk in a way that helps them to keep calm.

sensitivity (of a test): the ratio of true positive tests to the total number of positive cases expressed as a percentage; for example, a sensitive test may have 95 per cent success in detecting a disease among patients known to have that disease. A test with high sensitivity has few false negatives.

sick role behaviour: the activities undertaken by a person diagnosed as sick in order to try to get well.

social capital: feelings of social cohesion, solidarity and trust in one's neighbours.

social cognition: a model of social knowledge and behaviour that highlights the explanatory role of cognitive factors (e.g. beliefs and attitudes).

social comparison: the process by which a person or group of people compare themselves (their behaviour or characteristics) with others.

social desirability bias: the tendency to answer questions about oneself or one's behaviour in a way that is thought likely to meet with social (or interviewer) approval.

social identity: a person's sense of who they are at a group, rather than personal and individual, level (e.g. you are a student, possibly a female).

socialisation: the process by which a person learns – from family, teachers, peers – the rules, norms and moral codes of behaviour that are expected of them.

social learning theory: a theory that has at its core the belief that a combination of outcome expectancy and outcome value will shape subsequent behaviour. Reinforcement is an important predictor of future behaviour.

socio-economic status: a measure of the social class of an individual. Different measures use different indicators, including income, job type or years of education. Higher status implies a higher salary or higher job status.

Socratic dialogue: exploration of an individual's beliefs, encouraging them to question their validity.

specificity (of a test): the ratio of true negative tests to the total number of negative cases expressed as a percentage; for example healthy people are correctly identified as not having the condition being tested for. A test with high specificity has few false positives.

stages of change model: developed by Prochaska and di Clemente, this identifies five stages through which an individual passes when considering behavioural change: pre-contemplation, contemplation, preparation, change and maintenance/relapse.

statins: drugs designed to reduce cholesterol levels.

stem cell: a 'generic' cell that can make exact copies of itself indefinitely. In addition, such cells have the ability to produce specialised cells for various tissues in the body, including blood, heart muscle, brain and liver tissue. Found in the bone marrow.

stem cell transplant: procedure in which stem cells are replaced within the bone marrow following radiotherapy or chemotherapy or diseases such as leukaemia where they may be damaged.

stress inoculation training: a form of stress-reducing intervention in which participants are taught to control stress by rehearsing prior to going into stressful situations. Participants are taught to relax and use calming self-talk. The approach was developed by Donald Meichenbaum.

stress management training: a generic term for interventions designed to teach participants how to cope with stress.

stress reactivity: the physiological arousal, such as increased heart rate or blood pressure, experienced during a potentially stressful encounter.

stroke: damage to the brain either as a result of a bleed into the brain tissue or a blockage in an artery, which prevents oxygen and other nutrients reaching parts of the brain. More scientifically known as a cerebrovascular accident (CVA).

subjective: personal, i.e. what a person thinks and reports (e.g. excitement) as opposed to what is **objective**. Subjective is generally related to internal interpretations of events rather than observable features.

subjective expected utility (seu) theory: a decision-making model where an individual evaluates the expected utility (cf. desirability) of certain actions and their outcomes and selects the action with the highest seu.

subjective norm: a person's beliefs regarding whether important others (referents) would think that they should or should not carry out a particular action. An index of social pressure, weighted generally by the individual's motivation to comply with the wishes of others (see theory of planned behaviour).

sympathetic nervous system: the part of the autonomic nervous system involved in mobilising energy to activate and maintain arousal (e.g. increased heart rate).

synapse: junction between two neurons or between a neuron and target organ. Nerve impulses cross a synapse through the action of neurotransmitters.

systolic blood pressure: the maximum pressure of blood on the artery walls, which occurs at the end of the left ventricle output/contraction (measured in relation to **diastolic blood pressure**).

T

tachycardia: high heart rate – usually defined as greater than 100 beats per minute.

T cell: a cell that recognises antigens on the surface of a virus-infected cell, binds to that cell and destroys it.

temporomandibular disorder pain: a variety of conditions that cause tenderness and pain in temporomandibular joint (hinge joint of the jaw).

thalamus: area of the brain that links the basic functions of the hindbrain and midbrain with the higher centres of processing, the cerebral cortex. Regulates attention and contributes to memory functions. The portion that enters the limbic system is involved in the experience of emotions.

theory: a general belief or beliefs about some aspect of the world we live in or those in it, which may or may not be supported by evidence. For example, women are worse drivers than men.

transdermal patch: a method of delivering a drug in a slow release form. The drug is impregnated into a patch, which is stuck to the skin and gradually absorbed into the body.

transient ischaemic attacks: short periods of reduced blood flow to the brain, resulting in symptoms including short periods of confusion, weakness and other minor neurological symptoms.

treadmill test: a test of cardiovascular fitness in which participants gradually increase the level of exercise on a treadmill while having their heart monitored with an electrocardiogram.

trigeminal neuralgia: a painful inflammation of the trigeminal nerve that causes sharp and severe facial pain.

Type A behaviour (TAB): a constellation of characteristics, mannerisms and behaviour including competitiveness, time urgency, impatience, easily aroused hostility, rapid and vigorous speech patterns and expressive behaviour. Extensively studied in relation to the aetiology of coronary heart disease, where hostility seems central.

Type C personality: a cluster of personality characteristics manifested in stoic, passive and non-emotionally expressive coping responses. Thought to be associated with an elevated cancer risk.

Type D personality: a personality type characterised by high negative affectivity and social inhibition.

type 1 diabetes: see **diabetes**.

type 2 diabetes: see **diabetes**.

U

ulcerative colitis: a chronic inflammatory disease of the large intestine, characterised by recurrent episodes of abdominal pain, fever and severe diarrhoea.

ultrasound: the use of ultra high-frequency sound waves to create images of organs and systems in the body.

unrealistic optimism: also known as 'optimistic bias', whereby a person considers themselves as being less likely than comparable others to develop an illness or experience a negative event.

V

variable: (noun) something that can be measured or is reported and recorded as data, such as age, mood, smoking frequency or physical functioning.

vasospasm: a situation in which the muscles of artery walls in the heart contract and relax rapidly, resulting in a reduction of the flow of blood through the artery.

vicarious learning: learning from observation of others.

volition: action or doing (the post-intentional stage highlighted in the HAPA model of health behaviour change).

W

written emotional expression: a writing technique in which participants write about upsetting incidents either in their past or related to specific issues.

References

Aaronson, N.K., Ahmedzai, S., Bergman, B. *et al.* (1993). The European Organisation for Research and Treatment of Cancer QLQ-C30: a quality of life instrument for use in international clinical trials in oncology. *Journal of the National Cancer Institute*, 85: 365–76.

Abbott, S. (1988). Talking about AIDS. Report for AIDS Action Council, Canberra. *National Bulletin*, August, 24–7.

Abdullahi, A., Copping, J., Kessel, A. *et al.* (2009). Cervical screening: Perceptions and barriers to uptake among Somali women in Camden. *Public Health*, 123: 680–5.

Abraham, C., Krahé, B., Dominic, R. *et al.* (2002). Do health promotion messages target cognitive and behavioural correlates of condom use? A content analysis of safer sex promotion leaflets in two countries. *British Journal of Health Psychology*, 7: 227–46.

Abraham, C. and Michie, S. (2008). A taxonomy of behavior change techniques used in interventions. *Health Psychology*, 27: 379–87.

Abraham, S.C.S., Sheeran, P., Abrams, D. *et al.* (1996). Health beliefs and teenage condom use: a prospective study. *Psychology and Health*, 11: 641–55.

Abramsky, L. and Fletcher, O. (2002). Interpreting information: what is said, what is heard – a questionnaire study of health professionals and members of the public. *Prenatal Diagnosis* 22: 1188–94.

Absetz, P., Aro, A.R. and Sutton, S.R. (2003). Experience with breast cancer, pre-screening perceived susceptibility and the psychological impact of screening. *Psycho-Oncology*, 12: 305–18.

Acharya, S.D., Elci, O.U., Sereika, S.M. *et al.* (2009). Adherence to a behavioral weight loss treatment program enhances weight loss and improvements in biomarkers. *Journal of Patient Preference and Adherence*, 3: 151–60.

Achat, H., Kawachi, I., Byrne, C. *et al.* (2000). Prospective study of job strain and risk of breast cancer. *International Journal of Epidemiology*, 29: 622–8.

Acheson, D. (1998). Independent inquiry into inequalities in health. Report. London: HMSO.

Adams, G. and Salter, P.S. (2009). Health psychology in African settings: a cultural-psychological analysis. *Journal of Health Psychology*, 12: 539–51.

Adams, J. and White, M. (2005). Why don't stage-based activity promotion interventions work? *Health Education Research*, 20: 237–43.

Ader, R. (2001). Psychoneuroimmunology. *Current Directions in Psychological Science*, 10: 94–8.

Ader, R. (2007). *Psychoneuroimmunology*, 4th edn. New York: Academic Press.

Ader, R. and Cohen, N. (1993). Psychoneuroimmunology: conditioning and stress. *Annual Review of Psychology*, 44: 53–85.

Adler, N.E. and Matthews, K.A. (1994). Health psychology: why do some people get sick and some stay well? *Annual Review of Psychology*, 45: 229–59.

Affleck, G., Tennen, H., Croog, S. *et al.* (1987). Causal attributions, perceived benefits, and morbidity after a heart attack: an 8-year study. *Journal of Consulting and Clinical Psychology*, 55: 29–35.

Affleck, G., Tennen, H., Zautra, A. *et al.* (2001). Women's pursuit of personal goals in daily life with fibromyalgia: a value-expectancy analysis. *Journal of Consulting and Clinical Psychology*, 69: 587–96.

Agency for Health Care Policy and Research (1992). *Acute Pain Management, Clinical Practice Guideline*. Silver Spring, MD: AHCPR.

Ager, A., Carr, S., Maclachlan, M. *et al.* (1996). Perceptions of tropical health risks in Mponda, Malawi: attributions of cause, suggested means of risk reduction and preferred treatment. *Psychology and Health*, 12: 23–31.

Agostinelli, G. and Grube, J.W. (2002). Alcohol counter-advertising and the media: a review of recent research. *Alcohol Research and Health*, 26: 15–21.

Ahmad, W. (2000) (ed.). *Ethnicity, Disability and Chronic Illness*. Buckingham: Open University Press.

Ai, A.L., Park, C.L., Huang, B. *et al.* (2007). Psychosocial mediators of religious coping styles: a study of short-term distress following cardiac surgery. *Personality & Social Psychology Bulletin*, 33: 867–82.

Aitken, J.F., Youl, P.H., Janda, M. *et al.* (2006). Increases in skin cancer screening during a community-based randomized intervention trial. *International Journal of Cancer*, 118: 1110–16.

Ajzen, I. (1985). From intentions to actions: a theory of planned behavior. In J. Kuhl and J. Beckman (eds), *Action-control: From Cognition to Behavior*. Heidelberg: Springer Verlag.

Ajzen, I. (1991). The theory of planned behaviour. *Organizational Behavior and Human Decision Processes*, 50: 179–211.

Ajzen, I. and Fishbein, M. (1970). The prediction of behavior from attitudinal and normative beliefs. *Journal of Personality and Social Psychology*, 6: 466–87.

Ajzen, I. and Madden, T.J. (1986). Prediction of goal-directed behavior: attitudes, intentions, and perceived behavioral control. *Journal of Experimental Social Psychology*, 22: 453–74.

Alaranta, H., Rytokoski, U., Rissanen, A. *et al.* (1994). Intensive physical and psychosocial training program for patients with chronic low back pain. *Spine*, 19: 1339–49.

Albarracín, D., Gillette, J.C., Earl, A.N., Glasman, L.R., Durantini, M.R. and Ho, M.-H. (2005). A test of major assumptions about behaviour change: a comprehensive look at the effects of passive and active HIV-prevention interventions since the beginning of the epidemic. *Psychological Bulletin*, 131: 856–97.

Alexander, F. (1950). *Psychosomatic Medicine: Its Principles and Application*. New York: W.W. Norton.

Alexander, S.C., Keitz, S.A., Sloane, R. *et al.* (2006). A controlled trial of a short course to improve residents' communication with patients at the end of life. *Academic Medicine*, 81: 1008–12.

Alfredsson, L., Spetz, C.-L. and Theorell, T. (1985). Type of occupational and near-future hospitalization for myocardial infarction and some other diagnoses. *International Journal of Epidemiology*, 4: 378–88.

Allan, J.L., Farquharson, B., Choudhary, C. *et al.* (2009). Stress in telephone helpline nurses. *Journal of Advanced Nursing*, 65: 2208–15.

Allen, J.D., Stoddard, A.M., Mays, J. *et al.* (2001). Promoting breast and cervical cancer screening at the workplace: results from the Woman to Woman study. *American Journal of Public Health*, 91: 584–90.

Allen, J.K., Scott, L.B., Stewart, K.J. *et al.* (2004). Disparities in women's referral to and enrollment in outpatient cardiac rehabilitation. *Journal of General Internal Medicine*, 19: 747–53.

Allied Dunbar National Fitness Survey (1992). *A Report on Activity Patterns and Fitness Levels*. London: Sports Council and Health Education Authority.

Alloy, L.B., Abramson, L.Y. and Francis, E.L. (1999). Do negative cognitive styles confer vulnerability to depression? *Current Directions in Psychological Science*, 8: 128–32.

Allport, G.W. (1920). The influence of the group upon association and thought. *Journal of Experimental Psychology*, 3: 159–82.

Allport, G.W. (1935). Attitudes. In C. Murchison (ed.), *Handbook of Social Psychology*. Worcester, MA: Clark University Press.

Allport, G.W. (1961). *Pattern and Growth in Personality*. New York: Holt, Rinehart & Winston.

Allport, G.W. (1966). Traits revisited. *American Psychologist*, 21: 1–10.

Al-Moamary, M.S. (2008). Experience with pulmonary rehabilitation program in a tertiary care center in Saudi Arabia. *Saudi Medical Journal*, 29: 271–6.

Aloise-Young, P.A., Hennigan, K.M. and Graham, J.W. (1996). Role of self-image and smoker stereotype in smoking onset during early adolescence: a longitudinal study. *Health Psychology*, 15: 494–7.

Al-Smadi, J., Warke, K., Wilson, I. *et al.* (2003). A pilot investigation of the hypoalgesic effects of transcutaneous electrical nerve stimulation upon low back pain in people with multiple sclerosis. *Clinical Rehabilitation*, 17: 742–9.

Amelang, M. and Schmidt-Rathjens, C. (1996). Personality, cancer and coronary heart disease: further evidence on a controversial issue. *British Journal of Health Psychology*, 1: 191–205.

American Agency for Health Care Policy (1992). *Acute Pain Management: Operative or Medical Procedures and Trauma. Clinical Practice Guideline No. 1*. Washington, DC: AAHCP.

American Cancer Society (2008). *Cancer Facts and Figures 2008*. Atlanta, GA: American Cancer Society.

American Heart Association (1995). *Heart and Stroke Facts: 1995 Statistical Supplement*. Dallas, TX: American Heart Association.

American Psychiatric Association (2000). *Diagnostic and Statistical Manual of Mental Disorders*, 4th edn with revised text. Washington, DC: American Psychiatric Association.

Ames, G.M. and Janes, C.R. (1987). Heavy and problem drinking in an American blue-collar population: implications for prevention. *Social Science and Medicine*, 25: 949–60.

Amirkhanian, Y.A., Kelly, J.A., Kabakchieva, E. *et al.* (2005). A randomized social network HIV prevention trial with young men who have sex with men in Russia and Bulgaria. *AIDS*, 19: 1897–905.

Andersen, B.L., Cacioppo, J.T. and Roberts, D.C. (1995). Delay in seeking a cancer diagnosis: delay stages and psychophysiological comparison processes. *British Journal of Social Psychology*, 34: 33–52.

Anderson, M.R., Drescher, C.W., Zheng, Y.Y. *et al.* (2007). Changes in cancer worry associated with participation in ovarian cancer screening. *Psycho-Oncology*, 16: 814–20.

Andersen, R. and Newman, F. (1973). Societal and individual determinants of medical care utilization in the United States. *Millbank Memorial Fund Quarterly*, 51: 95–107.

Anderson, R.J., Friedland, K.E., Clouse, R.E. *et al.* (2001). The prevalence of comorbid depression in adults with diabetes: a meta-analysis. *Diabetes Care*, 24: 1069–78.

Andersson, G. (1996). The benefits of optimism: a meta-analytic review of the Life Orientation Test. *Personality and Individual Differences*, 21: 719–25.

Andrasik, F. (2007). What does the evidence show? Efficacy of behavioural treatments for recurrent headaches in adults. *Neurological Sciences*, 28: S70–7.

André, M., Borgquist, L. and Molstad, S. (2002). Asking for 'rules of thumb': a way to discover tacit knowledge in general practice. *Family Practice*, 19: 617–22.

Andreasson, S., Holder, H.D., Norström, T. *et al.* (2006). Estimates of harm associated with changes in Swedish alcohol policy: results from past and present estimates. *Addiction*, 101: 1096–105.

Annema, C.M., Luttik, M.L. and Jaarsma, T. (2009). Reasons for readmission in heart failure: perspectives of patients, caregivers, cardiologists and heart failure nurses. *Heart & Lung*, 38: 427–34.

Ansari, M., Shlipak, M.G., Heidenreich, P.A. *et al.* (2003). Improving guideline adherence: a randomized trial evaluating strategies to increase beta-blocker use in heart failure. *Circulation*, 107: 2799–804.

Antoni, M.H. (1987). Neuroendocrine influences in psychoimmunology and neoplasia: a review. *Psychology and Health*, 1: 3–24.

Antoni, M.H., Baggett, L., Ironson, G. *et al.* (1991). Cognitive behavioral stress management intervention buffers distress responses and immunological changes following notification of HIV-1 seropositivity. *Journal of Consulting and Clinical Psychology*, 59: 906–15.

Antoni, M.H., Cruess, S., Cruess, D.G. *et al.* (2000). Cognitive-behavioral stress management reduces distress and 24-hour urinary free cortisol output among symptomatic HIV-infected gay men. *Annals of Behavioral Medicine*, 22: 29–37.

Antoni, M.H., Cruess, D.G., Klimas, N. *et al.* (2002). Stress management and immune system reconstitution in symptomatic HIV-infected gay men over time: effects on transitional naive T-cells (CD4+CD45RA+CD29+). *American Journal of Psychiatry*, 159: 143–5.

Antoni, M.H., Lehman, J., Kilbourn, K. *et al.* (2001). Cognitive-behavioral stress management intervention decreases depression and enhances optimism and the sense of positive contributions among women under treatment for early-stage breast cancer. *Health Psychology*, 20: 20–32.

Antonovsky, A. (1987). *Unravelling the Mystery of Health: How People Manage Stress and Stay Well*. San Francisco, CA: Jossey-Bass.

Appels, A., Bar, F., Lasker, J. *et al.* (1997). The effect of a psychological intervention program on the risk of a new coronary event after angioplasty: a feasibility study. *Journal of Psychosomatic Medicine*, 43: 209–17.

Appleton, S., Watson, M., Rush, R. *et al.* (2004). A randomised controlled trial of a psychoeducational intervention for women at increased risk of breast cancer. *British Journal of Cancer*, 90: 41–7.

Arefjord, K., Hallarakeri, E., Havik, O.E. and Maeland, J.G. (1998). Myocardial infarction: emotional consequences for the wife. *Psychology and Health*, 13: 135–46.

Armitage, C.J. (2003). The relationship between multidimensional health locus of control and perceived behavioural control: how are distal perceptions of control related to proximal perceptions of control? *Psychology and Health*, 18: 723–38.

Armitage, C. and Conner, M. (1998). Extending the theory of planned behaviour: a review and avenues for further research. *Journal of Applied Social Psychology*, 28: 1429–64.

Armitage, C.J. and Conner, M. (2000). Social cognition models and health behaviour: a structured review. *Psychology & Health*, 15: 173–89.

Armitage, C.J. and Conner, M. (2002). Reducing fat intake: interventions based on the theory of planned behaviour. In D. Rutter and L. Quine (eds), *Changing Health Behaviour*. Buckingham: Open University Press.

Armitage, C.J., Conner, M., Loach, J. *et al.* (1999). Different perceptions of control: applying an extended theory of planned behaviour to legal and illegal drug use. *Basic and Applied Social Psychology*, 21: 301–16.

Arora, N.K. and McHorney, C.A. (2000). Patient preferences for medical decision making: who really wants to participate? *Medical Care*, 38: 335–41.

Arrigo, I., Brunner-LaRocca, H., Lefkovits, M. *et al.* (2008). Comparative outcome one year after formal cardiac rehabilitation: the effects of a randomized intervention to improve exercise adherence. *European Journal of Cardiovascular Prevention and Rehabilitation*, 15: 306–11.

Asamoah-Adu, A., Weir, S., Pappoe, M. *et al.* (1994). Evaluation of a targeted AIDS prevention intervention to increase condom use among prostitutes in Ghana. *AIDS*, 8: 239–46.

Ashton, L., Karnilowicz, W. and Fooks, D. (2001). The incidence and belief structures associated with breast self examination. *Social Behavior and Personality*, 29: 223–9.

Aspinwall, L.G. and Brunhart, S.M. (1996). Distinguishing optimism from denial: optimistic beliefs predict attention to health threats. *Personality and Social Psychology Bulletin*, 22: 993–1003.

Aspinwall, L.G. and Taylor, S.E. (1997). A stitch in time: self-regulation and proactive coping. *Psychological Bulletin*, 121: 417–36.

Astin, J.A. (1998). Why patients use alternative medicine: results of a national study. *Journal of the American Medical Association*, 279: 1548–53.

Astrom, M. (1996). Generalized anxiety disorder in stroke patients: a 3 year longitudinal study. *Stroke*, 17: 270–5.

Attari, A., Sartippour, M., Amini, M. *et al.* (2006). Effect of stress management training on glycemic control in patients with type 1 diabetes. *Diabetes Research and Clinical Practice*, 73: 23–8.

Atkinson, R.M. (1994). Late onset problem drinking in older adults. *International Journal of Geriatric Psychiatry*, 9: 321–6.

Audrain, J., Boyd, N.R., Roth, J. *et al.* (1997). Genetic susceptibility testing in smoking-cessation treatment: one-year outcomes of a randomized trial. *Addictive Behaviors*, 22: 741–51.

Aujoulat, I., Marcolongo, R., Bonadiman, L. and Deccache, A. (2008). Reconsidering patient empowerment in chronic illness: a critique of models of self-efficacy and bodily control, *Social Science & Medicine*, 66: 1228–39.

Austoker, J. (1994). Screening for ovarian, prostrate and testicular cancers. *British Medical Journal*, 309: 315–20.

Australian Bureau of Statistics (2005). *The Health and Welfare of Australia's Aboriginal and Torres Strait Islander Peoples*. Canberra: Australian Bureau of Statistics.

Ayanian, J.Z., Cleary, P.D., Weissman, J.S. *et al.* (1999). The effect of patients' preferences on racial differences in access to renal transplantation. *New England Journal of Medicine*, 341: 1661–9.

Bacharach, S.B., Bamberger, P.A., Sonnenstuhl, W.J. *et al.* (2004). Retirement, risky alcohol consumption and drinking problems among blue-collar workers. *Journal of Studies in Alcohol*, 65: 537–45.

Bachiocco, V., Scesi, M., Morselli, A.M. *et al.* (1993). Individual pain history and familial pain tolerance models: relationships to post-surgical pain. *Clinical Journal of Pain*, 9: 266–71.

Back, A.L., Arnold, R.M., Baile, W.F. *et al.* (2007). Efficacy of communication skills training for giving bad news and discussing transitions to palliative care. *Archives of Internal Medicine*, 167: 453–60.

Badr, H., Acitelli, L.K. and Carmack Taylor, C.L. (2007). Does couple identity mediate the stress experienced by caregiving spouses? *Psychology & Health*, 22: 211–30.

Badr, H. and Taylor, C.L.C. (2008). Effects of relationship maintenance on psychological distress and dyadic adjustment among couples coping with lung cancer. *Health Psychology*, 27: 616–27.

Bagozzi, R.P. (1993). On the neglect of volition in consumer research: a critique and proposal. *Psychology and Marketing*, 10: 215–37.

Baider, L., Andritsch, E., Uziely, B. *et al.* (2003). Effects of age on coping and psychological distress in women diagnosed with breast cancer: review of literature and analysis of two different geographical settings. *Critical Reviews in Oncology/Hematology*, 46: 5–16.

Bair, M.J., Robinson, R.L., Katon, W. *et al.* (2003). Depression and pain comorbidity: a literature review. *Archives of Internal Medicine*, 163: 2433–45.

Baker, A.H. and Wardle, J. (2003). Sex differences in fruit and vegetable intake in older adults. *Appetite*, 40: 269–75.

Bala, M., Strzeszynski, L. and Cahill, K. (2008). Mass media interventions for smoking cessation in adults. *Cochrane Database of Systematic Reviews*, 1: CD004704.

Balarajan, R. and Raleigh, V. (1993). *Ethnicity and Health in England*. London: HMSO.

Balaswamy, S., Richardson, V. and Price, C.A. (2004). Investigating patterns of social support used by widowers during bereavement. *The Journal of Men's Studies*, 13: 67–84.

Balldin, J., Berglund, M., Borg, S. *et al.* (2003). A 6-month controlled naltrexone study: combined effect with cognitive behavioral therapy in outpatient treatment of alcohol dependence. *Alcoholism Clinical and Experimental Research*, 27: 1142–9.

Baltes, P.B. and Baltes, M.M. (1990). *Successful Aging: Perspectives from the Behavioral Sciences*. New York: Cambridge University Press.

Bandolier (1999). Transcutaneous electrical nerve stimulation (TENS) in postoperative pain. *Bandolier*, July. Available from www.bandolier.com.

Bandolier (2003). Acute pain. *Bandolier* extra, February. Available from www.ebandolier.com.

Bandura, A. (1977). Self-efficacy: toward a unifying theory of behavioral change. *Psychological Review*, 84: 191–215.

Bandura, A. (1986). *Social Foundations of Thought and Action*. Upper Saddle River, NJ: Prentice Hall.

Bandura, A. (1997). *Self-Efficacy: The Exercise of Control*. New York: W.H. Freeman.

Bandura, A. (2001). Social cognitive theory: an agentic perspective. *Annual Review of Psychology*, 52: 1–26.

Banks, S.M., Salovey, P., Greener, S. *et al.* (1995). The effects of message framing on mammography utilization. *Health Psychology*, 14: 178–84.

Banthia, R., Malcarne, V.L., Varni, J.W. *et al.* (2003). The effects of dyadic strength and coping styles on psychological distress in couples faced with prostrate cancer. *Journal of Behavioral Medicine*, 26: 31–52.

Bardia, A., Tleyjeh, I.M., Cerhan, J.R., Sood, A.K., Limburg, P.J. *et al.* (2008). Efficacy of antioxidant supplementation in reducing primary cancer incidence and mortality: a systematic review and meta-analysis. *Mayo Clinic Proceedings*, 83: 23–34.

Barefoot, J.C., Dahlstrom, G. and Williams, R.B. (1983). Hostility, CHD incidence, and total mortality: a 25-year follow-up study of 255 physicians. *Psychosomatic Medicine*, 45: 59–63.

Barlow, J., Turner, A.P. and Wright, C.C. (2000). A randomised controlled study of the Arthritis Self-Management Programme in the UK. *Health Education Research Theory and Practice*, 15: 665–80.

Barlow, J.H., Wright, C., Sheasby, J. *et al.* (2002). Self-management approaches for people with chronic conditions: a review. *Patient Education and Counselling*, 48: 177–87.

Barnard, D., Street, A., Love, D.W. *et al.* (2006). Relationships between stressors, work support and burnout among cancer nurses. *Cancer Nursing*, 29: 338–45.

Barnett, M.M., Fisher, J.D., Cooke, H. *et al.* (2007). Breaking bad news: consultants' experience, previous education and views on educational format and timing. *Medical Education*, 41: 947–56.

Baron-Epel, O. and Kaplan, G. (2001). General subjective health status or age-related subjective health status: does it make a difference? *Social Science and Medicine*, 53: 1373–81.

Barrett, S. and Heubeck, B.G. (2000). Relationships between school hassles and uplifts and anxiety and conduct problems in Grades 3 and 4. *Journal of Applied Developmental Psychology*, 21: 537–54.

Barth, J., Schneider, S. and von Känel, R. (2010). Lack of social support in the etiology and the prognosis of coronary heart disease: a systematic review and meta-analysis. *Psychosomatic Medicine*, 72: 229–38.

Bartley, C.E. and Roesch, S.C. (2011). Coping with daily stress: the role of conscientiousness *Personality and Individual Differences*, 50: 79–83.

Bartley, M., Sacker, A. and Clarke, P. (2004). Employment status, employment conditions, and limiting illness: prospective evidence from the British household panel survey 1991–2001. *Journal of Epidemiology and Community Health*, 58: 501–6.

Barton, M.B., Morley, D.S. and Moore, S. (2004). Decreasing women's anxieties after abnormal mammograms: a controlled trial. *Journal of the National Cancer Institute*, 96: 529–38.

Bashir, S.A. (2002). Home is where the harm is: inadequate housing as a public health crisis. *American Journal of Public Health*, 92: 733–8.

Baum, A. (1990). Stress, intrusive imagery and chronic distress. *Health Psychology*, 9: 665–75.

Baum, A., Garofalo, J.P. and Yali, A.M. (1999). Socioeconomic status and chronic stress. Does stress account for SES effects on health? *Annals of the New York Academy of Science*, 896: 131–44.

Baum, A., Gatchel, R.J. and Krantz, D.S. (1997). *An Introduction to Health Psychology*, 3rd edition, New York: McGraw-Hill.

Baum, A. and Grunberg, N.E. (1991). Gender, stress and health. *Health Psychology* 10: 80–5.

Bauman, B. (1961). Diversities in conceptions of health and fitness. *Journal of Health and Human Behavior*, 2: 39–46.

Beach, S.R., Schulz, R., Lee, J.L. *et al.* (2000). Negative and positive health effects of caring for a disabled spouse: longitudinal findings from the Caregiver Health Effects study. *Psychology and Aging*, 15: 259–71.

Beadsmoore, C.J. and Screaton, N.J. (2003). Classification, staging and prognosis of lung cancer. *European Journal of Radiology*, 45: 8–17.

Beasley, M., Thompson, T. and Davidson, J. (2003). Resilience in response to life stress: the effects of coping style and cognitive hardiness. *Personality and Individual Differences*, 34: 77–95.

Beaver, K., Bogg, J. and Luker, K.A. (1999). Decision-making role preferences and information needs: a comparison of colorectal and breast cancer. *Health Expectations*, 2: 266–76.

Beaver, K., Luker, K.A., Owens, R.G. *et al.* (1996). Treatment decision making in women newly diagnosed with breast cancer. *Cancer Nursing*, 19: 8–19.

Beck, A.T. (1976). *Cognitive Therapy and the Emotional Disorders*. New York: International Universities Press.

Beck, A. (1977). *Cognitive Therapy of Depression*. New York: Guilford Press.

Beck, A.T., Ward, C.H., Mendelson, M. *et al.* (1962). Reliability of psychiatric diagnoses: 2. A study of consistency of clinical judgements and ratings. *American Journal of Psychiatry*, 119: 351–7.

Beck, A.T., Wight, F.D., Newman, C.F. and Liese, B.S. (1993). *Cognitive Therapy for Substance Abuse*. New York: Guilford Press.

Becker, M.H. (ed.) (1974). The health belief model and personal health behavior, *Health Education Monographs*, 2: 324–508.

Becker, M.H., Haefner, D.P. and Maiman, L.A. (1977). The health belief model in the prediction of dietary compliance: a field experiment. *Journal of Health and Social Behavior*, 18: 348–66.

Becker, M.H. and Maiman, L.A. (1975). Socio-behavioral determinants of compliance with health and medical care recommendations. *Medical Care*, 13: 10–14.

Becker, M.H. and Rosenstock, I.M. (1984). Compliance with medical advice. In A. Steptoe and A. Mathews (eds), *Health Care and Human Behavior*. London: Academic Press.

Becker, M.H. and Rosenstock, I.M. (1987). Comparing social learning theory and the health belief model. In W.B. Ward (ed.), *Advances in Health Education and Promotion*. Greenwich, CT: JAI Press.

Beecher, H.K. (1946). Pain in men wounded in battle. *Annals of Surgery*, 123: 96–105.

Bell, D.E. (1982). Regret in decision-making under uncertainty. *Operations Research*, 21: 961–81.

Bellaby, P. (2003). Communication and miscommunication of risk: understanding UK parents' attitudes to combined MMR vaccination. *British Medical Journal*, 327: 725–8.

Belloc, N.B. and Breslow, L. (1972). Relationship between physical health status and health practices. *Preventive Medicine*, 1: 409–21.

Bendsten, L., Evers, S., Linde, M. *et al.* (2010). EFNS guideline on the treatment of tension-type headache – report of an EFNS task force. *European Journal of Neurology*, 17: 1318–25.

Benedetti, F., Lanotte, M., Lopiano, L. *et al.* (2007). When words are painful: unraveling the mechanisms of the nocebo effect. *Neuroscience*, 147: 260–71.

Benight, C.C., Ironson, G., Klebe, K. *et al.* (1999). Conservation of resources and coping self-efficacy predicting distress following a natural disaster: a causal model analysis where the environment meets the mind. *Anxiety, Stress and Coping*, 12: 107–26.

Bennett, P. (2000). *Introduction to Clinical Health Psychology*. Oxford: Oxford University Press.

Bennett, P. (2003). *Abnormal and Clinical Psychology: An Introductory Text*. Buckingham: Open University Press.

Bennett, P. (2005a). Gastric and duodenal ulcers. In S. Ayers, A. Baum, C. McManus, S. Newman, K. Wallston, J. Weinman and R. West (eds), *Cambridge Handbook of Psychology, Health and Medicine*, 2nd edn. Cambridge: Cambridge University Press.

Bennett, P. (2005b). Irritable bowel syndrome. In S. Ayers, A. Baum, C. McManus, S. Newman, K. Wallston, J. Weinman and R. West (eds), *Cambridge Handbook of Psychology, Health and Medicine*, 2nd edn. Cambridge: Cambridge University Press.

Bennett, P. (2006). *Abnormal and Clinical Psychology: An Introductory Text*, 2nd edn. Buckingham: Open University Press.

Bennett, P. and Connell, H. (1999). Dyadic responses to myocardial infarction. *Psychology, Health and Medicine*, 4: 45–55.

Bennett, P. and Murphy, S. (1997). *Psychology and Health Promotion*. Buckingham: Open University Press.

Bennett, P., Owen, R.L., Koutsakis, S. *et al.* (2002). Personality, social context and cognitive predictors of post-traumatic stress disorder in myocardial infarction patients. *Psychology and Health*, 17: 489–500.

Bennett, P., Parsons, E., Brain, K. *et al.* (2010). Living at risk: a long-term follow-up study of women at intermediate risk of familial breast cancer. *Psycho-Oncology*, 19: 390–8.

Bennett, P., Phelps, C. *et al.* (2007). A randomised controlled trial of a brief self-help coping intervention designed to reduce distress when awaiting genetic risk information. *Journal of Psychosomatic Research*, 63, 59–64.

Bennett, P. and Smith, C. (1992). Parents' attitudinal and social influences on childhood vaccination. *Health Education Research: Theory and Practice*, 73: 341–8.

Bennett, P., Smith, P. and Gallacher, J.E.J. (1996). Vital exhaustion, neuroticism and symptom reporting in cardiac and non-cardiac patients. *British Journal of Health Psychology*, 1: 309–13.

Bennett, P., Wilkinson, C., Turner, J. *et al.* (2008). Psychological factors associated with emotional responses to receiving genetic risk information. *Journal of Genetic Counseling*. Published online, 8th February.

Bennett, P., Williams, Y., Page, N. *et al.* (2004). Levels of mental health problems among UK emergency ambulance personnel. *Emergency Medical Journal*, 21: 235–6.

Bensing, J.M., Tromp, F., van Dulmen, S. *et al.* (2006). Shifts in doctor–patient communication between 1986 and 2002: a study of videotaped general practice consultations with hypertension patients. *BMC Family Practice*, 25: 62.

Benyamini, Y., Leventhal, E.A. and Leventhal, H. (2003). Elderly people's ratings of the importance of health-related factors to their self-assessments of health. *Social Science and Medicine*, 56: 1661–7.

Beran, M.S., Cunningham, W., Landon, B.E. *et al.* (2007). Clinician gender is more important than gender concordance in quality of HIV care. *Gender Medicine*, 4: 72–84.

Berg, A.I., Hassing, L., McClearn, G.E. and Johansson, B. (2006). What matters for life satisfaction in the oldest-old? *Aging and Mental Health*, 10: 257–64.

Bergner, M., Bobbitt, R.A., Carter, W.B. *et al.* (1981). The sickness impact profile: development and final revision of a health status measure. *Medical Care*, 19: 787–805.

Berkman, L.F. (1984). Assessing the physical health effects of social networks and social support. *Annual Review of Public Health*, 5: 413–32.

Berkman, L.F., Blumenthal, J., Burg, M. *et al.* (2003). Effects of treating depression and low perceived social support on clinical events after myocardial infarction: the Enhancing Recovery in Coronary Heart Disease (ENRICHD) patients randomized trial. *Journal of the American Medical Association*, 289: 3106–16.

Berkman, L.F. and Syme, S.L. (1979). Social networks, lost resistance and mortality: a nine-year follow-up of Alameda County residents. *American Journal of Epidemiology*, 109: 186–204.

Bernal, I., Domènech, E., Garcia-Planella, E. *et al.* (2006). Medication-taking behavior in a cohort of patients with inflammatory bowel disease. *Digestive Diseases and Sciences*, 51: 2165–9.

Bernstein, S.L., Cabral, L., Maantay, J. *et al.* (2009). Disparities in access to over-the-counter nicotine replacement products in New York City pharmacies. *American Journal of Public Health*, 99: 1699–704.

Bethune, G.R. and Lewis, H.J. (2009). Let's talk about smear tests: social marketing for the National Cervical Screening Programme. *Public Health*, 123 Suppl 1: e17–22.

Bhopal, R., Hayes, L., White, M. *et al.* (2002). Ethnic and socio-economic inequalities in coronary heart disease, diabetes and risk factors in Europeans and South Asians. *Journal of Public Health Medicine*, 24: 95–105.

Bhopal, R., Unwin, N., White, M. *et al.* (1999). Heterogeneity of coronary heart disease risk factors in Indian, Pakistani, Bangladeshi, and European origin populations: cross-sectional study. *British Medical Journal*, 319: 215–20.

Bibace, R., Schmidt, L.R. and Walsh, M.E. (1994). Children's perceptions of illness. In G.N. Penny, P. Bennett and M. Herbert (eds), *Health Psychology: A Lifespan Perspective*. Switzerland: Harwood Academic Publishers.

Bibace, R. and Walsh, M.E. (1980). Development of children's conceptions of illness. *Pediatrics*, 66: 912–17.

Biddle, S. (1995). Exercise and psychosocial health. *Research Quarterly for Exercise and Sport*, 66: 292–7.

Biddle, S., Fox, K. and Boutcher, S. (2000). *Physical Activity and Psychological Wellbeing*. London: Routledge.

Biddle, S. and Murtrie, N. (1991). *Psychology of Physical Activity: A Health Related Perspective*. London: Springer Verlag.

Biddle, S.J.H. and Mutrie, N. (2008). *Psychology of Physical Activity: Determinants, Wellbeing and Interventions*, 2nd edn. London: Routledge.

Bieber, C., Müller, K.G., Blumenstiel, K. *et al.* (2006). Long-term effects of a shared decision-making intervention on physician–patient interaction and outcome in fibro-myalgia: a qualitative and quantitative 1 year follow-up of a randomized controlled trial. *Patient Education and Counseling*, 63: 357–66.

Biener, L., McCallum-Keeler, G. and Nyman, A.L. (2000). Adults' response to Massachusetts anti-tobacco television advertisements: impact of viewer and advertisement characteristics. *Tobacco Control*, 9: 401–7.

Biggam, F.H., Power, K.G., MacDonald, R.R. *et al.* (1997). Self-perceived occupational stress and distress in a Scottish police force. *Work and Stress*, 11: 118–33.

Bigman, C.A., Cappella, J.N. and Hornik, R.C. (2010). Effective or ineffective: attribute framing and the human papillomavirus (HPV) vaccine. *Patient Education and Counseling*, 81(suppl.): S70–6.

Bijttebier, P., Vercruysse, T., Vertommen, H. *et al.* (2001). New evidence on the reliability and validity of the pediatric oncology quality of life scale. *Psychology and Health*, 16: 461–9.

Billings, A.G. and Moos, R.H. (1981). The role of coping responses and social resources in attenuating the stress of life events. *Journal of Behavioural Medicine*, 4: 139–57.

Billings, A.G. and Moos, R.H. (1984). Coping, stress, and resources among adults with unipolar depression. *Journal of Personality and Social Psychology*, 46: 877–91.

Bird, J.E. and Podmore, V.N. (1990). Children's understanding of health and illness. *Psychology and Health*, 4: 175–85.

Birmingham Health Authority (1995). *Birmingham Annual Public Health Report: Closing the Gap*. Birmingham: Birmingham Health Authority.

Birmingham, P.K., Wheeler, M., Suresh, S. *et al.* (2003). Patient-controlled epidural analgesia in children: can they do it? *Anesthesia and Analgesia*, 96: 686–91.

Bishop, G.D. and Teng, C.B. (1992). Cognitive organization of disease information in young Chinese Singaporeans. Paper presented at First Asian Conference in Psychology, Singapore.

Bishop, R., Lau, M., Shapiro, S. *et al.* (2004). Mindfulness: a proposed operational definition. *Clinical Psychology: Science and Practice*, 11: 230–41.

Bjordal, J.M., Johnson, M.I. and Ljunggreen, A.E. (2002). Transcutaneous electrical nerve stimulation (TENS) can reduce postoperative analgesic consumption: a meta-analysis with assessment of optimal treatment parameters for postoperative pain. *European Journal of Pain*, 7: 181–8.

Bjørge, T., Engeland, A., Tverdal, A. *et al.* (2008). Body mass index in adolescence in relation to cause-specific mortal-ity: a follow-up of 230,000 Norwegian adolescents. *American Journal of Epidemiology*, 168: 30–7.

Black, J.L., Allison, T.G., Williams, D.E. *et al.* (1998). Effect of intervention for psychological distress on rehospitalization rates in cardiac rehabilitation patients. *Psychosomatics*, 39: 134–43.

Blair, S. and Brodney, S. (1999). Effects of physical inactivity and obesity on morbidity and mortality: current evidence and research issues. *Medicine and Science in Sports and Exercise*, 31(suppl.): S646–62.

Blalock, J.E. (1994). The syntax of immune-neuroendocrine communication. *Immunology Today*, 15: 504–11.

Blane, D., Higgs, P., Hyde, M. and Wiggins, R.D. (2004). Life course influences on quality of life in early old age. *Social Science and Medicine*, 58: 2171–9.

Blaxter, M. (1987). Evidence on inequality in health from a national survey, *The Lancet*, ii: 30–3.

Blaxter, M. (1990). *Health and Lifestyles*. London: Routledge.

Blenkinsop, S., Boreham, R. and McManus, S. (NFER) (2003). *Smoking, Drinking and Drug Use among Young People in England in 2002*. London: Stationery Office.

Blume, S. (2006). Anti-vaccination movements and their interpretations. *Social Science & Medicine*, 62: 628–42.

Blumenthal, J.A., Jiang, W., Babyak, M.A. *et al.* (1997). Stress management and exercise training in cardiac patients with myocardial ischemia. *Archives of Internal Medicine*, 157: 2213–17.

Blumenthal, J.A., Sherwood, A., Babyak, M.A. *et al.* (2005). Effects of exercise and stress management training on markers of cardiovascular risk in patients with ischemic heart disease: a randomized controlled trial. *Journal of the American Medical Association*, 293: 1626–34.

Blyth, F.M., March, L.M. and Cousins, M.J. (2003). Chronic pain-related disability and use of analgesia and health services in a Sydney community. *Medical Journal of Australia*, 179: 84–7.

Boersma, S.N., Maes, S. and van Elderen, T.M.T. (2005a). Goal disturbance predicts health-related quality of life and depression four months after myocardial infarction. *British Journal of Health Psychology*, 10: 615–30.

Boersma, S.N., Maes, S. and Joekes, K. (2005b). Goal disturbance in relation to anxiety, depression, and health-related quality of life after myocardial infarction. *Quality of Life Research*, 14: 2265–75.

Boini, S., Briançon, S., Guillemin, F. *et al.* (2004). Impact of cancer occurrence on health-related quality of life: a longitudinal pre-post assessment. *Health and Quality of Life Outcomes*, 2: 4–19.

Bogg, T. and Roberts, B.X. (2004). Conscientiousness and health-related behaviours: a meta-analysis of the leading behavioral contributors to mortality. *Psychological Bulletin*, 130: 887–919.

Bokan, J.A., Ries, R.K. and Katon, W.J. (1981). Tertiary gain and chronic pain. *Pain*, 10: 331–5.

Bolas, H., van Wersch, A. and Flynn, D. (2007). The well-being of young people who care for a dependent relative: an interpretative phenomenonological analysis. *Psychology & Health*, 22: 829–50.

Bolejko, A., Sarvik, C., Hagell, P. and Brinck, A. (2008). Meeting patient information needs before magnetic resonance imaging: development and evaluation of an information booklet. *Journal of Radiology Nursing*, 27: 96–102.

Boniol, M. and Autier, P. (2010). Prevalence of main cancer lifestyle risk factors in Europe in 2000. *European Journal of Cancer*, 46: 2534–44.

Booth-Kewley, S. and Friedman, H.S. (1987). Psychological predictors of heart disease: a quantitative review. *Psychological Bulletin*, 101: 343–62.

Booth-Kewley, S. and Vickers, R.R., Jr (1994). Associations between major domains of personality and health behaviour. *Journal of Personality*, 62: 281–98.

Boreham, R. and Shaw, A. (2001). *Smoking, Drinking and Drug Use Among Young People in England in 2000*. London: Stationery Office.

Borgia, P., Marinacci, C., Schifano, P. *et al.* (2005). Is peer education the best approach for HIV prevention in schools? Findings from a randomized controlled trial. *Journal of Adolescent Health*, 36: 508–16.

Borland, R. (1997). Tobacco health warnings and smoking related cognitions and behaviours. *Addiction*, 92(11): 1427–35.

Bosch, J.A., Fischer, J.E. and Fischer, J.C. (2009). Psychologically adverse work conditions are associated with CD8+ T cell differentiation indicative of immunesenescence. *Brain Behavior and Immunity*, 23: 527–34.

Bouhuys, A.L., Flentge, F., Oldehinkel, A.J. and van den Berg, M.D. (2004). Potential psychosocial mechanisms linking depression to immune function in elderly subjects. *Psychiatry Research*, 127: 237–45.

Bourbeau, J. and Bartlett, S.J. (2008). Patient adherence in COPD. *Thorax*, 63: 831–8.

Bourdeaudhuij, I. de. and Van Oost, P. (1998). Family characteristics and health behaviours of adolescents and families. *Psychology and Health*, 13: 785–804.

Boureaudhuij, I.D. (1997). Family food rules and healthy eating in adolescents. *Journal of Health Psychology*, 2: 45–56.

Bourgeois, M., Schulz, R. and Burgio, L. (1996). Interventions for caregivers of patients with Alzheimer's disease: a review and analysis of content, process and outcomes. *International Journal of Aging and Human Development*, 43: 35–92.

Bouteyre, E., Maurel, M. and Bernaud, J-L. (2007). Daily hassles and depressive symptoms among first year psychology students in France: the role of coping and social support. *Stress & Health*, 23: 93–9.

Bowden, A. and Fox-Rushby, J.A. (2003). A systematic and critical review of the process of translation and adaptation of generic health-related quality of life measures in Africa, Asia, Eastern Europe, the Middle East, South America. *Social Science and Medicine*, 57: 1289–306.

Bowland, L., Cockburn, J., Cawson, J. *et al.* (2003). Counselling interventions to address the psychological consequences of screening mammography: a randomised trial. *Patient Education and Counseling*, 49: 189–98.

Bowling, A. (1991). *Measuring Health: A Review of Quality of Life*. Buckingham: Open University Press.

Bowling, A. (1995a). *Measuring Disease: A Review of Disease-specific Quality of Life Measurement Scales*. Buckingham: Open University Press.

Bowling, A. (1995b). The most important things in life. Comparisons between older and younger population age groups by gender. Results from a national survey of the public's judgements. *International Journal of Health Sciences*, 6: 169–75.

Bowling, A. (2005). *Measuring Health: A Review of Quality of Life Scales*, 3rd edn. Milton Keynes: Open University Press.

Bowling, A. and Iliffe, S. (2006). Which model of successful ageing should be used? Baseline findings from a British longitudinal survey of ageing. *Age and Ageing*, 35: 607–14.

Brabin, L., Roberts, S.A., Farzaneh, F. *et al.* (2006). Future acceptance of adolescent human papillomavirus vaccination: a survey of parental attitudes. *Vaccine*, 24: 3087–94.

Bracken, P. and Thomas, P. (2002). Time to move beyond the mind–body split (editorial). *British Medical Journal*, 325: 1433–4.

Brain, K., Gray, J., Norman, P. *et al.* (2000). Randomized trial of a specialist genetic assessment service for familial breast cancer. *Journal of the National Cancer Institute*, 92: 1345–51.

Braithwaite, D., Emery, J., Walter, F. *et al.* (2004). Psychological impact of genetic counselling for familial cancer: a systematic review and meta-analysis. *Journal of the National Cancer Institute*, 96: 122–33.

Braithwaite, D., Sutton, S. and Steggles, N. (2002). Intention to participate in predictive genetic testing for hereditary cancer: the role of attitude toward uncertainty. *Psychology and Health*, 17: 761–72.

Brändli, H. (1999). The image of mental illness in Switzerland. In J. Guimon, W. Fischer and N. Sartorius (eds), *The Image of Madness: The Public Facing Mental Illness and Psychiatric Treatment*. Basel: Karger, pp. 29–37.

Brataas, H.V., Thorsnes, S.L. and Hargie, O. (2009). Themes and goals in cancer outpatient-cancer nurse consultations. *European Journal of Cancer Care*, 19: 184–91.

Bratzler, D.W., Oehlert, W.H. *et al.* (2002). Smoking in the elderly – It's never too late to quit. *Journal of the Oklahoma State Medical Association*, 95: 185–91.

Braverman, M.T., Aarø, L.E. and Hetland, J. (2007). Changes in smoking among restaurant and bar employees following Norway's comprehensive smoking ban. *Health Promotion International*, 23: 5–15.

Brawley, O.W. and Freeman, H.P. (1999). Race and outcomes: is this the end of the beginning for minority health research? *Journal of the National Cancer Institute*, 91: 1908–9.

Brena, S.F. and Chapman, S.L. (1983). *Management of Patients with Chronic Pain*. Great Neck, NY: PMA Publications.

Breslow, L. (1983). The potential of health promotion. In D. Mechanic (ed.), *Handbook of Health, Health Care and the Health Professions*. New York: Free Press.

Brewer, B.W., Manos, T.M., McDevitt, A.V. *et al.* (2000). The effect of adding lower intensity work on the perceived aversiveness of exercise. *Journal of Sport and Exercise Psychology*, 22: 118–30.

Brewer, N.T., Salz, T. and Lillie, S.E. (2007). Systematic review: the long-term effects of false-positive mammograms. *Annals of Internal Medicine*, 146: 502–10.

Brewin, C., Dalgleish, T. and Joseph, S. (1996). A dual representation theory of post-traumatic stress disorder. *Psychological Review*, 103: 670–86.

Brewin, C.R. and Holmes, E.A. (2003). Psychological theories of posttraumatic stress disorder. *Clinical Psychology Review*, 23: 339–76.

Brewster, A.E., Morrison, V., Hackett, P., *et al.* (2006). Attitudes of the general public and professional health care staff towards cancer treatment: the influence of age, quality of life, survival and side effects. *British Geriatric Society*, Spring meeting.

Bridle, C., Riemsma, R.P., Pattenden, J. *et al.* (2005). Systematic review of the effectiveness of health behavior interventions based on the transtheoretical model. *Psychology & Health*, 20: 283–301.

British Medical Association (2003a). *Adolescent Health*. British Medical Association, Board of Science and Education: BMA Publications Unit.

British Medical Association (2003b). *Childhood Immunisation: A Guide for Healthcare Professionals*. British Medical Association, Board of Science and Education: BMA Publications Unit.

British Thoracic Society (1997). Guidelines for the management of chronic obstructive pulmonary disease. *Thorax*, 52(suppl. 5): 1–26.

Briviba, K., Pan, L. and Rechkemmer, G. (2002). Red wine polyphenols inhibit the growth of colon carcinoma cells and modulate the activation pattern of mitogen-activated protein kinases. *Journal of Nutrition*, 132: 2814–18.

Broadbent, E., Petrie, K.J., Alley, P.G. and Booth, R.J. (2003). Psychological stress impairs early wound repair following surgery. *Psychosomatic Medicine*, 65: 865–9.

Broers, S., Kaptein, A.A., Le Cessie, S. *et al.* (2000). Psychological functioning and quality of life following bone marrow transplantation: a 3-year follow-up study. *Journal of Psychosomatic Research*, 48: 11–21.

Bronfenbrenner, U. (1972). *Two Worlds of Childhood*. New York: Simon & Schuster.

Brosschot, J.F., Gerin, W. and Thayer, J.F. (2006). Worry and health: the perseverative cognition hypothesis. *Journal of Psychosomatic Research*, 60: 113–24.

Brosschot, J.F., Pieper, S. and Thayer, J.F. (2005). Expanding stress theory: prolonged activation and perseverative cognition. *Psychoneuroendocrinology*, 30: 1043–9.

Brosschot, J.F. and Thayer, J.F. (1998). Anger inhibition, cardiovascular recovery, and vagal function: a model of the link between hostility and cardiovascular disease. *Annals of Behavioral Medicine*, 20: 326–32.

Brown, J., Cooper, C. and Kirkcaldy, B. (1996). Occupational stress among senior police officers. *British Journal of Psychology*, 87: 31–41.

Brown, J.S.L., Cochrane, R. and Hancox, T. (2000). Large-scale health promotion stress workshops for the general public: a controlled evaluation. *Behavioural and Cognitive Psychotherapy*, 28: 139–51.

Brown, R. (2004). Psychological mechanisms of medically unexplained symptoms: an integrative conceptual mode. *Psychological Bulletin*, 130: 793–813.

Bruce, J. and van Teijlingen, E. (1999). A review of the effectiveness of Smokebusters: community-based smoking prevention for young people. *Health Education Research*, 14: 109–20.

Brug, J., Conner, M., Harre, N. *et al.* (2005). The transtheoretical model and stages of a change: a critique. Observations by five commentators on the paper by Adams, J. and White, M. Why don't stage-based activity promotion interventions work? *Health Education Research*, 20: 244–58.

Brunton, G., Harden, A., Rees, R. *et al.* (2003). *Children and Physical Activity: A Systematic Review of Barriers and Facilitators*. London: EPPI-Centre, Social Science Research Unit, Institute of Education, University of London.

Bryan, A.D., Aiken, L.S. and West, S.G. (1996). Increasing condom use: evaluation of a theory-based intervention to prevent sexually transmitted diseases in young women, *Health Psychology*, 15: 371–82.

Bryan, A.D., Aiken, L.S. and West, S.G. (1997). Young women's condom use: the influence of acceptance of sexuality, control over the sexual encounter, and perceived susceptibility to common STDs. *Health Psychology*, 16: 468–79.

Bryon, M. (1998). Adherence to treatment in children. In L.B. Myers and K. Midence (eds), *Adherence to Treatment in Medical Conditions*. Netherlands: Harwood Academic Publishers.

Buckman, R. (1992). Who's for CPR? *Journal of the Royal College of Physicians of London*, 26: 461–2.

Budd, R.J. (1987). Response bias and the theory of reasoned action. *Social Cognition*, 5: 95–107.

Budd, R. and Rollnick, S. (1996). The structure of the readiness to change questionnaire: a test of Prochaska and di Clemente's transtheoretical model. *Health Psychology*, 15: 365–76.

Buick, D. and Petrie, K. (2002). 'I know just how you feel': the validity of healthy women's perceptions of breast cancer patients receiving treatment. *Journal of Applied Social Psychology*, 32: 110–23.

Bullinger, M. (1997). The challenge of cross-cultural quality of life assessment. *Psychology and Health*, 12: 815–26.

Bundy, C., Carroll, D., Wallace, L. *et al.* (1994). Psychological treatment of chronic stable angina pectoris. *Psychology and Health*, 10: 69–77.

Burack, J.H., Barrett, D.C., Stall, R.D. *et al.* (1993). Depressive symptoms and CD4 lymphocyte decline among HIV infected men. *JAMA*, 270(21): 2568–73.

Burell, G. (1996). Group psychotherapy in project New Life: treatment of coronary-prone behaviors for patients who had coronary bypass graft surgery. In S. Scheidt and R. Allan (eds), *Heart and Mind*. American Psychological Association.

Burgess, C., Cornelius, V., Love, S. *et al.* (2005). Depression and anxiety in women with early breast cancer: five-year observational cohort study. *British Medical Journal*, 330: 702–5.

Burgoyne, R. and Renwick, R. (2004). Social support and quality of life over time among adults living with HIV in the HAART era. *Social Science and Medicine*, 58: 1353–66.

Burke, V., Beilin, L., Cutt, H., Mansour, J. and Mori, T. (2007). Moderators and mediators of behaviour change in a lifestyle program for treated hypertensives: a randomized controlled trial (ADAPT). *Health Education Research*, B: 583–91.

Burns, J.W., Kubilus, A., Bruehl, S., Harden, R.N. and Lofland, K. (2003). Do changes in cognitive factors influence outcome following multidisciplinary treatment for chronic pain? A cross-lagged panel analysis. *Journal of Consulting and Clinical Psychology*, 71: 81–91.

Burns, V.E., Carroll, D., Drayson, M. *et al.* (2003). Life events, perceived stress and antibody response to influenza vaccination in young, healthy adults. *Journal of Psychosomatic Research*, 55: 569–72.

Burton, D., Graham, J.W., Johnson, C.A. *et al.* (2010). Perceptions of smoking prevalence by youth in countries with and without a tobacco advertising ban. *Journal of Health Communication*, 15: 656–64.

Bury, J., Morrison, V. and MacLachlan, S. (1992). *Working with Women and AIDS: Medical, Social and Counselling Issues*. London: Routledge.

Bush, D.E., Ziegelstein, R.C., Tayback, M. *et al.* (2001). Even minimal symptoms of depression increase mortality risk after acute myocardial infarction. *American Journal of Cardiology*, 88: 337–41.

Buunk, B.P., Zurriaga, R. and González, P. (2006). Social comparison, coping and depression in people with spinal cord injury. *Psychology & Health*, 21: 791–807.

Buzdar, A.U. (2004). Hormonal therapy in early and advanced breast cancer. *Breast Journal*, 10(suppl. 1): S19–21.

Byrne, D.G. and Espnes, G.A. (2008). Occupational stress and cardiovascular disease. *Stress & Health*, 24: 231–8.

Byrne, D.G. and Mazanov, J. (2003). Adolescent stress and future smoking behaviour: a prospective investigation. *Journal of Psychosomatic Research*, 54: 313–21.

Byrne, P. and Long, B. (1976). *Doctors Talking to Patients: A Study of the Verbal Behaviour of General Practitioners Consulting in their Surgeries*. London: HMSO.

Cabral, A.L., Conceicao, G.M., Saldiva, P.H. and Martins, A. (2002). Effect of asthma severity on symptom perception in childhood asthma. *Brazilian Journal of Medical and Biological Research*, 35: 319–27.

Cacioppo, J.T., Andersen, B.L., Turnquist, D.C. *et al.* (1986). Psychophysiological comparison processes: interpreting cancer symptoms. In B.L. Andersen (ed.), *Women with Cancer: Psychosocial Perspectives*. New York: Springer Verlag.

Cacioppo, J.T., Andersen, B.L., Turnquist, D.C. *et al.* (1989). Psychophysiological comparison theory: on the experience, description and assessment of signs and symptoms. *Patient Education and Counselling*, 13: 257–70.

Cacioppo, J.T. and Patrick, B. (2008). *Loneliness: Human Nature and the Need for Social Connection*. New York: W.W. Norton.

Cacioppo, J.T., Poehlmann, K.M., Kiecolt-Glaser, J.K. *et al.* (1998). Cellular immune responses to acute stress in female caregivers of dementia patients and matched controls. *Health Psychology*, 17: 182–9.

Cahill, S.M. (1999). Caring in families: what motivates wives, daughters, and daughters-in law to provide dementia care? *Journal of Family Studies*, 5: 235–47.

Cai, Y., Hong, H., Shi, R. *et al.* (2008). Long-term follow-up study on peer-led school-based HIV/AIDS prevention among youths in Shanghai. *International Journal of STD and AIDS*, 19: 848–50.

Caldwell, T.M., Rodgers, B., Clark, C. *et al.* (2008). Life course socioeconomic predictors of midlife drinking patterns, problems and abstention: findings from the 1958 British Birth Cohort Study. *Drugs and Alcohol Dependence*, 95: 269–78.

Calhoun, L.G. and Tedeschi, R.G. (eds) (2007). *Handbook of Post-traumatic Growth: Research and Practice*. London: Lawrence Erlbaum Associates.

California Department of Health Services (2003). *Alcohol Use During Pregnancy*. Sacramento, CA: CDHS.

Callaghan, P. and Li, H.C. (2002). The effect of pre-operative psychological interventions on post-operative outcomes in Chinese women having an elective hysterectomy. *British Journal of Health Psychology*, 7: 247–52.

Calnan, M. (1987). *Health and Illness: The Lay Perspective*. London: Tavistock.

Cameron, L. (2008). Illness risk representations and motivations to engage in protective behavior: the case of skin cancer risk. *Psychology & Health*, 23: 91–112.

Cameron, L.D. and Leventhal, H. (eds) (2003). *The Self-regulation of Health and Illness Behaviour*. London: Routledge.

Campbell, J.D., Mauksch, H.O., Neikirk, H.J. and Hosokawa, M.C. (1990). Collaborative practice and provider styles in delivering health care. *Social Science and Medicine*, 30: 1359–65.

Campbell, L.A., Kirkpatrick, S.E., Berry, C.C. and Lamberti, J.J. (1992). Psychological preparation of mothers of pre-school children undergoing cardiac catheterization. *Psychology and Health*, 7: 175–85.

Campbell, M.K., Carr, C., Devellis, B. *et al.* (2009). A randomized trial of tailoring and motivational interviewing to promote fruit and vegetable consumption for cancer prevention and control. *Annals of Behavioral Medicine*, 38: 71–85.

Campbell, M.K., Tessaro, I., DeVellis, B. *et al.* (2002). Effects of a tailored health promotion program for female blue-collar workers: health works for women. *Preventive Medicine*, 4: 313–23.

Campbell, R., Starkey, F., Holliday, J. *et al.* (2008). An informal school-based peer-led intervention for smoking prevention in adolescence (ASSIST): a cluster randomised trial. *Lancet*, 371: 1595–602.

Canada, A., Fawzy, N. and Fawzy, F. (2005). Personality and disease outcome in malignant melanoma. *Journal of Psychosomatic Research*, 58: 19–27.

Cancer Research UK (2011). http://info.cancerresearchuk.org/cancerstats/types/prostate/screening

Cannon, W.B. (1932). *The Wisdom of the Body*. New York: W.W. Norton.

Cantril, H. (1967). *The Pattern of Human Concerns*. New Brunswick, NJ: Rutgers University Press.

Carballo, E., Cadarso-Suarez, I., Carrera, J. *et al.* (2010). Assessing relationships between health-related quality of life and adherence to antiretroviral therapy. *Quality of Life Research*, 13: 587–99.

Cardano, M., Costa, G. and Demaria, M. (2004). Social mobility and health in the Turin longitudinal study. *Social Science and Medicine*, 58: 1563–74.

Cardinal, B.J., Lee, J.Y., Kim, Y.H. *et al.* (2009). Behavioral, demographic, psychosocial, and sociocultural concomitants of stage of change for physical activity behavior in a mixed-culture sample. *American Journal of Health Promotion*, 23: 274–8.

Carels, R.A., Darby, L., Cacciapaglia, H.M. *et al.* (2007). Using motivational interviewing as a supplement to obesity treatment: a stepped-care approach. *Health Psychology*, 26: 369–74.

Carers UK (2007). Facts about carers. [Brochure]. London: Carers UK.

Carers UK (2009). Facts about carers. [Brochure]. London: Carers UK.

Carling, C.L., Kristoffersen, D.T., Oxman, A.D. *et al.* (2010). The effect of how outcomes are framed on decisions about whether to take antihypertensive medication: a randomized trial. *Public Library of Science One*, 5: e9469.

Carlson, N. (2003). *Physiology of Behaviour*, 8th edn, Boston, MA: Allyn and Bacon.

Carlson, L.E., Taenzer, P., Koopmans, J. *et al.* (2003). Predictive value of aspects of the transtheoretical model on smoking cessation in a community-based, large-group cognitive behavioral program. *Addictive Behaviors*, 28: 725–40.

Caro, J.J., Speckman, J.L., Salas, M. *et al.* (1999). Effect of initial drug choice on persistence with antihypertensive therapy: the importance of actual practice data. *Canadian Medical Association Journal*, 160: 41–6.

Carod-Artal, J., Egido, J.A., González, J.L. *et al.* (2000). Quality of life among stroke survivors evaluated 1 year after stroke. *Stroke*, 31: 2995–3005.

Caron, F., Godin, G., Otis, J. *et al.* (2004). Evaluation of a theoretically based AIDS/STD peer education program on postponing sexual intercourse and on condom use among adolescents attending high school. *Health Education and Research*, 19: 185–97.

Carr, A.J. and Higginson, I.J. (2001). Are quality of life measures patient centred? *British Medical Journal*, 32: 1357–60.

Carr, D. (2003). A 'good death' for whom? Quality of spouse's death and psychological distress among older widowed persons. *Journal of Health and Social Behavior*, 44: 215–32.

Carrico, A.W., Antoni, M.H., Weaver, K.E. *et al.* (2005). Cognitive-behavioural stress management with HIV-positive homosexual men: mechanisms of sustained reductions in depressive symptoms. *Chronic Illness*, 1: 207–15.

Carroll, D., Davey-Smith, G. and Bennett, P. (1996a). Some observations on health and socioeconomic status. *Journal of Health Psychology*, 1: 1–17.

Carroll, D., Ebrahim, S., Tilling, K. *et al.* (2002). Admissions for myocardial infarction and World Cup football: database survey. *British Medical Journal*, 325: 1439–42.

Carroll, D., Moore, R.A., McQuay, H.J. *et al.* (2001). Transcutaneous electrical nerve stimulation (TENS) for chronic pain. In *The Cochrane Library*, issue 4. Oxford: Update Software.

Carroll, D., Tramèr, M., McQuay, H. *et al.* (1996b). Randomization is important in studies with pain outcomes: systematic review of transcutaneous electrical nerve stimulation in acute postoperative pain. *British Journal of Anaesthesia*, 77: 798–803.

Carroll, K.M., Libby, B., Sheehan, J. *et al.* (2001). Motivational interviewing to enhance treatment initiation in substance abusers: an effectiveness study. *American Journal of Addiction*, 10: 35–9.

Cartagena, R.G., Veugelers, P.J., Kipp, W. *et al.* (2006). Effectiveness of an HIV prevention program for secondary school students in Mongolia. *Journal of Adolescent Health*, 39: 9–16.

Carver, C.S. and Antoni, M.H. (2004). Finding benefit in breast cancer during the year after diagnosis predicts better adjustment 5–8 years after diagnosis. *Health Psychology* 26: 595–8.

Carver, C.S., Pozo, C., Harris, S.D. *et al.* (1993). How coping mediates the effect of optimism on distress: a study of women with early stage breast cancer. *Journal of Personality and Social Psychology*, 65: 375–90.

Carver, C.S. and Scheier, M.F. (1981). *Attention and Self-Regulation: A Control Theory Approach to Human Behavior*. New York: Springer.

Carver, C.S. and Scheier, M.F. (1998). *On the Self-regulation of Behaviour*. New York: Cambridge University Press.

Carver, C.S. and Scheier, M.F. (2005). Optimism. In C.R. Snyder and S.J. Lopez (eds), *Handbook of Positive Psychology* (pp. 231–43). Oxford: Oxford University Press.

Carver, C.S., Scheier, M.F. and Pozo, C. (1992). Conceptualizing the process of coping with health problems. In H.S. Friedman (ed.), *Hostility, Coping and Health*. Washington: American Psychological Association.

Carver, C.S., Scheier, M.F. and Weintraub, J.K. (1989). Assessing coping strategies: a theoretically based approach. *Journal of Personality and Social Psychology*, 56: 267–83.

Casey, D., De Civita, M. and Dasgupta, K. (2010). Understanding physical activity facilitators and barriers during and following a supervised exercise programme in Type 2 diabetes: a qualitative study. *Diabetic Medicine*, 27: 79–84.

Cassel, J. (1974). An epidemiological perspective of psychosocial factors in disease etiology. *American Journal of Public Health*, 64: 1040–3.

Cassell, E.J. (1976). Disease as an 'it': concepts of disease revealed by patients' presentation of symptoms. *Social Science and Medicine*, 10: 143–6.

Cassell, E.J. (1982). Paracetamol plus supplementary doses of codeine. An analgesic study of repeated doses. *European Journal of Clinical Pharmacology*, 23: 315–19.

Cassell, J.A., Mercer, C.H., Imriel, J. *et al.* (2006). Who uses condoms with whom? Evidence from national probability sample surveys. *Sexually Transmitted Infections*, 82: 467–73.

Cassileth, B.R., Lusk, E.J., Brown, L.L. and Cross, P.A. (1985). Psychosocial status of cancer patients and next of kin: normative data from the profile of mood states. *Journal of Psychosocial Oncology*, 3: 99–105.

Castillo-Richmond, A., Schneider, R.H., Alexander, C.N. *et al.* (2000). Effects of stress reduction on carotid atherosclerosis in hypertensive African Americans. *Stroke*, 31: 568–73.

Catz, S.L., Gore-Felton, C. and McClure, J.B. (2002). Psychological distress among minority and low-income women living with HIV. *Behavioral Medicine*, 28: 53–60.

Cavelaars, A.E.J.M., Kunst, A.E. and Mackenbach, J.P. (1997). Socio-economic differences in risk factors for morbidity and mortality in the European Community. *Journal of Health Psychology*, 2: 353–72.

Cella, D.F., Tulsky, D.S., Gray, G. *et al.* (1993). The Functional Assessment of Cancer Therapy scale: development and validation of the general measure. *Journal of Clinical Oncology*, 11: 570–9.

Centers for Disease Control and Prevention (1996). Community-level prevention of human immuno-deficiency virus infection among high-risk populations: the AIDS Community Demonstration Projects. *MMWR Morbidity and Mortality Weekly Reports*, 45(RR-6): 1–24.

Cesaroni, G., Forastiere, F., Agabiti, N. *et al.* (2008). Effect of the Italian smoking ban on population rates of acute coronary events. *Circulation*, 117: 1183–8.

Chacham, A.S., Maia, M.B., Greco, M. *et al.* (2007). Autonomy and susceptibility to HIV/AIDS among young women living in a slum in Belo Horizonte, Brazil. *AIDS Care*, 19(suppl. 1): S12–22.

Chadha, N.K. and Repanos, C. (2004). How much do healthcare professionals know about informed consent? A Bristol experience. *Surgeon*, 2: 328–33, 360.

Chadha, N.K. and Repanos, C. (2006). Patients' understanding of words used to describe lumps: a cross-sectional study. *Journal of Laryngology and Otology*, 120: 125–8.

Chaix, B., Rosvall, M. and Merlo, J. (2007). Neighborhood socioeconomic deprivation and residential instability: effects on incidence of ischemic heart disease and survival after myocardial infarction. *Epidemiology*, 18: 104–11.

Chalmers, B. (1996). Western and African conceptualisations of health. *Psychology and Health*, 12: 1–10.

Champion, V.L. (1990). Breast self-examination in women 35 and older: a prospective study. *Journal of Behavioural Medicine*, 13: 523–38.

Champion, V.L. and Miller, T.K. (1992). Variables related to breast self-examination. *Psychology of Women Quarterly*, 16: 81–96.

Chan, D.S., Callahan, C.W., Hatch-Pigott, V.B. *et al.* (2007). Internet-based home monitoring and education of children with asthma is comparable to ideal office-based care: results of a 1-year asthma in-home monitoring trial. *Pediatrics*, 119: 569–78.

Chan, D.S. and Fishbein, M. (1993). Determinants of women's intentions to tell their partner to use condoms. *Journal of Applied Social Psychology*, 23: 1455–70.

Chandrashekara, S., Jayashree, K., Veeranna, H.B. *et al.* (2007). Effects of anxiety on TNF-a levels during psychological stress. *Journal of Psychosomatic Research*, 63: 65–9.

Chapman, S. and Martin, M. (2011). Attention to pain words in irritable bowel syndrome: increased orienting and speeded engagement. *British Journal of Health Psychology*, 16: 47–60.

Charmaz, K. (1983). Loss of self: a fundamental form of suffering in the chronically ill. *Sociology of Health and Illness*, 5: 168–95.

Charmaz, K. (1991). *Good Days, Bad Days: The Self in Chronic Illness and Time*. New Brunswick, NJ: Rutgers University Press.

Charmaz, K. (1994). Identity dilemmas of chronically ill men. *Sociological Quarterly*, 35: 269–88.

Chassin, C., Presson, C.C., Rose, J.S. *et al.* (1996). The natural history of cigarettes from adolescence to adulthood: demographic predictors of continuity and change. *Health Psychology*, 15: 478–84.

Chatkin, J.M., Blanco, D.C., Scaglia, N. *et al.* (2006). Impact of a low-cost and simple intervention in enhancing treatment adherence in a Brazilian asthma sample. *Journal of Asthma*, 43: 263–6.

Cheing, G.L. and Hui-Chan, C.W. (1999). Transcutaneous electrical nerve stimulation: nonparallel antinociceptive effects on chronic clinical pain and acute experimental pain. *Archives of Physical Medicine and Rehabilitation*, 80: 305–12.

Cheing, G.L., Tsui, A.Y., Lo, S.K. *et al.* (2003). Optimal stimulation duration of TENS in the management of osteoarthritic knee pain. *Journal of Rehabilitation Medicine*, 35: 62–8.

Chen, J.Y., Fox, S.A., Cantrell, C.H. *et al.* (2007). Health disparities and prevention: racial/ethnic barriers to flu vaccinations. *Journal of Community Health*, 32: 5–20.

Chen, S.-L., Tsai, J.-C., Lee, W.-L. (2008). Psychometric validation of the Chinese version of the Illness Perceptin Questionnaire-Revised for patients with hypertension. *Journal of Advanced Nursing*, 64: 524–34.

Chen, S.Y., Gibson, S., Katz, M.H. *et al.* (2002). Continuing increases in sexual risk behavior and sexually transmitted diseases among men who have sex with men: San Francisco, Calif., 1999–2001. *American Journal of Public Health*, 92: 1387–8.

Cheng, C. (2000). Seeking medical consultation: perceptual and behavioural characteristics distinguishing consulters and nonconsulters with functional dyspepsia. *Psychosomatic Medicine*, 62: 844–52.

Cheng, T.L., Savageau, J.A., Sattler, A.L. *et al.* (1993). Confidentiality in health care: a survey of knowledge, perceptions, and attitudes among high school students. *Journal of the American Medical Association*, 269: 1404–7.

Chesney, M.A. (2003). Adherence to HAART regimes. *AIDS Patient Care and STDs*, 17: 169–77.

Chesney, M.A., Folkman, S. and Chambers, D. (1996). Coping effectiveness training for men living with HIV: preliminary findings. *International Journal of STDs and AIDS*, suppl. 2: 75–82.

Cho, H. and Salmon, C.T. (2006). Fear appeals for individuals in different stages of change: intended and unintended effects and implications on public health campaigns. *Health Communication*, 20: 91–9.

Chochinov, H.M., Hack, T., Hassard, T. *et al.* (2002). Dignity in the terminally ill: a cross-sectional, cohort study. *The Lancet*, 360: 2026–30.

Chochinov, H.M., Tataryn, D.J., Wilson, K.G. *et al.* (2000). Prognostic awareness and the terminally ill. *Psychosomatics*, 41: 500–4.

Choi, W.S., Harris, K.J., Okuyemi, K. *et al.* (2003). Predictors of smoking initiation among college-bound high school students. *Annals of Behavioral Medicine*, 26: 69–74.

Choinière, R., Lafontaine, P. and Edwards, A.C. (2000). Distribution of cardiovascular disease risk factors by socioeconomic status among Canadian adults. *Canadian Medical Association Journal*, 162(9 suppl.): S13–24.

Chou, R., Huffman, L.H. American Pain Society; American College of Physicians (2007). Nonpharmacologic therapies for acute and chronic low back pain: a review of the evidence for an American Pain Society/American College of Physicians clinical practice guideline. *Annals of Internal Medicine*, 147: 492–504.

Christensen, A.J., Edwards, D.L., Wiebe, J.S. *et al.* (1996). Effect of verbal self-disclosure on natural killer cell activity: moderating influence of cynical hostility. *Psychosomatic Medicine*, 58: 150–5.

Christensen, C., Larson, J.R., Jr, Abbott, A. *et al.* (2000). Decision making of clinical teams: communication patterns and diagnostic error. *Medical Decision Making*, 20: 45–50.

Chronister, J. and Chan, F. (2006). A stress process model of caregiving for individuals with traumatic brain injury. *Rehabilitation Psychology*, 51: 190–201.

Chun, M., Knight, B.G. and Youn, G. (2007). Differences in stress and coping models of emotional distress among Korean, Korean American and White-American caregivers. *Aging and Mental Health*, 11: 20–9.

CIA Central Intelligence Agency (2008). *World Factbook, 2008*. Washington, DC: CIA.

Cioffi, D. (1991). Beyond attentional strategies: a cognitive-perceptual model of somatic interpretation. *Psychological Bulletin*, 109: 25–41.

Clark, A. (2003). 'It's like an explosion in your life . . .': lay perspectives on stress and myocardial infarction. *Journal of Clinical Nursing*, 12: 544–53.

Clark, R. and Gochett, P. (2006). Interactive effects of perceived racism and coping responses predict a school-based assessment of blood pressure in black youth. *Annals of Behavioral Medicine*, 32: 1–9.

Clark, D.B. and Sayette, M.A. (1993). Anxiety and the development of alcoholism: clinical and scientific issues. *American Journal on Addictions*, 2: 59–76.

Clark, K.L., Loscalzo, M., Trask, P.C. *et al.* (2010). Psychological distress in patients wth pancreatic cancer – an understudied group. *Psycho-Oncology*, 19: 1313–20.

Clark, S.L. and Stephens, M.A.P. (1996). Stroke patients' well-being as a function of caregiving spouses' helpful and unhelpful actions. *Personal Relationships*, 3: 171–84.

Clark-Carter, D. (2003). Effect sizes: the missing piece in the jigsaw. *The Psychologist*, 16: 636–8.

Clarke, R. (2000). Perceptions of interethnic group racism predict increased vascular reactivity to a laboratory challenge in college women. *Annals of Behavioral Medicine*, 22: 214–22.

Clays, E., Leynen, F., De Bacquer, D. *et al.* (2007). High job strain and ambulatory blood pressure in middle-aged men and women from the Belgian job stress study.

Journal of Occupational and Environmental Medicine, 49: 360–7.

Clayton, J.M., Butow, P.N., Tattersall, M.H. *et al.* (2007). Randomized controlled trial of a prompt list to help advanced cancer patients and their caregivers to ask questions about prognosis and end-of-life care. *Journal of Clinical Oncology*, 25: 715–23.

Clifford, S., Barber, N. and Horne, R. (2008). Understanding different beliefs held by adherers, unintentional non-adherers, and intentional non-adherers: application of the Necessity-Concerns Framework. *Journal of Psychosomatic Research*, 64: 41–6.

Clow, A. (2001). The physiology of stress. In F. Jones and J. Bright (eds), *Stress: Myth, Theory and Research*. Harlow: Pearson, pp. 47–72.

Coates, T.J., McKusick, L., Kuno, R. *et al.* (1989). Stress management training reduced numbers of sexual partners but did not improve immune function in men infected with HIV. *American Journal of Public Health*, 79: 885–7.

Cobb, S. (1976). Social support as a moderator of life stress. *Psychosomatic Medicine*, 38: 300–14.

Coburn-Litvak, P.S., Pothakos, K., Tata, D.A. *et al.* (2003). Chronic administration of corticosterone impairs spatial reference memory before spatial working memory in rats. *Neurobiology, Learning & Memory*, 80: 11–23.

Cockburn, J., Paul, C., Tzelepis, F. *et al.* (2003). Delay in seeking advice for symptoms that potentially indicate bowel cancer. *American Journal of Health Behavior*, 27: 401–7.

Cocks, K., King, M.T., Velikova, G. *et al.* (2008). Quality, interpretation and presentation of European Organisation for Research and Treatment of Cancer quality of life questionnaire core data in randomised controlled trials. *European Journal of Cancer*, 44: 1793–8.

Cocquyt, V.F., Blondeel, P.N., Depypere, H.T. *et al.* (2003). Better cosmetic results and comparable quality of life after skin-sparing mastectomy and immediate autologous breast reconstruction compared to breast conservative treatment. *The British Association of Plastic Surgeons*, 56: 462–70.

Cohen, F. and Lazarus, R. (1979). Coping with the stresses of illness. In G.C. Stone, F. Cohen and N.E. Adler (eds), *Health Psychology: A Handbook*. San Francisco, CA: Jossey-Bass.

Cohen, H.J., Pieper, C.F., Harris, T., Rao, K. and Currie, M.M.K. (1997). The association of plasma IL-6 levels with functional disability in community-dwelling elderly. *Journal of Gerontology. A: Biological Science and Medical Science*, 52: M201–8.

Cohen, L.A. (1987). Diet and cancer. *Scientific American*, 102: 42–8.

Cohen, M., Hoffman, R.G., Cromwell, C. *et al.* (2002). The prevalence of distress in persons with human immunodeficiency virus infection. *Psychosomatics*, 43: 10–15.

Cohen, S. (1988). Psychosocial models of the role of social support in the etiology of physical disease, *Health Psychology*, 7: 269–97.

Cohen, S. (2004). Social relationships and health. *American Psychologist*, 59: 676–84.

Cohen, S. (2005). Keynote presentation at the eighth International Congress of Behavioral Medicine. *Journal of Behavioral Medicine*, 12: 123–1.

Cohen, S., Doyle, M.J., Skoner, D.P. *et al.* (1995). State and trait negative affect as predictors of objective and subjective symptoms of respiratory viral infections. *Journal of Personality and Social Psychology*, 68: 159–69.

Cohen, S., Doyle, W.J., Turner, R. *et al.* (2003). Sociability and susceptibility to the common cold. *Psychological Science*, 14: 389–95.

Cohen, S., Evans, G.W., Stokols, D. and Krantz, D.S. (1986). *Behavior, Health and Environmental Stress*. New York: Plenum.

Cohen, S., Frank, E., Doyle, W.J. *et al.* (1998). Types of stressors that increase susceptibility to the common cold in healthy adults. *Health Psychology*, 17: 214–23.

Cohen, S. and Herbert, T.B. (1996). Health psychology: psychological factors and physical disease from the perspective of human psychoneuroimmunology. *Annual Review of Psychology*, 47: 113–42.

Cohen, S. and Hoberman, H. (1983). Positive events and social support as buffers of life change stress. *Journal of Applied Social Psychology*, 13: 99–125.

Cohen, S., Kamarck, T. and Mermelstein, R. (1983). A global measure of perceived stress. *Journal of Health and Social Behaviour*, 24: 385–96.

Cohen, S., Tyrell, D.A. and Smith, A.P. (1993a). Life events, perceived stress, negative affect and susceptibility to the common cold. *Journal of Personality and Social Psychology*, 64: 131–40.

Cohen, S., Tyrell, D.A. and Smith, A.P. (1993b). Psychological stress and susceptibility to the common cold. *New England Journal of Medicine*, 325: 606–12.

Cohen, S. and Williamson, G.M. (1991). Stress and infectious disease in humans. *Psychological Bulletin*, 109: 5–24.

Cohen, S. and Wills, T.A. (1985). Stress, social support and the buffering hypothesis. *Psychological Bulletin*, 98: 310–57.

Cole, S.W., Kemeny, M.E., Taylor, S.E. *et al.* (1996). Elevated physical health risk among gay men who conceal their homosexual identity. *Health Psychology*, 15: 23–51.

Coleman, D.L. (1979). Obesity genes: beneficial effects in heterozygous mice. *Science*, 203: 663–5.

Coleman, P.G. (1999). Identity management in later life. In R.T. Woods (ed.), *Psychological Problems of Ageing: Assessment, Treatment and Care*. Chichester: Wiley.

Collicutt, J. (2011). Psychology, religion and spirituality. *The Psychologist*, 24: 250–51.

Collins, S. (2005). Explanations in consultations: the combined effectiveness of doctors' and nurses' communication with patients. *Medical Education*, 39: 785–96.

COMMIT (1995). Community intervention trial for smoking cessation (COMMIT): II. Changes in adult cigarette smoking prevalence. *American Journal of Public Health*, 85: 193–200.

Committee on Understanding and Eliminating Racial and Ethnic Disparities in Health Care, Institute of Medicine, National Academy of Sciences, Smedley, B.D., Stith, A.Y. and Nelson, A.R. (eds) (2002). *Unequal Treatment: Confronting Racial and Ethnic Disparities in Health Care.* Washington, DC: National Academy Press.

Compas, B.E., Stoll, M.F., Thomsen, A.H. *et al.* (1999). Adjustment to breast cancer: age-related differences in coping and emotional distress. *Breast Cancer Research and Treatment*, 54: 195–203.

Conner, M. and Armitage, C.J. (1998). Extending the theory of planned behaviour: a review and avenues for further research. *Journal of Applied Social Psychology*, 28: 1429–64.

Conner, M. and Godin, G. (2007). Temporal stability of behavioural intention as a moderator of intention-health behaviour relationships. *Psychology & Health*, 22: 875–97.

Conner, M. and Higgins, A.R. (2010). Long-term effects of implementation intentions on prevention of smoking uptake among adolescents: a cluster randomized controlled trial. *Health Psychology*, 29: 529–38.

Conner, M. and Norman, P. (1996). *Predicting Health Behaviour: Research and Practice with Social Cognition Models.* Buckingham: Open University Press.

Conner, M. and Sparks, (2005). Theory of planned behaviour and health behaviour. In M. Conner and P. Norman (eds), *Predicting Health behaviour*. London: Open University Press, pp.170–222.

Conner, M., Sutherland, E., Kennedy, F., Grearly, C. and Berry, C. (2008). Impact of alcohol on sexual decision making: intentions to have unprotected sex. *Psychology & Health*, 23: 909–34.

Connor, J.L., Kypri, K., Bell, M.L. *et al.* (2010). Alcohol outlet density, levels of drinking and alcohol-related harm in New Zealand: a national study. *Journal of Epidemiology and Community Health*, 2010 Oct 14.

Consedine, N.S., Horton, D., Magai, C. *et al.* (2007). Breast screening in response to gain, loss, and empowerment framed messages among diverse, low-income women. *Journal of Health Care for the Poor and Underserved*, 18: 550–66.

Constans, J.I., Mathews, A., Brantley, P.J. *et al.* (1999). Attentional reactions to an MI: the impact of mood state, worry, and coping style. *Journal of Psychosomatic Research*, 46: 415–23.

Cook, B.J. and Hausenblas, H.A. (2008). The role of exercise dependence for the relationship between exercise behavior and eating pathology: mediator or moderator? *Journal of Health Psychology*, 13: 495–502.

Cook, R.F., Billings, D.W., Hersch, R. *et al.* (2007). A field test of a web-based workplace health promotion program to improve dietary practices, reduce stress, and increase physical activity: randomized controlled trial. *Journal of Medical Internet Research*, 9: e17.

Cooper, C.L. and Payne, R. (eds) (1988). *Causes, Coping and Consequences of Stress at Work.* Chichester: Wiley.

Cooper, M.L., Agocha, V.S. and Sheldon, M.S. (2000). A motivational perspective on risky behaviours: the role of personality and affect regulatory processes. *Journal of Personality*, 68: 159–69.

Cope, C.D., Lyons, A.C., Donovan, V. *et al.* (2003). Providing letters and audiotapes to supplement a prenatal diagnostic consultation: effects on later distress and recall. *Prenatal Diagnosis*, 23: 1060–7.

Cordova, M., Andrykowski, M., Kenady, D. *et al.* (1995). Frequency and correlates of posttraumatic-stress-disorder-like symptoms after treatment for breast cancer. *Journal of Consulting and Clinical Psychology*, 63: 981–6.

Costa, P.T., Jr and McCrae, R.R. (1987). Neuroticism, somatic complaints and disease: is the bark worse than the bite? *Journal of Personality*, 55: 299–316.

Costa, P.T. and McCrae, R.R. (1992a). Four ways five factors are basic. *Personality and Individual Differences*, 13: 653–65.

Costa, P.T. and McCrae, R.R. (1992b). *Revised NEO Personality Inventory (NEO PI-R) and NEO Fivefactor Inventory (NEO FFI) Professional Manual.* Odessa, FL: Psychological Assessment Resources.

Costanzo, E.S., Lutgendorf, S.K. and Roeder, S. (2011). Common-sense beliefs about cancer and health practices among women completing treatment for breast caner. *Psycho-Oncology*, 20: 53–61.

Costanzo, E.S., Lutgendorf, S.K., Bradley, S.L., Rose, S. and Anderson, B. (2005). Cancer attributions, distress, and health practices among gynaecologic cancer survivors. *Psychosomatic Medicine*, 67: 972–80.

Costanzo, E.S., Lutgendorf, S.K., Mattes, M.L. *et al.* (2007) Adjusting to life after treatment: distress and quality of life following treatment for breast cancer, *British Journal of Cancer*. 97: 1625–31.

Cotman, C.W. and Engesser-Cesar, C. (2002). Exercise enhances and protects brain function. *Exercise Sport Science Reviews*, 30: 75–9.

Courtenay, W.H. (2000). Constructions of masculinity and their influence on men's well-being: a theory of gender and health. *Social Science and Medicine*, 50: 1385–401.

Covic, T., Adamson, B., Spencer, D. and Howe, G. (2003). A biopsychosocial model of pain and depression in rheumatoid arthritis: a 12-month longitudinal study. *Rheumatology*, 42: 176–85.

Cowburn, G. and Stockley, L. (2005). Consumer understanding and use of nutrition labelling: a systematic review. *Public Health & Nutrition*. 8: 21–8.

Cowburn, G. and Stockley, L. (2006). Consumer understanding and use of nutrition labelling: a systematic review. *Journal of the American Dietetic Association*, 106: 917–20.

Cox, D.S., Cox, A.D., Sturm, L. and Zimet, G. (2010). Behavioural interventions to increase HPV vaccination acceptability among mothers of young girls. *Health Psychology*, 29: 29–39.

Cox, K. (2003). Assessing the quality of life of patients in phase I and II anti-cancer drug trials: interviews versus questionnaires. *Social Science and Medicine*, 56: 921–34.

Cox, K.L., Gorely, T.J., Puddey, I.B., Burke, V. and Beilin, L.J. (2003). Exercise behaviour change in 40- to 65-year-old women: the SWEAT study (Sedentary Women Exercise Adherence Trial). *British Journal of Health Psychology*, 8: 477–95.

Cox, W.M. and Klinger, E. (2004). A motivational model of alcohol use: determinants of use and change. In W.M. Cox and E. Klinger (eds), *Handbook of Motivational Counselling: Concepts, Approaches, and Assessments*. Chichester: John Wiley, pp. 121–38.

Coyne, J. and Fiske, V. (1992). Couples coping with chronic and catastrophic illness. In T.J. Akamatsu, M.A.P. Stephens, S.E. Hobfoll and J.H. Crowther (eds), *Family Health Psychology*. Washington, DC: Hemisphere Publishing.

Coyne, J.C., Benazon, N.R., Rohrbaugh, M.J. *et al.* (2003). Patient and spousal attitude in couples living with chronic heart failure. Symposium paper presented at the 17th Conference of the European Health Psychology Society, September, Kos.

Coyne, J.C. and Racioppo, M.W. (2000). Never the twain shall meet? Closing the gap between coping research and clinical intervention research. *American Psychologist*, 55: 655–64.

Coyne, J.C. and Smith, D.A.F. (1991). Couples coping with a myocardial infarction: a contextual perspective on wive's distress. *Journal of Personality and Social Psychology*, 61: 404–12.

Cramer, J.A. (1998). Enhancing patient compliance in the elderly. Role of packaging aids and monitoring. *Drugs and Aging*, 12: 7–15.

Cramer, J.A. (2004). A systematic review of adherence with medications for diabetes. *Diabetes Care*, 27: 1218–24.

Cramp, F. and Daniel, J. (2008). Exercise for the management of cancer-related fatigue in adults. *Cochrane Database of Systematic Reviews*, issue 2, art. no.: CD006145. doi: 10.1002/14651858.CD006145.

Crepaz, N., Pasin, W.F., Herbst, J.H. *et al.* (2008). Meta-analysis of cognitive behavioural interventions on HIV positive persons' mental health and immune functioning. *Health Psychology*, 27: 4–14.

Creuss, D.G., Antoni, M.H., McGregor, B.A. *et al.* (2000). Cognitive-behavioral stress management reduces serum cortisol by enhancing benefit finding among women being treated for early stage breast cancer. *Psychosomatic Medicine*, 62: 304–8.

Crisp, A., Sedgwick, P., Halek, C. *et al.* (1999). Why may teenage girls persist in smoking? *Journal of Adolescence*, 22: 657–72.

Crossley, M.L. (2000). *Rethinking Health Psychology*. Buckingham: Open University Press.

Crossley, M.L. and Small, N. (1998). Evaluation of HIV/AIDS Education Training Services Provided by London Lighthouse at St. Ann's Hospice. Stockport Health Authority.

Crowe, F.L., Key, T.J., Appleby, P.N. *et al.* (2008). Dietary fat intake and risk of prostate cancer in the European: prospective investigation into cancer and nutrition. *American Journal of Clinical Nutrition*, 87: 1405–13.

Croyle, R.T. and Barger, S.D. (1993). Illness cognition. In S. Maes, H. Leventhal and M. Johnston (eds), *International Review of Health Psychology*, Vol. II. Chichester: Wiley.

Croyle, R.T. and Ditto, P.M. (1990). Illness cognition and behavior: an experimental approach. *Journal of Behavioral Medicine*, 13: 31–52.

Csof, R.-M., Hood, R., Keler, B. *et al.* (2009). *Deconversion*. Goettingen: Vandenhoech & Ruprecht.

Culver, J.L., Arena, P.L., Antoni, M.H. and Carver, C.S. (2002). Coping and distress among women under treatment for early stage breast cancer: comparing African Americans, Hispanics and non-Hispanics whites. *Psycho-Oncology*, 11: 495–504.

Cummings, J.H. and Bingham, S.A. (1998). Diet and the prevention of cancer. *British Medical Journal*, 317: 1636–40.

Curbow, B., Somerfield, M.R., Baker, F. *et al.* (1993). Personal changes, dispositional optimism, and psychological adjustment to bone marrow transplantation. *Journal of Behavioral Medicine*, 16: 423–43.

Curry, S.J. and Emmons, K.M. (1994). Theoretical models for predicting and improving compliance with breast cancer screening. Mini-series: advances in behavioural medicine research on breast cancer. *Annals of Behavioral Medicine*, 16: 302–16.

Cutrona, C.E. (1996). *Social Support in Couples*. Thousand Oaks, CA: Sage.

Cutrona, C.E. and Russell, D.W. (1987). The provision of social relationships and adaptation to stress. In W.H. Jones and D. Perlman (eds), *Advances in Personal Relationships*, Vol. 1. Greenwich, CT: JAI Press.

Cutrona, C.E. and Russell, D.W. (1990). Type of social support and specific stress: toward a theory of optimal matching. In B.A. Sarason, I.G. Sarason and G.R. Pierce (eds), *Social Support: An Interactional View*. New York: Wiley.

Currow, D.C., Agar, M., Plummer, J.L. *et al.* (2010). Chronic pain in South Australia – population levels that interfere extremely with activities of daily living. *Australia and New Zealand Journal of Public Health*, 34: 232–9.

Culver, J.L., Arena, P.L., Wimberly, S.R., Antoni, M.H. and Carver, C.S. (2004). Coping among African American, Hispanic, and non-Hispanic white women recently treated for early stage breast cancer. *Psychology and Health*, 19: 157–66.

Dababneh, A.J., Swanson, N. and Shell, R.L. (2001). Impact of added rest breaks on the productivity and well being of workers. *Ergonomics*, 44: 164–74.

Dagan, M., Sanderman, R., Schokker, M.C. *et al.* (2011). Spousal support and changes in distress over time in couples coping with cancer: the role of personal control. *Journal of Family Psychology*, 25: 310–18.

Dalton, S.O., Boesen, E.H., Ross, L. *et al.* (2002). Mind and cancer: do psychological factors cause cancer? *European Journal of Cancer*, 38: 1313–23.

Daly, J.M., Hartz, A.J., Xu, Y. *et al.* (2009). An assessment of attitudes, behaviors, and outcomes of patients with type 2 diabetes. *Journal of the American Board of Family Medicine*, 22: 280–90.

Damjanovic, A.K., Yang, Y., Glaser, R. *et al.* (2007). Accelerated telomere erosion is associated with a declining immune function of caregivers of Alheimer's disease patients. *Journal of Immunology*,179: 4249–54.

Dancey, C.P., Taghavi, M. and Fox, R.J. (1998). The relationship between daily stress and symptoms of irritable bowel: a time-series approach. *Journal of Psychosomatic Research*. 44(5): 537–45.

Dantzer, R. and Kelley, K.W. (1989). Stress and immunity: an integrated view of relationships between the brain and the immune system. *Life Sciences*, 44: 1995–2008.

Darnley, S.E., Kennedy, T., Jones, R. *et al.* (2002). A randomised controlled trial of the addition of cognitive behavioural therapy (CBT) to antispasmodic therapy for irritable bowel syndrome (IBS) in primary care. *Gastroenterology*, 122: A-69.

Dauchet, L., Amouyel, P. and Dallongeville, J. (2009). Fruits, vegetables and coronary heart disease. *Nature Reviews Cardiology*, 6: 599–608.

Davey-Smith, G., Ebrahim, S. and Frankel, S. (2001). How policy informs the evidence: 'evidence-based' thinking can lead to debased policy making (editorial). *British Medical Journal*, 322: 184–5.

Davey-Smith, G., Wentworth, D., Neaton, J.D. *et al.* (1996). Socio-economic differentials in mortality risk among men screened for the Multiple Risk Factor Intervention Trial, 2: black men. *American Journal of Public Health*, 86: 497–504.

David, J.P. and Suls, J. (1996). Coping efforts in daily life: role of big five traits and problem appraisals. *Journal of Personality*, 67: 265–94.

Davidson, K.W., Gidron, Y., Mostofsky, E. and Trudeau, K.J. (2007). Hospitalization cost offset of a hostility intervention for coronary heart disease patients. *Journal of Consulting and Clinical Psychology*, 75: 657–62.

Davidson, K.W., MacGregor, M.E., Stuhr, J. *et al.* (2000). Constructive anger verbal behaviour predicts blood pressure in a population-based sample. *Health Psychology*, 19: 55–64.

Davidson, P.R. and Parker, K.C.H. (2001). Eye movement desensitization and reprocessing (EMDR): a meta-analysis. *Journal of Consulting and Clinical Psychology*, 69: 305–16.

Davies, J.B. and Baker, R. (1987). The impact of self-presentation and interviewer bias on self-reported heroin use. *British Journal of Addiction*, 82: 907–12.

Deary, I.J., Clyde, Z. and Frier, B.M. (1997). Constructs and models in health psychology: the case of personality and illness reporting in diabetes mellitus. *British Journal of Health Psychology*, 2: 35–54.

DeBoer, M.F., Ryckman, R.M., Pruyn, J.F. *et al.* (1999). Psychosocial correlates of cancer relapse and survival: a literature review. *Patient Education and Counselling*, 37: 215–30.

Deci, E.L. and Ryan, R.M. (2000). The 'what' and 'why' of goal pursuits: human needs and the self-determination of behavior. *Psychological Inquiry*, 11: 227–68.

Deeg, D.J.H. and Kriegsman, D.M.W. (2003). Concepts of self-rated health: specifying the gender difference in mortality risk. *The Gerontologist*, 43: 376–86.

DeFriese, G. and Woomert, A. (1983). Self-care among the US elderly. *Research on Aging*, 5: 3–23.

De Haes, H. and Koedoot, N. (2003). Patient centered decision making in palliative cancer treatment: a world of paradoxes. *Patient Education and Counselling*, 50: 43–9.

Dehghani, M., Sharpe, L. and Nicholas, M.K. (2003). Selective attention to pain-related information in chronic musculoskeletal pain patients. *Pain*, 105: 37–46.

Deimling, G.T., Bowman, K.F., Sterns, S. *et al.* (2006) Cancer-related health worries and psychological distress among older adult long-term cancer survivors. *Psycho-Oncology*, 15: 306–20.

de Lange, A.H., Taris, T.W., Kompier, M.A. *et al.* (2003). The very best of the millennium: longitudinal research and the demand–control–(support) model. *Journal of Occupational Health Psychology*, 8: 282–305.

Delaney-Black, V., Chiodo, L.M., Hannigan, J.H. *et al.* (2010). Just say 'I don't': lack of concordance between teen report and biological measures of drug use. *Pediatrics*, 126: 887–93.

De Longis, A., Folkman, S. and Lazarus, R.S. (1997). The impact of daily stress on health and mood: psychologiocal and social resources as mediators. *Journal of Personality and Social Psychology*, 54: 486–95.

Dembrowski, T.M., MacDougall, J.M., Costa, P.T. *et al.* (1989). Components of hostility as predictors of sudden death and myocardial infarction in the Multiple Risk Factor Intervention Trial. *Psychosomatic Medicine*, 51: 514–22.

Dempster, M. and McCorry, N.K. (2011). The factor structure of the Revised Illness Perception Questionnaire in a population of oesophageal cancer survivors. *Psycho-Oncology*, doi: 10.1002/pon.1927.

De Moor, C., Sterner, J., Hall, M. *et al.* (2002). A pilot study of the effects of expressive writing on psychological and behavioral adjustment in patients enrolled in a phase II trial of vaccine therapy for metastatic renal cell carcinoma. *Health Psychology*, 21: 615–19.

De Neve, K.M. and Cooper, H. (1998). The happy personality: A meta-analysis of 137 personality traits and subjective wellbeing. *Psychological Bulletin*, 124: 197–229.

Denollet, J. (1998). Personality and coronary heart disease: the type-D scale-16 (DS16). *Annals of Behavioral Medicine*, 20: 209–15.

Denollet, J. and dePotter, B. (1992). Coping subtypes for men with coronary heart disease: relationship to well-being, stress and type-A behavior. *Psychological Medicine*, 22: 667–84.

Denollet, J., Pedersen, S.S., Vrints, C.J. and Conraads, V.M. (2006). Usefulness of Type D personality in predicting five-year cardiac events above and beyond concurrent symptoms of stress in patients with coronary heart disease. *The American Journal of Cardiology*, 97: 970e3.

Denollet, J., Sys, S.U., Stroobant, N. *et al.* (1996). Personality as an independent predictor of long-term mortality in patients with coronary heart disease. *The Lancet*, 347: 417–21.

Denscombe, M. (2001). Peer group pressure, young people and smoking: new developments and policy implications. *Drugs: Education, Prevention and Policy*, 8: 7–32.

de Nooijer, J., de Vet, E., Brug, J. and de Vries, N.K. (2006). Do implementation intentions help to turn good intentions into higher fruit intakes? *Journal of Nutrition Education and Behavior*, 38: 25–9.

de Nooijer, J., Lechner, L. and de Vries, H.A. (2001). Qualitative study on detecting cancer symptoms and seeking medical help: an application of Andersen's model of total patient delay. *Patient Education and Counseling*, 42: 145–57.

Department of Health (1991). *The Health of the Nation*. London: HMSO.

Department of Health (1992). *The Health of the Nation: A Strategy for Health in England.* London: HMSO.

Department of Health (1995). *Obesity: Reversing the Increasing Problem of Obesity in England.* Report from the Nutrition and Physical Activity Task Forces. London: HMSO.

Department of Health (1999) *Saving Lives: Our Healthier Nation*. London: Department of Health.

Department of Health (2000a). *Health Survey for England.* London: National Centre for Social Research & the National Foundation for Educational Research.

Department of Health (2000b) Statistics on smoking: England 1978 onwards. *Statistical Bulletin* 200/17. London: Department of Health.

Department of Health (2001a). *The 2000 Health Survey for England: The Health of Older People (aged 65+).* London: Department of Health.

Department of Health (2001b). *The Expert Patient: A New Approach to Chronic Disease Management for the 21st Century.* London: Department of Health.

Department of Health (2001c). *Involving Patients and the Public in Healthcare.* Available from: www.dh.gov.uk/Policy AndGuidance/OrganisationPolicy/PatientAndPublic Involvement/InvolvingPatientsPublicHealthcare/fs/en.

Department of Health (2003). *Tackling Health Inequalities: A Programme for Action.* London: Department of Health.

Department of Health (2004). *At Least Five a Week: Evidence on the Impact of Physical Activity and its Relationship to Health.* A Report from the Chief Medical Officer. London: Department of Health.

Department of Health (2007). *Tackling Health Inequalities: 2007 Status Report on the Programme for Action.* London: Department of Health.

Department of Health and Human Services (1996). Report of final mortality statistics, 1994. *Monthly Vital Statistics Report*, 45(3 suppl.). Hyattsville, MD: Public Health Service.

Department of Health and Human Services (1998). *Health, United States, 1998: Socio-economic Status and Health Chartbook.* Hyattsville, MD: National Center for Health Statistics.

Derbyshire, S.W. (2000). Exploring the pain 'neuro-matrix'. *Current Reviews of Pain*, 4: 467–77.

De Ridder, D., Fournier, M. and Bensing, J. (2004). Does optimism affect symptom report in chronic disease? What are its consequences for self-care behaviour and physical functioning? *Journal of Psychosomatic Research*, 56: 341–50.

De Ridder, D. and Schreurs, K. (2001). Developing interventions for chronically ill patients: Is coping a helpful concept? *Clinical Psychology Review*, 21: 205–40.

Descartes, R. (1664). *Traite de l'homme*. Paris: Angot.

Deshler, A.M., Fee-Schroeder, K.C., Dowdy, J.L. *et al.* (2006). A patient orientation program at a comprehensive cancer center. *Oncology Nursing Forum*, 33: 569–78.

Detmar, S.B., Aaronson, N.K., Wever, L.D. *et al.* (2000). How are you feeling? Who wants to know? Patients' and oncologists preferences for discussing health-related quality of life issues. *Journal of Clinical Oncology*, 18: 3295–301.

Devanesen, D. (2000). Traditional Aboriginal medicine practice in the Northern Territory. In *International Symposium on Traditional Medicine*, Awaji Islands, Japan. Available from: www.nt.gov.au/health/comm_health/abhealth_ strategy?Traditional%20Aboriginal%20Medicine%20- %20Japan%20Paper.pdf.

De Vellis, R.F., Lewis, M.A. and Sterba, K.R. (2003). Interpersonal emotional processes in adjustment to chronic illness. In J. Suls and K.A. Wallston (eds), *Social Psychological Foundations of Health and Illness*. Malden, MA: Blackwell.

De Vet, E., De Nooijer, J., DeVries, N.K. and Brug, J. (2007). Comparing stage of change and behavioral intention to understand fruit intake. *Health Education Research*, 22: 599–608.

De Vet, E., Gebhardt, W.A., Sinnige, J. *et al.* (2011). Implementation intentions for buying, carrying, discussing and using condoms: the role of the quality of the plans. *Health Education Research*, 26: 443–55.

Devine, C.M., Jastran, M., Jabs, J. *et al.* (2006). 'A lot of sacrifices': work–family spillover and the food choice coping strategies of low-wage employed parents. *Social Science and Medicine*, 63: 2591–603.

Devins, G.M., Mendelssohn, D.C., Barré, P.E. *et al.* (2003). Predialysis psychoeducational intervention and coping styles influence time to dialysis in chronic kidney disease. *American Journal of Kidney Diseases*, 42: 693–703.

de Vries, H., Candel, M., Engles, R. *et al.* (2006). Challenges to the peer influence paradigm: results for 12–13 year olds from six European countries from the European Smoking Prevention Framework Approach study. *Tobacco Control*, 15: 83–9.

Dew, M.A., Di Martini, A.F., Dabbs, A., de V. *et al.* (2007). Rates and risk factors for nonadherence to the medical regimen after adults solid organ transplantation. *Transplantation*, 83: 858–73.

Dey, P., Bundred, N., Gibbs, A. *et al.* (2002). Costs and benefits of a one stop clinic compared with a dedicated breast clinic: randomised controlled trial. *British Medical Journal*, 324: 507.

Deyo, R.A. (1986). Early diagnostic evaluation of lower back pain. *Journal of General Internal Medicine*, 1: 328–38.

Deyo, R.A. (1991). Fads in the treatment of low back pain. *New England Journal of Medicine*, 325: 1039–40.

Deyo, R.A., Walsh, N.E., Martin, D.C. *et al.* (1990). A controlled trial of transcutaneous electrical nerve stimulation (TENS) and exercise for chronic low back pain. *New England Journal of Medicine*, 322: 1627–34.

di Clemente, C.C. and Prochaska, J.O. (1982). Self-change and therapy change of smoking behavior: a comparison of processes of change in cessation and maintenance. *Addictive Behaviours*, 7: 133–42.

di Clemente, C.C., Prochaska, J.O., Fairhurst, S.K. *et al.* (1991). The process of smoking cessation: an analysis of precontemplation, contemplation, and preparation stages of change. *Journal of Consulting and Clinical Psychology*, 59: 295–304.

di Clemente, C.C. and Velicer, W.F. (1997). The transtheoretical model of health behavior change. *American Journal of Health Promotion*, 12: 11–12.

Didlake, R.H., Dreyfus, K., Kerman, R.H. *et al.* (1988). Patient noncompliance: a major cause of late graft failure in cyclosporine-treated renal transplants. *Transplant Proceedings*, 20: 63–9.

Diefenbach, M.A., Leventhal, E.A., Leventhal, H. *et al.* (1995). Negative affect relates to cross-sectional but not longitudinal symptom reporting: data from elderly adults. *Health Psychology*, 15: 282–8.

Diener, E., Emmons, R.A., Larsen, R.J. and Griffen, S. (1985). The satisfaction with life scale. *Journal of Personality Assessment*, 49: 71–5.

Diener, E., Lucas, R.E. and Scollon, C.N. (2006). Beyond the hedonic treadmill: revising the adaptation theory of well-being. *American Psychologist*, 61(4): 305–14.

Digiusto, E. and Bird, K.D. (1995). Matching smokers to treatment: self-control versus social support. *Journal of Consulting and Clinical Psychology*, 63: 290–95.

Dijkstra, A., Conijn, B. and DeVries, H. (2006). A match–mismatch test of a stage model of behavior change in tobacco smoking. *Addiction*, 101: 1035–43.

Dijkstra, P.U., Geertzen, J.H., Stewart, R. *et al.* (2002). Phantom pain and risk factors: a multivariate analysis. *Journal of Pain Symptom Management*, 24: 578–85.

Dillay, J.W., McFarland, W., Woods, W.J. *et al.* (2002). Thoughts associated with unprotected anal intercourse among men at high risk in San Francisco 1997–1999. *Psychology and Health*, 17: 235–46.

DiMatteo, M.R. (2004a). Variations in patients' adherence to medical recommendations: a quantitative review of 50 years of research. *Medical Care*, 42: 200–9.

DiMatteo, M.R. (2004b). The role of effective communication with children and their families in fostering adherence to pediatric regimes. *Patient Education and Counselling*, 55: 339–44.

DiMatteo, M.R., Haskard, K.B. and Williams, S.L. (2007). Health beliefs, disease severity, and patients adherence: a meta-analysis. *Medical Care*, 45: 521–8.

DiMatteo, M.R., Lepper, H.D. and Croghan, T.W. (2000). Depression is a risk factor for non-compliance with medical treatment: meta-analysis of the effects of anxiety and depression on patient adherence. *Archives of Internal Medicine*, 160: 2101–7.

Dimigen, G. and Ferguson, K. (1993). An investigation into the relationship of children's cognitive development and their concepts of illness. *Psychologia*, 36: 97–102.

Ding, A. (2003). Youth are more sensitive to price changes in cigarettes than adults. *Yale Journal of Biology and Medicine*, 76: 115–24.

Ditto, P.H., Druley, J.A., Moore, K.A. *et al.* (1996). Fates worse than death: the role of valued life activities in health state evaluations. *Health Psychology*, 15: 332–43.

Ditto, T.T. and Jemmott, J.B., III (1989). From rarity to evaluative extremity: effects of prevalence information on evaluations of positive and negative characteristics. *Journal of Personality and Social Psychology*, 57: 16–26.

Dodds, J. and Mercey, D. (2002). *London Gay Men's Survey: 2001 Results*. London: Department of STDs, Royal Free and University College Medical School.

Dodds, J.P., Mercey, D.E., Parry, J.V. *et al.* (2004). Increasing risk behaviour and high levels of undiagnosed HIV infection in a community sample of homosexual men. *Sexually Transmitted Infections*, 80: 236–40.

Doherty, S.R., Jones, P.D., Davis, L. *et al.* (2007). Evidence-based implementation of adult asthma guidelines in the emergency department: a controlled trial. *Emergency Medicine Australasia*, 19: 31–8.

Dohrenwend, B.S. and Dohrenwend, B.P. (1982). Some issues in research on stressful life events. In T. Millon, C. Green and R. Meagher (eds), *Handbook of Clinical Health Psychology*. New York: Plenum.

Dolansky, M.A., Stepanczuk, B., Charvat, J.M. *et al.* (2010). Women's and men's exercise adherence after a cardiac event. *Research in Gerontological Nursing*, 3: 30–8.

Doll, R. and Hill, A.B. (1954). The mortality of doctors in relation to their smoking habits: a preliminary report. *British Medical Journal*, 1: 1451–5.

Doll, R. and Peto, R. (1981). *The Cause of Human Cancer*. Oxford: Oxford University Press.

Doll, R., Peto, R., Boreham, J. and Sutherland, I. (2004). Mortality in relation to smoking: 50 years' observations on male British doctors. *British Medical Journal*, 328: 1519–28.

Doll, R., Peto, R., Hall, E. *et al.* (1994). Mortality in relation to consumption of alcohol: 13 years' observation on male British doctors. *British Medical Journal*, 309: 911–18.

Dooley, D., Fielding, J. and Levi, L. (1996). Health and unemployment. *Annual Review of Public Health*, 17: 449–65.

Doyal, L. (2001). Sex, gender, and health: the need for a new approach. *British Medical Journal*, 323: 1061–3.

Dragano, N., Verde, P.E. and Siegrist, J. (2005). Organisational downsizing and work stress: testing synergistic health effects in employed men and women. *Journal of Epidemiology and Community Health*, 59: 694–9.

Droomers, M., Schrijvers, C.T.M. and Mackenbach, J.P. (2002). Why do lower educated people continue smoking? Explanations from the longitudinal GLOBE study. *Health Psychology*, 21: 263–72.

Drossaert, C.H., Boer, H. and Seydel, E.R. (1996). Health education to improve repeat participation in the Dutch breast cancer screening programme: evaluation of a leaflet tailored to previous participants. *Patient Education and Counselling*, 8: 121–31.

Duff, A.J. (2001). Psychological interventions in cystic fibrosis and asthma. *Paediatric Respiratory Reviews*, 2: 350–7.

Duffy, L.C., Zielezny, M.A., Marshall, J.R. *et al.* (1991). Relevance of major stress events as an indicator of disease activity prevalence in inflammatory bowel disease. *Behavioral Medicine*, Fall: 101–10.

Duncan, S.C., Strycker, L.A. and Duncan, T.E. (1999). Exploring association in developmental trends of adolescent substance use and risky sexual behavior in a high risk population. *Journal of Behavioral Medicine*, 22: 21–34.

Dundas, R., Morgan, M. and Redfern, J. (2001). Ethnic differences in behavioural risk factors for stroke: implications for health promotion. *Ethnicity and Health*, 6: 95–103.

Dunbar-Jacob, J., Burke, L.E. and Pucznski, S. (1995). Clinical assessment and management of adherence to medication regimens. In P.M. Nicassio and T.W. Smith (eds), *Managing Chronic Illness: A Bio-psychosocial Perspective.* Washington, DC: American Psychological Association.

Dunton, G.F. and Vaughan, E. (2008). Anticipated affective consequences of physical activity adoption and maintenance. *Health Psychology*, 27: 703–10.

Dusseldorp, E., van Elderen, T., Maes, S. *et al.* (1999). A meta-analysis of psycho-educational programs for coronary heart disease patients. *Health Psychology*, 18: 506–19.

Dutta-Bergman, M.J. (2003). A descriptive narrative of healthy eating: a social marketing approach using psychographics in conjunction with interpersonal, community, mass media and new media activities. *Health Marketing Quarterly*, 20: 81–101.

Dzewaltowski, D.A. (1989). Toward a model of exercise motivation. *Journal of Sport and Exercise Psychology*, 11: 251–69.

Eagly, A.H. and Chaiken, S. (1993). *The Psychology of Attitudes*. Orlando, FL: Harcourt Brace Jovanovich.

Eaker, E.D., Sullivan, L.M., Kelly-Hayes, M. *et al.* (2004). Does job strain increase the risk for coronary heart disease or death in men and women? *American Journal of Epidemiology*, 159: 950–8.

Earl, A. and Albarracín, D. (2007). Nature, decay, and spiraling of the effects of fear-inducing arguments and HIV counseling and testing: a meta-analysis of the short- and long-term outcomes of HIV-prevention interventions. *Health Psychology*, 26: 496–506.

Eccleston, C. and Crombez, G. (1999). Pain demands attention: a cognitive-affective model of the interruptive function of pain. *Psychological Bulletin*, 125: 356–66.

Echabe, A.E., Guillen, C.S. and Ozamiz, J.A. (1992). Representations of health, illness and medicines: coping strategies and health promoting behaviour. *British Journal of Clinical Psychology*, 31: 339–49.

Echteld, M.A., Maes, S. and van Elderen, T.M.T. (1998). Predictors of quality of life in PTCA* patients: avoiding stressors increases quality of life. In R. Schwarzer (ed.), *Advances in Health Psychology Research*. Berlin: Berlin Free University. [*percutaneous transluminal coronary angioplasty]

Echteld, M.A., van Elderen, T.M.T. and van der Kamp, L.J.T. (2001). How goal disturbance, coping and chest pain relate to quality of life: a study among patients waiting for PTCA. *Quality of Life Research*, 10: 487–501.

Echteld, M.A., van Elderen, T. and van der Kamp, L.J.Th. (2003). Modeling predictors of quality of life after coronary angioplasty. *Annals of Behavioral Medicine*, 26: 49–60.

Edelmann, R. (1999). *Psychosocial Aspects of the Health Care Process*. Harlow: Prentice Hall.

Edwards, A. and Elwyn, G. (2009). *Shared Decision-making in Health Care. Achieving Evidence-based Patient Choice*. Oxford: Oxford University Press.

Edwards, A., Elwyn, G., Covey, J. *et al.* (2001). Presenting risk information: a review of the effects of 'framing' and other manipulations on patient outcomes. *Journal of Health Communication*, 6: 61–82.

Edwards, W. (1954). The theory of decision making. *Psychological Bulletin*, 51: 380–417.

Egan, G. (1998). *The Skilled Helper: Models, Skills, and Methods for Effective Helping*. Monterey, CA: Brooks/Cole.

Egan, G. (2006). *The Skilled Helper: A Problem-management and Opportunity Development Approach to Helping*. Belmont, CA: Wadsworth.

Eiser, C. (1985). *The Psychology of Childhood Illness*. New York: Springer Verlag.

Eiser, C. (1990). *Chronic Childhood Disease: An Introduction to Psychological Theory and Research*. Cambridge: Cambridge University Press.

Eiser, C. (2004). *Children with Cancer: Their Quality of Life*. NJ: Lawrence Erlbaum.

Eiser, C. and Havermans, T. (1992). Mothers' and fathers' coping with chronic childhood disease. *Psychology and Health*, 7: 249–57.

Eiser, C. and Morse, R. (2001). The measurement of quality of life in children: past and future perspectives. *Journal of Developmental and Behavioral Pediatrics*, 22: 248–56.

Eiser, C., Patterson, D. and Tripp, J.H. (1984). Diabetes and developing knowledge of the body. *Archives of Disease in Childhood*, 59: 167–9.

Eiser, J.R. (1996). Reconnecting the individual and the social in health psychology. *Psychology and Health*, 11: 605–18.

Eiser, J.R., Eiser, C. and Pauwels, C. (1993). Skin cancer: assessing perceived risk and behavioral attitudes. *Psychology and Health*, 8: 393–404.

Ekkekakis, P., Hall, E.E. and Petruzello, S.J. (2008). The relationship between exercise intensity and affective responses demystified: to crack the 40-year-old nut, replace the 40-year-old nutcracker! *Annals of Behavioural Medicine*, 35: 136–49.

Elfström, M.L. and Kreuter, M. (2006). Relationships between locus of control, coping strategies, and emotional well-being in persons with spinal cord injury. *Journal of Clinical Psychology in Medical Settings*, 13: 93–103.

Ellaway, A., McKay, L., Macintyre, S., Kearns, A. and Hiscock, R. (2004). Are social comparisons of homes and cars related to psychosocial health? *International Journal of Epidemiology*, 33: 1065–71.

Ellington, L. and Wiebe, D.J. (1999). Neuroticism, symptom presentation, and medical decision making. *Health Psychology*, 18: 634–43.

Ellis, A. (1977). The basic clinical theory of rational–emotive therapy. In A. Ellis and R. Grieger (eds), *Handbook of Rational–Emotive Therapy*. New York: Springer Verlag.

Elmer, P.J., Grimm, R., Jr, Laing, B. *et al.* (1995). Lifestyle intervention: results of the Treatment of Mild Hypertension Study (TOMHS). *Preventive Medicine*, 24: 378–88.

Elstein, A.S. and Schwarz, A. (2002). Clinical problem solving and diagnostic decision making: selective review of the cognitive literature. *British Medical Journal*, 324: 729–32.

Elwyn, G., Edwards, A., Kinnersley, P. *et al.* (2000). Shared decision making and the concept of equipoise: the competences of involving patients in healthcare choices. *British Journal of General Practice*, 50: 892–9.

Emanuel, L., Bennett, K. and Richardson, V.E. (2007). The dying role. *Journal of Palliative Medicine*, 10: 159–68.

Emery, S., Wakefield, M.A., Terry-McElrath, Y. *et al.* (2007). Using message framing to promote acceptance of the human papillomavirus vaccine. *Health Psychology*, 26: 745–52.

Emler, N. (1984). Delinquency and reputation. *Progress in Experimental Personality Research*, 13: 174–230.

Endler, N.S. and Parker, J.D.A. (1993). The multi-dimensional assessment of coping: concepts, issues, measurement. In G.L. Van Heck, P. Bonaiuto, I.J. Deary and W. Nowack (eds), *Personality Psychology in Europe*, Vol. 4. Netherlands: Tilburg University Press.

Endler, N.S., Parker, J.D.A. and Summerfeldt, L.J. (1998). Coping with health problems: developing a reliable and valid multidimensional measure. *Psychological Assessment*, 10: 195–205.

Eng, J.J. and Martin-Ginis, K.A. (2007). Using the theory of planned behaviour to predict leisure time physical activity among people with chronic kidney disease. *Rehabilitation Psychology*, 52: 435–42.

Engbers, L.H., van Poppel, M.N., Chin, A. *et al.* (2006). The effects of a controlled worksite environmental intervention on determinants of dietary behavior and self-reported fruit, vegetable and fat intake. *BMC Public Health*, 6: 253.

Engel, G.L. (1977). The need for a new medical model: a challenge for biomedicine. *Science*, 196: 129–36.

Engel, G.L. (1980). The clinical application of the bio-psychosocial model. *American Journal of Psychiatry*, 137: 535–44.

Engler, M.B. and Engler, M.M. (2006). The emerging role of flavonoid-rich cocoa and chocolate in cardiovascular health and disease. *Nutrition Reviews*, 64: 109–18.

Epton, T. and Harris, P.R. (2008). Self-affirmation promotes health behavior change, *Health Psychology*, 27: 746–52.

Erens, B., McManus, S., Prescott, A. *et al.* (2003). *National Survey of Sexual Attitudes and Lifestyles II: Reference Tables and Summary Report*. London: National Centre for Social Research.

Eriksen, H.R., Ihlebaek, C., Mikkelsen, A. *et al.* (2002). Improving subjective health at the worksite: a randomized controlled trial of stress management training, physical exercise and an integrated health programme. *Occupational Medicine*, 52: 383–91.

Eriksen, J., Jensen, M.K., Sjogren, P. *et al.* (2003). Epidemiology of chronic non-malignant pain in Denmark. *Pain*, 106: 221–8.

Erikson, E.H. (1959). Identity and the life cycle. *Psychological Issues*, 1: 1–171.

Erikson, E.H. (1980). *Identity and the Life Cycle: A Reissue*. New York: W.W. Norton.

Erikson, E.H., Erikson, J.M. and Kivnick, H.Q. (1986). *Vital Involvement in Old Age: The Experience of Old Age in Our Time*. New York: W.W. Norton.

Esterling, B.A., L'Abate, L., Murray, E.J. *et al.* (1999). Empirical foundations for writing in prevention and psychotherapy: mental and physical health outcomes. *Clinical Psychology Review*, 19: 79–96.

European Commission (1999). *A Pan-EU Survey of Consumer Attitudes to Physical Activity, Body Weight and Health*. Luxembourg: EC. DGV/F.3.

European Commission (2006) FACTSHEET: Alcohol-related harm in Europe – key data. Brussels, European Communities.

Euroqol Group (1990). Euroqol: a new facility for the measurement of health related quality of life. *Health Policy*, 16: 199–208.

Eurostat (2007). GP Utilisation. Retrieved from http://www.euphix.org

Evandrou, M. (2006). Inequalities among older people in London: the challenge of diversity. In V.R. Rodwin and M.K. Gusmano (eds), *Growing Older in World Cities: New York, London, Paris and Tokyo*. Nashville, TN: Vanderbilt University Press, pp. 173–98.

Evans, D. and Norman, P. (2002). Improving pedestrian road safety among adolescents: an application of the theory of planned behaviour. In D. Rutter and L. Quine (eds), *Changing Health Behaviour*. Buckingham: Open University Press.

Evans, G.W. and Stecker, R. (2004). Motivational consequences of environmental stress. *Journal of Environmental Psychology*, 24: 143–65.

Evans, R.L. and Bishop, D.S. (1990). Psychosocial outcomes in stroke survivors. *Stroke*, 21(suppl. II): II-48–II-49.

Evans, S., Fishman, B., Spielman, L. and Haley, A. (2003). Randomized trial of cognitive behaviour therapy versus supportive psychotherapy for HIV-related peripheral neuropathic pain. *Psychosomatics*, 44: 44–50.

Evans-Whipp, T.J., Bond, L., Ukoumunne, O.C. *et al.* (2010). The impact of school tobacco policies on student smoking in Washington State, United States and Victoria, Australia. *International Journal of Environmental Research and Public Health*, 7: 698–710.

Evers, A.W., Kraaimaat, F.W., Geenen, R. *et al.* (2003). Pain coping and social support as predictors of long-term functional disability and pain in early rheumatoid arthritis. *Behaviour Research and Therapy*, 41: 1295–310.

Evers, A.W., Kraaimaat, F.W., van Riel, P.L. and de Jong, A.J. (2002). Tailored cognitive-behavioral therapy in early rheumatoid arthritis for patients at risk: a randomized controlled trial. *Pain*, 100: 141–53.

Everson, S.A., Goldberg, D.E., Kaplan, G.A. *et al.* (1996). Hopelessness and risk of mortality and incidence of myocardial infarction and cancer. *Psychosomatic Medicine*, 58: 113–24.

Everson, S.A., McKey, B.S. and Lovallo, W.R. (1995). Effects of trait hostility on cardiovascular responses to harassment in young men. *International Journal of Behavioral Medicine*, 2: 172–91.

Eves, F.F., Webb, O.J. and Mutrie, N. (2006). A workplace intervention to promote stair climbing: greater effects in the overweight. *Obesity (Silver Spring)*, 14: 2210–6.

Expert Group (2004). Research in the behavioural and social sciences to improve cancer control and care: a strategy for development. *European Journal of Cancer*, 40: 316–25.

Ey, S., Hadley, W., Allen, D.N. *et al.* (2005). A new measure of children's optimism and pessimism: the youth life orientation test. *Journal of Child Psychology & Psychiatry*, 46: 548–58.

Eysenck, H.J. (1970). *The Structure of Human Personality*, 3rd edn. London: Methuen.

Eysenck, H.J. (1982). *Personality, Genetics and Behaviour*. New York: Praeger.

Eysenck, H.J. (1985). Personality, cancer and cardiovascular disease: a causal analysis. *Personality and Individual Differences*, 6: 535–56.

Eysenck, H.J. (1991). Dimensions of personality: 16, 5, or 3? Criteria for a taxonomic paradigm. *Personality and Individual Differences*, 12: 773–90.

Eysenck, H.J. and Grossarth-Maticek, R. (1989). Prevention of cancer and coronary heart disease and the reduction in the cost of the National Health Service. *Journal of Social, Political and Economic Studies*, 14: 25–47.

Ezer, H., Chachamovich, J.L.R. and Chachamovich, E. (2011). Do men and their wives see it the same way? Congruence within couples during the first year of prostate cancer. *Psycho-Oncology*, 20: 155–64.

Fadardi, J.S. and Cox, W.M. (2009). Reversing the sequence: reducing alcohol consumption by overcoming alcohol attentional bias. *Drug & Alcohol Dependence*, 101: 137–45.

Fagerli, R.A., Lien, M.E. and Wandel, M. (2007). Health worker style and trustworthiness as perceived by Pakistani-born persons with type 2 diabetes in Oslo, Norway. *Health (London)*, 11: 109–29.

Fahrenwald, N.L. and Walker, S.N. (2003). Application of the transtheoretical model of behavior change to the physical activity behavior of WIC mothers. *Public Health Nursing*, 20: 307–17.

Faller, H. and Bülzebruck, H. (2002). Coping and survival in lung cancer: a 10-year follow-up. *American Journal of Psychiatry*, 159: 2105–7.

Faller, H., Schilleing, S. and Lang, H. (1995). Causal attribution and life threatening disease. *Journal of Psychosomatic Research* 39: 619–27.

Fallowfield, L.J., Hall, A., Maguire, G.P. *et al.* (1990). Psychological outcomes of different treatment policies in women with early breast cancer outside a clinical trial. *British Medical Journal*, 301: 575–80.

Fallowfield, L. and Jenkins, V. (2004). Communicating sad, bad, and difficult news in medicine. *Lancet*, 363: 312–19.

Fallowfield, L., Jenkins, V., Farewell, V. *et al.* (2002). Efficacy of a Cancer Research UK communication skills training model for oncologists: a randomised controlled trial. *The Lancet*, 359: 650–6.

Fallowfield, L., Ratcliffe, D., Jenkins, V. and Saul, J. (2001). Psychiatric morbidity and its recognition by doctors in patients with cancer. *British Journal of Cancer*, 84: 1011–15.

Family Heart Study Group (1994). Randomised controlled trial evaluating cardiovascular screening and intervention in general practice: principal results of British family heart study. *British Medical Journal*, 308: 313–20.

Farber, N.J., Urban, S.Y., Collier, V.U. *et al.* (2002). The good news about giving bad news to patients. *Journal of General Internal Medicine*, 17: 914–22.

Farquhar, J., Fortmann, S., Flora, J. *et al.* (1990a). Effects of community-wide education on cardiovascular disease risk factors. *Journal of the American Medical Association*, 264: 359–65.

Farquhar, J.W., Fortmann, S.P., Flora, J.A. *et al.* (1990b). Effects of community-wide education on cardiovascular disease risk factors. The Stanford Five-City Project. *Journal of the American Medical Association*, 264: 359–65.

Farquhar, J., Maccoby, N. and Wood, P. (1977). Community education for cardiovascular disease. *The Lancet*, 1: 1192–5.

Faulkner, A. (1998). *When the News is Bad*. Cheltenham: Stanley Thorne.

Faulkner, A., Argent, J., Jones, A. and O'Keeffe, C. (1995). Improving the skills of doctors in giving distressing information. *Medical Education*, 29: 303–7.

Fauerbach, J.A., Lawrence, J.W., Haythornthwaite, J.A. and Richter, L. (2002). Coping with the stress of a painful medical procedure. *Behaviour Research and Therapy*, 40: 1003–15.

Fawzy, F.I., Canada, A.L. and Fawzy, N.W. (2003). Malignant melanoma: effects of a brief, structured psychiatric intervention on survival and recurrence at 10-year follow-up. *Archives of General Psychiatry*, 60: 100–3.

Fawzy, F.I. and Fawzy, N.W. (1998). Psychoeducational interventions. In J. Holland (ed.), *Textbook of Psycho-Oncology*. New York: Oxford University Press.

Fawzy, F.I., Fawzy, N.W., Hyun, C.S., Elashoff, R. *et al.* (1993). Malignant melanoma: effects of an early structured psychiatric intervention, coping, and affective state on recurrence and survival 6 years later. *Archives of General Psychiatry*, 50: 681–9.

Fedele, L., Marchini, M., Acaia, B. *et al.* (1989). Dynamics and significance of placebo response in primary dysmenorrhea. *Pain*, 36: 43–7.

Feldman, C.T., Bensing, J.M. and de Rujter, A. (2007). Worries are the mother of many diseases: General practitioners and refugees in the Netherlands on stress, being ill, and prejudice. *Patient Education and Counselling*, 65: 369–80.

Feldman, P.J., Cohen, S., Doyle, W.J. *et al.* (1999). The impact of personality on the reporting of unfounded symptoms and illness. *Journal of Personality and Social Psychology*, 77: 370–8.

Felsten, G. (2004). Stress reactivity and vulnerability to depressed mood in college students. *Personality and Individual Differences*, 36: 789–800.

Fenton, K.A., Korovessis, C., Johnson, A.M. *et al.* (2001). Sexual behaviour in Britain: reported sexually transmitted infections and prevalence of genital *Chlamydia trachomatir* infection. *The Lancet*, 358: 1851–4.

Ferguson, E. (2000). Hypochondriacal concerns and the five factor model of personality. *Journal of Personality*, 68: 705–24.

Ferrie, J.E., Martikainen, P., Shipley, M.J. *et al.* (2001). Employment status and health after privatisation in white collar civil servants: prospective cohort study. *British Medical Journal*, 322: 647.

Ferro, J.M. and Crespo, M. (1994). Prognosis after transient ischemic attack and ischemic stroke in young adults. *Stroke*, 25: 1611–16.

Ferruci, L., Baldasseroni, S., Bandinelli, D. *et al.* (2000). Disease severity and health-related quality of life across different chronic conditions. *Journal of the American Geriatrics Society*, 48: 1490–95.

Festinger, L. (1954). A theory of social comparison processes. *Human Relations*, 7: 117–40.

Festinger, L. (1957). *A Theory of Cognitive Dissonance*. Stanford, CA: Stanford University Press.

Figueiras, M.J. and Weinman, J. (2003). Do similar patient and spouse perceptions of myocardial infarction predict recovery? *Psychology and Health*, 18: 201–16.

Figueiras, M.J., Cortes, M.A., Marcelino, D. and Weinman, J. (2010). Lay views about medicines: the influence of the illness label for the use of generic versus brand. *Psychology & Health*, 25: 1121–8.

Filakti, H. and Fox, J. (1995). Differences in mortality by housing tenure and by car access from the OPCS Longitudinal Study. *Population Trends*, 81: 27–30.

Fine, P.G., Roberts, W.J., Gillette, R.G. and Child, T.R. (1994). Slowly developing placebo responses confound tests of intravenous phentolamine to determine mechanisms underlying idiopathic chronic low back pain. *Pain*, 56: 235–42.

Finkelstein, D.M., Kubzansky, L.D., Capitman, J. *et al.* (2007). Socioeconomic differences in adolescent stress: the role of psychological resources. *Journal of Adolescent Health*, 40: 127–34.

Finnegan, J.R., Jr, Meischke, H., Zapka, J.G. *et al.* (2000). Patient delay in seeking care for heart attack symptoms: findings from focus groups conducted in five U.S. regions. *Preventive Medicine*, 31: 205–13.

Finney, L.J. and Iannotti, R.J. (2002). Message framing and mammography screening: a theory-driven intervention. *Behavioral Medicine*, 28: 5–14.

Fischer, M., Scharloo, M., Abbink, J. *et al.* (2010). The dynamics of illness perceptions: testing assumptions of Leventhal's common-sense model in a pulmonary rehabilitation setting. *British Journal of Health Psychology*, 15: 887–903.

Fishbein, M. (1967). Attitude and the prediction of behavior. In M. Fishbein (ed.), *Readings in Attitude Theory and Measurement*. New York: Wiley.

Fishbein, M. and Ajzen, I. (1985). *Belief, Attitude, Intention and Behavior: An Introduction to Theory and Research*. Reading, MA: Addison-Wesley.

Fisher, J.D., Bell, P.A. and Baum, A. (1984). *Environmental Psychology*, 2nd edn. New York: Holt, Rinehart & Winston.

Fisher, K. and Johnston, M. (1996a). Emotional distress as a mediator of the relationship between pain and disability: an experimental study. *British Journal of Health Psychology*, 1: 207–18.

Fisher, K. and Johnston, M. (1996b). Experimental manipulation of perceived control and its effect on disability. *Psychology and Health*, 11: 657–69.

Fisher, K. and Johnston, M. (1998). Emotional distress and control cognitions as mediators of the impact of chronic pain on disability. *British Journal of Health Psychology*, 3: 225–36.

Fiske, S.T. and Taylor, S.E. (1991). *Social Cognition*, 2nd edn. New York: McGraw-Hill.

Fitzell, A. and Pakenham, K. (2010). Application of a stress-coping model to positive and negative adjustment outcomes in colorectal cancer caregiving. *Psycho-Oncology*, 19: 1171–8.

Fleishman, J.A., Sherbourne, C.D., Cleary, P.D. *et al.* (2003). Patterns of coping among persons with HIV infection: configurations, correlates, and change. *American Journal of Community Psychology*, 32: 187–204.

Fletcher, S.W., Black, W., Harris, R. *et al.* (1993). Report of the international workshop on screening for breast cancer. *Journal of the National Cancer Institute*, 85: 1644–56.

Fletcher, S.W., Harris, R.P., Gonzalez, J.J. *et al.* (1993). Increasing mammography utilization: a controlled study. *Journal of the National Cancer Institute*, 20: 112–20.

Flor, H., Breitenstein, C., Birbaumer, N. and Fuerst, M. (1995). A psychophysiological analysis of spouse solicitousness towards pain behaviours, spouse interaction and physical consequences. *Behavior Therapy*, 26: 255–72.

Flynn, B.S., Worden, J.K., Bunn, J.Y. *et al.* (2007). Youth audience segmentation strategies for smoking-prevention mass media campaigns based on message appeal. *Health Education and Behavior*, 34: 578–93.

Foa, E.B., Rothbaum, B.O., Riggs, D.S. and Murdock, T.B. (1991). Treatment of posttraumatic stress disorder in rape victims: a comparison between cognitive and behavioural procedures and counselling. *Journal of Consulting and Clinical Psychology*, 59: 715–23.

Foley, E., Baillie, A., Huxter, M. *et al.* (2010). Mindfulness-based cognitive therapy for individuals whose lives have been affected by cancer: a randomized controlled trial. *Journal of Consulting and Clinical Psychology*, 78: 72–9.

Folkman, S. (1984). Personal control and stress and coping processes: a theoretical analysis. *Journal of Personality and Social Psychology*, 46: 839–52.

Folkman, S. (2008). The case for positive emotions in the stress process. *Anxiety, Stress and Coping*, 21: 3–14.

Folkman, S. (2010). Stress, coping and hope. *Psycho-Oncology*, 19: 901–8.

Folkman, S. and Chesney, M. (1995). Coping with HIV infection. In M. Stain and A. Baum (eds), *Chronic Diseases. Perspectives in Behavioral Medicine*. Hillsdale, NJ: Lawrence Erlbaum.

Folkman, S. and Lazarus, R.S. (1980). An analysis of coping in a middle-aged community sample. *Journal of Health and Social Behavior*, 21: 219–39.

Folkman, S. and Lazarus, R.S. (1985). If it changes it must be a process: study of emotion and coping during three stages of a college examination. *Journal of Personality and Social Psychology*, 48: 150–70.

Folkman, S. and Lazarus, R.S. (1988). *Manual for the Ways of Coping Questionnaire*. Palo Alto, CA: Consulting Psychologists Press.

Folkman, S.K. and Moskowitz, J.T. (2000). Positive affect and the other side of coping. *American Psychologist*, 55: 647–54.

Folkman, S. and Moskowitch, J.T. (2004). Coping: pitfalls and promise. *Annual Review of Psychology*, 55: 745–74.

Food Standards Agency (2000). *National Diet and Nutrition Survey: Young People Aged 4–18 Years*. London: Stationery Office.

Ford, S., Fallowfield, L. and Lewis, S. (1996). Doctor–patient interactions in oncology. *Social Science and Medicine*, 42: 1511–19.

Ford, S., Schofield, T. and Hope, T. (2003). What are the ingredients for a successful evidence-based patient choice consultation? A qualitative study. *Social Science and Medicine*, 56: 589–602.

Fordyce, W.E. (1976). *Behavioural Methods for Chronic Pain and Illness*. St Louis, MO: Mosby.

Fordyce, W.E. (1982). The modification of avoidance learning in pain behaviors. *Journal of Behavioral Medicine*, 5: 405–14.

Fordyce, W.E. (1986). Learning processes in pain. In R.A. Sternbach (ed.), *The Psychology of Pain*, 2nd edn. New York: Raven Press.

Forrest, G., Plumb, C., Ziebland, S. *et al.* (2006). Breast cancer in the family-children's perceptions of their mother's cancer and its initial treatment: qualitative study. *British Medical Journal*, 332: 998–1003.

Forsberg-Wärleby, G., Möller, A. and Blomstrand, C. (2001). Spouses of first-ever stroke patients: psychological well-being in the first phase after stroke. *Stroke*, 32: 1646–56.

Forwell, G.D. (1993). *Glasgow's Health: Old Problems – New Opportunities*. A report by the Director of Public Health. Glasgow: Department of Public Health.

Fournier, M., de Ridder, D. and Bensing, J. (2002). Optimism and adaptation to chronic disease: the role of optimism in relation to self-care options in type 1 diabetes mellitus, rheumatoid arthritis and multiple sclerosis. *British Journal of Health Psychology*, 7: 409–32.

Frankl, V.E. (2006). *Man's Search for Meaning* (Lasch, I. Trans., 5th edn). Boston, MA: Bacon Press (original work published in 1946).

Franzkowiak, P. (1987). Risk taking and adolescent development. *Health Promotion*, 2: 51–60.

Frasure-Smith, N. (1991). In-hospital symptoms of psychological stress as predictors of long-term outcome after acute myocardial infarction in men. *American Journal of Cardiology*, 67: 121–7.

Frasure-Smith, N., Lespérance, F., Gravel, G. *et al.* (2000). Social support, depression, and mortality during the first year after myocardial infarction. *Circulation*, 101: 1919–24.

Frasure-Smith, N., Lespérance, F., Gravel, G. *et al.* (2002). Long-term survival differences among low-anxious, high-anxious and repressive copers enrolled in the Montreal heart attack readjustment trial. *Psychosomatic Medicine*, 64: 571–9.

Frasure-Smith, N., Lespérance, F., Prince, R.H. *et al.* (1997). Randomised trial of home-based psychosocial nursing intervention for patients recovering from myocardial infarction. *The Lancet*, 350: 473–9.

Frasure-Smith, N., Lespérance, F. and Talajic, M.E. (1995). Coronary heart disease/myocardial infarction: depression and 18-month prognosis after myocardial infarction. *Circulation*, 91: 999–1005.

Frasure-Smith, N. and Prince, R. (1985). The ischemic heart disease life stress monitoring program: impact on mortality. *Psychosomatic Medicine*, 47: 431–45.

Frattaroli, J. (2006). Experimental disclosure and its moderators: a meta-analysis. *Psychological Bulletin*, 132: 823–65.

Frayling, T.M., Timpson, N.J., Weedon, M.N. *et al.* (2007). A common variant in the FTO gene is associated with body mass index and predisposes to childhood and adult obesity. *Science*, 316: 889–94.

Freda, M.C. (2005). The readability of American Academy of Pediatrics patient education brochures. *Journal of Pediatric Health Care*, 19: 151–6.

Fredman, L., Hawkes, W.G., Black, S. *et al.* (2006). Elderly patients with hip fracture with positive affect have better functional recovery over 2 years. *Journal of the American Geriatric Society*, 54: 1074–81.

Fredrickson, B.L. (1998). What good are positive emotions? *Review of General Psychology*, 2: 300–19.

Fredrickson, B.L. (2001). The role of positive emotions in positive psychology: the broaden-and-build theory of positive emotions. *American Psychologist*, 56: 218–26.

Fredrickson, M. and Matthews, K.A. (1990). Cardiovascular responses to behavioral stress and hypertension: a meta-analytic review. *Annals of Behavioral Medicine*, 12: 30–9.

Freedland, K.E., Carney, R.M., Hance, M.L. *et al.* (1996). Cognitive therapy for depression in patients with coronary artery disease. *Psychosomatic Medicine*, 58: 93.

Freedman, L.S., Kipnis, V., Schatzkin, A. *et al.* (2008). Methods of epidemiology: evaluating the fat-breast cancer hypothesis: comparing dietary instruments and other developments. *Cancer Journals* 14: 69–74.

Freidson, E. (1961). *Patients' Views of Medical Practice*. New York: Russell Sage Foundation.

French, D.P., Cooper, A. and Weinman, J. (2006). Illness perceptions predict attendance at cardiac rehabiltation following acute myocardial infarction: a systematic review with meta-analysis. *Journal of Psychosomatic Research*, 61: 757–767.

French, D.P., Senior, V., Weinman, J. and Marteau, T. (2001). Causal attributions for heart disease. *Psychology and Health*, 16: 77–98.

French, D.P., Marteau, T., Senior, V. *et al.* (2002). The structure of beliefs about the causes of heart attack: a network analysis. *British Journal of Health Psychology*, 7: 463–79.

French, J.R.P., Jr, Caplan, R.D. and Van Harrison, R. (1982). *The Mechanisms of Job Stress and Strain*. Chichester: Wiley.

French, S.A., Perry, C.L., Leon, G.R. and Fulkerson, J.A. (1994). Weight concerns, dieting behaviour, and smoking initiation among adolescents: a prospective study. *American Journal of Public Health*, 84: 1818–20.

Freud, S. and Breuer, J. (1895). Studies on hysteria. In J. Strachey (ed.), *The Standard Edition of the Complete Psychological Works of Sigmund Freud*. London: Hogarth Press.

Friedman, H.S. (2003). Healthy life-style across the life-span: the heck with the Surgeon General! In J. Suls and K.A. Wallston (eds), *Social Psychological Foundations of Health and Illness*. Malden, MA: Blackwell.

Friedman, H.S. and Booth-Kewley, S. (1987). The 'disease-prone personality'. A meta-analytic view of the construct. *American Psychologist*, 42: 539–55.

Friedman, H.S., Tucker, J.S., Schwartz, J.E. *et al.* (1995). Childhood conscientiousness and longevity: health behaviors and cause of death. *Journal of Personality and Social Psychology*, 68: 696–703.

Friedman, M. and Rosenman, R.H. (1959). Association of specific overt behavior pattern with blood and cardiovascular findings. *Journal of American Medical Association*, 169: 1286–97.

Friedman, M. and Rosenman, R.H. (1974). *Type A Behavior and Your Heart*. New York: A.A. Knopf.

Friedman, M., Thoresen, C.E., Gill, J.J. *et al.* (1986). Alteration of Type A behavior and its effect on cardiac recurrences in post myocardial infarction patients: summary results of the Recurrent Coronary Prevention Project. *American Heart Journal*, 112: 653–65.

Friesner, S., Curry, D. and Moddeman, G. (2006). Comparison of two pain-management strategies during chest tube removal: relaxation exercise with opioids and opioids alone. *Heart and Lung*, 35(4): 269–76.

Fromm, K., Andrykowski, M.A. and Hunt, J. (1996). Positive and negative psychosocial sequelae of bone marrow transplantation: implications for quality of life assessment. *Journal of Behavioral Medicine*, 19: 221–40.

Fukui, S., Kugaya, A., Okamura, H. *et al.* (2000). A psychosocial group intervention for Japanese women with primary breast carcinoma. *Cancer*, 89: 1026–36.

Fulkerson, J.A. and French, S.A. (2003). Cigarette smoking for weight loss or control among adolescents: gender and racial/ethnic differences. *Journal of Adolescent Health*, 32: 306–13.

Funk, S.C. (1992). Hardiness: a review of theory and research. *Health Psychology*, 11: 335–45.

Furnham, A. (1990). The Type A behaviour pattern and perception of self. *Personality and Individual Differences*, 11: 841–51.

Furnham, A. (1997). Lay theories of work stress. *Work & Stress*, 11: 68–78.

Gadsby, J.G. and Flowerdew, M.W. (2000). Transcutaneous nerve stimulation and acupuncture-like transcutaneous nerve stimulation for chronic low back pain. In *The Cochrane Library*, issue 2. Oxford: Update Software.

Galavotti, C., Pappas-DeLuca, K.A. and Lansky, A. (2001). Modeling and reinforcement to combat HIV: the MARCH approach to behavior change. *American Journal of Public Health*, 91: 1602–7.

Gall, T.L. and Cornblatt, M.W. (2002). Breast cancer survivors give voice: a qualitative analysis of spiritual factors in long-term adjustment. *Psycho-Oncology*, 11: 524–35.

Gall, T.L., Miguez de Renart, R.M. and Boonstra, B. (2000). Religious resources in long-term adjustment to breast cancer. *Journal of Psychosocial Oncology*, 18: 21–37.

Gallacher, J.E.J., Hopkinson, C.A., Bennett, P. *et al.* (1997). Effect of stress management on angina. *Psychology and Health*, 12: 523–32.

Gallacher, J.E.J., Yarnell, J.W.G., Sweetnam, P.M. *et al.* (1999). Anger and incident heart disease in the Caerphilly study. *Psychosomatic Medicine*, 61: 446–53.

Gamble, J., Fitzsimons, D., Lynes, D. *et al.* (2007). Difficult asthma: people's perspectives on taking corticosteroid therapy. *Journal of Clinical Nursing*, 16: 59–67.

Gander, P.H., Merry, A., Millar, M.M. *et al.* (2000). Hours of work and fatigue-related error: a survey of New Zealand anaesthetists. *Anaesthetics and Intensive Care*, 28: 178–83.

Gardner-Nix, J., Backman, S., Barbati, J. *et al.* (2008). Evaluating distance education of a mindfulness-based meditation programme for chronic pain management. *Journal of Telemedicine and Telecare*, 14: 88–92.

Garratt, A., Schmidt, L., Mackintosh, A.M. and Fitzpatrick, R. (2002). Quality of life measurement: bibliographic study of patient assessed health outcome measures. *British Medical Journal*, 324: 1417–21.

Garssen, B. (2004). Psychological factors and cancer development. Evidence after 30 years of research. *Clinical Psychology Review*, 24: 115–338.

Gascoigne, P., Mason, M.D. and Roberts, E. (1999). Factors affecting presentation and delay in patients with testicular cancer: results of a qualitative study. *Psycho-Oncology*, 8: 144–54.

Gauce, A.M., Comer, J.P. and Schwartz, D. (1987). Long-term effect of a systems orientated school prevention program. *American Journal of Ortho-psychiatry*, 57: 127–31.

Gaughler, J.E., Davey, A., Pearlin, L.I. *et al.* (2000). Modeling caregiver adaptation over time: the longitudinal impact of behaviour problems. *Psychology and Aging*, 15: 437–50.

Gawande, A.A., Zinner, M.J., Studdert, D.M. *et al.* (2003). Analysis of errors reported by surgeons at three teaching hospitals. *Surgery*, 133: 614–21.

Geirdal, A.Ø., Reichelt, J.G., Dahl, A.A. *et al.* (2005). Psychological distress in women at risk of hereditary breast/ovarian or HNPCC cancers in the absence of demonstrated mutations. *Family Cancer*, 4: 121–6.

Gellert, G., Maxwell, R.M. and Siegel, B.S. (1993). Survival of breast cancer patients receiving adjunctive psychosocial support therapy: a 10-year follow-up study. *Journal of Clinical Oncology*, 11: 66–9.

General Medical Council (2002). *Tomorrow's Doctors, Recommendations on Undergraduate Medical Education*. London: General Medical Council.

Gerbert, B. (1984). Perceived likeability and competence of simulated patients: influence on physician's management plans. *Social Science and Medicine*, 18: 1053–60.

Gerend, M.A., Aiken, L.S. and West, S.G. (2004). Personality factors in older women's perceived susceptibility to diseases of aging. *Journal of Personality*, 72: 243–70.

Gerend, M.A. and Shepherd, J.E. (2007) Using message framing to promote acceptance of the human papillomavirus vaccine. *Health Psychology*, 26: 745–52.

German, J.B. and Walzem, R.L. (2000). The health benefits of wine. *Annual Review of Nutrition*, 20: 561–93.

Gibbons, C., Dempster, M. and Moutray, M. (2008). Stress and eustress in nursing students. *Journal of Advanced Nursing*, 61: 282–29.

Gibson, P.G., Coughlan, J., Wilson, A.J. *et al.* (2000). Limited (information only) patient education programs for adults with asthma. *Cochrane Database Systematic Review*, issue 1, art. no.: CD001005. doi: 10.1002/14651858. CD001005.

Giese-Davis, J., Koopman, C., Butler, L.D. *et al.* (2002). Change in emotion-regulation strategy for women with metastatic breast cancer following supportive-expressive group therapy. *Journal of Consulting and Clinical Psychology*, 70: 916–25.

Gifford, A.L., Laurent, D.D., Gonzales, V.M. *et al.* (1998). Pilot randomized trial of education to improve self-management skills of men with symptomatic HIV/AIDS. *Retrovirology*, 18: 136–44.

Gil, K.M., Keefe, F.J., Crisson, J.E. *et al.* (1987). Social support and pain behavior. *Pain*, 29: 209–17.

Gil, K.M., Williams, D.A., Keefe, F.J. *et al.* (1990). The relationship of negative thoughts to pain and psychological distress. *Behavior Therapy*, 21: 349–62.

Gill, P., Kaur, J.S., Rummans, T. *et al.* (2003). The hospice patient's primary caregiver. What is their quality of life? *Journal of Psychosomatic Research*, 55: 445–51.

Gillam, S., Jarman, B., White, P. and Law, R. (1989). Ethnic differences in consultation rates in urban general practice. *British Medical Journal*, 299: 953–7.

Gillies, P.A. (1991). HIV infection, alcohol and illicit drugs. *Current Opinion in Psychiatry*, 4: 448–53.

Gilpin, E.A., Pierce, J.P., Johnson, M. *et al.* (1993) Physician advice to quit smoking: results from the 1990 California Tobacco Survey. *Journal of General Internal Medicine*, 8: 549–53.

Ginandes, C., Brooks, P., Sando, W. *et al.* (2003). Can medical hypnosis accelerate post-surgical wound healing? Results of a clinical trial. *American Journal of Clinical Hypnosis*, 45: 333–51.

Giummarra, M.J., Gibson, S.J., Georgiou-Karistianis, N. *et al.* (2007). Central mechanisms in phantom limb perception: the past, present, and future. *Brain Research Reviews*, 54: 219–32.

Glanz, K., Grove, J., Lerman, C. *et al.* (1999). Correlates of intentions to obtain genetic counseling and colorectal cancer gene testing among at-risk relatives from three ethnic groups. *Cancer Epidemiology Biomarkers and Prevention*, 8: 329–36.

Glanz, K., Lankenau, B., Foerster, S. *et al.* (1995). Environmental and policy approaches to cardiovascular disease prevention through nutrition: opportunities for state and local action. *Health Education Quarterly*, 22: 512–27.

Glaser, R. and Kiecolt-Glaser, J.K. (2005). Stress-induced immune dysfunction: implications for health. *National Reviews in Immunology*, 5: 243–51.

Glaser, R., Rice, J., Sheridan, J. *et al.* (1987). Stress-related immune suppression: health implications. *Brain, Behavior and Immunity*, 1: 7–20.

Glasgow, R.E., Boles, S.M., McKay, H.G. *et al.* (2003). The D-Net diabetes self-management program: long-term implementation, outcomes, and generalization results. *Preventive Medicine*, 36: 410–19.

Glasgow, R.E., Hollis, J.F., Ary, D.V. *et al.* (1993). Results of a year-long incentives based worksite smoking cessation program. *Addictive Behaviors*, 18: 209–16.

Glasgow, R.E., Toobert, D.J. and Hampson, S.E. (1996). Effects of a brief office-based intervention to facilitate diabetes dietary self-management. *Diabetes Care*, 19: 835–42.

Glenister, D. (1996). Exercise and mental health: a review. *Journal of the Royal Society of Health*, 116: 7–13.

Glenton, C. (2002). Developing patient-centred information for back pain sufferers. *Health Expectations*, 5: 319–29.

Goddard, E. (2006). *The General Household Survey: Smoking and Drinking Among Adults 2005*. London: Office of National Statistics.

Goddard, M. and Smith, P. (1998). *Equity of Access to Health Care*. York: University of York.

Godin, G., Bélanger-Gravel, A., Eccles, M. and Grimshaw, J. (2008). Healthcare professionals' intentions and behaviours: A systematic review of studies based on social cognitive theories. *Implementation Science*, 3: 36.

Godin, G. and Kok, G. (1996). The theory of planned behavior: a review of its applications to health-related behaviours. *American Journal of Health Promotion*, 11: 87–98.

Godin, G., Lambert, L.-D., Owen, N. *et al.* (2004). Stages of motivational readiness for physical activity: a comparison of different algorithms of classification. *British Journal of Health Psychology*, 9: 253–67.

Godin, G., Sheeran, P., Conner, M. and Germain, M. (2008). Asking questions changes behavior: mere measurement effects on frequency of blood donation. *Health Psychology*, 27: 179–84.

Godin, G., Valois, P., Lepage, L. and Desharnais, R. (1992). Predictors of smoking behaviour: an application of Ajzen's theory of planned behaviour. *British Journal of Addiction*, 87: 1335–43.

Gokee LaRose, J., Tate, D.F., Gorin, A.A. *et al.* Preventing weight gain in young adults: a randomized controlled pilot study. *American Journal of Preventive Medicine*, 39: 63–8.

Goldberg, D. (1997). *General Health Questionnaire (GHQ-12)*. Windsor: NFER-Nelson.

Goldberg, D. and Williams, P. (1988). *A User's Guide to the General Health Questionnaire*. Windsor: NFER-Nelson.

Goldberg, L.R. and Strycker, L.A. (2002). Personality traits and eating habits: the assessment of food preferences in a large community sample. *Personality and Individual Differences*, 32: 49–65.

Goldberg, R.J., Steg, P.G., Sadiq, I. *et al.* (2002). Extent of, and factors associated with, delay to hospital presentation in patients with acute coronary disease (the GRACE registry). *American Journal of Cardiology*, 89: 791–6.

Goldman, S.L., Whitney-Saltiel, D., Granger, J. *et al.* (1991). Children's representations of 'everyday' aspects of health and illness. *Journal of Pediatric Psychology*, 16: 747–66.

Gollwitzer, P.M. (1999). Implementation intentions: strong effects of simple plans. *American Psychologist*, 54: 493–503.

Gollwitzer, P.M. and Brandstätter, V. (1997). Implementation intentions and effective goal pursuit. *Journal of Personality and Social Psychology*, 73: 186–99.

Gollwitzer, P.M. and Oettingen, G. (1998). The emergence and implementation of health goals. *Psychology and Health*, 13: 687–715.

Gollwitzer, P.M. and Oettingen, G. (2000). The emergence and implementation of health goals. In P. Norman and C. Abraham (eds), *Understanding and Changing Health Behaviour: From Health Beliefs to Self Regulation* . Amsterdam: Harwood Academic Press, pp. 229–60.

Gollwitzer, P.M. and Schaal, B. (1998). Metacognition in action: the importance of implementation intentions. *Personality and Social Psychology Review*, 2: 124–36.

Gollwitzer, P.M. and Sheeran, P. (2006). Implementation intentions and goal achievement: a meta-analysis of effects and processes. *Advances in Experimental Social Psychology*, 38: 69–119.

Gomel, M., Oldenburg, B., Simpson, J.M. et al. (1993). Work-site cardiovascular risk reduction: a randomized trial of health risk assessment, education, counseling, and incentives. *American Journal of Public Health*, 83: 1231–8.

Gomez, C.R., Nomellini, V., Faunce, D.E. and Kovacs, E.J. (2008). Innate immunity and aging. *Experimental Gerontology*, 43: 718–28.

Good, A. and Abraham, C. (2007). Measuring defensive responses to threatening messages: a meta-analysis of measures, *Health Psychology Review*, 1: 208–29.

Goode, K.T., Haley, W.E., Roth, D.L. et al. (1998). Predicting longitudinal changes in caregiver physical and mental health: a stress process model. *Health Psychology*, 17: 190–8.

Goodkin, K., Feaster, D.J., Asthana, D. et al. (1998). A bereavement support group intervention is longitudinally associated with salutary effects on the CD4 cell count and number of physician visits. *Clinical and Diagnostic Laboratory Immunology*, 5: 382–91.

Goodkin, K., Baldewicz, T.T., Asthana, D. et al. (2001). A bereavement support group intervention affects plasma burden of human immunodeficiency virus type 1. Report of a randomized controlled trial. *Journal of Human Virology*, 4: 44–54.

Goodwin, D., Boggs, S. and Graham-Pole, J. (1994). Development and validation of the Pediatric Oncology Quality of Life Scale. *Psychological Assessment*, 6: 321–8.

Goodwin, P.J., Leszcz, M., Ennis, M. et al. (2001). The effect of group psychosocial support on survival in metastatic breast cancer. *New England Journal of Medicine*, 345: 1719–26.

Gordon, C.L., Arnette, R.A.N.M. and Smith, R.E. (2011). Have you thanked your spouse today? Felt and expressed gratitude among married couples. *Personality and Individual Differences*, 50: 3339–43.

Gottlieb, B.H. and Bergen, A.E. (2010). Social support concepts and measures. *Journal of Psychosomatic Research*, 69: 511–20.

Gouin, J.P., Kiecol-Glaser, J.K., Malarkey, W.B. and Glaser, R. (2008). The influence of anger expression on wound healing. *Brain, Behavior and Immunity*, 22: 699–708.

Goyder, E.C., McNally, P.G. and Botha, J.L. (2000). Inequalities in access to diabetes care: evidence from a historical cohort study. *Quality in Health Care*, 9: 85–9.

Graham, H. (1994). Gender and class as dimensions of smoking behaviour in Britain: insights from a survey of mothers. *Social Science and Medicine*, 38: 691–8.

Graham, J., Ramirez, A., Love, S. et al. (2002). Stressful life experiences and risk of relapse of breast cancer: observational cohort study. *British Medical Journal*, 324: 1420–3.

Graham, J.E., Christian, L.M. and Kiecolt-Glaser, J.K. (2006). Stress, age and immune function: toward a lifespan approach. *Journal of Behavioral Medicine*, 29: 389–400.

Gratton, L., Povey, R. and Clark-Carter, D. (2007). Promoting children's fruit and vegetable consumption: interventions using the Theory of Planned Behaviour as a framework. *British Journal of Health Psychology*, 12: 39–50.

Gray, S.E. and Rutter, D.R. (2007). Illness representations in young people with Chronic Fatigue Syndrome. *Psychology and Health*, 22: 159–74.

Greco, P., Pendley, J.S., McDonell, K. et al. (2001). A peer group intervention for adolescents with type 1 diabetes and their best friends. *Journal of Pediatric Psychology*, 26: 485–90.

Green, B.L., Rowland, J.H., Krupnick, J.L. et al. (1998). Prevalence of posttraumatic stress disorder in women with breast cancer. *Psychosomatics*, 39: 102–11.

Green, C.R., Baker, T.A., Sato, Y. et al. (2003). Race and chronic pain: a comparative study of young black and white Americans presenting for management. *Journal of Pain*, 4: 176–83.

Greenglass, E., Fiksenbaum, L. and Eaton, J. (2006). The relationship between coping, social support, functional disability and depression in the elderly. *Anxiety, Stress, and Coping*, 19: 5–31.

Greenwood, C.R., Carta, J.J. and Kamps, D. (1990). Teacher versus peer-mediated instruction: a review of educational advantages and disadvantages. In H. Foot, M. Morgan and R. Shute (eds), *Children Helping Children*. Chichester: Wiley.

Greenwood, D.C., Muir, K.R., Packham, C.J. et al. (1996). Coronary heart disease: a review of the role of psychosocial stress and social support. *Journal of Public Health Medicine*, 18: 221–31.

Greer, S. (1999). Mind–body research in psycho-oncology. *Advances in Mind–Body Medicine*, 15: 236–81.

Greer, S., Morris, T. and Pettingale, K. (1979). Psychological responses to breast cancer: effect on outcome. *The Lancet*, 2: 940–9.

Greer, S., Morris, T., Pettingale, K. and Haybittle, J. (1990). Psychological response to breast cancer and 15 year outcome. *The Lancet*, 335: 49–50.

Grey, M., Boland, E.A., Davidson, M. et al. (2000). Coping skills training for youths with diabetes mellitus has long-lasting effects on metabolic control and quality of life. *Journal of Pediatrics*, 137: 107–13.

Griffin-Blake, C.S. and DeJoy, D.M. (2006). Evaluation of social-cognitive versus stage-matched, self-help physical activity interventions at the workplace. *American Journal of Health Promotion*, 20: 200–9.

Griffith, G.L., Morrison, V., Williams, J.M.G. and Tudor Edwards, R. (2009). Can we assume that research participants are utility maximisers? *European Journal of Health Economics*, 10: 187–96.

Grigsby, A.B., Anderson, R.J., Freedland, K.E. et al. (2002). Prevalence of anxiety in adults with diabetes. A systematic review. *Journal of Psychosomatic Research*, 53: 1053–60.

Griva, K., Myers, L.B. and Newman, S. (2000). Illness perceptions and self-efficacy beliefs in adolescents and young adults with insulin dependent diabetes mellitus. *Psychology and Health*, 15: 733–50.

Grodstein, F., Chen, J. and Willett, W.C. (2003). High-dose antioxidant supplements and cognitive function in community-dwelling elderly women. *American Journal of Clinical Nutrition*, 77: 975–84.

Gross, C.R., Kreitzer, M.J., Thomas, W. *et al.* (2010). Mindfulness-based stress reduction for solid organ transplant recipients: a randomized controlled trial. *Alternative Therapies in Health and Medicine*, 16: 36–44.

Grossardt, B.R., Bower, J.H., Geda, Y.E. *et al.* (2009). Pessimistic, anxious, and depressive personality traits predict all-cause mortality: the Mayo Clinic cohort study of personality and ageing. *Psychosomatic Medicine*, 71: 491–500.

Grossarth-Maticek, R., Bastiaans, J. *et al.* (1985). Psychosocial factors as strong predictors of mortality from cancer, ischemic heart disease and stroke: the Yugoslav prospective study. *Journal of Psychosomatic Research*, 29: 167–76.

Grundy, E. and Bowling, A. (1999). Enhancing the quality of extended life years: identification of the oldest old with a very good and very poor quality of life. *Aging and Mental Health*, 3: 199–212.

Grunfeld, E.A., Hunter, M.S., Ramirez, A.J. *et al.* (2003). Perceptions of breast cancer across the lifespan. *Journal of Psychosomatic Research*, 54: 141–6.

Gudbergsson, S.B., Fosså, S.D., Sanne, B. *et al.* (2007). A controlled study of job strain in primary-treated cancer patients without metastases. *Acta Oncologica*, 46: 534–44.

Gudmunsdottir, H., Johnston, M., Johnston, D. *et al.* (2001). Spontaneous, elicited and cued causal attributions in the year following a first myocardial infarction. *British Journal of Health Psychology*, 6: 81–96.

Gulland, A. (2002). BMA steps up call for ban on smoking in public places. *British Medical Journal*, 325: 1058.

Guthrie, R.M. (2001). The effects of postal and telephone reminders on compliance with pravastatin therapy in a national registry: results of the first myocardial infarction risk reduction program. *Clinical Therapeutics*, 23: 970–80.

Gutteling, J.J., Darlington, A-S.E., Janssen, H.L.A. *et al.* (2008). Effectiveness of health-related quality of life measurement in clinical practice: a prospective, randomized controlled trial in patients with chronic liver disease and their physicians. *Quality of Life Research*, 17: 195–205.

Haan, M.H. (2003). Can vitamin supplements prevent cognitive decline and dementia in old age? (editorial). *American Journal of Clinical Nutrition*, 77: 762–3.

Haan, M.N. and Kaplan, G.A. (1985). The contribution of socio-economic position to minority health. In M. Heckler (ed.), *Report of the Secretary's Task Force on Black and Minority Health: Crosscutting Issues in Health and Human Services*. Washington, DC: US Department of Health and Human Services.

Haas, D.C., Davidson, K.W., Schwartz, D.J. *et al.* (2005). Depressive symptoms are independently predictive of carotid atherosclerosis. *American Journal of Cardiology*, 95: 547–50.

Haberman, D. and Bloomfield, D.S.F. (1988). Social class differences in mortality in Great Britain around 1981. *Journal of the Institute of Actuaries*, 115: 495–517.

Habra, M.E., Linden, W., Anderson, J.C. *et al.* (2003). Type D personality is related to cardiovascular and neuroendocrine reactivity to acute stress. *Journal of Psychosomatic Research*, 55: 235–45.

Hack, T.F. and Degner, L.F. (2004). Coping responses following breast cancer diagnosis predicts psychological adjustment 3 years later. *Psycho-Oncology*, 13: 235–47.

Hagedoorn, M., Dagan, M., Puterman, E. *et al.* (2010). Relationship satisfaction in couples confronted with colorectal cancer: the interplay of past and current spousal support. *Journal of Behavioral Medicine*, doi: 10.1007/s10865-010-9311-7

Hagedoorn, M., Dagan, M., Puterman, E. *et al.* (2011). Relationship satisfaction in couples confronted with colorectal cancer: the interplay of past and current spousal support. *Journal of Behavioral Medicine* [Epub ahead of print]. doi:10.1007/s10865-010-9311-7.

Hagedoorn, M., Sandermann, R., Buunk, B.P. *et al.* (2002). Failing in spousal caregiving: the 'identity-relevant stress' hypothesis to explain sex differences in caregiver distress. *British Journal of Health Psychology*, 7: 481–94.

Hagger, M. (2010). Editorial: Self-regulation: an important construct in health psychology research and practice. *Health Psychology Review*, 4: 57–65.

Hagger, M., Chatzisarantis, N., Biddle, S.J.H. *et al.* (2001). Antecedents of children's physical activity intentions and behaviour: predictive validity and longitudinal effects. *Psychology and Health*, 16: 391–407.

Hagger, M., Chatzisarantis, N., Biddle, S.J.H. (2002). A meta-analytic review of the theories of reasoned action and planned behavior in physical activity: predictive validity and the contribution of additional variables. *Journal of Sport and Exercise Psychology*, 24: 3–28.

Hagger, M.S. and Orbell, S. (2003). A meta-analytic review of the common-sense model of illness representations. *Psychology and Health*, 18: 141–84.

Hagger, M.S., Wood, C., Stiff, C. and Chatzisarantis, N.L.D. (2009). The strength model of self-regulation failure and health-related behaviour. *Health Psychology Review*, 3: 208–38.

Hagger, M., Wood, C., Stiff, C. and Chatzisarantis, N.L. (2010). Ego depletion and the strength model of self-control: a meta-analysis. *Psychological Bulletin*, 136: 495–525.

Hajek, P., Taylor, T.Z. and Mills, P. (2002). Brief intervention during hospital admission to help patients to give up smoking after myocardial infarction and bypass surgery: randomised controlled trial. *British Medical Journal*, 324: 87–9.

Hakama, M., Coleman, M.P., Alexe, D.M. and Auvien, A. (2008). Cancer screening: evidence and practice in Europe 2008. *European Journal of Cancer*, 44: 1404–13

Hakim, A.A., Petrovitch, H., Burchfield, C.M. *et al.* (1998). Effects of walking on mortality among non-smoking retired men. *New England Journal of Medicine*, 338: 94–9.

Hale, G. (1996). The social construction of grief. In N. Cooper, C. Stevenson and G. Hale (eds), *Integrating Perspectives on Health*. Buckingham: Open University Press.

Hale, S., Grogan, S. and Willott, S. (2007). Patterns of self-referral in men with symptoms of prostate disease. *British Journal of Health Psychology*, 12: 403–19.

Halford, J.C.G. and Blundell, J.E. (2000). Serotonin drugs and the treatment of obesity. In T.G. Heffner and D.H. Lockwood (eds), *Obesity: Pathology and Therapy*. Berlin: Springer Verlag.

Hall, A.M., Kamper, S.J., Maher, C.G. *et al.* (2011). Symptoms of depression and stress mediate the effect of pain on disability, *Pain*, 152: 1044–51.

Hall, E.E., Ekkekakis, P. and Petruzzello, S.J. (2002). The affective beneficence of vigorous exercise revisited. *British Journal of Health Psychology*, 7: 47–66.

Hall, J.A., Roter, D.L. and Katz, N.R. (1988). Meta-analysis of correlates of provider behavior in medical encounters. *Medical Care*, 26: 657–75.

Hall, J.A. and Roter, D.L. (2002). Do patients talk differently to male and female physicians? A meta-analytic review. *Patient Education and Counseling*, 48: 217–24.

Hall, K.L. and Rossi, J.S. (2008). Meta-analytic examinations of the strong and weak principles across 48 health behaviours. *Preventive Medicine*, 46: 266–74.

Hall, P.A. and Fong, G.T. (2007). Temporal self-regulation theory: a model for individual health behavior. *Health Psychology Review*, 1: 6–52.

Hall, S.M., Humfleet, G.L., Muñoz, R.F. *et al.* (2009). Extended treatment of older cigarette smokers. *Addiction*, 104: 1043–52.

Hall, S. and Marteau, T.M. (2003). Causal attributions following serious unexpected negative events: a systematic review. *Journal of Social and Clinical Psychology*, 22: 515–36.

Hall, S.M., Tunstall, C., Rugg, D., Jones, R.T. and Benowitz, N. (1985). Nicotine gum and behavioral treatment in smoking cessation. *Journal of Consulting and Clinical Psychology*, 53: 256–8.

Hallal, P.C., Victora, C.G., Azevedo, M.R. *et al.* (2006). Adolescent physical activity and health: a systematic review. *Sports Medicine*, 36: 1019–30.

Hallaråker, E., Arefjord, K., Havik, O.E. and Maeland, J.G. (2001). Social support and emotional adjustment during and after a severe life event: a study of wives of myocardial infarction patients. *Psychology and Health*, 16: 343–56.

Halstead, M.T. and Fernsler, J.I. (1994). Coping strategies of long-term cancer patients. *Cancer Nursing*, 17: 94–100.

Hamer, M. and Karageorghis, C. (2007). Psychological mechanisms of exercise dependence. *Sports Medicine*, 37: 477–85.

Hammerfald, K., Eberle, C., Grau, M. *et al.* (2006). Persistent effects of cognitive-behavioral stress management on cortisol responses to acute stress in healthy subjects: a randomized controlled trial. *Psychoneuroendocrinology*, 31: 333–9.

Hämmig, O., Gutzwiller, F. and Bauer, G. (2009). Work–life conflict and associations with work- and nonwork-related factors and with physical and mental health outcomes: a nationally representative cross-sectional study in Switzerland. *BMC Public Health*, 30: 435.

Hampson, S.E., Glasgow, R.E. and Toobert, D.J. (1990). Personal models of diabetes and their relation to self-care activities. *Health Psychology*, 9: 632–46.

Hampson, S.E., Glasgow, R.E. and Zeiss, A. (1994). Personal models of osteoarthritis and their relation to self-management activities and quality of life. *Journal of Behavioural Medicine*, 17: 143–58.

Han, K.S. (2002). The effect of an integrated stress management program on the psychologic and physiologic stress reactions of peptic ulcer in Korea. *International Journal of Nursing Studies*, 39: 539–48.

Hankonen, N., Absetz, P., Ghisletta, P., Renner, B. and Uutela, A. (2010). Gender differences in social cognitive determinants of exercise adoption. *Psychology & Health*, 25: 55–69.

Hanson, R.W. and Gerber, K.E. (1990). *Coping with Chronic Pain. A Guide to Patient Self-management*. New York: Guilford Press.

Harburg, E.J.C., Chape, C., Erfurt, J.C. *et al.* (1973). Socio-ecological stressor areas and black and white blood pressure: Detroit. *Journal of Chronic Disease*, 26: 595–611.

Harcourt, D., Ambler, N., Rumsey, N. *et al.* (1998). Evaluation of a one-stop breast lump clinic: a randomised controlled trial. *The Breast*, 7: 314–19.

Harcourt, D., Rumsey, N. and Ambler, N. (1999). Same-day diagnosis of symptomatic breast problems: psychological impact and coping strategies. *Psychology, Health & Medicine*, 4: 57–71.

Harding, S. and Maxwell, R. (1997). Differences in mortality of migrants. In F. Drever and M. Whitehead (eds), *Health Inequalities: Decennial Supplement*. London: HMSO.

Härkäpää, K., Järvikoski, A., Mellin, G., Hurri, H. and Luoma, J. (1991). Health locus of control beliefs and psychological distress as predictors for treatment outcome in low-back pain patients: results of a 3-month follow-up of a controlled intervention study. *Pain*, 46: 35–41.

Harland, J., White, M., Drinkwater, C., Chinn, D., Farr, L. and Howel, D. (1999). The Newcastle Exercise Project: a randomised controlled trial of methods to promote physical activity in primary care. *British Medical Journal*, 319: 828–32.

Harris, A.H., Thoresen, C.E., Humphreys, K. *et al.* (2005). Does writing affect asthma? A randomized trial. *Psychosomatic Medicine*, 67: 130–6.

Harris, D.M. and Guten, S. (1979). Health-protective behaviour: an exploratory study. *Journal of Health and Social Behavior*, 20: 17–29.

Harris, P. and Middleton, W. (1994). The illusion of control and optimism about health: on being less at risk but no more in control than others. *British Journal of Social Psychology*, 33: 369–86.

Harris, T., Ferrucci, L., Tracy, R. *et al.* (1999). Associations of elevated interleukin-6 and C-reactive protein levels with mortality and the elderly. *American Journal of Medicine*, 106: 506–12.

Harrison, J.A., Mullen, P.D. and Green, L.W. (1992). A meta-analysis of studies of the health belief model with adults. *Health Education Research, Theory and Practice*, 7: 107–16.

Harrison, M.O., Koenig, H.G., Hays, J.C. *et al.* (2001). The epidemiology of religious coping: a review of recent literature. *International Reviews in Psychiatry*, 13: 86–93.

Hart, C.L., Davey-Smith, G., Hole, D.J. and Hawthorne, V.M. (1999). Alcohol consumption and mortality from all causes, coronary disease, and stroke: results from a prospective cohort study of Scottish men with 21 years of follow-up. *British Medical Journal*, 318: 133–40.

Hart, H., Bilo, H., Redekop, W. *et al.* (2003). Quality of life in patients with type 1 diabetes mellitus. *Quality of Life Research*, 12: 1089–97.

Hartford, K., Wong, C. and Zakaria, D. (2002). Randomized controlled trial of a telephone intervention by nurses to provide information and support to patients and their partners after elective coronary artery bypass graft surgery: effects of anxiety. *Heart and Lung*, 31: 199–206.

Haste, H. (2004). *My Body, My Self: Young People's Values and Motives about Healthy Living*, Report 2. London: Nestlé Social Research Programme.

Hatava, P., Olsson, G.L. and Lagerkranser, M. (2000). Preoperative psychological preparation for children undergoing ENT operations: a comparison of two methods. *Paediatric Anaesthesia*, 10: 477–86.

Hathaway, D. (1986). Effect of preoperative instruction on postoperative outcomes: a meta-analysis. *Nursing Research*, 35: 269–75.

Hausenblas, H.A. and Symons Downs, D. (2002). How much is too much? The development and validation of the Exercise Dependence Scale. *Psychology and Health*, 17: 387–404.

Havik, O.E. and Maeland, J.G. (1988). Changes in smoking behavior after a myocardial infarction. *Health Psychology*, 7: 403–20.

Hayes, N. and Joseph, S. (2003). Big 5 correlates of three measures of subjective wellbeing. *Personality and Individual Differences*, 34: 723–27.

Hayes, L., White, M., Unwin, N. *et al.* (2002). Patterns of physical activity and relationship with risk markers for cardiovascular disease and diabetes in Indian, Pakistani, Bangladeshi and European adults in a UK population. *Journal of Public Health Medicine*, 24: 170–8.

Hayes, S.C., Strosahl, K.D., Bunting, K. *et al.* (2004). What is acceptance and commitment therapy? In S.C. Hayes and K.D. Strosahl (eds), *A Practical Guide to Acceptance and Commitment Therapy*. New York: Springer.

Haynes, B. and Haines, A. (1998). Barriers and bridges to evidence-based clinical practice. *British Medical Journal*, 317: 273–6.

Haynes, G. and Feinleib, M. (1980). Women, work, and coronary heart disease: prospective findings from the Framingham heart study. *American Journal of Public Health*, 70: 133–41.

Haynes, R.B., Ackloo, E., Sahota, N. *et al.* (2008). Interventions for enhancing medication adherence. *Cochrane Database of Systematic Reviews*, issue 4, art. no.: CD000011. doi: 10.1002/14651858.CD000011.

Haynes, R.B., McKibbon, A. and Kanani, R. (1996). Systematic review of randomized trials of interventions to assist patients to follow prescriptions for medications. *The Lancet*, 384: 383–5.

Haynes, S.G., Feinleib, M. and Kannel, W.B. (1980). The relationship of psychosocial factors to coronary heart disease in the Framingham study. III. Eight year incidence of coronary heart disease. *American Journal of Epidemiology*, 111: 37–58.

Health Development Agency Magazine (2005). *Smoking Out Pregnant Teenagers*, Issue 25, Feb/March.

Health Education Authority (1997). *Guidelines: Promoting Physical Activity with Black and Minority Ethnic Groups*. London: Health Education Authority.

Health Education Authority (1998). *Young and Active? Policy Framework for Young People and Health – Enhancing Physical Activity*. London: Health Education Authority.

Health Promotion Authority for Wales (1996). *Lifestyle Changes in Wales. Health in Wales Survey 1996*, Technical Report no. 27. Cardiff: Health Promotion Authority for Wales.

Health Protection Agency (2010). *HIV in the United Kingdom: 2010 Report*. HPA. Also available online at: www.hpa.org.uk/topics/infectiousdiseases/infectionsAZ/HIV.

Health Survey for England (2006). http://www.ic.nhs.uk/statistics-and-data-collections/healthand-lifestyles-related-surveys/health-survey-for-england/health-survey-for-england-2006-latest-trends.

Health Survey for England (2007). Leeds: Health and Social Care Information Centre (2008), available from www.ic.nhs.uk.

Health Survey for England (2008). Trend Tables. The NHS Information Centre, 2009. http://www.ic.nhs.uk/webfiles/publications/HSE/HSE08trends/Health_Survey_for_england_trend_tables_2008.pdf.

Health Utilisation Research Alliance (2006). Ethnicity, socio-economic deprivation and consultation rates in New Zealand general practice. *Journal of Health Service Research and Policy*, 11: 141–9.

Healy, C.M. and McKay, M.F. (2000). Nursing stress: the effects of coping strategies and job satisfaction in a sample of Australian nurses. *Journal of Advanced Nursing*, 31: 681–8.

Heather, N. and Robertson, I. (1997). *Problem Drinking*. Oxford: Oxford University Press.

Heaven, C.M. and Maguire, P. (1998). The relationship between patients' concerns and psychological distress in a hospice setting. *Psycho-Oncology*, 7: 502–7.

Hedges, J.R., Mann, N.C., Meischke, H. *et al.* (1998). Assessment of chest pain onset and out-of-hospital delay using standardised interview questions: the REACT pilot study. *Academic Emergency Medicine*, 5: 773–80.

Heider, F. (1958). *The Psychology of Interpersonal Relations*. New York: Wiley.

Heijmans, M. (1998). Coping and adaptive outcome in chronic fatigue syndrome: importance of illness cognitions. *Journal of Psychosomatic Research*, 45: 39–51.

Heijmans, M. and de Ridder, D. (1998). Structure and determinants of illness representation in chronic disease: a comparison of Addison's disease and chronic fatigue syndrome. *Journal of Health Psychology*, 3: 523–37.

Heijmans, M., de Ridder, D. and Bensing, J. (1999). Dissimilarity in patients' and spouses' representations of chronic illness: explorations of relations to patient adaptation. *Psychology and Health*, 14: 451–66.

Heim, E., Augustiny, K., Blaser, A. and Burki, C. (1987). Coping with breast cancer: a longitudinal prospective study. *Psychotherapy and Psychosomatics*, 48: 44–59.

Heine, S.J. and Lehman, D.R. (1995). Cultural variation in unrealistic optimism: does the West feel more invulnerable than the East? *Journal of Personality and Social Psychology*, 68: 595–607.

Helder, D.I., Bakker, B., deHeer, P., van der Veen, F., Vossen, J.M.J.J., Wit, J.M. and Kaptein, A.A. (2004). Quality of life in adults following bone marrow transplantation during childhood. *Bone Marrow Transplantation*, 33: 329–36.

Helgeson, V.S., Reynolds, K.A. and Tomich, P.L. (2006). A meta-analytic review of benefit-finding and growth. *Journal of Consulting and Clinical Psychology*, 74: 797–816.

Helman, C. (1978). Feed a cold starve a fever: folk models of infection in an English suburban community and their relation to medical treatment. *Culture, Medicine and Psychiatry*, 2: 107–37.

Henderson, L., Gregory, J. and Swan, G. (2002). *The National Diet and Nutrition Survey: Adults Aged 19 to 64 years*. London: HMSO.

Henselmans, I., Fleer, J., de Vries, J. *et al.* (2010). The adaptive effect of personal control when facing breast cancer: cognitive and behavioural mediators. *Psychology & Health*, 25: 1023–40.

Heloma, A. and Jaakola, M.S. (2003). Four-year follow-up of smoke exposure, attitudes and smoking behaviour following enactment of Finland's national smoke-free work-place law. *Addiction*, 98: 1111–17.

Hemingway, H. and Marmot, M. (1999). Psychosocial factors in the aetiology and prognosis of coronary heart disease: systematic review of prospective cohort studies. *British Medical Journal*, 318: 1460–7.

Hendry, L.B. and Kloep, M. (2002). *Lifespan Development: Resources, Challenges, Risks.* London: Thomson Learning.

Hennessy, D.A., Lanni-Manley, E. and Maiorana, N. (2006). The effects of fatal vision goggles on drinking and driving intentions in college students. *Journal of Drug Education*, 36: 59–72.

Hennrikus, D.J., Jeffery, R.W., Lando, H.A. *et al.* (2002). The SUCCESS project: the effect of program format and incentives on participation and cessation in worksite smoking cessation programs. *American Journal of Public Health*, 92: 274–9.

Herbert, T.B. and Cohen, S. (1993). Stress and immunity in humans: a meta-analytic review. *Psychosomatic Medicine*, 55: 364–79.

Herman, P.M. and Walsh, M.E. (2010). Hospital admissions for acute myocardial infarction, angina, stroke, and asthma after implementation of Arizona's comprehensive Statewide Smoking Ban. *American Journal of Public Health*, 101: 491–6.

Herrman, C. and Wortman, C. (1985). Action control and the coping process. In J. Kuhl and J. Beckman (eds), *Action Control: From Cognition to Behavior*. New York: Springer-Verlag.

Herzlich, C. (1973). *Health and Illness: A Social Psychological Analysis*. London: Academic Press.

Herzog, T.A. (2008). Analysing the transtheoretical model using the framework of Weinstein, Rothman and Sutton (1998): the example of smoking cessation. *Health Psychology*, 27: 548–56.

Hewitt, D., McDonald, M., Portenoy, R., Rosenfield, B., Passik, S. and Breitbart, W. (1997). Pain syndromes and etiologies in ambulatory AIDS patients. *Pain*, 70: 117–23.

Higginson, I.J. and Carr, A.J. (2001). Using quality of life measures in the clinical setting. *British Medical Journal*, 322: 1297–300.

Hillier, S.M. and Jewell, J.A. (1983). *Health care and traditional medicine in China, 1800–1982*. London: Routledge.

Hingson, R.M., Heeren, T., Winter, M.R. and Wechsler, H. (2003). Early age of first drunkenness as a factor in college students' unplanned and unprotected sex attributable to drinking. *Pediatrics*, 111: 34–41.

Hinton, J. (1999). The progress of awareness and acceptance of dying assessed in cancer patients and their caring relatives. *Palliative Medicine*, 13: 19–35.

Ho, S.M.Y., Chan, C.L.W. and Ho, R.T.H. (2004). Post-traumatic growth in Chinese cancer survivors. *Psycho-Oncology*, 13: 377–89.

Hoare, J. and Flatley, J. (2008). *Drug Misuse Declared: Findings from the 2007/08 British Crime Survey*. Home Office Statistical Bulletin 13/08. London: Home Office. Available from: http://www.homeoffice.gov.uk/rds/pdfs08/hosb1308.pdf.

Hobfoll, S.E. (1989). Conservation of resources: a new attempt at conceptualizing stress. *American Psychologist*, 44: 513–24.

Hobfoll, S. (1991). Traumatic stress: a theory based on rapid loss of resources. *Anxiety Research*, 4: 187–97.

Hobfoll, S.E. (2001). The influence of culture, community, and the nested-self in the stress processes: advancing conservation of resources theory. *Applied Psychology: An International Review*, 50: 337–421.

Hobfoll, S.E., Jackson, A.P., Lavin, J., Britton, P.J. and Shepherd, J.B. (1994). Women's barriers to safer sex. *Psychology and Health*, 9: 233–52.

Hobfoll, S.E. and Lilly, R.S. (1993). Conservation of resources; a new attempt at conceptualising stress. *American Psychologist*, 44: 513–24.

Hodgson, S. and Maher, E. (1999). *A Practical Guide to Human Cancer Genetics.* Cambridge: Cambridge University Press.

Hoffman, S., O'Sullivan, L.F., Harrison, A. *et al.* (2006). HIV risk behaviors and the context of sexual coercion in young adults' sexual interactions: results from a diary study in rural South Africa. *Sexually Transmitted Diseases*, 33: 52–8.

Hofmann, W., Friese, M. and Wiers, R.W. (2007). Impulsive versus reflective influences on health behavior: a theoretical framework and empirical review. *Health Psychology Review*, 2: I11–37.

Hogbin, B. and Fallowfield, L. (1989). Getting it taped: the 'bad news' consultation with cancer patients. *British Journal of Hospital Medicine*, 41: 330–3.

Holick, M.F. (2004). Sunlight and vitamin D for bone health and prevention of autoimmune disease, cancers and cardiovascular disease. *American Journal of Clinical Nutrition*, 80(suppl.6), S1678–1688.

Holland, J.C. and Gooen-Piels, J. (2000). Principles of psycho-oncology. In J.C. Holland and E. Frei (eds), *Psychological Care of the Patient with Cancer.* New York: Oxford University Press.

Holland, W.W. and Stewart, S. (2005). *Screening in Disease Prevention: What Works?* Oxford: Radcliffe.

Hollis, J.F., Connett, J.E., Stevens, V.J. and Greenlick, M.R. (1990). Stressful life events, Type A behaviour, and the prediction of cardiovascular disease and total mortality over six years. *Journal of Behavioral Medicine*, 13: 263–81.

Holmes, T.H. and Rahe, R.H. (1967). The social readjustment rating scale. *Journal of Psychosomatic Research*, 11: 213–18.

Holmes, T.H. and Masuda, M. (1974). Life change and illness susceptibility. In B.S. Dohrenwend and B.P. Dohrenwend (eds), *Stressful Life Events: Their Nature and Effects*. New York: Wiley.

Holroyd, K.A. and Lipchik, G.L. (1999). Psychological management of recurrent headache disorders: progress and prospects. In R.J. Gatchel and D.C. Turk (eds), *Psychosocial Factors in Pain*. New York: Guilford Press.

Holroyd, K.A., O'Donnell, F.J., Stensland, M. *et al.* (2001). Management of chronic tension-type headache with tricyclic antidepressant medication, stress management therapy, and their combination. *Journal of the American Medical Association*, 285: 2208–15.

Holtzman, S., Newth, S. and DeLongis, A. (2004). The role of social support in coping with daily pain among patients with rheumatoid arthritis. *Journal of Health Psychology*, 9: 749–67.

Holzner, B., Kemmler, G., Cella, D. *et al.* (2004). Normative data for functional assessment of cancer therapy: general scale and its use for the interpretation of quality of life scores in cancer survivors. *Acta Oncologica*, 43: 153–60.

Hood, K.K., Peterson, C., Rohan, J.M. and Drotar, D. (2009). Association between adherence and glycemic control in pediatric Type 1 diabetes: a meta-analysis. *Pediatrics*, 24: e1171–e1179.

Hooker, K., Monahan, D., Shifren, K. *et al.* (1992). Mental and physical health of spouse caregivers: the role of personality. *Psychology and Aging*, 7: 367–75.

Hooper, L., Bartlett, C., Davey-Smith, G. *et al.* (2002). Systematic review of long-term effects of advice to reduce dietary salt in adults. *British Medical Journal*, 325: 628–32.

Hoorens, V. and Buunk, B.P. (1993). Social comparisons of health risks: locus of control, the person-positivity bias, and unrealistic optimism. *Journal of Applied Social Psychology*, 23: 291–302.

Hopwood, P. (1997). Psychological issues in cancer genetics: current research and future priorities. *Patient Education and Counselling*, 32: 19–31.

Horgan, R.P. and Kenny, L.C. (2007). Management of teenage pregnancy. *The Obstetrician and Gynaecologist*, 9: 153–8.

Horne, P.J., Hardman, C.A., Lowe, C.F. *et al.* (2009). Increasing parental provision and children's consumption of lunchbox fruit and vegetables in Ireland: the Food Dudes intervention. *European Journal of Clinical Nutrition*, 63: 613–18.

Horne, P.J., Tapper, K., Lowe, C.F., Hardman, C.A., Jackson, M.C. and Woolner, J. (2004). Increasing children's fruit and vegetable consumption: a peer modelling and rewards-based intervention. *European Journal of Clinical Nutrition*, 58: 1649–60.

Horne, R. (1997). Representations of medication and treatmen: advances in theory and measurement. In K.J. Petrie and J. Weinman (eds), *Perceptions of Health and Illness*. Chur, Switzerland: Harwood.

Horne, R. (2001). Compliance, adherence and concordance. In K. Taylor and G. Harding (eds). *Pharmacy Practice*. London: Taylor & Francis, pp. 165–84.

Horne, R. (1999). Patients' beliefs about treatment: the hidden determinant of treatment outcome? *Journal of Psychosomatic Research*, 47: 491–5.

Horne, R. and Weinman, J. (1999). Patients' beliefs about prescribed medicines and their role in adherence to treatment in chronic physical illness. *Journal of Psychosomatic Research*, 47: 555–67.

Horne, R. and Weinman, J. (2002). Self-regulation and self-management in asthma: exploring the role of illness perceptions and treatment beliefs in explaining non-adherence to preventer medication. *Psychology and Health*, 17: 17–32.

Hosking, S.G., Marsh, N.V. and Friedman, P.J. (1996). Post-stroke depression: prevalence, course and associated factors. *Neuropsychological Review*, 6: 107–33.

Hoth, K.F., Wamboldt, F.S., Bowler, R. *et al.* (2011). Attributions about cause of illness in chronic obstructive pulmonary disease. *Journal of Psychosomatic Research*, 70: 465–72.

Hotopf, M., Chidgey, J., Addington-Hall, J. and Ly, K.L. (2002). Depression in advanced disease: a systematic review. Part 1: Prevalence and case finding. *Palliative Medicine*, 16: 81–97.

House, A., Dennis, M., Mogridge, L., Warlow, C., Hawton, K. and Jones, L. (1991). Mood disorders in the year after first stroke. *British Journal of Psychiatry*, 2: 211–21.

House, J.S. (1987). Chronic stress and chronic disease in life and work: conceptual and methodological issues. *Work and Stress*, 1: 129–34.

House, J.S., Kessler, R., Herzog, A.R., Mero, R., Kinney, A. and Breslow, M. (1991). Social stratification, age, and health. In K.W. Scheie, D. Blazer and J.S. House (eds), *Aging, Health Behaviours, and Health Outcomes*. Hillsdale, NJ: Lawrence Erlbaum.

House, J.S., Robbins, C. and Metzner, H.L. (1982). The association of social relationships and activities with mortality: prospective evidence from the Tecumseh Community Health Study. *American Journal of Epidemiology*, 116: 123–40.

Houston, B.K., Chesney, M.A., Black, G.W., Cates, D.S. and Hecker, M.H.L. (1992). Behavioral clusters and coronary heart disease. *Psychosomatic Medicine*, 54: 447–61.

Houston, M. (2004). Commissioner denies plans for a Europe-wide smoking ban. *British Medical Journal*, 328: 544.

Hu, F.B. (2003). Overweight and obesity in women: health risks and consequences. *Journal of Women's Health* 12: 163–72.

Hu, F.B., Willett, W.C., Colditz, G.A., Ascherio, A., Speizer, F.E., Rosner, B., Hennekens, C.H. and Stampfer, M.J. (1999). Prospective study of snoring and risk of hypertension in women. *American Journal of Epidemiology*, 150: 806–16.

Hu, F.B., Willett, W.C., Manson, J.E., Colditz, G.A., Rimm, E.B., Speizer, F.E., Hennekens, C.H. and Stampfer, M.J. (2000). Snoring and risk of cardiovascular disease in women. *Journal of the American College of Cardiology*, 35: 308–13.

Hu, T.-W., Sung, H.-Y. and Keeler, T.E. (1995). Reducing cigarette consumption in California: tobacco taxes vs. an anti-smoking media campaign. *American Journal of Public Health*, 85: 1218–22.

Huberty, J.L., Ransdell, L.B., Sidman, C. *et al.* (2008). Explaining long-term exercise adherence in women who complete a structured exercise program. *Research Quarterly for Exercise & Sport*, 79: 374–84.

Hudson, M.M., Mertens, A.C., Yasui, Y. *et al.* (2003). Health status of adult long-term survivors of childhood cancer: a report from the Childhood Cancer Survivor Study. *JAMA*, 290: 1583–92.

Huerta, M.C. and Borgonovi, F. (2010). Education, alcohol use and abuse among young adults in Britain. *Social Science & Medicine*, 71: 143–51.

Hughes, G., Bennett, K.M. and Hetherington, M. (2004). Old and alone: barriers to healthy eating in older men living on their own. *Appetite*, 43: 269–276.

Huijbrechts, P., Duivenvoorden, H.J., Deckers, J.W. *et al.* (1996). Modification of smoking habits five months after myocardial infarction: relationship with personality characteristics. *Journal of Psychosomatic Research*, 40: 369–78.

Humphrey, N. (2002). Great expectations: the evolutionary psychology of faith-healing and the placebo effect. In C. von Hofsten and L. Bäckman (eds), *Psychology at the Turn of the Millennium*, Vol. 2: Social, Developmental, and Clinical Perspectives. Hove: Psychology Press.

Hunt, S.M. and Martin, C.J. (1988). Health related behaviour change: a test of a new model. *Psychology and Health*, 2: 209–30.

Hunt, S.M., McEwan, J. and McKenna, S.P. (1986). *Measuring Health Status*. Beckenham: Croom Helm.

Hunter, M.S., Grunfeld, E.A. and Ramirez, A.J. (2003). Help-seeking intentions for breast-cancer symptoms: a comparison of self-regulation model and the theory of planned behaviour. *British Journal of Health Psychology*, 8: 319–34.

Huskisson, E.C. (1974). Measurement of pain. *Lancet*, Nov 9; 2(7889): 1127–31.

Hyland, A., Wakefield, M., Higbee, C. *et al.* (2006). Anti-tobacco television advertising and indicators of smoking cessation in adults: a cohort study. *Health Education Research*, 21: 296–302.

Hyland, M.E., Bellesis, M., Thompson, P.J. and Keenyon, C.A.P. (1996). The constructs of asthma quality of life: psychometric, experimental and correlational evidence. *Psychology and Health*, 12: 101–21.

Illinois Racial and Ethnic Health Disparities Council. http://app.idph.state.il.us/iphi/docs/DraftFinal.pdf.

Ingledew, D.K. and Ferguson, E. (2007). Personality and riskier sexual behaviour: motivational mediators. *Psychology & Health*, 22: 291–315.

Ingledew, D.K. and McDonagh, G. (1998). What coping functions are served when health behaviours are used as coping strategies? *Journal of Health Psychology*, 3: 195–213.

Ingraham, B.A., Bragdon, B. and Nohe, A. (2008). Molecular basis for the potential of vitamin D to prevent cancer. *Current Medical Research and Opinion*, 24: 139–49.

Ingram, K.M., Jones, D.A., Fass, R.J., Neideig, J.L. and Song, Y.S. (1999). Social support and unsupportive social interactions: their association with depression among people living with HIV. *AIDS Care*, 11: 313–29.

Ingram, L., Morrison, V., Soulsby, J. *et al.* (2008). Mindfulness-based cognitive therapy for oncology outpatients and their family carers: a qualitative evaluation.

Inoue, S., Saeki, T., Mantani, T., Okamura, H. and Yamawaki, S. (2003). Factors related to patients' mental adjustment to breast cancer: patient characteristics and family functioning. *Support Care Cancer*, 11: 178–84.

Inouye, J., Flannelly, L. and Flannelly, K.J. (2001). The effectiveness of self-management training for individuals with HIV/AIDS. *Journal of the Association of Nurses in AIDS Care*, 12: 71–82.

International Center for Alcohol Policies (ICAP) (1998). *Report 5*. Washington, DC: ICAP.

International Obesity Taskforce and European Association for the Study of Obesity (2002). *Obesity in Europe: The Case for Action*. London: International Obesity Taskforce.

Iribarren, C., Darbinian, J.A., Lo, J.C. *et al.* (2006). Value of the sagittal abdominal diameter in coronary heart disease risk assessment: Cohort study in a large, multiethnic population. *American Journal of Epidemiology*, 164: 115–59.

Isen, A.M. (1987). Positive affect, cognitive processes, and social behaviour. In L. Berkowitz (ed.), *Advances in Experimental Social Psychology 20*. New York: Academic Press.

Isikhan, V., Comez, T., Danis, M.Z. (2004). Job stress and coping strategies in health care professionals working with cancer patients, *European Journal of Oncology Nursing*, 8: 234–44.

Ison, E. (2009). The introduction of health impact assessment in the WHO European Healthy Cities Network. *Health Promotion International*, 24(suppl. 1): i64–i71.

Iversen, M.D., Hammond, A. and Betteridge, N. (2010). Self-management of rheumatic diseases: state of the art and future perspectives. *Annals of Rheumatic Disease*, 69: 955–63.

Iwasaki, M., Otani, T., Sunaga, R. *et al.* (2002). Social networks and mortality based on the Komo–Ise cohort study in Japan. *International Journal of Epidemiology*, 31: 1208–18.

Jackson, R., Scragg, R. and Beaglehole, R. (1991). Alcohol consumption and risk of coronary heart disease. *British Medical Journal*, 303: 211–16.

Jacobs, D.R., Jr, Luepker, R.V., Mittelmark, M.B., Folsom, A.R., Pirie, P.L., Mascioli, S.R., Hannan, P.J., Pechacek, T.F., Bracht, N., Carlaw, R., Kline, F.G. and Blackburn, H. (1986). Community-wide prevention strategies: evaluation design of the Minnesota Heart Health Program. *Journal of Chronic Diseases*, 39: 775–88.

Jacobs, S.A., de Beer, H. and Larney, M. (2010). Adult consumers' understanding and use of information on food labels: a study among consumers living in the Potchefstroom and Klerksdorp regions, South Africa. *Public Health Nutrition*, 13: 1–13.

Jacobsen, P.B. and Hahn, D.M. (1998). Cognitive behavioral programmes. In J. Holland (ed.), *Textbook of Psycho-Oncology*. New York: Oxford University Press.

Jacobson, E. (1938). *Progressive Relaxation*. Chicago, IL: University of Chicago Press.

Jaffe, H. (1997). Dying for dollars. *Men's Health*, 12: 132–7.

Jaffe, L., Lutter, J.M., Rex, J., Hawkes, C. and Bucaccio, P. (1999). Incentives and barriers to physical activity for working women. *American Journal of Health Promotion*, 13(4): 215–18.

Jago, R., Baranowski, T., Zakeri, I. *et al.* (2005). Observed environmental features and the physical activity of adolescent males. *American Journal of Preventive Medicine*, 29: 98–104.

James, J.E. (2004). Critical review of dietary caffeine and blood pressure: a relationship that should be taken more seriously. *Psychosomatic Medicine*, 66: 63–71.

James, J.E. and Hardardottir, D. (2002). Influence of attention focus and trait anxiety on tolerance of acute pain. *British Journal of Health Psychology*, 7: 149–62.

James, J., Thomas, P. and Kerr, D. (2007). Preventing childhood obesity: two year follow-up results from the Christchurch obesity prevention programme in schools (CHOPPS). *British Medical Journal*, 335: 841.

James, S.A., LaCroix, A.Z., Kleinbaum, D.G. and Strogatz, D.S. (1984). John Henryism and blood pressure differences among black men. II. The role of occupational stressors. *Journal of Behavioral Medicine*, 7: 259–75.

Janlert, U., Asplund, K. and Weinehall, L. (1992). Unemployment and cardiovascular risk indicators. Data from the MONICA survey in northern Sweden. *Journal of Social Medicine*, 20: 14–18.

Janse, A.J., Gemke, R.J.B.J., Uiterwaal, C.S.P.M., van der Tweel, I., Kimpen, J.L.L. and Sinnema, G. (2004). Quality of life: patients and doctors don't always agree. *Journal of Clinical Epidemiology*, 57: 653–61.

Janz, N.K. and Becker, M.H. (1984). The health belief model: a decade later. *Health Education Quarterly*, 11: 1–17.

Janz, N.K., Zimmerman, M.A., Wren, P.A., Israel, B.A., Freudenberg, N. and Carter, R.J. (1996). Evaluation of 37

AIDS prevention projects: successful approaches and barriers to program effectiveness. *Health Education Quarterly*, 23: 80–97.

Janzon, E., Hedblad, B., Berglund, G. and Engstrom, G. (2004). Changes in blood pressure and body weight following smoking cessation in women. *Journal of Internal Medicine*, 255: 266–72.

Jarvis, M.J. (2004). Why people smoke. *British Medical Journal*, 328: 277–9.

Jatoi, I., Zhu, K., Shah, M. *et al.* (2006). Psychological distress in U.S. women who have experienced false-positive mammograms. *Breast Cancer Research and Treatment*, 100: 191–200.

Jay, S.M., Elliott, C.H. and Fitzgibbons, I. (1995). A comparative study of cognitive behavior therapy versus general anaesthesia for painful medical procedures in children. *Pain*, 62: 3–9.

Jellinek, E.M. (1960). *The Disease Concept of Alcoholism*. New Haven, CT: Hillhouse Press.

Jemmott, J.B., Croyle, R.T. and Ditto, P.H. (1988). Commonsense epidemiology: self-based judgements from laypersons and physicians. *Health Psychology*, 7(1): 55–73.

Jenkins, P.R., Jenkins, R.A., Nannis, E.D., McKee, K.T., Jr and Temoshok, L.R. (2000). Reducing risk of sexually transmitted disease (STD) and human immunodeficiency virus infection in a military STD clinic: evaluation of a randomized preventive intervention trial. *Clinical Infectious Diseases*, 30: 730–5.

Jenkins, R.L., Lewis, G. and Bebbington, P. (1997). The National Psychiatric Morbidity Surveys of Great Britain: initial findings from the household survey. *Psychology and Medicine*, 27: 775–89.

Jenkinson, C., Fitzpatrick, R., Garrat, A., Peto, V. and Stewart-Brown, S. (2001). Can item response theory reduce patient burden when measuring health status in neurological disorders? Results from Rasch analysis of the SF36 physical functioning scale (PF-10). *Journal of Neurology, Neurosurgery and Psychiatry*, 71: 220–4.

Jensen, M.P., Turner, J.A. and Romano, J.M. (2001). Changes in beliefs, catastrophizing, and coping are associated with improvement in multidisciplinary pain treatment. *Journal of Consulting and Clinical Psychology*, 69: 655–62.

Jerant, A., Chapman, B., Duberstein, P. *et al.* (2011). Personality and medication non-adherence among older adults enrolled in a six-year trial. *British Journal of Health Psychology*, 16: 151–69.

Jerram, K.L. and Coleman, P.G. (1999). The big five personality traits and reporting of health behaviours and health problems in old age. *British Journal of Health Psychology*, 4: 181–92.

Jerusalem, M. and Schwarzer, R. (1992). Self-efficacy as a resource factor in stress appraisal process. In R. Schwarzer (ed.), *Self Efficacy: Thought Control of Action*. Washington, DC: Hemisphere.

Jessop, D.C., Herberts, C. and Soloman, L. (2005). The impact of financial circumstances on student mental health. *British Journal of Health Psychology*, 10: 421–39.

Jessor, R. and Jessor, S.L. (1977). *Problem Behavior and Psychosocial Development: A Longitudinal Study of Youth*. New York: Academic Press.

Jewell, J. and Hupp, S.D. (2005). Examining the effects of fatal vision goggles on changing attitudes and behaviors related to drinking and driving. *Journal of Primary Prevention*, 26: 553–65.

Jirojanakul, P., Skevington, S.M. and Hudson, J. (2003). Predicting young children's quality of life. *Social Science and Medicine*, 57: 1277–88.

Johnson, C.L. and Barer, B.M. (1997). *Life Beyond 85 Years: The Aura of Survivorship*. New York: Springer.

Johnson, J.V., Hall, E.M. and Theorell, T. (1989). Combined effects of job strain and social isolation on cardiovascular disease morbidity and mortality in a random sample of the Swedish male working population. *Scandinavian Journal of Work, Environment, and Health*, 15: 271–9.

Johnson, M.I. (2001). Transcutaneous electrical nerve stimulation (TENS) and TENS-like devices: do they provide pain relief? *Pain Reviews*, 8: 121–58.

Johnson, S.B. (1999). Commentary: psychologists' resistance to showcasing the profession's accomplishments: What is all the fuss about? *Journal of Pediatric Psychology*, 24: 329–30.

Johnsson, K.O. and Berglund, M. (2003). Education of key personnel in student pubs leads to a decrease in alcohol consumption among patrons: a randomized controlled trial. *Addiction*, 98: 627–33.

Johnston, D.W. (2002). Acute and chronic psychological processes in cardiovascular disease. In K.W. Schaie, H. Leventhal and S.L. Willis (eds), *Effective Health Behavior in Older Adults*. New York: Springer, pp. 55–64.

Johnston, D.W. (2007). Emotions and the heart: psychological risk factors for cardiovascular disease. *European Health Psychologist*, 1: 9–11.

Johnston, M., Bonetti, D., Joice, S. *et al.* (2007). Recovery from disability after stroke as a target for a behavioural intervention: results of a randomsed controlled trial. *Disability and Rehabilitation*, 29: 1117–27.

Johnston, M., Foster, M., Shennan, J. *et al.* (2008). The effectiveness of an Acceptance and Commitment Therapy self-help intervention for chronic pain. *Clinical Journal of Pain*, 26: 393–402.

Johnston, M., Foster, M., Shennan, J.N.J. *et al.* (2010). The effectiveness of an Acceptance and Commitment Therapy self-help intervention for chronic pain. *Clinical Journal of Pain*, 26: 393–402.

Johnston, M. and Kennedy, P. (1998). Editorial: special issue on clinical health psychology in chronic conditions. *Clinical Psychology and Psychotherapy*, 5: 59–61.

Johnston, M., Morrison, V., MacWalter, R. and Partridge, C. (1999). Perceived control, coping and recovery from disability following stroke. *Psychology and Health*, 14: 181–92.

Johnston, M. and Pollard, B. (2001). Consequences of disease: testing the WHO International Classification of Impairments, Disability and Handicap (ICIDH) model. *Social Science and Medicine*, 53: 1261–73.

Johnston, M., Pollard, B., Morrison, V. and MacWalter, R. (2004). Functional limitations and survival following stroke: psychological and clinical predictors of 3 year outcome. *International Journal of Behavioral Medicine*, 11: 187–96.

Johnston, M. and Vogele, K. (1993). Benefits of psychological preparation for surgery: a meta-analysis. *Annals of Behavioral Medicine*, 15: 245–56.

Joice, S., Johnston, M., Bonetti, D., Morrison, V. *et al.* (2010) Stroke survivors' evaluations of a stroke workbook-based intervention designed to increase perceived control over recovery. *Health Education Journal*, doi: 10.1177/0017896910383555.

Joint Health Surveys Unit (2001). *Health Survey for England: The Health of Minority Ethnic Groups 1999*. London: HMSO.

Jolly, K., Taylor, R., Lip, G.Y. *et al.* (2007). The Birmingham Rehabilitation Uptake Maximisation Study (BRUM). Home-based compared with hospital-based cardiac rehabilitation in a multi-ethnic population: cost-effectiveness and patient adherence. *Health Technology Assessment*, 11: 111–18.

Jonas, B.S. and Mussolino, M.E. (2000). Symptoms of depression as a prospective risk factor for stroke. *Psychosomatic Medicine*, 62: 463–71.

Jones, B.A., Reams, K., Calvocoressi, L. *et al.* (2007). Adequacy of communicating results from screening mammograms to African American and White women. *American Journal of Public Health*, 97: 531–8.

Jones, E. and Morrison, V. (2004). Patient–carer interactions following stroke: the effect on distress. BPS Division of Health Psychology Annual Conference, Edinburgh, September.

Jones, F.A., Burke, R.J. and Westman, M. (eds) (2006). *Work Life Balance: A Psychological Perspective*. New York: Psychology Press.

Jones, J.M., Haslam, S.A., Jetten, J. *et al.* (2011). That which doesn't kill us can make us stronger (and more satisfied with life): the contribution of personal and social changes to well-being after acquired brain injury. *Psychology & Health*, 26: 353–69.

Jones, M.A. and Johnston, D.W. (2000). A critical review of the relationship between perception of the work environment, coping and mental health in trained nurses, and patient outcomes. *Clinical Effectiveness in Nursing*, 4: 74–85.

Jones, M., Jolly, K., Raftery, J. *et al.* (2007). 'DNA' may not mean 'did not participate': a qualitative study of reasons for non-adherence at home- and centre-based cardiac rehabilitation. *Family Practice*, 24: 343–57.

Jones, J.R., Huxtable, C.S., Hodgson, J.T. *et al.* (2003). *Self-reported Illness in 2001/02: Results from a Household Survey*. London: Health and Safety Executive.

Jones, R., Pearson, J., McGregor, S. *et al.* (2002). Does writing a list help cancer patients ask relevant questions? *Patient Education and Counseling*, 47: 369–71.

Jones, R.A. (1990). Expectations and delay in seeking medical care. *Journal of Social Issues*, 46: 81–95.

Jørgensen, K.J. and Gøtzsche, P.C. (2004). Presentation on websites of possible benefits and harm from screening for breast cancer: a cross-sectional study. *British Medical Journal*, 328: 148–53.

Jousilahti, P., Vartiainen, E., Tuomilehto, J., Pekkenen, J. and Puska, P. (1995). Effect of risk factors and changes in risk factors on coronary mortality in three cohorts of middle aged people in eastern Finland. *American Journal of Epidemiology*, 141: 50–60.

Joyce, C., Hickey, H., McGee, H. *et al.* (2003). A theory-based method for the evaluation of individual quality of life: the SEIQoL. *Quality of Life Research*, 12: 275–80.

Julien, R.M. (1996). *A Primer of Drug Action: A Concise, Nontechnical Guide to the Actions, Uses and Side Effects of Psychoactive Drugs*, 7th edn. New York: W.H. Freeman.

Kabat-Zinn, J. (2001). *Full Catastrophe Living: How to Cope with Stress, Pain and Illness Using Mindfulness Meditation*. London: Piatkus Books.

Kagee, A. and Deport, T. (2010). Barriers to adherence to antiretroviral treatment: The perspectives of patient advocates. *Journal of Health Psychology*, 15: 1001–11.

Kahn, K.L., Pearson, M.L., Harrison, E.R. *et al.* (1994). Health care for black and poor hospitalized Medicare patients. *Journal of the American Medical Association*, 271: 1169–74.

Kalichman, S.C., Benotsch, E.G., Weinhardt, L. *et al.* (2003). Health-related internet use, coping, social support, and health indicators in people living with HIV/AIDS: preliminary results from a community survey. *Health Psychology*, 22: 111–16.

Kalichman, S.C., Cherry, C. and Browne-Sperling, F. (1999). Effectiveness of a video-based motivational skills-building HIV risk-reduction intervention for inner-city African American men. *Journal of Consulting and Clinical Psychology*, 67: 959–66.

Kalichman, S.C., Cherry, C., Cain, D. *et al.* (2006). Internet-based health information consumer skills intervention for people living with HIV/AIDS. *Journal of Consulting and Clinical Psychology*, 74: 545–54.

Kalnins, I.H.C., Ballantyne, P. and Quartaro, G. (1994). School based community development as a health promotion strategy for children. *Health Promotion International*, 9: 269–79.

Kalra, L., Evans, A., Perez, I. *et al.* (2004). Training carers of stroke patients: randomised controlled trial. *British Medical Journal*, 328: 1099–104.

Kang, J.H., Cook, N.R., Manson, J.E., Buring, E., ScD; Albert, C.M. and Grodstein, F. (2009). Vitamin E, vitamin C, beta carotene, and cognitive function among women with or at risk of cardiovascular disease: the Women's Antioxidant and Cardiovascular Study. *Circulation*, 119: 2772–80.

Kanner, A.D., Coyne, J.C., Schaefer, C. and Lazarus, R.S. (1981). Comparison of two models of stress management: daily hassles and uplifts versus major life events. *Journal of Behavioral Medicine*, 4: 1–39.

Kaplan, G. and Baron-Epel, O. (2003). What lies behind the subjective evaluation of health status? *Social Science and Medicine*, 56: 1669–76.

Kaplan, G.A. and Reynolds, P. (1988). Depression and cancer mortality and morbidity: prospective evidence from the Alameda County study. *Journal of Behavioral Medicine*, 11: 1–14.

Karasek, R.A. (1979). Job demands, job decision latitude and mental strain: implications for job redesign. *Administrative Science Quarterly*, 24: 285–308.

Karasek, R. (1996). Lower health risk with increased job control among white collar workers. *Journal of Organizational Behavior*, 11: 171–85.

Karasek, R.A., Baker, D., Marxer, F., Ahlbom, A. and Theorell, T. (1981). Job decision latitude, job demands and cardiovascular disease: a prospective study of Swedish men. *American Journal of Public Health*, 71: 694–705.

Karasek, R.A. and Theorell, T. (1990). *Healthy Work: Stress, Productivity and the Reconstruction of Working Life*. New York: Basic Books.

Karasz, A. and McKinley, P.S. (2007). Cultural differences in conceptual models of fatigue. *Journal of Health Psychology*, 12: 613–26.

Karlamangla, A.S., Merkin, S.S., Crimmins, E.M. *et al.* (2010). Socioeconomic and ethnic disparities in cardiovascular risk in the United States, 2001–2006. *Annals of Epidemiology*, 20: 617–28.

Kasl, S.V. (1996). Theory of stress and health. In C.L. Cooper (ed.), *Handbook of Stress, Medicine and Health*. London: CRC Press.

Kasl, S.V. and Cobb, S. (1966a). Health behavior, illness behavior, and sick role behavior I. Health and illness behavior. *Archives of Environmental Health*, 12: 246–66.

Kasl, S.V. and Cobb, S. (1966b). Health behavior, illness behavior, and sick role behavior II. Sick role behavior. *Archives of Environmental Health*, 12: 531–41.

Katbamna, S., Ahmad, W., Bhakta, P. *et al.* (2004). Do they look after their own? Informal support for the South Asian carer. *Health & Social Care in the Community*, 12: 398–406.

Katz, M.H. (1997). AIDS epidemic in San Francisco among men who report sex with men: successes and challenges of HIV prevention. *Journal of Acquired Immune Deficiency Syndrome and Human Retrovirology*, 14: S38–S46.

Kauff, N.D., Satagopan, J.M., Robson, M.E. *et al.* (2002). Risk-reducing Salpingo-oophorectomy in women with a BRCA1 or BRCA2 mutation. *New England Journal of Medicine*, 346: 1609–15.

Kawachi, I., Kennedy, B.P., Lochner, K. *et al.* (1997). Social capital, income inequality, and mortality. *American Journal of Public Health*, 87: 1491–8.

Kearins, O., Walton, J., O'Sullivan, E. *et al.* (2009). Invitation management initiative to improve uptake of breast cancer screening in an urban UK Primary Care Trust. *Journal of Medical Screening*, 16: 81–4.

Keating, N.L., Guadagnoli, E., Landrum, M.B. *et al.* (2002). Treatment decision making in early-stage breast cancer: should surgeons match patients' desired level of involvement? *Journal of Clinical Oncology*, 20: 1473–9.

Keats, M.R., Culos-Reed, S.N., Courneya, K.S. *et al.* (2007). Understanding physical activity in adolescent cancer survivors: an application of the theory of planned behavior. *Psycho-Oncology*, 16: 448–57.

Keefe, F.J., Caldwell, D.S., Williams, D.A. *et al.* (1990). Pain coping skills training in the management of osteoarthritic knee pain – II: follow-up results. *Behavior Therapy*, 21: 435–47.

Keinan, G., Carmil, D. and Rieck, M. (1991). Predicting women's delay in seeking medical care after discovery of a lump in the breast: the role of personality and behaviour patterns. *Behavioral Medicine*, 17: 177–83.

Kelly, J.A., Murphy, D.A., Sikkema, K.J. *et al.* (1993). Psychological interventions to prevent HIV infection are urgently needed. *American Psychologist*, 48: 1023–34.

Kelly, J.A., Murphy, D.A., Sikkema, K.J. *et al.* (1997). Randomised, controlled, community-level HIV-prevention intervention for sexual-risk behaviour among homosexual men in US cities. *The Lancet*, 350: 1500–5.

Kelly, J.A., Murphy, D.A., Washington, C.D. *et al.* (1994). The effects of HIV/AIDS intervention groups for high-risk women in urban clinics. *American Journal of Public Health*, 84: 225–37.

Kelly, J.M., Rowe, A.K., Onikpo, F. *et al.* (2007). Care takers' recall of Integrated Management of Childhood Illness counselling messages in Benin. *Tropical Doctor*, 37: 75–9.

Kelly, J.A., St Lawrence, J.S., Stevenson, L.Y. *et al.* (1992). Community AIDS/HIV risk reduction: the effects of endorsements by popular people in three cities. *American Journal of Public Health*, 82: 1483–9.

Kelly, P.A. and Haidet, P. (2007) Physician overestimation of patient literacy: a potential source of health care disparities. *Patient Education and Counseling*, 66: 119–22.

Kemeny, M.E. (2003). The psychobiology of stress. *Current Directions in Psychological Science*, 12: 124–9.

Kemeny, M.E., Weiner, H., Taylor, S.E. *et al.* (1994). Repeated bereavement, depressed mood, and immune parameters in HIV seropositive and seronegative homosexual men. *Health Psychology*, 13: 14–24.

Kennedy, T., Jones, R., Darnley, S., Seed, P., Wessely, S. and Chalder, T. (2005). Cognitive behaviour therapy in addition to antispasmodic treatment for irritable bowel syndrome in primary care: randomised controlled trial. *British Medical Journal*, 331: 435.

Kentsch, M., Rodemerk, U., Muller-Esch, G., Schnoor, U., Munzel, T., Ittel, T.H. and Mitusch, R. (2002). Emotional attitudes toward symptoms and inadequate coping strategies are major determinants of patient delay in acute myocardial infarction. *Zeitschrift zu Kardiologie*, 91: 147–55.

Kern, M.L. and Friedman, H.S. (2008). Do conscientious individuals live longer? A quantitative review. *Health Psychology*, 27: 505–12.

Kerns, R.D., Haythornwaite, J., Southwick, S. and Giller, E.L. (1990). The role of marital interaction in chronic pain and depressive symptom severity. *Journal of Psychosomatic Research*, 34: 401–8.

Kerr, T., Small, W., Buchner, C. *et al.* (2010). Syringe sharing and HIV incidence among injection drug users and increased access to sterile syringes. *American Journal of Public Health*, 100: 1449–53.

Key, T.J., Fraser, G.E., Thorogood, M. *et al.* (1998). Mortality in vegetarians and non-vegetarians: a collaborative analysis of 8,300 deaths among 76,000 men and women in five prospective studies. *Public Health Nutrition*, 1: 33–41.

Khadilkar, A., Milne, S., Brosseau, L. *et al.* (2005). Transcutaneous electrical nerve stimulation (TENS) for chronic low-back pain. *Cochrane Database of Systematic Reviews*, issue 4, art. no.: CD003008. doi: 10.1002/14651858.CD003008.

Khantzian, E.J. (2003). Understanding addictive vulnerability: an evolving psychodynamic perspective. *Neuro-psychoanalysis*, 5: 3–35.

Khaw, K.T., Wareham, N., Bingham, S., Welch, A., Luben, R. and Day, N. (2008). Combined impact of health behaviours and mortality in men and women: the EPIC-Norfolk prospective population study. *PLoS Medicine*, 5: e12.

Kickbusch, I. (2003). The contribution of the World Health Organization to a new public health and health promotion. *American Journal of Public Health*, 93: 383–8.

Kiechl, S., Egger, G., Mayr, M. *et al.* (2001). Chronic infections and the risk of carotid atherosclerosis: prospective results from a large population study. *Circulation*, 103: 1064–70.

Kiecolt-Glaser, J.K., Dura, J.R., Speicher, C.E., Trask, C.E. and Glaser, R. (1991). Spousal caregivers of dementia victims: longitudinal changes in immunity and health. *Psychosomatic Medicine*, 53: 345–62.

Kiecolt-Glaser, J.K., Garner, W., Speicher, C. *et al.* (1984). Psycho-social modifiers of immunocompetence in medical students. *Psychosomatic Medicine*, 46: 7–14.

Kiecolt-Glaser, J.K. and Glaser, R. (1995). Psychological influences on immunity. *Psychosomatics*, 27: 621–4.

Kiecolt-Glaser, J.K. and Glaser, R. (1999). Psycho-neuroimmunology and cancer: fact or fiction? *European Journal of Cancer*, 35: 1603–7.

Kiecolt-Glaser, J.K., Glaser, R., Gravenstein, S., Malarkey, W.B. and Sheridan, J. (1996). Chronic stress alters the immune response to influenza virus vaccination in older adults. *Proceedings of the National Academy of Science USA*, 93: 3043–7.

Kiecolt-Glaser, J.K., Glaser, R., Williger, D. *et al.* (1985). Psychosocial enhancement of immunocompetence in a geriatric population. *Health Psychology*, 4: 25–41.

Kiecolt-Glaser, J.K., Malarkey, W.B., Cacioppo, J.T. and Glaser, R. (1994). Stressful personal relationships: immune and endocrine function. In R. Glaser and J.K. Kiecolt-Glaser (eds), *Handbook of Human Stress and Immunity*. San Diego, CA: Academic Press.

Kiecolt-Glaser, J.K., Marucha, P.T., Malarkey, W.B., Mercado, A.M. and Glaser, R. (1995). Slowing wound healing by psychosocial stress. *The Lancet*, 4: 1194–6.

Kiecolt-Glaser, J.K., McGuire, L., Robles, T.F. *et al.* (2002). Psychoneuroimmunology: psychological influences on immune function and health. *Journal of Consulting and Clinical Psychology*, 70: 537–47.

Kiecolt-Glaser, J.K. and Newton, T.L. (2001). Marriage and health: his and hers. *Psychological Bulletin*, 127: 472–503.

Kiecolt-Glaser, J.K., Preacher, K.J., MacCallum, R.C. *et al.* (2003). Chronic stress and age-related increases in the pro-inflammatory cytokine IL-6. *Proceedings of the National Academy of Science*, 10: 9090–5.

Kiernan, P.J. and Isaacs, J.B. (1981). Use of drugs by the elderly. *Journal of the Royal Society of Medicine*, 74: 196–200.

Kim, H.S., Sherman, D.K. and Taylor, S.E. (2009). Culture and social support. *American Psychologist*, 63: 518–26.

Kinman, G. and Jones, F. (2005). Lay representations of work stress: what do people really mean when they say they are stressed? *Work & Stress*, 19: 101–20.

Kinmonth, A.L., Woodcock, A., Griffin, S., Spiegal, N. and Campbell, M.J. (1998). Randomised controlled trial of patient-centred care of diabetes in general practice: impact on current wellbeing and future disease risk. The Diabetes Care from Diagnosis Research Team. *British Medical Journal*, 317: 1202–8.

Kinney, J.M., Stephens, M.A.P., Franks, M.M. and Norris, V.K. (1995). Stresses and satisfactions of family caregivers to older stroke patients. *The Journal of Applied Gerontology*, 14: 3–21.

Kirby, S.D., Ureda, J.R., Rose, R.L. and Hussey, J. (1998). Peripheral cues and involvement level: influences on acceptance of a mammography message. *Journal of Health Communication*, 3: 19–35.

Kirkcaldy, B.D., Athanasou, J.A. and Trimpop, R. (2000). The idiosyncratic construction of stress: examples from medical work settings. *Stress Medicine*, 16: 315–26.

Kirkcaldy, B.D. and Cooper, C.L. (1992). Managing the stress of change: occupational stress among senior police officers in Berlin. *Stress Medicine*, 8: 219–31.

Kitayama, S. and Cohen, D. (eds) (2007). *Handbook of Cultural Psychology*. New York: Guildford Press.

Kittleson, M.M., Meoni, L.A., Wang, N.Y. *et al.* (2006). Association of childhood socioeconomic status with subsequent coronary heart disease in physicians. *Archives of Internal Medicine*, 166: 2356–61.

Kivimäki, M., Elovainio, M., Kokko, K. *et al.* (2003). Hostility, unemployment and health status: testing three theoretical models. *Social Science and Medicine*, 56: 2139–52.

Kivimäki, M., Ferrie, J.E., Brunner, E. *et al.* (2005). Justice at work and reduced risk of coronary heart disease among employees: The Whitehall II Study. *Archives of Internal Medicine*, 165(19): 2245–51.

Kivimäki, M., Lawlor, D.A., Davey Smith, G. *et al.* (2007). Socioeconomic position, co-occurrence of behavior-related risk factors, and coronary heart disease: the Finnish Public Sector study. *American Journal of Public Health*, 97: 874–9.

Kivimäki, M., Leino-Arjas, P., Luukkonem, R. *et al.* (2002). Work stress and risk of cardiovascular mortality: prospective cohort study of industrial employées. *British Medical Journal*, 325: 857–60.

Kivimäki, M., Vahtera, J., Kosekenvuo, M., Uutela, A. and Pentti, J. (1998). Response of hostile individuals to stressful changes in their working lives: test of a psychosocial vulnerability model. *Psychological Medicine*, 28: 903–13.

Klatsky, A.L. (2008). Alcohol, wine, and vascular diseases: an abundance of paradoxes. *American Journal of Physiology: Heart and Circulatory Physiology*, 63: 582–3.

Klein, C.T.F. and Helweg-Larsen, M. (2002). Perceived control and the optimistic bias: a meta-analytic review. *Psychology and Health*, 17: 437–46.

Kline, K.N. and Mattson, M. (2000). Breast self-examination pamphlets. A content analysis grounded in fear appeals research. *Health Communication*, 12: 1–21.

Kline, P. (1993). *Personality: the Psychometric View*. London: Routledge.

Klonoff, E.A. and Landrine, H. (1994). Culture and gender diversity in commonsense beliefs about the causes of six illnesses. *Journal of Behavioral Medicine*, 17: 407–18.

Knapp, P., Raynor, D.K. and Jebar, A.H. *et al.* (2005). Interpretation of medication pictograms by adults in the UK. *Annals of Pharmacotherapy*, 39: 1227–33.

Knowler, W.C., Barrett-Connor, E., Fowler, S.E. *et al.* (2002). Reduction in the incidence of type 2 diabetes with lifestyle intervention or metformin. *New England Journal of Medicine*, 346: 393–403.

Kobasa, S.C. (1979). Stressful life events, personality and health: an inquiry into hardiness. *Journal of Personality and Social Psychology*, 37: 1–11.

Kobasa, S.C., Maddi, S. and Kahn, S. (1982). Hardiness and health: a prospective study. *Journal of Personality and Social Psychology*, 42: 168–77.

Koenig, H.G., McCullough, M.E. and Larson, D.B. (2001). *Handbook of religion and health*. Oxford: Oxford University Press.

Koenig, H.G., George, L.K., Stangl, D. and Tweed, D.L. (1995). Hospital stressors experienced by elderly medical inpatients: Developing a hospital stress index. *International Journal of Psychiatry in Medicine*, 25: 103–22.

Koffman, D.M., Lee, J.W., Hopp, J.W. *et al.* (1998). The impact of including incentives and competition in a workplace smoking cessation program on quit rates. *American Journal of Health Promotion*, 13: 105–11.

Kohl, H.W. (2001). Physical activity and cardiovascular disease: evidence for a dose–response. *Medicine and Science in Sports and Exercise*, 33: S472–S487.

Koikkalainen, M., Lappalainen, R. and Mykkanen, H. (1996). Why cardiac patients do not follow the nutritionist's advice: barriers in nutritional advice perceived in rehabilitation. *Disability and Rehabilitation*, 13: 619–23.

Koinis-Mitchell, D., McQuaid, E.L., Seifer, R. *et al.* (2009). Symptom perception in children with asthma: cognitive and psychological factors. *Health Psychology*, 28: 226–37.

Kok, G. and Schaalma, H. (1998). Theory-based and data-based health education intervention programmes. *Psychology and Health*, 13: 747–51.

Kole-Snijders, A.M.J., Vlaeyen, J.W.S. and Goossens, M.E.J. *et al.* (1999). Chronic low back pain: what does cognitive coping skills training add to operant behavioural treatment? Results of a randomized trial. *Journal of Consulting and Clinical Psychology*, 67: 931–44.

Kolk, A.M., Hanewald, G.J.F.P., Schagen, S. and Gijsbers van Wijk, C.M.T. (2003). A symptom perception approach to common physical symptoms. *Social Science and Medicine*, 57: 2343–54.

Konkolÿ Thege, B., Bachner, Y.G., Kushnir, T. and Kopp, M. (2009). Relationship between meaning in life and smoking status: results of a national representative survey. *Addictive Behaviours*, 34: 117–20.

Koob, G.F. (1999). Corticotropin-releasing factor, norepinephrine, and stress. *Biological Psychiatry*, 46: 1167–1180

Koordeman, R., Kuntsche, E., Anschutz, D.J. *et al.* (2009). Do we act upon what we see? Direct effects of alcohol cues in movies on young adults' alcohol drinking. *Alcohol and Alcoholism*, 46: 393–8.

Kop, N., Euwema, M. and Schaufeli, W. (1999). Burnout, job stress and violent behaviour among Dutch police officers. *Work and Stress*, 13: 3226–340.

Kop, W.J. and Krantz, D.S. (1997). Type A behaviour, hostility and coronary artery disease. In A. Baum, S. Newman, J. Weinman, R. West and C. McManus (eds), *Cambridge Handbook of Psychology, Health and Medicine*. Cambridge: Cambridge University Press.

Kornblith, A.B., Herndon, J.E., II, Weiss, R.B. *et al.* (2003). Long-term adjustment of survivors of early-stage breast carcinoma, 20 years after adjuvant chemotherapy. *Cancer*, 98: 679–89.

Korotkov, D. and Hannah, T.E. (2004). The five factor model of personality: strengths and limitations in predicting health status, sick role and illness behaviour. *Personality and Individual Differences*, 36: 187–99.

Kosmider, S., Shedda, S., Jones, I.T. *et al.* (2009). Predictors of clinic non-attendance: opportunities to improve patient outcomes in colorectal cancer. *Internal Medicine Journal*, 40: 757–63.

Kosmider, S., Shedda, S., Jones, I. *et al.* (2010). Predictors of clinic non-attendance-opportunities to improve patient outcomes in colorectal cancer. *Internal Medicine Journal*, 40: 757–63.

Kraft, P., Sutton, S. and McCreath-Reynolds, H. (1999). The transtheoretical model of behaviour change: are the stages qualitatively different? *Psychology and Health*, 14: 433–50.

Kramer, B.J. (1997). Gain in the caregiving experience. Where are we? What next? *The Gerontologist*, 37: 218–32.

Krantz, D.S., Glass, D.C., Shaeffer, M.A. and Davia, J.E. (1982). Behavior patterns and coronary disease: a critical evaluation. In J.T. Cacioppo and R.E. Petty (eds), *Perspectives in Cardiovascular Psycho-physiology*. New York: Guilford Press.

Krantz, D.S. and Manuck, S.B. (1984). Acute psychophysiological reactivity and risk of cardiovascular disease: a review and methodological critique. *Psychological Bulletin*, 96: 435–64.

Krantz, G. and Lundberg, U. (2006). Workload, work stress, and sickness absence in Swedish male and female white-collar employees. *Scandinavian Journal of Public Health*, 34: 238–46.

Krantz, G. and Orth, P. (2000). Common symptoms in middle-aged women: their relation to employment status, psychosocial work conditions and social support in a Swedish setting. *Journal of Epidemiology and Community Health*, 54: 192–9.

Krause, N.M. and Jay, G.M. (1994). What do global self-rated health items measure? *Medical Care*, 32: 930–42.

Krieger, N., Quesenberry, C. and Peng, T. (1999). Social class, race/ethnicity, and incidence of breast, cervix, colon, lung, and prostate cancer among Asian, black, Hispanic, and white residents of the San Francisco Bay area. *Cancer Causes Control*, 10: 525–37.

Krigsman, K., Nilsson, J.L. and Ring, L. (2007). Adherence to multiple drug therapies: refill adherence to concomitant use of diabetes and asthma/COPD medication. *Pharmacoepidemiology and Drug Safety*, 16: 1120–8.

Krischer, M.M., Xu, P., Meade, C.D. *et al.* (2007). Self-administered stress management training in patients undergoing radiotherapy. *Journal of Clinical Oncology*, 25: 4657–62.

Kriska, A. (2003). Can a physically active lifestyle prevent type 2 diabetes? *Exercise and Sport Science Review*, 31: 132–7.

Kristensen, T.S. (1995). The demand–control–support model: methodological challenges for future research. *Stress Medicine*, 11: 17–26.

Krohne, H.W. (1993). Vigilance and cognitive avoidance as concepts in coping research. In H.W. Krohne (ed.), *Attention and Avoidance: Strategies in Coping with Aversiveness*. Seattle, WA: Hogrefe and Huber.

Krol, Y., Grootenhuis, M.A., Destrée-Vonk, A. *et al.* (2003). Health-related quality of life in children with congenital heart disease. *Psychology and Health*, 18: 251–60.

Krones, T., Keller, H., Sönnichsen, A. *et al.* (2008). Absolute cardiovascular disease risk and shared decision making in primary care: a randomized controlled trial. *Annals of Family Medicine*, 6: 218–27.

Krukowski, R.A., Harvey-Berino, J. and Kolodinsky, J. (2006). Consumers may not use or understand calorie labeling in restaurants. *Journal of the American Dietetic Association*, 107: 33–4.

Kubler-Ross, E. (1969). *On Death and Dying*. New York: Macmillan.

Kuchler, T., Henne-Bruns, D., Rappat, S., Graul, J., Holst, K. and Williams, J.I. (1999). Impact of psychotherapeutic support on gastrointestinal cancer patients undergoing surgery: survival results of a trial. *Hepato-gastro-enterology*, 46: 322–35.

Kuenzler, A., Hodgkinson, K., Zindel, A., Bargetzi, M. and Znoj, H.J. (2010). Who cares, who bears, who benefits? Female spouses vicariously carry the burden after cancer diagnosis. *Psychology and Health*. Advance online publication.

Kuntzleman, C.T. (1985). Enhancing cardiovascular fitness of children and youth: the Feelin' Good Program. In J.E. Zins, D.I. Wagner and C.A. Maher (eds), *Health Promotion in the Schools: Innovative Approaches to Facilitating Physical and Emotional Well-being*. New York: Hawthorn Press.

Kuper, H., Adams, H.O. and Trichopoulos, D. (2000). Infections as a major preventable cause of human cancer. *Journal of Internal Medicine*, 248: 171–83.

Kuper, H. and Marmot, M. (2003). Job strain, job demands, decision latitude, and risk of coronary heart disease within the Whitehall II study. *Journal of Epidemiology and Community Health*, 57: 147–53.

Kuper, H., Singh-Manoux, A., Siegrist, J. *et al.* (2002). When reciprocity fails: effort–reward imbalance in relation to coronary heart disease and health functioning within the Whitehall II study. *Occupational and Environmental Medicine*, 59: 777–84.

Kurtz, M.A., Kurtz, J.C., Given, C.W. and Given, B.A. (2008). Patient optimism and mastery – do they play a role in cancer patients' management of pain and fatigue? *Journal of Pain and Symptom Management*, 36: 1–10.

Kurtz, S. and Silverman, J. (1996). The Calgary–Cambridge observation guides: an aid to defining the curriculum and organising the teaching in communication training programmes. *Medical Education*, 30: 83–9.

Kyngaes, H., Mikkonen, R., Nousiainen, E.M. *et al.* (2001). Coping with the onset of cancer. Coping strategies and resources of young people with cancer. *European Journal of Cancer Care*, 10: 6–11.

Lachman, M.E. and Weaver, S.L. (1998). The sense of control as a moderator of social class differences in health and well-being. *Journal of Personality and Social Psychology*, 74: 763–73.

Lahelma, E., Martikainen, P., Rahkonen, O. and Silventoinen, K. (1999). Gender differences in ill-health in Finland: patterns, magnitude and change. *Social Science and Medicine*, 48: 7–19.

Lai, D.T., Cahill, K., Qin, Y. *et al.* (2010). Motivational interviewing for smoking cessation. *Cochrane Database of Systematic Reviews*, issue 3, art. no.: CD006936. doi: 10.1002/14651858.CD006936.

Lamden, K.H. and Gemmell, I. (2008). General practice factors and MMR vaccine uptake: structure, process and demography. *Journal of Public Health*. 30: 251–7.

Lancaster, T., Silagy, C., Fowler, G. and Spiers, I. (1999). Training health professionals in smoking cessation. In *The Cochrane Library*, issue 1. Oxford: Update Software.

Landmark, B.T. and Wahl, A. (2002). Living with newly diagnosed breast cancer: a qualitative study of 10 women with newly diagnosed breast cancer. *Journal of Advanced Nursing*, 49: 112–21.

Landolt, M.A., Vollrath, M., Ribi, K., Gnehm, H.E. and Sennhauser, F.H. (2003). Incidence and associations of parental and child posttraumatic stress symptoms in pediatric patients. *Journal of Child Psychology and Psychiatry*, 44: 1199–207.

Landrine, H. and Klonoff, E.A. (1992). Culture and health-related schema: a review and proposal for interdisciplinary integration. *Health Psychology*, 11: 267–76.

Landrine, H. and Klonoff, E.A. (1994). Cultural diversity in causal attributions for illness: the role of the supernatural. *Journal of Behavioral Medicine*, 17: 181–93.

Lane, D., Beevers, D.G. and Lip, G.Y. (2002a). Ethnic differences in blood pressure and the prevalence of hypertension in England. *Journal of Human Hypertension*, 16: 267–73.

Lane, D., Carroll, D., Ring, C. *et al.* (2000). Effects of depression and anxiety on mortality and quality-of-life 4 months after myocardial infarction. *Journal of Psychosomatic Research*, 49: 229–38.

Lane, D., Carroll, D., Ring, C. *et al.* (2001). Predictors of attendance at cardiac rehabilitation after myocardial infarction. *Journal of Psychosomatic Research*, 51: 497–501.

Lane, D., Carroll, D., Ring, C. *et al.* (2002b). The prevalence and persistence of depression and anxiety following myocardial infarction. *British Journal of Health Psychology*, 7: 11–21.

Lang, E.V., Berbaum, K.S., Faintuch, S. *et al.* (2006). Adjunctive self-hypnotic relaxation for outpatient medical procedures: a prospective randomized trial with women undergoing large core breast biopsy. *Pain*, 126: 155–64.

Lang, E.V., Joyce, J.S., Spiegel, D. *et al.* (1996). The role of pain behaviors in the modulation of marital conflict in chronic pain couples. *Pain*, 65: 227–33.

Lang, T., Nicaud, V., Slama, K. *et al.* (2000). Smoking cessation at the workplace. Results of a randomised controlled intervention study. Worksite physicians from the AIREL group. *Journal of Epidemiology and Community Health*, 54: 349–54.

Langer, S.L., Rudd, M.E. and Syrjala, K.L. (2007). Protective buffering and emotional desynchrony among spousal caregivers of cancer patients. *Health Psychology* 26: 635–43.

Langewitz, W., Wossmer, B., Iseli, J. and Berger, W. (1997). Psychological and metabolic improvement after an outpatient teaching program for functional intensified insulin therapy. *Diabetes Research and Clinical Practice*, 37: 157–64.

Larsen, R.J. and Kasimatis, M. (1991). Day-to-day physical symptoms: individual differences in the occurrence, duration, and emotional concomitants of minor daily illnesses. *Journal of Personality*, 59: 387–423.

Larson, J. (1999). The conceptualization of health. *Medical Care and Review*, 56: 123–236.

Larsson, G., Mattsson, E. and von Essen, L. (2010). Aspects of quality of life, anxiety and depression among persons diagnosed with cancer during adolescence: a long-term follow-up study. *European Journal of Cancer*, 46: 1062–8.

Larsson, M., Boëthius, G., Axelsson, S. *et al.* (2008). Exposure to environmental tobacco smoke and health effects among hospitality workers in Sweden: before and after the implementation of a smoke-free law. *Scandinavian Journal of Work, Environment & Health*, 34: 267–77.

Latimer, P. (1981). Irritable bowel syndrome: a behavioral model. *Behaviour Research and Therapy*, 19: 475–83.

Latimer, P., Sarna, S., Campbell, D., Latimer, M., Waterfall, W. and Daniel, E.E. (1981). Colonic motor and myoelectric activity: a comparative study of normal subjects, psychoneurotic patients and patients with the irritable bowel syndrome. *Gastro-enterology*, 80: 893–901.

Lau, R.R. and Hartman, K.A. (1983). Common sense representations of common illnesses. *Health Psychology*, 2: 167–85.

Lau, R.R., Bernard, T.M. and Hartman, K.A. (1989). Further explorations of common sense representations of common illnesses. *Health Psychology*, 8(2): 195–219.

Lauby, J.L., Smith, P.J., Stark, M., Person, B. and Adams, J. (2000). A community-level HIV prevention intervention for inner-city women: results of the Women and Infants Demonstration Projects. *American Journal of Public Health*, 90: 216–22.

Laugesen, M. and Meads, C. (1991). Tobacco restrictions, price, income and tobacco consumption in OECD countries, 1960–1986. *British Journal of Addiction*, 86: 1343–54.

Laux, L. and Weber, H. (1991). Presentation of self in coping with anger and anxiety: an intentional approach. *Anxiety Research*, 3: 233–55.

Law, M.R., Frost, C.D. and Wald, N.J. (1991). By how much does dietary salt lower blood pressure? I – Analysis of observational data among populations. *British Medical Journal*, 302: 811–15.

Law, M.R., Wald, N.J. and Thompson, S.G. (1994). By how much and how quickly does reduction in serum cholesterol concentration lower risk of ischemic heart disease? *British Medical Journal*, 308: 367–72.

Lawlor, D.A., Ebrahim, S. and Davey Smith, G. (2002). Role of endogenous oestrogen in aetiology of coronary heart disease: analysis of age related trends in coronary heart disease and breast cancer in England and Wales and Japan. *British Medical Journal*, 325: 311–2.

Lawrence, D., Fagan, P., Backinger, C.L. *et al.* (2007). Cigarette smoking patterns among young adults ages 18–24 in the U.S. *Nicotine & Tobacco Research*, 9: 687–97.

Lawrence, E., Bunde, M., Barry, R.A. *et al.* (2008). Partner support and marital satisfaction: support amount, adequacy, provision and solicitation. *Personal Relationships*, 15: 445–63.

Lawrence, V., Murray, J., Samsi, K. and Banarjee, S. (2008). Attitudes and support needs of Black Caribbean, Asian and White British carers of people with dementia in the UK. *The British Journal of Psychiatry*, 193: 240–6.

Lawson, V.L., Lyne, P.A., Bundy, C. *et al.* (2007). The role of illness perceptions, coping and evaluation in care-seeking among people with type 1 diabetes. *Psychology and Health*, 22: 175–91.

Lazarus, R.S. (1966). *Psychological Stress and the Coping Process*. New York: McGraw-Hill.

Lazarus, R.S. (1984). Puzzles in the study of daily hassles. *Journal of Behavioral Medicine*, 7: 375–89.

Lazarus, R.S. (1991a). *Emotion and adaptation*. New York: Oxford University Press.

Lazarus, R.S. (1991b). Psychological stress in the workplace. In P. Perrewe (ed.), *Handbook on Job Stress*. Special issue of *Journal of Social Behavior and Personality*, 6: 1–13.

Lazarus, R.S. (1993a). From psychological stress to the emotions: a history of changing outlooks. *Annual Review of Psychology*, 44: 1–21.

Lazarus, R.S. (1993b). Coping theory and research: past, present and future. *Psychosomatic Medicine*, 55: 234–47.

Lazarus, R.S. (1999). *Stress and Emotion: A New Synthesis*. New York: Springer Verlag.

Lazarus, R.S. (2000). Toward better research on stress and coping. *American Psychologist*, 55: 665–73.

Lazarus, R.S. and deLongis, A. (1983). Psychological stress and coping in aging. *American Psychologist*, 38: 245–54.

Lazarus, R.S. and Folkman, S. (1984). *Stress, Appraisal, and Coping*. New York: Springer Verlag.

Lazarus, R.S., Kanner, A.D. and Folkman, S. (1980). Emotions: A cognitive-phenomenological analysis. In R. Plutchik and H. Kellerman (eds), *Theories of emotions* (pp. 189–217). New York: Academic Press.

Lazarus, R.S. and Launier, R. (1978). Stress related transactions between person and environment. In L.A. Pervin and M. Lewis (eds), *Perspectives in International Psychology*. New York: Plenum.

Lear, S.A. Ignaszewski, A., Linden, W. *et al.* (2003). The Extensive Lifestyle Management Intervention (ELMI) following cardiac rehabilitation trial. *European Heart Journal*, 24: 1920–7.

Lechner, S.C., Antoni, M.H., Lydston, D. *et al.* (2003). Cognitive-behavioral interventions improve quality of life in women with AIDS. *Journal of Psychosomatic Research*, 54: 253–61.

Lee, A., Cheng, F.F., Fung, Y. *et al.* (2006). Can health promoting schools contribute to the better health and well-being of young people? The Hong Kong experience. *Journal of Epidemiology and Community Health*, 60: 530–6.

Lee, B.T., Chen, C., Yueh, J.H. *et al.* (2010). Computer-based learning module increases shared decision making in breast reconstruction. *Annals of Surgical Oncology*, 17: 738–43.

Lee, C. (1999). Health, stress and coping among women caregivers: a review. *Journal of Health Psychology*, 4: 27–40.

Lee, C. (2001). Experiences of family caregiving among older Australian women. *Journal of Health Psychology*, 6: 393–404.

Lee, E.-H., Chun, M., Kang, S. *et al.* (2004). Validation of the Functional Assessment of Cancer Therapy-General (FACT-G) scale for measuring the health-related quality of life in Korean women with breast cancer. *Japanese Journal of Clinical Oncology*, 34: 393–9.

Lee, I.-M., Rexrode, K.M., Cook, N.R., Manson, J.E. and Buring, J.E. (2001). Physical activity and coronary heart disease in women: is 'no pain, no gain' passé? *Journal of the American Medical Association*, 285: 1447–54.

Lee, S.J., Back, A.L., Block, S.D. and Stewart, S.K. (2002). Enhancing physician–patient communication. *Hematology*, 464–83.

Lee, V., Cohen, S.R., Edgar, L. *et al.* (2006). Meaning-making intervention during breast and colorectal cancer treatment improves self-esteem, optimism, and self-efficacy. *Social Science & Medicine*, 62: 3133–45.

Leeks, K.D., Hopkins, D.P., Soler, R.E. *et al.* (2010). Worksite-based incentives and competitions to reduce tobacco use: a systematic review. *American Journal of Preventive Medicine*, 38(2 Suppl): S263–74.

Lefkowitz, R.J. and Willerson, J.T. (2001). Prospects for cardiovascular research. *Journal of the American Medical Association*, 285: 581–7.

Leon, D.A. and McCambridge, J. (2006). Liver cirrhosis mortality rates in Britain from 1950 to 2002: an analysis of routine data. *The Lancet*, 367: 52–6.

Lépine, J.P. and Briley, M. (2004). The epidemiology of pain in depression. *Human Psychopharmacology*, 19: S3–7.

Lerman, C. and Croyle, R. (1994). Psychological issues in genetic testing for breast cancer susceptibility. *Archives of Internal Medicine*, 154: 609–16.

Lerman, C., Hughes, C., Croyle, R.T. *et al.* (2000). Prophylactic surgery and surveillance practices one year following BRCA1/2 genetic testing. *Preventative Medicine*, 1: 75–80.

Lerman, C., Marshall, J. and Caminerio, A. (1996). Genetic testing for colon cancer susceptibility: anticipated reactions of patients and challenges to providers. *International Journal of Cancer*, 69: 58–61.

Leserman, J., Jackson, E.D., Petitto, J.M. *et al.* (1999). Progression to AIDS: The effects of stress, depressive symptoms, and social support. *Psychosomatic Medicine* 61(3): 397–406.

Leskin, G.A., Kaloupek, D.G. and Keane, T.M. (1998). Treatment for traumatic memories: review and recommendations. *Clinical Psychology Review*, 18: 983–1002.

Leslie, W.S., Hankey, C.R., Matthews, D. *et al.* (2004). A transferable programme of nutritional counselling for rehabilitation following myocardial infarction: a randomised controlled study. *European Journal of Clinical Nutrition*, 58: 778–86.

Letherman, C., Blackburn, D. and Davidhizar, R. (1990). How postpartum women explain their lack of obtaining adequate prenatal care. *Journal of Advanced Nursing*, 15: 256–67.

Leung, P.Y., Chan, C.L.W. and Ng, S.M. (2007). Tranquil acceptance coping: Eastern cultural beliefs as a source of strength among Chinese women with breast cancer. Paper presented at the International Psycho-Oncology Society (IPOS) conference, London, September 2007.

Leveälahti, H., Tishelman, C. and Öhlén, J. (2007). Framing the onset of lung cancer biographically: narratives of continuity and disruption. *Psycho-Oncology*, 16: 466–73.

Leventhal, E.A. and Crouch, M. (1997). Are there differences in perceptions of illness across the lifespan? In K.J. Petrie and J. Weinman (eds), *Perceptions of Health and Illness*. Amsterdam: Harwood Academic, pp. 77–102.

Leventhal, E.A., Hansell, S., Diefenbach, M., Leventhal, H. and Glass, D.C. (1996). Negative affect and self-report of physical symptoms: two longitudinal studies of older adults. *Health Psychology*, 15: 193–9.

Leventhal, E.A. and Prohaska, T.R. (1986). Age, symptom interpretation and health behavior. *Journal of the American Geriatric Society*, 34: 185–91.

Leventhal, H. and Coleman, S. (1997). Quality of life: a process view. *Psychology and Health*, 12: 753–67.

Leventhal, H. and Diefenbach, M. (1991). The active side of illness cognition. In J.A. Skelton and R.T. Croyle (eds), *Mental Representations in Health and Illness*. New York: Springer Verlag.

Leventhal, H., Diefenbach, M. and Leventhal, E. (1992). Illness cognition: using common sense to understand treatment adherence and effect cognitive interactions. *Cognitive Therapy and Research*, 16(2): 143–63.

Leventhal, H., Easterling, D.V., Coons, H., Luchterhand, C. and Love, R.R. (1986). Adaptation to chemotherapy treatments. In B. Anderson (ed.), *Women with Cancer*. New York: Springer Verlag.

Leventhal, H., Meyer, D. and Nerenz, D. (1980). The common sense model of illness danger. In S. Rachman (ed.), *Medical Psychology*, Vol. 2. New York: Pergamon.

Leventhal, H., Nerenz, D.R. and Steele, D.J. (1984). Illness representations and coping with health threats. In A. Baum, S.E. Taylor and J.E. Singer (eds), *Handbook of Psychology and Health: Social Psychological Aspects of Health*, Vol. 4. Hillsdale, NJ: Lawrence Erlbaum.

Leventhal, H., Patrick-Miller, L. and Leventhal, E.A. (1998). It's long-term stressors that take a toll: comment on Cohen *et al.* (1998). *Health Psychology*, 17: 211–13.

Leventhal, H. and Tomarken, A. (1987). Stress and illness: perspectives from health psychology. In S.V. Kasl and C.L. Cooper (eds), *Research Methods in Stress and Health Psychology*. London: Wiley.

Levinson, D.J., Darrow, C.N., Klein, E.B., Levinson, M.H. and McKee, B. (1978). *The Seasons of a Man's Life*. New York: A.A. Knopf.

Levine, R.M. and Reicher, S. (1996). Making sense of symptoms: self categorization and the meaning of illness/injury. *British Journal of Social Psychology*, 35: 245–56.

Levy, L., Patterson, R.E., Kristal, A.R. and Li, S.S. (2000). How well do consumers understand percentage daily value of food labels? *American Journal of Health Promotion*, 14: 157–60.

Lewin, B., Robertson, I.H., Irving, J.B. and Campbell, M. (1992). Effects of self-help post-myocardial-infarction rehabilitation on psychological adjustment and use of health services. *The Lancet*, 339: 1036–40.

Lewin, R.J., Furze, G., Robinson, J., Griffith, K., Wiseman, S., Pye, M. and Boyle, R. (2002). A randomised controlled trial of a self-management plan for patients with newly diagnosed angina. *British Journal of General Practice*, 52: 194–6, 199–201.

Lewis, C.L. and Brown, S.C. (2002). Coping strategies of female adolescents with HIV/AIDS. *The Association of Black Nursing Faculty*, 13: 72–7.

Lewis, G., Bebbington, P., Brugha, T., Farrell, M., Gill, B., Jenkins, R. and Meltzer, H. (1998). Socioeconomic status, standard of living, and neurotic disorder. *The Lancet*, 352: 605–9.

Lewis, S.C., Dennis, M.D., O'Rourke, S.J. and Sharpe, M. (2001). Negative attitudes among short-term stroke survivors predict worse long-term survival. *Stroke*, 32: 1640–5.

Ley, P. (1997). Compliance among patients. In A. Baum, S. Newman, J. Weinman, R. West and C. McManus (eds), *Cambridge Handbook of Psychology, Health and Medicine.* Cambridge: Cambridge University Press.

Ley, P. (1988). *Communicating with Patients. Improving Communication, Satisfaction, and Compliance.* London: Chapman Hall.

Lichtenstein, P. and Pedersen, N.L. (1995). Social relationships, stressful life events, and self-reported physical health: genetic and environmental influences. *Psychology and Health*, 10: 295–319.

Lim, A.S.H. and Bishop, G.D. (2000). The role of attitudes and beliefs in differential health care utilisation among Chinese in Singapore. *Psychology and Health*, 14: 965–77.

Lincoln, K.D., Chatters, L.M. and Taylor, R.J. (2003). Psychological distress among Black and White Americans: differential effects of social support, negative interaction and personal control. *Journal of Health and Social Behavior*, 44: 390–407.

Linden, W., Gerin, W. and Davidson, K. (2003). Cardiovascular reactivity: status quo and a research agenda for the new millennium. *Psychosomatic Medicine*, 65: 5–8.

Linden, W., Stossel, C. and Maurice, J. (1996). Psychosocial treatment for cardiac patients: a meta-analysis. *Archives of Internal Medicine*, 156: 745–62.

Lindsay, S., Smith, S., Bellaby, P. *et al.* (2009). The health impact of an online heart disease support group: a comparison of moderated versus unmoderated support. *Health Education Research*, 24: 646–54.

Linegar, J., Chesson, C. and Nice, D. (1991). Physical fitness gains following simple environmental change. *American Journal of Preventive Medicine*, 7: 298–310.

Linn, S., Carroll, M., Johnson, C. *et al.* (1993). High density lipoprotein cholesterol and alcohol consumption in US white and black adults: data from NHANES II. *American Journal of Public Health*, 83: 811–16.

Liossi, C., White, P., Franck, L. *et al.* (2007). Parental pain expectancy as a mediator between child expected and experienced procedure-related pain intensity during painful medical procedures. *The Clinical Journal of Pain*, 23: 392–9.

Liossi, C., White, P. and Hatira, P. (2006). Randomised clinical trial of a local anaesthetic versus a combination of self-hypnosis with a local anaesthetic in the management of paediatric procedure-related pain. *Health Psychology*, 25: 307–15.

Liossi, C., White, P. and Hatira, P. (2009). A randomized clinical trial of a brief hypnosis intervention to control venepuncture-related pain of paediatric cancer patients. *Pain*, 142: 255–63.

Lipkus, I.M., Barefoot, J.C., Williams, R.B. *et al.* (1994). Personality measures as predictors of smoking initiation and cessation in the UNC Alumni heart study. *Health Psychology*, 13: 149–55.

Lipton, A.A. and Simon, F.S. (1985). Psychiatric diagnosis in a state hospital: Manhattan state revisited. *Hospital and Community Psychiatry*, 36: 368–73.

Litt, M.D., Nye, C. and Shafer, D. (1995). Preparation for oral surgery: evaluating elements of coping. *Journal of Behavioral Medicine*, 18: 435–59.

Little, M. and Sayers, E.-J. (2004). While there's life . . . hope and the experience of cancer. *Social Science and Medicine*, 59: 1329–37.

Livingston, G. and Hinchliffe, A.C. (1993). The epidemiology of psychiatric disorders in the elderly. *International Review of Psychiatry*, 5: 317–29.

Llewellyn, C.D., McGurk, M. and Weinman, J. (2007). The relationship between the Patient Generated Index (PGI) and measures of HR-QoL following diagnosis with head and neck cancer: are illness and treatment perceptions determinants of judgment-based outcomes? *British Journal of Health Psychology*, 12: 421–37.

Lo, B. (2006). HPV vaccine and adolescents' sexual activity. *British Medical Journal*, 332: 1106–7.

Lo, B. (2007). Human papillomavirus vaccination programmes. *British Medical Journal*, 335: 357–8.

Lo, R. (1999). Correlates of expected success at adherence to health regimen of people with IDDM. *Journal of Advanced Nursing*, 30: 418–24.

Lobb, E.A., Butow, P.N., Kenny, D.T. and Tattersall, M.H. (1999). Communicating prognosis in early breast cancer: do women understand the language used? *Medical Journal of Australia*, 171: 290–4.

Lobchuk, M.M. and Vorauer, J.D. (2003). Family care-giving, perspective-taking, and accuracy in estimating cancer patient symptom experiences. *Social Science and Medicine*, 57: 2379–84.

Lock, K., Pomerleau, J., Causer, L., Altmann, D.R. and McKee, M. (2005). The global burden of disease attributable to low consumption of fruit and vegetables: implications for the global strategy on diet. *Bulletin of the World Health Organization*, 83: 100–8.

Locke, E.A. and Latham, G.P. (2002). Building a practically useful theory of goal setting and task motivation: a 35-year odyssey. *American Psychologist*, 57: 705–17.

Locke, G.R., III, Weaver, A.L., Melton, L.J., III and Talley, N.J. (2004). Psychosocial factors are linked to functional gastrointestinal disorders: a population based nested case-control study. *American Journal of Gastroenterology*, 99: 350–7.

Lodder, L., Frets, P.G., Trijsburg, R.W. *et al.* (2001). Psychological impact of receiving a BRCA1/BRCA2 test result. *American Journal of Medical Genetics*, 98: 15–24.

Loewenthal, K.M. (2007). *Religion, culture and mental health.* Cambridge: Cambridge University Press.

Löf, M., Sardin, S. Lagiou, P. *et al.* (2007). Dietary fat and breast cancer risk in the Swedish women's lifestyle and health cohort. *British Journal of Cancer*, 97: 1570–6.

Logan, T.K., Cole, J. and Leukefeld, C. (2002). Women, sex, and HIV: social and contextual factors, meta-analysis of published interventions, and implications for practice and research. *Psychological Bulletin*, 128: 851–85.

Lok, C.F. and Bishop, G.D. (1999). Emotion control, stress, and health. *Psychology and Health*, 14: 813–27.

Lomas, J. (1991). Words without action? The production, dissemination, and impact of consensus recommendations. *Annual Reviews in Public Health*, 12: 41–65.

Longabaugh, R. and Morgenstern, J. (1999). Cognitive-behavioural coping-skills therapy for alcohol dependence. *Alcohol Research and Health*, 23: 78–85.

Longo, D.R., Johnson, J.C., Kruse, R.L., Brownson, R.C. and Hewett, J.E. (2001). A prospective investigation of the impact of smoking bans on tobacco cessation and relapse. *Tobacco Control*, 10: 267–72.

Lorentzen, C., Ommundsen, Y. and Hole, I. (2007). Psychosocial correlates of stages of change in physical activity in an adult community sample. *European Journal of Sports Science*, 7: 93–106.

Lorenz, F.O., Wickrama, K.A.S., Conger, R.D. and Elder, G.H. Jr. (2006). The short-term and decade-long effects of divorce on women's midlife health. *Journal of Health and Social Behavior*, 47: 111–25.

Lorig, K. (1996). *Patient Education: A Practical Approach*. Newbury Park, CA: Sage.

Lorig, K. and Holman, H. (1989). Long-term outcomes of an arthritis self-management study: effects of reinforcement efforts. *Social Science and Medicine*, 29: 221–4.

Lorig, K., Ritter, P.L., Villa, F.J. *et al.* (2009). Community-based peer-led diabetes self-management: a randomized trial. *Diabetes Education*, 35: 641–51.

Lorig, K., Sobel, D.S., Stewart, A.L., Brown, B.W., Jr, Bandura, A., Ritter, P. *et al.* (1999). Evidence suggesting that a chronic disease self-management program can improve health status while reducing hospitalisation. *Medical Care*, 37: 5–14.

Lotrean, L.M., Dijk, F., Mesters, I. *et al.* (2010). Evaluation of a peer-led smoking prevention programme for Romanian adolescents. *Health Education Research*, 25: 803–14.

Louria, D. (1988). Some concerns about educational approaches in AIDS prevention. In R. Schinazi and A. Nahmias (eds), *AIDS Children, Adolescents and Heterosexual Adults*. New York: Elsevier Science.

Louw, Q.A., Morris, L.D. and Grimmer-Somers, K. (2007). The prevalence of low back pain in Africa: a systematic review. *BMC Musculoskeletal Disorders*, 8: 105.

Lovallo, W.R. (1997). *Stress and Health: Biological and Psychological Interactions*. Newbury Park, CA: Sage.

Lovallo, W.R., Pincomb, G.A., Brackett, D.J. *et al.* (1990). Heart rate reactivity as a predictor of neuroendocrine responses to aversive and appetitive challenges. *Psychosomatic Medicine*, 52: 17–26.

Lovegrove, E., Rumsey, N., Harcourt, D. *et al.* (2000). Factors implicated in the decision whether or not to join the tamoxifen trial in women at high familial risk of breast cancer. *Psycho-Oncology*, 9: 193–202.

Low, C.A., Stanton, A.L. and Danoff-Burg, S. (2006). Expressive disclosure and benefit finding among breast cancer patients: mechanisms for positive health effects. *Health Psychology*, 25: 181–9.

Lowe, C.F., Horne, P.J., Tapper, K. *et al.* (2004). Effects of a peer-modelling and rewards based intervention to increase fruit and vegetable consumption in children. *European Journal of Clinical Nutrition*, 58: 510–22.

Lowe, R., Norman, P. and Bennett, P. (2000). Coping, emotion and perceived health following myocardial infarction. *British Journal of Health Psychology*, 5: 337–50.

Lowe, R., Vedhara, K., Bennett, P. *et al.* (2003). Emotion-related primary and secondary appraisals, adjustment and coping associations in women awaiting breast disease diagnosis. *British Journal of Health Psychology*, 8: 377–91.

Lowes, J. and Tiggemann, M. (2003). Body dissatisfaction and dieting awareness in young children. *British Journal of Health Psychology*, 8: 135–47.

Lox, C.L., Martin Ginis, K.A. and Petruzzello, S.J. (2006). *The Psychology of Exercise: Integrating Theory and Practice*, 2nd edn. Scottsdale, AZ: Holcomb Hathaway.

Luck, A., Pearson, S., Maddern, G. *et al.* (1999). Effects of video information on pre-colonoscopy anxiety and knowledge: a randomised trial. *Lancet*, 354: 2032–5.

Lundberg, U., de Chateau, P., Winberg, J. *et al.* (1981). Catecholamine and cortisol excretion patterns in three year old children and their parents. *Journal of Human Stress*, 7: 3–11.

Luszczynska, A., Diehl, M., Gutiérrez-Doña, B. *et al.* (2004). Measuring one component of dispositional self-regulation: attention control in goal pursuit. *Personality and Individual Differences*, 37: 555–66.

Luszczynska, A. and Cieslak, R. (2009). Mediated effects of social support for healthy nutrition: fruit and vegetable intake across 8 months after myocardial infarction. *Behavioral Medicine*, 35: 30–8.

Luszczynska, A. and Schwarzer, R. (2003). Planning and self-efficacy in the adoption and maintenance of breast self-examination: a longitudinal study on self-regulatory cognitions. *Psychology and Health*, 18: 93–108.

Luszczynska, A., Sobczyk, A. and Abraham, C. (2007). Planning to lose weight: randomized controlled trial of an implementation intention prompt to enhance weight reduction among overweight and obese women. *Health Psychology*, 26: 507–12.

Lyonette, C. and Yardley, L. (2003). The influence on carer wellbeing of motivations to care for older people and the relationship with the care recipient. *Ageing & Society*, 23: 487–506.

MacBryde, C.M. and Blacklow, R.S. (1970). *Signs and Symptoms: Applied Pathologic Physiology and Clinical Interpretation*, 5th edn. Philadelphia, PA: Lippincott.

Macdonald, S., McMillan, T.M. and Kerr, J. (2010). Readability of information leaflets given to attenders at hospital with a head injury. *Emergency Medicine Journal*, 27: 279–82.

MacFadyen, L., Amos, A., Hastings, G. *et al.* (2002). They look like my kind of people: perceptions of smoking images in youth magazines. *Social Science and Medicine*, 56: 491–9.

Macintyre, S. (1986). The patterning of health by social position in contemporary Britain: directions for sociological research. *Social Science and Medicine*, 23: 393–415.

Macintyre, S. (1993). Gender differences in the perceptions of common cold symptoms. *Social Science and Medicine*, 36: 15–20.

Macintyre, S. and Ellaway, A. (1998). *Ecological Approaches: Rediscovering the Role of the Physical and Social Environment*. Oxford: Oxford University Press.

Mackay, D., Haw, S., Ayres, J.G. *et al.* (2010). Smoke-free legislation and hospitalizations for childhood asthma. *New England Journal of Medicine*, 363: 1139–45.

MacKellar, D., Gallagher, K.M., Finlayson, T., Sanchez, T., Lansky, A. and Sullivan, P.S. (2007). Surveillance of HIV risk and prevention behaviors of men who have sex with men – a national application of venue based, time-space sampling. *Public Health Reports*, 122 (Suppl.1), 39–47.

MacNee, W. (2004). Guidelines for chronic obstructive pulmonary disease (editorial). *British Medical Journal*, 329: 361–3.

MacNicol, S.A.M., Murray, S.M. and Austin, E.J. (2003). Relationships between personality, attitudes and dietary behaviour in a group of Scottish adolescents. *Personality and Individual Differences*, 35: 1753–64.

Macrodimitris, D. and Endler, N.S. (2001). Coping, control, and adjustment in Type 2 diabetes. *Health Psychology*, 20: 208–16.

Maes, S., Kittel, F., Scholten, H. and Verhoeven, C. (1990). Effects of the Brabantia project, a Dutch wellness-health programme at the worksite. *American Journal of Public Health*, 88: 1037–41.

Maes, S., Leventhal, H. and de Ridder, D.T. (1996). Coping with chronic disease. In M. Zeidner and N.S. Endler (eds), *Handbook of Coping*. New York: Wiley.

Maes, S. and van der Doef, M. (2004). Worksite health promotion. In A. Kaptein and J. Weinman (eds), *Health Psychology*. Oxford: BPS Blackwell, pp. 358–83.

Magar, E.C.E., Phillips, L.H. and Hosie, J.A. (2008). Self-regulation and risk-taking. *Personality & Individual Differences*, 45: 153–9.

Magarey, A., Daniels, L., Boulton, T. *et al.* (2003). Predicting obesity in early adulthood from childhood and parental obesity. *International Journal of Obesity*, 27: 505–13.

Magarey, A., Daniels, L.A. and Smith, A. (2001). Fruit and vegetable intakes of Australians aged 2–18 years: an evaluation of the 1995 National Nutrition Survey data. *Australian and New Zealand Journal of Public Health*, 25: 155–61.

Mager, W.M. and Andrykowski, M.A. (2002). Communication in the cancer 'bad news' consultation: patient perceptions and psychological adjustment. *Psycho-Oncology*, 11: 35–46.

Maggiolo, F., Ripamonti, D., Arici, C., Gregis, G., Quinzan, G., Camacho, G.A., Ravasio, L. and Suter, F. (2002). Simpler regimens may enhance adherence to antiretrovirals in HIV-infected patients. *HIV Clinical Trials*, 3: 371–8.

Magni, G., Moreschi, C., Rigatti-Luchini, S. and Merskey, H. (1994). Prospective study on the relationship between depressive symptoms and chronic musculoskeletal pain. *Pain*, 56: 289–97.

Magnusson, J.E. and Becker, W.J. (2003). Migraine frequency and intensity: relationship with disability and psychological factors. *Headache*, 43: 1049–59.

Magri, F., Cravello, L., Barili, L. *et al.* (2006). Sress and dementia: the role of the hypothalamic-pituitary-adrenal axis. *Aging & Clinical Experimental Research*, 18: 167–70.

Maguire, P. and Faulkner, A. (1988). How to improve the counselling skills of doctors and nurses in cancer care. *British Medical Journal*, 297: 847–9.

Maguire, P. and Pitceathly, C. (2002). Key communication skills and how to acquire them. *British Medical Journal*, 325: 697–700.

Mahajan, L., Wyllie, R., Steffen, R., Kay, M., Kitaoka, G., Dettorre, J., Sarigol, S. and McCue, K. (1998). The effects of a psychological preparation program on anxiety in children and adolescents undergoing gastrointestinal endoscopy. *Journal of Pediatric Gastroenterology and Nutrition*, 27: 161–5.

Mahalik, J.R., Burns, S.M. and Syzdek, M. (2007). Masculinity and perceived normative health behaviors as predictors of men's health behaviors. *Social Science & Medicine*, 64: 2201–9.

Maisto, S.A. and Connors, G.J. (1992). Using subject and collateral reports to measure alcohol consumption. In R.Z. Litten and J.P. Allen (eds), *Measuring Alcohol Consumption: Psychosocial and Biochemical Methods*. New Jersey: Humana Press.

Malfetti, J. (1985). Public information and education sections of the report of the Presidential Commission on Drunk Driving: a critique and a discussion of research implication. *Accident Analysis and Prevention*, 17: 347–53.

Maliski, S.L., Heilemann, M.V. and McCorkle, R. (2002). From 'death sentence' to 'good cancer': couples' transformation of a prostate cancer diagnosis. *Nursing Research*, 51: 391–7.

Malkin, C.J., Pugh, P.J., Jones, R.D. *et al.* (2003). Testosterone as a protective factor against atherosclerosis–immunomodulation and influence upon plaque development and stability. *Journal of Endocrinology*, 178: 373–80.

Maly, M.R., Costigan, P.A. and Olney, S.J. (2007). Self-efficacy mediates walking performance in older adults with knee osteoarthritis. *Journal of Gerontology A: Biological Sciences and Medical Sciences*, 62: 1142–6.

Mandelblatt, J. and Kanesky, P.A. (1995). Effectiveness of interventions to enhance physician screening for breast cancer. *Journal of Family Practice*, 40: 162–71.

Maniadakis, N. and Gray, A. (2000). The economic burden of back pain in the UK. *Pain*, 84: 95–103.

Manne, S.L., Norton, T.R., Ostroff, J.S. *et al.* (2007). Protective buffering and psychological distress among couples coping with breast cancer: the moderating role of relationship satisfaction. *Journal of Family Psychology* 21: 380–88.

Manning, P.K. and Fabrega, H. (1973). The experience of self and body: health and illness in the Chiapas Highlands. In G. Psathas (ed.), *Phenomenological Sociology: Issues and Applications*. New York: Wiley.

Mannino, D.M. (2003). Chronic obstructive pulmonary disease: definition and epidemiology. *Respiratory Care*, 48: 1185–91.

Manson, J.E., Greenland, P., LaCroix, A.Z., Stefanick, M.L., Mouton, C.P., Oberman, A., Perri, M.G., Sheps, D.S., Pettinger, M.B. and Siscovick, D.S. (2002). Walking compared with vigorous exercise for prevention of cardiovascular events in women. *New England Journal of Medicine*, 347: 716–25.

Manstead, A.S.R. (2000). The role of moral norm in the attitude–behavior relationship. In D.J. Terry and M.A. Hogg (eds), *Attitudes, Behavior and Social Context: The Role of Norms and Group Membership*. Mahwah, NJ: Lawrence Erlbaum.

Mantyselka, P., Kumpusalo, E., Ahonen, R., Kumpusalo, A., Kauhanen, J., Viinamaki, H., Halonen, P. and Takala, J. (2001). Pain as a reason to visit the doctor: a study in Finnish primary health care. *Pain*, 89: 175–80.

Marcell, A.V., Ford, C.A., Pleck, J.H. *et al.* (2007). Masculine beliefs, parental communication, and male adolescents' health care use. *Pediatrics*, 119: 966–75.

Marcus, B.H., Rakowski, W. and Rossi, J.S. (1992). Assessing motivational readiness and decision-making for exercise. *Health Psychology*, 22: 3–16.

Marcus, B.H., Selby, V.C., Niaura, R.S. and Rossi, J.S. (1992). Self-efficacy and the stages of exercise behaviour change. *Research Quarterly in Exercise and Sport*, 63: 60–6.

Marinus, J., Ramaker, C., van Hilten, J.J. and Stiggelbout, A.M. (2002). Health related quality of life in Parkinson's disease: a systematic review of disease specific instruments. *Journal of Neurology, Neurosurgery and Psychiatry*, 72: 241–8.

Markovitz, J.H., Matthews, K.A., Kannel, W.B., Cobb, J.L. and D'Agostino, R.B. (1993). Psychological predictors of hypertension in the Framingham study: is there tension in hypertension? *Journal of the American Medical Association*, 270: 2439–43.

Marks, D.F. (ed.) (2002). *The Health Psychology Reader*. London: Sage.

Marks, D.F., Murray, M., Evans, B. and Willig, C. (2000). *Health Psychology: Theory, Research and Practice*. London: Sage.

Marks, I., Lovell, K., Noshirvani, H., Livanou, M. and Thrasher, S. (1998). Treatment of post-traumatic stress disorder by exposure and/or cognition restructuring. *Archives of General Psychiatry*, 55: 317–25.

Marks, J.T., Campbell, M.K., Ward, D.S. *et al.* (2006). A comparison of Web and print media for physical activity promotion among adolescent girls. *Journal of Adolescent Health*, 39: 96–104.

Marlatt, A. (1996). Taxonomy of high-risk situations for alcohol relapse: evolution and development of a cognitive-behavioral model. *Addiction*, 91: 37–50.

Marlatt, G.A., Baer, J.S., Donovan, D.M. and Kivlahan, D.R. (1986). Addictive behaviors: etiology and treatment. *Annual Review of Psychology*, 39: 223–52.

Marmot, M. (2005). Social determinants of health inequalities. *Lancet*, 365: 1099–104.

Marmot, M., Atinmo, T., Byers, T. *et al.* (2007). *Food, Nutrition, Physical Activity, and the Prevention of Cancer: A Global Perspective*. Washington, DC: American Institute for Cancer Research.

Marmot, M.G., Davey-Smith, G. and Stansfield, S. (1991). Health inequalities among British civil servants: the Whitehall Study II. *The Lancet*, 337: 1387–93.

Marmot, M.G., Fuhrer, R., Ettner, S.L., Marks, N.F., Bumpass, L.L. and Ryff, C.D. (1998). Contribution of psychosocial factors to socioeconomic differences in health. *The Milbank Quarterly*, 76: 403–448.

Marmot, M.G. and Madge, N. (1987). An epidemiological perspective on stress and health. In S.V. Kasl and C.L. Cooper (eds), *Research Methods in Stress and Health Psychology*. London: Wiley.

Marmot, M., Ryff, C.D., Bumpass, L.L., Shipley, M. and Marks, N.F. (1997). Social inequalities in health: next questions and converging evidence. *Social Science and Medicine*, 44: 901–10.

Marmot, M.G., Shipley, M.J. and Rose, G. (1984). Inequalities in health: specific explanations of a general pattern? *The Lancet*, i, 1003–6.

Marsh, A., Smith, L., Piek, J. and Saunders, B. (2003). The Purpose in Life scale: psychometric properties for social drinkers and drinkers in alcohol treatment. *Educational & Psychological Measurement*, 63: 859–71.

Marshall, A.L., Leslie, E.R., Bauman, A.E. *et al.* (2003). Print versus website physical activity programs: a randomized trial. *American Journal of Preventive Medicine*, 25: 88–94.

Marsland, A.L., Bachen, E.A., Cohen, S. *et al.* (2002). Stress, immune reactivity and susceptibility to infectious diseases. *Physiology & Behaviour*, 77: 711–16.

Marteau, T.M., Kidd, J., Cuddeford, L. and Walker, P. (1996). Reducing anxiety in women referred for colposcopy using an information booklet. *British Journal of Health Psychology*, 1: 181–9.

Marteau, T.M. and Kinmouth, A.L. (2002). Screening for cardiovascular risk: public health imperative or matter for individual informed choice? *British Medical Journal*, 325: 78–80.

Martin, J., Sabugal, G.M., Rubio, R., Sainz-Maza, M., Blanco, J.M., Alonso, J.L. and Dominiguez, J. (2001). Outcomes of a health education intervention in a sample of patients infected by HIV, most of them injection drug users: possibilities and limitations. *AIDS Care*, 13: 467–73.

Martin, L.M., Calle, E.E., Wingo, P.A. and Heath, C.W., Jr (1996). Comparison of mammography and Pap test use from the 1987 and 1992 National Health Interview Surveys: are we closing the gaps? *American Journal Preventive Medicine*, 12: 82–90.

Martin, P., Rosa, G., Siegler, I.C. *et al.* (2006). Personality and longevity: findings from the Georgia centenarian study. *Age*, 28: 343–52.

Martin, R. and Leventhal, H. (2004). Symptom perception and health-care seeking behavior. In J.M. Raczynski and L.C. Leviton (eds), *Handbook of Clinical Health Psychology* (Volume 2, pp. 299–328). Washington, DC: American Psychological Association.

Martin, R., Lemos, C., Rothrock, N., Bellman, S.B., Russell, D. *et al.* (2004). Gender disparities in common-sense models of illness among myocardial infarction victims. *Health Psychology*, 23: 345–53.

Martin, R., Rothrock, N., Leventhal, H. and Leventhal, E. (2003). Common sense models of illness: implications for symptom perception and health-related behaviours. In J. Suls and K.A. Wallston (eds), *Social Psychological Foundations of Health and Illness*. Oxford: Blackwell.

Martin Ginis, K.A., Burke, S.M. and Gauvin, L. (2007). Exercising with others exacerbates the negative effects of mirrored environments on sedentary women's feeling states. *Psychology & Health*, 22: 945–62.

Marucha, P.T., Kiecolt-Glaser, J.K. and Favgehi, M. (1998). Mucosal wound healing is impaired by examination stress. *Psychosomatic Medicine*, 60: 362–5.

Maslach, C. (1982). *Burnout: The Cost of Caring*. Englewood Cliffs, NJ: Prentice Hall.

Maslach, C. (1997). Burnout in health professionals. In A. Baum, S. Newman, J. Weinman, R. West and C. McManus (eds), *Cambridge Handbook of Psychology, Health and Medicine*. Cambridge: Cambridge University Press.

Massie, M.J. (2004). Prevalence of depression on patients with cancer. *Journal of the National Cancer Institute Monographs*, 32, 57–71.

Masui, Y., Gondo, Y., Inagaki, H., Hirose, N. (2006). Do personality characteristics predict longevity? Findings from the Tokyo centenarian study. *Age*, 28: 353–61.

Matano, R.A., Futa, K.T., Wanat, S.F., Mussman, L.M. and Leung, C.W. (2000). The Employee Stress and Alcohol Project: the development of a computer-based alcohol abuse prevention program for employees. *Journal of Behavioral Health Services Research*, 27: 152–65.

Matarazzo, J.D. (1982). Behavioral health's challenge to academic, scientific and professional psychology. *American Psychologist*, 37: 1–14.

Matarazzo, J.D. (1984). Behavioral health: a 1990 challenge for the health sciences professions. In J.D. Matarazzo, N.E. Miller, S.M. Weiss, J.A. Herd and S.M. Weiss (eds), *Behavioral Health: A Handbook of Health Enhancement and Disease Prevention*. New York: Wiley.

Mathews, C., Guttmacher, S.J., Coetzee, N., Magwaza, S., Stein, J., Lombard, C., Goldstein, S. and Coetzee, D. (2002). Evaluation of a video based health education strategy to improve sexually transmitted disease partner notification in South Africa. *Sexually Transmitted Infections*, 78: 53–7.

Matthews, K.A., Siegel, J.M., Kuller, L.H., Thompson, M. and Vanat, M. (1983). Determinants of decision to seek medical treatment by patients with acute myocardial infarction symptoms. *Journal of Personality and Social Psychology*, 44: 1144–56.

Mattocks, C., Ness, A., Deere, K. *et al.* (2008). Early life determinants of physical activity in 11 to 12 year olds: cohort study. *British Medical Journal*, 336: 26–9.

Matza, L.S., Swensen, A.R., Flood, E.M. *et al.* (2004). Assessment of health-related quality of life in children: a review of conceptual, methodological, and regulatory issues. *Value in Health*, 7: 79–92.

McCabe, K.M., Yeh, M., Lau, A. *et al.* (2005). Racial/ethnic differences in caregiver strain and perceived social support among parents of youth with emotional and behavioral problems. *Mental Health Services Research*, 5: 137–47.

McCaffery, J.M., Papandonatos, G.D., Stanton, C. *et al.* (2008). Depressive symptoms and cigarette smoking in twins from the National Longitudinal Study of Adolescent Health. *Health Psychology*, 27: S207–S215.

McCann, B.S., Retzlaff, B.M., Dowdy, A.A., Walden, C.E. and Knopp, R.H. (1990). Promoting adherence to low-fat, low-cholesterol diets: review and recommendations. *Journal of the American Dietetic Association*, 90: 1408–14.

McCann, J., Stockton, D. and Goddard, S. (2002). Impact of false-positive mammography on subsequent screening attendance and risk of cancer. *Breast Cancer Research*, 4: R11.

McCarron, P., Davey-Smith, G. and Wormsley, J. (1994). Deprivation and mortality in Glasgow: changes from 1980 to 1992. *British Medical Journal*, 309: 1481–2.

McClenahan, R. and Weinman, J. (1998). Determinants of carer distress in non-acute stroke. *International Journal of Language and Communication Disorders*, 33: 138–43.

McCorkle, R., Strumpf, N., Nuamah, I., Adler, D.C., Cooley, M.E., Jepson, C., Lusk, E.J. and Torosian, M. (2000). A specialized home care intervention improves survival among older post-surgical cancer patients. *Journal of the American Geriatric Society*, 48: 1707–13.

McCracken, L. (1998). Learning to live with the pain: acceptance of pain predicts adjustment in persons with chronic pain. *Pain*, 74: 21–7.

McCracken, L.M. and Eccleston, C. (2003). Coping or acceptance: what to do about chronic pain? *Pain*, 105: 197–204.

McCrae, R.E. and Costa, P.T. (1987). Validation of the five-factor model of personality across instruments and observers. *Journal of Personality and Social Psychology*, 52: 81–90.

McCrae, R.E. and Costa, P.T. (1990). *Personality in Adulthood*. New York: Guilford Press.

McCrae, R.E., Costa, P.T., Ostendorf, F., Angleitner, A., Hrebickova, M., Avia, M.D., Sanz, J., Sancez-Bernardos, M.L., Kusdil, M.E., Woodfield, R., Saunders, P.R. and Smith, P.B. (2000). Nature over nurture: temperament, personality and life-span development. *Journal of Personality and Social Psychology*, 78: 173–86.

McCrae, R.R. (1990). Controlling neuroticism in the measurement of stress. *Stress Medicine*, 6: 237–40.

McCubbin, H.I. and Patterson, J.M. (1982). Family adaptations to crisis. In H.I. McCubbin, A. Cauble and J. Patterson (eds), *Family Stress, Coping and Social Support*. Springfield, IL: Charles Thomas.

McCubbin, H.I. and Patterson, J.M. (1983). The family stress process: the double ABCX model of adjustment and adaptation. In H.I. McCubbin, M.B. Sussman and J.M. Patterson (eds), *Social Stress and the Family: Advances and Developments in Family Stress Theory and Research*. New York: Haworth Press.

McDermott, M.M., Schmitt, B. and Wallner, E. (1997). Impact of medication non-adherence on coronary heart disease outcomes. *Archives of Internal Medicine*, 157: 1921–9.

McDonald, H.P., Garg, A.X. and Haynes, R.B. (2002). Interventions to enhance patient adherence to medication prescriptions: scientific review. *Journal of the American Medical Association*, 288: 2868–79.

McElnay, J. and McCallion, C.R. (1998). Adherence and the elderly. In L.B. Myers and K. Midence (eds), *Adherence to Treatment in Medical Conditions*. Amsterdam: Harwood Academic.

McEwan, M.J., Espie, C.A. and Metcalfe, J. (2004). A systematic review of the contribution of qualitative research to the study of quality of life in children and adolescents with epilepsy. *Seizure*, 13: 3–14.

McEwen, B.S. (2008). Central effects of stress hormones in health and disease: understanding the protective and damaging effects of stress and stress mediators. *European Journal of Pharmacology*, 583: 174–85.

McGill, H.C. and Stern, M.P. (1979). Sex and athero-sclerosis. *Atherosclerosis Review*, 4: 157–248.

McGregor, B.A., Antoni, M.H., Boyers, A. *et al.* (2004). Cognitive-behavioral stress management increases benefit finding and immune function among women with early-stage breast cancer. *Journal of Psychosomatic Research*, 56: 1–8.

McGuire, W. (1985). Attitudes and attitude change. In G. Lindzey and E. Aronson (eds), *Handbook of Social Psychology*, Vol. 2. New York: Random House.

McHugh, P., Lewis, S., Ford, S., Newlands, E., Rustin, G., Coombes, C., Smith, D., O'Reilly, S. and Fallowfield, L. (1995). The efficacy of audiotapes in promoting psychological well-being in cancer patients: a randomised, controlled trial. *British Journal of Cancer*, 71: 388–92.

McKenna, M.C., Zevon, M.A., Corn, B. and Rounds, J. (1999). Psychosocial factors and the development of breast cancer: a meta-analysis. *Health Psychology*, 18: 520–31.

McKenna, S.P. (2004). Assessing the quality of life in phases I and II anti-cancer drug trials: interviews versus questionnaires by Cox K (letter to the editor). *Social Science and Medicine*, 58: 659–60.

McKenna, S.P., Whalley, D. and Doward, L.C. (2000). Which outcomes are important in schizophrenia trials? *International Journal of Methods in Psychiatric Research*, 9 (suppl. 1): S58–67.

McKiernan, F.M. (1996). Bereavement and attitudes to death. In R.T. Woods (ed.), *Handbook of the Clinical Psychology of Ageing*. Chichester: Wiley.

McKirnan, D.J., Tolou-Shams, M., Courtenay-Quirk, C. *et al.* (2010). The treatment advocacy program: a randomized controlled trial of a peer-led safer sex intervention for HIV-infected men who have sex with men. *Journal of Consulting and Clinical Psychology*, 78: 952–63.

McLeod, J.D. and Kessler, R.C. (1990). Socioeconomic status differences in vulnerability to undesirable life events. *Journal of Health and Social Behaviour*, 31: 162–72.

McNair, D., Lorr, M. and Droppelman, L. (1971). *Manual for the Profile of Mood States*. San Diego, CA: Educational and Industrial Testing Service.

McNeil, B.J., Pauker, S.G., Sox, H.C., Jr and Tversky, A. (1982). On the elicitation of preferences for alternative therapies. *New England Journal of Medicine*, 306: 1259–62.

McNeill, L.H., Viswanath, K., Bennett, G.G. *et al.* (2007). Feasibility of using a web-based nutrition intervention among residents of multiethnic working-class neighborhoods. *Preventing Chronic Disease*, 4: A55.

McPherson, K.M., McNaughton, H. and Pentland, B. (2000). Information needs of families when one member of the family has a severe brain injury. *International Journal of Rehabilitation Research*, 23: 295–301.

McQuaid, E.L., Koinis-Mitchell, D., Walders, N. *et al.* (2007). Pediatric asthma morbidity: the importance of symptom perception and family response to symptoms. *Journal of Pediatric Psychology*, 32: 167–77.

McQuay, H.J. and Moore, R.A. (2005). Placebo. *Postgraduate Medical Journal*, 81: 155–60.

McVey, D. and Stapleton, J. (2000). Can anti-smoking television advertising affect smoking behaviour? Controlled trial of the Health Education Authority for England's anti-smoking TV campaign. *Tobacco Control*, 9: 273–82.

McVicar, A. (2003). Workplace stress in nursing: a literature review. *Journal of Advanced Nursing*, 44: 633–42.

Mechanic, D. (1962). The concept of illness behavior. *Journal of Chronic Disease*, 15: 189–94.

Mechanic, D. (1972). Social psychological factors affecting the presentation of bodily complaints. *New England Journal of Medicine*, 286: 1132–9.

Mechanic, D. (1978). *Medical Sociology*, 2nd edn. New York: Free Press.

Meechan, G., Collins, J. and Petrie, K. (2002). Delay in seeking medical care for self-detected breast symptoms in New Zealand women. *New Zealand Medical Journal*, 115: U257.

Meenan, R.F. and Mason, J.H. (1990). *AIMS2 Users Guide*. Boston University School of Medicine, Department of Public Health.

Meeske, K.A., Ruccione, K. and Globe, D.R. (2001). Posttraumatic stress, quality of life, and psychological distress in young adult survivors of childhood cancer. *Oncology Nursing Forum*, 28: 481–9.

Meeuwesen, L., Harmsen, J.A., Bernsen, R.M. *et al.* (2006). Do Dutch doctors communicate differently with immigrant patients than with Dutch patients? *Social Science and Medicine*, 63: 2407–17.

Mehta, V. and Langford, R.M. (2006). Acute pain management for opioid dependent patients. *Anaesthesia*, 61: 269–76.

Meichenbaum, D. (1985). *Stress Inoculation Training*. New York: Pergamon Press.

Meijer, S.A., Sinnema, G., Bijstra, J.O. *et al.* (2002). Coping style and locus of control as predictors for psychological adjustment of adolescents with a chronic illness. *Social Science and Medicine*, 54: 1453–61.

Meiser, B. (2005). Psychological impact of genetic testing for cancer susceptibility: an update of the literature. *Psycho-Oncology*, 14: 1060–74.

Melchior, M., Berkman, L.F., Niedhammer, I. *et al.* (2003). Social relations and self-reported health: a prospective analysis of the French Gazel cohort. *Social Science and Medicine*, 56: 1817–30.

Mellins, C.A., Brackis-Cott, E., Dolezal, C. *et al.* (2004). The role of psychosocial and family factors in adherence to antiretroviral treatment in human immunodeficiency virus-infected children. *Pediatric Infectious Disease Journal*, 23: 1035–41.

Mel'nikova, T.S. (1993). Thresholds of pain responses to electrical stimuli in patients with endogenous depression. *Patologichskaia Fiziologiia I Eksperimentalnaia Terapiia*, 4: 19–21.

Melzack, R. (1973). *The Puzzle of Pain*. London: Penguin Education.

Melzack, R. (1975). The McGill pain questionnaire: major properties and scoring methods. *Pain*, 1: 277–99.

Melzack, R. (1999). From the gate to the neuromatrix. *Pain*, suppl. 6: S121–6.

Melzack, R. (2005). Evolution of the neuromatrix theory of pain. The Prithvi Raj Lecture: presented at the third World Congress of World Institute of Pain, Barcelona 2004. *Pain Practice*, 5: 85–94.

Melzack, R. and Wall, P.D. (1965). Pain mechanisms: a new theory. *Science*, 50: 971–9.

Mendlowicz, M.V. and Stein, M.B. (2001). Quality of life in individuals with anxiety disorders. *American Journal of Psychiatry*, 157: 669–82.

Mendoza, S.A., Gollwitzer, P.M. and Amodio, D.M. (2010). Reducing the expression of implicit sterotypes: reflexive control through implementation intentions. *Personality and Social Psychology Bulletin*, 36: 512–23.

Mercken, L., Candel, M., Willems, P. and de Vries, H. (2007). Disentangling social selection and social influence effects on adolescent smoking: the importance of reciprocity of friendships. *Addiction*, 102: 1483–92.

Merkes, M. (2010). Mindfulness-based stress reduction for people with chronic diseases. *Australian Journal of Primary Health*, 16: 200–10.

Merritt, M.M., Bennett, G.G., Williams, R.B. *et al.* (2004). Low educational attainment, John Henryism, and cardiovascular reactivity to and recovery from personally relevant stress. *Psychosomatic Medicine*, 66: 49–55.

Merzel, C. and D'Afflitti, J. (2003). Reconsidering community-based health promotion: promise, performance, and potential. *American Journal of Public Health*, 93: 557–74.

Meyer, J.M. and Stunkard, A.J. (1993). Genetics and human obesity. In A.J. Stunkard and T.A. Wadden (eds), *Obesity: Theory and Therapy*. New York: Raven Press.

Meyer, T.J. and Mark, M.M. (1995). Effects of psychosocial interventions with adult cancer patients: a meta-analysis of randomized experiments. *Health Psychology*, 12: 101–8.

Meyer-Weitz, A., Reddy, P., Van Den Borne, H.W. *et al.* (2000). The determinants of health care seeking behaviour of adolescents attending STD clinics in South Africa. *Journal of Adolescence*, 23: 741–52.

Michell, L. and Amos, A. (1997). Girls, pecking order, and smoking. *Social Science and Medicine*, 44: 1861–9.

Michie, S., Dormandy, E. and Marteau, T.M. (2004). Increasing screening uptake among those intending to be screened: the use of action plans. *Patient Education and Counselling*, 55: 218–22.

Michie, S., Smith, J.A., Senior, V. and Marteau, T.M. (2003). Understanding why negative genetic test results sometimes fail to reassure. *American Journal of Medical Genetics*, 119A: 340–7.

Mikkelsen, A. and Saksvik, P.O. (1999). Impact of a participatory organizational intervention on job characteristics and job stress. *International Journal of Health Services Research*, 29: 871–93.

Miller, G.E. and Cohen, S. (2001). Psychological interventions and the immune system: a meta-analytic review and critique. *Health Psychology*, 20: 47–63.

Miller, R. and Miller, Y.D. (2003). Nifty after fifty: evaluation of a physical activity directory for older people. *Australia and New Zealand Journal of Public Health*, 27: 524–8.

Miller, S.M. (1987). Monitoring and blunting: validation of a questionnaire to assess styles of information seeking under threat. *Journal of Personality and Social Psychology*, 52: 345–53.

Miller, S.M., Brody, D.S. and Summerton, J. (1987). Styles of coping with threat: implications for health. *Journal of Personality and Social Psychology*, 54: 142–8.

Miller, S.M., Fang, C.Y., Manne, S.L. *et al.* (1999). Decision making about prophylactic oophorectomy among at-risk women: psychological influences and implications. *Gynaecological Oncology*, 75: 406–12.

Miller, S.M., Rodoletz, M., Mangan, C.E., Schroeder, C.M. and Sedlacek, T.V. (1996). Applications of the monitoring process model to coping with severe long-term medical threats. *Health Psychology*, 15: 216–25.

Miller, T.Q., Smith, T.W., Turner, C.W. *et al.* (1996). A meta-analytic review of research on hostility and physical health. *Psychological Bulletin*, 119: 322–48.

Miller, W. and Rollnick, S. (2002). *Motivational Interviewing: Preparing People to Change Addictive Behaviour*. New York: Guilford Press.

Miller, W., Rollnick, S. and Butler, C. (2008). *Motivational Interviewing in Health Care: Helping Patients Change Behavior*. New York: Guilford Press.

Milne, S., Welch, V., Brosseau, L. *et al.* (2001). Transcutaneous electrical nerve stimulation (TENS) for chronic low back pain. In *The Cochrane Library*, issue 4. Oxford: Update Software.

Mills, E.J., Nachega, J.B., Bangsberg, D.R. *et al.* (2006). Adherence to HAART: a systematic review of developed and developing nation patient-reported barriers and facilitators. *PLoS Medicine*, 3: e438.

Ming, E.E., Adler, G.K., Kessler, R.C. *et al.* (2004). Cardiovascular reactivity to work stress predicts subsequent onset of hypertension: the Air Traffic Controller Health Change Study. *Psychosomatic Medicine*, 66: 459–65.

Ministry of Health (2003). *A Longer Healthy Life* (in Dutch). Den Haag: Ministry of Health, Welfare and Sport.

Mino, Y., Babazono, A., Tsuda, T. *et al.* (2006). Can stress management at the workplace prevent depression? A randomized controlled trial. *Psychotherapy and Psychosomatics*, 7: 177–82.

Mishra, S., Bhatnagar, S., Gupta, D. *et al.* (2007). Incidence and management of phantom limb pain according to World Health Organization analgesic ladder in amputees of malignant origin. *American Journal of Hospice and Palliative Care*, 24: 455–62.

Misra, R., Crist, M. and Burant, C.J. (2003). Relationships among life stress, social support, academic stressors, and reactions to stressors of international students in the United States. *International Journal of Stress Management*, 10: 137–57.

Mitchell, A.J. and Kakkadasam, V. (2011). Ability of nurses to identify depression in primary care, secondary care and nursing homes: a meta-analysis of routine clinical accuracy. *International Journal of Nursing Studies*, 48: 359–68.

Mitchell, A.J. and Kumar, M. (2002). Influence of psychological coping on survival: review is not systematic (letter to the editor). *British Medical Journal*, 326: 598.

Mitchell, J.B., Ballard, D.J., Matchar, D.B. *et al.* (2000). Racial variation in treatment for transient ischemic attacks: impact of participation by neurologists. *Health Services Research*, 34: 1413–28.

Moens, V., Baruch, G. and Fearon, P. (2003). Opportunistic screening for chlamydia at a community based contraceptive service for young people. *British Medical Journal*, 326: 1252–5.

Moldofsky, H. and Chester, W.J. (1970). Pain and mood patterns in patients with rheumatoid arthritis: a prospective study. *Psychosomatic Medicine*, 32: 309–18.

Molyneux, A., Lewis, S., Leivers, U. *et al.* (2003). Clinical trial comparing nicotine replacement therapy (NRT) plus brief counselling, brief counselling alone, and minimal intervention on smoking cessation in hospital inpatients. *Thorax*, 58: 484–8.

Molloy, G.J., Dixon, D., Hamer, M. and Sniehotta, F.F. (2010). Social support and regular physical activity: does planning mediate this link? *British Journal of Health Psychology*, 15: 859–70.

Molloy, G.J., Johnston, M., Johnston, D.W. *et al.* (2008). Spousal caregiver confidence and recovery from ambulatory activity limitations in stroke survivors. *Health Psychology* 27: 286–90.

Molloy, G.J., Stamataki, E., Randall, G. and Harmerm, M. (2009). Marital status, gender, and cardiovascular mortality: behavioural, psychological distress and metabolic explanations. *Social Science & Medicine*, 69: 223–8.

Mommersteeg, P.M., Vermetten, E., Kavelaars, A. *et al.* (2008). Hostility is related to clusters of T-cell cytokines and chemokines in healthy men. *Psychoneuro-endicrinology*, 33: 1041–50.

Montazeri, A., Jarvandi, S., Haghighat, S. *et al.* (2001). Anxiety and depression in breast cancer patients before and after participation in a cancer support group. *Patient Education and Counseling*, 45: 195–8.

Montgomery, C., Lydon, A. and Lloyd, K. (1999). Psychological distress among cancer patients and informed consent. *Journal of Psychosomatic Research*, 46: 241–5.

Montgomery, C., Pocock, M., Titley, K. and Lloyd, K. (2003). Predicting psychological distress in patients with leukaemia and lymphoma. *Journal of Psychosomatic Research*, 54: 289–92.

Montgomery, R.J.V. and Kosloski, K.D. (2000). Family caregiving: change, continuity and diversity. In P. Lawton and R. Rubenstein (eds), *Alzheimer's Disease and Related Dementias: Strategies in Care and Research*. New York: Springer.

Montpetit, M.A. and Bergeman, C.S. (2007). Dimensions of control: mediational analyses of the stress-health relationship. *Personality and Individual Differences*, 43: 2237–48.

Moody, L.E. and McMillan, S. (2003). Dyspnoea and quality of life indicators in hospice patients and their caregivers, *Health and Quality of Life Outcomes*, 1: 9.

Moore, D., Aveyard, P., Connock, M. *et al.* (2009). Effectiveness and safety of nicotine replacement therapy assisted reduction to stop smoking: systematic review and meta-analysis. *British Medical Journal*, 338.

Moore, L. (2001). Are fruit tuck shops in primary schools effective in increasing pupils' fruit consumption? A randomised controlled trial. Abstract available from http://www.cf.ac.uk/socsi/whoswho/moore-tuckshop.html

Moore, L., Paisly, C.M. and Dennehy, A. (2000). Are fruit tuck shops in primary schools effective in increasing pupils' fruit consumption? A randomised controlled trial. *Nutrition and Food Science*, 30: 35–8.

Moore, S., Murphy, S., Tapper, K. *et al.* (2010). From policy to plate: barriers to implementing healthy eating policies in primary schools in Wales. *Health Policy*, 94: 239–45.

Moore, S. and Rosenthal, D. (1993). *Sexuality in Adolescence*. London: Routledge.

Moore, S.M., Barling, N.R. and Hood, B. (1998). Predicting testicular and breast self-examination behaviour: a test of the theory of reasoned action. *Behaviour Change*, 15: 41–9.

Moorey, S., Greer, S., Bliss, J. and Law, M. (1998). A comparison of adjuvant psychological therapy and supportive counselling in patients with cancer. *Psycho-Oncology*, 7: 218–28.

Moorey, S., Greer, S., Watson, M. (1994). Adjuvant psychological therapy for patients with cancer: outcome at one year. *Psycho-oncology*, 3: 39–46.

Moos, R.H. and Schaefer, A. (1984). The crisis of physical illness: an overview and conceptual approach. In R.H. Moos (ed.), *Coping with Physical Illness: New Perspectives*, Vol. 2. New York: Plenum.

Mor, V., Malin, M. and Allen, S. (1994). Age differences in the psychosocial problems encountered by breast cancer patients. *Journal of the National Cancer Institute Monographs*, 16: 191–7.

Morgan, J., Roufeil, L., Kaushik, S. *et al.* (1998). Influence of coping style and precolonoscopy information on pain and anxiety of colonoscopy. *Gastrointestinal Endoscopy*, 48: 119–27.

Morley, S., Eccleston, C. and Williams, A. (1999). Systematic review and meta-analysis of randomized controlled trials of cognitive behaviour therapy and behaviour therapy for chronic pain in adults, excluding headache. *Pain*, 80: 1–13.

Morone, N.E., Greco, C.M. and Weiner, D.K. (2008). Mindfulness meditation for the treatment of chronic low back pain in older adults: a randomized controlled pilot study. *Pain*, 134: 310–9.

Morris, B.A. and Shakespeare-Finch (2010). Rumination, post-traumatic growth, and distress: structural equation modelling with cancer survivors. *Psycho-Oncology*, doi: 10.1002/pon.1827.

Morris, C.D. and Carson, S. (2003). Routine vitamin supplementation to prevent cardiovascular disease: a summary of the evidence for the US Preventive Services Task Force. *Annals of Internal Medicine*, 139: 56–70.

Morris, D.B. (1999). Sociocultural and religious meanings of pain. In R.J. Gatchel and D.C. Turk (eds), *Psychosocial Factors in Pain.* New York: Guilford Press.

Morris, J.N., Clayton, D.G., Everitt, M.G. *et al.* (1990). Exercise in leisure time: coronary attack and death rates. *British Heart Journal*, 63: 325–34.

Morris, P.L.P., Robinson, R.G., Andrzejewski, P., Samuels, J. and Price, T.R. (1993). Association of depression with 10-year poststroke mortality. *American Journal of Psychiatry*, 150: 124–9.

Morrison, M.F., Petitto, J.M., Ten Have, T. *et al.* (2002). Depressive and anxiety disorders in women with HIV infection. *American Journal of Psychiatry*, 159: 789–96.

Morrison, V. (1988). Observation and snowballing: useful tools for research into illicit drug use? *Social Pharmacology*, 2: 247–71.

Morrison, V. (1999). Predictors of carer distress following a stroke. *Reviews in Clinical Gerontology*, 9: 265–71.

Morrison, V. (2001). The need to explore discrepant illness cognitions when predicting patient outcomes. *Health Psychology Update*, 10: 9–13.

Morrison, V. (2003). Furthering the socio-cognitive explanation of addiction. *Neuro-Psychoanalysis*, 5: 39–42.

Morrison, V., Ager, A. and Willock, J. (1999). Perceived risk of tropical diseases in Malawi: evidence of unrealistic pessimism and the irrelevance of beliefs of personal control? *Psychology, Health and Medicine*, 4: 361–8.

Morrison, V., Cottrell, L., Dawson, J. *et al.* (2002). Police force stress: psychological and job feature characteristics. Paper presented at the *Annual Conference of the European Health Psychology Society*, September.

Morrison, V., Henderson, B.J., Zinovieff, F. *et al.* (2011). Common, important, and unmet needs of cacer patients. *European Journal of Oncology Nursing*, doi:10.1016/j.ejon.2011.04.004.

Morrison, V., Hutchinson, A. and McCarthy, M. (2000a). Illness perceptions, perceived control and adherence in child asthmatics: are child–parent beliefs discrepant? Poster presentation at European Health Psychology Society annual conference, Leiden, The Netherlands.

Morrison, V., Johnston, M. and MacWalter, R. (2000b). Predictors of distress following an acute stroke: disability, control cognitions and satisfaction with care. *Psychology and Health*, 15: 395–407.

Morrison, V. and Plant, M.A. (1991). Licit and illicit drug initiations and alcohol related problems among illicit drug users in Edinburgh. *Drug and Alcohol Dependence*, 27: 19–27.

Morrison, V., Pollard, B., Johnston, M. and MacWalter, R. (2005). Anxiety and depression 3 years following stroke: demographic, clinical and psychological predictors. *Journal of Psychosomatic Research*.

Morrison, V.L. (1991a). The impact of HIV upon injecting drug users: a longitudinal study. *AIDS Care*, 3: 197–205.

Morrison, V.L. (1991b). Starting, switching, stopping: users' explanations of illicit drug use. *Drug and Alcohol Dependence*, 27: 213–17.

Morrison, V., Henderson, B., Taylor, C., A'ch Dafydd, N. and Unwin, A. (2010). The impact of information order on intentions to undergo predictive genetic testing: an experimental study. *Journal of Health Psychology*, 15(7): 1082–92.

Morse, J.M. and Johnson, J.L. (1991). Towards a theory of illness. The illness constellation model. In J.M. Morse and J.L. Johnson (eds), *The Illness Experience: Dimensions of Suffering*. Newbury Park, CA: Sage.

Morse, S.R. and Fife, B. (1998). Coping with a partner's cancer: adjustment at four stages of the illness trajectory. *Oncology Nursing Forum*, 25: 751–60.

Morwitz, V.G., Johnson, E., Schmittlein, D. (1993). Does measuring intent change behavior? *Journal of Consumer Research*, 20: 46–61.

Moskowitz, J.T., Hult, J.R., Busolari, C. and Acree, M. (2009). What works in coping with HIV? A meta-analysis with implications for coping with serious illness. *Psychological Bulletin*, 135: 121–41.

Moss, S., Thomas, I., Evans, A. *et al.* (2005). Randomised controlled trial of mammographic screening in women from age 40: predicted mortality based on surrogate outcome measures. *British Journal of Cancer*, 92: 955–60.

Moss-Morris, R. and Chalder, T. (2003). Illness perceptions and levels of disability in patients with chronic fatigue syndrome and rheumatoid arthritis. *Journal of Psychosomatic Research*, 55: 305–8.

Moss-Morris, R., McAlpine, L., Didsbury, L.P. *et al.* (2010). A randomized controlled trial of a cognitive behavioural therapy-based self-management intervention for irritable bowel syndrome in primary care. *Psychological Medicine*, 40: 85–94.

Moss-Morris, R., Weinman, J., Petrie, K.J. *et al.* (2002). The revised Illness Perception Questionnaire (IPQ-R). *Psychology and Health*, 17: 1–16.

Mott, J., Bucolo, S., Cuttle, L. *et al.* (2008). The efficacy of an augmented virtual reality system to alleviate pain in children undergoing burns dressing changes: a randomised controlled trial. *Burns*, 34: 803–8.

Motl, R.W., Gliottoni, R.C. and Scott, J.A. (2007). Self-efficacy correlates with leg muscle pain during maximal and submaximal cycling exercise. *Journal of Pain*, 8: 583–7.

Mowery, R.L. (2007). The family, larger systems, and end-of-life decision making. In D. Balk, C. Wogrin, G. Thornton and D. Meagher (eds), *Handbook of Thanatology: The Essential Body of Knowledge for the Student of Death, Dying, and Bereavement*. Northbrook, IL: Association for Death Education and Counseling, pp. 93–102.

Munaf, M.R. and Johnstone, E.C. (2008). Genes and cigarette smoking. *Addiction*, 103: 893–904.

Murgraff, V., McDermott, M.R., White, D. *et al.* (1999). Regret is what you get: the effects of manipulating anticipated affect and time perspective on risky single occasion drinking. *Alcohol and Alcoholism*, 34: 590–600.

Murnaghan, D.A., Blanchard, C.M., Rodgers, W.M. *et al.* (2010). Predictors of physical activity, healthy eating and being smoke-free in teens: a theory of planned behaviour approach. *Psychology & Health*, 25: 925–41.

Murphy, D., Lindsay, S. and Williams, A.C. de C. (1997). Chronic low back pain: predictions of pain and relationship to anxiety and avoidance. *Behaviour Research and Therapy*, 35: 231–8.

Murphy, M.H., Nevill, A.M., Murtagh, E.M. and Holder, R.L. (2007). The effect of walking on fitness, fatness and resting blood pressure. *Preventive Medicine*, 44: 377–85.

Murray, C.J.L. and Lopez, A.D. (1997). Alternative projections of mortality and disability by cause 1990–2020: Global Burden of Disease Study. *The Lancet*, 349: 1498–504.

Murray, D.F., Marks, M., Evans, B. and Willig, C. (2000). *Health Psychology: Theory, Research and Practice*. London: Sage.

Murray, M. (1997). A narrative approach to health psychology: background and potential. *Journal of Health Psychology*, 2: 9–20.

Murray, M. and Campbell, C. (2003). Beyond the sidelines: towards a more politically engaged health psychology. *Health Psychology Update*, 12: 12–17.

Murrell, R. (2001). Assessing the quality of life of individuals with neurological illness. *Health Psychology Update*, 10.

Myers, L.B. (1998). Repressive coping, trait anxiety and reported avoidance of negative thoughts. *Personality and Individual Differences*, 24: 299–303.

Myers, L.B. and Reynolds, D. (2000). How optimistic are repressors? The relationship between repressive coping, controllability, self-esteem and comparative optimism for health-related events. *Psychology and Health*, 15: 677–87.

Myers, J., Froelicher, V., Do, D. *et al.* (2002). Exercise capacity and mortality among men referred for exercise testing. *New England Journal of Medicine*, 346: 793–801.

Myrtek, M. (2001). Meta-analyses of prospective studies on coronary heart disease, type A personality, and hostility. *International Journal of Cardiology*, 79: 245–51.

Nachega, J.B., Mugavero, M.J., Zeier, M. *et al.* (2010). Treatment simplification in HIV-infected adults as a strategy to prevent toxicity, improve adherence, quality of life and decrease healthcare costs. *Journal of Patient Preference and Adherence*, 5: 357–67.

Nagasako, E.M., Oaklander, A.L. and Dworkin, R.H. (2003). Congenital insensitivity to pain: an update. *Pain*, 101: 213–19.

Naish, J., Brown, J. and Denton, B. (1994). Intercultural consultations: investigation of factors that deter non-English speaking women from attending their general practitioners for cervical screening. *British Medical Journal*, 309: 1126–8.

Naliboff, B.D., Munakata, J., Chang, L. *et al.* (1998). Toward a biobehavioral model of visceral hypersensitivity in irritable bowel syndrome. *Journal of Psychosomatic Research*, 45: 485–93.

Narevic, E. and Schoenberg, N.E. (2002). Lay explanations for Kentucky's 'Coronary Valley'. *Journal of Community Health*, 27: 53–62.

Nathan, J.P., Zerilli, T., Cicero, L.A. *et al.* (2007). Patients' use and perception of medication information leaflets. *Annals of Pharmacotherapy*, 41: 777–82.

National Collaborating Centre for Chronic Conditions (2004). Chronic obstructive pulmonary disease. National clinical guidelines on management of chronic obstructive pulmonary disease in adults in primary and secondary care. *Thorax*, 59(suppl. 1): 1–232.

National Diet and Nutrition Survey: Adults aged 19–64, Vol. 1 (2000). Carried out in 2000 on behalf of the Food Standards Agency and Department of Health by the Social Survey Division of the Office for National Statistics and Medical Research Council Human Nutrition Research. London: Stationery Office.

National Diet and Nutrition Survey Report. www.food.gov.uk/multimedia/pdfs/.../ndnsreport0809year1results.pdf.

National Institutes of Health Technology Assessment Panel (1996). Integration of behavioral and relaxation approaches into the treatment of chronic pain and insomnia. *Journal of the American Medical Association*, 276: 313–18.

Navas-Nacher, E.L., Colangelo, L., Beam, C. *et al.* (2001). Risk factors for coronary heart disease in men 18 to 39 years of age. *Annals of Internal Medicine*, 134: 433–9.

Nazroo, J. (1997). *The Health of Britain's Ethnic Minorities: Findings from a National Survey*. London: Policy Studies Institute.

Nazroo, J.Y. (1998). *Genetic, Cultural or Socioeconomic Vulnerability? Explaining Ethnic Inequalities in Health*. Oxford: Blackwell.

Neal, R.D., Ali, N., Atkin, K. *et al.* (2006). Communication between South Asian patients and GPs: comparative study using the Roter Interactional Analysis System. *British Journal of General Practice*, 56: 869–75.

Neff, L.A. and Karney, B.R. (2005). Gender differences in social support: a question of skill or responsiveness? *Journal of Personality & Social Psychology*, 88: 79–90.

Nelson, D.V., Baer, P.E. and Cleveland, S.E. (1998). Family stress management following acute myocardial infarction: an educational and skills training intervention program. *Patient Education and Counseling*, 34: 135–45.

Ness, A.R., Frankel, S.J., Gunnell, D.J. *et al.* (1999). Are we really dying for a tan? *British Medical Journal*, 319: 114–16.

Ness, A.R. and Powles, J.W. (1997). Fruit and vegetables, and cardiovascular disease: a review. *International Journal of Epidemiology*, 26: 1–13.

Nestle, M. (1997). Alcohol guidelines for chronic disease prevention: from prohibition to moderation. *Nutrition Today*, 32: 86–92.

New, S.J. and Senior, M. (1991). 'I don't believe in needles': qualitative aspects of a study into the uptake of infant immunisation in two English health authorities. *Social Science and Medicine*, 33: 509–18.

Newhagen, J. and Reeves, B. (1987). Emotion and memory responses for negative political advertising: a study of television commercials used in the 1988 presidential campaign. In F. Biocca (ed.), *Television and Political Advertising*, Vol. 1. Hillsdale, NJ: Lawrence Erlbaum.

Newton, T.L., Watters, C.A., Philhower, C.L. *et al.* (2005). Cardiovascular reactivity during dyadic social interaction: the roles of gender and dominance. *International Journal of Psychophysiology*, 57: 219–28.

Ng, B., Dimsdale, J.E., Rollnick, J.D. and Shapiro, H. (1996). The effect of ethnicity on prescriptions for patient-controlled anaesthesia for post-operative pain. *Pain*, 66: 9–12.

NHS Centre for Reviews and Dissemination (1999). *Effective Healthcare: Getting Evidence into Practice*. NHS CRD, Vol. 5, No. 1. London: Royal Society of Medicine Press.

NHS Executive (1996). *Patient Partnership: Building a Collaborative Strategy*. Leeds: NHS Executive.

NICE (2009a). *Clinical Guideline 76: Medicines Adherence: Involving Patients in Decisions about Prescribed Medicines and Supporting Adherence*. London: National Institute for Health and Clinical Excellence.

NICE (2009b). *Costing Statement: Medicines Adherence: Involving Patients in Decisions about Prescribed Medicines and Supporting Adherence* London: National Institute for Health and Clinical Excellence.

Nichols, K. (2003). *Psychological Care for the Ill and Injured: A Clinical Handbook*. Maidenhead: Open University Press.

Nicholson, N., Soane, E., Fenton-O'Creevy, M. *et al.* (2005). Personality and domain-specific risk-taking. *Journal of Risk Research*, 8: 157–76.

Nicolson, N.A. and van Diest, R. (2000). Salivary cortisol levels in vital exhaustion. *Journal of Psychosomatic Research*, 49: 335–42.

Niederhoffer, K.G. and Pennebaker, J.W. (2005). Sharing one's story: on the benefits of writing or talking about emotional experience. In C. Snyder and S.J. Lopez, *Handbook of Positive Psychology*. New York: Oxford University Press, pp. 573–83.

Niemcryk, S.J., Speer, M.A., Travis, L.B. *et al.* (1990). Psychosocial correlates of haemoglobin A1c in young adults with type I diabetes. *Journal of Psychosomatic Research*, 34: 617–27.

Niemi, M., Laaksonen, R., Kotila, M. and Waltimo, O. (1988). Quality of life 4 years after stroke. *Stroke*, 19: 1101–7.

Nijboer, C., Tempelaar, R., Triemstra, M., Sanderman, R. and van den Bos, G.A.M. (2001). Dynamics in cancer caregiver's health over time: gender-specific patterns and determinants. *Psychology and Health*, 16: 471–88.

Nnoaham, K.E. and Kumbang, J. (2010). Transcutaneous electrical nerve stimulation (TENS) for chronic pain. *Cochrane Database of Systematic Reviews*, issue 3, art. no.: CD003222. doi: 10.1002/14651858.CD003222.

Noble, L.M. (1998). Doctor–patient communication and adherence to treatment. In L.B. Myers and K. Midence (eds), *Adherence to Treatment in Medical Conditions*. Amsterdam: Harwood Academic.

Noblet, A.J. and LaMontagne, A. (2006). The role of workplace health promotion in addressing job stress. *Health Promotion International*, 21: 346–53.

Nolen-Hoeksema, S. (1991). Responses to depression and their effects on the duration of depressive episodes. *Journal of Abnormal Psychology*, 100: 569–82.

Nolen-Hoeksema, S., Wisco, B.E. and Lyubomirsky, S. (2008). Rethinking rumination. *Perspectives on Psychological Science*, 3: 400–24.

Noguchi, K., Albarracín, D., Durantini, M.R. *et al.* (2007). Who participates in which health promotion programs? A meta-analysis of motivations underlying enrolment and retention in HIV-prevention interventions. *Psychological Bulletin*, 133: 955–75.

Norberg, A.L., Lindblad, F. and Boman, K.K. (2005). Coping strategies in parents of children with cancer. *Social Science and Medicine*, 60: 965–75.

Nordstrom, C.K., Dwyer, K.M., Merz, C.N., Shircore, A. and Dwyer, J.H. (2001). Work-related stress and early atherosclerosis. *Epidemiology*, 12: 180–5.

Norman, P. and Bennett, P. (1996). Health locus of control. In M. Conner and P. Norman (eds), *Predicting Health Behaviour*. Buckingham: Open University Press.

Norman, P., Bennett, P., Smith, C. and Murphy, S. (1998). Health locus of control and health behaviour. *Journal of Health Psychology*, 3: 171–80.

Norman, P. and Brain, K. (2005). An application of an extended health belief model to the prediction of breast self examination among women with a family history of breast cancer, *British Journal of Health Psychology*, 10: 1–16.

Norman, P., Conner, M. and Bell, S. (1999). The theory of planned behaviour and smoking cessation. *Health Psychology*, 18: 89–94.

Norman, P. and Smith, L. (1995). The theory of planned behaviour and exercise: an investigation into the role of prior behaviour, behavioural intentions and attitude variability. *European Journal of Social Psychology*, 25: 403–15.

Normandeau, S., Kalnins, I., Jutras, S. *et al.* (1998). A description of 5 to 12 year old children's conception of health within the context of their daily life. *Psychology and Health*, 13(5): 883–96.

Norris, V.K., Stephens, M.A. and Kinney, J.M. (1990). The influence of family interactions on recovery from stroke: help or hindrance? *The Gerontologist*, 30: 535–42.

Norris, S.L., McNally, K., Zang, X. *et al.* (2011). Published norms underestimate the health-related quality of life among persons with type 2 diabetes. *Journal of Clinical Epidemiology*, 64: 358–65.

Norrsell, U., Finger, S. and Lajonchere, C. (1999). Cutaneous sensory spots and the 'law of specific nerve energies': history and development of ideas. *Brain Research Bulletin*, 48: 457–65.

Norström, T. and Skog, O.J. (2005). Saturday opening of alcohol retail shops in Sweden: an experiment in two phases. *Addiction*, 100: 767–76.

Northouse, L., Kershaw, T., Mood, D. *et al.* (2005). Effects of a family intervention on the quality of life of women with recurrent breast cancer and their family caregivers. *Psycho-oncology*,14: 478–91.

Northouse, L.L., Mood, D.W., Schafenacker, A. *et al.* (2007). Randomized clinical trial of a family intervention for prostate cancer patients and their spouses. *Cancer*, 110: 2809–18.

Nouwen, A., Cloutier, C., Kappas, A. *et al.* (2006). The effects of focusing and distraction on cold-pressor induced pain in chronic back pain patients and controls. *Journal of Pain*, 7: 62–71.

Noyes, R., Jr (2001). Hypochondriasis: boundaries and comorbidities. In G.J.G. Asmundson, S. Taylor and B.J. Cox (eds), *Health Anxiety: Clinical and Research Perspectives on Hyponchondriasis and Related Conditions*. New York: John Wiley & Sons, pp. 132–60.

Nutbeam, D., Smith, C., Moore, L. *et al.* (1993). Warning! Schools can damage your health: alienation from school and its impact on child behaviour. *Journal of Paediatrics and Child Health*, 29(suppl. 1): S25–30.

Nyklícek, I. and Kuijpers, K.F. (2008). Effects of mindfulness-based stress reduction intervention on psychological well-being and quality of life: is increased mindfulness indeed the mechanism? *Annals of Behavioral Medicine*, 35: 331–40.

Oaten, M. and Cheng, K. (2006). Improved self-control: the benefits of a regular program of academic study. *Basic & Applied Social Psychology*, 28(1): 1–16.

O'Boyle, C.A., McGee, H., Hickey, A. *et al.* (1992). Individual quality of life in patients undergoing hip replacement. *The Lancet*, 339: 1088–91.

O'Boyle, C.A., McGee, H., Hickey, A. *et al.* (1993). *The Schedule for the Evaluation of Individual Quality of Life (SEIQoL): Administration Manual*. Dublin: Department of Psychology, Royal College of Surgeons.

O'Brien, M.K., Petrie, K. and Raeburn, J. (1992). Adherence to medication regimens: updating a complex medical issue. *Medical Care Review*, 49: 435–54.

O'Carroll, R.E., Smith, K.B., Grubb, N.R. *et al.* (2001). Psychological factors associated with delay in attending hospital following a myocardial infarction. *Journal of Psychosomatic Research*, 51: 611–14.

O'Cleirigh, C., Ironson, G., Antoni, M. *et al.* (2003). Emotional expression and depth processing of trauma and their relation to long-term survival in patients with HIV/AIDS. *Journal of Psychosomatic Research*, 54: 225–35.

O'Connell, K., Skevington, S. and Saxena, S. *et al.* (2003). Preliminary development of the World Health Organization's Quality of Life HIV instrument (WHOQOL-HIV): analysis of the pilot version. *Social Science and Medicine*, 57: 1259–75.

O'Connor, A.P., Wicker, C.A. and Germino, B.B. (1990). Understanding the cancer patient's search for meaning. *Cancer Nursing*, 13: 167–75.

O'Connor, D.B., Jones, F., Conner, M., McMilan, B. and Ferguson, E. (2008). Effects of daily hassles and eating styles on eating behavior, *Health Psychology*, 27(1): S20–S31.

Odgers, P., Houghton, S. and Douglas, G. (1996). Reputation Enhancement Theory and adolescent substance use. *Journal of Child Psychology, Psychiatry and Allied Disciplines*, 37: 1015–22.

O'Donnell, L., San Doval, A., Duran, R. and O'Donnell, C.R. (1995). The effectiveness of video-based interventions in promoting condom acquisition among STD clinic patients. *Sexually Transmitted Diseases*, 22: 97–103.

O'Farrell, T.J. and Fals-Stewart, W. (2000). Behavioral couples therapy for alcoholism and drug abuse. *Journal of Substance Abuse Treatment*, 18: 51–4.

Office for National Statistics (1997). *Smoking Among Secondary School Children in 1996: England*. London: Stationery Office.

Office for National Statistics (1998). *1996 Mortality Statistics: Cause*. Series DH2, 23. London: Stationery Office.

Office for National Statistics (1999). *Social Trends 29*. London: Stationery Office.

Office for National Statistics (2000). *Results from the 1998 General Household Survey*. London: Stationery Office.

Office for National Statistics (2001). *Smoking Related Behaviour and Attitudes*. Series OS No.17. London: ONS.

Office for National Statistics (2009). *Alcohol-related Deaths in the United Kingdom 1991–2007*. Statistical Bulletin, 28 January 2009. Cardiff: ONS.

Office for National Statistics (2009). *Population Trends, Autumn 2009*. Cardiff: ONS.

Office for National Statistics (2010). *Death Registrations by Cause in England and Wales 2009*. Statistical Bulletin. Cardiff: ONS.

Ogden, J. (2003). Some problems with social cognition models: a pragmatic and conceptual analysis. *Health Psychology*, 22: 424–8.

Ogden, J., Fuks, K., Gardner, M. *et al.* (2002). Doctors' expressions of uncertainty and patient confidence. *Patient Education and Counselling*, 48: 171–6.

Ogden, J. and Mtandabari, T. (1997). Examination stress and changes in mood and health related behaviours. *Psychology and Health*, 12: 288–99.

Ogden, J., Veale, D. and Summers, Z. (1997). The development and validation of the Exercise Dependence Questionnaire. *Addiction Research*, 5: 343–56.

Ohayon, M.M., Guilleminault, C., Priest, R.G. *et al.* (2000). Is sleep-disordered breathing an independent risk factor for hypertension in the general population (13,057 subjects)? *Journal of Psychosomatic Research*, 48: 593–601.

O'Hegarty, M., Pederson, L.L., Nelson, D.E. *et al.* (2006). Reactions of young adult smokers to warning labels on cigarette packages. *American Journal of Preventive Medicine*, 30: 467–73.

Okamoto, K. (2006). Life expectancy at the age of 65 years and environmental factors: an ecological study in Japan. *Archives of Gerontology and Geriatrics*, 43: 85–91.

O'Keefe, D.J. and Jensen, J.D. (2007). The relative persuasiveness of gain-framed and loss-framed messages for encouraging disease prevention behaviors: a meta-analytic review. *Journal of Health Communication*, 12: 623–44.

Okelo, S.O., Wu, A.W., Merriman, B. *et al.* (2007). Are physician estimates of asthma severity less accurate in black than in white patients? *Journal of General Internal Medicine*, 22: 976–81.

Oldenburg, B., Glanz, K. and French, M. (1999). The application of staging models to the understanding of health behaviour change and the promotion of health. *Psychology and Health*, 14: 503–16.

Oldenburg, B. and Harris, D. (1996). The workplace as a setting for promoting health and preventing disease. *Homeostasis*, 37: 226–32.

Oliver, G., Wardle, J. and Gibson, E.L. (2000). Stress and food choice: a laboratory study. *Psychosomatic Medicine*, 2: 853–65.

Olson, D.H. and Stewart, K.L. (1991). Family systems and health behaviours. In H.E. Schroeder (ed.), *New Directions in Health Psychology Assessment*. New York: Hemisphere.

O'Malley, P.M., Johnston, L.D., Chaloupka, F.J. and Flay, B. (2005). Televised state-sponsored antitobacco advertising and youth smoking beliefs and behavior in the United States, 1999–2000. *Archives of Pediatric and Adolescent Medicine*, 159: 639–45.

O'Neill, M. and Simard, P. (2006). Choosing indicators to evaluate Healthy Cities projects: a political task? *Health Promotion International*, 21: 145–52.

Onwuanyi, A.E., Clarke, A. and Vanderbush, E. (2003). Cardiovascular disease mortality. *Journal of the National Medical Association*, 95: 1146–51.

Onwuteaka-Phillipsen, B., van der Heide, A., Koper, D. *et al.* (2003). Euthanasia and other end-of-life decisions in The Netherlands in 1990, 1995 and 2001. *The Lancet*, 362: 395–9.

Orbell, S. and Gillies, B. (1993). What's stressful about caring? *Journal of Applied Social Psychology*, 23: 272–90.

Orbell, S., Hopkins, N. and Gillies, B. (1993). Measuring the impact of informal caregiving. *Journal of Community and Applied Social Psychology*, 3: 149–63.

Orbell, S., Hodgkins, S. and Sheeran, P. (1997). Implementation intentions and the theory of planned behaviour. *Personality and Social Psychology*, 23: 945–54.

Orbell, S. and Sheeran, P. (2002). Changing health behaviours: the role of implementation intentions. In D. Rutter and L. Quine (eds), *Changing Health Behaviour*. Buckingham: Open University Press.

Orford, J. (2001). *Excessive Appetites: A Psychological View of Addictions*, 2nd edn. Chichester: Wiley.

Orth-Gomér, K., Undén, A.-L. and Edwards, M.-E. (1988). Social isolation and mortality in ischemic heart disease. *Acta Medica Scandinavica*, 224: 205–15.

Orth-Gomér, K. and Undén, A.-L. (1990). Type A behaviour, social support, and coronary risk: interaction and significance for mortality in cardiac patients. *Psychosomatic Medicine*, 52: 59–72.

Osborne, R.H., Wilson, T., Lorig, K.R. *et al.* (2007). Does self-management lead to sustainable health benefits in people with arthritis? A 2-year transition study of 452 Australians. *Journal of Rheumatology*, 34: 1112–7.

Osse, B.H.P., Myrra, J.F.J., Vernooij-Dassen, E.S. *et al.* (2002). Problems to discuss with cancer patients in palliative care: a comprehensive approach. *Patient Education and Counseling*, 47: 195–204.

Ossip-Klein, D.J., McIntosh, S. *et al.* (2000). Smokers aged 50+: who gets physician advice to quit? *Preventive Medicine*, 31: 364–9.

OXCHECK Study Group (1994). Effectiveness of health checks conducted by nurses in primary care: results of the OXCHECK study after one year. Imperial Cancer Research Fund OXCHECK Study Group. *British Medical Journal*, 308: 308–12.

OXCHECK Study Group (1995). Effectiveness of health checks conducted by nurses in primary care: final results of the OXCHECK study. Imperial Cancer Research Fund OXCHECK Study Group. *British Medical Journal*, 310: 1099–104.

Oxman, A.D., Davis, D., Haynes, R.B. *et al.* (1995). No magic bullets: a systematic review of 102 trials of interventions to improve professional practice. *Canadian Medical Association Journal*, 153: 1423–31.

Pachter, L.M. (1994). Culture and clinical care: folk illness beliefs and behaviours and their implications for health care delivery. *Journal of the American Medical Association*, 7: 690–4.

Paffenbarger, R.S., Hyde, J.T., Wing, A.L. *et al.* (1986). Physical activity, all-cause mortality, and longevity of college alumni. *New England Journal of Medicine*, 314: 605–12.

Page-Shafer, K.A., Satariano, W.A., Winkelstein, W. Jr. (1996) Comorbidity and HIV disease progression in homosexual/bisexual men: the San Francisco Men's Health Study. *Annals of Epidemiology 1996*, 6: 420–30.

Pakenham, K.I., Dadds, M.R. and Lennon, H.V. (2002). The efficacy of a psychosocial intervention for HIV/AIDS caregiving dyads and individual caregivers: a controlled treatment outcome study. *AIDS Care*, 14: 731–50.

Pakenham, K.I., Pruss, M. and Clutton, S. (2000). The utility of sociodemographics, knowledge and health belief model variables in predicting reattendance for mammography screening: a brief report. *Psychology and Health*, 15: 585–91.

Palesh, O., Butler, L.D., Koopman, C. *et al.* (2007). Stress history and breast cancer recurrence. *Journal of Psychosomatic Research*, 63: 233–9.

Palmer, S. and Glass, T.A. (2003). Family function and stroke recovery: a review. *Rehabilitation Psychology*, 48: 255–65.

Panagopoulou, E., Kersbergen, B. and Maes, S. (2002). The effects of emotional (non-) expression in (chronic) disease: a meta-analytic review. *Psychology and Health*, 17: 529–45.

Panagopoulou, E., Vedhara, K., Gaintarzti, C. *et al.* (2006). Emotionally expressive coping reduces pregnancy rates in patients undergoing in vitro fertilization. *Fertility and Sterility*, 86: 672–677.

Pandey, M., Sarita, G.P., Devi, N. *et al.* (2006). Distress, anxiety and depression in cancer patients undergoing chemotherapy. *World Journal of Surgical Oncology*, 4: 68.

Papanicolaou, D.A., Wilder, R.L., Manolagas, S.C. and Chrousos, G.P. (1998). The pathophysiologic roles of interleukin-6 in human disease. *Archives of Internal Medicine*, 128: 127–37.

Pargament, K.I., Koenig, H.G. and Perez, L.M. (2000). The many methods in religious coping: development and initial validation of the RCOPE. *Journal of Clinical Psychology*, 56: 519–43.

Paris, W., Muchmore, J., Pribil, A. *et al.* (1994). Study of the relative incidences of psychosocial factors before and after heart transplantation and the influence of post-transplantation psychosocial factors on heart transplantation outcome. *Journal of Heart Lung Transplantation*, 13: 424–30.

Park, C.L. (2006). Exploring relations among religiousness, meaning, and adjustment to lifetime and current stressful encounters in later life. *Anxiety, Stress, and Coping*, 19: 33–45.

Park, C.L. and Folkman, S. (1997). Meaning in the context of stress and coping. *Reviews in General Psychology*, 2: 115–44.

Park, C.L. and Lechner, S.C. (2007). Measurement issues in assessing growth following stressful life experiences. In L.G. Calhoun and R.G. Tedeschi (eds) (2007), *Handbook of Post-traumatic Growth: Research and Practice*. London: Lawrence Erlbaum Associates, pp. 47–67.

Park, D.C., Morrell, R.W., Frieske, D. *et al.* (1992). Medication adherence behaviors in older adults: effects of external cognitive supports. *Psychology and Aging*, 7: 252–6.

Park, P., Simmons, R.K., Prevost, A.T. *et al.* (2010). A randomized evaluation of loss and gain frames in an invitation to screening for type 2 diabetes: effects on attendance, anxiety and self-rated health. *Journal of Health Psychology*, 15: 196–204.

Parkes, K. (1984). Locus of control, cognitive appraisal, coping appraisal and coping in stressful episodes. *Journal of Personality and Social Psychology*, 46: 655–68.

Parle, M., Maguire, P. and Heaven, C. (1997). The development of a training model to improve health professionals' skills, self-efficacy and outcome expectancies when communicating with cancer patients. *Social Science and Medicine*, 44: 231–40.

Parsons, T. (1951). *The Social System*. New York: Free Press.

Partridge, C. and Johnston, M. (1989). Perceived control of recovery from physical disability: measurement and prediction. *British Journal of Clinical Psychology*, 28: 53–9.

Parveen, S. and Morrison, V. (2009) Predictors of familism in the caregiver role: a pilot study. *Journal of Health Psychology*, 14: 1135–43.

Parveen, S. (2011). Ethnicity, mediators and caregiver outcomes: a systematic review. Unpublished PhD thesis, Bangor University.

Parveen, S. and Morrison, V. (2011a in review). Predicting caregiver anxiety and depression.

Parveen, S. and Morrison, V. (2011b in review) Predicting caregiver gains.

Parveen, S., Morrison, V. and Robinson, C. (2011). Ethnic variations in the caregiver role: a qualitative study. *Journal of Health Psychology*, doi: 10.1177/1359105310 392416.

Pasterfield, D., Wilkinson, C., Finlay, I.G. *et al.* (2006). GPs' views on changing the law on physician-assisted suicide and euthanasia, and willingness to prescribe or inject lethal drugs: a survey from Wales. *British Journal of General Practice*, 56: 450–52.

Patenaude, A.F., Guttmacher, A.E. and Collins, F.S. (2002). Genetic testing and psychology: new roles, new responsibilities. *American Psychologist*, 57: 271–82.

Paton, A. (1999). Reflections on alcohol and the young. Invited commentary. *Alcohol and Alcoholism*, 34: 502–5.

Patterson, D.R. and Jensen, M.P. (2003). Hypnosis and clinical pain. *Psychological Bulletin*, 129: 495–521.

Patrick, D.L. and Peach, H. (1989). *Disablement in the Community*. Oxford: Oxford University Press.

Paunonen, S.V. and Ashton, M.C. (2001). Big five factors and facets and the prediction of behavior. *Journal of Personality and Social Psychology*, 91: 524–37.

Payne, N. (2001). Occupational stressors and coping as determinants of burnout in female hospice nurses. *Journal of Advanced Nursing*, 33: 396–405.

Payne, S. (2006). *The Health of Men and Women*. Buckingham: Open University Press.

Pbert, L., Osganian, S.K., Gorak, D. *et al.* (2006). A school nurse-delivered adolescent smoking cessation intervention: a randomized controlled trial. *Preventive Medicine*, 43: 312–20.

Pearlin, L.I. (1983). Role strains and personal stress. In H.B. Kaplan (ed.), *Psychosocial Stress: Trends in Theory and Research*. New York: Academic Press.

Pearlin, L.I. and Mullan, J.T. (1992). Loss and stress in ageing. In M.L. Wykle, E. Kahara and J. Kowal (eds), *Stress and Health among the Elderly*. New York: Springer Verlag.

Pearlin, L.I. and Schooler, C. (1978). The structure of coping. *Journal of Health and Social Behavior*, 19: 2–21.

Pearson, S., Maddern, G. and Hewett, P. (2005). Interacting effects of pre-operative information and patient choice in adaptation to colonoscopy: a randomised trial. *Diseases of the Colon and Rectum*. 48: 2047–54.

Peay, M.Y. and Peay, E.R. (1998). The evaluation of medical symptoms by patients and doctors. *Journal of Behavioral Medicine*, 21: 57–81.

Pederson-Fischer, A., Zacchariae, R. and Bovbjerg-Howard, D. (2009). Pychological stress and antibody response to influenza vaccination: a meta-analysis. *Brain, Behavior and Immunity*, 23: 427–33.

Pelosi, A.J. and Appleby, L. (1992). Psychological influences on cancer and ischaemic heart disease (for debate). *British Medical Journal*, 304: 1295–8.

Pelosi, A.J. and Appleby, L. (1993). Personality and fatal diseases. *British Medical Journal*, 306: 1666–7.

Peltola, H., Patja, A., Leinikkii, P. *et al.* (1998). No evidence for measles, mumps and rubella vaccine-associated inflammatory bowel disease or autism in a 14-year prospective study. *The Lancet*, 351: 1327–8.

Pendleton, D.A. (1983). Doctor–patient communication: a review. In D. Pendleton and J. Hasler (eds), *Doctor–Patient Communication*. London: Academic Press.

Pendleton, D., Schofield, T., Tate, P., Havelock, P. (1984). *The Consultation: An Approach to Learning and Teaching*. Oxford: Oxford University Press.

Penedo, F.J., Molton, I., Dahn, J.R. *et al.* (2006). Randomized clinical trial of group-based cognitive-behavioral stress management in localized prostate cancer: development of stress management skills improves quality of life and benefit finding *Annals of Behavioral Medicine*, 31: 261–70.

Pennebaker, J.W. (1982). Social and perceptual factors affecting symptom reporting and mass psychogenic illness. In M.J. Colligan, J.W. Pennebaker and L.R. Murphy (eds), *Mass Psychogenic Illness: A Social Psychological Analysis*. Hillsdale, NJ: Lawrence Erlbaum.

Pennebaker, J.W. (1992). *The Psychology of Physical Symptoms*. New York: Springer Verlag.

Pennebaker, J.W. (1993). Putting stress into words: health, linguistic and therapeutic implications. *Behavioral Research Therapy*, 31: 539–48.

Pennebaker, J.W. and Beall, S. (1986). Confronting a traumatic event: toward an understanding of inhibition and disease. *Journal of Abnormal Psychology*, 95: 274–81.

Pennebaker, J.W., Colder, M. and Sharp, L.K. (1990). Accelerating the coping process. *Journal of Personality and Social Psychology*, 58: 528–37.

Pennebaker, J.W., Kiecolt-Glaser, J. and Glaser, R. (1988). Disclosure of trauma and immune function: health implications for psychotherapy. *Journal of Consulting and Clinical Psychology*, 56: 239–45.

Pennebaker, J.W. and Skelton, J.A. (1981). Selective monitoring of bodily sensations. *Journal of Personality and Social Behaviour*, 35: 167–74.

Penninx, B., Guralnik, J.M., Pahor, M. *et al.* (1998). Chronically depressed mood and cancer risk in older persons. *Journal of the National Cancer Institute*, 90: 1888–93.

Penninx, B.W.J.H., van Tilburg, T., Kriegsman, D.M.W. *et al.* (1999). Social network, social support, and loneliness in older persons with different chronic diseases. *Journal of Ageing and Health*, 11: 151–68.

Penny, G.N., Bennett, P. and Herbert, M. (eds) (1994). *Health Psychology: A Lifespan Perspective*. Switzerland: Harwood Academic.

Penwell, L.M. and Larkin, K.T. (2010). Social support and risk for cardiovascular disease and cancer: a qualitative review examining the role of inflammatory processes. *Health Psychology Review*, 4: 42–55.

Perkins, H.W., Haines, M.P. and Rice, R. (2005). Misperceiving the college drinking norm and related problems: a nationwide study of exposure to prevention information, perceived norms and student alcohol misuse. *Journal of Studies on Alcohol*, 66: 470–8.

Perloff, L.S. and Fetzer, B.K. (1986). Self–other judgements and perceived vulnerability to victimization. *Journal of Personality and Social Psychology*, 50: 502–10.

Perna, F.M., Craft, L., Carver, C.S. and Antoni, M.H. (2008). Negative affect and barriers to exercise among early stage breast cancer patients. *Health Psychology*, 27: 275–9.

Perry, C.L. and Grant, M. (1988). Comparing peer-led to teacher-led youth alcohol education in four countries. (Australia, Chile, Norway and Swaziland). *Alcohol Health and Research World*, 12: 322–6.

Perry, K., Petrie, K.J., Ellis, C.J. *et al.* (2001). Symptom expectations and delay in acute myocardial infarction patients. *Heart*, 86: 91–2.

Persky, V.W., Kempthorne-Rawson, J. and Shekelle, R.B. (1987). Personality and risk of cancer: 20 year follow-up of the Western Electric study. *Psychosomatic Medicine*, 49: 435–49.

Perugini, M. and Bagozzi, R.P. (2001). The role of desires and anticipated emotions in goal-directed behaviours: broadening and deepening the theory of planned behaviour. *British Journal of Social Psychology*, 40: 79–98.

Peterson, T.R. and Aldana, S.G. (1999). Improving exercise behaviour: an application of the stages of change model in a worksite setting. *American Journal of Health Promotion*, 13: 229–32.

Peto, R., Darby, S., Deo, H., Silcocks, P., Whitley, E. and Doll, R. (2000). Smoking, smoking cessation, and lung cancer in the UK since 1950: combination of national statistics with two case-control studies. *British Medical Journal*, 321: 323–9.

Peto, R. and Lopez, A.D. (1990). Worldwide mortality from current smoking patterns. In B. Durston and K. Jamrozik (eds), *Tobacco and Health 1990: The Global War*. Proceedings of the 7th World Conference on Tobacco and Health. Perth: Health Department of Western Australia.

Peto, R., Lopez, A.D., Borehan, J., Thun, M. and Heath, C., Jr (1994). *Mortality from Smoking in Developed Countries 1950–2000*. Oxford: Oxford University Press.

Petrak, J.A., Doyle, A.-M., Smith, A. *et al.* (2001). Factors associated with self-disclosure of HIV serostatus to significant others. *British Journal of Health Psychology*, 6: 69–79.

Petrie, K.J., Buick, D.L., Weinman, J. and Booth, R.J. (1999). Positive effects of illness reported by myocardial infarction and breast cancer patients. *Journal of Psychosomatic Research*, 47: 537–43.

Petrie, K.J., Fontanilla, I., Thomas, M.G. *et al.* (2004). Effects of written emotional expression on immune function in patients with human immunodeficiency virus infection: A randomized trial. *Psychosomatic Medicine*, 66: 272–5.

Petrie, K.J., Jago, L.A. and Devcich, D.A. (2007). The role of illness perceptions in patients with medical conditions. *Current Opinion in Psychiatry*, 20: 163–7.

Petrie, K.J. and Weinman, J. (2003). More focus needed on symptom appraisal (editorial). *Journal of Psychosomatic Research*, 54: 401–3.

Petrie, K.J., Weinman, J., Sharpe, N. *et al.* (1996). Role of patients' view of their illness in predicting return to work and functioning after a myocardial infarction. *British Medical Journal*, 312: 1191–4.

Petrie, K.P., Cameron, L.D., Ellis, C.J., Buick, D. and Weinman, J. (2002). Changing illness perceptions after myocardial infarction: an early intervention randomized controlled trial. *Psychosomatic Medicine*, 64: 580–6.

Petruzzello, S.J., Jones, A.C. and Tate, A.K. (1997). Affective responses to acute exercise: a test of opponent-process theory. *Journal of Sports Medicine and Physical Fitness*, 37: 205–11.

Petticrew, A., Fraser, J. and Regan, M. (1999). Adverse life events and risk of breast cancer: a meta-analysis. *British Journal of Health Psychology*, 4: 1–17.

Petter, M., Blanchard, C., Kemp, K.A. *et al.* (2009). Correlates of exercise among coronary heart disease patients: review, implications and future directions. *European Journal of Cardiovascular Prevention and Rehabilitation*, 16: 515–26.

Petticrew, M., Bell, R. and Hunter, D. (2002). Influence of psychological coping on survival and recurrence in people with cancer: a systematic review. *British Medical Journal*, 325: 1066.

Petty, R. and Cacioppo, J. (1986). The elaboration likelihood model of persuasion. In L. Berkowitz (ed.), *Advances in experimental social psychology*, Vol. 19. Orlando, FL: Academic Press.

Petty, R.E. and Cacioppo, J.T. (1996). *Attitudes and Persuasion: Classic and Contemporary Approaches.* Boulder, CO: Westview Press.

Peveler, R., Carson, A. and Rodin, G. (2002). Depression in medical patients. *British Medical Journal*, 325: 149–52.

PHLS Communicable Disease Surveillance Centre (2002). *HIV and AIDS in the United Kingdom 2001. An Update: November 2002*. London: PHLS, ICH (London) and SCIEH.

Piaget, J. (1930). *The Child's Conception of Physical Causality*. London: Routledge and Kegan Paul.

Piaget, J. (1970). Piaget's theory. In P.H. Mussen (ed.), *Carmichael's Manual of Child Psychology*, 3rd edn, Vol. 1. New York: Wiley.

Piette, J.D., Weinberger, M. and McPhee, S.J. (2000). The effect of automated calls with telephone nurse follow-up on patient-centered outcomes of diabetes care: a randomized controlled trial. *Medical Care*, 38: 218–30.

Pinel, J.P.J. (2003). *Biopsychology*, 5th edn. Boston, MA: Allyn and Bacon.

Pinel, J.P.J., Assanand, S. and Lehman, D.R. (2000). Hunger, eating and ill-health. *American Psychologist*, 55: 1105–16.

Pinerua-Shuhaibar, L., Prieto-Rincon, D., Ferrer, A. *et al.* (1999). Reduced tolerance and cardiovascular responses to ischemic pain in minor depression. *Journal of Affective Disorders*, 56: 119–26.

Pinquart, M. and Sörensen, S. (2003). Differences between caregivers and noncaregivers in psychological health and physical health: a meta-analysis. *Psychology and Aging*, 18: 250–67.

Pinquart, M. and Sörensen, S. (2005). Ethnic differences in stressors, resources, and psychological outcomes of family caregiving: a meta-analysis. *The Gerontologist*, 45: 90–106.

Pirozzo, S., Summerbell, C., Cameron, C. and Glasziou, P. (2003). Advice on low-fat diets for obesity. In *The Cochrane Library*, issue 1. Oxford: Update Software.

Pisinger, C. and Jorgensen, T. (2007). Weight concerns and smoking in a general population: The Inter99 study. *Preventive Medicine*, 44: 283–9.

Pisters, M.F., Veenhof, C., de Bakker, D.H. *et al.* (2010). Behavioural graded activity results in better exercise adherence and more physical activity than usual care in people with osteoarthritis: a cluster-randomised trial. *Journal of Physiotherapy*, 56: 41–7.

Plante, T.G. and Rodin, J. (1990). Physical fitness and enhanced psychological health. *Current Psychology Research and Reviews*, 9: 3–24.

Plassman, B.L., Williams, J.W., Burke, J.R. *et al.* (2010). Systematic review: factors associated with risk for and possible prevention of cognitive decline in later life. *Annals of Internal Medicine*, 153(3): 182–93.

Plotnikoff, R.C., Brunet, S., Courneya, K.S. *et al.* (2007). The efficacy of stage-matched and standard public health materials for promoting physical activity in the workplace: the Physical Activity Workplace Study (PAWS). *American Journal of Health Promotion*, 21: 501–9.

Plotnikoff, R.C., Lippke, S., Courneya, K. *et al.* (2010). Physical activity and diabetes: an application of the theory of planned behaviour to explain physical activity for type 1 and type 2 diabetes in an adult population sample. *Psychology & Health*, 25: 7–23.

Plotnikoff, R.C., McCargar, L.J., Wilson, P.M. *et al.* (2005). Efficacy of an e-mail intervention for the promotion of physical activity and nutrition behavior in the workplace context. *American Journal of Health Promotion*, 19: 422–9.

Pollock, K., Wilson, E., Porock, D. *et al.* (2007). Evaluating the impact of a cancer supportive care project in the community: patient and professional configurations of need. *Health and Social Care in the Community*, 15: 520–9.

Polsky, D., Doshi, J.A., Marcus, S. *et al.* (2005). Long-term risk for depressive symptoms after a medical diagnosis. *Archives of Internal Medicine*, 165: 1260–66.

Post, S.G. (ed.) (2007). *Altruism and Health: Perspectives From Empirical Research*. New York, NY: Oxford University Press.

Potter, J., Hami, F., Bryan, T. and Quigley, C. (2003). Symptoms in 400 patients referred to palliative care services: prevalence and patterns. *Palliative Medicine*, 17: 310–14.

Potter, J.D., Slattery, M.L., Bostick, R.M. and Gapstur, S.M. (1993). Colon cancer: a review of the epidemiology. *Epidemiological Review*, 15: 499–545.

Poulin, M.J., Brown, S.L., Ubel, P. *et al.* (2010). Does a helping hand mean a heavy heart? Helping behavior and well-being among spouse caregivers. *Psychology and Aging*, 25: 108–17.

Pound, P., Bury, M., Gompertz, P. and Ebrahim, S. (1994). Views of survivors of stroke on the benefits of physiotherapy. *Quality in Health Care*, 3: 69–74.

Powell, H. and Gibson, P.G. (2003). Options for self-management education for adults with asthma. *Cochrane Database of Systematic Reviews*, CD004107.

Powell-Griner, E., Anderson, J.E. and Murphy, W. (1997). State and sex-specific prevalence of selected characteristics behavioural risk factor surveillance system,

1994 and 1995. *Morbidity and Mortality Weekly Report*, Centres for Disease Control, surveillance summaries, 46: 1–31.

Power, R., Koopman, C., Volk, J. *et al.* (2003). Social support, substance use, and denial in relationship to antiretroviral treatment adherence among HIV-infected persons. *AIDS Patient Care and STDs*, 17: 245–52.

Pradhan, E.K., Baumgarten, M., Langenberg, P. *et al.* (2007). Effect of mindfulness-based stress reduction in rheumatoid arthritis patients. *Arthritis and Rheumatism*, 57: 1134–42.

Prentice, A.M. and Jebb, S.A. (1995). Obesity in Britain: gluttony or sloth. *British Medical Journal*, 311: 437–9.

Prescott-Clarke, P. and Primatesta, P. (1998). *Health survey for England: The Health of Young People 1995–97.* London: The Stationery Office.

Price, R.A. and Gottesman, I.I. (1991). Body fat in identical twins reared apart: roles for genes and environment. *Behavioral Genetics*, 21: 1–7.

Price, D.D., Finniss, D.G. and Benedetti, F. (2008). A comprehensive review of the placebo effect: recent advances and current thought. *Annual Review of Psychology* 59: 565–90.

Price, V.A. (1988). Research and clinical issues in treating Type A behavior. In B.K. Houston and C.R. Snyder (eds), *Type A Behavior Pattern: Research, Theory, and Practice.* New York: Wiley.

Prochaska, J.O. (1994). Strong and weak principles for progressing from precontemplation to action based on twelve problem behaviours. *Health Psychology*, 13: 47–51.

Prochaska, J.O. and di Clemente, C.C. (1984). *The Transtheoretical Approach: Crossing Traditional Boundaries of Therapy.* Homewood, IL: Dow Jones Irwin.

Prochaska, J.O. and di Clemente, C.C. (1986). Towards a comprehensive model of change. In B.K. Houston and N. Heather (eds), *Treating Addictive Behaviours: Processes of Change.* New York: Plenum.

Prochaska, J.O. and Marcus, B.H. (1994). The trans-theoretical model: applications to exercise. In R.K. Dishman (ed.), *Advances in Exercise Adherence.* Champaign, IL: Human Kinetics.

Prochaska, J.O., Norcross, J.C., Fowler, J.L. and Follick, M.J. (1992). Attendance and outcome in a worksite weight control program: processes and stages of change as process and predictor variables. *Addictive Behaviors*, 17: 35–45.

Prochaska, J.O. and Velicer, W.F. (1997). The Transtheoretical Model of health behavior change, *American Journal of Health Promotion*, 12: 38–48.

Prochaska, J.O., Velicer, W.F., Rossi, J.S. *et al.* (1994). Stages of change and decisional balance for 12 problem behaviours. *Health Psychology*, 13: 39–46.

Prohaska, T.R., Funch, D. and Blesch, K.S. (1990). Age patterns in symptom perception and illness behaviour among colorectal cancer patients. *Behavior, Health and Aging*, 1: 27–39.

Prohaska, T.R., Keller, M.L., Leventhal, E.A. *et al.* (1987). Impact of symptoms and aging attribution on emotions and coping. *Health Psychology*, 6: 495–514.

Project MATCH Research Group (1998). Matching alcoholism treatments to client heterogeneity: Project MATCH three-year drinking outcomes. *Alcoholism: Clinical and Experimental Research*, 22: 1300–11.

Ptacek, J.T.P. and Eberhardt, T.L. (1996). Breaking bad news: a review of the literature. *Journal of the American Medical Association*, 276: 496–502.

Ptacek, J.T., Ptacek, J.J. and Ellison, H. (2001). 'I'm sorry to tell you' – physicians' reports of breaking bad news. *Journal of Behavioral Medicine*, 24: 205–17.

Puccio, J.A., Belzer, M., Olson, J. *et al.* (2006). The use of cell phone reminder calls for assisting HIV-infected adolescents and young adults to adhere to highly active antiretroviral therapy: a pilot study. *AIDS Patient Care and STDS*, 20: 438–44.

Puska, P., Tuomilehto, J., Nissinen, A. *et al.* (1985). *The North Karelia Project: 20 Year Results and Experiences.* Helsinki: National Public Health Institutem.

Quah, S.-H. and Bishop, G.D. (1996). Seeking help for illness: the roles of cultural orientation and illness cognition. *Journal of Health Psychology*, 1: 209–22.

Quentin, W., Neubauer, S., Leidl, R. *et al.* (2007). Advertising bans as a means of tobacco control policy: a systematic literature review of time-series analyses. *International Journal of Public Health*, 52: 295–307.

Quick, J.D., Nelson, D.L., Matuszek, P.A.C. *et al.* (1996). Social support, secure attachments and health. In C.L. Cooper (ed.), *Handbook of Stress, Medicine and Health.* London: CRC Press.

Quinlan, K.B. and McCaul, K.D. (2000). Matched and mis-matched interventions with young adult smokers: Testing a stage theory. *Health Psychology*, 19: 165–71.

Quinn, K., Kaufman, J.S., Siddiqi, A. and Yeatts, K.B. (2010). Stress and the city: housing stressors are associated with respiratory health among low socioeconomic status Chicago children. *Journal of Urban Health*, 87: 688–702.

Qureshi, M., Thacker, H.L., Litaker, D.G. *et al.* (2000). Differences in breast cancer screening rates: an issue of ethnicity or socioeconomics? *Journal of Women's Health and Gender Based Medicine*, 9: 1025–31.

Radley, A. (1994). *Making Sense of Illness: The Social Psychology of Health and Disease.* London: Sage.

Radley, A. (1996). Social psychology and health: framing the relationship. *Psychology and Health*, 11: 629–34.

Rafferty, Y., Friend, R. and Landsbergis, P.A. (2001). The association between job skill discretion, decision authority and burnout. *Work and Stress*, 15: 73–85.

Raftery, K.A., Smith-Coggins, R. and Chen, A.H. (1995). Gender-associated differences in emergency department pain management. *Annals of Emergency Medicine*, 26: 414–21.

Ragland, D.R. and Brand, R.J. (1988). Type A behaviour and mortality from coronary heart disease. *New England Journal of Medicine*, 318: 65–9.

Rahe, R. (1974). Life change and subsequent illness reports. In E.K.E. Gunderson and R. Rahe (eds), *Life Stress and Illness*. Springfield, IL: Charles Thomas.

Rahimi, A.R., Spertus, J.A., Reid, K.J. *et al.* (2007). Financial barriers to health care and outcomes after acute myocardial infarction. *Journal of the American Medical Association*, 297: 1063–72.

Rains, J.C., Penzien, D.B., McCrory, D.C. *et al.* (2005). Behavioral headache treatment: history, review of the empirical literature, and methodological critique. *Headache*, 45: S91–S108.

Ramel, W., Goldin, P.R., Carmona, P.E. and McQuaid, J.R. (2004). The effects of mindfulness meditation on cognitive processes and affect in patients with past depression. *Cognitive Therapy and Research*, 28: 433–55.

Ramirez, A., Craig, T., Watson, J. *et al.* (1989). Stress and relapse of breast cancer. *British Medical Journal*, 298: 291–3.

Ramirez, A.J., Westcombe, A.M., Burgess, C.C. *et al.* (1999). Factors predicting delayed presentation of symptomatic breast cancer: a systematic review. *The Lancet*, 353: 1119–26.

Ramnarayan, P., Roberts, G.C., Coren, M. *et al.* (2006). Assessment of the potential impact of a reminder system on the reduction of diagnostic errors: a quasi-experimental study. *BMC Medical Informatics and Decision Making*, 6: 22.

Rampersaud, E., Mitchell, B.D., Pollin, T.I. *et al.* (2008). Physical activity and the association of common FTO gene variants with body mass index and obesity. *Archives of Internal Medicine*, 168: 1791–7.

Rand, C.S. and Wise, R.A. (1994). Measuring adherence to asthma medication regimens. *American Journal of Respiratory and Critical Care Medicine*, 149 (suppl.): 69–76.

Rapp, S.R. and Chao, D. (2000). Appraisals of strain and of gain: effects on psychological wellbeing of caregivers of dementia patients. *Aging & Mental Health*, 4: 142–7.

Rasulo, D., Bajekal, M. and Yar, M. (2007). Inequalities in health expectancies in England and Wales: small area analysis from the 2001 Census. *Health Statistics Quarterly*, 34: 35–45.

Rawl, S.M., Given, B.A., Given, C.W. *et al.* (2002). Intervention to improve psychological functioning for newly diagnosed patients with cancer. *Oncology Nursing Forum*, 29: 967–75.

RCN (2002). Royal College of Nursing Congress 2002 Report summaries. *Nursing Standard*, 16: 4–9.

Reddy, D.M., Fleming, R. and Adesso, V.J. (1992). Gender and health. In S. Maes, H. Leventhal and M. Johnston (eds), *International Review of Health Psychology*, Vol. 1. Chichester: Wiley.

Rees, K., Bennett, P., Vedhara, K. *et al.* (2004). Stress management for coronary heart disease. *The Cochrane Library*.

Reeve, J., Menon, D. and Corabian, P. (1996). Transcutaneous electrical nerve stimulation (TENS): a technology assessment. *International Journal of Technology Assessment in Health Care*, 12: 299–324.

Reich, J. and Schatzberg, A. (2010). Personality traits and medical outcome of cardiac illness. *Journal of Psychiatric Research*, 44: 1017–20.

Rennemark, M. and Hagberg, B. (1999). What makes old people perceive symptoms of illness? The impact of psychological and social factors. *Aging & Mental Health*, 3: 79–87.

Renner, B., Kwon, S., Yang, B.-H. *et al.* (2008). Social-cognitive predictors of dietary behaviors in South Korean men and women. *International Journal of Behavioral Medicine*, 15(1): 4–13.

Renner, B. and Schwarzer, R. (2003). Social-cognitive factors in health behaviour change. In J. Suls and K. Wallston (eds), *Social Foundations of Health and Illness*. Oxford: Blackwell.

Renner, B., Spivak, Y., Kwon, S. and Schwarzer, R. (2007). Does age make a difference? Predicting physical activity of South Koreans, *Psychology & Ageing*, 22: 482–93.

Renzi, C., Peticca, L. and Pescatori, M. (2000). The use of relaxation techniques in the perioperative management of proctological patients: preliminary results. *International Journal of Colorectal Diseases*, 15: 313–16.

Resendes, L.A. and McCorkle, R. (2006). Spousal responses to prostate cancer: an integrative review. *Cancer Investigations*, 24: 192–8.

Resnick, R.J. and Rozensky, R.H. (eds) (1997). *Health Psychology Through the Life Span: Practice and Research Opportunities*. Washington, DC: American Psychological Association.

Resnicow, K., Jackson, A., Wang, T. *et al.* (2001). Motivational interviewing intervention to increase fruit and vegetable intake through black churches: results of the Eat for Life trial. *American Journal of Public Health*, 91: 1686–93.

Rhodes, F. and Wolitski, B. (1990). Perceived effectiveness of fear appeals in AIDS education: relationship to ethnicity, gender, age and group membership. *AIDS Education and Prevention*, 2: 1–11.

Rhodewalt, F. and Zone, J.B. (1989). Appraisal of life change, depression, and illness in hardy and nonhardy women. *Journal of Personality and Social Psychology*, 56: 81–8.

Ricciardelli, L.A. and McCabe, M.P. (2001). Children's body image concerns and eating disturbance: a review of the literature. *Clinical Psychology Review*, 21: 325–44.

Rice, P.L. (1992). *Stress and Health*. Pacific Grove, CA: Brooks/Cole.

Richard, R., van der Pligt, J. and de Vries, N. (1996). Anticipated regret and time perspective: changing sexual risk-taking behaviour. *Journal of Behavioural Decision Making*, 9: 185–99.

Richards, J., Fisher, P. and Conner, F. (1989). The warnings on cigarette packages are ineffective. *Journal of the American Medical Association*, 261: 45.

Richards, M.A., Westcombe, A.M., Love, S.B. *et al.* (1999). Influence of delay on survival in patients with breast cancer: a systematic review. *The Lancet*, 353: 1119–26.

Richardson, J. (2000). The use of randomised control trials in complementary therapies: exploring the issues. *Journal of Advanced Nursing*, 32: 398–406.

Richardson, K.M. and Rothstein, H.R. (2008). Effects of occupational stress management intervention programs: A meta-analysis. *Journal of Occupational Health Psychology*, 13: 69–93.

Richmond, R.L., Kehoe, L. and de Almeida Neto, A.C. (1997). Effectiveness of a 24-hour transdermal nicotine patch in conjunction with a cognitive behavioural programme: one year outcome. *Addiction*, 92: 27–31.

Ridgeway, V. and Mathews, A. (1982). Psychological preparation for surgery: a comparison of methods. *British Journal of Clinical Psychology*, 21: 271–80.

Riemsma, R.P., Taal, E. and Rasker, J.J. (2003). Group education for patients with rheumatoid arthritis and their partners. *Arthritis and Rheumatism*, 49: 556–66.

Rigby, K., Brown, M., Anagnostou, P. *et al.* (1989). Shock tactics to counter AIDS: the Australian experience. *Psychology and Health*, 3: 145–59.

Riley, J.L., III, Wade, J.B., Myers, C.D. *et al.* (2002). Racial/ethnic differences in the experience of chronic pain. *Pain*, 100: 291–8.

Ringström, G., Abrahamsson, H., Strid, H. and Simrén, M. (2007). Why do subjects with irritable bowel syndrome seek health care for their symptoms? *Scandinavian Journal of Gastroenterology*, 42: 1194–203.

Rivis, A. and Sheeran, P. (2003). Social influences and the theory of planned behaviour: evidence for a direct relationship between prototypes and young people's exercise behaviour. *Psychology and Health*, 18: 567–83.

Rivis, A., Sheeran, P. and Armitage, C. (2010). Explaining adolescents' cigarette smoking: a comparison of four modes of action control and a test of the role of self-regulatory mode. *Psychology & Health*, 25: 893–909.

Robb, K.A., Bennett, M.I., Johnson, M.I. *et al.* (2008). Transcutaneous electric nerve stimulation (TENS) for cancer pain in adults. *Cochrane Database of Systematic Reviews*, 3: CD006276.

Robb, K., Oxberry, S.G., Bennett, M.I. *et al.* (2009). A Cochrane systematic review of transcutaneous electrical nerve stimulation for cancer pain. *Journal of Pain and Symptom Management*, 37: 746–53.

Roberts, C.S., Cox, C.E., Reintgen, D.S. *et al.* (1994). Influence of physician communication on newly diagnosed breast patients' psychologic adjustment and decision-making. *Cancer*, 74: 336–41.

Roberts, J. and Rowland, M. (1981). *Hypertension in Adults 25–74 Years of Age, United States, 1971–1975*. Hyattsville, MD: National Center for Health Statistics (Vital and Health Statistics, Series II: Data from the National Health Survey, No. 221). DHHS publication No. 81-1671.

Robinson, M.S. and Alloy, L.B. (2003). Negative cognitive styles and stress-reactive rumination interact to predict depression: a prospective study. *Cognitive Therapy and Research*, 27: 275–92.

Robinson, R.G. (1998). *The Clinical Neuropsychiatry of Stroke*. Cambridge: Cambridge University Press.

Roesch, S.C., Adams, L., Hines, A. *et al.* (2005). Coping with prostate cancer: a meta-analytic review. *Journal of Behavioural Medicine*, 28: 281–93.

Roesch, S.C. and Weiner, B. (2001). A meta-analytic review of coping with illness: do causal attributions matter? *Journal of Psychosomatic Research*, 50: 205–19.

Rogers, C.R. (1961). *On Becoming a Person*. Boston, MA: Houghton Mifflin.

Rogers, E. (1983). *Diffusion of Innovations*. New York: Free Press.

Rogers, G., Curry, M., Oddy, J. *et al.* (2003). Depressive disorders and unprotected casual anal sex among Australian homosexually active men in primary care. *HIV Medicine*, 4: 271–5.

Rogers, R.W. (1983). Cognitive and physiological responses to fear appeals and attitude change: a revised theory of protection motivation. In J.T. Cacioppo and R.E. Petty (eds), *Social Psychophysiology: A Source Book*. New York: Guilford Press.

Rogers, R.W. and Prentice Dunn, S. (1997). Protection motivation theory. In D.S. Goffman (ed.), *Handbook of Health Behavior Research 1: Personal and Social Determinants*. New York: Plenum, pp. 113–32.

Romelsjö, A. and Branting, M. (2000). Consumption of illegal alcohol among adolescents in Stockholm county. *Contemporary Drug Problems*, 27: 315–33.

Ropka, M.E., Wenzel, J., Phillips, E.K. *et al.* (2006). Uptake rates for breast cancer genetic testing: a systematic review. *Cancer Epidemiology, Biomarkers and Prevention*, 15: 840–55.

Rosch, P.J. (1994). Can stress cause coronary heart disease? (Editorial). *Stress Medicine*, 10: 207–10.

Rosch, P.J. (1996). Stress and cancer: disorders of communication, control and civilization. In Cooper, C.L. (ed.), *Handbook of Stress, Medicine and Health*. Boca Raton, FL: CRC Press, pp. 27–60.

Rosco, J.A., Morrow, G.R., Aapro, M.S. *et al.* (2010). Anticipatory nausea and vomiting. *Supportive Care in Cancer*, doi: 10. 1007/s00520-010-0980-0.

Rose, J.S., Chassin, L., Presson, C.C. and Sherman, S.J. (1996). Prospective predictors of quit attempts and smoking cessation in young adults. *Health Psychology*, 15: 261–8.

Rose, S., Bisson, J. and Wessely, S. (2001). Psychological debriefing for preventing post traumatic stress disorder (PTSD). *Cochrane Database Systematic Review*, 3.

Rosenfeld, B., Breitbart, W., McDonald, M.V. *et al.* (1996). Pain in ambulatory AIDS patients II: impact of pain on psychological functioning and quality of life. *Pain*, 68: 323–8.

Rosengren, A., Hawken, S., Ounpuu, S. *et al.* (2004). Association of psychosocial risk factors with risk of acute myocardial infarction in 11119 cases and 1364 controls from 52 countries (the INTERHEART study): case-control study. *Lancet*, 364: 953–92.

Rosengren, A., Orth-Gomér, K., Wedel, H. and Wilhelmsen, L. (1993). Stressful life events, social support, and mortality in men born in 1933. *British Medical Journal*, 307: 1102–5.

Rosenman, R.H. (1978). Role of Type A pattern in the pathogenesis of ischaemic heart disease and modification for prevention. *Advances in Cardiology*, 25: 34–46.

Rosenman, R.H. (1996). Personality, behavior patterns, and heart disease. In C. Cooper (ed.), *Handbook of Stress, Medicine and Health*. Boca Raton, FL: CRC Press.

Rosenman, R.H., Brand, R.J., Jenkins, C.D. *et al.* (1975). Coronary heart disease in the Western Collaborative Group study; follow-up experience after 8 and a half years. *Journal of the American Medical Association*, 233: 872–7.

Rosenman, R.H., Brand, R.J., Sholtz, R.I. *et al.* (1976). Multivariate prediction of coronary heart disease during 8.5 year follow-up in the Western Collaborative Group study. *The American Journal of Cardiology*, 37: 903–10.

Rosenstock, I.M. (1966). Why people use health services. Milbank *Memorial Fund Quarterly*, 44: 94–124.

Rosenstock, I.M. (1974). The health belief model and preventive health behaviour. *Health Education Monographs*, 2: 354–86.

Rosenzweig, S., Greeson, J.M., Reibel, D.K. *et al.* (2010). Mindfulness-based stress reduction for chronic pain conditions: variation in treatment outcomes and role of home meditation practice. *Journal of Psychosomatic Research*, 68: 29–36.

Ross, D.A., Dick, B. and Ferguson, J. (eds) (2006). *Preventing HIV/AIDS in young people. A systematic review of the evidence from developing countries*. Geneva: World Health Organisation.

Ross, L., Boesen, E.H., Dalton, S.O. and Johansen, C. (2002). Mind and cancer: does psychosocial intervention improve survival and psychological well-being? *European Journal of Cancer*, 38: 1447–57.

Roth, M.L., Tripp, D.A., Harrison, M.H. *et al.* (2007). Demographic and psychosocial predictors of acute perioperative pain for total knee arthroplasty. *Pain Research and Management*, 12: 185–94.

Roth, S. and Cohen, L.J. (1986). Approach avoidance and coping with stress. *American Psychologist*, 41: 813–19.

Rothermund, K. and Brandstädter, J. (2003). Coping with deficits and losses in later life: from compensatory action to accommodation. *Psychology & Aging*, 18: 896–905.

Rotter, J.B. (1966). Generalized expectancies for the internal versus external control of reinforcement. *Psychological Monographs*, 90: 1–28.

Rovelli, M., Palmeri, D., Vossler, E. *et al.* (1989). Noncompliance in organ transplant recipients. *Transplant Proceedings*, 21: 833–4.

Roy, R., Symonds, R.P., Kymar, D.M. *et al.* (2005). The use of denial in an ethnically diverse British cancer population: a cross-sectional study. *British Journal of Cancer*, 91: 1–5.

Royal College of Physicians (1995). *Alcohol and the Public Health*. London: Macmillan.

Royal College of Psychiatrists (2003). *The Mental Health of Students in Higher Education*. London: RCPsych.

Roye, C., Perlmutter Silverman, P. and Krauss, B. (2007). A brief, low-cost, theory-based intervention to promote dual method use by black and Latina female adolescents: a randomized clinical trial. *Health Education and Behavior*, 34: 608–21.

Ruberman, W., Weinblatt, E., Goldberg, J.D. *et al.* (1984). Psychosocial resilience and protective mechanisms. *American Journal of Orthopsychiatry*, 57: 316–30.

Rudat, K. (1994). *Black and Minority Ethnic Groups in England: Health and Lifestyles*. London: Health Education Authority.

Ruiter, R.A.C. and Kok, G. (2005). Saying is not (always) doing: cigarette warning labels are useless. *European Journal of Public Health*, 15: 329.

Ruiter, R.A.C. and Kok, G. (2006). Response to Hammond *et al.* Showing leads to doing, but doing what? The need for experimental pilot-testing. *European Journal of Public Health*, 16: 225.

Russell, M.A., Wilson, C. and Baker, C.D. (1979). Effect of general practitioners' advice against smoking. *British Medical Journal*, 2: 231–5.

Rutter, D.R. (2000). Attendance and reattendance for breast cancer screening: a prospective 3-year test of the theory of planned behaviour. *British Journal of Health Psychology*, 2: 199–216.

Rutter, D.R., Steadman, L., Quine, L. (2006). An implementation intentions intervention to increase uptake of mammography. *Annals of Behavioral Medicine*, 32: 127–34.

Rutter, D. and Quine, L. (2002). *Changing Health Behaviour*. Buckingham: Open University Press.

Rystedt, L.W., Devereux, J. and Furnham, A.F. (2004). Are lay theories of work stress related to distress? A longitudinal study in the British workforce. *Work & Stress*, 18: 245–54.

Sabaté, E. (2003). *Adherence to Long-term Therapies: Evidence for Action*. Geneva: World Health Organzation.

Sackett, D.L. and Haynes, R.B. (eds) (1976). Compliance with therapeutic regimens. Baltimore, MD: Johns Hopkins University Press.

Safer, M.A., Tharps, Q.J., Jackson, T.C. *et al.* (1979). Determinants of three stages of delay in seeking care at a medical setting. *Medical Care*, 7: 11–29.

Safren, S.A., Otto, M.W. and Worth, J.L. (2001). Two strategies to increase adherence to HIV antiretroviral medication: Life-Steps and medication monitoring. *Behaviour Research and Therapy*, 39: 1151–62.

Safren, S.A., Radomsky, A.S., Otto, M.W. *et al.* (2002). Predictors of psychological well-being in a diverse sample of HIV-positive patients receiving highly active antiretroviral therapy. *Psychosomatics*, 43: 478–84.

Salander, P. (2007). Attributions of lung cancer: my own illness is hardly caused by smoking. *Psycho-Oncology*, 16: 587–92.

Salovey, P., Rothman, A.J., Detweiler, J.B. *et al.* (2000). Emotional states and physical health. *American Psychologist*, 55: 110–21.

Sallis, J.F., King, A., Sirard, J. and Albright, C. (2007). Perceived environmental predictors of physical activity over 6 months in adults: activity counseling trial. *Health Psychology*, 26: 701–9.

Samkoff, J.S. and Jacques, C.H. (1991). A review of studies concerning effects of sleep deprivation and fatigue on residents' performance. *Academic Medicine*, 66: 687–93.

Sandblom, G., Varenhorst, E., Rosell, J. *et al.* (2011). Randomised prostate cancer screening trial: 20 year follow-up. *British Medical Journal*, 342: d1539.

Sanders, S.H., Brena, S.F., Spier, C.J. *et al.* (1992). Chronic low back pain patients around the world: cross-cultural similarities and differences. *Journal of Clinical Pain*, 8: 317–23.

Sanderson, C. and Jemmott, J. (1996). Moderation and mediation of HIV-prevention interventions: relationship status, intentions, and condom use among college students. *Journal of Applied Social Psychology*, 26: 2076–99.

Sanderson, C.A. and Yopyk, D.J. (2007). Improving condom use intentions and behavior by changing perceived partner norms: an evaluation of condom promotion videos for college students. *Health Psychology*, 26: 481–7.

Sapolsky, R. (1986). Glucocorticoid toxicity in the hippocampus: reversal by supplementation with brain fuels. *Journal of Neuroscience*, 6: 2240–4.

Sapolsky, R.M. (1994). *Why Zebras Don't Get Ulcers*. New York: W.H. Freeman.

Sapolsky, R.M. (1996). Why stress is bad for your brain. *Science*, 273: 749–50.

Sapolsky, R.M., Krey, L.C. and McEwan, B.S. (1986). The neuroendocrinology of stress and ageing: the glucocorticoid cascade hypothesis. *Endocrine Reviews*, 7: 284–301.

Sapolsky, R.M., Romero, L.M. and Munck, A.U. (2000). How do glucocorticoids influence stress responses? Integrating permissive, suppressive, stimulatory, and preparative actions. *Endocrine Reviews*, 21: 55–89.

Sarason, B.R., Sarason, I.G. and Pierce, G.R. (1990). Traditional views of social support and their impact on assessment. In B.R. Sarason, I.G. Sarason and G.R. Pierce (eds), *Social Support: An Interactional View*. New York: Wiley.

Saremi, A., Hanson, R.L., Tulloch-Reid, M., Williams, D.E. and Knowler, W.C. (2004). Alcohol consumption predicts hypertension but not diabetes. *Journal of Studies of Alcohol*, 65: 184–90.

Sargent-Cox, K.A., Anstey, K.J. and Luszcz, M.A. (2010). Patterns of longitudinal change in older adults' self-rated health: the effect of the point of reference. *Heath Psychology*, 29: 143–52.

Sargent, J.D., Dalton, M. and Beach, M. (2000). Exposure to cigarette promotions and smoking uptake in adolescents: evidence of a dose-response relation. *Tobacco Control*, 9: 163–8.

Sarkar, U., Piette, J.D., Gonzales, R. *et al.* (2007). Preferences for self-management support: findings from a survey of diabetes patients in safety-net health systems. *Patient Education and Counseling*, 70: 102–10.

Sarkeala, T., Heinavaara, S. and Anttila, A. (2008). Organised mammography screening reduces breast cancer mortality: a cohort study from Finland. *International Journal of Cancer*, 122: 614–9.

Sarkisian, C.A., Liu, H.H., Ensrud, K.E. *et al.* (2001). Correlates of attribution of new disability to 'old age'. *Journal of the American Geriatric Society*, 49: 134–41.

Saunders, C. and Baines, M. (1983). *Living with Dying: The Management of Terminal Disease*. Oxford: Oxford University Press.

Saunders, R.P., Pate, R.R., Felton, G. *et al.* (1997). Development of questionnaires to measure psychosocial influences on children's physical activity. *Preventive Medicine*, 26: 241–7.

Sausen, K.P., Lovallo, W.R., Pincomb, G.A. *et al.* (1992). Cardiovascular responses to occupational stress in medical students: a paradigm for ambulatory monitoring studies. *Health Psychology*, 11: 55–60.

Savage, R. and Armstrong, D. (1990). Effect of a general practitioner's consulting style on patients' satisfaction: a controlled study. *British Medical Journal*, 301: 968–70.

Savage, S.A. and Clarke, V.A. (1996). Factors associated with screening mammography and breast self-examination intentions. *Health Education Research*, 11: 409–21.

Savundranayagam, M.Y. and Montgomery, R.J.V. (2010). Impact of role discrepancies on caregiver burden among spouses. *Research on Aging*, 32: 175–99.

Scharloo, M. and Kaptein, A. (1997). Measurement of illness perceptions in patients with chronic somatic illness: a review of the literature. In K.J. Petrie and J. Weinman (eds), *Perceptions of Health and Illness: Current Research and Applications*. London: Harwood Academic.

Scharloo, M., Kaptein, A.A., Weinman, J. *et al.* (1998). Illness perceptions, coping and functioning in patients with rheumatoid arthritis, chronic obstructive pulmonary disease, and psoriasis. *Journal of Psychosomatic Research*, 44: 573–85.

Scheffler, R.M., Brown, T.T., Syme, L. *et al.* (2008). Community-level social capital and recurrence of acute coronary syndrome. *Social Science and Medicine*, 66: 1603–13.

Scheier, M.F. and Carver, C.S. (1985). Optimism, coping and health: assessment and implications of generalized outcome expectancies. *Health Psychology*, 4: 219–47.

Scheier, M.F. and Carver, C.S. (1992). Effects of optimism on psychological and physical well-being: theoretical overview and empirical update. *Cognitive Therapy Research*, 16: 201–28.

Scheier, M.F., Weintraub, J.K. and Carver, C.S. (1986). coping with stress: divergent strategies of optimists and pessimists. *Journal of Personality and Social Psychology*, 51: 1257–1264.

Scherwitz, L., Perkins, L., Chesney, M. *et al.* (1992). Hostility and health behaviours in young adults: the CARDIA study. *American Journal of Epidemiology*, 136: 136–45.

Schiaffino, K.M. and Cea, C.D. (1995). Assessing chronic illness representations: the implicit models of illness questionnaire. *Journal of Behavioral Medicine*, 18: 531–48.

Schiaffino, K.M. and Revenson, T.A. (1992). The role of perceived self-efficacy, perceived control, and causal attributions in adaptation to rheumatoid arthritis: distinguishing mediator vs moderator effects. *Personality and Social Psychology Bulletin*, 18: 709–18.

Schlenk, E.A., Dunbar-Jacob, J. and Engberg, S. (2004). Medication non-adherence among older adults: a review of strategies and interventions for improvement. *Journal of Gerontological Nursing*, 30: 33–43.

Schmaling, K.B., Smith, W.R. and Buchwald, D.S. (2000). Significant other responses are associated with fatigue and functional status among patients with chronic fatigue syndrome. *Psychosomatic Medicine*, 62: 444–50.

Schmid Mast, M., Hall, J.A., Roter, D.L. (2007). Disentangling physician sex and physician communication style: their effects on patient satisfaction in a virtual medical visit. *Patient Education and Counseling*, 68: 16–22.

Schneiderman, N., Antoni, M.H. and Saab, P.G. (2001). Health psychology: psychosocial and bio-behavioral aspects of chronic disease management. *Annual Review of Psychology*, 52: 555–80.

Schnipper, H.H. (2001). Life after breast cancer. *Journal of Clinical Oncology*, 19: 3581–4.

Schofield, M.J., Lynagh, M. and Mishra, G. (2003). Evaluation of a Health Promoting Schools program to reduce smoking in Australian secondary schools. *Health Education and Research*, 18: 678–92.

Schofield, P.E., Butow, P.N., Thompson, J.F. *et al.* (2003). Psychological responses of patients receiving a diagnosis of cancer. *Annals of Oncology*, 14: 48–56.

Scholte op Reimer, J., de Haan, R.J., Rijners, P.T. *et al.* (1998). The burden of caregiving in partners of long-term stroke survivors. *Stroke*, 29: 1605–11.

Schou, I., Ekeberg, Ø. and Ruland, C.M. (2005). The mediating role of appraisal and coping in the relationship between optimism–pessimism and quality of life. *Psycho-Oncology*, 14: 718–27.

Schou, I., Ekeberg, O., Rulan, C.M. *et al.* (2004). Pessimism as a predictor of emotional morbidity one year following breast cancer surgery. *Psycho-Oncology*, 13: 309–20.

Schouten, B.C., Hoogstraten, J. and Eijkman, M.A. (2003). Patient participation during dental consultations: the influence of patients' characteristics and dentists' behavior. *Community and Dental Oral Epidemiology*, 31: 368–77.

Schrimshaw, E.W., Siegel, K. and Lekas, H.M. (2005). Changes in attitudes toward antiviral medication: a comparison of women living with HIV/AIDS in the pre-HAART and HAART Eras. *AIDS and Behavior*, 9: 267–9.

Schröder, C., Johnston, M., Morrison, V. *et al.* (2007). Health condition, impairment, activity limitations: relationship with emotions and control cognitions in people with disabling conditions. *Rehabilitation Psychology*, 52: 280–9.

Schroevers, M., Kraaij, V. and Garnefski, N. (2008). How do cancer patients manage unattainable personal goals and regulate their emotions? *British Journal of Health Psychology*, 13: 551–62.

Schulz, R., Bookwala, J., Knapp, J.E. *et al.* (1996). Pessimism, age, and cancer mortality. *Psychology and Aging*, 11: 304–9.

Schulz, R., O'Brien, A., Bookwala, J. *et al.* (1995). Psychiatric and physical morbidity effects of dementia caregiving: prevalence, correlates and causes. *The Gerontologist*, 35: 771–91.

Schulz, R. and Quittner, A.L. (1998). Caregiving for children and adults with chronic conditions: introduction to the special issue. *Health Psychology*, 17: 107–11.

Schulz, R., Tompkins, C.A. and Rau, M.T. (1988). A longitudinal study of the psychosocial impact of stroke on primary support persons. *Psychology and Aging*, 3: 131–41.

Schulz, U. and Mohamed, N.E. (2004). Turning the tide: benefit finding after cancer surgery. *Social Science and Medicine*, 59: 653–62.

Schur, E.A., Sanders, M. and Steiner, H. (2000). Body dissatisfaction and dieting in young children. *International Journal of Eating Disorders*, 27: 74–82.

Schwartz, B.S., Stewart, W.F., Simon, D. *et al.* (1998). Epidemiology of tension-type headache. *Journal of the American Medical Association*, 279: 381–3.

Schwartz, C., Sprangers, M., Carey, A. *et al.* (2004). Exploring response shift in longitudinal data. *Psychology & Health*, 9: 161–80.

Schwartz, G.E. and Weiss, S. (1977). What is behavioral medicine? *Psychosomatic Medicine*, 36: 377–81.

Schwarzer, R. (1992). Self efficacy in the adoption and maintenance of health behaviours: theoretical approaches and a new model. In R. Schwarzer (ed.), *Self Efficacy: Thought Control of Action*. Washington, DC: Hemisphere.

Schwarzer, R. (1994). Optimism, vulnerability, and self-beliefs as health-related cognitions: a systematic overview. *Psychology and Health*, 9: 161–80.

Schwarzer, R. (2001). Social-cognitive factors in changing health-related behavior. *Current Directions in Psychological Science*, 10: 47–51.

Schwarzer, R., Jerusalem, M. and Hahn, A. (1994). Unemployment, social support and health complaints: a longitudinal study of stress in East German refugees. *Journal of Community and Applied Social Psychology*, 4: 31–45.

Schwarzer, R. and Knoll, N. (2007). Functional roles of social support within the stress and coping process: a theoretical and empirical overview. *International Journal of Psychology*, 42: 243–52.

Schwarzer, R. and Leppin, A. (1991). Social support and health: a theoretical and empirical overview. *Journal of Social and Personal Relationships*, 8: 99–127.

Schwarzer, R. and Luszczynska, A. (2008). How to overcome health-Compromising behaviours: the Health Action Process approach. *European Psychologist*, 13(2): 141–51.

Schwarzer, R., Luszczynska, A., Ziegelmann, P. *et al.* (2008). Social-cognitive predictors of physical exercise adherence: three longitudinal studies in rehabilitation. *Health Psychology*, 27: 854–63.

Schwarzer, R. and Renner, B. (2000). Social-cognitive predictors of health behavior: action self-efficacy and coping self-efficacy. *Health Psychology*, 19: 487–95.

Scollay, P., Doucett, M., Perry, M. *et al.* (1992). AIDS education of college students: the effect of an HIV-positive lecturer. *AIDS Education and Prevention*, 4: 160–71.

Scottish Executive (1999). *Fair Shares for All.* Report of the National Review of Resource Allocation for the NHS in Scotland, chaired by Professor Sir John Arbuthnott, principal and vice-chancellor of Strathclyde University. Edinburgh: HMSO.

Scully, J.A., Tosi, H. and Banning, K. (2000). Life events checklists: revisiting the Social Readjustment Rating Scale after 30 years. *Educational and Psychological Measurement*, 60: 864–76.

Seale, C. and Kelly, M. (1997). A comparison of hospice and hospital care for the spouses of people who die. *Palliative Care*, 11: 101–6.

Searle, A. and Bennett, P. (2001). Psychological factors and inflammatory bowel disease: a review of a decade of literature. *Psychology, Health and Medicine*, 6: 121–35.

Searle, B., Bright, J.E.H. and Bochner, S. (2001). Helping people to sort it out: the role of social support in the Job Strain Model. *Work and Stress*, 15: 328–46.

Sears, S.F., Sowell, L.D., Kuhl, E.A. *et al.* (2007). The ICD shock and stress management program: a randomized trial of psychosocial treatment to optimize quality of life in ICD patients. *Pacing and Clinical Electrophysiology*, 30: 858–64.

Segal, Z.V., Williams, J.M.G. and Teasdale, J.D. (2002). *Mindfulness-Based Cognitive Therapy for Depression: A New Approach to Preventing Relapse*. New York: Guilford.

Segan, C.J., Borland, R. and Greenwood, K.M. (2002). Do transtheoretical model measures predict the transition from preparation to action in smoking cessation? *Psychology and Health*, 17: 417–35.

Segerstrom, S.C. and Smith, T.W. (2006). Physiological pathways from personality to health: the cardiovascular and immune systems. In M.E. Vollrath (ed.), *Handbook of Personality and Health*. Chichester: Wiley, pp. 175–94.

Segestrom, S.C. and Miller, G.E. (2004). Psychological stress and the human immune system: a meta-analytic study of 30 years of enquiry. *Psychological Bulletin*, 130: 601–30.

Segestrom, S.C., Taylor, S.E., Kemeny, M.E. *et al.* (1998). Optimism is associated with mood, coping, and immune change in response to stress. *Journal of Personality and Social Psychology*, 74: 1646–55.

Seligman, M.E.P. (2003). Positive psychology: fundamental assumptions. *The Psychologist*, 16: 126–7.

Seligman, M.E.P. and Csikszentmihalyi, M. (2000). Positive psychology: an introduction. *American Psychologist*, 55: 5–14.

Selye, H. (1956). *The Stress of Life*. New York: McGraw-Hill.

Selye, H. (1974). *Stress without Distress*. Philadelphia, PA: Lipincott.

Selye, H. (1991). History and present status of the stress concept. In A. Monat and R.S. Lazarus (eds), *Stress and Coping*. New York: Columbia University Press.

Semmer, N.K. (2006). Personality, stress, and coping. In M.E. Vollrath (ed.), *Handbook of Personality and Health*. London: Wiley, pp. 73–113.

Serour, M., Alqhenaei, H., Al-Saqabi, S. *et al.* (2007). Cultural factors and patients' adherence to lifestyle measures. *British Journal of General Practice*, 57: 291–5.

Shaffer, J.W., Graves, P.L., Swank, R.T. and Pearson, T.A. (1987). Clustering of personality traits in youth and the subsequent development of cancer among physicians. *Journal of Behavioral Medicine*, 10: 441–7.

Shakeshaft, A.P., Bowman, J.A. and Sanson-Fisher, R.W. (1999). A comparison of two retrospective measures of weekly alcohol consumption: diary and quantity/frequency index. *Alcohol and Alcoholism*, 34: 636–45.

Shankar, A., McMunn, A. and Steptoe, A. (2010). Health-related behaviors in older adults' relationships with socioeconomic status. *American Journal of Preventive Medicine*, 38: 39–46.

Shaper, A.G., Wannamethee, G. and Walker, M. (1994). Alcohol and coronary heart disease: a perspective from the British Regional Heart Study. *International Journal of Epidemiology*, 23: 482–94.

Shapiro, F. (1995). *Eye Movement Desensitisation and Reprocessing: Basic Principles*. New York: Guilford Press.

Shapiro, S.L., Oman, D., Thoresen, C.E. *et al.* (2008). Cultivating mindfulness: effects on well-being. *Journal of Clinical Psychology*, 64: 840–62.

Sharma, S., Malarcher, A.M., Giles, W.H. *et al.* (2004). Racial, ethnic and socioeconomic disparities in the clustering of cardiovascular disease risk factors. *Ethnicity and Disease*, 14: 43–8.

Sharp, T.J. (2001). Chronic pain: a reformulation of the cognitive-behavioural model. *Behaviour Research and Therapy*, 39: 787–800.

Sheeran, P. (2002). Intention–behaviour relations: a conceptual and empirical review. In M. Hewstone and W. Stroebe (eds), *European Review of Social Psychology*, Vol. 11. Chichester: Wiley.

Sheeran, P. and Abraham, C. (1996). The health belief model. In M. Conner and P. Norman (eds), *Predicting Health Behaviour*. Buckingham: Open University Press.

Sheeran, P., Abraham, C.S. and Orbell, S. (1999). Psychosocial correlates of heterosexual condom use: a meta-analysis. *Psychological Bulletin*, 125: 90–132.

Sheeran, P. and Orbell, S. (1996). How confidently can we infer health beliefs from questionnaire responses? *Psychology and Health*, 11: 273–90.

Sheeran, P. and Orbell, S. (1998). Do intentions predict condom use? Meta-analysis and examination of six moderator variables. *British Journal of Social Psychology*, 37: 231–50.

Sheeran, P. and Orbell, S. (1999). Implementation intentions and repeated behaviour: augmenting the predictive validity of the theory of planned behaviour. *European Journal of Social Psychology*, 29: 349–69.

Sheeran, P. and Orbell, S. (2000). Using implementation intentions to increase attendance for cervical cancer screening. *Health Psychology*, 19: 283–9.

Sheffield, D., Biles, P.L., Orom, H., Maixner, W. and Sheps, D.S. (2000). Race and sex differences in cutaneous pain perception. *Psychosomatic Medicine*, 62: 517–23.

Sheps, D.S. (2007). Psychological stress and myocardial ischemia: Understanding the link and implications. *Psychosomatic Medicine*, 69: 491–492.

Sherbourne, C.D., Hays, R.D., Ordway, L. *et al.* (1992). Antecedents of adherence to medical recommendations: results from the Medical Outcomes Study. *Journal of Behavioral Medicine*, 15: 447–68.

Sherman, A.C. and Simonton, S. (2001). Coping with cancer in the family. *The Family Journal: Counselling and Therapy for Couples and Families*, 9: 193–200.

Sherr, L. (1987). An evaluation of the UK government health education campaign on AIDS. *Psychology and Health*, 1: 61–72.

Sherr, L., Lampe, F.C., Clucas, C. *et al.* (2010). Self-reported non-adherence to ART and virological outcome in a multi-clinic UK study. *AIDS Care*, 23: 1–7.

Sherwood, A. and Turner, J.R. (1992). A conceptual and methodological overview of cardiovascular reactivity research. In J.R. Turner, A. Sherwood and K.C. Light (eds), *Individual Differences in Cardiovascular Responses to Stress*. New York, Plenum.

Shewchuck, R.M., Richards, J.S. and Elliott, T.R. (1998). Dynamic processes in health outcomes among caregivers of patients with spinal cord injuries. *Health Psychology*, 17: 125–9.

Shifren, K. and Hooker, K. (1995). Stability and change in optimism: a study among spouse caregivers. *Experimental Aging Research*, 21: 59–76.

Shilts, R. (2000). *And the Band Played on: Politics, People and the AIDS Epidemic*. New York: St Martin's Press.

Shinar, D., Schechtman, E. and Compton, R. (1999). Trends in safe driving behaviors and in relation to trends in health maintenance behaviors in the USA: 1985–1995. *Accident Analysis and Prevention*, 31: 497–503.

Shipley, B.A., Weiss, A., der, G., Taylor, M.D. and Deary, I.J. (2007). Neuroticism, extraversion and mortality in the UK Health and Lifestyle Survey: a 21-year prospective cohort study. *Psychosomatic Medicine*, 69: 923–31.

Siegel, K. and Gorey, E. (1997). HIV infected women: barriers to AZT use. *Social Science and Medicine*, 45: 15–22.

Siegel, K. and Schrimshaw, E.W. (2005). Stress, appraisal, and coping: a comparison of HIV-infected women in the pre-HAART and HAART eras. *Journal of Psychosomatic Research*, 58: 225–33.

Siegel, K., Karus, D.G., Raveis, V.H. *et al.* (1996). Depressive distress among the spouses of terminally ill cancer patients. *Cancer Practice*, 4: 25–30.

Siegel, K., Scrimshaw, E.W. and Dean, L. (1999). Symptom interpretation and medication adherence among late middle-age and older HIV-infected adults. *Journal of Health Psychology*, 4: 247–57.

Siegert, R.J. and Abernethy, D.A. (2005). Depression in multiple sclerosis: a review. *Journal of Neurology, Neurosurgery and Psychiatry*, 76: 469–75.

Siegrist, J., Dagmar Starke, D., Chandola, T. *et al.* (2004). The measurement of effort–reward imbalance at work: European comparisons. *Social Science and Medicine*, 58: 1483–99.

Siegrist, J., Peter, R., Junge, A. *et al.* (1990). Low status control, high effort at work and ischemic heart disease: prospective evidence from blue collar men. *Social Science and Medicine*, 35: 1127–34.

Sieverding, M., Weidner, G., von Volkmann, B. *et al.* (2005). Cardiovascular reactivity in a simulated job interview: the role of gender role self-concept. *International Journal of Behavioral Medicine*, 12: 1–10.

Sikkema, K.J., Kelly, J.A., Winett, R.A. *et al.* (2000). Outcomes of a randomized community-level HIV-prevention intervention for women living in 18 low-income housing developments. *American Journal of Public Health*, 90: 53–7.

Silverman, D. (1987). *Communication and Medical Practice: Social Relations and the Clinic*. London: Sage.

Simon, J.A., Carmody, T.P., Hudes, E.S. *et al.* (2003). Intensive smoking cessation counseling versus minimal counseling among hospitalized smokers treated with transdermal nicotine replacement: a randomized trial. *American Journal of Medicine*, 114: 555–62.

Simoni, J.M., Pantalone, D.W., Plummer, M.D. *et al.* (2007). A randomized controlled trial of a peer support intervention targeting antiretroviral medication adherence and depressive symptomatology in HIV-positive men and women. *Health Psychology*, 26: 488–95.

Singh, R.B., Sharma, J.P., Rastogi, V. *et al.* (1997). Prevalence of coronary artery disease and coronary risk factors in rural and urban populations of north India. *European Heart Journal*, 18: 1728–35.

Singh, R.K., Panday, H.P. and Singh, R.H. (2003). Irritable bowel syndrome: challenges ahead. *Current Science*, 84: 1525–33.

Sivell, S., Iredale, R., Gray, J. and Coles, B. (2007). Cancer genetic risk assessment for individuals at risk of familial breast cancer. *Cochrane Database of Systematic Reviews*, issue 2, art. no.: CD003721. doi 10.1002/14651858.CD003721.

Skarstein, J., Aass, N., Fossa, S.D. *et al.* (2000). Anxiety and depression in cancer patients: relation between the Hospital Anxiety and Depression Scale and the European Organization for Research and Treatment of Cancer Core Quality of Life Questionnaire. *Journal of Psychosomatic Research*, 49: 27–34.

Skelton, D.A., Young, A., Walker, A. *et al.* (1999). *Physical Activity in Later Life: Further Analysis of the Allied Dunbar National Fitness Survey and the Health Education Authority National Survey of Activity and Health*. London: Health Education Authority.

Skevington, S.M. (1990). A standardised scale to measure beliefs about controlling pain (BPCQ): a preliminary study. *Psychology and Health*, 4: 221–32.

Skoffer, B. (2007). Low back pain in 15- to 16-year-old children in relation to school furniture and carrying of the school bag. *Spine*, 32: E713–7.

Slavin, S., Batrouney, C. and Murphy, D. (2007). Fear appeals and treatment side-effects: an effective combination for HIV prevention? *AIDS Care*, 19: 130–7.

Sloper, P. (2000). Predictors of distress in parents of children with cancer: a prospective study. *Journal of Pediatric Psychology*, 25: 79–92.

Sluijs, E.M., Kok, G.J. and van der Zee, J. (1993). Correlates of exercise compliance in physical therapy, *Physical Therapy*, 73: 771–782.

Smedslund, G. and Rundmo, T. (1999). Is Grossarth-Maticek's coronary prone type II an independent predictor of myocardial infarction? *Personality and Individual Differences*, 27: 1231–42.

Smee, C., Parsonage, M., Anderson, R. *et al.* (1992). *Effects of Tobacco Advertising on Tobacco Consumption: A discussion Document Reviewing the Evidence*. London: Department of Health.

Smith, A. and Roberts, K. (2003). Interventions for post-traumatic stress disorder and psychological distress in emergency ambulance personnel: a review of the literature. *Emergency Medical Journal*, 20: 75–8.

Smith, B.W., Shelley, B.M., Dalen, J. *et al.* (2008). A pilot study comparing the effects of mindfulness-based and cognitive-behavioral stress reduction. *Journal of Alternative and Complementary Medicine*, 14: 251–8.

Smith, C.A. and Lazarus, R.S. (1993). Appraisal components, core relational themes, and the emotions. *Cognition and Emotion*, 7: 233–69.

Smith, C.A., Wallston, K.A., Dwyer, K.A. *et al.* (1997). Beyond good or bad coping: a multi-dimensional examination of coping with pain in persons with rheumatoid arthritis. *Annals of Behavioral Medicine*, 19: 11–21.

Smith, D.A., Ness, E.M., Herbert, R. *et al.* (2005). Abdominal diameter index: a more powerful anthropometric measure for prevalent coronary heart disease risk in adult males. *Diabetes, Obesity and Metabolism*, 7: 370–80.

Smith, D.M., Loewenstein, G., Jankovic, A. and Ubel, P.A. (2009). Happily hopeless: adaptation to a permanent, but not to a temporary, disability. *Health Psychology*, 28: 787–91.

Smith, H., Gooding, S., Brown, R. *et al.* (1998). Evaluation of readability and accuracy of information leaflets in general practices for patients with asthma. *British Medical Journal*, 317: 264–5.

Smith, J.A. (1995). Semi-structured interviewing and qualitative analysis. In J.A. Smith, R. Harre and L. van Langerhove (eds). *Rethinking Methods in Psychology*. London: Sage, pp. 9–26.

Smith, J.A. (1996). Beyond the divide between cognition and discourse: using interpretative phenomenological analysis in health psychology. *Psychology and Health*, 11: 261–71.

Smith, L.A. and Foxcroft, D.R. (2009). The effect of alcohol advertising, marketing and portrayal on drinking behaviour in young people: systematic review of prospective cohort studies. *BMC Public Health*, 9: 51.

Smith, M.Y., Redd, W.H., Peyer, C., Peyser, C. and Vogl, D. (1999). Post-traumatic stress disorder in cancer: a review. *Psycho-Oncology*, 8: 521–37.

Smith, T.W. (1994). Concepts and methods on the study of anger, hostility and health. In A.W. Siegman and T.W. Smith (eds), *Anger, Hostility and the Heart*. Hillsdale, NJ: Lawrence Erlbaum.

Smith, T.W., Gallo, L.C. and Ruiz, J.M. (2003). Toward a social psychophysiology of cardiovascular reactivity: interpersonal concepts and methods in the study of stress and coronary disease. In J. Suls and K. Wallston (eds), *Social Psychological Foundations of Health and Illness*. Oxford: Blackwell.

Smolderen, K.G. and Vingerhoets, A. (2010). Hospitalisation and stressful medical procedures. In D. French, K. Vedhara, A.A. Kaptein and J. Weinamn (eds), *Health Psychology*, 2nd edn. Chichester: Wiley, pp. 232–44.

Smyth, J.M., Stone, A.A., Hurewitz, A. and Kaell, A. (1999). Effects of writing about stressful experiences on symptom reduction in patients with asthma or rheumatoid arthritis: a randomized trial. *Journal of the American Medical Association*, 281: 1304–9.

Snell, J.L. and Buck, E.L. (1996). Increasing cancer screening: a meta analysis. *Preventive Medicine*, 25: 702–7.

Sniehotta, F.F., Scholz, U., Schwarzer, R. (2005). Bridging the intention–behavior gap: planning, self-efficacy and action control in the adoption and maintenance of physical exercise. *Psychology & Health*, 20: 143–60.

Sniehotta, F.F., Scholz, U., Schwarzer, R. (2006). Action plans and coping plans for physical exercise: a longitudinal intervention study in cardiac rehabilitation. *British Journal of Health Psychology*, 11: 23–37.

Sniehotta, F.F., Scholz, U., Schwarzer, R., Fuhrmann, B., Kiwus, U. and Voller, H. (2005). Long-term effects of two psychological interventions on physical exercise and self-regulation following coronary rehabilitation. *International Journal of Behavioral Medicine*, 2: 244–55.

Snoek, H.M., Engels, R.C., Janssen, J.M. *et al.* (2007). Parental behaviour and adolescents' emotional eating. *Appetite*, 49: 223–30.

Snow, P.C. and Bruce, D.D. (2003). Cigarette smoking in teenage girls: exploring the role of peer reputations, self concept and coping. *Health Education Research*, 18: 439–52.

Snyder, C. and Lopez, S.J. (2005). *Handbook of Positive Psychology*. New York: Oxford University Press.

Snyder, C.R. (1989). Reality negotiation: from excuses to hope and beyond. *Journal of Social and Clinical Psychology*, 8: 130–57.

Snyder, C.R., Irving, L.M. and Anderson, J.R. (1991). Hope and health. In D.R. Forsyth and C.R. Snyder (eds), *Handbook of Social and Clinical Psychology: The Health Perspective*. Elmsford, NY: Pergamon Press, pp. 285–305.

Snyder, C.R., Lehman, K.A., Kluck, B. *et al.* (2006). Hope for rehabilitation and vice versa. *Rehabilitation Psychology*, 51: 89–112.

Soames-Job, R.F. (1988). Effective and ineffective use of fear in health promotion campaigns. *American Journal of Public Health*, 78: 163–7.

Solberg Nes, L., Carlson, C.R., Crofford, L.J. *et al.* (2011). Individual difference and self-regulatory fatigue: optimism, conscientiousness, and self-consciousess. *Personality and Individual Differences*, 50: 475–80.

Solberg Nes, L. and Segestrom, S.C. (2006). Dispositional optimism and coping: a meta-analytic review. *Personality and Social Psychology Review*, 10: 235–51.

Solmes, M. and Turnbull, O.H. (2002). *The Brain and the Inner Mind: An Introduction to the Neuroscience of Subjective Wellbeing*. New York: Other Press/Karnac.

Solomon, R.L. (1977). Addiction: an opponent-process theory of acquired motivation: the affective dynamics of addiction. In J.D. Maser (ed.), *Psychopathology: Experimental Models*. San Francisco, CA: W.H. Freeman.

Soo, H., Burney, S. and Basten, C. (2009). The role of rumination in affective distress in people with a chronic physical illness: a review of the literature and theoretical formulation. *Journal of Health Psychology*, 14: 956–66.

Soons, P. and Denollet, J. (2009). Medical psychology services in Dutch general hospitals: state of the art developments and recommendations for the future. *Journal of Clinical Psychology in Medical Settings*, 16: 161–8.

Sorensen, G., Morris, D.M., Hunt, M.K. *et al.* (1992). Work-site nutrition intervention and employees' dietary habits: the Treatwell program. *American Journal of Public Health*, 82: 877–80.

Sorensen, G., Stoddard, A., Hunt, M.K. *et al.* (1998). The effects of a health promotion–health protection intervention on behavior change: the WellWorks Study. *American Journal of Public Health*, 88: 1685–90.

Sorensen, G., Stoddard, A., Peterson, K. *et al.* (1999). Increasing fruit and vegetable consumption through worksites and families in the Treatwell 5-a-day study. *American Journal of Public Health*, 89: 54–60.

Sorensen, G., Stoddard, A., Quintiliani, L. *et al.* (2010). Tobacco use cessation and weight management among motor freight workers: results of the gear up for health study. *Cancer Causes and Control*, 21(12): 2113–22.

Soria, R., Legido, A., Escolano, C. *et al.* (2006). A randomised controlled trial of motivational interviewing for smoking cessation. *British Journal of General Practice*, 56: 768–74.

Sorlie, P.D., Backlund, E. and Keller, J.B. (1995). US mortality by economic, demographic, and social characteristics: the National Longitudinal Mortality Study. *American Journal of Public Health*, 85: 949–56.

Sparks, P., Conner, M., James, R. *et al.* (2001). Ambivalence about health-related behaviours: an exploration in the domain of food choice. *British Journal of Health Psychology*, 6: 53–68.

Sparks, P. and Shepherd, R. (1992). Self-identity and the theory of planned behaviour: assessing the role of identification with green consumerism. *Social Psychology Quarterly*, 55: 388–99.

Speca, M., Carlson, L.E., Goodey, E. *et al.* (2000). A randomized wait-list controlled clinical trial: the effect of mindfulness meditation-based stress reduction program on mood and symptoms of stress in cancer patients. *Psychosomatic Medicine*, 62: 613–22.

Speisman, J.C., Lazarus, R.S., Mordkoff, A. *et al.* (1964). Experimental reduction of stress based on ego defense theory. *Journal of Abnormal and Social Psychology*, 68: 367–80.

Spence, M.J. and Moss-Morris, R. (2007). The cognitive behavioural model of irritable bowel syndrome: a prospective investigation of patients with gastroenteritis. *Gut*, 56: 1066–71.

Spiegel, D. (1992). Effects of psychosocial support on patients with metastatic breast cancer. *Journal of Psychosocial Oncology*, 10: 113–20.

Spiegel, D. (2001). Mind matters: coping and cancer progression. *Journal of Psychosomatic Research*, 50: 287–90.

Spiegel, D. and Giese-Davis, J. (2003). Depression and cancer: mechanisms and disease progression. *Biological Psychiatry*, 54: 269–82.

Spiegel, D., Butler, L.D., Giese-Davis, J. *et al.* (2007). Effects of supportive-expressive group therapy on survival of patients with metastatic breast cancer: a randomized prospective trial. *Cancer*, 110: 1130–8.

Spiegel, D., Bloom, J.R. and Yalom, I. (1981). Group support for patients with metastatic cancer: a randomized outcome study. *Archives of General Psychiatry*, 38: 527–33.

Spiegel, D., Bloom, J.R., Kraemer, H.C. *et al.* (1989). Effect of psychosocial treatment on survival of patients with metastatic breast cancer. *The Lancet*, 14(2): 888–91.

Spiller, R., Aziz, Q., Creed, F. *et al.* (2007). Clinical Services Committee of The British Society of Gastroenterology. Guidelines on the irritable bowel syndrome: mechanisms and practical management. *Gut*, 56: 1770–98.

Spolentini, I., Gianni, W., Repetto, L. *et al.* (2008). Depression and cancer: an unexplored and unresolved emergent issue in elderly patients. *Critical Reviews in Oncology/Hematology*, 65: 143–55.

Sreeramareddy, C.T., Shankar, R.P., Sreekumaran, B.V. *et al.* (2006). Care seeking behaviour for childhood illness: a questionnaire survey in western Nepal. *BioMedCentre International Health & Human Rights*, 6: 7. Published online 23 May 2006, doi: 10.1186/1472-698X-6-7.

Stainton Rogers, W. (1991). *Explaining Health and Illness: An Exploration of Diversity*. London: Wheatsheaf.

Stamler, J., Daviglus, M.L., Garside, D.B. *et al.* (2000). Relationship of baseline serum cholesterol levels in 3 large cohorts of younger men to long-term coronary, cardiovascular and all-cause mortality, and to longevity. *Journal of the American Medical Association*, 19: 284(3): 311–18.

Stansfeld, S.A., Bosma, H., Hemingway, H. *et al.* (1998). Psychosocial work characteristics and social support as predictors of SF-36 health functioning: the Whitehall II study. *Psychosomatic Medicine*, 60: 247–55.

Stanton, A.L., Collins, C.A. and Sworowski, L.A. (2001). Adjustment to chronic illness: theory and research. In A. Baum, T.A. Revenson and J.E. Singer (eds), *Handbook of Health Psychology*. Maah, NJ: Lawrence Erlbaum, pp. 387–403.

Stanton, A.L., Danoff-Burg, S. and Huggins, M.E. (2002a). The first year after breast cancer diagnosis: hope and coping strategies as predictors of adjustment. *Psycho-Oncology*, 11: 93–102.

Stanton, A.L., Danoff-Burg, S., Sworowski, L.A. *et al.* (2002b). Randomized, controlled trial of written emotional expression and benefit finding in breast cancer patients. *Journal of Clinical Oncology*, 20: 4160–8.

Stanton, A.L., Ganz, P.A., Rowland, J.H. *et al.* (2005). Promoting adjustment after treatment for cancer. *Cancer*, 104: 2608–13.

Stanton, A.L., Kirk, K.B., Cameron, C.L. *et al.* (2000). Coping through emotional approach: scale construction and validation. *Journal of Personality and Social Psychology*, 78: 1150–69.

Stanton, A.L., Revenson, T.A. and Tennen, H. (2007). Health psychology: psychological adjustment to chronic disease. *Annual Review of Psychology*, 58: 565–92.

Stanton, A.L. and Snider, P.R. (1993). Coping with a breast cancer diagnosis: a prospective study. *Health Psychology*, 12: 16.

Starace, F., Bartoli, L., Aloisi, M.S. *et al.* (2000). Cognitive and affective disorders associated to HIV infection in the HAART era: findings from the NeuroICONA study. Cognitive impairment and depression in HIV/AIDS. *Acta Psychiatria Scandinavica*, 106: 20–6.

Stead, L.F., Bergson, G. and Lancaster, T. (2008). Physician advice for smoking cessation. *Cochrane Database of Systematic Reviews*, 2: CD000165.

Stead, M., Hastings, G. and Eadie, D. (2002). The challenge of evaluating complex interventions: a framework for evaluating media advocacy. *Health Education Research*, 17: 351–64.

Steadman, L. and Quine, L. (2004). Encouraging young males to perform testicular self-examination: a simple, but effective, implementations intervention. *British Journal of Health Psychology*, 9: 479–88.

Steadman, L., Rutter, D.R. and Field, S. (2002). Individually elicited versus modal normative beliefs in predicting attendance at breast screening: examining the role of belief salience in the theory of planned behaviour. *British Journal of Health Psychology*, 7: 317–30.

Steffen, L.M., Arnett, D.K. and Blackburn, H. (2006). Population trends in leisure-time physical activity: Minnesota Heart Survey, 1980–2000. *Medicine and Science in Sports and Exercise*, 38: 1716–23.

Steinbrook, R. (2006). The potential of human papillomavirus vaccines. *New England Journal of Medicine*, 354: 1109–12.

Stenner, P.H.D., Cooper, D. and Skevington, S. (2003). Putting the Q into quality of life: the identification of subjective constructions of health-related quality of life using Q methodology. *Social Science and Medicine*, 57: 2161–72.

Stephens, C., Long, N. and Miller, N. (1997). The impact of trauma and social support on post traumatic stress disorder: a study of New Zealand police officers. *Journal of Criminal Justice*, 25: 303–14.

Stephens, M.R., Gaskell, A.L., Gent, C. *et al.* (2008). Prospective randomised clinical trial of providing patients with audiotape recordings of their oesophagogastric cancer consultations. *Patient Education and Counselling*, 72: 218–22.

Stephenson, J., Bauman, A., Armstrong, T. *et al.* (2000). *The Costs of Illness Attributable to Physical Inactivity in Australia: A Preliminary Study*. Canberra: Commonwealth Government of Australia.

Steptoe, A., Doherty, S., Rink, E. *et al.* (1999). Behavioural counselling in general practice for the promotion of healthy behaviour among adults at increased risk of coronary heart disease: randomised trial. *British Journal of Medicine*, 319: 943–7.

Steptoe, A., O'Donnell, K., Marmot, M. and Wardle, J. (2008). Positive affect and psychosocial processes related to health. *British Journal of Psychology*, 99: 211–27.

Steptoe, A., Owen, N., Kunz-Ebrecht, S.R. and Brydon, L. (2004b). Loneliness and neuroendocrine, cardiovascular, and inflammatory stress responses in middle-aged men and women. *Psychoneuroendocrinology*, 29: 593–611.

Steptoe, A., Pollard, T. and Wardle, J. (1995). Development of a measure of the motives underlying the selection of food: the food choice questionnaire. *Appetite 1995*, 25: 267–84.

Steptoe, A., Siegrist, J., Kirschbaum, C. and Marmot, M. (2004a). Effort–reward imbalance, overcommittment, and measures of cortisol and blood pressure over the working day. *Psychosomatic Medicine*, 66, 323–9.

Steptoe, A., Wardlaw, J. and Marmot, M. (2005). Positive affect and health-related neuroendocrine, cardiovascular, and inflammatory processes. *Proceedings of the National Academy of Sciences USA*, 102: 6508–12.

Steptoe, A., Wardle, J., Fuller, R. *et al.* (1997). Leisure-time physical exercise: prevalence, attitudinal correlates and behavioural correlates among young Europeans from 21 countries. *Preventive Medicine*, 26: 845–54.

Steptoe, A., Willemsen, G., Owen, N. *et al.* (2001). Acute mental stress elicits delayed increases in circulating inflammatory cytokines. *Clinical Science* (London), 101: 185–92.

Sterba, K.R., DeVellis, R.F., Lewis, M. *et al.* (2008). Effect of couple illness perception congruence on psychological adjustment in women with rheumatoid arthritis. *Health Psychology*, 27: 221–9.

Sterling, P. and Eyer, J. (1988). Allostasis: a new paradigm to explain arousal pathology. In S. Fisher and J. Reason (eds), *Handbook of Life Stress, Cognition and Health*. Oxford: John Wiley, pp. 629–49.

Sterne, J.A.C. and Davey-Smith, G. (2001). Sifting the evidence – what's wrong with significance tests? *British Medical Journal*, 322: 226–31.

Stevenson, M., Palamara, P., Rooke, M. *et al.* (2001). Drink and drug driving: what's the skipper up to? *Australia and New Zealand Journal of Public Health*, 25: 511–13.

Stewart, A.L. and Ware, J.E. (eds) (1992). *Measuring Functioning and Well-being: The Medical Outcomes Study Approach*. Durham, NC: Duke University Press.

Stewart, M., Davidson, K., Meade, D. *et al.* (2000). Myocardial infarction: survivors' and spouses' stress, coping, and support. *Journal of Advanced Nursing*, 31: 1351–60.

Stewart-Knox, B.J., Sittlington, J., Rugkasa, J. *et al.* (2005). Smoking and peer groups: results from a longitudinal qualitative study of young people in Northern Ireland. *British Journal of Social Psychology*, 44: 397–414.

Stice, E., Presnell, K. and Sprangler, D. (2002). Risk factors for binge eating onset in adolescent girls: a 2-year prospective investigation. *Health Psychology*, 21: 131–8.

Stiegelis, H.E., Hagedoorn, M., Sanderman, R. *et al.* (2004). The impact of an informational self-management intervention on the association between control and illness uncertainty before and psychological distress after radiotherapy. *Psycho-Oncology*, 13: 248–59.

Stirling, A.M., Wilson, P. and McConnachie, A. (2001). Deprivation, psychological distress, and consultation length in general practice. *British Journal of General Practice*, 51: 456–60.

Stoate, H.G. (1989). Can health screening damage your health? *Journal of the Royal College of General Practitioners*, 39: 193–5.

Stocks, N.P., Ryan, P., McElroy, H. *et al.* (2004). Statin prescribing in Australia: socioeconomic and sex differences. A cross-sectional study. *Medical Journal of Australia*, 180: 229–31.

Stolzenberg, L. and D'Alessio, S.J. (2007). Is nonsmoking dangerous to the health of restaurants? The effect of California's indoor smoking ban on restaurant revenues. *Evaluation Review*, 31: 75–92.

Storch, M., Gaab, J., Küttel, Y. *et al.* (2007). Psychoneuroendocrine effects of resource-activating stress management training. *Health Psychology*, 26: 456–63.

Stokols, D. (1992). Establishing and maintaining health environments. *American Psychologist*, 47: 6–22.

Stone, A.A., Bovbjerg, D.H., Neale, J.M. *et al.* (1993). Development of common cold symptoms following experimental rhinovirus infection is related to prior stressful life events. *Behavioral Medicine*, 8: 115–20.

Stone, D.H. and Stewart, S. (1996). Screening and the new genetics: a public health perspective on the ethical debate. *Journal of Public Health Medicine*, 18: 3–5.

Stone, G.C. (1979). Health and the health system: a historical overview and conceptual framework. In G.C. Stone, F. Cohen and N.E. Adler (eds), *Health Psychology: A Handbook*. San Francisco, CA: Jossey-Bass.

Stone, S.V. and McCrae, R.R. (2007). Personality and health. In S. Ayers *et al.* (eds). *Cambridge Handbook of Psychology, Health and Medicine*, 2nd edn. Cambridge: Cambridge University Press, pp. 151–5.

Stoudemire, A. and Hales, R.E. (1991). Psychological and behavioral factors affecting medical conditions and DSM-IV: an overview. *Psychosomatics*, 32: 5–12.

Strack, F. and Deutsch, R. (2004). Reflective and impulsive determinants of social behavior. *Personality and Social Psychology Review*, 220–47.

Strang, S. and Strang, P. (2002). Questions posed to hospital chaplains by palliative care patients. *Journal of Palliative Medicine*, 5: 857–64.

Strauss, A. and Corbin, J. (1998). *Basics of Qualitative Research Techniques and Procedures for Developing Grounded Theory*, 2nd edn. London: Sage Publications.

Strauss, R.S. (2000). Childhood obesity and self esteem. *Pediatrics*, 105: e15.

Strecher, V.J., Champion, V.L. and Rosenstock, I.M. (1997). The health belief model and health behaviour. In D.S. Gochman (ed.), *Handbook of Health Behavior Research I: Personal and Social Determinants*. New York: Plenum.

Strecher, V.J. and Rosenstock, I.M. (1997). The health belief model. In A. Baum, S. Newman, J. Weinman, R. West and C. McManus (eds), *Cambridge Hand-book of Psychology, Health and Medicine*. Cambridge: Cambridge University Press.

Strike, P.C. and Steptoe, A. (2005). Behavioral and emotional triggers of acute coronary syndromes: a systematic review and critique. *Psychosomatic Medicine*, 67: 179–86.

Stroebe, W., Zech, E., Stroebe, M.S. *et al.* (2005). Does social support help in bereavement? *Journal of Social and Clinical Psychology*, 24: 1030–50.

Stronks, K., VandeMheen, H., VandenBos, J. *et al.* (1997). The interrelationship between income, health and employment status. *International Journal of Epidemiology*, 16: 592–600.

Strosahl, K.D., Hayes, S.C., Wilson, K.G. *et al.* (2004). An ACT primer. Core therapy processes, intervention strategies, and therapist competencies. In S.C. Hayes and K.D. Strosahl (eds), *A Practical Guide to Acceptance and Commitment Therapy*. New York: Springer.

Stuckey, S.J., Jacobs, A. and Goldfarb, J. (1986). EMG biofeedback training, relaxation training, and placebo for the relief of chronic back pain. *Perceptual and Motor Skills*, 63: 1023–36.

Stunkard, A.J. and Wadden, T. (1993). *Obesity: Theory and Therapy*, 2nd edn. New York: Raven Press.

Stürmer, T., Hasselbach, P. and Amelang, M. (2006). Personality, lifestyle, and risk of cardiovascular disease and cancer: follow-up of population based cohort. *British Medical Journal*, 332: 1359.

Suarez, E.C., Kuhn, C.M., Schanberg, S.M. *et al.* (1998). Neuro-endocrine, cardiovascular, and emotional responses of hostile men: the role of interpersonal challenge. *Psychosomatic Medicine*, 60: 78–88.

Suarez, E.C. and Williams, R.B. (1989). Situational determinants of cardiovascular and emotional reactivity in high and low hostile men. *Psychosomatic Medicine*, 51: 404–18.

Suchman, A.L. and Ader, R. (1992). Classic conditioning and placebo effects in crossover studies. *Clinical Pharmacology and Therapeutics*, 52: 372–7.

Suchman, C.A. (1965). Stages of illness and medical care. *Journal of Health and Social Behavior*, 6: 114–28.

Sullivan, M.J.L., Rodgers, W.M. and Kirsch, I. (2001). Catastrophizing, depression and expectancies for pain and emotional distress. *Pain*, 91: 147–54.

Suls, J. and Bunde, J. (2005). Anger, anxiety and depression as risk factors for cardiovascular disease: the problems and implications of overlapping affective dispositions. *Psychological Bulletin*, 131: 260–300.

Suls, J. and Fletcher, B. (1985). The relative efficacy of avoidant and nonavoidant coping strategies: a meta-analysis. *Health Psychology*, 4: 249–88.

Suls, J. and Martin, R. (2005). The daily life of the garden-variety neurotic: reactivity, stressors exposure, mood spillover, and maladaptive coping. *Journal of Personality*, 73: 1–25.

Suls, J. and Rittenhouse, J.D. (eds) (1987). Personality and Physical Health (Special Issue). *Journal of Personality*, 55: 155–393.

Suls, J., Wan, C.K. and Costa, P.T., Jr (1995). Relationship of trait anger to resting blood pressure: a meta-analysis. *Health Psychology*, 14: 444–56.

SuperioCabuslay, E., Ward, M.M. and Lorig, K.R. (1996). Patient education interventions in osteo-arthritis and rheumatoid arthritis: a meta-analytic comparison with nonsteroidal antiinflammatory drug treatment. *Arthritis Care and Research*, 9: 292–301.

Surtees, P.G., Wainwright, N.W.J., Luben, R.N. *et al.* (2008). Depression and ischemic heart disease mortality: evidence from the EPIC-Norfolk United Kingdom Prospective Cohort Study. *American Journal of Psychiatry*, 165: 515–23.

Surwit, R.S. and Schneider, M.S. (1993). Role of stress in the etiology and treatment of diabetes mellitus. *Psychosomatic Medicine*, 55: 380–93.

Surwit, R.S., van Tilburg, M.A., Zucker, N. *et al.* (2002). Stress management improves long-term glycemic control in type 2 diabetes. *Diabetes Care*, 25: 30–4.

Suter, P.B. (2002). Employment and litigation: improved by work, assisted by verdict. *Pain*, 100: 249–57.

Sutherland, I. and Shepherd, J.P. (2001). Social dimensions of adolescent substance use. *Addiction*, 96: 445–58.

Sutton, S. (1996). Can 'stages of change' provide guidance in the treatment of addictions? A critical examination of Prochaska and DiClemente's model. In G.E. Edwards and C. Dare (eds), *Psychotherapy, Psychological Treatments and the Addictions*. Cambridge: Cambridge University Press.

Sutton, S. (2000). A critical review of the trans-theoretical model applied to smoking cessation. In P. Norman, C. Abraham and M. Conner (eds), *Understanding and Changing Health Behaviour*. Amsterdam: Harwood Academic.

Sutton, S. (2001). Back to the drawing board? A review of applications of the transtheoretical model to substance use. *Addiction*, 96: 175–86.

Sutton, S. (2002). Using social cognition models to develop health behaviour interventions: problems and assumptions. In D. Rutter and L. Quine (eds), *Changing Health Behaviour*. Buckingham: Open University Press.

Sutton, S. (2004). Determinants of health-related behaviours: Theoretical and methodological issues. In S. Sutton, A. Baum and M. Johnston (eds). *The Sage Handbook of Health Psychology*. London: Sage, pp. 94–126.

Sutton, S. (2005). Another nail in the coffin of the transtheoretical model? A comment on West (2005). *Addiction*, 100: 1043–6.

Sutton, S. (2010). Using social cognition model to develop health behaviour interventions: the theory of planned behaviour as an example. In *Health Psychology*, 2nd edn. Oxford: BPS/Blackwell Publishing Ltd, pp. 122–34.

Sutton, S., McVey, D. and Glanz, A. (1999). A comparative test of the theory of reasoned action and the theory of planned behaviour in the prediction of condom use intentions in a national sample of English young people. *Health Psychology*, 18: 72–81.

Suurmeijer, T.P.B.M., Reuvekamp, M.F. and Aldenkamp, B.P. (2001). Social functioning, psychological functioning, and quality of life in epilepsy. *Epilepsia*, 42: 1160–8.

Swami, V., Arteche, A., Chamorro-Premuzic, T., Maakip, I., Stanistreet, D. and Furnham, A. (2009). Lay perceptions of current and future health, the causes of illness, and the nature of recovery: explaining health and illness in Malaysia. *British Journal of Health Psychology* 14: 519–40.

Swami, V., Furnham, A., Kannan, K. and Sinniah, D. (2008). Lay beliefs about schizophrenia and its treatment in Kota Kinabalu. Malaysia. *International Journal of Social Psychiatry*, 54: 164–79.

Swan, G.E., McClure, J.B., Jack, L.M. *et al.* (2010). Behavioral counseling and varenicline treatment for smoking cessation. *American Journal of Preventive Medicine*, 38: 482–90.

Swartz, L.H., Noell, J.W., Schroeder, S.W. *et al.* (2006). A randomised control study of a fully automated internet based smoking cessation programme. *Tobacco Control*, 15: 7–12.

Swartzman, L.C. and Lees, M.C. (1996). Causal dimensions of college students' perceptions of physical symptoms. *Journal of Behavioral Medicine*, 19(2): 85–110.

Taaffe, D.R., Harris, T.B., Ferrucci, L. *et al.* (2000). Cross-sectional and prospective relationships of interleukin-6 and C-reactive protein with physical performance in eld-erly persons: MacArthur Studies of Successful Aging. *Journal of Gerontology. A: Biological Science and Medical Science*, 55: M709–15.

Tak, N.I., Te Velde, S.J. and Brug, J. (2007). Ethnic differences in 1-year follow-up effect of the Dutch Schoolgruiten Project: promoting fruit and vegetable consumption among primary-school children. *Public Health Nutrition*, 10: 1497–507.

Tak, N.I., Te Velde, S.J. and Brug, J. (2009). Long-term effects of the Dutch Schoolgruiten Project: promoting fruit and vegetable consumption among primary-school children. *Public Health Nutrition*, 12: 1213–23.

Takao, S., Tsutsumi, A., Nishiuchi, K. *et al.* (2006). Effects of the job stress education for supervisors on psychological distress and job performance among their immediate subordinates: a supervisor-based randomized controlled trial. *Journal of Occupational Health*, 48: 494–503.

Takeuchi, D.T., Leaf, P.J. and Kuo, H. (1988). Ethnic differences in the perception of barriers to help-seeking. *Social Psychiatry & Psychiatric Epidemiology*, 23: 273–80.

Takkouche, B., Regueira, C., Gestal-Otero, J.J. and Jesus, J. (2001). A cohort study of stress and the common cold. *Epidemiology*, 12: 345–9.

Tan, P.E.H. and Bishop, G.D. (1996). Disease representations and related behavioural intentions among Chinese Singaporeans. *Psychology and Health*, 11: 671–83.

Tang, P.C. and Newcomb, C. (1998). Informing patients: a guide for providing patient health information. *Journal of the American Medical Informatics Association*, 5: 563–70.

Tapper, K., Horne, P. and Lowe, C.F. (2003). The Food Dudes to the rescue! *The Psychologist*, 16: 18–21.

Targ, E.F. and Levine, E.G. (2002). The efficacy of a mind–body–spirit group for women with breast cancer: a randomized controlled trial. *General Hospital Psychiatry*, 24: 238–48.

Taylor, A., Goldberg, D., Hutchinson, S. *et al.* (2001). High risk injecting behaviour among injectors from Glasgow: cross sectional community wide surveys 1990–1999. *Journal of Epidemiology and Community Health*, 55: 766–7.

Taylor, B., Miller, E., Farrington, C.P. *et al.* (1999). Autism and measles, mumps and rubella vaccine: no epidemiological evidence for a causal association. *The Lancet*, 2026–9.

Taylor, B., Miller, E., Lingam, R. *et al.* (2002). Measles, mumps and rubella vaccination and bowel problems or developmental regression in children with autism: population study. *British Medical Journal*, 324: 393–6.

Taylor, C., Graham, J., Potts, H.W. *et al.* (2005). Changes in mental health of UK hospital consultants since the mid 1990s. *The Lancet*, 366: 742–4.

Taylor, C.B., Bandura, A., Ewart, C.K. *et al.* (1985). Exercise testing to enhance wives' confidence in their husbands' cardiac capability soon after clinically uncomplicated acute myocardial infarction. *American Journal of Cardiology*, 55: 635–8.

Taylor, S. (1983). Adjustment to threatening events: a theory of cognitive adaptation. *American Psychologist*, 38: 1161–73.

Taylor, S.E. (2006). Tend and befriend: biobehavioral bases of affiliation under stress. *Current Directions in Psychological Science*, 15: 273–7.

Taylor, S.E. (2007). Social support. In H.S. Friedman and R.C. Silver (eds), *Foundations of Health Psychology*. New York: Oxford University Press, pp. 145–71.

Taylor, S.E. and Armor, D.A. (1996). Positive illusions and coping with adversity. *Journal of Personality*, 64: 873–98.

Taylor, S.E., Klein, L.C., Grunewald, T.L. *et al.* (2003). Affiliation, social support, and biobehavioral responses to stress. In J. Suls and K.A. Wallston (eds), *Social Psychological Foundations of Health and Illness*. Oxford: Blackwell.

Taylor, S.E., Repetti, R.L. and Seeman, T. (1997). Health psychology: what is an unhealthy environment and how does it get under the skin? *Annual Reviews in Psychology*, 48: 411–47.

Taylor, S.E. and Seeman, T.E. (1999). Psychosocial resources and the SES–health relationship. *Annals of the New York Academy of Science*, 896: 210–25.

Taylor, S.E., Sherman, D.K., Kim, H.S. *et al.* (2004). Culture and social support: who seeks it and why? *Journal of Personality and Social Psychology*, 87: 354–62.

Taylor, S.E., Welch, W., Kim, H.S. and Sherman, D.K. (2007). Cultural differences in the impact of social support on psychological and biological stress responses. *Psychological Science*, 18: 831–7.

Tedeschi, R.G. and Calhoun, L.G. (2004). Post-traumatic growth: conceptual foundations and empirical evidence. *Psychological Enquiry*, 15: 1–18.

Tedeschi, R.G. and Calhoun, L.G. (2008). Beyond the concept of recovery: growth and the experience of loss. *Death Studies*, 32: 27–39.

Temoshok, L. (1987). Personality, coping style, emotion and cancer: towards an integrative model. *Social Science and Medicine*, 20: 833–40.

Temoshok, L. and Dreher, H. (1993). *The Type C connection: The Behavioral Links to Cancer and Your Health*. New York: Penguin.

Temoshok, L. and Fox, B.H. (1984). Coping styles and other psychosocial factors related to medical status and to prognosis in patients with cutaneous malignant melanoma. In B.H. Fox and B. Newberry (eds), *Impact of Psychoendocrine Systems in Cancer and Immunity*. Toronto: C.J. Hogrefe.

Tennant, C. (2002). Life events, stress and depression: a review of recent findings. *Australia and New Zealand Journal of Psychiatry*, 36: 173–82.

Tennen, H., Affleck, G., Armeli, S. *et al.* (2000). A daily process approach to coping: linking theory, research, and practice. *American Psychologist*, 55: 620–5.

Terracciano, A. and Costa, P.T. Jr (2004). Smoking and the five-factor model of personality. *Addiction*, 99: 472–81.

Terry, D.J. (1992). Stress, coping and coping resources as correlates of adaptation in myocardial infarction patients. *British Journal of Clinical Psychology*, 31: 215–25.

The Global Youth Tobacco Survey Collaborative Group (2002). Tobacco use among youth: a cross-country comparison. *Tobacco Control*, 11, 252–70.

The Information Centre (2008). *Health Survey for England 2006 Latest Trends*. London: The Information Centre, Lifestyles Statistics.

Theisen, M.E., MacNeill, S.E., Lumley, M.A. *et al.* (1995). Psychosocial factors related to unrecognized acute myocardial infarction. *American Journal of Cardiology*, 75: 1211–13.

Theorell, T. and Karasek, R.A. (1996). Current issues relating to psychosocial job strain and cardiovascular disease research. *Journal of Occupational Health Psychology*, 1: 9–26.

Theunissen, N.C.M., de Ridder, D.T.D., Bensing, J.M. *et al.* (2003). Manipulation of patient–provider interaction: discussing illness representations or action plans concerning adherence. *Patient Education and Counselling*, 51: 247–58.

Theunissen, N.C.M., Vogels, T.G.C., Koopman, H.M. *et al.* (1998). The proxy problem: child report versus parent report in health-related quality of life research. *Quality of Life Research*, 7: 387–97.

Thoits, P.A. (1995). Stress, coping and social support processes. Where are we? What next? *Journal of Health and Social Behavior* (extra issue), 36: 53–79.

Thomas, D.B., Gao, D.L., Ray, R.M. *et al.* (2002). Randomized trial of breast self-examination in Shanghai – final results. *Journal of the National Cancer Institute*, 94: 1445–57.

Thomas, M., Walker, A., Wilmot, A. *et al.* (1998). *Living in Britain: Results from the 1996 General Household Survey*. London: Stationery Office.

Thompson, A., Brennan, K., Cox, A. *et al.* (2008). Evaluation of the current knowledge limitations in breast cancer research: a gap analysis. *Breast Cancer Research*, 10: R26, doi:10.1186/bcr1983.

Thompson, S.C. (1981). Will it hurt less if I can control it? A complex answer to a simple question. *Psychological Bulletin*, 90: 89–101.

Thompson, S.C., Galbraith, M., Thomas, C., Swan. J. and Vrungos, S. (2002). Caregivers of stroke patient family members: behavioural and attitudinal indicators of overprotective care. *Psychology and Health*, 17: 297–312.

Thompson, S.C. and Pitts, J.C. (1992). In sickness and in health: chronic illness, marriage and spousal caregiving. In S. Spacapan and S. Oskamp (eds), *Helping and Being Helped: Naturalistic Studies*. Newbury Park, CA: Sage.

Thompson, S.C., Sobolew-Shubin, A., Galbraith, M.E. *et al.* (1993). Maintaining perceptions of control: finding perceived control in low-control circumstances. *Journal of Personality and Social Psychology*, 64: 293–304.

Thompson, W.G., Longstreth, G. and Drossman, D.A. (2000). Functional bowel disorders and functional abdominal pain. In D.A. Drossman, E. Corazziari, N. Talley *et al.* (eds), *Rome II: The Functional Gastrointestinal Disorders*, 2nd edn. McLean, VA: Degnon Associates.

Thrasher, J.F., Hammond, D., Fong, G.T. *et al.* (2007). Smokers' reactions to cigarette package warnings with graphic imagery and with only text: a comparison between Mexico and Canada. *Salud Publica Mexico*, 49 Suppl 2: S233–40.

Thuné-Boyle, I.C.V., Stygall, J., Keshtgar, M.R.S. and Newman, S.P. (2006). Do religious/spiritual coping strategies affect illness adjustment in patients with cancer? A systematic review of the literature. *Social Science & Medicine*, 63: 151–64.

Thurstone, L.L. (1928). Attitudes can be measured. *American Journal of Sociology*, 33: 529–44.

Timko, C. and Janoff-Bulman, R. (1985). Attributions, vulnerability and psychological adjustment: the case of breast cancer. *Health Psychology*, 4: 521–44.

Tobias, M. and Yeh, L.C. (2006). Do all ethnic groups in New Zealand exhibit socio-economic mortality gradients? *Australian and New Zealand Journal of Public Health*, 30: 343–9.

Tobin, D.L., Holroyd, K.A., Baker, A. *et al.* (1988). Development and clinical trial of a minimal contact, cognitive-behavioral treatment for tension headache. *Cognitive Therapy and Research*, 12: 325–39.

Todorova, I.L., Falcón, L.M., Lincoln, A.K. *et al.* (2010). Perceived discrimination, psychological distress and health. *Sociology of Health and Illness*, 32: 843–61.

Toljamo, M. and Hentinen, M. (2001). Adherence to self care and social support. *Journal of Clinical Nursing*, 10: 618–27.

Tomich, P.L. and Helgeson, V.S. (2004). Is finding something good in the bad always good? Benefit-finding among women with breast cancer. *Health Psychology*, 23: 16–23.

Toroyan, T. and Reddy, P.S. (2005–2006). Participation of South African youth in the design and development of AIDS photocomics: 1997–98. *International Quarterly of Community Health Education*, 25: 149–63.

Touzet, S., Réfabert, L., Letrilliart, L. *et al.* (2007). Impact of consensus development conference guidelines on primary care of bronchiolitis: are national guidelines being followed? *Journal of Evaluation of Clinical Practice*, 13: 651–6.

Tov, W. and Diener, E. (2007). Culture and subjective well-being. In S. Kitayama and D. Cohen (eds), *Handbook of Cultural Psychology*. New York: Guilford Press, pp. 697–713.

Triandis, H.C. (1977). *Interpersonal Behavior*. Monterey, CA: Brooks/Cole.

Triandis, H.C. (1995). *Individualism and Collectivism*. Boulder, CO: Westview.

Tromp, D.M., Brouha, X.D.R., DeLeeuw, J.R.J. *et al.* (2004). Psychological factors and patient delay in patients with head and neck cancer. *European Journal of Cancer*, 40: 1509–16.

Troy, A.S., Wlhelm, F.H., Shallcross, A.J. and Mauss, I.B. (2010). Seeing the silver lining: cognitive reappraisal ability moderates the relationship between stress and depressive symptoms. *Emotion*, 10: 783–95.

Trufelli, D.C., Bensi, C.G., Garcia, J.B. *et al.* (2008). Burnout in cancer professionals: a systematic review and meta-analysis. *European Journal of Cancer Care*, 17: 524–31.

Tsarenko, Y. and Polonsky, M.J. (2011). 'You can spend your life dying or you can spend your life living': identity transition in people who are HIV-positive. *Psychology & Health*, 26: 465–83.

Tschuschke, V., Hertenstein, B., Arnold, R. *et al.* (2001). Associations between coping and survival time of adult leukaemia patients receiving allogenic bone marrow transplantation: results of a prospective study. *Journal of Psychosomatic Research*, 50: 277–85.

Tubiana-Rufi, N., Moret, L., Czernichow, P. *et al.* (1998). The association of poor adherence and acute metabolic disorders with low levels of cohesion and adaptability in families with diabetic children: the PEDIAB Collaborative Group. *Acta Paediatrica*, 87: 741–6.

Tudor-Smith, C., Nutbeam, D., Moore, L. *et al.* (1998). Effects of the Heartbeat Wales programme over five years on behavioural risks for cardiovascular disease: quasi-experimental comparison of results from Wales and a matched reference area. *British Medical Journal*, 316: 818–22.

Turk, D.C. (1986). Workshop on Pain Management. Birmingham, UK.

Turk, D.C., Litt, M.D., Salovey, P. *et al.* (1985). Seeking urgent pediatric treatment: factors contributing to frequency, delay and appropriateness. *Health Psychology*, 4: 43–59.

Turk, D.C. and Okifuji, A. (1999). Assessment of patients' reporting of pain: an integrated perspective. *The Lancet*, 353: 1784–8.

Turk, D.C., Rudy, T.E. and Salovey, P. (1986). Implicit models of illness. *Journal of Behavioral Medicine*, 9: 453–74.

Turner, J.A. and Clancy, S. (1988). Comparison of operant behavioral and cognitive-behavioral group treatment for chronic low back pain. *Journal of Consulting and Clinical Psychology*, 56: 261–6.

Turner, J.A., Holtzman, S. and Mancl, L. (2007). Mediators, moderators, and predictors of therapeutic change in cognitive-behavioral therapy for chronic pain. *Pain*, 127: 276–86.

Turner, J., Page-Shafer, K., Chin, D.P. *et al.* (2001). Adverse impact of cigarette smoking on dimensions of health-related quality of life in persons with HIV infection. *AIDS Patient Care and STDs*, 15: 615–24.

Turner, J.C., Hogg, M.A., Oakes, P.J. *et al.* (1987). *Rediscovering the Social Group: A Self-categorization Theory*. Oxford: Blackwell.

Turner-Cobb, J.M., Gore-Felton, C., Marouf, F. *et al.* (2002). Coping, social adjustment, and attachment style as psychosocial correlates of adjustment in men and women with HIV/AIDS. *Journal of Behavioral Medicine*, 25: 337–53.

Turner-Cobb, J.M., Sephton, S.E., Koopman, C. *et al.* (2000). Social support and salivary cortisol in women with metastatic breast cancer. *Psychosomatic Medicine*, 62: 337–45.

Turunen, J.H., Mäntyselkä, P.T., Kumpusalo, E.A. *et al.* (2005). Frequent analgesic use at population level: prevalence and patterns of use. *Pain*, 115: 374–81.

Tversky, A. and Kahneman, D. (1981). The framing of decisions and the psychology of choice. *Science*, 211: 453–8.

Tyas, S.L. and Pederson, L.L. (1998). Psychological factors related to adolescent smoking: a critical review of the literature. *Tobacco Control*, 7: 409–20.

Tyczynski, J.E., Bray, F., Aareleid, T. *et al.* (2004). Lung cancer mortality patterns in selected Central, Eastern and Southern European countries. *International Journal of Cancer*, 109: 598–610.

Uchino, B.N. (2006). Social support and health: a review of physiological processes potentially underlying links to disease outcomes. *Journal of Behavioral Medicine*, 29: 377–87.

UK Central Statistics Office (1980). A change in revenue from an indirect tax change. *Economic Trend*, March: 97–107.

UNAIDS (2008). http://www.unaids.org/en/.

United Nations Secretariat (2002). *The Ageing of the World's Population*. Population Division, Department of Economic and Social Affairs, United Nations Secretariat. Available from: http://www.un.org/esa/socdev/ageing/agewpop.htm.

United Nations (2006). *World Population Prospects: The 2006 Revision and World Urbanization Prospects: The 2005 Revision*. Population Division of the Deparment of Economic and Social Affairs of the united Nations Secretariat. Available from: http://esa.un.org/unpp.

Unrod, M., Smith, M., Spring, B. *et al.* (2007). Randomized controlled trial of a computer-based, tailored intervention to increase smoking cessation counseling by primary care physicians. *Journal of General Internal Medicine*, 22: 478–84.

Uman, L.S., Chambers, C.T., McGrath, P.J. and Kisely, S. (2008). A systematic review of randomized controlled trials examining psychological interventions for needle-related procedural pain and distress in children and adolescents: an abbreviated Cochrane review. *Journal of Pediatric Psychology*, 33: 842–54.

Urquhart-Law, G. (2002). Dissimilarity in adolescent and maternal representations of type 1 diabetes: exploration of relations to adolescent well-being. *Child Health Care and Development*, 28: 369–78.

US Bureau of the Census (1999). *Statistical Abstracts of the United States: 1998*, 118th edn. Retrieved (2.10.2002) from: http://www.census.gov.

US Centers for Disease Control and Prevention (1996). Community-level prevention of human immuno-deficiency virus infection among high-risk populations: the AIDS Community Demonstration Projects. *MMWR Morbidity and Mortality Weekly Reports*, 45 (RR-6): 1–24.

US Department of Health and Human Services (1997). *Ninth Special Report to the U.S. Congress on Alcohol and Health, June 1997*. US Department of Health and Human Services, NIH, NIAAA.

US Department of Health and Human Services (2000). *Healthy People 2010*. Washington, DC: US Department of Health and Human Services.

US Department of Health and Human Services (2006). *The Health Consequences of Involuntary Exposure to Tobacco Smoke: A Report of the Surgeon General*. Atlanta, GA: US Department of Health and Human Services.

US Institute of Medicine (2002). *Unequal Treatment: Confronting Racial and Ethnic Disparities in Health Care*. Washington, DC: Institute of Medicine.

US Preventive Services Task Force (USPSTF) (2003). Routine vitamin supplementation to prevent cancer and cardio-vascular disease: recommendations and rationale. *Annals of Internal Medicine*, 139: 51–5.

Ussher, J.M. and Sandoval, M. (2008). Gender differences in the construction and experience of cancer care. The consequence of gender positioning of carers. *Psychology and Health*, 23, 945–63.

Vaillant, G.E. (1998). Natural history of male psychological health XIV: relationship of mood disorder, vulnerability and physical health. *American Journal of Psychiatry*, 155: 184–91.

Valente, S.M. (2003). Depression and HIV disease. *Journal of Association of Nurses in AIDS Care*, 14: 41–51.

Van Dammme, S., Legrain, V., Vogt, J. *et al.* (2010). Keeping pain in mind: a motivational account of attention to pain. *Neuroscience and Biobehavioral Reviews*, 34: 204–13.

Van de Creek, L., Paget, S., Horton, R. *et al.* (2004). Religious and non-religious coping methods among persons with rheumatoid arthritis. *Arthritis and Rheumatology*, 51: 49–55.

van den Arend, I.J., Stolk, R.P. *et al.* (2000). Education integrated into structured general practice care for type 2 diabetic patients results in sustained improvement of illness knowledge and self-care. *Diabetes Medicine*, 17: 190–7.

van den Heuvel, E.T.P., de Witte, L.P., Schure, L.M. *et al.* (2001). Risk factors for burn-out in caregivers of stroke patients, and possibilities for intervention. *Clinical Rehabilitation*, 15: 669–77.

van den Hout, J.H.C., Vlaeyen, J.W.S., Peters, M.L. *et al.* (2000). Does failure hurt? The effects of failure feedback on pain report, pain tolerance and pain avoidance. *European Journal of Pain*, 4: 335–46.

van der Doef, M. and Maes, S. (1998). The job demand–control(–support) model and physical health outcomes: a review of the strain and buffer hypotheses. *Psychology and Health*, 13: 909–36.

van der Doef, M. and Maes, S. (1999). The job demand–control(–support) model and psychological well-being: a review of 20 years empirical research. *Work and Stress*, 13: 87–114.

van der Geest, S. and Whyte, S. (1989). The charm of medicines: metaphors and metonyms. *Medical Anthropology Quarterly*, 3: 345–67.

Van Hecke, A., Grypdonck, M. and Defloor, T. (2009). A review of why patients with leg ulcers do not adhere to treatment. *Journal of Clinical Nursing*, 18: 337–49.

van der Heide, A., Deliens, L., Faisst, K. *et al.* (2003). End-of-life decision-making in six European countries: descriptive study. *The Lancet*, 361: 345–50.

van der Meer, V., van Stel, H.F., Detmar, S.B. *et al.* (2007). Internet-based self-management offers an opportunity to achieve better asthma control in adolescents. *Chest*, 132: 112–9.

van der Pligt, J. and de Vries, N.K. (1998). Expectancy-value models of health behaviour: the role of salience and anticipated affect. *Psychology and Health*, 13: 289–305.

van der Velde, F.W., Hooykaas, C. and van der Pligt, J. (1992). Risk perception and behaviour: pessimism, realism and optimism about AIDS-related health behaviour. *Psychology and Health*, 6: 23–38.

van Eck, M., Berkhof, H., Nicolson, N. *et al.* (1996). The effects of perceived stress, traits, mood states, and stressful daily events on salivary cortisol. *Psychosomatic Medicine*, 58: 508–14.

Vangeli, E. and West, R. (2008). Sociodemographic differences in triggers to quit smoking: findings from a national survey. *Tobacco Control*, 17: 410–15.

van Koningsbruggen, G.M., Das, E. and Rosos-Ewoldse, D.R. (2009). How self-affirmation reduces defensive processing of threatening heath information: evidence at the implicit level. *Health Psychology*, 28: 563–8.

van Stralen, M.M., De Vries, H., Mudde, A.N., Bolman, C. and Lechner, L. (2009). Determinants of initiation and maintenance of physical activity among older adults: a literature review. *Health Psychology Review*, 3: 147–207.

van Strien, T., Engels, R.C.M.E., van Leeuwe, J. and Snoek, H.M. (2005). The Stice model of overeating: tests in clinical and non-clinical samples. *Appetite*, 45: 205–13.

van Strien, T., Frijters, J.E.R., Bergers, G.P.A. and Defares, P.S. (1986). The Dutch Eating Behavior Questionnaire (DEBQ) for assessment of restrained, emotional and external eating behavior. *International Journal of Eating Disorders*, 5: 295–315.

van Strien, T., van de Laar, F.A., van Leeuwe, J.F.J. *et al.* (2007). The dieting dilemma in patients with newly diagnosed Type 2 diabetes: does dietary restraint predict weight gain 4 years after diagnosis? *Health Psychology*, 1: 105–12.

van 't Riet, J., Ruiter, R.A. *et al.* (2010). Investigating message-framing effects in the context of a tailored intervention promoting physical activity. *Health Education Research*, 25: 343–54.

van Tulder, M.W., Ostelo, R.W.J., Vlaeyen, J.W.S. *et al.* (2003). Behavioural treatment for chronic low back pain. In *The Cochrane Library*, issue 1. Oxford: Update Software.

van Vegchel, N., de Jonge, J., Bosma, H. and Schaufeli, W. (2005). Reviewing the effort–reward imbalance model: drawing up the balance of 45 empirical studies. *Social Science and Medicine*, 60: 1117–31.

van Wijk, C.M.T.G. and Kolk, A.M. (1997). Sex differences in physical symptoms: the contribution of symptom perception theory. *Social Science & Medicine*, 45: 231–46.

van Zuuren, F.J. and Dooper, R. (1999). Coping style and self-reported health promotion and disease detection behaviour. *British Journal of Health Psychology*, 4: 81–9.

Vaughan, P.W., Rogers, E.M., Singhal, A. *et al.* (2000). Entertainment-education and HIV/AIDS prevention: a field experiment in Tanzania. *Journal of Health Communication*, 5: 81–100.

Vedhara, K., Cox, N.K.M., Wilcock, G.K. *et al.* (1999). Chronic stress in elderly carers of dementia patients and antibody responses to influenza vaccination. *The Lancet*, 353: 627–31.

Vedhara, K. and Irwin, M.R. (eds), *Human Psychoneuroimmunology*. Oxford: Oxford University Press.

Vedhara, K., McDermott, M.P., Evans, T.G. *et al.* (2002). Chronic stress in nonelderly caregivers. Psychological, endocrine and immune implications. *Journal of Psychosomatic Research*, 53: 1153–61.

Vedhara, K., Shanks, N., Anderson, S. *et al.* (2000). The role of stressors and psychosocial variables in the stress process: a study of chronic caregiver stress. *Psychosomatic Medicine*, 62: 374–85.

Vedhara, K., Tallon, D., Gale, L. *et al.* (2003). Psychological determinants of wound healing in diabetic patients with foot ulceration. Paper presented at the European Health Psychology conference, Kos, August 2003.

Vedhara, K., Wang, E.C.Y., Fox, J.D. *et al.* (2001). The measurement of stress-related immune dysfunction in humans: an introduction to psychoneuro-immunology. In *Assessments in Behavioural Medicine*. Hove: Brunner-Routledge, pp. 441–80.

Veenhoven, R. (2003). Happiness. *The Psychologist*, 16: 128–9.

Verbrugge, L.M. and Steiner, R.P. (1985). Prescribing drugs to men and women. *Health Psychology*, 4: 79–98.

Verdugo, R.J. and Ochoa, J.L. (1994). Sympathetically maintained pain. I. Phentolamine block questions the concept. *Neurology*, 44: 1003–10.

Vestling, M., Tfvesson, B. and Iwarsson, S. (2003). Indicators for return to work after stroke and the importance of work for subjective well-being and life satisfaction. *Journal of Rehabilitation Medicine*, 35: 127–31.

Vickrey, B.G., Samuels, M.A. and Ropper, A.H. (2010). How neurologists think: a cognitive psychology perspective on missed diagnoses. *Annals of Neurology*, 67: 425–33.

Vikman, S., Airaksinen, K.E., Tierala, I. *et al.* (2004). Improved adherence to practice guidelines yields better outcome in high-risk patients with acute coronary syndrome without ST elevation: findings from nationwide FINACS studies. *Journal of Internal Medicine*, 256: 316–23.

Vilhauer, R.P., McClintock, M.K. and Matthews, A.K. (2010). Online support groups for women with metastatic breast cancer: a feasibility pilot study. *Journal of Psychosocial Oncology*, 28: 560–86.

Viner, R., McGrath, M. and Trudinger, P. (1996). Family stress and metabolic control in diabetes. *Archives of Diseases of Childhood*, 74: 418–21.

Vingerhoets, A.J.J.M. and Perski, A. (2000). The psychobiology of stress. In A.A. Kaptein, A.W.P.M. Appels and K. Orth-Gomér (eds), *Psychology in Medicine*. Houten: Wolters Kluwer International, pp. 34–49.

Vinkeles Melchers, N.V., Gomez M. *et al.* (2009). Do socio-economic factors influence supermarket content and shoppers' purchases? *Health Promotion Journal of Australia*, 20: 241–6.

Visser, M.J. (2007). HIV/AIDS prevention through peer education and support in secondary schools in South Africa. *Sahara Journal*, 4: 678–94.

Visser, de R.O. and Smith, J.A. (2007). Alcohol consumpton and masculine identity among young men. *Psychology & Health*, 22: 595–614.

Visser-Meily, A., van Heugten, C., Post, M. *et al.* (2005). Intervention studies for caregivers of stroke survivors: a critical review. *Patient Education and Counselling*, 56: 257–67.

Vitolins, M.Z., Rand, C.S., Rapp, S.R., Ribisl, P.M. and Sevick, M.A. (2000). Measuring adherence to behavioral and medical interventions. *Controlled Clinical Trials*, 21(5 suppl.): 188S–94S.

Vlaeyen, J.W., Kole-Snijders, A.M., Boeren, R.G. *et al.* (1995). Fear of movement/(re)injury in chronic low back pain and its relation to behavioral performance. *Pain*, 62: 363–72.

Voerman, G.E., Sandsjö, L., Vollenbroek-Hutten, M.M. *et al.* (2007). Changes in cognitive-behavioral factors and muscle activation patterns after interventions for work-related neck–shoulder complaints: relations with discomfort and disability. *Journal of Occupational Rehabilitation*, 17: 593–609.

Vögele, C. (1998). Serum lipid concentrations, hostility and cardiovascular reactions to mental stress. *International Journal of Psycophysiology*, 28: 167–79.

Vögele, C., Jarvis, A. and Cheeseman, K. (1997). Anger suppression, reactivity, and hypertension risk: gender makes a difference. *Annals of Behavioral Medicine*, 19: 61–9.

Vögele, C. and Steptoe, A. (1993). Anger inhibition and family history as moderators of cardiovascular responses to mental stress in adolescent boys. *Journal of Psychosomatic Research*, 37: 503–14.

Vogt, T.M., Mullooly, J.P., Ernst, D. *et al.* (1992). Social networks as predictors of ischemic heart disease, cancer, stroke and hypertension: incidence, survival and mortality. *Journal of Clinical Epidemiology*, 45: 659–66.

Vollrath, M. (2006). *Handbook of Personality and Health*. Chichester: Wiley.

Vosvick, M., Koopman, C., Gore-Felton, C. *et al.* (2003). Relationship of functional quality of life to strategies for coping with the stress of living with HIV/AIDS. *Psychosomatics*, 44: 51–8.

Wade, D.T. and Halligan, P.W. (2004). Do biomedical models of illness make for good healthcare systems? *British Medical Journal*, 329: 1398–401.

Wagenaar, A.C., Salois, M.J. and Komro, K.A. (2009). Effects of beverage alcohol price and tax levels on drinking: a meta-analysis of 1003 estimates from 112 studies. *Addiction*, 104: 179–90.

Wakefield, A.J., Murch, S.H., Anthony, A. *et al.* (1998). Ileal-lymphoid nodular hyperplasia, non-specific colitis and pervasive developmental disorder in children. *The Lancet*, 351: 637–41.

Wakefield, M.A., Chaloupka, F.J., Kaufman, N.J. *et al.* (2000). Effect of restrictions on smoking at home, at school, and in public places on teenage smoking: cross-sectional study. *British Medical Journal*, 321: 333–7.

Wakefield, M.A., Loken, B. and Hornik, R.C. (2010). Use of mass media campaigns to change health behaviour. *Lancet*, 376: 1261–71.

Waljee, J.F., Rogers, M.A. and Alderman, A.K. (2007). Decision aids and breast cancer: do they influence choice for surgery and knowledge of treatment options? *Journal of Clinical Oncology*, 25: 1067–73.

Walker, C., Papadopoulos, L., Lipton, M. *et al.* (2006). The importance of children's illness beliefs: the Children's Illness Perception Questionnaire (CIPQ) as a reliable assessment tool for eczema and asthma. *Psychology, Health & Medicine*, 11: 100–7.

Walker, J.G., Jackson, H.J. and Littlejohn, G.O. (2004). Models of adjustment to chronic illness: using the example of rheumatoid arthritis. *Clinical Psychology Review*, 24: 461–88.

Walker, L.G., Heys, S.D. and Eremin, O. (1999). Surviving cancer: do psychosocial factors count? *Journal of Psychosomatic Research*, 47: 497–503.

Walker, Z.A.K. and Townsend, J. (1999). The role of general practice in promoting teenage health: a review of the literature. *Family Practice*, 16: 164–72.

Wall, P.D. (1979). On the relation of injury to pain. The John J. Bonica Lecture. *Pain*, 6: 253–64.

Wallander, J.L. and Varni, J.W. (1998). Effects of pediatric chronic physical disorders on child and family adjustment. *Journal of Child Psychology and Psychiatry*, 39: 29–46.

Wallston, K.A. (1991). The importance of placing measures of health locus of control beliefs in a theoretical context. *Health Education Research*, 6: 251–2.

Wallston, K.A. and Smith, M.S. (1994). Issues of control and health: the action is in the interaction. In G. Penny, P. Bennett and M. Herbert (eds), *Health Psychology: A Lifespan Perspective*. London: Harwood Academic.

Wallston, K.A., Wallston, B.S. and deVellis, R. (1978). Development of the multidimensional health locus of control (MHLC) scale. *Health Education Monographs*, 6: 160–70.

Walsh, D.A. and Radcliffe, J.C. (2002). Pain beliefs and perceived physical disability of patients with chronic low back pain. *Pain*, 97: 23–31.

Walton, K.G., Schneider, R.H. and Nidich, S. (2004). Review of controlled research on the transcendental meditation program and cardiovascular disease: risk factors, morbidity, and mortality. *Cardiology Review*, 12: 262–6.

Wamala, S., Merlo, J., Bostrom, G. *et al.* (2007). Socioeconomic disadvantage and primary non-adherence with medication in Sweden. *International Journal for Quality in Health Care*, 19: 134–40.

Wang, H.W., Leineweber, C., Kirkeeide, R. *et al.* (2007). Psychosocial stress and atherosclerosis: family and work stress accelerate progression of coronary disease in women: the Stockholm Female Coronary Angiography Study. *Journal of Internal Medicine*, 261(3): 245–54.

Wang, J.L., Lesage, A., Schmitz, N. and Drapeau, A. (2008). The relationship between work stress and mental disorders in men and women: results from a population-based study. *Journal of Epidemiology and Community Health*, 62: 42–7.

Warburton, D.M., Revell, A.D. and Thompson, D.H. (1991). Smokers of the future. Special issue: Future directions in tobacco research. *British Journal of Addiction*, 86: 621–5.

Ward, S.E., Leventhal, H. and Love, R. (1988). Repression revisited: tactics used in coping with a severe health threat. *Personality and Social Psychology Bulletin*, 14: 735–46.

Ward, M.M., Mefford, I.N., Parker, S.D. *et al.* (1983). Epinephrine and norepinephrine responses in continuously collected human plasma to a series of stressors. *Psychosomatic Medicine*, 45: 471–86.

Wardle, J., Cooke, L.J., Gibson, E.L., Sapochnik, M., Sheiham, A. and Lawson, M. Increasing children's acceptance of vegetables; a randomized trial of parent-led exposure. *Appetite*, 40: 155–62.

Wardle, J. and Johnson, F. (2002). Weight and dieting: examining levels of weight concern in British adults. *International Journal of Obesity*, 26: 1144–9.

Wardle, J. and Steptoe, A. (2003). Socioeconomic differences in attitudes and beliefs about healthy lifestyles. *Journal of Epidemiology and Community Health*, 57: 440–3.

Warner, B.J., Curnow, L.J., Polglase, A.L. and Debinski, H.S. (2005). Factors influencing uptake of genetic testing for colorectal cancer risk in an Australian Jewish population. *Journal of Genetic Counselling*, 14: 387–94.

Warner, L., Klausner, J.D., Rietmeijer, C.A. *et al.* (2008). Effect of a brief video intervention on incident infection among patients attending sexually transmitted disease clinics. *Public Library of Science Medicine*, 5: e135.

Warner, L.J., Lumley, M.A., Casey, R.J. *et al.* (2006). Health effects of written emotional disclosure in adolescents with asthma: a randomized, controlled trial. *Journal of Pediatric Psychology*, 31: 557–68.

Warren, L. and Hixenbaugh, P. (1998). Adherence and diabetes. In L. Myers and K. Midence (eds), *Adherence to Treatment in Medical Conditions*. The Netherlands: Harwood Academic.

Watson, D. and Clark, L.A. (1984). Negative affectivity: the disposition to experience aversive emotional states. *Psychological Bulletin*, 96: 465–90.

Watson, D., David, J.P. and Suls, J. (1999). Personality, affectivity, and coping. In C.R. Snyder (ed.), *Coping: The Psychology of What Works*. Oxford: Oxford University Press, pp. 119–40.

Watson, D. and Pennebaker, J.W. (1989). Health complaints, stress and distress: exploring the central role of negative affectivity. *Psychological Review*, 96: 234–54.

Watson, D. and Pennebaker, J.W. (1991). Situational, dispositional and genetic bases of symptom reporting. In J.A. Skelton and R.T. Croyle (eds), *Mental Representation in Health and Illness*. New York: Springer Verlag.

Watson, M., Buck, G., Wheatley, K. *et al.* (2004a). Adverse impact of bone marrow transplantation on quality of life in acute myeloid leukaemia patients: analysis of the UK Medical Research Council AML 10 Trial. *European Journal of Cancer*, 40: 971–8.

Watson, M., Davidson-Homewood, J., Haviland, J. *et al.* (2002). Influence of psychological coping on survival and recurrence: a response to the systematic review (letter to the editor). *British Medical Journal*, 325: 598.

Watson, M., Foster, C., Eeles, R. *et al.* (2004b). Psychosocial impact of breast/ovarian (BRCA1/2) cancer-predictive genetic testing in a UK multi-centre clinical cohort. *British Journal of Cancer*, 91: 1787–94.

Watson, M., Haviland, J.S., Greer, S. *et al.* (1999a). Influence of psychological response on survival in breast cancer: a population-based cohort study. *The Lancet*, 9187: 1331–6.

Watson, M., Homewood, J., Haviland, J. *et al.* (2005). Influence of psychological response on breast cancer survival: 10-year follow-up of a population-based cohort. *European Journal of Cancer*, 41: 1710–14.

Watson, M., Lloyd, S., Davidson, J. *et al.* (1999b). The impact of genetic counselling on risk perception and mental health in women with a family history of breast cancer. *British Journal of Cancer*, 79: 868–74.

Webb, O.J. and Eves, F.F. (2007). Effects of environmental changes in a stair climbing intervention: generalization to stair descent. *American Journal of Health Promotion*, 22: 38–44.

Webb, O.J., Eves, F.F. *et al.* (2010). Investigating behavioural mimicry in the context of stair/escalator choice. *British Journal of Health Psychology*, 16: 373–85.

Weber, A. and Lehnert, G. (1997). Unemployment and cardio-vascular diseases: a causal relationship? *International Archives of Occupational and Environmental Health*, 70: 153–60.

Weber, B.A., Roberts, B.L., Yarandi, H. *et al.* (2007). The impact of dyadic social support on self-efficacy and depression after radical prostatectomy. *Journal of Aging and Health*, 19: 630–45.

Weber, M.A. and Julius, S. (1998). The challenge of very mild hypertension: should treatment be sooner or later? *American Journal of Hypertension*, 11: 1495–6.

Weiner, B. (1986). *An Attributional Theory of Motivation and Emotion*. New York: Springer.

Weinman, J., Ebrecht, M., Scott, S. *et al.* (2008). Enhanced wound healing after emotional disclosure intervention. *British Journal of Health Psychology*, 13: 95–102.

Weinman, J. and Petrie, K.J. (1997). Illness perceptions: a new paradigm for psychosomatics? (editorial). *Journal of Psychosomatic Research*, 42: 113–16.

Weinman, J., Petrie, K.J., Moss-Morris, R. *et al.* (1996). The Illness Perception Questionnaire: a new method for assessing the cognitive representation of illness. *Psychology and Health*, 11: 431–55.

Weinman, J., Petrie, K.J., Sharpe, N. *et al.* (2000). Causal attributions in patients and spouses following first-time myocardial infarction and subsequent life changes. *British Journal of Health Psychology*, 5: 263–74.

Weinstein, N.D. (1982). Unrealistic optimism about suscepti-bility to health problems. *Journal of Behavioral Medicine*, 2: 125–40.

Weinstein, N. (1984). Why it won't happen to me: percep-tions of risk factors and susceptibility. *Health Psychology*, 3: 431–57.

Weinstein, N. (1987). Unrealistic optimism about illness sus-ceptibility: conclusions from a community-wide sample. *Journal of Behavioral Medicine*, 10: 481–500.

Weinstein, N.D. (1988). The precaution adoption process. *Health Psychology*, 7: 355–86.

Weinstein, N.D. (2003). Exploring the links between risk per-ception and preventive health behaviour. In J. Suls and K.A. Wallston (eds), *Social Psychological Foundations of Health and Illness*. Malden, MA: Blackwell.

Weinstein, N.D., Rothman, A.J. and Sutton, S.R. (1998). Stage theories of health behavior: conceptual and meth-odological issues. *Health Psychology*, 17: 290–9.

Weinstein, N.D. and Klein, W.M. (1996). Unrealistic optimism: present and future. *Journal of Social and Clinical Psychology*, 15: 1–8.

Weinstein, N.D., Lyon, J.E., Sandman, P.M. and Cite, C.L. (1998). Experimental evidence for stages of precaution adoption. *Health Psychology*, 17: 445–53.

Weinstein, N.D. and Sandman, P.M. (1992). A model of the precaution adoption process: evidence from home radon testing. *Health Psychology*, 11: 170–80.

Weinstein, N. and Sandman, P.M. (2002). Reducing the risk of exposure to radon gas: an application of the Precaution Adoption Process model. In D. Rutter and L. Quine (eds). *Changing Health Behaviour* (pp. 66–86). Buckingham: Open University Press.

Weinstein, N.D., Sandman, P.M. and Blalock, S.J. (2008). The precaution adoption process model. In K. Glanz, B.K. Rimer and K. Wiswanath (eds), *Health Behavior and Health Education: Theory, Research and Practice*, 4th edn. San Francisco, CA: Jossey-Bass, pp. 123–47.

Weisenberg, M., Raz, T. and Hener, T. (1998). The influence of film-induced mood on pain perceptions. *Pain*, 76: 365–75.

Weisse, C.S., Turbiasz, A.A. and Whitney, D.J. (1995). Behavioral training and AIDS risk reduction: overcoming barriers to condom use. *AIDS Education and Prevention*, 7: 50–9.

Weller, D. (2004). Behavioural and social science research in cancer: time for action (editorial comment). *European Journal of Cancer*, 40: 314–15.

Weller, S.C. and Davis-Beaty, K. (2007). Condom effective-ness in reducing heterosexual HIV transmission. *Cochrane Database of Systematic Reviews*, issue 4, art. no.: CD003255. doi: 10.1002/14651858.CD003255.

Wellings, K., Field, S., Johnson, A.M. *et al.* (1994). Studying sexual lifestyles. In K. Wellings, S. Field, A.M. Johnson and J. Wadsworth (eds), *Sexual Behaviour in Britain*. London: Penguin.

Wellings, K., Nanchahal, K., Macdowall, W. *et al.* (2001). Sexual behaviour in Britain: early heterosexual experi-ence. *The Lancet*, 358/9296: 1843–50.

Wells, A. (2000) *Emotional Disorders and Metacognition: Innovative Cognitive Therapy*. Chichester: Wiley.

Wells, A. and Matthews, G. (1996). Modelling cognition in emotional disorder: the S-REF model. *Behaviour Research and Therapy*, 34: 881–8.

Wells, D. (2011). The value of pets for human health. *The Psychologist*, March: 172–6.

Wells, M.E., McQuellon, R.P., Hinkle, J.S. *et al.* (1995). Reducing anxiety in newly diagnosed cancer patients: a pilot program. *Cancer Practice*, 3: 100–4.

Wells, Y.D. (1999). Intentions to care for a spouse: gender differences in anticipated willingness to care and expected burden. *Journal of Family Studies*, 5: 220–34.

Wen, L.M., Thomas, M., Jones, H. *et al.* (2002). Promo-ting physical activity in women: evaluation of a 2-year community-based intervention in Sydney, Australia. *Health Promotion International*, 17: 127–37.

Wessely, S., Rose S. and Bisson, J. (1999). A systematic review of brief psychological interventions ('debriefing') for the treatment of immediate trauma related symptoms and the prevention of post-traumatic stress disorder. In *The Cochrane Library*. Oxford: Update Software.

West, R. (1992). Nicotine addiction: a re-analysis of the arguments. *Psychopharmacology*, 108: 408–10.

West, R. (2005). Time for a change: putting the trans-theoretical (stages of change) model to rest. *Addiction*, 100: 1036–9.

West, R. and Shiffman, S. (2007). *Smoking Cessation*, 2nd edn. Oxford: Health Press.

West, R., Edwards, M. and Hajek, P.A. (1998). Randomized controlled trial of a 'buddy' system to improve success at giving up smoking in general practice. *Addiction*, 93: 1007–11.

Westman, M., Eden, D. and Shirom, A. (1985). Job stress, cigarette smoking and cessation: conditioning effects of peer support. *Social Science and Medicine*, 20: 637–44.

Whelan, E.M. (1988). The truth about Americans' health. In R. Yarian (ed.), *Annual Editions*: *Health*, 9th edn. Guilford, CT: McGraw-Hill/Dushkin, pp. 25–9.

White, A. (2007). A global projection of subjective well-being: a challenge to positive psychology? *Psychtalk* 56: 17–20.

White, A., Nicolaas, G., Foster, K. *et al.* (1993). *Health Survey for England 1991*. London: HMSO.

White, P.D., Goldsmith, K.A., Johnson, A.L. *et al.* on behalf of the PACE trial management group. (2011). Comparison of adaptive pacing therapy, cognitive behaviour therapy, graded exercise therapy, and specialist medical care for chronic fatigue syndrome (PACE): a randomised trial. *The Lancet, Early Online Publication*, 18 February 2011, doi:10.1016/S0140-6736(11)60096-2.

Whiteman, M.C. (2006). Personality, cardiovascular disease and public health. In M.E. Vollrath (ed.), *Handbook of Personality and Health*. Chichester: John Wiley & Sons, pp. 13–34.

Whiteman, M.C., Fowkes, F.G.R., Deary, I.J. *et al.* (1997). Hostility, smoking, and alcohol consumption in the general population. *Social Science & Medicine*, 44: 1089–96.

Whooley, M. and Browner, W.S. (1998). Associations between depressive symptoms and mortality on older women. *Archives of Internal Medicine*, 158: 2129–35.

WHOQOL Group (1993). Study protocol for the World Health Organisation project to develop a quality of life assessment instrument (WHOQOL). *Quality of Life Research*, 2: 153–9.

WHOQOL Group (1994). Development of the WHOQOL: rationale and current status. Monograph on quality of life assessment: cross-cultural issues 2. *International Journal of Mental Health*, 23: 24–56.

WHOQOL Group (1998). The World Health Organization Quality of Life Assessment (WHOQOL): development and psychometric properties. *Social Science and Medicine*, 46: 1569–85.

Widows, M.R., Jacobsen, P.B. and Fields, K.K. (2000). Relation of psychological vulnerability factors to posttraumatic stress disorder symptomatology in bone marrow transplant recipients. *Psychosomatic Medicine*, 62: 873–82.

Wiers, R.W. and Hofmann, W. (2010). Implicit cognition and health psychology: changing perspectives and new interventions. *The European Health Psychologist*, 12: 4–6.

Wilbert-Lampen, U., Leistner, D., Greven, S. *et al.* (2008). Cardiovascular events during World Cup soccer. *New England Journal of Medicine*, 358: 475–83.

Wild, S. and McKeigue, P. (1997). Cross sectional analysis of mortality by country of birth in England and Wales, 1970–92. *British Medical Journal*, 314: 705–10.

Wiles, R., Ashburn, A., Payne, S. *et al.* (2004). Discharge from physiotherapy following stroke: the management of disappointment. *Social Science and Medicine*, 59: 1263–73.

Wilkinson, M. (1992). Income distribution and life expectancy. *British Medical Journal*, 304: 165–8.

Wilkinson, R.G. (1990). Income distribution and mortality: a 'natural' experiment. *Sociology of Health and Illness*, 12: 391–412.

Wilkinson, R. and Pickett, K. (2010). *The Spirit Level: Why More Equal Societies Almost Always Do Better*. London: Penguin.

Williams, J., Wake, M., Hesketh, K. *et al.* (2005). Health-related quality of life of overweight and obese children. *Journal of the American Medical Association*, 293: 1–5.

Williams, K., Robinson, C. and Morrison, V. (2011, in review). The role of illness perceptions and anticipatory coping on willingness to provide care in the future.

Williams, P.G. (2006). Personality and illness behaviour. In M.E. Vollrath (ed.), *Handbook of Personality and Health*. Chichester: Wiley, pp. 157–73.

Williams, J.E., Paton, C.C., Siegler, I.C. *et al.* (2000). Anger proneness predicts coronary heart disease risk: prospective analysis from Atherosclerosis Risk in Communities (ARIC) study. *Circulation*, 1010: 2034–9.

Williams, M.T. and Hord, H.G. (2005). The role of dietary factors in cancer prevention: beyond fruits and vegetables. *Nutrition in Clinical Practice*, 20: 451–9.

Williams, N.H., Hendry, M., France, B. *et al.* (2007). Effectiveness of exercise-referral schemes to promote physical activity in adults: systematic review. *British Journal of General Practitioners*, 57: 979–86.

Williamson, D., Robinson, M.E. and Melamed, B. (1997). Pain behaviour, spouse responsiveness, and marital satisfaction in patients with rheumatoid arthritis. *Behavioral Modification*, 21: 97–118.

Williamson, G.M., Shaffer, D.R. and Schulz, R. (1998). Activity restriction and prior relationship history as contributors to mental health outcomes among middle-aged and older spousal caregivers. *Health Psychology*, 17: 152–62.

Williamson, S. and Wardle, J. (2002). Increasing participation with colorectal cancer screening: the development of a psychoeducational intervention. In D. Rutter and L. Quine (eds), *Changing Health Behaviour*. Buckingham: Open University Press.

Wills, T.A. (1981). Downward comparison principles in social psychology. *Psychological Bulletin*, 90: 245–71.

Wills, T.A. and Ainette, M.G. (2007). Social support and health. In S. Ayers *et al.* (eds), *Cambridge Handbook of Psychology, Health & Medicine*, 2nd edn. Cambridge: Cambridge University Press, pp. 202–7.

Wilson, J.F., Moore, R.W., Randolph, S. and Hanson, B.J. (1982). Behavioral preparation of patients for gastrointestinal endoscopy: information, relaxation and coping style. *Journal of Human Stress*, 8: 13–23.

Wilson, P.W.F., D'Agostino, R.B., Sullivan, L., Parise, H. and Kannel, W.B. (2002). Overweight and obesity as determinants of cardiovascular risk. *Archives of Internal Medicine*, 162: 1867–72.

Wimbush, E., MacGregor, A. and Fraser, E. (1998). Impact of a national mass media campaign on walking in Scotland. *Health Promotion International*, 13: 45–53.

Windle, G. and Woods, R.T. (2004). Variations in subjective well-being: the mediating role of a psychological resource. *Ageing & Society*, 24: 583–602.

Winett, R.A., Anderson, E.S., Wojcik, J.R. *et al.* (2007). Guide to health: nutrition and physical activity outcomes of a group-randomized trial of an Internet-based intervention in churches. *Annals of Behavioral Medicine*, 33: 251–61.

Wing, R.R., Phelan, S. and Tate, D. (2002). The role of adherence in mediating the relationship between depression and health outcomes. *Journal of Psychosomatic Research*, 53: 877–81.

Winkleby, M., Fortmann, S. and Barrett, D. (1990). Social class disparities in risk factors for disease: eight year prevalence patterns by level of education. *Preventive Medicine*, 19: 1–12.

Wise, R.A. (1998). Drug activation of brain reward pathways. *Drug and Alcohol Dependence*, 51: 13–22.

Witham, M.D., Crighton, L.J. and McMurdo, M.E. (2007). Using an individualised quality of life measure in older heart failure patients. *International Journal of Cardiology*, 16: 40–5.

Witte, K. (1992). Putting the fear back into fear appeals: the extended parallel process model. *Communication Monographs*, 59: 329–49.

Witte, K. and Allen, M. (2000). A meta-analysis of fear appeals: implications for effective public health campaigns. *Health Education and Behavior*, 27: 591–615.

Wolf, R.L., Lepore, S.J., Vandergrift, J.L. *et al.* (2008). Knowledge, barriers, and stage of change as correlates of fruit and vegetable consumption among urban and mostly immigrant black men. *Journal of the American Dietetic Association*, 108: 1315–22.

Wollin, S.D. and Jones, P.J. (2001). Alcohol, red wine and cardiovascular disease. *Journal of Nutrition*, 131: 1401–4.

Wong, Y.J., Ho., R.M., Shin, M. and Tsai, P. (2011). Chinese Singaporeans' lay beliefs, adherence to Asian values, and subjective well-being. *Personality and Individual Differences*, 50: 822–7.

Wood, F., Robling, M., Prout, H. *et al.* (2010). A question of balance: a qualitative study of mothers' interpretations of dietary recommendations. *Annals of Family Medicine*, 8: 51–7.

Woods, R. (2008). Introduction. In R. Woods and L. Clare (eds), *Handbook of the Clinical Psychology of Ageing*, 2nd edn. London: Wiley, pp. 1–16.

Woods, R.T. (ed.) (1999). *Psychological Problems of Ageing: Assessment, Treatment and Care*. Chichester: Wiley.

Woodward, M., Oliphant, J., Lowe, G. *et al.* (2003). Contribution of contemporaneous risk factors to social inequality in coronary heart disease and all causes mortality. *Preventive Medicine*, 36: 561–8.

Woolf, S.H. (1996). Immunizations. In S.H. Woolf, S. Jonas and R.S. Lawrence (eds), *Health Promotion and Disease Prevention in Clinical Practice*. Baltimore, OH: Williams & Wilkins.

World Cancer Research Fund (1997). *Food Nutrition and the Prevention of Cancer: A Global Perspective*. Washington, DC: American Institute for Cancer Research.

World Health Organization (1947). Constitution of the World Health Organization. Geneva: WHO.

World Health Organization (1980). *International Classification of Impairments, Disabilities and Handicaps (ICIDH). A Manual of Classification Relating to the Consequences of Disease*. Geneva: WHO.

World Health Organization (1981). *Global Strategy for Health for All by the Year 2000*. Geneva: WHO.

World Health Organization (1988). *Healthy Cities Project: Five Year Planning Framework*. Copenhagen: WHO Regional Office for Europe.

World Health Organization (1995). *World Health Report*. Geneva: WHO.

World Health Organization (1996). *Health Promoting Schools. Report of a WHO Expert Committee on Comprehensive School Health Education and Promotion*. Geneva: WHO.

World Health Organization (1999). *Health 21: Health for All in the 21st Century*. Copenhagen: WHO Regional Office for Europe.

World Health Organisation (2001). *International Classification of Functioning, Disability and Health (ICF)*. Geneva: WHO.

World Health Organization (2002). *The World Health Report: Reducing Risks, Promoting Healthy Life*. Copenhagen: WHO Regional Office for Europe.

World Health Organization (2003). *Gender, Health and Tobacco*. Geneva: WHO.

World Health Organization (2004). *Young People's Health in Context: Health Behaviour in School-aged Children (HBSC) Study*. International report from the 2001/2002 survey. C. Currie, C. Roberts, A. Morgan, R. Smith, W. Settertobulte, O. Samdal and V.B. Rasmussen (eds). Available from: www.euro.who.int.

World Health Organization (2008). *WHO Report on the Global Tobacco Epidemic: The MPOWER Report*. Geneva: WHO.

World Health Organization (2010). *World Health Statistics 2010*. Geneva: WHO.

World Health Organization Expert Committee (1990). *Cancer Pain Relief and Palliative Care*, Technical Report Series No. 84. Geneva: WHO.

World Health report (2008). http://www.who.int/research/en/.

Wortley, P. and Fleming, P. (1997). AIDS in women in the United States: recent trends. *Journal of the American Medical Association*, 278: 911–16.

Wright, A.J. (2010). The impact of perceived risk on risk-reducing behaviours. In D. French, K. Vedhara, A.A. Kaptein and J. Weinman (eds), *Health Psychology*, 2nd edn. London: BPS Blackwell, pp. 111–21.

Wu, A.W., Snyder, C.F., Huang, I.C. *et al.* (2006). A randomized trial of the impact of a programmable medication reminder device on quality of life in patients with AIDS. *AIDS Patient Care and STDS*, 20: 773–81.

Wysocki, T., Harris, M.A., Buckloh, L.M. *et al.* (2007). Randomized trial of behavioral family systems therapy for diabetes: maintenance of effects on diabetes outcomes in adolescents. *Diabetes Care*, 30: 555–60.

Yan, H. and Sellick, K. (2004). Quality of life of Chinese patients newly diagnosed with gastrointestinal cancer: a longitudinal study. *International Journal of Nursing Studies*, 41: 309–19.

Yang, L., Sahlqvist, S., McMinn, A., Griffin, S.J. and Ogilvie, D. (2010). Interventions to promote cycling: systematic review. *British Medical Journal*, Oct 18: 341.

Yardley, L. and Dibb, B. (2007). Assessing subjective change in chronic illness: an examination of response shift in health-related and goal-oriented subjective status. *Psychology & Health*, 22: 813–28.

Ye, X.X., Huang, H., Li, S.H. *et al.* (2009). HIV/AIDS education effects on behaviour among senior high school students in a medium-sized city in China. *International Journal of STD and AIDS*, 20: 549–52.

Yee, J.L. and Schulz, R. (2000). Gender differences in psychiatric morbidity among family caregivers: a review and analysis. *The Gerontologist*, 40: 147–64.

Yip, Y.B., Sit, J.W., Fung, K.K. *et al.* (2007). Impact of an arthritis self-management programme with an added exercise component for osteoarthritic knee sufferers on improving pain, functional outcomes, and use of health care services: an experimental study. *Patient Education and Counseling*, 65: 113–21.

Yorke, J. and Shuldham, C. (2005). Family therapy for chronic asthma in children. *Cochrane Database Systematic Review*, 2: CD000089.

Young, J.M., D'Este, C. and Ward, J.E. (2002). Improving family physicians' use of evidence-based smoking cessation strategies: a cluster randomization trial. *Preventive Medicine*, 35: 572–83.

Yusuf, S., Hawken, S., Ôunpuu, S. *et al.* (2004). Effects of potentially modifiable risk factors associated with myocardial infarction in 52 countries (the INTERHEART study): case-control study. *The Lancet*, 364: 937–52.

Yzer, M.C., Fisher, J.D., Bakker, A.B. *et al.* (1998). The effects of information about AIDS risk and self-efficacy on women's intentions to engage in AIDS preventive behavior. *Journal of Applied Social Psychology*, 28: 1837–52.

Yzer, M.C., Siero, F.W. and Buunk, B.P. (2001). Bringing up condom use and using condoms with new sexual partners: intention or habitual? *Psychology and Health*, 16: 409–21.

Zabora, J., BrintzenhofeSzoc, K., Curbow, B., Hooker, C. and Piantadosi, S. (2001). The prevalence of psychological distress by cancer site. *Psycho-Oncology*, 10: 19–28.

Zachariae, R., Pedersen, C.G., Jensen, A.B., Ehrnrooth, E., Rossen, P.B. and von der Maase, H. (2003). Association of perceived physician communication style with patient satisfaction, distress, cancer-related self-efficacy, and perceived control over the disease. *British Journal of Cancer*, 88: 658–65.

Zakowski, S.G., Ramati, A., Morton, C. and Flanagan, R. (2004). Written emotional disclosure buffers the effects of social constraints on distress in cancer patients. *Health Psychology*, 23: 555–63.

Yang, L., Sahlqvist, S., McMinn, A. *et al.* (2010). Interventions to promote cycling: systematic review. *British Medical Journal*, 341: c5405.

Zakowski, S. (1995). The effects of stressor predictability on lymphocyte proliferation in humans. *Psychology and Health*, 10: 409–25.

Zakowski, S.G., McAllister, C.G., Deal, M. and Baum, A. (1992). Stress, reactivity, and immune function in healthy men. *Health Psychology*, 11: 223–32.

Zarit, S., Reever, K. and Bach-Peterson, J. (1980). Relatives of the impaired elderly: correlates of feelings of burden. *The Gerontologist*, 20: 649–55.

Zautra, A.J., Davis, M.C., Reich, J.W. *et al.* (2008). Comparison of cognitive behavioral and mindfulness meditation interventions on adaptation to rheumatoid arthritis for patients with and without history of recurrent depression. *Journal of Consulting and Clinical Psychology*, 76: 408–21.

Zaza, C. and Baine, N. (2002). Cancer pain and psychosocial factors: a critical review of the literature. *Journal of Pain and Symptom Management*, 24: 526–42.

Zborowski, M. (1952). Cultural components in response to pain. *Journal of Social Issues*, 8: 16–30.

Zeidner, M. and Saklofske, D. (1996). Adaptive and maladaptive coping. In M. Zeidner and N. Endler (eds), *Handbook of Coping: Theory, Research, Application*. New York: Wiley.

Zelter, L. and LeBaron, S. (1982). Hypnosis and nonhypnotic techniques for reduction of pain and anxiety during painful procedures in children and adolescents with cancer. *Journal of Pediatrics*, 101: 1032–5.

Zervas, I.M., Augustine, A. and Fricchione, G.L. (1993). Patient delay in cancer: a view for the crisis model. *General Hospital Psychiatry*, 15: 9–13.

Zhang, Y., Proenca, R., Maffie, M., Barone, M., Leopold, L. and Friedman, J.M. (1994). Positional cloning of the mouse obese gene and its human homologue. *Nature*, 372: 425–32.

Zimmers, E., Privette, G., Lowe, R.H. and Chappa, F. (1999). Increasing use of the female condom through video instruction. *Perceptual and Motor Skills*, 88: 1071–7.

Zinovieff, F., Morrison, V., Coles, A. and Cartmell, R. (2005). Are the needs of cancer patients and their carers generic? Paper presented to the European Health Psychology Society annual conference, Galway, September.

Zohar, D. and Dayan, I. (1999). Must coping options be severely limited during stressful events: testing the interaction between primary and secondary appraisals. *Anxiety, Stress and Coping*, 12: 191–216.

Zola, I.K. (1973). Pathways to the doctor: from person to patient. *Social Science and Medicine*, 7: 677–89.

Zorrilla, E.P., McKay, J.R., Luborsky, L. and Schmidt, K. (1996). Relation of stressors and depressive symptoms to clinical progression of viral illness. *American Journal of Psychiatry*, 153(5): 626–35.

Zucker, A. (2007). Ethical and legal isues and end-of-life decision making. In D. Balk, C. Wogrin, G. Thornton and D. Meagher (eds), *Handbook of Thanatology: The Essential Body of Knowledge for the Student of Death, Dying, and Bereavement*. Northbrook, IL: Association for Death Education and Counseling, pp. 103–12.

Zucker, D., Hopkins, R.S., Sly, D.F. *et al.* (2000). Florida's 'truth' campaign: a counter-marketing, anti-tobacco media campaign. *Journal of Public Health Management Practice*, 6: 1–6.

Zuckerman, M. (1979). *Sensation Seeking: Beyond the Optimal Level of Arousal*. Hillsdale, NJ: Lawrence Erlbaum.

Zuckerman, M. (1984). Sensation seeking: a comparative approach to a human trait. *Behavioral and Brain Sciences*, 7: 413–17.

Index